Psychology: An Introduction

Fifth Edition

Psychology: An Introduction

Fifth Edition

Jerome Kagan
Harvard University

Ernest Havemann

Julius Segal

Harcourt Brace Jovanovich, Publishers
San Diego New York Chicago Washington, D.C. Atlanta London Sydney Toronto

Copyrights and Acknowledgments for textual material and Illustration credits appear on pages 623–50, which constitute a continuation of the copyright page.

Cover Design: Ron Miriello

Requests for permission to make copies of any part of the work should be mailed to: Permissions, Harcourt Brace Jovanovich, Publishers, Orlando, Florida 32887.

ISBN: 0–15–572633–1

Library of Congress
Catalog Card Number: 83–81023

Printed in the United States of America

Preface

So swift has been the recent pace of psychological research that each revision of *Psychology: An Introduction* is in essence a brand-new book. Perhaps the most eloquent evidence of the knowledge explosion will be found in the index of this Fifth Edition, where a very high proportion of the topics listed—all essential to an understanding of what psychology is all about in the mid-1980s—were not even a part of any psychologist's vocabulary when the first edition appeared. Thus our chief task in preparing this edition was to answer some urgent questions raised by the rapid advance of the science.

We have always aimed to serve instructors and students receptive to a book that, as one journal review of the Fourth Edition put it, "combines brevity, clarity, rigor, and relevance." But how could we preserve brevity while still doing justice to all the new knowledge plus the abiding basics of the old? How could we preserve rigor and relevance without sacrificing clarity?

To keep the book brief, we have continued to seek extreme economy in writing style and to concentrate more than ever on the main thrust and meaning of psychology—the basic principles that the Tyler study (page 135) found were remembered longest by students—rather than the unnecessary terminology and extraneous details that Tyler found to be quickly forgotten. To keep the book rigorous and relevant, we have constantly asked ourselves: Of all the knowledge that now exists, what elements are *most* important to students—both those preparing themselves for advanced courses and those who will have no further exposure to psychology?

We have made it our top priority to foster an appreciation of such momentous findings as the brain's marvelous complexity and versatility, the ingenious ways people learn and remember, the way individual differences contribute to humanity's richness and create many of its misunderstandings, and the basic message of social psychology—which is that no person is an island and that who you are depends largely on whom you are with. If we can help students grasp the significance of these principles—and disabuse them of some of the false and often harmful beliefs about human behavior popular among people who have never taken a psychology course—we will be gratified.

Because doing all this has become such a formidable task, the two original authors are happy to be joined in this Fifth Edition by a third collaborator, Julius Segal.

Changes in the Fifth Edition

Besides adding many scores of new studies that have pushed psychology's frontiers into new ground since 1980, we have made substantial changes in the structure and presentation of the book. In particular, we have taken a new approach to two topics that have always confounded textbook authors—the marvels of the human brain and the problem of abnormal behavior.

The brain and the wondrous ways it processes and stores information are the very core of modern psychology, and it is impossible to grasp the thrust of the science without a basic knowledge of what the brain does and how it operates. On the other hand, its structures are so complex that any discussion runs the danger of sounding like pure physiology and alienating students who expect something very different from the course. We have therefore reorganized and almost completely rewritten Chapter 2 ("Brain and Body") to center the presentation on the many essential functions performed by the brain. The structural details of the nervous system and other bodily influences on behavior thus fall naturally into perspective as the tools that facilitate all these stunning accomplishments.

Abnormal psychology poses difficulties because it is a subject that students usually expect to find fascinating—but that often turns out to be mostly terminology for disorders that can seem remote from ordinary experience. In the past we have confined the discussion to a section of a chapter. Recent advances in the field, however, now make it possible to treat the subject not as a mere list of terms but as a continuum of unfortunate but widespread reactions to more stress than individuals can tolerate, given their own particular biological structures and their psychological and social backgrounds. We have therefore added a new Chapter 12 devoted entirely to abnormal psychology. Although the chapter emphasizes that every case is unique, it describes through specific examples and case histories the five major classes now listed in the diagnostic manual (DSM-III) of the American Psychiatric Association—namely, schizophrenia, affective disorders, anxiety disorders, personality disorders, and substance abuse.

Many other sections of the book have been rewritten in the light of new developments. To cite some major examples, the brief history of psychology in Chapter 1 has been revised from the new perspective in which current trends place the work of James, Watson, Skinner, and the Gestalt school. The chapters on learning (Chapter 3), memory (Chapter 4), and perception (Chapter 8) have been recast to reflect the growing view of these matters as related steps in human information processing. The discussion of development (Chapter 14) has been augmented by new views of how rapidly intellectual skills grow in infancy as the size of the brain increases, the role of classmates and teachers in social and emotional development in the early school years, and the surprising ability of the human personality to change and grow throughout the life span. Chapter 15 on social psychology has been reorganized to provide a unified view of the interrelationships among socialization, conformity, attitudes, interpersonal attraction, and attribution theory.

At the request of many instructors, we have moved the section on "How to Study This Book" to Chapter 1, where it can now be more conveniently assigned at the very start of the course. We have also enlarged it considerably to present the SQ3R study method in greater detail. For help in following SQ3R's review step, chapter summaries are now divided into the major sections of the chapter, each section identified by the heading used in the text. (The *Study Guide* that accompanies the book has been restructured and rewritten in toto for additional assistance in using the SQ3R method.)

"How to Study This Book" is one of the chapter supplements that can be assigned or omitted at the discretion of the instructor. These chapter supplements, containing materials that are pertinent and useful but not absolutely essential to a basic understanding of the science, were introduced in the previous edition to provide additional coverage and greater flexibility. Other topics discussed in supplements are test construction (Chapter 6), altered states of consciousness (Chapter 8), sexual feelings and behavior (Chapter 9), sex roles and conflicts in today's world (Chapter 10), personality tests (Chapter 13), and aggression and altruism (Chapter 15). In Chapter 7 a supplement is used to present additional information on the sense of vision.

Even with the supplements, this edition remains a brief book—and by omitting the supplements, instructors can readily make the book even briefer. A number of instructors report they have shaped the course to the needs of their particular students by assigning the supplements to a class section that shows good progress but skipping some or all of them with another section that has problems. This, in effect, makes for two books—a *very* short volume that nonetheless covers all the fundamentals of the science, or a somewhat longer volume with varying lengths and levels of enrichment that may better fit the requirements of the class.

Jerome Kagan
Ernest Havemann
Julius Segal

Acknowledgments

Classroom consultants

The following people, who have been teaching the introductory course, have provided us with many helpful suggestions in this and in past editions:

Leonore Loeb Adler, The College of Staten Island, CUNY
Mary J. Allen, California State College
J. R. Arneson, South Dakota School of Mines & Technology
Heesoon Aust, Centralia College
Vergie Lee Behrens, Scottsdale Community College
Otto A. Berliner, SUNY, Alfred State College
James Bickley, Pasadena City College
Jack Blakemore, Monterey Peninsula College
Sue Bowen, Cleveland State Community College
James Brandt, Minot State College
Myron Brender, Kingsborough Community College, CUNY
Thomas Brothen, University of Minnesota
Dean Brysen, South Dakota School of Mines & Technology
Patrick Butler, San Jose City College
Roland Calhoun, Humboldt State University
Susie C. Campbell, Davidson County Community College
W. John Cannon, Columbia Union College
Michael Ceddia, Massachusetts Bay Community College
Louis G. Cesaratto, Ulster County Community College
Carol E. Chandler, McHenry County College
Garvin Chastain, Boise State University
William Coggan, Massasoit Community College
David Stewart-Cohen, California State College
Francis B. Colavita, University of Pittsburgh
Betty T. Conover, Miami-Dade Community College
Alice M. Crichlow, Massasoit Community College
Anne Louise Dailey, Community College of Allegheny County
Anne G. English, University of Toledo
Elliot E. Entin, Ohio University
Paul E. Finn, Saint Anselm's College
Bess Fleckman, Miami-Dade Community College, North Campus
B. L. Garrett, DePauw University
Robert Gibson, Centralia College
Jon Gosser, Delta College
Mary Hamilton, Highline Community College
Judith Roes Hammerle, Adrian College
Gordon Hammerle, Adrian College
James M. Hammond, Columbia Union College
Francis J. Hanrahan, Hudson Valley Community College

W. Bruce Haslam, Weber State College
Roy K. Heintz, California State University, Long Beach
Judy Hensley, Otero Junior College
Faunie Hewlett, Cleveland State Community College
Annette Hiedemann, West Virginia Wesleyan College
Robert R. Higgins, Oakland Community College
John E. Hoffman, East Los Angeles College
Richard D. Honey, Transylvania University
Philip Howard, Enterprise State Junior College
Michael Hughmanick, West Valley College
Morton Isaacs, Rochester Institute of Technology
Charles W. Johnson, University of Evansville
James L. Johnston, Madison Area Technical College
Richard Kellogg, SUNY, Agricultural & Technical College
Kenneth A. Koenigshofer, Chaffey College
Charlton R. Lee, Cypress College
Edward E. Leech, Cleveland State Community College
Tim Lehmann, Valencia Community College
Diane Leroi, College of San Mateo
Harold List, Massachusetts Bay Community College
Cameron Marshman, Rio Hondo College
William A. Marzano, Illinois Valley Community College
Ann B. McNeer, Polk Community College
Douglas Miller, Miami University
Donald H. Millikan, San Diego Mesa College
Elizabeth Morelli, Henry Ford Community College
C. Thomas Musgrave, Weber State College
Dennis L. Nagi, Hudson Valley Community College
Edward F. O'Day, San Diego State University
Dan E. Perkins, Richland College
F. A. Perry, Jr., Erie Community College
David W. Prull, Community College of the Finger Lakes
David L. Quinby, Youngstown State University
Bob Rainey, Florida Junior College
Robert L. Ramlet, Elgin Community College
Mary Renfer, Mt. View College
Sue H. Rhodamer, Cleveland State Community College
O. L. Riner, Gulf Coast Community College
Carol Roberts, San Diego Mesa College
John C. Roehr, Hudson Valley Community College
Steve Rosengarten, Middlesex County College
Frank M. Rosenkrans, III, Eastern Washington University
Joel Rosevelt, Golden West College
Douglas A. Ross, Indiana University of Pennsylvania
Alva Sachs, College of San Mateo
Ganus Scarborough Jr., Jefferson State Junior College
Gary Schaumberg, Cerritos College
Jerome Seidman, Montclair State College
Michael B. Sewall, Mohawk Valley Community College
Ruth B. Shapiro, John Jay College

Jack P. Shilkret, Ann Arundel Community College
Charlotte Simon, Montgomery College
Lora S. Simon, Holyoke Community College
Ronald E. Siry, University of Cincinnati
David Skinner, Valencia Community College
Joseph L. Slosser, Chemeketa Community College
Leo V. Soriano, Winona State University
Donovan Swanson, El Camino College
Givens L. Thornton, Clarion State College
Jerome D. Tietz, Santa Barbara City College
William K. Trinkaus, South Connecticut State College
Luis Vazquez, Cleveland State College
Jerry L. Vogt, Stanford University School of Medicine
Albert C. Widhalm, Kankakee Community College
Michael Witmer, Skagit Valley College
Sherman Yen, Essex Community College

Reviewers

We have also had the benefit of advice from scholars who provided us with critiques of individual chapters. Some of the following reviewed the Fourth Edition chapters and provided us with suggestions for additional new materials. Some reviewed preliminary drafts of the new chapters, and some did both. The authors, of course, take full responsibility for any defects that may nonetheless appear.

John Altrocchi, University of Nevada
Allen E. Bergin, Brigham Young University
Ellen S. Berscheid, University of Minnesota
James A. Briley, Jefferson State Junior College
Parnell W. Cephus, Jefferson State Junior College
Eve V. Clark, Stanford University
Herbert H. Clark, Stanford University
Margaret J. Gatz, University of Southern California
Julian Hochberg, Columbia University
Bartley Hoebel, Princeton University
W. E. Kintsch, University of Colorado
Stephen Kosslyn, Harvard University
Leon Rappaport, Kansas State University
Sandra Scarr, University of Virginia
James R. Stellar, Harvard University

Besides the consultants and reviewers, we are indebted and grateful to Joan Lawson, Whitney Walton, and Joyce R. Wasserstein for their valuable help.

Contents

PART 1

Psychology: A New Approach to Old Questions 2

CHAPTER 1

The Scope, Goals, and Methods of Psychology 4

Psychology's two aims and many interests 6

How psychology studies human behavior 11

The ultimate method: experimentation 18

Psychology in the past, present, and future 22

How behavior is guided by heredity and environment 29

Summary 35

Supplement: How to study this book (and others) 39

The SQ3R system of study: a method that works 39

CHAPTER 2

Brain and Body: The Physical Foundations of Human Behavior 46

The supreme brain, its intricacy, and its "beautiful relationships" 47

Brain function no. 1: sensing the world and taking action 52

Brain function no. 2: thinking, planning, and remembering 55

Brain function no. 3: managing our emotional and physical lives 61

How the brain performs its functions: the neurons and their messages 68

Summary 73

PART 2

How Learning and Memory Shape Our Lives 78

CHAPTER 3

The Universal Laws of Learning 80

Classical conditioning 82

Operant conditioning 90

Operant escape, punishment, and learned helplessness 99

The cognitive view: learning as a step in information processing 108

Summary 114

CHAPTER 4

Memory: The Storehouse of Information 118

Remembering for just an instant—or for a lifetime 120

The mystery of the memory trace: there must be one—but what is it? 125

Why we forget 128

The encoding and transfer process 135

Encoding and learning 141

Some aids to encoding 147

Summary 154

PART 3

Using Information from Memory: Speaking, Thinking, and Learning 158

CHAPTER 5

Language and Concepts 160

The structure and rules of language 162

Producing messages and understanding them 165

How we learn language 169

The doubly useful words called concepts 177

Thinking and problem solving 185

Summary 195

CHAPTER 6
Intelligence: What Is It? How Well Can It Be Measured? 198
Theories of the nature of intelligence 199
Intelligence tests: what they do and don't do 209
IQ and the nature-nurture question 219
Intelligence, age, creativity, and the brain versus the computer 227
Summary 231
Supplement: The science of test construction 235

PART 4
Knowing About the World: The Senses and Perception 240

CHAPTER 7
The Senses: Our Source of Information 242
How the senses operate 244
Taste, smell, touch, and the two forgotten senses 246
Sound waves and hearing 252
Light waves and vision 258
Summary 263
Supplement: Retinal coding, visual sharpness, and color mixing 266

CHAPTER 8
Perception: The First Step in Information Processing 272
How the nervous system is "wired" for survival 273
Selection and attention 279
Perceptual organization 283
What does the information mean?—the element of interpretation 291
Summary 293
Supplement: Perception and altered states of consciousness 296
Sleep, dreams, hypnosis, and meditation 296
Drugs 301

PART 5
Human Feelings and Aspirations 310

CHAPTER 9
Emotions and Drives 312
Emotions and the body: "stirred up" or "toned down" 313
Emotions and the brain 322
Individual differences in emotion 326
The drives and behavior 328
Stimulus needs as a driving force 336
Summary 339
Supplement: Sexual feelings and behavior 342

CHAPTER 10
Motives, Frustration, and Conflict 352
The goals of success and friendship 353
Some other powerful motives 362
How and why motives affect behavior 368
Frustration and conflict 372
Summary 377
Supplement: Sex roles and the conflicts they create 379
What it means to be masculine or feminine 379
The built-in problems of being female 386
The built-in problems of being male 390

PART 6
Human Personality: Sources, Problems, and Strengths 394

CHAPTER 11
Anxiety, Stress, and Coping 396
Anxiety and its effect on behavior 398
The wear and tear of stress 405
Successful coping and normal behavior 414
Defense mechanisms and other questionable forms of coping 418
Summary 425

CHAPTER 12
Abnormal Psychology 428
The scope of abnormal behavior 429
Origins and types of abnormal behavior 431
Schizophrenia: no. 1 crippler 436
Affective disorders: abnormalities of mood 439
Anxiety disorders 445
Personality disorders 449
Substance abuse: abnormal use of alcohol and drugs 443
Attitudes toward abnormal behavior: how they can hurt or heal 460
Summary 463

CHAPTER 13
Personality and Psychotherapy 466
Personality theories 468
Freud's psychoanalytic theory 471
Humanistic theories of personality 479
Social learning theories and behavior therapy 482
Other therapies (including medical) 486
Summary 493
Supplement: Tests of personality 497

PART 7
Becoming a Person and Relating to Others 502

CHAPTER 14
Human Development 504
Babies at birth: alike yet different 506
Physical and mental development 513
Personality development: birth to eighteen months 518
The first social demands: eighteen months through three years 521
The preschool years: four and five 524
The period of teachers and peers: six to ten 525
Adolescence: fun or fury? 529
Development—and sometimes about-face—in adulthood 536
The challenges and triumphs of growing old 541
Summary 543

CHAPTER 15
Social Psychology 546
Learning—and conforming to—the ways of society 547
Our attitudes toward life: how we acquire, cling to, and sometimes change them 557
"Persuasive communications" and attitude change 562
Our search for the reasons people act as they do: attribution theories 566
How we form our social relationships: the forces of attraction and liking 572
Summary 577
Supplement: Aggression, altruism, and bystander apathy 580

Appendix: Statistical Methods 584
Glossary 607
References and Acknowledgments 623
Name Index 651
Subject Index 659

Psychology: An Introduction

Fifth Edition

PART 1

Psychology: A New Approach to Old Questions

As you start this course you are embarking on an exciting journey into the mysteries and marvels of human existence. The pathway leads through territory that fascinated your ancestors throughout written history—and probably long before that—but remained uncharted until very recently. Now it has been opened up for exploration by the science of psychology, much as outer space has been made accessible by modern-day scientists who have created rocket engines and capsules that fly to the moon.

Our concern is the vast and varied realm of human behavior—the workings of the body and brain, the ways in which we human beings resemble and differ from one another, our physical actions, and our thoughts, emotions, dreams, aspirations, loves, hates, worries, and joys. The goal we seek is an answer to the questions: Why do we act as we do, for better or for worse? What are the forces that shape our lives? Or, to put this in the simplest and most personal terms, *what makes us tick?*

From what little we know about our earliest ancestors, it appears they were so baffled by these questions that they could only resort to supernatural explanations. Their fate seemed at the mercy of "good spirits" who sometimes blessed them with health, happiness, and success in their hunt for food, and "bad spirits" who sometimes plagued them with sickness, sadness, and misfortune.

By the time of the ancient Greeks, the science of mathematics was flourishing, physicians had learned a great deal about the human body, and philosophers took a more sophisticated view of human experience. One puzzle that fascinated the Greeks was the human senses—our ability to see a person standing many yards away, totally unconnected in any apparent way with our own body, or to hear that person speak. One philosopher speculated that all objects must give off some kind of invisible substance that penetrates our eyes or ears, then travels to the brain. (As you will find later in the course, this was a pretty good guess.) Another puzzle was human temperament. Why are some people so melancholy? Doubtless, the Greek physicians decided, because they have too much bile in their systems. Why are others so optimistic, happy, and warm-hearted? Doubtless because they have an especially rich flow of blood. (These guesses were at least on the right track in suggesting an interaction between body, brain, and mood.)

By around the year 1600, most leading

thinkers of the Western world had decided that behavior was largely dictated by inborn characteristics, somehow present at the moment of birth. Babies are born with strong tendencies to be either gloomy, optimistic, generous, greedy, ambitious, or lazy. Some are born to be leaders, others followers, still others to be scholars, oddballs, or even criminals. But a little later the philosopher John Locke popularized a different view, namely that a baby at birth is simply a *tabula rasa,* or blank tablet, on which anything at all can be written by experience and learning. The two opposite views posed another puzzle: Are our lives governed by heredity or by environment?

And so through the centuries humanity remained absorbed in the attempt to explain human nature. The philosophers speculated. Literary giants wrote of human passions, struggles, triumphs, and tragedies. But the facts were not available—only personal opinion and guesswork. It was impossible to know for sure how we see and hear until modern science learned about light and sound waves and the way they affect nerve endings within the body. Human moods and emotions could not be analyzed until science identified the substances secreted by the human glands and the complex way the glands interact with the brain. The process of heredity could not be understood until biologists discovered the chromosomes, genes, and the chemical key to life called DNA. The influence of environment was unclear until psychologists established the facts about learning and about development from infant to adult.

Even today we do not know the full story—and perhaps we never will, for human behavior is so complex that it may forever defy complete understanding. But psychologists aided by the progress of other scientists have found some of the answers, and they are making new discoveries all the time. When you finish this course you will know more about the human experience than anybody in the world did a century ago, when the science of psychology opened its first laboratory.

In this introductory section of the book Chapter 1 discusses the methods psychology uses to study behavior and describes some of its landmark findings, including the way heredity operates and helps shape our lives. Chapter 2 describes the biological equipment of body and brain that makes possible the variety and richness of our lives.

CHAPTER 1

Psychology's two aims and many interests 6
- The goals of psychology
- "Pure" and "applied" psychology
- Clinical psychology and counseling

How psychology studies human behavior 11
- Observation
- Interviews and case histories
- Questionnaires and opinion surveys
- Tests and measurements
- Measurements, individual differences, and the normal curve
- The method of correlation
- The advantages and pitfalls of correlation

The ultimate method: experimentation 18
- Independent and dependent variables
- Experimental and control groups
- Single-blind and double-blind experiments

Psychology in the past, present, and future 22
- William James, "mental life," and the era of introspection
- John Watson, conditioned reflexes, and the behaviorist revolution
- B. F. Skinner and the behaviorist era
- The Gestalt school of thought
- The rise of the cognitive school
- Cognitive psychology and our "mental models of reality"
- The humanistic school
- Other approaches

How behavior is guided by heredity and environment 29
- The key to heredity: chromosomes and genes
- Where we get our genes
- Being born male or female
- How heredity affects behavior
- How environment affects behavior

Summary 35

Important terms 38

Supplement: How to study this book (and others) 39

The SQ3R system of study: a method that works 39
1. Survey
2. Question
3. Read
4. Recite
5. Review

Summary of Supplement 43

Recommended readings 44

The Scope, Goals, and Methods of Psychology

Have you read the introduction to this section of the book on pages 2–3? If not, you will find it helpful to turn back and look at it now before starting the chapter. The book is divided into seven parts, each preceded by an introduction that serves as a guide to what will be found in the section. These introductory discussions will tell you what to expect—and how each part of the book relates to the entire field of psychology.

A definition of psychology takes only a few brief words: It is *the systematic study of behavior and the factors that influence behavior.* Yet that simple statement covers a range of subject matter so vast that, like the universe itself, its boundaries defy imagination.

Just the single word *behavior* means many things. Our physical actions begin each morning when we wake, yawn, stretch, dress, and eat breakfast, and do not end until we go back to bed and fall asleep—after a long day in which we walk, talk, study, work, play, and sometimes laugh or cry. Inside ourselves is another world of activity. We think, learn, remember, and forget. We feel hunger and thirst—and such emotions as anger, fear, joy, and sadness. We have stirrings of desire for accomplishment and success, friendship, and sometimes revenge. We worry over our problems and seek ways to cope with them.

The *factors that influence behavior* are also many and varied. The most important is the human brain, but the brain itself is immensely complex—made up of 10 billion nerve cells, of scores of different kinds performing different functions, that are intricately connected and interconnected and constantly exchanging messages coded into little jolts of electricity and chemical activity. The brain would be useless without the help it gets from other parts of the body. It would not know anything about the environment without the specialized nerve cells of the sense organs, sensitive to light, sound, smell, taste, and pressure. It would not even know when we are hungry or thirsty without signals provided by the bloodstream and some of the visceral organs. It would not experience emotions without the aid of various chemicals produced by the human glands.

To understand behavior, psychology must study all these many relationships between the brain and the rest of the body. It must also ponder the workings of heredity—and the extent to which our conduct is governed by traits and tendencies handed down to us from the countless generations of forebears from whom we are descended. At the same time it must examine the influence of environment, including the many ways we learn from our experiences, remember them, and apply them.

In particular it must look at the way the actions of other people affect our own behavior—which turns out to be much more significant and far-reaching than one might ever suspect.

Psychology's two aims and many interests

Our definition includes the words *systematic study* because psychology uses the rigorous and highly disciplined methods of science. It does not rely on some mysterious and supernatural explanation for human behavior, as our early ancestors presumably did. It is not content to describe behavior as some philosopher of the past, however brilliant, may have imagined it to be. Psychology is skeptical and demands proof. It is based on controlled experiments and on observations made with the greatest possible precision and objectivity (meaning freedom from personal prejudices or preconceived notions).

Without taking the scientific approach, it is difficult to reach valid conclusions about human behavior. The nonscientist is almost bound to commit numerous mistakes of observation and interpretation and to make judgments based on faulty or insufficient evidence. All of us tend to generalize from our own feelings and experiences—though what we see in ourselves is not necessarily characteristic of people in general. (Psychology has established conclusively that there is a wide range of individual differences in almost all human traits.) Or we generalize from the actions and opinions of the people we know, which again are not necessarily universal. (Psychology has shown that we tend to surround ourselves with people whose opinions, interests, and tastes are similar to our own.)

Thus the findings of psychology often come as a surprise—even to psychologists. You will encounter many facts in this course that seem to go contrary to common-sense observation and many of the views of human nature expressed in literature and in old adages. For example:

Does *practice make perfect*? Certainly not if you practice the wrong way, as you will discover in the chapters on learning and memory—and many things are learned and remembered without any practice at all.

Is it wise to *hitch your wagon to a star*? On the contrary, as the chapter on motives shows, you are asking for trouble if you set your goals too high.

Is it true that *the child is father to the man*? No, as you will find in the chapter on developmental psychology—for traits exhibited in early childhood often change radically by adolescence, and indeed people do about-faces throughout life.

Does *familiarity breed contempt*? No, as is explained in the chapter on social psychology—for the more familiar we are with other people, the more likely we are to be attracted to them.

The goals of psychology

In the study of behavior and the factors that influence it, psychology has two goals: (a) *to understand behavior* and (b) *to predict behavior.* Indeed understanding and predicting are the goals of all sciences. Chemists, for example, have sought from the beginning to understand why wood burns and gold does not—and to predict what will happen when a chemical substance is subjected to flame or combined with another chemical in a test tube. Psychologists seek, among other things, to understand why individuals behave as they do in a classroom or in social situations—and to predict what would happen if certain changes were made in the school or social environment.

Most scientists seek not only to understand and predict events but to control them as well. Chemists want to be able to control the substances they deal with so that they can produce new chemicals to serve useful new purposes, such as the various synthetics now used in clothing and automobiles. To a certain extent, psychologists also look for ways to control human behavior. This is especially true of those who devote their careers to helping people overcome mental and emotional problems. They want to control the behavior of the people who consult them by trying to relieve an unreasonable fear of going out in public, an inability to establish satisfactory sexual relationships, or alcohol addiction.

But dealing with human beings is far different from mixing chemicals in a test tube. The possibility of controlling human behavior raises thorny questions of moral and social policy. Therefore psychologists have mixed feelings about whether control of behavior should or should not be considered a third goal of the science. Some psychologists have argued that human behavior is always under some kind of control—by the ways in which parents rear their children, the school systems, the rewards and punishments provided in the business world, and the nation's laws—and that it would be better to have the control exercised in a scientific fashion by scientists dedicated to improving the human condition (Skinner, 1971). Most psychologists, however, shun the awful responsibility—and the dangers of abuse—inherent in efforts to manipulate human behavior.

"Pure" and "applied" psychology

Many psychologists are concerned only with *pure science*—that is, knowledge for the sake of knowledge. Their chief activities are teaching and research. Some of their investigations are scarcely distinguishable from the work of their colleagues in the older sciences. Like physicists, they are interested in the physical aspects of the environment, particularly the way various forms of energy affect our sense organs and therefore the way we perceive the world. Like physiologists, they seek further information about the structure and functioning of the body and brain. Like chemists and medical researchers, they examine chemical substances that influence our nervous system and our emotions. They are interested in lower organisms as well as people—*organism* meaning any living creature—because many studies can be made with animals that would be unethical with human beings. An example is research on punishment, which has shown that its effects can be much more complex and harmful than was ever suspected.

Most of the "pure" psychologists, however, deal directly with all the

Figure 1-1 The field of environmental psychology *Study of how such things as water pollution, dirty air, and noise affect behavior and the quality of life.*

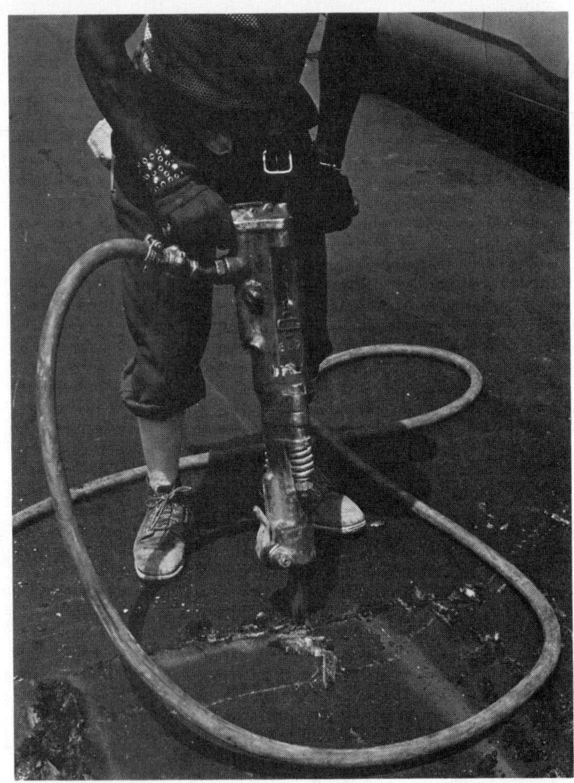

many forms that human behavior takes. They study the ways people act under different circumstances—and have found that our behavior depends to a surprising degree on where we are and whom we are with. They examine the various ways people learn, remember or forget, acquire motives, get along or clash with other people, encounter conflict and stress, and either cope successfully with their problems or lapse into abnormal behavior.

Many psychologists are chiefly concerned not so much with pure science, or the discovery of knowledge, as with *applied science,* or using the knowledge to help society carry on its everyday tasks, tackle its problems, and improve the quality of life. *School psychologists* test pupils, analyze learning problems, and evaluate teaching methods, the curriculum, textbooks, and educational films. *Industrial psychologists* help select and train workers and improve working conditions, employee morale, and staff cooperation.

Environmental psychologists are especially concerned with ecological problems like smog, water pollution, crowding, and noise (see Figure 1-1)—and with helping our industrial society maintain an environment that preserves the balance of nature and enables humanity and other organisms to continue to thrive. *Community psychologists,* sometimes called specialists in *community mental health,* are concerned with the social environment and the way schools and other institutions might better serve individual human needs.

Clinical psychology and counseling

Most applied psychologists, indeed the largest single group of psychologists of all, use the findings of the science to help people solve the various problems that trouble so many in our society from time to time—everything from deciding on a suitable line of work to coping with sexual maladjustments and crippling anxieties. Of all professionally trained psychologists in the nation, nearly half are in this particular field of applied psychology (Jones, 1969).

A psychologist administers a personality test—one of the procedures in counseling and clinical psychology.

A clinical psychologist (wearing a tie) conducts a session in group therapy.

Some members of this group practice *psychological counseling,* which is assistance to people who need guidance on such temporary problems as difficulties in school or choice of a vocation. In their search for the best solution, counselors often administer tests that have been developed by psychology, for everything from general intelligence to aptitude for specific tasks. One of psychology's most important findings, as you will see in Chapter 6, is that people are usually very good at doing some things but only mediocre to poor at others—and one secret of success, in both school and jobs, is to take advantage of your own particular strengths. Psychological counselors attempt to discover and encourage these strengths.

Some counselors specialize in helping married couples overcome difficulties that are caused not by deep-seated personality problems but by poor communication or inability to agree on financial or recreational priorities. These marriage counselors sometimes work with individual couples, sometimes with groups.

Clinical psychology is the diagnosis and treatment of psychological disorders of a more pervasive nature—all the symptoms that are popularly labeled "neurotic." Clinical psychologists, like marriage counselors, sometimes work with individuals, sometimes with groups. They use the technique called *psychotherapy*—or treatment through discussing problems, trying to get at the root of them, and modifying attitudes, emotional responses, and behavior.

Psychotherapy began with Sigmund Freud, an Austrian physician and neurologist, who asked his troubled patients to lie on a couch (see Figure 1-2) and talk about themselves, their experiences, and what was troubling them, simply letting their thoughts roam in any direction. By analyzing the patients' flow of discussion as described in Chapter 13, Freud tried to discover the origin of the problems and eventually lead his patients to understand and overcome them.

Psychotherapy was originally the sole province of specialists who, like

Figure 1-2 The birthplace of psychotherapy *It was in this room, on this couch, that psychoanalysis began. The photograph was made in the office of Sigmund Freud about 1895.*

Freud, were physicians with advanced training in *psychoanalysis,* as Freud's method is called. The first psychologists who entered the field also used Freud's technique, and many of today's clinical psychologists continue to be strongly influenced by Freudian theory. But others have developed different methods of approaching the special problems of the individuals they are trying to help. There are now far more clinical psychologists than psychoanalysts in the United States, using a wide array of techniques that will also be described in Chapter 13.

How psychology studies human behavior

In any science, the methods of investigation depend largely on the subject matter. Chemistry, dealing with substances that can be seen, felt, tasted, and manipulated, uses very direct methods. The chemist can simply put two substances together in a test tube, see what happens, and measure and analyze the result. Astronomy has to use more indirect methods. It cannot in any way manipulate the stars and planets. It must be content to observe them through telescopes or through the eyes of cameras and television equipment sent on space capsules to Venus and Mars.

Because behavior takes such a wide variety of forms, psychologists have had to improvise. No single method can be applied to all the activities that interest the science. Therefore psychologists have had to adopt a number of different ways of studying their subject matter—and they are constantly seeking new ways. The most prominent methods of study now in use are described in the following pages.

Observation

In many cases, psychologists do what astronomers do—that is, observe events pertinent to the science, such as the actual behavior of people in various kinds of social situations. To what extent, for example, is the way we behave toward other people dictated by how wealthy or important we think they are? One clue was found in a study in which psychologists observed how motorists behaved toward another driver who was slow to start and held up traffic when the light changed from red to green. If the offending driver was in an old rattletrap, it was found that the motorist behind was quick to honk in protest. If the slow-moving driver was in a shiny new luxury car, other motorists were much more patient (Doob and Gross, 1968).

In a sense all human beings constantly use the technique of observation. Everybody observes the behavior of other people and draws some conclusions from their actions. If we note that a woman student rarely speaks up in class and blushes easily in social situations, we conclude that she is shy, and we treat her accordingly. (We may try to put her at ease, or, if we feel so inclined, we may enjoy embarrassing her and making her squirm.) Psychologists make their observations in a more disciplined fashion. They try to describe behavior objectively and exactly, and they are loath to jump to conclusions about the motives behind it.

In studying behavior through observation, psychologists usually try to remain aloof from what is going on in order to avoid influencing events in any way. They practice what is called *naturalistic observation,* in which they try to be as inconspicuous and anonymous as possible, lest their very presence affect the behavior they are studying. Sometimes they even arrange to be unseen, as illustrated in Figure 1-3. Some of our most valuable knowledge about the behavior of infants and the way they develop has come from observers who used this method. The famous Masters and Johnson findings on sexual response were obtained in part in this manner.

At other times, psychologists engage in *participant observation.* They take an active part in a social situation—sometimes deliberately play-acting to see how other people behave toward someone who seems unusually withdrawn or hostile. Or they may participate in an encounter group to study their own as well as other people's reactions.

Interviews and case histories

Another way to discover how people behave and feel is to ask them—and therefore psychologists often use the *interview method,* questioning subjects in depth about their life experiences. Perhaps the best-known studies made through interviews are those of Alfred Kinsey, who became interested in human sexual behavior when some of his students at Indiana University asked him for advice. When he went to the university library for information, he found many books of opinion about sexual behavior but almost none that shed any light on the kind and frequency of sexual experiences men and women actually had in real life. So Kinsey determined to find out, and the only possible way seemed to be to interview as many men and women as he could and ask them about their sexual feelings and experiences from childhood on, as he is

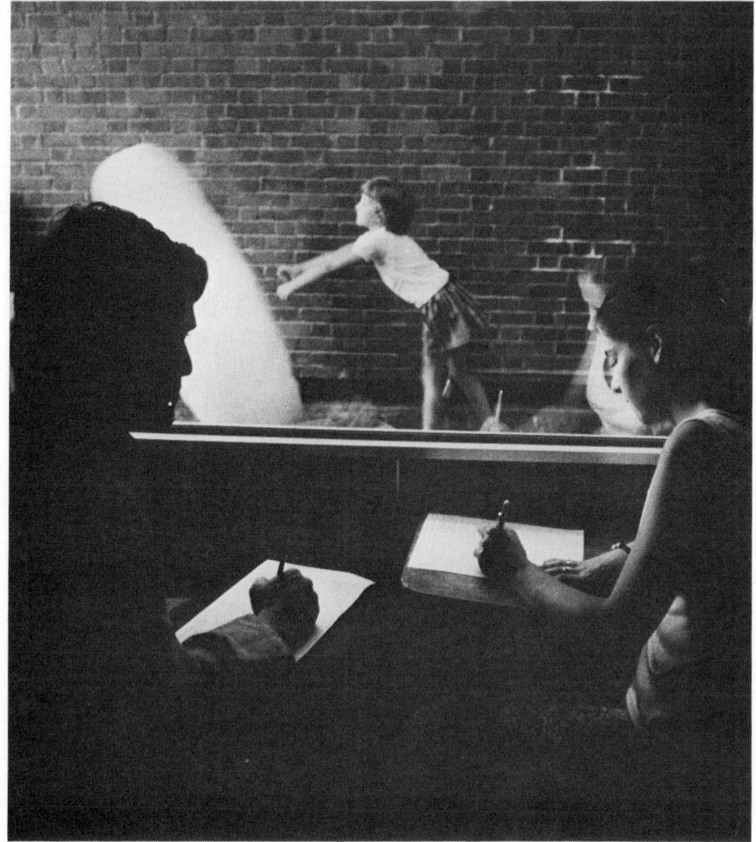

Figure 1-3 Invisible observers study child behavior *Unseen behind a one-way mirror, investigators use the method of naturalistic observation to study a child at play. To the observers outside the room, the wall panel looks like a sheet of clear glass. To the child inside, it looks like a mirror.*

shown doing in Figure 1-4. His well-known reports on male and female sexual behavior, discussed in Chapter 9, were the result.

A special application of the interview method is the *case history,* in which many years of a person's life are reconstructed to show how various behavior patterns have developed. Case histories are particularly useful in revealing the origins of abnormal behavior. Indeed some forms of psychotherapy rely on building up a long and detailed case history as an aid to understanding and correcting the client's problems.

Questionnaires and opinion surveys

Closely related to the interview is the *questionnaire,* which is especially useful in gathering information quickly from large numbers of people. A questionnaire is a set of written questions that can be answered easily, usually with a check mark. To produce accurate results, a questionnaire must be worded with extreme care. Indeed the creation of a reliable questionnaire is a fine art, for the slightest change in the way the questions are worded may completely distort the results.

Questionnaires and interviews are sometimes challenged on the ground that people may not respond truthfully. Kinsey's work, for example, has been attacked by critics who doubt that people would be honest

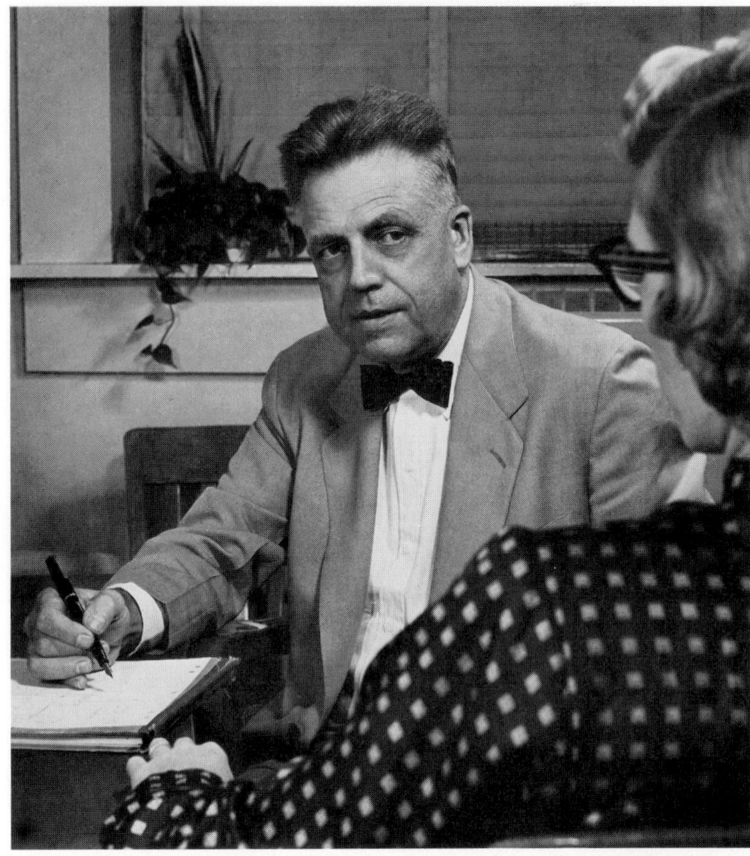

Figure 1-4 A Kinsey interview *Alfred Kinsey conducts one of the nearly 8,000 interviews on which he based his monumental book* Sexual Behavior in the Human Female.

about their sexual behavior. But experienced investigators have many ways of spotting people who are lying or exaggerating. Perhaps interviews and questionnaires do not always reveal the complete truth. When carefully planned and conducted, however, they can be extremely useful.

Questionnaires and interviews find a special use in the study of public opinion, in which psychologists are also active. Scientific methods of choosing a sample of people to poll, and analyzing the results, have made it possible to show how all the people in the United States are divided on any controversial issue, within a few percentage points of possible error, by questioning a mere 1,500 or so.

Public opinion surveys are a valuable contribution to the democratic process because they provide an accurate picture of how citizens actually feel about such issues as taxation, defense expenditures, foreign policy, abortion, and laws regulating sexual conduct and the use of drugs. Before such information was available, there was no accurate way to gauge public opinion—and often small but vociferous minorities, by waging intense publicity campaigns, were able to convince politicians that they represented the majority view. Now many congressmen and other political leaders base their votes on the will of the majority (which is often unorganized and silent) as expressed in the polls.

Some well-known, though less important, uses of public opinion surveys include predictions of election results and the Nielsen ratings of the popularity of television shows. Business firms use surveys to measure public response to new products and to sales and advertising campaigns.

Tests and measurements

Among the oldest tools of psychology are the *tests* it has developed for many human characteristics, abilities, and achievements. You have probably taken a number of such tests—for example, the Scholastic Aptitude Tests, or SAT, which is a form of intelligence test, or examinations that showed your elementary and high school teachers how your progress in reading or mathematics compared with the national average. When applying for a job you may be asked to take tests that psychologists have devised for ability at specific tasks, ranging from clerical work to being an astronaut. If you have occasion to visit a clinical psychologist, you may be tested for various personality traits.

The construction of truly scientific tests—which actually measure what they are supposed to measure and do so accurately and consistently—is much more difficult than is commonly supposed. Many of the so-called psychological tests in newspapers and magazines, which claim to tell you how happy, self-fulfilled, or neurotic you are, or how good you are likely to be as a husband, wife, or parent, have no value at all. They are simply parlor games dreamed up out of thin air by some nonpsychologist—and any score you may make on them, good or bad, is not to be taken seriously. Even psychology's best tests have weaknesses despite all the scientific knowledge and effort that have gone into them. But they also have their uses, and the search goes on constantly for new and better versions.

Besides trying to develop tests of psychological traits, psychologists are also interested in the *measurement* of any and all physical characteristics that may have a bearing on behavior. They have found, for example, that feelings of hunger are caused not by activity of the stomach, as popularly supposed, but by measurable changes in the composition of the bloodstream. They have measured the size and activity of the glands that help create emotions, and the way emotional arousal produces changes in heart rate, blood pressure, and breathing. They have identified some of the chemicals, produced in nerve endings, that transmit nervous impulses—and have found how irregularities in the production of these chemicals play a part in mood, strange states of consciousness like those produced by using marijuana or LSD, and abnormal behavior.

Measurements, individual differences, and the normal curve

Psychology's tests and measurements have been particularly helpful in adding to our knowledge of *individual differences.* They have shown that every person is indeed unique and that all kinds of physical and psychological traits, from height and muscular strength to intelligence and emotional sensitivity, vary over a wide range from small to large, low to high, and weak to strong.

In studying what tests and measurements show about individual dif-

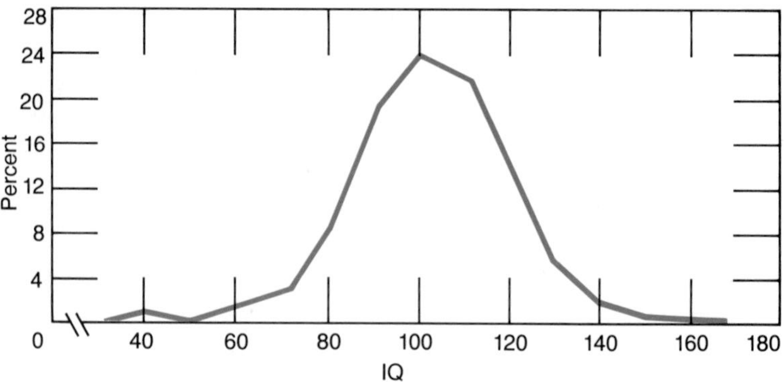

Figure 1-5 Individual differences in IQ *The graph was obtained by testing the IQs of a large number of people in the United States. Note how many people scored right around the average of 100. (A total of 46.5 percent showed IQs between 90 and 109.) Note also how the number falls off rapidly from the midpoint to the lower and upper extremes. Fewer than 1 percent of all people showed IQs under 60 and only 1.33 percent were at 140 or over (Terman and Merrill, 1937).*

ferences, the science relies heavily on mathematical techniques known as *psychological statistics,* which are described in an appendix to the book. One of the most important findings has been the discovery that almost all human traits, from height and weight to intelligence, fall into a similar pattern. In height, for example, the measurements for adult American men range all the way from around 3 feet to around 8 feet. But most cluster around the average, which is now about 5 feet 9 inches, and the number found at each point in the range goes down steadily with each inch up or down from the average. Note the graph in Figure 1–5, which shows how IQs as measured by intelligence tests range from below 40 to above 160—but with the majority falling close to the average of 100, and only a very few at the extreme low or high levels.

The graph line in Figure 1-5 is so typical of the results generally found in all tests and measurements that it is known as the *normal curve of distribution.* The message of the curve is that in almost all measurable traits, physical and psychological, most people are average or close to it, some are a fair distance above or below, and a few are very far above or below. Those who are about average have a lot of company. Those who are far removed from the average—in intelligence the geniuses and the mentally retarded, in height the seven-footers and the four-footers—are rare.

The curve of normal distribution helps explain a great deal about behavior, including the general similarities displayed by most people and the wide deviations shown by a few others. The curve applies to performance in school. (Most students have to do an average amount of struggling; some can make A's without turning a hair; some cannot handle the work at all.) It applies to musical talent, athletic skill, and interest or lack of interest in sex—as well as to the intensity of emotional arousal and the strength of motives for achievement, power, and friendship. These and many other individual differences are the reason you cannot generalize about humanity as a whole from your own traits—especially on a matter where you happen to fall at an unusually low or high point in the curve.

The method of correlation

One question that has interested psychologists almost from the beginning of the science is: Do children resemble their parents in intelligence? This is a question that has many implications for study of the part played in human behavior by heredity and environment—which, as will be seen a little later, is one of the basic issues in psychology. How would you try to go about answering it?

A person totally untrained in the methods of science might jump to conclusions based on personal experience: "No, obviously not. My neighbors the Smiths are both smart people—they went to college and have good jobs—but their two kids are having a terrible time in school." Or, "Certainly. My neighbors the Joneses are geniuses and their two daughters are the smartest kids in their school."

A more sophisticated approach would be to look at a much larger sample of children and parents than provided by just the Smiths or the Joneses—and give both generations intelligence tests rather than to rely on personal impression of how smart they seemed to be. This would be a good start toward a scientific answer. But the results would be difficult to interpret, because the tests would show all kinds of contradictions. One mother and father, both with IQs of 120, turn out to have an only child whose IQ is also 120—but another couple with the same IQ has an only child with an IQ of 90. One mother at 95 and father at 85 have an only child with an IQ of 90—but a similar couple has a child at 125. Even in the same family the tests would sometimes show three children with IQs as far apart as 85, 115, and 135. Without some method of analyzing and interpreting the test results, any scientific answer to the question would still be elusive.

In this type of situation, psychologists apply another statistical tool called *correlation.* This is a mathematical method used to examine two different measurements (such as the IQs of parents and the IQs of their children)—and to determine, from what would otherwise seem hopelessly jumbled numbers, what relationship if any actually exists between the two. The method, which is explained in the appendix on statistics, boils down the figures into a *coefficient of correlation* ranging from 0.00 (no relationship at all) to 1.00 (a one-to-one or absolutely perfect relationship). In the case of parents and children, the coefficient of correlation between IQs has generally been found to indicate a fairly high though by no means perfect relationship.

The advantages and pitfalls of correlation

The method of correlation has provided a great deal of psychological knowledge that would not otherwise be available. For example, it has given developmental psychologists many clues about the relationship of childhood behavior to behavior in later life. Do children who are passive at the ages of 6 to 10 tend to be withdrawn in adulthood? The correlation is around .28 for males, .48 for females. Do children who are prone to displays of anger tend to exhibit disorganized behavior as adults? The correlation is about .42 for males, only about .12 for females.

You will find many correlations mentioned throughout the book—but one word of caution is in order. Correlations reveal the existence and extent of relationships, but they do not necessarily indicate cause and effect. Unless carefully interpreted, they can be misleading. There is a high correlation between the number of permanent teeth in children and their ability to answer increasingly difficult questions on intelligence tests. But this does not mean that having more teeth causes increased mental ability. The correlation is high because increasing age accounts for both the new teeth and the mental development.

The ultimate method: experimentation

One other method of investigation is so important and productive that it deserves a separate section of the chapter. This is the *experiment*—in which the psychologist makes a careful and rigidly controlled examination of cause and effect. The experimenter sets up one set of conditions and determines what kind of behavior takes place under those conditions. Then the conditions are changed—and the effect of the changes, if any, is measured.

The experimental method has many applications. It has been used to study numerous aspects of how we learn or fail to learn—for example, the effect of practice of various kinds under various conditions and the question of whether devoting study time to recitation as well as to reading a textbook is an effective technique. The experimental method has also disclosed much of our present knowledge about the part played by familiarity in our likes and dislikes for other people, as well as many other factors in our social relationships. Experiments on animals, where the activity of the nervous system can be measured with electrodes, have produced many findings about the functions of brain structures and the sense organs.

Independent and dependent variables

Every psychological experiment is an attempt to discover whether behavior—in any of its many forms—changes when conditions change. Both the possible behavior change and the change in conditions are called *variables.* The change in conditions is set up and controlled by the experimenter. Note the example illustrated in Figure 1-6, where the change in conditions is the fact that the experimenter or an assistant deliberately sits down right next to a person seated on a park bench. Since the change is manipulated by the experimenter and in no way dependent on anything the subject does or does not do, it is called the *independent variable.*

The behavior that occurs in response to the independent variable—in this case the fact that the subject almost immediately got up and went away—is called the *dependent variable.* In all experiments, the experimenter arranges to change the independent variable, then measures the dependent variable as exhibited by a group of subjects. The results for the bench-sitting subjects are illustrated in Figure 1-7. The graph shows that changing the independent variable caused a pronounced change in the behavior of a significant number of the subjects—indicating that many people like to have "elbow room" and get uncomfortable when crowded.

Figure 1-6 An experiment in crowding produces a two-minute drama *At top, a man who is about to become the subject of the experiment sits alone on a park bench, enjoying his newspaper. Middle, an experimenter sits down beside him. Bottom, the man with the newspaper has left. The photos reconstruct what happened frequently in a study of how much "elbow room" people prefer and the effects of crowding, the full results of which are illustrated in Figure 1-7.*

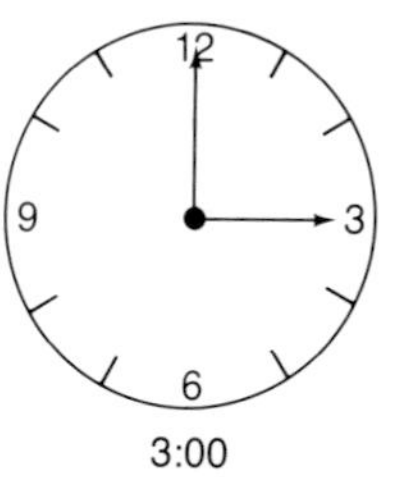

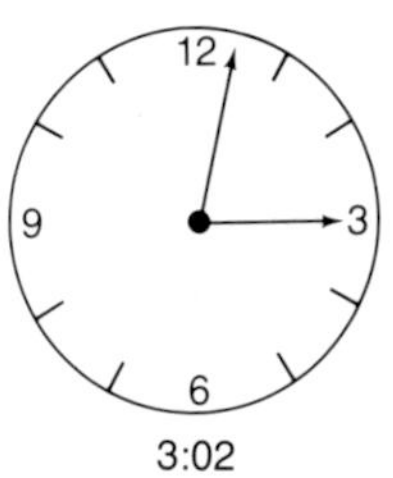

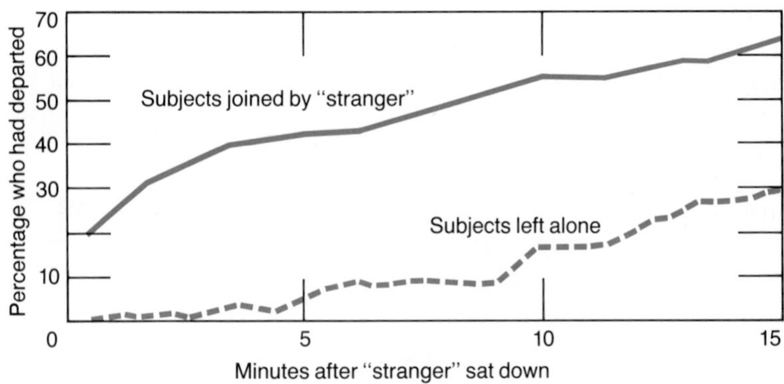

Figure 1-7 How the unwanted experimenter drove the bench-sitters away *In the study illustrated in Figure 1-6, it turned out that 40 percent of people sitting alone on a park bench left within 3 minutes after the experimenter or an assistant sat down beside them. By the end of 15 minutes, 60 percent had moved on. Their departures were clearly prompted by the unwanted "stranger"—because almost all similar bench-sitters observed at the same time, but left alone, remained for at least 5 minutes and 70 percent were still there after 15 minutes (after Sommers, 1969).*

The bench-sitting study is a good example of the way psychological experiments can be conducted outside the confines of a laboratory—often, as in this case, with the help of the technique of observation. Such experiments, which are becoming increasingly common because they offer a direct approach to "the problems and insights that a study of the everyday world provides," frequently produce findings that go far beyond those obtained under laboratory conditions where all the influential factors in a real-life situation cannot be duplicated—or that may even be at odds with laboratory results (Baddeley, 1981).

Experimental and control groups

It is important to note that the graph in Figure 1-7 has two lines—one for the bench-sitters who were joined by the "stranger," the other for bench-sitters who were left alone. This is because the findings would not mean much if only the first of these two groups had been observed. True, many of these bench-sitters moved away, often very quickly. But how many of them were planning to leave anyway—and would have walked off even if no one had joined them?

The problem was solved by observing the second group and timing how long they remained on the bench. Thus there were (a) an *experimental group* for whom the independent variable was the intrusion by the stranger, and (b) a *control group* who were left alone. The wide difference in behavior between the experimental group and the control group became a clear indication of the effect of the independent variable.

In the bench-sitting experiment the subjects in both groups had to be selected by chance, since they were unknown to the experimenter and were not even aware they were taking part in a psychological study. In most experiments, however, the experimental and control subjects are chosen with great care. Note, for example, Figure 1-8, showing the results of an experiment that demonstrated the value of recitation as a study technique. The results would have been meaningless if the experimental group, which used recitation, had been made up entirely of good students and the control group of poor students. Instead the experimenter had to make sure that the two groups were evenly matched. In experiments on learning, the subjects have to be approximately equal in such matters as average age, years of school completed, grades, and IQ, and they have to study for the same amount of time and under similar conditions. Often it is also important to match the experimental and control groups for sex, race, and social background. Only in this way can experimenters make sure that the independent variable they are trying to study (in Figure 1-8, the use of recitation) is the only one that could have produced the change in the dependent variable (in Figure 1-8, the number of syllables remembered).

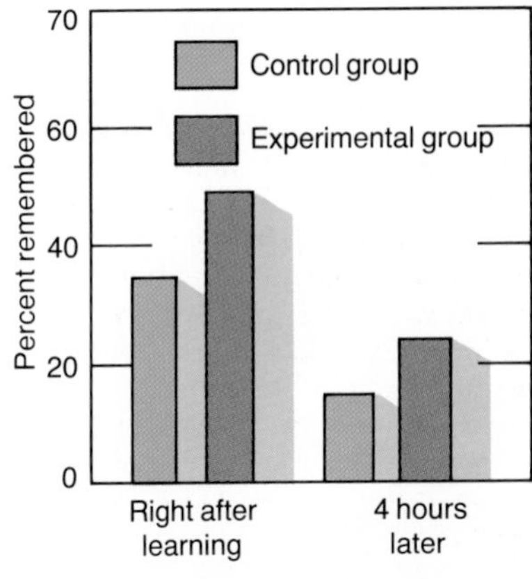

Figure 1-8 Experimental group (recitation) versus control group (no recitation) *In an experiment on the effectiveness of recitation, both groups spent the same amount of time studying a list of nonsense syllables (like KOV, TUS, and PIM). But the experimental group devoted 20 percent of the time to reciting the syllables, while the control group did no reciting at all. As the bars show, the experimental group demonstrated significantly greater memory for the list, both immediately after the study period and several hours later (Gates, 1917). For the precautions that had to be taken in selecting the two groups, see the text.*

Single-blind and double-blind experiments

In an experiment on the effects of marijuana on driving ability, psychologists would divide their subjects into an experimental group that was under the influence of the drug and a control group that was not. But a further precaution would be necessary—for the subjects' performance might be affected by their knowledge that they had taken the drug and their expectations of how it might affect them. To avoid this possibility, it would be important to keep the subjects from knowing whether they had received the drug. This could be done by giving half the subjects an injection of the drug's active ingredient, THC, and the other half an injection of a salt solution that would have no effect, without telling them which was which. This method, in which subjects cannot know whether they belong to the experimental group or the control group, is called the *single-blind technique.*

There is the further danger that the experimenter's own ratings of the subjects' performance might be affected by knowing which of them had taken the drug and which had not. To make the experiment foolproof, the drug or salt solution would have to be injected by a third party, so that even the experimenter would have no way of knowing which subjects had received which kind of injection. This method, in which neither the subject nor the experimenter knows who is in the experimental group and who is in the control group, is called the *double-blind technique.* It is particularly valuable in studying the effects of drugs, including the tranquilizers and antidepressants used to treat mental disturbances. It is also used in any other experiment where knowledge of the conditions might affect the judgment of the experimenter as well as the performance of the subjects.

As developed and refined over the years, and with the checks provided by such methods as use of a control group and the double-blind technique, the experiment is psychology's most powerful tool. For one thing, an experiment can be repeated by another experimenter at another time and in another place, ruling out the possibility that the results were accidental or influenced by the first experimenter's personality or preconceived notions of what would happen. (In this connection, a word frequently found in psychological literature is *replicate;* to replicate an experiment is to perform it again in the same manner and obtain the same results.) When facts have been established by the experimental method and verified time and again by other experimenters with other subjects, we can have great faith in their validity.

Wundt

Psychology in the past, present, and future

The psychological experiment—and psychology itself—has come a long way since the science began. At the start, the idea of taking a scientific approach to the study of behavior required a radical shift in human thinking and invention of brand-new techniques of study. Though chemists had been experimenting with the composition and transformation of elements and compounds, and physicists with the forces of motion, gravity, and electricity, no one had ever tried to experiment with human behavior. Moreover the early psychologists lacked the tools necessary for sophisticated exploration. They had no way of analyzing the activity of individual nerve cells or of the glands. They had no means of testing intelligence, motivation, or personality traits.

The year the science was founded is usually put at 1879, when Wilhelm Wundt opened the first psychological laboratory at Germany's University of Leipzig. Wundt had studied to be a physician, then, instead of practicing medicine, taught as a professor of physiology. But he soon lost interest, because he was much more concerned with human consciousness than with the workings of the body. His experiments, in retrospect, seem rather trivial. For example, he and his students spent hours in the laboratory listening to the click of a metronome—sometimes set fast and sometimes set slow, sounding only a few times or many—and analyzed their conscious reactions. They decided that a rapid series of clicks produced excitement and a slow series made them relaxed, and that they had slight feelings of tension before each click and of relief afterward.

Despite this modest beginning, the new science of psychology found an immediate and enthusiastic response. Wundt was the most popular professor at his university, and no classroom was big enough to hold all the students who wanted to hear his lectures. A few years later, similar acclaim came to Sir Francis Galton, one of the first British psychologists. Galton, who was interested in individual differences, invented numerous devices to test such traits as hearing, sense of smell, color vision, and ability to judge weights. At one time he set up his equipment at an International Health Exhibition in London—and people flocked in to be his subjects, gladly paying an entrance fee for the privilege. Even in those early years, when psychology was just taking a few tentative steps into the vast realm of human behavior, it captured the public's imagination.

Galton

William James, "mental life," and the era of introspection

Like Wundt, most of the pioneers concentrated on an attempt to discover the nature, origins, and significance of conscious experiences. Their chief method of investigation was *introspection*, or looking inward. They tried to analyze the processes that went on inside their minds, asked their subjects to do the same, and recorded their findings, as objectively as possible, for comparison with other observers.

The most prominent of the early American psychologists was William James, who came to the science from an unusual background. Like Wundt, he studied medicine but never practiced. Indeed he had a difficult time finding his true vocation. At one time he wanted to be an artist, then a chemist, and once he joined a zoological expedition to Brazil. In his late twenties he suffered a mental breakdown and went through a prolonged depression in which he seriously thought of committing suicide. But he recovered—largely, he believed, through what he called "an achievement of the will"—and went on to become a Harvard professor and prolific writer on psychology and philosophy.

James

James had no doubt about the mission of the new science. A textbook he wrote began with the words: "Psychology is the study of mental life." The distinguishing feature of this mental life, he felt, was that human beings constantly seek certain end results and must constantly choose among various methods of achieving them. In one passage he wrote:

> I would . . . if I could, be both handsome and fat and well-dressed, and make a million a year, be a wit, a *bon vivant,* and a lady-killer, as well as a philosopher, a philanthropist, statesman, warrior, and African explorer, as well as a "tone poet" and saint. But the thing is simply impossible. The millionaire's work would run counter to the saint's; the *bon vivant* and the philanthropist would trip each other up; the philosopher and the lady-killer could not well keep house in the same tenement of clay. Such different characters may conceivably at the outset of life be possible. But to make any of them actual, the rest must more or less be suppressed. . . . This is as strong an example as there is of selective industry of the mind (James, 1890).

As those words indicate, James was interested in the broad pattern of human strivings—the cradle-to-grave progress of human beings as thinking organisms who adopt certain goals and ambitions, including spiritual ones, and struggle in various ways to attain the goals or become reconciled to failure.

John Watson, conditioned reflexes, and the behaviorist revolution

Was William James perhaps more philosopher than psychologist? Was introspection really scientific or just another form of mere speculation about the human condition? These questions raised some nagging doubts as the years went on—and in 1913 another American, John Watson, revolutionized psychology by breaking completely with the school of introspection and founding the movement called *behaviorism.*

Watson

Watson declared that "mental life" is something that cannot be seen or measured and thus cannot be studied scientifically. Instead of trying to examine any such vague thing as "mental life" or consciousness, he concluded, psychologists should concentrate on actions that are plainly visible. In other words, he wanted the science to study what people *do,* not what they think.

Watson did not believe in anything like "free will," or the ability to control our own destiny. Instead he believed that everything we do is predetermined by our past experiences. He considered all human behavior to be a series of actions in which a *stimulus,* that is, an event in the environment, produces a *response,* that is, an observable muscular movement or some physiological reaction, such as increased heart rate or glandular secretion, that can also be observed and measured with the proper instruments. (For example, shining a bright light into the eye is a stimulus that causes an immediate response in which the pupil of the eye contracts. A loud and unexpected noise is a stimulus that usually causes the response of muscular contraction, or jumping, and increased heart rate.) Watson believed that through establishment of *conditioned reflexes,* a type of learning discussed in Chapter 3, almost any kind of stimulus can be made to produce almost any kind of response. Indeed he once said that he could take any dozen babies at birth and, by conditioning them in various ways, turn them into anything he wished—doctor, lawyer, beggar, or thief.

Even the existence of a human mind was doubted by Watson. He conceded that human beings had thoughts, but he believed that these were simply a form of talking to oneself, by making tiny movements of the vocal cords. He also conceded that people have what they call feelings, but he believed that these were only some form of conditioned response to a stimulus in the environment.

B. F. Skinner and the behaviorist era

For many decades behaviorism was the dominant force in psychology. Watson was succeeded as leader of the movement by B. F. Skinner, who has been chiefly interested in the learning process and has revised and expanded Watson's ideas. He has made many important contributions to our knowledge of how patterns of rewards and punishments produce and modify connections between many kinds of stimuli and responses and thus help control the organism's behavior—often in the most complex ways.

Skinner's best-known book is *Beyond Freedom and Dignity,* published in 1971. Here he argues that people possess neither of the two attributes mentioned in his title. To Skinner, people are not responsible for their conduct, neither to blame for their failures nor deserving of credit for their achievements. They are simply the creatures of their environment. Their behavior depends on the kinds of learning to which they have been subjected, particularly which of their actions have been rewarded. A "social engineer" aware of all the principles of learning could mold people into any form desired, whether for good or for evil.

Skinner

The behaviorists in general, in their effort to avoid introspective speculation and confine their investigations to forms of behavior that can be seen and measured, have tended to experiment with lower animals. Skinner built his principles of learning on the behavior of rats and pigeons. Other behaviorists have worked with various animals to explore such matters as motives, aggression, cooperation, conflicts, and even abnormal behavior. The thrust of the science was to find universal laws that applied to all organisms, rather than just to some unique and perhaps imaginary mental quality, spiritual superiority, or "achievement of the will" possessed by human beings.

The great contribution of the behaviorists has been to pull psychology back from the danger of becoming a mere branch of philosophic speculation, relying solely on an inward examination of a mental life that nobody but its possessor can see or examine. The behaviorists, with their search for simple, universal, and observable knowledge, pushed psychology into more disciplined channels—and the realization that a science must be objective and based on controlled experiments and measurements of behavior.

On the other hand, behaviorism was always controversial. Many psychologists rejected the idea that human beings are like mere pieces of machinery that automatically perform in a certain way whenever a certain button is pushed. In particular, they disagreed with Skinner's belief that we have no real freedom of choice or responsibility for our own actions. We do seem, as William James pointed out, to make choices. We have complicated thoughts, feelings, emotions, and attitudes that are difficult to explain through a simple push-button theory. Even in learning, there would appear to be a wide gap between a rat trying to run a maze and a college student studying a textbook containing all the rich meanings of human language. By ruling out any consideration of James's "mental life," behaviorism seemed to its critics to have put psychology into a straitjacket.

The Gestalt school of thought

One movement of considrable historic importance in the opposition to behaviorism was *Gestalt psychology*, which originated in Germany at about the same time Watson's ideas were becoming influential in the United States. The movement took its name from a German word that has no exact English equivalent. *Gestalt* is roughly translated as "pattern" or "configuration," but it means something more than that. The Gestalt school believed that in studying any psychological phenomenon, from a perceptual process to the human personality, it is essential to look at events considered *as a whole.* Indeed the Gestalt theories have often been summarized as maintaining that "the whole is greater than the sum of its parts."

On the matter of perception, for example, note Figure 1-9. If you look at the panel marked *a* in the upper left-hand corner, you see merely four miscellaneous lines. If asked to describe them, you might call them just "an arrangement of lines," or "four sticks," or "four sticks with spaces between them." These lines, however, can be put together in

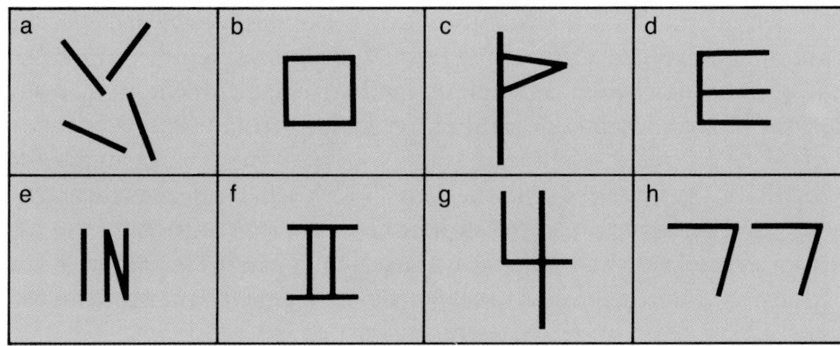

Figure 1-9 Some Gestalts that are far greater than the sum of their parts *The four little lines in a make no sense at all. But note how many significant forms they can take when rearranged into patterns, or Gestalts, as described in the text. You can probably create some other meaningful patterns from the same four-line raw materials.*

Figure 1-10 How the context, or surrounding, influences the Gestalt *What do you see in the left-hand drawing when you look where the arrow points? Certainly you do not say to yourself: "I see a head, a body, two arms, and two legs—and therefore I see a person." Instead, as the Gestalt psychologists emphasized, you take in the whole pattern and see the person without any effort at all. Moreover the drawing illustrates another Gestalt principle—the fact that the uniform, taxi, and hotel make you immediately aware that the person is a doorman. In the right-hand drawing, the same man in a different context becomes a military officer.*

various other ways. In *b* they become clearly and unmistakably a square, and in *c* a pennant or a flag on a golf course. In *d* they strike the eye immediately as a letter in the English alphabet, and in *e* they become a word. Or they can be seen as a Roman numeral (*f*), the number 4 (*g*), or even 77 (*h*). When you see these configurations, you no longer even think about the four basic parts from which they are constructed.

The Gestalt psychologists stressed not only the whole rather then the parts but also the importance of the entire situation, or context, in which the "whole" is found. A demonstration is shown in Figure 1-10. Note how your interpretation of the man pointed to by the arrows is dictated by the rest of what you see in the drawings. Though the Gestalt movement is no longer active, many of its ideas survive in today's emerging view of mental activity and human behavior in general as a pattern and a unity.

The rise of the cognitive school

In a sense the opposite directions taken by the behaviorists and the introspectionists were like the efforts of a gunner who first aims too far to the left, next too far to the right—and then, with the target bracketed, scores a direct hit. Both schools of thought were somewhat wide of the mark, yet both were essential to the growth of psychology into its present form. Many aspects of "mental life" have now been drawn back into the field of study—and psychologists in recent years have been busy exploring the human use of language, thinking, and memory, as well as human emotions, motives, and social relationships. Yet at the same time, thanks to the influence of Watson and Skinner, the study has become much more disciplined and systematic, relying on observations of actual behavior rather than mere speculation.

The trend today is toward what is called *cognitive psychology*—"cognitive" referring to all the ways in which we learn about our environment, store the knowledge in memory, think about it, and use it to act intelligently in new situations. These various forms of mental activity are often referred to as *information processing,* a term borrowed from computer science. They begin with what in a computer would be called the inputs—the raw data about the environment that we gather through our sense organs as they respond to light and sound waves, the mechanical forces of pressure and heat, and the chemical forces that cause sensations of taste and smell. Our brain then tries to make sense out of all this jumble of stimuli, comparing it to previous information and interpreting its significance (through the process of perception as described in Chapter 8). The information, thus transformed into meaningful patterns, is then stored in memory, where it is associated with other information to which it bears some relationship. We call on the information whenever we need it—as a computer would tap its memory bank—to help us think, understand, and solve problems.

Cognitive psychology and our "mental models of reality"

The cognitive psychologists reject the behaviorist proposal that people are mere passive creatures of the environment, responding unthinkingly to the world's stimuli. Instead they view the human organism as "an active seeker of knowledge and processor of information," from which it actively builds "mental representations of the world" (Klatzky, 1980). These *mental models of reality* are a core idea in cognitive psychology. Kenneth Craik, one of the founders of the school, has said that our mental picture of the world, plus our knowledge of our own possible actions, enables us to "try out various alternatives, conclude which is the best of them, react to future situations before they arise, use the knowledge of past events in dealing with the future, and in every way react in a much fuller, safer, and more competent manner" (Craik, 1952).

To put this another way, the cognitive psychologists think of the human mind as a sort of mental executive that organizes the world's stimuli into perceptual patterns (for example, perceiving a girl or a boy rather than a collection of arms, legs, and body), makes comparisons, and processes the information it receives into new forms and categories. It discovers meanings and uses its stored knowledge to find new principles that aid in constructive thinking, making judgments, and deciding on appropriate behavior. These ideas have influenced most of today's psychologists in one way or another, in all the branches of the science from the study of the senses to psychotherapy.

The humanistic school

Psychology has of course taken many other directions since Wundt opened the first laboratory, as would be expected in a science embracing such a wide field of inquiry. One of today's prominent movements is *humanistic psychology,* which also stems in part from the Gestalt school. Like the Gestalt psychologists, the humanists prefer to view the human personality as a pattern and an entity. To try to study human behavior by breaking it down into fragments, such as individual responses to individual stimuli, is regarded as futile and indeed a display of "disrespect" for the unique quality of the human spirit (Matson, 1971).

Humanistic psychologists take the view that we human beings are totally different from other organisms. We are distinguished by the fact that we have values and goals and seek to express ourselves, grow, fulfill ourselves, and find peace and happiness. Our thoughts and aspirations, which Watson considered inappropriate for study, appear to the humanistic psychologists to be the most important of all aspects of behavior.

The humanists take a broad and very hopeful view of the true quality of human nature, its accomplishments, and its potentialities. They believe that human beings are strongly motivated to realize their possibilities for creativity, dignity, and self-worth. The techniques of psychotherapy used by humanistic psychologists are built around the assumption that people will always grow in a constructive way if their environment permits them to do so.

The humanistic psychologists are in some ways more oriented toward philosophy, literature, and religion than toward the investigative methods of the sciences. Many humanistic psychologists have been associated with efforts to expand consciousness and achieve unity of mind and body through encounter groups, sensitivity training, and other kinds of mental and physical "reaching out."

Other approaches

A school of thought related in many ways to the humanistic movement is *existential psychology,* which also emphasizes the quality of the human spirit. The existential psychologists, in direct contrast to Skinner, believe strongly in the importance of free will. They maintain that the events in our lives do not control our destinies—for what really counts is our own attitude toward the events, which we are free to choose for ourselves. We are all responsible for our own behavior since we can make our own decisions and thus control our own attitudes and thoughts and rise above even the most adverse events in our environment. The techniques of psychotherapy used by existential psychologists are designed to create a sense of identity and self-determination that fosters commitment and love. (If you want to learn more about the existential approach, which is difficult to summarize, see the book by Rollo May cited in the list of recommended readings at the end of the chapter.)

Many psychologists, past and present, have been influenced in various ways by the *psychoanalytic school* established by Sigmund Freud. Even those who are skeptical of the value of psychoanalysis in therapy accept some of his ideas about personality and the way it is formed. Particularly influential has been his idea that behavior is often influenced by *unconscious processes,* especially motives of which we are unaware.

All in all the science has had a remarkably rich history, and it would be impossible to list all the prominent figures and influential ideas that have made important contributions. The progress has been especially rapid in recent years, as knowledge has built on knowledge, and many of the facts and terms you will find in the course were unknown even a few decades ago. Each new finding, of course, raises new questions and demands new explanations, and it is unlikely that psychologists will ever complete their exploration of the vast domain they have entered. But they have gone a long way toward probing the very core of human nature and human experience, including mental processes and behavior in all their great variety from a baby's first faltering attempts at learning to an adult's complex emotions, strivings, conflicts, and social adjustments or maladjustments.

How behavior is guided by heredity and environment

One of the important advances in our understanding of behavior has come through the rapid strides made in this century by *behavior genetics*, the study of the way organisms inherit traits that help control their conduct. Among these inherited traits are the structure of the brain, the ability of the nervous system to produce various chemicals essential to the transmission of nervous impulses and normal functioning of the brain, and the way the glands manufacture substances that affect the nervous system and help create emotions and mood.

It is obvious that the inherited structure of the human body and brain is responsible for many aspects of our behavior. It enables us, unlike lower animals, to speak a rich language that we use to communicate with one another. It gives us a superior skill at most forms of information processing. On the other hand, it also sets limits. Because of the way our brain operates, with its messages traveling at only a tiny fraction of the speed of electricity, we cannot possibly make complex mathematical calculations as fast as a computer. Because of the way our nervous systems and glands cooperate, we cannot possibly live our lives without experiencing emotions—which, though they often exhilarate us, may also plunge us into fear or despair and make us incapable of performing with the computer's cold accuracy. Our sense organs, which are part of the nervous system, are incapable of detecting certain kinds of light waves that are visible even to a bee or high-pitched sounds that are clearly audible to a dog. The structure of our bodies makes it impossible for us to live underwater like a fish or fly like a bird. Heredity has provided us with our own kind of physical equipment, and we have to live our lives within its bounds.

Psychologists—and philosophers before them—have always been interested in the question of just how much influence heredity has on our behavior. Do the traits with which we are born have a lifelong effect on our actions, learning ability, intelligence, and indeed entire personality, including tendencies toward emotional and mental disturbances? Or do the inborn traits just provide the raw material of our behavior, which is then shaped into its eventual form by our environment (which is the sum total of all the varying influences exerted from the moment of birth by our families, society as a whole, and the physical circumstances of our lives)?

Does intelligence run in families? It does in this New York family in which all six children have IQs at the genius level.

The relative importance of heredity and environment has been a topic of considerable debate. William James, for example, believed that much of our behavior is regulated to a great extent by powerful human instincts present at birth—including pugnacity, rivalry, sociability, shyness, curiosity, acquisitiveness, and love. Watson, on the other hand, believed the newborn child can be turned into almost any kind of adult through conditioned reflexes established by the environment. The debate is often called the *nature-nurture* controversy, and will be referred to often by that term throughout the book. It still continues—though it has been modified greatly by modern findings about heredity.

The key to heredity: chromosomes and genes

We now have considerable knowledge about the mechanics of heredity, which explain how life is passed on from one generation to the next. A new life begins, of course, when the egg cell produced by the mother is penetrated and fertilized by the sperm cell of the father, as shown in Figure 1-11. The two join into a single cell—and this single cell eventually grows into a human baby. It does so by a process of division. The single cell splits and becomes two living cells, then each of these in turn splits to make four, and so on.

Thus the original fertilized egg cell must somehow contain the whole key of life. Something inside it must direct the entire development from single cell to the baby at birth (whose body contains about 200 billion cells organized into the various specialized parts of the body) and beyond that from infant to fully matured adult. Something in it must also determine the inherited characteristics of the individual to be born—the color of the eyes, the facial features, the potential size, and possibly the psychological characteristics.

This "something" is the *chromosomes*—the tiny structures shown in Figure 1-12 as seen under a powerful microscope. The original fertilized cell contains 46 chromosomes. When the cell splits, the chromosomes also divide. Thus each cell of the newborn baby as well as of the fully grown human body contains exactly the same 46 chromosomes that were present in the fertilized egg with which life began. The chromosomes hold the key to the development of the human being and are the carriers of heredity.

Each chromosome, though tiny in itself, is composed of hundreds of even smaller structures called *genes,* each of which is a molecule of a complex chemical called DNA (deoxyribonucleic acid). Scientists have managed to extract a single gene from a chromosome of one of the lower

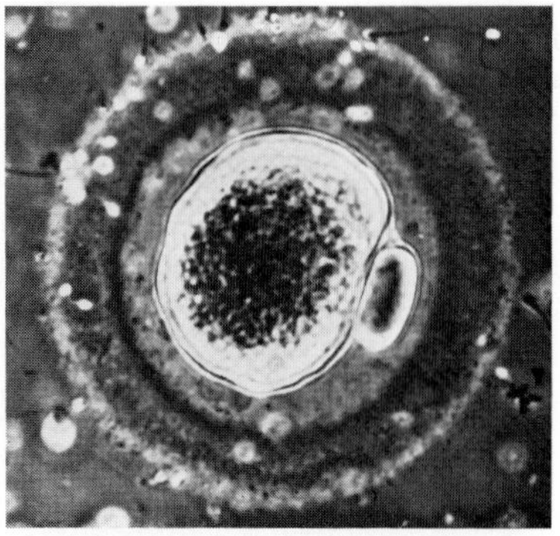

Figure 1-11 The moment of conception *The large round object is a human egg cell. At this moment it is being fertilized by a male sperm cell that has worked its way deep inside and can no longer be seen. Other sperm cells, with small heads and long tails, are also attempting to pierce the egg but have arrived too late.*

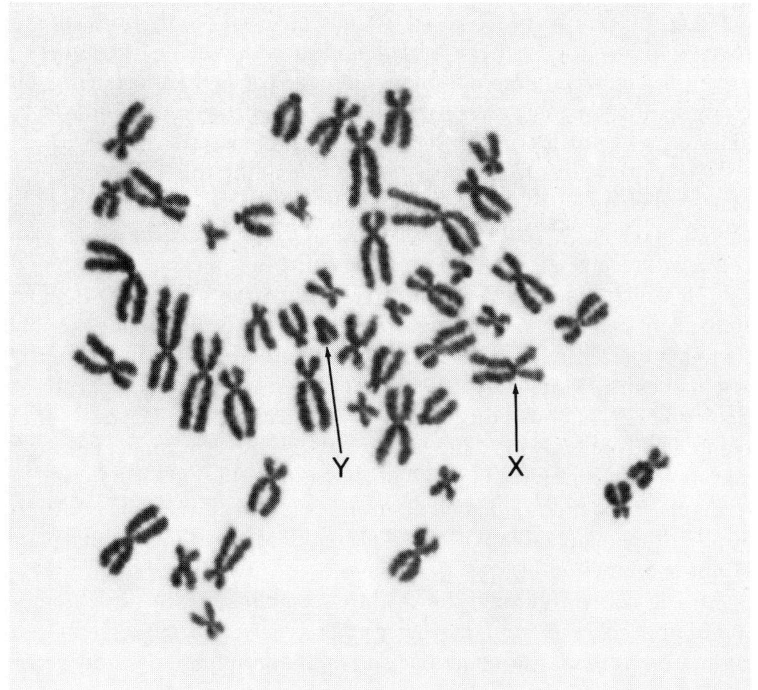

Figure 1-12 The human chromosomes *When enlarged 750 times, human chromosomes look like this. These are from a man's skin cell, broken down and spread out into a single layer under the microscope. The labels point out the X and Y chromosomes, which determine sex as will be explained later in the chapter.*

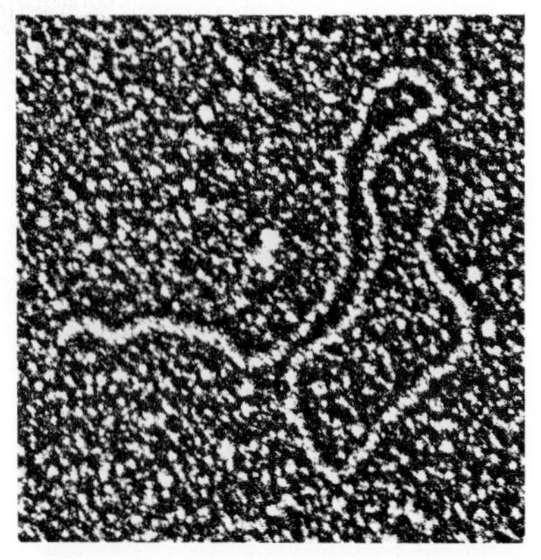

Figure 1-13 A single gene *The first gene ever isolated and photographed under high magnification was this twisted strand taken from one of the bacteria frequently found in the human intestinal tract. It is 55 millionths of an inch long (Shapiro et al., 1969).*

organisms and, through a microscope, take the photograph of it shown in Figure 1-13.

Human genes have not yet been isolated, examined, or counted. But it is believed that there are at least 20,000 of them in each human cell and perhaps as many as 125,000. Each gene is believed to be responsible—sometimes by itself but more often in combination with other genes—for some particular phase of development. The genes direct the process by which some cells of the body grow into skin and others grow into nerves or muscles, also the process by which cells become grouped into organs such as the heart, the stomach, and the liver. They control such characteristics as the color of the eyes and the length of the bones. Our heredity depends on those many thousands of genes, organized into our 46 chromosomes. It is the particular kinds of genes we possess that make us develop into human beings and into the individual human being that each of us is.

Where we get our genes

In the living cell, the 46 chromosomes are not arranged as they were shown in Figure 1-12, where they were deliberately separated and spread out to pose for their microscopic portrait. Instead they are arranged in 23 pairs. In each pair the two chromosomes are similar in structure and function and are composed of genes of similar structure and function. For purposes of exposition, we can think of them as pairs A1-A2, B1-B2, C1-C2, D1-D2, and so on.

In growth, the 23 pairs of chromosomes with their matched genes duplicate themselves exactly, so that each new cell also has pairs A1-A2, B1-B2, C1-C2, D1-D2, and so on. But the cells of reproduction—the mother's egg cell and the sperm cell of the father—are formed in very different fashion. Here the pairs split up. Half of each pair goes into one egg or sperm cell, the other half into another cell. Thus each egg or sperm cell has only 23 chromosomes, not 23 pairs.

When two cells of reproduction are formed by this process, it is a matter of chance whether cell 1 will receive A1 or A2, B1 or B2, C1 or C2, and so on. Cell 1 may receive A1, B2, and C1, in which case cell 2 will receive A2, B1, and C2. Or cell 1 may receive A2, B2, and C1, in which case cell 2 will receive A1, B1, and C2. This random splitting of the 23 pairs can itself result in 8,388,608 different possible reproductive cells with different combinations of the two halves of the original pairs. Moreover, the splitting has a further complication. Sometimes A1, in breaking away from A2, leaves some of its own genes behind and pulls away some of the A2 genes. Any one of the 23 chromosomes can and often does behave in this way, with anywhere from one to several hundred genes from its paired chromosomes. All in all, there are many billions of possible combinations of the original pairs of chromosomes and genes.

An egg cell containing one of these combinations of the chromosomes and genes present in the mother is fertilized by a sperm cell containing one of the combinations of the chromosomes and genes present in the father. The chromosomes and genes pair up, and life begins for another unique human being. Never before, unless by a

These twins were reunited after years of separation when one was raised by a German family and the other by a Jewish family. Because they have inherited exactly the same genes, they look alike and probably are similar in many other respects, despite having been reared in different environments.

chance so mathematically remote as to be almost impossible, did the same combination of genes ever exist. Never again is it likely to be repeated.

The one exception to the fact that each human being is unique is in the case of identical twins. Here a single egg cell, fertilized by a single sperm cell, develops into two individuals. They have the same chromosomes and genes in the same combination, and they tend to be very much alike in every basic respect.

Being born male or female

One of the 23 pairs of chromosomes present in the fertilized egg cell plays a particularly significant role in development: It determines whether the fertilized egg will be a girl or boy. If you look back at Figure 1-12 you will note that two chromosomes are pointed out by arrows. One of them, as the caption states, is called an *X chromosome,* the other a *Y chromosome.* Despite their different appearances, they constitute a pair—the only exception to the rule that paired chromosomes are similar in structure. You will also note that the chromosomes in Figure 1-12 are from a cell taken from a male. The X-Y pairing always produces a male. When there is an X-X pair, the result is always a female.

This, then, is how sex is determined. When the mother's X-X pair of chromosomes splits to form an egg cell, the result is always a cell containing an X chromosome. When the father's X-Y pair splits to form two sperm cells, however, the X chromosome goes to one of the cells, the Y chromosome to the other. If the sperm cell with the X chromosome fertilizes the egg, the result is an X-X pairing and a girl. If the sperm cell with the Y chromosome fertilizes the egg, the result is an X-Y pairing and a boy.

How heredity affects behavior

People are born, live their lives, and die. But their chromosomes and genes are passed on from generation to generation, from parent to child. All of us carry around, in every cell of our bodies, the genes that have influenced human development and behavior since the appearance of humans on earth. They guarantee that we will grow up in the image of our ancestors rather than into apes or fish. Yet the particular combination of genes that each of us carries is unique, coming from a grandfather here, a great-grandmother there, and so on back through countless individuals in countless generations.

Studies in behavior genetics have demonstrated that the particular combination we inherit plays a considerable part in our behavior. There is now evidence that inherited tendencies help determine whether we will be *extroverted,* that is, inclined to be sociable and outgoing, or *introverted,* that is, withdrawn and inclined to be preoccupied with our own selves (Scarr, 1969). Our inborn characteristics may also incline us toward shyness, and inherited differences in the structure and functioning of the nervous system and the glands (Williams, 1956) appear to influence emotional and sexual behavior.

Various forms of emotional and mental disturbance also appear to depend at least in part on the gene pattern. The extreme mental disorder called *schizophrenia,* which occurs in only about one person out of a hundred, has been found considerably more likely to afflict people who have a parent or a brother or sister who suffers from the problem. This finding cannot be attributed—at least not entirely—to the effect of living around someone who is schizophrenic. One investigator, who studied only children who had been reared away from their own family in a foster home, found that about 10 percent whose real mothers were schizophrenic developed schizophrenia themselves, while no cases of schizophrenia occurred in a control group of adopted children who had been born to normal mothers (Heston, 1970). There is also evidence that genetic factors produce tendencies toward depression and perhaps other less extreme forms of abnormal behavior as well (Tsuang and Vandermey, 1980).

On the matter of intelligence, there is a correlation of close to .50 between the IQs of children and their parents, and a similar relationship between the IQs of brothers and sisters. It has also been found that defective genes or gene combinations cause some types of mental retardation.

How environment affects behavior

All the findings just cited support the nature side of the nature-nurture debate. There is also considerable evidence, however, to support the nurture side. For example, it has been found that not all the people who may inherit a tendency toward schizophrenia actually develop the disorder. Presumably the factor that determines which will fall prey and which will escape is environment. Statistical studies have shown that schizophrenia is most common among people living in the slum or near-slum areas of big cities (Hollingshead and Redlich, 1958), where they are likely to experience poverty and frustration. The disorder is less likely to occur among people who live in more favorable circumstances.

It is also known that intelligence is affected by nurture—for a baby's mental capacity, regardless of what its genes decree, has been found to flourish in a stimulating environment and to be stunted by an unfavorable environment. There are significant correlations between the IQs of foster parents and their adopted children, and also between the IQs of children unrelated by blood but brought up in the same foster home.

Among today's psychologists, it would be difficult to find any who believe that an individual's psychological future is preordained by inherited traits—or, on the other hand, who agree with Watson's contention that the newborn baby is shaped into adult form solely by the environment. The prevailing view is that both nature and nurture play a part. Heredity seems to set tendencies and limitations. But then environment takes over to encourage or discourage the development and effect of the inborn traits. The debate today is mostly over the relative importance of nature and nurture—the question of not whether but how much each of them influences such individual aspects of behavior and personality as the way we perceive and interpret the world around us, our intelligence and ability to learn from experience, our emotional behavior, and our reactions (normal or abnormal) to frustrations and stress.

SUMMARY

Psychology's two aims and many interests

1. Psychology is *the systematic study of behavior and the factors that influence behavior.*
2. The goals of psychology are (a) *to understand behavior* and (b) *to predict behavior.*
3. Many psychologists are concerned only with *pure science,* or knowledge for the sake of knowledge. Others are chiefly interested in *applied science,* or the use of psychological findings to help society carry on its everyday tasks, tackle its problems, and improve the quality of life.
4. Fields of applied psychology include:
    a. *School psychology,* which tests pupils, analyzes learning problems, and evaluates teaching methods.
    b. *Industrial psychology,* which includes the selection and training of employees and the study of workers' morale and cooperation.
    c. *Environmental psychology,* which deals with ecological problems like pollution and overcrowding.
    d. *Community psychology,* which deals with the social environment and how it could better serve human needs.

e. *Psychological counseling,* which gives assistance to people who need guidance on such temporary problems as school difficulties, choice of a vocation, or marriage conflicts.
f. *Clinical psychology,* which helps diagnose more deep-seated psychological problems and treat such problems through *psychotherapy.*

How behavior is guided by heredity and environment

5. The methods used by psychology to study behavior include *naturalistic observation, participant observation, interviews* and *case histories, questionnaires, tests* and *measurements,* and *experiments.*
6. The results of tests and measurements are analyzed through mathematical techniques called *psychological statistics.*
7. Psychological statistics have greatly enhanced our knowledge of *individual differences* by showing that almost all physical traits (like height) and psychological characteristics (like intelligence) follow the *normal curve of distribution*—with most measurements clustering around the average and only a few falling at the lowest or highest extremes.
8. *Correlation* is a statistical tool used to determine how much relationship, if any, exists between two different measurements—such as the IQs of parents and the IQs of their children.

The ultimate method: experimentation

9. The *experimental method,* which is the science's most powerful tool, is an attempt to discover cause and effect through a rigidly controlled examination of whether behavior changes when conditions change.
10. The experimenter controls the *independent variable,* which is set up independently of anything the subject does or does not do, and then studies the *dependent variable,* which is a change in the subject's behavior resulting from a change in the independent variable.
11. Experiments often use both an *experimental group,* whose behavior is studied under new conditions, and a *control group,* who are not placed under the new conditions.
12. In a *single-blind* experiment, the subjects do not know whether they belong to the experimental group or the control group. In a *double-blind* experiment, neither the subjects nor the experimenter knows.
13. An experiment is *replicated* when it is performed again in the same manner by another experimenter who obtains the same results—thus ruling out the possibility that the original results were accidental or influenced in some way by the first experimenter.

Psychology in the past, present, and future

14. Psychology was founded in 1879 when the first laboratory was opened by Wilhelm Wundt at a German university. The early

psychologists, including the American William James, were chiefly interested in human consciousness, which they studied through *introspection,* looking inward at mental processes.

15. The school of *behaviorism,* a rebellion against introspective studies, was founded by John Watson, who declared that mental processes cannot be seen or measured and therefore cannot be studied scientifically. Watson believed that psychologists should study what people do, not what they think.
16. Watson held that human behavior is a series of actions in which a *stimulus*—that is, an event in the environment—produces a *response*—that is, an observable muscular movement or some physiological reaction, such as increased heart rate or glandular secretion, that can also be observed and measured with the proper instruments. He believed that through establishment of *conditioned reflexes,* a type of learning, almost any kind of stimulus could be made to produce almost any kind of response.
17. B. F. Skinner, who succeeded Watson as leader of the behaviorist school, agrees that human beings are creatures of their environment whose behavior depends on the kinds of learning to which they have been subjected—and who are therefore not to blame for their failures or deserving of credit for their achievements.
18. *Gestalt psychology,* which takes its name from a German word meaning "pattern" or "configuration," maintained that events must be considered as a whole in studying any psychological phenomenon—from a perceptual process to personality—because "the whole is greater than the sum of its parts." The Gestalt school also stressed the entire situation, or context, in which the "whole" is found.
19. Many of the Gestalt ideas survive in today's trend toward *cognitive psychology,* which is interested in all the ways we learn about our environment, store the knowledge in memory, and use it to think and act intelligently in new situations. These various forms of mental activity are often called *information processing.*
20. A core idea in cognitive psychology is that we build *mental models of reality* from information about the world provided by our sense organs, which we can then examine for meanings and guidance in behavior.
21. Today's *humanistic psychology* also stems in part from the Gestalt school. The humanists believe we are unique organisms because we have values and goals and seek to express ourselves, grow, fulfill ourselves, and find peace and happiness.
22. Other schools of thought include *existential psychology* and the *psychoanalytic school* established by Sigmund Freud.

How psychology studies human behavior

23. *Behavior genetics* is the study of the way organisms inherit traits that help control their conduct.
24. There is a continuing debate, often called the *nature-nurture* con-

troversy, over the relative importance of heredity and environment in establishing behavior.

25. The mechanisms of human heredity are the 23 pairs of *chromosomes,* 46 in all, found in the fertilized egg cell and repeated through the process of division in every cell of the body that grows from the egg.
26. Each chromosome is made up of a large number of *genes,* which are composed of a chemical called DNA. The genes direct the growth of cells into parts of the body and also account for the individual differences we inherit.
27. Being female or male is determined by the *X chromosome* and the *Y chromosome.* An X-X pairing in the fertilized egg cell creates a female. An X-Y pairing creates a male.
28. There is evidence that inherited gene patterns set limits on the possible range of behavior in many ways including intelligence, emotionality, sexual behavior, and tendencies toward extroversion or introversion and various forms of abnormal behavior—but that environment then determines whether these tendencies will prevail and where within the possible range our behavior will actually fall.

IMPORTANT TERMS

applied science
behavior genetics
behaviorism
case history
chromosome
clinical psychology
cognitive psychology
community psychology
conditioned reflexes
control group
correlation
counseling
dependent variable
double-blind
environment
environmental psychology
existential psychology
experiment
experimental group
extroverted
gene
Gestalt psychology
heredity
humanistic psychology
independent variable
individual differences
industrial psychology
information processing
interviews
introspection
introverted
measurements
mental models of reality
naturalistic observation
nature-nurture
normal curve of distribution
participant observation
psychoanalysis
psychological statistics
psychotherapy
public opinion survey
pure science
questionnaire
replication
response
school psychology
single-blind
stimulus
tests
X chromosome
Y chromosome

SUPPLEMENT:

How to Study This Book (and Others)

For students, some of psychology's most useful findings have been in the field of learning, particularly on the most effective ways to study and remember what is in a textbook. Learning and memory are such important aspects of information processing that they require two chapters of full discussion a little later in the course. But many of the practical implications can be summarized in advance, here at the start, for your guidance in using this book to the best possible advantage.

To begin, let us say that you have six hours to devote to learning a chapter and that reading through the chapter carefully takes two hours. What should you do? Read the chapter three times?

To spend the six hours reading sounds logical, but actually it is the worst possible way to approach the task. You will learn and remember much better if you cut down the amount of reading and spend the rest of the time reciting what you have learned. Indeed you might find it best to spend *most* of your time in recitation. This fact was established many years ago in the experiment that was illustrated in part in Figure 1-8 on page 21. The full results are illustrated here in Figure 1-14. They demonstrate clearly that in at least some forms of learning the most efficient method is to spend as much as 80 percent of study time in recitation.

There are many reasons for the value of recitation. For one thing it helps motivate you—for just knowing that you will try to recite what you read stimulates the desire to learn what is on the printed page. It also provides immediate feedback, telling you how much you remember. And it is good practice in recall, the ability to bring out the knowledge you have stored in memory when you need it.

The SQ3R system of study: a method that works

Recitation is a key point in a well-known method of studying that has produced excellent results and improved grades for students who have applied it. This is the SQ3R system (Robinson, 1962), an abbreviation for the five steps it suggests: survey, question, read, recite, and review. Since there are many individual differences in the ways students find it most convenient and effective to approach a textbook, you may want to experiment with them and adapt them to your own particular style. But you will almost surely find it useful to follow them in one way or

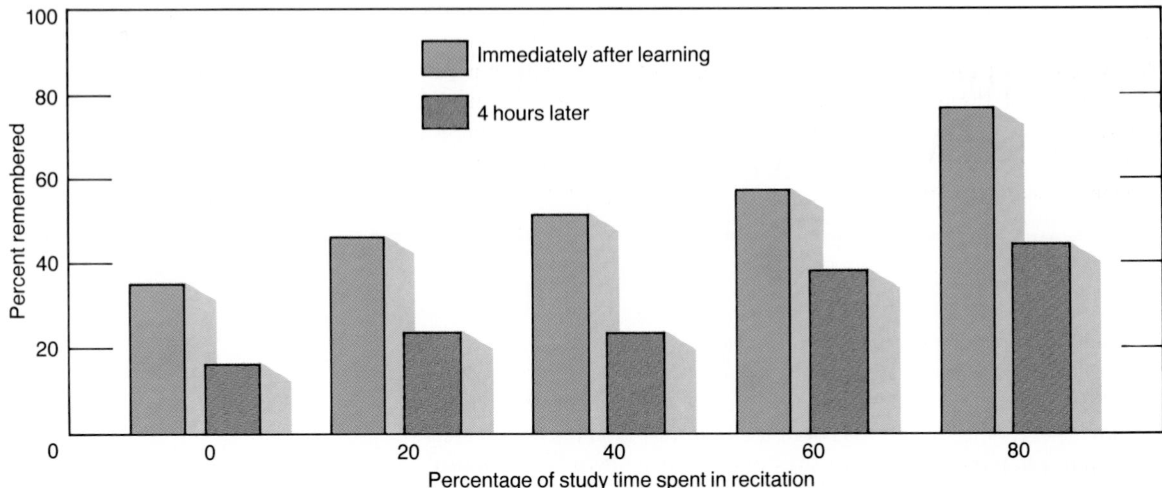

Figure 1-14 Recitation: it beats reading hands down *The bars show the results of an experiment in which students of various ages studied nonsense syllables for the same amount of time but in different ways. Some subjects spent the entire time reading the syllables, while others spent 20 to 80 percent of the time reciting. Tests made immediately afterward and again 4 hours later showed that their ability to remember the syllables went up in direct proportion to how much time they had spent in recitation (Gates, 1917).*

another, going about them in your own way and devoting as much time to each of them as you prefer.

The steps as applied to this book, which is designed for maximum convenience in using SQ3R, are described in the following pages.* The system can also be used, with any necessary variations, in studying most other textbooks—although the task, as you will see, is more difficult with books that lack chapter outlines and do not organize the materials into sections and subsections identified by distinctive and meaningful headings.

1. Survey

Before starting to read a chapter, you should have a general notion of what it contains and the key points it makes. The survey need not take long. Note the title (for Chapter 1, *The Scope, Goals, and Methods of Psychology*), which is in itself a very brief description of what is to come. Then look at the outline that precedes each chapter (as on page 4 for Chapter 1). The section headings, found there in colored type, list the approximately five main points covered in each chapter. (In Chapter 1, the first two are *Psychology's two aims and many interests* and *How psychology studies human behavior.*)

This may be enough of a survey, for it will tell you that you can expect to be studying (a) psychology's aims and interests; (b) the methods it uses to study behavior, with special emphasis on (c) the experiments psychologists perform; (d) the history, present status, and future prospects of the science; and (e) the part played in behavior by heredity and environment. Or you may want to take a little more time and thumb through the chapter, noting how much space is devoted to each of the main sections, some of the secondary headings found under each, and

*If you have the Study Guide that accompanies the book, you will find instructions there for using it as a further help in the SQ3R steps.

the illustrations (which help illuminate some of the points). You might also want to look at the list of important terms at the end of the chapter. You will not yet know the meaning of many of these terms, but just being aware of them is another clue to what to expect. The whole purpose of the survey is to provide a framework that will help you organize the chapter's facts and ideas as you encounter them.

Make a similar survey at the start of each major section of the chapter, which you will find identified by a heading in this type style:

Psychology's two aims and many interests (p. 6)

How psychology studies human behavior (p. 11)

Thumb through the section and examine the words printed in italics for emphasis and the points that are made in the illustrations. Note especially the secondary headings, marking subsections of the discussion, which are in this type style:

The goals of psychology (p. 6)

"Pure" and "applied" psychology (p. 7)

In other words, take a few moments to get a general idea of what this particular section of the book is going to tell you.

2. Question

This step applies to the secondary headings in the book. Each time you come to a new subsection and before you start reading it, turn its heading into a question that will pique your curiosity and orient you toward finding the answer. For the secondary heading *The goals of psychology* you might ask yourself: "What is this science trying to accomplish, and why?" Or you can put the question in any other way that makes you wonder why the book is going to discuss the matter and eager to learn more about it.

The wording is not important, and you should not spend much time or effort. The idea is just to ask yourself what you will be looking for as you start to read, which in turn will help you find the gist of the subsection and organize your thoughts about it. Stopping to ask the question also reminds you to pay attention to the headings—which are valuable guides to the discussion but are ignored by many readers.

3. Read

How much to read in one chunk is largely a matter of individual preference. Some students find it best to study the entire chapter as a whole, a technique they find helpful in understanding the pattern of the materials and the way the individual topics and facts relate to one another. Some study one major section at a time (usually about five to ten pages), others only a subsection (seldom more than a single page). You may want to experiment with what works best for you—and vary the size of the chunk for various parts of the book. Some parts are more or less familiar and can be taken in fairly easily. In others new ideas may tend to crowd together and get confusing if taken in too large a dose.

Whatever you decide, read with the idea that you will make an active search for the answer to the question you have asked for each secondary heading, and that you want to comprehend and remember it. As the author of the SQ3R system has pointed out, "Reading textbooks is work"—and readers must know what they are looking for, find it, and then organize their thoughts about it.

4. Recite

You can recite what you have read by talking, either out loud or in your mind—which is what the term means to most people. But a much better way is to jot down notes summarizing what you have read. The notes should be brief—just a single word or a very few at most—and in your own language. They should be written *after* you have finished reading, not while you are in the process. (Many students make the mistake of taking notes as they go along, often in the same words used in the book and without really comprehending their meaning.)

Regardless of the size of chunk you prefer to handle, the best method is to stop at the end of each subsection, look away from the book, and try to recite the gist of what you have just read—the answer to the question you asked at the beginning and any other important information you have learned. Then jot down a brief note that summarizes the subsection. For the subsection headed *The goals of psychology,* your notes might be:

A. Goals
   1. understand behavior
   2. predict "
   Question of control?

In taking notes for the subsections, you will find one small complication. Each chapter and each major section begin with some preliminary paragraphs before you come to the heading that marks the first of the subsections. Sometimes these paragraphs are merely a general introduction to what will follow. At other times—and Chapter 1 is an example—they serve not only to set the stage but also to present some important information. When this occurs, you can regard the paragraphs as a sort of subsection for recital and note-taking purposes. For these paragraphs in Chapter 1, your notes might be:

A. Psychology defined
   1. many types behavior
   2. many influences on behavior
   3. systematic (scientific) study

A possible alternative to taking notes is to go back and underline the key words and key points in the subsection. This works for some students but is generally less helpful, in part because it does not force you to put the point into your own words. Moreover it may lead to reading just for the sake of finding important sentences and marking them without any real attention to the meaning. Some students fall into the mistake of making so many underlines, before they finish the subsection, of words and sentences that seem important at the time but later prove otherwise, that the page becomes a jumble of repetitions and sometimes even contradictions. You can, of course, use both techniques—first make notes, then underline the words in the book that relate to your notes, as well as details that you want to remember.

5. Review

When you get to the end of a major section of the book—for example when the heading *How psychology studies human behavior* signals the start of a new major section on page 11—look over the notes you have jotted down on the subsections and find how the various points are organized and related to one another. Or, if you have used underlines instead of notes, go back through the section and examine the points you have marked. Then, since this step is closely related to the previous one, cover up your notes or look away from the book and recite the points. If you have trouble recalling any of them, or what any of them means, take another look at your notes or the book and try again.

Turn also to the summary at the end of the chapter, where the most important points are presented briefly. For convenience in applying the SQ3R system, the summary is divided into the major sections of the chapter, with each identified by the same heading used in the text. Read the summary for the section you have been studying and make sure you are aware of all the ideas it contains, understand them, and can explain them. If not, go back to the chapter and do some more reading of what you have missed. Your review will probably take no more than five minutes in all—but it will be of tremendous value in making sure you have grasped all the points made in the section and fixing them in your memory.

When you have completed the chapter and your review of the final major section, make another review of the chapter as a whole. Here the list of important ideas will help. Go through the list and make sure you know and can explain all the terms it contains. If you can—and can also recall the points made in the summary—you have such a deep understanding of the overall meaning of the chapter that many of its details (like the kind of work done by the early psychologists Wundt, Galton, and James) should stay with you almost automatically.

SUMMARY OF SUPPLEMENT

The SQ3R system of study: a method that works

1. *Recitation* is of great value in studying. It is better to spend as much as 80 percent of study time in an active attempt to recite than to devote the entire time to reading and rereading.

2. A study method that emphasizes recitation—and has proved effective—is the *SQ3R system.*
3. The first step in SQ3R is to *survey* the entire chapter to get a general idea of what it contains—and to do the same for each major section as you come to it.
4. The second step, performed as you start each subsection, is to turn the heading into a *question* that will pique your curiosity and orient you toward finding the answer.
5. Next *read* as big a chunk of the chapter as you find best suited to your own individual preferences—with the idea of making an active search for the answer to the question or questions you have asked, comprehending the answer, and remembering it.
6. Next, stop at the end of each subsection to *recite* the gist of what you have just read. The best method is to jot down notes—in your own words and as brief as possible—that summarize the subsection.
7. When you come to the end of a major section, *review* what is in it. Look over the notes you have taken on the subsections and find how the various points are organized and related to one another. Then cover up your notes and recite the points. Examine the chapter summary for that section to make sure you know all the key ideas, understand them, and can explain them. If not, go back to the chapter to study what you have missed.
8. After you have completed the five steps for each major section, make another review of the chapter as a whole. The summary will again help, as will the list of important terms you should know and be able to explain.

RECOMMENDED READINGS

Chaplin, J. P., and Krawiec, T. C. *Systems and theories of psychology,* 3d ed. New York: Holt, Rinehart & Winston, 1974.

Christensen, L. B. *Experimental methodology,* 2d ed. Boston: Allyn & Bacon, 1980.

Evans, R. I. *The making of psychology: discussions with creative contributors.* New York: Knopf, 1976.

Hall, C. S., and Lindzey, G. *Theories of personality,* 3d ed. New York: Wiley, 1978.

May, R. *Psychology and the human dilemma.* Princeton, N.J.: Van Nostrand Reinhold, 1967.

Meyers, L. S., and Grossen, N. E. *Behavioral research: theory, procedure, and design,* 2d ed. San Francisco: Freeman, 1978.

Murphy, G., and Kovach, J. K. *Historical introduction to modern psychology,* 3d ed. New York: Harcourt Brace Jovanovich, 1972.

Rogers, C. *Freedom to learn: a view of what education might become.* Columbus, Ohio: Merrill, 1969.

Watson, R. I. *The great psychologists: from Aristotle to Freud.* Philadelphia: Lippincott, 1978.

Wertheimer, M. A. *A brief history of psychology.* New York: Holt, Rinehart & Winston, 1979.

Wood, G. *Fundamentals of psychological research,* 2d ed. Boston: Little, Brown, 1977.
Woods, P. J. *The psychology major: training and employment strategies.* Washington, D.C.: American Psychological Association, 1979.

CHAPTER 2

The supreme brain, its intricacy, and its "beautiful relationships" 47
- The secret of being human: the cerebral cortex
- The brain's many types of nerve cells and their functions
- The brain's own chemical factory
- The nervous system: linkages of brain, body, and behavior

Brain function no. 1: sensing the world and taking action 52
- Receiving and interpreting what goes on in the environment
- Where our body movements originate
- The brain's information processing and relay station
- The miracle of coordination and balance

Brain function no. 2: thinking, planning, and remembering 55
- The storehouse of memory
- The cortex and intellectual development
- Left brain and right brain
- Left for logic, right for hunches

Brain function no. 3: managing our emotional and physical lives 61
- The production and control of emotions
- Keeping the body alive
- The autonomic nervous system: the brain's able assistant

How the brain performs its functions: the neurons and their messages 68
- The neuron's "receivers" and "senders"
- How neurons speak to one another: synapses and neurotransmitters
- To fire or not to fire?
- How neurons give their all—or nothing at all
- Turning beeps into meanings and feelings
- Neurotransmitters, mental problems, and drugs

Summary 73

Important terms 76

Recommended readings 77

Psychology and society
- Is the right brain neglected? 60
- Will brain research make psychology obsolete? 72

Brain and Body: The Physical Foundations of Human Behavior

It sits just beneath your skull, perched on the top end of your spine, about the size of a grapefruit and weighing about three pounds. It is grey-pink in color, and is covered with a seemingly endless maze of folds and wrinkles. On its underside, where it connects with the spine, are some odd looking structures whose shapes give no hint whatsoever of what they could possibly be for.

That just about describes what you would see if you could somehow peek inside your head and get a look at your brain. It certainly does not seem like much. Yet this flabby, unimpressive looking handful of matter is what governs all of your behavior and gives you your special identity as a person. The brain—through an incredibly intricate web of connections both within itself and with other parts of the body—literally runs your life. All the human capacities you will read about in this book—to gather information, learn and remember, act intelligently, move about, develop skills, feel emotions, cope with stress, relate to others—are managed by the brain. Think of all the things you did in the last 24 hours. Whatever you did—sleep, dream, wake up, shower, get dressed, drive your car, play tennis, study, get angry, make love—you accomplished through the powers of your brain.

The energy to operate this marvelous instrument comes from the activity of billions of nerve cells that are in constant communication with each other and with their counterparts throughout the body. The result is a network of brain-and-body systems that is surely one of the great miracles of nature. Knowledge of how these systems work—and exactly what they accomplish—is essential to an understanding of the entire field of psychology.

The supreme brain, its intricacy, and its "beautiful relationships"

The brain has aptly been called "a very privileged organ" (Calne, 1981). Nature has conspired to guard it from harm and to give it preferential treatment over every other organ of the body. The brain is encased in thick bone that protects its soft tissue, and it is surrounded by a fluid that cushions it from injury in case of sudden impact. If the body is deprived of food, it is the first to get its share of whatever nutrients are coursing through the blood. And though the brain makes up only 2 percent or less of the average person's total weight, it gets 20 percent of the body's total oxygen supply.

The brain has won its supreme status for good reason. Its re-

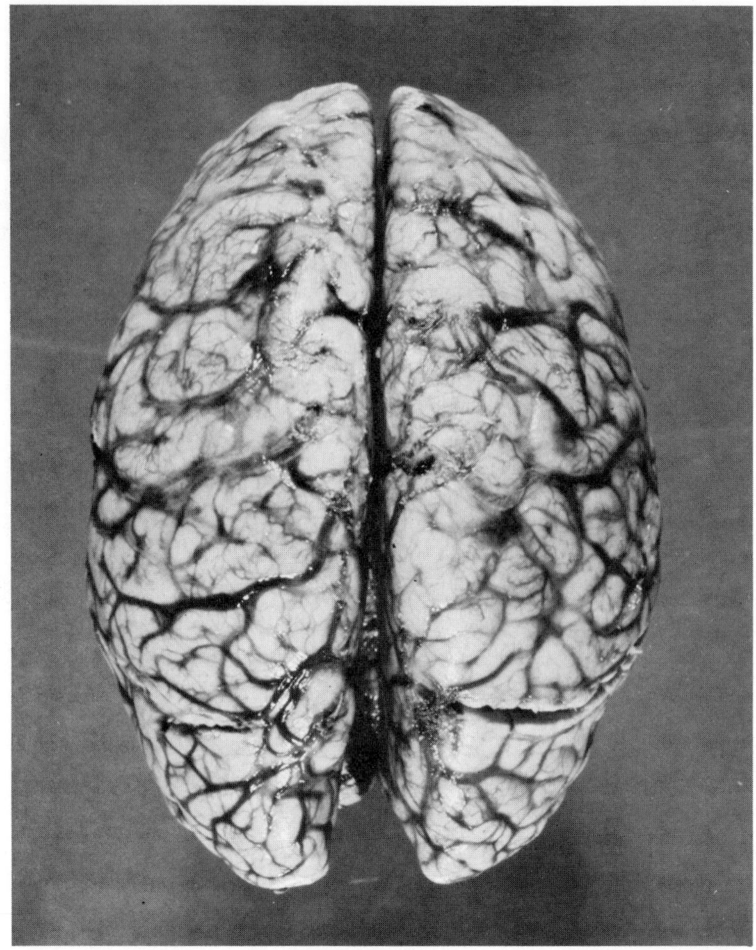

Figure 2-1 A topside view of the brain *The photograph shows the human brain as seen from above, displaying the elaborate folds and creases described in the text. Note especially the vertical line, resembling a narrow ditch, running down the middle from the top of the photo (which is the front of the brain) to the bottom. This is a deep fissure that divides this top part of the brain into two separate halves, or* hemispheres, *as discussed in the text.*

sponsibilities are vast and complex, and they critically affect all our psychological and physical functions. If the brain is severely injured—in an auto accident, for example, or from a gunshot wound—the victim's capacities, behavior, and basic personality can be dramatically altered. Though much still remains a mystery about the brain's operations, psychologists have learned a great deal about the tasks assigned to this organ, and how they are carried out. The key is the brain's intricate connections—its "many beautiful relationships" (Miller, 1969).

The secret of being human: the cerebral cortex

Seen from above, as if the top of your head were transparent, the brain looks as shown in Figure 2-1—a mass of grey tissue so rich in blood-filled arteries that it takes on a pinkish cast. Its surface resembles a piece of heavy cloth. This is the part of the brain that is chiefly responsible for your remembering, thinking, and planning—the activities that make you more intelligent than other animals. It is called the *cerebral*

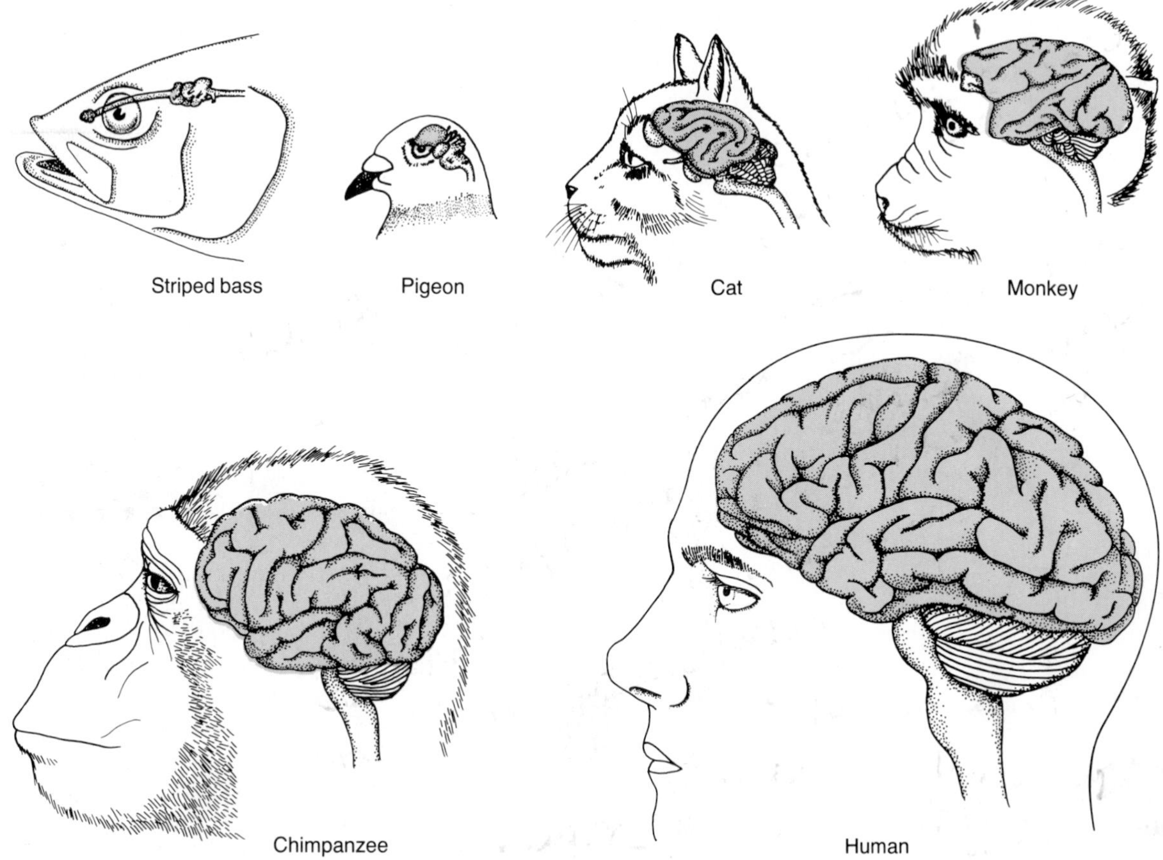

cortex, and as shown in Figure 2-2, nature has made it larger in human beings than in any other species. Indeed it is really too large to fit comfortably into the human head, for it measures about 1.5 square feet (.14 square meters) in area. All the convolutions you see in Figure 2-1—the intricate foldings and refoldings—are needed to squeeze it into the skull. What you see in the photograph is only about a third of the cerebral cortex. All the rest is hidden in the creases.

The cortex is the surface—like the thick wrinkled skin of a prune—of the human brain's largest single structure, the *cerebrum,* which lies massively atop all the other parts of the brain. As Figure 2-1 shows, the cortex and the cerebrum are split down the middle into a left half, or *left hemisphere,* and a right half, or *right hemisphere,* Thus in a sense we have two brains doing our thinking—a fact raising some interesting questions that will be discussed later.

Beneath the cerebrum, and totally hidden by its bulk when the brain is viewed from above, lie a number of other structures with their own special roles to play in our behavior. We share with lower forms of animal life a number of these structures—those, for example, that

Figure 2-2 The evolution of the human brain *The size of the cerebral cortex increases dramatically as we go up the evolutionary ladder—from fish to mammals—and reaches its greatest proportional size in human beings. The brains of some large creatures weigh more than ours. (The whale's is eight times heavier.) But our brain is by far the largest in relation to body size (Hubel, 1979).*

generate our emotions and maintain our basic life functions. But it is the cerebrum and its cortex, comprising 80 percent of the human brain, that make us special. Without them, we humans are "almost a vegetable, speechless, sightless, senseless" (Hubel and Wiesel, 1979).

The brain's many types of nerve cells and their functions

Within the brain's three pounds (1.4 kilograms) of tissue are about 10 billion separate *neurons*, or nerve cells, all connected and interconnected in a most complex fashion. Each of these fiberlike cells may receive messages from thousands of other neurons, process these messages in various ways, then pass its own messages along to thousands more. The total number of possible connections is so great that it totally defies the imagination (Lewin, 1974).

No two neurons are precisely identical in form (Stevens, 1979)—and one reason the brain is so versatile is that the cells are also of many different types, with their own specialized functions. Depending on how finely the differentiations are made, there are at least 100 types and perhaps as many as 500 (Hubel, 1978), far more cell types than other organs of the body possess. The liver, for example, has no more than two different kinds of cells.

The primary job of most brain cells is transmitting messages. Others, however, perform different tasks. The brain, for example, has some cells that operate very much like sense organs—serving as its "eyes" and "ears" to observe changes in the bloodstream and thus detect when the body needs food or water. Others are sensitive to changes in the body's internal temperature. The brain also has neurons that operate like miniature glands, producing complicated chemicals called *hormones* (named after the Greek word meaning "activators" or "exciters"). These hormones are released into the bloodstream and travel through the body, stimulating many kinds of physical activity.

The brain's own chemical factory

The ability of certain brain cells to produce hormones, discovered only a few years ago, has opened up one of the most exciting scientific fields of investigation. Recent findings, which may lead to great advances in our knowledge of behavior, show that the brain manufactures hormonelike chemicals that can be as powerful in their effects as synthetically manufactured drugs prescribed by doctors. They seem to affect parts of the brain associated with pain and with emotion and mood (Edelson, 1981).

Does acupuncture work? If so, its success results from spurring the brain to produce hormones resembling morphine.

One group of brain chemicals has been named *endorphins*—from Greek words meaning "the morphine within"—because they are similar in structure and effect to the powerful painkiller morphine (Snyder, 1980). The endorphins may help explain the mystery of acupuncture, or the sticking of needles into nerves in various parts of the body, an ancient technique that has been widely used by Chinese physicians to reduce pain and promote the cure of physical ailments. Applying needles in this way, it has been found, seems to increase production of the brain's own brand of morphine—as if a natural pain barrier is set up when the needle is inserted (Facklam and Facklam, 1982). A few investigators have reported that treatment with substances derived from endorphins can also produce improvement in certain patients suffering from the mental illness called schizophrenia (Snyder, 1982). Further studies may shed considerable light on mental disturbances, emotional well-being and upset, and addiction to heroin—which, like morphine, is a derivative of the poppy plant.

In addition to endorphins, the brain's versatile cells produce other hormonelike substances that appear to have profound influences on behavior—including, for example, drinking behavior, muscular movement, and memory (Iversen, 1982). More and more brain chemicals are rapidly being identified, and their number is likely one day to exceed 200 (Snyder, 1980).

The nervous system: linkages of brain, body, and behavior

The neurons of the brain can affect our behavior only because there are links between them and other parts of the body. These links are forged by the rest of the human nervous system, composed of neurons of various kinds that connect with the brain. The neuron fibers of the nervous system extend throughout the body as shown in Figure 2-3. The outlying neurons comprise the *peripheral nervous system,* a network that extends to the fingertips, feet, eyes, and ears. All the neurons of the peripheral nervous system eventually connect to the *central nervous system*—made up of the *spinal cord,* which is a sort of master cable to the brain, and the brain itself. The central nervous system roughly resembles a huge telephone exchange. The peripheral system is like the wires carrying messages to and from the central exchange, extending to the far reaches of the town it serves.

Neurons differ in length as well as kind. Some, especially in the brain, are only the tiniest fraction of an inch in length. Others are more than three feet (about one meter) long. For example, the neurons that enable you to wiggle your toes extend all the way from the lower part of the spinal cord to the muscles of the toes. Neurons can be grouped into three classes:

1. *Afferent neurons* are neurons of the senses. The word afferent is derived from the Latin word *ad,* which means "to" or "toward," and *ferre,* which means "to bear" or "to carry." The afferent neurons of the peripheral nervous system carry messages from our eyes, ears, and other sense organs toward the central nervous system. When they reach the brain, they are translated into our experiences of vision, hearing, touch, taste, and smell.
2. *Efferent neurons* carry messages from the central nervous system in an outward direction—ordering muscles to contract and directing the activity of the body's organs and glands.
3. *Connecting neurons* are communications neurons that carry messages between other neurons. They are stimulated only by another neuron. They do not end in muscle or gland tissue but only at junctions

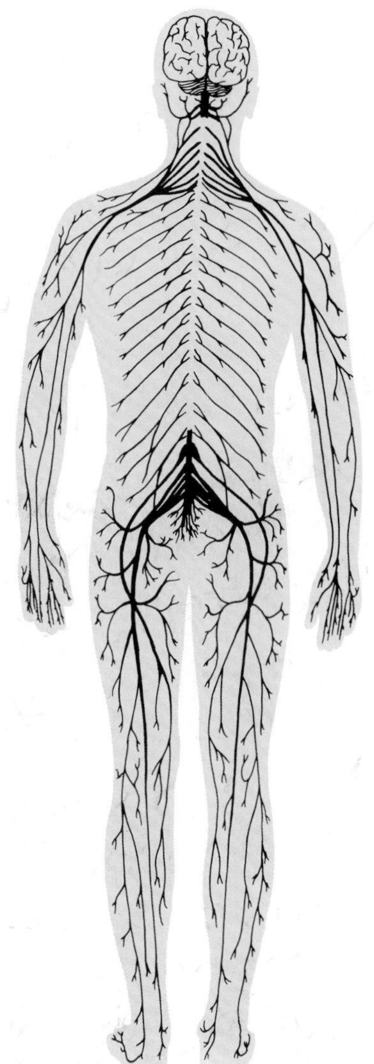

Figure 2-3 The human nervous system *Like the tributaries that form a river, individual neuron fibers at all the far reaches of the body join together to form small nerves, which is the name for bundles of neuron fibers. The small nerves join with others to form larger nerves, at last becoming the very large ones that join with the central nervous system—the brain and the spinal cord.* Twelve cranial nerves, *in pairs going to the left and right sides of the head, connect directly with the brain. There are also 31 pairs of large spinal nerves, connected with the spinal cord at the spaces between the bones of the spine.*

with other neurons, which they either stimulate or inhibit from sending their own messages. Most of these connecting neurons, though not all, are found in the brain and spinal cord.

Every moment of our lives, day and night, afferent neurons carry information to the brain, and efferent neurons dispatch the brain's decisions and directions. As the center of this ceaseless activity of the nervous system, the brain performs all the essential and wondrous functions that will be discussed in this chapter.

Brain function no. 1: sensing the world and taking action

You are driving down the street, and a child darts into the path of your car. In a twinkling, the muscles of your right leg tense and your foot hits the brake, bringing your car safely to a stop. Or you are in bed sound asleep. Suddenly there are shouts of "Fire!" You awake with a start, jump out of bed, run down the hall, pick up your child, and head out of the house to safety.

Though we tend to take our behavior in such situations for granted, it is actually quite remarkable. Such acts must be orchestrated by millions of neurons, receiving and sending messages with blinding speed. Our capacities to get information from the world, process that information, and take appropriate action all depend on the intricate functioning of the brain—both the cerebral cortex and the related structures lying below it.

Receiving and interpreting what goes on in the environment

All the information picked up by our sense organs is eventually transmitted, by way of the brain's many pathways, to the cerebral cortex. As shown in Figure 2-4, the cortex has specialized areas that receive the sensory messages for vision and hearing, also a long strip that receives messages of bodily sensations from the feet (at the top) to the head (at the bottom). In these specialized areas the messages are analyzed and interpreted. The brain decides which messages are important and what they mean. The sounds of speech—which are of particular importance because language plays such a large role in human behavior—have an area of their own especially concerned with understanding the meaning of words and sentences.

The importance of the cerebral cortex in registering and processing sensory information becomes dramatically clear in cases of harm to any of these portions of the brain (Williams, 1979). Depending on the location and extent of injury to the back part of the cortex responsible for vision, for example, an individual might suffer varying degrees of blindness, even though the eye and its own muscles and nerves remain perfectly intact. If the area for understanding speech is injured, an individual might no longer be able to interpret what is being said, even though all parts of the ear are perfectly healthy and the sounds of the words spoken are clearly heard. In such cases, the afflicted persons literally cannot get the words "through their heads."

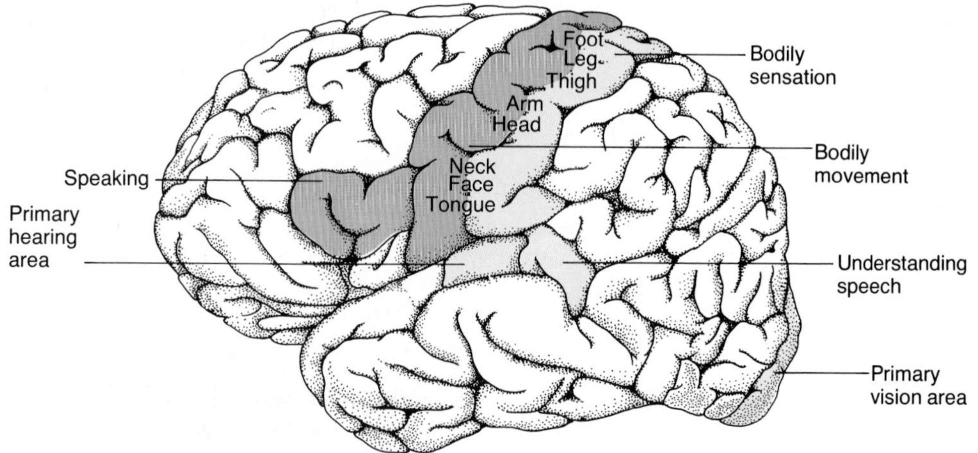

Figure 2-4 Some areas of the cerebral cortex with special functions
On this drawing of the cerebral cortex as it would be seen from the left side of the body, the colored portions represent areas that are known to perform some of the special jobs described in the text (Geschwind, N. The specialization of the brain. Scientific American, *1979, 186).*

Where our body movements originate

The messages from our sense organs often call for us to take appropriate action—and the cortex has another specialized strip also shown in Figure 2-4, that controls body movements from feet to head. It is from here that the brain sends out signals for the body to accomplish the vast range of movements of which we are capable—not only the gross muscular adjustments of the arms and legs used in lifting or running, but also the tiny adjustments of the finger muscles used in threading a needle or playing the guitar (Evarts, 1979).

The cortex also has an area for speaking that moves the vocal cords and muscles associated with them in a way that produces meaningful sounds. When a stroke damages this area of the cortex, the result is often a loss of the incomparable human gift of speech—the ability to formulate and utter precisely the words that convey our ideas. It is from this portion of the brain also that you are able to manufacture the sounds that give voice to your feelings—a shriek of delight when you see your home team score a winning touchdown, a groan of despair when you hear about the death of a friend, or a sigh of contentment when you feel the embrace of a loved one.

The brain's information processing and relay station

Serving as a central switchboard for messages passed between the cortex and the body is a structure called the *thalamus,* shown in Figure 2-5. The thalamus has aptly been described as an "information processing center" (Lewin, 1974). Messages from the various sense organs eventually arrive at the thalamus, where they are organized and sent on upward to the cerebral cortex. The thalamus also acts as a relay station for nervous impulses traveling in the opposite direction, especially some of the messages from the cerebral cortex calling for motor activity.

One part of the thalamus is in a network of brain circuits called the *reticular activating system,* which is related in a strange way to the processing of sensory information. The network gets its name from the

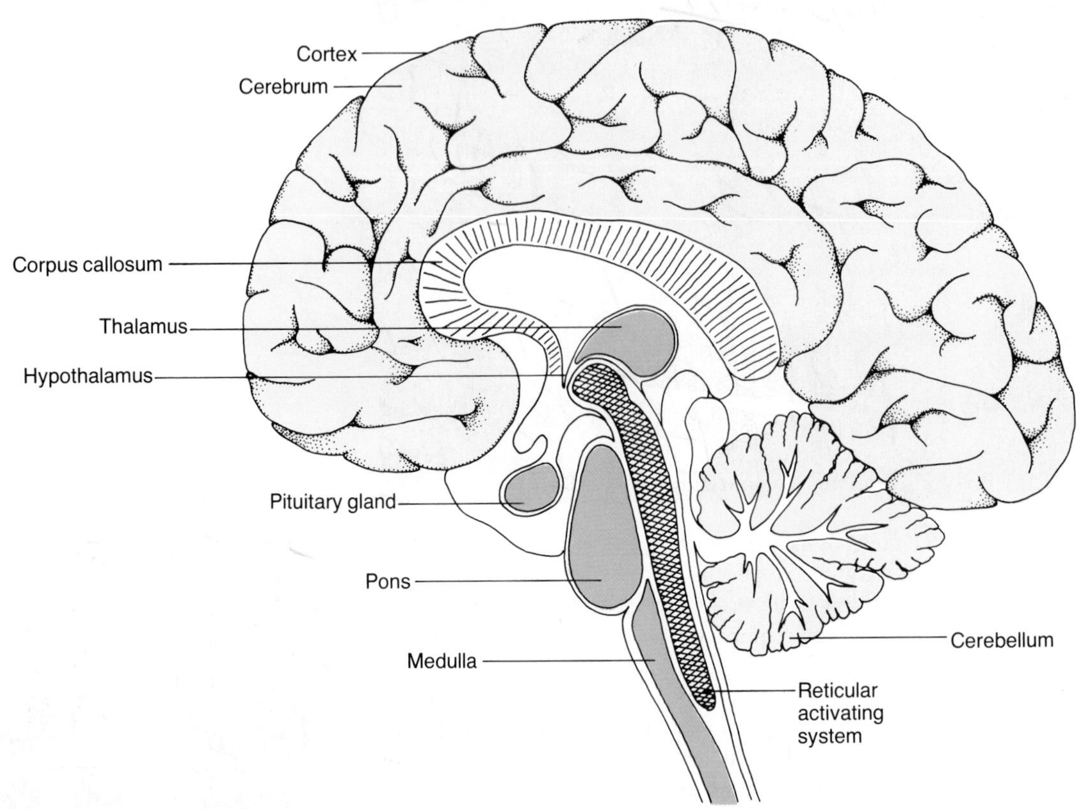

Figure 2-5 A sectional view of the brain *Individual parts of the human brain are shown here as they would be seen if the brain were divided down the middle from front to back. The functions of the various structures are described in the text (London, P.* Beginning psychology. *The Dorsey Press, 1978).*

fact that it appears under a microscope as a crisscrossed (or reticulated) pattern of nerve fibers. As shown in Figure 2-5, it extends downward to the bottom part, or stem, of the brain, where brain and spinal cord join together.

Nerve pathways carrying messages from the sense organs to the highest parts of the brain have side branches that enter the circuits in the reticular activating system. These side branches stimulate the system to send impulses of its own in an upward direction, thus arousing the top part of the brain to a general state of alertness and activity. For lack of such arousal, an animal in which the reticular activating system has been destroyed may remain permanently unconscious. Similarly, a sleeping animal can be awakened immediately by electrical stimulation of the reticular activating system (Moruzzi and Magoun, 1949).

The miracle of coordination and balance

Of special importance in regulating the body's movements is the *cerebellum,* which, as shown in Figure 2-5, is attached to the back of the brain stem. The cerebellum, a "magnificently patterned, orderly and fantastically complex piece of machinery" (Hubel, 1979), has many connections with the parts of the cerebral cortex that initiate muscular activity. Its role is to coordinate all the various finely regulated muscular movements of which we are capable, such as typing and playing a flute.

The cerebellum controls the intricate muscular movements of the musician.

If the cerebellum is damaged, movements become jerky, and great effort and concentration are required to perform even what was once such an automatic activity as walking. Victims of damage to the cerebellum also have difficulty speaking, which requires well-coordinated movements of the muscles of the vocal cords, windpipe, and mouth.

The cerebellum also controls body balance and is the part of the brain that keeps us right side up. It plays an important role in allowing us to do things that require great equilibrium. An example is shooting a pistol at a target. Studies of champion marksmen in the Russian Army showed that, although many parts of their body moved, the pistol remained virtually immobile (Evarts, 1979). With millions of neurons sending their messages to and fro—from the eyes, the cerebral cortex, the arms and fingers—somehow the brain, thanks largely to the cerebellum, is able to integrate all these messages into an act of exquisite balance and precision. Like the cerebrum, the cerebellum is divided into two lobes, or hemispheres. The left and right lobes are connected by the *pons,* which gets its name from the Latin word for bridge. The neurons of the pons serve as a bridge or cable that transmits messages between the two hemispheres of the cerebellum.

The muscular coordination and balance of this athlete are also by courtesy of the cerebellum.

Brain function no. 2: thinking, planning, and remembering

The brain areas responsible for our sensations and movements make up only about a quarter of the cerebral cortex. The rest of it, all the parts that were left unshaded in Figure 2-4 (p. 53) seems to account for the way the brain "plans for the future, thinks, and reasons creatively" (Miller, 1969)—in other words, all the cognitive processes that raise us far above the level of other organisms.

These unspecified areas of the cortex are the seat of our consciousness—our awareness of ourselves and what is going on in the world, our ability to think about our past and imagine our future. Though we take consciousness for granted, it is a strange and wonderful thing. We sometimes say, after making some kind of glaring mistake, "I think I'm losing my mind"—as if the human brain is like a house that somehow knows when it is falling down.

This man has or will have a faulty memory—for alcohol damages a brain structure (hippocampus) that plays an important part in remembering.

The storehouse of memory

It is in these unspecified areas of the cortex, presumably, that the brain stores our memories of what has happened to us—and thus helps us learn from experience. In performing this function, the brain seems to call on another of its structures known as the *hippocampus* (Zola-Morgan, Squire, and Mishkin, 1982). The hippocampus lies beneath the cortex and is impossible to illustrate clearly. Although the way it operates is not exactly known, it appears to be essential to the establishment of long-lasting memories. For example, a case has been reported of a 29-year-old man whose hippocampus was surgically severed for medical reasons. He retained all his old memories but apparently could not establish any new ones. He could not learn the address of the new house to which his family had moved. He read the same magazines over and over again, and worked the same jigsaw puzzles, without ever realizing that he had seen them before (Milner, 1959).

It has been found that long-term consumption of alcohol by animals decreases the number of connections among the neurons of the hippocampus—a fact that may explain the memory failures of human alcoholics (Riley and Walker, 1978). There are also indications that deterioration of nerve cells in the hippocampus may account for the loss of memory in very old people (Scheibel et al., 1975)—although some investigators doubt that aging in itself has much significant effect so long as people remain mentally active and continue using their brain cells (Diamond, 1978).

The cortex and intellectual development

Although the cortex cannot operate independently of other brain structues such as the hippocampus, its central role in memory and other cognitive functions is clearly apparent in the way its size and development are related to human intellectual abilities. Even before birth, in the darkness of the womb, the human cerebrum and its cortex grow so rapidly that they almost seem to explode (see Figure 2-6). Growth continues after birth—at such a pace that the baby's brain triples in weight in the first 6 months of life. By the age of 2 the brain reaches three quarters of its ultimate weight, and it is precisely during these opening years that the child makes remarkable strides in motor skills, speech, and the first displays of the human capacity to remember and reflect.

In monkeys at the age of 2 years, the cerebral cortex seems to function about as well as it ever will (Goldman, 1974). But for human babies, the cortex still has considerable growing to do, and parents watching their children in the preschool years can see the growth reflected in behavior. Young children display ever-expanding abilities

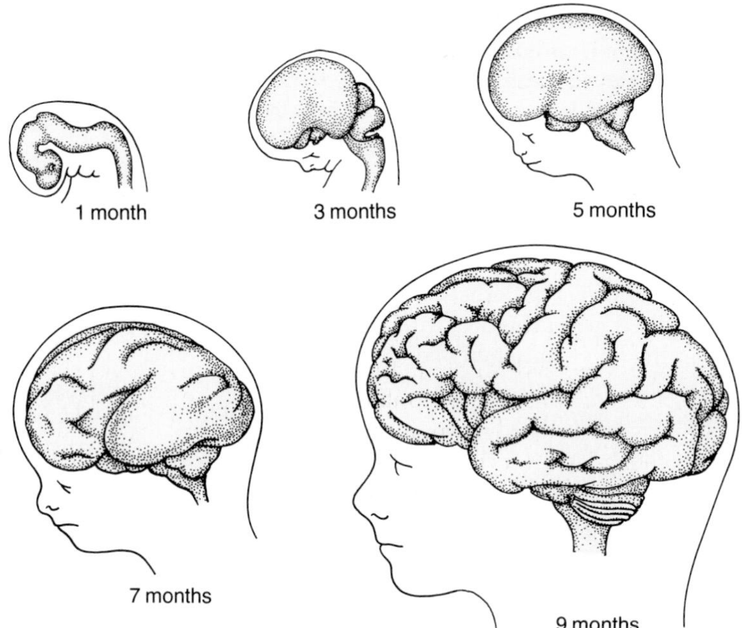

Figure 2-6 The brain's explosive growth before birth *During each minute in the womb, the brain of the infant-to-be gains tens of thousands of new brain cells. The folds on the brain's surface begin to appear at about the middle of pregnancy—as the cortex grows rapidly to fill the top of the tiny fetus skull (Cowan, W. M. Development of the brain.* Scientific American, *1979).*

to think, plan, and remember. From an infant who could see, hear, smell, and cry well enough at birth, the child in the first grade has become a person who can begin to read, understand, question, and wonder. Indeed all the various stages of children's intellectual development described later in the book are dependent on the progressive growth and maturation of the cerebral cortex (Tanner, 1978).

Do rich early learning experiences influence the rate of growth of the brain? This question has attracted the interest of a number of psychologists, and the answer seems to be yes. Almost all the neurons of the brain are present at birth. The number increases by only a small amount, if at all, in later years (Greenough, 1982). Yet the brain quadruples in weight from birth to adulthood. Some of the added weight comes from the growth of supporting tissue. But the increased weight is also caused by the fact that the neurons grow and develop new offshoots—much as a young tree develops new branches—that interconnect with other neurons and receive messages from them. Experiments have shown that animals raised in an enriched environment, containing numerous toys and visual stimuli, develop heavier brains than animals raised in ordinary bare cages (Bennett et al., 1964)—and that the neurons of their brains have more such interconnecting offshoots (Schapiro and Vukovich, 1970).

Left brain and right brain

As was noted in Figure 2-1 (p. 48), the topmost and most characteristically human part of the brain—the cerebrum and cerebral cortex—is divided into two hemispheres. Most of the nerve fibers connecting the brain with all the various parts of the body, either directly or through

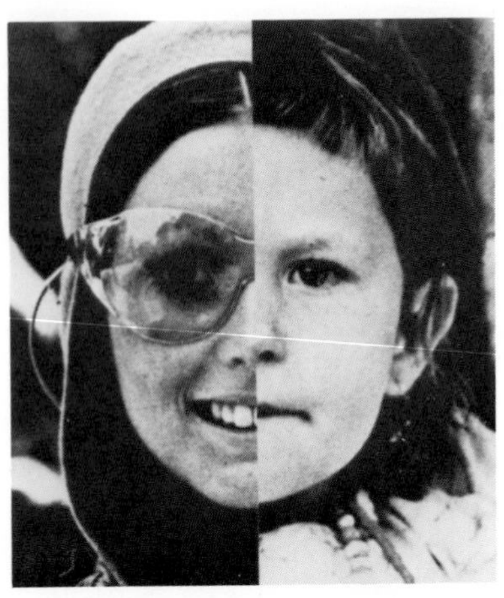

Figure 2-7 Whose face is this? Can you pick it out of the "lineup" shown below? *If you saw this composite face and were asked to match it against the eight faces shown in Figure 2-8, you would have no trouble. But if you had a split brain your answer would be very different, as explained in the text.*

the spinal cord, cross from one side to the other. This means that the left hemisphere ordinarily receives sensory messages from and controls movement in the right side of the body. The right hemisphere deals with the left side of the body. If like most people you write with your right hand, it is your left hemisphere that directs the movements. The left hemisphere also controls the use of language—speaking and understanding the speech of others. Thus in most people the left hemisphere is the dominant one—the one we most often use and rely on.

Though we really have two brains—one for language and the right side of the body, the other for the left side of the body—we are not ordinarily aware of this dual thinking mechanism inside us. One reason is that the two hemispheres cooperate very closely. They have numerous interconnections, especially through a structure called the *corpus callosum* (shown in Figure 2-5, p. 54) that resembles a thick telephone cable between the two hemispheres. Thus each half of the cerebrum and cerebral cortex ordinarily knows exactly what is going on in the other half.

What would happen if the corpus callosum were missing and the two halves of the brain lacked this important channel of intercommunication? We do not have to guess the answer. We know—because surgeons sometimes cut the corpus callosum for medical reasons. (The surgery is performed as a last resort to relieve patients suffering from one type of epilepsy, a condition in which abnormal patterns of brain activity sometimes cause crippling seizures.) The operation has been found to produce some strange results. Patients may exhibit little change in intelligence, personality, and general behavior—yet careful testing reveals that in some ways they act as if they possess two separate brains functioning independently.

One of the most striking demonstrations of this fact has been obtained by using the photographs shown in Figures 2-7 and 2-8. The composite photo in Figure 2-7 is shown to "split-brain" subjects—as those with a severed corpus callosum are known—in such a manner that the right side of the photo is transmitted to the left hemisphere.

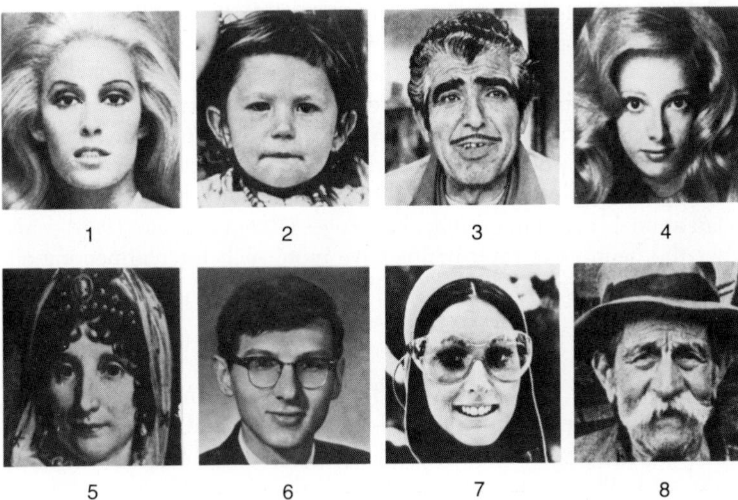

Figure 2-8 The "lineup" of faces for comparison *These are the eight faces to be matched against the composite photo in Figure 2-7. Your own whole brain will see at a glance that no. 2 is the right half of the Figure 2-7 photo and no. 7 is the left half.*

The left half of the photo is transmitted to the right hemisphere. When split-brain subjects are asked to say whose photo they see, they answer that it is the child whose full photograph is no. 2 in Figure 2-8. But if they are asked to *point* to whose photo is shown, they select no. 7—the young woman with the large glasses (Levy, Trevarthen, and Sperry, 1972).

Why should this be? Why should these subjects say so confidently that the photo is no. 2—yet *point* with equal confidence to no. 7? To find the reason, we must look to another split-brain experiment.

Left for logic, right for hunches

This other experiment is illustrated in Figure 2-9. The results show that the left brain of the split-brain subject did not seem to have much conception of form or spatial relationships. It produced only separate details of the model drawings, without putting them together into a whole. The right brain seemed to have a much better idea of the total pattern of the model drawings—but it had only a shaky grasp of many of the details. Neither brain, working separately, could reproduce the model drawings with much accuracy. Try reproducing the cross and cube yourself, using your left hand if you are normally right-handed, your right hand if you are left-handed. You will find that your own intact brain, with the hemispheres cooperating through the corpus callosum, enables you to do a fairly good job even with the hand that you do not ordinarily use in this way.

The split-brain experiments indicate that the two hemispheres may operate in different ways and perform different functions. Such a difference in functioning would not be surprising, for the two hemispheres are not exactly alike even in structure. Numerous asymmetries—or differences in the sizes of various areas—have been found. These variations, with some areas substantially larger on the left side and others on the right, have been observed even in unborn babies, an indication that they are inborn rather than acquired as the result of experience and learning (Galaburda et al., 1978).

A number of psychologists have concluded that the left hemisphere is specialized to deal with individual items of information, considered

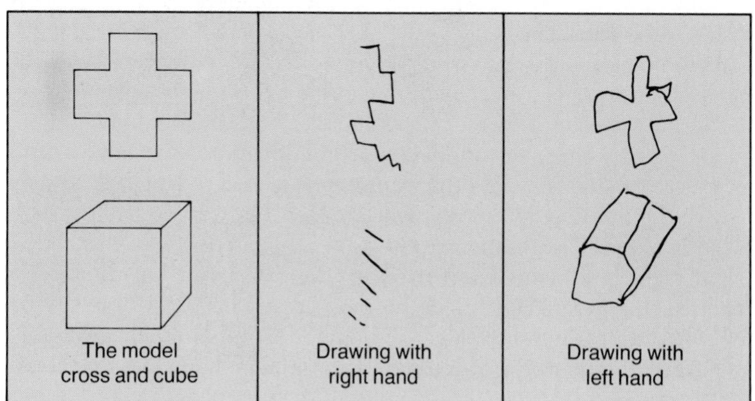

Figure 2-9 Drawings by a split-brain subject: the right brain does better *When a split-brain patient was asked to reproduce the drawings at the left, he could create only parts of the figures with his right hand, controlled by his left brain. He did better at reproducing the drawings as a whole with his left hand, controlled by the right brain—though he was still far from perfect (Bogen, 1969).*

Psychology and Society: Is the right brain neglected?

In terms of the brain's two hemispheres and their different functions, the United States and other modern industrialized nations are strictly left-brain societies. Our schools emphasize reading, writing, mathematics, and science. Our most esteemed leaders—in industry, the professions, and government—are those who excel at the ability to focus sharply on the facts, analyze them, reason about them logically, and express their conclusions in convincing language.

Even our definition of intelligence has this same basis. Most intelligence tests require subjects to read written questions or follow spoken instructions. Most of the test questions measure the ability to remember facts, draw logical inferences, and manipulate words and mathematical symbols. It is these skills—all ordinarily residing in the left hemisphere—that determine whether a person's IQ is high, low, or average.

Because of our emphasis on left-hemisphere functions, some members of our society have a difficult time. Some children for example, suffer from a conditon of the nervous system called *dyslexia* that makes it very hard for them to read. They are seriously handicapped at getting along in society even though they sometimes have superior abilities of other kinds—drawing, for example. Had they been born into a society without a written language, some of them might be considered unusually talented because of their skill at manipulating form and space—while many of us who find it easy to read might be held in very low regard in such a society because we lack those talents (Geschwind, 1980).

Robert Ornstein is one of a number of psychologists who are concerned that our educational system and society as a whole have been unduly one-sided in training and valuing only "half our minds." Ornstein suggests that overemphasis on the left hemisphere, which tends to think about separate items of information in isolation from the big picture, may account for many of today's social problems. He points out that our society has made many brilliant technological advances, but often these individual advances have produced grave dislocations. Knowledge of atomic energy has led to an arms race and the threat of nuclear destruction. Advances in medicine have lengthened individual life expectancy but have also created overpopulation and the danger of famine.

As a result of our "preoccupation with isolated facts," says Ornstein, we have created many social problems "whose solutions depend upon our ability to grasp the relationship of parts to wholes. . . . The problem is not that technology is leading us to destruction, but that technical progress has outstripped our perspective and judgment." Perhaps it is time to "reinstate a balance"—and use the long-neglected talents of our right brains to gain an intuitive understanding of the grand pattern of human life and society (Ornstein, 1978).

one by one in logical sequence—especially in the kind of thinking that we call reasoning, or arriving step by step at logical conclusions. It seems to be particularly adept at language, where sounds are put together in logical order into words, then words into sentences. The right hemisphere appears to specialize in considering things as a whole, taking account of many different items at once. Thus the right hemisphere excels in processing many kinds of visual information, especially of form and space, and music and other sounds not related to language. It may also be the intuitive half of the brain. Albert Einstein, in making such great discoveries as the theory of relativity, apparently used this ability of the right half of his brain to view "the big picture" of things. He reported that he managed to do his most creative work by disregarding logic, letting his mind wander, and doing his thinking not in orderly language but in patterns of spatial relationships and hunches that could not be put into language at all. Einstein's experiences—and what has been learned in general about the differences between the right brain and the left brain—raise some profound questions about human life and civilization that are discussed in a box on Psychology and Society.

Studies of the functions of the left brain and right brain have helped psychology begin to translate "the mental forces of the conscious mind" into "objective science" (Sperry, 1982). Our knowledge about the two brain hemispheres, however, remains incomplete. One group of investigators, for example, found evidence of different functioning of the two hemispheres in a normal subject, with an intact corpus callosum, as shown in Figure 2-10. When the subject was trying to master the toy shown in the photo (a spatial task), measurements of the electrical activity of his brain indicated his right hemisphere was doing most of the work. When he switched to writing a letter (language), the waves showed more activity in the left hemisphere (Ornstein, 1978). But the findings of other investigators suggest that the differences in activity between the two hemispheres are not so easily measured, and that there is still much to be learned about the specialized roles of each hemisphere in various human functions (Gevins et al., 1979).

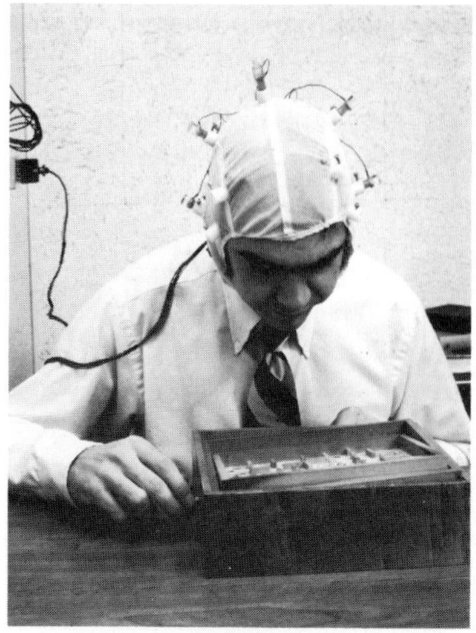

Figure 2-10 A normal subject tackles a spatial task. What do his brain waves show? *This subject, a graduate student, has been fitted with a skull cap that holds electrodes against various parts of his skull. The electrodes are hooked up to an* electroencephalograph, *or* EEG *for short, that records the electrical activity (or brain waves) occurring beneath them. For what the waves showed when the subject was trying to perform a delicate feat of judging space and movement to get a steel ball through a labyrinth, see the text.*

Brain function no. 3: managing our emotional and physical lives

The workings of the brain described thus far—allowing us to make sense out of our environment, to move about in the world, and to think as human beings—are impressive in their own right. But even with them, our lives would be flat and barren were it not for the deeply moving experiences we call emotions. True, the emotions of fear and danger are often upsetting and sometimes destructive. However, they also help us cope with the world and meet its crises. And there are other emotions that greatly enrich our lives—love, the joy of accomplishment, the spiritual glow we experience when we are in the presence of beauty and truth. All these are also the products of our brain.

Still another responsibility of the brain, making all else possible, is the management of our physical well-being—that is, keeping us alive and our bodies in working order. The brain decides when we need food or drink. It keeps body chemistry in balance. It governs our breathing, the pumping of the heart, and blood pressure. Indeed our lives are finally at an end only when the brain ceases its last flicker of activity.

The production and control of emotions

Of special importance in emotional behavior is the *limbic system,* a network of brain structures and pathways illustrated in Figure 2-11. A prominent part of the network is the *hypothalamus,* which is the brain's most direct link to the body glands that are active in fear, anger, and other emotions. Indeed, as can be seen by turning back to Figure 2-5 (p. 54), the master gland, the *pituitary,* is attached to the hypothalamus. Thus the hypothalamus, working in concert with other portions of the limbic system, delivers messages that help produce the "stirred-up" bodily processes that accompany emotion. The actual feel-

Figure 2-11 **The brain's limbic system** *The word* limbic *means "bordering," and the limbic system is so named because its parts form a border, or loop, around the deepest core of the cerebrum. The functions of the system and some of its key parts are described in the text (Zimbardo, P. G.* Psychology and life, *10th ed. © 1979 Scott, Foresman and Company).*

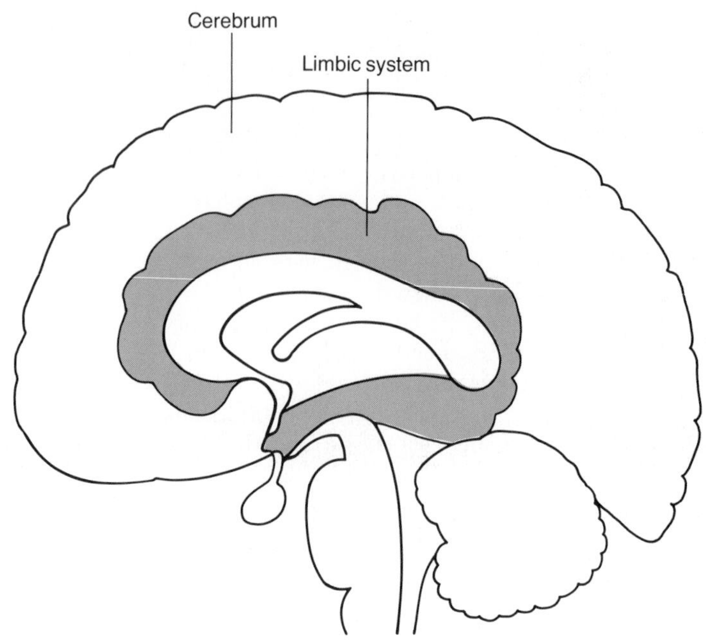

ings we experience are another aspect of the human consciousness for which the cerebral cortex is responsible. In one way or another, it is the brain that accounts for our vivid appreciation of life's pleasures and our sorrow over its tragedies.

In lower mammals, the limbic system appears to contain the programing that directs the instinctive patterns in which they feed, mate, fight, and escape from danger. Laboratory experiments have shown that surgery or electrical stimulation at various parts of the limbic system can cause animals to behave in ways that appear unusually docile or unusually aggressive, as illustrated in Figure 2-12.

We cannot be sure, of course, whether the behavior shown in Figure

In displays of emotion—perhaps aggression in particular—the brain structure of special importance is the limbic system.

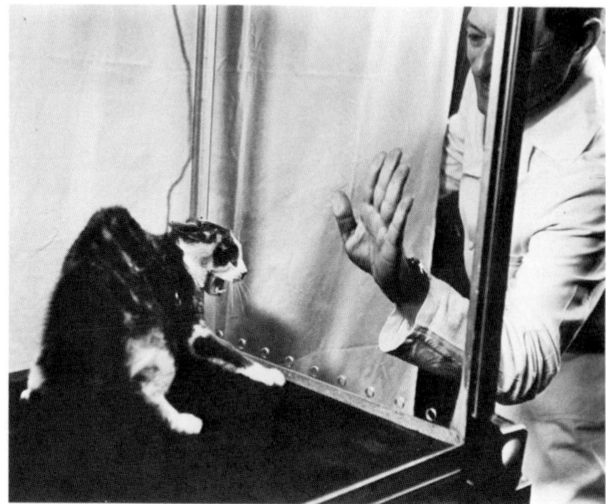

Figure 2-12 The limbic system and aggression *The photographs show the effect of electrical stimulation of the brain through electrodes planted in or around the limbic system of the cat. At left, under stimulation at one particular spot, the cat calmly ignores its traditional prey, the rat. At right, stimulation at another spot makes the cat assume a hostile posture toward a laboratory assistant with whom it is ordinarily on friendly terms.*

2-12 represents genuine docility and rage or simply some other kind of change in the operation of the brain. One school of thought holds that abnormalities in the limbic system account for the fact that some people are easily provoked into violent rages and physical violence. But other scientists disagree.

Keeping the body alive

Unlike human beings, who are dependent on the brain for physical well-being, some organisms manage to live their lives, feed themselves, and reproduce without the help of any nervous system at all. An example is the one-celled paramecium, which you may have seen under a microscope in a biology laboratory. Its entire single-celled "body" is somehow sensitive to heat and light and capable of initiating its own movements.

Animals a little higher in the evolutionary scale have specialized nerve cells but no brains. In the tiny sea creature called the coral, for example, there is simply a scattered network of nerve fibers with no central management. The neurons and the various parts of the body work together much like a loose federation of states, each preserving considerable independence. This haphazard arrangement is enough to serve the coral's needs, but it would be totally incapable of running the human body.

In discussions of how the human body is maintained in a condition of well-being and efficiency, the key word is *homeostasis*—meaning a state of stability in such matters as internal temperature and chemical balance, with a proper supply of oxygen, water, and all the various other substances that the cells require. The air we breathe, the water we drink, and the food we eat are like the raw materials required to keep a factory busy. We need a central management system to order them, make sure they arrive on time, distribute them where they are needed, and see that they are processed properly.

The hypothalamus, besides being a center for emotional behavior, plays a role in homeostasis by helping signal when the body needs more food or water and by regulating states of wakefulness and sleep. It also acts like a highly accurate thermostat, turning on the instant the temperature inside the body gets a little too low and off again when the temperature gets a shade too high.

One brain structure—the *medulla,* shown in Figure 2-5 (p. 54) is responsible for coordinating such vital bodily processes as breathing and the beating of the heart. The medulla is also a major relay station, containing neurons that transmit messages between the spinal cord and the upper parts of the brain.

The autonomic nervous system: the brain's able assistant

In controlling bodily processes, the brain has an effective assistant in the form of the *autonomic nervous system,* or ANS for short. The word *autonomic* means independent or self-sufficient—and in many ways the autonomic nervous system operates on its own, as its name suggests, without much if any conscious control. Even if we try we cannot ordinarily command our stomach muscles to make the movements that help digest food. We cannot order the muscles of the blood vessels to

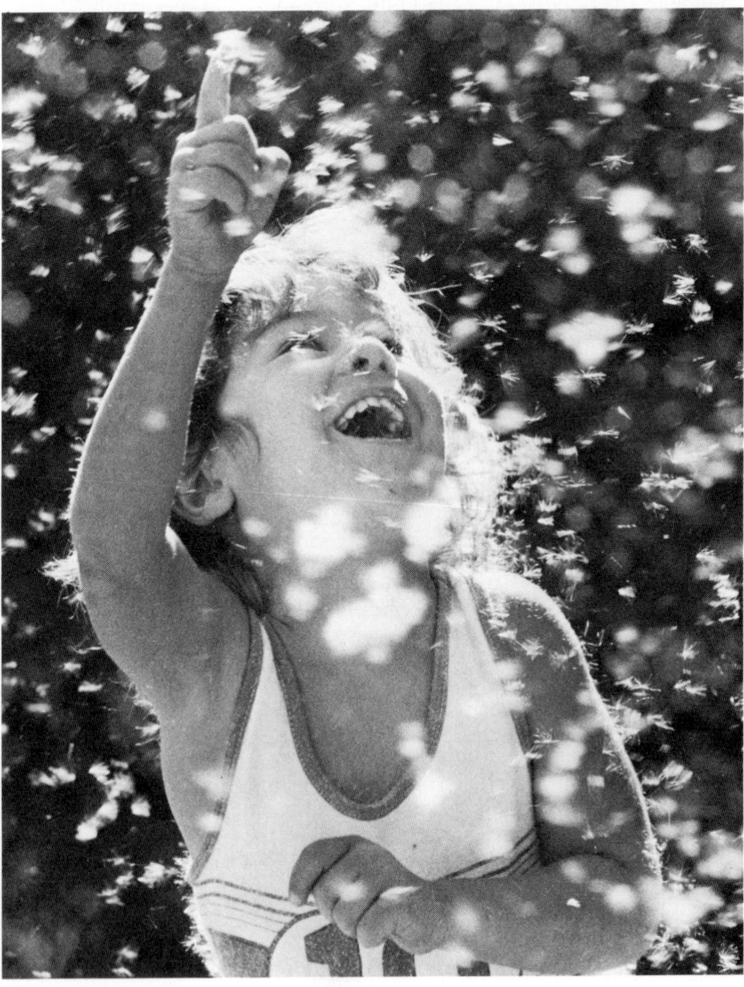

Joy is the most glorious of the emotions controlled by the ANS.

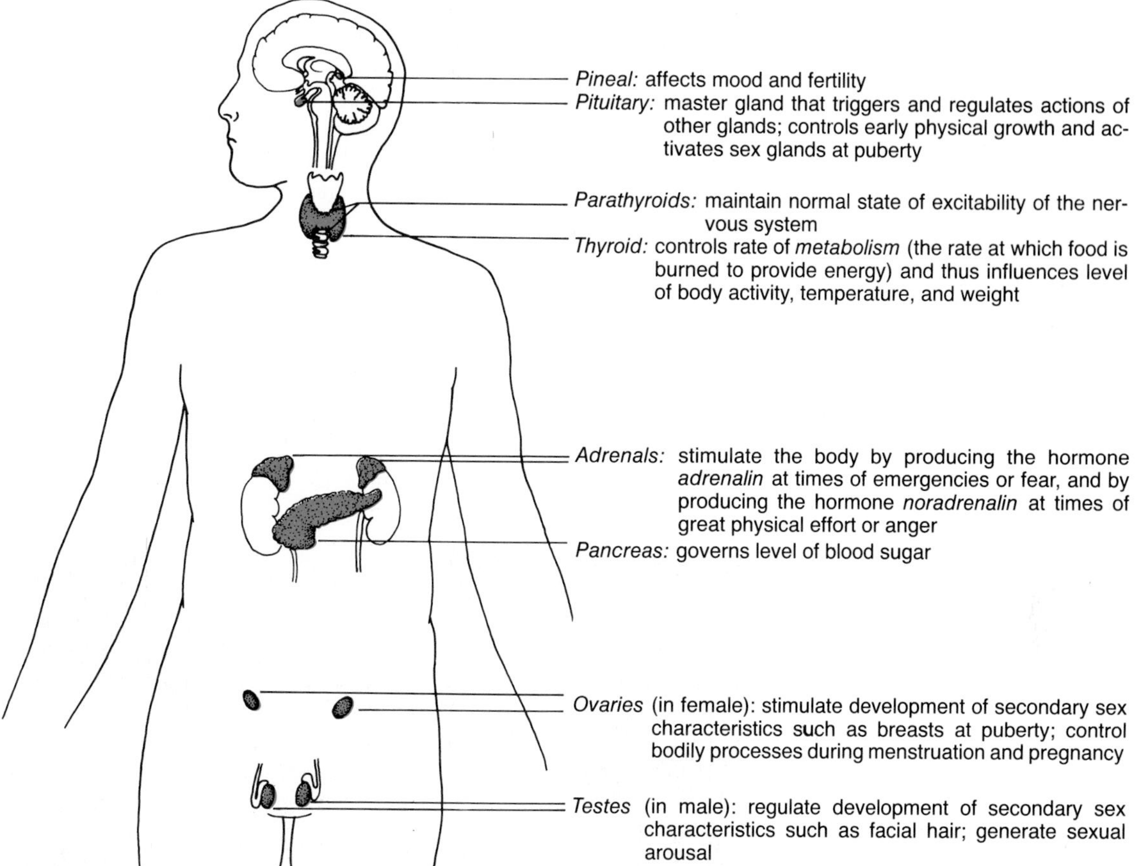
Pineal: affects mood and fertility
Pituitary: master gland that triggers and regulates actions of other glands; controls early physical growth and activates sex glands at puberty
Parathyroids: maintain normal state of excitability of the nervous system
Thyroid: controls rate of *metabolism* (the rate at which food is burned to provide energy) and thus influences level of body activity, temperature, and weight
Adrenals: stimulate the body by producing the hormone *adrenalin* at times of emergencies or fear, and by producing the hormone *noradrenalin* at times of great physical effort or anger
Pancreas: governs level of blood sugar
Ovaries (in female): stimulate development of secondary sex characteristics such as breasts at puberty; control bodily processes during menstruation and pregnancy
Testes (in male): regulate development of secondary sex characteristics such as facial hair; generate sexual arousal

Figure 2-13 The human endocrine glands *The endocrine glands receive messages from the brain and ANS that make them spring into action or sometimes slow down. The glands influence the excitability of the brain and the rest of the nervous system, helping create emotional experiences.*

channel a strong flow of blood to the stomach to aid digestion—or to redirect the flow of blood toward the muscles of the arms or legs when we have to do physical work. We cannot make our hearts pump faster or slower. But the ANS can do all these things—and does so constantly, even when we are asleep or in a deep coma caused by an anesthetic or a brain injury.

In addition, the ANS exercises considerable independent influence on important bodily structures called *endocrine glands,* or glands of internal secretion, which are also resistant to conscious control. Unlike the sweat glands that deliver perspiration to the skin, or the salivary glands that deliver fluids to the mouth, the endocrine glands discharge their products directly into the bloodstream. These substances, as mentioned earlier, are called hormones. They influence many bodily activities, including those associated with emotional behavior. The endocrine glands and their functions are listed in Figure 2-13.

The autonomic nervous system exerts its impact on important body processes through a number of centers called *ganglia,* as shown in Figure 2-14. These are like small brains scattered throughout the body. They consist of masses of nerve cells packed together and connected with one another—just as in the brain itself but on a much smaller scale. Some

The sympathetic division of the autonomic nervous system is at work to help the animal meet an emergency—either by fighting or running away.

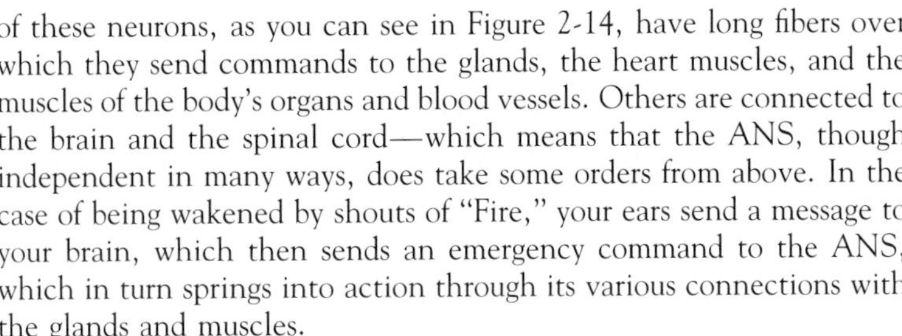

of these neurons, as you can see in Figure 2-14, have long fibers over which they send commands to the glands, the heart muscles, and the muscles of the body's organs and blood vessels. Others are connected to the brain and the spinal cord—which means that the ANS, though independent in many ways, does take some orders from above. In the case of being wakened by shouts of "Fire," your ears send a message to your brain, which then sends an emergency command to the ANS, which in turn springs into action through its various connections with the glands and muscles.

As shown in Figure 2-14, there are two divisions of the ANS, differing in structure and function.

The parasympathetic division: running the ordinary business of living The *parasympathetic division* connects with the stem of the brain and the lower part of the spinal cord. It is made up of a number of widely scattered ganglia, most of which lie near the glands or muscles of organs to which it delivers its messages. Because it is so loosely constructed, it tends to act in piecemeal fashion, delivering its orders to one or several parts of the body but not necessarily to all at once.

In general, the parasympathetic division seems to play its most important role during those frequent periods when no danger threatens and the body can relax and go about the ordinary business of living. It tends to slow down the work of the heart and lungs. It aids digestion by stimulating our salivary glands, producing wavelike motions of the muscles of the stomach and intestines, and encouraging the stomach to produce digestive acid and the liver to produce the digestive fluid called bile. It also brings about elimination of the body's waste products from the intestines and bladder. At times, however, the parasympathetic division abandons these usual tasks and helps mobilize the body for emergency action. When it does this—operating in ways that are not yet understood—it seems to assist and supplement the work of the other part of the autonomic system, the sympathetic division.

The child's wide eyes are one of the bodily signs of strong emotion.

The sympathetic division: meeting emergencies The *sympathetic division* is shown in Figure 2-14 as a long chain of ganglia extending down the side of the spinal cord. There is a similar chain, not shown, on the other side of the cord. All the many ganglia of the sympathetic division are elaborately interconnected. Note that many of the nerve fibers going out from the chains of ganglia meet again in additional ganglia in other parts of the body, where they again form complicated interconnections with nerve cells that finally carry commands to the glands and smooth muscles. For this reason the sympathetic division, unlike the parasympathetic, tends to function as a unit.

When the sympathetic division springs into action, as when you experience fear or anger, it does many things all at once. Most notably, it commands the adrenal glands to spill their powerful stimulants into the blood stream. By acting on the adrenal glands, liver, and pancreas, it increases the level of blood sugar, thus raising the rate of metabolism and providing additional energy. It causes the spleen, a glandlike organ in which red corpuscles are stored, to release more of these corpuscles into the bloodstream, thus enabling the blood to carry more oxygen to

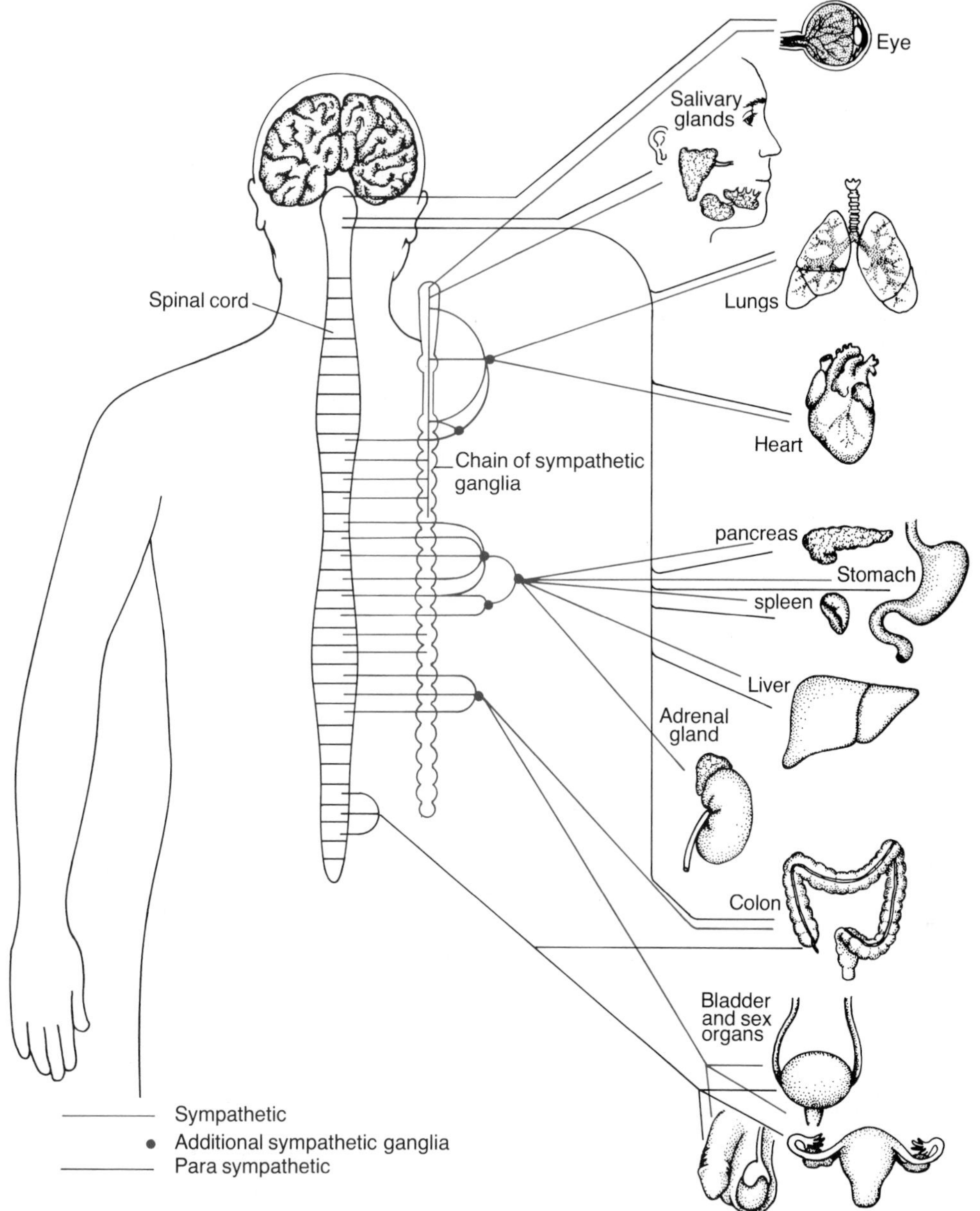

Figure 2-14 Autonomic nervous system *The long chain of ganglia of the* sympathetic division *extends down the side of the spinal cord, to which it makes many connections. (There is a similar chain on the other side of the body.) The* parasympathetic division *has small ganglia near the glands and smooth muscles that both divisions help control, though in different ways, (after Crosby, Humphrey, and Lauer, 1962).*

the body's tissues. It changes the size of the blood vessels—enlarging those of the heart and muscles of body movement and constricting those of the muscles of the stomach and intestines. It makes us breathe harder. It enlarges the pupils of the eyes, which are controlled by muscles, and slows the activity of the salivary glands. ("Wide eyes" and a dry mouth are characteristic of a number of strong emotions such as fear.) It also activates the sweat glands and contracts the muscles at the base of the hairs on the body, causing the hair to rise on animals and producing goose flesh in human beings. In general, the changes prepare the body for emergency action—such as fighting or running away.

How the brain performs its functions: the neurons and their messages

The brain carries out its many duties through a constant exchange of messages, flashing through its own untold billions of pathways and also to and from the rest of the nervous system. The messages take the form of nervous impulses that resemble tiny electrical charges, each barely strong enough to jiggle the needle of the most sensitive recording device.

The nervous impulses are produced by the neurons, which have been aptly described as the "building blocks" of the brain (Stevens, 1979). Indeed they are the basic units in the entire nervous system. The neurons start sending their messages long before birth and continue humming with activity throughout life. If every neuron in the brain fired off its impulse at the same instant, the entire amount of electricity produced would be just about enough to power a small transistor radio. Yet these tiny impulses somehow account for all the accomplishments of the brain and the rest of the nervous system.

The neuron's "receivers" and "senders"

Although neurons show many variations, they all resemble the drawing in Figure 2-15 in a general way. The *dendrites* are the "receivers." When they are properly stimulated, they set off the nervous impulse, which travels the fiberlike length of the neuron to the other end. In between is the *cell body,* which has a *nucleus,* or core, containing the chromosomes and genes that caused the cell to grow into a neuron in the first place. The cell body performs the process of metabolism, converting food supplied by the blood steam into energy. Moreover the surface of the cell body is dotted with numerous *receptor sites* that are also capable of responding to stimulation, like the dendrites, and setting off nervous impulses, which travel down the fiberlike *axon* to the *end branches,* which are the neuron's "senders."

The axon's *myelin sheath,* found in many but not all neurons, is a whitish coating of fatty protective tissue that increases the speed at which the nervous impulse travels. Transmission is further improved by the *nodes,* which are constrictions of the sheath acting as little booster stations that help nudge the impulse along to the end branches, the "senders" that deliver the neuron's message.

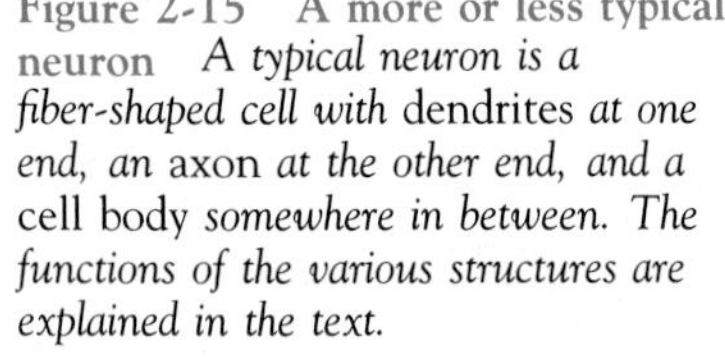

Figure 2-15 A more or less typical neuron *A typical neuron is a fiber-shaped cell with* dendrites *at one end, an* axon *at the other end, and a* cell body *somewhere in between. The functions of the various structures are explained in the text.*

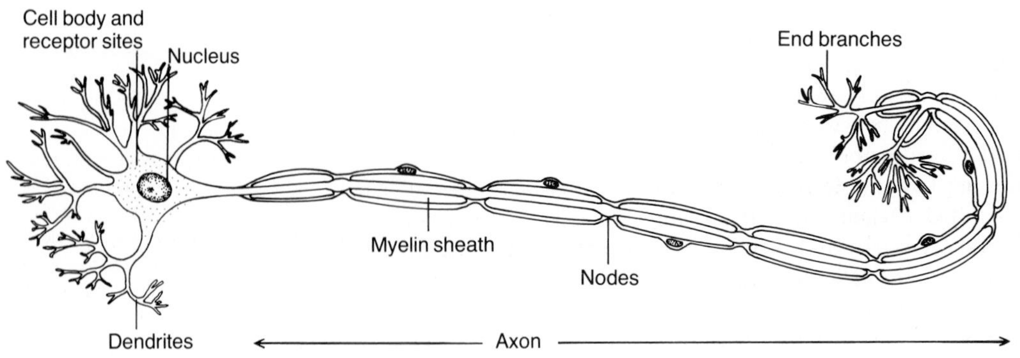

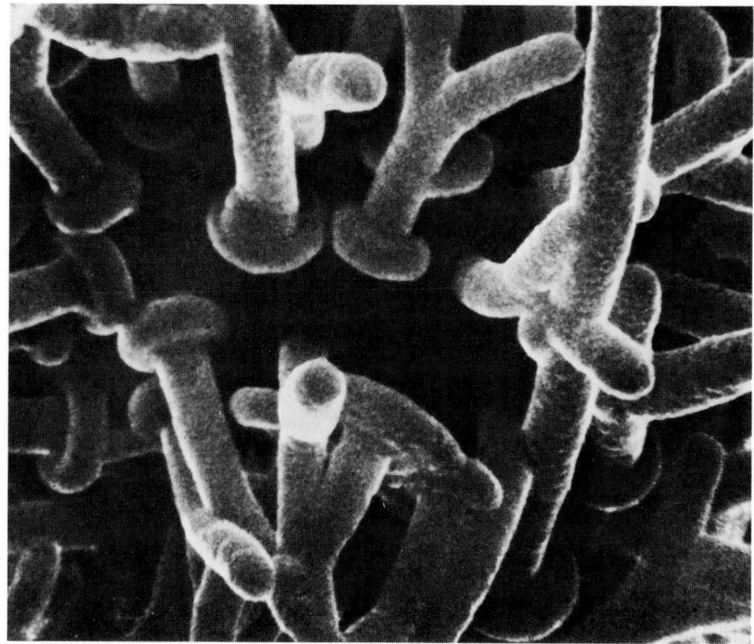

Figure 2-16 The synaptic knobs *This photograph, taken at a magnification of about 2,000 times life size, was the first ever made of the synaptic knobs. It shows some of the structures in a snail (Lewis, Zeevi, and Everhart, 1969).*

Some neurons have their end branches in glands or muscles, which their impulses stimulate into action. Most neurons, however, particularly in the brain, have end branches that connect with other neurons. Their job is communication—passing messages along to other neurons.

How neurons speak to one another: synapses and neurotransmitters

The nervous impulse can only travel the length of the neuron that produces it—from dendrites or receptor sites to the end branches of the axon. There it stops. It can go no farther. It can, however, influence other neurons by delivering its message.

The key to transmission of the message is the *synapse,* the connecting point where an end branch-sender of one neuron is separated by only a microscopic distance—a millionth of an inch—from a dendrite-receiver of another neuron. At the synapse, where the two neurons almost touch, the first can influence the second in various ways. Sometimes the electrical charge arriving at the synapse is enough in itself to produce an effect. Usually, however, the action is chemical. The senders of the axon contain small amounts of chemical substances called *neurotransmitters.* When the neuron fires, a burst of these substances is released at the synapse (Eccles, 1964). The chemicals flow across the tiny gap between the two neurons and act on the second neuron.

Figure 2-16 is a photograph of parts of the neuron that play an especially important role in the transmission of messages—the little swellings called *synaptic knobs* at the very tips of the branches of the axon. It is these knobs that actually form synapses with other neurons at their dendrites or cell-body receptor sites. An enlarged drawing of a synapse is shown in Figure 2-17.

In the first neuron the neurotransmitter is produced in the cell body

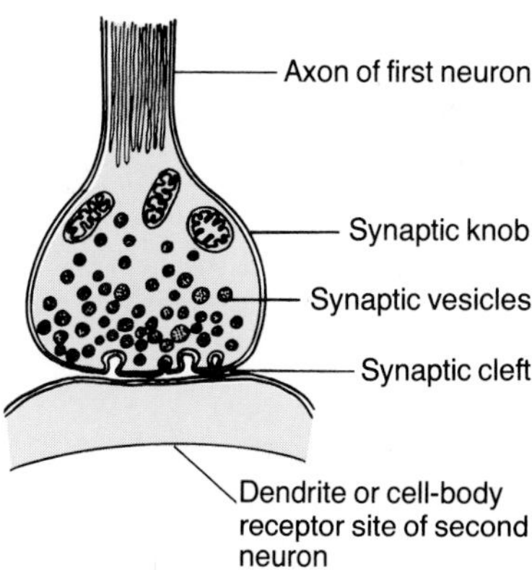

Figure 2-17 Where neuron meets neuron: the synapse *The axon of the first neuron ends in a synaptic knob, separated from the second neuron by only a tiny gap called the* synaptic cleft. *What happens at the cleft is described in the text.*

and delivered down the length of the fiber to the *synaptic vesicles,* where it is stored until called upon. When the neuron fires, the nervous impulse reaching the synaptic knob causes the vesicles to release their transmitter chemicals. These neurotransmitters flow across the *synaptic cleft* and act on the second neuron. Some of the neurotransmitters act as stimulants, urging the second neuron to fire off its own nervous impulse. Others, however, do the opposite, instructing the second neuron to refrain from action. They act to *inhibit* any activity in the second neuron.

To fire or not to fire?

Will the second neuron fire—or will it not? On this question, it must be emphasized that the neuron has synapses with as many as several thousand others whose axon end branches are in close contact with its dendrites or cell-body receptor sites. At any given instant, the neuron may be receiving messages from a few, many, or all of these axons. Some of the messages are delivered by neurotransmitters that tell it to fire, others by neurotransmitters that do the opposite. Moreover the neuron itself responds in different ways depending on where the message arrives. Some of its receptor sites are like switches that signal "on." Stimulation at these points tends to make the neuron fire. Other receptor sites are like "off" switches. Stimulation of these points tends to inhibit the neuron from firing (Lewin, 1974).

Thus whether the neuron fires or not depends on the whole pattern of messages it receives. Ordinarily it will not fire in response to a single message arriving at one of its many dendrites or on its cell body. Instead the firing process requires multiple stimulation—a whole group of messages arriving at once or in quick succession from the other neurons with which it has synaptic contact. Moreover the messages that represent signals to fire must outweigh the messages that inhibit it from firing.

In the brain, with all its multiple interconnections, activity goes on constantly at many thousands of synapses all at the same time. Each neuron in the network is receiving messages from hundreds or thousands of other neurons. The nervous impulses it receives may have no effect at all. They may be too few in number or too far apart in time to make it fire. Or the incoming messages urging it to fire may be canceled out by messages that inhibit firing. Then the messages it receives may not get through at all. On the other hand, the messages may make it fire anywhere from just once to many times in rapid succession—and in turn influence all the many other neurons with which its own axons form connections.

At each of these new synapses, the process is repeated. The message may get through or not. It may inhibit other neurons or it may cause them to fire—again just a single time or many times in quick succession. Thus once a message gets started through the brain, its possible pathways are virtually unlimited. One neuron's impulses may stimulate a few or many other neurons into action. The new impulses may travel in any one of many directions or in a number of directions at once. They may be few or many, slow or rapid. And at each new switching point the process is repeated, introducing thousands of possible new pathways.

Small wonder that the human nervous system is capable of so many accomplishments. By comparison with the brain, the nation's telephone network is just a child's toy.

How neurons give their all—or nothing at all

The nervous impulse—the tiny charge of electricity that passes down the length of the neuron fiber—can best be compared to the glowing band of fire that travels along a lighted fuse. In the neuron, however, no combustion takes place. What actually happens is that there is an exchange of chemical particles from inside and outside the nerve fiber, creating different electrical charges between them. Once the nervous impulse created by this change of electrical charges has passed down the length of the fiber, the neuron quickly returns to its normal state and is ready to fire off another impulse.

The neuron ordinarily operates on what is called the *all or none principle.* That is to say, if it fires at all it fires as hard as it can, given its physiological condition at the moment (which, in complex ways, can be altered by the messages it is receiving from other neurons). All stimuli of sufficient power set off the same kind of impulse—as strong as the neuron is capable of producing at that moment.

After the neuron has fired, it requires a brief recovery period before it can fire again. This recovery period has two phases. During the first phase the neuron is incapable of responding at all. During the second phase it is still incapable of responding to all the stimuli that would ordinarily make it fire, but it can respond if the stimuli are powerful enough. The length of the recovery period varies. Some neurons recover slowly and can fire only a few times per second. A few recover so swiftly that they can fire as often as 1,000 times a second when sufficiently stimulated. Most are in between, with a maximum firing rate of several hundred times a second.

Figure 2-18 shows the actual sequence of nervous impulses fired off by a neuron over a period of several tenths of a second, under three different kinds of stimulation. These tracings of the neuron's activity demonstrate that stronger stimulation makes the neuron fire more often but not with greater strength.

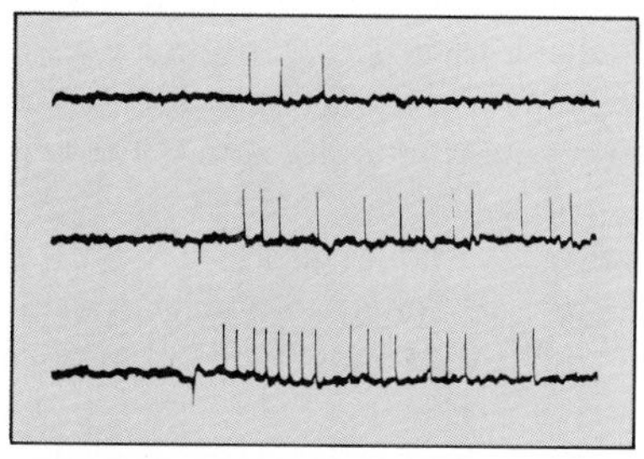

Figure 2-18 A neuron's messages: alike but in different patterns
These are the tracings from an electrode that was attached to the neuron of a rat. Each upward movement of the lines shows a separate impulse. The neuron was from the rat's tongue, and the stimulus was salt solution in varying strengths. The response of the neuron to the weakest salt solution is shown in the top line. In the center line the stimulus was ten times stronger and in the bottom line a hundred times stronger. Note that the neuron's responses to these different intensities of stimulation varied only in rate and pattern, not in the strength of its individual impulses (Pfaffman, 1955).

Turning beeps into meanings and feelings

Those little jolts of electricity shown in Figure 2-18 represent the basic activity that goes on inside the nervous system, in human beings as well as other animals. Each neuron ordinarily produces only one kind of impulse, its own little unvarying "beep." Yet somehow these monotonous beeps—by the rate at which they are produced, the patterns they form, and the way they are routed through the brain—manage to perform all the miracles of human cognition and consciousness. They tell us what our eyes see and our ears hear. They enable us to learn and to think. They direct our glands and internal organs to function in harmony. They direct our muscles to perform such intricate and delicate feats as driving an automobile or playing a violin.

Different neurons, in transmitting their nervous impulses, release

Psychology and Society: Will brain research make psychology obsolete?

Advances in brain research have led some scientists to conclude that everything we experience and do will one day be explained by the electrical and chemical operations of the brain. Even psychologists sometimes wonder if "psychology is in danger of losing its status as an independent body of knowledge" (Peele, 1981).

The findings about the brain are indeed impressive. Many experiments with animals have shown that behavior can be greatly influenced by chemical stimulants, using substances that resemble the brain's neurotransmitters. Injecting one kind of chemical into the hypothalamus will make an animal stop eating, even if it is hungry. A different chemical makes the animal eat, even if it is already gorged with food (Leibowitz, 1970). Chemical stimulation has also been found to change human behavior. Various drugs that influence brain activity (notably tranquilizers and stimulants such as amphetamines) affect human perception, thinking, and moods. Some recent studies even suggest that memory can be improved by chemical means (Weingarten et al., 1981).

Experiments with animals have also shown that behavior can be greatly influenced by electrical stimulation through electrodes planted in the brain or by destruction of some of the brain tissue. When a particular small area of the hypothalamus is destroyed, animals stay awake until they die of exhaustion. When another part of the hypothalamus is destroyed, animals spend most of their time sleeping (Nauta, 1946). Surgery has pronounced effects on human behavior as well—as in the case of split-brain patients with a severed corpus callosum. And efforts to transplant healthy brain tissue to replace diseased portions of the brain now appear possible (Wyatt and Freed, 1983).

Does all this mean that we can dispense with psychology? Will human behavior—and its control—one day be reducible to the brain's nervous impulses and neurochemical juices?

Most scientists, biologists as well as psychologists, think not. For one thing, the workings of the brain are so complex as to defy complete understanding. Neuropsychologist Elliot Valenstein, for example, has pointed out that a given drug does not always produce one specific effect. He believes that the circuits regulating behavior are so widespread, and the possible pathways so numerous, that the brain will probably always remain something of a mystery—and elude any attempts at control.

More important, no matter how complete our understanding of the brain, its structures and circuits cannot be made to work independently, as if in a vacuum. The brain works instead as an instrument through which behavior is modified by experience. It is the pathways of learning somehow laid down in the brain that really determine most of our behavior. They influence how we will interpret and respond to the stimuli that reach our senses. They influence what we find pleasant and what we find unpleasant. They determine what we find psychologically stressful and what we react to emotionally. They, even more than real physical needs, determine our habits of sleep, hunger, thirst, and sexual behavior. Neuropsychologist Roger Sperry, when he received the Nobel prize for his work on the split brain, emphasized this point. We cannot depend on the brain as an isolated organ, he said, to tell us about the operation of the conscious mind (Sperry, 1982).

Biologists themselves have put advances in brain research into clearest perspective. Seymour Kety, for decades a leading investigator of the physical foundations of behavior, acknowledges that remarkable progress has been made in our understanding of the structures of the brain, the relationships among its parts, and how brain chemistry affects behavior. But he maintains that biology can hardly presume to be able with its tools alone to unravel the mysteries of human personality and experience (Kety, 1982). And Nobel prize-winning brain scientist John Eccles has observed: "I go all the way with my fellow scientists in understanding the brain physically. But it doesn't explain me, or human choice, delight, courage, or compassion. I think we must go beyond. . . . There is something apart from all the electricity and chemistry we can measure" (Facklam and Facklam, 1982).

No matter how much we learn about the operations of the human brain, it is psychology that must ultimately explain what it is that makes you what you are.

split-brain patients—indicate that the left hemisphere specializes in individual items of information, logic, and reasoning, while the right hemisphere specializes in information about form, space, music, and entire patterns and is the intuitive half of the brain.

Brain function no. 3: managing our emotional and physical lives

20. The *limbic system,* a network of brain structures and pathways, helps regulate emotional behavior.
21. A prominent part of the limbic system is the *hypothalamus*—the brain's most direct link to the body glands that are active in emotions. The master gland, the pituitary, is attached to the hypothalamus.
22. The hypothalamus also plays a role in maintaining the body's *homeostasis,* the state of stability in such matters as internal temperature and chemical balance.
23. The *medulla* is responsible for a number of essential bodily processes including breathing and heartbeat. It is also a relay station between the spinal cord and the upper parts of the brain.
24. The *autonomic nervous system* exercises a more or less independent control over the glands, the heart muscles, and the muscles of the body's organs and blood vessels. It helps regulate breathing, heart rate, blood pressure, and digestion. In times of emergency it works in conjunction with the endocrine glands to mobilize the body's resources for drastic action.
25. The *endocrine glands,* or *ductless glands,* influence behavior by secreting *hormones* (or activators) into the bloodstream. The most important endocrine glands are:
    a. the *pineal,* which affects mood and fertility
    b. the *pituitary,* which is the master gland, producing hormones that control growth, cause sexual development at puberty, and regulate other glands
    c. the *parathyroids,* which maintain a normal state of excitability of the nervous system
    d. the *thyroid,* which regulates metabolism and affects levels of body activity, temperature, and weight
    e. *adrenals,* which secrete the powerful stimulants *adrenalin* (active in states of emergency or fear) and *noradrenalin* (active during physical effort or anger)
    f. the *pancreas,* which governs blood sugar level
    g. the female *ovaries* and male *testes,* which regulate sexual characteristics and behavior
26. The autonomic nervous system is composed of two parts: (a) the *parasympathetic division,* which is most active under ordinary circumstances; and (b) the *sympathetic division,* which is active in emergencies.

How the brain performs its functions: the neurons and their messages

27. Each neuron in the nervous system is a fiberlike cell with receivers called *dendrites* at one end and senders called *end branches* at the

other. Stimulation of the neuron at its dendrites—or at *receptor sites* on its cell body—sets off a nervous impulse that travels the length of the fiber, or *axon,* to the end branches, where the impulse activates other neurons, muscles, or glands.

28. The key to the transmission of nervous messages is the *synapse,* a junction point where a sender of one neuron is separated by only a microscopic distance from a receiver of another neuron.
29. The sending neuron can stimulate the receiving neuron electrically at times, but it usually releases chemical *neurotransmitters* that flow across the tiny gap of the synapse and act on the receiving neuron.
30. A neuron ordinarily fires on the *all or none principle*—if it fires at all, it fires as hard as it can. Most neurons have a maximum firing rate of several hundred times a second.
31. Since each neuron usually produces only its own little unvarying impulse, the miracles of human consciousness and cognition are determined by the rate at which the impulses are produced, the patterns they form, and the way they are routed through the brain.
32. Anything that alters the amount and effectiveness of neurotransmitters in the brain is likely to have a great impact on thinking and moods. Mind-altering drugs like marijuana and heroin act on the neurotransmitters, as do medications used to treat mental illnesses and depression.

IMPORTANT TERMS

adrenalin
adrenals
afferent neuron
all or none principle
autonomic nervous system
axon
brain
cell body
central nervous system
cerebellum
cerebral cortex
cerebrum
connecting neuron
corpus callosum
dendrite
ductless glands
efferent neuron
end branches
endocrine gland
endorphins
ganglia
hippocampus
homeostasis
hormone
hypothalamus
left hemisphere
limbic system
medulla
metabolism
myelin sheath
neuron
neurotransmitter
nodes
noradrenalin
ovaries
pancreas
parasympathetic division
parathyroids
peripheral nervous system
pineal
pituitary
pons
receptor site
reticular activating system
right hemisphere
spinal cord
sympathetic division
synapse
synaptic cleft
synaptic knobs
synaptic vesicles

RECOMMENDED READINGS

Brown, T. S., and Wallace, P. *Physiological psychology.* New York: Academic Press, 1980.

Bunge, M. *The mind-body problem: a psychobiological approach.* New York: Pergamon Press, 1980.

Cotman, C. W., and McGaugh, J. L. *Behavioral neuroscience: an introduction.* New York: Academic Press, 1980.

Eccles, J. C. *The understanding of the brain,* 2d ed. New York: McGraw-Hill, 1977.

Oakley, D. A., and Plotkin, H. C., eds. *Brain, behaviour, and evolution.* New York: Methuen, Inc., 1979.

Powell, G. *Brain and personality.* New York: Praeger Publishers, 1979.

Valenstein, E. S. *Brain control.* New York: Wiley, 1973.

Wittrock, M. C., ed. *The brain and psychology.* New York: Academic Press, 1980.

PART

2

How Learning and Memory Shape Our Lives

In a psychology classroom two young women sit side by side taking notes. Like all of us, they have inherited the same basic human structure of bone, muscle, internal organs, and nervous system. Moreover, it happens that they are about the same height and weight and have the same color eyes and hair. They made almost identical scores on the Scholastic Aptitude Tests, an indication that they are about equal in intelligence. They grew up in similar homes in the same neighborhood and went to the same high school. In all these ways they are much alike—but there the resemblance ends.

One has no career ambitions and is not especially interested in her college work. She is really just marking time, getting C's in her courses, until she marries her longtime boyfriend, who is just a year away from graduation and a job. She wants to be a full-time housewife and mother, preferably with three or four children. She is shy and avoids company but has a trusting disposition and seldom says an unkind word about anyone. When she is criticized, she becomes embarrassed and apologetic.

The other wants to be a famous lawyer. She studies hard and gets straight A's. She has many friends but none who is very close, and she is not sure she ever wants to be married. Although she is outgoing, witty, and popular, she is basically suspicious of other people and is frequently sarcastic.

When she is criticized, she gets angry and fights back.

Nature has provided these two women with similar physical and psychological capacities and limitations, but *nurture* has turned them into two quite opposite sorts of people. In one way or another, they have acquired their own very different motives, ambitions, attitudes toward people, and ways of reacting to criticism and to other events in their lives. True, some of the personality characteristics they display may be influenced by inborn tendencies. But to a considerable extent these women have *learned* to be what they are.

Because learning shapes our lives in so many significant ways, it has always been a major concern of psychology. Recently, the rise of the cognitive school has given both learning and the related phenomenon of memory a new emphasis as two of the major steps in information processing. In cognitive terms, learning is the way we acquire information about the environment. Memory is the way we store that information and keep it available so that we can call on it and use it to our advantage. Although these two steps are closely intertwined and mutually dependent, the most convenient way to discuss them is in separate chapters—Chapter 3, on the universal laws of learning, and Chapter 4, on the vast and cunningly organized storehouse of information called human memory.

CHAPTER 3

Classical conditioning 82
- Learning unreasonable fears, unreasonable preferences
- Pavlov and the drooling dogs
- Learning to fear Santa Claus
- Conditioning comas and asthma attacks
- Conditioning, physical upsets, and treatment
- The elements of classical conditioning
- Reinforcement, extinction, and spontaneous recovery
- Stimulus generalization and discrimination
- Learning to be neurotic

Operant conditioning 90
- B. F. Skinner and his magic box
- Some principles of operant conditioning
- Shaping behavior
- Learning to be superstitious
- Some facts about reinforcement
- Applications of operant conditioning: a look at behavior modification
- Token economies
- Conditioning, biofeedback, and medicine

Operant escape, punishment, and learned helplessness 99
- Escape and avoidance in human behavior
- Punishment and its effect on behavior
- Punishment works with animals
- But does punishment work with people?
- The sad case of the helpless dogs
- Learned helplessness in human beings
- Helplessness as the result of failure
- When you fail, whom do you blame?
- Therapy—and self-therapy—for helplessness

The cognitive view: learning as a step in information processing 108
- The case of the ingenious chimps
- Learning without reinforcement
- Learning without a response
- Cognitive maps, expectancies, and knowledge
- Observation learning
- Some limits on learning: species-specific behavior

Summary 114

Important terms 117

Recommended readings 117

Psychology and society
- The question of scientific ethics 86
- Does behavior modification threaten human freedom? 98
- Learned helplessness and the schools 106

The Universal Laws of Learning

Some of the creatures that inhabit our earth manage to live their lives without learning much of anything. Everything they need to know is already present in the wiring of the nervous system with which they are born. Guided solely by these built-in patterns of behavior, or *instincts,* they can find food, build shelters, mate, and survive to what for their species is a ripe old age. Without any training, spiders spin their characteristic webs, birds construct their nests, salmon migrate from their river birthplace to the ocean and back to the river to spawn. Some creatures—ants, for example—even have an instinctive knowledge of how to establish elaborate societies and maintain them with a highly efficient division of labor.

But human beings are altogether different. We have few if any instincts. No inborn blueprint in the nervous system steers us automatically through life. We have to learn how to find food, keep warm, build shelters. We must learn to form social arrangements that provide the safety of numbers and enrich our lives by providing through joint effort what no individual could manage alone.

The difference between instinctive and learned behavior is dramatically apparent in the contrast between the rigidly limited existence of the spider and the great variety of human experience. Each spider lives exactly the way its species has lived for countless generations,

Instincts provide the spider with full instructions for spinning this web, which is exactly the same as its ancestors have spun. The spider—unlike human beings—can live out its life without ever learning anything.

spinning the same kind of web to serve as its home and a trap for the other insects it eats. Human beings have lived in everything from caves to condominiums. We have hunted for meat to eat—with spear, bow and arrow, or high-powered rifles—or have raised herds of steers, hogs, sheep, and poultry. We have cultivated the soil—with crude wooden plows pulled by oxen and with sophisticated machinery—and grow everything from artichokes to zucchini. We have transported ourselves and our goods in donkey carts, rafts, trains, diesel-powered ships, and spacecraft.

The spider, when it pops out of its egg, is forever destined to behave like all other spiders. In contrast, the human baby can learn to behave in an almost infinite variety of ways. In body and brain, all babies everywhere are more or less alike—yet a baby born in the United States will live a far different life from a baby born in a South American jungle. The child's future depends on what kind of knowledge the environment offers and how well that knowledge is learned and used.

Over the years, psychology has taken two notably different approaches to the study of learning. In the period when most psychologists preferred to study observable actions and ignore such vague and elusive matters as mental life and human consciousness, learning was generally regarded as a process that produced clear-cut and readily apparent changes in behavior. Many psychologists concentrated on lower animals—rats, pigeons, dogs, indeed everything from tiny flatworms to gorillas—and the way their behavior could be altered by experience. The science searched for universal laws that applied not just to human beings but to all forms of animal life.

Even during this period, however, there were some psychologists who believed learning could not be fully understood without considering the subtle workings of the brain—and most especially the superior brain of the human organism. The rise of the cognitive school has popularized this view of learning as the acquisition of knowledge—one of the steps in "the human being's active interaction with information about the world" (Klatzky, 1980).

Both these approaches have been fruitful, and both are represented in what is today the generally accepted definition: *Learning is any relatively permanent change in behavior (or behavior potential) produced by experience* (Tarpy and Mayer, 1978). The words "behavior potential" refer to the knowledge we acquire and remember—like the nursery rhyme *Old Mother Hubbard*—without necessarily displaying any change in the way we act. The definition also covers the universal laws of learning that psychologists have established by observing the actual behavior of human beings and lower animals.

Classical conditioning

This chapter concentrates on the universal laws that apply to all organisms. The next chapter discusses the cognitive aspects of learning—notably the way we human beings manage to pile all kinds of information into our storehouse of memory, with the items neatly sorted into bins so that we can find what we need when we need it.

These chapters on learning and memory are a general summary of findings about which most but not all psychologists would agree. To become acquainted with everything that is known and all the various ways in which different psychologists have interpreted the findings, you would have to start with the recommended readings listed at the end of the chapter, take advanced courses—and then spend a lifetime of concentrated study. (Many people have done just that—and have found their lives endlessly fascinating and rewarding.) With this caution that there is more to be learned about learning than any introductory course can ever hope to convey—or than has yet been discovered—let us start with one of the simplest and most universal forms of learning, *classical conditioning,* a process that accounts for many of the things you do without knowing why.

Learning unreasonable fears, unreasonable preferences

Suppose you suffer from a strange reluctance to be in any kind of small, enclosed place. It frightens you to step into an elevator or a closet. You breathe faster; you feel a sinking sensation in your stomach; your hands tremble. You know that this fear, which is called *claustrophobia,* makes no sense. But you cannot help it. You are frightened without knowing why.

Unreasonable fears of this kind trouble many people. Some are afraid of being in open spaces, as on a broad prairie or on a lake *(agoraphobia)*. Some are afraid of heights *(acrophobia)*, and it frightens them to look out

If looking at this construction worker makes you dizzy, you probably have acrophobia, or fear of heights—from which this man is obviously free.

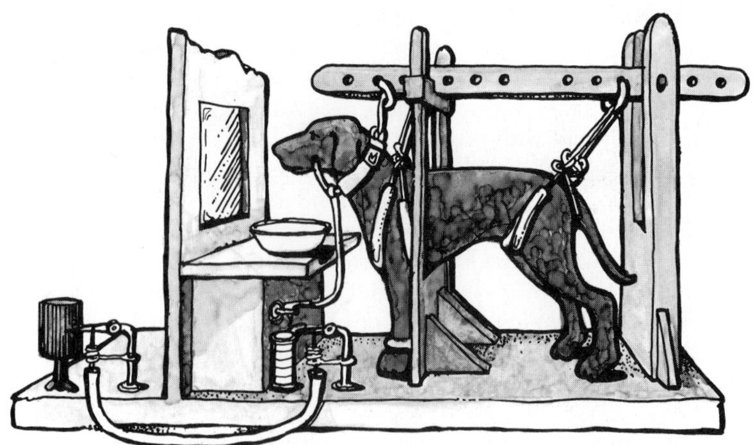

Figure 3-1 Pavlov's dog *A tube attached to the dog's salivary gland collects any saliva secreted by the gland, and the number of drops from the tube is recorded on a revolving drum outside the chamber. The experimenter can watch the dog through a one-way mirror and deliver food to the dog's feed pan by remote control. Thus there is nothing in the chamber to distract the dog's attention except the food, when it is delivered, and any other stimulus that the experimenter wishes to present, such as the sound of a metronome. For the discoveries Pavlov made with this apparatus, see the text (Yerkes and Morgulis, 1909).*

the window of a tall building or climb to the top of a football stadium. Some are thrown into mild panic by hearing a telephone ring, or driving past a cemetery, or even getting into an automobile.

Similarly, many of us have equally unreasonable preferences for certain things, especially certain kinds of people. We may be instantly attracted to men who have mustaches or men who are bald, or to small women or women who are tall and broad shouldered. We may feel unexplained warmth toward a certain tone of voice or the way a person walks, gestures, or dresses. We know that these matters have nothing to do with what the person is really like, yet we find ourselves irresistibly drawn.

These unreasonable fears and preferences are learned responses—though often we do not know how we have learned them. In many cases they seem to be the result of classical conditioning, which can best be explained by discussing the work of Ivan Pavlov, a Russian scientist who performed the most famous experiment in the history of psychology.

Pavlov and the drooling dogs

Pavlov made his experiment—indeed a whole series of experiments—in the early years of this century. His subjects were dogs, and his experimental apparatus was the simple but effective device illustrated in Figure 3-1.

Pavlov's concern was the type of behavior called a *reflex,* an automatic action exhibited by all organisms that possess a nervous system. One such reflex is the knee jerk. When you have your legs crossed, with one foot dangling in the air, a sharp tap just below the kneecap makes the foot jump. (If not, there may be something wrong with your nervous system.) Another reflex makes your pupils smaller whenever a bright light strikes your eyes. Another pulls your hand away from a hot coffee pot. The bodily changes associated with emotions are also reflex responses. For example, when a baby hears a sudden loud noise, this stimulus automatically triggers the nervous system into producing the changes in heartbeat and glandular activity that are characteristic of fear.

All reflex responses take place without conscious effort, because our

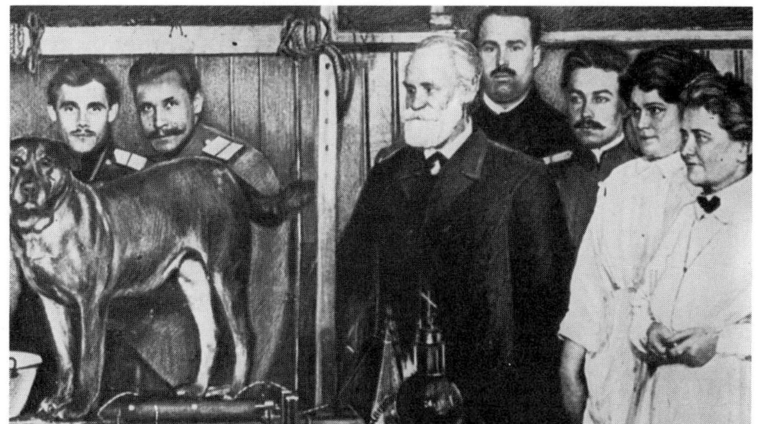

Pavlov (at center, foreground), assistants, and subject.

nervous system is wired in such a way that the stimulus automatically produces the response. The reflexes are built in, not learned. The question that interested Pavlov was this: Can they be modified by learning?

He set about answering the question by investigating the salivary reflex—which results in secretions by the salivary glands of the mouth when food is presented. He strapped a dog into the harness shown in Figure 3-1 and then introduced a sound, such as the beat of a metronome. The dog made a few restless movements, but there was no flow of saliva. This was what Pavlov had expected. The stimulus for reflex action of the salivary glands is the presence of food in the mouth—not the sound of a metronome, which is a neutral stimulus that has no effect one way or the other. When food was delivered and the dog took it into its mouth, saliva of course flowed in quantity.

Now Pavlov set about trying to connect the neutral stimulus of the sound with the reflex action of the salivary glands. While the metronome was clicking, he delivered food to the dog, setting off the salivary reflex. After a time he did the same thing again—sounded the metronome and delivered food. When he had done this many times, he tried something new. He sounded the metronome but did not deliver any food. Saliva flowed anyway. The sound alone was a sufficient stimulus to produce the salivary response (Pavlov, 1927). The dog had learned—through the form of learning now called classical conditioning—to exhibit the salivary reflex in response to a totally new kind of stimulus.

Learning to fear Santa Claus

How Pavlov's drooling dogs relate to more complicated forms of human behavior was demonstrated in another famous experiment—this one performed by John Watson, the founder of behaviorism. Watson's subject was an 11-month-old boy named Albert. His experiment was an attempt to establish whether the reflex response of fear produced in infants by a loud noise could be conditioned to take place in response to other and previously neutral stimuli.

At the start Albert had no fear of a white rat. But every time he

Psychology and Society: The question of scientific ethics

Put yourself for a moment in the shoes of John Watson—a psychologist with a chance to perform an experiment in conditioning a fear reaction in 11-month-old Albert. Would you do it? Or would you worry about the possibility of doing long-term harm to the child? What if the fear actually did generalize to Santa Claus, thus depriving Albert of a childhood pleasure? What if he felt uncomfortable all his life around white animals, white rugs, and white-haired people?

The Albert experiment was performed at a time when psychology, in its early excitement over obtaining the first scientific understanding of human behavior, was inclined to ignore such questions. Now the science is much more concerned about the risks to its subjects. The great majority of today's psychologists would never undertake such an experiment. Any who did would be very careful to make sure that Albert's conditioned fear was promptly eliminated through further learning—a precautionary measure that Watson omitted (Harris, 1979).

The question of ethics has been the subject of much soul-searching among psychologists. Some methods of studying behavior seem to be clearly unacceptable. For example, no psychologist would consider urging a brain operation just for the sake of studying its effects. But in other cases, the line is difficult to draw. Are psychologists ever justified in deceiving their subjects—such as by telling them they are administering electric shocks to another person, when in fact the other person is a confederate who is only pretending to be shocked? Some psychologists defend the use of little white lies when necessary to achieve important findings (Cooper, 1976). Others consider experiments that rely on deception to be "confidence games" that the science should scorn (Forward, Canter, and Kirsch, 1976). There has been debate even over the propriety of using the technique of naturalistic observation to study people going about their usual activities—a technique that some feel may often be an invasion of privacy.

The American Psychological Association, to which most practitioners of the science belong, has drawn up a set of guidelines to ethical experimentation—and is prepared to expel any member who clearly violates them. But there are many borderline cases that psychologists can decide only by weighing any possible harm to their subjects against the value to humanity of the knowledge they may discover. This is a problem that will probably always plague a science that deals with human beings.

touched the animal, a loud noise was sounded. After a number of pairings of animal and sound, Albert began to cry when he saw the rat. He also showed strong signs of fear toward some other furry objects, including a dog and a fur coat, and a suspicious attitude toward a bearded mask of Santa Claus (Watson and Rayner, 1920). If the fear persisted, Albert may have come to be afraid of sidewalk Santa Clauses at Christmas—without ever knowing why. Unfortunately no information is available about Albert's future life because Watson lost touch with him—a fact that raises some questions of scientific ethics (see the box on Psychology and Society).

The Albert experiment, despite its unsatisfactory conclusion, casts considerable light on the unexplained fears we often display as adults. In many cases, they are simply conditioned responses, learned in childhood through some long-forgotten pairing of stimuli—indeed through an experience that may not even have impressed us very much at the time. Similarly, the experiment helps explain many of our unreasonable preferences. A liking for people of a certain type may go back to a childhood experience in which a person with that kind of face or body build or mannerisms elicited reflex responses of warmth and pleasure.

Conditioning comas and asthma attacks

Other experiments have shown that many kinds of bodily reactions can be conditioned to occur in response to previously neutral stimuli. Would you believe, for example, that a mere injection of salt solution, which has no effect on the body, could make animals lose consciousness and go into a coma? Or that human beings, prone to asthma attacks because of an allergy to dust or pollen, could suffer an attack when exposed to a harmless substance to which they had no allergy at all?

Such things can in fact be made to happen. In one experiment, rats were put into a coma with a heavy dose of insulin, producing the drastic reaction known as insulin shock. The drug was administered with a hypodermic needle while a bright light was shining. The association of needle, light, and coma resulted in a spectacular kind of conditioning. The same kind of light was turned on, the same needle was used to inject a harmless shot of salt water—and the animals went into a coma characteristic of insulin shock (Sawrey, Conger, and Turrell, 1956).

In an experiment on asthma, people allergic to certain kinds of dust or pollen were exposed to these substances—and responded with their usual symptoms of allergy—at the same time as other neutral and harmless substances were also presented. Eventually these neutral substances alone were enough to cause asthma attacks. In some cases, even a picture of the previously neutral substance was enough to produce an attack (Dekker, Pelser, and Groen, 1957).

Conditioning, physical upsets, and treatment

The experiments on coma and asthma indicate the ways in which classical conditioning can produce some of the strange physical symptoms that may bother us as adults. An asthma sufferer may have been conditioned—not in the laboratory but by some real-life experience—to have an attack when walking into a particular room or seeing a particular person or even looking at a certain kind of picture on a television screen. Events that occur in our lives, unimportant in themselves but associated with past experiences, may make us have headaches or become sick to our stomachs. We may suddenly and inexplicably show all the symptoms of having a cold, or we may experience heart palpitation, high blood pressure, dizziness, cramps, or loss of muscular control.

Another experiment points to a way in which the unfortunate effects of conditioning—whether physical symptoms or unreasonable fears—can be counteracted. The subject was a 3-year-old boy named Peter, who had a strange fear of rabbits. Though the origin of the fear was not known, presumably it was developed through classical conditioning in much the same way as Albert's fear of rats and beards. Could it be eliminated? A psychologist approached the problem by gradually associating rabbits with a pleasant event—eating—instead of with fear responses. While Peter was enjoying a meal, a caged rabbit was brought within sight but at a safe distance. On subsequent days, again while Peter was eating, the rabbit was moved closer and closer. Eventually the fear disappeared—to the point where Peter petted the rabbit and let it nibble at his fingers (Jones, 1924).

This kind of treatment, as you will find later in the book, is now one of the standard tools that psychotherapists use to treat physical and psychological symptoms that result from early conditioning. How the original conditioning occurred need not be known. The symptoms can often be eliminated through a reconditioning process that establishes different associations.

The elements of classical conditioning

With these facts in mind about the far-reaching effects that classical conditioning can have on our lives, let us now return to Pavlov's experiment and discuss this type of learning in more detail. To understand the process we must first consider its five basic elements, using the terms that Pavlov himself used to describe them.

1. The food used in the experiment was the *unconditioned stimulus*—the stimulus that naturally and automatically produces the salivary response, without any learning.
2. The sound of the metronome was the *conditioned stimulus*—neutral at the start but eventually producing a similar response.
3. Pairing the unconditioned stimulus of food with the conditioned stimulus of sound was the *reinforcement*—the key to conditioning.
4. The reflex action of the salivary glands when food was placed in the dog's mouth was the *unconditioned response*—the response that is built into the wiring of the nervous system and takes place automatically, without any kind of learning.
5. The response of the glands to the sound of the metronome was the *conditioned response*—resulting from some kind of change in the dog's nervous system produced by pairing the conditioned stimulus with the unconditioned stimulus and therefore with the salivary response.

These elements are common to all cases of classical conditioning. In Watson's Albert experiment, the unconditioned stimulus was the loud noise; the conditioned stimulus was the rat; the reinforcement was the pairing of the loud noise with the rat; the unconditioned response was the automatic display of fear toward the noise; and the conditioned response was the learned display of fear toward the rat.

Reinforcement, extinction, and spontaneous recovery

Once Pavlov had established the conditioned salivary response, he wanted to find out how long and under what circumstances it would persist. When he merely kept sounding the metronome without ever again presenting food—in other words, when he removed the reinforcement—he found that in a very short time the flow of saliva in

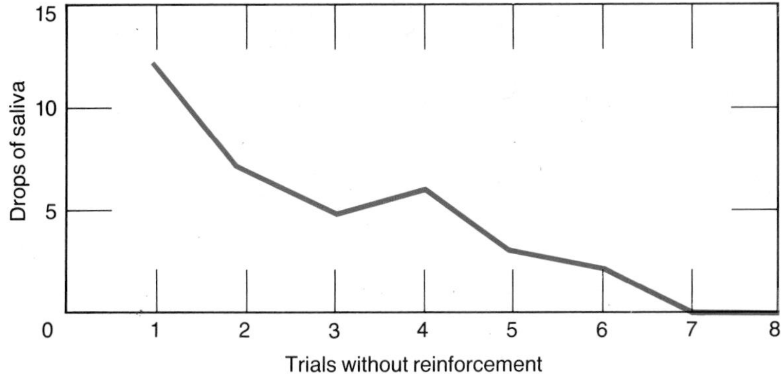

Figure 3-2 The conditioned reflex: going, going, gone *The graph shows what happened to Pavlov's dog when the conditioned stimulus of sound was no longer accompanied by the unconditioned stimulus of food. The conditioned salivary response, very strong at first, gradually grew weaker. By the seventh time the metronome was sounded, the conditioned response had disappeared. Extinction of the response was complete.*

response to the sound began to decrease, and soon it stopped altogether, as shown in Figure 3-2. In Pavlov's terminology, this disappearance of the conditioned response is called *extinction.* When he occasionally followed the sound with food—thus providing reinforcement not every time but sometimes—he found that he could make the conditioned response continue indefinitely.

Pavlov also tried another approach. He withheld reinforcement and let the conditioned response undergo extinction, then gave the dog a rest away from the experimental apparatus, and later tried again to see if there would be any response to the metronome. Under these circumstances, the conditioned response that had seemed to be extinguished reappeared. Pavlov called this *spontaneous recovery*—a phenomenon that may account for real-life situations in which unreasonable fears or preferences, learned originally through conditioning, suddenly crop up again after seeming to have vanished.

Stimulus generalization and discrimination

In Pavlov's experiments, it must be noted, there was nothing magic about the sound produced by the metronome. Indeed he later used many other kinds of stimuli—and found that he could just as easily condition the salivary response to the sound of a bell or to the flash of a light. He also discovered that a dog conditioned to the sound of a bell would salivate just as readily to the sound of a different bell or even a buzzer. This phenomenon is called *stimulus generalization*—meaning that once an organism has learned to make a response to a particular stimulus, it tends to display that behavior toward similar stimuli as well. Stimulus generalization explains why little Albert feared not only rats but also a bearded man.

After Pavlov had established the principle of stimulus generalization, he went on to demonstrate its opposite, *stimulus discrimination.* Here, by continuing to reinforce salivation to the bell by presenting food and omitting food when he sounded a different bell or a buzzer, Pavlov soon taught the dog to salivate only to the sound of the original bell, not to the other sounds. The dog had learned to discriminate between the stimulus of the bell and the other stimuli. If the experiment is carried far enough, it can be shown that a dog is capable of quite delicate stimulus discrimination. For example, it can learn to respond to the tone of middle C, yet not to respond to tones that are only a little higher or a little lower on the scale.

Learning to be neurotic

Pavlov also discovered that by taking advantage of the stimulus discrimination effect he could condition a dog to behave as if it was seriously neurotic. First, he projected a circle and an ellipse on a screen and conditioned the dog to discriminate between the two. Then he gradually changed the shape of the ellipse so that it looked more and more like a circle. Even when the difference in appearance was very slight, the dog still make the discrimination successfully. But when the difference became too small for the dog to recognize, and discrimination was impossible, the dog acted strangely disturbed.

Pavlov repeated this experiment with a number of different dogs, and the effects were always drastic. The dogs became restless, destructive, or apathetic—sometimes all these things—and developed muscle tremors and tics (Pavlov, 1927). Pavlov's experiments suggest that human neuroses may also result from problems and difficulties that occur through classical conditioning. This possibility will be explored later in the chapter in connection with *learned helplessness,* a phenomenon that has been shown to have profound effects on human behavior.

Operant conditioning

Classical conditioning, as has been seen, changes reflex behavior that, in the absence of any learning, would occur only in response to specific stimuli—like salivation to the presence of food. But reflexes are not the only form of behavior. For example, if a rat is placed in a cage, it exhibits many types of behavior that seem to be spontaneous and self-generated, not mere predetermined responses to any kind of stimulus. The rat may sniff at the cage, stand up to get a better look at things, scratch itself, wash itself, and touch various parts of the cage. Similarly, babies in their cribs display many spontaneous actions. They move their arms and legs, try to turn over or grasp a blanket or the bars of the crib, turn their heads and eyes to look at various objects, and make sounds with their vocal cords.

Such actions are not reflexes set off by some outside stimulus. The actions are initiated by the rat or the baby—put in motion by the organism itself. So instead of having something in the environment produce a response, we have here just the opposite. The rat or the baby is acting on the environment. It might be said that the organism is "operating" on the world around it—and often bringing about some kind of change in the environment. Hence this type of activity is called *operant behavior.*

Like inborn reflexes, operant behavior can also be modified through learning. One way is through a form of learning that, since it resembles

An example of operant behavior—by both human infant and kitten.

classical conditioning in a number of respects, is called *operant conditioning.*

B. F. Skinner and his magic box

The classic demonstration of operant conditioning was performed by B. F. Skinner with the special kind of cage shown in Figure 3-3. When Skinner first placed a rat in the cage, it engaged in many kinds of spontaneous operant behavior. Eventually, besides doing other things, it pressed the bar. A pellet of food automatically dropped into the feeding cup beneath the bar. Still no learning took place. In human terms, we might say that the animal did not "notice" any connection between the food and the bar, and it simply ate the food and continued its random movements as before. Eventually it pressed the bar again, causing another pellet to drop. After several such occurrences the animal "no-

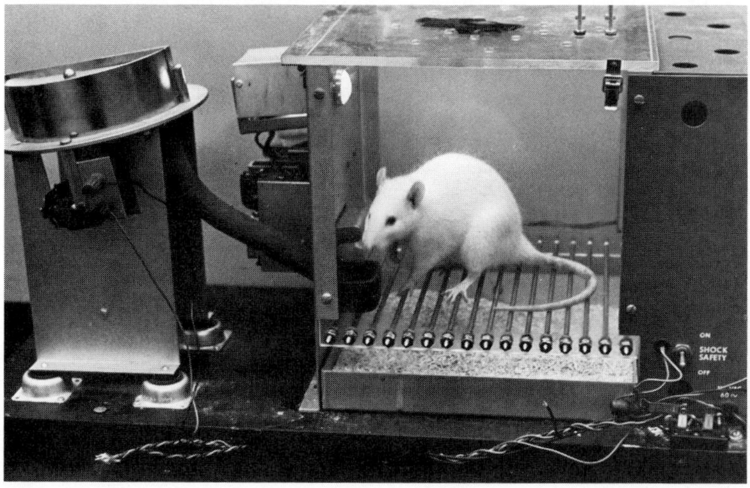

Figure 3-3 Learning in the Skinner box *With this simple but ingenious invention, a box in which pressure on the bar automatically releases a pellet of food or a drop of water, Skinner demonstrated many of the rules of operant behavior. For what happens to a rat in the box, see the text.*

Figure 3-4 Shaping a pigeon's behavior *How can a pigeon be taught to peck at that little black dot in the middle of the white circle on the wall of its cage? When first placed in the box, the bird merely looks about at random (A). When it faces the white circle (B), it receives the reinforcing stimulus of food in the tray below (C). Step by step, the pigeon is first rewarded for looking at the circle (D), then not until it approaches the circle (E), then not until it pecks at the circle (F). The next step, not illustrated here, is to withhold the reward until the pigeon pecks at the dot.*

ticed" what had happened and formed an association between the act of pressing the bar and the appearance of food. The rat now began pressing the bar as fast as it could eat one pellet and get back to the bar to release another (Skinner, 1938).

To put this another way, the rat operated on the cage (now famous as the "Skinner box") in various ways. One particular kind of operant behavior, pressing the bar, had a rewarding result—it produced food. Therefore the rat repeated that behavior. Using the same language that is applied to classical conditioning, we say that the presentation of the food was a reinforcement of the bar-pressing behavior. The rule in operant conditioning is that operant behavior that is reinforced tends to be repeated—while operant behavior that is not reinforced tends to be abandoned.

Some principles of operant conditioning

The Skinner box prompted a host of new studies of learning. It was found that operant conditioning followed many of the laws laid down by Pavlov for classical conditioning. Conditioned operant behavior, like the conditioned reflex response, was subject to *extinction.* That is, if the rat was no longer rewarded with food for pressing the bar, it eventually stopped pressing. *Spontaneous recovery* also occurred: After a rest away from the Skinner box, the rat started pressing again.

Experiments with pigeons, which are especially good subjects in their own version of the Skinner box, clearly showed *stimulus generalization.* A pigeon that had learned to obtain food by pecking at a white button would also peck at a red or green button. But if only the operant behavior toward the white button was reinforced, the pigeon displayed *stimulus discrimination.* In that case the pigeon learned to peck only at the white button and to ignore the red and green ones.

Shaping behavior

Psychologists interested in operant conditioning have developed a method of teaching animals many complicated and unusual forms of behavior, a process called *shaping.* Figure 3-4 illustrates one way this process can be used. A pigeon is led step by step, through reinforcement by food as it gets closer and closer to performing the desired activity, to exhibit a form of behavior that it might never have hit upon spontaneously. Pigeons shaped in this manner have become excellent quality control inspectors in manufacturing plants—watching drug capsules roll by on a conveyer belt and signaling when a defective one appears (Verhave, 1966). Shaping is also the technique used to train animals to perform unusual and spectacular tricks.

Learning to be superstitious

Do you have a "lucky" sweater that you always wear to exams because it helps you get good grades? Do you win more tennis matches if you wear the same pair of socks and carefully pull on the right one before

These elephants would never have tried to sit on a stool as a form of operant behavior—had they not been taught through the process of shaping.

the left one? Do you avoid stepping on sidewalk cracks to prevent disaster?

If so, you are probably exhibiting the effects of operant conditioning—and have more in common with Skinner's pigeons than you might suspect. Pigeons, too, sometimes learn to be superstitious. Skinner showed this by retooling one of his boxes so that it delivered food from time to time without any rhyme or reason, and regardless of what the pigeon in the box did or did not do. As a result, the birds developed some strange and unusual habits. A bird that happened to be flapping its wings when the food appeared might continue to flap incessantly, as if it "believed" that this produced food. Some pigeons learned to crane their necks, or to peck at a blank wall, or to keep moving in circles.

This kind of superstition, it has been suggested, often influences the behavior of animals in the wild (Neuringer, 1970). Animals engage in all kinds of random behavior, and their actions can be operantly conditioned very quickly through reinforcement. Nature provides many kinds of reinforcement that occur independently of anything the animal does—for example, rain that falls when the animal is thirsty, fruit that drops off a tree when it is hungry. If the environment just happens to provide food immediately after the animal has scratched an ear, the animal may acquire a lasting superstition that makes it scratch its ear regularly. Conversely, if an animal is scratching an ear just before being struck by a falling tree branch, it may behave afterward as if it had decided that scratching means bad luck.

Many human superstitions, not only our own individual quirks but those common to many people, probably originated in the same manner. One widely held superstition may have been started by a boy who walked under a ladder and promptly fell into a mud puddle. Another may have been started by a girl who found a clover with an extra leaf, then promptly found a penny.

Figure 3-5 The chimp and the poker chip *Why is the chimp dropping the chip into the slot? The reason is that the chip was used as a secondary reinforcer in a learning experiment—and now, when placed in a vending machine, it produces a primary reinforcement by making food drop into the tray.*

Some facts about reinforcement

The term reinforcement, as you have probably noticed, keeps cropping up in these discussions of operant conditioning. Indeed it lies at the very core of the process and has therefore been the subject of a great deal of research. With animals, it is easy to provide reinforcement. Food and water constitute an obvious kind of reward, and experimenters in operant conditioning call them *primary reinforcers.* But human beings seldom do any learning in order to receive food or water. Instead they usually seem to learn for less tangible rewards, such as praise or acceptance. Indeed even animal trainers often use the reward of affection rather than anything so elementary as food. Such rewards are called *secondary reinforcers,* and it has been assumed that they have gained their value through some kind of conditioning process that linked them originally with primary reinforcers. A simple example of secondary reinforcement is illustrated in Figure 3-5.

The effects of the timing of reinforcements have been studied in great detail. In most animal experiments, it has been found, immediate

To the baby—and to most adults—affection is one of the most powerful secondary reinforcers.

reinforcement produces the most rapid learning. Any delay reduces the amount of learning, and too long a delay usually produces no learning at all, as is shown in Figure 3-6. The same thing holds true for young children. It is almost impossible to teach a 4-year-old to stay out of the street, for example, if the child is not rewarded at once for doing so, or punished for not doing so (Wickelgren, 1977). For adults, however, immediate reinforcement is not so important. They can associate behavior engaged in at one time with a reward that comes much later—for example, a grade given at the end of a course.

Experimenters have also studied the effects of *constant reinforcement* (reward for each performance) as compared with *partial reinforcement* (reward on some occasions but not on others). They found that while learning generally takes place more rapidly with constant reinforcement, the behavior is more persistent (that is, more resistant to extinction) with partial reinforcement (Robbins, 1971). This finding has many applications to real-life situations. For example, parents who want their children to acquire a lasting tendency to work hard in school and get good grades will probably accomplish more with partial than with constant reinforcement. The trick is not to offer reinforcement for

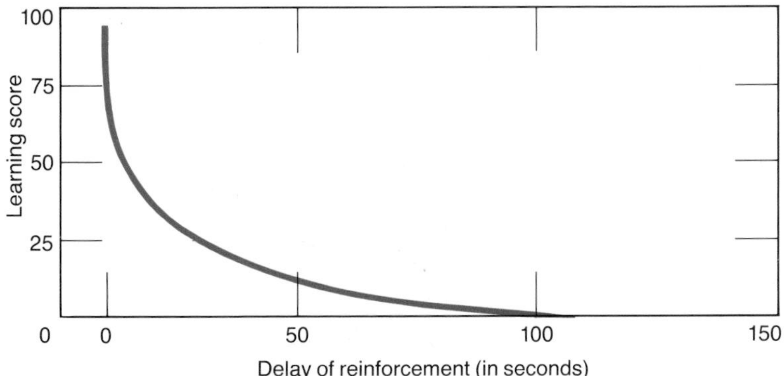

Figure 3-6 Oops . . . the reinforcement came too late *The steep drop in the curve shows how rapidly learning fell in an experiment in which reinforcement—food presented when rats pressed the bar in a Skinner box—was delayed for intervals ranging from a few seconds to about two minutes. Note that there was no learning at all when reinforcement was delayed for slightly more than 100 seconds (Perin, 1943).*

every good grade, but rather to bestow praise and affection (and possibly material rewards as well) a little more sparingly.

The long-lasting effects of partial reinforcement may also create problems in bringing up children. Suppose a little girl starts having temper tantrums whenever she asks for something and it is denied. Her parents try to ignore her behavior—but every once in a while, just to quiet her down, they give in and let her have what she wants. What they have done is set up a situation where the operant behavior of temper tantrums (the very thing they would like to eliminate) produces the reward of candy, or whatever it is the girl wants, on a schedule of partial reinforcement (the very thing most likely to make the behavior resist extinction and occur over and over again).

Applications of operant conditioning: a look at behavior modification

Parents who want their children to stop throwing temper tantrums and animal trainers who want their dolphins to jump through hoops have something in common: both are trying to mold behavior. Indeed all of us are constantly trying to influence behavior—our own actions as well as those of the people around us (Stolz, Wienckowski, and Brown, 1975). We try to lose weight, quit smoking, get higher grades, perform better on the job, be more cheerful, generous, and thoughtful. We try to influence other people to give us a good grade or a raise, show us more appreciation and respect, or stop doing things that annoy us. In so doing we often practice what psychologists call *behavior modification,* based largely on operant conditioning and the use of secondary reinforcement.

As psychologists use the term, behavior modification means any deliberate program designed to influence and change behavior through learning. The assumption is that behavior is controlled to a considerable degree by its consequences. If a certain type of behavior "works"—that is, if it results in reinforcement through some tangible reward or praise or even just a feeling of self-esteem—it is likely to be learned and repeated. If it does not produce satisfactory results, it will be abandoned. This of course is a basic principle of operant conditioning.

Experiments in behavior modification have produced some dramatic results. One of the first attempts was made with a 3-year-old girl in a nursery school who was too shy and withdrawn to take part in any of the group activities. Instead she tried to hide by staying on the floor, either motionless or crawling. How could she be led to get up, start moving around, and join the other children? The secret turned out to be very simple. As long as she was on the floor, her teachers ignored her. As soon as she got up on her feet, they flattered her with attention. Given this reinforcement, she quickly became an active member of the group (Harris et al., 1965).

The same kind of behavior modification—ignoring undesirable actions and rewarding desirable ones—has since been successful in many situations. It has been used to help other withdrawn children become more sociable and to produce normal conversation from children who refused to talk. In schools it has proved effective with pupils who were disrupting their classes and falling behind in achievement (O'Leary, 1972). Children who seemed well on the road to becoming delinquents have been led to cooperate with their families, take care of their rooms, and become less hostile and aggressive (Baer, 1973). Adults have learned to eliminate stuttering and unreasonable fears—and, to some extent, overcome such problems as sexual impotence or frigidity and insomnia (Stolz, Wienckowski, and Brown, 1975).

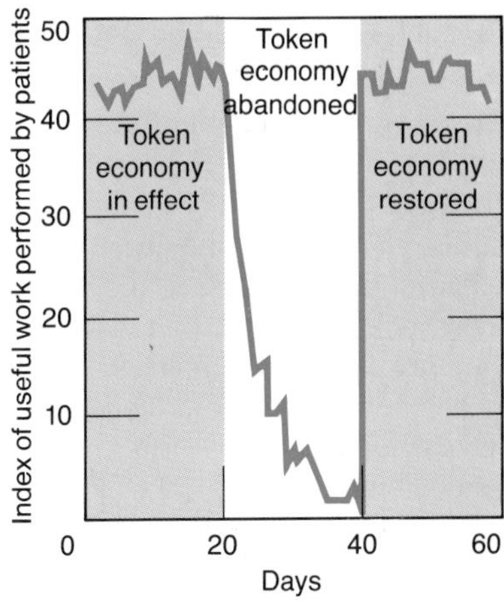

Figure 3-7 Behavior modification revolutionizes a hospital *Under a token economy, patients worked actively at useful jobs and helped run the hospital (line in colored area at left). From the 20th to 40th days of the experiment, the token economy was abandoned and the patients quickly went back to their old passive ways (line in center area). As soon as the token economy was put back in effect, they again pitched in as shown by the line in the colored area at right (Ayllon and Azrin, 1968).*

Token economies

One special kind of behavior modification, in which the reinforcement is a sort of make-believe cash payment for desirable behavior, is called a *token economy.* It is widely used in mental hospitals, where it was originated as an attempt to improve the general atmosphere and the daily lives of patients. For dressing properly, eating in an acceptable manner, and working at useful jobs, patients are rewarded with tokens that they can use like money to "buy" such privileges as movies, rental of radios or television sets, cigarettes, candy, and opportunities for privacy. These token economies have produced some remarkable changes in behavior, as can be seen in Figure 3-7.

Token economies have also been used successfully in schools, particularly to help retarded or emotionally disturbed children and those with learning problems (O'Leary and Drabman, 1971). In one interesting experiment, a psychologist used actual cash instead of tokens in dealing over a period of years with a group of about 400 teenage boys who had done so badly in school that they were considered "uneducable." To get them interested in learning, he paid them small sums of money for any accomplishments. This seemed to get the boys going, to such an extent that later he could reward them successfully simply by permitting them to study favorite subjects. On the average the boys managed to cover between two and three years of schoolwork in a single year, and even their scores on intelligence tests improved substantially (Cohen, 1970). Token economies and behavior modification in general are not infallible and indeed have inspired some fears, as discussed in a box on Psychology and Society—but they have been found clearly effective in many situations.

Conditioning, biofeedback, and medicine

Another attempt to apply the principles of conditioning—in this case to the field of medicine—has added a new word to the English language. The word is *biofeedback,* which did not appear in dictionaries published even 10 years ago but is now widely used. Newspapers, magazines, and television programs have acclaimed biofeedback as a revolutionary new tool capable of curing everything from headaches to high blood pressure, crippled muscles, and epilepsy.

An example of biofeedback: When the subject produces a certain kind of brain wave, the flowers appear on the screen.

Attempts have been made to apply biofeedback to all the various bodily activities over which we ordinarily have no conscious control, including heart rate, blood pressure, and the movements of the stomach

Psychology and Society: Does behavior modification threaten human freedom?

To many people the term *behavior modification* conjures up visions of a totalitarian society in which the rulers, by cynically manipulating rewards and punishments, turn the citizenry into a docile flock of sheep meekly obeying their masters. One experimenter showed subjects a videotape of a teacher who was using reinforcement techniques to influence the classroom behavior of students. Subjects who saw the tape after being told it was a demonstration of behavior modification expressed a good many objections to the teacher's methods. Obviously the term had prejudiced them—because subjects who saw the tape after hearing it described as a demonstration of "humanistic education" praised the teacher for the very same actions (Woolfolk, Woolfolk, and Wilson, 1977).

Are people's fears justified? Could unscrupulous use of the laws of learning produce knee-jerk acceptance of a dictator's oppression? The answer is almost certainly no.

One indication comes from the type of behavior modification called behavior therapy, described later in the book. People who undertake behavior therapy not just willingly but in fact eagerly—hoping to learn to give up cigarettes or lose weight or free themselves from some unreasonable fear—sometimes fail completely. In other words, even the most expert application of learning principles, on an individualized basis and on people who want it to work, cannot always succeed.

Moreover actions learned through behavior modification tend to be abandoned once the rewards stop. This happened in the token hospital economy shown in Figure 3-7, and it has also been demonstrated in other experiments. In one of them, two groups of nursery school children began a new activity—drawing for the first time with felt-tipped pens. Group A was encouraged to master the new technique with the promise of a fancy certificate of merit with a gold star and red ribbon. Group B merely drew for the fun of drawing. Several weeks later, after Group A's quest for the certificate of merit was over, these pupils seemed to have lost much of their interest in the new pens—but the pupils in Group B were as enthusiastic as ever (Lepper, Greene, and Nisbett, 1973). Such findings have led some psychologists to question the long-term effectiveness of behavior modification even for the most laudable purposes. The problem is that "token rewards may lead to token learning" (Levine and Fasnacht, 1974).

Rewards can indeed backfire, as was once clearly demonstrated in a way that was as amusing as it was convincing. A monkey watched while an experimenter put a piece of banana under one of two identical containers. Then a screen was placed between the containers and the monkey. After a brief period the screen was removed and the monkey was permitted to choose between the two containers. It was not surprising that the monkey went directly for the one containing the banana. The surprising thing was the monkey's behavior when the experimenter secretly substituted a lettuce leaf for the banana while the screen hid the view. Ordinarily a monkey is happy to get a piece of lettuce, but a banana is a much greater delicacy—like a juicy steak compared with a dry hamburger for human beings. And in this case the poor monkey, having expected a banana, was outraged, refused to have anything to do with the lettuce, and screamed in anger at the experimenter (Tinklepaugh, 1928). A dictator bent on controlling the populace through behavior modification would have to be careful to keep supplying bananas instead of lettuce—and hope that the citizenry never tired of bananas.

muscles. Perhaps one reason we cannot control these activities is that we are not usually aware of them. We do not know how fast our hearts are beating, whether our blood pressures are high or low, or whether our alimentary canals are busy digesting food. Nor are we aware of many other bodily events—for example, tenseness in our foreheads and neck muscles (which appears to be the cause of tension headaches), spasms of the blood vessels in our heads (migraine headaches), or the patterns of our brain waves (which may be related to epilepsy and also, in another form, to feelings of relaxation, peace of mind, and happiness).

Biofeedback procedures attempt to give us control over these activities by providing a moment-to-moment reading of what is going on in our bodies. With headache patients, for example, electrodes are attached to the muscles of the forehead and neck and connected to a device that clicks rapidly when the muscles are tense, more slowly when they begin to relax. Given this knowledge of what is going on, patients may learn to control the activity of their muscles. Similarly, through devices that monitor and report the volume of blood in the forehead, migraine sufferers may learn to direct the flow of blood away from the vessels in the head that cause the problem (Tarler-Benlolo, 1978).

However, even in the treatment of headaches, where biofeedback has had its greatest successes, the results have varied from patient to patient and have not always been satisfactory. One reason may be that people show wide individual differences in the ability to learn to control their bodily activities, just as they differ in other skills. Although the technique has not yet proved nearly so spectacular as the publicity often suggests, biofeedback is being studied further by many psychologists and researchers in numerous hospitals and medical schools.

Operant escape, punishment, and learned helplessness

Another finding made in studies of operant conditioning has many implications for real-life behavior. This is the finding that operant conditioning can be established with two very different kinds of reinforcement. The first, called *positive reinforcement,* has already been described. It takes the form of such desirable rewards as food, praise, and valuable tokens. The other kind, called *negative reinforcement,* is the termination of something painful or otherwise unpleasant—for example, an electric shock.

When negative reinforcement is used in the laboratory, animals usually learn very quickly. This has best been demonstrated by placing dogs in a device called a hurdle box that has two compartments separated by a barrier. The barrier is high enough to discourage the animal but low enough to jump over when there is a real incentive. One of the compartments has a wire mesh floor through which a shock can be administered; the other does not.

When the dog is placed in the wired compartment and the electricity turned on, the animal quickly learns to jump across the hurdle to the other side. This behavior is called *operant escape.* If some kind of warning is given, such as a light turned on or off a few seconds before the shock is administered, the animal will quickly learn to jump the hurdle when the light changes and thus miss the shock entirely. This behavior is called *operant avoidance.*

Escape and avoidance in human behavior

A great deal of everyday human behavior seems to represent some form of operant escape and avoidance, learned through negative reinforcement. For example, a young boy finds the presence of a stranger in his home distasteful—and he wants to escape. He may make a series of random movements and eventually hide his head in his mother's lap, thus shutting out the sight and sound of the stranger. Having once discovered this kind of escape, he may generalize the behavior to other situations—and conceivably turn into the kind of adult who stays away from social functions and remains as inconspicuous as possible in the most inconspicuous kind of job.

Many defenses against events that arouse unpleasant anxiety appear to be forms of operant escape and avoidance. You may have noticed that many people who are made anxious by criticism become overapologetic. This may very well be a form of conditioned operant behavior that in some way served as a successful escape from anxiety in the past—perhaps with a mother who stopped criticizing and instead showed affection when her child apologized.

You may also know people who try to avoid anxiety by deliberately insulating themselves from situations that might upset them—for example, social events, travel, or difficult jobs. The price they pay for this form of operant avoidance is often a limited life-style with few adventures or satisfactions.

The child is practicing operant escape. Alarmed by a stranger, he has blotted out the sight by burying his head in his mother's skirt, but he now feels brave enough to take another look.

Punishment and its effect on behavior

Operant behavior can also be conditioned—in some cases and to some extent—through the use of *punishment.* Here the goal is not to reinforce a response, and therefore make it likely to occur again in the future, but to eliminate a response. Most people and indeed society as a whole seem to believe in the effectiveness of punishment as a form of behavior modification. Toddlers are punished by a slap on the hand if they grab at a fragile lamp or by a slap on the bottom if they whine too much. Older children are punished if they are "sassy," get into fights or into the cookie jar, or refuse to do their homework.

Teachers punish pupils by keeping them after school, by making them write essays on the evils of laziness, and by sending them to the principal's office for a stern lecture. In college, poor grades are themselves a form of punishment, and being flunked out is the ultimate. Employers punish workers by bawling them out or firing them. Society as a whole levies fines or prison sentences on people who drive too fast or without a license, create a public nuisance, or do any of hundreds of other things prohibited by law. There is even considerable public support for the death sentence for such crimes as murder. The popular belief is that punishment or the threat of punishment stops bad behavior and encourages good behavior.

Students of marriage have found that it is not uncommon for one or both partners to use punishment in an attempt to change the other's behavior. Note this case: A husband is annoyed because his wife is often in a bad mood and has the habit of swearing at the children when they misbehave. In an effort to change her behavior, he throws a tantrum and yells at her, or storms out of the house for the evening, or stops doing household chores. The wife, in turn, is annoyed because the husband always leaves the den in a mess—with newspapers, magazines, and books scattered over the floor and on top of the television set. In an effort to change *his* behavior, *she* throws out his magazines, stops talking to him, and rejects his sexual approaches (Patterson, Hops, and Weiss, 1975). Both are saying, in effect, "Yes, I'm punishing you by being as unpleasant as I can—and I'll do it until you change your ways."

The question is: Does punishment really work? In the case of the sour-tempered wife and the messy husband, it did not. They wound up taking their problems to a marriage counselor. But the question cannot always be answered with a simple yes or no. It is surrounded by many complications, all bearing on our attempts to get along in society and with our fellow human beings.

Punishment works with animals

Because ethical considerations limit experiments with human beings, most laboratory studies of punishment use animals as subjects. In general, punishment often results in rapid and long-lasting learning by animals (Solomon, 1964). As might be expected from what was said earlier about delayed reinforcement, the punishment is most effective if administered as soon as possible after the behavior that the experimenter wants to eliminate (Campbell and Church, 1969).

The punishment is most effective of all when combined with reward—that is, when the "wrong" behavior is punished and the "right" behavior is rewarded. This has been shown by placing a rat in a simple T-shaped maze. The animal starts at the bottom of the T and has the choice, when it reaches the top, of turning either right or left. The rat will learn the "correct" turn very quickly if rewarded with food when it turns right and punished with shock when it turns left. A real-life demonstration of the same principle is provided by the housebreaking of a young puppy, which, as countless dog owners have discovered, is best accomplished by punishing the animal immediately by slapping it with a rolled-up newspaper when it wets the rug and showing it that the same act is praiseworthy when performed outdoors.

But does punishment work with people?

In at least some cases, punishment also helps babies and small children to learn. Indeed its use is sometimes unavoidable. A slap on the hand when a child reaches toward a forbidden object may be the only way to prevent damage, as when the object is a fragile lamp, or even serious injury, if the object happens to be a sharp knife.

With older children and adults, however, the effectiveness of punishment is not at all clear. One reason is that it is impossible to say how any given individual feels about any particular kind of supposedly punishing treatment. If that statement strikes you as peculiar, consider this situation: A mother and father make it a regular practice, when their children misbehave, to raise a great fuss. They yell at the children, call them to task, bawl them out, threaten them with everything from being sent to bed without supper to a thorough spanking. They believe that this punishment will make the children mend their ways. The children, however, may view the situation in an entirely different light. Let us say

This scene is eloquent proof that threats and punishments do not always work as well as generally believed.

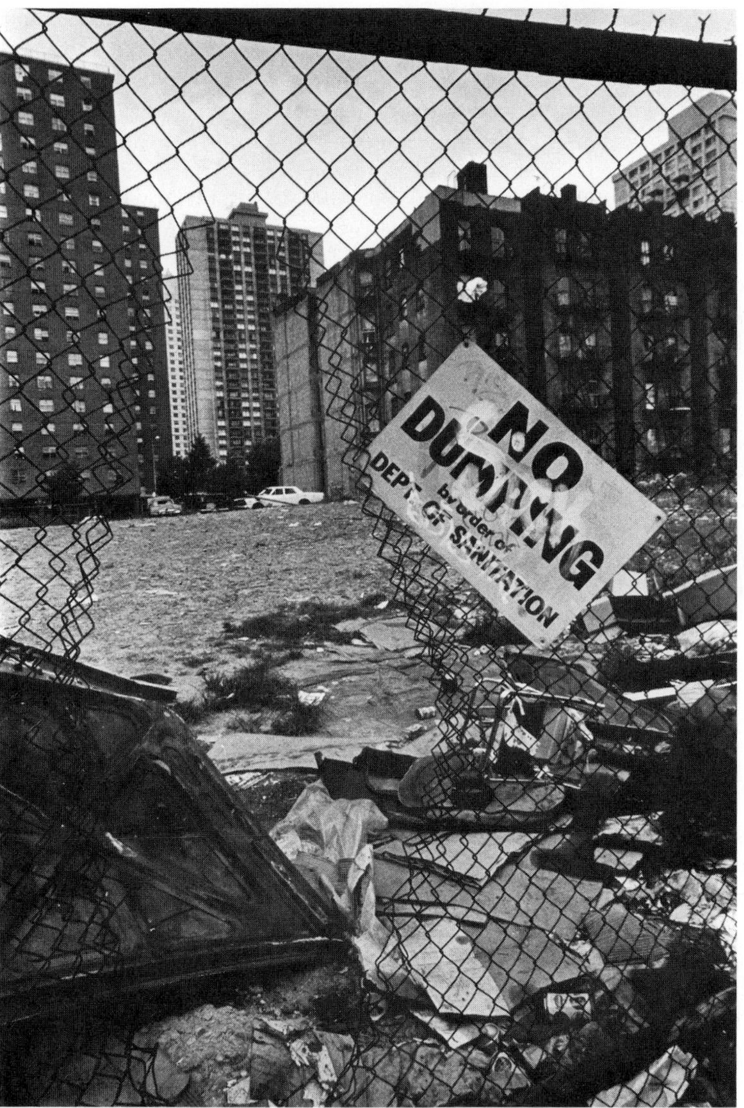

that their parents ordinarily ignore them, displaying very few signs of interest or affection. Thus, to the children, the intended punishment is actually a form of attention, which they desperately crave. It constitutes a positive reinforcement that they are likely to seek again and again. In these cases even a spanking may be regarded as a positive reinforcement.

Psychologists are well aware that punishment often achieves exactly the opposite of its intended effect. It can create a vicious circle within a family: The child misbehaves, the parent punishes, and the punishment leads to further misbehavior (Miller, 1975). Punishment may also have far-reaching side effects. Studies of children who received drastic verbal or physical punishment have shown that they tend to acquire a dislike for the people who punish them, such as their parents or teachers (Munn, Fernald, and Fernald, 1969). These children often become aggressive and punishing toward other children—and as adults frequently are cruel to their own offspring.

The sad case of the helpless dogs

Even with animals, punishment may produce unfortunate results. This was demonstrated in an experiment in which a dog was strapped into the kind of harness used by Pavlov. The dog then received a series of 64 electrical shocks, each lasting five seconds, delivered at random intervals. There was no way the dog could avoid the shocks or escape from them before the five seconds were up. The next day the dog was placed in a hurdle box. From time to time the light inside the box was dimmed, and a few seconds later a shock was administered through the floor of the compartment in which the dog had been placed. The animal could avoid the shock altogether by jumping over the hurdle into the other compartment when the warning light was dimmed, or it could escape the shock by jumping after the electricity was turned on. If the dog did not jump into the other compartment, the shock continued—this time for a full 50 seconds.

The results of the experiment, shown in Figure 3-8, were dramatic. A number of dogs were used in the experiment. All had 10 trials in the hurdle box during which they could learn to avoid or escape the shock. But the amount of learning that took place was small. Most of the animals simply accepted the shock for the full 50 seconds, making no attempt to leap over the hurdle. They behaved in totally different fashion from a control group of dogs which had not previously received inescapable shocks. In accordance with what was said earlier about operant escape and avoidance, these "normal" dogs learned very quickly to leap the hurdle in time to avoid the shock or to escape in a hurry once the shock had begun.

How are we to account for the failure of the experimental dogs to learn—for their passive acceptance of a severe and long-lasting shock? The experimenters attribute it to what they have called *learned helplessness.* That is, while the dogs were in the Pavlov harness they learned that nothing they could do would have any effect on whether they received a shock or for how long. In human terms, they had no hope

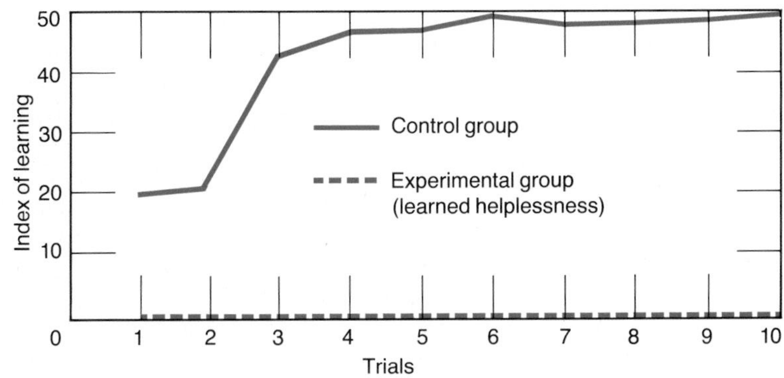

Figure 3-8 Results of an experiment in learned helplessness *The rapid rise in the solid line shows how quickly "normal" dogs learned how to cope with an electric shock delivered in a hurdle box, as explained in the text. The shaded line shows the very different behavior of animals that had acquired learned helplessness—and therefore seemed incapable of learning how to do anything about the shock.*

that they could do anything about the shock, even when moved to the hurdle box, and they therefore had no incentive to try to escape (Maier, Seligman, and Solomon, 1969).

Learned helplessness in human beings

It has been shown that human beings as well as animals can be led to acquire learned helplessness through simple laboratory procedures. In one experiment, for example, college volunteers were subjected to an earsplitting noise. They were told that they could stop the noise by learning how to manipulate some control devices—but actually these devices had no effect. Later, when placed in another situation where it would have been easy to move a control lever and turn off the noise, the subjects made no effort and simply put up with the noise until the experimenter called a halt (Hiroto, 1974).

The experiments on learned helplessness suggest that attempts to change human behavior through punishment are fraught with danger. Many parents who believe in the old adage "Spare the rod and spoil the child" are quick to punish almost any kind of behavior of which they disapprove. Often they do so with the same degree of verbal or physical intensity regardless of how major or minor the child's transgressions may be. Some parents seem to operate by whim. Depending on their moods, they may at times severely punish exactly the same behavior that they ignore at other times.

Children who are continually bawled out or spanked—especially if the punishment is inconsistent—may very well acquire learned helplessness. They may decide that they have no control over when, how, or why they are punished. They may give up trying to learn what their parents are trying to teach them, in which case the attempts to punish them into learning the difference between good behavior and bad become self-defeating. Such children may even become seriously neurotic—exhibiting behavior similar to that displayed by Pavlov's dogs in his stimulus discrimination experiments. The same unfortunate results may occur when elementary school teachers who are unsympathetic to the slow learners in their classes constantly berate them for their stupidity.

Helplessness as the result of failure

The original experiment on learned helplessness, performed with dogs in the late 1960s, opened up a new line of psychological investigation in which many important developments have been occurring. Punishment, it has been found, is not the only possible cause of learned helplessness. An even more common cause is failure—at any of the tasks we face throughout life, in the classroom or in the outside world.

In laboratory experiments, many of the symptoms of a temporary kind of learned helplessness have been produced by giving students problems that they were told could be solved but that were in fact impossible (Tennen and Eller, 1977). In real-life situations, children have been found to display learned helplessness as a result of failure in a school assignment, such as mathematics (Dweck, Goetz, and Strauss, 1977). They may then fail at other subjects and take a pessimistic attitude toward their general abilities and prospects for the future. (For a discussion of the serious social problem this creates, see the box on Psychology and Society.) Adults may acquire similar feelings because of failure to find or hold a job or to establish satisfactory social relationships.

These findings are of great practical importance to all of us because failure is an inevitable part of life. We cannot always succeed at everything. In college, only a few students get all A's and only one is at the top of the class. Not all would-be athletes make the team, and only one is chosen most valuable player. In the world of jobs, a dozen people may be competing for a promotion that only one of them can get. In our social relations, not all of us can be the most popular or the best looking. Even if we have many friends who like us, there will always be others who ignore us or view us with distaste.

Thus all of us experience failure of one kind or another at one time or another. If failure produces learned helplessness, we may become as passive and psychologically crippled as the dogs in the Pavlov harness. We may become victims of a deep depression—a "blue funk"—that a psychiatrist would classify as highly neurotic or even psychotic (Depue and Monroe, 1978). But, though everyone experiences failure, not everybody suffers drastic consequences. One of the great contributions of studies of learned helplessness has been to offer some clues as to when, how, and why this unhappy result is likely to occur—a matter that deserves discussion here even though it digresses from simple conditioning.

When you fail, whom do you blame?

To understand any symptoms of learned helplessness you ask yourself this question: When you fail, where do you place the blame?

Suppose you are in love—but the object of your affections rejects you. It makes a great deal of difference whether you blame yourself, blame her (him), or blame women (men) in general. Blaming yourself usually results in a serious loss of self-esteem and is closely associated with lack of confidence in the future (Garber and Hollon, 1977). Sometimes it produces serious depression (Rizley, 1978). The particular way in which you blame yourself is also important. If you merely blame your behavior in that one particular relationship, your feelings of helplessness will probably be less severe. But if you blame yourself in general—your own character, so to speak—you are much more likely to be in trouble (Peterson, Schwartz, and Seligman, 1981). Thus it is better to think, "Well, I just did the wrong thing that time," than to decide, "That's the way I am and it seems I'm just plain unattractive to women (men)."

If you blame the other party or the other sex in general—thereby attributing your failure to outside factors—you preserve your self-esteem. But this does not necessarily exempt you from the symptoms of helplessness. Again it appears that if you make a sweeping condemnation—of all women (or all men)—your helplessness is likely to generalize and handicap you in other situations. If you blame one particular person—"She (he) is overly competitive and reject-

Psychology and Society: Learned helplessness and the schools

The American school system is both a pride and a puzzlement. In keeping with our policy of free education for all, we spend about $100 billion a year on our elementary schools and high schools (U.S. National Center for Education Statistics, 1983). About 77 percent of our young people finish high school (Bureau of the Census, 1982). Yet national surveys have clearly established that our elementary and secondary schools turn out many students who are not adequately prepared either to go on to college or hold any but the most unskilled jobs (Silberman, 1970). Despite all those years in the classroom, these students have not mastered the basic skills of reading, writing, and arithmetic.

Why? Some people blame television, claiming that its diet of spoon-fed entertainment discourages reading. Some blame the parents, saying that a lack of discipline in the home produces unruly classrooms. And some blame the schools, arguing that they pay more attention to frills than to the ABC's. But studies of learned helplessness suggest there may be a more basic explanation than any of these.

It has been known for a long time that children from low-income homes are the most likely to leave school without acquiring the basic skills. Even by the sixth grade, the average child from a low-income home is two years behind middle-income children in scholastic achievement. By the eighth grade the gap has grown to three years. Children from low-income homes are much more likely to drop out without finishing high school and much less likely to go to college even if they get a diploma (Hess and Bear, 1968).

It is also known that people at low-income levels are especially likely to experience the feelings associated with learned helplessness. When social scientists speak of levels of society, ranging from upper-upper to lower-lower classes, they often use income and years of education as their guidelines—but an even more accurate indication is the extent to which people believe they have power or access to power in the society and control over their own and their children's lives (Strauss, 1979). Low-income people generally lack these feelings of power and control—a lack that is characteristic of learned helplessness—and so do their children (Coles, 1971).

Pupils from these homes enter school without the benefit of two characteristics that have been found especially important to success—namely a good "self-concept" (meaning confidence in their own abilities) and a belief that they can control their destinies through their own efforts (Coleman,

ing"—there is less likelihood that the incident will affect other relationships (Abramson, Seligman, and Teasdale, 1978).

Any form of learned helplessness can cause serious problems. One group of investigators has cited the example of an accountant who gets fired from his job. If his symptoms do not generalize to other situations, he may continue to be a good husband and father and to function well in social situations. But the symptoms may cripple him nonetheless. He may be unable to prepare his own income tax return or try for a new job in accounting. If the helplessness becomes generalized, his entire life may be affected. He may become sexually impotent, neglect his children, and avoid any social contacts (Abramson, Seligman, and Teasdale, 1978).

Therapy—and self-therapy—for helplessness

Though most of us suffer at times from learned helplessness—when failure makes us question our own abilities and call ourselves incompetent, lazy, unattractive, and generally good for nothing—our pessimistic attitudes fortunately do not usually last very long. We have trouble with math but overcome it by working a little harder—or make

1966). Their feelings of learned helplessness are then likely to be aggravated by failure to keep up with the classroom work. The result is a vicious circle. Many of these pupils, unequipped with the basic skills, will probably spend their adult lives in marginal jobs or on public assistance—and at a poverty level that probably destines their own children to repeat the cycle.

One of the most pressing social questions of the day is whether this vicious circle can be broken—and if so, how. The answer seems elusive, though many educators are trying to find it. Some schools are experimenting with attempts to make the curriculum and environment more flexible, to take account of individual differences. It has been found, for example, that pupils differ in the way their progress is affected by such variables as noise level, lighting conditions, and working alone versus working in groups. Some learn best from materials they read or see in charts, others from listening to the teacher's words or to tape cassettes (Dunn, 1983). An individual's daily energy cycle also seems to be a factor. Some schools have found that many pupils are dull and lethargic in the morning—and have cut the truancy rate by rearranging their schedules to avoid difficult classes at the opening 9 A.M. bell. Many high schools have instituted remedial programs, especially in reading, in an effort to help students who have fallen behind in the earlier grades.

One of the most successful approaches has been to deal with the problem early, before children ever go to school (National Assessment of Educational Progress, 1981). The outstanding example is a project that provided two years of preschool training to 3-year-olds in a ghetto district of Ypsilanti, Michigan, with one dedicated teacher to every five or six children. Staff members also worked with the children and their mothers in the home for an hour and a half a week, 30 weeks of the year.

At the age of 14, these children were well ahead of a control group from the same neighborhood on many measures of achievement, including reading, mathematics, and the use of language. They also seemed more committed to learning and were less likely to misbehave in class or become delinquent (Schweinhart and Weikart, 1980). Such a program, however, would cost about $8,000 per child at today's prices—and there is some question whether even this amount of training can fully counteract all the other influences in the low-income environment.

up for our lack of mathematical ability by doing well in another subject. Though one person of the opposite sex rejects us, we soon find someone else who likes us a great deal. After being fired, we find another job at which we are more efficient—and we end up feeling much better about ourselves and the world.

When we do this, we provide our own very effective therapy—for we are doing exactly what a therapist would try to do if our problems were so severe that we had to seek help. The best treatment for learned helplessness, it has been found, is to give people some evidence that they do have the ability to succeed (Teasdale, 1978). Sometimes they have set their goals impossibly high and have to be taught to be more realistic. Sometimes they have to work at developing their skills at performing their jobs or conducting their social relationships. But mostly therapists seek to provide situations in which people who suffer from learned helplessness can and do succeed, thereby discovering that they are more competent at more things than they thought they were. This new confidence generalizes to other situations (Bandura, Jeffery, and Gajdos, 1975), and they begin to feel a growing faith in their ability to control their own futures.

Figure 3-9 You can't keep a good chimp down *Faced with the problem of reaching a banana suspended high overhead, the chimpanzee at top has managed by balancing a long stick beneath it and quickly climbing up. The chimpanzee at bottom has hit upon the "insight" of piling three boxes one atop another as a makeshift step stool (Köhler, 1925)*

The cognitive view: learning as a step in information processing

For many years the laws of classical and operant conditioning dominated psychologists' view of learning. Indeed the behaviorist school thought of all human behavior in terms of conditioning, produced more or less automatically by events in the environment. It was widely accepted that classical conditioning stamps certain kinds of responses into us. Operant conditioning leads us to repeat actions that are rewarded and to refrain from actions that are unsuccessful or result in punishment. Thus we humans are all pretty much the creatures of our environment.

The prevailing view was that there is little difference between human beings going about their daily lives and a rat negotiating its way through a simple T maze. The rat's behavior can be accurately predicted if we know in which arm of the T it has previously been rewarded with food and in which arm it has been punished by a shock. Human beings, of course, have had much more complex experiences, and their environment constitutes a much more elaborate kind of maze. But the theory was that we could also predict their behavior fairly well if we simply knew which of their actions had been rewarded in the past and which had been punished, and in what way and to what extent (Miller and Dollard, 1941).

Even during the heyday of this viewpoint, however, there were dissenters. Some psychologists objected on theoretical grounds, maintaining that the rich variety of human activities defies full explanation in terms of simple conditioning. Others kept coming up with experimental results, even with lower animals, that seemed impossible to fit into the laws of conditioning. It was this line of thinking and these experiments that led to the rise of today's cognitive view of learning as one of the steps in *information processing*—with the human organism, far from being a passive product of experience, actively interacting with the environment.

The case of the ingenious chimps

One of the first influential experiments along cognitive lines was reported by the German psychologist Wolfgang Köhler as far back as the 1920s. Köhler worked with chimpanzees, creating situations in which they had to demonstrate considerable ingenuity to get at a banana placed tantalizingly out of reach. Sometimes the food was just a little farther than arm's length away from a chimp behind a barrier. Sometimes it was suspended overhead, too high to reach by jumping. So near and yet so far.

Could the chimpanzees learn to get the food? As it turned out, they managed in a number of clever ways. The animals behind the barrier found they could use sticks, available within arm's reach, to rake in the banana. The animals who saw the food overhead hit upon several strategies, two of which are illustrated in Figure 3-9. To Köhler, this kind of learning went far beyond any stimulus-response connections established by conditioning. He held that the animals had learned through *insight*—or what today would be called cognition. That is, they evaluated the situation, called on their past knowledge about sticks and boxes, and processed all this information in terms of cause and effect.

Learning without reinforcement

Another influential experiment, reported in 1930 and performed with rats in a maze, produced results that cast doubt on the theory that reinforcement is essential to learning. The rats were divided into three groups. Group 1 always found food at the end of the maze—a clear-cut and immediate reinforcement. The Group 2 rats were simply placed in the maze and permitted to move around in any way they chose, never finding any food. Group 3 was treated the same way as Group 2 for the first 10 days, receiving no reinforcement. Then, after the tenth day, food was placed at the end of the maze, as it had been all along with Group 1.

How the three groups performed, as measured by how direct a route they took without entering blind alleys, is illustrated in Figure 3-10. Note that the rats in Group 1 learned rapidly, as the laws of operant conditioning would have predicted, improving every day right from the beginning. As might also have been predicted, the rats in Group 2, which were never reinforced, did not display much learning. But note the strange behavior of Group 3. For the first 10 days this group also showed little learning. Then, on the eleventh day, when a reward was provided at the end of the maze, the rats immediately began running the course like veterans. Even in just wandering about the maze for 10 days, without any reinforcement, they apparently had learned a great deal about the correct path. As soon as a reward was provided, they began to demonstrate this knowledge.

To describe the behavior of the Group 3 rats, the experimenters used the term *latent learning*—meaning learning that lies latent and unused

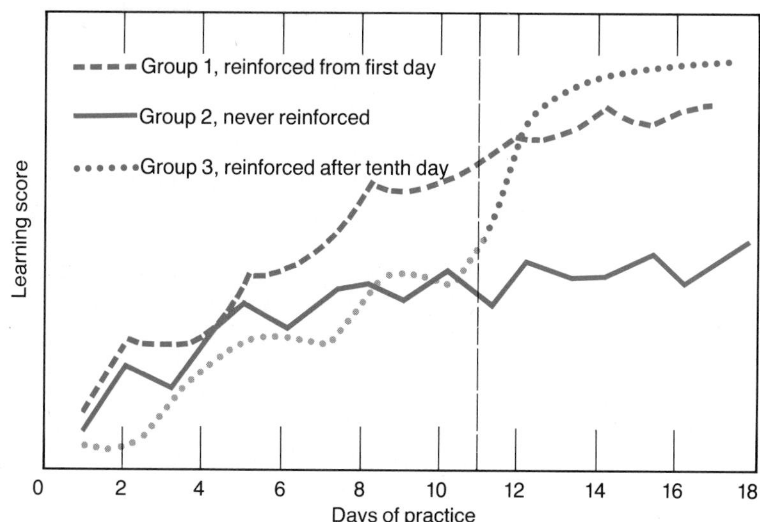

Figure 3-10 A funny thing happened on the way through the maze *The graph shows the surprising behavior of three groups of rats placed in a maze under different conditions of reinforcement. For the meaning of the lines, which chart the rats' progress in learning the way through the maze, see the text (Tolman and Honzik, 1930).*

until there is some reason to apply it. The experiment seemed to show that even lower animals can learn without the immediate reinforcement considered essential to classical and operant conditioning—and in fact without any reinforcement at all. In cognitive terminology, the rats moving around the maze without any reward had acquired and stored knowledge about the pathway, which they could call on as soon as it was useful in helping them get to food as rapidly as possible.

Latent learning is an everyday experience in human behavior. For example, you have undoubtedly traveled along a city street or highway lined with business establishments, seen a shop in which you had no special interest at the time, then later recalled exactly where to find the shop when you needed a pair of shoes, a stereo repair, or a bicycle. You learned the shop's location without any reinforcement. Much of the information you have stored in memory and are not using at the moment represents latent learning. There was no apparent reinforcement for acquiring such knowledge as what you ate for breakfast yesterday, a joke you read in a magazine five years ago, or the color of a textbook you used as a high school freshman.

Learning without a response

Just as the last experiment demonstrated that learning is possible without reinforcement, other experiments have shown that learning can take place without a response. In one of the most famous studies the subject was a dog in a Pavlov-type harness. The unconditioned stimulus was an electric shock to the paw, the unconditioned response the pulling away of the paw, and the conditioned stimulus a high tone sounded just before the shock was delivered. The animal, of course, was quickly conditioned to pull its paw away at the sound of this tone—and it also showed stimulus discrimination by ignoring a low tone that was never followed by shock. So far just a routine example of classical conditioning and stimulus discrimination.

But now the experimenter did the same thing with another dog—except that this dog's leg was paralyzed with a drug, so that it would not be pulled away. When the high tone was sounded and the shock delivered, the animal could not respond. Yet when the process was repeated later, after the drug had worn off, the dog pulled its paw away immediately at the sound of the high tone while ignoring the low tone. It had learned to avoid the shock and to discriminate between the two tones—even though the establishment of a stimulus-response connection was impossible during the conditioning trials (Solomon and Turner, 1962).

A number of other studies have also demonstrated that performing a specific response is not always essential to learning. For example, rats that have learned to run through a maze to get food will take the same path even when the maze is flooded and they have to swim—an entirely different kind of motor activity (MacFarlane, 1930). A rat that has learned to press the bar in a Skinner box with its right paw will manage to press the bar anyway if that paw is immobilized. It will use the left paw if possible—and, if that one is also immobilized, it will press the bar with its nose or body (Kimble, 1961).

As a human analogy, one psychologist has suggested the behavior of children who learn to pick up their toys at the end of a play period, perhaps for the reward of pleasing their parents. The children do not just learn "a particular set of muscle movements." In other circumstances they will use different movements or pick up clothing instead of toys—and thus "perform the response in different but functionally equivalent ways" (Wickelgren, 1977).

Cognitive maps, expectancies, and knowledge

The various experiments just described—Köhler's chimpanzees and their "insight," the rats that acquired latent learning without any reinforcement, and the paralyzed dog that learned to avoid a shock—led many psychologists to seek a new definition of learning. Granted, human beings as well as lower animals often establish a simple stimulus-response connection through classical and operant conditioning, with reinforcement a part of the process. But in cases where some other kind of learning occurs, in ways not accounted for by the laws of conditioning, just what is it that the organism learns—and how does the learning take place?

Edward Tolman, who collaborated on the latent learning experiment, suggested the term *cognitive map* (Tolman, 1948). From many studies of behavior in mazes, Tolman concluded that even animals learn not just mere responses that propel them to a reward but a knowledge of the spatial features of the environment—of where things are and "what leads to what." Reinforcement does not produce the learning but instead merely leads animals to use what they already know. If a reward is provided in one part of the cognitive map, they will manage to go there, in one way or another. If there is punishment, they will avoid that spot.

Subsequent experimenters, working with types of learning that did not pose the spatial problems found in mazes, enlarged Tolman's terminology into the idea of acquiring *expectancies* (Bolles, 1972). Even in classical conditioning, they suggested, Pavlov's dogs learned to salivate to the sound of the metronome because they expected the sound to be followed by food. In operant conditioning, rats in a Skinner box learn to press the bar because they expect the action to be followed by food. These investigators agreed with Tolman that the animals learn "what leads to what"—but pointed out that learning can include more than just the spatial relationships implied by the term cognitive map.

Today's cognitive psychologists have expanded these suggestions into the all-embracing term *knowledge.* What is learned, according to the cognitive school, is all sorts of knowledge—the "maps" of pathways acquired by Tolman's rats, the expectancies about food acquired by Pavlov's dogs, and a human's knowledge that Main Street is one block north of Broadway, an aspirin can be expected to relieve a headache, $2 \times 4 = 8$, the past tense of *swim* is *swam,* and the earth is round.

The cognitive psychologists regard "the human organism as an active seeker of knowledge and processor of information"—with learning being the step in which we acquire information that we then modify, manipulate, store, and use in various ways (Klatzky, 1980). They view learning as one element in a closely related series of processes that will be discussed later in the book—notably memory (Chapter 4), language and cognition (Chapter 5), and perception (Chapter 8).

Observation learning

One way of acquiring knowledge that has been widely studied is *learning through observation* (or, as some psychologists prefer, *learning through modeling* or *learning by imitation*). All three terms refer to the process through which we learn by observing the behavior of others.

It has been known for some time that even lower animals learn by observation and imitation. In one of the early experiments, a cat was taught in a Skinner box to obtain food by pressing the bar when a light went on. Another cat, which had been watching, was then placed in the box. This second cat began very quickly to press the bar when the light went on. Through observation, it had learned much faster than the first cat (John et al., 1968). Subsequent experiments have demonstrated many kinds of observation learning by many animals, from mice to dolphins.

With human beings, one of the most dramatic examples of observation learning was recorded on film by Albert Bandura. In this experiment, children watched a movie showing an adult striking a large doll with a hammer. When the children then had an opportunity to play with the doll themselves, they showed remarkably similar behavior. The photographs of this experiment, some of which are shown in Figure 3-11, have greatly influenced psychologists' attitudes toward observation learning. (They have also raised some serious questions about the effects of the violence shown in the movies and on television.)

Cognitive theorists do not think of observation learning as merely an automatic and unthinking imitation of what one has seen. Rather they believe that we begin in early childhood, and continue throughout our lives, to observe what goes on around us and to store up the information

A prime example of learning through observation.

that this observation provides. We observe what other people seem to value, how they go about getting what they value, their behavior in general, and the results of their behavior. At the same time, we make judgments. We may or may not decide to value what they value. We may imitate their behavior, adopt some but not all of it, or reject it entirely. As Bandura has stated, learning by observation is "actively judgmental and constructive rather than a mechanical copying" (Bandura, 1974).

Closely akin to observation learning, of course, is the kind of learning you are doing at this moment—and that people do in many ways in many situations. This is learning by receiving instruction from someone else, as when reading a textbook (or a recipe) or listening to a teacher in the classroom (or to a tennis pro telling you how to improve your serve). The cognitive psychologists would say that in our information processing we have the benefit not only of the knowledge stored in our own memories but, through language, of all the knowledge possessed by our fellow human beings and indeed the wisdom of the ages as recorded in our libraries.

Some limits on learning: species-specific behavior

Though recent studies have greatly expanded the definition of learning and enriched our understanding of the process, they have also reduced psychology's once boundless expectations for what learning can accomplish. When it was generally believed that events in the environment automatically stamp in the behavior of organisms, John Watson was thoroughly confident that he could condition a newborn baby to be anything he wished—doctor, lawyer, beggar, or thief. Indeed behaviorists in general assumed at the time that any organism, human or otherwise, could be conditioned to display almost any kind of behavior in response to almost any stimulus.

But note what happened when a husband-wife team of psychologists decided to become animal trainers. They assumed that their knowledge of conditioning and shaping would enable them to teach almost any kind of beast to do almost anything. But after trying with some 6,000 animals of 38 different species—including raccoons, cockatoos, reindeer, pigs, chickens, and whales—they were forced to admit they had been grossly overoptimistic.

The animals' learning, they found, was limited by which is called *species-specific behavior.* Chickens have an inborn tendency to scratch for their food, pigs to root for it, racoons to wash it. Thus the two psychologist–animal-trainers never were able to teach raccoons to pick up coins and drop them into a piggy bank. The animals insisted on going through their natural washing motions—rubbing the coins together, dipping them into the bank, then rubbing them together again. The pigs insisted on rooting, the chickens on scratching (Breland and Breland, 1961).

One experiment that added a strange twist to our knowledge of species-specific behavior was performed in the following fashion: A rat was permitted to drink some sweet-flavored water while a bright light was flashed and a noise was sounded. Later the rat was made sick to its

Figure 3-11 See aggression, learn aggression *Why are the boy and girl above acting so aggressively toward the toy? And why does their aggressive behavior take such remarkably similar form? The answer is reminiscent of the old saying "Monkey see; monkey do." The children were imitating the behavior of a model—the woman below, who had behaved in exactly this fashion in a movie they had seen.*

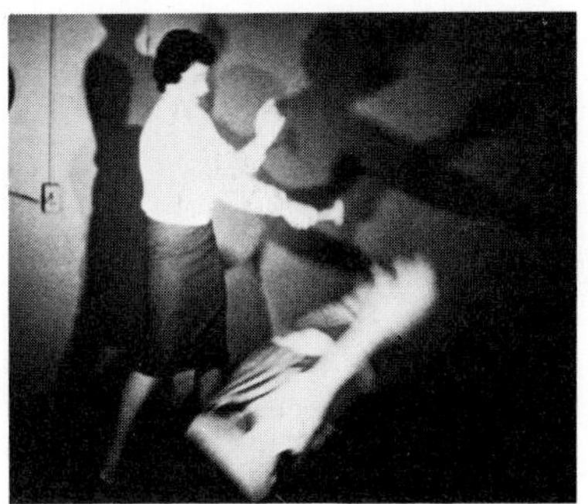

stomach through X-ray irradiation. Under these circumstances, what did the rat learn? It turned out that the animal learned to avoid sweet-tasting water. It did not learn to avoid the light or the noise (Garcia and Koelling, 1966). This raises an interesting question—because a rat placed in the same situation, except with an electric shock substituted for the subsequent illness, quickly learns to avoid the flashing light and the sound as well as the food.

The answer seems to be that rats have a species-specific tendency to associate taste—but not other kinds of stimuli—with feelings of being sick. Indeed variations of the experiment have shown that a rat that gets sick after eating a certain kind of food does not avoid the dish from which the food was eaten, nor foods similar in appearance or texture—but only foods with that particular taste (Rozin and Kalat, 1971). This characteristic of rats and some other animals, which is known as "bait shyness," has obvious survival value, since illness ordinarily means they have eaten poisonous food. Bait shyness is another indication that not all responses can become associated with all stimuli.

Bait shyness may have a human counterpart of sorts in the phobias mentioned early in the chapter. The most common phobias are about objects or situations that presented real danger during many centuries of human history—for example heights, open spaces, darkness, and certain kinds of insects and animals. People seldom acquire troublesome fears of lawn mowers, power tools, or bathtubs, though today these things are potentially much more dangerous than darkness or open spaces (Seligman, 1971). Our tendency to shun some objects and events but not others may be a form of species-specific human behavior that once had survival value. Certainly our use of language is species-specific behavior—dictated by the structure and dynamics of the human brain—that greatly enhances our range of learning and helps account for some of the marvels of memory, as will be discussed in the next chapter.

SUMMARY

Classical conditioning

1. Learning is *any relatively permanent change in behavior (or behavior potential) produced by experience.*
2. One of the simplest and most universal forms of learning concerns the *reflex,* which is an inborn and built-in response to a stimulus.
3. Through learning, a reflex response can become attached to a stimulus that did not originally cause the response. The process was demonstrated when Pavlov taught a dog to respond to a sound with the salivary reflex, which originally was caused only by the presence of food in the mouth. This type of learning is called *classical conditioning.*
4. In classical conditioning, the stimulus that naturally sets off the reflex (in Pavlov's experiment, the food) is called the *unconditioned stimulus.* The previous neutral stimulus to which the reflex becomes attached (the sound) is called the *conditioned stimulus.*
5. The original reflex response (in Pavlov's experiment, salivation) is called the *unconditioned response.* The response to the conditioned stimulus is the *conditioned response.*

6. The pairing of the unconditioned stimulus and the conditioned stimulus is called *reinforcement.* When reinforcement is no longer provided (in Pavlov's experiment, if food no longer accompanies the sound), the conditioned response tends to disappear—a process called *extinction.* After a rest period, however, the conditioned response may reappear—a process called *spontaneous recovery.*
7. When a response has been conditioned to one stimulus, it is also likely to be aroused by similar stimuli—a process called *stimulus generalization.* Through further conditioning, however, the organism can learn to respond to one particular conditioned stimulus but not to other stimuli that closely resemble it—a process known as *stimulus discrimination.*
8. Classical conditioning by past events accounts for many of the unreasonable fears and preferences displayed by human adults—also for such strange physical symptoms as unexplained headaches or nausea.

Operant conditioning

9. Another type of learning, demonstrated by Skinner, concerns *operant behavior*—the random or exploratory activities in which organisms engage, not in reflex response to a stimulus but as a self-generated way of "operating" on the world around them.
10. Skinner showed that a rat in a cage containing a bar would eventually press the bar as part of its operant behavior—and would learn to keep pressing if rewarded with food. This form of learning is called *operant conditioning.*
11. In operant conditioning, the *reinforcement* is the reward (in Skinner's experiment, the food). The rule is that operant behavior that is reinforced by a reward tends to be repeated, while operant behavior that is not reinforced tends to take place only at random intervals or is abandoned.
12. Like classical conditioning, operant conditioning also displays *extinction, spontaneous recovery, stimulus generalization,* and *stimulus discrimination.*
13. Through operant conditioning, animals can be taught to perform complex tasks by rewarding them for the successful completion of each step that leads to the desired behavior. This process is called *shaping.*
14. Rewards that the organism finds basically satisfying, such as food and water, are *primary reinforcers.* The less tangible rewards for which human beings often learn, such as praise or acceptance, are *secondary reinforcers.*
15. Operant learning usually takes place fastest with *constant reinforcement,* or reward for each performance. But learning is usually more resistant to extinction with *partial reinforcement,* or rewards on some occasions and not on others.
16. The use of rewards to influence human activities—for example, praising a withdrawn nursery school child to encourage sociable behavior—is called *behavior modification.*
17. A special form of behavior modification, widely used in mental

hospitals, provides reinforcement in the form of tokens that can be spent like money for goods and privileges. This method is called a *token economy.*

18. *Biofeedback* is an operant conditioning technique that attempts to relieve physical ailments through devices that provide the subject with moment-by-moment readings of such bodily activities as muscle tension and blood flow.

Operant escape, punishment, and learned helplessness

19. Operant conditioning can be established through either *positive reinforcement,* in the form of desirable rewards, or *negative reinforcement,* which is the termination of something painful or otherwise unpleasant, like an electric shock.
20. Experiments with negative reinforcement have shown that animals are very quick to learn *operant escape,* or how to get away from the shock, and *operant avoidance,* or how to prevent the shock by taking some kind of action before it occurs. Many human defenses against events that arouse unpleasant anxiety appear to be forms of operant escape or avoidance.
21. In *punishment,* the goal is not to reinforce a response, and therefore make it more likely to occur in the future, but to eliminate a response. Although punishment often produces rapid learning in animals, it is of questionable value in influencing human behavior.
22. One result of punishment, in both animals and human beings, may be *learned helplessness*—a tendency to believe that events cannot be controlled and to give up trying to learn.
23. Learned helplessness can be caused not only by punishment but also by failure. The effects depend partly on whether victims blame themselves or outside factors.
24. Learned helplessness may apply only to one kind of activity or situation, or it may become generalized and affect the victim's entire approach to life.
25. Therapists try to treat learned helplessness, which can result in seriously neurotic behavior, by persuading victims that they have more ability to succeed than they realize.

The cognitive view: learning as a step in information processing

26. Cognitive psychologists regard learning as one of the steps in *information processing*—with the human organism, far from being a passive product of experience, actively interacting with the environment.
27. Among the experiments that helped lead to the cognitive view are (a) Köhler's finding that chimpanzees seem to learn through *insight,* (b) the discovery that rats in a maze may display *latent learning,* which takes place without reinforcement and lies dormant until there is a reason to use it, and (c) the temporarily paralyzed dog that learned how to escape from a shock even though it could not make a response during the learning trials.
28. Various psychologists have suggested that what is learned is not just

a simple stimulus-response connection but a *cognitive map* (of a maze, for example) or an *expectancy* (for example, that food will follow the sound of a metronome). The cognitive view now includes both these theories in the all-embracing idea that what we learn is *knowledge* of many kinds.

29. One form of acquiring knowledge is *learning through observation* (also called *learning through modeling* or *learning by imitation*). Closely akin to observation learning is the familiar process of learning through instruction, for instance by listening to a teacher or reading a book.
30. The ability of organisms to learn is limited by *species-specific behavior*—or the strong tendency to behave in ways dictated by inherited characteristics. For human beings the use of language is a species-specific behavior that greatly enhances our range of learning.

IMPORTANT TERMS

behavior modification
biofeedback
classical conditioning
cognitive map
conditioned response
conditioned stimulus
constant reinforcement
expectancy
extinction
information processing
insight
knowledge
latent learning
learned helplessness
learning through observation (or modeling or imitation)
negative reinforcement
operant avoidance
operant behavior
operant conditioning
operant escape
partial reinforcement
positive reinforcement
primary reinforcer
punishment
reflex
reinforcement
secondary reinforcer
shaping
species-specific behavior
spontaneous recovery
stimulus discrimination
stimulus generalization
token economy
unconditioned response
unconditioned stimulus

RECOMMENDED READINGS

Hilgard, E. R., and Bower, G. H. *Theories of learning,* 4th ed. New York: Appleton-Century-Crofts, 1975.
Hulse, S. H., Egeth, H., and Deese, J. *The psychology of learning,* 5th ed. New York: McGraw-Hill, 1980.
Kintsch, W. *Memory and cognition,* 2d ed. New York: Wiley, 1977.
Pavlov, I. P. *Conditioned reflexes.* New York: Oxford University Press, 1927.
Schwartz, B. *Psychology of learning and behavior.* New York: Norton, 1978.
Seligman, M. E. P. *Helplessness.* San Francisco: Freeman, 1975.
Skinner, B. F. *The behavior of organisms.* New York: Appleton-Century-Crofts, 1938.
Wickelgren, W. A. *Learning and memory.* Englewood Cliffs, N.J.: Prentice-Hall, 1977.

CHAPTER 4

Remembering for just an instant—or for a lifetime 120
- Sensory memory: gone in a second
- Short-term memory: a half minute at best
- Information processing in short-time memory
- Long-term memory: often for life
- The process of retrieval

The mystery of the memory trace: there must be one—but what is it? 125
- Memory and the brain's neurotransmitters
- Forming new synapses
- RNA and the possibility of "learning pills"

Why we forget 128
- How remembering and forgetting are measured
- Theories of forgetting
- Theory 1: fading of the memory trace
- Theory 2: failure in retrieval
- Theory 3: interference
- Theory 4: motivated forgetting

The encoding and transfer process 135
- Chunking—or putting many little facts into one neat package
- The "tip of the tongue" experience as a clue to encoding
- Tip of the tongue and levels of processing
- The associative network theory
- Forming links between new and old
- The question of what we encode, remember, and retrieve

Encoding and learning 141
- The search for meaning and organization
- Learning by rule versus learning by rote
- Moral for learners: take your time
- How learning builds on learning

Some aids to encoding 147
- How categories help
- Categories, chunking, and clustering
- Clustering, cause-and-effect, and made-up stories
- Storing visual information in memory
- Mnemonic devices

Summary 154

Important terms 157

Recommended readings 157

Psychology and Society
- Is memory infinite or limited? 124
- The witnesses swear they saw it—but did it really happen? 140
- "As the old saying goes, familiarity breeds . . . well, I guess I forget what it breeds" 142

Memory: The Storehouse of Information

If you are like most people, you are not altogether happy with your memory. There must have been many times when you said, "I'm sorry. I've forgotten your name. I have a terrible memory for names." Or, "I meant to send you a birthday card, but I just plain forgot." Or, after an exam, "I knew the answer but I couldn't remember it."

Human memory is often blamed, maligned, apologized for, and agonized over. Yet, no matter how forgetful or absentminded you may consider yourself at times, there is an enormous amount of knowledge stored somewhere—and somehow—within your nervous system. Adult human beings do not have to be prize-winning scholars to know the meanings of many thousands of English words and perhaps some foreign words as well, plus the multiplication tables, rules of mathematics, and many basic facts about geography, science, and history. Not to mention such practical matters as how to drive a car, read a map, operate a calculator, make a phone call, and shop for food and clothing. The marvel is not how much we forget but how much we remember.

To cognitive psychologists, with their emphasis on knowledge as a key part of the human experience, learning and memory are of course closely related. Learning is the way we acquire all the many forms of knowledge we possess and utilize. Memory is the storehouse in which we keep all this information—carefully sorted into various rooms, aisles, and bins so that we can find it quickly when we need it.

At least we try, in the learning and memory steps of information processing, to stow the knowledge away in readily accessible form. We do not always succeed. Sometimes we let a piece of information slip through our hands, so to speak, like the cook who carelessly drops his container of black pepper into a wastebasket and never sees it again. Sometimes we seem to stow a fact away in the wrong place, like the cook who mistakenly puts his pepper can into the refrigerator and cannot find it when he needs it. Either way, we say we have forgotten—perhaps permanently, perhaps just for the time being.

As the analogy of the cook and his pepper suggests, how well we remember information depends in large part on how carefully we have stored it away—or, in other words, how well we have learned it in the first place. If we have done the job properly, the information will be there in the storehouse of our memory when we need it—and usually we manage to lay our hands on it in a hurry.

Remembering for just an instant—or for a lifetime

One approach to understanding the mysteriously efficient process of memory is to consider this example: A young woman is driving across the country to Denver. She is on her way to the home of some friends, where she will have dinner and spend the night. She is expected at about 5 P.M. As she nears the city, however, her car develops engine trouble. A mechanic at a roadside garage tells her the repairs will take an hour or two. So she goes to a phone booth to call her friends and explain that she will be late.

In the phone book she finds her friends' number, which is 629-1965. But at that moment there is a loud squeal of brakes on the highway. Startled, she glances toward the road and sees that there has been a near collision. Turning back to the phone, she finds that she has completely forgotten the number. Indeed it seems that the number never registered at all in her memory. She looks it up again and this time starts repeating it to herself—*six, two, nine, one, nine, six, five*—as she turns from the book and drops a coin into the phone. She remembers the number but gets a busy signal. By the time she has fished the coin out of the return slot, dropped it back into the phone, and waited for the tone, she finds that she has forgotten the number again. She remembered it longer this time—but not long enough.

So she looks up the number again. This time, while repeating it to herself, she notices that it is exactly the same as her birth date, for she was born on June 29, or 6/29, in 1965. Now she remembers the number no matter how many times she gets a busy signal and has to try again. In fact she may remember it the rest of her life.

As this example indicates, memories may persist over a time span that varies over an extremely wide range, from a mere fraction of a second to a lifetime. For convenience, psychologists divide the range into three stages of memory, illustrated in Figure 4-1. It will be helpful to refer to the figure as you read the description of the three stages in the following pages.

The young woman's experiences in a phone booth tell a great deal about human memory, as explained in the text.

Sensory memory: gone in a second

Everything that impinges on our sense organs seems to be remembered for at least a brief instant, but sometimes no longer. Thus the young woman in the phone booth remembered the numbers 629-1965 between the time she looked at them in the directory and the time she heard the squeal of brakes. Then she forgot them completely.

These very brief recollections are known as *sensory memory*, containing just the lingering traces of information sent to the brain by the sense organs. These traces—the *echo* of sounds we hear and the *icon* of sights we see—begin to deteriorate rapidly. Ordinarily they disappear completely within a single second (Sperling, 1960) unless they are somehow transferred to the next of the three memory categories.

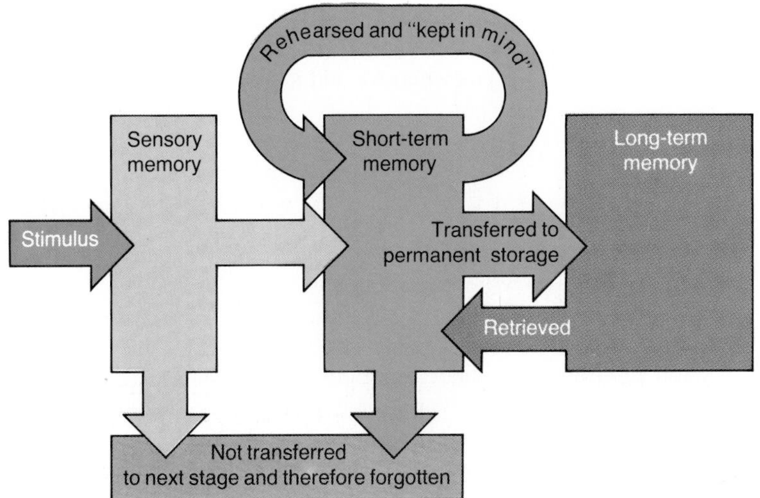

Figure 4-1 The three stages of memory *This diagram offers a quick summary of how the three stages of memory operate. The sights, sounds, and other stimuli in the environment register briefly in* sensory memory. *Some are promptly lost but others are transferred to* short-term memory. *There again some are lost but others are rehearsed and "kept in mind" long enough to be transferred to* long-term memory—*a more or less permanent storehouse from which they can later be retrieved (Shiffrin and Atkinson, 1969). The three stages are described in detail in the text.*

Short-term memory: a half minute at best

The second of the three stages is *short-term memory,* into which some but not all of the information that arrives in sensory memory is transferred. In the case of the woman at the telephone, her second look at the phone book resulted in the transfer of the number 629-1965 to short-term memory. There it remained long enough for her to try the call once—but, when she tried again after getting a busy signal, it had already disappeared.

Unless some processing takes place within short-term memory, information held there deteriorates as shown in Figure 4-2 and seems to be forgotten completely within about 30 seconds (Shiffrin and Atkinson, 1969). So much information is lost in this way that one psychologist has described short-term memory as a "leaky bucket" (Miller, 1964). However, this is not entirely a disadvantage. For example, a bank teller remembers only briefly that he is cashing a customer's paycheck for $150.89. By the time the next customer steps up to the window, the figure $150.89 has already vanished from his memory. This is just as

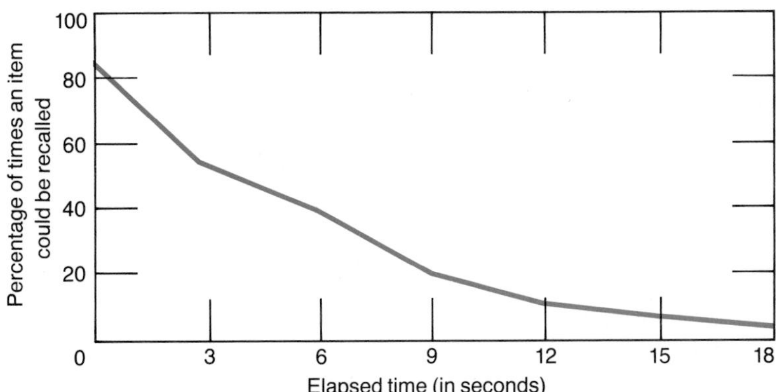

Figure 4-2 The brief lifespan of short-term memory *In a study of how long short-term memory lasts, experimenters gave subjects a grouping of letters and a number, such as KRG 297. Subjects were asked to begin immediately to count aloud, going backward by three's from the number (297, 294, 291, and so on). At various intervals, a light was flashed informing them to stop counting and to try to recall the letters (KRG). Under these circumstances, which kept them too busy counting to rehearse or do any other kind of processing of their information about the letters, the subjects' recall dropped rapidly and was down to nearly zero after a mere 18 seconds (Peterson and Peterson, 1959).*

well—for he would be totally confused by the end of the day if he recalled every transaction starting with the first one of the morning.

The same thing happens when we add a column of figures, such as

37
49
65
22

We say to ourselves (adding the right-hand digits from the top down) 16, 21, 23. Then we write down the 3 and start over on the left-hand numbers, 5, 9, 15, 17. Thus we get the answer 173. All the intermediary numbers that flash through our consciousness—the 16, 21, 23, 5, 9, and 15—disappear almost as rapidly as they are formed. If they did not, we would find it almost impossible to add the columns. We would get the numbers hopelessly jumbled.

Indeed it appears that much of the forgetting we do from short-term memory is intentional (Bjork, 1972). We have no need to remember the information. We do not want to remember it—and it would only get in our way, for the capacity of the short-term memory is quite small in terms of amount of information as well as time span. On the average, it holds seven items—exactly the number of digits in a phone number—although for some people the limit is only five and for others it is as many as nine (Miller, 1956). When short-term memory is full to capacity with its five to nine items, new information can be added only by dropping some of the old. Therefore we often throw out the old items deliberately. We do so by manipulating the processes that go on in short-term memory, which will now be described.

Information processing in short-term memory

A number of information-processing activities seem to take place in short-term memory (Sperling, 1967). First, there must be some kind of *scanning* of the information that is being held briefly in sensory memory. From the constant flow of sights, sounds, and other messages from the sense organs, some particular items must be *selected* as worthy of attention. (This scanning and selection process is closely related to the psychological phenomenon of perception and will be discussed more fully in Chapter 8.)

If the information selected for attention is to be held for any length of time, some sort of *rehearsal system* must be set up. That is, the information must be deliberately kept in mind and prevented from slipping out of the "leaky bucket." Through rehearsal, information can be kept in short-term memory as long as desired—though the amount of information that can be kept alive, as has been stated, is quite small.

To help with the processing, the information held in short-term memory is usually transformed in some way that makes it as simple and easy to handle as possible. This process is called *encoding*—for it resembles the manner in which a business machine can take complicated facts (such as a customer's name and address, past-due balance, and new purchases) and code them into a series of holes on a punch card. When the information in short-term memory is language or numbers, the encoding is usually done in acoustical terms—that is, the information is encoded into sounds (Kintsch, 1970).

Finally, if the information is to be remembered more or less permanently, it must be passed along and stored in *long-term memory.* The process seems to take place somewhat as follows. The new information, held in short-term memory and kept alive through rehearsal, is associated with any relevant pieces of information that already exist in long-term memory. Comparisons are made and relationships sought. Further encoding and recoding take place. When this so-called *transfer process* is successful, the new information is more or less permanently fitted into long-term memory, like a new item dropped into the appropriate bin in a warehouse.

Long-term memory: often for life

In the case of the woman in the phone booth, the transfer of the number 629-1965 into lasting memory included all the processes just described. Visual images of the numbers in the directory arrived in sensory memory. These images were scanned, encoded into sounds, and held in short-term memory through rehearsal. While rehearsing the numbers, the woman noted that they were the same as her birth date. With the help of this association between new and old information, the transfer to long-term memory became easy and effective.

How long is long? As you surely have discovered to your sorrow at times, it is not always as long as we would wish. We often forget things we would like to remember—for reasons that will be discussed later. But

"The matters about which I'm being questioned, Your Honor, are all things I should have included in my long-term memory but which I mistakenly inserted in my short-term memory."

Psychology and Society: Is memory infinite or limited?

All psychologists agree that human memory is a remarkable storehouse with a vast capacity for words, numbers, facts, and details, as well as relationships, rules, and general principles. Most psychologists, indeed, believe that we use only a fraction of our abilities—and that many rooms and bins in the storehouse remain empty and waiting, an untapped resource. The majority view is that, although we know and remember a great deal, we have the potential to accomplish much more.

A minority view—which raises some provocative questions for society and for the way we plan our lives—comes from Wayne A. Wickelgren, a psychologist at the University of Oregon. Wickelgren believes that the human capacity to learn and remember, though very large, has definite limits. Moreover, he believes that most of the time most of us operate fairly close to capacity. We learn and remember about as much as the workings of our nervous systems permit. We would all be happier if we recognized our limitations and took a more charitable view of our own accomplishments and those of other people. The schools would do a better job if they recognized that students cannot learn everything all at once. Thus he questions the value of such educational practices as asking elementary school pupils to learn the names of European capitals and high school students to learn a foreign language.

Wickelgren believes that *what* we learn—in school or in our life experiences—is far more important than *how much* we learn. In the educational system, "emphasis should be on the quality rather than the amount of knowledge that students are required to learn." The schools should concentrate on information that "we can *use* to achieve some important goal"—such as the general principles that provide "insight and understanding" of our universe, our society, and the workings of the human organism: "It is of far less general value to know the superficial physical characteristics of various plants and animals than to know about nutrition, disease, first aid, the anatomy and physiology of the human body, and the general principles of living systems." Wickelgren concedes that learning a foreign language may provide some personal, social, and intellectual satisfactions—but questions whether this is as valuable in the early school years as acquiring a broader understanding of human experience.

In planning your own life, Wickelgren suggests, it is wise to set priorities, concentrate on learning what is really important to you, and avoid attempting the impossible. Moreover, he suggests that there has to be a trade-off between time spent studying and time spent applying what you do know: "Some people who know more than others have accomplished less as a direct result of their learning."

Recognizing the limitations of memory, Wickelgren believes, can also help us understand and sympathize with other people: "It is unreasonable to tell a co-worker or friend in a five-minute period ten things you want that person to do and expect him or her to remember it all without mistakes. . . . One source of friction in personal relations and of inefficiency in job performance could be eliminated if we remembered that the capacity for learning and memory is limited" (Wickelgren, 1977).

many long-term memories persist for a lifetime. As for how much information we can store in long-term memory, there is really no way of knowing. Certainly the capacity is very large.

Most people have the meanings of tens of thousands of words stored in memory. Some have vocabularies that run into the hundreds of thousands. With the help of these words we accumulate all kinds of facts and rules about the way the world operates. It has been estimated that the items of information and relationships held in memory must number in the tens of millions. It may even be that the memory storehouse has an absolutely unlimited capacity—though this is a matter of debate with some important implications for our educational system and our own life plans, as discussed in a box on Psychology and Society.

The process of retrieval

We cannot possibly be conscious at any given moment of all the millions of items of information we hold in long-term memory. Most of the information just lies there, like the unused items in storage bins. We have no need for it. We do not think about it. But then there comes a time when the situation we face calls for us to use a particular piece of information. Let us say that we are reading one evening by the light of a single lamp. Suddenly the light goes out—and we are left in the dark. The situation calls for action, and for the use of the knowledge we have stored in long-term memory about lamps, electricity, and alternative sources of light. Did the bulb burn out, as bulbs sometimes do? Did a fuse or circuit breaker cut off the current—and how can we check? Is the electricity off all through the building—and if so what can we do about it? Have the lights also gone out in nearby buildings, indicating a neighborhood power failure? Should we call the utility company—and if so how can we do this in the dark?

An order has arrived at memory's storage house, calling for the immediate delivery of some of the items held in the bins. We need information, and to be able to use it we must engage in the process called *retrieval.* That is, we must find the right bin, pull out the right items, and deliver them to short-term memory, where we can actively think about them.

Look back at Figure 4-1 and note the two arrows showing the interaction between short-term and long-term memory. One arrow indicates the process in which new information is transferred from short-term memory into more or less permanent storage. The other arrow indicates the retrieval process, in which information that has been stored in long-term memory is called back into short-term memory, or in other words back into consciousness, where we can think about it and use it.

Unless the retrieval process is successful, and we find the right items of information in the right bins, the knowledge we have stored in long-term memory is of no use to us. (It does no good to know that we have a flashlight and candle somewhere if we cannot remember where we put them.) Fortunately, the human retrieval process operates in wondrous ways, more directly and efficiently than most computers. We do not have to rummage through all the storage rooms and all the bins in every room to find what we need. Instead we are capable of what has been called *direct-access retrieval* (Wickelgren, 1981). Our storehouse is organized in such a way that we can ordinarily go directly to the right room and the right bin, put our hands on the items we need, and deliver them promptly to short-term memory. The way we accomplish this highly efficient organization is discussed later in the chapter.

The mystery of the memory trace: there must be one—but what is it?

Every time we store a new piece of information in long-term memory, we are somehow changed. We can do something—recall a new fact or engage in a new kind of behavior—that we could not do before. Obviously something has happened inside us. But what?

Psychologists do not know for sure. They must confine themselves to saying that a *memory trace* has been established. They can only speculate as to what this memory trace is, how it is created, and why it sometimes persists and results in long-lasting memories and sometimes vanishes. Some psychologists believe there are several kinds of memory traces, perhaps corresponding to the three different stages of memory. Others believe that just a single type of trace, which may last anywhere from a fraction of a second to a lifetime, accounts for all forms of memory (Wickelgren, 1981).

Whatever the nature and number may be, the memory trace surely represents some kind of change in the nervous system. Sometimes the change seems to take place inside the spinal cord. At least experiments with animals have shown that simple reflexes can be conditioned through the spinal cord when it has been disconnected from the brain (Patterson, Cegavske, and Thompson, 1973). More often, however, the change takes place in the brain, especially in the highest part, or cortex, of the brain. It probably occurs at the switching points, or synapses. When we learn something, we route nervous impulses over a particular pathway, passing through a number of synapses in a particular pattern. The various kinds of nervous activity that take place along this pathway presumably have a lasting effect that makes it possible to reactivate the pattern on future occasions—thus enabling us to remember what we have learned.

Memory and the brain's neurotransmitters

Establishment of the memory trace seems to depend at least in part on the brain's *neurotransmitters,* the chemicals that pass messages along from one neuron to another. Studies of lower animals indicate that when one neuron stimulates another neuron to fire, by releasing its

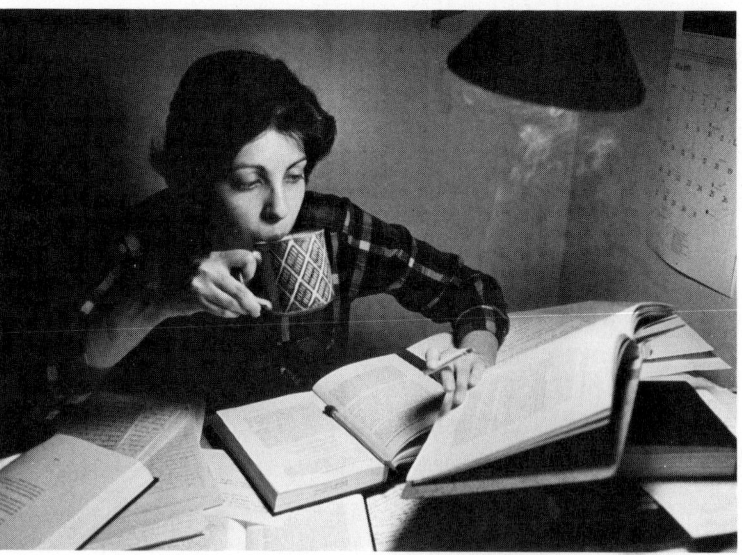

There's caffeine in the coffee and nicotine in the cigarette. Will these mild stimulants help the student remember?

neurotransmitters into the synapse between them, these chemicals produce a lasting change in the efficiency of the synapse (Kandel, 1970). The second neuron becomes more likely to fire again in the future, thus making it easier for nervous impulses to travel the same pathway again.

In the case of human beings, it has been observed that drugs that influence the way brain cells produce their neurotransmitters have some pronounced effects on memory. Investigators have found that human subjects often show an increased ability to store information in long-term memory after they have received even small doses of a drug that increases the brain's active supply of the neurotransmitter called acetylcholine (Davis, 1978). Indeed almost any drugs that stimulate the chemical activity of the brain tend to improve the establishment of memories. Among such drugs are caffeine, nicotine, and amphetamines (McGaugh and Dawson, 1971)—provided they are taken in doses small enough to avoid arousal that is so intense as to produce confusion. Likewise, drugs that slow down the brain's chemical activity interfere with learning. This is true of alcohol (Goodwin et al., 1970), tranquilizers (Johnson, 1969), and even mild doses of such anesthetics as ether or laughing gas (Leukel, 1957).

Forming new synapses

The establishment of memory traces also appears to depend at times on the formation of new synapses—resulting in new connections between neurons that did not previously influence one another (Moore, 1976). The formation of new synapses presumably can continue throughout life. It is especially apparent in the development of the brain from birth, when it weighs only about 11 ounces, to adulthood, when it weighs about 3 pounds. Most of the neurons of the brain are present at birth; the number increases only slightly.* But the neurons increase in size and develop new dendrites (making possible new synaptic connections) much as a young tree develops new branches.

The effect of learning on the brain has been demonstrated by experiments in which young animals have been raised under conditions offering different kinds of opportunities to learn. For example, one group of rats was brought up in ordinary cages, another in an environment enriched by various kinds of visual stimuli and toys. Examination after death showed that the animals from the enriched environments had heavier brains (Bennett et al., 1964). Encouraging animals to learn has also been found to result in an increased number of dendrites in the brain, indicating that more new synapses were formed (Greenough, 1976). The brains of animals from enriched environments have also been found to contain more neurotransmitter chemicals (Bennett et al., 1964)—another indication that the establishment of memory traces may depend on both formation of new synapses and greater chemical activity and efficiency at the synapses.

---

*Until recently it was believed that we possess at birth all the brain neurons we will ever have. Indications have now been found, however, that a small number can appear later (Greenough, 1982).

RNA and the possibility of "learning pills"

But how and why synaptic changes take place remains a mystery. Some investigators have suggested that they may depend on a chemical called *RNA*, similar to the DNA that makes up the genes and serves as the carrier of heredity. These investigators point out that in every cell of the body, including the nerve cells, the DNA manufactures various forms of RNA that act as its "messengers," controlling the growth and functioning of the cell. Their theory is that learning changes the amount and type of RNA produced in nerve cells (Hyden, 1967) and that the RNA then operates to establish new synapses or change the efficiency of existing synapses. But the evidence linking RNA to learning has been seriously challenged (Byrne et al., 1966)—and, even if true, it would not shed much light on the mystery of the memory trace. You may have heard the suggestion that someday we might all be able to become mathematical geniuses instantly by taking RNA extracted from the brain of an Einstein—but this is a notion that few psychologists take seriously.

The establishment of long-term memories—all those tens of millions of them that we may accumulate in a lifetime—is another example of how the human brain operates in marvelous ways that challenge understanding. Despite what has been discovered about the relationships among learning, the neurotransmitters, and the synapses, we still are not even sure whether any specific memory trace represents a change in a specific pattern of part of the brain or a more generalized change affecting widespread parts of the nervous system (Wickelgren, 1977). The process is far too complex to offer much hope of quick and easy results from any kind of "learning pill." We will just have to reconcile ourselves to the fact that laying down long-term memories usually requires the kind of work that will be described later in the chapter.

Why we forget

Memory cannot be discussed without also discussing forgetting. They are opposite sides of the same coin. We learn something—that is, we store some piece of information in our memory. Sometimes this information persists and we can call on it whenever we need it. We say that we remember. Sometimes the information seems to disappear or elude us—and we say we have forgotten. Why do we remember some things and forget others?

How remembering and forgetting are measured

Attempts to investigate the twin processes of remembering and forgetting face many obstacles. There is no way psychologists can examine the nervous system to see what kinds of changes have been laid down in it by learning and how well these changes persist. They can only devise tests to determine how much is remembered and how much is forgotten. Unfortunately, these tests can never make a direct measure of memory. All they can measure is how well people *perform* on the tests—and their performance may not be an entirely accurate indication of how much they remember.

Let us say that two girls in elementary school are taking the same arithmetic course. They listen to the same explanations by their teacher and study the same textbooks. Now one day the teacher gives a written examination. Girl A gets 90. Girl B gets 70. The logical conclusion is that girl A learned her arithmetic very well and remembered it and that girl B either learned it poorly or quickly forgot it.

The truth, however, is that we do not really know. All we can say for sure is that girl A *performed* much better on the examination than did girl B. It may very well be that girl B had learned addition, subtraction, and the multiplication tables backward and forward and did badly on the examination because these subjects were so old hat to her that she was bored when asked to show how well she could perform.

Performance on tests of memory can be adversely affected not only by poor motivation but also by anxiety, distractions, and many other factors. Thus tests of remembering and forgetting must always be viewed with reservations. But psychologists, in their effort to do the best they can, have adopted three standard methods of measurement.

Recall One way to prove you have learned the Gettysburg Address is to recite it—which demonstrates that you can *recall* it, or bring it out intact from wherever it is stored in your memory. In school, a common use of recall is in the essay type of examination. When teachers ask, "What is classical conditioning?" they are asking you to recall and write down what you have learned.

Recognition Often we cannot recall what we have learned, at least not completely, but we can prove that we remember something about it by being able to *recognize* it. For example, you may not be able to recall the Gettysburg Address. But if someone asked you what begins with the words "Fourscore and seven years ago," you might immediately recognize the speech, thus demonstrating that you certainly remember something about it.

In multiple-choice examinations you are asked to choose the right answer from among several possible answers and thus prove that you recognize it. Because recognition is easier than recall, many students would rather take a multiple-choice test than an essay examination.

Relearning The most sensitive method of measuring memory is one that is seldom used. This is the method of *relearning,* which is accurate but cumbersome. All of us once learned the Gettysburg Address, or, if not that, then some other well-known piece of writing (anything from a nursery rhyme to Hamlet's soliloquy). We may not be able to recite these pieces now; so we would fail on the recall test. We might recognize them if we saw or heard them again. This would prove that we remember something but would not be a very precise measure of how much. If we set about relearning them, however, the length of time this took us would serve as a highly accurate measure.

Theories of forgetting

Relearning was the measurement used in one of psychology's earliest and most famous studies of forgetting, made by a nineteenth-century German named Hermann Ebbinghaus. For his experiments, Ebbinghaus

BIK TAF
ROP GOK
DAF MIK
PEM BUL
FUM HAN
NIF RIN
GOR KUF
MEF JUN
JAL LEP
KUL DAL
LUF FOM
HIR REL
WOX TUR

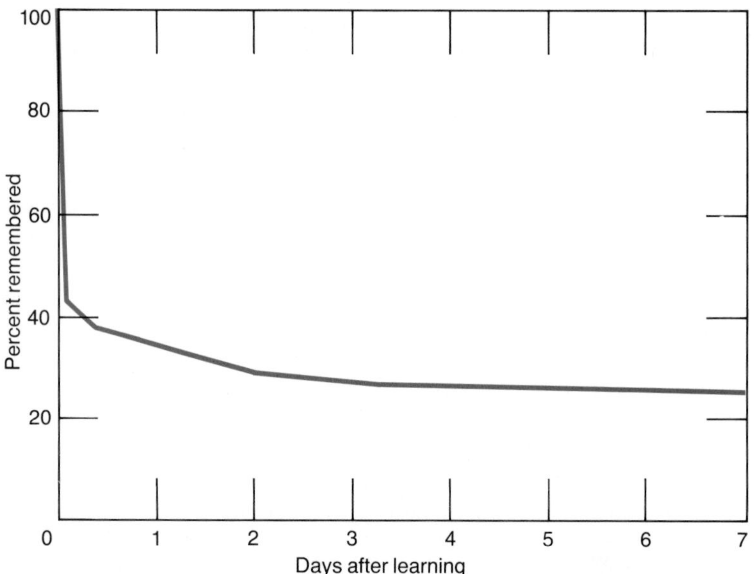

Figure 4-3 Ebbinghaus's famous curve of forgetting *Ebbinghaus memorized lists of 13 nonsense syllables similar to those shown here, then measured how much he could remember after various intervals. After 20 minutes, he remembered only 58 percent and after about an hour only 44 percent. After the initial sharp dip, however, the curve flattened out. After one day he remembered about 34 percent and after two days about 28 percent. Although the graph line does not extend that far, he recalled 21 percent after a month (Ebbinghaus, 1913).*

invented the nonsense syllable. He learned lists of such syllables and then measured how long it took him to relearn the lists to perfection after various intervals. He came up with the *curve of forgetting* shown in Figure 4-3. The curve does not always apply, because we learn some things so thoroughly that we never forget them. However, it tells a great deal about the forgetting of such varied kinds of learning as motor skills, poems we have memorized, and college courses we have taken. Its message is this: *When we learn something new, often we quickly forget much of it, but we remember at least some of it for a long time.*

As to why we forget, the answer is not yet fully known. But there are a number of theories worth considering. In fact all the theories may be correct at least in part, for forgetting may be such a complex process that it takes place in different ways under different circumstances.

Theory 1: fading of the memory trace

One of the oldest theories of forgetting assumes that the memory trace, whatever its physical nature, is subject to decay—that it begins to fade as time goes on and sometimes disappears entirely. The theory regards the memory trace as resembling the marks of a pencil on a piece of paper, or a path worn into a plot of grass. It can be kept functioning through use, as a pencil mark can be emphasized by tracing and retracing and a pathway can be kept clear by continuing to walk over it. But without use the memory trace may vanish, as a pencil mark fades with time and a pathway becomes overgrown when abandoned.

Many of today's memory theorists continue to believe that the memory trace has some physical quality that changes with the passage of time, often reducing the likelihood that it can be retraced or reactivated. Indeed they think of it as having two qualities. The first is its *strength*—meaning how likely it is to "pop into mind." This quality, the strength of the memory trace, is at its peak immediately after learning and declines with the passage of time. The second quality is *resistance to extinction,* meaning how well the trace can manage to survive and become immune to fading or decay (Wickelgren, 1977).

Establishing resistance to extinction is believed to take a certain amount of time. It requires what memory theorists call *consolidation,* a period during which the trace undergoes a process that might be compared with the hardening or "setting" of a newly laid sidewalk. (During the consolidation period whatever changes are produced at the synapses by learning may somehow become more permanent, or perhaps new synapses may have time to form.) The consolidation process takes place most rapidly in the first minutes after learning—but it continues, though at a gradually slowing rate, as long as the memory trace exists. Thus, though the memory trace may decrease in strength with the passage of time, it may also become more and more resistant to extinction as the years go by.

The idea that time affects both the strength and resistance of the memory trace is based in part on studies of people who have suffered amnesia, or loss of memory, because of head injuries. This type of amnesia often takes a very strange form. Patients may be unable to remember anything that happened in the past five years yet have a normal memory for events that happened earlier. As they begin to get over the effects of their injuries, their memories return on a predictable time schedule. First they recover their memory for events that are five years old, then for four-year-old events, and so on until their recovery is complete (Weiskrantz, 1966). It would appear that the older their memory traces, the more resistant the traces were to temporary disruption by injury.

Theory 2: failure in retrieval

Other psychologists take a different view. They believe that the memory trace, once it has been established as part of long-term memory, probably persists for as long as we live. But information held in memory is of no use to us unless it remains not only stored but available. If for one reason or another we cannot retrieve it, we say we have forgotten it. Thus forgetting may be not a failure in memory but rather a failure in retrieval. As one psychologist has put it: "In this respect memory is like a huge warehouse in which all sorts of things are stored but which is less than perfectly organized, so that it is not always easy to find a given item upon demand" (Kintsch, 1977).

Temporary forgetting caused by failure in retrieval is an everyday experience. There undoubtedly have been many occasions when you found yourself unable to remember some item of information, then later on recalled it perfectly, especially if something happened to "jog your memory." Whether retrieval failure can cause a permanent loss, as if the item were so hopelessly mislaid somewhere in the storehouse that it could never be found, is a matter of debate.

Many experiments have been performed in search of factors that might affect retrieval for better or worse. It has been found, for example, that at least some kinds of information are more easily retrieved in the

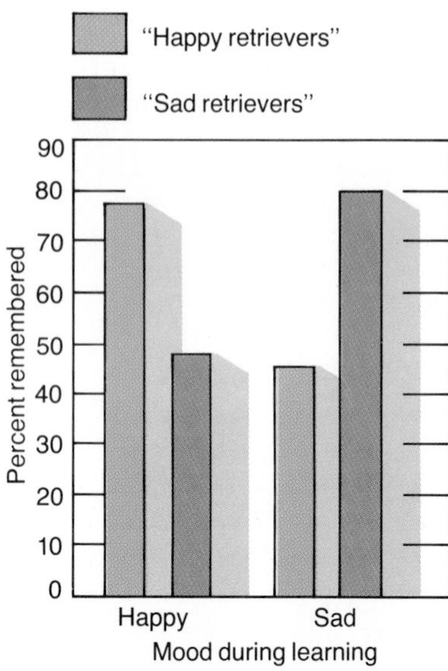

Figure 4-4 Being in the right mood as an aid to retrieval *These are the results of an experiment, described in the text, in which subjects tried to recall word lists under two different conditions: (1) when they were in the same mood as when they studied the list, and (2) when they were in the opposite mood. Note how much better both the "happy retrievers" and the "sad retrievers" did on the list they learned while in the same mood as when they were tested (after Bower, 1981).*

same physical setting in which the learning took place (for example the same classroom)—or even through visualizing the setting (Smith, 1979). This suggests that we may find it helpful, when trying to remember a name, to try to recall the physical circumstances in which we met or last saw that person.

It has also been found that retrieval is more effective when we are in the same mood as when we first acquired the information. In one experiment the emotional state of the subjects was manipulated through hypnosis and they learned two lists of words, one when they were happy and another when they were sad. Later they were tested for their recall, some when they were in the same hypnotically induced mood as during the learning and some when they were in the opposite mood. As is shown in Figure 4-4, mood was found to have a striking effect on the subjects' ability to retrieve the words. The "happy retrievers" made a much better score on the list they learned when they were happy than on the one they learned while sad. The "sad retrievers" did much better on the list they learned while sad than on the list they learned while happy. It was also found that when subjects were hypnotized into a happy mood then asked to recall events of their childhood, they remembered many pleasant incidents and only a few unpleasant ones. Subjects hypnotized into a sad mood recalled more unpleasant than pleasant events (Bower, 1981).

Indeed almost any important similarity between conditions at the time of retrieval and at the time of learning and encoding may serve as a cue that "jogs the memory." The principle has been stated in these words: "When the conditions of encoding and recall are most similar, then recall will be best" (Klatzky, 1980).

Theory 3: interference

Another possible explanation for forgetting is that our ability to remember any given piece of information is interfered with by other information stored in memory. This theory holds that our memory for what we learn today is often adversely affected by what we have learned in the past and also by what we will learn in the future. The various pieces of information compete for attention and survival—and not all of them can prevail.

Proactive interference When old information causes us to forget new information, the process is called *proactive interference.* The phenomenon of proactive interference can be demonstrated through simple laboratory procedures, such as asking subjects to try to learn and remember several lists of words. The results of one such experiment are illustrated in Figure 4-5. Note the steady decline in the subjects' ability to remember new materials caused by more and more proactive interference from prior learning.

Proactive interference is greatest when we try to learn new materials that are similar to old materials already stored in memory—as was the case with the word lists used in the experiment shown in Figure 4-5. Proactive interference is considerably less troublesome when the new

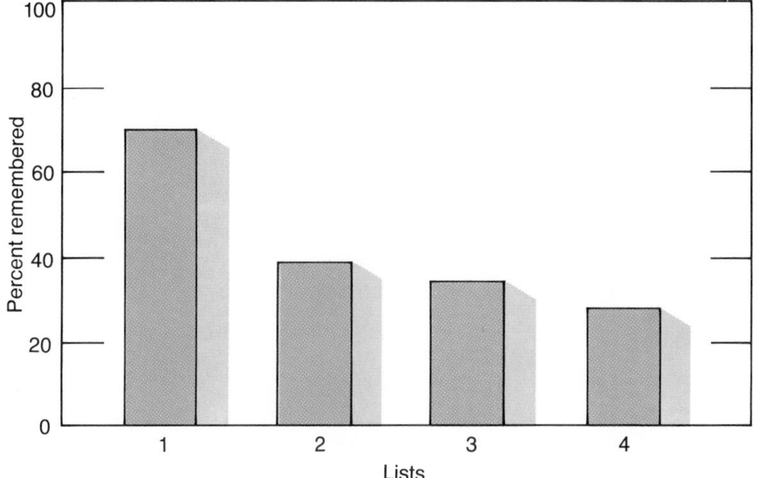

Figure 4-5 How the old interferes with the new *In one of the classic experiments on proactive interference, subjects learned a list of paired adjectives. Two days after learning, they were tested for their recall of list 1 and asked to learn list 2. After a similar interval they were tested on list 2 and learned list 3. Two days later they were tested on list 3 and learned list 4. Finally, after another two-day interval, they were tested on list 4 and the experiment ended. The steady decline in the height of the bars shows how learning list 1 interfered with memory for list 2, how learning lists 1 and 2 interfered with memory for list 3, and so on (Underwood, 1957).*

materials are substantially different from the old, as illustrated in Figure 4-6. In this experiment, one group of subjects watched four videotaped broadcasts of news items that all fell into the same general category, for example national political developments. Another group watched similar news items on the first three tapes. But the fourth tape abruptly switched the subject, for example from national politics to foreign affairs. As the figure shows, both groups remembered less and less over the first three trials. On the final tape, the first group continued to display a decline caused by proactive interference—but the second group, with proactive interference reduced because of the change to a different topic, did much better.

Exactly how proactive interference operates is a matter of debate. The majority opinion seems to be that the old materials interfere with retrieval of the new (Watkins and Watkins, 1975)—a suggestion that would make the interference theory of forgetting very similar to the

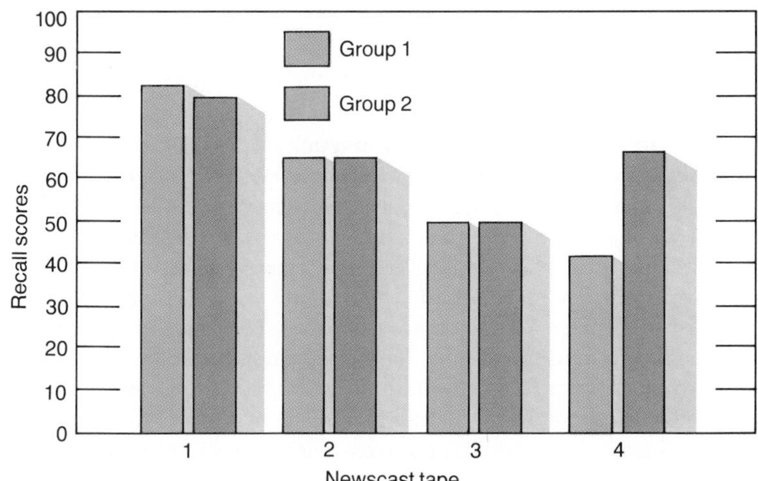

Figure 4-6 Changing the subject as an antidote to proactive interference *The bars show the results of an experiment in which subjects watched a series of four videotapes of old news broadcasts. After each tape they were tested on how much of it they remembered. For both groups, the recall scores began a steady decline as listening to tape 1 interfered with their ability to remember tape 2 and listening to tapes 1 and 2 interfered with their memory for tape 3. But note the discrepancy between the two groups on tape 4. Group 1 subjects continued to show a decline, but group 2 suddenly displayed a sharp improvement (Gunter, Berry, and Clifford, 1981). For the reason, see the text.*

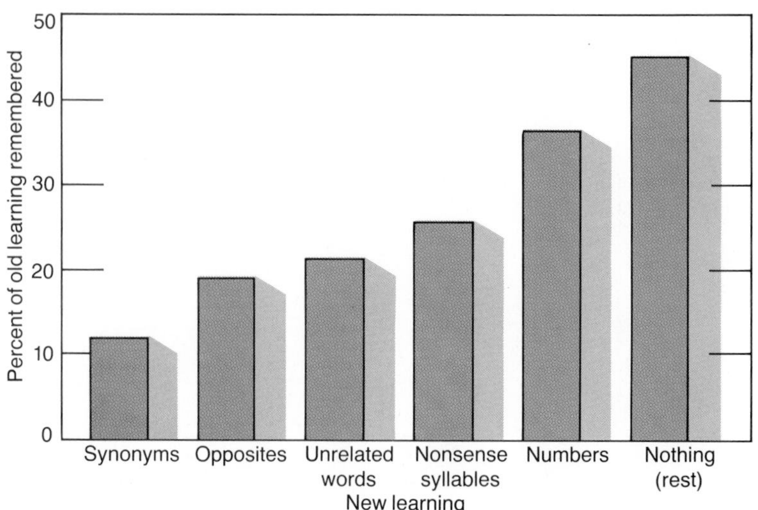

Figure 4-7 How the new interferes with the old *The bars show the results of an experiment in which subjects were asked to learn a list of adjectives, then tested 10 minutes later on how many they could remember. During the 10 minutes some subjects were kept busy at various new learning tasks—such as learning synonyms for the adjectives—and some were just permitted to do nothing. The fact that the subjects who worked at new learning tasks recalled fewer of the adjectives than the "do nothing" group demonstrates the effect of retroactive interference. The more similar the new learning was to the old, the greater was the amount of retroactive interference (McGeoch and McDonald, 1931).*

retrieval theory. But some psychologists believe that proactive interference simply makes it more difficult to learn new materials and encode them into long-term memory (Radtke and Grove, 1977). Others believe that the effect somehow takes place within the memory storehouse, after encoding but before the attempt at retrieval (Chechile and Butler, 1975).

Retroactive interference In proactive interference, old information gets in the way of remembering new information. The opposite situation—when new information causes us to forget old information—is called *retroactive interference.* This phenomenon has also been demonstrated through simple laboratory procedures, as in the experiment illustrated in Figure 4-7. Note that similarity between old and new materials again plays an important role in recall. When subjects learned a new list of words with the same meaning as the words in the previous list (synonyms), they experienced more retroactive interference than when the new list contained very different materials, such as nonsense syllables or numbers.

Perhaps the most interesting—and consoling—fact about retroactive interference is that it has a greater effect on unimportant materials that are not worth remembering anyway (like lists of words learned in a laboratory) than on important and meaningful materials. Retroactive interference often makes us forget the specific details of what we have learned, especially if the details are not essential, but it is not nearly so likely to make us forget the basic theme and meaning of what we have learned (Christiaansen, 1980). Thus you will probably forget some of the things you learn in this course because of retroactive interference from information you will learn in future courses and from your life experiences. You may not remember the exact meaning of such terms as classical conditioning and reinforcement, but you will probably always remember the general principles of learning and of how memory operates. A study that shows what students are likely to remember is illustrated in Figure 4-8.

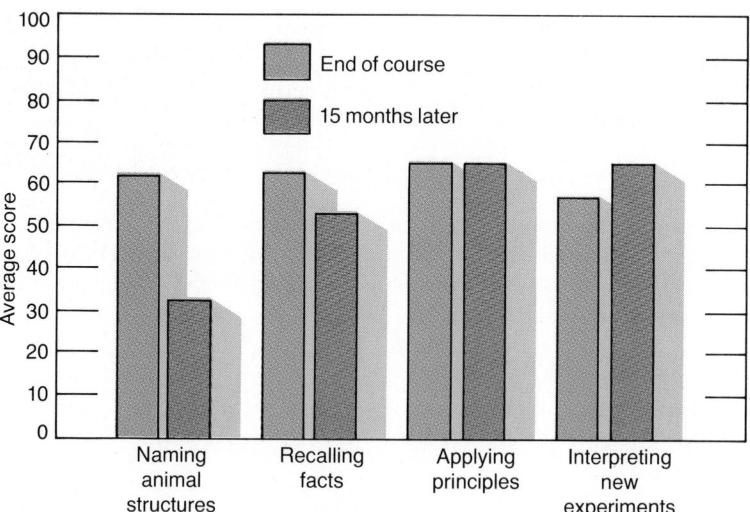

Figure 4-8 What college students forget—and what they remember *The scores represented by the bars were obtained by testing college students on their knowledge of zoology—first immediately after they had finished a course then 15 months later. By the time of the second test the students had forgotten about half the terminology they had learned for animal structures and many specific facts. But they still knew the principles as well as ever and could apply them to new situations. On the matter of interpreting experiments that they had never heard of before, they were actually better than at the end of the course. The improvement was probably due to the greater general knowledge and maturity the students acquired in an additional year of college (Tyler, 1933).*

Theory 4: motivated forgetting

The fact that we seem to forget some things deliberately was mentioned earlier in connection with the processes that take place in short-term memory. Many theorists believe that at times we also forget information stored in long-term memory simply because we want to forget it. For example, we forget the name of a person we dislike, or we forget the problems we had at a certain stage of life and look back to that period as a time when we were ideally happy. People who gamble are notoriously prone to remember the times they won and to forget the times they lost, often building up a totally false impression of how well they have done over the years.

Motivated forgetting has been widely studied by psychoanalysts, who have found that it often plays a part in abnormal or neurotic behavior. It is less important in the lives of more or less normal people. Indeed most of us are troubled by persistent memories of embarrassing and painful events that we would gladly forget if only we could. Motivated forgetting does seem to occur at times—but less often than most of us would wish. It accounts for only a small part of our forgetting.

The encoding and transfer process

The four theories of why we forget, all of which may be correct at least in part and at times, offer some valuable hints on how we can avoid the handicap and embarrassment of forgetting. The motivation theory suggests that we are more likely to remember when we want to remember. The other theories indicate that we will be most efficient at remembering if we can manage to store information in such a way that the memory traces will not fade away with the passage of time, that the information can be retrieved when we want it, and that it will remain more or less intact despite interference from previous and future learning.

All these matters depend on how we encode and transfer information to long-term memory. Thus the key to remembering lies in two related questions: What is the nature of the encoding process that creates our store of knowledge and how can we do the processing more effectively—and learn and remember to greater advantage?

Chunking—or putting many little facts into one neat package

One of the important elements in encoding can best be explained by taking another look at short-term memory, with its capacity of about seven items. Note what happens if you look briefly at this string of letters:

tvfBIYmcasATNbcnASA

You will probably find it impossible to remember all 19 letters, or indeed anywhere near that number. But note what happens with just a slight change:

tvFBIymcaSATnbcNASA

The 19 letters are now turned into a mere six units—each containing familiar combinations of initials—and fall well within the limits of short-term memory. You would have no trouble remembering them after a mere few seconds of study (after Bower, 1970).

This process, in which a number of individual units of information are combined into one—wrapped together securely, so to speak, in a single neat package—is called *chunking* (Miller, 1956). Chunking greatly increases the scope of short-term memory, which can hold about seven big packages of information just about as well as it can handle seven small individual items. We encode many forms of information into chunks—letters into words (as illustrated in Figure 4-9), words into phrases *(frying pan, chicken chow mein),* phrases into sentences *(Mary had a little lamb),* individual digits into memorable dates (1492, 1776), and so on.

Obviously chunking requires some interaction between short-term and long-term memory. We could not readily form the chunks TV and FBI, for example, unless we were already familiar with these combinations of letters. And obviously much of the information in long-term memory has been encoded and stored there in chunks. In this respect memory is something like a storehouse that gets a request for, say, a radio. We do not have to rummage around in different parts of the storehouse for all the various transistors, wires, dials, and speakers. Instead we reach right into the appropriate bin and immediately pull out the entire set, all assembled and boxed.

The "tip of the tongue" experience as a clue to encoding

Another aspect of encoding has been demonstrated in a study based on a commonplace experience that you have doubtless had many times. You are trying to remember something—somebody's name, a word you want to use in a letter or term paper, a fact that you need to answer an exam question. You are sure you know it. You have it "on the tip of the tongue." But, at the moment, you cannot quite bring it to mind.

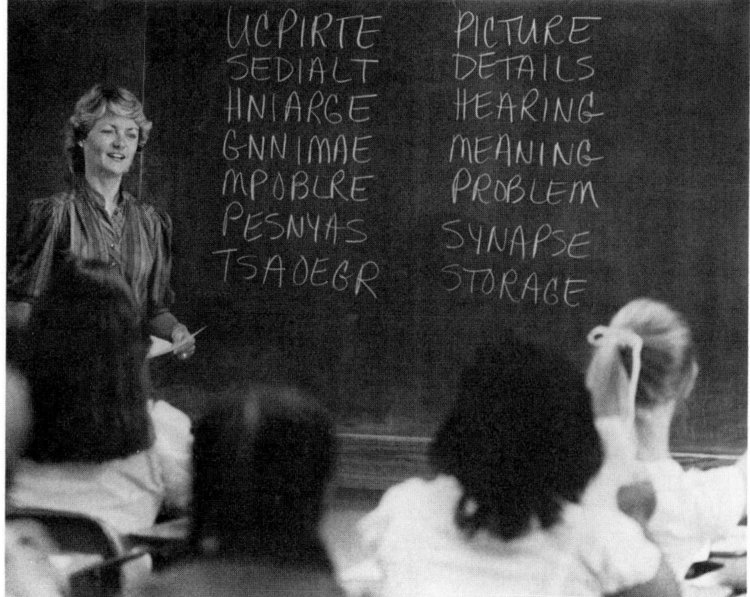

Figure 4-9 A classroom demonstration of chunking *The instructor first shows the blackboard as in the upper photo. How many of the 49 letters can the class possibly remember after studying the board for a minute or two? Not many, because each line in the column contains seven letters—and seven is about the capacity of short-term memory. But then she shows the board in the photo below. The task becomes much easier, for each line of letters has been rearranged into a familiar word that constitutes a single chunk, and there are now just seven chunks to deal with instead of 49 individual letters.*

This "tip of the tongue" phenomenon was investigated by asking university students to try to recall, from hearing the definitions, such words as *sampan, sextant, nepotism,* and *ambergris*—all fairly unusual words that they probably once had an opportunity to learn but would not have had many occasions to use. As was expected, it turned out that often they could not remember the word but felt they had it "on the tip of the tongue." What exactly did this mean? It was found that the students could often—indeed in 57 percent of the cases—guess the first

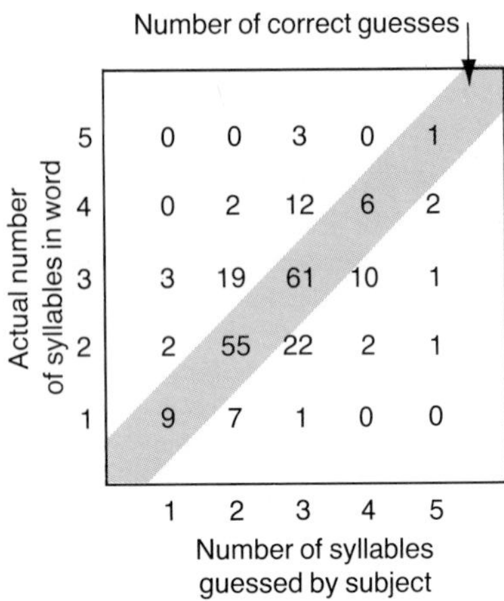

Number of correct guesses
Actual number of syllables in word
5 | 0 0 3 0 1
4 | 0 2 12 6 2
3 | 3 19 61 10 1
2 | 2 55 22 2 1
1 | 9 7 1 0 0
1 2 3 4 5
Number of syllables guessed by subject

Figure 4-10 "I can't remember the word—but I do know how long it is" *Students who had a word on "the tip of the tongue" but could not quite recall it, in the experiment described in the text, were asked to guess how many syllables it had. As shown by the figures in the shaded band, their guesses were more right than wrong unless the word had more than three syllables.*

letter of the word they were seeking. They also demonstrated considerable recall for the last letter of the word. Often they thought of words that had a similar sound. When trying to remember *sampan,* for example, they thought of such words as *Saipan, Siam, Cheyenne,* and *sarong,* and even such made-up words as *sanching* and *sympoon.* Moreover, as is shown in Figure 4-10, they usually knew how many syllables were in the word—at least if the number of syllables, as in the great majority of everyday English words, was no more than three. There was even some indication that they knew which syllable the accent was on. Most important of all, they often thought of words with a similar meaning. For example, in the case of *sampan,* which is defined as a small Chinese boat, they thought of *barge, houseboat,* and *junk* (Brown and McNeill, 1966).

Tip of the tongue and levels of processing

The tip-of-the-tongue experiment and other findings have led to the *levels-of-processing theory,* which holds that the way words are encoded into memory takes place on a number of different levels, ranging from the most superficial to the deepest and most significant (Craik and Lockhart, 1972). We process words at one level by noting the way they look in writing—such visual characteristics as the letters with which they begin and end. We also take into account the way they sound when spoken and the number of syllables they contain. At the deepest level we encode their meaning—and associate them with other words that mean more or less the same thing.

Psychologists are generally agreed that encoding takes the various forms described by the levels-of-processing theory. But most students of memory reject the notion that the process can be divided into levels, with the deepest producing longer-lasting memory than the others. There is considerable evidence that all forms of encoding can be useful—and that the most effective method in any given case depends on the material we are trying to encode and the particular features we find it important to remember (Baddeley, 1978).

The associative network theory

Most researchers now believe that memory can best be described and explained as an immensely complicated network in which thousands upon thousands of words and ideas are all connected and interconnected by long and far-reaching strands of association (Anderson and Bower, 1973). As new information is encoded into the network, new linkages are formed to old information already contained there. Some of these links or associations are direct, others more roundabout. Some are strong, some weak. Some are long-lasting, resistant to forgetting, and easy to retrieve. Others are weaker and less likely to be recalled.

This view of memory, called the *associative network theory,* accounts for the extraordinary human ability at direct retrieval. Leading to every fact or chunk of information in the network are countless linkages. Through one link or another we can usually find a quick and direct route to what we need—and, once we have it, we can then also pull out any or all the other chunks with which it is connected.

We encode new information into long-term memory by noting how it relates to what we have already stored—and thus we add it to the network along with all the appropriate associations to existing information. A new fact or chunk of facts is woven into the network, attached by many far-reaching new strands through which, if they are solid and strong enough, we can reach and retrieve it when we need it.

Forming links between new and old

The vital role of associations or linkages between new information and old has been demonstrated in an ingenious experiment in which subjects were asked to read a paragraph that at first glance seems so unusual that it is difficult to follow, let alone understand and remember. Try reading the paragraph yourself, as slowly as you like, then turn away from the book and see how much you can recall.

> With hocked gems financing him, our hero bravely defied all scornful laughter that tried to prevent his scheme. "Your eyes deceive," he had said. "An egg, not a table, correctly typifies this unexplored planet." Now three sturdy sisters sought proof. Forging along, sometimes through calm vastness, yet more often over turbulent peaks and valleys, days became weeks as many doubters spread fearful rumors about the edge. At last from nowhere welcome winged creatures appeared, signifying momentous success (Dooling and Lachman, 1971).

In all probability you can remember very little of the paragraph, in which all kinds of unusual details come thick, fast, and without much apparent rhyme or reason. But suppose you had been told, before reading the paragraph, that it was a fanciful description of Columbus's voyage to America in 1492. In that case you could have fitted it into what you already know about the discovery of America—and undoubtedly, like one group of subjects in the experiment, you would have been able to encode and remember much of it.

The question of what we encode, remember, and retrieve

In the encoding process we add something new to the associative network. But just what is it that we add? Is it an exact copy of something we have done, seen, or heard—like a movie or a tape recording? Or is it something else?

In some cases what we encode is clearly a faithful copy. An experimenter once asked college students to recite the words to *The Star Spangled Banner,* Hamlet's soliloquy, and other familiar passages of verse and prose. Whatever they remembered at all, it turned out, was almost a word-by-word reproduction (Rubin, 1977). But this kind of verbatim encoding and retrieval is rare. In most cases we seem to engage in what is called *constructive processing.* We encode and retrieve not an exact copy of the information we receive—as from a printed page or a lecture

Psychology and Society: The witnesses swear they saw it—but did it really happen?

In a courtroom one witness after another takes the stand and swears under oath that the defendant was the man seen leaving the scene of a murder, a revolver still in his hand. The defendant claims he was miles away at the time. The prosecution case is strong. The defense case is weak. Verdict: guilty. Sentence: life imprisonment.

Has justice been done? Maybe. But maybe not. There have been a number of cases in which innocent people have been identified, tried, and convicted for crimes they did not commit. The fact that eye witness accounts can be grossly unreliable was observed many years ago (Stern, 1904). New studies of how memories are often the products of constructive processing, as described in the text, cast additional doubt on courtroom testimony and pose the question of how often our system of justice may go wrong—not only in criminal cases but in all kinds of lawsuits, from accident claims to antitrust proceedings.

A number of expriments have been performed by showing subjects videotapes or slides of such events as automobile accidents and asking them later what they saw. The results have demonstrated that "eyewitness accounts" are often wrong about important details. For example, subjects are sometimes sure they saw a stop sign at the scene of the accident, when in fact there was only a yield sign. Errors are particularly likely to occur if the experimenter talks to the subjects immediately after the pictures have been shown, before the test of recollections, and asks questions that suggest a false possibility—for example, "Did the car stop at the stop sign?" when there was no stop sign (Loftus, Miller, and Burns, 1978). The recollections of real-life eyewitnesses may be similarly distorted by any questions they answer for police at the scene of an accident, or later for their acquaintances or for the lawyers. Even the way a question is worded may influence what they think happened, though the questioner may have no intention of misleading them.

An unusual opportunity to check on the accuracy of some actual sworn testimony was provided by the Watergate hearings that led to President Nixon's resignation in 1974. A prominent member of Nixon's staff, John Dean, testified before a congressional committee about various meetings he had with Nixon and others in the White House, and his testimony could later be compared with actual tape recordings that had been made of those conversations. Dean was not trying to mislead the congressional committee, and he was in all probability telling the truth as he remembered it, but he was woefully wrong about many details of what he swore he said to the President and what the President said to him. Indeed a side-by-side comparison of his transcribed testimony and the transcriptions of the tapes "shows that hardly a word of Dean's account is true" (Neisser, 1981).

One has to wonder. How many defendants have been found guilty or innocent of crimes, how many verdicts have been reached by juries in lawsuits of all kinds, on the basis of witnesses' confident descriptions of what they saw or heard—though it never really happened?

or a conversation—but whatever meanings and associations we have found. We remember not "what was out there" but what we ourselves "*did* during encoding"—that is, the way we processed the information and related it to the knowledge already held in long-term memory (Craik and Tulving, 1975).

In most cases, therefore, we remember what we consider important—the theme or underlying meaning—and forget or distort many of the details, such as the exact wording. One study has suggested this analogy: When we read or hear something, we make mental notes—like the brief reminders you might jot down in your notebook while listening to a lecture. It is these notes, not the actual words we read or heard, that we store in some appropriate "pigeonhole, in memory" until we need them. While stored in the pigeonhole, the various factors that cause forgetting may cause some of the notes to become smudged. Some of them may even get lost. Thus, when we try to retrieve the information, we find that it is incomplete—only a sketchy reminder of what we actually read or heard. All we can do is "fetch the notes from their pigeonhole and from this fragmentary information reconstruct what . . . was in the original message"—or rather what we now have come to believe was in it (Clark and Clark, 1977).

With the brief and sometimes smudged or incomplete notes, we do the best we can. We try to make sense out of them. We fill in the missing details—sometimes accurately and sometimes not. Thus a great deal of what we think we remember never really happened—or, if it did, it was different in many respects from the way we remember it. Memory, as one scholar has said, is often "unreliable, given to invention, and even dangerous" (Bower, 1978).

The omissions and distortions pose serious problems at times—especially, as is discussed in a box on Psychology and Society, in legal trials where precise details may be crucial to the outcome. Nevertheless, the associative network serves as well in most cases, particularly in remembering and retrieving the most basic and important meanings and the general principles of the information we have processed.

Encoding and learning

The associative network of long-term memory is so large and complex, and its linkages so intricately connected and interconnected, that tugging at one strand can produce far-reaching and sometimes unpredictable results. Suppose, for example, that you are asked to retrieve everything you remember about the word *angel.* You might begin by pulling out information from paintings you have seen of winged figures in white robes, with halos and playing harps. From there you might move on to describe the churches you have seen, the prayers you have learned, and the principles underlying the world's major religions. You might go on to talk about morality, then about a priest or rabbi who played a significant part in your life.

Your progression of associations may lead almost anywhere—and if you are asked to do the same thing tomorrow the pathway may take an entirely different route. Of course the associations vary from person to person. To another individual, the word *angel* may immediately suggest the California baseball team and lead to a discussion of Yankee Stadium, Babe Ruth, candy bars, and eventually some unsuccessful personal experiences with dieting.

As these examples of retrieval indicate, every item of information in long-term memory is associated with many other items, which in turn lead to innumerable other associations. How likely you are to remember and retrieve any new information depends on how well you manage to add it to this network—that is, how many strong associations you form to linkages that already exist. Effective encoding sometimes takes place without much effort. You do not have to make any deliberate attempt, for example, to remember important events in your life or the names and faces of people who have played significant parts in it. But often—

Psychology and Society: "As the old saying goes, familiarity breeds . . . well, I guess I forget what it breeds"

You are thoroughly familiar, of course, with the U.S. penny. But how much do you know about it? Without looking, try to answer these questions: Does the legend 1¢ appear on it? The words ONE PENNY? What motto is on the front? What motto is on the back? Where is the year of coinage? Which if any of the following words appear on it: FREEDOM, LIBERTY, EQUALITY?

Now take a look at a penny and see how well you did. If you could answer very few of the questions—and if most of the answers you did venture were wrong—you have a lot of company. A study found that Americans, though they have seen and handled many pennies, have only the haziest idea of what the coin really looks like (Nickerson and Adams, 1979). It appears that familiarity breeds, if not contempt, at least a remarkable inability to remember.

This phenomenon was also demonstrated in an unusual study made in England when the BBC changed the wavelengths of its radio stations in accord with a new international agreement in the late 1970s. The change was one of the best-advertised events of all time. For weeks the BBC stations broadcast announcements of the new wavelengths every few minutes, often in the form of jingles to attract special attention. The new numbers were also widely advertised in television and newspaper ads. Yet a survey of radio listeners produced some peculiar findings. All the subjects knew there was going to be a change, and more than four out of five knew the date the change would take place. But only a few could even attempt to guess what the new wavelengths were going to be, and most of the guesses were far wide of the mark (Bekerian and Baddeley, 1980).

It is not known exactly why we encode so little information about familiar matters. Perhaps familiarity produces boredom, and we quit paying attention. Perhaps we chunk only enough information about a penny to enable us to recognize one, ignoring the details as unimportant. Perhaps we tune in radio stations not so much by the number of the wavelength as by feel or the position of the needle on the set.

At any rate the facts clearly indicate that many of the efforts spent to get people to encode information into memory are not very successful. One has to wonder how many radio and television commercials have no more effect than the BBC announcements. Or how many speeches by a political figure who keeps harping on the same message. Or how many newspaper editorials, health warnings, safe driving tips, and books on how to lose weight, stop worrying, and achieve social popularity and happiness. Or for that matter protest marches: You may remember there was a giant rally last year, but can you remember what the protest was about?

and especially in school or when trying to master a new skill, like chess or repairing electronic equipment—you have to work hard to form the associations.

Thus memory is closely related to learning. How well we remember generally depends on how well we learn in the first place—that is, on how many links or associations we establish between new information and information already stored in the network. This kind of encoding depends in turn on how thoroughly we analyze and understand the new information and how many relationships we can find between the new and the old. The richer and more elaborate our analysis, the more likely we are to form a long-lasting memory that will resist forgetting and be easy to retrieve (Kintsch, 1977).

The search for meaning and organization

In studying a page like this one, it is futile just to read and re-read the words without making any attempt to understand them. The words may eventually begin to seem familiar, like old friends—but mere familiarity, without careful attention and analysis, is no guarantee of successful encoding. Indeed, as is discussed in a box on Psychology and Society, we sometimes learn and remember surprisingly little about familiar objects and events. What counts in learning is something quite different:

> The critical thing for most of the material you learn in school is to understand it, which means encoding it in a way that makes it distinctive from unrelated material and related to all the things it ought to be related to in order for you to use it. . . . The time you spend thinking about material you are reading and relating it to previously stored material is about the most useful thing you can do in learning any new subject matter (Wickelgren, 1977).

To put this another way, the key to successful encoding is to figure out the meaning of new information and organize it into some unified and logical pattern that can be readily associated with other information. Because meaning is so important, some things are just naturally easier to learn and encode into memory than others. If the materials themselves make sense—that is, if they are intrinsically meaningful—we have a good head start on our processing. Thus it is much easier to remember lists of actual three-letter words (such as SIT, HAT, BIN, COW) than lists of three-letter nonsense syllables. In fact it is easier to remember lists of nonsense syllables that resemble real words than syllables that are truly nonsensical. An experiment performed many years ago showed that subjects are about 50 percent better at remembering syllables like DOZ, SOF, LIF, and RUF, all of which remind most people of actual words, than totally unfamiliar syllables like ZOJ, JYQ, GIW, and VAF (McGeoch, 1930).

In an even earlier experiment, subjects were asked to learn and remember 200 items or words that were in four different forms: lists of nonsense syllables, lists of random digits, passages of prose writing, and passages of poetry. The results of the experiment are shown in Figure 4-11. Note how much better the subjects remembered the prose or poetry than the nonsense syllables or the nonsense arrangements of digits. Poetry—which has both meaning and a kind of internal logic and organization provided by the cadence and rhymes—proved the easiest of all to encode and remember.

Learning by rule versus learning by rote

Both meaning and organization help account for the fact that we usually remember longer if we learn by *rule* or logic (that is, if we try to understand the underlying principles) than if we learn by *rote* (or simply try to memorize materials by repeating them mechanically, without any regard to what they mean). A simple classroom demonstration of this fact is shown in Figure 4-12.

In the class shown in the upper photo, the students learned by rote. By simply repeating the numbers over and over, they managed to get them into memory after a fashion. But this kind of encoding produced

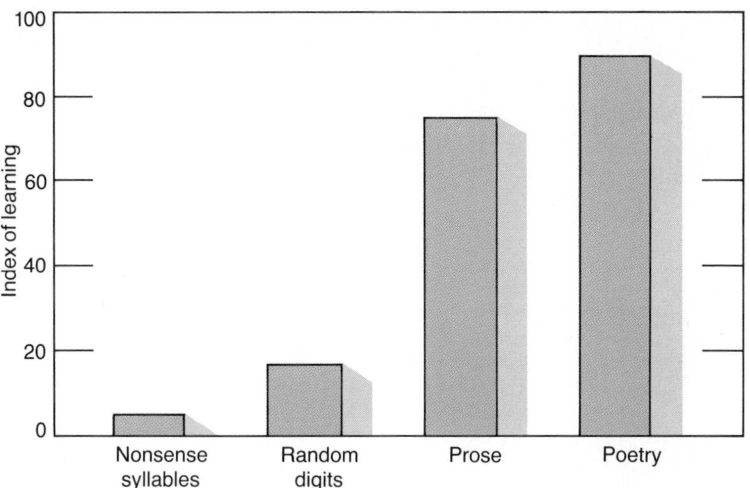

Figure 4-11 Meaningful materials: so much easier to remember *The height of the bars shows how little subjects could remember of lists of meaningless nonsense syllables or random digits—and how much they remembered of equally long lists of more meaningful materials (after Lyon, 1914).*

only short-lived memory. When they were tested three weeks later, not one of them remembered the numbers correctly. Most members of the class in the lower photo, alerted to the fact that the numbers could be learned by finding a logical rule, managed to do a much more effective job of encoding—and therefore remembered the numbers much better after three weeks had passed (Katona, 1940). If you try the experiment yourself as suggested in the caption beside the photos, or on some of your friends, you will probably get the same convincing results.

Some things, of course, simply have to be learned by rote. There is no other way to learn the multiplication tables or the sequence of letters in the alphabet. And, as these examples suggest, some information learned by rote is never forgotten. But most college courses would be almost impossible to encode into lasting memory by rote—and fortunately most courses readily lend themselves to learning by rule. They have patterns of meaning and organization, built around underlying principles, and are presented by instructors and in textbooks in ways designed to help you find, understand, and analyze those patterns. They can be studied and encoded effectively through logical approaches like the SQ3R system that was described in the supplement to Chapter 1.

Moral for learners: take your time

Learning ordinarily depends more on the kind of cognitive processing and encoding we do than on the amount of time we spend (Craik and Tulving, 1975). Thus even a small amount of time spent finding meaning, organization, and relationships is generally more effective than a great deal of time devoted merely to rehearsing what is on a page more or less verbatim. It did not take the woman in the phone booth long to associate the phone number 629-1965 with her birth date, yet she formed a linkage strong enough to last for life.

In most cases, however, effective encoding requires deliberate effort—we have to work at it—and a certain amount of time. Indeed the more time we spend the more likely we are to remember, provided

Figure 4-12 A classroom demonstration of rule versus rote *The instructor is asking two different classes to try to learn and remember the numbers she has written on the blackboard. The numbers are the same in both cases. In the class above, however, she suggests that the numbers can be most easily remembered in groups of three, as she has arranged them. In the class below, she explains that the digits are not in random order but fall into a definite and logical pattern in both lines. She does not say what the pattern is, leaving the students to find out for themselves. Most of them did find the pattern, and this had an important effect on how well they learned and remembered the numbers, as described in the text. Try the experiment yourself before you read the explanation in the footnote on page 146.*

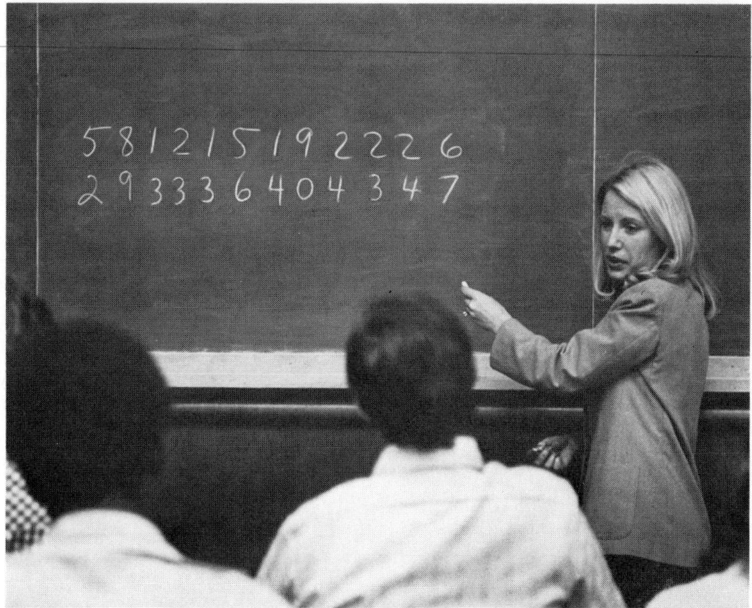

of course that we use the time effectively. There are no short cuts in learning. For example, nothing is gained through "speed reading," which is the popular name for techniques that are supposed to enable you to read a printed page much faster while still comprehending everything the words mean. In fact studies have shown that the faster you read the less you are likely to understand or remember (Graf, 1973).

There are certain advantages, of course, in saving time through the rapid scanning of materials that you do not need to remember, or when you are glancing through a long and complicated article or book in which there are only a few specific pieces of information that you want to seek out and concentrate on. But in general any increase in reading speed, beyond your normal rate, saves time only at the expense of remembering. The kind of encoding that results in long-lasting memory, like the weaving of a strong and far-flung net, simply cannot be rushed.

Even after new information has been encoded into memory, it usually pays to spend some more time studying it—possibly because practice and repetition somehow increase the strength and retrievability of the memory traces in the network. This fact is expressed in the *law of overlearning,* which states: After you have learned something, further study tends to increase the length of time you will remember it. The law of overlearning seems to explain why we never forget such childhood jingles as "Twinkle, twinkle little star," or the stories of Cinderella and Goldilocks and the Three Bears. Long after we knew these things by heart, we continued to recite or listen to them over and over again. We not only learned but overlearned.

The law of overlearning also explains why cramming is not a satisfactory way to learn the contents of a college course. By cramming students may learn enough to get a passing grade on an examination, but they are soon likely to forget almost everything they learned. A little overlearning, on the other hand, is like time spent thinking about new materials and trying to understand them and relate them to previous information. It is a good investment in the ability to remember for a long time.

How learning builds on learning

Another practical implication of psychology's studies of encoding is this: The more we already know, the easier it is to learn and remember something new. As we go through school and college, we acquire a bigger vocabulary, more mathematical symbols and rules, more knowledge of the general principles of science, human behavior, and the workings of our society. All this previously stored information helps us understand the new information, relate it to past knowledge, and encode it solidly into our memory network.

The fact that learning builds on learning has never been expressed more eloquently than by William James, even though James lived and wrote many years before the discovery of most of what is now known about encoding and memory.

> *The more other facts a fact is associated with in the mind, the better possession of it our memory retains.* Each of its associates becomes a hook to which it hangs, a means to fish it up by when sunk beneath the surface. Together, they form a network of attachments by which it is woven into

---

The blackboard figures are arranged in this logical pattern: The numbers following the first one, which is 5, are obtained by regularly adding 3-4-3-4-3-4-3-4 to the preceding number. Thus 5 is followed by 8 (5 plus 3); 8 is followed by 12 (8 plus 4); 12 by 15 (12 plus 3); and 15 by 19 (15 plus 4). Number 26 at the end of the first line is followed by 29 (26 plus 3) to start the second line, and 29 is then followed by 33 (29 plus 4), and so on.

> the entire tissue of our thought. The "secret of a good memory" is thus the secret of forming diverse and multiple associations with every fact we care to retain. . . . Most men have a good memory for facts connected with their own pursuits. The college athlete who remains a dunce at his books will astonish you by his knowledge of men's records in various feats and games, and will be a walking dictionary of sporting statistics. The reason is that he is constantly going over these things in his mind, and comparing and making series of them. They form for him not so many odd facts but a concept-system—so they stick. So the merchant remembers prices, the politican other politicians' speeches and votes, with a copiousness which amazes outsiders, but which the amount of thinking they bestow on these subjects easily explains. The great memory for facts which a Darwin and a Spencer reveal in their books is not incompatible with the possession on their part of a brain with only a middling degree of physiological retentiveness [by which James means inborn ability for remembering]. Let a man early in life set himself the task of verifying such a theory as that of evolution, and facts will soon cluster and cling to him like grapes to their stem. Their relations to the theory will hold them fast; and the more of these the mind is able to discern, the greater the erudition will become (James, 1890).

Of course the possession of a great deal of information increases the possibility of proactive and retroactive interference. But any tendency to forgetting that this may create is more than offset by the increased chances of finding more associations between new and old and thus weaving the new information more solidly into the network.

Figure 4-13 What is this monkey learning? *All the monkey seems to be learning is that it will find food under one of the two objects in front of it but not under the other. When the photo was taken, the food was always under a funnel and never under a cylinder, regardless of which was on the left or right. At other times, the food was under a circle but not a rectangle, a cube but not a sphere, a black object but not a white object, and so on. At first the monkey had trouble learning where to find the food. But after the experiment had gone on long enough—with several hundred pairs of objects—the monkey learned to learn. Thus when a new pair of objects was presented, the monkey mastered the problem on the very first trial. Whether or not it found the food under the first object it examined, it went almost unerringly to the correct object the next time the pair was presented (Harlow, 1949).*

Some aids to encoding

The fact that learning builds on learning helps explain what would otherwise be a baffling aspect of schoolwork. Insofar as can be measured, children entering high school have matured to the point where they possess all the nervous system equipment that makes learning possible. Their innate ability to learn will not increase much, if at all. They are already about as smart, to use the popular term, as they will ever be. Yet everybody knows that high school seniors can learn things that would be beyond high school freshmen—and college students can go a long step further. People who go back to college when they are in their 40s or older, as many do nowadays, are often surprised to find how much easier the work seems than when they were younger. They are better at learning because they already know more.

The information stored in memory is not, however, the entire explanation. There is another reason all of us get better and better at encoding and remembering new information as time goes on: Our classroom work and our life experiences provide us with something that is perhaps even more valuable than facts and general principles. We learn how to learn.

One need not be a great scholar. Even the monkey shown in Figure 4-13 learned to learn. Asked to perform a long series of learning tasks that were similar in general but different in detail, the monkey showed remarkable improvement. It developed what is called a *learning set*—a successful strategy for approaching the learning task. In an experiment with human beings, using a similar but more difficult series of problems,

The words arranged at random:

Slate	Emerald	Diamond	Steel	Sapphire	Brass
Bronze	Gold	Lead	Limestone	Aluminum	Ruby
Iron	Granite	Marble	Platinum	Silver	Copper

The words organized into categories:

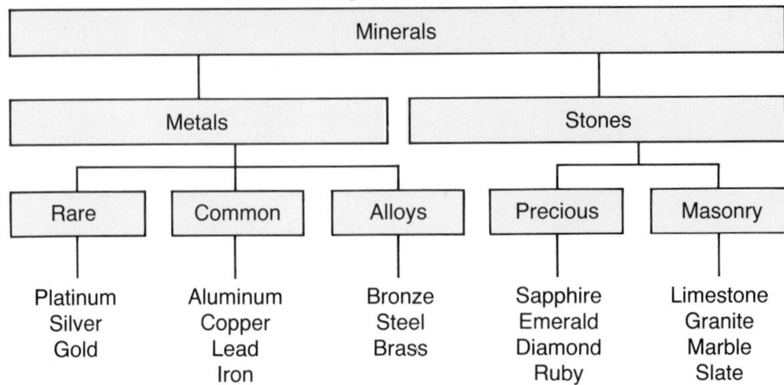

Figure 4-14 An experiment on categories as an aid to encoding *The control group saw the list of 18 words presented at random. The experimental group saw them as arranged in the diagram. For how well the two groups learned and remembered, see the text and Figure 4-15.*

the results were much the same. It was also found, as might be expected, that college students were quicker to develop effective learning sets or strategies than fifth-graders. In turn the fifth-graders were quicker than preschool children (Levinson and Reese, 1967).

How categories help

One useful strategy that all of us adopt, in one way or another, helps us deal with materials that do not at first glance seem to hang together of their own accord. We often manage to organize and encode this type of information by breaking it down into *categories*—a method best explained by the example shown in Figure 4-14. Note that the 18 words on the list, presented at random, do not seem to have much in common. They do not fall into any kind of obvious pattern—and you might think that, if you wanted to encode them into memory, you would have to learn them by rote. This is the way the experimenter's control group went about trying to memorize them—painfully and, as will be seen in a moment, without much lasting success.

Another group of subjects, however, got some help. To these subjects, the words on the list were presented in the manner shown in the diagram of Figure 4-14. The subjects were helped to see that all the words fell into the general category of minerals, that this category could be broken down into the subcategories of metals and stones, and that these subcategories could again be divided into three different kinds of metals (rare, common, and alloys) and two different kinds of stones (precious stones and stones used in masonry).

The control group and the experimental group were both asked to try to learn several such lists, containing 112 words in all, within four trials. The difference in the amounts learned by the two groups was striking. As Figure 4-15 shows, the subjects who had been helped to organize the words into categories proved far superior. Indeed they remembered all

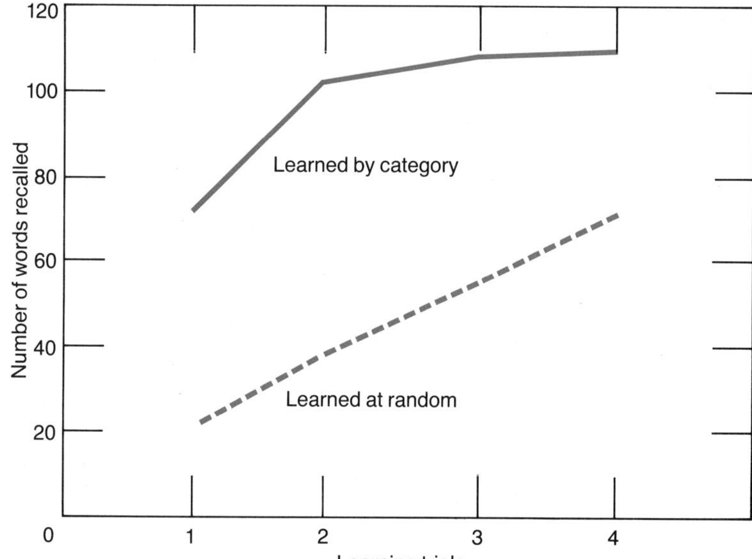

Figure 4-15 Did the categories make a difference? Yes, indeed. *The colored line shows how rapidly the experimental subjects were able to learn as a result of seeing the words in Figure 4-14 arranged in categories. Subjects who tried to memorize the words by rote (black line) did not do nearly so well.*

112 words perfectly on the third and fourth trials—a level never even approached by the subjects who tried to learn the words by rote (Bower et al., 1969).

Categories, chunking, and clustering

Organizing materials into categories bears considerable resemblance to the chunking process that enables us to hold seven large packages of information in short-term memory as readily as seven small individual items. In both cases a number of small units of information are lumped together into a single unit. When the process refers to short-term memory, it is called *chunking;* and when it relates to long-term memory, it is called *clustering.* Information can be organized into clusters formed by categories, by meanings, by logic, or in other ways. And information stored in some form of cluster tends to hang together in a solid unit that becomes a strong part of the associative network.

Clustering also aids retrieval. Within each tightly bound and cohesive cluster there are a number of individual items of information. In the search of memory that goes on during retrieval, we have a much better chance of finding one of many items than any single item. And when we manage to find this one item, we can pull the whole cluster of information out with it.

An example might occur on an essay examination where you are asked to define the term *stimulus generalization.* At first the meaning of the term eludes you. You seem to have forgotten it. But then, as you continue to search through your memory network, the word *stimulus* leads you to the term *conditioned stimulus*—and thus to the whole package of information that falls into the category of classical conditioning. Out pour all the facts you have clustered there, including the meaning of *stimulus generalization.*

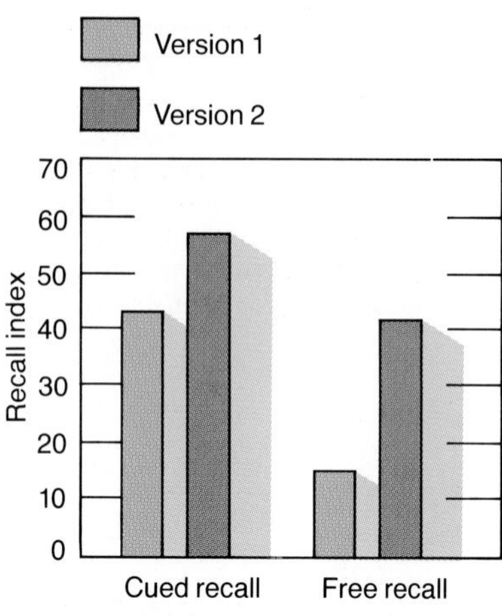

Figure 4-16 If one event causes another, you are likely to remember both *The bars show the results of the experiment, described in detail in the text, with two versions of the same story. Note how much more was remembered by subjects who read version 2 (the cause-and-effect version) than subjects who read version 1—when tested for either "free recall" (how much they remembered without prompting) or "cued recall" (how well they could remember the second of two sentences after the first was read to them).*

Clustering, cause-and-effect, and made-up stories

One interesting way we encode clusters into long-term memory is demonstrated by how much we remember of the things we read, such as stories. If the story moves in a straight line, with one event leading logically to the next, we can usually remember a good deal of it. If the story jumps around, switching from one point of view to another, we are less likely to remember it (Black, Turner, and Bower, 1979).

We seem particularly adept at clustering together materials that have a cause-and-effect relationship that binds them into a logical entity. An indication comes from an experiment in which two groups of college students studied slightly different versions of the same story. Version 1 contained pairs of sentences like these:

> He lowered the flames and walked over to the refrigerator, seeing a bowl he had left on the table. Suddenly it fell off the edge and broke.
>
> While he was sitting on a huge log he found an old pocket knife. He felt sad as they took a few more pictures and headed back.

In version 2 the sentence pairs were changed to read like this:

> He lowered the flames and walked over to the refrigerator, bumping a bowl he had left on the table. Suddenly it fell off the edge and broke.
>
> While he was sitting on a huge log he lost an old pocket knife. He felt sad as they took a few more pictures and headed back.

Note that the changes, though small, create a cause-and-effect relationship in the version 2 sentence pairs that does not occur in version 1. *Bumping a bowl* (version 2) is a logical reason for the bowl to fall off the table; *seeing a bowl* (version 1) is not. Someone who *lost an old pocket knife* is likely to have felt sad, while someone who *found an old pocket knife* is not. As is illustrated in Figure 4-16, establishing the cause-and-effect relationship produced a significantly better memory for the version 2 sentences (Black and Bern, 1981).

Similarly, it has been demonstrated that one good way to remember a list of unrelated items is to make up a story about them that ties them all together. Let us say, for example, that you are going to a supermarket to buy the following 10 items, listed in the order you would find them along the route you take through the aisles:

1. coffee	6. light bulbs
2. hamburger	7. matches
3. charcoal	8. facial tissues
4. milk	9. broom
5. paper cups	10. dog food

One way you can be almost sure of remembering everything in proper order is to make up a story like the one presented in Figure 4-17. Such stories have been found remarkably helpful. The experiment in Figure

Figure 4-17 Remembering a shopping list *The 10 supermarket items listed in the text can be easily recalled in order by making up this story: I was sitting in my kitchen one evening drinking a cup of* coffee *when my neighbor came in with her child to invite me to a Saturday cookout. She said we would grill* hamburgers *over* charcoal. *I asked her to sit down and join me for coffee, and I poured the child some* milk *in a* paper cup. *While we were talking the* light bulb *burned out, and my neighbor lit some* matches *to help me replace the bulb. In the darkness the child spilled some milk, and we wiped it up with* facial tissues. *I heard my dog at the door and went to let it in. There was another dog that wanted to enter, but I chased it away with a* broom *and fed my pet its* dog food *while my neighbor and I finished our coffee (after Bower, 1978).*

4-18, for example, found an extremely large difference in recall of work lists between subjects who wove the words into stories and subjects who did not.

Storing visual information in memory

Made-up stories are particularly helpful if you try to form a mental picture or image of the events, like the drawings in Figure 4-17. Indeed studies have shown that there are many situations in which the use of *imagery* helps to encode, remember, and retrieve information (Bower, 1972). One reason seems to be that we have an extraordinary ability to remember visual information. This was demonstrated in a famous experiment in which subjects looked at a set of over 600 colored pictures—then were tested on how many they could recognize when the pictures were shown again, now paired with another picture they had not seen before. In all the subjects spotted 97 percent of the original pictures—a far better performance than could ever be attained with the same large number of words (Shepherd, 1967).

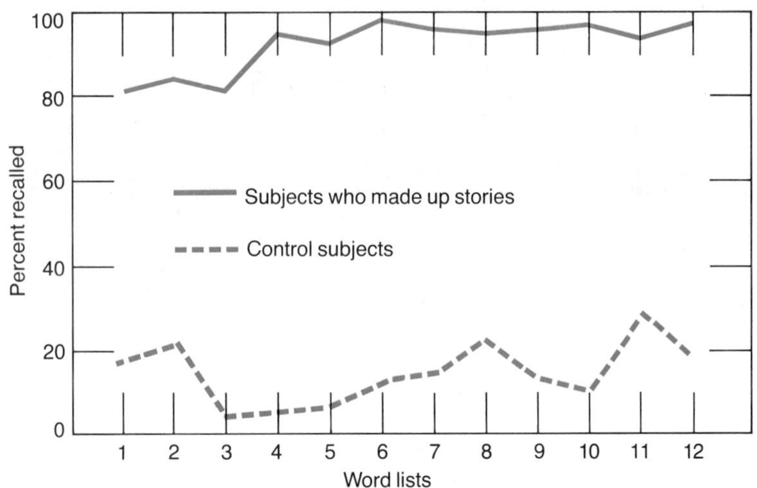

Figure 4-18 How well do made-up stories work? *Extremely* well. *The graph lines show the results of an experiment in which one group of students made up stories to help them remember a dozen lists of words, while a control group was merely asked to try to memorize the lists. When tested later, the subjects who made up stories remembered their lists almost perfectly. The other subjects had forgotten most of their words (Bower and Clark, 1969).*

Many other experiments have shown that we remember a good deal about the visual characteristics of information we have seen, such as whether an item in a list of words or sentences was printed in type or written by hand (Hintzman, Block, and Inskeep, 1972). We also seem to encode some other physical aspects of information, such as whether an item on a list of words on a tape recording was spoken in a woman's voice or a man's (Craik and Kirsner, 1974). Such findings have led some psychologists to believe we have two separate ways of encoding and storing information, one for the physical attributes we note through our senses and the other for knowledge that can be put into words (Paivio, 1971). This theory would help explain the fact that imagery aids encoding, but it raises many complex problems and ambiguities and it may prove impossible ever to verify or disprove.

One interesting sidelight is that lower animals encode considerable amounts of information into memory without the help of language—which makes possible the search for meaning and organization that characterizes so much of human encoding. Indeed studies show that even a monkey, an animal far lower in intellectual development than its cousin the chimpanzee, can perform much like a human being on a test of memory for pictures (Sands and Wright, 1982). Encoding visual characteristics seems to be a more fundamental skill than the human encoding of verbal information—but we do not know whether the two are different in kind or merely in degree.

Mnemonic devices

The ability to encode visual information and imagery is the basis of most techniques called *mnemonic devices,* after the Greek word for memory. Like the term itself, these devices date back to ancient Greece (Yates, 1966), where they were developed by orators who needed reminders of the points they wanted to make during their long speeches. Their method was based on the spatial arrangement of a temple with which they were thoroughly familiar—that is, the order in which they walked past the doorways, rooms, statues, and other objects within the temple

Figure 4-19 Using "one is a bun" to remember the shopping list *The drawings show a set of images that might be built on the "one is a bun" device to help remember the same shopping list that was in the Figure 4-17 story. If you spend a few minutes studying and thinking about the drawings, thus encoding the images into your own memory, you will probably be surprised to find how long you can remember the list—probably for days or even weeks. You will remember it still longer if you think up a set of images of your own (after Bower, 1978).*

walls. For each location, they created a mental image associating the spot with a topic in their speech. For example, if they wanted to start by discussing medicine, they might visualize a famous physician of the day pushing through the temple entrance. To try this method yourself, you can base it on the layout of your home, its rooms, and its prominent pieces of furniture.

A somewhat more complicated mnemonic system, for remembering things like shopping lists or chores to be done during the day, has been used in a number of psychological experiments and found extremely helpful. You begin by memorizing this jingle:

> One is a bun; two is a shoe;
> Three is a tree; four is a door;
> Five is a hive; six is sticks;
> Seven is heaven; eight is a gate;
> Nine is wine; ten is a hen.

To use this device to help remember the supermarket shopping list mentioned earlier, the trick is to form a mental image connecting the items on the list (coffee, hamburger, and so on) with the words in the jingle that rhyme with the numbers (bun-one, shoe-two, and so on). One way such images might be formed is illustrated in Figure 4-19. The process usually takes only a few seconds and has been found to result in almost perfect recall (Bugelski, Kidd, and Segmen, 1968).

Similar systems, more elaborate in that they can provide memory hooks for as many as 100 items, are the secret behind the seemingly incredible feats performed by the "memory experts" who quickly learn long lists of objects or people's names. For remembering things that do not hang together through any organization or logic, mnemonic devices are unquestionably useful. One reason is that they take advantage of the well-established value of imagery. Another is that they provide a ready-made framework into which the new information can be clustered.

Some simple little mnemonic devices with which you are probably familiar include the jingle that begins "Thirty days hath September" (for remembering how many days there are in each month), the sentence "Every good boy does fine" (for remembering the notes in music), and "I left port" (for remembering the difference between the port, or left side, of a ship and the starboard, or right side). Note that the value of all mnemonic aids is limited to materials that would otherwise have to be encoded and stored by rote. For most of the knowledge we acquire, there is no substitute for the kind of information processing that seeks meanings, organization, relationships, and rules.

SUMMARY

Remembering for just an instant—or for a lifetime

1. Memories may last from a fraction of a second to a lifetime. The range is divided into three stages of memory: (a) *sensory,* (b) *short-term,* and (c) *long-term.*
2. *Sensory memory* is made up of the lingering traces of information sent to the brain by the senses. The information is forgotten within a second unless transferred to short-term memory.
3. *Short-term memory* has a capacity of about seven items of information, which are forgotten within about 30 seconds unless further processing takes place.
4. The information processing in short-term memory includes: (a) *scanning* of the information in sensory memory and selection of some items as worthy of attention, (b) *rehearsal* (to keep information in mind for more than 30 seconds), (c) *encoding* of information (to make it simple and easy to handle), and (d) further encoding that results in *transfer* of the information to long-term memory.
5. *Long-term memory* is a more or less permanent storehouse of information.
6. *Retrieval* is the process that recalls information held in long-term memory back to short-term memory, where we can actively think about it and use it.

The mystery of the memory trace: there must be one—but what is it?

7. Exactly what happens inside the nervous system when we store information in long-term memory is not known. Psychologists say

that a *memory trace* has been established, but they can only speculate as to what this trace is, how it is formed, and why it sometimes seems to persist forever and sometimes seems to vanish.

8. Formation of the memory trace seems to depend at least in part on the brain's *neurotransmitters,* the chemicals that pass messages along from one neuron to another. It appears that the neurotransmitters increase the efficiency of the *synapse* between two neurons.
9. Formation of the memory trace may also depend on the establishment of new synapses, resulting in new connections between neurons that did not previously influence one another.
10. Some psychologists have suggested that changes at the synapses may be caused by a chemical called *RNA,* which is similar to the DNA that makes up the genes and serves as the carrier of heredity.

Why we forget

11. How well people remember and how much they forget cannot be measured directly but only by how well they *perform* on tests of memory. Three methods used by psychologists to test performance are: (a) *recall,* (b) *recognition,* and (c) *relearning.*
12. Tests of performance show that we often quickly forget much of what we have just learned, but remember at least some of it for a long time. The fact that we forget rapidly at first but more slowly later on is shown by the *curve of forgetting.*
13. There are four theories of why we forget, all of which may be true at least in part and at times: (a) *fading of the memory trace,* (b) *failure in retrieval,* (c) *interference from other information stored in memory, and* (d) *motivated forgetting,* or forgetting because we want to forget.
14. When old information causes us to forget new information, the process is called *proactive interference.* The opposite, where new information causes us to forget old information, is called *retroactive interference.*

The encoding and transfer process

15. The manner in which we encode and transfer information to long-term memory determines how well we will be able to remember and retrieve it.
16. In the process called *chunking* we combine a number of individual units of information into one package—such as when we combine the seven letters UCPIRTE into the single word PICTURE. Chunking increases the scope of short-term memory, which can hold around seven big packages of information about as well as it can handle seven small items. In the interaction between short-term and long-term memory, information is often transferred to storage in chunks.
17. Studies have shown that words are encoded into long-term memory in several ways—how they look in writing and sound to the ear, the number of syllables they contain, and their meaning. These findings have led to the *levels-of-processing theory,* which holds that encoding occurs at levels ranging from the most superficial to the deepest and most significant. Most psychologists agree that en-

coding takes various forms, but they reject the notion that the process can be divided into levels that affect how long we remember.

18. The prevailing view is the *associative network theory,* which describes memory as a complex network in which countless items of information are connected and interconnected by long and far-reaching strands of association.
19. The theory holds that we encode new information into long-term memory by noting how it relates to what we have already stored—and thus add it to the network with all the appropriate associations ot existing information.
20. Sometimes we encode and can retrieve a faithful copy of the information—as when we recite a familiar poem word for word. More frequently we engage in *constructive processing*—encoding and retrieving the theme or underlying meaning and trying to fill in the details, sometimes accurately and sometimes not. It has been said that memory is often "unreliable, given to invention, and even dangerous."

Encoding and learning

21. How well we remember generally depends on how well we have learned in the first place—that is, on how thoroughly we understand new information and how many associations we find between new and old.
22. Since finding meaning and organization is useful in forming associations, it is generally more effective to learn by *rule* than by *rote.*
23. The *law of overlearning* states: After you have learned something, continuing to work at learning it tends to increase the length of time you will remember it.

Some aids to encoding

24. *Clustering* is the encoding and storing into long-term memory of information organized into packages composed of a number of small units (like chunking in short-term memory). Clusters of information can be formed by categories, meaning, logic, or in other ways.
25. *Made-up stories* are a method of clustering items of information that would not otherwise hang together. Made-up stories are particularly helpful if you try to form a mental picture or image of the events.
26. *Imagery* is helpful because we have an extraordinary ability to remember visual information—a fact that has led some psychologists to believe we have two separate ways of encoding and storing information—one for physical attributes and the other for knowledge that can be put into words.
27. *Mnemonic devices* are tricks, like the "Thirty days hath September" jingle, that help provide a memory framework for materials that otherwise would have to be learned by rote. Many mnemonic devices rely on imagery for their effectiveness.

IMPORTANT TERMS

associative network
categories
chunking
clustering
consolidation
constructive processing
curve of forgetting
encoding
imagery
learning set
levels of processing
long-term memory
made-up stories
memory trace
mnemonic devices
motivated forgetting
neurotransmitter
overlearning
proactive interference
recall
recognition
rehearsal
relearning
retrieval
retroactive interference
RNA
rote
rule
scanning
sensory memory
short-term memory
synapse
transfer

RECOMMENDED READINGS

Anderson, J. R., and Bower, G. H. *Human associative memory.* Washington, D.C.: Winston, 1973.

Estes, W. K., ed. *Handbook of learning and cognitive processes,* Vol. 6. Hillsdale, N.J.: Erlbaum, 1979.

Kintsch, W., *Memory and cognition.* New York: Wiley, 1977.

Klatzky, R. L. *Human memory: structures and processes,* 2d ed. San Francisco: W. H. Freeman, 1980.

Lindsay, P. H., and Norman D. A. *Human information processing: an introduction to psychology,* 2d ed. New York: Academic Press, 1977.

Nilsson, L. G., ed. *Memory problems and processes.* Hillsdale, N.J.: Erlbaum, 1979.

Norman, D. A. *Memory and attention: an introduction to human information processing,* 2d ed. New York: Wiley, 1976.

Wickelgren, W. A. *Learning and memory.* Englewood Cliffs, N.J.: Prentice-Hall, 1977.

PART 3

Using Information From Memory: Speaking, Thinking, and Learning

Learning brings us all kinds of information about the world we live in. Memory serves as a storehouse in which we hold the information for future use, organized in a highly effective system for finding and retrieving whatever items we need. We have learned and can recall a myriad of facts and rules of great potential value in understanding and dealing with our environment—that is, with the objects, events, and other people around us. The question now becomes: How do we *use* this information?

One way we use our knowledge is to communicate with other human beings—and thus engage in the cooperative activities essential to carry on the basic tasks of human society. We human beings, in every society ever known, have developed a language that conveys messages understood by all of us, enabling us to work, play, and live together. We use language to tell each other how we feel, what we need, what we desire. We use it to amuse ourselves in conversation, to form friendships, and to help one another grow and transport food, build houses and office skyscrapers, and manu-

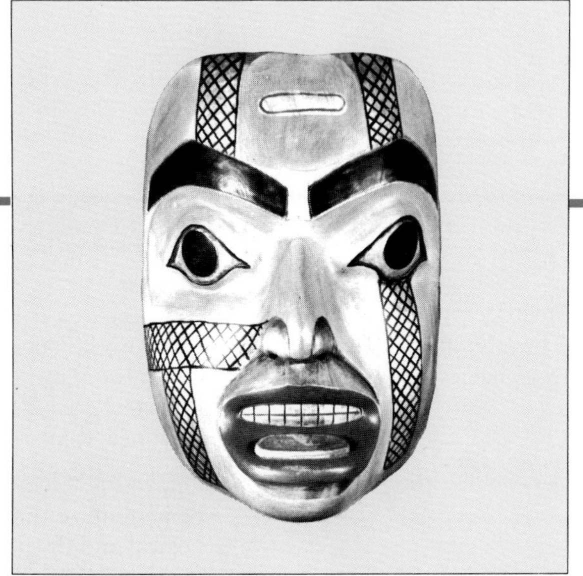

facture and distribute clothing. With language we can express everything from a child's simple request for a glass of water to the most complex scientific theories.

We also use our stored knowledge to think about the world we live in, understand and solve its problems, and act accordingly. Our information processing—learning about the environment, remembering what we have learned, and applying our knowledge to new situations—is the source of what is called human intelligence, or the ability to adapt to our environment and in many ways even control it. Thanks to human intelligence, our species has managed to thrive in climates as diverse as the equatorial jungles and the arctic ice—and to explore outer space through visits to the moon and camera expeditions to Saturn.

These aspects of information processing are the subjects of Part 3. Chapter 5 describes the versatile and all-important role of language and the ways it helps us learn, think, and solve problems. Chapter 6 discusses human intelligence and its marvels and mysteries.

CHAPTER 5

The structure and rules of language 162
- Language structure: the basic sounds
- Units of meaning: the morphemes
- The rules of grammar
- The rules of syntax

Producing messages and understanding them 165
- The speaker's problem
- The listener's problem
- The listening processes

How we learn language 169
- Can television replace mother?
- The child's struggle to convey meaning
- Acquiring the rules of grammar
- Parents help—but children are fine pupils
- Theories of language learning
- Can apes learn language?

The doubly useful words called concepts 177
- Concepts without words
- How language enriches our concepts—and concepts enrich our language
- Concepts and inferences
- Concepts, categories, learning, and memory
- A continuing mystery: what exactly is a concept?
- Family resemblances and "fuzzy" boundary lines
- Language as a pair of eyeglasses for viewing the world: does it distort our vision?
- Or do we design the eyeglasses to fit our vision?
- How new thinking produces new language

Thinking and problem solving 185
- Some tools of thinking: rules and premises
- Logical and illogical thinking
- Problem solving: the four steps
- Using algorithms and heuristics
- Pitfall 1: failure to analyze the problem
- Pitfall 2: thinking what we would like to think
- Pitfall 3: functional fixedness
- Pitfall 4: relying on the readily available

Summary 193

Important terms 195

Recommended readings 196

Psychology and Society
- A flexible language for a complex society 166
- How can we give equal education to children of families who do not speak "standard English"? 171

Language and Concepts

If you should ever happen to be in a foreign country, not knowing a word of the native tongue and unable to find anyone who speaks English, you will soon appreciate the importance of language. You cannot ask or receive directions. You cannot order food, except by pointing. You cannot ask for a physician, except by making gestures of distress. If you do find a doctor, you cannot describe your symptoms. You might be able to communicate to some extent through facial expressions and gestures—but otherwise you are almost as helpless as a baby who has not yet learned to talk.

Language, being such an all-important part of human behavior, has always been one of psychology's central concerns. Many studies have been made of how and why we use language (its function), how we put sounds and words together to form such a marvelously useful communications system (its structure), and the ways in which we send our own signals and understand those that other people send to us (the processes of producing and comprehending language). Psychologists have also been interested in the question of how in the world children ever manage to acquire mastery of such a complicated signaling system—so quickly and easily that they know many of the rules and can convey their own messages as early as the age of two.

In terms of information processing, language performs many services. It helps us acquire information by providing labels for the objects and events in the environment. It helps us encode information into memory by providing many of the linkages in the associative network of memory. It helps us think and solve problems. Indeed much of the thinking we do would be impossible without the use of words and the ideas they represent.

In evolutionary terms, language is a "uniquely human activity," made possible by the structure and dynamics of the human brain, that gives us a tremendous advantage over all other organisms (Miller, 1981). In coping with the environment we need not discover everything all by ourselves. Instead we can profit from the knowledge that our fellow human beings have acquired. Indeed written language makes available to us the recorded learning of the past—the philosophies of the ancient Greeks, the mathematical systems of the ancient Arabs, the scientific discoveries of Galileo. Thanks to language, each of us knows more than any one person, starting from scratch, could discover in a thousand lifetimes. As one psychologist has said, language "makes life experiences cumulative . . . [and therefore] cultural evolution takes off at a rate that leaves biological evolution far behind" (Brown, 1970).

This European road sign acknowledges the fact that people—except in their own language—are "almost as helpless as a baby who has not yet learned to talk."

The structure and rules of language

The origin of human language is lost in the mists of antiquity. But we can assume that its first purpose was to exchange messages of vital concern to survival—to enable people to *communicate* with one another about food supplies and how to obtain them, about danger and how to avoid it. Other animals, lower on the evolutionary scale, also manage to do this in one way or another. Bees that have found a new food supply go back to the hive and perform a dance, the nature and speed of which tell the other bees how to get to the food (Von Frisch, 1950). Birds sing their characteristic songs to attract mates and discourage interlopers. Chimpanzees use sounds and gestures to warn their friends of danger and to threaten their enemies. But no other organism has ever developed a method of exchanging so many messages of so many varied and complex meanings.

Communication, of course, is still the basic function of language. Our utterances are designed, as one study has put it, "to inform listeners, warn them, order them to do something, question them about a fact, or thank them for a gift or act of kindness." We "intend to have some effect on our listeners"; we "want to convey certain ideas" and expect our listeners to recognize our intention and "act accordingly" (Clark and Clark, 1977). Written language, likewise, aims to communicate and in some way influence. Its purpose may be to inform (a textbook), to change an opinion (a newspaper editorial), to urge action

In this dialogue, the animated manner of the woman at left indicates a strenuous attempt to communicate—the basic function of a language.

(a letter to a congressman), to present a demand (a letter requesting immediate payment of an overdue bill), or perhaps just to amuse (a mystery novel).

We now use language to convey a great deal more than simple messages about food and danger. But our language, for all its richness, continues to be characterized by a kind of elegant simplicity. Basically it is simply an agreement among those of us who speak the same language that certain sounds used by all of us, strung together according to rules that all of us know, convey messages intended by the speaker and understood by the listener.

Language structure: the basic sounds

The sounds constitute the structure of language—and it is a very simple structure indeed. All spoken language depends on the number of sounds that can be produced by the human vocal cords, and the number is limited. This may seem hard to believe, in view of the apparent complexity and variety of all the sentences that can be heard in the halls of the United Nations—English, French, Spanish, German, Russian, and the many languages of Asia and Africa—but it is true. No language contains more than 85 different basic sounds, and some contain as few as 15. English has about 40, or a few more depending on regional dialects.

The basic sounds, called *phonemes,* might be described as the building blocks of language. In English, the phonemes include such sounds as the short *a* in *pat,* the long *a* in *pate,* the consonant *p* as in either *pat* or *pate,* the *ch* in *chip,* the *th* in *the,* and the *sh* in *shop.* Thus the word *pat* contains three phonemes. By changing any of the three, you can produce many different words. Changing the first phoneme will give you *bat, cat, chat,* and so on. Changing the second creates *pate, pet, pit, pout,* and others. A new sound at the end creates *pack, pad, pal, pan,* and more. If you play around with the word *pat* in this way, changing just one of the three phonemes at a time, you will find that you can produce more than 30 different words.

Units of meaning: the morphemes

By themselves, the phonemes usually have no meaning. (Although some meaningful units, like the first person pronoun *I,* are made up of a single phoneme.) But they can be put together, in combinations of two or more, to form units that do have meaning. For example, we can start with the phoneme *t,* add the phoneme pronounced as *ee,* then add the phoneme *ch,* and arrive at the combination *teach.* The result is called a *morpheme*—a combination of phonemes that possesses meaning in and of itself. Like *teach,* many morphemes are words. Others are prefixes or suffixes, which can in turn be combined with other morphemes to form words. For example, we can combine the three morphemes *un* (a prefix), *teach* (a word in itself), and *able* (a suffix) to form the word *unteachable.* Or we can start with the same morpheme *teach,* add *-er* (meaning *one who*) and *-s* (to denote the plural), and form the word *teachers*. The plural *-s* is one of the most commonly used morphemes, as is *-ed* to indicate the past tense of a verb (walk*ed*, talk*ed*).

Some very long words represent a single morpheme—for example, *hippopotamus*. But most long words are combinations of morphemes and therefore of meanings. Note the following:

1 2
pitiful

1 2 3
disjointed

1 2 3 4
insurmountable

Or consider *antidisestablishmentarianism*, which you may have heard cited as the longest word in the English language. This is a combination of no fewer than seven meaningful morphemes:

1 2 3 4 5 6 7
antidisestablishmentarianism

The building blocks of language, though simple, make possible a tremendous variety of expression. The 40 English phonemes (which are written using only the 26 letters of the alphabet) are combined in various ways to produce more than 100,000 morphemes. These are in turn combined with one another to produce the 600,000 or more words found in the largest dictionaries.

The rules of grammar

Words alone, however, are not enough to make language possible. True, we must understand and agree on what is called *semantics*, or the meaning of the morphemes and words in our language. But, in addition, we must know how to string the words together into meaningful sentences. Thus every language has two essential elements: (a) a *vocabulary* of meaningful sounds and words; and (b) a set of rules, called *grammar*, for combining the words into an almost infinite number of sentences that can be constructed to express an almost infinite variety of semantic meanings.

Vocabularies differ from one language to another, of course, and often greatly. The English word *house* is *maison* in French and *casa* in Spanish, and in Chinese it is pronounced something like *ook*. The rules of grammar, however, though they vary in detail, share some basic similarities in all languages—including the dead languages of the past as well as those spoken today. Presumably this is because people everywhere have the same abilities and limitations in the use of language (Clark and Clark, 1977).

Even these ancient Hittite inscriptions follow the same rules of grammar we use today.

The rules of syntax

Among the most important rules of grammar are those called *syntax*, which relate to sentence structure. The rules of syntax regulate the manner in which nouns, verbs, adjectives, and adverbs are placed in proper order to form phrases—and the way the phrases are combined in turn into sentences that convey a meaning readily understood by anyone who speaks the language. Without these rules, language would be a jumble. For example, even very young children know the meaning of the individual names and words *Bill, quickly, who, the, down, was, street, saw, walking, John, a, sweater, his, in, yellow, friend.* But when presented in that order, the words do not convey any message. Rearranged according to the rules of syntax, they become the meaningful sentence:

> John, who was walking quickly down the street, saw his friend Bill in a yellow sweater.

If that is the message you want to convey about John and Bill, you have to arrange the words in that order. Any change in the arrangement might convey an entirely different meaning, as for example:

> *John, who was in a yellow sweater, quickly saw his friend Bill walking down the street.*
>
> *Bill saw his friend John, who was walking quickly down the street in a yellow sweater.*

You will find that you can use the 16 words to express several other meanings, simply by altering the syntax.

The rules of syntax very somewhat from language to language. Thus we place adjectives before nouns (*red house*), while the French place them after the nouns (*maison rouge*). But the pattern is always logical. The basic rule is that "what belongs together mentally is placed close together syntactically" (Vennemann, 1975).

As will be noted later, we acquire a knowledge of syntax and other rules of grammar during early childhood. We may not be aware of all the rules either as children or as adults, but we follow them even if we cannot explain what they are. In combination with the agreed-on meanings of morphemes and words, rules are the magic key to human communication (Chomsky, 1965). As you will see in a box on Psychology and Society, they probably form the only kind of system that could meet the needs of our civilization.

Producing messages and understanding them

The use of language is a form of information processing that entails a great deal of skill and work. Producing language—speaking or writing new sentences created on the spot—requires thinking and planning. Understanding language also demands the most complex kind of mental activity.

Especially in the case of the spoken word, communication depends on close cooperation between speaker and listener. The speaker, having a purpose in mind, must carefully choose words and produce sentences that will "get the message across." The listener then must interpret the meaning and intention of the combination of sounds reaching the ear.

The flags shown here are three of the signals used in an international system of communication among ships at sea. Each of them conveys a single, simple message—in two cases a request for a specific kind of help, in the other a specific warning.

Suppose that your language, which is your own communications system, worked the same way. For each idea that you wanted to express—everything from "Let's eat" to "Psychology is the systematic study of behavior"—you would need a separate "flag" of some kind, in the form of a spoken or written word. How many flags or spoken words—each conveying only one simple message—would you need to convey everything that you now say in the course of an ordinary day? How long would it take just to tell a classmate that you would like to go along to a movie but have a history examination tomorrow and must study, and besides you have to do some laundry and return a book to the library—so all in all, though you appreciate the invitation and would like a rain check, you feel you must say no.

How long would it take to write a letter to a relative explaining what you have been studying in this psychology course? How many pages would the letter run, and how much postage would it cost?

The number of flags you would need, each conveying its own message, is almost beyond imagination. In fact, no matter how many flags you had, you would not be able to communicate more than a fraction of what you now do. Most of the thoughts you express in the course of an ordinary day take the form of sentences you have never used or heard before. You make the messages up on the spot. Your listeners, in most cases, have never before heard the same combination of words. If you were a ship captain, you would be constantly designing and sewing up new flags. Your listeners, never having seen the flags before, would not have the faintest idea what they meant.

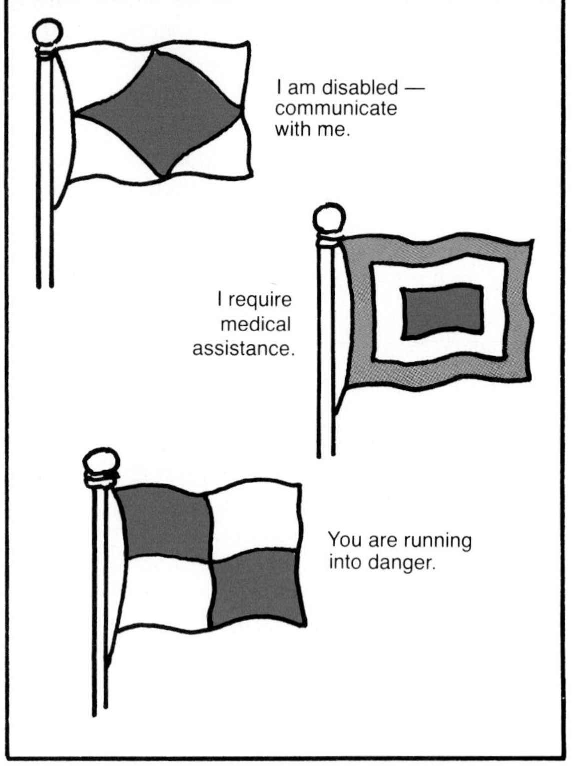
I am disabled — communicate with me.
I require medical assistance.
You are running into danger.

Thus the flags used by ship captains, though valuable in their own specific way, lack the all-purpose flexibility of human language. Our system, combining the simple building blocks of a small number of phonemes according to the established rules of grammar, enables us to exchange an unlimited number and variety of messages. It would be difficult indeed to imagine any other system that could possibly enable us to live in the complex societies we have developed.

Suppose, for example, you are in a room with a friend who is sitting near a window. You want the window opened wider. How, exactly, shall you phrase the suggestion? From all the possible words and syntactic arrangements available, you decide to say, "It's hot in here." Now your friend has to do some processing—for the words "It's hot in here" can be interpreted in a number of different ways. Your friend has to decide: Were you merely stating a fact? Do you mean that you want the window opened wider—or shut? Are you perhaps suggesting that both of you move to a different room? The possibilities have to be considered and accepted or rejected. Your friend will probably get the message, but not without working at it. For both speaker and listener, the use of language "makes full contact with our full cognitive abilities" (Clark and Clark, 1977).

The speaker's problem

One way to get some idea of the difficulty of producing language is to make a tape recording of some of your own utterances, especially when you are trying to explain something fairly complicated. Hearing the tape afterward, you will probably be shocked at how tongue-tied you sound. Or listen carefully to someone else's conversation, paying attention not to the meaning but to the flow of words.

The spoken word is not nearly so smooth and fluent as is generally believed. As we talk, we often have to stop and think. Our speech is full of long pauses, *and-uhs,* and *ers.* We make mistakes or fail to express ourselves clearly and have to amend our utterances with phrases like *I mean* or *that is to say.* Sometimes we stop in the middle of a sentence, leave it unfinished, and start all over. We make "slips of the tongue"—as was shown by one language scholar who, listening carefully to the utterances of the people around her, collected such amusing errors as these words that popped out in the middle of a marriage ceremony: *With this wing I thee red.* Or the case of a mother who wanted to say *David, feed the pooch* but actually said *David, food the peach.* Or the person who apparently thought simultaneously of the adjectives *grizzly* and *ghastly,* so that the actual utterance came out *grastly* (Fromkin, 1973).

These errors in spoken language point to the problems we face when we produce sentences. First we have to think of the meaning we want to convey—perhaps a message that will be several sentences long. Then we have to plan each sentence and each part of a sentence. We have to find the right words to flesh out the sentence and then put the words in their proper places. Finally we have to command all the muscles we use in speech to carry out the program we have planned—even as we are mentally racing ahead to what we want to say next (Clark and Clark, 1977).

Writing poses the same problems, though writers can correct their errors and have second thoughts before they put their language on public exhibition. Even the most experienced writers often start a sentence, cross the words out, and start over. After finishing the sentence they may go back and add new phrases or reword old ones. Many noted authors find that it takes a full day's work to produce, in final form, a page as long as this one.

The listener's problem

When you listen to someone speak, and try to interpret the meaning and intent, you have to engage in what is probably an even more difficult form of information processing. The only raw data you have are the sound waves produced by the speaker's voice and transmitted through the air to your ears. Ordinarily these waves meet with considerable competition from other sounds elsewhere in the vicinity. Other people are carrying on conversations in the same room. Footsteps thud against the floor. Noisy automobiles go by. A telephone rings. A door slams. A whistle blows. You may think you hear every word and every syllable uttered by the speaker—but in fact you do not. Many of the sounds are blotted out.

Even if you heard all the words, your ears could not immediately identify them. Many English words sound pretty much alike—for example *writer* and *rider*, *wave* and *waif*. Moreover, most of us are very careless about the way we pronounce words. We say not *I'm going to* but *I'm gonna*, not *Won't you* but *Woncha?*, not *Give me* but *Gimme*. Regional accents further confuse matters. Bostonians say not *Harvard* but *Havad*. Many Southerners say not *whether* but *whethah*.

Two psychologists once made high-fidelity tape recordings of some everyday conversations, then cut up the tapes so that they could play back separate portions—anything from a single word to longer phrases. Listeners to these excerpts had a hard time recognizing what they heard. When they listened to a single word, they failed to identify it more than half the time. Even when they heard a phrase three words long, they missed it nearly 30 percent of the time (Pollack and Pickett, 1964). What this shows is that making sense out of the sound waves that strike our ears is as difficult as trying to read a page on which paint has been splattered, making it impossible to recognize many of the words.

The listening processes

How do we manage this seemingly impossible task? One clue comes from a study made with some doctored tape recordings of speech. A simple sentence was recorded just as it was spoken, for example:

It was found that the wheel was on the axle.

Then the phoneme *wh* was masked, as if by a cough, leaving the sound of (?)*eel*. Next some other words were spliced into the tape in place of *axle*. The experimenters now had four tapes in all, presenting these sounds:

It was found that the (?)eel was on the { axle. / shoe. / orange. / table. }

The last word, it turned out, made all the difference. Subjects who listened to the first tape were sure they heard a *wheel* was on the *axle*, but other subjects were equally sure a *heel* was on the *shoe*, a *peel* was on the *orange*, and a *meal* was on the *table* (Warren and Warren, 1970).

The interesting thing here is that the clue to the unintelligible sound (?)*eel* came after the sound itself—indeed four words later. Somehow, in processing the sentence, the listeners managed to hold up judgment until they had the clue. Then they were absolutely sure they had heard

As they translate the proceedings, the United Nations interpreters in the foreground have a special problem first in active processing when they listen to the words and second in producing language when they convert the words into a second language.

a word that fit logically into the sentence. The evidence indicates that in listening we carry out many mental processes all at the same time. We simultaneously try to recognize sounds, identify words, look for syntactic patterns, and search for semantic meaning. When sounds and words are in themselves vague or unintelligible—as so often happens in everyday speech—the processing for syntax and semantics creates order out of chaos (Clark and Clark, 1977) . All this takes place so smoothly that we are not even aware of the mental work we do when listening or the handicaps we overcome.

How we learn language

Considering all the mental processing required to produce or understand language, it seems almost a miracle that children ever learn to use it. Yet learn they do—and very quickly. By the age of 2, many are already speaking such sentences as "Baby drink milk." By the age of 5, they understand the meaning of about 2,000 words (Smith, 1926). By about the age of 6, they have learned virtually all the basic rules of grammar. They can string words together according to the rules to create meaningful new sentences of their own. And they understand the meaning of sentences they have never heard before.

Everything about the use of language must be learned except how to create the sounds, which is an inborn ability common to all normal children. Early in life, all babies begin to produce many sounds that resemble the phonemes of language—presumably because of movements of the muscles of the mouth, throat, and vocal cords associated with breathing, swallowing, and hiccupping. This "*babbling*" occurs spontaneously. It is not an attempt to imitate sounds that have been heard—as was demonstrated by observations of a deaf baby whose parents were deaf and mute. This baby never heard a sound, yet did the same kind of babbling as any other child (Lenneberg, 1967).

Indeed it appears that children of all nationalities make the same sounds in their earliest babbling. It has been found, for example, that there are no differences among the babbling sounds of infants born to families that speak English, Russian, or Chinese (Atkinson, MacWhinny, and Stoel, 1970). American infants have been observed to utter sounds that are not used by English-speaking adults but only by people who speak French or German (Miller, 1951). Soon, however, babies begin to concentrate on the sounds appropriate to their own language, which they hear from their parents and others around them. The other sounds, not used in English, fade away through disuse.

Sadly for those of us who try to learn foreign languages after we have grown up, these other sounds often disappear completely. Many of us who try to learn French or German are never able to pronounce some of the phonemes properly, even though we may have done so quite naturally when we were babies. This fact has an important bearing on one of the current debates over public policy in education, as explained in a box on Psychology and Society.

Can television replace mother?

As for how children learn all the many other things required for the use of language, psychologists have some clues and some theories—but as yet they have found no single and totally satisfactory explanation. About all that can be said for certain is that people can learn semantics and grammar only through exposure to language as used by other people—plus interaction with people.

Mere exposure to language does not appear to be enough. A case has been reported of a boy named Jim, the son of deaf parents who used only sign language. As deaf parents often do, they encouraged him to listen frequently to radio and television, to make up for their own inability to provide him with the sounds of speech. Although Jim had normal hearing and speech ability, he did not seem to profit much from his experiences with television. In his preschool years he knew only a few advertising jingles and some words he had probably picked up from playmates. He lagged far behind other children his age until arrangements were made for an adult from outside the home to engage him regularly in direct, two-way conversation (Sachs and Johnson, 1976). Similarly, it has been noted that children in the Netherlands who listen regularly to nearby German television stations do not ordinarily learn any German as a result (Snow et al., 1976).

Interaction between child and mother, or some other intimate caretaker, appears to be the crucial factor (Bruner, 1978.) The two seek to communicate. And somehow, as a result of this mutual effort, the child quickly acquires an understanding of the structure of language and a mastery of the processes of producing and understanding it. The first accomplishment of young babies is to speak a few meaningful words: *baby, mama, milk.* Soon afterward, within a few months, they begin to string words together: *baby walk, see mama.* The average length of their utterances increases as shown in Figure 5-1. Some children learn more quickly than others—but all of them, if normal, show steady and consistent progress.

Psychology and Society: How can we give equal education to children of families who do not speak "standard English"?

The United States, as a melting pot for people from all over the world and with many different language backgrounds, has always faced a serious educational problem. Today the problem centers mostly on the Spanish-speaking population. We have more than 11 million citizens of Hispanic origin—including many children who have grown up in homes where only Spanish is spoken. These children—like their predecessors from homes where only Italian or German or Polish or Yiddish was spoken—often face serious difficulties in acquiring knowledge in English-speaking schools.

How can these children receive the American ideal of equal educational opportunity? One possible way—urged by many Spanish-speaking parents—is to have them taught in Spanish by Spanish-speaking teachers. It has been suggested that this should be done throughout the early grades of elementary school. Later, English would be introduced and taught as a second language (as many English-speaking American children are now taught Spanish or French). Even after the children began to learn English, they would continue to devote as much time to Spanish and Latin-American history and culture as to United States history and English literature.

The suggestion has considerable appeal. It would preserve a cultural heritage—that is, fluency in the language of origin and familiarity with the traditions and customs of the Spanish-speaking world. Especially for children in the early grades, it would avoid the dislocations and handicaps of attending schools that use an unfamiliar language—and possibly the learned helplessness caused by failure.

But to function fully and efficiently as members of our English-speaking society, all children must eventually become adept at English. And psychological findings raise some serious questions about the wisdom of delaying the process. As the text states, the ability to pronounce unused phonemes decreases with age. Most people who acquire a new language after childhood never manage to speak it without an accent (Labov, 1970; Oyama, 1973). Indeed learning a new language at all becomes more difficult, for reasons that are not entirely understood. One study has cited the case of a professor from a foreign nation who visited the United States. Though he had spent many years studying English, he had great difficulty making himself understood—while his 5-year-old child, with no previous instruction, picked up English so fast as to begin laughing at the father's mistakes (de Villiers and de Villiers, 1978).

Thus Spanish-speaking schools represent a trade-off, with certain advantages but also some dangers that would not be apparent without psychology's studies of language. The same findings apply to children from homes where American Indian languages are spoken, and also to black children whose parents speak what is sometimes called "Black English" as opposed to "standard English." Black English is almost a language of its own, with its own rules of pronunciation and grammar. Where standard English calls for the sentence *I asked John if he played baseball,* for example, Black English calls for *I asked John do he play baseball.* In the way it applies its rules, Black English is just as consistent as any other language (Farb, 1974). Indeed some linguists feel that it is more direct and expressive than standard English as spoken by many middle-class Americans. It does, however, create problems for children who, though fluent in Black English, must cope with schools—and later with a society—in which a very different language is demanded. How can education be best tailored to such students?

The child's struggle to convey meaning

From the beginning, children use speech in an attempt to send a message. They are not trying to copy adult grammar. They do not yet know how to string their words together in accordance with the rules of syntax. As one study stated, "The child is not reciting sentence types but is conveying meanings" (de Villiers and de Villiers, 1978).

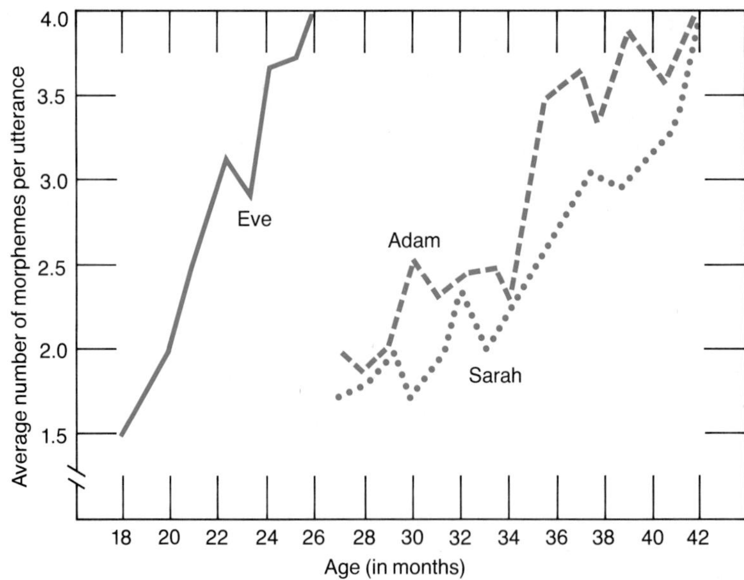

Figure 5-1 Children's speech: from simple to complex *Charted here is the increasing complexity of the language spoken by three children whose utterances were carefully recorded over a period of months to determine the average number of morphemes they strung together in each burst of speech. The fastest progress was made by Eve, who was observed from the time she was 18 months old. Less quick to use longer strings of words were Adam and Sarah, both of whom were studied beginning at 27 months. Although the three children progressed at different rates, there were some remarkable similarities in their development (after Brown, Cazden, and Bellugi-Klima, 1969).*

At first, children seem to throw their words together haphazardly, and the adults around them may sometimes have trouble understanding the meaning. For example, a child of about two may say, "Put suitcase for?" when an adult would say, "What did you put it in the suitcase for?" Or the child may say, "Who dat . . . somebody pencil?" when an adult would say, "Whose pencils are they?" (Brown and Bellugi, 1964). Yet the meaning is there. Children are constantly struggling to express themselves as best they can, within the limits of their knowledge of grammar. When they want to say something but do not know the proper words or phrases, they make up their own way of expressing it. Note these examples of the speech of children at about the age of 3:

> By a child struggling to take off a sweater: *I wanta be it off.*
>
> By a child who is trying to smooth down a piece of paper and has been urged by the mother to "make it nice and flat": *How would you flat it?*
>
> By a child who is holding a piece of paper over a baby sister's head and plans to drop it: *I'm gonna fall this on her* (Bowerman, 1974).

If you are like most people, your first impulse is to laugh at such childish awkwardness. But, on second thought, might it not be more appropriate to marvel at the children's ingenuity?

Acquiring the rules of grammar

Even at an early age, children acquire some of the rules of grammar practiced by the adults around them. At about the age of 2, for example, children are likely to say such things as *gooses swimmed.* Even though the statement is not put correctly, it shows that they have learned something about the rules. They have discovered that ordinarily a noun can be made plural by adding an *-s* and a verb can be turned into the past tense by adding an *-ed*. We can hardly blame them for the fact that our language is not always consistent and decrees that the plural of *goose* is *geese* and the past tense of *swim* is *swam*.

Children learn the rules of grammar in a remarkably consistent pattern. Whether they are fast learners or slow, and regardless of the size or nature of their vocabularies, they seem to acquire their knowledge in a predictable order. In the study of the three children presented in Figure 5-1, for example, a careful record was kept of the age at which they showed an ability to use morphemes that change the meaning of words. The first such morpheme generally used was *-ing,* added to a verb to denote an action going on at the moment (in the phraseology of grammarians, the present progressive tense). One of the girls, trying to explain that her father was at work, said he was "making pennies."

Somewhat later came the addition of an *-s* to words to make them plural. And still later—again for all three children—the use of an *-'s* to indicate possession. They learned to use some of the articles (*the, a, an*) before they added an *-ed* to a verb to convey the past tense (Brown, 1973).

Learning the rules seems to proceed in much the same fashion the world over. With minor variations, the first two-word utterances of children are similar regardless of whether they are learning to speak English, Russian, or Samoan (Slobin, 1971). Children everywhere seem to go about learning the rules in much the same way (Slobin, 1973)—with the ultimate aim of using them to make sense.

Parents help—but children are fine pupils

Adults help children learn in a number of ways. They speak to children slowly, with many pauses (Broen, 1972). They use short sentences (Newport, 1975) and often repeat words or phrases to help the child understand. Their sentences, however, are well formed and readily understandable (Cross, 1977). All in all, by gearing their speech to the child's level of ability to follow and comprehend the words, they provide what have been called "language lessons in miniature" (Clark and Clark, 1977)—helping the child pick up not only meaning but grammar (Vorster, 1974).

As far as meaning is concerned, parents usually make a deliberate effort at clarity. Thus mothers have been found to repeat and clarify as in these utterances to a child: *Put the red truck in the box now. The red truck. No, the red truck. The red truck in the box* (Snow, 1972). Perhaps these repetitions also help children acquire knowledge of syntax by breaking utterances down into separate phrases, thus emphasizing how words are strung together into phrases and phrases into sentences. But such utterances serve only as models. They do not explain the rules, which children have to figure out for themselves.

On the matter of the grammatical rules, parents seldom provide feedback that would let children know whether their own utterances are put together properly or not. Indeed it has been found that mothers almost never correct or punish errors in syntax. They ignore mistakes of this kind although they usually correct children for speaking in a way that gets the facts wrong. Thus when one of the children in the study illustrated in Figure 5-1 said, *Mama isn't boy; he a girl*—a statement that was factually correct though grammatically all wrong—the mother replied approvingly, *That's right.* When another of the children said of a television program, *Walt Disney comes on Tuesday*—a statement grammatically correct but factually wrong—the mother was quick to point out the error with the firm comment, *No, he does not* (Brown, 1973).

Nonetheless, even without any direct guidance, children learn the rules quickly. They are much more likely to wind up using correct syntax, on which they have received no feedback, than always telling the truth, on which they have received a great deal of feedback.

Theories of language learning

At one time most psychologists believed that the manner in which language is learned could be explained fully in terms of operant conditioning. They thought that some of the sounds babies make in their early babbling are reinforced by their parents' smiles, fondling, or other forms of approval. These sounds tended to be repeated. Other sounds, not appropriate to the language, are not reinforced and tend to disappear. The same process of reinforcement, or lack of it, was believed to account for the manner in which babies start to string sounds together into meaningful sentences (Skinner, 1957).

Later, some psychologists who became impressed by the importance of learning through observation proposed a different theory. They suggested that language is learned not through operant conditioning but through imitation of the way parents combine phonemes into meaningful morphemes, then string morphemes together into meaningful words and sentences.

Both these theories may account at least in part for how language is learned, yet neither seems to offer a complete explanation. It is difficult to see how operant conditioning can lead children to acquire rules that will enable them to create new sentences of their own—especially since they may receive positive reinforcement in the form of approval for grammatically incorrect utterances (*Mama isn't boy; he a girl*) and disapproval when their grammar is correct (*Walt Disney comes on Tuesday*). It is also difficult to see how imitation can result in completely new and original sentences—and in fact there is evidence that children who do very little imitating learn language just as well as children who do a lot of it (de Villiers and de Villiers, 1978).

A totally different theory has been proposed by Noam Chomsky, a linguist at the Massachusetts Institute of Technology. Chomsky suggests that the human brain is wired in such a way that we are born with some kind of "innate mechanism" for learning and using language. This innate mechanism enables us as children to do some rapid information processing on the language we hear from our elders. We quickly develop our own theories of how adults string sounds together to convey meaning. Later we modify and expand these theories as we get more experience at communicating with others—and soon we are using the rules of grammar in such a sophisticated fashion that we can understand or express almost anything. The Chomsky theory holds that, in a sense, we cannot help learning language and using it the way we do. This is simply the way our brains operate—a species-specific behavior dictated by our biological inheritance. Even as little children, it has been observed, we have "minds like little vacuum pumps designed by nature to suck up words" (Miller, 1981). Just as fish are born to swim and moles to burrow, we may be born to speak.

Can apes learn language?

Many attempts have been made in recent years to explore the question of whether any other animals, especially chimpanzees and other apes, may possibly share the human talent for language. One problem is that even the apes seem unable to use their vocal cords to make the sounds of human speech. Therefore experimenters have tried substitutes—for example, the sign language used by deaf people, which was the basis of an early study made by Beatrice and Allen Gardner with the chimpanzee named Washoe shown in Figure 5-2.

After about four years of training, Washoe had learned a vocabulary of more than 130 signs, including *you, please, cat, enough,* and *time.* Moreover, she could string the signs together into statements like *hurry gimme toothbrush* (Gardner and Gardner, 1972). She even made up a word of her own using the signs available to her—*water-bird* to describe a duck. The Gardners are convinced that Washoe learned sign language in much the same way a human child learns the spoken word—and indeed that she displayed about as much command of language as a 3-year-old child.

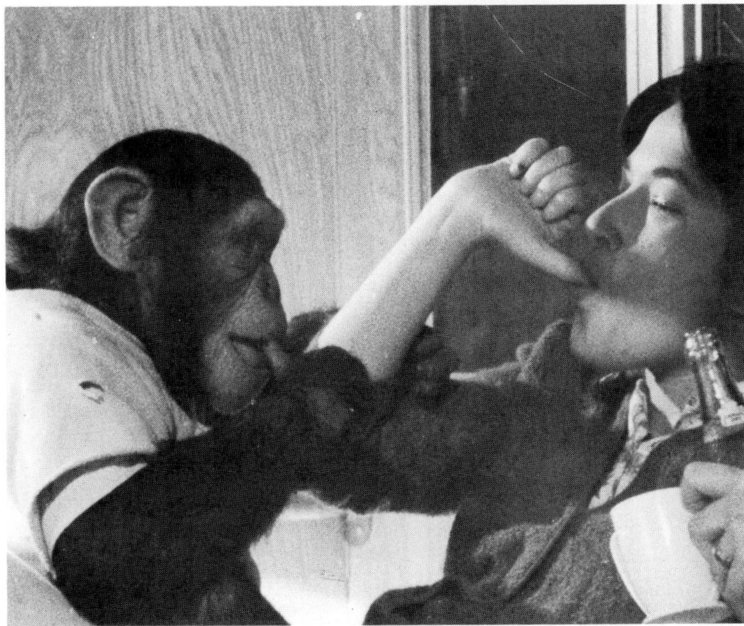

Figure 5-2 A chimpanzee "talks" *At the age of 2½, the chimpanzee named Washoe makes the sign language signal for "drink."*

Figure 5-3 The first chimp "conversation" *These two chimpanzees have learned at Emory University to communicate through a keyboard that flashes symbols on a projector—and here they conduct what is believed to be the first two-way exchange between animals using symbols like human language. Herman, at left, complies with Austin's signaled request for bread, then licks his own fingers.*

Another approach was taken by David Premack with a chimpanzee named Sarah, who was taught to communicate by using symbols made of plastic cut into various shapes. The pieces each represented a word, and the words could be arranged in order on a magnetized board. Sarah learned the meanings of numerous words and sentences like *Mary give apple Sarah.* Once she understood the meaning of the words *take, dish,* and *red,* she obeyed a command expressed in a sentence she had never seen before: *Sarah take red dish.* When her caretaker showed her two foods she liked, chocolate and a banana, she spontaneously created the sentence *Mary give Sarah banana chocolate*—which needs only an *and* between the two food names to be exactly the way a human child might ask for two things at once (Premack, 1976).

For a time many psychologists believed that the Washoe and Sarah experiments—and later studies like the one illustrated in Figure 5-3 (Savage-Rumbaugh, Rumbaugh, and Boysen, 1978)—cast serious doubt on Chomsky's theory that the ability to use language is a species-specific activity confined to human beings. It is now generally accepted, however, that the experiments show only that apes are capable of understanding symbols, communicating with them, and using them in various kinds of information processing, not that they can use language in any human sense.

Premack himself has reached this conclusion, despite the accomplishments he observed in Sarah. So has another psychologist, Herbert Terrace, who conducted a more recent long-term study of a chimpanzee playfully named Nim Chimpsky. Terrace began with high hopes of showing that Nim could acquire human facility with language. After five years, however, he reached the reluctant conclusion that most of Nim's communication was little more than a "subtle imitation" of his teachers, learned for the sake of obtaining rewards. There seemed to be no indication of any knowledge about syntax or of the human child's growing ability to produce longer and more complex messages. To take the most pessimistic view, Nim never greatly surpassed the performance of a dog that learns to obey the spoken commands of *sit* or *heel* (Terrace, 1979).

The doubly useful words called concepts

One feature of our language deserves special attention because it makes possible our great flexibility in the use of words for both communication and information processing in general. This is the fact that only a few of the words we use are the names of specific, one-of-a-kind objects—for example, the planets Mars and Venus. Most words, on the contrary, represent whole groups of objects, events, actions, and ideas. Even a simple word like *water* means not only the colorless fluid in the glass we hold in our hands but also any somewhat similar substances anywhere, including the salty contents of the oceans and the raindrops that fall from the sky. *Justice* represents many different abstract ideas held by people around the world at various times in history and embodied in various legal codes and practices.

Such words are called *concepts*—which can be defined roughly as notions of some kind of similarity between matters that we realize are also different from one another. For example, the concept *water* represents an awareness that the substances in drinking glasses, oceans, and raindrops, though they take different forms, are in fact similar. Many kinds of similarities can contribute to the formation of concepts. Some concepts grow out of the physical attributes of objects as they appear to our senses—for example, similarities in the appearance of roses and tulips (*flowers*), the sound of a singing voice and a brass band (*music*), and the feel of a piece of paper and a windowpane (*smooth*). Some are based on similarities in relationships between physical attributes: *bigger* applies to such diverse pairs of objects as fly-to-gnat, adult-to-child, and Texas-to-Delaware, and *louder* applies to shout versus whisper or thunderclap versus shout. Other concepts take note of similarities in function. Dwelling, for example, embraces a one-family house, a high-rise apartment, a tepee, and an igloo. An abstract concept like *justice* lumps together ideas that are in some way similar.

Concepts without words

Though words that express concepts make up a large part of our vocabulary, concepts can be formed without using any language at all. Many learning experiments have shown that animals, which have no language, can acquire concepts of triangles, as shown in Figure 5-4, and other qualities. Dogs obviously have a concept of *tree,* and will behave toward a tree they have never seen before just as they behave toward more familiar trees. Pigeons have been found to display a high level of skill at lumping similar objects together (Herrnstein and de Villiers, 1980).

Human babies acquire concepts before they learn how to talk. The first similarities they note are of physical attributes like color and shape (Linn et al., 1982), and one of their first concepts is of the human face. By the time they are a year old, they already seem to lump objects together by similarities in function, creating concepts like furniture and

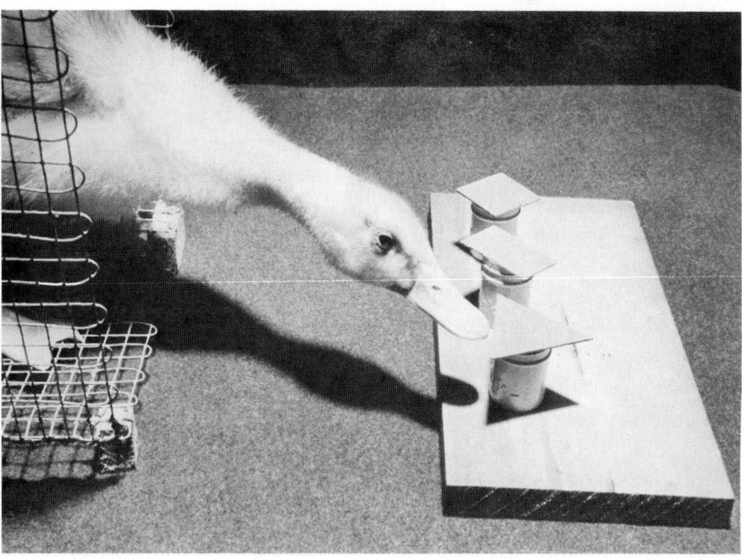

Figure 5-4 The duck can't say "triangle"—but knows one when it sees it *The duck has learned that food is always found beneath some kind of three-sided figure, never beneath a four-sided figure. Even if the size and exact shape of the figures are changed, the duck will look under the triangle. It must have some concept of triangularity—gained, as explained in the text, without the use of language.*

food (Ross, 1980). Indeed children seem almost addicted to finding concepts, and this helps account for their remarkable ability to acquire language. Presumably they must have some concept of things like *furniture* and *food* before they can understand and use those words.

How language enriches our concepts— and concepts enrich our language

If language is not essential for acquiring concepts, however, it is certainly a great help. Much of our communication and thinking depends on words that represent complex concepts embedded within other concepts, in a way that would be impossible without language. Note, for example, the term *human being.* What the term means to us goes far beyond any physical attributes (two legs, erect posture, and so on) or functions (being students, working at jobs). We have a far richer concept of *human being* as the highest (which is itself a concept) of mammals (another concept)—a mammal being a particular kind of organism (still another concept) that produces (another) its young (another) inside (another) the body (another) of the mother (another), which nurses (another) the baby (another) after (another) birth (still another).

Language helps us find meanings, relationships, and similarities—and thus build concepts on top of concepts. Without language, it would be difficult to find much resemblance between a two-legged human being walking on the land and a whale swimming in the ocean. Our concept word *mammal,* however, includes both of them.

Just as our language enriches our concepts, so do our concepts enrich our language. It is concept words that make it possible to use the 26 letters and 40-odd phonemes of the English language to express an unlimited number of messages. Suppose we lacked the concept *people* and had to talk about each individual by a different and distinct name. Or had no concept *dwelling* and had to use a different word for each place where someone lives—and the same for every item of furniture and food. We would find ourselves as limited as the ship captains using the flags that were shown on page 166. Indeed we would be more limited—for even the flags, as you will note if you look back at them, depend on the concept words *disabled, assistance, danger,* and others.

Concepts and inferences

The use of concepts lends a tremendous variety and versatility to the kind of information processing we call thinking. When we encounter a new object or experience, we do not ordinarily have to deal with it as a unique event of which we have no prior knowledge and must learn about from scratch. Instead we can fit it into some already existing concept (Bruner, Goodnow, and Austin, 1956). A dog of a species we have never seen before is instantly recognizable as a dog. A strange new sculpture by a modern artist is immediately recognizable as a piece of art. Concepts "give our world stability. They capture the notion that many objects or events are alike in some important respect, and hence can be thought about and responded to in ways we have already mastered" (Smith and Medin, 1981).

One important way concepts help us think can be demonstrated by this example: Someone says to you, "There is a bird in Brazil called a cariama. Does it have wings?" Almost immediately, you answer, "Yes." You do not know this from your own experience, but have reached your answer through the useful form of thinking called *inference*—or drawing logical conclusions from facts already known. You have been told that a cariama fits into the concept bird. Your concept of bird includes the fact, previously learned and stored in memory, that birds have wings. Therefore it is reasonable to infer, even though you have never seen a cariama, that it too has wings.

The process of inference enables you to think about many matters without having any direct knowledge of the situation (Collins and Quillian, 1972). At the end of a long day's drive, you feel confident that you will find a motel room if you push on another 50 miles toward Atlanta. You can make this inference because, even though you have never been there before, you know Atlanta is a big city and your concept of cities includes the presence of motels on their outskirts. If someone sends you a new kind of pocket calculator as a present, and nothing happens when you turn it on, you can infer from your concept of portable electronic devices that it probably needs batteries.

Our inferences are sometimes wrong. Suppose, for example, that the question about the Brazilian bird was, "Does a cariama fly?" Again you would probably answer yes, because your concept of birds includes flight. But there are a few birds that do not fly, and the cariama may just happen to be one of them.

Most of our inferences, however, are correct and valuable. Just as the rules of grammar enable us to generate sentences we have never spoken before and to understand sentences we have never heard before, so does the process of inference enable us to think about all kinds of matters we have never actually encountered. We can generalize about the new and unfamiliar from what we have observed about similar objects or events. Indeed most of what we know—or think we know—is based on inference rather than on direct observation.

Concepts, categories, learning, and memory

While reading these pages on concepts, you may have been reminded of the topic discussed in the previous chapter on memory—that is, the way categories help us organize information and encode it into long-term memory. Concepts and categories are closely related. Many concepts represent categories, and many concept words describe categories. Note Figure 5-5 (a condensed version of an illustration used in Chapter 4 to show how students learned and remembered a word list much more easily when the words were arranged in categories). You will see that all the words representing the categories and subcategories are terms for concepts. *Minerals* embraces all inorganic chemical elements or compounds that occur naturally in the world, usually substances mined from the earth. *Metals* and *stones,* though more difficult to define precisely, are types of minerals that have their own distinctive qualities and often

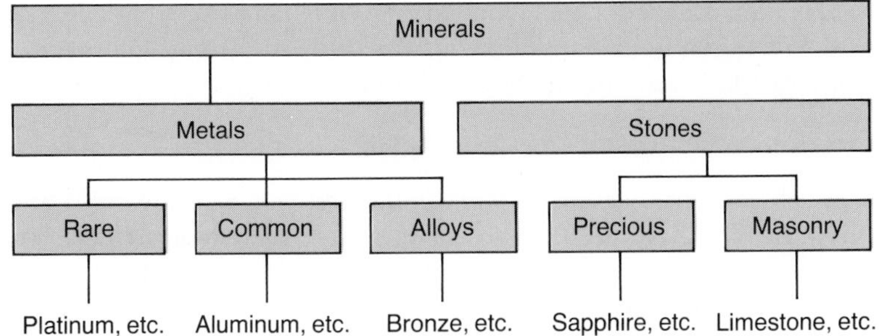

Figure 5-5 Concepts and learning by categories *You will recognize this list from Chapter 4, where it illustrated an experiment in committing information to long-term memory through the use of categories and subcategories. For its significance to this chapter's discussion of concepts, see the text.*

appearance. The other key words in the chart—rare, common, alloys, precious, and masonry—all represent concepts that are used in this case to form subcategories of various kinds of metals and stones that can be lumped together because they bear certain similarities.

Concepts and categories are one of the ways language helps us learn and remember. They make possible all kinds of chunking and clustering that help us process information in short-term memory and encode it efficiently into a network of long-term memory. As we acquire more information, we change our concepts in many ways—refining or enlarging them and forming new ones. Out of our simplest concepts, like faces, food, and furniture, we build increasingly complex concepts that serve as high-level clusters of related information and ideas. Thanks to these new "and ever more complex combinations of simpler ideas," we can remember and "think about complex subject matter just about as easily and efficiently as we could previously think about simpler subject matter" (Wickelgren, 1981).

Language accounts to a great extend for the fact that learning builds on learning—or, in William James's words, that new items of information "cluster and cling like grapes to a stem." It does so both by helping us acquire concepts and giving us specific words that help us remember and think about specific details. It is difficult to imagine, for example, how a surgeon could be trained without all the words that medical science has developed over the years to describe the human body—some representing the general principles of how the body is put together and functions, other identifying specific anatomical structures. Effective surgery would probably be impossible without an "effective language" (Bross, 1973).

The relation between language and learning and memory is a two-way street. As one study stated, "Learning new words enables children to conquer new areas of knowledge, and these new areas enable them to learn new words, and so on" (Clark and Clark, 1977). This is one reason, unfortunately, that children from poorly educated families often have a difficult time in school, thus continuing a vicious circle that leads one generation after another to have trouble getting along in society. Children whose parents have very little formal education and use a limited vocabulary start school with a severe handicap. There are hundreds of words and concepts that they have never heard of but that are already familiar to children whose parents are better educated. They simply do not have the same kind of "effective language" that makes it easy to find similarities and relationships between the new information presented in school and their prior knowledge.

A continuing mystery: what exactly is a concept?

Though concepts play such a large and useful part in our learning and thinking, and have been studied extensively by psychologists and linguists, they continue to be something of a puzzle. Earlier it was stated that concepts "can be defined roughly as notions of some kind of similarity between matters that we realize are also different from one another." The word *roughly* must now be emphasized—for the exact nature of concepts is not clear and there are a number of conflicting theories.

One theory, dating back to Aristotle, is that our concepts lump together groups of objects or ideas that all share some common properties. For example, the concept *cup* would apply to a (a) concrete object that (b) is concave, (c) holds liquids, (d) has a handle, and (e) can be used for drinking hot liquids. That seems to describe most cups—but unfortunately it fails to cover all of them. The cups used in Chinese restaurants do not have handles, and using a tin cup to drink a very hot liquid is likely to result in burnt lips and fingers. True, all cups have the other three properties in common, at least if we ignore the exception in which a cup is full of holes and any liquid would leak right out. But there are many things that are concrete objects, concave and capable of holding liquids, that are not cups—a bowl, for example (Smith and Medin, 1981).

The old theory runs into many such problems, even with simple concepts of very familiar things. The outstanding characteristics of *bird* are flying and feathers—but penguins and chickens cannot fly, and a turkey on the Thanksgiving table, with its feathers removed, is still a bird. Therefore many of today's scholars are tying to develop new explanations allowing for the fact that items grouped in a concept vary in the extent to which they share certain properties—and that some members of the group may lack some of the properties altogether.

Family resemblances and "fuzzy" boundary lines

One of the new theorists, Eleanor Rosch, has suggested that from our observations of events in the world we form a notion of a typical bird (or vegetable or fruit or anything else). For most Americans, the typical bird seems to be a robin—which is rather small, has two short legs and two wings, flies, sits in trees, and sings. Then we lump other living creatures into our concept of bird, or reject them, depending on how much family resemblance they bear to our typical bird the robin. We know immediately that thrushes and song sparrows, which are very similar to robins, fit into our concept of birds. We need a little more time to decide that a chicken is a bird, because it is a good deal larger than a robin and does not fly or sit in trees (Rosch and Mervis, 1975).

Sometimes, Rosch has pointed out, the boundary lines for family resemblances are extremely "fuzzy." Therefore we may have trouble deciding whether a bat fits the concept of bird or animal and whether a tomato is a vegetable or a fruit (Rosch, 1973). The same "fuzziness" in the way we form concepts makes it difficult to classify a 16-year-old female as a girl or a woman, and rheumatism as a disease or something else. Our concepts and categories—and indeed our thinking in general—are not always so neat as we would like them to be. But perhaps this simply reflects the fact that our world is itself a rather messy place, not easy to describe in cut-and-dried terms.

Even simple concepts like bird, animal, vegetable, and fruit continue to pose unanswered questions. The origin and nature of our more abstract concepts—justice, integrity, beauty, selfishness, evil, and all the many others—are even more difficult to study. Many of today's psychological research efforts are directed toward finding new insights that will add to our knowledge of not only language and concepts but human thinking in general.

Language as a pair of eyeglasses for viewing the world: does it distort our vision?

One of the interesting questions about language and thinking is this: Is it possible that language restricts our information-processing abilities? Does it perhaps serve as a pair of faulty eyeglasses through which we get only a limited and sometimes distorted view of the world?

One prominent language student, Benjamin Whorf, suggested that people who use different languages have very different ways of looking at the world and different concepts about the similarities and relationships that it displays. In studying many languages, Whorf found one group of American Indians who lump together with a single word things that fly—insects, airplanes, and even airplane pilots. He found other languages that do not have any devices for distinguishing the past, present, and future tenses of verbs (Whorf, 1956). In Whorf's view, such differences are bound to affect the way people who speak these languages conceive the world, organize it, and think about it.

This is an intriguing theory—and it seems to receive a certain amount of support from some of the matters discussed in the last few pages. The trained surgeon, with an "effective language" of anatomy, looks at and thinks about the human body differently from the rest of us. Children who start school with impoverished vocabularies probably conceive of the world in more limited fashion than their more fortunate classmates. It would appear that information processing can be influenced not only by the use of different languages but also by differences in the vocabularies of people who speak the same language.

Or do we design the eyeglasses to fit our vision?

There is a great deal of evidence, however, that language is usually tailored to human thinking, rather than vice versa. Among all the many languages of the world, there are more basic similarities than differences. Certainly on the matter of the physical objects and everyday events found in the world, people everywhere seem to perceive them, find names for them, organize them into concepts and categories, and think about them in ways that are often very similar.

Some colors, for example, seem particularly striking—doubtless because of the way the sense organs of the eye and the process of perception operate (as will be explained in Chapters 7 and 8). And, though languages differ in the number of colors for which they have names, the names always refer to the colors that "hit the eye," like red and yellow, not to all the many other hues and shades found in nature (Kay, 1975). Similarly, most languages have terms for shapes that human perception seems to find compelling, such as squares and circles. Most languages also have terms indicating that people all over the world think in much the same fashion about the dimensions of objects (like the English *height* and *length*) and distance and direction (Clark and Clark, 1977).

Eleanor Rosch has suggested that our concepts about the physical world are based on what is actually "out there" in nature. That is to say, they are molded by and reflect the physical realities of the environment. Objects just naturally fall into groups like birds and animals, vegetables and fruits—and our language acknowledges this fact (Rosch, 1977). Our brains are wired to notice certain attributes of the objects and events we encounter—and family resemblances in these attributes form the basis of our concepts.

How new thinking produces new language

Another indication that language is tailored to human thinking is the fact that language changes when people's thinking changes. Note, for example, all the new words that football has created while developing to its present highly technical level. There were no such terms in the English language, even a few years ago, as *cornerback, noseguard,* and *safety blitz.* All grew out of the need to find new terms for new concepts developed by inventive coaches.

When we need a new word, we coin it—or borrow it from another language. (Many everyday "English" words are borrowed—*goulash* from Hungarian, *whiskey* from Gaelic, *sabotage* from French.) And as additions to the language become more and more widely used, we often shorten them to make them more convenient (Zipf, 1949). Thus the original term *moving picture* has been condensed to *movie, gasoline* to *gas, telephone* to *phone.* Specialists in certain areas of knowledge, such as surgeons, coin or borrow their own vocabulary and often engage in their own form of shortening terms for simplicty and convenience.

All in all, though thinking may in some ways be molded and limited by language, as Whorf has pointed out, the human brain seems remarkably capable of adapting this useful tool to its own advantage. One study stated: "Apparently when people lack a word for a useful concept, they soon find one. . . . What this suggests is that language differences reflect the culture and not the reverse" (Clark and Clark, 1977). The moral for all of us is that we have in language a tool of virtually infinite possibilities—limited, for all practical purposes, only by how well we learn to handle it.

Thinking and problem solving

Sometime when you are engaged in thinking—about anything at all, from your plans for the next meal to your ideas about religion and politics—stop yourself and examine what kind of process has been going on. Most likely you will find you have been talking to yourself—thinking through the use of language, and especially words that represent concepts.

Thinking is one of those terms that everybody understands but nobody quite knows how to define. It is probably best described as the *mental manipulation of information.* In the learning and memory stages of information processing, we build a store of knowledge about the objects and events we have encountered—a sort of mental representation of the world and the way it operates. In the thinking stage, we process this inner representation in various ways to add to our understanding of the world and solve the problems it presents. Our thinking is entirely independent of physical objects and actual events. We can think about objects that are not present at the moment (like an architect planning

The artist thinks not in language but in mental images of what he wants to convey.

a house that does not yet exist), about events that occurred in the past (a childhood birthday party), or about abstract concepts that have no physical reality at all (religion and politics).

Thinking does not necessarily require language. Animals obviously do some kind of thinking, and so do human babies before they have learned to speak. An artist working on a painting thinks in terms of mental images—a mind's-eye picture of what the details and final results should look like. Musicians compose and orchestrate by manipulating "sounds" that they hear only inside themselves. Mathematicians manipulate their own symbols and formulas. But most of us think mostly in words most of the time, and language greatly enlarges the scope of our thinking.

We think about many things in many ways. As we observe the world around us, we seek to find some kind of order in its objects and events. We look for meanings and relationships that enable us to form concepts and categories. As we accumulate more knowledge, these concepts change and become more and more refined and elaborate. The mind, it has been said, is constantly working on its knowlege (Bowerman, 1978)—trying to understand and absorb the new and revising the old in light of the new.

We think about what we have learned about our world in the past and what we plan to do in the world tomorrow. We think about our food, clothing, and shelter, about our classes and job, about the people we know and our relationships with them. We also think about ideas—and develop our own set of beliefs about religion, politics, and what is good and bad in our society.

Some tools of thinking: rules and premises

Among the important pieces of information we process during our thinking are the *rules* that govern the relationships and interactions among the objects and events in the environment—in other words, the facts we have learned about the way the world operates. We have learned from experience that water, if heated enough, will boil and turn to steam. We have also discovered that an egg placed in boiling water will start to turn hard, and if left long enough will become hard-boiled. In thinking about cooking, these are some of the rules we manipulate.

Some of the rules we use come from our own observations. Others represent the pooled observations of many people—the kinds of information found in our libraries. When we think about the sky and the solar system, we utilize astronomy's rule that the moon revolves around the earth and the earth and other planets revolve around the sun. When we think about the distance around a circular lake that we know to be a half mile wide, we use the mathematician's rule that the circumference equals the diameter (here .5 mile) times π (3.1416).

We also base much of our thinking on what are called *premises*, or basic beliefs that we accept even though they cannot be proved. The line between a premise and a rule is often hazy and difficult to draw, for many generally accepted beliefs are really not probably true. Even in science, for example, such ideas as the theory of evolution and many advanced mathematical theories are still only premises, though they are in accord with the best observations currently possible and have at least a certain claim to validity.

Many premises are the result of individual experience. They are not necessarily based on objective observation, and they vary greatly from one person to another. Some of us, from what we have observed, believe that most people are honest—and much of our thinking about other people is based on this firmly held premise. Others hold just as firmly to the premise that most people are dishonest. Some think and act on the premise that it is wise to keep one's nose to the grindstone, others on the premise that all work and no play makes Jack a dull boy.

Logical and illogical thinking

When you express an opinion and explain why you have reached it, a friend may say, "That's logical. I agree." Or, on the contrary, "Your logic is wrong. I disagree." Logical thinking means drawing conclusions that follow inescapably from the rules we have learned and the premises we have adopted. A simple example would be in answering the question: *Does a whale nurse its young?* You have learned the rule that all mammals nurse their young. You know that a whale is a mammal. Therefore it follows that a whale must nurse its young.

Illogical thinking means drawing conclusions that are not justified by such evidence as rules, facts, and premises. For example, a young woman may decide to become a schoolteacher as a result of this line of thought: "My mother says she was extremely happy when she was teaching. Therefore I will be happy teaching." Her thinking is illogical because she may have very different tastes from her mother's and the teaching profession may have changed in the meantime. A man with a stomachache takes a pill that was once prescribed for a friend, thinking, "The pill helped him, and therefore it will help me." But his stomachache may be entirely different and may only be aggravated by the medicine.

When we accuse people of being illogical, we are often incorrect. Their logic is perfectly sound, granted their premises, and it is the premises that we disagree with. Was it illogical for Christopher Columbus's critics to believe he would fall off the earth if he kept sailing west? No, for they based their reasoning on the premise that the earth was flat—and, if so, Columbus's ships would indeed fall off like plates pushed to the edge of a table. Their logic was right but their premise was wrong, because the earth is not flat.

Was it illogical to think that the Niña, Pinta, and Santa Maria would fall into nothingness because the earth is flat? Strangely, it was not illogical at all—as the text explains.

Many arguments and misunderstandings among statesmen and nations as well as between husbands and wives are caused not so much by fallacies in logical thinking as by starting from different premises. One economist, using flawless logic, may conclude that taxes should be raised. An equally brilliant economist, using equally faultless logic, may conclude that taxes should be lowered. One person decides, after much reasonable thought, that capital punishment is wrong. Another person, after equal consideration, decides it is essential. Which of the economists and opinions on capital punishment is right and which is wrong?

We cannot really say, because we have no way of establishing the validity of the premises on which they are based.

We cannot be sure that a premise is wrong unless it clearly violates the truth, and this is seldom the case. We know for a fact, as the navigators of Columbus's time did not know, that the earth is spherical rather than flat. If a man claims to be Napoleon, we know he is unquestionably wrong and we doubt his sanity. But mostly we hold our premises more or less on faith. We can agree or disagree with another person's premises but cannot usually prove them right or wrong. Thus people whose thinking is totally logical can reach entirely different conclusions.

Problem solving: the four steps

Much human thinking is an attempt at *problem solving*, designed to cope with the innumerable problems faced by all human beings. As a student you must solve not only the theoretical problems in your math courses but also many everyday problems. You have a certain number of dollars available for tuition, books, clothes, housing, food, and entertainment. How can you best allot the dollars to these expenses? A person starting a long automobile trip must ask: What highways will provide the best route? How can the trip best be broken up into how many days on the road? A mechanic looking at a stalled automobile must ask: What is wrong? How can I fix it?

Many studies have been made of problem solving, the pitfalls to avoid, and the most effective ways to go about it. One finding is that the process requires four distinct steps. We have to undertake these steps whether we understand them or not, and knowing about them is one way to improve our skill. The four are:

1. *Defining the problem*—to clarify its nature and the solution or goal that we seek.
2. *Devising a strategy*—that is, a plan of attack that shows reasonable promise of reaching the goal.
3. *Carrying out the strategy*—by calling on any rules and other knowledge that may be useful and by avoiding distractions and focusing our attention on the task.
4. *Evaluating progress toward the goal*—by stopping from time to time to see if we are getting closer to the solution and should continue with our strategy or switch to a different approach (Wessells, 1982).

Using algorithms and heuristics

The most effective strategy, when it is available, is to use what is called an *algorithm*. The word originally was used to describe mathematical formulas and procedures—which of course guarantee a correct solution to any problem that deals with numbers, provided we understand the problem and know the proper algorithm to apply. The term has now been broadened to include any specific technique that can be followed step by step and will produce a correct solution without fail. An example would be the problem of calling a friend who is not listed in the phone book. You know the number begins 445-57—— but have forgotten the last two digits. You can use an algorithm by trying every possible number from 445-5700 through 445-5799. The method may keep you busy for a long time—especially if the correct number turns out to be 445-5799—but it cannot fail.

For most of the problems we face, no algorithm is available and we have to rely instead on what are called *heuristics.* These are rules of thumb—approaches that have worked for us in the past, in somewhat similar situations, and may work again though there is no guarantee. A driver who comes to a fork in an unfamiliar country road, while trying to get to a town known to be somewhere toward the west, chooses the path that seems from the position of the sun to head more westerly—though it may later curve and turn south. A chess player, who cannot possibly predict all the possible moves in the game, follows the rule of thumb of trying to control the center of the board—which does not guarantee winning but usually helps.

Pitfall 1: failure to analyze the problem

Among the dangers we face in problem solving, one of the most common is a failure to analyze the situation thoroughly—and instead jump to an incorrect view of the nature of the problem and the possible solution. This pitfall is beautifully illustrated by the experiment illustrated in Figure 5-6, which you should try for yourself before going on to the next paragraph.

The problem presented in the figure is fairly simple—yet few people manage to solve it. The answer is that you must turn over cards 1 and 3. If card 1 has a colored glove on the back, or if card 3 has a colored hat on the back, then the statement you are asked to prove or disprove is false. But if card 1 has a black glove on the back, and card 3 has a black hat on the back, then the statement is true.

Most people insist that the cards to turn over are 1 and 4. But in fact card 4 has no bearing on the problem. Regardless of whether the hat on the back is colored or black, this card cannot prove or disprove the statement. The reason people tend to fall into the error of picking this card seems to be that they take too much for granted in reading the problem. From the statement given in the experiment, *Every card that has a colored hat on one side has a black glove on the other side,* they assume that it is also true that every card that has a black glove on one side must have a colored hat on the other side. But this has never been stated and is not part of the problem. The psychologist who devised the experiment has made many similar studies and has found that most people have this tendency to jump to unwarranted assumptions about the nature of the problem (Wason, 1971).

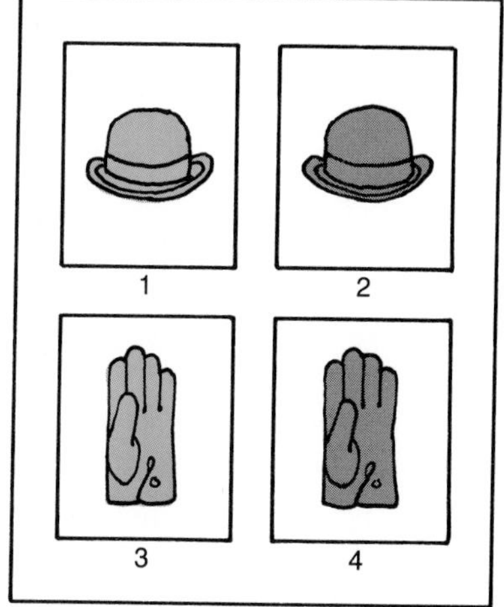

Figure 5-6 Can you solve this problem? *The four cards, which have symbols on both sides, lie on a table so that you can see them as shown here. You are told that each card has on one side a hat, which may be either colored or black, and on the other side a glove, which also may be either colored or black. You are asked to prove or disprove this statement:* Every card that has a colored hat on one side has a black glove on the other side. *How many cards—and which ones—would you have to turn over to find out whether the statement is true or false? For the answer, see the text (after Wason, 1971).*

Pitfall 2: thinking what we would like to think

Closely allied to the error of failing to analyze the problem and making unwarranted assumptions is the fact that we sometimes tend to let our personal biases get in the way. We try hard—and sometimes against all the weight of evidence and logic—to find the answer we would like to

Figure 5-7 **How did these horse trades turn out?** *This was the question posed to around 650 students taking an introductory psychology course. Each of the five possible answers was checked by at least four students. After you have reached your own answer, see the text and Figure 5-8 for the results of the experiment and what they tell us about a pitfall in problem solving.*

A man buys a horse for $60. A week later he sells it for $70. A few days later he buys it back for $80, only to sell it again for $90. What was the financial result of his transactions?

A. *He lost $10.*
B. *He broke even.*
C. *He made $10.*
D. *He made $20.*
E. *He made $30.*

find. The way our personality traits can affect problem solving has been demonstrated by the experiment shown in Figure 5-7, which you should try for yourself before going on to the next paragraph.

Fewer than half the students who took part in the experiment checked the correct answer, which is *D. He made $20.* But the most interesting development was that there turned out to be a significant difference between male and female students. As is shown in Figure 5-8, considerably more men than women got the correct answer. Almost twice as many women as men checked *B. He broke even.* In fact more women checked *B* than any of the other possibilities.

The experimenter concluded that women tend to favor the "broke even" answer because the female personality is less aggressive than the male—and more inclined to be "communal, selfless, and kind" (Hormuth, 1983). Many of the women students seemed to prefer to think of people as breaking even in financial transactions rather than taking risks and winding up with a profit or loss. We all have a tendency to reach conclusions agreeable to our own personality traits and opinions. It was established many years ago, by showing subjects a series of steps in a line of thinking in support of a statement, that people often find logic in even the most faulty reasoning if they agree with the statement it supports—and find flaws in even the most logical reasoning if they disagree with the conclusion (Janis and Frick, 1943).

Pitfall 3: functional fixedness

Another tendency we all share is to get into a rut in our view of the world and the way it operates. In particular, we tend to think of an object as functioning only in one certain way—and therefore to ignore its other possible uses. This pitfall, called *functional fixedness,* was best demonstrated in the famous old experiment illustrated in Figure 5-9. Examine the figure and see if you can solve the problem before you read on to the next paragraph. The problem is especially difficult when you

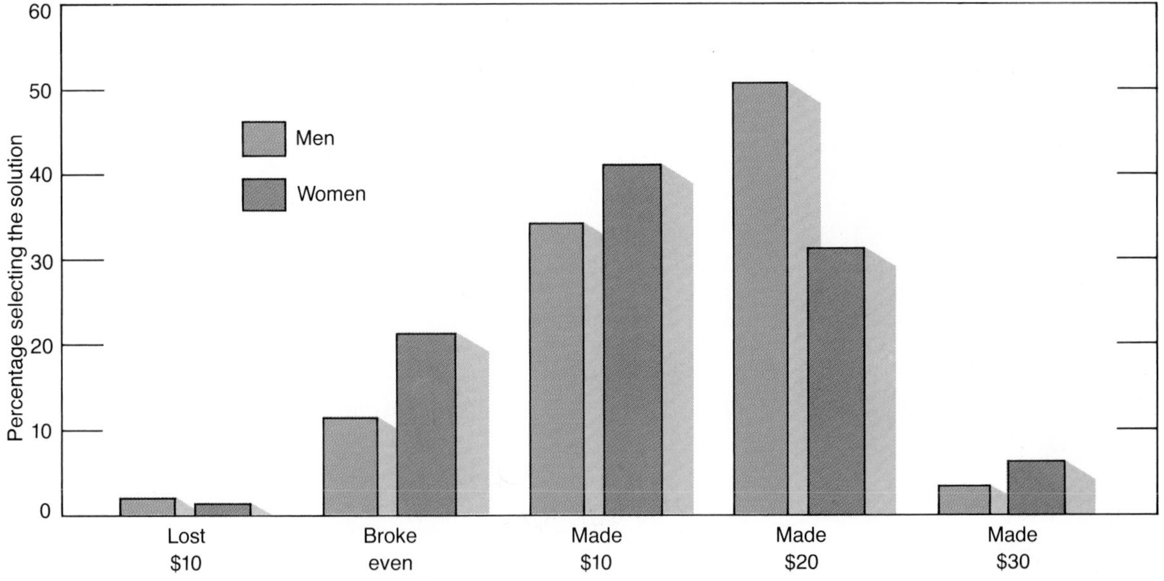

have only a photograph and cannot actually manipulate the objects—but, with effort and luck, you may find the answer.

The problem can be solved, as you will see when you turn the page to Figure 5-10, only by forgetting about the way a box is ordinarily used. You have to empty the box of all the matches, tack it to the door, and turn it into your candle stand. Though this seems simple enough once you know it, fewer than half the subjects thought of it when the experiment was first performed (Duncker, 1945).

Functional fixedness reduces our efficiency at solving many everyday problems. A nail file is for filing nails—and we may completely overlook the possibility of using it to tighten a screw and thus repair a broken

Figure 5-8 A strange case of sex differences in solving a horse-trading problem *The bars show the percentages of men and women college students who selected the various possible answers to the horse-trading problem shown in Figure 5-7. Note how many more women than men selected "broke even" and how many more men than women selected "made $20."*

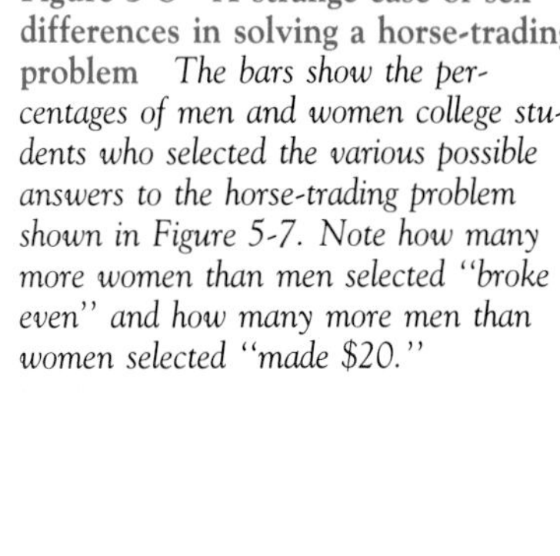

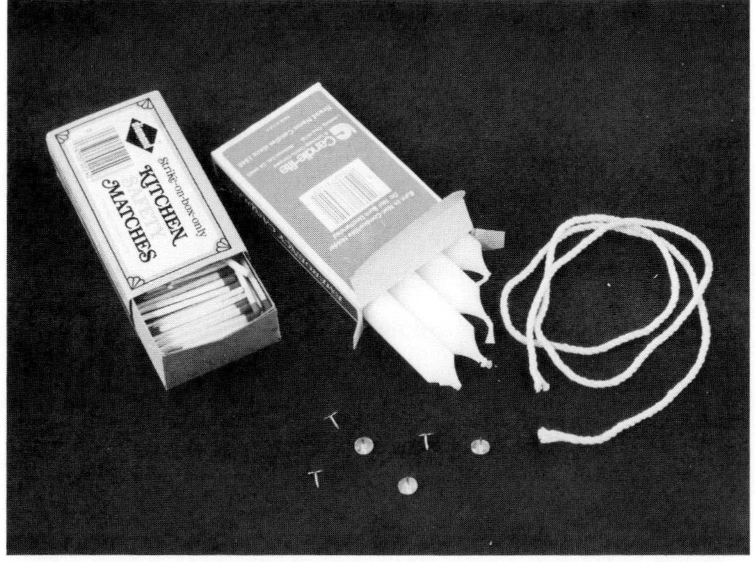

Figure 5-9 Problem: how to mount the candle on a door so it won't drip on the floor *These were the objects used in an experiment described in the text. Subjects were asked to figure out a way to turn them into an improvised candle stand. Try it yourself before turning to the next page for an illustration of how it can be done.*

Figure 5-10 The candle stand solution *The problem posed in Figure 5-9 can be solved only by finding an unusual way of using the box that held the matches. Just use the thumbtacks to fasten it to the door—and, lo, you have a candle stand to catch the drippings.*

lamp. A goldfish bowl is for holding fish—and the first person who converted one into a terrarium for growing house plants had to break some powerful old associations. We even have a tendency to think that things performing the same functions should look alike. As old photographs show, the first automobile manufacturers turned out cars that strongly resembled buggies.

Functional fixedness is one form of a more general phenomenon called *persistence of set.* Over the years we develop a mental set toward problems—that is, our own habitual way of approaching them. We tend to follow the same approach even in situations where other methods would be more appropriate. One almost sure way to improve your ability to solve new problems is to work at greater flexibility by trying at the very start to think of several possible ways to define the problem and the goal, as well as a number of different strategies that might work.

Pitfall 4: relying on the readily available

The fourth common pitfall is best explained by indulging in a bit of fantasy. Suppose your life depends on a modern-day version of one of those old mythical tests—like slaying a dragon—devised by a king seeking a worthy heir to his throne. The test is this: the king pulls a book from his library shelves. He turns at random to a page and circles the first word he finds that either begins with an *r* (like *road*) or has *r* as its third letter (like *carpenter*). You have to guess which. If you are right, the kingdom is yours. If you are wrong, off with your head.

How would you go about deciding? Most people, it has been found, start by trying to figure the odds. They see how many words they can recall that begin with an *r,* then how many they can recall with *r* as the third letter. They find it much easier to think of words starting with *r,* decide the chances are heavily weighted in that direction—and make the wrong guess. As it happens, there are more words in which *r* is the third letter rather than the first. But we pay much more attention to the first letter than any other when encoding words into memory, and therefore words like *road* and *rock* are more readily available than words like *cork* and *farm.* (Tversky and Kahneman, 1973).

Much of our real-life thinking and problem solving also depends on the availability of the information we have stored in memory. Availability is determined partly by our methods of encoding information and partly by other factors. Recent events are likely to have an especially strong influence on our thinking. (Most drivers slow down and are extra careful after seeing an overturned car, a tow truck, and an ambulance beside the road.) We are more influenced by an event that has a personal impact than by something we read in a newspaper. (A homeowner is more likely to buy additional fire insurance after watching a neighbor's house burn down than after watching televised fires in other parts of the city.)

Our reliance on the most readily available information often serves a useful purpose, because by and large our memory operates to make the most important information the easiest to recall. But there are times when relying on the readily available prevents us from solving a problem or causes an error (Tversky and Kahneman, 1974). Note this common occurrence: If we associate with people who lean strongly toward a certain life-style and opinions, we may accept their judgment as the representative wisdom of all humanity—and be influenced accordingly in important decisions about career, purchases, marriage, and morals. In actual fact, their behavior and beliefs may be just a minority phenomenon that is not typical of most people—and not at all suitable for us.

As in the case of functional fixedness, the availability pitfall can be avoided by being flexible in approaching the problem. Somewhere in your memory storehouse you have many kinds of information that might help. The first information that comes to mind, as you start searching your memory, may be all you need. On the other hand, it may not be enough to solve the problem, and concentrating on it may lead you into a blind alley from which it is difficult to escape. It may be useful to stop and think: What other information do I have that bears on the problem? How can I think about the problem in a way that will help me find this other information? Thinking, as has been said, is the manipulation of information—and, in problem solving, the more we manipulate the more information the better.

SUMMARY

The structure and rules of language

1. Language is a "uniquely human activity" made possible by the structure and dynamics of the human brain.
2. The basic function of language is *communication.* It enables us to exchange an unlimited number and variety of messages and pass knowledge along from one generation to the next.
3. Language also helps us acquire information (by providing labels for the objects and events in the environment), to encode information into memory, and to think and solve problems.
4. The building blocks of language are the basic sounds called *phonemes.* English has about 40 phonemes, and no language has more than 85.
5. Phonemes are combined into meaningful sounds called *morphemes,* which may be words, prefixes, or suffixes. English has more than 100,000 morphemes, which are combined in turn to produce more than 600,000 words.
6. *Semantics* is the meaning of a language's morphemes and words.
7. Every language has two essential elements: (a) a *vocabulary* (or set of morphemes and words with meanings dictated by semantics) and (b) a *grammar* (or set of rules for putting morphemes and words together).
8. An important part of grammar is the rules of *syntax,* which govern sentence structure.

Producing messages and understanding them

9. Speaking and writing are complex forms of information processing that require us to think of the meaning we want to convey, plan each sentence and each part of a sentence, find the right words to flesh out our thoughts, and put the words in their proper order.

10. When listening, we also carry out many mental processes. We simultaneously try to recognize sounds, identify words, look for syntactic patterns, and search for semantic meaning.
11. When we listen to speech, the individual sounds and words are often vague or unintelligible but our information processing makes order out of chaos—so smoothly that we are not even aware of the mental work we do or the handicaps we overcome.

How we learn language

12. Children display a remarkable ability to learn language. At the age of 2 most speak three-word sentences, at 5 understand the meaning of about 2,000 words, and at 6 have acquired virtually all the basic rules of grammar.
13. In learning language, the crucial factor appears to be communication and interaction between child and mother, or some other intimate caretaker.
14. Learning the rules of grammar appears to proceed in much the same fashion for babies the world over, regardless of what language they are learning to speak.
15. Some theorists have suggested that language is learned through operant conditioning, others that it is acquired through observation learning and imitation. More recently Noam Chomsky has proposed the theory that the human brain is wired in such a way that we have an "innate mechanism" for learning and using language.
16. At one time it appeared that apes are capable of using sign language in much the same way human beings use words. More recent evidence, however, suggests that their abilities are very limited.

The doubly useful words called concepts

17. Only a few words are names of specific, one-of-a-kind objects. Most are *concepts,* which can be defined roughly as notions of similarity between objects or ideas that are also different from one another.
18. Some concepts are based on similarities between physical attributes. Some are based on similarities in relationships between physical attributes (*bigger, louder*), and some on similarities in function (*dwelling, furniture*). Concepts like *justice* and *religion* lump together abstract ideas that are in some way similar.
19. Young babies and animals can acquire some concepts without language—but language enables us to build concepts on top of concepts and adds tremendous variety and versatility to our thinking and communication.
20. Our knowledge of concepts enables us to make useful *inferences* by drawing logical conclusions about new and unfamiliar objects and events from what we already know.
21. Many concepts represent *categories,* or groupings that help us organize information and encode it into long-term memory.
22. A number of theories have been proposed to explain the exact nature and formation of concepts. One theory, suggested by El-

eanor Rosch, is that from our observations of the world we form a notion of a typical object, for example, a robin that seems to be a typical bird—then lump other creatures into our concept of bird, or reject them, depending on how much family resemblance they show to a robin.

23. Benjamin Whorf has suggested that people who use different languages have different ways of looking at the world, organizing it, and thinking about it. There is considerable evidence, however, that we tailor our language to our thinking, adding new words whenever we need them.

Thinking and problem solving

24. *Thinking,* defined as *the mental manipulation of information,* can be accomplished without language—but language is chiefly responsible for the fact that our thinking is independent of physical objects and events and can range widely in space and time.
25. Among the important pieces of information we use in our thinking are the *rules* that we have learned govern the relationships and interactions among objects and events.
26. We also base our thinking on *premises,* which are basic beliefs that we accept even though they cannot be proved.
27. The four essential steps in *problem solving* are: (1) defining the problem, (2) devising a strategy, (3) carrying out the strategy, and (4) evaluating progress toward the goal.
28. The most effective strategy is an *algorithm*—a mathematical formula or other procedure that will guarantee a correct solution if followed step by step.
29. When an algorithm is not available, we use *heuristics,* or rules of thumb that have worked in similar situations and may work again.
30. Pitfalls in problem solving include: (1) failure to analyze the problem, (2) thinking what we would like to think, (3) functional fixedness, and (4) relying on the most readily available information.
31. The pitfalls can often be avoided by greater flexibility in analyzing the problem, thinking of several possible ways to define the problem and the goal, seeking a number of different strategies that might work, and searching memory for additional information that may help (instead of concentrating solely on the most readily available information).

IMPORTANT TERMS

algorithm
babbling
communication
concept
functional fixedness
grammar
heuristics
"innate mechanism"
morpheme
persistence of set
phoneme
premises
problem solving
rules
semantics
syntax
thinking
vocabulary

RECOMMENDED READINGS

Brown, R. *A first language.* Cambridge, Mass.: Harvard University Press, 1973

Chomsky, N. *Language and mind,* enl. ed. New York: Harcourt Brace Jovanovich, 1972.

Clark, H. H., and Clark, E. V. *Psychology and language.* New York: Harcourt Brace Jovanovich, 1977.

de Villiers, J. G., and de Villiers, P. A. *Language acquisition.* Cambridge, Mass.: Harvard University Press, 1978.

Johnson-Laird, P. N., and Wason, P. C., eds. *Thinking: readings in cognitive science.* Cambridge, England: Cambridge University Press, 1977.

Miller, G. A. *Language and speech.* San Francisco: Freeman, 1981.

Smith, E. E., and Medin, D. L. *Categories and concepts.* Cambridge, Mass.: Harvard University Press, 1981.

Wessells, M. G. *Cognitive psychology.* New York: Harper & Row, 1982.

CHAPTER 6

Theories of the nature of intelligence 199
- Is intelligence a general ability? The Spearman-Thurstone view
- Or is intelligence many separate skills? The Guilford view
- Piaget's theory of intelligence
- Piaget's four steps in mental growth:
- 1. The sensorimotor stage
- 2. The preoperational stage
- 3. The stage of concrete operations
- 4. The stage of formal operations
- Piaget and you

Intelligence tests: what they do and don't do 209
- Mental age, chronological age, and IQ
- Some well-known intelligence tests: individual and group
- The problem of measuring aptitude
- IQ, personality traits, and success in the classroom
- IQ and occupation
- Does IQ determine success? The case for a "yes" answer
- Does IQ determine success? The case for a "no" answer

IQ and the nature-nurture question 219
- How IQ "runs in families"
- But is it the family genes—or the family environment?
- How heredity and environment interact
- Some environmental influences
- IQ and family size
- How IQ sometimes leaps upward—or suffers a drastic decline
- The moral for parents and teachers

Intelligence, age, creativity, and the brain versus the computer 227
- What age does to the IQ
- IQ and creativity
- Tests of creativity
- "Artificial intelligence"—the computer's electronic brain

Summary 231

Important terms 234

Supplement: The science of test construction 235
- Requirement 1: objectivity
- Requirement 2: reliability
- Requirement 3: validity
- Requirement 4: standardization
- Vocational aptitude tests
- Interest tests
- Personality tests

Summary of supplement 238

Important terms 238

Recommended readings 239

Psychology and society
- Making the most of your IQ 203
- Intelligence testing, social policy, and the law 217
- Race and intelligence 222

Intelligence: What Is It? How Well Can It Be Measured?

What does it mean to be intelligent? David Wechsler, who constructed a number of the most widely used of today's tests, defined intelligence as *the capacity to understand the world and the resourcefulness to cope with its challenges.* That is to say, you are intelligent if you know what is going on around you, can learn from experience, and therefore act in ways that are successful under the circumstances. Your behavior has meaning and direction and is rational and worthwhile (Wechsler, 1975).

To the cognitive psychologists, intelligence is skill at information processing. It embraces all the steps described up to now in this book—learning, memory, use of language, thinking, and problem solving. It also includes an important matter that will be discussed in the next section of the book—that is, the role of the sense organs and perception in picking up information in the first place, thus providing the "inputs" on which information processing operates. From the cognitive viewpoint, it is all these various forms of information processing that enable us to understand our world and cope with it intelligently.

Intelligence is a complex phenomenon that raises many questions. Is intelligence a single ability or a combination of several different abilities? Can a person be highly intelligent in some respects but well below average in others? How—and how well—can intelligence be measured? If one of today's intelligence tests shows that a person has an IQ of 110 (or 90 or 100 or 120), how much does this tell us about that person's chances for getting along in school—and, more important, for leading a happy and successful life? A great deal of psychological research has been devoted to these questions. Many of them are still topics of debate. The old nature-nurture question, for example, has probably created more controversy in this field than in any other. Psychologists are agreed that some people certainly seem more intelligent than others—but they disagree, sometimes heatedly, on whether the differences are caused mostly by heredity or mostly by environment.

Theories of the nature of intelligence

One problem plaguing all investigators is that intelligence can mean different things to different people—and has done so from time to time and place to place throughout human history. The ancient Greeks considered intelligence to mean talent for oratory. The Chinese, until the Communist revolution, judged it to mean mastery of the written word, which is a different skill. (Many fluent conversationalists and eloquent speakers are poor writers—and many literary giants are tongue-tied in conversation or on the speaker's platform. (Some tribes in Africa measure intelligence in terms of hunting ability, many South Pacific islanders in terms of ability to navigate a boat.

There have been and still are places in the world where people who score high enough on today's American intelligence tests to be classified as geniuses would be considered hopelessly retarded because they are tone-deaf and cannot sing or play a musical instrument, or because they cannot run fast or hit a moving target with a spear. Even in our own nation, intelligent behavior can mean different things in academic circles, the business community, rural farm areas, and big-city ghettos.

Wechsler points out that the way we use the word *intelligence* represents a value judgment. That is to say, we call people intelligent when they have qualities that we ourselves—or our society as a whole, or the special part of society in which we live—consider resourceful and worthwhile. In general, our American culture admires fluency in language and talent for mathematics and science. The most intelligent people, according to the consensus, are those who can analyze facts, reason about them logically, and express their conclusions in convincing words. These are the very qualities that are associated with doing well in our schools—and, as will be seen later, our intelligence tests measure academic ability better than they measure anything else.

Is intelligence a general ability? The Spearman-Thurstone view

Despite the difficulties, many theories have been proposed—and all of them, though they continue to be argued pro and con, have made a contribution to our understanding of this complex phenomenon. One of the first influential theories was suggested many years ago by Charles Spearman, who applied sophisticated statistical analysis to the results of test scores on many kinds of abilities from reading comprehension to visualization of spatial relationships. Spearman concluded that the score on any test depends in part on an *s factor,* meaning a specific kind of skill at that particular kind of task. But people with a high level of s factor on one task also tend to make high scores at other tasks—a fact that Spearman believed could only be explained by a pervasive kind of mental ability that he called the *g factor,* for *general intelligence* (Spearman, 1927).

Another psychologist, L. L. Thurstone, disagreed with the idea of general intelligence and set out to disprove it. He too gave dozens of different tests to schoolchildren, measuring their ability at a wide range of tasks—and he, too, despite his original aim, wound up convinced that a g factor affects all kinds of mental processing. Thurstone proposed the theory that intelligence is composed of this general factor plus seven outstanding specific skills that he called *primary mental abilities:*

1. *Verbal comprehension*—indicated by size of vocabulary, ability to read, and skill at understanding mixed-up sentences and the meaning of proverbs.
2. *Word fluency*—the ability to think of words quickly, as when making rhymes or solving word puzzles.
3. *Number*—the ability to solve arithmetic problems and to manipulate numbers.

4. *Space*—the ability to visualize spatial relationships, as in recognizing a design after it has been placed in a new context.
5. *Associative memory*—the ability to memorize quickly, as in learning a list of paired words.
6. *Perceptual speed*—indicated by the ability to grasp visual details quickly and to observe similarities and differences between designs and pictures.
7. *General reasoning*—skill at the kind of logical thinking that was described in Chapter 5.

Or is intelligence many separate skills? The Guilford view

Today's intelligence tests measure performance at most or all of the seven primary mental abilities—and show, as did Thurstone, that people who are skillful at any one of them tend to do well on the others. The correlations among scores for the seven abilities are by no means perfect, but they are high enough to convince most psychologists that the g, or general factor, is important. Some psychologists, however, using different kinds of tests, have found so little correlation that they question the existence of any kind of general factor (Stevenson, Friedrichs, and Simpson, 1970).

One group of investigators, headed by J. P. Guilford of the University of Southern California, has concluded that intelligence seems to be made up of no less than 120 different kinds of ability. The 120-factor theory, illustrated in Figure 6-1, maintains that an individual may display a very high level of ability at some tasks, average ability at others, and low ability at still others. Guilford and his associates have devised finely differentiated tests for many of the 120 factors—and have found very little relationship between their subjects' scores on one test and their scores on many of the others (Guilford, 1967).

Among other things, Guilford has found that people differ widely in their abilities to deal with different kinds of materials (or *contents,* as they are termed in Figure 6-1). For example, some people are very good at handling what he labels semantic contents, or language and ideas.

Figure 6-1 Guilford's 120-factor theory of intelligence *The separate kinds of ability suggested by Guilford are represented by the small individual blocks contained in the cube. The theory maintains that each factor is the ability to perform one of five different types of mental* operations *on one of four different kinds of material, or* contents, *with the aim of coming up with one of six different kinds of end results, or* products. *Thus the total number of abilities that make up intelligence (or blocks in the cube) is 5 × 4 × 6, or 120. Followers of the theory measure the mental operation called "divergent thinking" by asking a question such as "How many uses can you think of for a brick?"—and noting how many different answers the individual can come up with and how imaginative the answers are. One test of the mental operation called "evaluation" is to present the four words* cat, cow, mule, *and* mare *and ask whether these are best categorized as: (a) farm animals, (b) four-legged animals, or (c) domestic animals. The answer will be found at the bottom of page 202.*

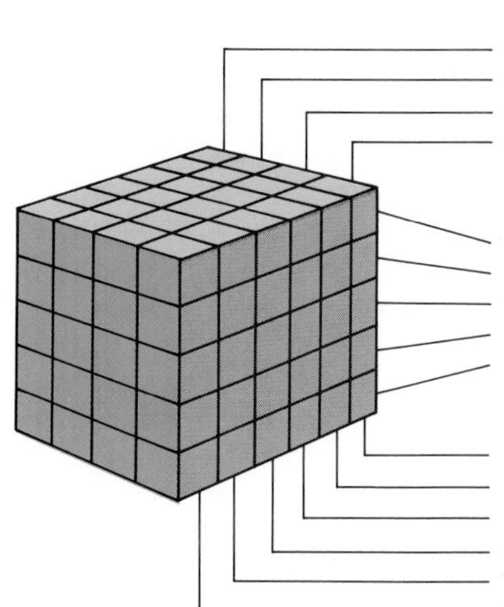

Piaget, with his customary beret and pipe, studies the playtime behavior of some children.

These people might be outstanding as writers or philosophers. Others excel at working with *symbolic contents,* such as numbers. These people might be most productive as mathematicians or accountants. Others do best with *figural contents,* such as pictures or specific objects. These people would seem best suited to become artists or master mechanics.

Guilford's theory and others that eliminate or minimize the importance of a g factor have their followers and their critics—and the search for new knowledge about the nature of intelligence continues. Meanwhile the present theories all offer useful guidance to people who are planning their lives and to the educational system that serves them, as will be seen in a box on Psychology and Society.

Piaget's theory of intelligence

Another view of intelligence comes from the Swiss psychologist Jean Piaget, who spent more than a half-century studying the mental development of his own and other children as they grew from infancy through adolescence. Piaget's observations have greatly influenced psychology's current position on how we think, reason, solve problems, and use our intelligence to understand and adapt to our world. He has been a major figure in the rise of the cognitive school, and no introduction to modern psychology would be complete without a discussion of the essential elements of his theory.

Piaget has concluded that our mental growth—which he defines as an increased ability to adapt to new situations—takes place because of two key processes that he calls *assimilation* and *accommodation.* Assimilation is the process of incorporating a new stimulus into one's existing cognitive view of the world. Accommodation is the process of changing one's cognitive view and behavior when new information dictates such a change.

Although all three of the answers to the question posed in Figure 6-1 are correct, the best answer is (c) domestic animals. This makes the finest and neatest distinction between the four animals and other kinds of animals. "Farm animals" is not the best answer because a cat is often found elsewhere. "Four-legged animals" is not the best answer because almost all animals have four legs.

Psychology and Society: Making the most of your IQ

Whatever the exact nature of intelligence is finally discovered to be—if indeed the mystery can ever be solved—there seems to be no doubt that all of us, at any given point in our lives, are gifted with a certain amount of it. Except for the most retarded, all human beings possess more information-processing ability, or "capacity to understand" and "resourcefulness to cope," or whatever one chooses to call it, than any of the lower animals. Within our own species we vary over a wide range. But whatever our own level may be, we can use psychology's knowledge to apply our intelligence to the best possible advantage. Our school systems, likewise, can use the findings to guide students into the most productive possible lives.

One of the most crucial decisions that everyone must make—and one that is especially urgent during the school years—is the choice of job and career. If you manage to find the right job, suited to your own particular abilities, you are likely to perform well and be successful and happy in your work. The wrong job can be a disaster. You probably know people who find life miserable because they are trying to adjust to jobs they find a constant struggle—where they have to work painfully hard, and run very fast, just to stay in place. No matter how hard they try, they never manage to get on top of the work they have chosen. They are always worried about mistakes and failure. Yet all the psychological theories about the nature of intelligence suggest that they might have found some other line of work easy, pleasant, and rewarding.

The general-factor theories suggest that two people, though the same in IQ, may perform very differently at different kinds of tasks. On test items that measure one of Thurstone's seven primary mental abilities—and on a job that utilizes that special ability—you may do as well as someone with an IQ as much as 15 points higher. At another, you may perform no better than someone with an IQ 15 points lower. Theories like Guilford's, based on specific abilities, suggest that the swing can be even greater.

Ability, of course, is not the only factor in determining your "fit" to a job. A lot depends on your own particular interests and personality traits. Of two jobs at which you are equally good, you might love one and hate the other. Other things being equal, however, you are likely to be comfortable and successful at a job that suits your talents. The school years—and especially college—provide an opportunity to learn your strong points and weaknesses. If you find mathematics difficult, the theories of intelligence would suggest that you quickly abandon any thought of being an engineer or accountant. Difficulty in English courses, especially composition, is a warning against attempts to find a career where fluency in language is important, such as journalism, teaching, the law, or politics. Similarly, the subjects you find easier and more interesting than others point to your best opportunities for a fruitful career. Many people, without ever having heard of a g factor or Guilford's work, have found that the best thing that happened to them in college was discovering that they were unusually good at something they had never suspected.

As a simple example, consider a young boy who has a number of toys. To these familiar old toys we add a new one, a magnet. The boy's initial impulse will be to assimilate the new toy into his existing knowledge of other toys; he may try to bang it like a hammer, throw it like a ball, or blow it like a horn. But once he learns that the magnet has a new and unprecedented quality—the power to attract iron—he accommodates his view of toys to include this previously unfamiliar fact. He now behaves on the revised assumption that some toys are not designed to bang, throw, or make noise with but to attract metal.

There is always tension, Piaget has concluded, between assimilation (which in essence represents the use of old ideas to meet new situations) and accommodation (which in essence is a change of old ideas to meet new situations). The resolution of this tension results in intellectual growth. Thus we can develop our cognitive skills only through active

The child in Piaget's sensorimotor stage has not yet learned to use symbols and language—but knows that if he can pull the cloth away he will see his mother's face.

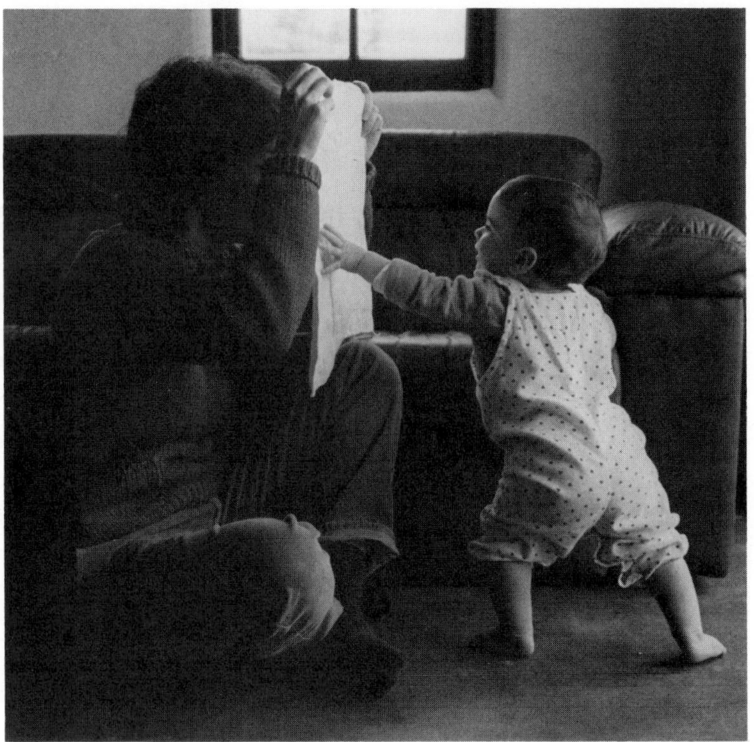

interaction with the objects and other people in our world. We need an environment that exposes us to new situations and new problems and thus challenges us to exercise and increase our mental skills.

Another key word in the Piaget theory is *operations.* The term is difficult to define. Roughly, an operation is a sort of dynamic mental rule for manipulating objects or ideas into new forms and back to the original, like the rule that four pieces of candy (or the mere figure 4) can be divided into two parts of two each, then put back again into the original four. The full meaning will become clearer as the discussion proceeds.

Piaget's four steps in mental growth: 1. The sensorimotor stage

Piaget has found that mental growth, beginning at birth, takes place in a series of four stages, in each of which the child thinks and behaves in quite different fashion than earlier. He maintains that the child grows intellectually not like a leaf, which simply gets larger every day, but like a caterpillar that is eventually transformed into a butterfly (Piaget, 1952).

In the first or *sensorimotor stage,* during about the first 18 months of life, children have not yet learned to use language and symbols to represent the objects and events in the environment. They know the world only in terms of their own sensory impressions of its sights, sounds, tastes, and smells and their own muscular movements and the effects these movements create. By the age of 4 to 6 months, babies are aware that they can produce results through physical activity. They will

Figure 6-2 The puzzle of liquid and jars: it baffles a child in Piaget's preoperational stage *The child points to both the squat jars to acknowledge that they contain an equal amount of liquid. But when the liquid is poured from one of these into a tall, thin jar, she thinks the tall jar contains more liquid. Not until she is around 7 will she realize that the amount of liquid remains the same regardless of the size or shape of the jar.*

repeatedly kick at toys hanging over their cribs, apparently to make them swing and thus produce a change of stimulus that they find interesting. By the age of 12 months they act as if they know that objects are permanent and do not mysteriously disappear. If a toy is shown to them and then is hidden behind two pillows side by side in the crib, they know how to find it. They look first behind one of the pillows. If the toy is not there, they look behind the other.

2. The preoperational stage

From about 18 months to around the seventh birthday, children are in what Piaget calls the *preoperational stage.* They have acquired language and can manipulate symbols. They may behave toward a doll as if it was a child and toward a stick as if it was a gun. They often put objects together in appropriate groups—for example, all their red blocks into one pile and the blue blocks into another. But their actions are still dictated largely by the evidence of their senses. They have not yet developed the kinds of concepts that would enable them to form meaningful categories. They are not yet capable of thinking in terms of the dynamic rules of operations.

Children of about 4 or 5, for example, can learn to select the middle-sized of three rubber balls. They have attained what Piaget has called an *intuitive understanding* that the middle-sized ball is bigger than the small one but smaller than the big one. But if three balls of very different size from the original three are then shown, they must learn to make the selection all over again (Stevenson and Bitterman, 1955)—because they have not yet grasped the operational rule that distinguishes all middle-sized objects, of whatever nature, from those larger or smaller. Until about 7 they are also fooled by the puzzle illustrated in Figure 6-2. Apparently the height of the jar is such an outstanding characteristic that they cannot help equating height with the amount of liquid the jar contains.

The child in the stage of concrete operations can reason logically and apply rules to the abacus, which he can see and feel—but would be less competent at manipulating language and ideas.

3. The stage of concrete operations

Some time between the ages of 6 and 8, American children enter the *stage of concrete operations*—the period at which, as the name implies, they first begin to understand the principles of operational rules. One of their accomplishments is becoming aware that the amount of fluid does not change in the experiment that was shown in Figure 6-2. They have discovered the important operational rule that Piaget calls *conservation*—that is, the fact that you can change the appearance of an object without changing such qualities as volume, mass, number, and weight (and, as in the case of the fluid, can usually change it back to the original).

They learn numerous operational rules. They now know, for example, that if object no. 1 is as heavy as object no. 2, and no. 2 is as heavy as no. 3, then nos. 1 and 3 must be equal in weight. They have also acquired considerable sophistication in the use of concepts and categories. They realize, for example, that "all the pets that are dogs" plus "all the pets that are not dogs" go to make up a category called "all pets." They also realize that objects or attributes can belong to more than one concept. They know that animals can be tame or wild, furry or feathered.

Thus children in the stage of concrete operations show an ability to reason logically and apply operational rules. But as Piaget's name for the stage implies, they reason more effectively about objects that they can see or feel than about verbal statements. Suppose, for example, that children of this age are asked: "A is the same size as B, but B is smaller than C; which is bigger, A or C?" They may not be able to answer—for the question requires thinking about a sentence rather than about concrete objects.

4. The stage of formal operations

The fourth and final period of mental growth—the *stage of formal operations*—begins at around the age of 12. In a giant leap toward intellectual skill, children in their adolescent years acquire the ability to reason logically not just about actual objects but about abstract ideas and possibilities. They acquire full mastery of the important rules that Piaget calls operations and can apply them to all kinds of situations, real or imagined. They can assume hypothetical conditions and make correct inferences, thus manipulating their own thoughts as readily as they once manipulated colored blocks.

The dramatic difference between the stages of concrete and formal operations is demonstrated by children's response to a question that requires them to analyze a theoretical situation—for example, "If all unicorns have yellow feet and I have yellow feet, am I a unicorn?" Younger children, still confined to the world of actual objects, cannot answer because they are incapable of reasoning about such nonexistent matters as unicorns and having yellow feet. Older children, having reached the stage of formal operations, can examine the logic of the hypothetical problem and quickly answer, "No."

In Piaget's words, "Thought takes wings." Adolescents no longer waste time trying to answer questions or solve problems with trial and error techniques. Instead they make definite plans to apply an operational rule. They systematically try to think of all the possible solutions, then reexamine their thinking to make sure they have indeed exhausted all the possibilities.

One prominent characteristic of the stage of formal operations is preoccupation with one's own information processing. Adolescents think about their own thoughts and are curious to learn how these thoughts are organized and where they will lead. All kinds of questions occur to them. As one adolescent put it, "I find myself thinking about my future, and then I begin to think about why I am thinking about my future, and then I begin to think about why I am thinking about why I am thinking about my future."

This inquiring attitude often causes conflict with the standards of the adult world. Adolescents become keenly aware that people do not always practice what they preach, and they begin to question such ideals as democracy, honesty, self-sacrifice, and turning the other cheek. They may decide that many of the beliefs and values they have been taught are "phony"—and to search instead for a different set of moral principles and a new philosophy of life.

Piaget and you

In one way or another you have progressed through the four stages of intellectual development as charted by Piaget. Your timing may have been on the fast side or the slow side, for there are considerable individual differences in the age at which children move from one stage to the next. But the transformation from sensorimotor infant to adolescent capable of formal operations seems to take place in the same manner for most people—even for children of different nationalities, and regardless of what kind of education they receive (Goodnow and Bethon, 1966).

You have probably forgotten the details of how your own mental abilities were transformed, in Piaget's terms, from "caterpillar to butterfly." But you may have the chance to observe the process in your own offspring or other children. One finding of importance to those who deal with children is that it appears impossible to speed up the process by trying to teach the reasoning skills appropriate to a more advanced period (Brown, 1965). It seems that children can understand only experiences and pieces of information that match what they already know about vocabulary, facts, and rules—or that are just a bit in advance of their existing information and cognitive skills. If a new experience or idea has no readily apparent connection with what they already know, they are not likely to learn much if anything about it. Indeed they may not even pay attention to it.

On the other hand, it appears that the progress of many children is retarded by learned helplessness acquired as the result of their home environment or failure and criticism in the early years of school. Children from low-income homes, in particular, may become so discouraged that they never take full advantage of the abilities they develop during the stage of formal operations. They may have a good deal more intelligence than they display or even realize. One reason is that their environment may lead them to make low scores on intelligence tests, which in turn leads both them and their teachers to have lower expectations for them, which leads to a further inhibition of their ability to display the skills measured by the tests. Hence the importance of taking a realistic look at intelligence tests, which is the next topic.

Alfred Binet and his daughters, some years before he created the first intelligence test.

Intelligence tests: what they do and don't do

Intelligence tests began as a psychologist's solution to a problem faced by Paris schools at the beginning of the century, when compulsory education began. Many classrooms were crowded, and slow students were holding up the progress of the faster ones. One solution, it seemed, would be to identify the children who lacked the mental capacity required by the standard curriculum and put them in a separate school of their own. But how could they be recognized?

A French psychologist named Alfred Binet who went to work on the problem realized that the task of identifying the poorer students could not safely be left to the teachers. There was too much danger that teachers would show favoritism toward children who had pleasant personalities and would be too harsh on those who were troublemakers. There was also the question of whether teachers could recognize children who appeared dull but in fact could have done the work if they had tried (Cronbach, 1949).

To avoid these pitfalls, Binet developed a test designed to measure potential ability at school tasks rather than performance in school—and to produce the same scores regardless of the personalities or prejudices of those who gave or took the test. Binet's test was first published in 1905, has been revised many times since, and is still widely used today. In fact all modern intelligence tests bear a considerable resemblance to Binet's original work.

In the United States, one of the best-known current versions of the original test is the *Stanford-Binet Intelligence Scale.* With the simple kind of physical equipment shown in Figure 6-3, it can be given successfully even to children who are too young to have developed a wide range of language skills. Older children and adults are asked questions that measure such things as vocabulary, memory span for sentences and

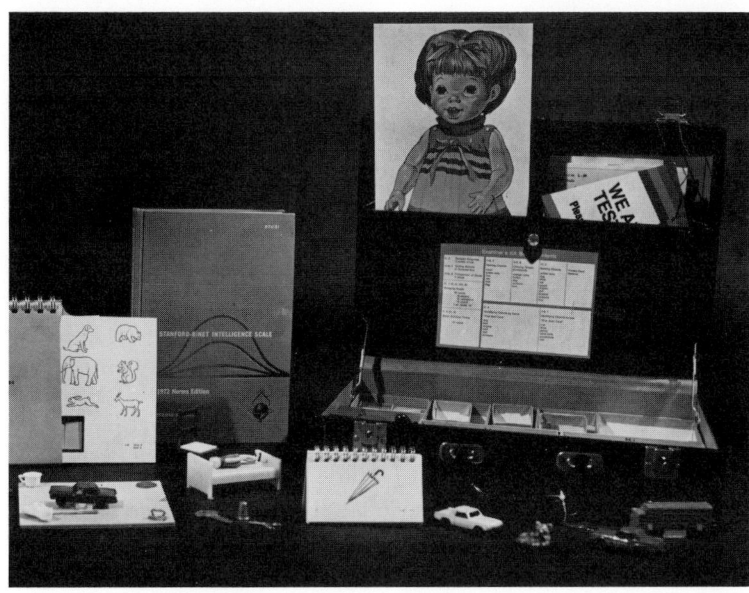

Figure 6-3 An examiner's bag of tricks for the Stanford-Binet test *Small children taking the Stanford-Binet Intelligence Scale are asked to perform various tasks with a paper doll and toys.*

Figure 6-4 Some Stanford-Binet test items *As shown by these examples, the questions asked very young children do not demand fluency in language. The questions increase in difficulty, particularly in matters of language and reasoning, at higher age levels.*

Two years old	On a large paper doll, points out the hair, mouth, feet, ear, nose, hands, and eyes. When shown a tower built of four blocks, builds one like it.
Four years old	Fills in the missing word when asked, "Brother is a boy; sister is a ______" and "In daytime it is light; at night it is ______."
Nine years old	Answers correctly when examiner says, "In an old graveyard in Spain they have discovered a small skull which they believe to be that of Christopher Columbus when he was about ten years old. What is foolish about that?" Answers correctly when asked, "Tell me the name of a color that rhymes with head." "Tell me a number that rhymes with tree."
Adult	Can describe the difference between laziness and idleness, poverty and misery, character and reputation. Answers correctly when asked, "Which direction would you have to face so your right hand would be toward the north?"

numbers, and reasoning ability. Some of the test items used at various age levels are shown in Figure 6-4.

Mental age, chronological age, and IQ

The scoring method originally used by Binet was based on the concept of *mental age,* or MA for short. As children mature, they are able to pass more and more of the items on tests of this type. The testing of large numbers of children has shown exactly how many items the average child is able to pass at the age of 6 or 7 or whatever the child's actual age happens to be. To examiners, actual age in years and months is known as *chronological age,* or CA for short.

For the average child, mental age and chronological age are equal. But children who have less intelligence than average are unable to pass all the items suitable to their age level and thus show an MA that is lower than their CA. Those who have more intelligence than average pass some of the items designed for older children and thus show an MA that is higher than their CA.

The relationship between mental age and chronological age was the original basis for that well-known term *intelligence quotient,* or IQ. The average IQ was arbitrarily set at 100, a convenient figure, and the individual child's IQ was determined by the formula

$$IQ = \frac{MA}{CA} \times 100$$

As an example of how the formula is applied, take the case of a child whose mental age works out on the test to 6 years and 8 months. To make the arithmetic easier, this mental age is converted into months; 6 years and 8 months equal 80 months. If the child's chronological age is also 80 months, the formula works out as follows:

$$IQ = \frac{80}{80} \times 100 = 1 \times 100 = 100$$

If the child is only 6 years old (72 months), the formula becomes

$$IQ = \frac{80}{72} \times 100 = \frac{10}{9} \times 100 = 111$$

If the child's actual age is 8 years (96 months), the formula becomes

$$IQ = \frac{80}{96} \times 100 = \frac{10}{12} \times 100 = 83$$

The intelligence quotient can still be thought of in terms of its original meaning. The average IQ is 100. The ability to pass items above one's age level indicates an IQ of more than 100, and the inability to pass all the items appropriate for one's age level results in an IQ of less than 100. In actual practice, the IQ of an individual taking the Stanford-Binet or other intelligence tests is now determined from tables that translate the individual's raw score on the test and chronological age into an IQ figure. The way IQs are distributed in the population, according to the Stanford-Binet test, is shown in Figure 6-5.

Some well-known intelligence tests: individual and group

The Stanford-Binet is only one of many tests now available. Even more widely used today are three devised by David Wechsler—the Wechsler Adult Intelligence Scale (or WAIS for short), another for children aged 7 to 16, and still another for children 4 to 6½. The distinguishing feature of the Wechsler tests is that they contain two separate kinds of items, called verbal and performance. The verbal items measure vocabulary, information, general comprehension, memory span, arithmetic

IQ	Classification	Percentage of people
Over 139	Very superior	1
120–139	Superior	11
110–119	High average	18
90–109	Average	46
80–89	Low average	15
70–79	Borderline	6
Below 70	Mentally retarded	3

Figure 6-5 IQs, what they mean, and how many people are found at each level *Administering the Stanford-Binet test to thousands of people has shown that one person in a hundred comes out with an IQ over 139 and can be classified as "very superior." (In popular terminology, this person is a "genius.") Three in a hundred come out with IQs below 70 and are classified as "mentally retarded." Almost half of all people have IQs in the "average" range of 90 to 109.*

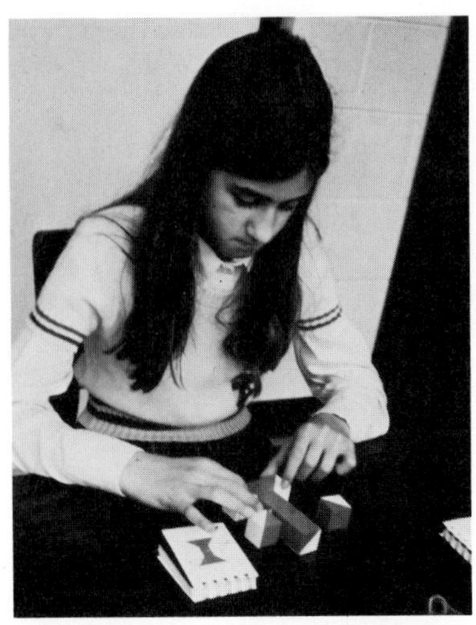

Figure 6-6 A performance item on a Wechsler test *With colored blocks of various patterns, the subject is asked to copy a design as one of the performance items on a Wechsler Intelligence Scale. The examiner notes how long the task takes as well as how accurately it is performed.*

reasoning, and ability to detect similarities between concepts. The performance items measure ability at completing pictures, arranging pictures, working puzzles, substituting unfamiliar symbols for digits, and making designs with blocks as shown in Figure 6-6.

A subject's IQ can be calculated for the test as a whole or for the verbal items and the performance items considered separately. This feature is often an advantage in testing people who lack skill in the use of the English language, for they may score much higher on the performance items than on the verbal items.

Both the Stanford-Binet and the Wechslers are *individual tests,* given to one person at a time by a trained examiner. The advantage of individual tests is that the examiner can readily detect if the results are being influenced by such factors as poor vision, temporary ill health, or lack of motivation. Their disadvantage, of course, is that they cannot conveniently be used to test large numbers of people, such as all the pupils in a big school.

Available for large-scale testing of many people at the same time are a number of *group tests*—typically taking the form of printed questions, such as those shown in Figure 6-7, which are answered by making penciled notations. Among the widely used group tests are the Scholastic Aptitude Tests, or SAT, taken each year by about a million high school seniors and used by many colleges and universities as one of the methods of judging applicants. The SAT has two parts, one for verbal ability and the other for mathematics, with the possible score on each part ranging from 200 to 800. In recent years the average scores have been around 425 on the verbal scale and 465 on the mathematical. Since the students taking the test are a selected group who have already proved their ability to get along in school, the 425 and 465 averages represent an IQ of well over 100.

It is well known that a number of colleges and universities have a cutoff point for SAT scores and will rarely admit a student who falls below that level. Therefore the SAT terrifies many high school seniors. Actually, however, the SAT affects college admissions less often than is generally supposed. A survey made around the start of this decade

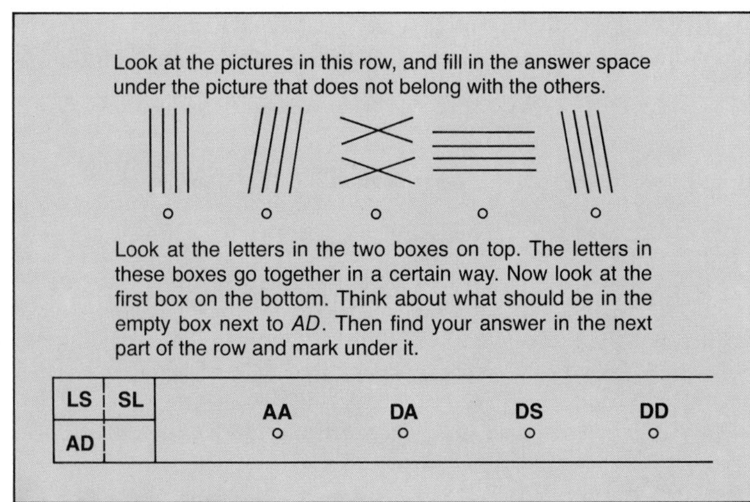

Figure 6-7 A group intelligence test for young children *These are sample items for second- and third-graders from the Otis-Lennon School Ability Test. Sample items demonstrate how the questions should be answered and are not counted in the actual scoring. The actual items in this test range from about as difficult as the sample items shown here to much more difficult. At this age level, the person administering the test reads the instructions to the children taking it. Older children and adults taking group tests read the instructions themselves, so that the tests can be given just by handing them out.*

The first mass application of a group intelligence test—with World War I recruits as the subjects.

found that only 48 percent of American institutions of higher learning even require all applicants to take the test. Only 2 percent listed SAT scores as the "most important" factor and another 43 percent as "very important." Many more institutions were found to give greater weight to grades in high school, which 31 percent called "most important" and another 34 percent "very important" (AACRAO and the College Board, 1980). High school grades, it has been established, do just as well as SAT scores in predicting success in college (Trusheim and Crouse, 1982).

The United States has so many institutions of higher learning, with such various admissions policies, that it is "not very difficult for even the minimally academically motivated student to gain admission to some college" (Hargadon, 1981). High school seniors in other nations would envy their American counterparts. In China, for example, college applicants have to take a three-day examination covering six different subjects—and of the 3 million students who take the exam only 300,000 are accepted (Butterfield, 1980).

The problem of measuring aptitude

From the beginning all intelligence tests have been what are called *aptitude tests,* measuring a person's ability to learn a new skill or perform an unfamiliar task. Such tests are, at least in theory, far different from *achievement tests,* which measure how much learning or skill a person has actually acquired. Intelligence tests attempt to determine how well the individual will be able to perform academic work in the future. Academic achievement tests, on the other hand, show how much the individual has accomplished in the past. For example the Iowa and Stanford achievement tests, widely used in elementary and high schools, show how much pupils have learned about such classroom subjects as reading and arithmetic—and how they compare with other pupils around the nation. Achievement tests in general measure how well the subjects have mastered some specific topic, usually a topic that has been studied recently. A final exam in college is in essence an achievement test, the purpose of which is to measure how much you have learned about the course.

In designing an ability test—of academic talent or anything else—one serious problem is that it is usually impossible to measure ability without any regard for past achievement. If you look back at the items from the Stanford-Binet test shown in Figure 6-4 (p. 210), you will see that many of them require at least some kind of prior learning. To answer correctly, a 2-year-old must have learned the meaning of the words *hair, mouth,* and *hands.* The 4-year-old must have acquired some fairly rich concepts of houses and books. The adult must have learned the points of the compass and the distinctions between such words as *laziness* and *idleness.* Thus measures of intelligence are no exception to the rule that "all tests reflect what a person has learned" (Anastasi, 1981).

Intelligence tests try to surmount the problem, insofar as possible, by measuring subjects' ability to use their existing knowledge in a novel way. Thus 2-year-olds are asked to apply to a paper doll their knowledge about their own mouth and hair. Adults are asked to make a novel spatial orientation based on their knowledge of the compass. Moreover in constructing intelligence tests an attempt is made to base all the questions on knowledge and skills that everyone has had an equal chance to obtain. It is assumed that every 2-year-old has had an opportunity to learn the meaning of *hair, mouth,* and *hands,* that every 4-year-old knows the meaning of *houses* and *books,* and that every adult should have been exposed to information about the points of the compass. No questions are asked that can be answered only by a child who has had nature study in summer camp, or only by an adult who has studied trigonometry or Spanish.

Nonetheless there is a certain amount of bias in intelligence tests. In a nation containing as many diverse social and ethnic groups as the United States, not all people are exposed to the same kinds of basic knowledge. The tests favor those who have acquired the knowledge and language skills typical of the middle and upper-middle classes and fostered by a school system largely staffed by middle-class teachers. Thus the tests produce some uneven results. Children from middle-class and upper-class homes make higher scores in general than children from lower-class homes (Janke and Havighurst, 1945). City children tend to make higher scores than children from rural areas (McNemar, 1942). Black children and children of ethnic groups from some other cultural backgrounds make lower average scores (Herzog and Lewis, 1970).

IQ, personality traits, and success in the classroom

Scores on intelligence tests, besides being affected by past learning, also depend to a considerable extent on many personality factors: "Whenever one measures a child's cognitive functioning, one is also measuring

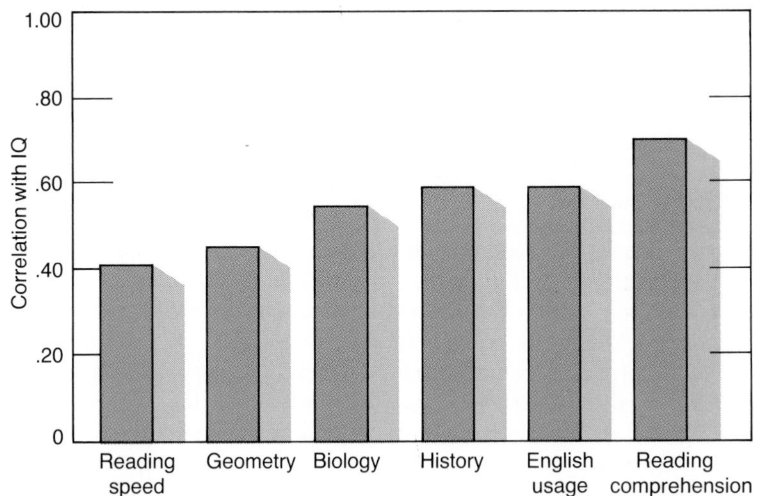

Figure 6-8 The relation of IQ to achievement in school *These correlations between IQ and performance in specific school subjects or skills were found in a study that used the Stanford-Binet Scale to measure intelligence (Bond, 1940). Note that the correlation was greatest for reading comprehension and lowest for reading speed.*

cooperation, attention, persistence, ability to sit still, and social responsiveness" (Scarr, 1981). Motivation is especially important—and therefore it is not surprising that middle-class children, who are strongly encouraged to take pride in the mastery of reading, writing, spelling, and arithmetic, make higher scores on the average than lower-class children who are less motivated toward academic success. Also important is what is often called adjustment, or psychological well-being—a fact that produces higher scores among children from stable and secure family backgrounds.

Thus intelligence tests cannot hope to measure, with pinpoint accuracy, an individual's sheer, disembodied skill at information processing (or Wechsler's "capacity to understand the world"). Nonetheless the IQ, as determined by any of the standard group or individual tests, is a good indication of how well a person is likely to do in school. Many studies have been made of the relationship between IQ and grades in classes all the way from elementary school to the university level, and all have shown correlations ranging from .40 to .60 or even higher (Wing and Wallach, 1971). The correlations are higher for some forms of school achievement than others, as shown in Figure 6-8. Students with low IQs usually have so much difficulty that they drop out of school before or immediately after the twelfth grade, leaving a group that is in general well above average to go on to college or other training above the high school level. A study made in the 1960s found that the average IQ of college freshmen was 115 (Conry and Plant, 1965). Those who went on to a doctoral degree averaged around 125 (Matarazzo, 1972).

The relationship between IQ and school achievement stems from Binet's basic aim in designing the original test, which was to predict how well an individual pupil could be expected to perform in the classroom. Binet tried many test items of many different kinds and kept only the items on which pupils who were successful in their classes did better than those who were failing. He deliberately avoided the use of any items, such as measures of physical dexterity or musical talent, that did not seem relevant to grades. It would perhaps be more fitting to say that his test and its modern counterparts measure an individual's AQ, or academic quotient, rather than IQ, or intelligence quotient. The fact that the tests are called measures of intelligence, rather than something more modest, is one reason they have come under attack in recent years by many psychologists as well as by outside critics and the legal system, as explained in a box on Psychology and Society.

IQ and occupation

Though the IQ is a good predictor of success in school, there is some question as to how well it predicts anything else. What about jobs, for example? Does a high IQ mean you are destined for a high-level occupation, a low IQ for a low-level job?

One massive body of evidence bearing on these questions comes from a study of the many thousands of men who took the Army's group intelligence test during the Second World War. The results, some of which are illustrated in Figure 6-9, indicate that there is indeed a relation between IQ and occupation—but less than one might expect. The average IQ of such professional people as accountants and engineers was around 120, and the average for truck drivers and miners was below 100. But there was a wide range of IQs in every occupation. The IQs of accountants ranged from about 95 to over 140. The IQs of

Figure 6-9 Jobs and IQs *The bars show the range of IQs of men in various occupations. Miners, for example, were found to have IQs from under 60 to nearly 130. The average IQ for each occupation is indicated by the vertical black lines inside the bar. For miners, the average was 93. For an interpretation of the figures, see the text (Harrell and Harrell, 1945).*

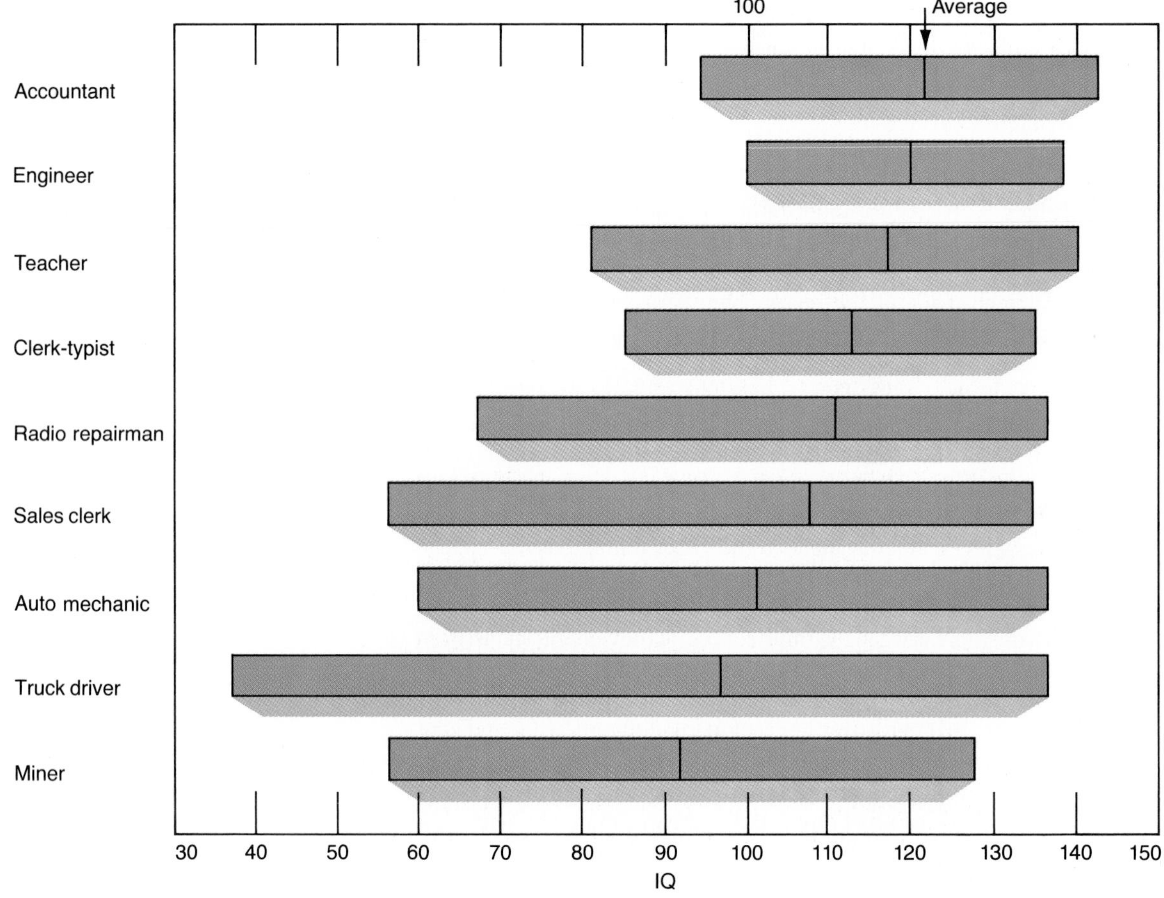

The history of intelligence testing has taken a curious twist. Until the 1960s it was "generally considered to be one of psychology's major success stories" (Tyler, 1976). Today it is one of the most controversial aspects of the science—passionately criticized by many "concerned citizens and parents, teacher organizations . . . psychologists . . . and consumer advocate groups" (Glaser and Bond, 1981), though also stoutly defended by many.

All kinds of tests have been attacked in the courts and by the nation's lawmakers. School boards have been sued for using IQ as a basis for assigning pupils to special classes for backward students, and employers for using aptitude tests to determine whom to hire and whom to promote. Some of the suits have been decided in favor of testing and others against—and, either way, the decisions have been appealed to higher courts. Several states and federal agencies have adopted laws or regulations that drastically limit and sometimes virtually forbid testing—and defenders of tests have promptly filed suits to prevent enforcement of the laws. Thus the legal status of testing is "currently in limbo" (Bersoff, 1981)—and may remain there for years while the controversy rages on.

The basic issue is as much a matter of social policy as of scientific validity. Critics question not only the accuracy of the tests and the way they are administered and scored but also the social consequences—on the ground that testing perpetuates the advantages now enjoyed by middle-class and upper-class Americans and is unfair and harmful to the lower classes and to minorities, notably blacks and Hispanics (Carroll and Horn, 1981). They point out that the lower average scores made by minority groups bar a disproportionate number of them from jobs and promotions in industry and civil service, and also cut off many educational opportunities.

In education, a particularly controversial issue is the assignment of young pupils to the special classes set up in many school systems for the "educable mentally retarded" found to have IQs of 50–70. Theoretically these classes protect the pupils from failure in the standard curriculum and provide remedial training that may enable them to resume a place in their suitable grade later on. Indeed one of Binet's purposes in creating his test was to find children whose intelligence was not developing properly and raise their IQ through special instruction. Critics maintain, however, that the instruction is often slipshod and the "retarded" label forever dooms the child to a second-rate education.

The complexities of the controversy were apparent in the conflicting views of two groups of eminent educators that were published almost simultaneously a few years ago. A panel appointed by the National Academy of Sciences, which concentrated on examining the scientific evidence for and against testing, concluded that tests have proved on the whole to be valid and useful in predicting how well an individual will do in the classroom or on a job. Although testing should not be the only criterion, said the Academy's panel, it is not in itself unfair to minorities, whose lower average scores merely reflect their disadvantaged background (National Research Council, 1982).

The opposite conclusion was reached by the Commission on the Higher Education of Minorities, which concentrated chiefly on the social consequences. The Commission found that all forms of testing as now practiced—including even classroom exams used to determine a student's grades—serve no real educational purpose and merely "pose special obstacles to the development of minority students." Instead of trying to rank students in comparison with one another, the Commission suggested, the schools should measure the progress and growth of the individual student—for the "principal function" of the educational system is to "increase the competence of students" and help them "lead more productive and fulfilling lives" (Astin, 1982).

truck drivers showed a particularly wide range—all the way from under 40 to nearly 140. Some accountants had IQs lower than the average for truck drivers—and a number of truck drivers (and miners and mechanics as well) had IQs higher than the average for accountants, engineers, and teachers.

One explanation for these findings undoubtedly is the amount of education the men in the study had received. Of two people with equal IQs, the one able to go to college may become an accountant or engineer. The other, unable for one reason or another to go to college or even complete high school, may have to settle for a job of much lower prestige. In fact other studies have shown that education is the chief factor in determining occupational status (Duncan, Featherman, and Duncan, 1972). In general, college graduates have better jobs than high school graduates, who in turn have better jobs than those who have not completed high school. The relation between IQ and job status, such as it is, seems to depend chiefly on the fact that people with higher IQs generally manage to acquire more education than others, barring such circumstances as illness or family financial problems. (Various studies have found correlations ranging as high as .70 between IQ and years of school completed.)

Does IQ determine success? The case for a "yes" answer

One of the most important questions about IQ is the extent to which it relates not just to classroom grades or choice of occupation but to successful living. This is a difficult question to answer, for success is an elusive concept. It can hardly be defined in terms of income, for many people have little interest in making a lot of money. Other types of success—efficiency and pleasure in one's job, good human relations, happiness in general—are hard to measure. Thus the answer has never been definitely established and is a matter of considerable dispute among psychologists.

One study that has led many psychologists to consider a high IQ to be a great asset in achieving success of any kind was made with a group of 1,500 California schoolchildren who qualified as mentally gifted, with IQs of 140 or more, putting them in the top 1 percent of the population. The study was begun in 1921 by Lewis M. Terman and continued by him and his associates for many years, as the children grew into adulthood and middle age.

As children, Terman's subjects were superior in many respects besides IQ. They were above average in height (by about an inch), weight, and appearance. They were better adjusted than average and showed superiority in social acitivity and leadership.

In later life, not all the gifted children lived up to their early promise. Some of them dropped out of school and wound up in routine occupations. Some, even though they went to college, turned out to be vocational misfits and drifters. But these were the exceptions, and their records tended to show problems of emotional and social adjustment and low motivation toward achievement. On the whole the group was outstandingly successful. A large proportion went to college, achieved above-average and often brilliant records, and went on to make important contributions in fields ranging from medicine and law to literature and from business administration to government service. Many earned the recognition of a listing in *Who's Who* or *American Men of Science.* The average level of accomplishment was far higher than could be expected of a group chosen at random. Terman's mentally gifted children also seemed to display a high level of physical and mental health, a death rate lower than average, and a lower divorce rate. One psychologist has expressed this view of the Terman study:

> Findings such as these establish beyond a doubt that IQ tests measure characteristics that are obviously of considerable importance in our present technological society. To say that the kind of ability measured by intelligence tests is irrelevant or unimportant would be tantamount to repudiating civilization as we know it (Jensen, 1972).

Does IQ determine success? The case for a "no" answer

There are, however, many dissenters. A number of investigators, after studying not just the mentally gifted but people in general, have reported finding little or no relationship between IQ and success outside the classroom. Grades in school, closely correlated with IQ, have been found to be unrelated to actual efficiency at such diverse jobs as bank teller, factory worker, or air traffic controller (Berg, 1970)—or even at scientific research (Taylor, Smith, and Ghiselin, 1963).

Some scholars have concluded that IQ bears on success only to the extent that an IQ in the lower ranges may make it impossible for a person to complete high school, perform successfully in college, or qualify for certain demanding jobs. (If you turn back to Figure 6-9, you will note that none of the men working as an accountant had an IQ under 95, and none of the engineers was below about 98). For people in or above the 100—110 range, differences in IQ do not seem to have much effect on achievement in later life (Wallach, 1976). Certainly success as measured in financial terms appears to depend mostly on other factors (Jencks, 1972). In the words of one study, a person "can obtain a very high IQ score and still not behave very admirably in the real world" (Zigler and Trickett, 1978).

IQ and the nature-nurture question

Like almost all other human traits and behaviors studied by psychology, intelligence is clearly influenced by both heredity and environment. This is a well-established fact on which all psychologists are in full agreement. Indeed it seems inevitable that the genes we inherit, which affect so many other aspects of our physical and psychological functioning, should influence the way our nervous system and brain operate—and therefore our intelligence. It also seems obvious that interaction with the environment—particularly all the learning we do—should help determine our ability to behave intelligently. But just how big a role does heredity play, and how big is the role of environment?

On this question psychologists are sharply divided. Some maintain heredity is as much as twice as important as environment (Eysenck, 1981). Others believe environment is more important than heredity, perhaps by a considerable margin (Kamin, 1981). On no other issue has the nature-nurture controversy been waged more heatedly. One reason

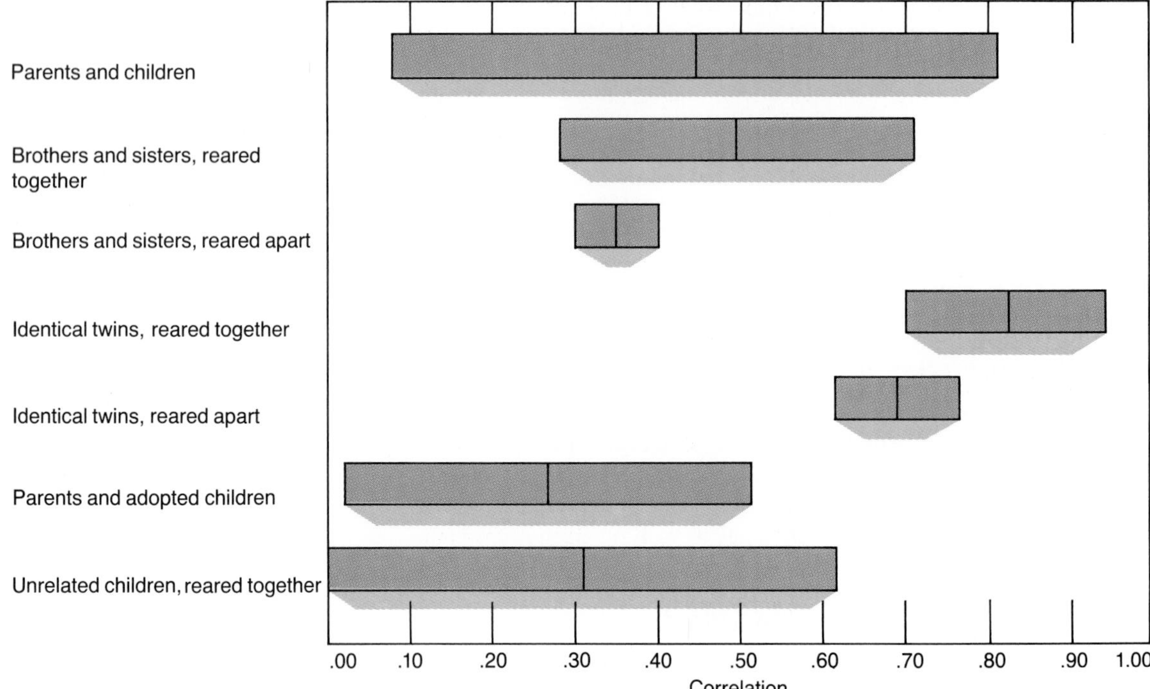

Figure 6-10 Family resemblances in IQ *The bars show the range of correlations—and the midpoint within the range—found in various studies of comparisons in IQ between blood relatives and also between people who lived in the same home even though they were not related. The correlation between unrelated people who grew up in different homes would of course be zero. For a discussion of the correlations shown here—and how they have been interpreted—see the text (Erlenmeyer-Kimling and Jarvik, 1963; Jencks et al., 1972; and Kamin, 1979).*

is that the evidence on both sides can be interpreted in so many different ways. Another is that the controversy bears on a number of social problems—for example, the question of whether intelligence can be changed through preschool and other programs designed to improve the environment in which children grow up.

How IQ "runs in families"

Many studies have indicated that the more closely related two people are—that is, the greater their similarity in genetic background—the more similar their IQs are likely to be. Correlations between the IQs of children and their parents, brothers and sisters, and even more distant relatives all seem to show that IQ tends to "run in families."

The studies are summarized in Figure 6-10. Note the top bar, which shows the relationships found between parents and children. Different investigators found different correlations, but the figures range up and down from a midpoint of about .50. The second bar from the top shows that the correlations between brothers and sisters living with their parents have also been found to cluster around .50. The third bar shows that children of the same parents, even when separated and brought up in different homes, still display a fairly high correlation, with the figures clustering around .35. Identical twins, who have inherited the same genes, show very high correlations when brought up together, and impressively high correlations even when separated and brought up apart from each other.

Much of the case for the nature side of the debate rests on those top five bars in the figure—and especially on the bar for identical twins reared in different homes. If people with exactly the same genes show a correlation of somewhere between .62 and .77 even when they grow up in different environments, then the influence of heredity on IQ would appear to be very strong indeed.

But is it the family genes—or the family environment?

The correlations, however, do not impress those who take the nurture side of the argument. The figures on identical twins who grew up in different homes, for example, have been challenged on a number of grounds—including the small number of subjects (such twins are difficult to find), the kinds of intelligence tests that were used, and possible bias in the way the tests were administered and scored. Leon Kamin of Princeton University, who has carefully examined the studies, has also concluded that the environments in which the twins grew up were probably much more similar than the term "reared apart" would imply. In many cases, he found, the two were brought up in families that were closely related—for example, one by the actual mother, the other by a grandmother or an aunt. Sometimes the two grew up in the same town and went to the same school, and in at least one case they actually lived next door to each other. This tendency toward similarity in environment, Kamin concluded, might be just as responsible as the identical genes for the high correlations in IQ (Kamin, 1981).

The pronurture side also points to the studies summarized in the bottom two bars of Figure 6-10. Note that some fairly substantial correlations, ranging up to .50, have been found between foster parents and adopted children to whom they were totally unrelated by blood. Note also the bar for unrelated children who were brought up together, usually through adoption into the same home. One study found a zero correlation for such children—the figure that would be expected for unrelated people chosen at random—but other findings have ranged as high as around .60. Both these bars, to the psychologists on the nurture side, indicate the strong influence of environment.

So the debate goes on and sometimes grows bitter, because it spills over into the issue of whether there are racial differences in IQ, as discussed in a box on Psychology and Society. But many psychologists—perhaps a substantial majority—have concluded that the argument is futile, as it is on most nature-nurture questions, and that there is no way of making a final judgment on whether heredity or environment, in their constant interaction, has the greater influence. One widely accepted suggestion is that the inherited genes probably set a top and bottom limit on an individual's possible IQ score—and the environment then determines where within this range the score will actually fall. Some believe that the range is around 20–25 points (Scarr-Salapatek, 1971)—in other words, that a more or less average person may wind up with an IQ of 85 if brought up in a deprived environment but 105 to 110 if brought up under ideal conditions. Some psychologists believe the range may be even greater, especially for individuals born with the possibility of superior intelligence (Gottesman, 1963).

Psychology and Society: Race and intelligence

One of the curious aspects of the nature-nurture debate is the vast amount of attention lavished in recent years on the question of possible racial differences in intelligence. Many dozens of scholarly articles have argued the question pro and con. Countless news stories have reported the newest scraps of evidence and the latest shifts in opinion, and countless editorials have commented with approval or outrage.

All this concern centers on the well-established fact that—on the average—blacks score 10 to 15 points lower on IQ tests than whites. The issue is why. Some psychologists and biologists have decided that in all probability there is an innate, genetically determined difference between the races (Jensen, 1969; Eysenck, 1981). Others have concluded that there is only a difference in the environment. Proponents of the two opposite views, nonscientists even more than scientists, have hailed each new finding that seemed to prove their case—or have attacked the finding as inconclusive, irrelevant, or both.

Almost ignored in the crossfire has been the majority opinion among psychologists, which is not nearly so newsworthy as the debate. Most psychologists believe there is really no way of deciding how much of the black-white difference in average scores can be explained by heredity and how much by environment (Loehlin, Lindzey, and Spuhler, 1975) or bias in the tests. It has been pointed out that we know so little about the complex ways cultural and environmental factors affect IQ that we can "say nothing about genetic differences" (Block and Dworkin, 1976) and can "make only wild speculations about racial groups" (Scarr-Salapatek, 1971).

To any of us as individuals, the argument is unimportant. Both blacks and whites show a wide and overlapping range of individual differences in IQ, and our own score is not affected by the average for the race or ethnic group to which we belong. As for the social significance of the argument, note this comment by Leon Kamin:

> There is no way of providing a definite answer to the question of black-white differences until and unless we are able to build a society in which blacks and whites are exposed to similarly favorable—and nondiscriminatory—environments. The irony is that if we succeed in building such a society, nobody will any longer be interested in answering the question (Kamin, 1981).

The effect of the interaction between heredity and environment on IQ has been compared to what happens when a mixture of seeds is planted in different kinds of soil (Lewontin, 1976). Since the seeds contain various combinations of genes, they attain a fairly wide range of differences in height under any growing conditions. When planted in ideal soil, as shown in Figure 6-11, they may vary from say 2 to 4 feet tall. But in poor soil they may grow only as high as about 1 to 3 feet. Looking at any single one of the plants, without full knowledge of the genes it inherited or the soil that provided its environment, how can anybody say why it is as tall or as short as it is?

How heredity and environment interact

We have no way of knowing how many genes play a part in helping determine an individual's IQ—or in what way these genes regulate the structure and dynamics of the human brain, the rest of the nervous system, and other traits that may also influence intelligence. Nor can we say for sure in what way and to what extent the influence of any or all of these genes can be enriched or stunted through interaction with the environment. One theory, of which Sandra Scarr of Yale is the chief

Figure 6-11 The analogy between IQ and plant growth *Like human IQs, the height of these plants shows a wide range of individual differences. Why? One reason is the genes they have inherited, which produce differences regardless of the growing conditions. Another is the environment, which makes the average height much larger for the plants grown in good soil than for the plants in poor soil.*

proponent, holds that many genetic traits play a part and that their interaction with the environment takes three important forms:

1. Parents who are themselves intelligent, and therefore likely to pass along to their offspring the genes associated with a high IQ, are also likely to provide a favorable environment. For example, "parents who read well and enjoy reading are likely to provide their children with books"—and in turn "their children are more likely to be skilled readers who enjoy the activity."
2. Children who have inherited favorable genes, for not only intelligence but appearance and personality, are more likely to evoke favorable responses from their environment: "Socially engaging, cheerful children get more social interaction than passive, sober children. In the intellectual arena, cooperative, attentive children receive more pleasant and instructional interactions from the adults around them than uncooperative, distractible children."
3. As children grow older, they take an active part in creating their own environments—and in choosing what aspects of the environment they will respond to and learn from. Again their inherited tendencies are related to their environment, and that environment in turn further encourages the tendencies (Scarr, 1981).

Thus children who grow up in advantaged homes tend to have what Scarr calls "a double dose of advantage"—a good genetic background plus a good environment. Children born into disadvantaged homes tend in general to have just the opposite—a less favorable genetic background plus an unfavorable environment.

Some environmental influences

One way environment affects IQ is reminiscent of the analogy of the seeds grown in barren soil. Poor nutrition, it has been shown, stunts the development of a child's nervous system as well as physical growth. In a study made in South Africa, undernourished children were found to have IQs that averaged 20 points lower than children who had received an adequate diet (Stock and Smythe, 1963).

An example of intellectual stimulation in the home—a factor that shows a high correlation with future IQ.

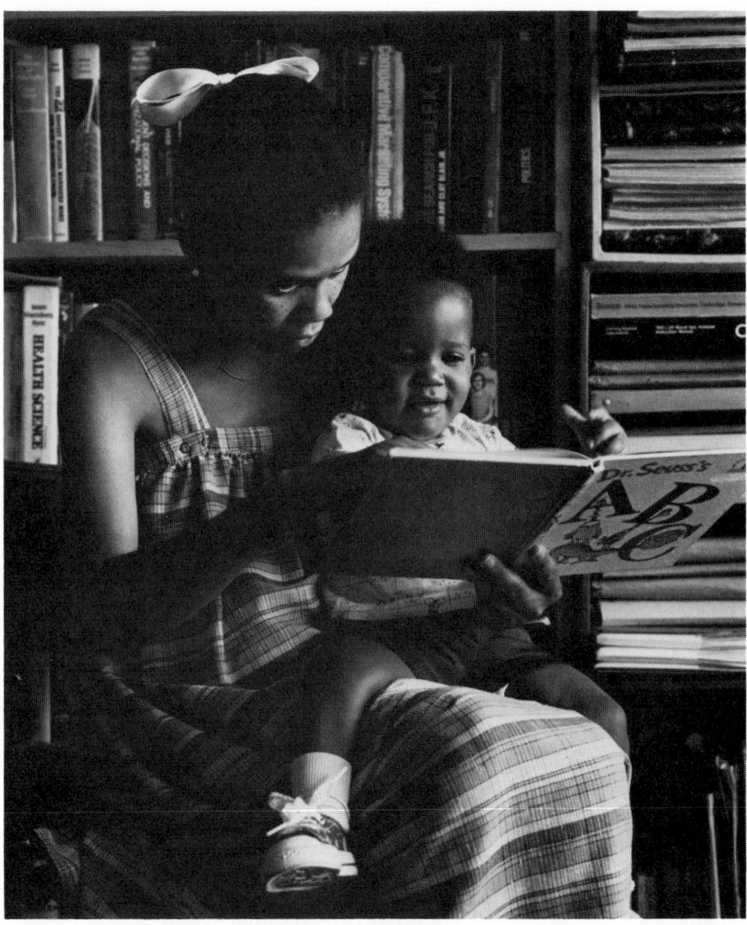

The psychological environment is also important. Indeed it plays a large part in the relation of IQ to social class and to the correlations of between .32 and .59 that have been reported between children's IQs and parents' educational level (Pearson, 1969). Middle-class mothers, it has been found, spend more time than lower-class mothers talking to their young children, playing with them, and encouraging them to learn and to solve problems on their own. A very high correlation of .76 has been found between children's IQ and parents' scores on a scale that measures how much encouragement and help they offer in using language and increasing vocabulary, how much motivation and reward they provide for intellectual accomplishment, and the opportunities for learning they provide in the home, including personal help, books and other forms of stimulation (Wolf, 1963).

The difference in average IQ between children born into lower-class homes and those born into middle-class and upper-class homes has been found to increase through early childhood (Bayley, 1970). On the other hand, children of lower-class parents, if adopted into families that are above average in education and income, wind up with higher IQs than might have been expected. A study made in France managed to compare a group of such adopted children with their blood brothers and sisters who remained in the original home with the parents. The adopted children had an average IQ of 111. Their brothers and sisters averaged only 95 (Schiff et al., 1978). Another study of black and interracial children adopted into above-average homes found that they had an average IQ of 106, considerably higher than would have been expected had they remained with their mothers (Scarr and Weinberg, 1976). The earlier the adoption takes place the better, indicating that the environment is important even during the earliest months of life—and perhaps especially so.

IQ and family size

Even the number of children in the family has been found to influence IQ, at least in part because the number is related to differences in environment and level of intellectual stimulation. A large-scale study made in the Netherlands showed that average IQ declines as the number of children goes up, and that this finding cannot be entirely explained by the fact that parents with above-average IQs tend to have fewer children than others. Indeed IQ was also found to depend on order of birth, with the average declining steadily from firstborn to last-born (Belmont and Marolla, 1973). The explanation seems to be that the older children in a large family enjoy more contact with and stimulation from the parents, while the younger ones spend more time in the company of other children.

On the basis of the Netherlands studies, it has been suggested that parents who want to provide their offspring with the best possible intellectual environment should have two children and no more (Zajonc and Markus, 1975). The spacing of the two children—whether they are born close together or several years apart—does not seem to matter (Belmont, Stein, and Zybert, 1978). Having an only child is dubious, for the Netherlands figures show that only children rank below other firstborns in average IQ. The reason may be that only children lack the mental stimulation that comes from interacting with and serving as teachers to others. The Netherlands study, incidentally, may offer a further explanation for the racial differences in IQ that were discussed in the box on Psychology and Society on page 222—for blacks have been much more likely than whites to grow up in large families.

How IQ sometimes leaps upward—or suffers a drastic decline

Many people think of IQ as remaining stable throughout life, like the temperature inside a building controlled by a thermostat that never lets the thermometer rise or fall more than a few degrees. In truth, however, children often show substantial changes in IQ over the years. They do so even when they continue to live in what seems to be an unchanging environment—that is, in the same home with the same parents and brothers and sisters, at the same level of social class.

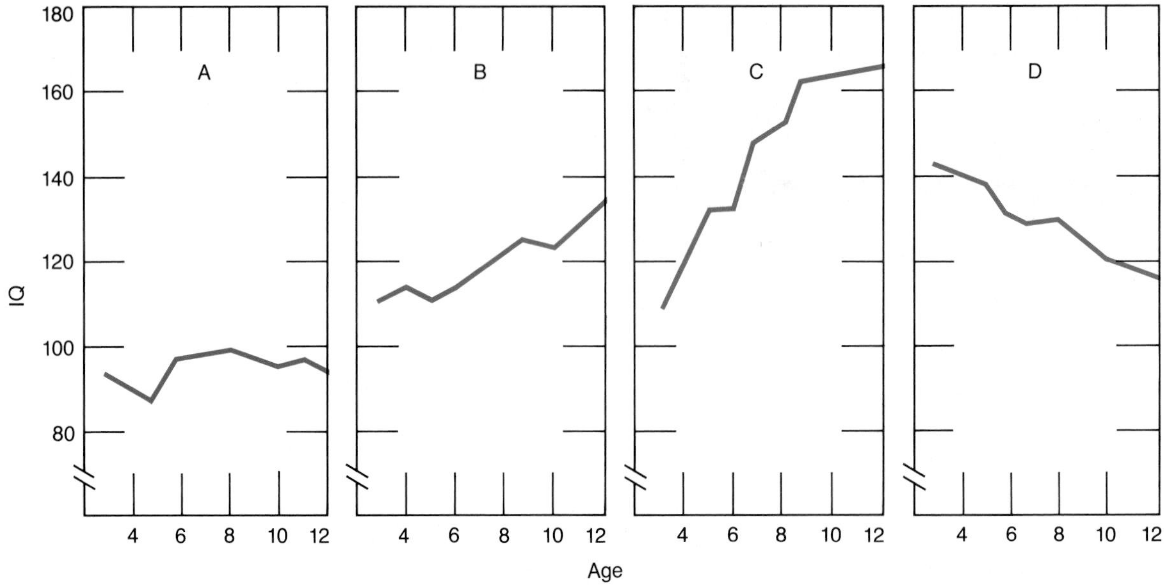

Figure 6-12 IQ from year to year: it may stay the same, rise, or fall *These graphs were obtained from annual tests of children's IQs as they grew up. About half the children showed nearly straight-line results as in* A, *with IQ remaining almost constant. Some showed substantial increases, such as the 20-point rise in* B. *A few showed very striking improvement, such as the 50-point rise in* C. *And some showed decreases of as much as 30 points, as in* D *(Sontag, Baker, and Nelson, 1958).*

This puzzling fact was demonstrated in a study in which the progress of 140 girls and boys was carefully followed over a 10-year period, from the time they were 2 years old until they were 12. Intelligence tests given every year indicated that about half the children showed just about the same IQ from one year to the next and indeed from the start of the 10-year period to the end. But for the other half there were changes upward or downward that in some cases reached striking proportions. In Figure 6-12, which illustrates some of the individual records from this study, note that one child's IQ rose from about 110 to 160, and another's dropped from about 140 to 110.

The study found some noteworthy personality differences between the children who showed increases and those who showed declines. The children whose IQ went up were more independent, competitive, and likely to take the lead in conversation. They showed strong motivation to master intellectual problems, worked harder in school, and persisted at even the most difficult tasks. These are personality traits that our society has encouraged in boys, while at the same time urging girls to be dependent and passive and not to seem smarter than their brothers. It is worthy of note that the study found boys more likely to show increases in IQ, girls more likely to show decreases.

A similar study of children between the ages of 2 and 18 also found striking changes in IQ, with over half the subjects varying by 15 or more points at some time during a 16-year period. The investigators noted that the subjects who showed the greatest changes up or down were those "whose life experiences had also fluctuated between disturbing and satisfying periods," indicating that health and emotional adjustment help account for the shifts. One girl, for example, showed a sharp decline at a time when she was suffering from asthma and poor vision and her family was undergoing considerable strain and economic hardship (Honzik, Macfarlane, and Allen, 1948).

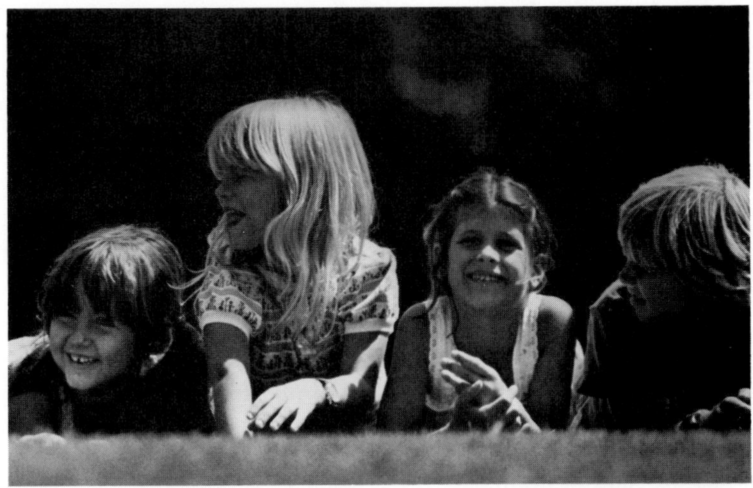

Some of the "socially engaging, cheerful children" who Scarr says get more social and intellectual interaction than others.

The moral for parents and teachers

The studies certainly indicate that the IQ is by no means a constant and unchanging trait like a person's fingerprints—and that a score made on any given day is by no means an unerring guide to the future. They constitute a warning to parents and teachers not to take the results of an intelligence test too seriously by giving up on a child who has made a low score or expecting too much from a child who has made a high score.

The studies also provide further evidence that IQ scores depend on motivation and adjustment as well as on cognitive skills. It seems that children are most likely to gain in IQ over the years if the parents provide a stable emotional climate, serve as models of intellectual achievement, and emphasize and reward intellectual accomplishment and independence. Teachers and schools striving toward Binet's goal of improving intelligence are most likely to succeed if they consider the child's personality as well as IQ. Especially in the case of low-scoring children, "interventions that address the motivational and adjustment aspects of learning may well be more effective than those that primarily address the cognitive lags" (Scarr, 1981).

For those of us past the age of childhood who are thinking of our own performance, the studies raise an interesting question: Does the influence of motivation on IQ mean that we can improve our IQ through a deliberate effort toward better achievement? The answer is not known. But certainly some college students who make poor grades as freshmen suddenly begin making much better grades later. It may be that retesting of these students would show an increase in IQ.

Intelligence, age, creativity, and the brain versus the computer

Much of psychology's study of intelligence has been devoted to the topics discussed thus far in the chapter—the attempt to describe it, chart its development through childhood, measure it, and examine the way it is influenced by heredity and environment. But the search has also taken many other approaches. Among the important and interesting questions that psychology has tackled are these: After the childhood years in which intelligence grows so rapidly, what happens as people move into adulthood and old age? What is the relationship, if any between intelligence and that rare talent called creativity—which has produced such remarkable accomplishments as breakthroughs in scientific knowledge, inventions like the airplane and television, and great works of art, music, and literature? What can today's computer science tell us about the workings of the human brain—and is it possible that the computer will someday perform so intelligently that the brain may become obsolete? What has been learned in these areas will make up this final section of the chapter.

What age does to the IQ

Older people frequently complain that they can no longer think as well or as fast as they once could. Their memory, they add, has begun to play tricks on them. They can recall events of years ago as vividly as ever—but have trouble remembering what happened yesterday. They are partly right. Studies have shown that some forms of mental agility—for example, thinking quickly of as many words as possible that begin with the letter *K*—begin to show a steep decline beginning as early as the age of 30 (Schaie and Strother, 1968). So does skill at tasks requiring close coordination between the eye and the hand (Baltes and Schaie, 1974)—like playing video games. But many of the popular beliefs about the effects of age on intelligence are false. Older people do not in fact remember long-ago events better than recent ones (Warrington and Sanders, 1971). They just think they do, because they have talked or thought about the old events on so many occasions. Many of their mental skills are just about as sharp or even sharper than in the past. On tests of vocabulary, for example, it has been found that people as old as 85 do just as well as younger people (Blum, Jarvik, and Clark, 1970).

Keeping mentally active—like Maggie Kuhn, founder of the Gray Panthers, here delivering an impassioned speech—helps maintain mental skills into old age.

In one important long-term study, nearly 100 men were tested as they moved from their late teens into their 60s. They began by taking a group intelligence test when they were college freshmen, with an average age of 19. They took a similar test when they were 50 and finally when they were 61. The results of the three tests are shown in Figure 6-13.

Scores on the arithmetic items in the test were highest at age 19 and went down steadily thereafter. Scores on items measuring reasoning ability, on the contrary, rose steadily and were highest at 61. Scores on items measuring verbal ability were substantially higher at 50 than at 19 but then declined slightly at 61. The total score rose markedly from 19 to 50 and afterward showed only a slight decline.

The subjects were all chosen from the college population and therefore doubtless had above-average IQs to begin with. Presumably they also led lives more favorable than average to continued intellectual stimulation and growth as they got older—and keeping mentally active appears to be important in maintaining cognitive skills throughout

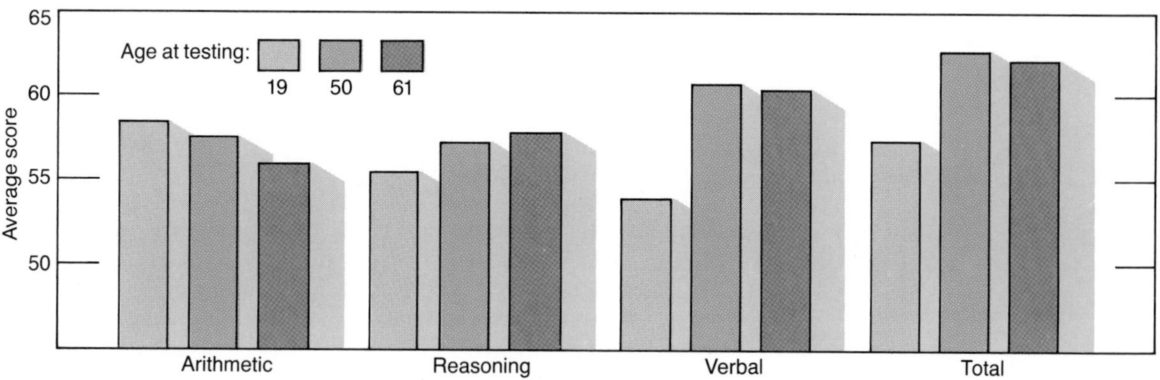

Figure 6-13 At what age are we smartest? *The bars show the raw scores (not IQ) for three of the skills measured by intelligence tests, as well as the total score, made by a group of college men as they grew older (Owens, 1966).*

adult life. Their histories seem to indicate that intelligence is by no means the monopoly of the young—and that there is no reason to despair, especially for those of us who have been to college, over what will happen to our mental abilities as we get older.

IQ and creativity

Since about 1 percent of subjects who take the Stanford-Binet test show IQs of 140 or more, as was shown in Figure 6-5 (p. 211), there are more than two million people in the United States who qualify as what are popularly known as "geniuses." They are capable of extraordinary feats of mental skill—but obviously not many of them will ever display the kind of outstanding originality that we associate with creative genius as displayed by a Shakespeare, Michelangelo, Beethoven, Einstein, or Edison. True creativity is extremely rare, and its relation to intelligence uncertain.

Having superior intelligence definitely "does not guarantee creativity" (MacKinnon, 1962). Indeed in some fields, for example painting and sculpture, there appears to be very little if any correlation between IQ and creative ability (Barron, 1968). Most fields seem to require what has been called a "threshold" IQ, higher in the sciences than in literature or music. Above that minimum requirement creativity depends less on intelligence than on other factors (Crockenburg, 1972).

A clue to the other factors comes from studies showing that creative people tend to have a number of traits in common that are not shared by most other people. Generally speaking, they were lone wolves in childhood. They either were spurned and rejected by other children or sought solitude themselves. If being different from other children caused them anxiety, they eventually overcame it. They grew up with no need to conform to the people and the ways of life around them. In fact creative people *want* to be different and original and to produce new things. They are not afraid of having irrational or bizarre thoughts, are willing to examine even the most foolish-seeming ideas, and are not worried about success or failure. Many of them are aggressive and hostile, not at all the kind of people who win popularity contests (MacKinnon, 1962).

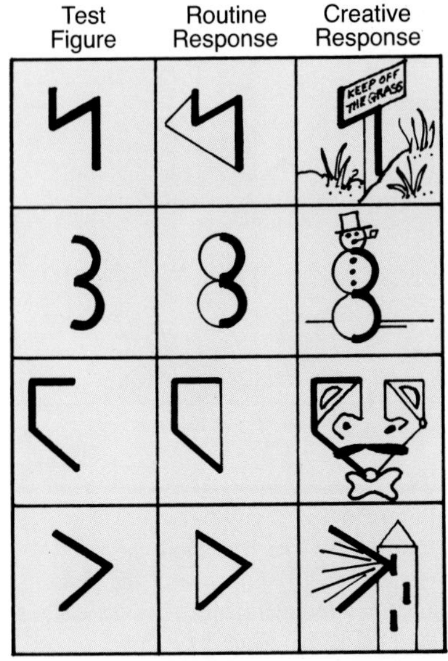

Figure 6-14 A test of creativity *Subjects are asked to start with the simple lines in the left-hand column and turn them into any kind of drawing the lines suggest. Most subjects produce the kinds of drawings shown in the middle column. Very creative people come up with imaginative elaborations like those in the right-hand column (Barron, 1958).*

Tests of creativity

Many attempts have been made to devise tests that will spot creative people so that they may receive special treatment to encourage their talents. One such test is illustrated in Figure 6-14. Other tests ask subjects to think up as many uses as possible for objects such as a brick or paper clip (Guilford, 1954), or ways to improve familiar objects like writing instruments, carpenters' tools, and children's toys (Torrance, 1966).

If potentially creative people could be spotted early and protected from pressures toward conformity—particularly in the elementary school classroom—perhaps more of them would actually flourish. But there are many difficulties in the testing and encouragement of creativity. For one thing, true creativity requires more than mere originality. Sheer novelty—or what might be called "offbeat" thinking—is not enough. Besides being new and unusual, a creative idea must also be *appropriate.* A new scientific theory must be in accord with the known facts. When we look at a painting or hear music we must have some perception of aptness, of a disciplined relationship to the world as we know it, if we are to consider the work of art esthetically pleasing and thus genuinely creative.

"Artificial intelligence"—the computer's electronic brain

A new approach to the study of human intelligence—and even of human creativity—is based on the way computers have managed to perform many of the accomplishments once believed to be the sole prerogative of the human brain. These electronic machines, with circuits programed to provide what is called *artificial intelligence,* can perform many tasks of great complexity. In the business world, they make out payrolls, write checks, keep track of immense inventories, and in some cases operate manufacturing plants with very little human help. In the medical field, they analyze a patient's symptoms and make a creditable diagnosis. They guide space ships to Mars and Venus and pilot the space shuttle back to a perfect landing. Along lighter lines, they play creditable games of checkers and chess—well enough, indeed, to beat most of us run-of-the-mill human players.

There seem to be a number of similarities between artificial intelligence and human intelligence. When one of today's sophisticated computers is presented with a problem to solve, it does many of the things a human being would do. It analyzes the problem and calls on the information stored in its memory bank to provide an appropriate solution. Indeed the first computer experts began by studying the way people report they approach a problem, then designing a program to guide the electronic brain through similar steps. Thus the way people think has contributed to the development of more intelligent computers, and in turn computer science has "contributed valuable hypotheses to cognitive psychology about human thought processes" (Simon, 1982).

Many psychologists look to the computer for further light or thinking and intelligence, and many computer scientists regar selves as psychologists. But just how much real resemblance between human and artificial intelligence is still an open questi circuits of the computer are very different from the pathways the multiple synapses of the brain. The electronic impulse through the computer at the speed of light travel at least three times faster than nervous impulses. Many of today's comput example, those that play the best game of chess—are designed take advantage of that speed than to "think" like a human pl

George Miller of Princeton, who devoted several years of st search for what computers can tell us about human thinking psychologist who has concluded that the resemblances are nc pursuing: "How computers work seems to have no real relevanc the mind works, any more than a wheel shows how peopl (Miller, 1983). It may be that the computer will eventually b with other machines that duplicate human behavior—but in a bearing no similarity to the way we ourselves perform the acts. (pitching machine used by baseball teams, which delivers every possible kind of pitch without in any way duplicating the muscle movements of a human player's back, shoulders, arms, and hands.) Even so—and many psychologists remain more hopeful—computers already serve as valuable assistants to human thinking.

SUMMARY

Theories of the nature of intelligence

1. Intelligence is the *capacity to understand the world and the resourcefulness to cope with its challenges*—or, in terms of cognitive psychology, *skill at information processing.*
2. One theory is that intelligence is composed of a pervasive mental ability called the *g factor,* for *general intelligence,* plus a number of *s factors,* or specific kinds of skill at a particular task.
3. Thurstone suggested that the specific skills are for verbal comprehension, word fluency, number, space, associative memory, perceptual speed, and general reasoning—which he called the seven *primary mental abilities.*
4. Guilford believes that intelligence is made up of no less than 120 different kinds of ability and that a person may rank high in some of them but low in others.
5. Both the Thurstone and the Guilford theories suggest that two people with the same intelligence may perform differently at different kinds of tasks—and that success and happiness on a job depend largely on choosing work that suits your own particular strengths and weaknesses.
6. Piaget, whose studies of intellectual development in children made him a major figure in the rise of the cognitive school, concluded that intellectual growth is basically an increased ability to adapt to new situations. The key processes in development, he found, are

assimilation (incorporating a new stimulus into one's existing cognitive view of the world) and *accommodation* (changing one's cognitive view and behavior when new information dictates such a change).

7. A key word in Piaget's theory is *operation*—meaning a sort of dynamic mental rule for manipulating objects or ideas into new forms and back to the original—like the rule that four pieces of candy (or the figure 4) can be divided into two parts of two each, then restored to the original four.
8. Piaget charted children's intellectual development through four stages: (a) the *sensorimotor stage,* birth to 18 months, in which they know the world only through their sensory impressions and the results of their motor (or muscular) movements: (b) the *preoperational stage,* 18 months to about 7 years, in which they have acquired language and can manipulate symbols, but do not yet grasp the dynamic rules of operation; (c) the *stage of concrete operations,* 3 to 7, when they can apply operational rules to objects they can see or feel; and (d) the *stage of formal operations,* beginning about 12, when they can apply operational rules and logical reasoning to abstract ideas and possibilities.

Intelligence tests: what they do and don't do

9. *Intelligence tests* provide a measure of *intelligence quotient,* or *IQ.* The intelligence quotient gets its name from the fact that it was originally determined by comparing a child's *mental age* (as shown by the ability to pass test items that can be passed by the average child of various ages) with *chronological age* (or actual age).
10. The average IQ is 100, and almost half of all people score between 90 and 109.
11. An *individual test* is given by a trained examiner to one person at a time. Two widely used individual intelligence tests are the *Stanford-Binet Intelligence Scale* and the *Wechsler Adult Intelligence Scale.*
12. A *group test* of intelligence can be given to many people at the same time. One well-known example is the *Scholastic Aptitude Tests* (SAT).
13. Intelligence tests are *aptitude tests,* which measure ability to learn a new skill or perform an unfamiliar task. In theory, aptitude tests are different from *achievement tests,* which measure how much skill or learning a person has actually acquired. However, it is usually impossible to measure ability without any regard for past achievement—and "all tests reflect what a person has learned."
14. Scores on intelligence tests also depend on motivation, adjustment, and other personality factors.
15. Thus intelligence tests are biased to some extent in favor of people who have acquired the knowledge, language skills, and motivation typical of the middle and upper-middle classes. Such children make higher average scores than children from lower-class homes. City children make higher scores than rural children. Blacks and members of other ethnic cultures make lower average scores.

16. Although the tests cannot hope to measure sheer, disembodied skill at information processing, they are good predictors of success in school. Studies have found correlations of .40 to .60 or even higher between IQ and grades in classes from the elementary through the college level.
17. Psychologists disagree about the extent to which IQ is related to occupation and success in general. Any correlation may depend on the fact that a certain minimum IQ is required to complete high school and college and to perform successfully in some of the more demanding occupations.

IQ and the nature-nurture question

18. Psychologists agree that intelligence is clearly influenced by both heredity and environment. But some believe that heredity is twice as important as environment, others that environment is more important.
19. One widely accepted suggestion is that inherited genes probably set a top and bottom limit on an individual's potential IQ score—and that environment then determines where within this range the score will actually fall. The possible difference between growing up in a deprived environment and an ideal environment has been estimated at around 20–25 points—and perhaps even greater for individuals born with the possibility of superior intelligence.
20. Scarr has suggested that many genetic traits play a part and that their interaction with the environment takes three forms: (a) parents likely to pass along favorable genes are also likely to provide a favorable environment; (b) children with favorable genes for intelligence, appearance, and personality are likely to evoke more favorable responses from the people around them; and (c) as children get older, they play an active part in creating their own environments.
21. Even when brought up in what seems to be an unchanging environment (same home, parents, and social class), children sometimes show changes in IQ over the years ranging as high as 50 points up or down. The shifts may be related to motivation and other personality factors, health, and emotional adjustment.

Intelligence, age, creativity, and the brain versus the computer

22. Studies indicate that some mental skills (especially speed at manipulating letters and numbers and eye-hand coordination) decline as early as the age of 30. But skill at reasoning increases at least into the 60s, and use of vocabulary is as good at 85 as earlier.
23. *Creativity* is extremely rare, even among people with superior IQs. Besides intelligence, it seems to depend on personality factors—for example, a disdain for conformity and success, a willingness to examine even the most foolish-seeming ideas, and a desire to be "different" and original.
24. Computer science, which has created electronic machines that perform many feats associated with the human brain, has created

a new approach to the study of intelligence. Many psychologists expect the *artificial intelligence* of the machine to shed new light on human thinking. But some have decided that there are so many differences between machine and brain that "how computers work seems to have no real relevance to how the mind works."

IMPORTANT TERMS

accommodation
achievement test
aptitude test
artificial intelligence
assimilation
chronological age
(stage of) concrete operations
conservation
creativity
(stage of) formal operations
g factor
individual test
intelligence
intelligence test
IQ
mental age
operational rules
preoperational stage
primary mental abilities
sensorimotor stage
s factor

SUPPLEMENT:

The Science of Test Construction

Informal tests of human characteristics go back to the beginnings of history. Mythology and literature are full of stories about young men who had to slay a dragon to prove they were brave enough to deserve the hand of the princess—or people who had to answer riddles posed by wise men to prove that they were intelligent enough to become rulers. The ancient Chinese used tests to select people for governmental posts. The ancient Greeks made selections on the basis of tests they developed for both physical and mental skills (Doyle, 1974).

Until very recently, however, tests were based largely on guesswork, and the results doubtless left a great deal to be desired. (Slaying a dragon does not necessarily make a man a good husband. Nor does answering a riddle necessarily indicate leadership ability.) Even today, a great many of the tests in newspapers and magazines have dubious value. If you want to take one of these popular tests for the fun of it, fine. But you cannot take seriously the claim that such tests will show how good a spouse or parent you are likely to be, or whether you are suffering from depression or in danger of becoming an alcoholic, or any of the other things they claim to tell you about yourself.

Constructing a test that will actually do a good job of measuring what it is supposed to measure is a science in itself—a difficult job to which many psychologists have devoted many years of study. The difficulties can best be explained by discussing the four strict requirements that a test must meet to qualify as scientifically sound.

Requirement 1: objectivity

A satisfactory test should be *objective*—that is, it should provide results that are not affected by the personal opinions or prejudices of the person who gives and grades it. The first intelligence test, as was mentioned earlier, was an attempt to obtain a more objective measure of a child's ability to profit from classes in school than could be provided by the opinion of the teacher, which might be colored by the child's personality, behavior in class, or family's position in the community.

Insofar as is possible, psychological tests are designed so that any qualified person can present them to the subject in the same manner and under the same testing conditions. A uniform method is provided for scoring the results. Thus the person taking the test should get the same score regardless of who administers and scores it.

Requirement 2: reliability

To show why a test must also be *reliable,* an analogy can be drawn between a test and an oven thermometer. If the thermometer is reliable—that is, if it gives the same reading every time for the same amount of heat—the cook can count on roasts and pies to come out of the oven in perfect shape. On the other hand, if the thermometer is damaged and unreliable, it may give a reading of 300 degrees on one occasion and 400 degrees on the next, even though the actual temperature is exactly the same. In this case the food is likely to be somewhat disappointing.

Just as a good thermometer must produce consistent temperature readings, a good test must produce consistent scores. One way of determining the reliability of a test is to compare the same person's score on all the odd-numbered items with the score on all the even-numbered items; these two scores should be similar. Or two versions of the test can be constructed and given to the same person on two different occasions. Again, the scores should be similar.

Requirement 3: validity

The most important requirement of all is *validity*. That is, a test must actually measure what it is intended to measure. There are a number of ways to determine this. Common sense is one of them; the items in the test must bear a meaningful relationship to the characteristic being measured. (The thought of trying to assess musical ability by asking questions on the rules of football does not make sense and must be rejected.) But common sense is not always enough. It would seem perfectly logical, for example, to assume that tests of finger dexterity would measure aptitude for dentistry—yet one scientific study found that finger dexterity actually shows a negative correlation with the income of dentists (Elton and Shevel, 1969).

A better way is to observe the behavior of people who have taken the test and determine whether they behave as their test scores predicted. Thus the validity of intelligence tests, as measures of academic ability, has been shown by the high correlations between IQ and school grades. A test of aptitude for dentistry could be proved valid or invalid by following the careers of people who took it—or, to save time, by determining the test scores of dentists who are already practicing and whose abilities and performance are already known.

Requirement 4: standardization

The final requirement of scientific testing can best be explained by imagining this situation: A psychologist has drawn up a 100-question test that can be given and scored objectively. It has proved reliable, and it seems to be a reasonable and valid measure of aptitude for working with computers. Another psychologist decides to use the test and gives it to a college student, who answers 60 of the items correctly. What does this score of 60 tell the psychologist? By itself, not very much. The psychologist cannot know, after giving the test to a single person, whether a score of 60 indicates exceptional aptitude, very low aptitude, or something in between.

As this example indicates, the results of a test are generally not very useful unless they can be compared with the scores of other people. Thus most tests, before they are considered ready for use, are themselves tested by administering them to a large and representative sample of the population. Records are kept of how many people score at all the possible levels from highest to lowest. This process, called *standardization,* makes it possible to determine whether the score made by an individual is average, low, or high. Indeed the individual's ranking can be pinpointed precisely. We can say that the score falls (let us say) on the 71st *percentile*—that is, the individual has done better than 71 percent of all people, while 29 percent of all people make the same or a higher score.

All the accepted intelligence tests have been standardized on large samples of the population. They meet the requirements of objectivity and reliability and have proved valid for predicting academic success (although, as you have seen, their validity for doing anything else is in question). Many other kinds of tests, devised for special purposes, have also been constructed with the greatest possible regard for scientific accuracy.

Vocational aptitude tests

Some tests attempt to measure specific talents that would be useful at specific kinds of jobs. These are called *vocational aptitude tests* and are widely used in counseling people on choice of career.

Tests have been developed for all kinds of special skills, among them musical ability, dealing with details as required in clerical jobs, manual dexterity, and the motor coordination required to operate complicated machinery. These tests are often used by industry in selecting job applicants and by the military services in assigning people to specific tasks such as radio operator or astronaut.

Some vocational aptitude tests attempt to measure several different skills and arrive at a sort of aptitude profile that shows where the test taker is strongest and weakest. One such test measures skill at spelling and grammar, dealing with numbers, clerical speed and accuracy, mechanical problems, and several types of thinking and reasoning. Those taking the test can be advised that they will probably do best in a job requiring the skills for which they score highest.

Interest tests

Also used in vocational guidance are *interest tests*—which attempt to measure how the subject feels about various activities. The tests try to establish whether the subject is interested in or bored by such activities as literature, music, the outdoors, mechanical equipment, art, science, social affairs, and all kinds of specific activities ranging from butterfly collecting to repairing a clock or making a speech. Tests of this type provide an indication of the sort of work in which subjects are likely to be happiest.

Personality tests

A great deal of time, energy, and ingenuity has gone into the creation of *personality tests,* which are potentially the most valuable of all. A test that could accurately distinguish between normal and neurotic personalities would enable clinical psychologists to find the people most in need of psychotherapy and perhaps lead to the discovery of new methods of treatment. It would make comparisons possible among people who have grown up in different environments and with different experiences and thus greatly add to the knowledge of child development. By spotting certain kinds of disturbed personalities, it could conceivably prevent such tragedies as assassination attempts.

Personality tests will be discussed in detail in Chapter 13. Suffice it to say here that they present as many difficulties as opportunities. Indeed few psychological tests at present are entirely satisfactory. Tests of vocational aptitudes and interests, for example, usually show a much lower correlation with actual success on a job than intelligence tests show with school achievement. Nonetheless the tests often offer valuable clues about an individual's personality, patterns of skills, and preferences for certain activities. They are often a helpful guide to clinical psychologists and vocational counselors.

SUMMARY OF SUPPLEMENT

1. To qualify as scientifically sound a test should be
   a. *Objective*—meaning that the subject will receive the same score regardless of who administers and scores the test.
   b. *Reliable*—yielding similar scores when the same person is tested on different occasions.
   c. *Valid*—actually measuring what it is supposed to measure.
   d. *Standardized*—pretested on a large and representative sample so that an individual's score can be interpreted by comparison with the scores of other people.
2. *Vocational aptitude tests* measure ability to perform the special tasks required in specific jobs.
3. *Interest tests* measure how much an individual likes or dislikes various activities—thus providing a clue to what sort of job might be most congenial.
4. *Personality tests* attempt to measure all the many traits that make up personality and to distinguish between normal and neurotic patterns.

IMPORTANT TERMS

interest test
objective
personality test
reliable
standardized
valid
vocational aptitude test

RECOMMENDED READINGS

Anastasi, A. *Psychological testing,* 4th ed. New York: Macmillan, 1976

Block, N. J., and Dworkin, G., eds. *The IQ controversy.* New York: Pantheon, 1976.

Buros, O. K., ed. *The mental measurements yearbook.* Highland Park, N.J.: Gryphon, published annually.

Cronbach, L. J. *Essentials of psychological testing,* 3d ed. New York: Harper & Row, 1970.

Eysenck, H. J., and Kamin, L. *The intelligence controversy.* New York: Wiley, 1981.

Loehlin, J. C., Lindzey, G., and Spuhler, J. N. *Race differences in intelligence.* San Francisco: Freeman, 1975.

Matarazzo, J. D., and Wechsler, D. *Wechsler's measurement and appraisal of adult intelligence,* 5th ed. New York: Oxford University Press, 1972.

Samuda, R. J. *Psychological testing of American minorities: issues and consequences.* New York: Dodd, Mead, 1975.

Sattler, J. M. *The assessment of children's intelligence.* Philadelphia: Saunders, 1974.

Terman, L. M., and Oden, M. H. *The gifted child grows up.* Stanford: Stanford University Press, 1974.

PART

4

Knowing About the World: The Senses and Perception

Out there in our world—beyond the envelope of skin that encases the human body—lies a wealth of information essential to our survival. We have to keep constantly aware of what exists in our environment just to move around without bumping into its objects or falling into its pits. We need to know about the presence of food and shelter and danger—and, in order to function in our kind of society, something of the great body of knowledge that humanity has accumulated over the ages and stored in its libraries.

All around us, the world is aflicker and abuzz with information. Within us is the marvelous information-processing equipment provided by the human brain, with its ability to learn, remember, manipulate language, and think. In our daily lives we experience such an effortless interaction between the sights and sounds of the environment and our inner psychological processes that we take it for granted. We seem to know just naturally what our world is like, and we deal with it confidently. But suppose there was no way for the outside information to penetrate that sheath of skin?

The answer is suggested by the famous case of Helen Keller, left blind and deaf by a childhood illness that struck before she had time to become aware of what goes on in the environment. In the years after her illness she lived in a dark and silent void. She could not communicate with other people, nor they with her. No information could penetrate, and she had no way of imagining how to cope with a world she did not even know was there. She was unable to feed or dress herself or behave in any other way like a human being.

Then a miracle occurred. When she was

6, Keller came under the care of a remarkable teacher named Anne Sullivan. Slowly and painfully, Keller began using her sense of touch—through signals pressed into the palm of her hand—to acquire the awareness of the environment ordinarily gained through eyes and ears. Once the information got in, she proved capable of processing it with great skill. She soon learned to use language—and eventually she became a *cum laude* college graduate, linguist, and author.

There has never been more dramatic evidence of the importance of the human senses. Without the input they provide, all the rest of our psychological capabilities would be useless. We would have nothing to learn or remember. We could never use language—and, even if we could, we would have nothing to talk or think about. Therefore the way the senses operate to inform us about the world, which is the topic of Chapter 7, has always been one of psychology's prime interests. Of equal concern has been the kindred matter of perception, or the way the nervous system organizes and interprets the raw evidence received from the senses, which is discussed in Chapter 8.

As you will see, the senses enable you to be aware of the world's sights, sounds, flavors, odors, and textures. Perception gives meaning to what you see, hear, taste, smell, and feel—to know immediately, for example, that the combination of whiteness with black lines and squiggles that you see at this moment is a page of a book. Together, the senses and perception tell you what exists in the environment and what it is doing, so that you can then use your other psychological strengths to act accordingly—utilizing your brain's "beautiful relationships" and ability to learn and remember.

CHAPTER 7

How the senses operate 244
The sensory thresholds
Sensory adaptation
The secret code of the sense organs
The pattern theory of the senses

Taste, smell, touch, and the two forgotten senses 246
Taste
Smell
The skin senses
The two forgotten senses: bodily movement and equilibrium

Sound waves and hearing 252
The physical nature of sound
The hearing receptors
How the hearing receptors work
Loudness and hearing damage
How do you know where the sound comes from?

Light waves and vision 258
The physical nature of light waves
The structure of the eye
The visual receptors
Color vision
Vision in bright sunlight and in a dark theater

Summary 263

Important terms 265

Supplement: Retinal coding, visual sharpness, and color mixing 266
Visual sensitivity and acuity
Adding and subtracting colors
Color blindness
Afterimages
Two famous old theories—and how well they have survived

Summary of supplement 270

Important terms 271

Recommended readings 271

Psychology and society
Noise pollution, deafness, high blood pressure, and ulcers 257

The Senses: Our Source of Information

In their own way, the information-gathering structures of the nervous system are as remarkable as the brain itself. All our awareness of the world's colors, shapes, and movements comes to us by way of just two little patches of nerve tissue inside the eyeballs. Each is only about the size of a quarter, yet they manage to inform us about an entire landscape and to distinguish about 350,000 different gradations of hue and brightness. All our awareness of the world's sounds comes to us through just two little harp-shaped collections of neurons buried in the inner part of the ear—which are versatile enough to inform us about everything from the merest rustle of a leaf to the loudest thunderclap, and from the deepest rumble of a foghorn to the highest tweet of a piccolo.

Our eyes are so sensitive that on a clear, black night they can spot a candle flame more than 30 miles away. Our noses can detect a single drop of perfume wafted through the air in a three-room apartment. Our skin senses can feel an object as small and fragile as the wing of a bee dropped gently on our cheek (McBurney and Collings, 1977). All through our waking hours—and to some extent while we sleep—these efficient input devices pick up a constant flow of information of all kinds.

True, we are not as superior to lower animals in sensory sensitivity as in brain power. In fact many creatures excel us. Hawks have better distance vision. Bees and other insects can detect ultraviolet light that we cannot see at all (the reason we sometimes get painfully sunburned on what looks like a hazy and harmless day). Bats have such a wide range of hearing that they use it as a sort of sonar system to guide them in the dark—sending out very high-pitched little noises, undetectable by the human ear, and then listening for the sounds to bounce back from objects around them. Bloodhounds and airport police dogs that can sniff out a bag of marijuana hidden in a suitcase have a far keener sense of smell than ours. Minnows, with taste organs all over their bodies, have a far sharper sense of taste.

Yet our senses are fully capable of bringing us all the information about the outer world that we need, and our information-processing abilities have enabled us to add greatly to their powers. Radio extends our range of hearing to the conversation of astronauts walking on the moon. Television enables us to see what is happening on the other side of the world. With X-ray equipment scientists can peer into the human body, and with microscopes into the structure of a human cell.

How the senses operate

All our sense organs, though they vary greatly in the sensations they produce, operate on the same basic principles. They have to be activated by a *stimulus*—some form of meaningful energy impinging on them. They must also have a *receptor* sensitive to that particular kind of stimulus. At the moment, the stimulus is the light waves reflecting off your book. The receptors are the light-sensitive cells in your eyes. You cannot see the book in a totally blackened room because there are no light waves, nor through your ears or fingertips because they have no receptors for light.

When receptor cells are activated by a stimulus, they set off bursts of nervous impulses. After being routed through various switching points, the receptors' messages reach the sensory areas of the cerebral cortex, where they are translated into our conscious sensations of vision, hearing, and the rest. Our brain never actually encounters light or sound. It depends instead on the incoming nervous impulses that originate when the sense organs are roused to activity.

The sensory thresholds

One principle that holds for all the senses is that they are activated only by a stimulus that is at or above their *absolute threshold,* or the minimum amount of stimulus energy to which their receptors can respond. Any weaker stimulus has no effect and therefore goes unnoticed. When a physician tests your hearing by noting how far you can follow the ticking of a watch, he is making a rough estimate of your absolute threshold of hearing. In scientific studies of the relationship between stimuli and sensations, more precise measurements are used. These show that stimuli of borderline strength are sometimes detected and sometimes missed. The absolute threshold is defined as the exact level at which a subject can detect the stimulus 50 percent of the time.

The senses also have a threshold for the ability to discriminate between two stimuli that are similar in strength but not exactly alike. For example, suppose you see a flash of light, followed immediately by a different flash. How much greater intensity would the second light require before you could notice a difference? The answer, it has been found, is 1.6 percent. This is the *difference threshold* for light, also known as the *just noticeable difference,* or j.n.d. For sound the difference threshold is 10 percent.

The rule that the difference threshold is a fixed percentage of the original stimulus is called *Weber's law,* in honor of the physiologist who discovered it more than a century ago. The law does not apply at very low intensities or at very high intensities, but it holds generally over a large part of the range of stimulation. In practical terms, it means this: The more intense the sensory stimulation to which the human organism is being subjected, the greater the increase in intensity required to produce a recognizable difference. In a room where there is no sound except the soft buzz of a mosquito, you can hear a pin drop. On a noisy city street you can hear the loud honk of an automobile horn but may be completely unaware of a friend shouting to you from down the block.

Sensory adaptation

When you undress, you sometimes notice marks on your skin caused by a wristwatch, belt, or elastic band in your clothing. Surely those areas of skin have been subjected all day to a considerable amount of pressure. Why did you not feel it?

The answer lies in the principle of *sensory adaptation,* which means that after a time our senses adjust to a stimulus—they get used to it, so to speak—and the sensation produced by the stimulus tends to disappear. If you hold salt water or a bitter fluid in your mouth, the taste goes away. The strong smell that greets you in a fish market soon seems to disappear. Your eyes may strike you as an exception, because your vision never goes blank no matter how long you stare at an object, but this is only because the eyes are never really still. The muscles controlling the eyeballs constantly produce spontaneous, pendulum-like motions at the rate of as many as 100 a minute, which means that light rays never keep stimulating the same receptor cells for very long. By attaching a miniature slide projector to the eyeball, casting a continuing image on the same receptor cells despite any movements, it has been found that the image quickly fades from sight (Pritchard, 1961).

The way sensory adaptation occurs is not completely understood. In some cases, notably the skin, it is known that the receptors themselves tend to stop responding. In other cases, the adaptation appears to occur somewhere farther along in the nerve pathways that carry sensory messages, perhaps even in the brain itself. Whatever the explanation, all the senses demonstrate adaptation in one way or another—though a new stimulus will produce an immediate new response. In practical terms, the principle of adaptation means that our sensory equipment is best equipped to inform us of changes in our environment—exactly the kind of information that is generally most valuable.

The secret code of the sense organs

The manner in which the sense organs send their information to the brain—and the way the sensory areas of the cortex manage to understand the messages and translate them into our conscious sensations—is another of the marvels of the nervous system. When a receptor cell is stimulated, all it can do is set off bursts of nervous impulses. These impulses are all of equal strength. They vary only in number and in the pattern of firing, close together in rapid succession or farther apart.

On their way to the brain the messages from the sensory receptors pass through a number of synapses—switching points at which the messages are often combined and processed into a kind of code. Each eye, for example, has about 127 million receptor cells. Right inside the eyeball, these receptors funnel their impulses into a mere one million neurons that make up the optic nerve that carries information toward the brain. Thus, on the average, the neurons of the optic nerve monitor the activity in well over 100 receptors and respond with their own impulses, which condense and summarize the information they have received. These messages are again processed and refined farther along the line, until finally they reach the cerebral cortex in a kind of coded shorthand that the brain cells quickly decipher.

All these complex events take place almost instantaneously and without any effort on our part. The physical properties of light waves—or of sounds, smells, tastes, and anything that touches our bodies—are detected by the sensory receptors and transformed into nervous impulses. These impulses are then combined, condensed, put into code, delivered to the topmost part of the brain, and translated—and we see, hear, smell, taste, and feel.

The pattern theory of the senses

When scientists first began to study the operation of the senses, many of them looked for receptors designed to detect some specific quality of a stimulus—for example, a visual receptor activated by a blue light wave or a hearing receptor activated by the tone from one particular piano string. But this search has been abandoned. Through modern techniques it is now possible to measure the impulses in a single sensory neuron of a laboratory animal, and these measurements show that the sensory receptors are not narrowly specialized but what one investigator has termed "broadly tuned" (Uttal, 1973). True, the eye of a monkey—and presumably the human eye as well—contains some receptor cells that show their greatest response to a blue light wave (MacNichol, 1964). The monkey's ear contains receptors that show their greatest response to a tone of C above middle C (Rose et al., 1971). But these receptors will also respond, to some extent and in one way or another, to a fairly wide range of light or sound waves. They are not specifically designed to detect just a single kind of stimulus, as Channel 2 on your television set is zeroed in on one station and one only.

The modern view of how the senses operate is called the *pattern theory*. This theory holds that stimuli for any of the senses affect a great many *broad-tuned receptors*. For example, blue light waves arouse some receptors of the eye to set off a vigorous burst of nervous impulses and at the same time stimulate other receptors to a lesser extent. The neurons of the optic nerve, monitoring a number of receptors, may in turn be stimulated vigorously or moderately by impulses received from these receptors, or may even be turned off and prevented from firing at all (Kuffler, 1953). As a result, any single neuron of the optic nerve may produce impulses of its own that vary greatly in number and rate—and the combined activity in all the million neurons can form an almost infinite number of patterns. It is these highly varied patterns of nervous impulses—the elaborate code in which information about a sensory stimulus reaches the cerebral cortex—that produce our highly varied sensations. The patterns depend, of course, on which receptors are stimulated and to what extent—but there is no one-to-one relationship between a specific receptor and a specific sensation.

Taste, smell, touch, and the two forgotten senses

Though the senses all operate on the same basic principles, they show a considerable variety in the location of their receptors, the stimuli to which they respond, and the sensations they produce. It is popularly assumed that we are gifted with five senses, and it is true that these five—vision, hearing, taste, smell, and touch—are our sole sources of inputs from the outer world. Yet we have two other senses that we seldom even consider but that bring us essential information about our own bodies. Without these two forgotten senses—bodily movement and equilibrium—we would find it difficult to walk or even keep from falling down, and impossible to play tennis or operate a typewriter.

All the seven senses are important contributors to the information processing we do. The rest of the chapter will describe them one by one, starting with taste, perhaps the simplest, and concluding with the intricate abundance of vision.

Taste

Though we can recognize a great variety of foods, and either relish or reject them, taste is probably the least efficient of our senses. The flavor of food actually depends only in small part on our taste receptors. Much of the sensation is produced by other factors—warmth, cold, the consistency of the food, the mild pain caused by certain spices, and above all smell. The next time your nose is stuffed up by a cold, notice that your meals seem almost tasteless.

The taste receptors are more or less out in the open. If you examine your tongue in a mirror, you will notice that it is covered with little bumps, some tiny, others a bit larger. Inside each of the bumps, a few of which are also found at the back of the mouth and in the throat, are the *taste buds*, which contain the receptors for the sense of taste. Each

The tea taster provides a good example of how much the sense of smell contributes to the flavor we attribute to the sense of taste.

Human taste buds, photographed under high magnification.

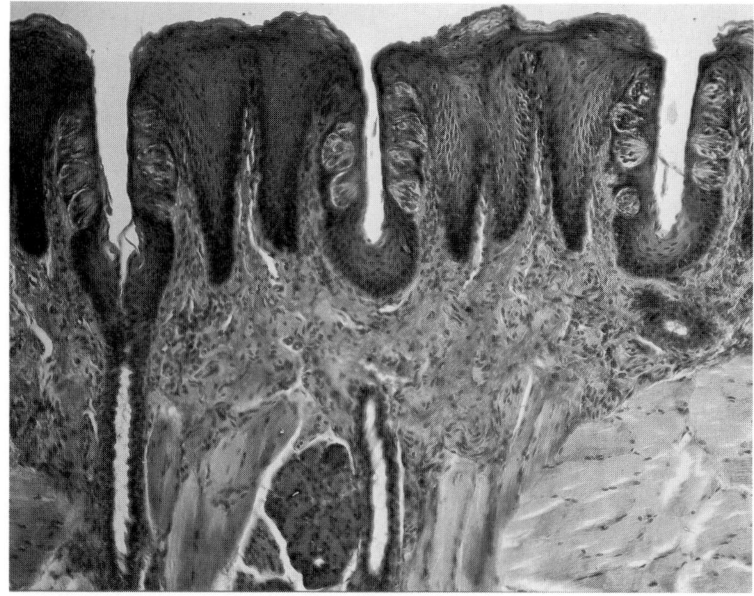

bump contains about 245 taste buds, and each taste bud contains about 20 receptors sensitive to chemical stimulation by food molecules. Food dissolved in saliva spreads over the tongue, enters small pores in the surface of the bumps, and sets off reactions in the receptors. These reactions trigger activity in adjacent neurons, which fire off nervous impulses toward the brain.

The taste receptors, as the pattern theory suggests, appear to be broadly tuned to respond to many kinds of chemical stimulation. But they seem to respond most vigorously to four basic taste qualities—some to stimuli that are sweet, others to stimuli that are sour, salty, or bitter. The receptors that are especially sensitive to sweetness are concentrated near the tip of the tongue, those most sensitive to sour stimuli at the sides toward the rear.

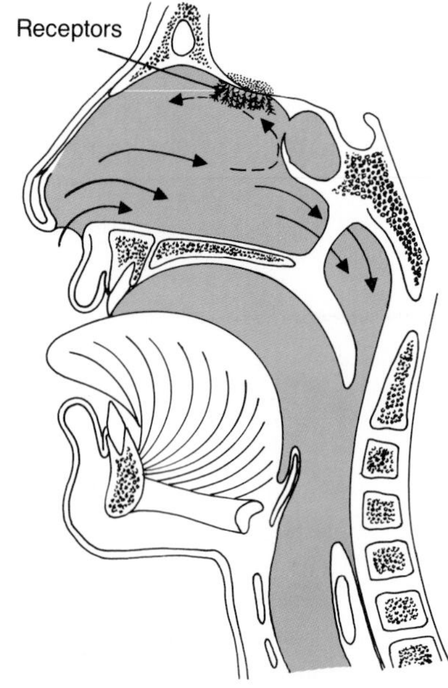

Figure 7-1 The nose and its receptors *This cross section of the human head shows the position of the receptors for the sense of smell, at the very top of the nasal passages. The arrows indicate how some of the air we breathe rises to touch the receptors.*

Smell

The receptors for the sense of smell, as shown in Figure 7-1, lie at the very top of the nasal passages leading from the nostrils to the throat. As we breathe normally, the flow of air from nostrils to throat takes a direct path, as the figure indicates, but a certain amount rises gently to touch the smell receptors. In some little-understood manner the receptors are stimulated by gases and by the molecules of chemical substances suspended in the air. Perhaps the molecules create a chemical reaction. Perhaps the receptors respond in some way to the shape of a molecule—like locks activated by one particular key.

Many lower animals rely on the sense of smell to track down their prey or to detect the approach of an enemy—and even as a means of communicating with one another. They "speak" by secreting chemical substances called *pheromones,* whose odor has a powerful effect on others of their species. Frightened rats, for example, produce a pheromone that serves as a warning signal to other rats (Valenta and Rigby,

1968). Dogs secrete a pheromone in their urine that tells other dogs to stay away from their territory.

Many female animals, including dogs and cats, secrete pheromones that signal when they are sexually receptive. The odor arouses and attracts males—in the case of some species of moth, from as far away as a mile or more. There are some indications that there may also be human pheromones that influence sexual behavior, through to a lesser extent and without our conscious awareness. Women can detect musk-like odors—which are characteristic of the sex pheromones secreted by male animals—much more readily than can men or sexually immature girls. Moreover their sensitivity to these odors is greatest during the time in their menstrual cycle when the amount of the hormone estrogen in their bodies is at its peak (Vierling and Rock, 1967).

One study of dormitory residents at a women's college produced provocative results. When the college term began, the subjects reported wide differences in the dates when their menstrual periods began. Six months later, however, those who were spending a lot of time together as roommates or close friends reported that the dates were considerably closer together, as if there was a growing tendency for their menstrual cycles to coincide (McClintock, 1971). Perhaps pheromones secreted during the cycle had a mutual effect on the timing. And perhaps the appeal of perfumes and men's colognes—even the fact that sometimes we are strongly attracted to another person without knowing why—also indicates some mysterious language that only the nose understands.

The skin senses

The receptors for the skin senses are nerve endings scattered throughout the body, just under the surface. They are sensitive to four basic types of stimulation—pressure, pain, cold, and warmth. As with the other senses, the sensation they produce appears to depend on the pattern of nervous impulses set off by a number of broad-tuned nerve endings. Indeed manipulation of the pattern can fool us into experiencing a sensation that is totally at odds with the actual stimulation. This has been demonstrated with the device illustrated in Figure 7-2. When cool water is passed through both coils, the device feels cool to the touch. When warm water is passed through both coils, it feels warm. But when one coil is warm and the other is cool, the device produces a sensation of heat—so great that anyone who grasps it immediately pulls away. Somehow the pattern of nervous impulses set up by this kind of stimulation completely fools the sense of touch.

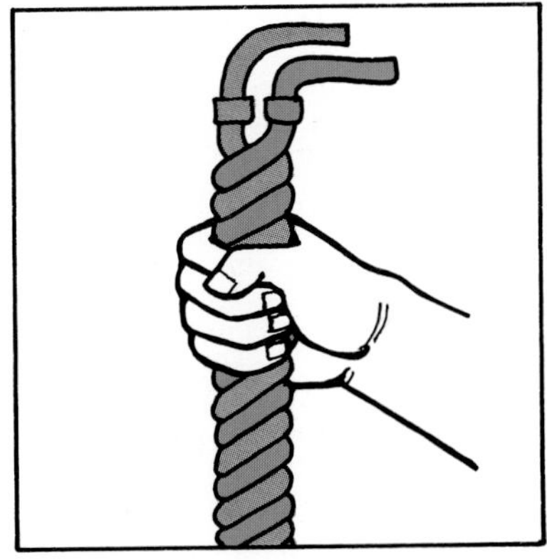

Figure 7-2 **When you touch this harmless coil, watch out!** *This device can fool the skin senses in startling fashion. The colored and gray coils are completely separate and can be connected to different sources of water. The surprising result described in the text is obtained by running cool water through one coil and pleasantly warm water through the other.*

Nerve endings that contribute to the sensation of pain are found not only in the skin but also in our muscles and internal organs. Indeed some of the most excruciating pains come from muscle cramps or from distention of the intestines by gas. Yet the receptors in most of the internal organs do not respond to stimuli that would cause pain if applied to the skin. The intestines, for example, can be cut or even burned without arousing any sensation of pain.

Pain sensations pose many baffling questions. Athletes in the heat of competition may suffer blows severe enough to produce deep bruises—yet feel no pain until later. People with intense and long-continued pain can sometimes be relieved through hypnosis (Goleman, 1977). Chinese surgeons often use no anesthetic, just the technique of acupuncture in which little needles are stuck in various spots of the patient's skin, often far removed from the part of the body undergoing the operation. Electrical stimulation applied to the spinal cord or brain—or for that matter even a placebo, which is a mere sugar pill with no medical effect—may make severe pain disappear. Why?

The answer is not known. One theory is that many of these phenomena occur because the brain is induced in one way or another to increase its output of the morphinelike painkillers it can produce (Iversen, 1979). Another theory is based on indications that there seem to be two different pathways carrying pain messages through the spinal cord and into the brain. One is made up of *"fast" fibers* that signal sharp, localized pains like a pinprick. The other consists of *"slow" fibers* that signal duller, more generalized pains like those produced by many illnesses (Liebeskind and Paul, 1977). Some investigators believe that these two kinds of fibers interact at some kind of *gate-control mechanism* in the spinal cord, either opening it to let pain messages through or shutting it to cut off the sensations (Melzack, 1973). Such a gate might be activated by nervous impulses set up through acupuncture or electrical stimulation. In the case of hypnosis or placebos, the brain itself might send signals to the control mechanism.

Though we can only theorize about the way pain operates, we do know that it serves a purpose. Without the warning provided by pain, we might hold a hand in a flame until the tissues were destroyed, or cut off a finger while peeling an apple. Even the pain of headache, though we cannot attribute it to any specific cause, is probably a warning that we have been under too much physical or psychological strain. By forcing us to slow down or even take a day off, the headache takes us away from a situation that, if continued, might cause some serious damage to the tissues of our bodies or to our mental stability.

The two forgotten senses: bodily movement and equilibrium

Even in a pitch-black room, you know exactly how to move your hand to point up, down, or to either side, and to touch the top of your head or your left knee. This may not seem like much of an accomplishment—but it would be completely impossible without the generally ignored and unappreciated sense of *bodily movement,* which keeps us constantly informed of the position and motion of our muscles and bones.

The receptors for the sense of bodily movement are nerve endings found in three parts of the body. The first are in the muscles, and they are stimulated when the muscles stretch. The second are in the tendons that connect the muscles to the bones and are stimulated when the muscles contract and put pressure on the tendons. The third, and apparently most important, are in the linings of the joints between the bones and are stimulated by movements of the joints. Without the information provided by these three receptors, we would have trouble performing any of the bodily movements we now take for granted. Even to walk, we would have to concentrate on using our eyes to guide our

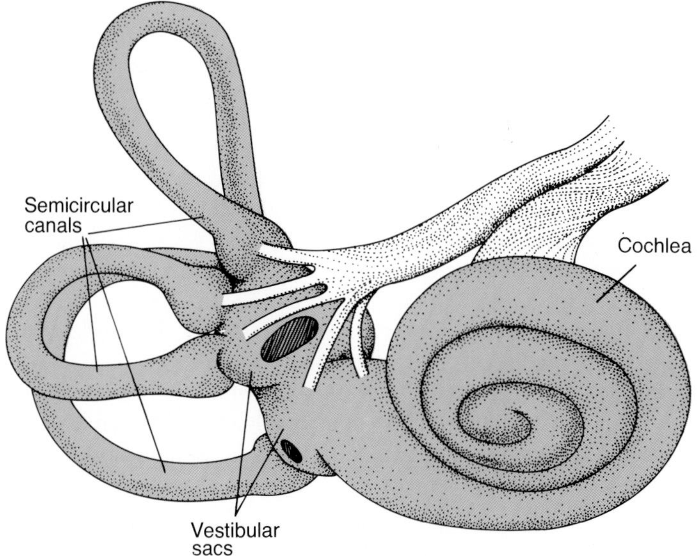

Figure 7-3 The sense organs for equilibrium *The receptors for the sense of equilibrium lie in these passages of the inner ear, next to the cochlea of the sense of hearing.*

legs and feet into the right position for each step.

The other forgotten sense is *equilibrium,* which keeps our bodies in balance and oriented to the force of gravity. Thanks to this sense, our bodies stay erect—and, if we should start to fall, we catch our balance through reflex action, without even thinking about it.

The receptors for the sense of equilibrium are hairlike cells found in fluid-filled passages that are part of the inner ear, as illustrated in Figure 7-3. The three *semicircular canals* lie at such angles to one another that any movement of the head moves the thick fluid in at least two of them, stimulating the receptors they contain. In the *vestibular sacs,* the receptors are matted together and tiny pieces of stonelike crystal are imbedded in the mattings. The crystals are heavy enough to be pulled downward by the force of gravity, putting pressure on the receptors. Thus the

This stunt would be impossible without the human sense of equilibrium.

receptors in the vestibular sacs keep us aware of being upright even when we are not moving.

Among them, the receptors for the sense of equilibrium constantly monitor the position of the head and any change in position. Besides keeping us right side up and in balance, they provide information essential to our sense of vision. By stepping toward a mirror, you can observe that your head bobs around when you walk—as it also does in many other circumstances. Unless the muscles controlling movement of the eyeballs made constant adjustments to hold your gaze steady, your field of vision would jiggle and blur. These adjustments are made by reflex action in response to messages from the sense of equilibrium. No matter how much you bob or shake your head, the world you see remains firmly in place.

Some people experience motion sickness when the various pathways of the sense of equilibrium become overloaded. Medicines such as Dramamine act to prevent motion sickness by inhibiting some of the nervous activity.

Sound waves and hearing

When you hit the key for middle C on a piano, a hammer strikes the string for middle C, the string vibrates, and you hear a sound. You can distinguish it from other notes, like the B just below it and the D just above it. You can also distinguish it from the middle C on any other musical instrument, even though the two sounds have a definite similarity. If you hit the key a little harder, the sound gets louder. Press the key more gently, and the sound gets softer.

Striking the piano key demonstrates some of the basic principles that govern the sense of hearing—and suggests the wide range of stimuli that our ears can detect and discriminate among. We can hear tones all the way from the deepest bass to the highest treble, and distinguish between tones that are just a tiny bit apart. We can hear anything from the merest hint of a whisper to the roar of a jet airplane, which has many millions of times more energy.

The physical nature of sound

The stimulus for hearing is sound waves, traveling unseen through the atmosphere. The waves are little ripples of contraction and expansion of the air, typically produced by the vibration of a piano string or the human vocal cords or by two objects banging together. They have three qualities that determine the sensations they produce:

1. *Frequency*, or the number of waves per second, determines the sensation of *pitch*. The lowest sounding note on a piano measures about 27 hertz, or Hz, the scientific term for the number of cycles of contraction and expansion per second. The highest is around 4,200 Hz. Our full range of hearing extends from about 20 to 20,000 Hz.
2. *Amplitude*, or the strength of the wave, determines the degree of loudness we hear, although not entirely. Our sense of hearing is most sensitive to the frequencies between about 400 and 3,000 Hz, which

is about the range of the human voice. Frequencies higher or lower than that do not sound as loud even when they have exactly the same amplitude. A wave of 1,000 Hz sounds louder than 10,000 Hz, which in turn sounds louder than 100 Hz, because we are least sensitive of all to low notes. The way waves vary in amplitude and frequency is illustrated in Figure 7-4.

3. *Complexity* determines the sensation of *timbre,* which is the quality that distinguishes a middle C on the piano from the same note on a clarinet or violin. Complexity results from the fact that virtually all sources of sound produce not just a single frequency but others as well. For example, while the middle C piano string is vibrating at 256 Hz, sections of the string also vibrate at higher frequencies though with lower amplitude. Each half vibrates at 512 Hz, twice the basic frequency, each third at 768 Hz, and so on. These additional vibrations are called overtones. All the various frequencies combine into a complex sound wave with the shape illustrated in Figure 7-5, which produces the sensation of a middle C with the timbre characteristic of its source.

The hearing receptors

What you call your ear—the flap of tissue at the side of the head—is in fact the least important part of your hearing equipment. The working parts, including the receptors, lie hidden inside the skull.

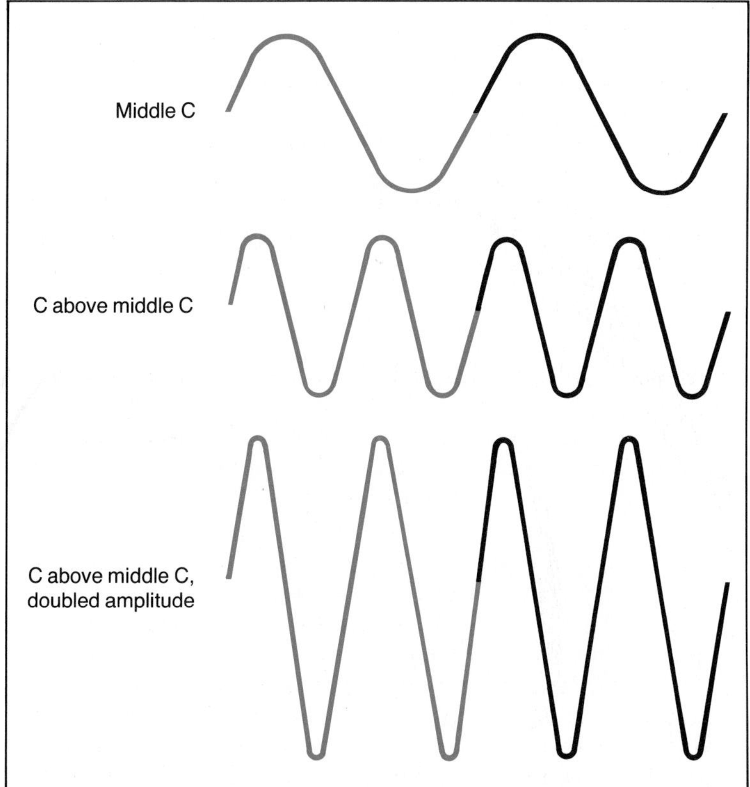

Figure 7-4 Sound waves: frequency and amplitude *The wave at the top, for the pure tone of middle C, has a frequency of 256 Hz. The wave in the middle, for the C above middle C, has twice as many cycles of contraction and expansion per second, or 512 Hz. Sounding this same note with twice the force produces the wave at the bottom, which continues at a frequency of 512 Hz but has double the amplitude, as indicated by the height of the wave. The colored portions of the wave show a single cycle of contraction and expansion.*

Figure 7-5 **A pattern of complexity and timbre** *Unlike the "pure" waves shown in Figure 7-4, the waves that usually reach our ears take this complex form. The note shown here comes from a violin. It maintains a basic frequency that produces our sensation of pitch, but each cycle of contraction and expansion is modified by overtones that change the pattern of the wave and result in our sensation of the violin's own special timbre.*

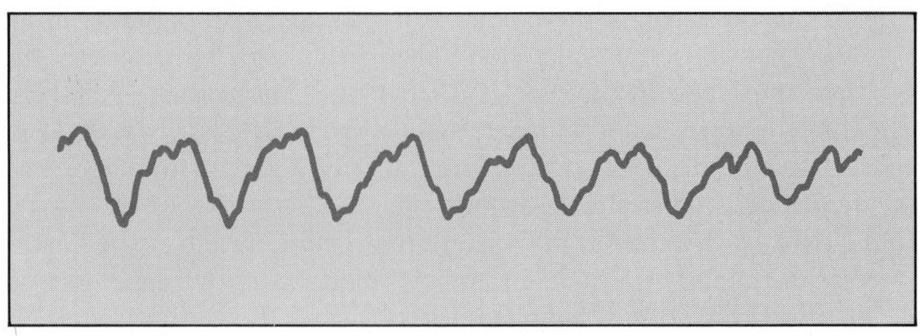

The structure is shown in Figure 7-6. The *outer ear,* or visible portion, merely collects sound waves. The waves create vibrations of the *eardrum* that are passed along through the *middle ear,* an air-filled cavity containing three small bones that conduct and amplify the vibrations. The last of the three bones transmits the vibrations to the *cochlea,* a bony structure shaped like a snail's shell, which contains the *inner ear's* receptors for hearing.

The cochlea is filled with fluid, and stretched across it, dividing it more or less in half, is a piece of tissue called the *basilar membrane.* When the vibrations of sound reach the cochlea, they set up motions of the fluid inside, thus bending the basilar membrane. Lying on the membrane is the *organ of Corti,* a collection of the receptors for hearing.

How the hearing receptors work

Sound waves cause the entire basilar membrane to respond with wave-like, up-and-down motions that travel along its length and breadth (Békésy, 1960). These motions in turn activate the hearing receptors, which are shaped like very fine hairs resting on the membrane. When the floor beneath the receptors moves, the hair-shaped cells jiggle like

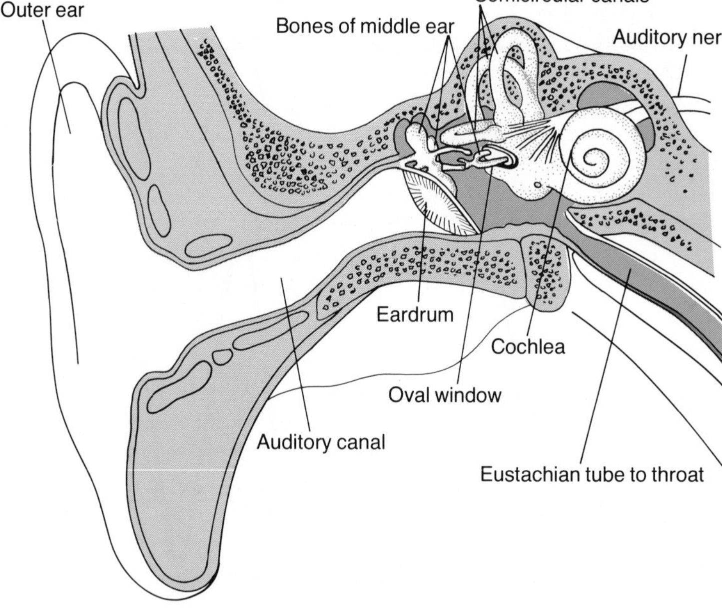

Figure 7-6 **A diagram of the hearing apparatus** *Sound waves enter the* outer ear, *pass through the* auditory canal, *and set up vibrations of the* eardrum. *The three bones of the middle ear transmit the vibrations to the* cochlea *through its* oval window. *The* auditory nerve *carries messages from the hearing receptors inside the cochlea to the brain. The* Eustachian *tube, traveling from middle ear to throat, keeps the air pressure inside the middle ear at the same level as outside. (When the tube is temporarily clogged, as sometimes happens when you have a cold or ride in an airplane or elevator, you can feel a difference in pressure against the eardrum.) The* semicircular canals *play no part in hearing but are responsible for our sense of equilibrium, as discussed earlier.*

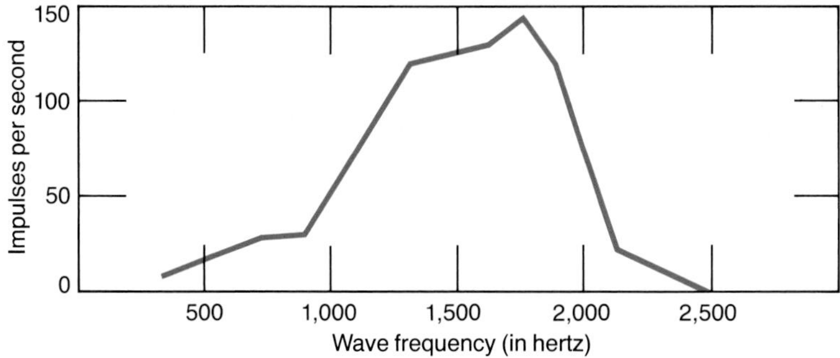

Figure 7-7 A hearing neuron and broad tuning *The graph line shows the number of nervous impulses produced by a single auditory neuron of a monkey, in response to the stimulation of a receptor cell by sound waves of different frequencies, all sounded at the same amplitude (between the level of conversation and the noise of an automobile). Note that the neuron was activated to some extent by frequencies anywhere within a range of more than 2,000 Hz. The range was even greater at higher amplitudes, smaller at lower amplitudes (after Rose et al., 1971).*

little dancers. This stimulates the neurons of the *auditory nerve,* to which the receptors connect, to produce nervous impulses that are routed toward the sensory areas of the cerebral cortex.

The basilar membrane is narrowest and stiffest at the end where vibrations caused by sound waves first enter the cochlea at its oval window. The membrane then becomes progressively wider and more flexible toward its other end. The narrower portions of the membrane—and the receptor cells at those points—move most vigorously in response to high-frequency sound waves. The wider portions and their receptors show a greater response to low frequencies. Thus the code of nervous impulses in which hearing messages eventually reach the cerebral cortex seems to depend in part on which receptors, at which locations along the membrane, are stimulated.

The hearing receptors, however, are excellent examples of broad tuning, for they generally respond to a considerable range of frequencies. Note Figure 7-7, which illustrates the activity of a single neuron associated with a single receptor cell. This particular neuron was stimulated to its most rapid-fire burst of impulses by a frequency of about 1,800 Hz. But it was also stimulated, though to a lesser degree, by frequencies anywhere from about as low as 300 Hz to about as high as 2,500 Hz.

Thus the code in which hearing messages reach the cerebral cortex—and are translated into our sensations of pitch, loudness, and timbre—appears to depend not only on which particular receptors are stimulated, but also on the number of them, the rate at which each sets off nervous impulses, and especially the entire pattern of the impulses (Uttal, 1973). In fact, for the very low frequencies—those below about 400 Hz—the code does not seem to depend at all on the exact location of the receptor, because these frequencies make the basilar membrane move as a unit, to an equal degree throughout its length and breadth.

Loudness and hearing damage

In studying the amplitude of sound waves, researchers use what is called the *decibel scale.* Their instruments measure the amount of energy in sound waves and convert it into numerical readings on the scale shown in Figure 7-8. Such measurements are useful in many ways, particularly to ecological psychologists interested in the effects of noisy environments.

There is evidence that exposure to noise can seriously interfere with

Figure 7-8 Noise ratings on the decibel scale *Some frequently heard sounds register on the decibel scale of amplitude all the way from about 12 for the rustle of leaves to 120 for a thunderclap and 150 for a jet plane warming up nearby. The scale, with 0 set at the absolute threshold for a sound at 1,000 Hz, is logarithmic, with each 10 points on the scale representing a tenfold increase in energy level. Thus the noise level in a typical business office (40 decibels) represents 10 times more energy or amplitude than a whisper heard from close by (30 decibels). Note the danger zone for hearing damage, also the point at which sounds become painful to the ear.*

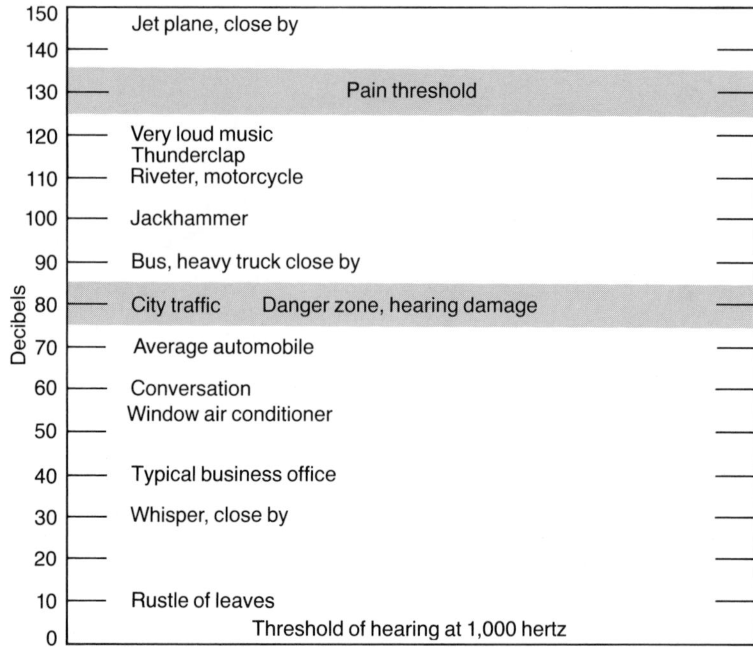

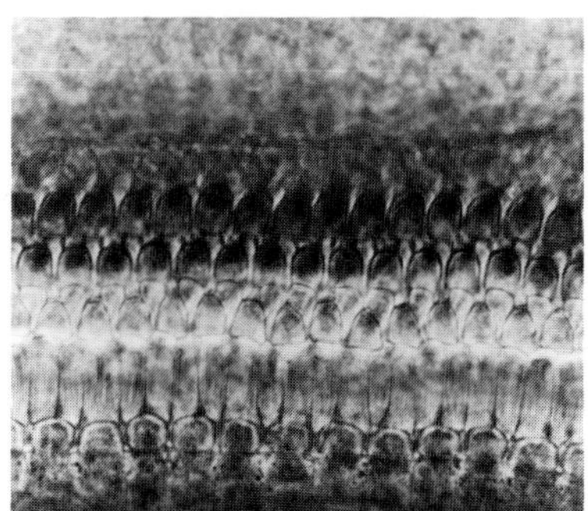

Figure 7-9 What noise can do to the hearing receptors *Normal receptor cells on the basilar membrane of an animal are shown above. The damaged cells below are from an animal exposed to prolonged noise.*

learning and thinking. One study found that children from a school near a busy airport, when tested for puzzle-solving ability, were generally less persistent and less successful than children from a quieter school (Cohen et al., 1980). Another study found that schoolchildren living on the lower floors of a high-rise apartment complex, where they received the full brunt of traffic noise from a busy highway, had generally lower reading skills than children living on the top floors (Cohen, Glass, and Singer, 1973). Noise seems to have a particularly harmful effect on information-processing abilities when it occurs at unpredictable intervals (Glass and Singer, 1973).

Prolonged exposure to sound above 85 decibels can cause hearing damage—a fact of considerable importance because the noise level in city streets often goes above that level. The damage is particularly likely to occur in the narrow portion of the basilar membrane, to the receptor cells chiefly responsible for detecting sounds of high frequency. The way these receptors may be affected is illustrated in Figure 7-9. This and some other problems created by a noisy environment are discussed in detail in a box on Psychology and Society.

How do you know where the sound comes from?

If someone sitting behind you coughs, you know immediately where the sound comes from. If you hear an automobile pass by, unseen, you can tell at once in which direction it is moving. Something about the sound waves and the manner in which they stimulate your hearing receptors tells you where they come from and in what direction they are moving.

The ability to determine location seems to depend on the fact that slightly different sound waves reach the two ears. A sound wave from the left arrives at the left ear a tiny fraction of a second before it strikes

Psychology and Society: Noise pollution, deafness, high blood pressure, and ulcers

Our society may be hazardous to our ears. Millions of Americans work at jobs—in airports, construction, mining, and many other occupations—that regularly expose them to noise that can cause hearing damage. Millions more regularly encounter a dangerous noise level from heavy traffic, or bring it on themselves through their fondness for motorcycles, speedboats, power mowers, and loud music.

Noise is a subtle pollutant, with effects that are usually not immediately apparent, and most people are unaware of the risk of hearing damage. Workers in noisy jobs often reject the protection offered to them. They discard their earplugs or wear them loose for greater comfort, or poke holes in their earmuffs to provide ventilation. People willingly go to discotheques where the sound regularly hits 120 decibels or more, and listen to music through stereo earphones at more than 100 decibels. Current musical tastes, indeed, seem to be the chief villain among young people. Tests of freshmen entering college have found that as many as 61 percent of them have already suffered at least some hearing loss, and that many of them can hear no better than the average 65-year-old (Lipscomb, 1969), an age at which parts of the basilar membrane and its receptor cells normally show deterioration.

Whether caused by age or earlier in life by noise, partial deafness can create serious psychological problems. Since the loss of hearing occurs gradually, over a period of time, those who suffer from it are often unaware that they can no longer hear sounds they have always taken for granted—and especially that they have trouble understanding ordinary conversation. They may begin to suspect that other people are whispering to exclude them from the conversation, possibly even making disparaging or threatening remarks about them.

The form of abnormal behavior called *paranoia*, in which victims have delusions that other people are plotting against them and persecuting them, is often displayed by elderly people suffering from deafness (Post, 1966), considerably less often by old people whose hearing is still reasonably good. Even if the result is less drastic, people with hearing difficulties often become suspicious, withdrawn, and hostile—to the point where others actually do avoid them. These problems are not necessarily related to age. Similar symptoms of confusion, agitation, irritability, and hostility have been observed in college students in whom a temporary and partial deafness was induced through hypnosis, without their realizing it. Other students who were aware that the hypnosis had affected their hearing proved much less likely to suffer any psychological consequences (Zimbardo, Andersen, and Kabat, 1981).

Hearing loss and its possible psychological consequences are only one of the dangers of a noisy environment. A survey of available medical evidence has found that noise is linked to a number of physical ailments, including dizziness, headache, digestive disturbances, ulcers, and high blood pressure (Raloff, 1982). The rule of thumb adopted by the Environmental Protection Agency is this: Whenever you have to raise your voice to be heard above the noise in your environment, you are running a physical and psychological risk. Self-preservation dictates that you had better do something about it or get away.

the right ear, and in a slightly earlier phase of its cycle of contraction and expansion. By the time the sound wave reaches the right ear it has slightly less amplitude because it has traveled farther. And because high frequencies are more likely than low ones to be absorbed by any object that gets in the path of sound waves, the pattern of overtones has been altered by contact with the head, thus slightly changing the timbre.

The structure of the outer ear also seems to play a part, because its intricate shape bounces sound waves around much as the walls and furniture in a room affect the music from a stereo set. The two outer ears, receiving waves from different directions, reflect them toward the eardrum in different ways. Thus in a number of ways the receptors in the two ears are stimulated somewhat differently and produce slightly differ-

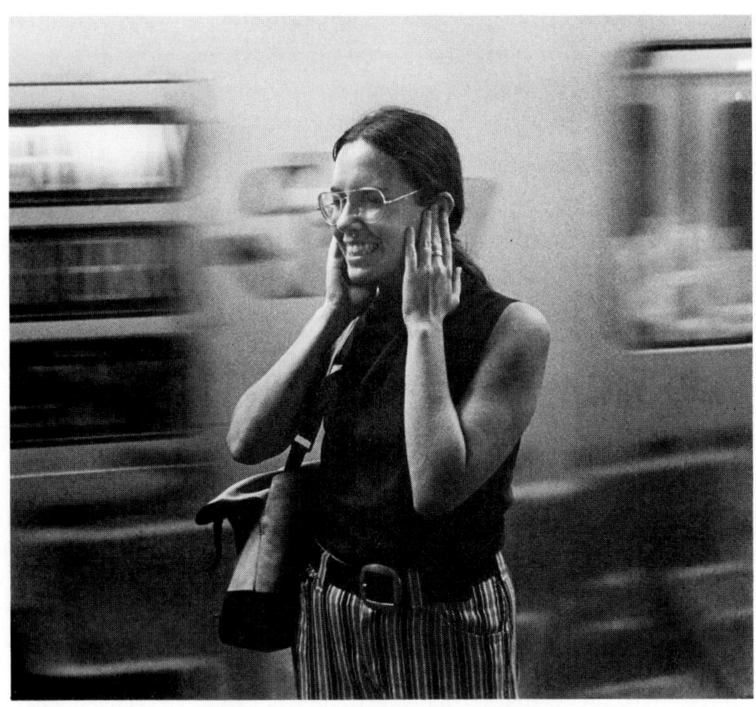

Too many decibels for comfort: the roar of the passing subway train makes the woman clench her teeth and try to shut out the painful noise.

ent patterns of nervous impulses, which the brain can usually decode into an instant judgment about the location of the sound. We are probably not so skillful at locating sounds as are animals with movable outer ears—like dogs and horses that prick their ears when curious about a noise—but we manage well enough.

Light waves and vision

The stimulus for vision is light waves, which are pulsations of electromagnetic energy. Unlike sound waves, they do not create any motion of the air and indeed can travel through a vacuum, as they do when light from a star reaches us across the vast expanses of empty space. If you could arrange to make two coins hit together inside a vacuum, you would hear no click because sound waves would not be formed. But the light waves from a filament inside a vacuum tube shine brightly. The waves travel at 186,000 miles (300,000 kilometers) a second, the fastest speed known and presumably the fastest possible. This is such a great velocity that a light wave, if you could manage to reflect it around the world, would make the long journey and get back to you in less than one-seventh of a second.

As can be seen in Plate I, light waves are closely related to many other forms of pulsating energy, ranging from infinitesimal cosmic rays to the huge waves of household electricity, which are 100 million meters long. In this vast spectrum of electromagnetic energy, light occupies only a very small niche. The little band of waves we can see ranges from about 380 billionths of a meter to about 780 billionths. The shortest waves, which are seen as violet, are just a little bit longer than the invisible ultraviolet rays that cause sunburn. The longest, which are seen as red, are just a little bit shorter than the invisible infrared waves produced by a heating lamp.

The physical nature of light waves

Although light waves are totally different from sound waves, there is a close parallel in the way the physical qualities of the two kinds of waves affect the senses. Like sound, light has three qualities that determine the sensations it produces:

1. *Wavelength,* the distance between the peaks of the waves, determines the *hue,* the scientific term for the color we see. White light is a mixture of all the hues. When a white light such as a sunbeam is broken down into its components by passing through a prism, the wavelengths are separated to form the visible spectrum shown in Plate I.
2. *Intensity,* the amount of energy in the light wave, determines the sensation of *brightness,* although not entirely. Just as the same amplitude of sound produces greater loudness at the frequencies between 400 and 3,000 Hz, the same intensity of light ordinarily produces greater brightness at the yellow and green wavelengths in the middle of the visible spectrum.
3. *Complexity,* the degree to which the predominant wavelength is somewhat masked by other wavelengths, determines the sensation called *saturation.* The purer the wavelength, the greater the saturation and the more vivid the hue. When other wavelengths are mixed in, we see a hue that we often describe as duller or muddier. A pure or saturated red is strikingly colorful. If other wavelengths are added to reduce the saturation, what we see is "less red."

The structure of the eye

If you have ever taken photographs—especially with a camera that must be properly set and focused before the shutter is snapped—you should feel right at home with the diagram of the eyeball in Figure 7-10. The *iris* and *pupil* serve the same purpose as the diaphragm in a camera. When the smooth muscles of the iris open to maximum size, as they do under dim conditions, the pupil admits about 17 times as much light as when it is contracted to its smallest size. The *lens* of the eye serves the same purpose as the lens of a camera but in a way that would not be possible with even the most carefully designed piece of glass. The lens of a camera has to be moved forward and backward to focus on nearby or faraway objects. The lens of the eye remains stationary but changes shape. The action of the *ciliary muscles* makes the lens thinner to bring faraway objects into focus and enables it to thicken to focus on nearby objects. Sharp images created by the lens are cast on the *retina,* the eye's equivalent of film.

Receptor cells in the retina trigger nervous impulses that leave the eyeball by way of the *optic nerve.* At the point where this cable of neurons exits, there is a small gap in the retina known as the *blind spot,*

Figure 7-10 The structure of the eye *Light waves first strike the* cornea, *a transparent bulge in the outer layer of the eyeball. The cornea serves as a sort of preliminary lens, gathering light waves from a much wider field of vision than would be possible if the eyeball merely had a perfectly flat window at the front. The light waves then pass through the* pupil, *which is an opening in the* iris, *a circular arrangement of smooth muscles that contract and expand to make the pupil smaller in bright light and larger in dim light. (When you look at your eyes in a mirror, the pupil is the dark, almost black circle at the center. The iris is the larger circle around it containing the pigments that determine eye color.) Behind the pupil lies the transparent* lens, *the shape of which is controlled by the* ciliary muscles. *The lens focuses the light rays on the* retina, *which contains the light-sensitive receptors of the eye. The receptors are most tightly packed in the* fovea, *where visual acuity is greatest. Messages from the receptors are transmitted to the brain by way of the* optic nerve, *which exits from the back of the eyeball, a little off center. Attached to the eyeball are muscles that enable us to look up, down, and sideways. The space inside the eyeball is filled with a transparent substance, as is the space between the cornea and the iris (Bloom and Fawcett, 1968).*

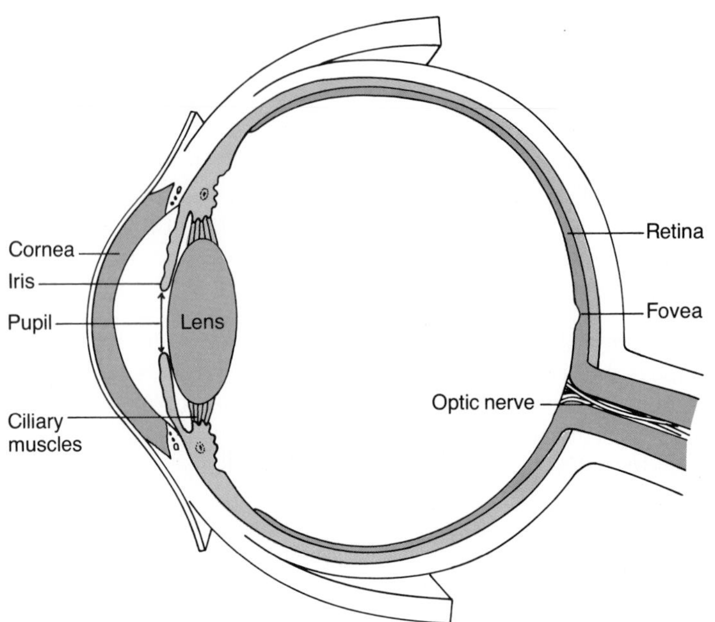

containing no receptors. We are never aware of this gap in our visual field in ordinary life, but you can discover it for yourself by examining Figure 7-11.

The visual receptors

Although a good camera has a sharper lens and a diaphragm with a much wider range than the iris, no photographic film can begin to compare with the efficiency of the retina. The receptors are sensitive to low intensities of light that would not register at all in a camera and can also function under high intensities that would burn out the film. Most important of all, the retina responds continuously, without any halt for winding from one frame of film to the next.

Each retina, if flattened out, would be an irregular ellipse with a total area of just about three-fourths of a square inch (slightly under five square centimeters). Packed into this small area are about 127 million receptors of the kind shown in Figure 7-12. The great majority of the receptors are long and narrow, a fact that has given them the name *rods.* The rest, numbering about 7 million, are somewhat thicker and tapered; these are called *cones.* The rods function chiefly under conditions of low illumination and send information to the brain about movement and about whites, grays, and blacks but not about hue. The cones

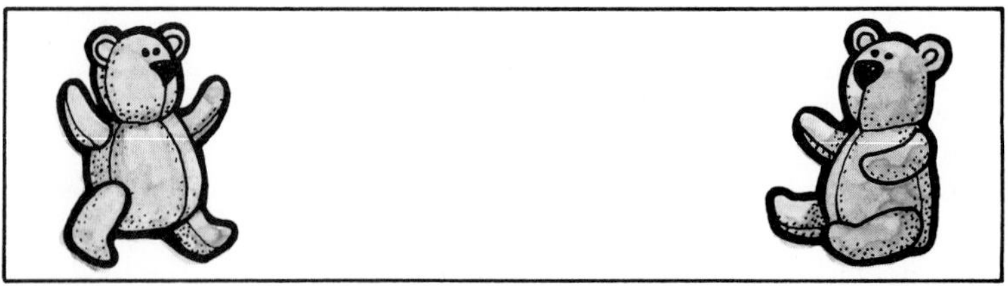

Figure 7-11 A demonstration of the blind spot *Hold the book at arm's length, close your right eye, and look at the teddy bear on the right. Now move the book slowly closer. When the image of the teddy bear at the left falls on the blind spot of your left eye, it will disappear. To demonstrate the blind spot of the right eye, repeat with the left eye closed and your gaze concentrated on the teddy bear at the left.*

function in strong illumination and provide sensations not only of movement and brightness from white to black but also of hue.

The cones are most numerous toward the middle of the retina. Indeed the area called the *fovea,* at the very center of the retina, contains only cones, packed together more tightly than anywhere else. This is where our vision is sharpest. When we read or do anything else that requires a very sharp image, we keep the object in the center of our field of vision so that its light waves fall on the fovea.

The manner in which light waves stimulate the receptors of the retina was discovered many years ago when physiologists managed to extract a substance called *visual purple* from the rods. Visual purple is a pigment that absorbs light, which bleaches it at a rate depending on intensity and wavelength. Thus light waves striking the retina produce chemical changes in the visual purple, and these changes act to stimulate the neurons next in the pathway that carries messages from receptors to brain (Wald, 1951).

The cones contain pigments akin to visual purple and operate in much the same way, except that there are three different types. One is most sensitive to blue wavelengths, another to green, and the third to waves in the red-yellow portion of the spectrum. As is shown in Figure 7-13, however, all three types are broadly tuned, and their pigments respond to some degree to many wavelengths.

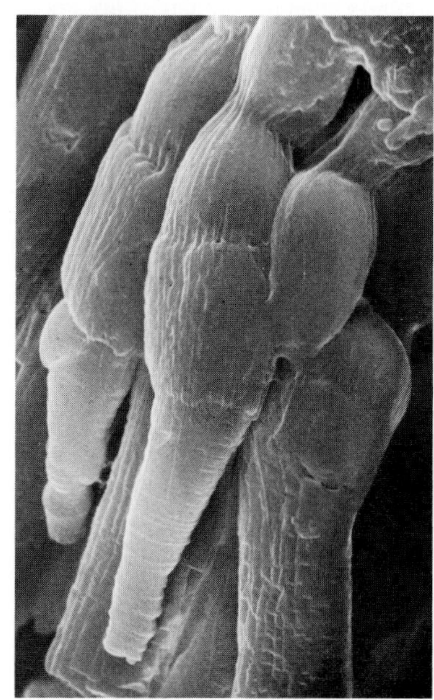

Figure 7-12 The retina's receptor cells *The shapes that give the names to the eye's light-sensitive rods and cones can be seen clearly in this photograph of the retina of a mud puppy, made with an electron microscope.*

Color vision

The three types of cones, each responding in its own way to different wavelengths, begin to account for our ability to distinguish all the hues of the rainbow. But the ability also depends on the coding that takes place in the complex pathway of neurons that leads from the eye to the sensory areas of the cerebral cortex, through a number of switching points including a major processing and relay station in the thalamus.

The pathway begins with neurons in the retina that make contact with the receptor cells—sometimes with just one, sometimes with a number of them—and are stimulated to a greater or lesser degree by the

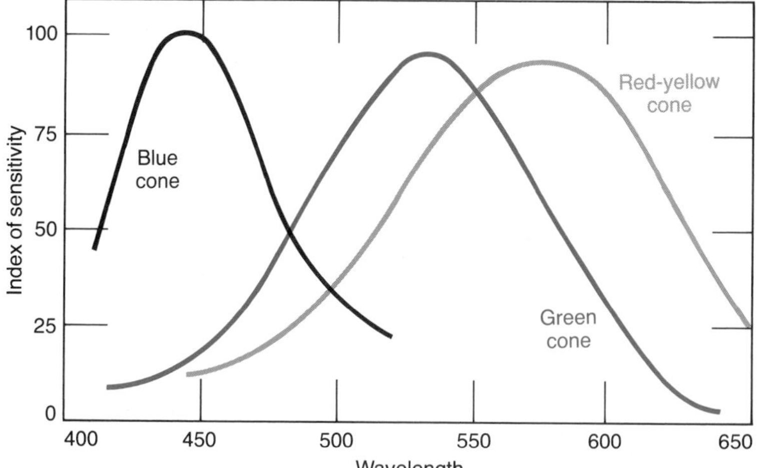

Figure 7-13 The three types of cones and how they react *The graph lines show the sensitivity of the three cones in the retina of a monkey to different wavelengths of light. For each, the sensitivity is greatest at one particular point along the color spectrum and grows progressively weaker at lower and higher wavelengths—but there is at least some response over a wide range. The cone most sensitive to green, for example, reacts to some extent to almost the entire spectrum, all the way from blue to orange. The measure of sensitivity used here was the amount of light absorbed by the pigments in the cone (after MacNichol, 1964).*

Figure 7-14 How an opponent-processing cell works *The graph line shows the nervous impulses produced by one of the opponent-processing neurons in the visual pathway of a monkey. In the absence of any stimulation, the neuron fires at an average rate of five impulses per second. A violet-blue stimulus induces a sharp burst of activity. A yellow stimulus almost completely stops any activity (after De Valois and De Valois, 1975).*

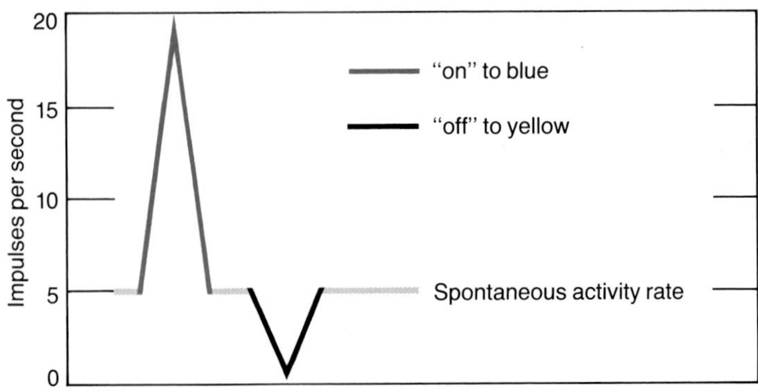

chemical activity of the receptors. Their nervous impulses, in turn, stimulate the neurons of the optic nerve, which send off their impulses to the next switching point. Among the nerve cells in the pathway there appear to be four kinds responsible for color vision, each behaving in a different way in response to the messages it receives.

One type of nerve cell fires a rapid burst of impulses in response to messages indicating a blue stimulus but is turned off by a yellow stimulus, as shown in Figure 7-14. Another does just the opposite—it shows a high rate of activity in response to yellow and is turned off by blue. The third type is activated by red and slowed down by green, the fourth type activated by green and slowed down by red. There are also two other types of neurons that appear to be responsible for black-and-white sensations and brightness. One is turned on by white or bright stimuli and turned off by black or dark stimuli. The other works in the opposite fashion, on for dark and off for bright (De Valois and Jacobs, 1968).

This modern explanation of vision is known as the *opponent-process theory*. It is of course a pattern theory. A visual stimulus sets up a pattern of chemical response in the rods and the three kinds of cones in the retina. This pattern in turn stimulates the neurons of the visual system into their own pattern of nervous activity, with the six opponent-process cells for blue-yellow, red-green, and bright-dark all behaving in different ways. It is this total pattern of nervous impulses, arriving at the visual centers of the brain, that determines what we see.

Vision in bright sunlight and in a dark theater

One of the most valuable aspects of our visual equipment is its ability to function under an extremely wide range of illumination. Note what happens when you walk through bright afternoon sunlight into a movie theater where there is hardly any light at all. At first the theater seems pitch-black, and you can hardly find your way down the aisle to an empty seat. But after a while your eyes undergo what is called *dark adaptation*—and you can clearly see the aisle, the seats, and the faces of the people around you.

Dark adaptation depends mostly on the rods, whose visual purple builds up to high levels when it goes unbleached for a time by strong light. (The production of visual purple, in turn, requires vitamin A—which is why people who suffer from night blindness, or inability to adapt, are advised to eat carrots.) Full adaptation to dark takes about a half hour, by which time the eyes are about 100,000 times more sensitive to light than they were in the bright sunlight. Note that you do not see colors in a dimly lighted place such as a theater—nothing but shades of gray. This is because the color-sensitive cones cannot function at low intensities of light. Only the rods respond.

SUMMARY

How the senses operate

1. The *senses* are the information-gathering structures of the nervous system.
2. The two requirements for sensation are (a) a *stimulus,* or some form of meaningful energy impinging on the body, and (b) a *receptor,* or nervous structure capable of responding to that particular stimulus.
3. To activate a sensory receptor, a stimulus must be above the *absolute threshold,* or minimum intensity required to make the receptor respond.
4. To be distinguished as different, two stimuli must vary by at least the amount of the *difference threshold,* also called *just noticeable difference,* or j.n.d. for short. *Weber's law* is that for each sense the difference threshold is a fixed percentage of the original stimulus (10 percent for sound, 1.6 percent for light).
5. All the senses display *sensory adaptation*—meaning that the sensation produced by a constant stimulus disappears after a time, though a new stimulus creates an immediate new response. Thus our senses are best equipped to provide information about change in the environment.
6. The modern view of how the senses operate is *pattern theory.* This theory holds that a stimulus affects a great many *broad-tuned receptors,* which set off nervous impulses carried to the brain by a pathway of neurons that process the information and encode it into patterns. The sensory areas of the cerebral cortex translate the patterns into our sensations.

Taste, smell, touch, and the two forgotten senses

7. The receptors for *taste* lie mostly in the *taste buds* of the tongue. They are broadly tuned to respond to chemical stimulation—but there are four types especially sensitive to either sweet, sour, salty, or bitter.
8. The receptors for *smell* lie at the top of the nasal passages leading from the nostrils to the throat. They are sensitive to gases and to molecules of chemical substances suspended in the air.
9. The receptors for the *skin senses* are nerve endings lying just beneath the surface. They account for our sensations of pressure, pain, cold, and warmth.
10. The *sense of bodily movement* keeps us informed of the position of our muscles and bones and is essential to such complex movements as walking. The receptors are nerve endings in the muscles, tendons, and joints.
11. The *sense of equilibrium* keeps us in balance and oriented to the force of gravity. The receptors are hairlike nerve cells in the inner ear's three *semicircular canals* and *vestibular sacs.*

Sound waves and hearing

12. The stimulus for *hearing* is *sound waves,* which are ripples of contraction and expansion of the air. Sound waves vary in *frequency, amplitude,* and *complexity.* The frequency determines our sensation of *pitch.* Amplitude determines *loudness* (though not entirely). Complexity determines *timbre.*
13. Sound waves are collected by the *outer ear,* or visible part. The waves create vibrations of the *eardrum,* which are then passed along by the three bones of the *middle ear* to the *cochlea* of the *inner ear.* In the cochlea, the vibrations set up complicated wavelike motions of the *basilar membrane.* These motions activate the hairlike receptors for hearing in the *organ of Corti,* lying on the basilar membrane.
14. The basilar membrane is narrowest and stiffest at the end where sound enters the cochlea, and the receptors at this end respond most vigorously to high-frequency waves. The membrane becomes progressively wider and more flexible toward the other end, which is most sensitive to low frequencies.
15. The amplitude of sound waves is measured on a *decibel scale* of loudness. Exposure to noise can have a harmful effect on information-processing abilities—and above 85 decibels can cause hearing damage.
16. Our ability to know which direction a sound comes from depends on the fact that the hearing receptors in the two ears receive a slightly different pattern of stimulation and send slightly different patterns of nervous impulses to the brain.

Light waves and vision

17. The stimulus for *vision* is *light waves,* a pulsating form of electromagnetic energy. Light waves vary in *wavelength, intensity,* and *complexity.* Wavelength determines *hue,* the term for the sensation produced by a colored object. Intensity determines *brightness* (though not entirely). Complexity determines *saturation,* or the sensation of a vivid or dull hue. White light is a mixture of all the wavelengths, as can be demonstrated by passing it through a prism and obtaining a spectrum of the hues.
18. Light waves occupy a small portion of the range of electromagnetic radiation, which extends from cosmic rays (the shortest) to household electricity (the longest). Violet waves are a little longer than the invisible ultraviolet waves that cause sunburn. Red waves are slightly shorter than the invisible infrared waves produced by a heating lamp.
19. Light waves enter the eyeball through the *pupil,* which is an opening in the *iris.* They then pass through a transparent *lens,* which can change shape by the action of the *ciliary muscles* to focus the waves sharply on the *retina* at the back of the eyeball. The retina contains the receptors for vision—nerve structures called *rods* and *cones.*
20. The rods function chiefly under low illumination and send information to the brain about movements and about whites, grays, and

blacks but not about color. The rods contain *visual purple,* a pigment that is bleached by light.

21. The cones function in strong illumination and send information to the brain about not only movement and brightness but also color. There are three kinds of cones, containing pigments that are broad tuned but most sensitive to either blue, green, or red-yellow.
22. The modern explanation of vision is *opponent-process theory.* This holds that nervous impulses set off by the rods and three types of cones enter a pathway to the brain containing six different types of neurons. One shows a burst of activity when the receptors respond to a red stimulus but is lowered in activity when the receptors respond to a green stimulus. Another type does exactly the opposite. It is turned on by a green stimulus but turned off by a red stimulus. Another pair of neurons responds in opposite ways to a blue or yellow stimulus. Another responds in opposite ways to white (or brightness) and black (or darkness). The total pattern of nervous impulses—activated by the response of the rods and cones to a stimulus, then carried to the visual area of the brain by the six types of neurons—accounts for our visual sensations.
23. *Dark adaptation,* which makes the eyes about 100,000 times more sensitive under low illumination than in strong light, depends mostly on the rods. At low intensities only the rods function. Because the cones do not respond, color vision is absent.

IMPORTANT TERMS

absolute threshold
amplitude
auditory nerve
basilar membrane
blind spot
bodily movement
brightness
broad-tuned receptors
ciliary muscles
cochlea
complexity
cones
cornea
dark adaptation
decibel scale
difference threshold
eardrum
equilibrium
Eustachian tube
"fast" fibers
fovea
frequency
gate-control mechanism
hue
inner ear
intensity
iris
just noticeable difference
lens
middle ear
opponent-process theory
optic nerve
organ of Corti
outer ear
oval window
overtones
pattern theory
pheromone
pitch
pupil
receptor
retina
rods
saturation
semicircular canals
sensory adaptation
"slow" fibers
stimulus
taste buds
timbre
vestibular sacs
visual purple
wavelength
Weber's law

SUPPLEMENT:

Retinal Coding, Visual Sharpness, and Color Mixing

As an input for our information processing, the eye works in wondrous ways. The retina is much more than just a passive receiving device, responding mechanically to the presence of light waves. Besides its rods and cones, it contains many more millions of neurons that are connected and interconnected into an elaborate network capable of performing very much like a little brain. As was said early in the chapter, the eye has 127 million receptor cells but only about one million neurons in the optic nerve that runs from the eye toward the brain. Thus the retina's own network of neurons must act as a sort of funnel, channeling information from a wide range of receptors into a much narrower transmission cable. To do this the retinal network must perform a great deal of processing and interpretation. It monitors activity in the rods and cones, condenses the information, and encodes it into meaningful patterns of nervous impulses that are sent along to the cerebral cortex.

Some idea of how all this is accomplished within that little patch of tissue at the back of the eyeball can be gained from Figure 7-15, although the diagram is by necessity just a simplified representation of the actual complexity of the retinal network. Every rod and cone connects to a very short *bipolar cell* that in turn connects to a *ganglion cell* of the optic nerve. Thus the route for information can be summarized as

1. Bleaching of pigment in receptor cell
   stimulates
2. Nervous impulses in bipolar cell
   stimulates
3. Nervous impulses in ganglion cell

But there are many complications. At step 2 in the route a single bipolar cell may make direct contact with just one receptor cell or with many. It may also have indirect contact with some or many other receptors through a *horizontal cell.* Thus it may be stimulated to produce nervous impulses by the activity of only one receptor or in various ways by the activity of many receptors. Likewise at step 3 a ganglion cell has direct contact with just one bipolar cell or with many—and may also have indirect contact with some or many others through an *internal association cell.* It can be stimulated through any of the possible connections. Moreover the impulses it receives often have different effects depending on what pathway has produced them. By measuring the activity of a single ganglion neuron of animals, it has been found that light striking one part of the retina may stimulate the neuron to produce

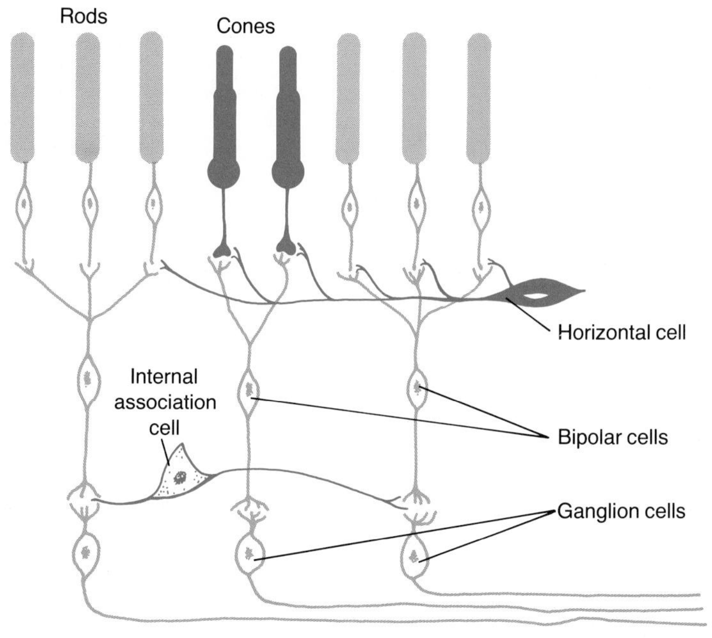

Figure 7-15 The retina's processing network *This is a much simplified diagram of the complex connections and interconnections between nerve cells in the retina that process visual information and funnel it toward the brain. The direct connections run from rods and cones to* bipolar cells *to* ganglion cells *of the optic nerve. The indirect connections are made through* horizontal cells *and* internal association cells. *The way the network operates is explained in the text.*

a burst of impulses, while light at an adjacent part of the retina turns it off (Kuffler, 1953).

All in all, the retinal network is constructed in a way that permits a great amount of processing of visual information before any messages ever leave the eye. In effect, the network monitors what is going on in the receptor cells, compares the activity in one receptor with the activity in others, and extracts and summarizes many kinds of information. The number of possible patterns of nervous impulses created by the intricate network—the coded messages carried by the optic nerve toward the brain—is almost beyond imagination.

Visual sensitivity and acuity

The retinal network, though it always bears a general resemblance to the diagram that was shown in Figure 7-15, varies in its detailed structure at different parts of the retina. At the outer part of the retina, where there are far more rods than cones and in some places no cones at all, several thousand receptors may feed into a single ganglion cell. This helps account for the far greater sensitivity of the outer part of the retina to very low intensities of light—a phenomenon you can observe for yourself by finding a very dim star in the skies at night. If you look directly at the star, so that its light waves fall at the center or fovea of the retina, it will disappear. But if you glance at it from the side, so that its waves fall on the outer part of the retina, you will see it again. One or more ganglion cells serving the outer part of the retina—and picking up messages from thousands of rods—gathered in enough stimulation to fire off a message.

The greater sensitivity to light at the outer part of the retina, however, is accompanied by a considerable loss of sharpness of vision, or *acuity*. The message sent to the brain by the ganglion cell could have originated in the stimulation of any one of the thousands of receptors it serves. Therefore the exact spot at which the retina was stimulated and the exact nature of the stimulus cannot be specified (De Valois, 1966).

At the fovea, the network takes a very different form. The ganglion cells serving the densely packed cones in this part of the retina get messages from only one or a few receptors. Thus acuity is greatest at the fovea. When you read or do anything else that requires a very sharp image, you automatically focus your eyes so that the light waves fall directly on the fovea—where there is a direct line, so to speak, from cone to optic nerve.

Adding and subtracting colors

One question that has interested researchers over the years is this: What happens to our visual sensations when various wavelengths of the spectrum are mixed together? The answer, it turns out, is not at all what everyday experiences would indicate. For example, every schoolchild who owns a paint set knows that if you have no green, you can produce it by combining blue and yellow. But every schoolchild is wrong. Mixing blue and yellow paints does not *combine* the two colors. It does something very different.

This may sound startling, but there is a simple explanation. Blue paint looks blue because it absorbs most of the wavelengths found in the white light provided by sunshine or artificial illumination. It reflects only the waves in and around the blue portion of the spectrum, including, since no paint is a pure blue, some of the green. Yellow paint absorbs most of the wavelengths of white light except those in and around the yellow part of the spectrum, again including some of the green. When you put blue and yellow paint together, you get a mixture that absorbs all the wavelengths except the ones in the green area that both paints happen to reflect. But this is not combining light waves. It is more like subtracting them.

Adding light waves together cannot be done with paint, but only with special equipment. One way is to use color filters that permit only waves of a certain length to get through, like those producing sensations of blue or yellow. When two slide projectors are equipped with different filters, two wavelengths can be thrown on the same white screen and thus actually mixed. The results are as shown in Plate II. Note that the combination of blue and yellow produces not green but a neutral gray.

The laws of *color mixture*—the true blending of light waves, not the mixture of paints—are summarized in Plate III. The combination of any two hues opposite each other in the circle produces gray—and such opposites are known as *complementary colors* because they cancel each other out. Two waves not opposite each other combine into the sensation of a hue somewhere between them in the circle.

Color blindness

A few people—believed to number about 5,000 in the United States—never experience the sensation of hue at all. These people are totally *color blind* and see the world only in shades of gray, like a black-and-white photograph. Perhaps as many as another 1.5 million Americans are color blind to some extent. The most common difficulty is distinguishing reds and greens. Less common is reduced sensitivity to blues and yellows.

Most people who are color blind do not even know it. One reason is that light waves reaching the eye are seldom a fully saturated single wavelength. Both blue and yellow paints, as has been mentioned, reflect some green. Most red objects reflect some yellow waves, and most green objects some blue rays. (Traffic lights are deliberately designed this way, to help people with red-green difficulties.) Color-blind people learn to use subtle differences in saturation—as well as brightness and other clues—to recognize and name hues they never see as the normal eye experiences them. Their deficiencies can readily be detected, however, with tests like the one shown in Plate IV. The tests are useful in steering people away from jobs in which color blindness would be a handicap (or, as in the case of flying an airplane, an actual hazard).

Afterimages

Another visual phenomenon is *afterimages,* which are demonstrated in Plate V. (Experiment with the illustration, according to the instructions, before you go on to the next paragraph.)

What happens when you look at Plate V is this: By staring fixedly at the pattern of colors, you provide a prolonged stimulus to the receptors in the retina and the neurons that carry their messages to the brain. When the stimulus is then withdrawn (as you transfer your gaze to another part of the page) you see an afterimage that is in complementary hues to the original stimulus. If you follow the instructions carefully, this afterimage should be so vivid as to startle you—if not on the first try, at least after you have made a few practice attempts.

Actually there are two afterimages, although this is difficult to demonstrate except under laboratory conditions. Immediately after the stimulus is withdrawn you see a *positive afterimage,* in the same color as before. But this quickly vanishes and is replaced by a longer-lasting *negative afterimage,* in which the complementary colors appear.

Two famous old theories—and how well they have survived

All the phenomena just mentioned—afterimages, color blindness, and the laws of color mixture—have played a part in the long search for an explanation of how the sense of vision operates. The fact that a mixture of red and green waves produces yellow, as was shown in Plate II, was incorporated into the famous *Young-Helmholtz theory,* which was proposed nearly two centuries ago. Young and Helmholtz, working independently, concluded that all our sensations of hue are produced by just three types of color receptors: for red, green, and blue. The sensation of yellow, with no receptor of its own, is produced by simultaneous stimulation of the red and green receptors.

The Young-Helmholtz theory, though developed long before the discovery of the retina's light-sensitive pigments, was in remarkable accord with what is now known about the receptors. It is still valid about the operation of the cones, except that what the theory held to be a red receptor has turned out to be even more sensitive to yellow, and all the cones have been found more broad tuned than Young and Helmholtz suspected. The theory was never adequate, however, to explain color blindness or afterimages.

If a yellow sensation were indeed the result of combined activity of red-sensitive and green-sensitive cones, as the theory held, then people with red-green color blindness would be expected to have difficulty with yellows as well. Yet people with even extreme red-green deficiencies usually experience vivid sensations of yellow. Moreover yellow afterimages never result from red or green stimulation. Instead they follow blue.

For these reasons the Young-Helmholtz explanation was always suspect, and about a century ago another famous theory was proposed as an alternative. This was the *Hering theory,* which held that the visual system must somehow operate on the basis of nervous impulses paired as black-white, red-green, and blue-yellow. This theory provided a logical explanation for all the known facts about color blindness and afterimages. For example, blue would produce its afterimages because it stimulated the blue-yellow pair in the blue direction. This nervous activity would continue for an instant after the stimulus was removed, resulting in the brief afterimage of blue. Then the complementary yellow afterimage would be produced when the blue-yellow pair acted in the opposite direction as it returned to normal.

Today's view of color vision is of course a combination of the two old theories. Modern knowledge of the retina's light-sensitive pigments and activity in individual neurons of the visual pathway has shown that Young-Helmholtz was generally correct about the receptors, Hering about the neurons. The early theories, without the help of today's laboratory techniques, made some remarkably accurate guesses.

SUMMARY OF SUPPLEMENT

1. Processing of information picked up by the rods and cones begins in the retina, which contains an elaborate network of neurons. This network acts as a sort of funnel, channeling information from the 127 million rods and cones into the mere one million fibers of the optic nerve.
2. The direct route through the retina's network is from a receptor cell to a *bipolar cell* (which may make contact with only one or with many receptors) then to a *ganglion cell* of the optic nerve (which may make contact with one or many bipolar cells). The route may take many variations because of interconnections provided by *horizontal cells* and *internal association cells.*

3. The fovea provides our greatest sharpness, or *acuity,* of vision because its densely packed cones connect with only one or a few ganglion cells. The outer part of the retina is the most sensitive because as many as several thousand of its rods may feed into a single ganglion cell—and stimulation of any one of the rods may produce impulses in that ganglion cell.
4. The search for explanations of vision has always been influenced by the laws of *color mixture* and the phenomena of *color blindness* and *afterimages.* Two famous old explanations were the *Young-Helmholtz theory,* which attributed color vision to three types of cones, and the *Hering theory,* which held that vision depends on nervous impulses paired as black-white, red-green, and blue-yellow. Modern thinking is a combination of these two theories.

IMPORTANT TERMS

acuity
afterimage (positive, negative)
bipolar cell
color blindness
color mixing
complementary colors
ganglion cell
Hering theory
horizontal cell
internal association cell
Young-Helmholtz theory

RECOMMENDED READINGS

Carterette, E. C., and Friedman, M. P., eds. *Handbook of perception,* Vol. IV (Hearing) and Vol. V (Seeing). New York: Academic Press, 1975 and 1978.

Hochberg, J. *Perception,* 2d ed. Englewood Cliffs, N.J.: Prentice-Hall, 1978.

Kaufman, L. *Perception: the world transformed.* New York: Oxford University Press, 1979.

Levine, M. W., and Shefner, J. M. *Fundamentals of perception.* Reading, Mass.: Addison-Wesley, 1981.

Lindsay, P. H., and Norman, D. A. *Human information processing,* 2d ed. New York: Academic Press, 1977.

Ludel, J. *Introduction to sensory processes.* San Francisco: Freeman, 1978.

CHAPTER 8

How the nervous system is "wired" for survival 273
The nervous system's feature detectors
Levels of feature-detector processing
Perception as an inborn skill
Reality and illusion
Our perceptual specialty: detecting change and contrast

Selection and attention 279
Why we select as we do
How many inputs can you handle?
Selection and exploration

Perceptual organization 283
Some rules of organization
Perceiving a stable and consistent world
Perceiving distance and depth
The relationship between distance and size

What does the information mean?—the element of interpretation 291
Prototypes, feature analysis, and "global" processing
It's a face—but whose face?
Expectations, mental set, and context

Summary 293

Important Terms 295

Supplement: Perception and altered states of consciousness 296

Sleep, dreams, hypnosis, and meditation 296
Ordinary and paradoxical sleep
How much sleep do we need?
Why do we sleep at all?
Hypnosis
Meditation

Drugs 301
How widespread is drug use?
Marijuana
LSD (or "acid")
PCP (or "angel dust")
Stimulants
Cocaine
Sedatives and tranquilizers
Heroin

Summary of Supplement 307

Important Terms 309

Recommended Readings 309

Psychology and Society
Extrasensory perception—new frontier or human delusion? 297

Perception: The First Step in Information Processing

If you had to rely solely on the raw and unprocessed information that reaches your sense organs, the world would be a baffling expanse of confusion, bombarding you with an almost hopeless jumble of stimuli. Throughout your waking hours light waves bounce to your eyes from a multitude of surfaces, in all the wavelengths of the spectrum and a wide array of intensities. Sound waves pulsate against your eardrums in an overwhelming barrage of frequencies and amplitudes. The nerve endings in your skin react to the temperature of the air and the pressure of your clothing or the chair you sit on. Your senses of bodily movement and equilibrium react to even the slightest movement you make, your sense of smell to any trace of odor.

What a bewildering profusion of inputs you must cope with at any given moment—and how rapidly and relentlessly the pattern keeps changing. When someone speaks to you, for example, your hearing receptors are under a rapid-fire onslaught of 600 to 720 separate sounds and pauses every minute (Hochberg, 1978). The sounds flow "in a continuous and indivisible stream," and none of them has any real identity of its own. If you chopped up a tape recording of speech into the individual sounds, you would have no idea what the sounds represented—and could never splice any of the tiny bits of tape into another meaningful recording (Levine and Shefner, 1981).

Yet somehow we human beings manage to make sense of all the miscellaneous, ever-shifting, potentially confusing stimulation the world provides to our sense organs. Without any conscious effort we extract the precise information that is important to us (Gibson, 1969). We know almost instantaneously what it means. The key to this remarkable accomplishment is *perception,* which can be defined as *the process through which we become aware of our environment by selecting, organizing, and interpreting the evidence from our senses.*

How the nervous system is "wired" for survival

Without our skill at perception we would be in deep trouble. Much of our learning and thinking would be laborious and perhaps even impossible. For example, how long do you suppose it would take you to read this page if you had to work at deciphering every visual stimulus that reaches your eyes? That is to say, if you had to figure out each time that a vertical line with a little horizontal dash across it is a *t,* a vertical line with a curve an *h,* a partial circle with a horizontal line across it an *e*—and that a combination of *t, h,* and *e* means *the?* How long would you last in big-city traffic if you had to keep asking yourself: "That patch of blue light waves out there—is it an automobile or something else? Is it moving? How fast and in what direction? Is it dangerous or can I ignore it?"

But you do not have to stop to think. You perceive the automobile and its movement without even trying. Undoubtedly the process requires considerable work by the nervous system, but the work takes place quickly and effortlessly. In fact in most cases you cannot help perceiving what you do, even if you make a deliberate effort, because perception is a process over which we have little conscious control.

The process of perception enables you to move about confidently, taking for granted that you know what is going on around you and will immediately become aware of any danger. Perception is one of the psychological abilities that have enabled the human race to survive. Had our ancestors not been able to recognize immediately the approach of an enemy—had they been forced to stop and analyze every nervous impulse from their eyes, then painstakingly piece together all these bits of information—they would never have lived through the prehistoric ages.

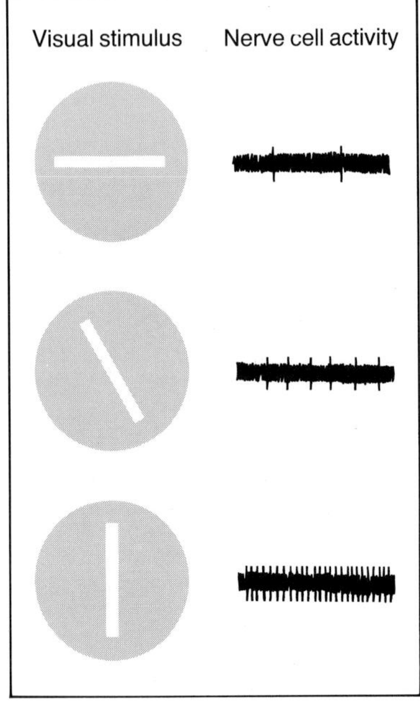

Figure 8-1 How a feature-detector cell works *The spikes in the graph lines are recordings of the nervous impulses in one of the feature-detector cells of a cat's brain. In response to a horizontal line, the cell displays only its normal amount of spontaneous activity. To an oblique line, there is a small response. To a vertical line—the kind of feature to which this cell is specifically sensitive—there is a sharp burst of activity (Hubel, 1963).*

The nervous system's feature detectors

Part of our skill at perception depends on the structure of the nervous system—the way it is "wired" to extract information from the environment. The nerve pathways from the sense organs to the brain, and the sensory areas of the brain itself, contain a great number of specialized cells that are quick to detect important features of the environment. In the visual system these cells, called *feature detectors,* are especially sensitive to patterns and to movement. In the system for hearing the feature detectors are especially sensitive to pitches and changes in pitch. Thus the cells are ideally suited to respond immediately to stimuli that represent such important information as the shapes of objects, motion, and the flow of conversation.

Much of our knowledge of feature detectors comes from the research of David Hubel and Torsten Wiesel, who shared a 1981 Nobel prize for their work. Hubel and Wiesel measured the nervous impulses in individual cells of the visual cortex of cats and monkeys, while the animals looked at a screen on which various kinds of stimuli were flashed. They found that some of the brain cells responded vigorously to a vertical line on the screen but did not respond at all to a horizontal line, as shown in Figure 8-1. Other cells acted in the opposite fashion, responding to a horizontal line but not to a vertical line. Others responded most vigorously to angles, and still others to movements (Hubel and Wiesel, 1965).

Similarly it has been found that the sensory areas in the brains of animals—and presumably of human beings as well—contain feature detectors specialized to respond to various characteristics of sound waves. Some are activated most strongly by low-pitched sounds, others by high-pitched sounds, and still others only by a change in pitch (Whitfield and Evans, 1965).

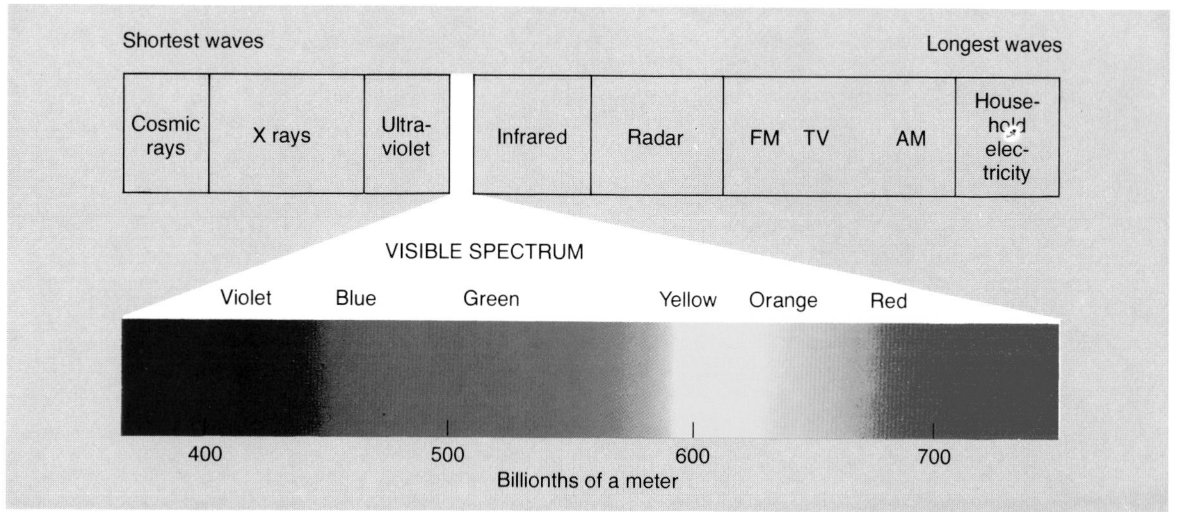

Plate I Electromagnetic energy and the visible spectrum *Various forms of electromagnetic radiation range from cosmic rays, the shortest waves, to ordinary household electricity, the longest. The visible spectrum of light, with waves ranging from about 380 to 780 billionths of a meter, occupies only a small portion of the band.*

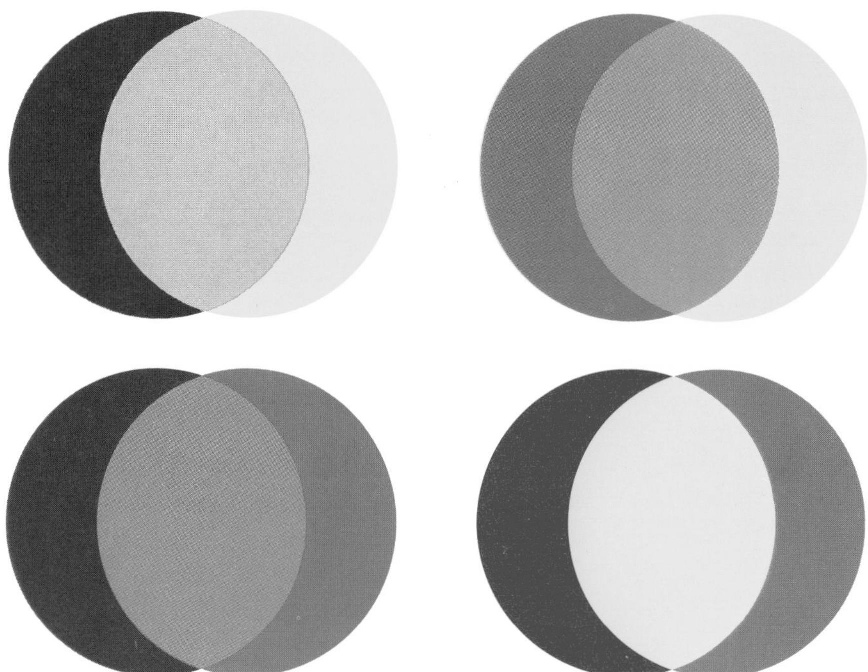

Plate II What happens when light waves are combined *The circles show what happens when two colors are projected through filters onto the same screen. When blue and yellow are combined, the result is gray—far different from the result of mixing blue and yellow paint. Note also that the combination of red and green produces yellow. This fact greatly influenced the development of theories of color vision, as will be explained in the text. It is also the principle by which color television operates. Television tubes produce three kinds of dots on the screen—blue, red, and green—which combine to create all the hues we see.*

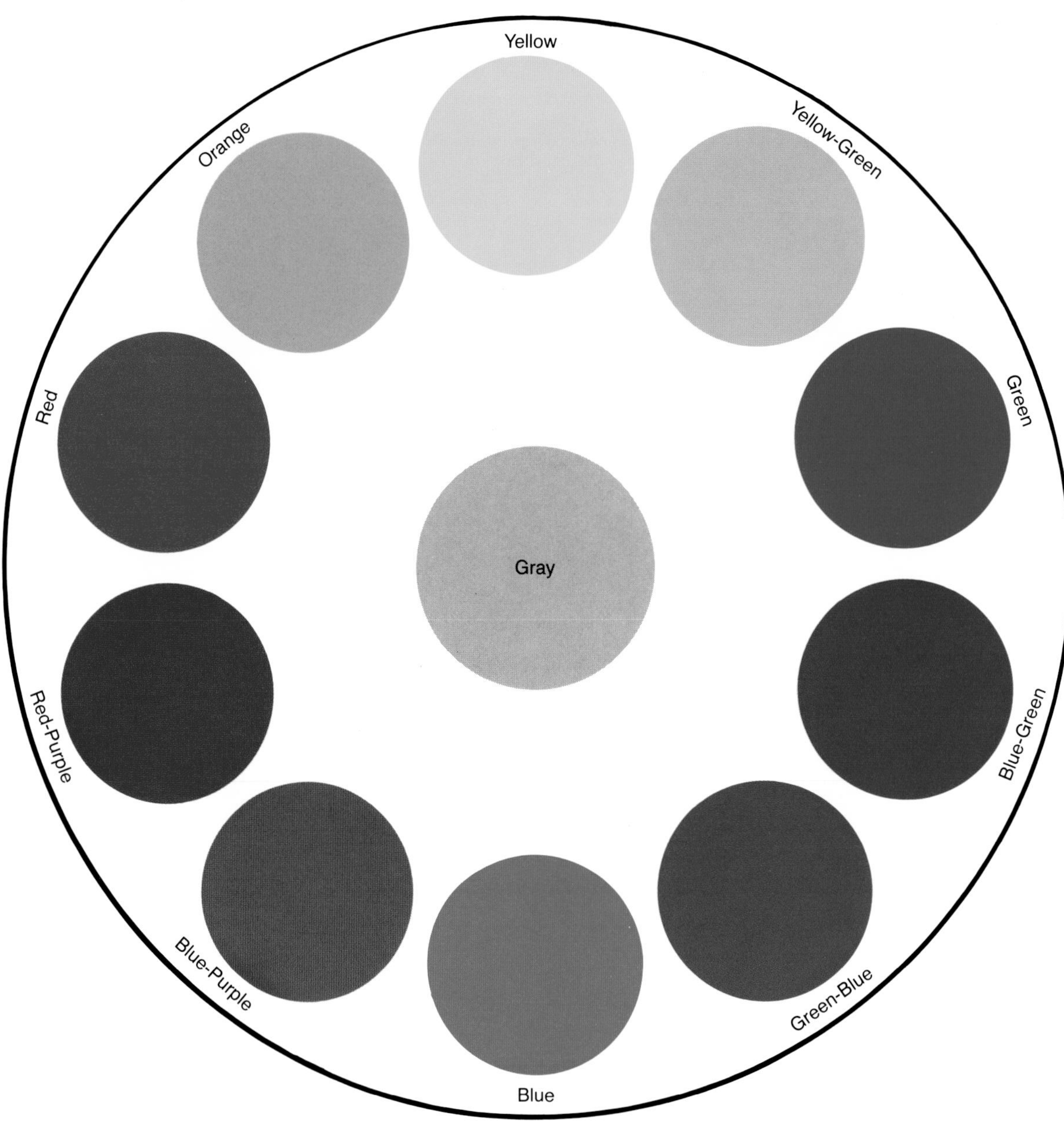

Plate III A circular guide to the hues *The laws of color mixture are summarized by this circle. To find what hue a combination of any two will produce, draw a line between them. If the line passes through the center of the circle, the result is gray. If not, the resulting hue lies in between—like a green-yellow or a blue-green.*

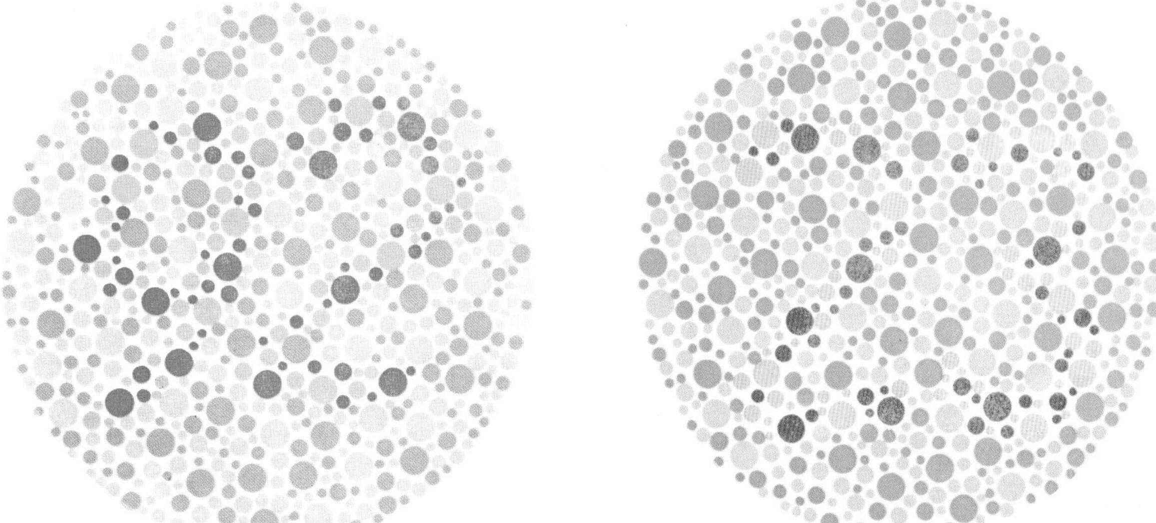

Plate IV A test of color blindness *What numbers, if any, do you see in the circles? People with normal color vision see a 92 at the left and a 23 at the right. People with various types of color blindness see something different: only partial numbers or no numbers at all.*

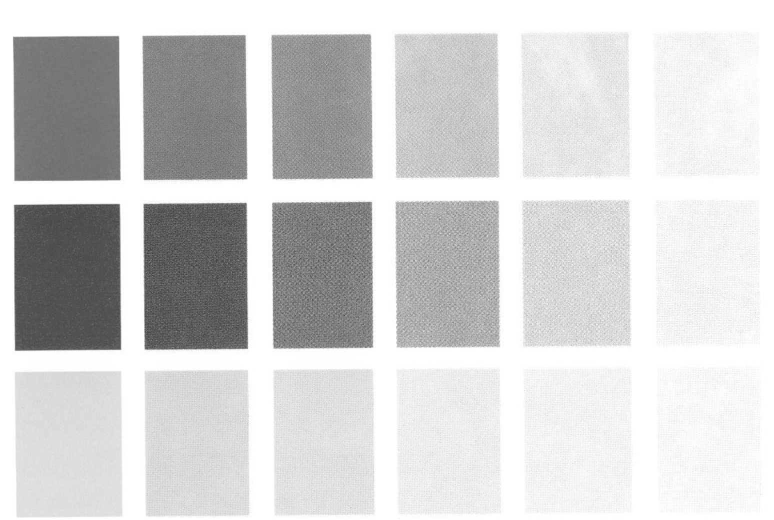

Plate V Saturated versus unsaturated color *The rows of rectangles show what happens if we start with the purest possible wavelength of one of the three pigment primary colors, then gradually mix in other wavelengths. The rectangles at the extreme left are said to be completely saturated. Those at the far right have very low saturation.*

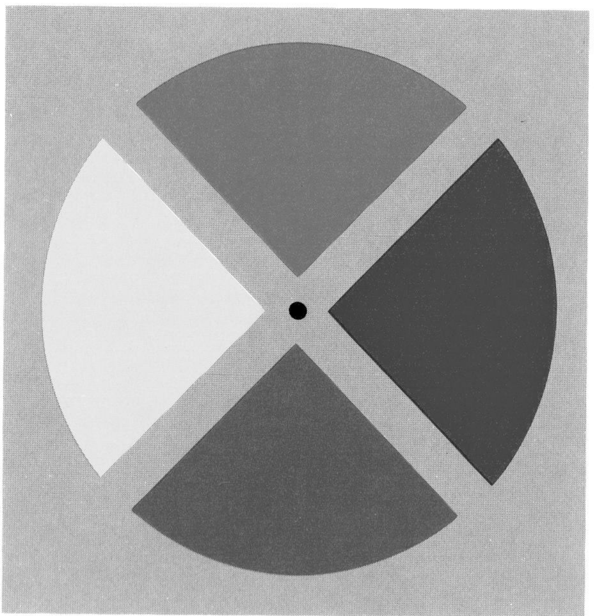

Plate VI A demonstration of after-images *Focus your eyes on the dot in the center of the circle at left and gaze steadily for a half minute or more. Then look quickly at the dot in the center of the square at right. You should see a startling change in hue.*

Plate VII The afterimage comes to modern art *This modern painting uses the principle of the afterimage to create a startling effect. To experience it, stare at the top rectangle for about half a minute, fixing your eyes on the white spot in the center. Then shift your eyes quickly to concentrate on the dark spot in the lower rectangle. The painting,* Flags, *is by* Jasper Johns, 1965, *and is from the artist's collection.*

Levels of feature-detector processing

Hubel and Wiesel found that feature detectors range from the very simple to the very complex, performing a hierarchy of functions. At the lowest level of the visual system a *simple cell* reacts to a certain kind of stimulus in a certain part of the visual field—for example, a vertical line whose light waves strike the very center of the retina. If the same line is moved to one side, the cell stops its activity. At the next level a *complex cell,* which receives messages from a number of simple cells, continues to respond even when the stimulus appears at a different location. At the highest level a *hypercomplex cell,* which receives messages from a number of complex cells, makes very fine distinctions among various kinds of stimuli. To activate one such cell most vigorously, for example, a line must be not only vertical but one particular size in length and width.

Thus the processing becomes more and more refined at each level of the feature-detection wiring. The operation can best be explained by speaking for a moment as if the units of the nervous system had minds of their own. An individual receptor cell, stimulated only by the light waves striking its own tiny spot on the retina, cannot possibly know whether the light is part of a vertical line, a horizontal line, or anything else. But in the visual pathway between receptors and highest part of the brain, a simple feature detector cell, receiving messages that originated in a number of receptors, can begin to get an idea. At each subsequent step the processing continues—with a complex cell receiving and analyzing information from many simple cells, and a hypercomplex cell from many complex cells, until the information about the stimulus is fully developed and translated into a sensation. We are immediately aware of the shape of the object that is stimulating the eye's receptors, as well as where it is and how it is moving.

Perception as an inborn skill

This kind of perceptual skill does not have to be learned. It is simply an inborn characteristic of the nervous system. Hubel and Wiesel studied newborn monkeys—or in some cases very young monkeys kept away from any visual stimulation since birth—and found feature cells in full operation. Simple, complex, and hypercomplex cells were all activated by the very first stimulation of the eye's receptors, responding in much the same way as the cells of older animals with visual experience (Wiesel and Hubel, 1974). For at least some animals there is a period right after birth when lack of visual stimulation may cause permanent damage to the functioning of the feature-detector cells (Wiesel and Hubel, 1965)—but all the necessary wiring seems to be in place at birth, prepared to operate barring any unusual circumstances.

We cannot be sure, of course, that the Hubel and Wiesel findings apply to our own nervous system. Their experiments on the animal brain cannot be duplicated with human beings. There is considerable indirect evidence, however, that the human nervous system is wired in the same way (McCullough, 1965). It appears that the pathways of the sensory system not only receive the inputs provided by the sense organs but begin the information processing by making an initial selection and interpretation of these inputs. It has been said that they "condense the information present in the world down to certain specific features that are essential to the organism" (Levine and Shefner, 1981).

Reality and illusion

The process of perception, aided by the inborn characteristics of the nervous system, is the source of our first quick impressions of what is going on around us. The process is not perfect, and our first impressions are not always in accord with the facts. For example, you may have had the experience, when riding along a highway, of being sure you saw a dead dog at the side of the road—only to discover, as you got closer, that it was just a piece of rumpled cloth. Your perceptual process, in its effort to make sense out of the visual stimulation reaching your eyes, signaled *dog* when in fact there was no dog at all. Students of perception have shown that you can be fooled by many kinds of optical illusions, some of which are illustrated in Figure 8-2.

Sometimes we perceive motion where none exists. A stationary spot of light, viewed in darkness without any frame of reference, may seem to move of its own accord. This phenomenon, known as the *autokinetic illusion,* used to plague pilots flying at night, who had trouble judging the position of a beacon light or another plane visible only by the lights on its wingtips and tail. The problem has been solved by lights that flash on and off, greatly reducing the chances of error.

Another visual illusion, called *stroboscopic motion,* is illustrated in Figure 8-3. This one has been turned to advantage in motion pictures, which are actually a succession of still pictures flashed on the screen at the rate of about 24 a second, and in television, where still pictures are flashed at about 30 per second. What you actually see is a series of stationary shots similar to those in Figure 8-4. If you viewed these photos in rapid succession, as you view movies or television, your eyes would fill in the gaps and the horse would seem to jump smoothly over the hurdle.

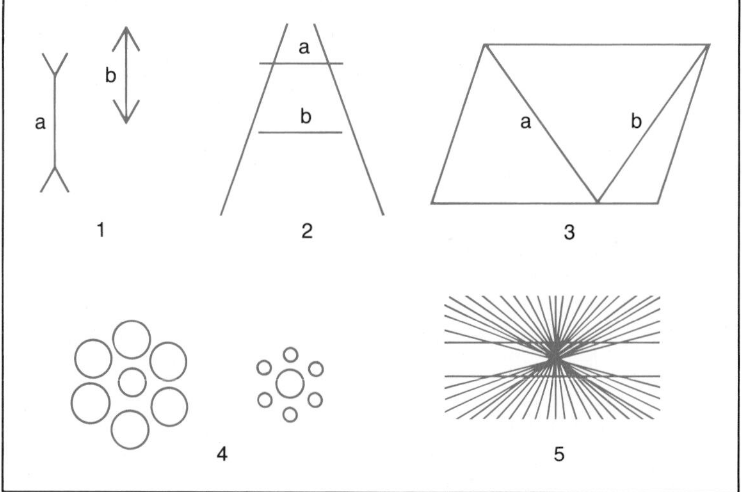

Figure 8-2 How do you perceive these drawings? *Is line* a *or line* b *longer in no. 1? In no. 2? In no. 3? Which of the two inner circles in no. 4 is larger? In no. 5, are the horizontal lines straight or curved? After you have made your judgments, you can discover with a ruler that all the lines* a *and* b *are the same size, and so are the two circles in no. 4. The lines in no. 5 are parallel.*

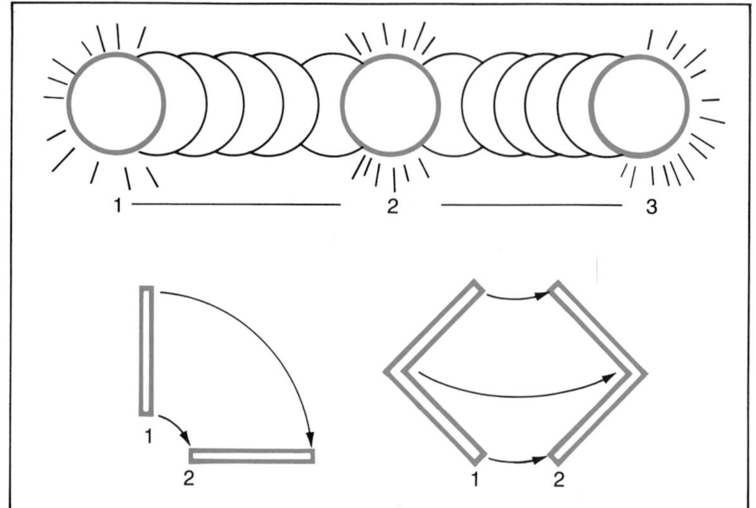

Figure 8-3 Stroboscopic motion *These are examples of the apparent motion produced by stationary objects. At top, lights 1, 2, and 3 are flashed briefly and in rapid succession. Nothing moves, and in fact there is nothing in the spaces between the lights. But the viewer perceives the light as moving smoothly from position 1 to position 3, as indicated by the shaded circles. At bottom, two slits of light shown in rapid succession appear to move as shown by the arrows. The bar at left seems to flop from vertical to horizontal. The slits at right seem to flip over and move in three dimensions, as when the page of a book is turned.*

Perceptual illusions may also occur during what are called *altered states of consciousness,* like those produced by drugs and hypnosis, as will be discussed in the chapter supplement. Indeed people in altered states of consciousness sometimes believe they see objects that do not even exist. In general, however, perception gives us a realistic view of what is going on in the world. Our first impressions, arrived at so quickly and automatically, are usually accurate and useful.

Our perceptual specialty: detecting change and contrast

Our inborn skills are particularly adept at spotting any *change* in stimulation, which is often the most useful information of all. Indeed our

Figure 8-4 A century-old forerunner of the motion picture industry *This famous 19th-century series of pictures was made by using a battery of cameras whose shutters could be tripped in rapid succession. They resemble the still photos now shown on motion picture and television screens to produce the effect of smooth motion.*

nervous system makes it almost impossible to ignore change. If a radio is playing softly in the background while you are reading, you may pay no attention to it—but cannot help noticing if the sound stops. You are instantly aware of the change if the light in the room becomes brighter because of a sudden surge in electricity, or dimmer because a filament has burned out.

Movement, which is a form of change, is such a compelling stimulus that even very young babies try hard to follow any moving object with their eyes. When you look at a pasture full of horses, you are most aware of those that are running. An advertising sign that uses stroboscopic motion demands your attention far more than a sign that remains stationary.

The reason movement leaps immediately to awareness probably also depends on inborn characteristics of the nervous system. It appears that the wiring of the visual system contains a separate pathway for motion, in addition to another route for patterns (Sekuler and Levinson, 1977). This is a characteristic of great potential value in survival, for there are many situations in which it is more important to detect and respond quickly to the movement of an object than to know what the object may be. To our ancestors, for example, the sudden approach of a wild animal meant danger regardless of whether the animal happened to be a lion or a bear.

Another compelling stimulus is *contrast*—like any sharp difference in the intensity of light reflected by two objects in the field of vision. Even babies are attracted by contrast. If a black triangle is placed in the field of vision of babies only 2 days old, they will spend most of their time focusing on one of the triangle's sides or angles—the places where there is the sharpest contrast between the black of the triangle and the light background (Salapatek and Kessen, 1966). Babies also show an early interest in the human face, especially the face of the mother. What they

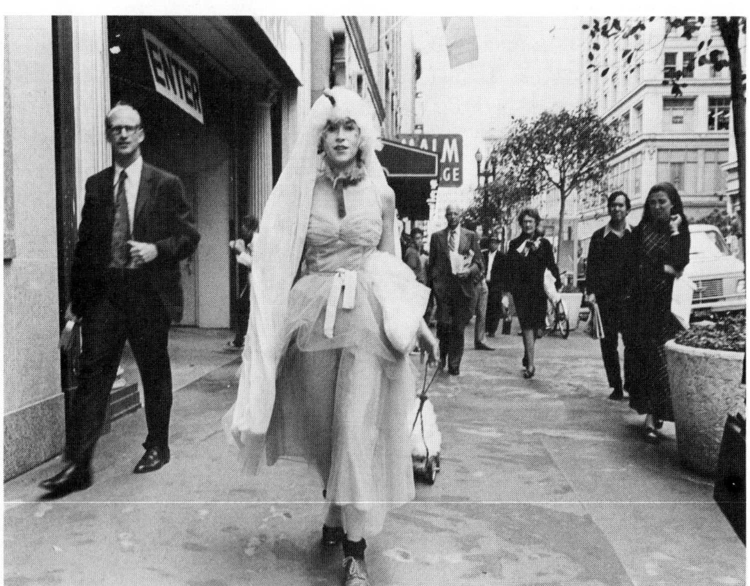

The compelling nature of contrast is apparent in the curious stares directed at the oddly-dressed pedestrian.

notice particularly is the high degree of contrast between a light face and dark eyes or hairline, or between a dark face and the whites of the eyes and the teeth.

Detecting contrast, of course, is an important element in determining the shape and nature of objects. The reason contrast leaps to attention, like movement, again appears to be the structure of the sensory system. It has been found that most cells in the optic nerve of animals, carrying messages from the eye's receptors toward the brain, are vigorously stimulated by light falling on one part of the retina but inhibited from producing nervous impulses by light striking adjoining areas (Kuffler, 1953). At the corner of a black triangle, for example, the white background would not only activate several such cells but also turn off the activity in other cells concerned with the adjacent black area. This phenomenon, called *lateral interaction* in the retina, provides an inborn mechanism for detecting contrast.

Besides change, movement, and contrast, there are two other stimulus characteristics that have a considerable effect on the process of perception. One is *size,* with large objects more compelling than small ones. When you look at the front page of a newspaper, you notice the biggest headlines first. The second is *intensity.* When you drive at night along a business street where all the signs are of equal size, the brightest one is the most compelling. When you stand on a crowded bus, you may ignore the pressure of the people pressed against you—but you notice at once if someone accidentally pokes an elbow into your ribs.

Selection and attention

Of the three elements that constitute perception—selection, organization, and interpretation—*selection* heads the list. This is because we cannot possibly cope with all the varied and ever-changing stimulation that bombards our sense organs. To avoid utter confusion, we have to select and pay attention to only a small part of it.

What we select depends on many factors, ranging from automatic and involuntary to conscious and deliberate. At one extreme are the choices dictated by the inborn tendencies of our sensory system, with its alertness to change, movement, and contrast. At the other extreme are the kinds of choices that might be made by a man working as a forest ranger, as he stands on a high observation tower looking out over a wide expanse of hills, valleys, open spaces, trees, and streams. Scanning the scene, he thinks he spots a plume of smoke. He raises his binoculars and focuses his eyes on this single aspect of the landscape. Only now, after selecting this one spot on which to concentrate, can he try to find some organization in the stimuli reaching his eyes (do they really represent a plume of smoke or something else?) and make an interpretation (if it is smoke is it coming from a cabin or is it the start of a forest fire?).

Between the two extremes are many gradations that are difficult to classify. The in-between choices seem to depend partly on inborn tendencies and partly on learning and experience, and often it is hard to say whether we make them consciously or unconsciously. They may reflect our entire personality or our mood of the moment. At any rate the process of preception must start in one way or another with which of all the environment's stimuli we select for further information processing.

Why we select as we do

Because so many factors can influence selection, people looking at the same event in the environment may percieve it in different ways. Julian Hochberg has pointed out that even looking at a page like this one can result in a number of varied impressions. As you read it now, you are probably paying attention sentence by sentence because you want to learn what the words have to say. You perceive the meaning of the words. But suppose this were somebody else's book, from a course you were not interested in, and you had merely picked it up for lack of anything better to do. In that case you might just look at it causally, with no intention of reading it, and perceive it merely as a page of printed matter. If you were a proofreader at a publishing house, you would ignore the meaning of the page and concentrate your attention instead on perceiving any typographical errors (Hochberg, 1978). To emphasize this point, three typographical errors have been planted on the page. You probably did not perceive them. But if you go back and read the page again, directing your attention to misspellings, you will find them.

As the possible ways of perceiving a page would indicate, we are likely to pay attention to events that interest us for one reason or another. When people look at words flashed only briefly for their inspection, they are better at recognizing terms related to their own special interests than unrelated terms. Subjects interested in religion are quick to perceive words like *sacred.* Subjects interested in economics are quick to perceive *income* (Postman, Bruner, and McGinnies, 1948).

Our motives also play a part. Ambitious people are especially quick to perceive words like *strive* and *perfect* (McClelland and Liberman, 1949). In fact the way we select stimuli may be influenced by our entire personality and also by our emotional state at the moment. You can observe for yourself how mood affects selection. When you are feeling out of sorts you are likely to pay attention to anything in the environment that is potentially irritating—a noise in the next room, a watchband that feels too tight, another person's frown. When you are feeling on top of the world you may be unusually aware that the sun is shining, everybody seems to be friendly to you, and there are a great many attractive people walking around. As the old saying goes, a pessimist sees a glass that is half empty, an optimist a glass that is half full.

How many inputs can you handle?

It is difficult to pay attention to more than one event in the environment at a time, and selecting one stimulus usually means losing perception of the other possible inputs. A frequent example occurs in driving an automobile. As you drive along a highway where the traffic is light, you are listening to the radio—to a football game or a news broadcast that is about to give a weather report. But now you come to a busy intersection. The traffic lights are changing. You have to slow down, veer into another lane, watch out for a car that has moved into your path. When all this activity ends, you find to your surprise that the score in the football game has changed or that the news is over and you have missed the weather report. While your attention was directed elsewhere the radio was on just as loud as before, but your perceptual processes missed it entirely.

Many laboratory experiments have shown that it is especially difficult to process two different inputs if they arrive in the same sensory channel. In studying sounds heard at the same time, experimenters have used earphones that deliver one spoken message to the right ear and a completely different one to the left ear. It has been found that subjects can pay attention to and understand either one of the two messages—but not both at once. Indeed subjects usually get very little information of any kind from the unattended ear. In one experiment, for example, they were asked to listen carefully to the message in the right ear and also to tap with a ruler any time they heard the word *the* in either ear. They caught most of the *the's* heard by the right ear but only a few of those heard by the left ear (Treisman, 1969).

For visual stimuli, the crucial importance of selection has been most effectively shown by the experiment illustrated in Figure 8-5. When subjects looking at the mirror were asked to follow the boxing match, they could not say what had happened in the ball game. Those who directed their attention to the ball game did not know what had happened in the boxing match (Neisser and Becklen, 1975).

It is somewhat easier to pay attention to two things at once when two different senses are being stimulated. You may have noticed, for example, that you can continue to read with fairly good comprehension while listening to a radio or a telephone conversation. Apparently the mental processes required for perception can operate more efficiently on two different kinds of sensory information than on two messages in the same sensory channel.

Selection and exploration

What selection does, in the last analysis, is help us perceive what is likely to be important to us, ignore all the many other inputs provided

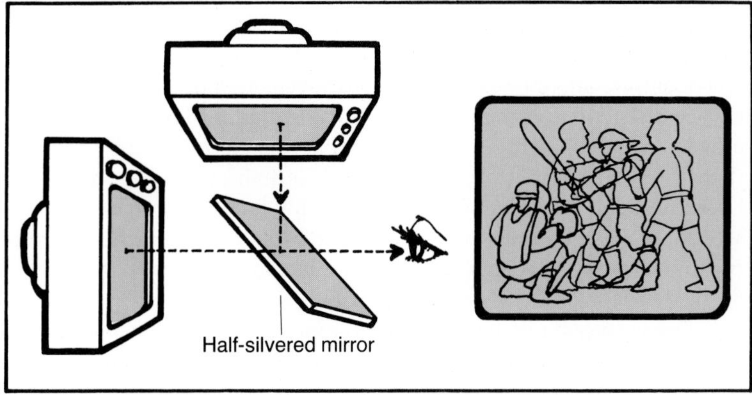

Figure 8-5 Boxing match or ball game—it can't be both *In the experiment on selective perception discussed in the text, one television set showed a videotape of a boxing match visible to subjects through a one-way mirror. Another set showed a tape of a baseball game, reflected off the mirror to the eyes of the subjects. Thus subjects saw two events occurring at the same time, as in the drawing at the left. For what they perceived, see the text (Hochberg, 1978).*

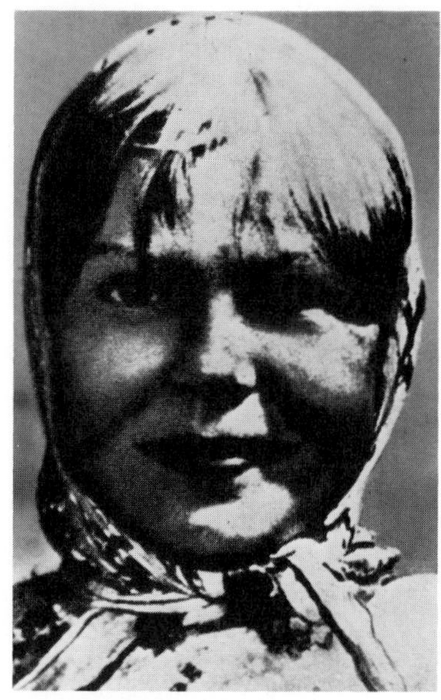

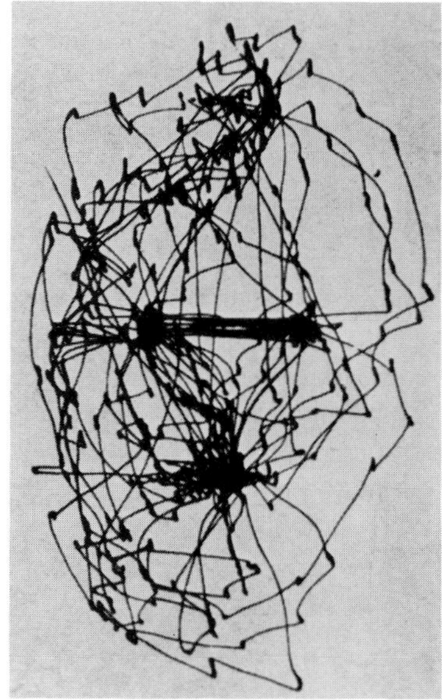

Figure 8-6 The scanning process *The pattern of lines was made by bouncing a light beam off the white of a man's eye, thus recording his eye movements as he looked for a few minutes at the photograph of the girl. Note how many movements took place and how they provided information about all the important elements of the photo (Yarbus, 1967).*

by our sense organs, and concentrate on using the rest of our information-processing talents to the best possible advantage. In lower animals, this function of selection can be observed in their behavior toward a new stimulus, which Pavlov called the *orienting reflex* (or, in his lighter moments, the *what-is-it? reflex*). Animals look, prick their ears, sniff, and often feel the object with their paws or their lips. They appear to be exploring for the maximum of information.

We human beings explore the world mostly with our eyes. When we notice something unusual out of the corner of the eye—usually because of movement or contrast—we move the eyeballs to bring the image to the center of the retina where our vision is sharpest. Then we make a series of scanning movements, as illustrated in Figure 8-6. These scanning movements occur even when we think we are staring fixedly at a stimulus like the Figure 8-6 photo, meaning that the eyes send the brain information about first one part of the photo, then another and still others. Somehow the brain manages to piece together this rapid succession of fragmentary bits of information into a perception of the photograph as a whole. The way this is done resembles the creation of a mosaic from tiny bits of tile—but how it is done is only dimly understood.

Though we are not aware of the eye movements, they somehow focus first on the most informative parts of the stimulus. The subject whose movements are shown in Figure 8-6 probably glanced first at the left eye, then the mouth, right eye, bright patch of hair at the top, and nose. Even these few scanning movements, taking hardly more than a single second, provided all the most essential information about the nature of the photograph. The later movements served only to verify, refine, and fill in the details of the first impression.

When we direct our attention to exploring a new stimulus, we human beings exhibit our own version of the orienting reflex. Many changes may take place in the body, all of such a nature that they facilitate perception and prepare for action if the stimulus calls for it. The pupils of the eye dilate and admit more light (Hess, 1965). The pattern of brain waves changes (Tecce, 1971). Heart rate and breathing speed up and the muscles of the body begin to tense. When we really pay attention, we are attentive all over.

Perceptual organization

When we select a stimulus in the environment for further exploration, the first thing we want to know is: *What is it?* To answer this question, we have to see or hear the stimulus as something that hangs together as a unit of some kind, separate and distinguishable from all the other stimuli the environment provides. We must see light waves organized into some kind of object—an animal, an automobile, a face, something. Or we must hear a string of sound waves organized into the meaningful pattern of human speech, or a rap at the door, or an approaching car.

In vision we organize stimuli into an object largely by the perceptual principle of *figure and ground.* As you read this page, for example, your eyes are stimulated by the white space and many little black lines, curves, squiggles, and dots. Your perceptual process organizes these stimuli into black figures—letters, words, and punctuation marks—seen against a white ground. This is also the way you perceive a chair, a face, or the moon in the sky. The figure hangs together, into an organized shape. The ground is a neutral and formless setting for the figure. What separates the two and sets the figure off from the ground is a clearly perceived dividing line called a *contour.* The separation depends in part on our inborn skill at perceiving contrast, probably because of the way feature detectors operate.

Some interesting examples of how we organize visual stimuli into figure and ground are shown in Figure 8-7. In the upper drawing you can perceive a white figure—the goblet—against a colored ground. Or you can perceive two colored figures—the faces—against a white ground. But you cannot perceive both at once. In the bottom drawing you can perceive some strange colored figures against a white ground. Or you can perceive the white figure TIE against a colored ground.

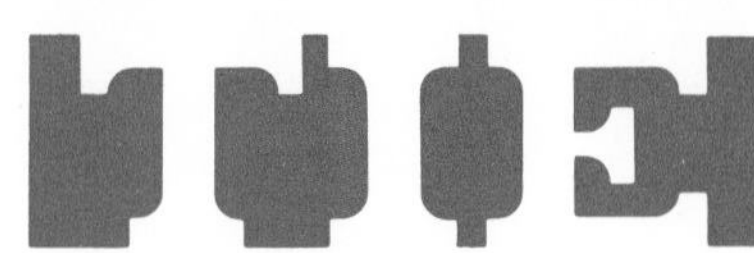

Figure 8-7 The principle of figure and ground *When you first look at the top drawing you probably perceive a white goblet. In the bottom drawing you probably perceive some colored figures that look a little like pieces of a jigsaw puzzle. But you can also perceive something quite different in the two drawings, as explained in the text.*

Some rules of organization

Although the same stimuli can sometimes be grouped into very different patterns, there are a number of rules of organization that generally apply. The most important are the following:

Closure refers to the fact that we do not need a complete and uninterrupted contour to perceive a figure. If part of the contour is missing, our perceptual processes fill in the gaps. This rule of perception is illustrated in Figure 8-8. The rule of closure also operates for sounds. A tape recording of a spoken message can be doctored so that many of the sounds are missing—consonants, vowels, syllables, or entire words. Yet if you heard the tape you would have no trouble perceiving the message.

Figure 8-8 Some examples of closure *Though the figures are incomplete in one way or another, we perceive them at once for what they are.*

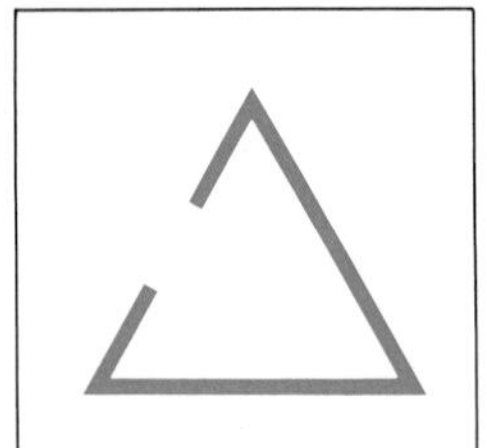

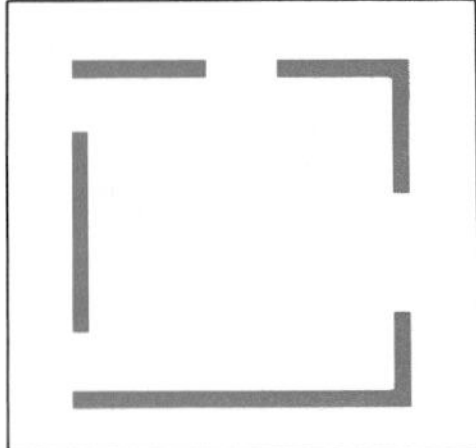

Continuity, which is closely related to closure, is the tendency to perceive continuous lines and patterns. An example is shown in Figure 8-9. The two lines at the left, seen separated in space, have their own continuity, but when they are put together as at the right, a different kind of continuity makes us perceive them quite differently. In looking at any kind of complex visual stimulus we are likely to perceive the organization dictated by the most compelling kind of continuity.

Similarity and proximity are illustrated in Figure 8-10. The checkerboard lettered A, with blocks all the same color and equal distances apart, has no real pattern inside it. If you keep looking at it and shift your eyes from one point to another, your tendency to find organization is likely to make you perceive some patterns—vertical rows, horizontal rows, or groups of squares arranged in pairs, squares, or rectangles—but these patterns are not compelling and are likely to keep shifting. In B, however, removing the color from some of the blocks makes a white cross fairly leap off the page. This demonstrates the rule of similarity, which is that we tend to group stimuli that are alike.

In variation C of the checkerboard some of the colored blocks have been moved closer together, and now you clearly perceive a pattern of four squares. This demonstrates the rule of proximity, which is that we tend to group together stimuli that are close together in space. The rule also applies to sounds. When we hear a series of sounds that are all alike, the pattern we hear depends on the timing. When we hear click-click . . . click-click . . . click-click (with the dots indicating a pause) the rule of proximity dictates that we organize the sounds into pairs. When we hear click-click-click . . . click-click-click we perceive patterns of three. Even different sounds presented this way—click-buzz-ring . . . click-buzz-ring—are perceived in groups of three.

Perceiving a stable and consistent world

In trying to answer the question *What is it?* we have to overcome some serious handicaps. Though the objects visible in the world may have a definite and unchanging shape, the light rays they reflect to our eyes

Figure 8-9 An example of continuity *At the left we clearly perceive two continuous lines that are combinations of straight and curved segments. When the two lines are put together as at the right, however, we find it difficult to perceive the original pattern. Instead we perceive a continuous wavy line running through another continuous line of straight horizontal and vertical segments.*

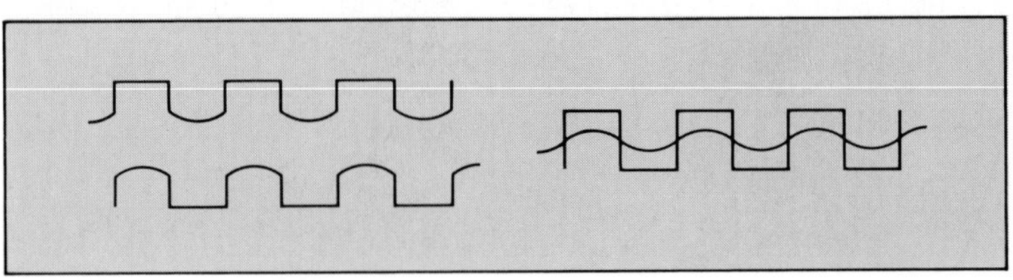

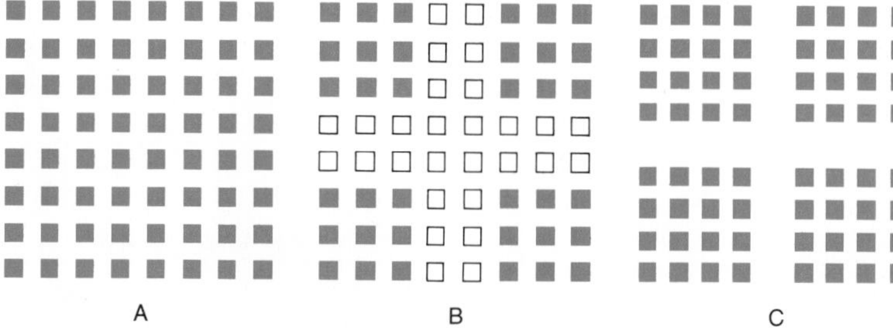

Figure 8-10 The effects of similarity and proximity *Drawing A has no pattern. But note what happens to your perception when some of the colored blocks are changed to white, as in B, or moved closer together, as in C.*

take many different patterns depending on the angle from which we view them. A dinner plate, for example, casts its true circular image only when we look straight down at it or hold it vertically in front of our eyes. From any other angle it casts different images—all sorts of ovals and ellipses. A door is a rectangle only when seen at right angles to the eyes. From other angles, as when it swings open or shut, it forms various images that are trapezoids.

This confusion seldom bothers us. Regardless of the shape of the image cast on our eyes, we know immediately that we are looking at a round plate or a rectangular door. Thanks to what is called *perceptual constancy*, we perceive a stable and consistent world. The form of perceptual constancy demonstrated by the plate and the door is called *shape constancy*. Some other forms are the following:

Size constancy refers to our tendency to recognize the actual size of an object regardless of whether the image it casts on the eye is large, as when seen close up, or small, as when seen from a distance. Figure 8-11 demonstrates how the actual size of the image creates a distorted view of the world on the film in a camera. We ourselves, viewing the same scene from the same place as the camera lens, would perceive everything in proper perspective. You can experience a perhaps even more

Figure 8-11 What the world would look like without size constancy *This is how two people on a beach look to a camera held at close range. If you were holding the camera, your eyes would see much the same kinds of images—hands of different sizes, exaggerated torsos, undersized heads. But you would not be aware of the distortion.*

The hydrant in the foreground casts a much larger image on the eye than the tall buildings in the background—yet you have no trouble perceiving the actual size.

convincing demonstration of size constancy by trying the experiment illustrated in Figure 8-12. If you follow the instructions, the images cast on your eyes by the small salad plate and the large dinner plate will be exactly the same size. Yet you will find that what you perceive—and in fact cannot help perceiving—is a small plate fairly close to you and a large plate farther away.

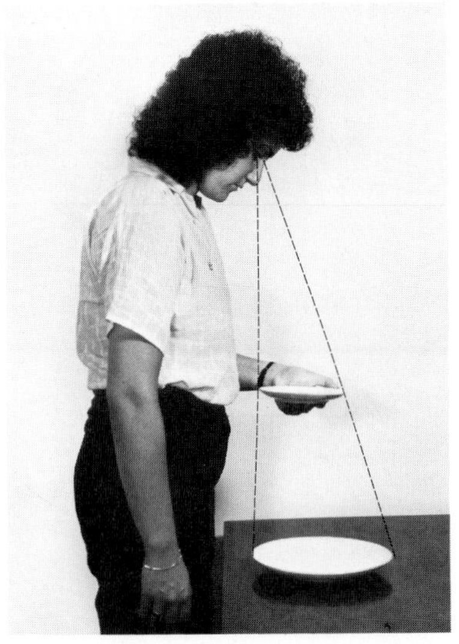

Figure 8-12 Salad plate or dinner plate? *For a clear demonstration of size constancy, put a dinner plate on the table. Then move a salad plate up and down until its image exactly blots out the dinner plate. Without changing the height at which you hold the salad plate, move it to one side. The images cast on your eyes by the two plates are exactly the same size—but what do you perceive?*

Brightness constancy can best be explained by the example of how we perceive a black shoe lying on a sidewalk in bright sunlight and the same shoe lying on a snowbank in deep shade on a cloudy winter day. In either case the shoe looks black, its background white. But if you made some measurements with a photographer's light meter you would discover something strange. The shoe in sunlight would register just as bright on the meter as the snow in the shade—perhaps even brighter. Regardless of the actual intensity of the light waves reaching our eyes, brightness constancy gives us consistent impressions of blacks, whites, and grays and the contrasts between them. Part of the explanation seems to be the ratio of light intensity, which is about the same between sunlit shoe and sidewalk as between cloudy-day shoe and shaded snow (Hochberg, 1978).

Perceiving distance and depth

Another important question, as we explore the world, is: *Where is it?* Merely to walk around without bumping into walls and other people, we must not only perceive objects organized into patterns and shapes but also know how far away they are. Before we step off a bus we must know how deep a drop there is to the pavement. Fortunately we perceive distance and depth without even thinking.

The ability seems to depend partly on inborn wiring, as has been demonstrated with the apparatus shown in Figure 8-13. This device, known as a "visual cliff," is a piece of heavy glass suspended above the floor. Across the middle of the glass is a board covered with checkered cloth. On one side of the board the same kind of cloth is attached to the bottom of the glass, making this look like the solid, or shallow, side

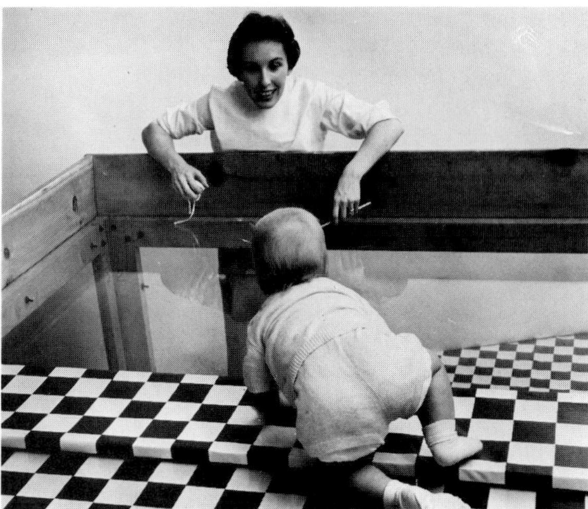

Figure 8-13 A baby avoids a fall on the visual cliff *At left a baby fearlessly crawls toward its mother on the glass covering the shallow-looking side of the visual cliff. But at right the baby stops—seeming afraid to cross the glass that covers the apparently deep side (Gibson and Walk, 1960).*

of the cliff. On the other side the cloth is laid on the floor, and to all appearances there is a drop on that side.

As the figure shows, a 9-month-old baby crawls without hesitation over the shallow-looking side but hesitates to crawl onto the deep side. Lower animals show this tendency before any kind of learning presumably has had time to take place. Baby lambs and goats tested as soon as they are able to walk avoid the deep side. This ability seems to be the secret of how even very young animals—particularly mountain goats born into an environment full of sharp and dangerous drops—manage to avoid falls.

An important clue to what happens on the visual cliff—and in depth and distance perception in general—appears to be a phenomenon called *motion parallax.* When we move our head, the images reaching our eyes from the visual field move across the retina. As the images swim in front of our eyes, so to speak, those from distant objects do not travel very far or fast. Those from nearby objects travel much faster. You can observe this for yourself the next time you ride in a bus, or even better a train where you are hardly conscious of your own motion. Nearby objects will seem to speed right by, while objects in the background remain almost stationary. As the images move, the signals sent to the brain originate in different parts of the retina—and the changing patterns of nervous impulses are translated by the brain into perceptions of distance.

Other factors that aid the perception of distance are difficult to classify as either inborn or learned. Indeed it seems most likely that they are a combination of the two (Hochberg, 1978). Some of the most influential factors are the following:

The eye muscles send their own messages to the brain. The muscles controlling the position of the eyeballs move to make the lines of vision from the two eyes converge on the object being viewed. At the same time, the muscles controlling the shape of the lenses operate to bring the object into the sharpest possible focus. These movements take place automatically and you are not ordinarily aware of them. But you can feel

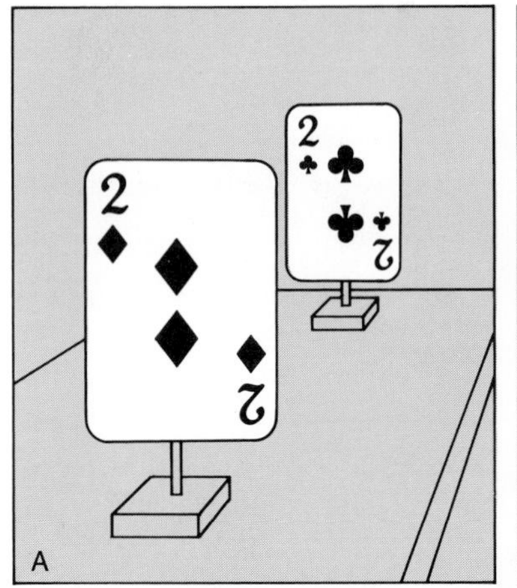

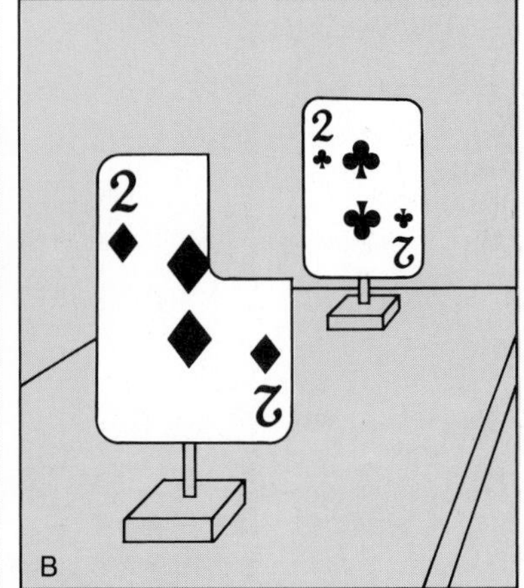

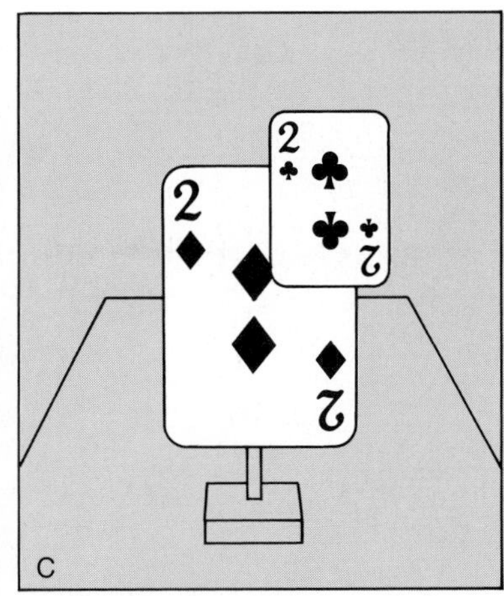

Figure 8-14 Fooling the eye with interposition *The drawings illustrate an experiment that shows how your perception of distance can be thrown off by manipulating the clue of interposition. Two ordinary playing cards are arranged as shown in A and are the only objects visible in an otherwise dark room. You perceive clearly that the two of clubs is farther away. Now a corner is clipped from the two of diamonds, as shown in B, and the stand holding this card is moved to the right. If you now look at the cards through one eye and see them as shown in C, you perceive a small two of clubs close by and a larger two of diamonds farther away (Krech, D. and Crutchfield, R. S.* Elements of psychology, *2d edition. © 1969 by Alfred A. Knopf, Inc. Reprinted by permission).*

them if you deliberately shift your gaze from the farthest object within view—preferably the distant horizon—and try to look at the tip of your nose. The attempt will be unsuccessful, of course, but it will demonstrate that the muscles produce messages—which the brain somehow manages to combine with other information to help determine distance and depth.

Binocular vision refers to the fact that the two eyes receive different images because of the distance between them, which is about 64 millimeters or 2½ inches. Like the two lenses of a three-dimensional camera, the eyes view objects in the visual field from slightly different angles. The images they receive are somehow put together by the brain into a three-dimensional pattern that greatly assists the perception of depth and distance.

Interposition is another clue to distance perception because nearby objects block off part of our view of more distant objects. If a child is standing in front of a tree, we see all of the child's body but only part of the tree. If the tree is closer, we see the entire tree but only part of the child. Interposition is so important a clue that it can be manipulated in the laboratory to completely fool the eye, as shown in Figure 8-14.

Perspective is a distance clue that has been used by artists for many centuries to create a three-dimensional impression on a flat piece of canvas. The three types of perspective are illustrated in Figure 8-15. *Linear perspective* refers to the fact that parallel lines, like the railroad tracks in the photo, seem to draw closer together as they recede into the distance. *Aerial perspective* refers to the fact that distant objects, because they are seen through air that is usually somewhat hazy, appear less distinct and less brilliant in color than nearby objects. If you have lived within sighting distance of mountains or city skyscrapers you may have noticed that the mountains or buildings seem much closer on days when the air is unusually clear.

The third type of perspective is *gradient of texture,* which you can best observe by looking at a large expanse of lawn. The grass nearby can be seen so well that every blade is distinct, and therefore its texture looks

Figure 8-15 Perspective and distance perception *The three-dimensional effect of this photograph results from all three types of perspective—linear, aerial, and gradient of texture.*

quite coarse. Farther away, the individual blades seem to merge and the texture becomes much finer.

Shadowing—or the pattern of light and shadow on the objects we see—also helps us perceive distance and depth. Our world is usually illuminated from above—by the sun in the daytime and overhead light fixtures at night. The top parts of three-dimensional objects receive the full force of the light waves, while the lower parts are more or less shadowed. The extent to which we use this clue is shown in Figure 8-16, where an unfamiliar pattern of shadowing creates an unusual illusion.

Figure 8-16 An illusion formed by shadowing *Compare what you perceive here with what you perceive when you turn the page upside down. The reason is the way distance and depth perception is affected by shadowing, as explained in the text. (The photograph is printed upside down on the page, reversing the way the shadows were actually cast.)*

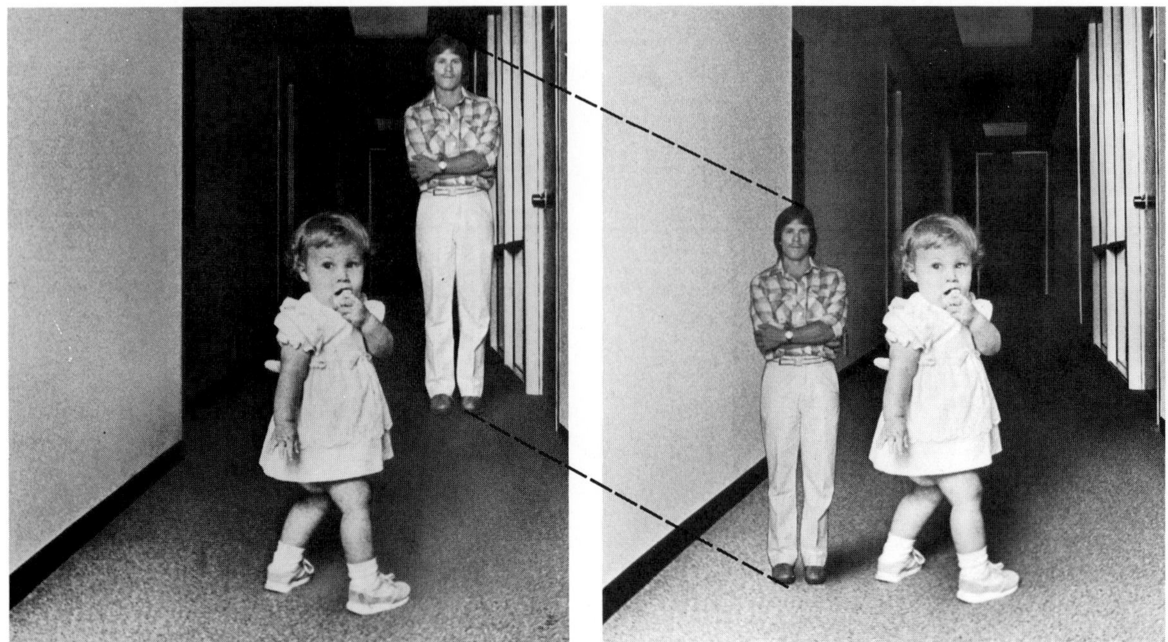

Figure 8-17 Size and distance perception *In the photograph at left, you clearly perceive a small child nearby and her father farther away. One reason is that you know the father is bigger. But the size of the images they cast on your eyes is almost exactly the same, as shown in the composite photo at the right, made by cutting the father out of the original picture and pasting him next to the child (after Boring, 1964).*

The relationship between distance and size

To a very considerable extent, our perception of distance also depends on our perception of size and the principle of size constancy. We know how big a basketball is, regardless of how large or how small an image it casts on our eyes. Thus, when we see it thrown down the court, we can judge how far away it is by how large it seems in relation to the other objects in the visual field. We know roughly how big another adult is, and this helps us determine the distance between us. In the photograph in Figure 8-17—as in any similar real-life situation—we immediately perceive that we are looking at a baby close up and an adult some distance away.

Perception of distance is thrown off if we misjudge size, as has been demonstrated in experiments conducted with playing cards much larger or smaller than those ordinarily used in bridge or poker. Seen in a room

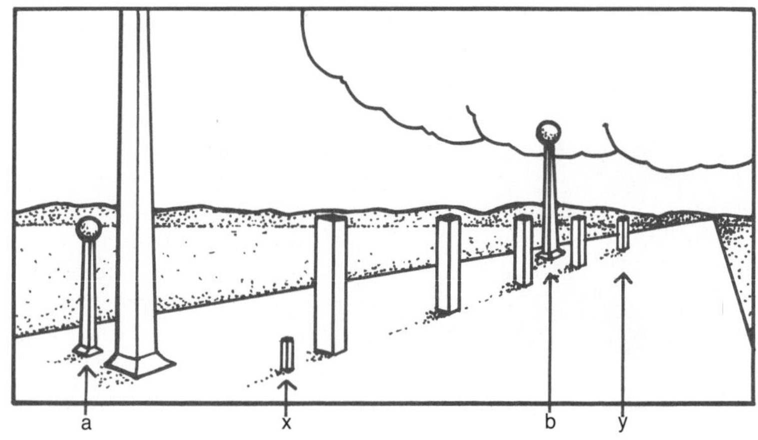

Figure 8-18 The case of the deceptive lampposts *There is no doubt in your mind—Is there?—that lamppost* a *is much smaller than lamppost* b. *Or that the wooden block* x *is much smaller than* y? *But measure them with a ruler and you will find that the two posts and the two blocks are exactly the same size. The perceived distance of the objects—with* b *and* y *seeming considerably farther away—affects your perception of their size (Beeler and Branley, 1951).*

that affords no other clues, the oversized cards always seem closer than they really are, the undersized cards much farther away. The relationship between perceived distance and perceived size works both ways, as is illustrated in Figure 8-18.

What does the information mean?—the element of interpretation

The two elements of perception discussed thus far provide a fast start for information processing. Selection answers the question: Which one of all the many objects and events in the environment is worthy of attention and exploration? Organization helps decide: What is it, and where is it? But one important question remains: *What does it mean?* Finding the answer requires the third element of perception, which is *interpretation.*

Of all the elements, interpretation is the most clearly dependent on learning rather than on any inborn characteristics of the nervous system. It is ordinarily made by comparing new information provided by the senses with old information that has been acquired in the past. Note for example the symbols in Figure 8-19. You probably have never seen anything exactly like them before—but you perceive at once that all of them are the letter *E.* You have stored in memory what students of perception call a *prototype* or *schema*—a sort of generalized model of what the letter *E* looks like. You can interpret and identify the new symbols because they resemble this prototype. Similarly, you have prototypes that help you recognize the human face, a tree, the animal called a dog, and all the other objects and events you have become familiar with.

Prototypes, feature analysis, and "global" processing

The way we match a new stimulus against our prototype has been the subject of considerable study and speculation. One school of thought has been that we engage in a feature-by-feature analysis and comparison. In looking at a letter, we might note whether it has horizontal or vertical lines or both, diagonal lines moving upward to the left or right, and so on. This kind of feature analysis can be programed into computers to enable them to recognize letters, and there is considerable evidence that it is also employed in human perception (Geyer and DeWald, 1973). You may have observed in your own experience that under difficult conditions, such as when looking at the small letters on an eye chart, you are more likely to mistake an *E* for an *F,* with which it shares several features, than for an *X,* with which it shares none.

Another possibility is that we base our comparisons not on mere features but on what has been termed "global" processing—that is, the total overall pattern formed by the various individual features, viewed as a single and well-integrated unit. This suggestion was first made by Gestalt psychologists, a school of thought that has been summarized as maintaining that "the whole is greater than the sum of its parts." The Gestalt psychologists pointed out, for example, that when we look at ∷ or □ we immediately perceive a square, not four independent dots or

Figure 8-19 You know what these are—but how do you know? *These symbols are unlike any E's you have seen before, yet you recognize them at a glance. For the explanation, see the discussion of prototypes in the text.*

two horizontal and two vertical lines. Similarly, the human face seems to leap into perception as a unit, without any feature-by-feature analysis of eyes, nose, and mouth. If you turn back to Figure 8-7 (p. 283) and look again at the drawing that can be seen as either a goblet or two faces, you will note that you see the faces before you notice such details as nose, lips, and chin.

Many psychologists now believe that we rely at times on global processing and at other times on feature analysis, depending on the nature of the stimulus and the conditions under which we view it (Hoffman, 1980). Some stimuli lend themselves readily to global processing because their individual features just naturally seem to hang together and form an integrated whole. Others do not (Treisman and Gelade, 1980) and are therefore more suitable for feature analysis. Often it appears that we combine the two processes, taking first a global view, then attending to some of the individual features, then again considering the stimulus in its entirety (Broadbent, 1977).

It's a face—but whose face?

In one way or another—through global processing or feature analysis or a combination of the two—we find a resemblance between a new stimulus and a prototype. Then we are likely to note the special features that distinguish the new stimulus, making it similar to but different from all other stimuli that match the prototype. Let us say that a woman student new to the class sits in front of you today. At first you see only the back of her head, then she turns. You perceive without effort a human face that matches your prototype of faces in general. But this new face has some features of its own that make it different from all other faces you have ever seen. You will probably note these special features and store a new and more specific pattern in memory, from which you can recognize her when you see her again.

Later you see her face in the distance, or shown very small in a photograph. You perceive immediately that you are looking at a stimulus matching your prototype of the human face. But whose face? To find out, you have to compare the specific features and pattern with some people you know who seem like strong possibilities. Is it your old friend Mary Smith? No, not quite. Tracy Johnson? Again, no, not quite. The woman who just joined your class? Ah, yes, everything matches.

Figure 8-20 A little perceptual magic: now it's a man, now it's a rat *Cover both rows of drawings, then ask a friend to watch while you uncover the faces in the top row one at a time, beginning at the left. The friend will almost surely perceive the final drawing as the face of a man. Then try the bottom row in similar fashion on another friend. This friend will almost surely perceive the final drawing as a rat. The psychologists who devised this experiment found that 85 to 95 percent of their subjects perceived the final drawing as a man if they saw the other human heads first, as a rat if they saw the animals first—though of course the final drawings are exactly alike (Bugelski and Alampay, 1961).*

Expectations, mental set, and context

All the testing of likely interpretations of the face—discarding Mary Smith, discarding Tracy Johnson, deciding on the new classmate—may take only an instant. The process will be especially fast and seemingly effortless if you see the woman in the classroom or on the campus nearby, where you might expect to find her. It will probably be more difficult if you see her in totally new and different circumstances—for example, working in uniform as a part-time traffic director at a city intersection. This is because experience has led us to expect certain events to happen in our world in certain familiar ways. We have a mental set toward the environment. What we perceive and how we interpret it depends to a considerable extent on this set—in other words, on our *perceptual expectations.*

Laboratory experiments have shown that manipulating people's expectations can greatly affect their perceptions. Would you believe, for example, that two people could look at exactly the same drawing—yet that one would see a man and the other would see a rat? To convince yourself, try the demonstration illustrated in Figure 8-20.

The drawing, of course, was specially designed. The final figure was deliberately made ambiguous, so that it looks both like a man's face and a rat. You can just as easily perceive one as the other. But many of the sights we encounter in real life are also ambiguous—and the way we perceive them is also likely to depend on what we expect to see.

In a similar way, interpretation also depends on the situation in which we encounter a stimulus—that is, the *context* in which it is found. For a demonstration, note Figure 8-21. There you see exactly the same unusual symbol in the middle of each of the two words. If you saw it set apart by itself, you would hardly know what it was supposed to be. You might even guess that it was a set of goal posts. In the context of the words, you immediately perceive the first of the identical symbols as an *H* and the second as an *A*.

THE CHT

Figure 8-21 Same symbol, different context, different interpretation
Most people looking at these two words, read them easily without ever realizing that the two "letters" in the middle of the words are identical—and in fact bear only a faint resemblance to any real letters (Selfridge and Neisser, 1960).

Interpretation—like all elements of perception—works in mysterious ways. It may even be affected by our mood or physical condition at the moment. An experimenter once asked subjects to describe pictures they were told they would see dimly on a screen. Actually there were no real pictures, only blurs and smudges. But hungry subjects, who had gone 16 hours without eating before the experiment, thought they saw all kinds of foods and food-related objects (McClelland and Atkinson, 1948). It appears that we begin our information processing by perceiving not only what we expect to see and what the situation indicates we are likely to see but also what we want to see.

SUMMARY

How the nervous system is "wired" for survival

1. Perception is *the process through which we become aware of our environment by selecting, organizing, and interpreting the evidence from our senses.*
2. Our skill at perception depends in part on the inborn structure of the nervous system and its specialized nerve cells called *feature*

detectors, found in the pathways from sense organs to brain and in the brain itself. In vision, some feature detectors respond sharply to patterns (such as vertical line, a horizontal line, or an angle) and others to movement. In hearing, some feature detectors are strongly activated by either low-pitched sounds, high-pitched sounds, or changes in pitch.

3. Feature detectors range from *simple cells* to *complex cells* to *hypercomplex cells.* At each level the processing of sensory information is refined and more fully developed.
4. Our perceptions of the world are usually—but not always—in accord with the facts. Among the exceptions are optical illusions and distortions during *altered states of consciousness* (like those produced by hypnosis or drugs).
5. Two optical illusions are the *autokinetic illusion,* in which a stationary spot of light seen in darkness seems to move of its own accord, and *stroboscopic motion,* in which two stationary objects viewed close together in space and time seem to be moving. Moving pictures and television are based on stroboscopic motion.
6. Because of the inborn wiring of the nervous system we are particularly adept at perceiving *movement, change, contrast,* and stimuli of substantial *size* and *intensity.*

Selection and attention

7. *Selection* is a key element in perception because we can perceive only a few of all the many stimuli that constantly bombard our senses. Selection depends on the inborn structure of the nervous system and on such learned factors as interests, motivation, emotional state, and personality.
8. When we select and pay attention to one event, we usually lose perception of other stimuli. It is especially difficult to process two different inputs if they arrive in the same sensory channel—for example, to pay attention to two conversations at the same time.
9. Selection helps us explore the environment, perceive what is likely to be most important, ignore the rest, and concentrate on using the rest of our information-processing talents to the best possible advantage.

Perceptual organization

10. *Organization* is a key element because, in order to answer the question *What is it?,* we have to see or hear a stimulus that hangs together in some kind of unit—a human face or a meaningful pattern of human speech.
11. An important factor in organization is *figure and ground,* which is the tendency to perceive an object as a meaningful unit set off from a neutral background by a dividing line called a *contour.*
12. Organization generally follows the rules of *closure, continuity, similarity,* and *proximity.*
13. *Perceptual constancy* is the tendency to perceive a stable and consistent world even though the stimuli that reach our eyes are incon-

sistent and potentially confusing. Perceptual constancy includes *shape constancy*, *size constancy*, and *brightness constancy.*

14. In perceiving distance and depth we rely on clues provided by *motion parallax,* sensations provided by movements of the *eye muscles, binocular vision, interposition, perspective,* and *shadowing.*
15. Perceived distance also depends on perceived size—and this relationship works both ways.

What does the information mean?—the element of interpretation

16. *Interpretation* is a key element because it answers the question *What does it mean?* Interpretation is ordinarily made by comparing new information provided by the senses with old information acquired in the past.
17. We interpret and identify a new stimulus by matching it against generalized models that we have stored in memory of familiar events and objects—like the letter *E* or the human face. Such a model is called a *prototype* or *schema.*
18. In matching a new stimulus to a prototype we may engage in *feature analysis* (in the case of the letter *E,* noting the three horizontal lines and the vertical line) or *global processing* (noting the overall pattern of the individual features, viewed as a single and well-integrated unit).
19. Our interpretations are influenced by *perceptual expectations,* or mental sets acquired because we have learned to expect certain events to occur in certain familiar ways. They are also influenced by the *context* in which the new stimulus is found and to some extent even by our mood, physical condition, and wishes.

IMPORTANT TERMS

aerial perspective
autokinetic illusion
binocular vision
brightness constancy
closure
complex cell
context
continuity
contour
contrast
depth perception
distance perception
feature analysis
feature detectors
figure and ground
global processing
gradient of texture
hypercomplex cell
interposition
interpretation
linear perspective
motion parallax
organization
perception
perceptual constancy
perceptual expectation
perspective
prototype
proximity
schema
selection
shadowing
shape constancy
similarity
simple cell
size constancy
stroboscopic motion
visual cliff

SUPPLEMENT: Perception and Altered States of Consciousness

The discussion thus far has concerned ordinary, everyday perception as it occurs during the waking hours when our sense organs and brain are functioning normally. But other forms of perception may occur at times when our brain is not working in the usual fashion, during *altered states of consciousness* like those produced by alcohol and other drugs. And some psychologists—as well as many nonpsychologists—believe that there are some strange and unexplained ways we can extract information from the world without using our ordinary senses, a possibility popularly known as ESP and discussed in a box on Psychology and Society.

One very common example of perception during an altered state of consciousness is sleep. Our eyes are closed and we see nothing. Our sense of hearing is turned off to the point where it would take a loud shout to wake us. Yet in our dreams we perceive all kinds of things. We see scenes and people, some familiar and some unlike anything or anybody we have ever really seen in our lives. We hear ourselves talk and other people answer. All these sights and sounds, though nonexistent, may be as vivid as any of our real-life perceptions. Like the events we actually experience when awake, they can move us to intense feelings of love, pleasure, hostility, anger, and fear.

Sleep, dreams, hypnosis, and meditation

Dreams presumably have always fascinated humanity, for they seem to free us from all limitations of space or time. Our early ancestors must have been baffled by dreams in which they seemed to move about in distant places and to talk to people long dead. The line between dream and reality must have been difficult to draw—and must have hinted at all sorts of mysteries of the human spirit and of a world beyond ordinary human understanding.

Dreams have often been regarded as portents of the future, for dreams sometimes come true. To a statistician, this is not surprising. There are more than four billion people in the world. The average adult, it has been found, dreams for nearly two hours a night (Williams, 1971). Thus there are bound to be numerous occasions when somebody dreams of the death of a friend and the friend actually does die soon afterward—or when a dream seems to accurately predict the receipt of an important letter, the result of a sports event, or a train wreck. Such coincidences are startling and memorable. The great majority of dreams that turn out to be mistaken go unnoticed.

Psychology and Society: Extrasensory perception—new frontier or human delusion

Can we human beings perceive events through channels other than our eyes, ears, and the rest of the senses? In other words, do we possess ESP, short for *extrasensory perception?* Are there at least some of us who can read other people's minds, or know what an object is without looking at it, or perhaps even know in advance what is about to happen?

The idea is attractive to many people and has been found to exist in virtually all known cultures (Scheils, 1978). Nothing that science has yet discovered can explain or even allow for the existence of ESP. But every possibility is worth examining—and therefore some investigators have been engaged for many years in the field of *parapsychology,* or the study of ESP and other psychological events that seem to go beyond normal limits and defy explanation in any normal scientific way. They have done research on three kinds of ESP that have been reported from time to time:

1. *Mental telepathy,* or what is commonly known as mind reading
2. *Clairvoyance,* or the ability to perceive an object without using the ordinary senses—such as knowing what card will be turned up next from a shuffled deck
3. *Precognition,* or the ability to perceive something that has not yet happened—such as how a pair of dice will turn up on the next roll

The field of parapsychology is too complex and controversial to be covered adequately here. About all that can be said is that some researchers have reported finding subjects who seemed to display abilities at telepathy, clairvoyance, and precognition. These subjects were by no means 100 percent accurate, but they did seem to produce results that could not be explained by sheer luck (Rhine and Pratt, 1957). Other researchers have reported telepathy experiments in which the dreams of "receivers" seemed to be influenced by the thoughts of "senders" who were some distance away, in one case by 40 miles (Krippner, 1972). Many of the experiments that seem to demonstrate ESP, however, have been attacked as poorly designed and lacking safeguards against cheating (Hansel, 1966). One survey found that only 5 percent of psychology professors believe that the existence of ESP has been established (Wagner and Monnett, 1979).

The controversy has some important implications for the future of society. If ESP actually exists—or is possible—then human abilities have some unexplored dimensions that may revolutionize human life and the future course of science. But if a belief in ESP is nothing more than wishful thinking and superstition, like the faith of the Greeks in their Delphic oracle, then the popular interest in it is a serious barrier to understanding human behavior. If you want to know more about the topic and judge the evidence for yourself, you can start with the books on ESP listed in the recommended readings.

Since the time of Sigmund Freud a different meaning has often been attached to dreams. Freud believed that dreams are an expression of wishes prohibited by the dreamer's conscience. Forbidden sexual desires in particular, he thought, are likely to crop up—often in a hidden form in which the male sexual organ is symbolized by a snake, a tower, or an airplane; the female organ by a basket or a flower.

Many psychoanalysts and other therapists have followed Freud's lead and try to analyze their patients' dreams in search of clues to hidden conflicts. Although different therapists use different methods of interpreting dreams, enough successes have been reported to indicate that the content of a dream may indeed reflect the dreamer's unconscious wishes at times (Hauri, 1976). An interesting sidelight is that there seem to be some differences in what men and women dream about. One study found that American men tend to dream more about such matters as achievement, hostility, and aggression. Women's dreams were found to be more emotional and friendly, often taking place in indoor settings and relating to home and family life (Winget, Kramer, and Whitman, 1972). Similar differences have been found among boys and girls aged 11 to 13. The boys dream more frequently about aggressive actions and situations that turn out badly, the girls about the home and happy occasions (Foulkes, 1982). This may be due to the different roles males and females have traditionally been taught to play in our society.

Ordinary and paradoxical sleep

The way sleep differs from the waking state of consciousness has been shown by studies of brain waves and muscle activity, measured by electrodes attached to people sleeping through the night in laboratories. The studies have shown quite clearly that sleep is by no means a state of suspended animation in which body and brain are shut down for a time. Sleep is not just a slowing down but a kind of activity in its own right. The brain continues to be highly active—though in a different way (Williams, 1971). Moreover it has been found that there are several different kinds of sleep.

Most of the night is spent in what is called *ordinary sleep.* As can be seen in Figure 8-22, the brain's activity during ordinary sleep differs considerably from the pattern during waking hours, and the muscles of the body are considerably more relaxed. Four stages of ordinary sleep, ranging from light to very deep, can be distinguished from tracings of brain and muscle activity. We move back and forth among these four stages during the night. Most people have three periods of the deepest sleep, the first starting within an hour after dropping off, the last ending after about three or four hours.

About a quarter of the night is spent in *paradoxical sleep*—which gets its name from the fact, also shown in Figure 8-22, that the brain's activity is very similar to the waking state but the bodily muscles are almost totally relaxed. When subjects who are in paradoxical sleep are awakened, about 80 to 85 percent of them report they have been dreaming (Berger, 1969). In fact during paradoxical sleep the eyes dart quickly about as if following a series of visual images. Therefore this stage is also known as *REM sleep*—REM standing for the *rapid eye movement* that can be observed.

How much sleep do we need?

Young adults sleep an average of 7½ hours a night (Webb and Cartwright, 1978), but there are wide individual differences. Some people

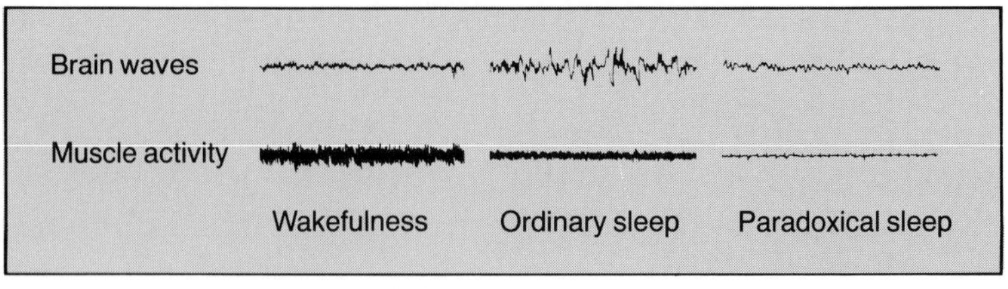

Figure 8-22 Brain and muscle activity during sleep *The tracings show typical patterns of brain waves and muscle activity during periods of wakefulness, ordinary sleep, and paradoxical (or REM) sleep. Note that during paradoxical sleep the brain waves resemble the pattern during wakefulness, but the muscles are most relaxed of all.*

prefer to sleep as long as 10 hours or more, others only a few hours. One woman was found to get along on 45 minutes of sleep a night (Meddis, Pearson, and Langford, 1973). Whatever your own sleeping habits may be, you are stuck with them. They cannot be comfortably changed. In one experiment some couples were asked to try to get along on less sleep by cutting down slowly—a half hour a week. None of them ever got below 5 hours a night and all of them eventually gave up the attempt (Johnson and MacLeod, 1973).

Most people are occasionally troubled by *insomnia,* or the inability to fall asleep, and some people suffer from it chronically. In one large-scale survey 6 percent of adult men and 14 percent of women reported that they experienced insomnia often or fairly often (Kripke and Simons, 1976)—an indication that perhaps 10 million or more adult Americans spend many nights tossing and turning before they drop off. Among the people most likely to experience insomnia are those suffering from depression (Kales et al., 1976) and those who have frequently used sleeping pills, which are occasionally helpful but can lead to chronic sleep disturbances if used too often (Kales et al., 1974).

Why do we sleep at all?

As you probably have observed for yourself, a sleepless night produces unpleasant aftereffects. Merely lying in bed and resting is no substitute for real sleep (Lubin et al., 1976). In fact any lack of sleep below your natural requirements, whether from insomnia or other causes, is likely to make you feel logy, irritable, and generally below par. Yet you can go without sleep entirely for remarkably long periods without suffering any real damage. Volunteers have gone more than a week. Often they developed shaky hands and a lowered tolerance for pain. Some of them began to have hallucinations, but this was rare and never occurred before 60 sleepless hours. Their breathing, heart rate, blood pressure, and body temperature remained normal. They showed a minor loss of ability to perform some kinds of tasks but none at other kinds (Webb and Cartwright, 1978).

These facts raise the question: Why do we sleep at all? The answer seems to lie in a sleep-producing chemical substance, called the *S factor,* that has been found in the brains of animals and most recently in human urine. When even very tiny amounts of this chemical are injected into the brains of other animals, it causes about a 50 percent increase in very deep, dream-free sleep (Maugh, 1982). If the S factor could be produced synthetically, it might solve the problems of people who experience sleep disorders. At present, however, investigators have to process more than 4 tons of urine to obtain about a millionth of an ounce.

There are some indications that other substances produced by animals and human beings may also induce sleep. Body chemistry as well as brain chemistry may play a part. Some investigators have suggested that ordinary sleep serves to restore the body's chemical balance, while REM sleep restores the brain's ability to function (Hartmann, 1973)—perhaps by somehow renewing the chemical substances that help transmit nervous impulses (Moruzzi, 1972).

Hypnosis

Like sleep in some ways, but totally unlike it in others, is the altered state of consciousness called *hypnosis.* This too may produce some strange perceptions. At the hypnotist's suggestion, the subject may see a chair where none exists and will carefully walk around the imaginary obstacle.

People under hypnosis may give vivid and detailed accounts of events they could not recall under ordinary circumstances, even incidents dating back to early childhood. Therapists sometimes use hypnosis to dredge up forgotten experiences that may have caused psychological problems, and law officials to help witnesses produce forgotten details that may solve a crime. There is considerable question, however, about the accuracy of such recollections. One psychiatrist has found that recollections of childhood experiences obtained under hypnosis often prove to be inaccurate (Orne, 1982). And almost all courtroom testimony by witnesses who had been hypnotized was barred in 1982 by the California Supreme Court, on the ground that they often come to believe in "pseudomemories or fantasies." There is an analogy here between hypnosis and sleep. Most of us have had the experience of not being quite sure whether something actually happened to us or occurred only in a dream.

The nature of the hypnotic state is unknown. Psychologists know only how to produce it, not what it is. The hypnotist may ask the subject to sit as relaxed as possible and stare fixedly at some small object, such as a key, the tip of a pencil, or a point of light. Meanwhile the hypnotist speaks in a quiet and repetitious monotone, suggesting that the subject is growing more and more relaxed, that the subject's eyes are tiring, and that the subject is becoming sleepy. Soon the subject seems to respond to the suggestions: The eyelids flutter and close. The body becomes limp. The head droops, and apparently the subject is sound asleep (Moss, 1965).

There is no similarity, however, between the hypnotic state and real sleep. The brain waves show a different pattern. So do many measures of bodily activity. Moreover the subject remains fully conscious of the hypnotist's voice and responds to the hypnotist's suggestions. Indeed one characteristic of the hypnotic state is an intense and sharply focused attention on the hypnotist's words and the perceptions and events that are suggested (Hilgard and Hilgard, 1975).

Not everybody can be hypnotized. Perhaps as many as 10 percent show almost no response at all. Only about 25 percent enter the deeper stages of the hypnotic experience and only about 5 to 10 percent enter the very deepest stages (Hilgard, 1965). Those who are most susceptible tend to be normal, outgoing people of the type who readily become imaginatively involved in events—"carried away" by books or movies, for example. Many of them say they were rather severely punished in childhood, an experience that perhaps inclines them to obey the hypnotist's suggestions (Hilgard, 1970).

Meditation

Many Americans are currently seeking another kind of altered state of consciousness through the practice of *meditation*, which has long been a part of philosophies and religions in Oriental civilizations. Among the methods followed are Yoga, Zen, and transcendental meditation. Though these vary somewhat, they all have as their goal a frame of mind in which ordinary thought processes are suspended and the mind is opened to enhanced perceptions of beauty and truth and perhaps religious insights that defy an attempt to put them into words.

Methods of meditation usually have four features in common (Benson, 1975):

1. They are practiced in a quiet atmosphere, free from distractions.
2. The meditator assumes a comfortable position, but not one likely to lead to sleep.
3. The meditator tries to achieve deep relaxation and freedom from intruding thoughts by concentrating on the breathing process (also, in transcendental meditation, by silently repeating a word called a mantra, usually taken from the Hindu holy books).
4. The meditator tries to be as passive as possible, not thinking or worrying about anything.

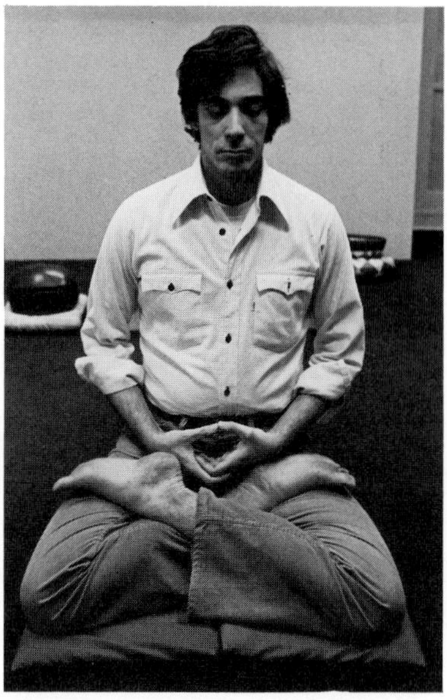

Yoga, with its positions conducive to relaxation, is one form of meditation.

After a time—perhaps 20 or 30 minutes—even consciousness of what the meditator has been concentrating on, breathing or the mantra, may disappear, leaving the mind in a sort of suspended state of nothingness (Ornstein, 1971). This is often accompanied by feelings of floating on air, timelessness, expanded awareness, and deep joy (Deikman, 1973).

Meditation has been found to change patterns of brain activity. In particular it increases the occurrence of what are called alpha waves (Banquet, 1973), which are associated with relaxation. The rate of breathing and consumption of oxygen by the body may decline by about 15 percent (Wallace and Benson, 1972), indicating a very deep kind of relaxation. It has been found that people who practice meditation regularly can cut down or eliminate the use of cigarettes or drugs (Benson and Wallace, 1972) and perhaps even free themselves from symptoms of high blood pressure (Benson, Rosner, and Marzetta, 1973). A recent study found that men in a prison who learned and practiced meditation became less aggressive, experienced less anxiety and depression, and were more likely than other inmates to stay out of trouble after being released (Alexander, 1982).

You can try meditation yourself simply by sitting in a quiet room with your eyes closed, paying close but relaxed attention to your breathing in and out, and saying to yourself the word *one* after each breath. This has been found to produce many of the effects of more elaborate techniques, especially the decrease in oxygen consumption and bodily activity (Beary and Benson, 1974).

Drugs

The use of drugs to alter states of consciousness goes far back in history. It would appear that humanity has always been interested in finding substances that relieve anxiety, produce feelings of contentment and happiness, and sometimes result in strange experiences that make the user perceive the world in distorted fashion, have hallucinations of imaginary sights and sounds, and perhaps attain a mystical religious sense of oneness with the universe.

Some of the mind-altering substances used today are so routine a part of our social scene that they are seldom even thought of as drugs. *Nicotine,* whose effects constitute the chief appeal of smoking, is a chemical that acts in several different ways—sometimes as a stimulant, sometimes as a sort of tranquilizer relieving feelings of anxiety. *Caffeine,* found in coffee and tea, is a powerful stimulant. *Alcohol* acts as a depressant to parts of the brain, relieving inhibitions and encouraging the talkativeness and laughter characteristic of cocktail parties. In large quantities alcohol sometimes releases feelings of hostility and aggressiveness (as in the barroom fight) and often interferes with motor coordination (causing the drunken person to stagger).

The substances ordinarily thought of as drugs include a number of substances whose use is illegal, ranging from marijuana to heroin, as well as prescription drugs like sleeping pills and stimulants taken for "kicks" rather than on a physician's orders. All the mind-altering drugs create their effects by temporarily changing the activity of the brain—certainly by assisting or hindering the transmission of messages at the brain's innumerable switching points, perhaps also by changing the circuits over which messages ordinarily flow.

Almost invariably, the effect depends not only on the drug itself and the amount used but also on the user's frame of mind, the circumstances in which the drug is used, and the behavior of companions. Certainly the user's expectations play an important part. It has been found that cocaine users, who expect to get "high" from sniffing the powder, may not know the difference when another substance that produces the same sensation in the nose is substituted for the real thing (Van Dyke and Byck, 1982).

How widespread is drug use?

The use of drugs increased rapidly in the United States during the 1960s and 1970s. The illegal traffic in marijuana and heroin, and later cocaine, became a multibillion-dollar business and a standard element in television and movie plots. The increase was especially pronounced among young people, who began experimenting with drugs at earlier and earlier ages. By the late 1970s 15 percent of the graduating classes of elementary schools had tried marijuana and many had experimented with LSD, angel dust, and other drugs. Among high school seniors, 60 percent had tried marijuana and nearly 11 percent were daily users (Johnston, Bachman, and O'Malley, 1981).

In recent years there appears to have been a sharp drop in the popularity of at least some drugs among young people. The number of high school seniors who used marijuana daily fell to 7 percent by 1981, perhaps because of a growing belief, then held by 58 percent of the seniors, that regular use is a "great risk" to health. The percentages who had ever tried angel dust or had used it within a year also declined

The most common of all illegal drug transactions: a sale of marijuana.

substantially, probably because of widespread publicity about its unpredictable and dangerous effects. There has been an increase, however, in the use of cocaine, Quaaludes, and amphetamines (Johnston, Bachman, and O'Malley, 1982).

The use of drugs among college students varies widely from one campus to another and often even from one year to the next on the same campus. Therefore few attempts have been made to measure it. One series of surveys at a university in New England found that 26 percent of the 1978 students used marijuana on a regular basis (defined as at least once a week), compared with 16 percent in 1969. The number of regular users of cocaine was 1.6 percent, compared with none in 1969. The study found that in the 1960s students who used drugs were more likely than others to be alienated from society, active in campus political groups, and vague about career plans. But by 1978 the drug users were "essentially indistinguishable" from nonusers except that they were more likely to be sexually active and to have consulted a psychiatrist while in college. For men the number who had sought psychiatric help was about 14 percent for users and 2 percent for nonusers, for women it was 24 percent and 15 percent (Pope, Ionescu-Pioggia, and Cole, 1981). There is no way of knowing whether these figures indicate that the use of drugs induces psychological problems or that students with problems are more likely to take up drugs.

In general the use of drugs, though widespread, has been less so than popularly believed. A large-scale survey made in the mid-1970s, of people in the 18-to-25-year-old bracket who are most likely to be users, found that marijuana was the only drug that had been used by as many as 25 percent within the past month. Of other drugs only stimulants had been used by even 5 percent within the past month, and from there the figures ranged downward to less than 0.5 percent for heroin (Abelson and Fishburn, 1976). Nonetheless drugs are a matter of concern to many psychologists and public health officials, because all of them affect the brain and body in complex ways that are not fully understood. None of them has been proved harmless and some have caused many fatalities, especially when two or more were used in combination.

Marijuana

Marijuana is the dried leaves and flowers of the hemp plant, usually smoked though sometimes swallowed. Its active ingredient is THC, which, when taken in pure and concentrated form, is a *psychedelic drug*—one that often produces hallucinations of imaginary sights and sounds and a sense of detachment from one's body. As marijuana is ordinarily used, however, the amount of THC that gets into the body and brain produces only a sort of intoxicating effect—feelings of well-being, friendliness, and often an unusually vivid perception of colors, music, and tastes.

In the laboratory, the drug seems to reduce the span of short-term memory and the ability to make decisions rapidly (Clark and Nakashima, 1968). On simulated tests of driving ability, subjects make more errors in judging speed (Hollister, 1971). The effects may last four to eight hours after the user has first experienced a "high." In fact the THC and other ingredients in marijuana tend to accumulate in the fatty tissues of the brain and body and remain there for several weeks, with an added buildup if more is used in the meantime.

The long-term effects of marijuana use have not been established, though more than a thousand studies have been made. After surveying all the available evidence, the Institute of Medicine of the National Academy of Sciences has concluded that the popularity of marijuana "justifies serious national concern," but that there is as yet no clear proof that it causes irreversible damage to the body or brain. Among the possible physical risks are lung cancer, high blood pressure, heart ailments, and damage to the reproductive system. The psychological risks are difficult to assess, but many members of the Institute believe they may be extensive (National Academy of Sciences, 1982).

LSD (or "acid")

The best-known of the clearly psychedelic drugs is *LSD,* often called "acid." Users may stare at a simple object for minutes on end, finding it unbelievably fascinating because they say they experience a richness of color and texture unknown to normal consciousness. When they close their eyes, they are likely to see imaginary designs, scenes, and faces and hear imaginary conversations and music. On a "bad trip," as an unpleasant experience with LSD is known, they may imagine that their bodies are distorted or rotting, that they are surrounded by darkness and gloom, or perhaps that they are dying (Barron, Jarvik, and Bunnell, 1972).

Even when users take LSD with the same companions and under much the same circumstances, they are likely to experience different effects on different occasions—sometimes pleasant, sometimes terrifying. Of the people who try LSD and similar drugs, only a very small number continue for very long—apparently because of the unpredictable effects and the fact that the perceptual distortions and hallucinations lose their novelty appeal (Brecher, 1972). Similar drugs are *mescaline,* which comes from a cactus plant, and *psilocybin,* found in a Mexican mushroom.

PCP (or "angel dust")

The strangest of all drugs used for kicks is *PCP* or *angel dust*—a compound that was developed in medical laboratories not as a stimulant or sedative but as an operating room anesthetic. Its real name is *phencyclidine,* and it is a psychedelic drug with drastic and often unpredictable effects on the brain. Taken in any strength or amount, it can make users lose their muscular coordination, forget where they are, and have bizarre hallucinations. When this happens they act as if they were psychotic—or in popular language, insane—and indeed they are psychotic until the effect wears off.

Cases have been reported in which people under the influence of angel dust did things they would ordinarily never have dreamed of doing—such as killing a good friend without even knowing or remembering it. The brain's functions may be so badly disorganized that the user falls into a coma or the heart stops beating, and there is no known antidote that will counteract these physical effects. One director of emergency hospital services has called it "the most dangerous drug to hit the streets in years" (Gallagher, 1983).

Stimulants

Another group of drugs, classified as *stimulants,* affect self-perception more than perception of the outer world. By increasing the activity of the brain, especially the centers for arousal and wakefulness, they create a sense of energetic well-being. Chief among them are various compounds chemically labeled *amphetamines,* known by the slang terms of "uppers," "bennies," "meth," and "speed." Used for kicks, or over long periods by truck drivers and athletes to mask fatigue, they are among the most dangerous of drugs. Many users build up a tolerance and must take ever-increasing amounts to achieve the same effect. The high they create may be accompanied by severe anxiety and irrational thinking that sometimes leads to violent behavior. The high is often followed by a deep depression in which the user may become suicidal. Prolonged abuse of the drug has been found to produce brain damage (Kales, 1969).

The use of stimulants has increased in recent years to the point where they now appear to be second only to marijuana among the drugs used with some regularity (Johnston, Bachman, and O'Malley, 1982). Their popularity has created a considerable traffic in counterfeit pills that look like and are sold as amphetamines—a potential threat to buyers who find they can take a large dose of these bogus pills without ill effect, then try to do the same thing with actual amphetamines.

Cocaine

The most widely publicized drug in recent years has been *cocaine,* a stimulant obtained from the leaves of two species of coca shrub that grow in South America. The drug has been used by people living in the Andes mountains for at least 5,000 years, but it was hardly known in the United States until the 1960s. Now it is estimated that perhaps as many as 50,000 kilograms (110,000 pounds) are smuggled into the nation every year.

Cocaine has become known as a "fashionable" drug, especially popular among people in the entertainment business. One reason is that it is extremely expensive. Sold as a white powder, which may be anywhere from 10 to 85 percent pure, it generally sells for $100 and up per gram (about 1/35 of an ounce). A gram provides about 10 doses, usually taken by sniffing the powder into the nose. The cocaine is absorbed by the membranes of the nose and quickly produces a high in which the user experiences a powerful surge of joy, confidence, and mental clarity. The feeling lasts about a half hour.

Cocaine is not addicting, in the strict sense of that word. That is, users do not have to keep increasing the dosage to get the same effect, and they suffer only minor withdrawal symptoms if they stop. It is, however, habit forming. Experiments have shown that even monkeys who have experienced the effects will choose cocaine in preference to food if they can have one or the other but not both—to the point where they are in danger of starvation (Aigner and Balster, 1978). The drug has been termed "relatively safe" in the medical sense but "severely habit-forming" and capable of leading to "self-destructive behavior" (Van Dyke and Byck, 1982). A number of entertainment figures have lost their careers because cocaine became more important than work, and at least one has been killed by an overdose of cocaine taken along with other drugs.

Sedatives and tranquilizers

The drugs called *sedatives,* popularly known as "downers," include barbiturates and other such sleep-producing compounds as *Quaaludes* and *Seconals.* By slowing down brain activity, they produce feelings of relaxation and abandonment—in which, according to their intended use, the user can quickly and blissfully fall asleep. People who take them for kicks fight off the urge to sleep and try to maintain the pleasant feelings, which in many ways resemble those produced by alcohol.

Also generally classed as "downers" are such mild tranquilizers as *Valium* and *Librium,* used medically for the relief of anxiety. Like sedatives, the tranquilizers produce a sense of relaxation, but without as much drowsiness. They are widely prescribed by physicians and are harmless if used in moderation, but they can be dangerously habit-forming when used in excess or for kicks.

Heroin

Considered so dangerous that its use even for medical purposes is prohibited in the United States is *heroin.* Like two similar but less potent drugs called *morphine* and *codeine,* it is a derivative of the poppy plant. All three drugs are *narcotics,* meaning they cut off some of the brain circuits and produce lethargy and profound sleep. Their medical value is to relieve even the most intolerable pain. Used for kicks, heroin produces an immediate rush of pleasure and freedom from anxiety—a high in which users forget their problems and feel on top of the world.

Many people who use heroin become addicted and need the drug desperately to avoid the painful withdrawal symptoms that occur when the effect wears off—shakes, cold sweats, and stomach convulsions. Moreover they need more and more of the drug as time goes on, and the habit may eventually cost $200 a day or more. Many addicts can support the habit only by turning to burglary or prostitution, and the half-million or so regular users in the United States are responsible for large numbers of crimes. A study in Baltimore found that 243 addicts had committed 500,000 crimes in 11 years. A study of prison inmates in California found that those who were heroin addicts had averaged 167 crimes a year, compared with just over two a year for other prisoners (Califano, 1982). Thus heroin is a serious social problem even though only a small percentage of people ever try it and fewer still experiment with it more than a few times, making it the least widely used drug of all.

SUMMARY OF SUPPLEMENT

1. Some psychologists and many nonpsychologists believe that we have a potential ability at *extrasensory perception* (ESP), or perceiving events through channels other than the five senses. ESP is one aspect of *parapsychology,* the study of psychological phenomena that seem to go beyond normal limits and to defy explanation in any normal scientific way.
2. Forms of ESP include *mental telepathy* (mind reading), *clairvoyance* (the ability to perceive an object without using the ordinary senses), and *precognition* (the ability to perceive something that has not yet happened).

Sleep, dreams, hypnosis, and meditation

3. *Altered states of consciousness,* in which brain activity and perception do not operate in the usual fashion, include *sleep, hypnosis,* and changes produced by *meditation* or *drugs.*
4. In *ordinary sleep,* which occurs through most of the night, brain waves show a different pattern from that of waking hours, and the muscles of the body are more relaxed. In *paradoxical sleep,* which occurs for about a quarter of the night, the brain's activity is very similar to the waking state but the bodily muscles are almost totally relaxed. Paradoxical sleep is also known as *REM sleep*—REM standing for the *rapid eye movement* that accompany it. Dreaming takes place during REM sleep.
5. Sleep appears to depend on brain chemistry and possibly body chemistry. Some psychologists believe that ordinary sleep restores the body's chemical balance, while REM sleep restores the brain's ability to function.

6. *Hypnosis* is a strange state of consciousness that resembles sleep, although brain waves and measures of bodily activity are different. Subjects often have imaginary perceptions suggested by the hypnotists and may recall long-ago events they cannot ordinarily remember, although the accuracy of these recollections is questionable.
7. *Meditation* produces changes in brain activity and reduces the rate of breathing and oxygen consumption. The mind seems to achieve a sort of suspended state of nothingness, often accompanied by feelings of timelessness, expanded awareness, and deep joy.

Drugs

8. Various *drugs* that change brain activity have been used since far back in history to relieve anxiety, produce feelings of contentment and happiness, create hallucinations of imaginary sights and sounds, and sometimes attain mystical religious experiences.
9. Legal and commonly used drugs are *nicotine* (in tobacco), *caffeine* (in coffee and tea), and *alcohol.*
10. The use of illicit drugs in the United States increased rapidly in the 1960s and 1970s and has become a multibillion-dollar business, although there are some indications that it may now be declining somewhat. Though the number of young Americans who use drugs is large, it has never been as large as generally believed. One survey found that the only drugs that had been used by as many as 5 percent of young people within the past month were marijuana (25 percent) and stimulants (about 5 percent).
11. *Marijuana* contains the active ingredient *THC,* which when taken in pure and concentrated form is a *psychedelic drug*—one that often produces hallucinations and a sense of detachment from one's body. The Institute of Medicine has concluded that the popularity of marijuana "justifies serious national concern," though the effects are difficult to assess and there is as yet no clear proof of damage to the brain or body.
12. Drugs that have a clearly psychedelic effect include *LSD* ("acid") and *PCP* ("angel dust"). Both produce strange hallucinations and PCP has been termed "the most dangerous drug to hit the streets."
13. *Stimulants*—notably *amphetamines*—increase brain activity and create a sense of energetic well-being, sometimes followed by depression as the effects wear off.
14. *Cocaine,* an expensive stimulant that is usually sniffed into the nose, has become a "fashionable" drug in recent years. It produces a surge of joy and confidence that lasts about a half hour. It is habit-forming and users may come to neglect all else.
15. *Sedatives* ("downers") include *barbiturates* and *Quaaludes. Tranquilizers* are similar in relieving anxiety but produce less sleepiness. All can be habit forming.
16. *Heroin* is a narcotic derived from the poppy plant. Although it is the least widely used of all drugs, it is considered a serious social problem because addicts need more and more to avoid painful withdrawal symptoms and may turn to crime to support the habit.

IMPORTANT TERMS

altered states of consciousness
clairvoyance
extrasensory perception
hypnosis
insomnia
meditation
mental telepathy
narcotics
ordinary sleep
paradoxical sleep
parapsychology
precognition
rapid eye movement (REM)
REM sleep
sedatives
stimulants
tranquilizers

RECOMMENDED READINGS

Carterette, E. C., and Friedman, M. P., eds. *Handbook of perception,* Vol. VIII (*Space and object perception*) and Vol. IX (*Perceptual processing*). New York: Academic Press, 1978.

Cartwright, R. D. *A primer on sleep and dreaming.* Reading, Mass.: Addison-Wesley, 1978.

Dember, W. N., and Warm, J. S. *Psychology of perception,* 2d ed. New York: Holt, Rinehart & Winston, 1979.

Goleman, D., and Davidson, R. J. eds. *Consciousness: brain states of awareness, and alternate realities.* New York: Irvington, 1979.

Hilgard, E. R. *Divided consciousness.* New York: Wiley, 1977.

Hochberg, J. *Perception,* 2d ed. Englewood Cliffs, N.J.: Prentice-Hall, 1978.

Kaufman, L. *Perception: the world transformed.* New York: Oxford University Press, 1979.

Neisser, U. *Cognition and reality.* San Francisco: Freeman, 1976.

Ray, O. S. *Drugs, society, and human behavior,* 2d ed. St. Louis: Mosby, 1978.

Wolman, B. *Handbook of dreams: research, theories, and applications.* New York: Van Nostrand, 1979.

On ESP:

Hansel, C. E. M. *ESP: a scientific evaluation.* New York: Scribners, 1966.

Rhine, J. B., and Brier, R., eds. *Parapsychology today.* New York: Citadel Press, 1968.

Tart, C. T. *Learning to use extrasensory perception.* Chicago: University of Chicago Press, 1976.

PART

5

Human Feelings and Aspirations

Thus far the book has concentrated on the superb ability of the human organism to process information—the way we gather knowledge of our world through our sensory equipment and the process of perception, store the knowledge in memory, manipulate it, think and communicate about it, and use it to understand and deal intelligently with our environment. But we human beings are far more than mere thinking machines. Unlike the computer, we do not function with cold and automatic precision. We have feelings—as vivid as towering rage and overwhelming joy. We have desires and hopes—from the meanest self-seeking to the most sublimely spiritual. Sometimes we fulfill our aspirations. Sometimes we find ourselves totally thwarted or torn by conflict.

The book now turns to this other realm of human experience—to what psychology has learned about such age-old concerns as love and hate, ecstasy and despair, greed and generosity, kindness and cruelty, ambition and sloth. In so doing, it will of necessity discuss the way people interact with one another and how the human personality is shaped by the human society. It will present psychol-

ogy's findings on how our lives are influenced from cradle to grave by the people around us, how others attract or repel us, and how we manage or fail to get along with them. It will deal with adjustment and maladjustment, wholesome and abnormal attempts to cope with life's problems, and the ways therapists have learned to help the unsuccessful.

The exploration of this rich aspect of the human experience, which will make up the rest of the book, begins in Chapter 9 with a discussion of emotions. Our emotions, as you will see, spring from interactions between the brain, the autonomic nervous system, and the body, particularly the bodily structures called glands. Chapter 9 also discusses the forces known as drives, originating in physical states like hunger and the need for sleep that demand relief.

Chapter 10 covers motives—the desires we acquire and the goals we learn to seek. It discusses the ways in which we sometimes fulfill our goals and sometimes meet with frustration or get caught in a tug-of-war between competing desires.

CHAPTER 9

Emotions and the body: "stirred up" or "toned down" 313
- Being emotional all over
- Emotions, the autonomic nervous system, and the glands
- The role of the facial muscles
- Left brain, right brain, and facial expressions
- The eyes as clues to emotions
- Feedback theories of emotions (James-Lange and others)

Emotions and the brain 322
- The Cannon-Bard theory
- The cognitive view of emotions
- Cannon-Bard and its cognitive updating
- James-Lange and its cognitive updating

Individual differences in emotion 326
- Learning to be different
- Some inborn differences
- Emotional stress—for better and for worse

The drives and behavior 328
- The signals for hunger
- Hunger and the hypothalamus
- Hunger and body weight
- Why do people get fat?
- Too many fat cells?
- Thirst
- Other drives

Stimulus needs as a driving force 336
- The need for sensory stimulation
- The need for stimulus variability
- Stimulus variability and survival
- Emotions, drives, stimulus needs, and motives

Summary 339

Important terms 341

Supplement: Sexual feelings and behavior 342
- Sex through the ages
- Today's attitudes: the sexual revolution and its aftermath
- The complexities of human sexuality
- Individual differences: the forgotten message of the Kinsey reports
- Sex and nature-nurture
- Living with the differences
- Sex and youth: a "lonely and . . . silent experience"
- Communication: the "absolute cornerstone"

Summary of supplement 350

Recommended readings 351

Psychology and society
- Do lie detectors ever lie? 315
- Why reading about sex can be injurious to your mental health 347

Emotions and Drives

Imagine if you can living in a world without emotions. You would feel much the same whether you suddenly inherited a fortune or lost all your savings, whether you were watching the climax of a passionately romantic movie or being followed down a dark street in the dead of night. No matter what happened, you would never be filled with happiness, touched by sadness, swept up in excitement, or seized by fear.

Life would be unbearably dreary and boring. What would there be to make events memorable—whether a surprise party or a funeral, a weekend outing, or a Monday morning exam? Moreover, chaos would soon overwhelm us. If people never felt sorry or ashamed, why would anyone hold back from harming others? If we never felt afraid, what would prompt us to protect ourselves in the face of danger?

Although emotional experiences give a unique flavor to our lives and help regulate our existence, they raise many difficult questions. Just what is an emotion? What happens when we become angry or sad, happy or ashamed? Why do some people lose control of their emotions and begin to behave in strange and irrational ways? The questions have always interested psychologists. Though all the answers are not yet in, their findings have shed considerable light on the relationships among our emotions, behavior, and what is happening inside our brain and body.

Emotions and the body: "stirred up" or "toned down"

One essential characteristic of emotions is that they are accompanied by bodily changes. The easiest cases to recognize are those in which the body is obviously "stirred up." We assume that people are emotional when their voices rise, when they blush or get pale, when their muscles grow tense or tremble. We know that we are emotional—even if we manage to conceal all outward signs—when we feel that we are inwardly shaking, or are "hot under the collar," or that our mouth is dry, our pulse racing, or our stomach "full of butterflies." But there are also quieter emotions in which the body seems to be "toned down." Such are the calm, peaceful, and contented feelings we experience when we enjoy a sunbath, a beautiful piece of music, or a satisfying meal. In these cases, too, the body is affected in some manner.

To be emotional usually means to be emotional all over. The obvious outward display shown here is accompanied by equally turbulent inner changes.

The relationship between mind and body in emotion seems to work both ways. Think about something very pleasant, such as inheriting a million dollars from an unknown relative. Quite possibly you will soon *feel* pleasant. Think of something that angers you, such as a bad grade, a social snub, being blamed for someone else's mistake. Soon you may *feel* angry. Or try the opposite. Make a smile, hold it, and see if you do not begin to feel happy and have pleasant thoughts. Clench your fist, keep clenching it, and see if you do not begin to feel angry and have aggressive thoughts.

A psychologist once demonstrated this relationship through an experiment in which college students were led to manipulate their facial muscles without realizing that what they were doing had any relationship to emotions. They were told that the experiment was a study of the effect of muscle movements on perception. Electrodes were attached to the facial muscles to make this explanation seem plausible. The subjects were then asked to contract or relax their muscles in a way that at times resembled a smile and at other times resembled a frown. To a very considerable extent, the subjects reported feeling happy when the muscles were in a smiling position and angry when the muscles were in a frowning position—though they were not consciously aware of their own facial expressions (Laird, 1974).

Being emotional all over

The fact that emotion is accompanied by changes affecting many parts of the body is most apparent in the behavior of lower animals, such as the cat pictured in Figure 9-1. It is less obvious among human beings, for most of us have learned to hide many of the outward signs of emotion. But the changes can readily be measured with laboratory equipment, like the device illustrated in Figure 9-2. This is an elaborate version of what is commonly called a lie detector, a controversial device

Figure 9-1 Displays of emotion in the cat *An angry or friendly cat shows many signs of a stirred-up bodily state. The angry cat* (left) *crouches and growls. Its hair stands on end, its ears are laid back, and its eyes are wide and staring. The friendly cat* (right) *arches its back, pricks its ears, narrows its eyes, and purrs (Young, 1961).*

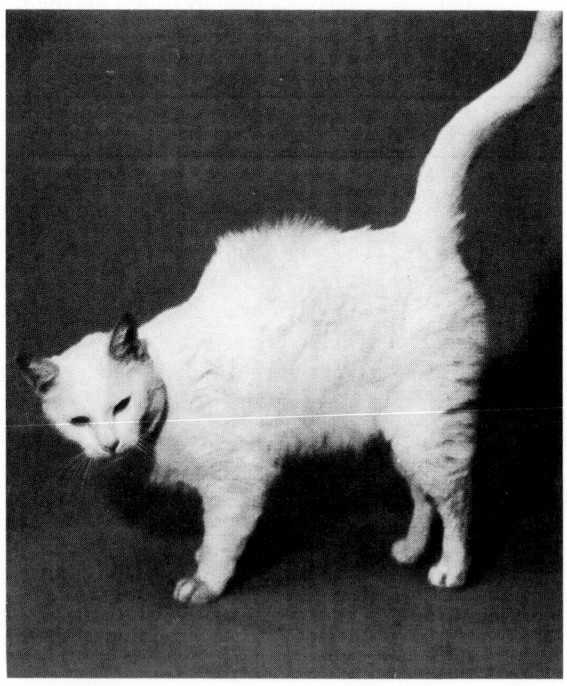

Psychology and Society: Do lie detectors ever lie?

It has been estimated that at least a million Americans a year are asked to take a lie detector test. Some are defendants, plaintiffs, or witnesses in legal cases. Others are job applicants or workers in chain stores, banks, supermarkets, or other companies that use the test to try to spot dishonesty. Still others are executives in industrial firms or government agencies that require periodic loyalty checks.

Many people believe the lie detector is an infallible scientific instrument and place absolute confidence in its results. The test is certainly based on a sound principle—namely that people are likely to become physiologically "stirred up" when they feel so threatened by a question that they answer it untruthfully. But psychology has found that a perfectly innocent person may react emotionally to a critical question—and thus appear to be lying when actually telling the truth. And career criminals who are veteran liars can feel no anxiety or guilt about anything—and can therefore tell outrageous untruths without showing the slightest emotional ripple. To complicate matters, scoring test results may be influenced by the purely subjective impressions of the examiners. Their interpretation of the tracings of physical reactions to test questions may be colored by personal biases about the subject's age, sex, social class, or race. All in all, the great weight of psychological evidence is that lie detector tests have no real claim to being "scientific" or infallible (Lykken, 1981).

Lie detector testing has become a thriving American industry, and it is likely that a significant number of legal and administrative decisions are unfairly influenced by the results. Perhaps this is a good example of how psychology can sometimes be misapplied—how the science can be bent out of shape when its findings are used without sufficient safeguards and caution.

that is discussed in a box on Psychology and Society. The changes can also be shown by chemical analysis of the composition of the blood.

When we experience a strong emotion, such as fear, our heartbeat may increase from the normal rate of around 72 per minute to as high as 180. Blood pressure may also rise sharply, and blood is often diverted from the digestive organs to the muscles of movement and to the surface of the body, resulting in flushed cheeks and the sensation of warmth. The composition of the blood changes. The number of red corpuscles, which carry oxygen, increases markedly. Secretion of hormones by the endocrine glands produces changes in the level of blood sugar, the acidity of the blood, and the amount of adrenalin and noradrenalin (powerful stimulants secreted by the adrenal glands) in the bloodstream.

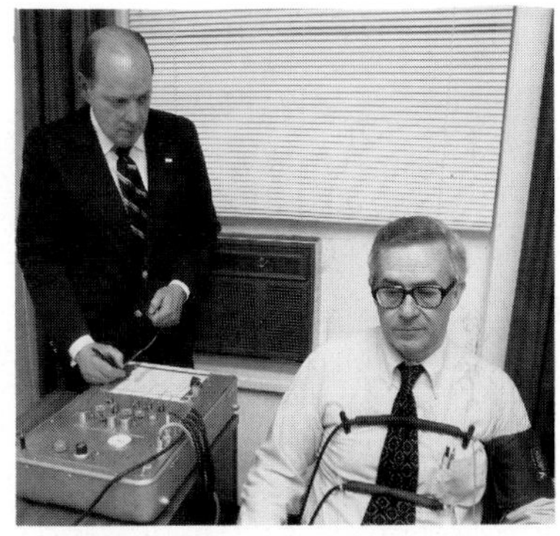

Figure 9-2 A machine that measures emotions *This device produces continuous tracings of bodily processes that often change during emotion. The bands around the man's body measure his rate and depth of breathing. The sleeve around his upper arm measures blood pressure. Electrodes attached to his hand, not shown in the photo, measure what is called the galvanic skin reflex, or changes in the electrical activity of the skin caused by activity of the sweat glands.*

The normal movements of the stomach and intestines, associated with the digestion and absorption of food, usually stop during anger and rage. In other emotional states they may show changes resulting in nausea or diarrhea (Shaffer, 1947). The body's metabolic rate tends to go up. Both the food molecules in the bloodstream and the body tissues themselves are burned off at a faster rate, creating additional energy. Breathing may change in rate, depth, and ratio between time spent breathing in and time spent breathing out. We may gasp or pant. The salivary glands may stop working, causing the feeling of dryness in the mouth often associated with fear and anger. The sweat glands, on the other hand, may become overactive, as shown by the dripping forehead that may accompany embarrassment or the "cold sweat" that sometimes accompanies fear. The tiny muscles at the base of the hairs may contract and raise goose flesh. Finally the pupils of the eyes may enlarge, causing the wide-eyed look that is characteristic of rage, excitement, and pain.

Emotions, the autonomic nervous system, and the glands

All these changes represent bodily activities regulated by the autonomic nervous system and the endocrine glands, over which we ordinarily have little if any conscious control. The autonomic nervous system, without any command from the "thinking" parts of the brain, controls such functions as breathing, heart rate, and blood pressure. The endocrine glands secrete powerful hormones like adrenalin into the bloodstream. And it is worthy of note that we do not seem to have much control over our emotions. They often seem to boil up of their own accord, and we feel them even if we manage to hide all outward signs. Even during situations in which we have determined in advance to remain calm, we often find ourselves unaccountably angry, frightened, or anxious.

In the case of fear and anger, two of the most powerful emotions, the adrenal glands seem to be unusually active. In one study, a chemical analysis was made of the urine of players on a professional hockey team to determine how their adrenal glands functioned before and after a game. The players who took an active part in the game, fighting to win, showed about six times as much noradrenalin after the game as beforehand. But two injured players, who were unable to play and were worried about their future with the team, showed increased amounts of adrenalin. The coach sometimes showed more noradrenalin and sometimes more adrenalin, depending on how well his team had done (Elmadjian, 1959).

Aside from detecting the presence of adrenalin in fear and noradrenalin in anger, however, psychologists have found it very difficult to match any particular bodily state with any particular emotional experience. The same person, on two separate occasions when reporting feelings of joyousness, may show a different pattern of bodily change. And a group of people who report feeling exactly the same emotion (say of joy or distress) may show a number of different patterns. Among students anxious over an examination, for example, one may tend to perspire a great deal, another to show muscle tension, another to have a rapid pulse (Lacey and Van Lehn, 1952; Lacey, Bateman, and Van Lehn, 1953). Certainly bodily changes are an important element in emotion. But the changes have been described as "rather diffuse and global in character" (Mandler, 1962). It is very hard to determine, through physiological measurement alone, what kind of emotion a person is experiencing. Indeed a similar physiological response occurs when we play tennis, make love, or face a crisis (Rose, 1980).

The role of the facial muscles

A number of other bodily changes that often accompany emotion have nothing to do with the autonomic nervous system, the glands, or the visceral organs. Instead these changes represent activity of the muscles of movement over which we do ordinarily have conscious control. You probably have been aware of some of them—for example, muscular tension (as when the teeth are clenched in anger) or trembling (which

Emotion	Tempo	Pitch	Volume
	Patterns of speech		
Happiness	Fast	High	Loud
Sadness	Slow	Low	Soft
Contempt	Slow	Low	Loud

Figure 9-3 Examples of speech patterns that reflect emotion *Speech patterns often vary sharply depending on the emotion experienced. The patterns are so consistent that some emotional states can be identified with surprising accuracy just from the sound of a person's voice (Scherer, 1981). From the opening "hello" of a telephone conversation, for example, we can often tell whether the person on the other end is happy or sad.*

occurs when two sets of muscles work against each other). When emotionally excited, many people have a tendency to blink their eyes or make nervous movements, such as brushing back their hair or drumming their fingers. Emotions are often expressed vocally in laughter, snarls, moans, and screams—or revealed by changes in the speed, pitch, and loudness of speech as shown in Figure 9-3. They are also revealed in such facial expressions as smiles, grimaces, and frowns. In fact even just thinking about experiences that are happy, sad, or infuriating can produce strikingly different patterns of activity in tiny muscles of the face. Though the changes are often too small to be seen, they can be detected by measuring the electrical activity of muscle cells (Schwartz, 1982), using instruments like the one shown in Figure 9-4.

One group of psychologists maintains that facial expressions are a key factor in emotional experience. They hold that every basic emotion is accompanied by a characteristic facial pattern that occurs automatically because of the manner in which our bodies and brains are programed by heredity (Izard, 1977). The various patterns, they believe, are the product of evolution, since an ability to communicate through facial expressions has considerable survival value. Especially for animals that do not have a spoken language, it is an advantage to be able to avert hostility through facial expressions of friendliness or submission. Expressions of fear can alert other members of the group to the presence of danger. Thus the process of natural selection has favored the survival of individuals carrying genes programing their facial expressions (Andrew, 1965).

This theory is based in part on a study that used the photographs shown in Figure 9-5. These photos and several others were shown to subjects in a number of different societies, and the subjects were asked to try to identify the emotions being displayed (as you are asked in the caption accompanying the faces). There was remarkable agreement about the emotions—not only among subjects in the United States, Argentina, Brazil, China, and Japan but among members of isolated societies in New Guinea (Ekman, 1971). The study indicates that the facial expressions that accompany at least some emotions seem to be universal and unlearned, as if they were indeed genetically programed—set by nature rather than nurture. A further indication comes from observations of the spontaneous facial expressions of very young babies (Izard and Dougherty, 1982), as shown in Figure 9-6.

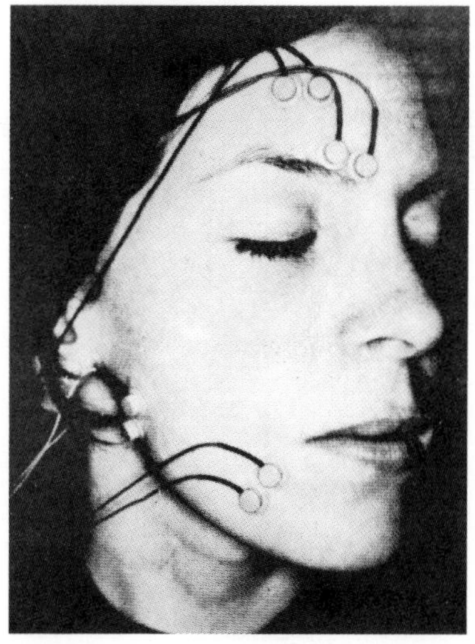

Figure 9-4 An emotion-detecting device *Electrodes placed on the forehead and cheeks measure the activity of muscles responsible for facial expressions. They can detect changes in emotion not apparent to the eye.*

Figure 9-5 Facial expressions of emotion: can you identify them? *Try to match these faces with the emotions of anger, disgust, fear, happiness, sadness, and surprise. The answers will be found at the bottom of the page.*

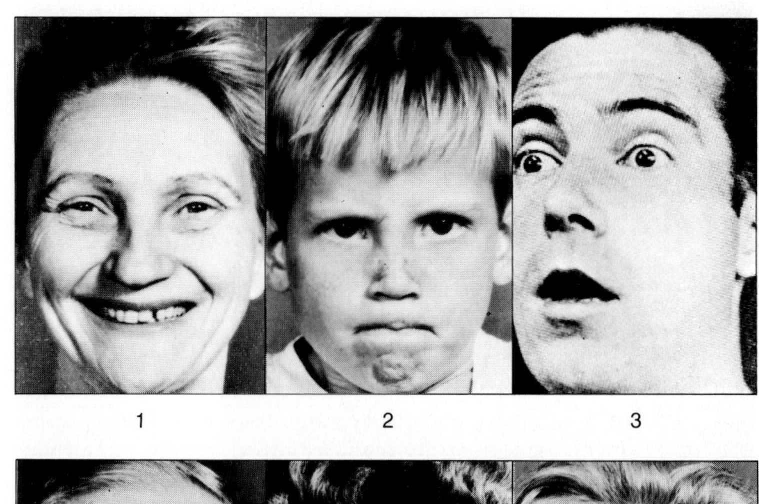

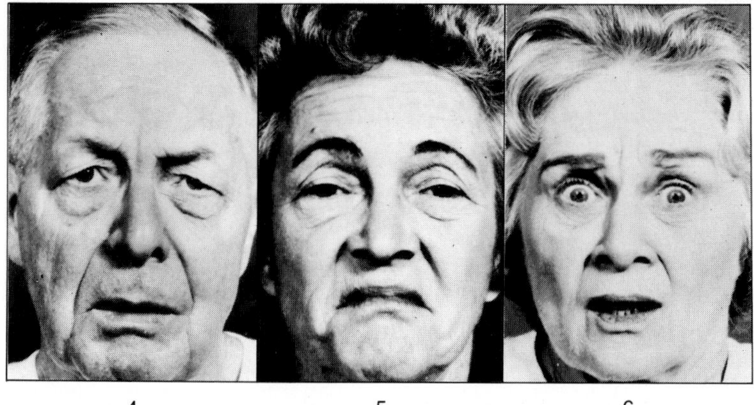

Left brain, right brain, and facial expressions

A provocative finding about facial expressions was made in an experiment that used the three photographs shown in Figure 9-7. Before you read the next paragraph, look at the photos and try to determine your answer to the question posed in the caption.

If the three photos struck you as being alike yet somehow different, there is a reason. A is an undoctored photograph of the man. The other two are composites, made by splitting the original photo down the middle and flopping the two halves. In *B*, you see the man as he would appear if his entire face was like the right side. C shows the face as if it was made up of two left sides. If you found that C seemed to display the most intense emotion, you have considerable company. When the experimenters showed the three photographs—and similar ones of other people displaying various other emotions—they found that subjects tended to agree that the left-face composites gave the most intense impression (Sackheim, Gur, and Saucy, 1978).

The experiment is in line with what is known about the differences between the left brain and right brain. The left hemisphere of the brain

---

The emotions being expressed in Figure 9-5 are: (1) happiness, (2) anger, (3) surprise, (4) sadness, (5) disgust, and (6) fear.

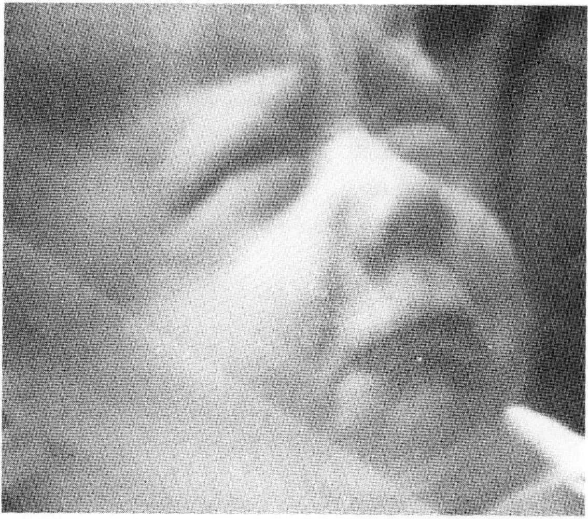

seems to specialize in language, logic, and details. The right hemisphere seems to specialize in spatial relationships, form, music, and in achieving intuitive understanding of "the big picture" instead of concentrating on details. There is also some evidence that the right hemisphere plays a dominant role in activating the muscles of the face (Gatz, 1970; Peele, 1961) and in emotional reactions (Davidson and Schwartz, 1976). Thus it seems possible, as the experiment with the composite photographs suggests, that expressions on the left side of our face give the best indication of the emotion we are experiencing. All this is still somewhat speculative—but it suggests that, if you want to know how other people really feel, you should concentrate on the expression on the left side of their face and ignore the right side. This is not as easy to do in the ordinary rapid flow of conversation and changes in facial expression as in a laboratory where photographs can be manipulated, but it may prove worth the effort.

Figure 9-6 Emotions of infants: written all over their faces *Notice the similarity of these facial expressions to those of the happy and sad adults pictured in photos 1 and 4 of Figure 9-5. For the significance of the photographs, see the text.*

Figure 9-7 Three expressions of emotion: which is the strongest? *In all three photographs the man is expressing disgust. In which one, would you say, is his expression clearest and strongest? The way most people answer this question is explained in the text.*

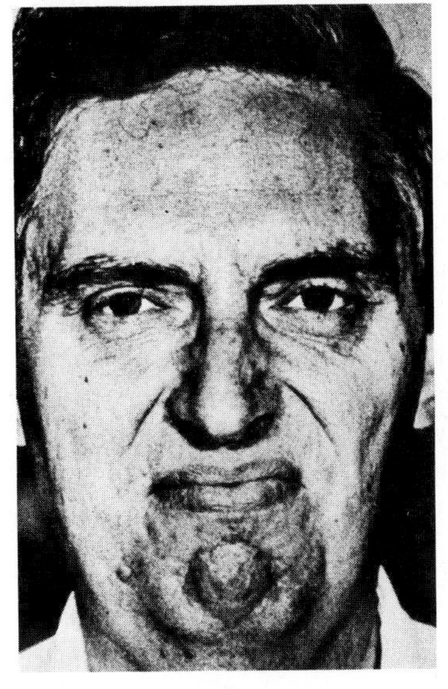

A

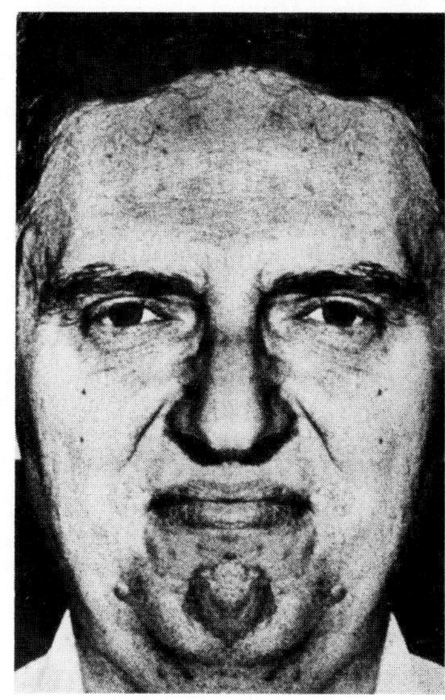

B

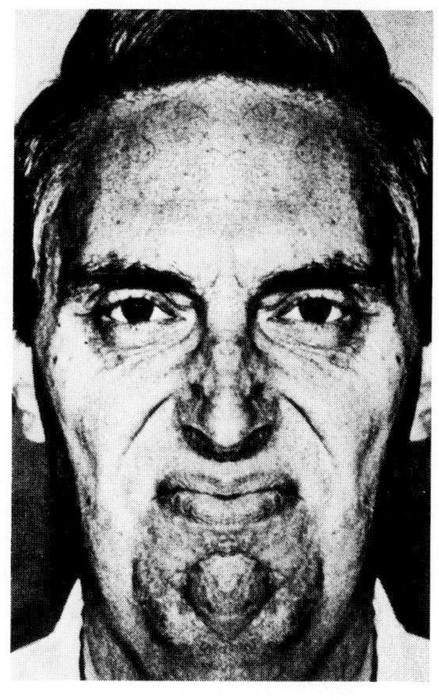

C

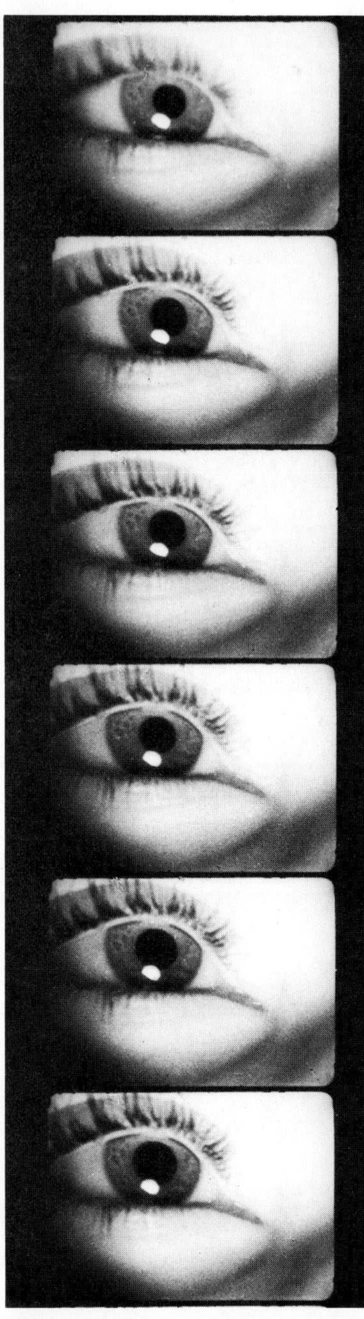

Figure 9-8 A photographic record of pupil response *This series of photographs, taken over a period of 4 seconds, shows a man's eye as he looked at a picture of a woman's face. Note the rapid increase in pupil size from the normal, at top, to the bottom, where the diameter was about 30 percent greater.*

The eyes as clues to emotion

Back in the sixteenth century a French poet wrote that the eyes are "windows of the soul." Modern psychology testifies that these words were more than a felicitous figure of speech. Studies have shown that one very sensitive measure of some emotions is the size of the pupil of the eye.

Pupil size is a good indication of even such a mild emotion as interest. One experiment that demonstrates this fact is illustrated in Figure 9-8. In general, it was found that subjects showed significant increases in pupil size when they looked at pictures they found interesting, but no increase when they looked at something they found unpleasant (Hess, 1965). In another experiment, male subjects looked at the two photographs shown in Figure 9-9, which you should examine before reading the next paragraph.

The only difference in the two photographs in Figure 9-9 is that the one at the left has been retouched to make the woman's pupils seem larger; the one at the right to make them seem smaller. Yet this slight difference made a considerable difference in the way subjects responded—and perhaps in the way you reacted. When the subjects were asked in which photo the woman seemed to be more sympathetic (or warmer, happier, or more attractive), they tended to pick the face with the large pupils. When they were asked in which one she seemed angrier (or more unfriendly or more selfish), they tended to pick the one with the small pupils (Hess, 1975). Moreover, their own pupils grew wider when they looked at the photo with the large pupils than when they looked at the other.

One experimenter, who worked with babies in their homes, used a drug that dilated her pupils on one visit, then a different drug that made her pupils artificially small on another visit. When the experimenter's pupils were large, she found that the babies smiled at her more often. The responses of the mothers were also affected. When the experimenter's pupils were large, the mothers described her in such terms as "soft," "gentle," and "open." When her pupils were small, they found her "harsh," "brassy," and "cold" (Ashear, 1975).

All in all, it appears that pupil size—which is controlled by the autonomic nervous system and the smooth muscles of the iris—not only reflects emotional states but serves as a clue that all of us use in assessing how other people feel. We may not even be conscious of the fact, but we seem to be somehow aware that large pupils indicate interest and therefore warmth and acceptance. Long before psychology began studying this matter, women used belladonna, a drug that dilates the pupils, as a standard part of their cosmetic equipment. They believed that putting drops of belladonna in their eyes made them more attractive—indeed the word *belladonna* means "beautiful lady." Perhaps they were right, though for reasons not understood at the time. Along similar lines, we speak warmly of children who are "wide-eyed" with wonder at Christmas—and we describe unfriendly and hostile people as being "sharp-eyed" or "gimlet-eyed."

It is interesting to note, however, that not everyone reacts more favorably to wide pupils under all circumstances. It has been found that

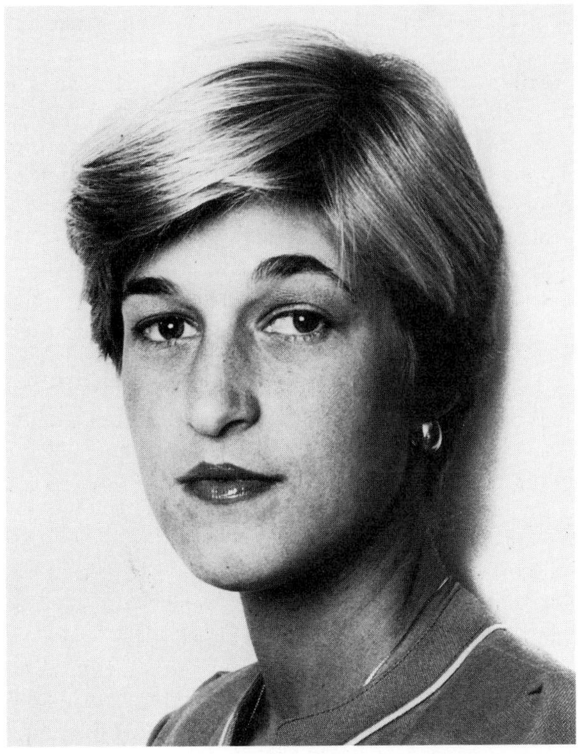

Figure 9-9 An experiment in judging facial expressions *Take a careful look at these two photographs. In which of them does the woman appear to be more sympathetic? In which does she seem to be angrier? Or do you find no difference? For the opinions of subjects who took part in an experiment using the photos, see the text.*

male homosexuals tend to prefer photos of women with small pupils to photos of women with wide pupils. The same seems to be true of Don Juans—men who are more interested in sexual conquests than in forming close relationships with women (Hess, 1975).

Feedback theories of emotion (James-Lange and others)

The various changes that take place in the body, welling up without conscious control and often despite our determination to suppress them, have naturally commanded the attention of psychology from its earliest days. They were the basis of the first important theory of emotions—which was proposed by William James, one of the science's founding fathers, and represented a radical change in thinking about emotional behavior. Common sense says that we cry because we are sad, strike out because we are angry, tremble and run because we are afraid. James made the suggestion—startling to the scientific world of his day and even now to someone who hears it for the first time—that things are exactly the opposite.

James said that emotion occurs in this fashion: Certain stimuli in the environment set off the physiological changes. These changes in turn stimulate the various sensory nerves leading from the visceral organs and other parts of the body to the brain. It is these sensory messages from our aroused bodies that we then perceive as emotion. In other words, we do not cry because we are sad. On the contrary, we feel sad because we are crying. Similarly, we do not tremble because we are afraid, but feel afraid because we are trembling (James, 1890).

This notion that the physiological changes come first and that the perceived emotion is a feedback from the changes was also proposed at about the same time by the Danish scientist Carl Lange. It persisted more or less unchallenged for many years as the *James-Lange theory of emotion.* The weakness of the theory is that it is so difficult to match any particular kind of bodily state (and whatever kind of feedback this might produce) with any particular emotion.

A more recent theory has been proposed by psychologists impressed with the role of the facial muscles. They too believe that our feelings of emotion represent a feedback of bodily sensations—but not so much from the visceral organs as from the muscles of the face, which, as has been said, they believe are programed by nature to respond in certain definite ways to certain stimuli in the environment (Tomkins, 1962). Again the question is whether specific facial expressions can be matched with specific emotions. Proponents of the facial feedback theory believe that the matching exists (Izard and Dougherty, 1982), but other psychologists are skeptical (McCaul, Holmes, and Soloman, 1982).

Emotions and the brain

Whether or not our feelings of emotion depend on feedback—either from the visceral organs, as the James-Lange theory presumed, or from the facial muscles—is just one of the many problems that continue to make emotions a topic of speculation and debate. But there is no doubt that emotions are accompanied by bodily changes of many kinds—ranging, as has been said, from pupil size to activity of the glands, digestive organs, heart muscles and even the chemical composition of the blood. Nor is there any doubt that the activity of the brain changes—a fact that many psychologists now believe is the real key to emotional behavior.

Certainly emotions must be numbered among our most intense conscious experiences. Strong emotions—of the kind that made Oedipus gouge out his eyes, Juliet renounce her family for Romeo, and Hamlet kill his uncle the king—have been the chief subject of literature in all cultures throughout history. In our own day-to-day lives, our emotions frequently command our attention. When they boil up, we cannot ignore them. Our pleasant emotions (joy, love) have us "walking on air." Our unpleasant emotions (anger, fear, shame, disgust) fill us with despair. Emotions sometimes make it impossible for us to choose our words carefully, concentrate on our work, or even read or listen to music. They may make us, for the moment, totally irrational. A study of how people act in emotional crises, such as being caught in a life-threatening fire, found that about 15 percent became so panicky that they were unable to take any appropriate action. Another 70 percent showed at least some signs of disorganization (Tyhurst, 1951).

The Cannon-Bard theory

The brain's activity was the basis of another famous theory of emotions—the *Cannon-Bard theory.* According to the Cannon-Bard view, certain stimuli in the environment cause the hypothalamus* to fire off patterns of nervous activity that have two simultaneous effects. One, the hypothalamus arouses the autonomic nervous system and thus triggers the various physiological changes associated with emotion. Two, at the same time, the hypothalamus sends messages to the cerebral cortex that result in our feelings of emotion. Note that the Cannon-Bard theory attaches no importance to the feedback of bodily sensations, which is the basic element of the James-Lange theory. It considers the physiological changes to be a sort of side effect—useful in preparing the body to take appropriate action but not essential to our conscious experience of emotion.

At first glance, the Cannon-Bard and James-Lange theories seem totally at odds. It would appear that if one is right, the other must be wrong. But, as so often happens in the study of human behavior, what seems to be true is not necessarily true at all. Many psychologists now believe that both theories are partially correct but also partially wrong, in that neither is a full explanation.

The cognitive view of emotions

A number of psychologists, all leaning more or less to the cognitive school, have contributed to a new view of emotions. Their ideas are still being formulated and refined and at present differ in many respects, as you will see if you take an advanced course in emotional behavior. For our present purposes, however, their ideas can be put together into a sort of composite picture of the *cognitive theory of emotion.* The discussion that follows ignores some of the fine points that are at issue, and perhaps no single psychologist would agree with all the generalities—but it will serve as an introduction to this important area of research.

The cognitive view emphasizes the conscious experience of emotion—that is, the mental processes that account for such feelings as joy, anger, and fear (Lazarus, 1982). Many factors contribute to this experience. One is information about events in the environment, delivered to the cortex (or highest part of the brain) from the sense organs. Another is the brain's storehouse of information about similar events in the past, which aids in appraising and interpreting the new stimuli. Another is patterns of nervous impulses in the hypothalamus and the rest of the brain's limbic system—which, acting through the autonomic nervous system and probably also directly on the pituitary gland, create the physiological changes of being stirred up or toned down. Still another is feedback from these physiological changes, delivered to the cortex via sensory neurons from the visceral organs and the muscles of the body and face. All these factors interact to produce the emotions we experience—and sometimes to initiate behavior that expresses our emotions, intensifies the pleasant ones, or helps us escape from the unpleasant ones.

---

*Actually Cannon believed that the thalamus was the key. But it has since been found that the hypothalamus, with its close relationship to the autonomic nervous system and the pituitary gland, is the important structure.

Indeed some psychologists think of emotional experiences as another of the altered states of consciousness such as those produced by hypnosis or drugs. People who strike back with unaccustomed vigor in anger or panic in fear sometimes say afterward, "I wasn't myself" or "I must have been out of my mind." And certainly emotions, like other altered states, do affect perception. To a joyous person, the world appears bright and cheerful. To a person caught up in distress and disgust, the world is full of gloom and disaster (Izard, 1977).

Cannon-Bard and its cognitive updating

The cognitive psychologists, you will have noted, agree with Cannon-Bard about the importance of the hypothalamus—but not with the theory that messages sent from the hypothalamus to the cortex account for our emotions. Though the exchange of messages between hypothalamus and cortex works in both directions, the new view holds that the cortex plays the commanding role by appraising events that occur in the environment. At any given moment, the information received by the cortex from the sense organs may be neutral in terms of emotional impact, in which case we make a cognitive decision that no emotional reaction is called for. The information may set off patterns of nervous impulses, traveling from cortex to hypothalamus, that are associated with the emotion of interest. The sense organs may convey what the cognitive process decides is good information that calls for joy, or bad information calling for distress, anger, or fear. Sometimes the sensory information compels our attention and creates an emotional reaction even when we are busy with other matters (Nielsen and Sarason, 1981). For example, while absorbed in study at a library table, we may respond to a sexually attractive person who happens to walk by. Also of course we may experience more than one emotion in response to an event (Polivy, 1981). We may feel both sad and angry, for example, after being rejected by a friend, or both fearful and excited while entering an airplane.

The cognitive appraisal of the environment is often immediate and almost automatic (Arnold, 1960)—something like the rapid first impression that occurs in perception. If we find a snake in our path, for example, everything seems to happen at once. Our hearts jump. We feel afraid. We leap back. All this seems to occur without any conscious decision making. At other times our appraisal is more complex and deliberate (Lazarus and Averill, 1972). An example is the "slow burn" we sometimes experience when we hear a remark and have no immediate reaction. But then we think about it, decide it was insulting, and get angry.

On some occasions the appraisal appears to follow rather than precede physiological arousal. For some reason that we do not understand at the moment, our bodies become stirred up or toned down. Perhaps stimuli in the environment have affected the unconscious workings of our minds. Perhaps we have exhibited a conditioned reaction—as in Watson's famous experiment in which the child Albert's fear response was conditioned to furry animals and men with beards. At any rate, we

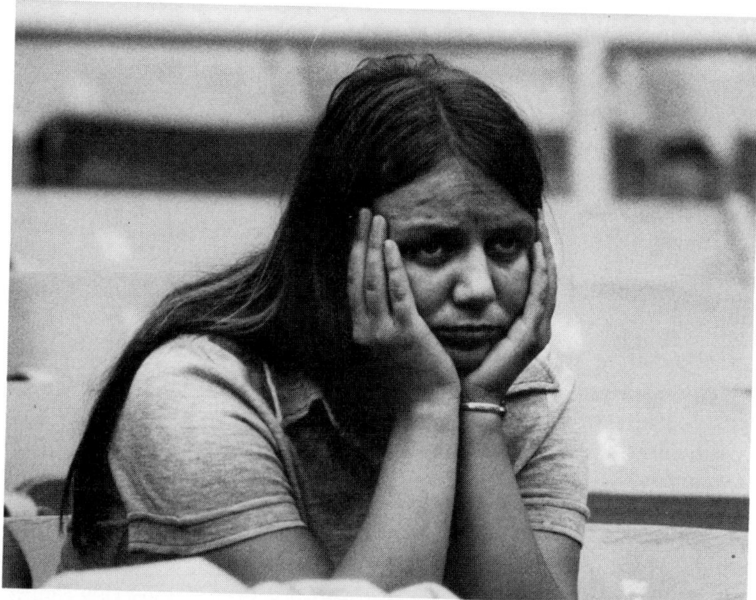

A blue mood, in wh... seems blue? Or is the p... tired? Perhaps she herself ... made the appraisal.

experience some kind of change in the nature and level of our internal sensations, which we must then try to appraise and interpret (Schachter and Singer, 1962). For example, a student sitting alone in a room at night may become aware of unusual bodily sensations and interpret them as feelings of loneliness. A student who has a similar pattern of sensations when a difficult examination is coming up may interpret them as anxiety. Another who has put in an unusually hard day's work may decide that they simply represent fatigue. Such cases of unexplained arousal are infrequent (Maslach, 1978), but they do occur.

James-Lange and its cognitive updating

Just as the cognitive view accepts the Cannon-Bard theory in part, so does it agree with the James-Lange theory that bodily sensations are an essential aspect of emotion. Indeed it maintains that the brain and body work together in many ways during emotional experiences. For example, the student who interprets bodily sensations as representing anxiety over an examination may, as a result of this interpretation and labeling, experience additional activity of the autonomic nervous system, intensified physiological changes, and greater feedback—all of which add to the feeling of anxiety. On the other hand, attributing the feelings to fatigue may reduce the activity of the autonomic nervous system, dampen the physiological activity, and thus lessen the bodily feedback and the feelings being experienced.

The cognitive view maintains, however, that bodily states are not enough in themselves to account for all the very different emotions we experience. Once we become aware that bodily changes are taking place, what really determines our feelings is our cognitive activity—our thinking about the stimulus that has produced the changes and the entire environmental situation in which it occurred.

Individual differences in emotion

If someone asked you how many different kinds of emotions a human being can experience, how would you answer? Our language contains hundreds of words that describe emotional feelings—and your answer might depend on how many of these words you are familiar with, also how many of them you use to appraise and label your own feelings. Other cultures use different labels. People in the Caroline Islands, for example, have two different words meaning anger—one for justified anger toward someone who has acted improperly, the other for anger that cannot readily be explained by another person's behavior (Lutz, 1982).

One psychologist has suggested that there are ten basic emotions, listed in Figure 9-10. Our other emotional experiences, according to this view, are combinations of two or more of these ten. The possible ways in which ten emotions can be combined, of course, run into the thousands. If feelings of interest are considered to be emotions, as in this listing, then it appears that we experience some amount of emotion during most or all our waking hours (Izard, 1977). But the more spectacular feelings that people usually think of as emotions (joy, anger, fear, and the like) occupy less of our time—probably under 10 percent for most of us.

Learning to be different

There are of course many individual differences in emotional experience. Some of these differences are the result of learning. Even simple classical conditioning, as was discussed in Chapter 3, can create unreasonable fears (as in the experiment in which 11-month-old Albert came to be afraid of dogs and other furry objects) and unreasonable prefer-

The ten basic emotions

anger	guilt
contempt	interest-excitement
disgust	joy
distress	shame
fear	surprise

Four important complex emotions

anxiety
(fear plus anger, distress, guilt, interest, or shame)

depression
(distress plus anger, contempt, fear, guilt, or shame)

hostility
(a combination of anger, contempt, and disgust)

love
(interest plus joy)

Figure 9-10 One psychological view of the range of emotions *The fundamental human emotions, according to one investigator, are those listed at the top of the table. Other emotions that we frequently experience, notably those at the bottom, are combinations of some of the fundamental feelings (after Izard, 1977).*

ences. Because of this kind of childhood conditioning, some individuals have intense emotional reactions to objects or events in the environment that leave other people entirely unmoved. Moreover, the more complex cognitive processes that help determine emotional experience vary greatly from one person to another, mostly because of associations laid down in long-term memory through learning.

Behavior resulting from emotion also shows many individual differences. Some people have learned to suppress many of the outward signs of emotion. (Such people are often called "poker-faced.") Others are quick to display their feelings. (They are said to "wear their hearts on their sleeves.") Displays of emotion vary from culture to culture, obviously because of what these cultures have taught their members about appropriate behavior. When Navaho or Apache Indians are angry, they do not raise but lower their voices. When inhabitants of the Andaman Islands want to show joy at greeting a visiting relative, they sit down in the visitor's lap and weep (Opler, 1967).

Some inborn differences

On the other hand, some differences appear to be inborn. Studies of very young children, who have not yet had the opportunity to do much learning, have shown that some are much more inclined to smile than others, while some have a pronounced tendency to be irritable and cry at the slightest provocation.

There is considerable evidence that one inborn difference affecting emotions is the sensitivity of the autonomic nervous system (ANS), which controls many of the bodily changes associated with emotion. It has been found, for example, that people differ widely in the way they respond to drugs that act directly on the ANS (Gellhorn and Miller, 1961). Some of us seem to react to weaker stimulation of the ANS than others—and to react more rapidly and with greater intensity. Patterns of ANS activity also vary. In the same kind of emotional situation, one person may consistently show a rapid heartbeat, while another may show only a small change in heart rate but a pronounced increase in skin temperature (Lacey and Lacey, 1958). Differences of this kind can be observed even in children (Tennes and Mason, 1982). Two-year-olds who are chronically anxious, timid, and shy have been found to have a heart rate that is unusually high but generally stable. Two-year-olds who are less fearful usually have a heart rate that is low and subject to considerably more variation.

There are also wide differences in the size and activity of the endocrine glands that play such an important part in emotion. A normal thyroid gland may weigh anywhere from 8 to 50 grams, the testes from 10 to 45 grams, the ovaries from 2 to 10 grams. The output of human adrenal glands under similar conditions has been found to vary from 7 to 20 grams, of pituitary glands from 250 to 1,100 milligrams (Williams, 1956). Presumably a person with large and active endocrine glands displays different physiological changes—and therefore has different emotional experiences—from a person with smaller or less active glands.

Certainly any abnormality of the glands or nervous system can have a drastic effect on emotional experience. One demonstration comes from a study of people who had suffered injuries to the spinal cord and had lost all bodily sensations below the point of damage. These people reported that their emotions were considerably less intense after the injury than before. The higher up the spine the damage had occurred, and thus the less feedback of bodily sensations they retained, the greater was the loss of emotional intensity (Hohmann, 1966).

Emotional stress—for better and for worse

Because the emotions are associated with so many physiological changes, often of a highly stirred-up nature, they put the body under considerable stress. They can be physically exhausting, as is evident from the "washed-out" feeling that often follows an outburst of anger or a serious scare. Wear and tear on the body are caused by pleasant as well as unpleasant emotions. As one investigator has stated, "A painful blow and a passionate kiss can be equally stressful" (Selye, 1976).

Up to a point, *emotional stress* is an unavoidable and even desirable aspect of life. Some of our most glorious moments arise from the tension and excitement of joy and love. The milder emotion of interest adds zest and meaning to our work, our recreation, and our social relationships. Without our emotions and their accompanying stress, our lives would be drab and colorless.

Even fear is useful. It helps us avoid or escape from situations that threaten our well-being and sometimes our lives. It makes us drive more carefully and plan more constructively for the future. Unless fear becomes so intense as to create panic, it can help us perform better in many situations. Many combat pilots, for example, have reported that mild fear made them more efficient. In one study, a third of the pilots said that even strong fear was helpful rather than disorganizing (Wickert, 1947). When the wear and tear of emotional stress persist too intensely and for too long a time, however, they can create disastrous effects. The topic of stress—and the various ways we attempt to cope with it—will be discussed in Chapter 11.

The drives and behavior

Besides emotions, there is another group of psychological conditions that are accompanied by physiological changes and have a pronounced effect on behavior. For example, as you know from experience, a state of hunger can make you jumpy, jittery, and unable to concentrate. The urge to find food, when the body lacks it, can be just as strong as the tendency to run away in fear or strike back in anger. In the famous case of a party of pioneers stranded by an 1846 blizzard in the Donner Pass, the urge overrode all moral and esthetic scruples and turned some of them into cannibals.

No clear dividing line exists between emotions and such states as hunger. Both depend on bodily activities. Both may produce strong sensations. Both may trigger behavior, sometimes of the most explosive kind. Yet there is a difference. In ordinary conversation, we would never think of referring to hunger as an emotion. Psychologists acknowledge a scientific difference by distinguishing between emotions and what they call *drives*.

The drives center on the process of homeostasis, or the maintenance of bodily stability. It is one of the brain's functions, as was explained in Chapter 2, to preserve homeostasis by making sure our bodies have a constant supply of all the substances our cells require to perform efficiently. When our bodies lack any of these substances, we experience a drive—which can be defined as *a pattern of brain activity resulting from physiological imbalances that threaten homeostasis.* Among the drives are *hunger* (caused by the lack of food), *thirst* (lack of water, which makes up two-thirds of our bodies), and *breathing* (the need for oxygen). The breathing drive goes unnoticed most of the time, but people who are drowning or being suffocated will fight as hard for air as they would fight for food when starving.

The pattern of brain activity that constitutes a drive makes us seek whatever our bodies need to maintain homeostasis. By so doing—for example, by finding food—we restore the physiological balance, change the pattern of brain activity, and thus satisfy the drive.

The signals for hunger

How do we know when we are hungry? Common-sense observation tells us we have hunger pangs that occur in the stomach, which feels empty and overactive and sometimes actually growls for food. This common-sense explanation is partially true. There are nerve fibers that carry messages to the brain from the stomach (Ball, 1974), and also from the mouth, throat, and intestines. But these messages do not seem essential. Experiments have shown that rats continue to show signs of hunger even if all the sensory neurons leading from the stomach to the brain are cut (Morgan and Morgan, 1940)—indeed even if the animal's entire stomach is removed (Tsang, 1938). There have also been cases in which the human stomach has been removed for medical reasons, without any pronounced effect on the desire for food (Wangensteen and Carlson, 1931).

More important than sensations from the stomach, it now appears, are hunger messages originating in that previously unsuspected organ the liver. It is the liver that does the chief job of receiving food supplies after they have been absorbed into the bloodstream from the intestines, then converting these foods into chemicals that provide energy for the cells of the body and brain. Apparently the liver is alert to any deficiencies in the body's food supplies and signals the brain when such deficiencies occur (Friedman and Stricker, 1976).

Hunger and the hypothalamus

Within the brain, the hypothalamus plays an important part in sensations of hunger. At one time, indeed, it was believed that the hypothalamus had two areas that acted as an on switch and an off switch for the hunger drive. This belief arose from experiments with animals. It

The hunger drive can be stimulated by the sight of attractive food.

was found that when an electrode is implanted in one part of the hypothalamus, and electrical stimulation is applied, an animal will start eating. If this same area is surgically destroyed, the animal loses virtually all interest in food (Anand and Brobeck, 1951). When an animal is stimulated through an electrode implanted in another part of the hypothalamus, it immediately stops eating. If this area is destroyed, the animal eats voraciously and becomes grossly fat (Hetherington and Ranson, 1940).

These experiments, however, do not tell the whole story. For one thing, a rat stimulated in what might seem to be the on switch of the hypothalamus does not necessarily eat. If no food is present, the animal will do something else. It may drink water or gnaw on wood (Valenstein, Cox, and Kakolewski, 1970), as if the stimulation merely produced some kind of general arousal. Moreover, animals can be made to start eating by electrical stimulation of brain areas outside the hypothalamus (Valenstein, 1973)—or sometimes even by just pinching a rat's tail (Valenstein, 1976).

It appears now that the hunger drive depends on brain patterns that are far more complex than mere on and off switches (Balagura, 1973). Some of the nerve cells in the hypothalamus seem to be sensitive to changes in the food supply present in the bloodstream, particularly the level of fatty compounds (Nisbett, 1972) and also the level of blood sugar. But the hypothalamus also responds to messages carried by nerve fibers from various parts of the alimentary canal and from the liver. The hunger drive is also affected by outside stimuli—such "incentive objects" as the smell of food from a restaurant kitchen or the sight of pastries in a bakery window—and by our eating habits and the social relationships we have built around eating. (We tend to feel hungry around our usual dinner time regardless of our physiological condition, and we usually eat more when we are with family or friends than when we are alone.)

Hunger and body weight

The hunger drive is closely related to the fact that the body contains a large number of cells, scattered throughout, that are especially designed for the storage of fatty compounds. In evolutionary terms, survival of the species presumably depended on the ability of these *fat cells* to store up energy that would tide the body over the prolonged periods of starvation that human beings once experienced frequently (and still do in many places). Under ordinary circumstances, the hunger drive keeps these cells filled to an appropriate level with fatty compounds. But when the body lacks other sources of food and energy, the fat cells are emptied and their contents used as fuel. This raises the level of fatty compounds in the bloodstream—a change that serves as one of the triggers for the hunger drive.

Since the amount of fat stored in the body largely determines a person's weight, it might be said that the hunger drive tends to keep our body weight at its ideal level (Stellar and Corbit, 1973). Ordinarily we eat enough to maintain our reserve stores of fat and keep our weight from falling too low (Nisbett, 1972). But we stop short of consuming an excess of food that would become fat deposits and make us too heavy (Hervey, 1969).

Even a slight change in food intake can have a drastic effect on weight. For example, adding as little as ten medium-sized potato chips a day to one's usual diet would result in a gain of about eleven pounds a year. Yet most of us stay at the same weight over long periods of time. One is reminded of the workings of a thermostat that manages, by turning a furnace on and off, to keep a building within a temperature range of one or two degrees.

In this connection, note the experiment illustrated in Figure 9-11. The animal in the experiment was fed artificially, with food delivered directly to the stomach. It never smelled, tasted, or swallowed the food. Nevertheless, it managed to maintain its body weight at the normal level. Indeed artificial feeding may have been an advantage in this respect—as will be seen in the following paragraphs about people who, despite the ordinarily fine-tuned workings of the hunger drive, become overweight.

Why do people get fat?

In the United States, it has been estimated, somewhere between a quarter and a third of all adults are at least 25 percent over their ideal weight—some by as much as 20 or 50 or even 100 pounds. The reason is a mystery that many psychologists have spent years trying to unravel—in part because obesity can lead to severe psychological problems as well as to physical disorders such as high blood pressure, diabetes, and heart disease (Grinker, 1982).

Figure 9-11 An animal that never eats—yet is properly fed *When the rat presses the bar, a squirt of liquid food is delivered directly to its stomach. It soon learns to press the bar just often enough to satisfy its hunger and maintain its normal intake of food (Epstein and Teitelbaum, 1962).*

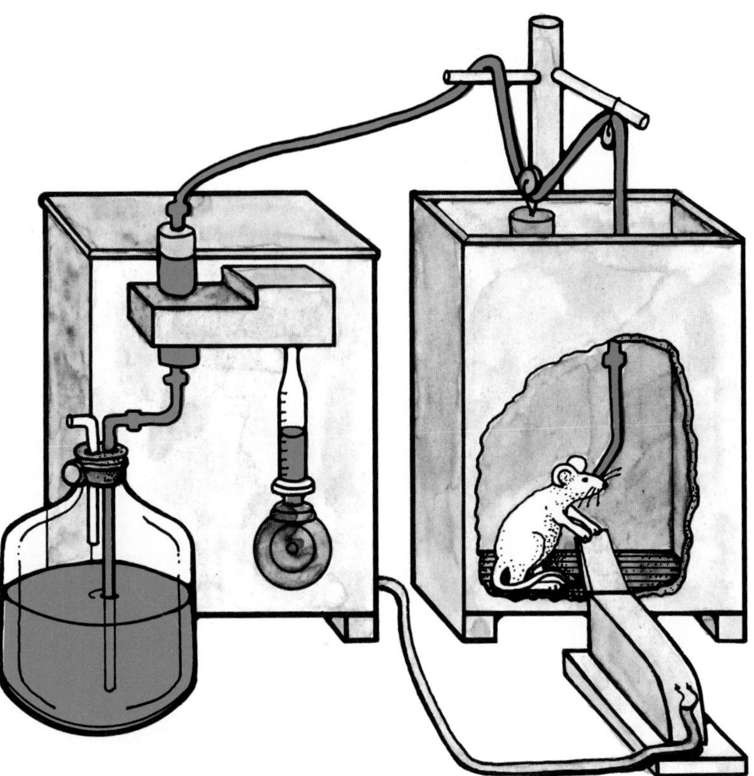

In some cases, obesity seems to stem from metabolic disturbances. Instead of turning food into energy at the normal rate, the body stores an excessive amount of it as fat deposits. In most cases, however, obesity is simply the result of eating too much and exercising too little (Miller, 1975).

But why do people eat too much? Sometimes there seem to be emotional reasons. Clinical psychologists have found that many overweight patients overeat to relieve anxieties over competition, failure, rejection, or sexual performance. And some people eat simply as a matter of habit—regardless of whether their hunger drive signals the need for food—or have a strong preference for such high-calorie foods as butter, cheese, ice cream, pastries, and candy.

Studies have found that the eating patterns of fat people are unusual in several respects. For one thing, fat people tend to eat whenever they have the opportunity, even if they have already had a meal and would not normally be hungry. This was demonstrated in striking fashion in the experiment illustrated in Figure 9-12. In another experiment, in which clocks were manipulated to make the subjects think that dinner was being served later than usual, fat people ate more than their customary amount, though people of normal weight did not (Schachter and Gross, 1968). Whenever overweight people sit down to a table, they tend to eat more and eat faster (Schachter, 1971). They are particularly likely to eat a lot when the food tastes unusually good—and more likely than people of normal weight to be turned off by food that tastes bad (Nisbett, 1968).

In all these respects, the eating habits of overweight people closely resemble those of animals that have become fat after surgical destruction of part of the hypothalamus. Moreover, overweight people behave in a number of other ways very much like animals with damage to this part of the brain. They tend to be emotional and irritable (Rodin, 1972; Rodin, Elman, and Schachter, 1972), to be more lethargic and less active than average (Bullen, Reed, and Mayer, 1964), and to have less interest in sex (Nisbett and Platt, 1972).

It is possible that overweight people have some kind of brain abnormality affecting regions of the hypothalamus—something akin to the surgical destruction in experimental animals (Schachter, 1971). Or it may be that the bloodstream of overweight people carries some kind of chemical, produced by a quirk in the manner in which their alimentary canals and livers process food, that overstimulates the hypothalamus and thus creates more frequent and more intense hunger. Investigators are trying to learn whether such a substance exists—and if so, what it is and how it might be controlled (Miller, 1975).

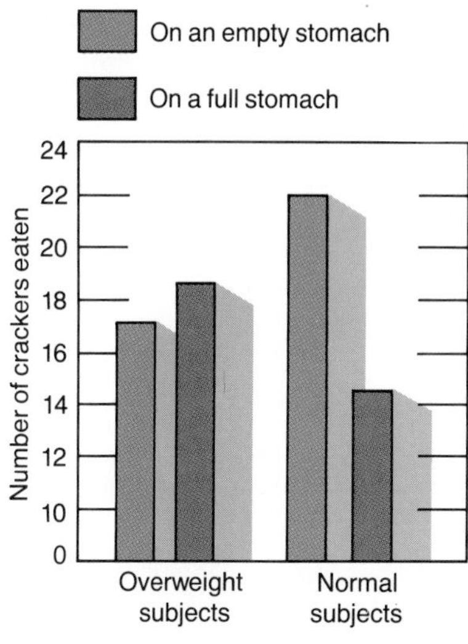

Figure 9-12 One clue to overeating *An experimenter worked with two groups of subjects, one group of normal weight and the other anywhere from 14 to 75 percent overweight. When the subjects arrived at the laboratory, having skipped the previous meal, half from each group were fed sandwiches, the other half nothing. They then took part in what they thought was an evaluation of the taste of five different kinds of cracker presented to them in separate bowls. They were told that they could eat as few or as many of the crackers as they wished in making their judgments. As the graph shows, the amount eaten by the subjects of normal weight was considerably lower if they had just eaten sandwiches. The overweight subjects, however, actually ate somewhat more on a full stomach than on an empty stomach. For a possible explanation of these results, see the text (Schachter, 1971).*

Too many fat cells?

Another theory of obesity blames the cells designed for storage of fatty compounds. It has been found that at least some overweight people have an unusually large number of these cells in their bodies (Björntorp, 1972). In extreme cases, they may have fully three times as many as people of normal weight (Knittle and Hirsch, 1968). The cells may be voracious consumers of fatty compounds carried by the bloodstream.

Thus overweight people, because of their excessive number of fat cells, may be more or less constantly hungry for reasons they cannot control by any act of will power. Their hunger may become particularly intense if they try to diet. Indeed it has been suggested that many fat people, because of the social pressure against obesity, are actually underweight rather than overweight in terms of the requirements of their own bodies (Nisbett, 1972).

Why do some people have more fat cells than others? The answer seems to lie partly in heredity. Breeding experiments with animals show that some strains are more likely than others to produce fat offspring generation after generation (Schemmel, Michelsen, and Gill, 1970). Similarly, overweight human parents tend to have overweight children.

Overeating in the period immediately after birth may also be a factor. Experiments with rats indicate that the number of fat cells in their bodies is increased by giving them excessive amounts of food in the first three weeks of life, after which overfeeding no longer has this effect. Similarly, the number of fat cells in the human body seems to be established during early childhood and to remain relatively constant from then on. Adults who go on starvation diets show a decrease in the size of these cells, as their contents are drawn on for fuel, but no decrease in the number of cells (Hirsch and Knittle, 1970). People who deliberately overeat to gain weight show an increase in the size of the cells but no increase in number (Sims et al., 1968). One approach to the obesity problem may be to urge mothers not to push babies to overeat during the early period when the number of fat cells is being

Does the tendency to be overweight run in families? The artist who produced this painting seems convinced that it does.

established. But of course this approach comes too late for overweight people beyond the age of childhood, who continue to have their difficulties despite everything that has been learned thus far about the hunger drive.

Thirst

The *thirst drive* resembles the hunger drive in many respects. The common-sense observation—that we get thirsty when our mouths are dry—again turns out to be partially true. The drive does depend in part on messages carried to the brain from the mouth—as well as from the throat, which seems to signal how much water has passed through, and from the stomach, which signals whether it is empty or full (Blass and Hall, 1976). But still this is not the full explanation. A person may feel thirsty even when nerve fibers from the mouth and throat are under anesthesia, sending out no messages at all (Cofer, 1972).

Again the hypothalamus plays an important part. A lack of water causes the cells of the body to become dehydrated, and certain nerve cells in the hypothalamus appear to be sensitive to this change. Moreover, a lack of water reduces the volume of blood flowing through the body, causing sensory receptors in the blood vessels and heart to send signals to the brain (Epstein, Kissileff, and Stellar, 1973). The reduced volume of blood also causes the kidneys to produce a chemical that stimulates the hypothalamus (Epstein, Fitzsimons, and Simons, 1969).

Thus the thirst drive is triggered by various signs of imbalance in the body's water supply. Much as in the case of hunger, the goal of the thirst drive is water, not the mere act of drinking. When the experiment that was illustrated in Figure 9-11 (p. 332) is changed, so that the animal receives water instead of food directly into the stomach, it soon learns to take in the normal amount of fluid even though it never drinks.

Other drives

The *sleep drive,* which plays an important part in the rhythm of our daily lives, was mentioned in Chapter 8 (pages 296–299) in the discussion of altered states of consciousness. This drive appears to be triggered by imbalances in brain chemistry, and possibly body chemistry as well, that build up while we are awake and active. When we sleep, we correct the chemical imbalances and wake up ready to function again at full efficiency. As in the case of hunger, it has been found that surgery on parts of the brain has drastic effects. Destruction of one area causes an animal to remain awake until it dies of exhaustion. Destruction of another area causes the animal to sleep almost constantly. But it is not clear whether this indicates that the brain contains an on switch and an off switch for sleep or whether the surgery merely interferes with a more complex circuitry that controls the drive.

The *temperature drive* is common to all warm-blooded animals. In human beings its goal is to maintain the body's inner temperature at about 98.6° Fahrenheit (37° centigrade). It appears to be controlled by cells in the brain that are sensitive to temperature changes. When stimulated by increased warmth, they send off messages that cause perspiration (which cools the body through evaporation) and that also cause more blood to move toward the surface of the body, where it loses

The sleep drive can be powerful enough to prevail even in the most uncomfortable circumstances, as on this park bench.

heat more quickly. When stimulated by cooling, these brain cells induce shivering (the constriction of blood vessels in the skin) and increased bodily activity and heat production (Miller, 1969).

The *elimination drive* serves to rid the body of its waste products.

The *pain drive* leads us to avoid events that would damage our bodies. It accounts for such learned behavior as keeping our hands away from flames, being careful with sharp objects, and resting or swallowing medicine to relieve a headache.

To this list some scientists would add a *sex drive.* But sexual activity, though essential for survival of the species, is not essential for survival of the individual. Sex, and whether it is a drive or something else, is discussed at length in a supplement to this chapter.

A relatively new school of scientific thought called *sociobiology* maintains that at least some forms of social behavior are also akin to drives and are dictated by inherited biological traits (Wilson, 1975). One example they cite is altruistic behavior—for example, the willingness of a father to risk his own life to save his children from a burning house. By doing this, the sociobiologists say, the father attempts to ensure the survival of others who can pass along the human genes, which are the chemical components of inheritance—and especially genes that he shares with his children because they descend from the same forebears. In other words, the theory states that altruism and other similar forms of cooperative behavior help preserve the pool of human genes—and genes dictating such behavior have been more likely to survive and be passed along through past generations. By stressing the role of the genes in determining social behavior, sociobiology takes an extreme pro-nature position in the nature-nurture debate. The theory is interesting but controversial, and many psychologists are skeptical.

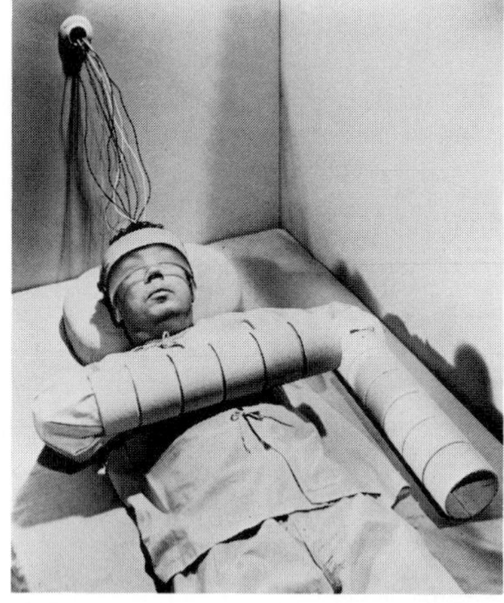

Figure 9-13 An experiment in sensory deprivation *This man is taking part in an experiment designed to show what happens when activity of the human senses is reduced as near as possible to zero. The eyeshade permits him to see nothing but a dim haze. The arm casts mask the sense of touch in his hands. The room is soundproofed, and he hears nothing but the soft hum of a fan. The wires at the top of the photo recorded his brain waves (Bexton, Heron, and Scott, 1954). For what happens to him under these conditions, see the text.*

Stimulus needs as a driving force

Drives are powerful forces. When they go unsatisfied, they may result in intense discomfort and eventually death. They have long been recognized and studied as primary sources for the energizing of behavior.

In recent years, psychologists have found that our innate nature seems to demand certain other satisfactions. Food, water, sleep, and the other goals that satisfy the drives are not enough. In addition, we seem to have inborn tendencies to seek certain kinds of stimulation. We display what have come to be known as *stimulus needs.* There appear to be at least two kinds of stimulus needs: the *need for sensory stimulation* and the *need for stimulus variability.*

The need for sensory stimulation

One famous experiment that shows what happens to people who are deprived of sensory stimulation is illustrated in Figure 9-13. Volunteers remained in bed, with their senses of sight, hearing, and touch masked. Except during meal periods, they tasted and smelled nothing. In other words, activity of their senses was held to almost zero. Soon many of them were unable to think logically. Their memories became disorganized. Sometimes they felt strangely happy. At other times they felt anxious or even panicky. Some of them began to develop symptoms associated with severe mental disturbance. They saw imaginary sights and heard imaginary sounds. The experience was so upsetting that nearly half of them had to beg off within 48 hours, even though they were being paid generously for each day they continued.

Other investigators, using similar techniques, have found less drastic effects. One study found that sensory deprivation may even produce some beneficial effects—for example, an increase in creative thinking and the discovery by heavy smokers that they can do without cigarettes when the usual incentive objects associated with smoking are removed (Suedfeld, 1975). The conflicting results determined by different experimenters suggest that the expectations of subjects may play a part in the results. If subjects fear adverse consequences, perhaps they are more likely to experience distress.

At any rate, we do seem to have some kind of need for sensory stimulation if we are to continue functioning in a normal fashion. Why this should be true is not known. One possible answer lies in what has been discovered about the reticular activating system of the brain. Nervous impulses from the sense organs pass through this system on their way to the sensory areas of the cerebral cortex, where they result in conscious sensations of sights and sounds. As they pass through, they seem to set off other impulses, which the reticular activating system sends to all parts of the cortex, keeping it in a state of activity and alertness. Without this barrage of impulses from the reticular activating system, it has been suggested, the cortex is handicapped (Magoun, 1963).

The need for stimulus variability

As was stated in the chapter on perception, there is something inherently attractive and compelling about a change of stimulus. Indeed human beings seem to have an innate need for what is called *stimulus variability.* When we have the opportunity, we show an innate preference for a change in stimulation and tend to seek it out. This is also true of other organisms, as was demonstrated in the experiment illustrated in Figure 9-14. Even in this simple T-shaped maze a rat shows a strong tendency to go to the arm that represents a change of stimulus—the dark arm that was originally white or the white arm that was originally dark.

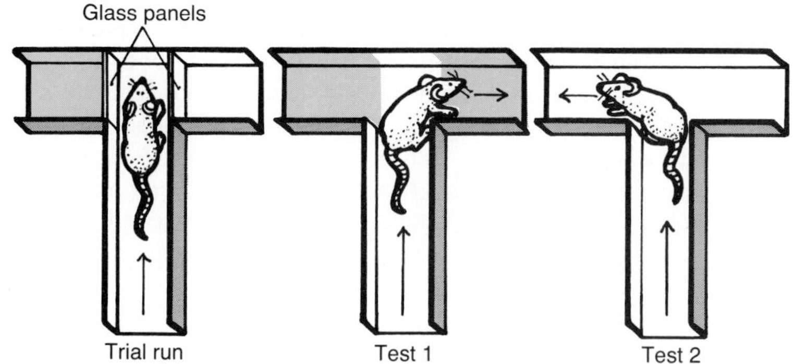

Figure 9-14 An animal's search for change *In the trial run a rat enters the T-shaped maze at the bottom and is stopped by the glass panels at a point where it can see that the left arm is dark and the right arm is white. In Test 1 the glass panels are removed and both arms are dark. The rat shows a strong tendency to enter the arm that was formerly white. If the trial run is followed by Test 2, where both arms are white, the rat shows a strong tendency to enter the arm that was formerly dark. As the text explains, this behavior seems to be dictated by a preference for a change in stimulus (Dember, 1965).*

Figure 9-15 The case of the curious monkey *The monkey, a prisoner in a dimly lit box, has learned to push open the window solely for the privilege of watching a toy train in operation for 30 seconds.*

Figure 9-16 Why is this monkey working so hard? *Do the latches unlock anything? No. Does the monkey know this? Yes. Then why does the monkey bother to open the latches? For the answer, see the text.*

The results of this experiment fit in with many other observations of animal and human behavior. Monkeys will learn to open a window, as in Figure 9-15, for the reward of seeing what is happening on the other side (Butler, 1953). Presented with the hooks and latches shown in Figure 9-16, a monkey will work hard to open them even though it has discovered that doing so leads nowhere. Human babies seem irresistibly attracted to rattles, toys hanging over the crib, and their own fingers. Adolescents and adults alike gladly pay for the stimulus change represented by the lights flashing on a video-game screen.

Stimulus variability and survival

The need for stimulus variability plays a useful role for the organism. Every stimulus change presents new information about the environment, and such information is often essential to successful adjustment and at times even survival. An organism with an inborn need for stimulus variability has a biological advantage over an organism without it.

One aspect of stimulus variability that deserves special mention is *stimulus complexity*. A young baby, to whom a toy rattle represents a strange and complicated stimulus, will play with it for a long time. An older infant will put it aside more quickly, and a schoolchild will not play with it at all. To a schoolchild a game of tag is endlessly fascinating, while a college student will be interested only in football. To satisfy the organism's needs, the stimulus must have a certain amount of complexity. On the other hand, a stimulus that is too complex is not attractive. A child is more attracted to a nursery rhyme than to a Shakespeare sonnet.

These facts about stimulus complexity may remind you of Piaget's observations of the child's stages of intellectual development. Piaget found that it is impossible to rush children from one stage to the next by trying to teach them the reasoning skills appropriate to the more advanced stage. At each level of development they can understand and profit from only such experiences and pieces of information as match what they already know—or that are just a little in advance of their existing information and skills. Similarly, all of us seek stimuli that are complex enough to intrigue us—but not so complex as to overwhelm and baffle us. It might be said that we have an innate curiosity—but only to the point where curiosity is rewarding rather than frustrating.

Is the child satisfying a need for stimulation?

Emotions, drives, stimulus needs, and motives

All the matters mentioned in this chapter have a strong influence on behavior. We seek out events that arouse pleasant emotions (joy, love) and avoid events that arouse unpleasant emotions (distress, fear). The drives impel us toward such incentive objects as food. The stimulus needs give us a curiosity and a zest for variety in the sights and sounds with which we surround ourselves.

Thus all these matters, based at least in part on the ways in which our brains and bodies are programed by nature, have a bearing on the goals we seek in our day-to-day activities. They are closely related to the way we are motivated to behave, not only in our daily experiences but in our long-range planning. Indeed the line between emotions, drives, and stimulus needs, on the one hand, and motives, on the other hand, is difficult to draw. It is partly for the sake of convenience—rather than because of any clear-cut distinction—that psychologists separate the topics that have been discussed in this chapter from their studies of motives, which will be the subject of the next chapter.

SUMMARY

Emotions and the body: "stirred up" or "toned down"

1. *Emotions* are always accompanied by bodily changes. The body may be stirred up or toned down.
2. Many of the bodily changes in emotion are controlled by the autonomic nervous system and the endocrine glands. These changes include: (a) heart rate, (b) blood pressure, (c) blood circulation, (d) the composition of the blood, (e) activity of the digestive organs, (f) metabolic rate, (g) breathing, (h) salivation, (i) sweating, (j) goose flesh, and (k) pupil size.
3. Other bodily changes in emotion are controlled by the muscles of movement. These changes include: (a) muscular tension, (b) trembling, (c) eye blinking and other nervous movements, (d) vocal expressions of emotion, and (e) facial expressions.
4. One theory holds that every basic emotion represents in part a characteristic pattern of facial expression programed by heredity.
5. Pupil size generally increases when a person experiences interest or pleasure.

6. The *James-Lange theory* held that emotions occur when a stimulus in the environment sets off physiological changes. Feedback from these changes, sent to the brain from the body's sensory nerves, is then perceived as emotion. We do not tremble because we are afraid, but feel afraid because we are trembling.

Emotions and the brain

7. The *Cannon-Bard theory* maintained that emotions occur when a stimulus in the environment sets off patterns of nervous activity in the hypothalamus. These patterns were considered to have two simultaneous effects: (a) they are sent to the autonomic nervous system, where they trigger the bodily changes of emotion; and (b) they are sent to the cerebral cortex, where they cause perception of emotion.
8. Today's cognitive psychologists regard emotions as composed of many complex factors. These include: (a) information about events in the environment, delivered to the cerebral cortex by the sense organs; (b) the brain's storehouse of information, which helps appraise and interpret new events; (c) patterns of nervous activity in the hypothalamus and the rest of the brain's limbic system, which trigger the autonomic nervous system into producing bodily changes; and (d) feedback from the bodily changes.
9. The cognitive view agrees with James-Lange that feedback of physiological changes is important—and with Cannon-Bard that activity of the hypothalamus plays a part. But it holds that neither theory is the full explanation. What really determines emotions is the cognitive activity resulting from the stimulus that has produced the bodily changes and the entire environmental situation in which it occurs. This cognitive activity shows wide individual differences because of prior experience and learning.

Individual differences in emotion

10. Inborn factors that help create individual differences in emotional experience include: (a) sensitivity of the autonomic nervous system, and (b) the size and activity of the endocrine glands.
11. Emotions can be physically exhausting and put the body under considerable stress. But they are also desirable and useful, adding interest to life and helping us to function more effectively.

The drives and behavior

12. A *drive* is a pattern of brain activity resulting from physiological imbalances that threaten homeostasis. The drives include *hunger, thirst, breathing, sleep, temperature, elimination,* and *pain.*
13. The *hunger drive* depends on: (a) nerve cells in the hypothalamus that are sensitive to changes in the food supply contained in the bloodstream, and (b) information sent to the hypothalamus from the alimentary canal and liver. The hunger drive is also affected by incentive objects in the environment (the sight or smell of food) and by eating habits and social relationships built around eating.

14. Although the hunger drive operates to keep most people at normal weight, more than one-fourth of American adults are at least 25 percent overweight. Possible explanations of obesity include: (a) metabolic disturbances; (b) overeating to relieve anxiety; (c) an unknown chemical in the blood stream, caused by abnormalities in the way the alimentary canal and liver process food; and (d) an excess of the bodily cells that store fatty compounds.
15. The *thirst drive* depends on: (a) nerve cells in the hypothalamus that are sensitive to dehydration, (b) signals sent to the brain from the heart and blood vessels when the volume of blood is lowered by lack of water, and (c) stimulation of the hypothalamus by a chemical produced by the kidneys.

Stimulus needs as a driving force

16. Closely allied to the drives are *stimulus needs*—or the organism's tendency to seek certain kinds of stimulation.
17. There are two stimulus needs: (a) the *need for sensory stimulation,* and (b) the *need for stimulus variability.*

IMPORTANT TERMS

Cannon-Bard theory
cognitive theory
drive
elimination drive
emotion
emotional stress
fat cells
hunger drive
incentive object
James-Lange theory
pain drive
sensory stimulation
sleep drive
sociobiology
stimulus complexity
stimulus needs
stimulus variability
temperature drive
thirst drive

SUPPLEMENT:
Sexual Feelings and Behavior

One of the most powerful forces in human behavior occupies a puzzling position in psychological thinking. Should sex, which pervades so many human activities, be classified as a drive? Perhaps—for among lower animals it has all the characteristics of a drive. Should it be regarded as an emotion? Perhaps—for sexual passion is one of the most intense human feelings and closely related to the emotion called love. Yet it does not quite fit into either of these categories. Nor does it exactly fit the definition of a motive, the subject of the next chapter.

Just as scientists have trouble with the proper classification of human sex, so do many human beings have trouble sorting out their own urges and feelings and finding their own sexual identity and fulfillment. Today's United States, after the celebrated "sexual revolution" of the 1960s and 1970s, is tilted strongly toward sexual permissiveness. Yet many people—young as well as old—seem uncomfortable with recent trends. In a public opinion poll made near the start of this decade, 61 percent agreed with the statement that "it's getting harder and harder to know what's right and what's wrong" and 76 percent that "permissiveness has led to a lot of things that are wrong with the country these days" (Yankelovich, Skelly, and White, 1977). Psychotherapists report an unusual number of clients who complain of loss of sexual desire—so many that the problem is now listed as a mental disorder by the American Psychiatric Association.

Sex through the ages

To a social historian, there is nothing surprising about sharp swings in public opinion about sexual behavior—or dissatisfaction with the results. Every conceivable attitude has been eagerly embraced at one time and place but roundly condemned at others. Homosexual acts were punishable by death among the ancient Hebrews, but accepted and even admired by the Greeks. Later the early Christians held that abstinence was the noblest form of sexual behavior, but at about the same time the Romans were indulging in their famous orgies in the Colosseum. In England at the time of Queen Elizabeth, sex was treated "with a frankness and frequently with a ribaldry that has no parallel in Western history." A little later, under Queen Victoria, it was regarded "with such great circumspection that among some groups of these very same Englishmen one would hardly have known that coitus ever took place" and any falls from propriety "were the cause of great scandal and disgrace" (Ehrmann, 1964).

England's about-face had its counterpart recently in the United States, only in reverse. In the early years of this century, a team of scientists visiting our planet from outer space would have found so little mention of sex, in either print or polite conversation, that they might have had trouble guessing how Americans produced their babies. Today there is almost complete freedom to discuss or write about sex, and books and movies often make it appear that Americans are programed by nature to spend most of their time engaging in sexual activity or preparing for it. Visiting scientists would be forced to wonder not how Americans reproduce—but how they manage to find time for anything else.

Today's attitudes: the sexual revolution and its aftermath

As recently as the 1960s, a considerable majority of Americans believed that sex before marriage was wrong. But a public opinion poll at the start of the 1980s found that 59 percent consider premarital sex either "not wrong at all" or "wrong only sometimes." The largest margins of approval were found among the young (82 percent of those 25 or under) and the best-educated (69 percent of those with at least a high school diploma), as well as in high-income groups (Singh, 1980). Attitudes have become much more permissive toward sex education in the schools, birth control, and such practices as oral sex (for which some married couples went to prison a few decades ago). Most people are no longer horrified when someone in public life, male or female, acknowledges homosexual behavior—and the gay liberation movement and organizations of gays are prominent in many cities and colleges.

Along with the changed attitudes has come an increase in sexual activity among the unmarried, especially young unmarried women. In the 1940s, only about 19 percent of teenage women engaged in premarital sex (Kinsey et al., 1953). Around the start of this decade the number had jumped to about 65 percent of women who had reached the age of 19 (Abernathy et al., 1979). The figures for teenage men have not increased nearly so much—from about 72 to 78 percent—but in recent years far fewer men have had their experience exclusively with prostitutes or "bad girls," far more with classmates or work associates. The new pattern has been accompanied by a sharp rise in teenage pregnancies. A survey of women between the ages of 15 and 19 living in metropolitan areas found that about 16 percent had become pregnant (Zelnick and Kantner, 1980).

Until very recently many observers of sexual attitudes and behavior—including some who helped create the revolution—were concerned that the pendulum of public opinion had swung too far toward permissiveness. Paul Gebhard, then director of the Institute for Sex Research founded by Alfred Kinsey, put the problem in these words:

> When we started our work there was far too much repression and hypocrisy. The old idea that sex is "dirty" was a very harmful thing. But now we worry that the move has gone too far. There is a lot of difference

between *freedom* to enjoy sex, which is what we always favored, and a *command* to enjoy sex, which seems to face people today. By putting a burden on people to display a constant sexuality—or seem to display it—today's atmosphere may be just as harmful as the old taboos (Gebhard, 1980).

It now appears, however, that the pendulum reached its maximum swing in the mid-1970s and is moving back to a more central position. The annual Yankelovich polls of public opinion have shown a consistent trend toward sexual conservatism since 1976 (Yankelovich, Skelly, and White, 1983). At the same time a number of sex counselors in colleges have noted a decline in promiscuity and a growing concern for commitment, marriage, and children (Stern, 1983).

Again the shift is hardly surprising in the light of history. There seems to be no magic formula that can guarantee sexual fulfillment for everyone—and every attempt to prescribe one has led to disillusionment and a move toward its opposite.

The complexities of human sexuality

If this were a text about lower animals, sex could be discussed in much simpler terms. Among nonhuman mammals sex is almost as direct a drive as hunger, though less frequently triggered. Usually the female sex drive is quiescent, and over long stretches of time the female is not sexually attractive to the male of her species. At regularly recurring periods, however, the ovaries release hormones that activate a sex control mechanism centered in the hypothalamus of the brain. During these periods, which vary in frequency and length from species to species, the female seeks sexual contacts and engages in the kind of courtship and copulation characteristic of the species. The female's readiness is apparent from such clues as odors, vocal signals (the sex "calls" of cats), or changes in the color and size of the genitals. These cues in turn prompt the male to initiate sexual behavior.

Sex in many animals also resembles a drive in that the behavior that satisfies it is largely unlearned. Even when rats are raised in total isolation, with no opportunity to learn about the anatomy of the opposite sex or about the species' characteristic sexual behavior, they usually copulate like other rats at the first opportunity. Farther up the evolutionary scale, however, some learning seems necessary. Male and female monkeys raised in isolation do not ordinarily know how to behave toward each other at the first meeting (Harlow and Harlow, 1962).

Among human beings, sex bears only slight resemblance to a drive. True, sexual activity is most frequent during the years when the concentration of sex hormones in the bloodstream is highest, from puberty into the middle years. But men and women of all ages can have the desire and ability to engage in sexual activity. The female's desires are not significantly dependent on her monthly hormone cycles. Nor is her sexual attractiveness to the male. Some people seek out sexual contacts frequently, without any particular stimulation by glandular cycles or

The emotion of love is molded by a host of desires, preferences, and attitudes that all of us begin to learn in childhood and early youth, then keep or sometimes revise throughout our lives.

external cues. Others never engage in sexual activity, even in the most provocative situations.

Human sexual behavior clearly does not depend on some "sex center" in the brain that operates like an on-off switch. Rather, it seems to result from a combination of many nervous pathways ranging all the way from the spinal cord to the cerebral cortex (Whalen, 1976). Some of these pathways may be programed by heredity. Some are influenced by the activity of the sex glands in complex ways that have thus far defied analysis (Beach, 1976). Others may not depend on glandular activity at all.

Sexual behavior is influenced by a whole array of desires and preferences that all of us begin to learn in childhood and may continue to revise throughout our lives. It is molded by our personalities, moral standards, and social relationships—the ways in which we have learned to regard our parents and brothers and sisters, establish friendships, and view marriage and some of the problems that occur in marriage. Some people, indeed, value sexual experiences less for the physical gratification they provide than as acts of communication, friendship, or even hostility. (Many rapists seem to be motivated less by sexual passion than by a hatred of the opposite sex.) The emotion of love, though often associated with sexual desire, may be felt just as strongly in nonsexual situations—as toward a child, a parent, or a close friend.

Individual differences: the forgotten message of the Kinsey reports

It is the complexity of all the physical and psychological wellsprings of human sexual behavior that makes the topic so puzzling to scientists, societies, and individuals. Indeed one problem with the sexual revolution—and one reason it may now have passed into history—is that it fostered an atmosphere that totally disregarded the complexities. The freedom of discussion spawned a whole new profession of "sex experts" who deluged the nation with what they claimed were the secrets of sexual happiness. Like the authors of books guaranteed to make you lose 20 pounds in 20 days, they promised magic results from recipes that seldom work and for many people may actually be harmful (see the box on Psychology and Society).

Much of the advice and alleged fact-finding offered at the peak of the revolution was based on the assumption that sex is the most urgent goal of human life for all people at all times—an assumption that seems to sell magazines and books but goes counter to the most important single finding of serious sex investigators. This is the fact that there seems to be a wider range of individual differences in sexual appetite, capacity, and preferences than in almost any other human trait.

For the best information on sexual characteristics, we are indebted to the Kinsey reports. Although Alfred Kinsey's books on male and female sexual behavior were written a generation ago, they remain the most solid surveys ever made, based on studies of more than 5,000 men and nearly 8,000 women—many of whom reported behaving in ways that Kinsey himself, who was stern and somewhat prissy by today's standards, at first found shocking.

Kinsey's greatest contribution, though it has been ignored by many of the recent popular writers, was the discovery that individual differences in sexual behavior are truly amazing. For men in their twenties and early thirties, Kinsey found that the median number of orgasms was two a week.* But at the lowest extreme he found men who never had an orgasm. At the other extreme he found men who were having as many as four a day or more, day in and day out (Kinsey, Pomeroy, and Martin, 1948).

Among women the individual differences were even greater. Kinsey found some women who had never in their lives experienced sexual excitement of any kind. He also found women who had been married for many years but had experienced only one or two orgasms in their lives. At the other extreme, he found women whose sexual desires were so frequent and intense that they could be satisfied only by masturbation—in some cases as many as thirty or more times a week, with numerous orgasms on each occasion (Kinsey et al., 1953).

Sex and nature-nurture

What causes these enormous differences? The answer is a matter of dispute—another aspect of the nature-nurture argument. And, as usual, there is a good deal to be said on both sides.

Nurture, in the form of learned attitudes toward sex, certainly plays a part. Growing up in a home where sex is thought of as "dirty"—spoken of only in terms of the evils of masturbation and the horror of venereal diseases—tends to produce inhibitions that can curtail behavior and responsiveness and perhaps reduce capacity as well. The general

*The median is the midway point. Half the men reported two or more a week, the other half two or fewer.

Psychology and Society: Why reading about sex can be injurious to your mental health

Browse through any bookstore or magazine rack and you will find enough sexual material to keep you busy—should you want to study it all—for weeks on end. You can read all kinds of advice on how to find ecstatic fulfillment and countless studies that give you the latest figures on how people feel and act, based on what are advertised as brand-new, comprehensive, and thoroughly scientific surveys of thousands of subjects. The statistics look impressive. They assure you that exactly 62.3 percent of all Americans are given to behavior A, 22.7 percent to behavior B, and so on down the line to a mere 1.2 percent who indulge in behavior K.

Unfortunately most of the books and magazine articles are written by people who have never attempted any truly scientific study of the facts—and who may have concocted their advice out of thin air in a frantic search for a new and previously unexploited angle. Even the "sex surveys" usually have no validity at all, since they disregard the rules carefully designed by psychologists to produce accurate sampling in public opinion polls. Magazines often survey only their own readers, who are a small and special group interested in the subject matter and viewpoint of that particular publication. Many book authors, untrained in psychology, mail out thousands of questionnaires but have to base their statistics on the relatively few who bother to answer (because the questions tickle their own particular fancy). One of the best-selling surveys was written by an author who mailed out 100,000 questionnaires but received only 3,019 replies.

Even the most serious researchers have to view their findings with caution. It is difficult to find a representative sample of people who will discuss their attitudes and behavior candidly and truthfully. It is difficult to know what to ask and how to phrase the questions to avoid influencing the responses. Kinsey, for all his painstaking efforts to be scientific, conceded that his results were only "approximations of the fact," though he felt they were "probably fair approximations" (Kinsey, Pomeroy, and Martin, 1948). Most of his popular imitators claim more but deliver much less. The latest so-called scientific survey may be interesting reading and may introduce you to some new viewpoints held by some people somewhere—but it is probably inaccurate in its statistics and certainly worthless as personal guidance.

Trying to imitate the way other people are said to behave—or to follow advice offered by someone who may or may not qualify as an expert—may actually be harmful. An anthropologist who has studied sexual behavior in many cultures has said:

> I like to think that sex should be enjoyed for the sheer magnificence of it—that this is what sex is all about. But sex can be magnificent only when you engage in it in your own way and at your own choosing—as much or as little of it as you please, and according to your own tastes and preferences. All the solid research on sex ever done shows that no two people are alike in how they feel about sex, how much capacity they have for it, or what they like and don't like. The kind of sex behavior that is successful for one person can be absolutely devastating for another person, and vice versa. But much of the popular writing totally ignores this fact (Messenger, 1979).

In other words, it seems that much of the sex literature should be labeled, somewhat like a package of cigarettes, with a warning that it may be injurious to your mental health.

attitude of society also has an effect. For example, many generations of females were doubtless influenced by the old notion that a "good" woman was supposed to find sex repugnant and engage in it if at all only as a concession to the "animal nature" of her husband. Among women who were born before the turn of the century and grew up when this idea was still widely accepted, Kinsey found that about a third of them never experienced orgasm in the first year of marriage and about a fifth of them were still having no orgasms in the tenth year of marriage (Kinsey et al., 1953). Among women born in this century, these figures have steadily declined as society has become more permissive.

Generally, most aspects of sexuality are established by the time of adolescence and persist throughout life.

Many sex researchers have concluded that our varying sexual capacities also depend on the fact that we inherit different patterns of glandular activity, sensitivity of the nervous system, and other physical characteristics that contribute to sexuality. It has been found that men who enter puberty early—showing the typical change of voice and rapid growth in height as early as the age of 11—tend to have the most insistent sexual appetites (Kinsey, Pomeroy, and Martin, 1948). Presumably their high level of sexuality, like their early onset of puberty, can be largely attributed to inborn factors.

Living with the differences

To some extent, levels of sexuality are subject to change. Kinsey found one woman, for example, who spent 28 years of marriage without an orgasm, then began experiencing sexual climax for the first time. This is probably an example of how childhood training and society's taboos can inhibit sexual response, and of how a person can break out of the inhibitions. Masters and Johnson, a well-known team of sex investigators and therapists, have reported frequent success in helping men who thought they were impotent and women who were unable to reach orgasm (Masters and Johnson, 1970).

In general, however, most aspects of sexuality seem to be well-established by the time of adolescence and to persist throughout life. This is true even of homosexual preferences, and especially true of sexual capacity. Most men and women have their own pattern of desire and ability for orgasm. They are physically incapable of exceeding this rate of activity, except perhaps for brief periods, and are likely to be physically or psychologically uncomfortable with a lower rate.

The individual differences, however, seem to have very little effect on fulfillment. The research institute founded by Kinsey has found that frequency of sexual relations has scant relation to happiness in marriage. If the partners have similar desires, they can be as happy having sex once a month as every night of the week (Gebhard, 1979). Moreover, fulfillment does not appear to depend on preferences in expressions of sexuality. It has been found that couples who enter into sex with shyness and reserve are just as happy as those who take the uninhibited approach recommended by most of today's sex manuals (Vincent, 1956).

Sex and youth: a "lonely and . . . silent experience"

Young people in particular face a difficult task in trying to determine their sexual identities at the very time they are facing all the other problems of entering adulthood. Despite today's more permissive atmosphere, the task is still surrounded by confusion and self-doubt. One group of investigators who has made many studies of the sexual behavior of young people has concluded: "Coping with sexual development remains a lonely and overly silent experience" (Simon, Berger, and Gagnon, 1972).

For many young people, the introduction to sexual intercourse is not nearly so glorious as they were led to believe. One striking bit of evidence comes from a survey made in Denmark, a nation that has been very permissive toward premarital sexual relations for a long time. You might suppose that sex would come naturally in Denmark if anywhere. But only 26 percent of the men and women in the study reported that their first sexual experience was satisfactory. About 20 percent recalled it with mixed emotions, and all the rest, a majority of 54 percent, had negative feelings (Hesselund, 1971). Note these comments:

> *By women*
> It was definitely no experience. Neither I nor my partner got an orgasm.
>
> I was curious and excited but it was horrible.
>
> I was disappointed, pessimistic.
>
> *By men*
> Very awkward. Everything went wrong.
>
> It was a great disappointment. An enormous failure. I was afraid of the next time and did not make new attempts for the following two years.

However, an unhappy introduction to sex did not by any means prove fatal to these young Danes. At the time they were interviewed, when their average age was 23, all but a few were either married or had established some satisfactory relationship. The study indicates that it is probably as unrealistic to expect glorious success in one's first attempts at sex as in one's first attempts at playing the piano. Indeed not all of us will ever in our lives attain the kind of glorious, mind-boggling success described in the sex manuals—any more than all of us will ever be invited to play piano concertos with a symphony orchestra.

Even among college students who are living together, sexual problems are not unusual. One study of such relationships found that 70 percent were troubled by the fact that one partner had a higher interest in sex than the other or that the times when they felt an interest did not match. In nearly two-thirds of the relationships, the woman was troubled by failure to reach orgasm as often as she would have liked (Macklin, 1972).

Communication: the "absolute cornerstone"

Most serious researchers agree that establishing a satisfactory sexual relationship is an immensely complicated task that takes time and effort. Above all else, most believe, it requires honest and unabashed communication about the partners' desires and preferences.

Masters and Johnson have termed open discussion of sexual likes and dislikes the "absolute cornerstone" of a successful relationship (Masters and Johnson, 1963). Indeed their treatment of sexually unsuccessful couples centers on the exchange of information, through gestures as well as words. Paul Gebhard says, "The chief stumbling block to sexual fulfillment is the fact that couples don't talk enough about their feelings. Even couples who have been married for 20 years—and know each other's preferences in food, reading, and music like the backs of their hands—often hesitate to tell each other what they like, dislike, or view with indifference in sexual matters" (Gebhard, 1979).

Unfortunately, open communication about sexual preferences is difficult for most people. It violates the popular belief that sexual performance is a natural gift and that everybody should automatically be "good in bed" without the need for any instruction, indeed even without giving the matter any thought. Or the idea that techniques picked up from a sex manual are sure to be effective with any partner under any circumstances, which is also untrue. The individual differences in tastes and responses are far too great to permit any magic formula for success. Moreover, many people find that too much attention to technique turns sex from a spontaneous expression of love into a mechanical performance that they find unsatisfactory or even distasteful (Vincent, 1956).

The evidence seems to indicate that every sexual relationship is unique, bringing together two partners who are themselves unique. Most researchers believe that the partners have to learn by themselves how to make the relationship work—and that this learning process depends mostly on the give and take of communication.

SUMMARY OF SUPPLEMENT

1. The human sexual urge is difficult to classify as either a drive, emotion, or motive, though it has some of the characteristics of all three. Similarly it appears difficult for many people to find their own sexual identity and fulfillment—regardless of whether the prevailing attitude of society is rigidly restrictive or highly permissive.
2. On all kinds of sexual behavior, history has seen many swings from repression to enthusiastic acceptance. In the United States, the "sexual revolution" of the 1960s and 1970s produced a much more liberal attitude toward open discussion, premarital sex, and birth control, and a sharp rise in teenage sexual activity (especially among young unmarried women) and teenage pregnancies.
3. There are now many indications that the revolution reached its peak about 1976 and that the swing is now back toward a more central position.
4. Among animals, sex is clearly a drive. In human beings sexual behavior depends on many nerve pathways and glandular influences, as well as on a whole array of learned preferences that people begin to learn early in childhood and may revise all their lives.
5. The Kinsey reports show a wider range of individual differences in sexual appetite, capacity, and preferences than exists in almost any other human trait.
6. The individual differences seem to be dictated in part by nature (glandular activity and sensitivity of the nervous system) and in

part by nurture (learned attitudes toward moral standards and social relationships).

7. Though patterns of sexuality are to some extent subject to change, most of them seem to be established by adolescence and to persist throughout life. It has been observed that "no two people are alike in how they feel about sex, how much capacity they have for it, or what they like and don't like."
8. The frequency and nature of sexual activity seem to have little effect on fulfillment, as long as both partners have similar desires.
9. For young people, trying to establish sexual identity while also facing all the other problems of entering adulthood has been called "a lonely and overly silent experience." First sexual experiences are often unsatisfactory.
10. Establishing a satisfactory sexual relationship takes time and effort. Honest and unabashed communication about the partners' desires and preferences, though difficult for many people, appears to be the key.

RECOMMENDED READINGS

Balagura, S. *Hunger: a biopsychological analysis.* New York: Basic Books, 1973.

Carlson, N. R. *Physiology of behavior,* 2d ed. Boston: Allyn and Bacon, 1981.

Darwin, C. *The expression of emotion in man and animals.* New York: AMS Press, 1972.

Gaylin, W. *Feelings.* New York: Harper & Row, 1979.

Grings, W. W., and Dawson, M. E. *Emotions and bodily responses: a psychophysiological approach.* New York: Academic Press, 1978.

Izard, C. E. *Human emotions.* New York: Plenum, 1977.

Plutchik, R., and Kellerman, H., eds. *Emotion: theory, research and experience.* New York: Academic Press, 1980.

Strongman, K. T. *The psychology of emotion,* 2d ed. New York: Wiley, 1978.

Suedfeld, P. *Restricted environmental stimulation: research clinical applications.* New York: Wiley, 1980.

CHAPTER 10

The goals of success and friendship 353
- The achievement motive
- The power motive
- Avoidance of power
- The affiliation motive
- The dependency motive
- Birth order and the motives for success and friendship

Some other powerful motives 362
- The motive for certainty
- The motive to live up to standards
- The hostility motive
- The motive for self-actualization
- Unconscious motives

How and why motives affect behavior 368
- Motive hierarchies and targets
- The effect of incentive value
- Gauging your chances of success
- Expectancy of success and locus of control
- Long-range plans, too much motivation, and running scared
- Fear of failure at a varsity swim meet

Frustration and conflict 372
- Sources of frustration
- Frustration and the eye of the beholder
- Conflicts as a source of frustration
- Competing motives and group conflict
- Approach and avoidance conflicts

Summary 377

Important Terms 378

Supplement: Sex roles and the conflicts they create 379

What it means to be masculine or feminine 379
- You're X-X (or X-Y) and stuck with it
- But nature doesn't do it all
- Some boy-girls and girl-boys
- Learning to act masculine or feminine
- How parents encourage sex typing without knowing it
- Pressure from television, books, and schools
- Getting the message early

The built-in problems of being female 386
- Putting women down
- The female inferiority complex
- Suppressing the achievement motive
- The housewife's conflict
- The liberated woman's conflict

The built-in problems of being male 390
- Suppressing the affiliation and dependency motives
- The male burden of proof
- The burden of being superior

Summary of Supplement 392

Important Terms 393

Recommended Readings 393

Psychology and Society
- Violence, movies, and television 366
- Making tough decisions: can psychology help? 375

Motives, Frustration, and Conflict

W*hy in the world would a person like that do such a thing?* The question leaps to mind when we hear that a famous actress committed suicide, a timid neighbor risked his life chasing an armed mugger, a senator with a reputation for selfless service to humanity accepted a bribe, or the leading student on the campus abruptly dropped out of college. In asking *Why?* we are like a mystery-novel detective trying to solve a crime. We are searching for the motive.

But the answer is harder to find in the real world than in novels. Perhaps the actress was overwhelmed by a conflict between the image of a confident and popular person she portrayed on the screen and her actual insecurity and loneliness. The timid neighbor may have been secretly yearning all his life for a chance at bravery and fame. The senator may have had a consuming desire to match his millionaire colleagues. The student may have hated academic work and made all A's just to please demanding parents. Or there may have been other explanations that would never occur to us. Though guessing other people's motives is a popular pastime, it is often futile. Indeed we cannot always be sure even of our own motives. "I can't believe I did that" is an admission we all make at times.

The goals of success and friendship

Though motives are difficult to pin down or to study scientifically, they seem to control much human behavior and have always been one of psychology's basic concerns. Many of the early psychologists believed motives could be explained in terms of inherited characteristics. These psychologists were impressed by the instinctive behavior displayed by many animals—for example, the way a spider spins its web and the way salmon migrate from river to ocean and back to the river to spawn. Since we human beings are also a form of animal life, why not assume that we too behave in accordance with instincts? The pioneer American psychologist William James theorized that there were no less than 17 powerful human instincts: imitation, rivalry, pugnacity, sympathy, hunting, fear, acquisitiveness, constructiveness (the urge to build), play, curiosity, sociability, shyness, secretiveness, cleanliness, jealousy, love, and mother love (James, 1890).

It is now known that human beings have few if any instincts. Certainly we do not exhibit any elaborate built-in patterns of behavior, determined by the inherited wiring of the nervous system, like the web-spinning behavior of spiders or the nest-building behavior of birds. Human habitations are a great deal more varied and flexible in design.

Yet there obviously are some forces within the human personality that initiate, energize, direct, and organize behavior. The drives and stimulus needs that were discussed in the preceding chapter often serve as such forces—but there are also others, such as the 17 urges that James thought of as instincts. These forces are now called motives. Most psychologists define a motive as *a desire to reach a goal that has value for the individual.*

In studying motives, psychologists ask these questions: Why do certain goals (success, power, friendship, helping others) have so much value that we devote vast amounts of effort and planning to reach them? And why do goals vary so greatly from person to person?

Most psychologists would agree that our goals and motives are determined in part by our biological characteristics and in part by learning. There is considerable disagreement, however, as to how these two factors operate and which is more important. In other words, the nature-nurture argument crops up once again.

Some psychologists believe that motives are based mostly on the biological demands of the drives and stimulus needs. The hunger drive, for example, might lead to attempts to attain success and power, thus making sure the drive will never go unsatisfied. Other psychologists believe that motives are cognitive processes that depend mostly on learning. Their view is based in part on the widespread individual differences that have been found in motivation. They hold that each of us, as a result of our individual life experiences and patterns of thinking, comes to value certain goals above others. Even in the same family, one brother may exhibit a strong tendency to be dependent on other people, another brother to be hostile to authority, a sister to achieve success in school and career. Certainly motives vary considerably from culture to culture. For the ancient Greeks, a strong motive was to achieve moderation in all things, especially in displaying emotion. For the Romans, it was to seem thoughtful and serious. For the Buddhists in classical India and China, it was to be without desire. Prominent in our own society are motives to attain success and friendship.

The achievement motive

The desire to succeed—to perform well at all kinds of tasks and in a career—is called the *achievement motive.* Very few people, of course, have a uniformly high standard of achievement in all their undertakings. For some people the achievement motive is directed mostly at athletic prowess, for others at intellectual mastery, musical skills, or making money. People with a strong achievement motive tend to work hard at the things they tackle and to make the most of their talents. When people who score high on tests designed to measure the achievement motive are matched with people of equal ability but lower in achievement motive, they do better on the average at many kinds of mathematical and verbal tasks (Lowell, 1952) and other intellectual problems (French and Thomas, 1958). They make better grades in high school (Sadacca, Ricciuti, and Swanson, 1956) and in college (Morgan, 1951). In their life work they are more likely to rise above their family origins and move upward in society. Figure 10-1 illustrates a

The strength of the achievement motive is clearly apparent in the triumphant face of this runner.

study in which men whose fathers all had middle-level jobs were divided into two groups, one that scored high and the other low on tests of achievement motive. As the graph shows, far more of the men high in achievement motive had risen to jobs above their father's level—and far fewer were in jobs below their father's level.

One reason people high in achievement motive are more successful in their careers appears to be that they are realistic about their abilities and the chances they are willing to take. They prefer jobs in which they have a reasonable chance of success and can obtain reasonable rewards. People low in achievement motive, on the other hand, are more inclined either to settle for an easier but low-paying job or to make a grandiose stab at a high-level job that is beyond their capacities (Morris, 1966). A study made in Germany showed that the achievement motive affects even the risks taken in driving an automobile. The study found that drivers high in achievement motive tend to commit only minor

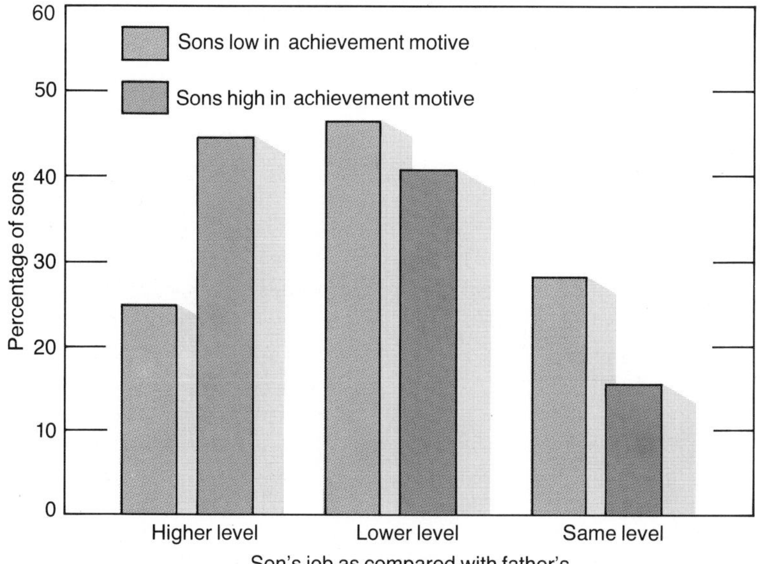

Figure 10-1 The achievement motive and rising in society *If you have a strong achievement motive, are you likely to wind up in a better job than your father's? The bars show the results of a study of fathers and sons, described in the text, that indicates you are about three times more likely to wind up at a higher level than at a lower level. If you are low in achievement motive, however, you are more likely to wind up at a lower than at a higher level (Crockett, 1962).*

A happy student, holding proof that she has reached the goal dictated by her achievement motive.

traffic offenses that represent calculated risks, such as illegal parking. Drivers low in achievement motive get into trouble for driving either too slowly or recklessly (Hoyos, 1965).

Why do some of us develop a stronger desire for achievement than others? There are many reasons relating to our experiences in home and school, what we read and what we see on television, and the people we come to admire (and therefore try to imitate) or dislike. Our estimate of our own abilities, which may be accurate or distorted, also plays a part.

One study indicates that the way our parents treated us in childhood may be a crucial factor. A group of boys was divided into those who scored high and those who scored low for achievement motive. Their mothers were then asked at what ages they had demanded that the boys start to show signs of independence—that is, go to bed by themselves, entertain themselves, stay in the house alone, make their own friends, do well in school without help, and later earn their own spending money and choose their own clothes. Questions were asked about 20 such forms of independent behavior. As Figure 10-2 shows, all the

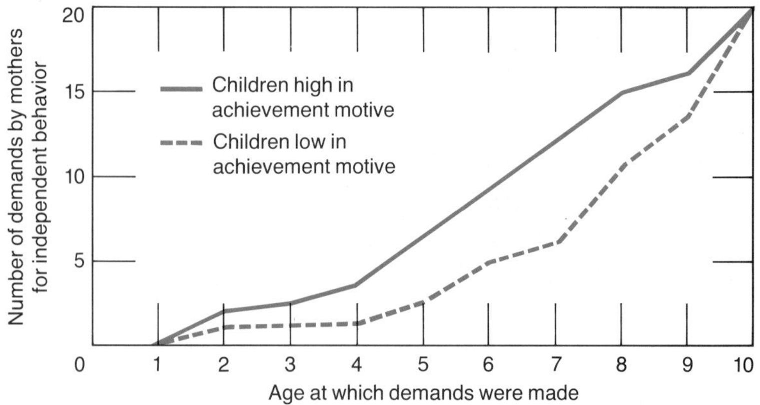

Figure 10-2 Early training and the achievement motive *Do parents who encourage young children to be independent also encourage the achievement motive? So it would appear from these results of a study, described in the text, of the ages at which mothers demanded 20 forms of independent behavior. The mothers of sons who turned out high in achievement motive made about as many demands at the age of 2 as the mothers of sons low in achievement motive made at the age of 4—and about as many by the age of 5 as the other mothers by the age of 7 (Winterbottom, 1953).*

mothers had made the 20 demands by the time their sons were 10 years old. But the boys who turned out to be high in achievement motive were urged to be independent at much earlier ages than the others. Encouraging independence in early childhood seems to strengthen the achievement motive—and parents who are overprotective seem to discourage it.

The power motive

The desire to be in a position of control—to be the boss, to give orders, to command respect and obedience—is called the *power motive.* At first glance, it may seem very much like the achievement motive. But the achievement motive is directed toward performing well at whatever one chooses to undertake. The power motive, on the other hand, has less to do with good performance than with being top dog. Studies of American presidents have shown that those who had a strong power motive (as judged from their speeches) tended to take strong and decisive actions and had a great impact on our society—but were not necessarily good presidents who made important and constructive contributions (Winter and Stewart, 1978).

It has been found that college students who have a strong power motive tend to be officers in campus organizations, serve on student-faculty committees, and work for the school newspaper and radio station. They like to have nameplates, credit cards, and possessions associated with prestige, such as tape recorders, television sets, and framed pictures. They are quick to take up new fashion trends (Winter, 1973).

Both on the campus and in later life, men high in power motive tend to do considerable drinking (Brown, 1975) and to be reckless when they gamble (McClelland and Teague, 1975).

Though people with a strong power motive often become leaders of their group, they do not necessarily serve the group's best interests. Evidence demonstrates that they provide the members with less information and fewer options than do leaders with a weaker urge for power. They also show less concern for moral issues raised by the group's activities and decisions (Fodor and Smith, 1982).

In men, the motive often seems to interfere with establishing satisfactory relationships with the opposite sex. A study of college students who were going together found that men who were high in power motive tended to be less satisfied than other men with their relationships, and so did their partners. Moreover, these couples were much more likely to break up (Stewart and Rubin, 1976). When men high in power motive do marry, they seem to prefer submissive wives (Winter and Stewart, 1978), and their marriages are less likely to be successful (McClelland et al., 1972).

In a complex society such as ours, the power motive doubtless serves a useful purpose. Somebody has to run the government, the corporations, and all the other organizations that are essential to the functioning of an industrial nation. Moreover, though people who aspire to positions of power may pay a price in their personal relationships, they seem to find many satisfactions. Among the United States presidents of this century, it appears that those highest in power motive were the ones who enjoyed the job the most (Barber, 1972). But the power motive probably also directs the behavior of dictators, gang leaders, and the builders of fraudulent financial empires.

Avoidance of power

Some people, instead of seeking power, seem strongly motivated to avoid it, as if they feared rather than admired it. They shun situations in which their actions can be controlled by other people, and they do not like to exercise control themselves. The motive to avoid power is especially likely to occur among men who were the youngest members of a large family—perhaps because of early experiences in which they felt pushed around by older and more powerful brothers and sisters.

People who fear power and are motivated to avoid it try very hard to preserve their independence from authority. In college, they dislike anything that smacks of regimentation—such as large lecture classes and required courses of study. They would rather be graded on a paper they have prepared on their own than on an examination (Winter, 1973). A study of college women who had this attitude toward power showed that they were more likely than other students to leave the campus before graduation, by either transferring to another school or sometimes dropping out altogether (Stewart, 1975).

People with a strong motive to avoid power are not very interested in such possessions as stereo sets and automobiles. When they do have material possessions, they are quick to lend to others. If they own cars, they are more likely than other people to have an accident—almost as if to show their lack of concern. They tend to be closemouthed about their own affairs, even to the point of lying, if necessary, to preserve their privacy. They shun careers in which they would have power over others and gravitate toward jobs in which they can help others, such as teaching (Winter and Stewart, 1978).

The affiliation motive

The desire to be around other people is the *affiliation motive.* All of us grow up with this motive, which makes us first seek close attachments with our parents and later establish friendly relationships with others. The strength of the motive, however, varies widely. Some people maintain close ties with their parents all their lives and are extremely sociable in general. They are "joiners" who always like to be in a group and prefer to work in jobs where they cooperate with and have the help of others. Other people prefer to spend their time alone and to be on their own in their work. Some display the affiliation motive so seldom that they appear to be loners who care very little for human companionship.

To at least some extent, however, the affiliation motive appears to operate in everyone. It is particularly noticeable in people who are experiencing unpleasant emotions, for there seems to be considerable truth in the adage that "misery loves company." This fact was demonstrated by an experiment in which university women were asked to visit a psychology laboratory. When they arrived, they found a frightening piece of apparatus awaiting them and were told it was designed to deliver severe electrical shocks. After having been made anxious about the nature of the experiment, they were told that they had their choice of waiting their turn alone or in company. Fully 63 percent preferred company, with most of the rest saying they did not care one way or the other. In a control group of women who had not been made anxious

These students, working together on a school publication, are probably motivated as much by affiliation as by achievement.

about the experiment, the number who preferred company while waiting was only 33 percent (Schachter, 1959).

In jobs that call for a group effort, it has been found that people high in affiliation motive would rather be with their friends even when they could work with strangers who were more competent and could offer more help. They are more pleased by signs that their group is getting along well emotionally than by its accomplishments. There is some evidence that students with a strong affiliation motive make better grades in classes where everyone is friendly and the instructor takes a personal interest and calls students by name (Tschukitscheff, 1930), although this seems to be far more true of men than of women.

The dependency motive

Closely allied to the desire for affiliation is the *dependency motive,* which also appears to exist in all of us. The dependency motive probably stems from our experiences as babies, when we are completely dependent on our parents. They give us food, drink, warmth, comfort, and relief from pain. This tendency to rely on others—at least at times and for certain things—never leaves us. We continue to have a strong urge to depend on others to organize our lives, set up our schedules, help us with our work, comfort us, and give us support and pleasure. Like affiliation, the dependency motive is especially prominent in troubling situations. Hospital patients, for example, often have mixed feelings. Despite their illness and worry, they may enjoy the opportunity to be dependent on their physicians and nurses.

Behavior that stems from the dependency motive has been found to be more common among women than men. But this is because our society, at least until recently, has considered dependency to be appropriate, feminine, and rather attractive in women. The motive itself is

Clinging to mother: a clear example of the dependency motive at work.

probably equally strong in men—but they are less likely to display it because society has frowned on dependent behavior on the part of males. Often the motive is gratified by men in subtle ways. They may take their problems to the teacher or to the boss (though usually under the guise of being logical rather than emotional). Or they may tend to rely on columnists and television commentators for an interpretation of world events—and to give enthusiastic allegiance to political leaders with strong personalities.

Birth order and the motives for success and friendship

Were you the firstborn in your family—or did you come along later? This may seem an odd question to ask in a discussion of motives, but it is more relevant than it may appear. Firstborn children are considerably more likely than others to have a strong motive for affiliation. In the study illustrated in Figure 10-3, for example, males and females ranging in age from 11 to 62 took tests designed to measure the affiliation motive. Men who were the firstborn (or only) children in their families were found to be about twice as likely as other men to make high scores. Firstborn women were about six times more likely than others to show a strong affiliation motive.

Similar findings have been reported for the achievement motive. For example, students who are firstborns set higher standards for themselves than later-borns. They are also more competitive and have higher educational aspirations (Falbo, 1981). Indeed the achievement motive has inspired many firstborns to become outstandingly successful. Any list of prominent people—eminent scholars, people listed in *Who's Who*, even presidents of the United States—contains an unusually high proportion of firstborns. The well-known people whose photos are shown in Figure 10-4 all were firstborn children.

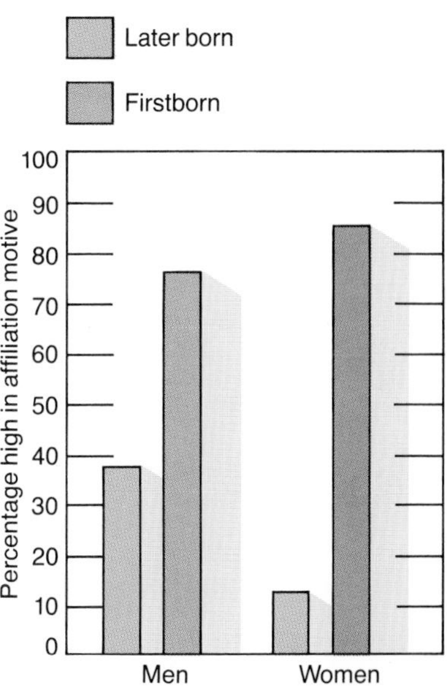

Figure 10-3 The affiliation motive: highest among firstborns *The bars show the percentages of males and females, from children to older people, who made high scores on a test measuring the affiliation motive. Note the wide discrepancy between firstborn children and others (Dember, 1964)*

Muhammad Ali

Jane Fonda

Harry S Truman

Margaret Mead

Theodore Roosevelt

Martin Luther King

Figure 10-4 Besides success, what do these people have in common? *All these people, whose careers would indicate a high level of achievement motive, share another attribute. What? For the answer, see the text.*

A possible explanation is that parents appear to treat a firstborn child differently from later children. Mothers devote more time to the firstborn, are more protective, take a greater part in the child's activities, interfere more, and are more extreme with both praise and criticism (Hilton, 1967). Thus the firstborn child is thrust from the start into an adult world and expected to conform to adult standards (Feshbach, 1971). Later children receive less attention and guidance from their parents and are more influenced by their relations with other children.

Firstborn children, again perhaps because of their early close interactions with their parents, have been found to be more trusting of authority than later-born children (Suedfeld, 1969). Firstborn men, though not women, have a strong tendency to conform to social pressures (Sampson and Hancock, 1967). Moreover, just as the youngest child in the family seems to fear and shun power, firstborns often rate high in the motive to attain power. There seems to be some truth in an observation made by the psychoanalyst Alfred Adler, who once described the firstborn child as a "power-hungry conservative" (Adler, 1928). There are of course many exceptions to these generalities.

Some other powerful motives

The motives that have just been discussed—achievement, power, affiliation, and dependency—are the easiest to study and have received the most attention from psychologists. Other motives, however, also seem to influence all of us, sometimes very strongly.

The motive for certainty

Even very young children display a strong *motive for certainty*—that is, a desire to feel at home in their world, to know where they stand, to avoid the discomfort of unfamiliar and surprising events. They clearly enjoy the certainty represented by their own bed, their own toys, the presence of familiar people and objects in their environment. As they grow a little older, they like to have rules set for their conduct; they like the certainty of knowing what they are permitted to do and what they are not permitted to do. The prospect of uncertainty—sleeping in a strange house, being taken care of by a strange baby-sitter, going to school for the first time—is likely to upset them.

Adults too tend to be motivated toward the known and away from the unknown. For some, such as explorers and astronauts, other motives prove stronger. In general, however, the desire for certainty operates strongly in most of us at most times. We like to feel that we know how our relatives and friends will act toward us, what is likely to happen tomorrow in the classroom or on the job, and where and how we will be living next year.

In some people, the motive for certainty is so strong that they seem to avoid any kind of change, even when the price of inaction is very high. You undoubtedly know people who continue to work in jobs they hate, or who persist in marriages they have long since decided are hopeless. Apparently they would rather stay with the known, no matter how unpleasant, than face the unknown. For most of us, however, the desire for certainty operates to keep our lives on an even keel. It takes three forms:

1. We like to think that we can predict what will happen next—that is, that future events will be orderly and foreseeable.
2. When unusual events surprise us, we like to understand them and relate them in some way to previous experiences.
3. We seek consistency among the various beliefs we hold and between our beliefs and our behavior.

The motive to live up to standards

All of us, as we grow up, begin to set rules for our own behavior. Through learning what society values and through identification with our parents and other adults, we acquire inner standards of many kinds. We also acquire a strong *motive to live up to our standards.* Most people want to be attractive, responsible, friendly, skillful, generous, honest, and fair. Some, because of a different early environment, have standards that call for them to be domineering, tough, and rebellious.

Our standards form what is called our *ego ideal*—our notion of how we would always think and act, if we were perfect. Many of us acquire such high standards that we cannot possibly live up to all of them at all times. In fact the motive to live up to inner standards often requires us to suppress other powerful motives. Our standards may tell us that we should not take food from another person even if we are hungry, that we should be kind even to people toward whom we feel hostile, that we should play fair no matter how much we want to win. As a result, we often feel shame and guilt, over our thoughts if not actually our conduct. In popular terms, our conscience hurts. When we fail to meet our standards, the pangs of conscience can be painful indeed. This is why people who commit crimes sometimes behave in such a way that they are almost sure to be caught. Apparently they prefer punishment by imprisonment to the self-punishment that results from a serious failure to live up to inner standards.

The hostility motive

Though most of us do not like to admit it, all of us have a *hostility motive.* Evidence first appears in children at about 2 years of age. Up to then, all they seem to want from other people is their presence and the stimulation, help, and approval they provide. But at this stage, children begin to want something else from others. They want—at times—to see other people display signs of worry, fears of discomfort, actual pain. Later they may hope that misfortune will befall others and that they will have the gratification of knowing about it.

Some scientists regard hostility as a biological trait that makes *aggression* as inevitable for human beings as fighting over territory is for baboons and other animals (Lorenz, 1966). Others, probably a majority, believe that the hostility motive is learned and that it stems from

A basketball coach finds it impossible to restrain the hostility motive.

the fact that children cannot have everything they want. Some of their desires are bound to be frustrated by the rules of society and by the conflicting desires of other people. They cannot always eat when they want to. They have to learn to control their drive for elimination except when they are in the bathroom. They cannot have the toy that another child owns and is playing with. Their mothers cannot always cater to their whims. Other children, bigger than they are, push them around.

Aggression resulting from hostility may take such forms as argumentativeness, sarcasm, physical and mental cruelty, and fighting. Yet, while all people are motivated at some time by hostility, not everyone displays aggression. Boys and men are more inclined to aggressive behavior than girls and women, for our society has traditionally approved of a certain amount of aggression in males, but has discouraged it in females. The social environment—especially the attitudes toward violence held by parents and by the community as a whole—seems to be a strong influence. Researchers recently studied a town in Mexico where violence was generally approved and admired. In this town violent incidents were very common. In another town public opinion disapproved of violence. Here violent incidents were rare (Paddock, O'Neill, and Haver, 1978). Researchers have also found numerous small societies, for example in isolated parts of New Guinea and the Philippine Islands, where aggressive behavior is almost unknown (Bandura, 1973).

There is considerable evidence that aggressive behavior is most likely to occur among people who, for whatever reason, happen to be in a high state of arousal. Experiments have shown that aggression seems to be provoked by the discomfort of being exposed to loud noise (Geen and

O'Neal, 1969) or working in an overheated room (Baron and Lawton, 1972)—even by the physical arousal created by brisk exercise (Zillman, Katcher, and Milavsky, 1972). Some psychologists have suggested that the high level of violence in our society can be explained at least in part by the fast pace of modern life and the noise and crowding that occur in our cities (Geen, 1976).

It has also been established that aggression is encouraged by watching other people behave aggressively—that is, through the kind of observation learning that was illustrated on page 113 with the photographs of children attacking a doll with a hammer after watching a movie of an adult doing this. Experiments on imitation of aggression raise the issue of how our society has been affected by all the violence depicted in the movies and on television, as discussed in a box on Psychology and Society.

The motive for self-actualization

A good deal of human history seems to revolve around the motive for hostility (leading to acts of violence, revenge, and war) and the motive for power (which has produced such despots as Hitler and Stalin). But should history lead us to take a pessimistic view of human nature? Among those who think otherwise are the humanistic psychologists—who believe that the most powerful motivating force in human beings is the aspiration toward benevolent and spiritual goals. The humanists' view of human motivation is called the *theory of self-actualization,* which holds that people will always pursue the highest and most idealistic aims unless their development is warped by a malevolent social environment.

The theory was formulated by Abraham Maslow, one of the leading humanists. Maslow believed that human beings are innately inclined to seek beauty, goodness, truth, and the fullest possible development of their own unique potentialities for perfection and creativity. Human motives, he theorized, take the form shown in Figure 10-5. The physiological motives at the bottom of the pyramid are the most urgent. People must satisfy their hunger and thirst drives before they can undertake the search for safety, which is the next step upward. And only in a safe and stable society can they then begin to seek the higher goals to which human nature aspires.

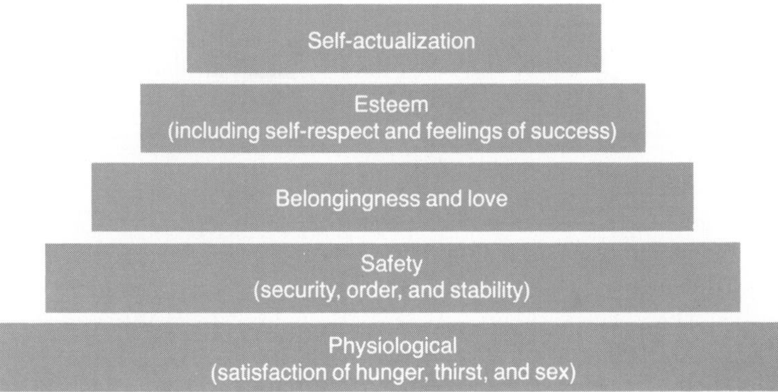

Figure 10-5 Maslow's pyramid of motives *Maslow's theory holds that human motives take the form of this pyramid. Once the* physiological motives *at the bottom have been satisfied, human beings are freed to pursue the* safety motives—*and so on up the higher levels. For the meaning of the self-actualization motive that is at the very top, see the text.*

Psychology and Society: Violence, movies, and television

During your lifetime, in the hours you have spent watching movies and television, how many acts of violence have you witnessed? How many fistfights, beatings, stabbings, shootings, gang wars, and rapes?

Even for the most casual moviegoer and television-watcher, the number would be staggering. One clue comes from a study of cartoon shows for children that appeared on television in the mid-1970s. Each hour of these cartoons, it was found, contained an average of 21.5 violent actions (Slaby, Quarforth, and McConnachie, 1976). And these were just kiddie shows, not adult fare. In recent years, despite objections by government agencies and concerned citizens, there appears to have been no significant reduction in television violence (Gerbner et al., 1980).

Do television and the movies help account for the increased violence revealed by today's crime statistics? In the past, some psychologists doubted that incidents seen on the screen have any real effect on behavior (Kaplan and Singer, 1976). Indeed some maintained that watching make-believe scenes of violence may have a cathartic effect—that is, it may enable viewers to release pent-up aggressive urges and therefore relieve any pressure to act (Dollard et al., 1939). There is now considerable evidence, however, that violence on the screen often encourages real-life aggression.

Some of the effects represent a subtle change in attitude. One study found that people who watch a great deal of television tend to become distrustful of others and afraid of being victims of crime. They often try to protect themselves with extra locks on their doors, guard dogs, and guns (Gerbner and Gross, 1976). At the same time, they seem to become hardened to violence and less likely to be emotionally upset by real-life incidents of aggression (Thomas et al., 1977). It might be said that they begin to take violence for granted, as a standard part of human behavior.

Other more direct effects have also been observed. One group of investigators found that preschool children who were heavy viewers of violent programs became more aggressive during their play periods at day-care centers (Singer and Singer, 1980). Another study, of elementary school children in the United States, Finland, and Poland, found that in all three countries children who regularly watched programs containing heavy doses of violence were rated by their peers as most aggressive. This was true of girls as well as boys (Eron and Huesmann, 1980). Still other studies revealed a significant increase in both verbal and physical aggression by children after television was introduced into their communities (Williams, 1978; Granzberg and Steinbring, 1980), though aggressive behavior seems to decrease in children who watch television shows in which the characters solve their problems constructively, without resorting to violence (Leiffer, Gordon, and Graves, 1974).

It has been found that adults also tend to behave more aggressively after watching films that show aggressive acts (Hartmann, 1969). Moreover a number of violent crimes appear to be real-life imitations of television or movie stories (Mankiewicz and Swerdlow, 1977). Professional criminals sometimes learn new techniques from watching crimes on the screen (Hendrick, 1977).

The weight of evidence is that the effects of violence in the movies and television are at least suspect—and, in the opinion of many psychologists, clearly damaging. Should the display of violence be stopped? This is an issue that society must decide. It is surrounded by many arguments pro and con about censorship and even freedom of the press—for news reports of actual crimes are often followed by a sharp rise in similar types of crime, as after the first hijacking of an airplane in 1967 (Bandura, 1973).

The goal at the very top of the pyramid, self-actualization, is a sort of all-encompassing self-fulfillment. Self-actualizing people have satisfied their search for such esthetic pleasures as order, symmetry, and beauty. They accept themselves and others and the realities of existence, and they rejoice in the experience of living. Self-actualizers are spontaneous and creative and have a keen sense of humor. They have made the most of their abilities and have become all they are capable of becoming (Maslow, 1970). All this, to Maslow, represents the goal toward which all human beings by their very nature are motivated—though deprivation and social pressures may prevent some of them from ever reaching this ideal level of development. Some of the people Maslow regarded as having attained the top of his pyramid are shown in Figure 10-6.

One study indicates that people who seem to be self-actualizing are likely to be free from tendencies to be neurotic (Knapp, 1965)—in other words, that self-actualization and what is often called "mental health" go hand in hand. But in general Maslow's theory does not lend itself to experimental proof or disproof. It must be taken largely on faith. To many psychologists the theory has the intuitive ring of truth. To others it seems too optimistic.

Figure 10-6 Some famous self-actualizers *These are some of the people whom Maslow regarded as having reached the very peak of human motivation. Above, Eleanor Roosevelt; center, Albert Einstein; below, Helen Keller.*

Unconscious motives

Another idea that has influenced many psychologists holds that human activities are often a response to *unconscious motives*—that is, to wishes and desires that we are not aware of, that in fact we might vehemently deny, but that influence our behavior nonetheless, sometimes to a striking degree. The idea of unconscious motives, first proposed by Sigmund Freud, raises some thorny psychological problems, among them the question of how a desire that is unconscious can operate to produce relevant behavior. But his idea does seem to explain some aspects of human behavior that would otherwise be baffling.

One example of what appears to be an unconscious motive is the phenomenon known as posthypnotic suggestion. While subjects are under hypnosis, they may be told that after they awaken from the trance they will go and raise a window the first time the hypnotist coughs—even though they will not remember having received this instruction. Later the hypnotist coughs, and, sure enough, the subjects do open a window. If asked why, they say that the room was getting stuffy or that they felt faint. They have no suspicion that the real reason was to comply with the hypnotist's demand.

Other examples are all around us. A mother may seem to believe in all sincerity that she has the most generous, affectionate, and even self-sacrificing motives toward her daughter. Yet an unprejudiced observer might say that the mother's real motives are to dominate the daughter, keep her from marrying, and hold on to her as a servant. A man may earnestly deny that he has any hostile motives. Yet we may see that he performs many subtle acts of aggression against his wife, his children, and his business associates. A person may feel genuinely motivated to go to the dentist or to keep a date with a friend, yet conveniently "forget" the appointment.

Although the notion of unconscious motives is puzzling, many psychologists agree that it is valid, including some who reject other aspects of Freud's theories. Accepting the idea leads to a rather startling conclusion: If motives can affect behavior even though they are completely unconscious, then we will often find it as difficult to analyze our own motives as to know the motives of others.

How and why motives affect behavior

One reason we are not very good at analyzing the motives of other people is that motives may not necessarily result in any behavior at all. For one thing, they may be thwarted by outside events—the circumstances of our lives—over which we have no control. The key here is *opportunity*—for we cannot fulfill any of our desires unless we have a chance to try. The achievement motive is often the victim of lack of opportunity. For example, a young woman wants very badly to have a professional career, but for lack of money she cannot get the necessary education. A young man wants very badly to work in advertising, but cannot find any advertising firm that will hire him.

Lack of opportunity may also thwart the affiliation motive. Young people eager for the companionship of the opposite sex may live in a community where young men greatly outnumber young women, or vice versa. For older people, the lack of opportunity is caused by the fact that women live much longer than men. Among Americans who are 45 or older, there are over 7 million more women than men (U.S. Bureau of the Census, 1980).

In other cases, motives are never gratified for reasons that lie within the self. Some people have a strong desire for achievement yet never show any sign of striving for success—though they do not lack opportunity. Others have strong motives for power yet merely go on their happy-go-lucky way, never trying to attain positions of power. Psychologists have found so many discrepancies between motivation and behavior that their approach has changed greatly in recent years. At one time most of them were interested in classifying, defining, and measuring motives. Now most of them are concerned with the ways in which people act or do not act on their motives—in other words, with all the factors that determine whether we try to satisfy them, how hard we try, and how we go about seeking satisfaction. These factors, in which there is a wide range of individual differences, are the subject of the rest of the chapter.

Motive hierarchies and targets

All of us seem to have motives for achievement, power (or avoidance of power), affiliation, dependency, certainty, living up to standards, hostility, and (if we accept Maslow's theory) self-actualization. But there are great differences in the strengths of these desires. Each of us has built up a highly individual *hierarchy of motives* in which some have a top priority, while others are much less urgent. Of course the strength of a motive—the position it occupies in the hierarchy—plays a considerable part in determining how hard, if at all, we try to satisfy it (Atkinson, 1974). Some of us have such a strong affiliation motive that we are willing to ignore a weaker desire for achievement to avoid making our friends jealous. On the other hand, some of us are so intent on achievement or power that we are willing to sacrifice the friendships dictated by a weaker affiliation motive.

Our hierarchy of motives does not operate in a vacuum. It changes from time to time with the situation of the moment. No matter how high the affiliation motive may be in the hierarchy, none of us is invariably eager for affiliation at all times and with all people. (Indeed most of us know people with whom we would not care to affiliate under any circumstances.) Nor are we always inclined to satisfy our motives for achievement or hostility, however strong they may be in general.

To a great extent, our desires of the moment depend on what psychologists call our *motive targets*—that is, the people to whom our various motives are directed. For example, a man may have strong motives for achievement toward his business associates, for power toward the members of his political club, for affiliation towards his parents, and for dependency toward his wife. His desires will change during the course of the day as he moves from one relationship to another. The motive targets, as well as the hierarchy, help determine which motive will prevail.

The effect of incentive value

As was mentioned in the last chapter, the hunger drive can be triggered by such incentive objects as the smell of food from a restaurant kitchen or the sight of pastries in a bakery window. In a somewhat similar way, motives are also triggered by incentives in the environment.

For example, a college woman goes home at the end of the day with no particular plans for the evening. A friend calls and suggests they go to an 8 p.m. tryout for parts in a school play. Going to the tryouts is a potential incentive to act on any one of a number of motives—for achievement, say, or for affiliation. Whether the student responds eagerly or turns down the suggestion will depend in large part on how much *incentive value* trying out for a play holds for her.

The incentive value of any event or object varies considerably from one person to another. Two students may have equally strong desires for achievement, but one student's motive may center on finishing school as quickly as possible and starting on a job, the other's on getting good grades. Indeed good grades are such a strong incentive for some students that they cheat on tests, although an A obtained in this manner is a dubious form of achievement (Johnson, 1981). As incentives for the affiliation motive, one student may place great value on joining a certain campus organization, while another may not value that organization at all.

Gauging your chances of success

Another factor that affects our decision to act or not to act on our motives is how much chance we have to get what we want. We are not likely to try very hard, if at all, unless we have a reasonable expectation of success. The college woman invited to try out for the campus play will probably turn down the suggestion if she believes that she has absolutely no chance—even though she places a high incentive value on getting a part. A male student may be highly motivated to call up a woman he has met in one of his classes, and he may place a high incentive value on going out with her. But if he feels shy and awkward around women and considers himself unattractive and uninteresting, he will probably take no action.

In gauging our chances of success, we try to make a realistic appraisal of the situation. We may decide not to try out for a campus play because we have never had any acting experience. We may abandon any thought of a career in accounting because we always have trouble in math courses. But often we are influenced not so much by the facts as by our self-image—our own perception of ourselves and our abilities. Some people have an exaggerated opinion of their talents and are inclined to try anything (a tendency that may bring them one disappointment after another). On the other hand, people who have acquired learned helplessness always tend to be pessimistic about their chances, whatever the situation. They may be capable of far more success—at fulfilling their motives for achievement, affiliation, and other goals—than they themselves believe. They give up without really trying.

Expectancy of success and locus of control

Closely related to learned helplessness is another phenomenon that has been studied in recent years by many psychologists interested in the relationships between motives and behavior. This is the matter of whether we believe that we are in control of our own lives or at the mercy of outside events (deCharms and Muir, 1978). It has been found that some people assume their chances of success depend largely on *internal factors*—their own abilities and efforts. Others feel that success depends more on *external factors*—sheer luck and the inherent difficulty of attaining whatever goal they seek (Weiner, 1974).

The psychological term for this phenomenon is *locus of control.* (*Locus* is the Latin word for *place.*) People who assume that the locus of control is internal tend to take responsibility for their own actions and to try hard to implement their motives. They also seem to feel that other people create their own successes and failures—and they are reluctant to give money or help to those who are in trouble (Phares and Lamiell, 1975). They are not easily influenced by the opinions of other people and are careful though not timid in the risks they are willing to take (Strickland, 1977).

People who assume that the locus of control is external are less likely to strive for the goals dictated by their motives. They tend to rely on luck—and to be sympathetic to others who are in trouble, whom they regard as "down on their luck." They are readily influenced by the opinions of others (Sherman, 1973) and inclined to be reckless. When things go badly for them, the effect on their mood seems to linger for a long time (Lefcourt et al., 1981). When they do succeed—in the classroom, a job, or marriage—they are less likely to take credit for their success than to consider themselves blessed by circumstances, or to decide that whatever they did right must have been pretty easy. All of these are of course general tendencies. None of us believes totally in external control or internal control.

Long-range plans, too much motivation, and running scared

All the factors just mentioned help determine how hard we try to implement a motive, if indeed we try at all. Moreover our behavior at any given moment also depends on our long-range thinking about our goals. If the college woman invited to the tryout aspires to become a professional actress—or if she seeks a long-term affiliation with a group of theater people—she is much more likely to act than if she regards the experience as just a momentary diversion. Psychology's findings about the relationship of motives to behavior have been summarized in the theory that our actions in any situation are influenced by the following interplay of forces (Atkinson and Raynor, 1974):

1. *The strength of our motive* (as determined by our hierarchy of motives and the target to which we are directing our actions)
2. *The way we perceive our chances of success* (influenced by our attitude toward locus of control and any feelings of learned helplessness we may have acquired)
3. *The incentive value* of what we are doing or could be doing at the moment
4. *The relationship of present to future actions*—in other words our judgments about the possibilities to which our behavior may lead, especially the incentive value of these future actions and the way we perceive our chances of future success

An interesting sidelight is the finding that a very high level of motivation does not always help attain a goal. On the contrary, a motive can be so strong as to be self-defeating (Atkinson, 1976). We may be so intent on the goal, so eager to attain it, that we lose our perspective and our performance suffers. This is often true of people who have a strong affiliation motive and want very badly to be liked. You have probably known people who tried so hard to win your friendship that their constant attentions, favors, and flattery became a nuisance.

Some evidence has also been found that attempts to implement a motive are often hampered by the fear of failure. This is especially true of the achievement motive. An example might be a college man who has long-range plans to become a lawyer. He takes a crucial examination that has great incentive value because he must meet the admission standards of the law school he wants to attend. His fear of failure may make him "run scared" and perform far below his capabilities.

Fear of failure at a varsity swim meet

The effect of fear of failure on the affiliation motive was demonstrated in an unusual experiment with the varsity swim teams at three universities. The members of the teams, men and women, were tested for motivation and divided into two groups. One had a high level of affiliation motive and a low fear of social rejection. The other group had a weaker affiliation motive and a greater fear of rejection. Later all the swimmers took part in a joint meet. Individual winners were determined by the time they made when swimming alone against the clock. There was also competition among groups of three swimming the course together, with their average time determining the winning trio.

The results were striking. On the average, the swimmers who were high in affiliation motive and low in fear of rejection swam more than 1.5 seconds faster in a group than when they were alone—as if the desire to win approval from their teammates spurred them to greater effort. The swimmers higher in fear of rejection did just the opposite. They were more than 1.5 seconds slower when swimming in a group—as if they did not want to outshine the other two members (Sorrentino and Sheppard, 1978). (The differences in performance were considerably greater for men, incidentally, than for women—a fact that may or may not indicate some sex differences in the way motives operate.) The experiment has some interesting implications for psychology-minded athletic coaches seeking improved performance in team and individual sports.

Frustration and conflict

Motives that rank near the top of the hierarchy can be powerful forces in directing behavior, not only at any given moment but over a lifetime. Indeed two of the most important aspects of human personality and adjustment are these: (a) To what extent are our strongest motives gratified—and to what extent do they go unfulfilled? (b) If we fail to fulfill our motives, in what manner and how successfully do we cope with the failure?

It is inevitable, given the nature of human aspirations and human society, that most of us will never gratify all our motives. We are almost bound to encounter what psychologists call *frustration.* This is one of life's most unpleasant experiences and can have extremely unfortunate results—for frustration is a frequent cause of the anxiety and abnormal behavior that will be discussed in the next two chapters.

Sources of frustration

Psychologists define frustration as *the blocking of motive satisfaction by some kind of obstacle.* On a very simple level, our motive to get somewhere on time may be blocked—therefore frustrated—by a flat tire. On a more complex level, any one of a number of obstacles may frustrate our motives to be actors, athletes, or successful in our relations with people we like.

In popular usage, the term *frustration* refers to the unpleasant feelings that result from the blocking of motive satisfaction—that is, the feelings we experience when something interferes with our wishes, hopes, plans, and expectations. But these feelings, which are really emotional responses to frustration, take so many forms that they cannot be de-

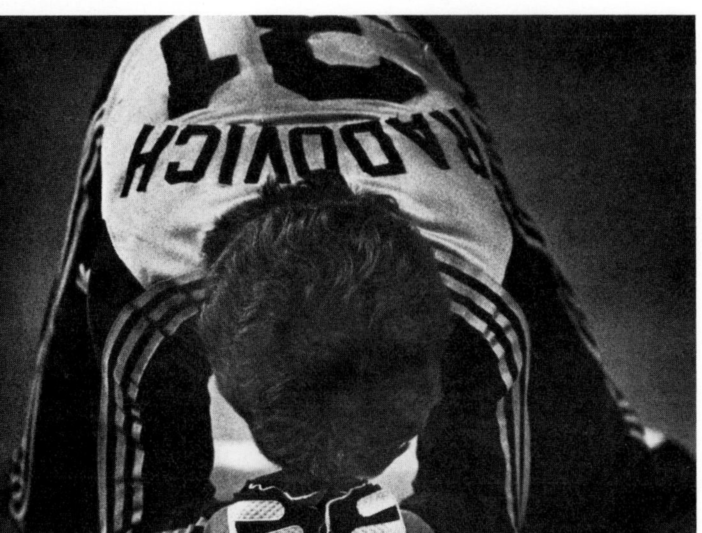

This soccer player is suffering the frustration of his hopes for victory.

scribed scientifically. They may range from mild surprise to murderous rage, from confusion to disappointment to anger to depression to apathy.

Frustration is a universal experience. Our environment is full of events that often seem especially designed to keep us from fulfilling our wishes. Even our own body and personality make frustration inevitable. The possible sources of frustration are usually broken down into four categories—but note how many possibilities exist in each:

1. *Physical obstacles*—such as a drought that frustrates a farmer's attempts to produce a good crop. Or a broken alarm clock, traffic jam, or flat tire that prevents us from getting to class on time.
2. *Social circumstances*—such as a refusal by another person to return our affection, social barriers against minority groups, or problems of society that frustrate our motive for certainty by raising the threat of economic dislocation or war.
3. *Personal shortcomings*—such as when we want to be musicians but find that we are tone deaf, or aspire to be Olympic champions but lack the physical equipment. None of us is as talented as we would like.
4. *Conflicts between motives*—for example, wanting to leave college for a year to try painting, but also wanting to please one's parents by remaining in school.

Frustration and the eye of the beholder

What kinds of physical obstacles, social circumstances, personal shortcomings, and conflicts are likely to be most frustrating? The answer is that frustration is entirely relative. It all depends on the situation.

A classic experiment was performed by observing the conduct of children aged 2 to 5 in a playroom equipped only with "half toys," such as a telephone without a transmitter and an ironing board without an iron. Despite the missing parts, the children played quite happily—until a dividing screen was removed and they saw much better toys in the other half of the room. Then, when a wire barrier was placed between them and the "whole toys," most of them showed signs of extreme frustration (Barker, Dembo, and Lewin, 1941).

As the experiment showed, "half toys" are fun to play with if there is nothing better at hand. When better toys lie just beyond reach, the "half toys" are no longer good enough. Adult frustrations are equally relative. A man may be perfectly happy with his old used car until his neighbor buys a new model. A woman may be perfectly happy with her job until her friend in the next office gets a promotion. Many people who are successful and well liked suffer pangs of frustration because a brother or sister is even more successful and popular.

There are wide individual differences in the ability to tolerate frustration. This has been found true even among young children (Hutt, 1947). Among adults, the evidence is all around us. You doubtless know men and women who carry on in normal fashion and even appear relatively cheerful despite serious physical handicaps or tragic disappointments. You probably know others who are reduced to tears or temper tantrums if the breakfast bacon is too crisp.

Conflict as a source of frustration

The most common of the four sources of frustration is *conflict*—which psychologists define as *the simultaneous arousal of two or more incompatible motives, resulting in unpleasant emotions.* The phrase "unpleasant emotions" is an essential part of the definition. A person whose motives are in genuine conflict experiences anxiety, uncertainty, and the feeling of being torn and distressed. This is why conflict is a potential threat to normal behavior.

One type of conflict occurs between the motive to live up to inner standards and some other motive. For example, most children acquire a desire to live up to a standard that calls for them to be obedient and respectful to their parents. Yet at times they may be motivated by hostility and want to strike out against their parents. Even though they do not actually commit any hostile act, the desire itself may produce shame or guilt. Adolescents and adults often experience similar conflict over what would happen to their self-respect and their image in society if they struck out angrily against a teacher or boss. Some are troubled by a conflict between an inner standard calling for independence and toughness and the motive to show signs of dependency or affection.

Another type of conflict occurs when two motives for different and incompatible goals are aroused at the same time. The achievement and affiliation motives are especially likely to pull in opposite directions. An example that you may have experienced is this: It is the night before an examination. The achievement motive, in the form of a desire for a

Psychology and Society: Making tough decisions: can psychology help?

All of us are faced from time to time with difficult decisions: the choice of a college, a career, a job, or a mate. The wrong decision can be disastrous—for one of life's most bitter experiences is to look back with regret at an action that can no longer be reversed. Moreover many of our decisions have long-lasting consequences for others as well as ourselves. Is there a right way to make decisions—to improve the odds of success—and a wrong way?

One promising suggestion comes from a study of the way people seem to go about making their decisions. Many people, it was found, are trapped into one or another of these four mistakes: (a) They are too complacent—and take the most comfortable course of action available without considering the possible risks. (b) They make the decision most highly recommended by their acquaintances, which may or may not be right for them. (c) They procrastinate, duck the responsibility, and shift it to someone else. (d) They act impulsively—jumping to any decision, right or wrong, that will end their painful conflict (Janis and Mann, 1977).

In contrast, it was found, the best approach is to search carefully for every scrap of information that may be relevant to the decision, evaluate this information without bias, and then weigh the alternatives in a systematic way before making a choice. One way is to write down on a sheet of paper answers to hard-nosed questions such as these: What are the practical gains and losses that are likely to follow each possible course of action? How will my decision affect the significant people in my life? How will it affect my own self-concept—the way I will feel about myself in the future? How will the rest of the world—family members, close friends, fellow workers—view my decision? People who take this approach, it was found, are far less likely to live to regret their decisions.

good grade, pulls you in the direction of locking yourself in your room and studying. But friends call and suggest going to a party. The affiliation motive now pulls strongly in the opposite direction. Only one of the two motives can be satisfied. An agonizing decision must be made.

To complicate the problem, the decision is likely to cause anxiety no matter which way you turn. If you decide to study, you risk anxiety over losing the goal of being with your friends—and perhaps over the possibility that their regard for you may suffer. If you decide instead to go out with your friends, you risk anxiety over your grade—and perhaps also over the possibility of rejection by your teachers or parents.

Life is full of conflicts over pairs of goals that cannot both be attained. Shall I marry now (and lose my chance for other social experiences with the opposite sex) or wait (and risk losing the person I think I love)? Shall I try for a well-paying but difficult job (and risk failure) or settle for a more modest job (and give up the idea of being rich)? Shall I spend everything I earn (and risk my future security) or save some of it (and miss out on things I want to buy now)? Shall I live in a city or in the country? Shall I have a small family or a large one? The list of conflicts could be expanded almost indefinitely. Some findings about the best way to resolve them are discussed in a box on Psychology and Society.

Competing motives and group conflict

The conflict over competing motives that we feel as individuals can sometimes beset groups as well. A business can be torn apart by conflict among its executives between achieving success and living up to certain standards of behavior. A school can be filled with dissension when some teachers strive for power while others strive to create a benign environment where the students can fully realize their potential.

One investigator studied conflict in a so-called cooperative Israeli community settled by American immigrants (Reisman, 1981). The underlying problem was a sharp clash of motives. For some members of the group, all that mattered was the economic success of the community. For others, economic success was far less important than establishing a community that favored warm affiliations among its members. The result was the same kind of tension we feel within ourselves when two incompatible motives vie with each other. In the words of one settler, a normally mild-mannered engineer: "It got to the point where I actually hated people from the other side. When I got up in the morning and thought of having to work with them or meet them in the street, I would get upset. For the sanity of my wife and me, we just had to leave." The stress of the conflict left its mark—as it sometimes does on individuals. Nearly a decade later, many of those who remained in the community seemed subdued and demoralized.

Approach and avoidance conflicts

Our conflicts are seldom simple. Indeed they are often so complex that we have trouble understanding them, much less coping with them. To help recognize the complexity, it is useful to note that some of our motives incline us to *approach* a desirable goal (as does the motive for achievement), while others make us seek to *avoid* something unpleasant (like the shame and guilt that result from failure to live up to our standards). Psychologists noted many years ago that these two desires to approach the good and avoid the bad can result in a truly bewildering array of conflicts (Lewin, 1935), all falling in general into the four following classes:

1. An *approach-approach conflict* takes place between two motives that both make us want to approach desirable goals. However, we cannot reach both goals, for attaining one of them means giving up the other. We cannot simultaneously satisfy the motive to watch the late movie on television and the motive to get a good night's sleep. We cannot simultaneously roam around the world and settle down in a career. Thus we are often torn between alternatives—each of which would be thoroughly pleasant except for our regret over losing the other.
2. An *avoidance-avoidance conflict* occurs between two motives that make us want to avoid two alternatives that are both unpleasant. For example, you are too keyed up over tomorrow's examination to get to sleep. You would like to avoid the unpleasantness of tossing and turning in bed, and you could do so by taking a sleeping pill. But you would also like to avoid the grogginess you will suffer tomorrow if you do take the sleeping pill.
3. An *approach-avoidance conflict* occurs when fulfilling a motive will have both pleasant and unpleasant consequences. For young people, the thought of getting married often creates an approach-avoidance

conflict. Being married has many attractions—but it also means added responsibilities and loss of freedom.

4. A *double approach-avoidance conflict,* the most complex and unfortunately the most common type of all, takes place when we are torn between two goals that will both have pleasant and unpleasant consequences. A college woman from a small community wants to become a certified public accountant. But she knows that the best opportunities in this field exist in large cities, and she is worried about the crowded and impersonal aspects of big-city life. Now she falls in love with a classmate who plans to go into business with his father, who runs a small-town automobile agency. She wants very much to marry this man and she likes the idea of living with him in a small community. But she knows that this community will give her very little opportunity for her chosen career as an accountant. Which way shall she turn?

To the double approach-avoidance conflict—so common in life—there is never a fully satisfactory solution. Whichever goal we choose, we are likely to feel at times that we made the wrong decision. Indeed making the decision can be so difficult that sometimes we are inclined to throw up our hands and abandon both goals. The various ways in which people cope with conflict are the subject of the next chapter.

SUMMARY

The goals of success and friendship

1. A motive is *a desire to reach a goal that has value for the individual.*
2. Some psychologists believe that motives are based largely on drives and stimulus needs (for example, that the hunger drive might lead to attempts to attain success and power, thus making sure the drive will never go unsatisfied).
3. Other psychologists believe that motives are cognitive processes that depend mostly on learning.
4. Among important motives are desires for *achievement, power, affiliation,* and *dependency.*

Some other powerful motives

5. Motives for *certainty, living up to inner standards,* and *hostility* can also strongly influence behavior.
6. Humanistic psychologists believe that human beings also have a *motive for self-actualization*—that is, to pursue the highest and most idealistic aims, rejoice in the experience of living, and make the most of their abilities.
7. Many psychologists agree with Freud's belief that we also have *unconscious motives* that influence our behavior even though we are unaware of them.

How and why motives affect behavior

8. All of us seem to possess all the human motives, but to a widely varying degree. An individual pattern of motives, from strongest to weakest, is a *hierarchy of motives.*

9. The strength of a motive at any given moment depends on the presence of *motive targets,* or the people to whom the various motives are directed.
10. Often a motive cannot be fulfilled because of lack of opportunity. In particular, we may never have the opportunity to gratify all our desires for achievement.
11. Other factors that help determine whether we will try to fulfill a motive include: (a) the strength of the motive (determined by the motive hierarchy and motive targets), (b) the way we perceive our chances of success, (c) the *incentive value* of any action we might take, and (d) the relationship of present to future actions (our judgment of long-term consequences).
12. Our perception of our chances of success depends in part on *locus of control*—or whether we believe success depends on *internal factors* (our own abilities and efforts) or *external factors* (such as luck).

Frustration and conflict

13. *Frustration* is the *blocking of motive satisfaction by some kind of obstacle.* The obstacles may be: (a) physical obstacles, (b) social circumstances, (c) personal shortcomings, or (d) conflict.
14. A *conflict* is the *simultaneous arousal of two or more incompatible motives, resulting in unpleasant emotions.*
15. Types of conflict are: (a) *approach-approach* (seeking two desirable goals), (b) *avoidance-avoidance* (seeking to prevent two undesirable alternatives), (c) *approach-avoidance* (over a goal that will have both pleasant and unpleasant aspects), and (d) *double approach-avoidance* (when we are torn between two goals that both have some desirable and some undesirable aspects).
16. Conflict between incompatible motives can affect groups as well as individuals.

IMPORTANT TERMS

achievement motive
affiliation motive
aggression
approach-approach conflict
approach-avoidance conflict
avoidance-avoidance conflict
certainty motive
conflict
dependency motive
double approach-avoidance conflict
frustration
hostility motive
incentive value
locus of control
motive hierarchy
motive targets
motive to live up to inner standards
power motive
self-actualization
unconscious motives

SUPPLEMENT:
Sex Roles and the Conflicts They Create

One conflict worthy of special note arises from the mixed motives and inner standards that most of us have about how men are expected to behave (simply because they are male) and how women are expected to behave (simply because they are female). This conflict has produced a great deal of debate over such issues as the women's liberation movement and the Equal Rights Amendment—with some women and men vigorously in favor and others bitterly opposed. It has caused disagreements between husbands and wives over such matters as whether the wife shall work (and if so whether her career should be considered as important as the husband's) and how to divide the housekeeping chores. It has also produced internal conflicts and self-doubts for members of both sexes—who, confused about their parts in modern society, sometimes hardly know how to regard themselves or each other.

Throughout history it has been assumed that men and women differ in important ways—almost as if they were members of two separate species (Tavris and Offir, 1977). Men have been expected to act *masculine* and women to act *feminine.* What these two words meant was never spelled out, but until recently everyone had a pretty good idea. Before reading on, stop to take the test offered in Figure 10-7 (p. 380), put together by a social psychologist to measure how people rate according to conventional standards of masculinity and femininity. What the score tells you will be explained in the next few paragraphs.

What it means to be masculine or feminine

The test is based on the fact that most people see far more contrasts than similarities between a typical man and a typical woman. In one study, for example, a group was asked to rate men on a scale ranging from "not at all aggressive" to "very aggressive," from "very illogical" to "very logical," and so on through a long list of personality traits. Then the subjects were asked to rate women on the same scale. Both male and female subjects agreed to a remarkable extent that men are generally aggressive, independent, dominant, competitive, logical, direct, adventurous, self-confident, and ambitious. Women were described as almost exactly the opposite—unaggressive, dependent, submissive, not competitive, illogical, sneaky, timid, lacking in self-confidence, and unambitious. Men were described as closemouthed and women as talkative, men as rough and women as gentle, men as sloppy in their habits and women as neat. The subjects agreed that men do not usually enjoy art and literature and cannot easily express any tender feelings, but that women do like art and literature and find it easy to express their feelings (Broverman et al., 1972).

The test in Figure 10-7 measures many of the traits generally considered to distinguish between men and women in our society. Most men would make high minus scores on the test, most women high plus scores. But this would be true chiefly among older people and the less educated. Younger people, especially the college trained, seem to be changing. When the test was given to students at Stanford University, where it originated, only half the males scored as masculine, likewise half the females as feminine. About 15 percent of both sexes wound up on the "wrong" side of the dividing point. These men had plus or feminine scores, the women minus or masculine scores. The other 35 percent fell in the gray area between +1 and −1.

This 35 percent was classified as *androgynous*—a word derived from a combination of the Greek *andros,* for *man,* and *gyne,* for *woman.* The androgynous students, both male and female, had some of the personality traits considered characteristic of men and some considered characteristic of women. In some situations they acted in typically masculine ways, in others in feminine ways.

The large number of students who scored in the androgynous range (as you may also have done—or as surely some of your classmates did) raises some interesting questions. Are men and women really as different as has always been assumed? Do our different bodies destine us to have different motives, emotions, interests, and personalities? Or do we behave differently (when we do) because somehow we have been taught to be different?

Figure 10-7 Are you masculine, feminine, or both? *Write down next to each item a number from 1 to 7 indicating how strongly you display that particular trait. On the first item, for example, put down a 1 if you believe that you are never or almost never self-reliant, a 7 if you believe that you are always or almost always self-reliant, or some other number in between to indicate how far you lean in the direction of self-reliance or lack of it. When you finish rating yourself on all 60 items, see the footnote on page 382 for scoring instructions (Bem, 1974).*

1. self-reliant
2. yielding
3. helpful
4. defends own beliefs
5. cheerful
6. moody
7. independent
8. shy
9. conscientious
10. athletic
11. affectionate
12. theatrical
13. assertive
14. flatterable
15. happy
16. strong personality
17. loyal
18. unpredictable
19. forceful
20. feminine
21. reliable
22. analytical
23. sympathetic
24. jealous
25. has leadership abilities
26. sensitive to the needs of others
27. truthful
28. will take risks
29. understanding
30. secretive
31. makes decisions easily
32. compassionate
33. sincere
34. self-sufficient
35. eager to soothe hurt feelings
36. conceited
37. dominant
38. soft spoken
39. likable
40. masculine
41. warm
42. solemn
43. willing to take a stand
44. tender
45. friendly
46. aggressive
47. gullible
48. inefficient
49. acts as a leader
50. childlike
51. adaptable
52. individualistic
53. does not use harsh language
54. unsystematic
55. competitive
56. loves children
57. tactful
58. ambitious
59. gentle
60. conventional

You're X-X (or X-Y) and stuck with it

The matter of masculinity versus femininity boils down to an aspect of the nature-nurture controversy that has been mentioned frequently in previous chapters. To start with the argument that nature may be the key factor, it must be pointed out that without question the workings of heredity have arranged for males and females to be different not only in their sexual apparatus but in every cell of their bodies. All the cells in a woman's body contain an X-X pair of chromosomes, while all the cells in a man's body contain an X-Y pair.

In some species the two chromosome pairs create startling physical differences. The male red-winged blackbird, for example, is a solid shiny black except for the bright red and yellow-edged patches on his wings. His mate is not black at all. She is brown, with no wing patches but a heavily striped breast. Looking at the two of them you have to wonder how they ever manage to figure out that nature intended for them to get together. But among human beings there are no such pronounced differences in appearance. Except for their sex organs, boy babies and girl babies look very much alike. If they are wearing as much as a diaper it is impossible to tell them apart. When adult males and females are dressed alike in jeans and shirts, with hair the same length, it can be difficult at first glance to tell which is which.

The chromosome pairings do, however, produce an invisible but important difference. The male sex glands produce large amounts of hormones called *androgens,* the female glands large amounts of a hormone called *estrogen.* Do the androgens make you act masculine? Or estrogen make you act feminine? The two hormones do seem to have some effects, starting even before birth. All fertilized eggs start out to grow into females. In the case of X-Y eggs, the Y chromosome then orders a flood of androgen—and this androgen bath triggers the development of the male sex organs (Money and Ehrhardt, 1973). Thus, in the early stages of pregnancy, Y chromosome produces androgen which produces male.

Many scientists believe that the two hormones may also affect the developing brain. Androgen may program the circuits of the brain into a tendency to operate in ways distinctively masculine, estrogen in ways typically feminine. One recent study, for example, shows striking differences between male and female monkeys in an area of the hypothalamus that influences sexual behavior. In this area the male neurons were found to have more numerous and more varied synapses than the female neurons—probably because of the "masculinizing influence" of the male hormone before birth (Ayoub, Greenough, and Juraska, 1983). Experiments with animals have also shown that changing the balance of the male and female hormones, before or just after birth, can make male monkeys and rats grow up acting like females and females grow up acting like males (Bardwick, 1971).

With human beings, a study was made of some young women who had been subjected to the influence of androgen before birth as an unexpected side effect of a new drug taken by their mothers. As a group these young women were more masculine than feminine in many respects. As children they were tomboys. They shunned dolls and preferred to play baseball and football. In adolescence they were not very interested in boys and felt uncomfortable acting as baby-sitters. They had doubts about marriage and motherhood (Ehrhardt and Baker, 1973).

But nature doesn't do it all

All in all, it seems quite probable that nature creates some inborn tendencies. But there is ample proof that heredity alone does not necessarily push men toward being independent and aggressive, nor women toward being passive and submissive. Whatever the effects of our X-X or X-Y chromosome pairs, our hormones, and the possible early programing of our brains, it has been found that the effects are by no means final and irreversible (Stoller, 1972).

The evidence started piling up years ago when an anthropologist, Margaret Mead, reported the strange—to us—behavior of three tribes with whom she had lived in the wilds of the South Pacific island of New Guinea. The men and women in these tribes, biologically the same as the rest of humanity, had notions of masculinity and femininity far different from those that have prevailed in our society and most others.

In tribe no. 1, both men and women were aggressive and violent. They were headhunters and cannibals. The women—perhaps because pregnancy interfered with their normal warlike habits—disliked having and caring for their children, especially the girl babies. In tribe no. 2, both men and women were what we would call highly feminine. Both sexes shunned aggression. Both were gentle, kind, passive, and warmly emotional. Both took care of and nurtured the children.

In tribe no. 3, the members of one sex spent all their time applying cosmetics, gossiping, pouting, engaging in emotional outbursts, and taking care of the children. Members of the other sex had clean-shaven heads, scorned any makeup or ornamentation, were active and domineering, and provided most of the tribe's food and other necessities. But the last sentence describes how the women behaved. The preceding sentence, about a fondness for cosmetics and emotional outbursts, describes the men (Mead, 1935).

Some boy-girls and girl-boys

In our own society some dramatic evidence comes from a study made by researchers at the Johns Hopkins University of a group of *hermaphrodites*—people born, through a quirk of nature, with some of the outward sexual characteristics of the male but also with some characteristics of the female. Until recently, when it was learned how to distinguish X and Y chromosomes under a microscope, there was no way to know for sure whether hermaphrodites were biologically male or female. Their parents and physicians could only guess. If they guessed

---

To score the test in Figure 10-7, first add up the numbers you have placed next to items 1, 4, 7, 10, 13, 16, 19, 22, 25, 28, 31, 34, 37, 40,43, 46, 49, 52, 55, and 58. Divide the total by 20. The result is your masculinity score. Next add up the numbers next to items 2, 5, 8, 11, 14, 17, 20, 23, 26, 29, 32, 35, 38, 41, 44, 47, 50, 53, 56, and 59. Divide the total by 20. The result is your femininity score. Now subtract the masculinity score from the femininity score and divide the result, which may be plus or minus, by 2.3. You now have your final score, which can be interpreted as follows: Over +2, traditionally feminine in tastes and behavior. Between +1 and +2, "near feminine." Between +1 and −1, mixed or androgynous (for the meaning of which see the text). Between −1 and −2, "near masculine." A minus figure below −2, traditionally masculine in tastes and behavior.

male, then usually the inappropriate female characteristics were surgically removed and the baby was brought up as a boy. If they guessed female, the male traces were removed and the baby was brought up as a girl.

The Johns Hopkins researchers found a number of people who had been born as hermaphrodites and gave them the chromosome test. It turned out that some who had been reared as boys had the X-Y combination and were therefore indeed biologically males—but others had the X-X combination and were actually females. Similarly some reared as girls were indeed X-X and female—but others had the X-Y combination and were actually males. As far as behavior was concerned, however, the chromosomes did not seem to matter. Those who had been brought up as boys acted masculine, whether they were X-Y or X-X. Those brought up as girls acted feminine, even if they were X-Y and biologically male. If you had met any of these people socially or at work, you would never have guessed that there was anything unusual about their sexual identity (Money and Ehrhardt, 1973).

Learning to act masculine or feminine

All in all the evidence seems to show that, despite any inborn tendencies, nurture is the crucial influence. We learn to act masculine or feminine through a process called *sex typing* that occurs throughout the world. Every society assigns different roles to men and women and expects them to behave in different ways and to have different duties, interests, and standing in the community. As the New Guinea example shows, the assigned roles may vary considerably from one society to another. But whatever the particular customs, men are expected to act like men and women like women. They are taught to do so from birth.

A group of psychologists once interviewed parents on the first day of their newborn babies' lives. Half the babies were boys, the other half girls. Tests at the hospital where they were born showed that, as a group, the boys and girls were remarkably alike in every measurable trait. They could not be told apart by appearance, muscle tone, reflexes, or even size. Yet the parents of the boys believed that their babies were outstandingly strong, firm, hardy, alert, and well-coordinated. The parents of the girls described their babies as more delicate, more finely featured, softer, and less inclined to pay attention (Rubin, Provenzano, and Luria, 1974). The psychologists who made the study concluded that the physical and psychological characteristics of babies are mostly "in the eye of the beholder"—and it so happens that the eyes of most beholders look at males and females very differently, not just in the cradle but throughout life.

Parents treat their offspring in many different ways depending on the sex. When cooing to a baby in a crib they use one tone of voice toward a girl, a different one toward a boy. Fathers playing with the baby are cautiously gentle toward a girl, more roughhouse toward a boy (Weitzman, 1975). Mothers in general feed boys more than girls, even on the first day of life (Lewis and Als, 1975). They dress the two sexes differently—even in the case of twins of opposite sex (Brooks and Lewis, 1974). They look at a baby girl more often and talk to her more frequently (Goldberg and Lewis, 1969).

Today's parents seem to be increasingly aware of their role in sex typing. A public opinion poll showed that a majority of Americans—about 56 percent—now believe that men act in masculine ways and women in feminine ways largely because of the "way they were raised and taught to act" rather than because of "basic physical differences between them." There has been a sharp increase in the number of mothers who ask their daughters to help with such traditionally male tasks as household repairs and mowing the lawn, and their sons to help with such traditionally female tasks as cooking and laundry (Roper, 1980). By and large, however, powerful forces are still pushing females in the direction of being "feminine" and males in the direction of being "masculine." Everyone who grows up in our society is bound to feel the pressure.

How parents encourage sex typing without knowing it

Even parents who say they believe in treating the two sexes in the same way make distinctions. Some convincing evidence comes from an experiment with young and theoretically liberated mothers. All these women claimed that boys and girls were alike and should be treated alike. Indeed almost all of them said that they encouraged their girls to be rough-and-tumble and their boys to play with dolls. But their conduct showed otherwise.

Half the mothers were introduced to a 6-month-old baby named Adam and were observed while playing with him in a room that contained a train (typically a male toy), a doll (typically female), and a toy fish (neuter). The mothers usually handed Adam the train.

The other half were observed while playing with a 6-month-old named Beth. These mothers usually handed Beth the doll—and afterward some of them remarked what a sweet and uncomplaining little girl she was. Actually, as you may have guessed, there was only one baby. (It happened to be a boy.) But 6-month-olds look so much alike that none of the mothers caught on. They gave "Adam" the traditional treatment for a boy, "Beth" the traditional treatment for a girl (Will, Self, and Datan, 1974).

Thus we start being sex typed while still in the cradle. As one study put it: "Wittingly or unwittingly, parents encourage and reinforce sex-appropriate behavior, and little boys and girls respond to parental encouragement and reward. So little boys learn to be independent, active, and aggressive; their sisters to be dependent and passive" (Weitzman, 1975).

Pressure from television, books, and schools

Television shows designed for children proclaim the same message: males are the world's movers and shakers, females their meek subordinates. A study of children's programs and the accompanying commercials showed that about three-fourths of all the characters on the screen were male, only one-fourth female. Little boys usually played football, went camping, and played with toy cars and construction sets. Little girls usually played at cooking and keeping house (O'Kelly, 1974).

In children's picture books girls are generally portrayed as passive and doll-like, winning attention and praise only for their attractiveness, working mostly at tasks designed to please and help their brothers and fathers. Boys, on the other hand, are mostly shown as adventuresome, admired for their skill and achievements, and engaging in all kinds of acts requiring independence and self-reliance (Weitzman et al., 1972).

Teachers in nursery schools have been found to follow a similar pattern. In one way or another, often through open praise, they encourage boys to be independent and aggressive, to defend themselves in fights, and in general to be "brave little men." But the girls are praised mostly for their appearance, especially when they wear nice dresses and look feminine (Joffe, 1971). Girls are viewed as considerably more altruistic and helpful than boys—despite the fact that their actual classroom behavior shows no marked differences (Shigetomi, Hartmann, and Gelfand, 1981). Teachers, like parents, often are unaware that they treat the two sexes differently (Serbin and O'Leary, 1975).

In kindergartens and elementary schools, teachers usually encourage boys to play a dominant role in the classroom and girls to take a back seat (Baumrind, 1972). They expect boys to be noisy and often troublesome, but girls to be quiet and well-behaved (Howe, 1971). When they assign chores, they ask boys to stack books and move furniture, girls to serve fruit juice and cookies (Pogrebin, 1972).

Getting the message early

Of course some parents are more likely than others to mold their offspring into the traditional roles of masculinity and femininity (Weitzman, 1975). There are also differences in schools—and in various communities, social classes, and ethnic and racial groups. For example, the early training of black girls seems to encourage considerably more independence than the early training of white girls (Ladner, 1971).

But by and large children have been brought up to believe that women should be pretty and preferably slim, while men should be tall and strong. Women should be passive, nonaggressive, and submissive toward men, while men should be active, aggressive, and dominant. The message sinks in very early. When offered a choice, girls as young as 3 and 4 display their femininity in the kinds of toys they select—the customary dolls, toy stoves, and dish sets. Boys shun such toys and prefer guns, trucks, and cowboy suits (Maccoby and Jacklin, 1974). When the opportunities arise, boys are more likely than girls to take risks (Ginsburg and Miller, 1982).

This girl is acting in accordance with society's expectations for her sex.

Thus from the beginning society has switched your development onto one track if you are female, an altogether different track if you are male. The results are likely to affect your entire cognitive style—the ways you perceive the world and process information (Bem, 1981). The collisions to which this can lead—especially today when the old masculine-feminine traditions are being questioned—will be described in the following sections.

The built-in problems of being female

Until recently in human history it probably was to everyone's advantage for males to act masculine and females to act feminine. In the primitive societies in which humanity lived for countless generations, in fact, survival depended on a division of labor between the sexes. The women, bearing and nursing one child after another, could not roam far from home. Their chief job was as mothers and homemakers. The men were free to range far and wide hunting for animals to provide food. Moreover the men, being physically stronger, protected the home against wild beasts and unfriendly strangers. The tradition was established early and served a purpose. Women were dependent. Men were dominant (Robertson, 1977).

Some social scientists believe that society still operates more smoothly when the sexes specialize in different roles—the male as breadwinner and link between the family and the outside world, the female as the source of affection and support within the family (Parsons and Bales, 1953). Many observers, however, have concluded that there is no longer any need in our modern society for men to be masculine and women to be feminine. They point out that physical strength is no longer important. Very few jobs in the industrial system cannot be performed as well by a woman as by a man. In a world of nuclear weapons, aggressiveness of the kind that can lead to warfare is disastrous. The population explosion has turned large families into a liability instead of an asset—and women, in this age of birth control, have fewer children and more years to live after the last of them has gone to school or left home. Because they are not necessarily immobilized by children and are free to enter the work force, they are no longer dependent on men to support them.

You may reject this argument and prefer to believe that the masculine and feminine roles do serve a purpose. But there can be little doubt that in today's world they do cause trouble and conflict for both sexes. To see how this happens, we can start with the problems the roles create for women.

Putting women down

History tells us that women have never shared equally in society's esteem, praise, privileges, and rewards. In one way or another they were treated as the inferior sex in ancient Egypt, Greece, and Rome—and, on our own continent, by the Indians (Tavris and Offir, 1977). In fact sexual discrimination may have been the first form of social inequality (Robertson, 1977), practiced before people ever thought of discriminating against one another on the basis of race or social class. The division of labor between the sexes has varied from society to society—but, no matter how the jobs were split up, those assigned to men have always been considered more important (Goode, 1965).

Although this pattern may be changing somewhat, it still continues. Note which sex dominates the following pairs of people likely to work together on a daily basis: physician-nurse, dentist-dental hygienist, bank officer-teller, airplane pilot-flight attendant, store manager-sales clerk (England, 1979). Among people in the nation's largest corporations who earn $40,000 a year or more, fewer than 5 percent are women—and no women at all occupy the position of executive officer (Kenny, 1980). Males, perhaps because of their higher status, tend to take prerogatives at work that women do not. They are much more likely to behave in a dominating fashion toward their female co-workers, and to use intimate gestures and sexual innuendos in their personal interactions on the job (Radecki and Jennings, 1980).

The female inferiority complex

Many females grow up with a sort of built-in inferiority complex. By the time they get to kindergarten many of them have already decided that their fathers are more intelligent than their mothers (Ollison, 1975)—an indication of how they feel about the two sexes in general. By high school age their inferiority complex is in full flower. A study made in Baltimore found that girls were much more inclined than boys to be self-conscious, worry about their appearance, have a low opinion of themselves, and wish they could have been members of the opposite sex (Simons and Rosenberg, 1975).

By the time women reach college age many are thoroughly down on themselves. In one study students were asked to predict their grades for the following term. The women were considerably less optimistic than the men—though in this particular group, as it turned out, the women actually did somewhat better (Crandall, 1969). In general college women seem to have less hope for the future, in later life as well as in classes, than men (Frieze, 1975).

Like most victims of an inferiority complex, women tend to have an external locus of control and believe that their fate is determined more by luck than by their own efforts. Some evidence comes from a study of their gambling preferences, in which observers watched what happened at booths at a county fair where customers had a chance to win prizes. It was found that a large majority of men preferred to try games of skill, such as tossing rings. Women, on the other hand, preferred games of sheer chance, such as bingo (Deaux, White, and Farris, 1975).

Suppressing the achievement motive

Perhaps the greatest problem of all for women results from the fact that they are encouraged to give full expression to their motives for affiliation and dependency, but are under pressure to suppress their motives for achievement and hostility. It is not considered feminine to be too

Who says a woman can't do a man's job?

successful, especially at the tasks and jobs that have been regarded as for men only. Nor is it feminine to be competitive and aggressive. And here is where many women find themselves in a bind.

In the past it was common for women, even the most capable ones, to conceal their intelligence, abandon any interest in such masculine subjects as mathematics and science, and either shun a career or settle for such a traditionally feminine job as nursing. Even today, despite affirmative action and scholarship programs, few women pursue careers in scientific and technical fields (U.S. Bureau of Labor Statistics, 1980). Although girls do as well as boys in mathematics in the early grades, fewer females take advanced high school or college math courses and become physicists, engineers, or computer scientists (Meece et al., 1982).

Many women still accept the idea of being second-class citizens, bound to defer and cater to men. Such behavior discourages a woman from becoming a self-reliant person, living by her own inner desires rather than by what society seems to expect and want. Indeed it has been suggested that the traditional standards for femininity call for a "compliant, dependent, self-effacing personality" that is likely to be accompanied by "neurotic needs and vulnerabilities" (Block, Von Der Lippe, and Block, 1973). One psychoanalyst has pointed out cases of women who become so crippled that they are afraid to assert themselves, be spontaneous, or try such new experiences as flying or driving an automobile (Symonds, 1974). To complicate matters, a woman seeking help often encounters a male psychotherapist who provides treatment "aimed at reducing her complaints about the quality of her life and promoting adjustment to the existing order" (Carmen, Russo, and Miller, 1981).

The housewife's conflict

Of course many women genuinely prefer to be housewives and full-time mothers (Gass, 1974). They are not self-effacing or neurotic at all. They simply would rather take care of a house and bring up their children than perform work of other kinds. They find that being a housewife-mother provides ample satisfaction for their achievement motives and the most gratifying kind of self-fulfillment.

A sociologist who made a large-scale study of housewives in the Chicago area found that many of them regarded their roles as "self-expressive and creative"—a chance to build a richer and more varied way of life than they could attain in most jobs available in the business world. They enjoyed the freedom and challenge of being their own bosses. They saw their relationships with their husbands as a matter not of domination and submission but of developing a deep intimacy "suited to the unique needs of both personalities." They found motherhood to be a stimulating challenge demanding skill, creativity, and leadership (Lopata, 1972).

It should be noted, however, that even the happy housewife is likely to experience conflict in today's world. So much has been written about the rebellion of modern women against the traditional feminine role that a woman who accepts any part of the role is almost bound to experience self-doubts. Perhaps she does not really enjoy being a housewife and mother. Perhaps she can never be as self-fulfilled as women who prefer careers to homemaking. She may even, by failing to take a more active part in the rebellion, be a traitor to her sex. She finds herself pulled in opposite directions—one by a tradition that seems also to gratify her own most basic desires, the other by today's emphasis on casting off the old feminine shackles. As Figure 10-8 shows, a substantial number of women actually oppose efforts to change women's status in society. Among them are women who believe on religious or philosophical grounds that the traditional sex roles and status are the natural order of things—or who, happy with their life-style, believe that any change would do them more harm than good.

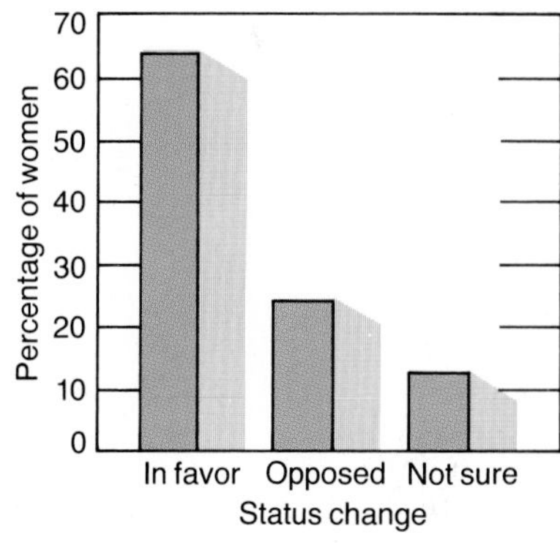

Figure 10-8 How women feel about women's status *In a 1980 public opinion poll, nearly two-thirds of all American women said they favored "efforts to strengthen and change women's status in society." But a surprisingly large minority of women—nearly one-fourth—were opposed. The figures for men were almost exactly the same (Roper, 1980).*

Many women, regardless of whether they have chosen the role of wife and mother or a career outside the home, seem to find their position unsatisfactory and regret the way they are living their lives. In one survey, 30 percent of women not employed outside the home said they would rather be working. But of the women with full-time jobs exactly the same 30 percent said they would rather be staying home (Roper, 1980). The two roles have such a profound effect on the way a woman lives that each has great advantages and grave disadvantages. Having to choose between them can lead to serious doubts and regrets.

The liberated woman's conflict

What about the women who are most dedicated to the ideas of liberation—those who have rebelled most sharply against traditional standards of femininity, who deplore the thought of devoting their lives to taking care of a house, a husband, and children, who want full independence both financially and psychologically? They too feel the pull of tradition. Brought up to be feminine, they developed inner standards calling for them to suppress the motives for achievement and hostility. These ingrained standards are hard to shake. Even the attempt to do so is likely to produce anxiety.

Thus even the most liberated women are likely to wonder at times if they would be more fulfilled if they became full-time housekeepers and mothers. They may also worry about how society in general—and men in particular—will react if they persist in being ambitious and competitive. This was shown in a study at a women's college in New Jersey that places strong emphasis on courses and issues related to the liberation movement. It was found that a considerable majority of the women at this school believed that a wife's career was as important as the husband's and that both should contribute equally to the family's finances. The majority wanted to work all their lives, wanted their husbands to share in the housekeeping, and rejected the idea that "the most important thing for a woman is to be a good wife and mother." But they also felt that men would not want to marry a woman who held such liberated views. Since most of them wanted marriage and children besides a career, they were caught in a conflict and "probably experiencing considerable anxiety about their futures" (Parelius, 1975).

Such anxiety seems to be justified—for relationships between men and women are currently surrounded by considerable doubt. A growing number of women—especially the young and college educated—are rebelling against their sex typing and determined to express their achievement motives by having careers. But American men, although most of them now say they favor a higher status for women (Roper, 1980), still are inclined to think of marriage in terms of the customary masculine and feminine roles.

The built-in problems of being male

Sex typing clearly creates conflicts for women in our society. Less well publicized is the fact that sex typing also creates conflicts for men. It is not easy to be as masculine as society has urged men to be. Nor is it easy to rebel against the masculine role—which for most men is as deeply ingrained an inner standard as femininity is for most women.

There is even more pressure on boys to be masculine than on girls to be feminine. Most families urge boys to be "little men" even before they have any idea what it means to be a man. They are constantly warned not to act like girls, not to cry, not to be "sissies." Most people have always considered it worse for a boy to be a sissy than for a girl to be a tomboy—and this opinion appears to persist among college students, both male and female (Feinman, 1974). The problem this creates for young male children has been summed up in these words:

> The little boy is asked to do something which is not clearly defined for him, based on reasons he cannot possibly appreciate, and enforced with threats, punishment, and anger by those who are close to him. . . . Anxiety frequently expresses itself in over-straining to be masculine, in virtual panic at being caught doing anything traditionally defined as feminine (Hartley, 1959).

Suppressing the affiliation and dependency motives

The male conflict between motives is exactly the opposite of the female conflict. Boys and men are encouraged—often overencouraged—to express their motives for achievement and hostility. They are expected to welcome every opportunity to leap into competition. But they are expected to suppress their motives for affiliation and dependency and to suppress or at least conceal their emotions, especially any tender or vulnerable feelings. They have to keep a stiff upper lip—avoiding any show of fear or grief—even in the face of the most drastic kind of disappointment or tragedy.

The struggle to play the masculine role can be fraught with anxieties. The motives for affiliation and dependency are universal. So are the emotions that accompany them. Society's demand to suppress them is in effect a demand to "transcend your humanity." And efforts to do so can never completely succeed: "Since it is impossible to program out all emotions, even the most extreme he-man can only approximate" the masculine ideal (Stevens, 1974). Thus every man—aware of the stirrings of the softer and weaker emotions he tries so dutifully to hide—is bound to worry about his own masculinity.

Some of these players may find that proving their masculinity is a heavy burden.

The male burden of proof

Girls and women are considered feminine unless they display overwhelming evidence to the contrary, but boys and men have to win the right to be called masculine. They have to *prove* their masculinity; they have to face and succeed in all kinds of "financial, intellectual, sexual, and physical tests" (Stevens, 1974). The testing process starts early and continues throughout life. At different ages and in different environments, the requirements vary. Boys may have to prove themselves by being athletic or by being tough, men by making a lot of money or by being a man's man in whatever way this is defined by their associates. But the burden of proof is always present—and the burden is heavier than most people think:

> It is a strain for women to have to act weaker, more dependent and submissive, and less competent than they really are, but it's probably a greater strain to have to act tougher, stronger, more dominant, and more competent than one really feels inside. It is also a strain to have one's masculine status constantly dependent on success at work and providing well for a family of dependents (Skolnick and Skolnick, 1974).

The burden of being superior

While women grow up with a tendency toward built-in inferiority complexes, men are sex typed into thinking of themselves as superior. For all the secret self-doubts they may have, they have been taught that they are the better of the two sexes, destined by birth to be lord and master. This has its obvious advantages—yet it too can be a burden. Robert Seidenberg, a psychoanalyst, has made these observations:

> It is quite probable that men become victims of their own advantages. An unearned superiority is thrust on them. This places a constant burden of

> proof upon them which causes distortions of character and personality which are tragic to behold. The man is placed, often through no need or desire of his own, in a position of proving why he, of two people, should automatically be the standard bearer of the family. Often, to prove his doubtful superiority, he must resort to pseudo self-enhancement such as uncalled-for bravery, cunning, tricks, and outmoded feats of courage. . . . Men ultimately suffer the corruption of unearned victories and ascendancy. Their personalities become warped by the myth of their own dominance and superiority (Seidenberg, 1970).

One study of senior men in a Midwest university found that many of them planned high-level and difficult careers even though they had not done well in their classes and had not received much encouragement from their teachers, counselors, or friends. Since their ambitions apparently exceeded their abilities, the study concluded, these men ran a considerable risk of "dissatisfaction and frustration with their chosen careers" (Stake and Levitz, 1979).

How is a man supposed to act toward a woman who is obviously as intelligent and well-educated as he is—perhaps even more so? A survey of Ivy League seniors showed that many of them felt extremely uncomfortable in such a situation. About 30 percent conceded that they had felt intellectually insecure or under strain. Some had simply decided to avoid such women. Others had mixed feelings. They wanted intellectual companionship with women but found it threatening (Komarovsky, 1973). It has been observed that the pressure to live up to the demands for male superiority may cause a man never to marry, lest his wife discover that he is all too human beneath his grandiose pretenses. If he does marry, he usually chooses an extremely submissive woman whom he can keep in a state of awe—and with whom, because he never exposes his own feelings, he never achieves any intimacy at all (Anderson, 1981).

It is perhaps as difficult to be automatically typed as superior as to be automatically typed as inferior. Men as well as women suffer anxieties over the way they are sex typed to perform—which may be totally at odds with their own motives and emotions, not to mention their physical strength and other capabilities. The traditional standards of masculinity and femininity may still serve a purpose or may have become obsolete—but as long as they continue to influence human behavior they will cause inner conflicts for both sexes, as well as some open conflicts between them.

SUMMARY OF SUPPLEMENT

What it means to be masculine or feminine

1. All societies expect men to be masculine and women to be feminine. Our society has traditionally defined masculine as being aggressive, independent, and dominant, feminine as being unaggressive, dependent, and submissive.
2. Differences in behavior between the two sexes may depend in part on the effects of the different hormones produced by the sex glands, including possibly early programing of the brain.

3. Most differences in behavior appear to be the result of *sex typing,* or learning what society expects of males and females. Although parents tend to treat boys and girls more equally than in the past, they still exert a powerful force in sex typing their children.
4. Sex typing begins at birth and is promoted by children's television, books, and schools.

The built-in problems of being female

5. The feminine role into which women are sex typed calls for what has been called a "compliant, dependent, self-effacing personality." As a result, many women acquire an inferiority complex and belief in external locus of control, and they suppress the achievement motive.

The built-in problems of being male

6. The masculine role into which men are sex typed calls for suppression of the affiliation and dependency motives and for constant proof of superiority.
7. The traditional standards of masculinity and femininity cause inner conflicts for both sexes and open conflicts between them.

IMPORTANT TERMS

androgens
androgynous
estrogen
feminine
masculine
sex typing

RECOMMENDED READINGS

Atkinson, J. W., and Raynor, J. O. *Personality, motivation, and achievement.* New York: Wiley, 1978

Buck R. *Human motivation and emotion.* New York: Wiley, 1976.

Cattell, R. B., and Kline, P. *The scientific analysis of personality and motivation.* New York: Academic Press, 1976.

Heilbrun, A. B. *Human sex-role behavior.* New York: Pergamon Press, 1981.

McClelland, D. C. *Power: the inner experience.* New York: Halsted, 1975.

Parsons, J. *The psychobiology of sex differences and sex roles.* New York: McGraw-Hill, 1980.

Toates, F. M., and Halliday, T. R., eds. *Analysis of motivational processes.* New York: Academic Press, 1981.

Weiner, B. *Achievement motive and attribution theory.* Morristown, N.J.: General Learning Press, 1974.

Winter, D. G. *The power motive.* New York: Free Press, 1973

Zillman, D. *Hostility and aggression.* New York: Wiley, 1979.

PART

6

Human Personality: Sources, Problems, and Strengths

Pat is a kind, friendly, and competent young woman. She is a good student and fine tennis player, loved by her family and admired by her friends—the kind of person most of us have in mind when we use the word "normal."

Mark is always the star performer in his class. But he is constantly tense and on guard, relentlessly striving for perfection. A "loner" whose days and nights are scarred by insecurity and self-doubt, he often feels that life is an uphill, anxiety-filled battle.

Helen is a high school dropout with a growing police record. She is awash in anger and suspicion, and her existence seems without meaning or purpose. Lately she has withdrawn from the world entirely. She spends most of her time in her room, unkempt and mumbling to herself.

How did these three human beings get that way? Was it an accident of heredity—a chance spin of the roulette wheel of genes and chromosomes? Or was it the environment into which they were thrust at birth?

This section of the book discusses what psychology has learned about the many factors—both hereditary and environmental—that tend to make people aggressive or passive, friendly or withdrawn, depressed or optimistic, focused on achievement or mired in self-criticism and defeat. It is concerned with the origins and complexities of the human personality, over the broad spectrum from the successful to the abnormal, and the reasons some people seem able to withstand

the most shattering misfortunes while others fall apart under far less pressure.

Chapter 11 describes the powerful effect on personality of two forces, anxiety and stress, that are closely related to emotions, motives, frustration, and conflict. These two potentially damaging factors, you will see, are a universal and unavoidable part of living. And our psychological well-being depends on how we cope with them, for better or for worse.

Chapter 12 discusses abnormal behavior, the unfortunate result of unsuccessful attempts to deal with anxiety and stress. The chapter explains how the symptoms, depending on the individual's physical and psychological characteristics, range all the way from mild peculiarities to total disintegration.

Chapter 13 discusses psychology's theories, many of them derived from studies of abnormal behavior, of the origins and nature of the human personality. The chapter also describes the many varied methods of psychotherapy that clinical psychologists and psychiatrists have developed in their attempts to help troubled people whose own efforts to cope with serious problems have failed. Together, the three chapters in this section summarize what psychology has discovered about the rich and variegated pattern of the human personality, its sources, its problems—and above all the surprising amount of strength and resiliency that it somehow manages to display, frequently against seemingly hopeless odds.

CHAPTER 11

Anxiety and its effect on behavior 398
- Some anxiety-provoking situations
- Uncertainty as a source of anxiety
- General and specific anxiety
- The effect of anxiety on social behavior
- The effect of anxiety on learning and grades
- Anxiety and risk taking

The wear and tear of stress 405
- Stress and the general adaptation syndrome
- Psychosomatic illnesses
- Who gets sick and who doesn't?—differences in stressful experiences
- Differences in resistance to stress
- High blood pressure, the power motive, and anger
- Selye's prescription for staying healthy
- The psychological effects of stress

Successful coping and normal behavior 414
- Assertive coping
- The normal personality

Defense mechanisms and other questionable forms of coping 418
- Rationalization
- Repression
- Sublimation
- Identification
- Reaction formation
- Projection
- The pro and con of defense mechanisms
- Aggression as a response to anxiety and stress
- Withdrawal and apathy
- Regression

Summary 425

Important terms 426

Recommended readings 427

Psychology and Society
- Stress, illness, and the role of the physician 410
- Wouldn't it be nice to be the kind of person who never suffers stress? (Or would it?) 412
- The Vietnam POWs, stress, and survival 416
- What it means to be normal: some comforting advice 419

Anxiety, Stress, and Coping

After weeks of anticipation, you face your first day on a new job. It is a job you fought hard to get, but now the prospect seems strangely ominous and bleak. Worse yet, you cannot understand why you should feel this way—so you try to think of plausible reasons. Will you succeed? Will you like the people you work with? Will your boss be fair? Will the work turn out to be as interesting as you thought? One by one, you easily dismiss these questions, but you cannot dismiss the threatening emotional cloud that follows you to work. As you leave your car and approach your new office, you would have little trouble describing how you feel: worried, wound up, nervous, tense, "jumpy." All these terms are attempts to label what psychologists call *anxiety,* an emotion that has far-reaching effects on human personality and behavior.

Anxiety is likely to arise whenever the future is shrouded in uncertainty and doubt. You may experience it when you come to class to take an important exam, sit in the doctor's office waiting to learn what your X rays and lab tests show, or drive on the highway and suddenly see the flashing light of a police car looming behind you. Even astronauts, trained for years to face their task, show evidence of anxiety as they sit at their controls, knowing that in a few seconds they will blast off into the void of space. Although everyone does not use the same words to describe anxiety, all of us know firsthand what it feels like—and that it can affect the way we function.

All of us have also encountered periods when the pressures and strains of life pile up and seem almost unbearable. A law school student described such a situation. "I have three exams next week, and I'm told my whole career can depend on the grades I get. But I have to spend precious time hunting for a summer job or else I'll never be able to pay my debts. Meanwhile I'm struggling with a big decision. My girlfriend wants us to get married now, but I think we should wait until I finish law school. Life seems almost too much for me." The familiar result for this student was distressing physical symptoms—a racing heart, shortness of breath, trembling hands, queasy stomach, and headaches. When this happens, we are experiencing what psychologists call *stress,* the body's reactions to outside pressures. When the strains of life become too severe or overwhelming, the stress they cause may take the form of physical illness and even death.

The psychological experience of anxiety and the physiological states of stress are two powerful influences on human behavior. Life being what it is, we cannot avoid them. We are bound to encounter them many times in the natural course of events. If we seriously fail to cope

This man, under pressure to decide on a course of action, is a likely victim of anxiety.

with them, we may get physically sick or lapse into the kinds of abnormal behavior described in the next chapter. Most of us, however, learn to cope—and thus not only keep our bodily well-being and our behavior within normal bounds, but even face life with reasonable optimism and zest. Our ability to do so is evidence of the surprising strength and resilience of the human personality.

Anxiety and its effect on behavior

Anxiety can be defined as *a vague, unpleasant feeling accompanied by a premonition that something undesirable is about to happen.* The feeling is closely related to the emotion of fear. Indeed it is very difficult to draw a sharp dividing line between them. The only difference is that usually fear is a reaction to a specific stimulus and has a "right now" quality about it. (We see a snake, know exactly what we are afraid of, and recognize that we are afraid right here and now.) Anxiety ordinarily does not have an obvious cause and is not so much concerned with the here and now as with some future unpleasantness. (When we arrive on a new job, we have no idea what lies in store for us or why we should worry about it.)

The vagueness of anxiety makes it particularly difficult to handle. We usually cannot explain why we feel as we do or what it is that we fear may happen. Yet, for some unexplained reason, we find ourselves in the grip of the most uncomfortable of emotions. Our feelings can be intensely painful or can become chronic like a dull toothache, interfering over long periods with our sleep, appetite, and moods. The word *jumpy*, often applied to the feelings, is especially apt—for people plagued by anxiety are likely to have a lower threshold for other kinds of emotional response. They may be irritable and quickly moved to anger, and they may also overreact to pleasurable stimuli. They tend to have wide swings of mood and their behavior is often unpredictable.

Some anxiety-provoking situations

Although the causes of anxiety are difficult to pinpoint, there appear to be five situations in which it is most likely to occur:

1. We have conflicting motives. (Such as wanting to dedicate our lives to helping others, yet at the same time wanting to make a lot of money.)
2. We experience a conflict between our behavior and an inner standard. (As when we do something we believe to be wrong.)
3. We encounter some unusual event that we cannot immediately understand and adjust to. (For example, when arriving on a new campus, not knowing what kind of behavior is expected.)
4. We are faced with events whose outcome is unpredictable. (For example, the score we will make on an important test.)
5. We confront the loss of a beloved person. (For example, when a spouse or parent becomes desperately ill.)

In all these cases, the emotion of anxiety is clearly related to motives. In situations 1 and 2, it is produced by a conflict between motives or between a motive and an inner standard. In situations 3 and 4 it is produced by frustration of the motive for certainty. And in situation 5, it is produced by frustration of the affiliation motive.

Uncertainty as a source of anxiety

Circumstances that provoke anxiety vary among individuals. But any situation that is clouded with uncertainty—not knowing what will happen, not knowing what is expected, not knowing the best course of action—has a built-in potential for creating anxiety. The most striking demonstration of this fact comes from an experiment that had totally unexpected and at first glance mysterious results. The subjects, all college men, were asked to listen to a voice counting to 15. At the count of 10, they were told, they might receive an electric shock. Whether or not this would happen depended on the draw of 1 card from a pack of 20, which was shown to them. For one group, the deck contained only 1 shock card and 19 no-shock cards—so that these subjects knew their chances of shock were only 1 in 20, or 5 percent. For the second group, the chances were 50 percent. For the third group, the chances were 95 percent.

As the counting began, measurements were made of the subjects' physiological arousal, which presumably indicated the amount of anxiety they experienced. Common sense suggested that the group with the 50 percent chance of shock would show the most anxiety. The 5 percent group would feel relatively safe, and the 95 percent group would consider themselves almost certain to receive a shock and would be reconciled to it. Even the experimenters expected this result. To their amazement, however, the 5 percent group showed by far the most anxiety, as illustrated in Figure 11-1.

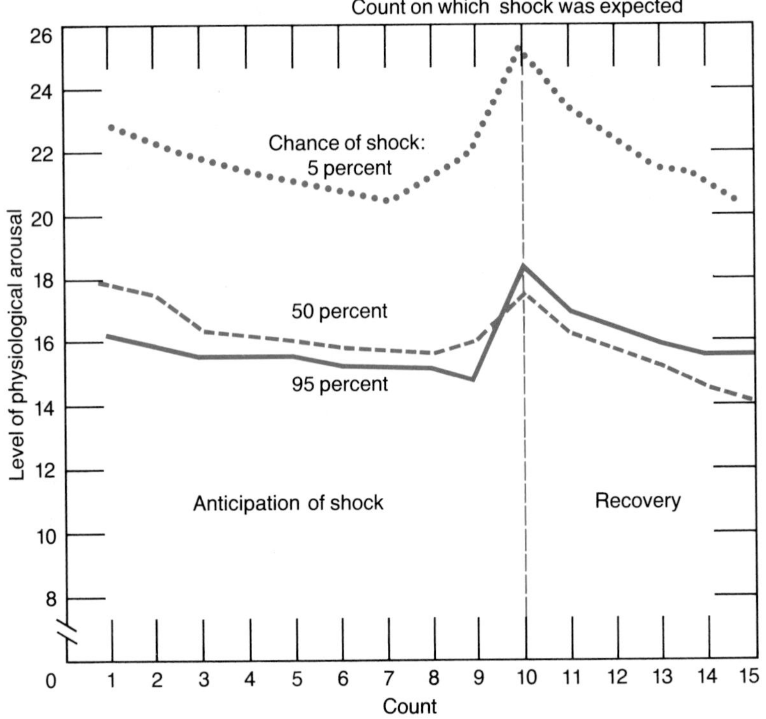

Figure 11-1 An experiment with surprising results *Subjects who had only a 5 percent chance of receiving a shock at the count of 10 showed more physiological arousal—hence presumably more anxiety—than subjects who had a 50 percent chance or a 95 percent chance. The measure of physiological arousal shown here is electrical conductivity of the skin, affected by activity of the sweat glands (Epstein and Roupenian, 1970). For an explanation of this unexpected result, see the text.*

Why should this have happened? The answer lies in the comments of the 50 percent group. These subjects said they decided that their chances of getting a shock were high enough to lead them to expect it—thus reducing the uncertainty—and merely to hope they would be spared. Thus they felt very much like the subjects in the 95 percent group, who were almost sure to get a shock. The subjects in the 5 percent group, on the other hand, experienced much more uncertainty. They felt that their chances of getting a shock were so low that they could not expect and reconcile themselves to it. Yet neither could they dismiss the possibility. It was this greater uncertainty that made them experience the greatest anxiety of all.

Another example of anxiety caused by uncertainty may occur in a noisy environment. Noise in itself does not usually create problems. We may find it distracting at first but usually adapt to it quickly. For most people, even exposure to frequent noise such as airplanes flying low overhead does not lead to serious difficulties (Tarnopolsky, Watkins, and Hand, 1980). But when we are working at a difficult task such as studying for an exam, noise can produce anxiety if it occurs at unpredictable intervals. We become vigilant and edgy—waiting, so to speak, for the other shoe to drop.

In general, the more information people have as they prepare to face an anxiety-provoking experience, the better they feel. But the result appears to depend to some degree on how apprehensive they are to begin with. For those who are very anxious, information about what lies in store may actually increase the problem. In one study, a group of women, about to have their hands immersed in painfully cold water, received detailed information about what to expect. The information helped reduce the anxiety of those who were not overconcerned about the experience—but it compounded the anxiety of women who approached the experiment with extreme foreboding (McCaul, 1980).

General and specific anxiety

Many studies have been made of anxiety and its effects. One finding is that some people seem to display anxiety in many of the situations they face. They feel anxious regardless of whether they are working in their classroom or job, taking part in a social event, picking up the telephone, shopping, or even starting a vacation. They worry about many things and have a vague uneasiness about all future events. Such people are victims of *general anxiety*. Others display only *specific anxiety* in some particular situation but not at other times (Spielberger, 1971). One well-known example is stage fright, which strikes many people who are otherwise generally free of anxiety. A type of specific anxiety often found among college students has to do with taking tests. *Test anxiety*, as it is called, is so common that it has been one of the most widely studied of all forms. Investigators have found that it can be relieved—and performance on tests can often be improved—by such measures as relaxation training and practice at concentrating on the test itself rather than on one's inner feelings (Wine, 1971).

Both general and specific anxiety seem to feed on themselves. The victim, having become anxious, is painfully aware of the signs of emotional arousal (increased heart rate, butterflies in the stomach)—and the very awareness increases the amount of anxiety. Relaxation training presumably counteracts this vicious circle. So do biofeedback techniques, which can be used to recognize and control internal bodily changes associated with anxiety (Rice and Blanchard, 1982). One experiment showed that even such a simple device as deliberately controlling one's breathing, to half the normal rate, can significantly lower some of the physiological signs of anxiety and the feelings of anxiety as well (McCaul, Solomon, and Holmes, 1979).

A class in relaxation training designed to relieve feelings of anxiety.

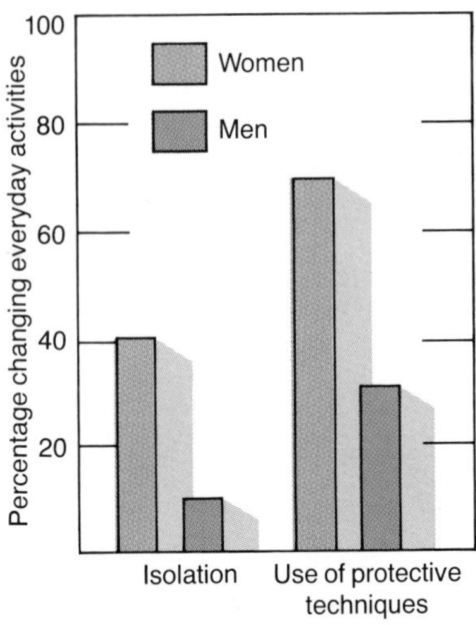

Figure 11-2 Anxiety: the difference it can make in everyday activities *The bars show that women—because they are more fearful of crime than men—are much more likely to alter their social behavior. They are four times more likely to isolate themselves—to avoid public transportation and parks and to stay home after dark. They are well over twice as likely to adopt unusual protective tactics such as wearing shoes that make it easier to run, or choosing their bus seat to avoid passengers who look dangerous (Riger and Gordon, 1981).*

Anxiety is also relieved by alcohol and by such tranquilizers as Valium and Librium, presumably because these drugs reduce the activity of the brain's neurotransmitter noradrenaline. However, researchers point out that the relief is obtained at a price. Any antianxiety drug reduces the ability to cope realistically with the environment by meeting changes and challenges (Gray, 1978).

The effect of anxiety on social behavior

Some people manage to hide any outward signs of anxiety, but it is such a powerful emotion that it often affects social behavior—at times to a significant extent. One timely study measured the way anxiety over crime influenced the everyday lives of people in Chicago, San Francisco, and Philadelphia. It was found that well over twice as many women as men were concerned about being harmed by criminals. (Fear of rape probably explains much of the difference.) Moreover, as is shown in Figure 11-2, women were twice as likely as men to isolate themselves from others and to take unusual measures to protect themselves when they were outside their home. Thus it appeared that fear of crime severely limited the women's social behavior, narrowing their choices of where to go and what to do in order to feel safe.

Behavior resulting from anxiety, of course, is not always logical or sensible. The precautions the women in this study were found to take did not necessarily guarantee their safety—for attacks often occur in the home (McDermott, 1979). Indeed anxiety can lead to behavior that is so far removed from reality that it must be considered abnormal, as will be explained in the next chapter.

The effect of anxiety on learning and grades

Of particular interest to college students is the influence of anxiety on the ability to learn and on grades. Does it promote learning by increasing the desire to learn? Or does it interfere with learning?

Insofar as the facts can be determined, it appears that people high in anxiety do better than others at simple learning tasks but more poorly than others at difficult learning tasks (O'Neil, Spielberger, and Hansen, 1969). Presumably their anxiety impairs the intense concentration required for the learning of complicated materials. They seem distracted, as if their anxiety forces them to focus on the way they feel rather than on the tasks at hand (Holyrod et al., 1978). People high in anxiety seem to do particularly badly at learning when someone is watching them. Their performance at even simple learning tasks usually goes down sharply in the presence of an observer, while people low in anxiety do just about as well when watched as when alone (Ganzer, 1968).

How does anxiety affect actual performance in college? This question was explored by an investigator who selected one group of male students who appeared to be relatively high in anxiety and another group relatively low in anxiety. He examined their college board scores, as an indication of their ability, and their actual grades in college. He found that students with the lowest levels of scholastic ability made approximately the same grades regardless of whether they were high or low in

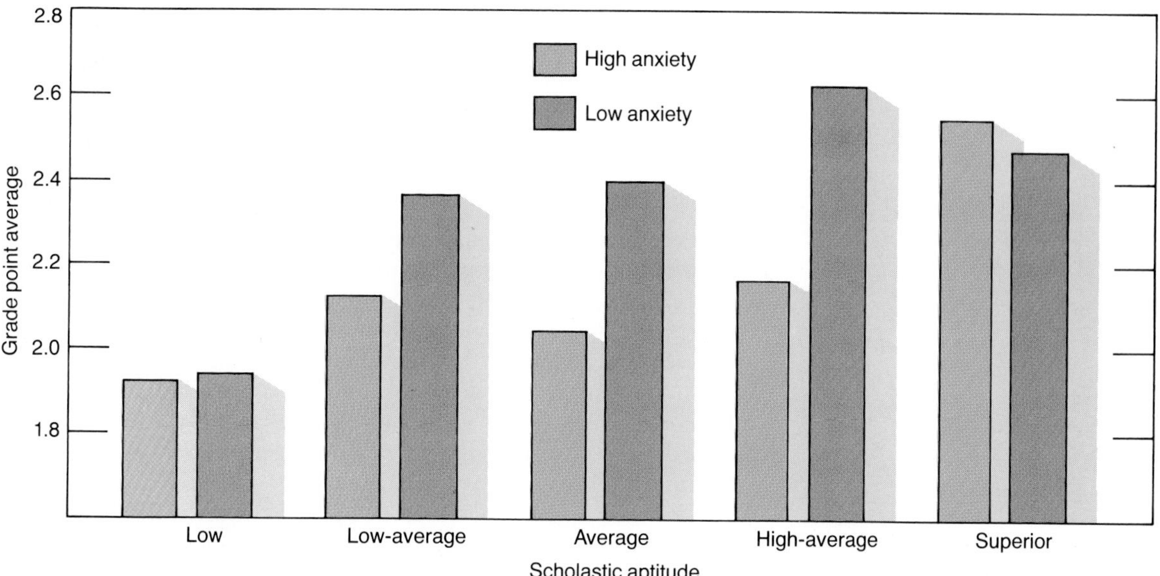

anxiety. So did students with the highest levels of scholastic ability. But at the in-between levels of ability—where, of course, most students fall—the students who were low in anxiety made significantly better grades than did the anxious students. Full results of the study appear in Figure 11-3.

Figure 11-3 Anxiety and performance in college *The bars show the average grades made by high-anxiety and low-anxiety students of different levels of scholastic ability as indicated by their college board scores. Note the pronounced differences found between the two groups at the middle ranges of scholastic ability (Spielberger, 1962).*

A follow-up study was made with anxious freshmen who were making such low grades that they were in danger of flunking out of college. One group of these freshmen took an active part in a counseling program in which they received advice about their problems in college, methods of study, campus life in general, and their relations with professors—advice that presumably would reduce their anxiety about the college situation. Another group, matched as closely as possible for college board scores, type of high school attended, and other factors that influence performance in college, did not receive counseling. From midterm to the end of the first semester the counseled group made an average improvement of more than half a grade point. The group that was not counseled improved by less than a tenth of a grade point (Spielberger, Denny, and Weitz, 1962). Anxiety about the college situation appears to be a frequent—though perhaps correctable—cause of failure in college. Anxiety about a particularly difficult subject such as mathematics can also be reduced with treatment, leading to improved performance (Bander, Russell, and Zamostny, 1982).

Another recent study suggests that the relationship between anxiety and learning can work in reverse as well—that we can become anxious because we are having trouble learning rather than the other way around. This study found that students in an advanced psychology course who were very anxious about tests did well enough on multiple-choice questions but had difficulty on short-answer questions, essay questions, and take-home exams—all of which require a more comprehensive recall of what has been learned. The students also reported problems in learning new material and picking out important points in reading assignments. The researchers concluded that the anxiety resulted from an inadequate grasp of the subject matter, and suggested that the students might be helped as much by acquiring new learning strategies as by practicing anxiety-reducing techniques (Benjamin et al., 1981).

Anxiety and risk taking

One characteristic that influences the way people live their lives is the amount of risk they are willing to take. Some people are very conservative and hate to go out on a limb. Others seem to be born gamblers who take all kinds of chances. There appears to be a strong relationship between this refusal or readiness to take risks and anxiety.

An experiment that demonstrates this fact is illustrated in Figure 11-4. Note that subjects who appeared to be relatively free from anxiety tended to scorn the "sure thing" in the game that was used in the experiment. They made very few throws from the close distances where they were almost certain to succeed but would receive only a low score. They also tended to avoid the high risk of gambling that they could score from the longest distances, where they would have received the highest scores. Subjects who appeared to be relatively high in test anxiety made many more shots from the short distances and also "went for broke" more often by trying from the longest distances.

The experiment suggests that people who are highly anxious about success and failure tend to adopt either a very conservative or a very risky strategy in life situations. They are inclined to settle for the sure thing and thus avoid failure that would add to their anxiety, or else they tend to take the chances at which success is so unlikely that they can readily excuse their failure. You have probably observed people who take few chances in life, settle for jobs that seem beneath their abilities, and yet take an occasional flier in a gambling casino or a risky investment. Less anxious people, on the other hand, seem to have enough confidence to take the middle-range risks that are most likely to lead to success in the long run.

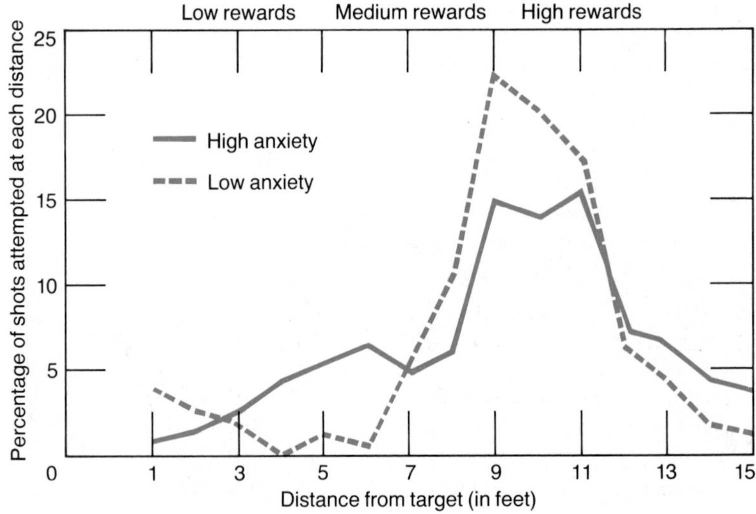

Figure 11-4 Anxiety, conservatism, and "going for broke" *Two groups of subjects played an experimental game in which they tossed rings at a peg, trying from any distance they chose. They were told that for ringing the peg from close distances they would receive low scores, from middle distances middle scores, and from far distances very high scores. Note that subjects who had been found low in anxiety chose a strategy of intermediate risks. Those who had been found high in anxiety tended to be either very conservative or to go for broke (Atkinson et al., 1960).*

Similarly, it has been observed that college students highly anxious about failure tend to leave examination rooms early (Atkinson and Litwin, 1960), as if to avoid the further anxiety of continued effort. This behavior, of course, only increases the probability that they will actually experience the failure they find such a disturbing prospect.

The wear and tear of stress

To psychologists, as has been said, the term *stress* applies to the body's reactions to outside pressures—in other words, to the physiological wear and tear caused by attempting to adjust to events that cause emotional and other forms of arousal. In everyday language, of course, the word is also applied to the events themselves. Psychologists often refer to such events as *stressors.* The fact that many situations place a serious burden on the human organism has gained popular recognition in all the references made today to the "stress and strain" of modern life. Even people who have never taken a psychology course acknowledge that our society puts all of us under severe and often painful pressure caused by competition (for acceptance to college, grades, jobs, and promotions) and by social demands, worries about economic security and the possibility of war, crowded streets, and many similar concerns. People disillusioned with modern life often use the contemptuous term "rat race"—implying that existence has become a constant, mindless struggle for a prize of dubious value.

There is no question that modern life is filled with stressors of various sorts. Many events that are commonplace in our daily lives have been found to produce signs of stress even in lower animals. Exposure to noise—a standard feature of city life—raises the blood pressure of rats. Dogs that are raised in isolation and then suddenly introduced into a normal environment exhibit a long-lasting fear that makes them incapable of appropriate behavior (Fuller, 1967). The human counterpart would be the abrupt shift of environment we experience when changing schools, jobs, or places of residence—or even the more general kinds

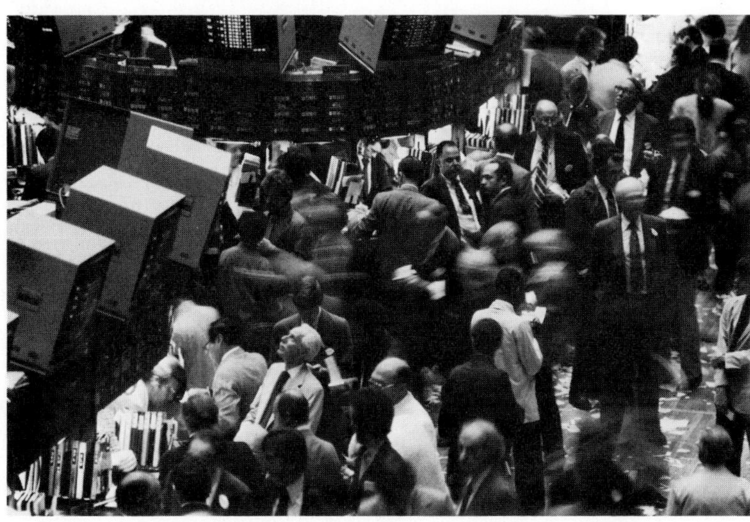

These people, whether making or losing money in the stock market, are being exposed to emotional tensions—a potential source of stress.

of rapid change that have been occurring in technology, economics, and politics.

Whether life is really more difficult today than in the past, however, is dubious. Human beings have always been subject to conditions that cause stress. At one time the pressures came from fighting the elements and the animals and scrambling frantically for the next meal. Throughout history our ancestors were beset by pain, illness, and the danger of violent death. Today's sources of stress, though different, may be no more burdensome than those of the past—and indeed may actually be less so for many people. There is no way of knowing for sure.

Psychologists define stress as *the body's reaction to anything that threatens to damage the organism.* Stress can be caused by a disease germ, air and noise pollution, or the physical danger faced by a football player or a steeplejack. It can accompany any situation that produces anxiety, frustration, or conflict and therefore the physical wear and tear of intense or prolonged emotion. Thus stress depends not only on outside events but on our own feelings as we react to them. One person may experience severe stress over an event that leaves another person relatively calm.

Stress and the general adaptation syndrome

The damaging potential of stress, whatever its origin, was dramatically demonstrated by Hans Selye, who experimented with animals and exposed them to stressful physical conditions, such as the injection of poison in doses not quite strong enough to kill. The results, however, seem to be much the same as those produced in human beings by any form of external or internal pressure, including prolonged anxiety or other emotional tension.

Selye found that when an animal was injected with poison, its body automatically tried to defend itself. Most notably, its endocrine glands immediately sprang into action (as they also do in human emotional arousal). The adrenal glands in particular showed striking changes. They became enlarged and produced more adrenalin. They also discharged their stored-up supply of the hormones known as steroids, which make many contributions to the body's well-being. Because of this high level of activity of the adrenal glands, numerous physical changes occurred in the animals. For example, tissue was broken down into sugar to provide energy. The amount of salt normally found in the bloodstream was sharply reduced.

After a few days of continued exposure to stress-producing conditions, the animals seemed to adapt. The adrenal glands returned to normal size and began to renew their supply of steroids. The salt level in the blood rose to normal or even higher. Apparently the animals had adjusted to the situation and were perfectly normal.

Their recovery, however, was only temporary. After several weeks of continued pressure, the adrenal glands again became enlarged and lost their stores of steroids. The level of salt in the blood fell drastically. The kidneys, as a result of receiving an excess of hormones, underwent some complicated and damaging changes. Eventually the animals died, as if from exhaustion. They had been killed, so to speak, by an excess of the hormones they had produced in their own defense.

Another of Selye's important findings was that even during the period of apparent recovery, the animals were not so normal as they seemed. If a second source of stress was introduced during this period, the animals quickly died. In attempting to adapt to the original source of stress, apparently they had used their defenses to the maximum and were helpless against a new form of pressure (Selye, 1956).

To describe the sequence of events that takes place during prolonged stress—the initial shock or alarm, the recovery or resistance period, and at last exhaustion and death—Selye coined the phrase *general adaptation syndrome.* (To physicians the word *syndrome* means the entire pattern of symptoms and events that characterize the course of a disease.)

Psychosomatic illnesses

There are many indications that the general adaptation syndrome found in animals also occurs in human beings. Stress caused by frustration and conflict—indeed by any kind of prolonged emotional upset—can be just as drastic as the kind Selye produced by injecting poison. The physical results often take the form of *psychosomatic illnesses,* meaning bodily ailments that stem at least in part from mental and emotional causes. Diseases that frequently seem to be psychosomatic include high blood pressure, heart attacks, stomach ulcers, diabetes, tuberculosis, multiple sclerosis, and possibly some forms of cancer (Miller, 1975)—as well as a host of minor illnesses including the common cold.

One study has suggested that perhaps all illnesses, not only those regarded as psychosomatic, usually are triggered by stress-producing situations. The study was made by compiling case histories of a group of patients suffering from a wide variety of physical ailments. It was found that all the patients had undergone some experience, shortly before the onset of the disease, that was psychologically distressing. (The experiences most frequently reported are listed in Figure 11-5). The study indicates that under ordinary conditions our bodies are able

Emotional state believed to have triggered illness	Percentage of cases
Resentment or hostility	17
Frustration or rejection	13
Depression, hopelessness	13
Anxiety	13
Feelings of helplessness	12
Separation from a loved one	9
Stressful changes in life situation or threatening situation	9
Difficulties in relationship with therapist or experimenter	4
Miscellaneous	10

Figure 11-5 The emotional background of illness *Case histories of patients suffering from physical illnesses showed that all of them had recently experienced some type of stressful situation. The most common trigger for the illnesses was feelings of resentment or hostility (Luborsky, Docherty, and Penick, 1973).*

to resist such external causes of illness as viruses and bacteria. When our usual defenses are weakened by stress, we are likely to get sick. This evidently applies to people at all ages, including youngsters. In one pioneering study, investigators followed 16 families—100 persons in all—for a year. The subjects were asked to keep a diary of upsetting experiences and were examined every two weeks for throat infections. The results were striking. Subjects who showed throat infections encountered a significantly increased number of stressful events in the previous two weeks (Meyer and Haggerty, 1962).

Can stress keep those who are sick from getting well? One team of researchers studied children with puzzling cases of diabetes, a metabolic disorder that can usually be kept in check with injections of the drug insulin. For these children, however, the medicine was totally ineffective. No matter how high a dose they received, their diabetic attacks could not be controlled. All these children, it turned out, were living in homes torn by conflict and tension and were constantly enmeshed in the quarrels of their parents. Eventually, they suffered near-fatal blood disturbances that required hospitalization. Once in the hospital, however, they could be treated successfully. As soon as they were removed from their stressful environment, even routine doses of insulin proved effective (Minuchin et al., 1975).

Can stress actually kill, as it killed Selye's animals? Some evidence that it can comes from a study of middle-aged men who died suddenly of heart attacks. Their backgrounds showed that four out of every five had been feeling depressed for periods ranging from a week to several months. (Depression, as will be seen later, is often a result of prolonged stress.) Just before the fatal attack, at least half of them had been in a situation likely to produce sudden and intense emotional arousal—in some cases an unusually heavy work load or other bustle of activity, in others circumstances creating a high level of anxiety or anger (Greene, Goldstein, and Moss, 1972). It seems likely that stress was at least a contributing factor in their deaths. (The findings about psychosomatic illness are highly pertinent to the practice of medicine as discussed in a box on Psychology and Society.)

Who gets sick and who doesn't?—differences in stressful experiences

Everybody undergoes stressful experiences—yet not everybody comes down with a psychosomatic illness. Why? One reason seems to be that no two people have the same experiences and that each experience has a sort of built-in potential for creating a certain level of stress, high or low. After studying the life experiences and medical records of large numbers of people, one group of investigators developed the Life Stress Scale shown in Figure 11-6, which assigns a numerical value to the amount of stress that adjusting to various new events seems to create. Note that these events include not only misfortunes but pleasurable happenings—such as getting married, achieving something outstanding, and even going on vacation or celebrating Christmas. Indeed getting married, assigned a figure of 50, was found fully half as stressful as the death of a husband or wife, which tops the list with 100.

Experience	Stress units
Death of spouse	100
Divorce	73
Separation	65
Jail term	63
Death of close family member	63
Getting married	50
Being fired	47
Reconciliation in marriage	45
Retiring	45
Getting pregnant	40
Sex problems	39
New member in family	39
Change in finances	38
Death of close friend	37
Change to new kind of work	36
Change in work responsibilities	29
Trouble with in-laws	29
An outstanding achievement	28
Wife starts job or stops	26
Begin or end school	26
Trouble with boss	23
Change in work conditions	20
Move to new residence	20
Changing schools	20
Changing social activities	18
Vacation	13
Christmas holidays	12
Minor law violation	11

Figure 11-6 A scale of stress produced by various events *These are some of the figures in the Life Stress Scale, discussed in the text (Holmes and Rahe, 1967).*

Happy event—but stressful nonetheless.

Psychology and Society: Stress, illness, and the role of the physician

The relationships that have been found between stress and physical ailments shed considerable light on what was previously a medical mystery. Part of the puzzle centered on the fact that until recently only a few medicines or medical techniques were physically effective in combating disease. Indeed some of the methods used in the past—such as drawing blood from an already weak patient by applying leeches—were actually harmful. Yet patients treated by the old methods often made spectacular recoveries. Even today, witch doctors in primitive societies cure many ailments as if by magic, as do faith healers in our own society.

Another part of the puzzle concerned that famous medical device called the placebo—a mere sugar pill, with no remedial value at all. Physicians have known for a long time that the number of people whose physical symptoms vanish after they take a placebo may be just as high as if real medicine had been prescribed. This phenomenon, called the *placebo effect,* causes great confusion in attempts to study the effectiveness of new drugs.

The key to the mystery now appears to be that any form of treatment comforts the patient, relieves stress, and thus helps the body mobilize its own defenses and throw off disease. The famous "bedside manner" of doctors in our great-grandparents' day may have been just as effective, in its own way, as today's techniques. Perhaps it would help today with the many people who complain that physicians—for all their blood tests, X rays, and wonder drugs—often take an impersonal approach to illness that makes patients feel more like case histories than like suffering human beings.

The likelihood of psychosomatic illness, the investigators concluded, is determined by the total number of stress units that occur within a single 12-month period. When the number exceeded 200, more than half the people in the study developed health problems. Thus the scale indicates that a person is more likely than not to become sick if a single year's experiences include divorce (73 units), losing a job (47), a change in finances (38), the death of a close friend (37), and a change to a new kind of work (36). When the total exceeded 300, nearly 80 percent of the subjects became ill.

Differences in resistance to stress

Although the Life Stress Scale serves as a guide to the potentially stressful effects of various experiences, critics regard it as too arbitrary to apply to all people under all circumstances (Rabkin and Struening, 1976). For one thing, any attempt to generalize ignores differences in attitudes toward life's events. Some people take a much calmer view than others of divorce, loss of a job, or the other matters listed in the stress scale. Even the death of a spouse may produce more relief than stress for someone it releases from an intolerable relationship (Rutter, 1983). In fact some people seem unmoved by anything at all that happens to them—a peculiar phenomenon discussed in a box on Psychology and Society.

There are widespread individual differences in physical as well as psychological reactions to outside pressures—another reason some people get sick while others do not. One study, for example, compared two groups of subjects, all of whom had been exposed to what appeared to be equal amounts of outside pressure (such as job difficulties, loss of a loved one, or financial problems). The group that developed illnesses of one kind or another turned out to have two characteristics: (a) a strong tendency to prolonged anxiety and worry, and (b) a past history of some kind of bodily weakness, such as a vulnerable stomach or heart. The group that did not get sick showed neither of these traits (Hinkle, 1974).

A recent study was made of executives of a Midwest utility company, all of whom had experienced various stressful situations, including transfer to a new job in a new city. An attempt was made to compare the personality traits of those who became ill and those who did not. Those who escaped illness turned out to have much more of what the researcher termed "hardiness." For one thing, they were more committed to themselves, their work, their families, and their social roles than were the illness-prone executives. They tended to have an internal locus of control (see Chapter 10) and a sense of being responsible for their own destiny. They made vigorous attempts to face and solve their problems, in contrast to the more passive approach of the illness-prone (Kobasa, 1979).

Though this study indicates that active efforts to cope with stressful situations reduce the likelihood of illness, there is also evidence that too intense an effort can be harmful. In assessing the chances of suffering a heart attack, some investigators have found that the greatest risk is among people they have termed Type A. These people have an extremely high achievement motive and believe they can overcome any obstacle if only they try hard enough. They are ambitious and competitive and have a sense of urgency about getting their tasks done on time. They usually work to the limits of their endurance, and sometimes beyond it. When thwarted, they react with hostility and aggression. (This description, of course, fits many hard-driving and successful people, including numerous corporation executives.) The chances of suffering a heart attack are considerably less among Type B people—who are more easygoing and place less value on success (Glass, 1977).

High blood pressure, the power motive, and anger

One remarkable study indicates that high blood pressure—another potentially crippling psychosomatic illness—is closely related to the motive for power (see Chapter 10). In this study, men in their early thirties were measured for motivation and for tendencies to gratify or inhibit their motives. Twenty years later, their patterns of blood pressure were measured. The study found that the early tests of motivation were remarkably accurate in predicting which of the subjects would have high blood pressure in later life. By far the greatest number of cases occurred among men who had been found, when in their thirties, to have a strong power motive that they tried to inhibit (McClelland, 1979). Presumably the strong motivation, kept bottled up, produced frequent anger and thus chronic stress. There is evidence that people whose power motive is frustrated are vulnerable to other psychosomatic illnesses as well (McClelland et al, 1981).

Many people with high blood pressure tend to conceal strong feelings of anger and resentment with submissive behavior—and thus avoid

Psychology and Society: Wouldn't it be nice to be the kind of person who never suffers stress? (Or would it?)

Some people sail blithely through life with hardly a hint of stress. No matter what happens to them, no matter what kind of crisis they face, they rarely seem to suffer any pressure or tension. On our own more jittery days we may consider them the most fortunate of people—and even envy them their composure. But are they really so lucky? Would we really like to be in their shoes?

A clue to the answer comes from a study of a number of people who were in the midst of unusually stressful experiences, including some who had been torn away from their families and uprooted from their native country (Hinkle, 1974). Among these people there were some who seemed unshaken by the loss of home, community, friends, and in some cases even marriage partner. But these stress-free individuals seemed to be a breed apart, with attitudes and feelings foreign to most of us.

For one thing, they seemed totally unconcerned about other people—and in no way responsible for anyone else. If a family member was in trouble, they refused to worry because "nothing can be done about it." Some declined to help a sick parent—or relative—because "it would be too much for me."

One might say they acted as if interested only in their own well-being—except that even their own welfare did not seem to concern them very much. No matter how difficult their circumstances, they saw no reason to be upset or bitter. If their lot in life turned out to be poverty-stricken and lonely, so be it. Such matters, they felt, were beyond their control. Indeed some of them turned down a chance to increase their income by working overtime because it might be too tiring, or a promising transfer to another job because it was too much trouble, or a promotion because it would mean too much responsibility.

They seemed to have made a trade-off. They avoided the wear and tear of stress by never letting themselves care much about anything. They avoided any attempt to extend themselves—in their own behalf or to help anyone else. They were content to avoid stress by ignoring life's exciting challenges, its precious opportunities, and what most of us would consider its obligations.

If we could all be like them, would we be happier? Would the human community be better off?

open confrontations with others (Weiner, 1982). It has been suggested that this may be one reason high blood pressure is twice as prevalent among blacks—many of whom have resented their status in society but have kept their anger in check—as among whites (Krantz et al., 1981).

Selye's prescription for staying healthy

Selye believed that we all have our own individual pattern of resistance to damage by stress. The limits to what we can withstand are set by two factors. One is our general ability to adjust to stressful situations, or what Selye called our "supply of adaptation energy." The other is the amount of wear and tear that the weakest part of the body can tolerate without succumbing to psychosomatic illness. (Some people have weak stomachs and are inclined to get ulcers. Some have heart structures that are susceptible to damage.)

The secret of a healthy and fulfilling life, according to Selye, is to live to the full extent of our capabilities—that is, to savor the excitement and emotionality of life but not to put undue strain on ourselves. The trick, he says, is to "determine our optimum speed of living, by trying various speeds and finding out which one is most agreeable" (Selye, 1976). If we find the pace damaging, we can pull back. If we thrive on it, we can venture a little further.

Selye believed that both the limiting factors in withstanding damage from stress—adaptation energy and the tolerance level of the weakest part of the body—are the result of heredity, determined by our genes. But this viewpoint may have been colored by his background in biology. Many psychologists hold that tolerance of distress also depends on nurture. They believe that we can learn to cope with anxiety and stress in a constructive way rather than letting them overwhelm and damage us (Miller, 1976).

The psychological effects of stress

Along with the physical wear and tear of stress, notably psychosomatic illness, go many psychological effects. Indeed the difference between normal behavior and abnormal behavior, which will be the topic of the next chapter, seems to depend in large part on the amount of anxiety and stress that people experience. The amount, in turn, depends on the type of event.

As in the case of physical illness, stressful life changes that are pleasurable—becoming engaged, getting married, being promoted at work—are not as damaging as unpleasant ones. One investigator, reviewing various studies, has identified three kinds of events that have been found to be especially harmful (Rutter, 1983): (a) events that mean the loss of an important relationship—for example, divorce (Paykel, 1978); (b) events that cannot be controlled and therefore produce a feeling of helplessness—for example, a tragic accident; and (c) events that pose a long-term threat because they have lasting consequences—for example, a lingering illness or the loss of a job (Brown and Harris, 1978).

The physical and psychological effects are sometimes difficult to separate. This is especially true in the case of *depression*, a common emotional disturbance that can range in severity from mild to crippling. One investigator has estimated that as many as 30 million Americans can expect to suffer from depression at some time in their lives (Kline, 1974). They may not even know what is wrong—for the milder form of depression does not necessarily cause them to feel unhappy or "blue." Nor do they necessarily appear depressed to their friends. Mild states of depression typically result in feelings of unexplained fatigue and lack of enthusiasm. Their victims may have trouble getting any work done and may lose interest in activities that once gave them pleasure. Often they think they must be suffering from some disease, such as mononucleosis, that causes a lack of energy. Yet physical tests show nothing wrong.

There is considerable evidence that depression is related to brain chemistry. In particular, it seems to be associated with low levels of the neurotransmitter noradrenalin or with reduced effectiveness in the way this neurotransmitter operates at the brain's synapses (Schildkraut, 1969). Animal experiments have shown that the amount of noradrenalin in the brain may decline substantially during stress (Weiss, Glazer, and Pohorecky, 1976).

A tendency toward depression, especially in its more extreme forms, appears to be at least partly the result of heredity (Winokur, 1981). Apparently some people are born with a type of brain chemistry that is prone to low levels of noradrenalin and thus depression, just as other people are born with weak stomachs or weak hearts that are vulnerable to damage by stress. At any rate depression is an emotional disturbance in which the physical and psychological aspects of stress appear closely intermingled. Many other psychological disturbances also seem to represent some form of failure to cope successfully with stressful experiences and their physical and emotional effect (Lazarus, 1978). If we have learned to handle stress and anxiety, our behavior remains within normal bounds. If not, we may slip across the line into abnormal behavior.

Successful coping and normal behavior

The photographs in Figure 11-7 show that even small children display different reactions to stressful situations. One child makes a strenuous effort to cope. Another quickly gives up.

Adults display an even wider range of differences. They may try to fight off the cause of the stress or throw up their hands. They may succeed in surmounting the stressful situation or they may fail. When they fail, as is sometimes inevitable, they may find a way of reconciling themselves to the situation—or, on the other hand, they may develop physical ailments or a crippling amount of anxiety, anger, or learned helplessness. To a considerable extent, all abnormal behavior is the result of unsuccessful coping. Some sort of maladjustment occurs between the individual and the environment (especially the social environment: family, friends, fellow workers, bosses, teachers). The individual experiences anxiety and stress and wants to relieve them—but does not know how (Lazarus, 1978).

Even in animal experiments, successful coping has been found an effective defense against stress. In one study, two groups of rats were subjected to the stress-producing stimulus of electric shocks. One group was permitted to learn a warning signal. In human terms, they discovered when the shock was coming and could prepare for it, and in the meantime they had nothing to fear. The other group received no warning at all. Though both groups were exposed to exactly the same number and intensity of shocks, the second group developed five times as many stomach ulcers as the other (Weiss, 1970). A similar experiment produced a significant finding about levels of noradrenalin in the brain. Animals that had no way of predicting or preparing for the shock showed a decrease, as would be expected from what was said earlier about stress, noradrenalin, and depression. But the animals that could cope after a fashion, because they knew when the shock was coming and could relax in the meantime, actually showed an increase (Weiss et al., 1975). It has been suggested that this experiment indicates "there may even be some psychological advantage from meeting and successfully coping with a manageable source of stress" (Miller, 1976).

Assertive coping

To constructive attempts to deal with anxiety and stress, psychologists often apply the term *assertive coping*. One form is a direct attempt to change the stressful situation. For example, let us say that we are

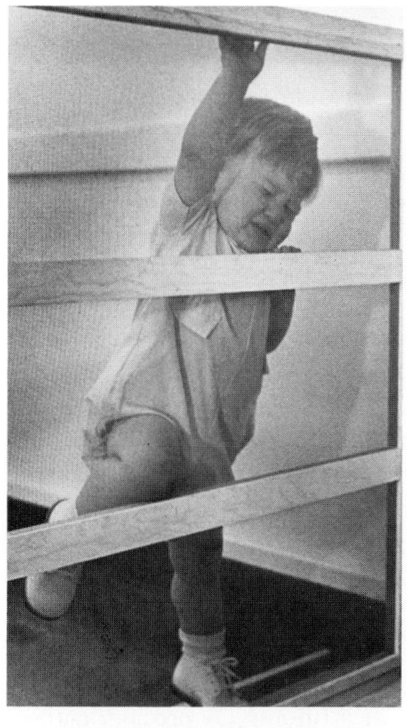

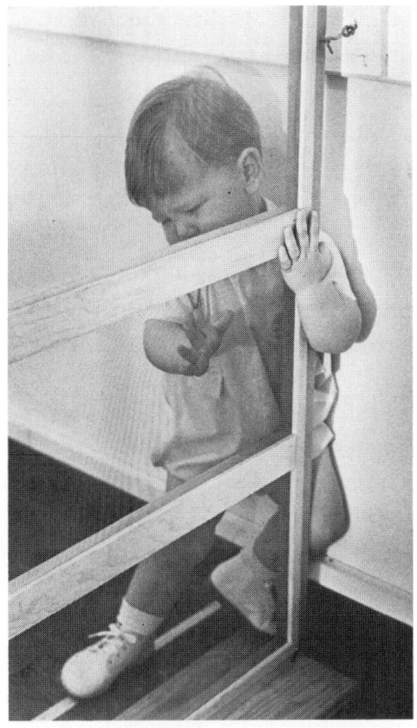

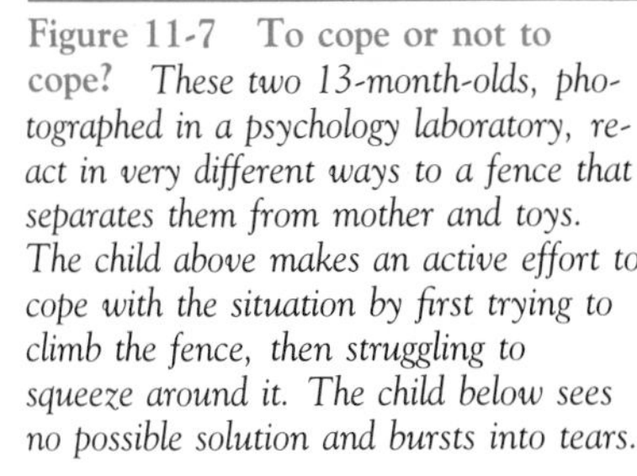

Figure 11-7 To cope or not to cope? *These two 13-month-olds, photographed in a psychology laboratory, react in very different ways to a fence that separates them from mother and toys. The child above makes an active effort to cope with the situation by first trying to climb the fence, then struggling to squeeze around it. The child below sees no possible solution and bursts into tears.*

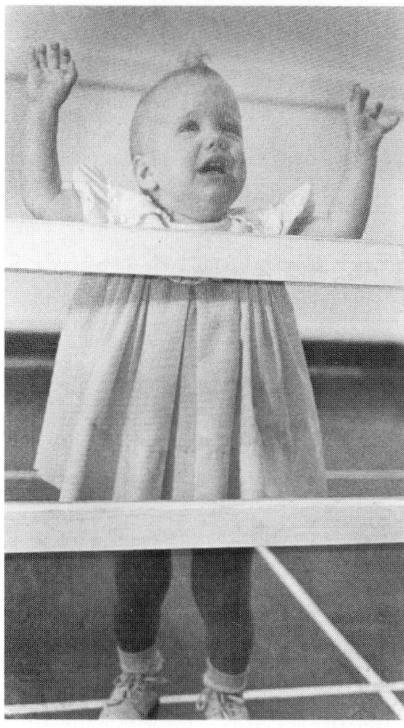

experiencing frustration. One of our motives has been blocked. We feel bad about the situation. We may even suffer anger so intense that it amounts to rage and sets the stomach churning. Yet, if we can keep our wits about us, perhaps we can somehow manage to overcome the obstacle. We can face up to the difficulty and try to find some way to overcome it. We can regard the situation as an exercise in problem solving and get busy seeking the answer, which may take one of the following three forms:

Psychology and Society: The Vietnam POWs, stress, and survival

Few people have ever undergone—much less endured—the kind of stress-laden experience of some of the Americans who were taken prisoner during the war in Vietnam. They were held captive for as many as nine years and spent as many as four of those years in solitary confinement. Some were chained to their cots for months at a time. They were kept awake and questioned for days on end. They suffered starvation, dysentery, cold, and physical torture. When they were at long last returned in 1973, they were met by a team of physicians and psychiatrists who fully expected to find them in a state of total physical and psychological collapse. Yet they turned out to be remarkably fit, considering what they had been through. A follow-up study of the Navy fliers among them showed that they have continued to do well by any standards—and much better than many POWs of past wars whose confinement was not nearly so long or brutal (Richlin et al., 1980). Indeed they seem to be doing better than many veterans of Vietnam who were not POWs. How did they manage?

For one thing, they were older and more mature than the typical soldier. Most of them were officers and pilots and their military training had prepared them to expect crises. They believed in the importance and righteousness of their mission and were highly motivated to survive. Most of all, they exhibited a strong spirit of group cooperation and support, helping each other as much as they could in their common ordeal.

Even in solitary confinement, they developed some effective methods of assertive coping. Some adopted a program of physical exercise. Others passed the time by inventing new games, or by memorizing stories. A few kept busy by keeping a careful census of the insects in their cells. Without toothbrushes to preserve their teeth they made picks out of bamboo sticks and wire and dental floss out of threads from their clothing or blankets.

Though their captors ordered them not to talk to each other, and punished them for violations, they developed a secret communications system in which taps on the wall, floor, or ceiling stood for letters of the alphabet. For short distances they tapped with their fingers, for longer distances with their fists or elbows or a tin cup. A prisoner ordered to sweep the prison compound used the strokes of his broom to tap messages to the men in their cells. A prisoner walking past another cell dragged his sandals in code. With these ingenious messages, the POWs encouraged each other to hold out and endure the captivity (Deaton et al., 1977).

The POWs coped with a situation more grievous than any of us will be likely to face. And they survived.

1. Changing the environment Even a hungry animal, barred from getting food by a closed door, often tries to outwit its environment by gnawing through the barrier. A motorist frustrated by a flat tire can get busy changing it or try to find a phone and seek help. A student who wants to be an accountant but is weak in certain areas of mathematics can tackle these subjects and try to master them. Couples frustrated by a bad marriage can engage in assertive coping by going to a marriage counselor—or, if necessary, by ending the marriage.

Assertive coping with the environment consists in a meaningful attempt to change the situation in a constructive way that has a reasonable chance of success. (For an extraordinary example, see a box on Psychology and Society.) Even though the attempt may fail, the effort itself seems to combat the damaging effects of stress.

2. Changing our own behavior In many cases, the stress we suffer comes not so much from the environment as from our own behavior. Failure in college can result from inattention in class or insufficient study. Social unpopularity may reflect a grumpy, timid, or overaggressive approach to other people. (The way people's behavior toward us is largely determined by our own actions is one of the concerns of Chapter 15.)

Thus at times the only effective way to reduce stress is to change our own behavior. For example, people with financial problems often can escape only by setting up a strict budget and resisting their urge to spend (Ilfield, 1980). The couple who undertake marriage counseling will probably find that both partners have to make readjustments in the ways they act toward each other. Indeed people who seek counseling or therapy of any kind are in effect asking for help in changing their own behavior and attitudes.

3. Managing the internal wear and tear Sometimes a stressful situation persists no matter how hard we try to change the environment or our own behavior. During severe economic recessions many people continue to suffer the strains of unemployment and lack of money no matter how hard they try or how far they travel in search of a job. Efforts to cope with the situation by changing their own behavior—such as training themselves for a new line of work—may fail. A person may also be helpless to do anything about such sources of stress as the illness of a family member or lack of talent for a chosen career.

In situations of genuine helplessness—not learned helplessness—there is just no escape from the source of stress. The only form assertive coping can take is an effort to control the effects. We must somehow keep the physical and emotional wear and tear within bounds, so that they do not destroy us physically or psychologically. There is no magic formula for this kind of coping, but many people have succeeded at it. Helen Keller was a conspicuous example. So are the hundreds of thousands of people who somehow kept their sanity and spirit in the concentration camps of the Second World War.

In talking about managing the internal effects, we are really discussing what is often called *mental health.* It is difficult even to define mental health, much less offer suggestions for attaining it. Perhaps it consists, as one psychologist has suggested, in harmony among physical well-being, effective functioning as a member of society, and a high level of personal morale (or sense of self-worth and self-reliance). Preserving mental health is possible even in the most difficult situations because the anxiety and stress we experience depend not so much on what the environment does to us as on the way we view ourselves and our relations to the environment (Lazarus, 1978). In exactly the same situation, a person with low self-esteem and an external locus of control suffers far more than a person with a positive self-image and an internal locus of control.

The normal personality

In attempting to define normal personality and normal behavior, psychologists for many years emphasized the word *adjustment.* Normal personality traits, it was generally believed, are those that help people adjust to the environment and to other people—in other words, to accept the realities of the physical world and of society and to behave in harmony with them. This description of the normal personality still persists to some extent. Indeed many colleges offer a course called the psychology of adjustment.

In recent years, however, many psychologists have come to believe that adjustment is too passive and negative a term, implying a self-effacing conformity to what other people are thinking and doing. Some have decided that adjustment, if taken to mean a more or less unquestioning acceptance of some aspects of society—such as mass killings in warfare and the spending of human resources on military equipment rather than on education—is itself abnormal (Laing, 1960).

Thus the emphasis has shifted. Growing numbers of psychologists now regard normal behavior not as mere adjustment but as an active effort to cope with the problems of life and achieve some kind of honest self-awareness, independence, and fulfillment. As was mentioned in Chapter 10, Maslow has suggested the term self-actualization. Other psychologists have defined normal people as those who maintain a stable sense of identity (Erikson, 1968)—or who possess the inner freedom to make their own decisions rather than yielding to pressures from the environment and from other people (Bühler, 1968). Some of the current thinking about being normal is summarized in a box on Psychology and Society.

Defense mechanisms and other questionable forms of coping

Besides assertive coping, people devise many other ways of trying to handle anxiety and stress. These other ways, by and large, are not nearly so effective. They may serve as stopgaps in an emergency. They may even be practiced over long periods, as a sort of life strategy, with some success and without serious damage. But they are questionable at best—and, when carried to extremes, they carry a serious risk. They lie in a sort of gray area between successful coping and downright failure to cope—or, in other words, between normal and abnormal behavior,

Prominent among them are certain devices, first described by Sigmund Freud, called *defense mechanisms.* Freud regarded these mechanisms as unconscious psychological processes, mental or symbolic, that people develop to relieve anxiety. Unlike assertive coping, they are not deliberate efforts to change the environment or one's own behavior or to deal realistically with anxiety and stress. Indeed all defense mechanisms are based to some degree on self-deception and distortion of reality. Yet everybody adopts some of them at one time or another. They are not necessarily harmful. But psychotic people often display them in exaggerated form.

Rationalization

One defense mechanism has been recognized ever since Aesop started the phrase sour grapes with his fable about the fox. (The fox, unable to

Psychology and Society: What it means to be normal: some comforting advice

Adding the term mental health to the English language—and its equivalent to languages around the world—has produced some unfortunate side effects. The term has often been misinterpreted and exaggerated, as have been the goals of Sigmund Freud and the newer schools of psychotherapy. Many people are intimidated by the concepts of mental health and the normal personality, which they see as demanding perfection beyond the reach of most ordinary mortals. They are vaguely dissatisfied because they worry that they—and life itself—should be far better than they are.

Actually, psychology's message to society is reassuring rather than frightening. Asked to describe the normal personality, most psychologists would probably agree on the following six points. Note especially the first of them.

1. Being normal does not mean being perfect. Everybody gets angry, has hostile thoughts, gets greedy at times, and does foolish things. Everybody encounters frustrations and conflicts and experiences anxiety and stress. Nobody can cope in a completely successful manner at all times. We can only do our best—which probably means to function more or less satisfactorily despite the inevitable problems of the human condition.
2. Normal people are realistic. They have learned not to expect perfection, either in themselves or in others. They are aware of their own limitations and accept the fact that other people also have limitations. Since they do not have unduly grandiose expectations, they are not surprised or overly ashamed or angry when they themselves fail or when others fail them.
3. Normal people can "roll with the punch." They may be unhappy at times over the state of the world or over personal disappointments, but they manage to live with these situations. They are flexible and can change their plans. They are confident of their ability to cope with whatever situations may arise—not necessarily as well as they would like, but at least after a fashion.
4. Normal people possess a certain amount of enthusiasm and spontaneity. They find things to do that give them pleasure, whether working productively or watching a sunset.
5. Normal people have a good deal of independence. They do not shift, like a weather vane, with every change in the wind, either in society as a whole or among their associates. They do not mind being alone. Indeed they enjoy a certain amount of privacy.
6. Normal people are capable of feeling and showing affection and of establishing close relationships with others—not necessarily many others, but a chosen few. They can love and be loved.

reach an inviting cluster of grapes, consoled itself by deciding they would have been sour anyway.) Freud's name for this defense mechanism is *rationalization*—an attempt to deal with stressful situations by claiming that they never really occurred.

People often resort to rationalization to explain away their frustrations. A man, rejected by a woman, convinces himself that she was not nearly so attractive or interesting as he had supposed. A woman, turned down when applying for employment, convinces herself that the job was not really worth having.

People also use rationalization to reduce the anxiety caused by conflicts between motives and inner standards. A mother's real reason for keeping her daughter from dating may be jealousy, a motive of which her conscience disapproves. She rationalizes by claiming she is acting for the daughter's own good. A student cheats on an examination and rationalizes by claiming that everybody cheats.

Repression

Some people who suffer anxiety and stress over their motives simply try to banish the motives from their conscious thoughts—to the point where they seem to be totally unaware of their desires. This defense mechanism is called *repression*. People who at one time suffered severe anxiety and stress over sexual motives may repress these motives so thoroughly that they no longer seem to be aware of any sexual feelings or desires at all. Other people seem oblivious to the fact that they have any desires for dependency or hostility. Some cases of *amnesia,* or loss of memory, appear to be exaggerated forms of repression.

Sublimation

A motive that causes anxiety may also be transformed unconsciously into a different but related motive that is more acceptable to society and to oneself. This defense mechanism is known as *sublimation,* a process that enables a "shameful" motive to find expression in a more noble form. Freud believed that works of art are often the result of sublimation—that the Shakespeares and Michelangelos of the world may very well have channeled forbidden sexual urges into artistic creativity. Similarly, Freud believed that people may sublimate their urges toward cruelty into a socially approved desire to become surgeons, prosecuting attorneys, or even teachers with the power to discipline the young.

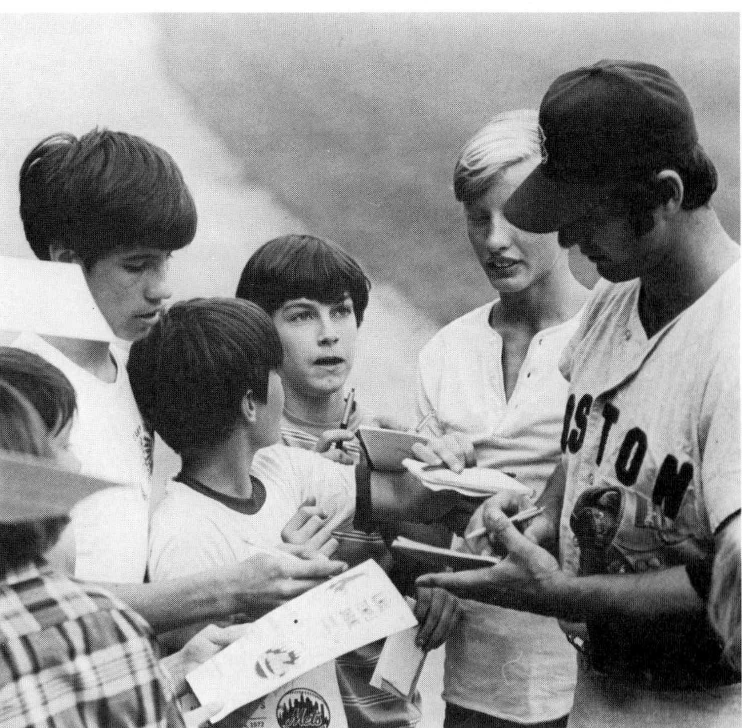

Could a young boy reduce his anxiety about his athletic skill by identifying with a baseball star?

Identification

Another mechanism for relieving anxiety is to take on the virtues of some admired person or group that seems free of such anxiety. This process is called *identification.* An example would be a man, anxious about his own lack of courage, who identifies with a swashbuckling movie star or a group of mountain climbers so that he can believe he too possesses their daring. A woman anxious about her lack of social acceptance may identify with a popular roommate.

In a more complex form, identification may be established with a figure of authority who is resented and feared. Thus a young man may defend himself against the anxiety aroused by hostile feelings toward his boss by identifying with the boss. He may imitate the boss's mannerisms and express the same opinions, thus persuading himself that he possesses the same power. This type of identification may also be made with a group. Young people, anxious about their feelings of envy and hostility toward an exclusive clique, may identify with the group and adopt its standards. A study of prisoners in German concentration camps during the Second World War showed that many of them imitated the characteristics of the very guards from whose brutality they were suffering (Bettelheim, 1943).

Reaction formation

People who display a trait to excess—that is, in an exaggerated form that hardly seems called for by the circumstances—may be using the defense mechanism called *reaction formation.* They are pretending to possess motives that are the exact opposite of the real motives that are causing their anxiety. For example, a man appears to be the soul of politeness. He is constantly holding doors for other people, saying "Yes, sir," and "Yes, ma'am," always smiling, agreeable, and apologetic for his mistakes. This exaggerated politeness and concern for others may simply be a defense mechanism he has adopted to conceal the fact that he has hostile motives and that his hostility is making him anxious. A woman who dresses in a provocative manner and is constantly flirting and telling risqué stories may be concealing her sexual inhibitions and fear of being unattractive.

Projection

The man who claims that everybody is dishonest and the woman who is convinced of the immorality of the younger generation may have reached their conclusions through honest examination of the evidence. On the other hand, they may be exhibiting another defense mechanism called *projection,* in which people foist off or project onto other people motives or thoughts of their own that cause them anxiety. The man who talks too much about dishonesty may be concealing his own strong tendencies toward dishonesty. The woman who talks too much about the immorality of young people may be concealing her own strong sexual desires.

Projection often plays a part in disagreements between marriage partners. Many husbands complain that their wives are extravagant, although a disinterested observer can clearly see that it is the husband himself who is wasting money. Wives who are torn by sexual conflicts and urges toward infidelity may falsely accuse their husbands of having affairs. A marriage counselor who hears accusations by husband or wife of bad conduct or improper motives always looks for the possibility that the complaints represent projection rather than truth. Projection is one of the most powerful and dangerous of the defense mechanisms. It works very effectively to reduce anxiety, but it does so at the risk of a completely distorted view of the truth about oneself and others.

The pro and con of defense mechanisms

The six defense mechanisms just discussed are the most common and easily recognizable. There are doubtless others. Indeed we human beings are remarkably ingenious at finding new ways to delude ourselves. In one way or another, we persuade ourselves that we did not really want the goals we cannot achieve, that our motives are completely admirable, that we are living up to our own and society's standards, and that our disappointments are somehow bearable.

Because anxiety and stress are so common, all of us use defense mechanisms from time to time—either those that have been mentioned or others of our own invention. Though these defense mechanisms are usually irrational, they often serve a useful purpose. They may help us through crises that would otherwise overwhelm and disable us. If nothing else, they may gain us time in which we can gather the strength, maturity, and knowledge needed to cope more realistically and constructively with our anxiety and stress. Only in extreme cases does

Behind the obvious aggression lie some hidden sources of anxiety and stress at which we can only guess.

the use of defense mechanisms slip over into the realm of abnormal psychology.

Aggression as a response to anxiety and stress

Other reactions to anxiety and stress also lie near the borderline between normal and abnormal behavior. One of the most common is *aggression,* which is often produced by frustration. Children frustrated by other children who take their toys often get angry and strike out with their fists. Frustrated adults may kick at a tire that has gone flat, break an offending golf club, hit a tennis ball into the next county, or shout insults to a driver who has cut them off. This kind of behavior, aimed specifically at the source of the frustration, is called *direct aggression.*

When a direct attack on the source of frustration is impossible, people may display *displaced aggression* and vent their emotions on an innocent bystander. A man angry at a powerful and overdemanding boss goes home and behaves aggressively toward his wife and children. (In everyday language, he uses them as scapegoats.) A little girl angry at her parents takes out her aggression on a smaller child or on a pet. Scapegoating accounts for a great deal of the prejudice displayed against minority groups and foreigners. The prime example occurred when Hitler made the Jews scapegoats, blaming them for all the frustrations and conflicts that Germany was suffering in a time of economic and political tension.

Withdrawal and apathy

Some individuals react to difficult situations by *withdrawal.* To avoid further anxiety and stress, they shun close contacts with other people

Lonely in a crowd—an example of withdrawal.

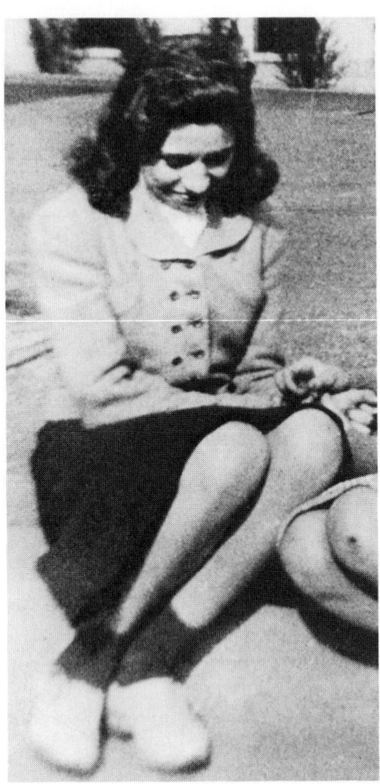
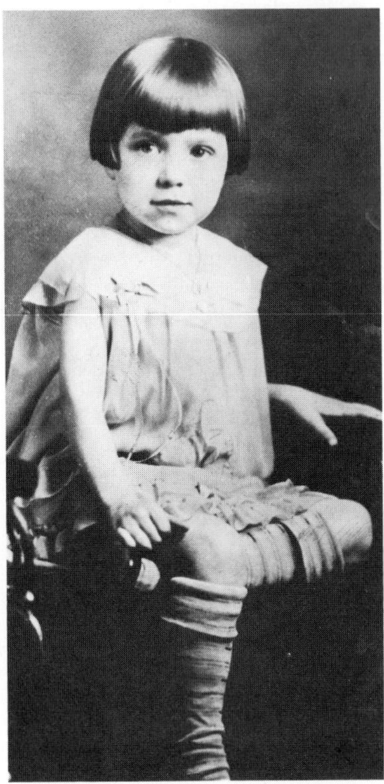
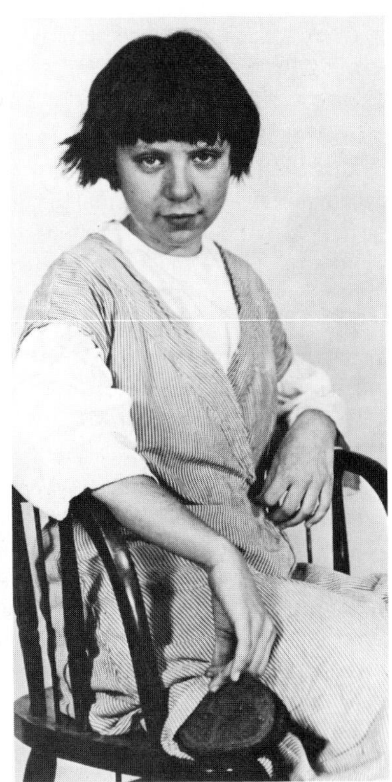

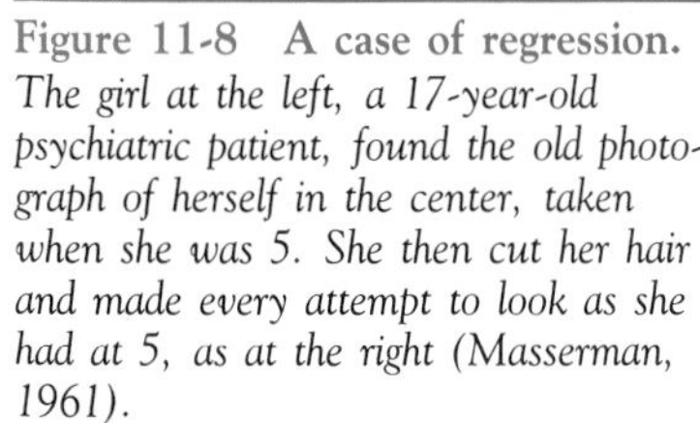

Figure 11-8 A case of regression. *The girl at the left, a 17-year-old psychiatric patient, found the old photograph of herself in the center, taken when she was 5. She then cut her hair and made every attempt to look as she had at 5, as at the right (Masserman, 1961).*

or any attempt to gratify their motives. We say of such people that they have "retreated into a shell" or that they have "quit trying." Rather than trying to cope assertively with their difficulties, they choose to escape by narrowing the horizons of their lives—often in drastic and self-limiting ways.

In similar fashion, some people display *apathy*. They are sad and listless, seem to lose all interest in what happens to them, and have a difficult time finding energy for the ordinary chores of life.

Regression

The experiment with the "half toys" described in Chapter 10—in which children aged 2 to 5 were frustrated by being separated by a barrier from desirable playthings—produced an interesting side effect. The children began to behave in a manner more appropriate to younger levels of development. Indeed they acted like children 17 months younger, on the average, than their actual ages. This type of behavior—retreating toward activities that usually characterize a lower level of maturity—is called *regression*.

Displays of regression as a reaction to frustration and stress are common among children. A firstborn child, upset by the arrival of a baby sister or brother, may go back to such forgotten habits as thumb sucking or may want to be fed from a bottle. Frustrated adults may regress to such childish behavior as weeping or throwing temper tantrums. People who are victims of extreme emotional disturbance sometimes display striking degrees of regression, as illustrated in Figure 11-8. They are among the types of people discussed in the next chapter—which describes in detail what happens when efforts to cope fail, and the human personality falls apart.

SUMMARY

Anxiety and its effect on behavior

1. *Anxiety* is a vague, unpleasant feeling accompanied by a premonition that something undesirable is about to happen.
2. Anxiety is closely related to motives, especially conflicts between motives and frustration of the motive for certainty. Any situation clouded with uncertainty has a built-in potential for creating anxiety.
3. People who display anxiety in many different situations are victims of *general anxiety*. Those who display it in some particular situation but not at other times have *specific* anxiety. A specific type common among college students is *test anxiety*. Some anxieties—for example about crime—can substantially affect social behavior.
4. People high in anxiety do better than others at simple learning tasks but more poorly at difficult learning tasks. In college, anxiety does not seem to affect the grades of students of either highest or lowest learning ability. Among students of in-between ability, those with high anxiety make significantly lower grades than those with low anxiety.
5. In their approach to life, people high in anxiety tend either to be very conservative and avoid risks or to "go for broke." People low in anxiety tend toward the middle-range risks that are most likely to lead to success in the long run.

The wear and tear of stress

6. *Stress* is the body's reaction to anything that threatens to damage the organism—from a disease germ to intense and prolonged emotion.
7. The damaging potential of stress was demonstrated by Hans Selye in experiments with animals subjected to small doses of poison. Selye found that the body automatically tries to defend itself in ways that include striking changes in activity of the endocrine glands, especially the adrenals. After a time the body seems to adapt and the glands return to normal. If the stressful conditions continue, however, the recovery proves to be only temporary and the animal dies—killed by an excess of hormones the body produced in its own defense. This sequence of events is called the *general adaptation syndrome*.
8. The bodily changes described by Selye also seem to occur in human beings, often as part of the stress caused by frustration, conflict, or

any prolonged emotional upset. They often take the form of *psychosomatic illnesses,* meaning bodily ailments that stem at least in part from mental and emotional causes.

9. Three kinds of stressful events are especially damaging psychologically: (a) the loss of an important relationship, (b) uncontrollable events, and (c) events that pose long-term threats.
10. The psychological effects of stress include *depression.* This appears to be associated with low levels or reduced effectiveness of the brain's supply of the neurotransmitter noradrenalin, which apparently can occur during stress.

Successful coping and normal behavior

11. *Assertive coping* is an effective defense against stress. It may take three forms: (a) an attempt to change the environment and relieve the stressful situation, (b) changing one's own behavior, or (c) keeping the emotional and physical wear and tear within bounds.
12. Assertive coping is one key to *normal behavior,* which many psychologists define in terms of honest self-awareness, independence, fulfillment, a stable sense of identity, and inner freedom.

Defense mechanisms and other questionable forms of coping

13. Among questionable forms of coping are the *defense mechanisms* described by Freud. These are unconscious psychological processes, mental or symbolic. They include: (a) rationalization, (b) repression, (c) sublimation, (d) identification, (e) reaction formation, and (f) projection.
14. Other questionable reactions to anxiety and stress include: (a) direct aggression, (b) displaced aggression, (c) withdrawal or apathy, and (d) regression.

IMPORTANT TERMS

adjustment
amnesia
anxiety
apathy
assertive coping
coping
defense mechanism
depression
direct aggression
displaced aggression
general adaptation syndrome
general anxiety
identification
mental health
normal behavior
placebo effect
projection
psychosomatic illness
rationalization
reaction formation
regression
repression
specific anxiety
stress
stressor
sublimation
test anxiety
withdrawal

RECOMMENDED READINGS

Christie, M., and Mellett, P. *Foundations of psychosomatics.* New York: Wiley, 1981.

Dohrenwend, B. S., ed. *Stressful life events: their nature and effects.* New York: Wiley, 1974.

Elliot, G. R., and Eisdorfer, C., eds. *Stress and human health.* New York: Springer Verlag, 1982.

Krohne, H. W., and Laux, L., eds. *Achievement, stress, and anxiety.* Washington, D.C.: Hemisphere, 1982.

Levine, S., and Ursin, H. *Coping and health.* New York: Plenum, 1980.

Neufeld, R. W. J., ed. *Psychological stress and psychopathology.* New York: McGraw-Hill, 1982.

Sarason, I. G., Spielberger, C. D., and Milgram, N. A., eds. *Stress and anxiety,* Vol. 8. Washington, D.C.: Hemisphere, 1982.

Steptoe, A. *Psychological factors in cardiovascular disorders.* New York: Academic Press, 1981.

CHAPTER 12

The scope of abnormal behavior 429
Characteristics of the abnormal personality
The prevalence of mental disorders

Origins and types of abnormal behavior 431
Biological influences
Psychological influences
Environmental influences
Varieties and shades of abnormality

Schizophrenia: no. 1 crippler 436
Behavior patterns of schizophrenics
The search for schizophrenia's roots

Affective disorders: abnormalities of mood 439
A case of depression—and how it differs from "the blues"
Escaping the pain through suicide
The two poles of manic-depressive illness
Origins of mood disorders
Sex differences in depression

Anxiety disorders 445
Generalized anxiety disorder
Panic disorder
Phobic disorder
Obsessive-compulsive disorder

Personality disorders 449
Antisocial personality: reckless and ruthless
Paranoid personality: always suspicious, always threatened
Narcissistic personality: loving yourself too much

Substance abuse: abnormal use of alcohol and drugs 453
The development of dependence
Alcoholism: trying to drown problems while creating more
From relaxation to blackouts
The heavy penalties of heavy drinking
Male and female drinking patterns
Origins of alcoholism
Slipping from drug use to abuse
The special hazards of mixing drugs

Attitudes toward abnormal behavior: how they can hurt or heal 460
The importance of family supports
The taint of mental disorder
Abnormal behavior and creativity

Summary 463

Important terms 464

Recommended readings 465

Psychology and society
Physical ailments: an underestimated cause of psychological disorders 433
Helping victims of schizophrenia decide about parenthood 438
Depression in childhood: how vulnerable are the young? 444
The emotional scars left by shocking life experiences 447

Abnormal Psychology

By the time you finish reading this chapter, you may very well decide you are the victim of a mental disorder. Just as medical students tend to think they may have the physical diseases they are learning to diagnose, students of abnormal psychology often see in themselves the symptoms of abnormal behavior.

There are two reasons. First, as you study the causes of mental disorders, you will probably find at least some of them in your own background. Most people, if you asked them to search their past for experiences that could have led to a psychological collapse, would have little trouble doing so. Second, you probably have in fact experienced to some degree a number of the symptoms you will be reading about. So have most of us. It is a rare person indeed who has not discovered how it feels to become anxious or depressed, how easy it is to feel physically ill when we are in conflict, or how we can become so frustrated and angry that the whole world seems to be against us.

Yet, while all of us may have had some of the same experiences and symptoms as persons clearly identified as abnormal, most of us go through life without ever suffering an actual breakdown in psychological functioning. The task of identifying that breaking point—where the human personality goes significantly awry—is among the most challenging in the field of psychology.

The scope of abnormal behavior

The wild-eyed, unkempt man on the street corner who constantly mumbles to himself and insists he is Jesus is clearly acting strange. So, too, is the woman who is so deeply depressed that she has withdrawn from the world and no longer even leaves her bed in the morning to get dressed or eat. Psychologists would not hesitate to describe their behavior as abnormal. Nor would psychologists hesitate to describe as distinctly normal people who are functioning at the peak of their powers and feeling good about themselves and others. Most people, however, fall well between these two extremes—in the gray area between what is clearly normal and what is not. It is virtually impossible, therefore, to arrive at an absolute definition of abnormal behavior.

Nevertheless, a working definition needs to be established. It would be impossible to study abnormal psychology without setting at least some standards for abnormal behavior—and for differentiating it from the normal.

This person shows signs of unusual, undesirable, and unhappy behavior typical of the abnormal personality.

Characteristics of the abnormal personality

Is it abnormal to believe in witches? It was not considered so by the American colonists. Is it abnormal for a young woman to faint from the excitement of attending a dance or the embarrassment of hearing profanity? It was not considered so in Victorian England. Is suicide abnormal? To most Americans, it may seem the ultimate in abnormality. Yet in the Far East a Buddhist priest who commits suicide as a form of political protest is regarded as exhibiting strength of character rather than abnormality.

From a statistical viewpoint, behavior can be called abnormal if it is uncommon and unusual—as popular terminology recognizes by referring to it as "odd." But this is not the whole story, for even unusual forms of behavior are not generally called abnormal unless they are regarded as undesirable by the particular society in which they occur. In our own society, the habit of working 18 hours a day is probably rarer than heroin addiction. Yet an 18-hour work day is generally considered admirable or at least acceptable and is therefore called normal. Heroin addiction is considered undesirable and therefore called abnormal.

Since personal happiness is highly valued in the United States, people who are happy are generally regarded as being free of any abnormality. Though this criterion is widely accepted, there are some notable exceptions. Many people who commit vicious acts that could hardly be considered normal—such as wartime atrocities and mass murders in peacetime—seem to be perfectly happy.

In general, however, a useful working definition of abnormal behavior embraces the three points that have been mentioned. An abnormal personality trait or type of behavior is: (a) statistically unusual, (b) considered undesirable by most people, and (c) a source of unhappiness to the person who possesses or displays it. It must be admitted that the definition is not very satisfactory from a scientific point of view and would not be accepted enthusiastically by many psychologists—chiefly on the ground that it sets up rigid standards that enable our society to label as abnormal anybody whose behavior is disliked or considered disruptive, whether or not that behavior can be judged abnormal by any scientific measure.

The prevalence of mental disorders

One way of estimating the extent of abnormal behavior is to identify how many people are actually diagnosed as having a mental disorder. A precise figure is not easy to obtain, but the current estimate, based on the results of several surveys, is that at least 15 percent of the United States population is affected by mental disorders during any one-year period. Each year a third of these are new cases (Regier and Taube, 1981). The economic cost—including loss of earnings and the expense of care and treatment—has been estimated at close to 40 billion dollars a year (President's Commission on Mental Health, 1978).

No statistical data, however, can portray the full impact of mental disorders in human terms. Anyone who has actually experienced periods of intense anxiety or depression knows how disabling they can be and how much agony they can cause. Patients in the throes of terminal cancer pain who also had a history of severe depression were asked to compare the two. Most reported that the physical pain was more bearable—and far preferable to the psychological pain of depression (Jamison, 1982).

Origins and types of abnormal behavior

The causes of abnormal behavior vary to some degree from one type of disorder to another. One dominating element common to all of them, however, appears to be stress. The relationship between stress and abnormal behavior has been clear ever since the time of Pavlov. In one experiment Pavlov conditioned a dog to discriminate between a circle and an ellipse projected on a screen. The dog learned to salivate to the circle but not to the ellipse. Then the shape of the ellipse was changed gradually so that it became more and more like a circle. Even when the difference in appearance was very small, the dog still made the discrimination. But when the difference became too tiny for the dog to perceive and the discrimination became impossible, the dog began to behave strangely. At various times animals placed in this situation became restless, hostile, destructive, and apathetic, and they developed muscle tremors and tics (Pavlov, 1927).

Many other studies have shown that animals begin to exhibit abnormal behavior when they experience greater stress—caused by frustration or in other ways—than they can tolerate (Masserman, 1943).

The early experiments in learned helplessness (see pp. 103–5) are in a sense a demonstration of how the stressful effect of electric shocks, delivered regardless of what the animal does or does not try to do, produces abnormal behavior.

Learned helplessness in human beings is clearly the product of stressful situations and the acquired belief that the victim had no way of escaping. Perhaps an even clearer example is the breakdown sometimes suffered by soldiers in combat—even those who have coped successfully with the difficulties of civilian life. The difference between normal and abnormal behavior seems to hinge on the amount of stress a person experiences and the person's ability to handle this amount. Both factors are influenced by (a) biological structure, (b) psychological traits, and (c) the environment.

Biological influences

Wide individual differences exist in glandular activity and sensitivity of the autonomic nervous system—perhaps also in the activity of the brain centers concerned with emotion. These individual differences may incline one person to be much more easily aroused and more intensely emotional than another. Thus some people, because of their inherited biological makeup, probably experience a great deal more emotional and physical wear and tear than others.

Certainly there is considerable evidence that heredity can contribute to tendencies toward the most severe forms of abnormal behavior. Schizophrenia, for example, is more common among the close relatives of schizophrenics than among people whose family background shows no other cases. Studies also indicate that hereditary factors may produce tendencies toward disabling forms of depression and perhaps toward other less extreme forms of abnormal behavior as well (Tsuang and Vandermey, 1980).

Psychological influences

Regardless of what kind of biological equipment we inherit, our acquired psychological traits also play a key role in determining how much anxiety and stress we are likely to experience and how much we can tolerate without lapsing into abnormal behavior. For example, if we acquire motives for achievement or power that we cannot gratify, or we have strong motives for affiliation and approval that are frustrated, we become extremely vulnerable.

Particularly significant are our inner standards. An event that produces little or no anxiety in a person with relatively low standards of mastery and competence may produce almost unbearable anxiety in a person with higher standards. Clinical psychologists often see people who have suffered a crippling amount of anxiety and stress over violations of standards of sexual behavior, honesty, hostility, or dependency that would seem trivial to most of us. However, the importance of psychological traits in abnormal behavior should not conceal the role that physical factors can sometimes play—as discussed in a box on Psychology and Society.

Psychology and Society: Physical ailments: an underestimated cause of psychological disorders

Doctors and psychiatrists have long recognized that stress and conflict can affect our physical well-being. Now it is clear that the reverse is equally true. Psychological symptoms, sometimes quite severe, can arise from ailments of the body rather than from disturbing life experiences. About 10 percent of patients treated in psychiatric clinics are found to suffer from hidden medical conditions that gave rise to their psychological complaints (Hall, 1980a). With appropriate medical treatment, their symptoms usually clear up rapidly.

Even those of us who never feel the need for psychotherapy may at times suffer what appears to be emotional distress but actually stems from physical problems. For example, a brilliant college sophomore became constantly anxious and downcast, stayed in bed instead of attending classes, dropped her social life, slept poorly, and became belligerent toward her family and suspicious of her friends. A perceptive physician ordered blood tests, which showed the patient was suffering the emotional distress typical in severe cases of mononucleosis, popularly known as "mono." This is a blood infection that responds quickly to medication—and six months later the student was back on top of her work and filled with a sense of well-being.

Such cases are not unusual. People suffering from anemia, a deficiency in red blood cells, often complain of being depressed, unmotivated, and unable to concentrate. So do many patients who have hepatitis, an inflammation of the liver (Schwab, 1980). A diseased thyroid gland can cause rapid swings of mood, uncontrollable restlessness and agitation, disturbed sleep, and anxiety to the point of panic and even hallucinations (Hall, 1980b). Hypoglycemia, an abnormally low level of blood sugar, has been known to produce similarly severe personality disturbances in children as well as adults.

Psychological complaints can even arise from physical conditions that are quite routine. Periods of deep melancholy often accompany cases of the flu, and in many women the metabolic changes produced by the menstrual cycle. Many medicines for common ailments can cause psychological disturbances as a side effect (Hall, Stickney, and Gardner, 1980). Two such medicines are cortisone, often used to treat "tennis elbow," and sedatives prescribed for insomnia. Both can trigger depression far more devastating than the original complaints.

For anyone who experiences emotional problems, an important first step is to have a doctor look carefully for possible physical causes, which are sometimes well concealed and difficult to uncover. More often than is generally supposed, appropriate medical treatment—without the need for psychotherapy—is the key to restoring mental health.

Environmental influences

Also important is the environment to which we have been exposed from birth, especially the social experiences we have encountered. Some environments are much more likely than others to produce abnormal behavior. Statistical studies show that severe mental disorders are most common among people living in poverty. Indeed those in the lowest socioeconomic classes appear to have more than the usual share of all kinds of mental health problems (Kelly, Snowden, and Munoz, 1977). Perhaps this is because people forced to live in an impoverished environment have a more stressful existence than people at more affluent levels of society. Or perhaps growing up under deprived conditions reduces the individual's tolerance for stress and anxiety.

Environmental influences also help determine the particular kind of abnormal behavior a person is most likely to display. The culture of middle-class and upper-class America has traditionally maintained that individuals are personally responsible for what happens to them—and therefore people in this culture who fail to live up to inner standards of

Figure 12-1 Some examples of abnormal behavior *The psychiatric profession has identified over 230 specific mental disorders. In contrast to the major disorders discussed in the text, most of the examples listed here affect relatively few people. However, they portray the great variety of ways in which the human personality can function abnormally (American Psychiatric Association, 1980).*

Category of disorders	Major symptoms	Examples
Somatoform disorders	Recurring physical disabilities for which there is apparently no physical cause	Paralysis of the arms or legs Blindness Loss of sensitivity in a part of the body
Dissociative disorders	Sudden loss or change in sense of identity	Amnesia (severe memory failure, especially the inability to recall significant personal information) Multiple personality (splitting of the individual into two or more completely different selves)
Psychosexual disorders	Problems of sexual functioning or identity that are caused by psychological factors	Impotence or premature ejaculation Inability by the female to feel sexual excitement Painful spasms of the vagina that preclude intercourse Voyeurism Child molestation Transsexualism (desperate wish to become a member of the opposite sex) Homosexuality—but only when it is unwanted or distressing to the individual

(continued)

Source: American Psychiatric Association, *DSM-III*, 1980.

achievement and virtue are likely to suffer intense feelings of guilt or depression. Americans with a less affluent background are more likely to display symptoms generated by feelings of anger, bitterness, and suspicion.

To summarize, the chances that people will display abnormal behavior—and the particular kinds of abnormal behavior to which they are most prone—depend in part on the biological equipment they have inherited, in part on the psychological traits they have acquired, and in part on the environment in which they find themselves both as children and adults. These three factors work together to make some people behave in ways that range from slightly to severely disturbed.

Category of disorders	Major symptoms	Examples
Organic mental disorders	Abnormalities of behavior associated with either temporary or permanent damage or malfunctioning of the brain	Dementia (impaired thinking, judgment, and impulse control as found among the aged) Delirium (disorientation, perceptual disturbances, nightmares and insomnia, and clouding of consciousness resulting from sudden withdrawal from alcohol or drugs)
Miscellaneous disorders of impulse control	Failure to resist an impulse or temptation to perform acts harmful to the individual or to others	Pathological gambling (so persistent that it disrupts family life or work) Kleptomania (irresistible impulse to steal) Pyromania (fire setting) Explosive episodes of aggressiveness and destructiveness for no reason
Factitious disorders	Psychological or physical symptoms that are voluntarily produced by the individual	Self-inflicted injuries or wounds Repeated attempts to be admitted to hospitals Simulation of severe psychological disturbances such as memory loss and hallucinations

Varieties and shades of abnormality

Abnormal behavior takes many forms. Some deviations from the normal are so slight that they are popularly termed mere quirks—strange little habits like eccentricities in dress or speech. People who have somehow picked up such habits may seem a bit odd at times, but they are not seriously discomforted or prevented from functioning effectively. At the other extreme are the serious forms of mental disturbance that render their victims out of touch with reality and incapable of conducting the ordinary affairs of life. These drastic forms of abnormal behavior are relatively rare. In a sort of twilight zone between normal behavior and extreme abnormality are long-lasting emotional disturbances characterized by high levels of stress and anxiety. Their victims usually manage to get along in school, hold jobs, and conduct more or less successful family and social relationships. But their chronic feeling of being anxious and distressed interferes with their effectiveness and their zest for life. They are the people who are most likely to seek relief through psychotherapy.

In a sense, every case of abnormal behavior is unique. Each person experiences an individual pattern of stressful situations and responds to them in individual ways dictated by an individual set of biological, psychological, and environmental factors. Thus any attempt to classify the symptoms has to be somewhat arbitrary. But some kind of classification is essential. Researchers everywhere must speak a common language in their studies of the causes of various types of abnormal behavior. A common terminology is also necessary for reliable diagnoses and appropriate treatments.

The classification scheme now used by most psychologists and other mental health professionals was established in 1980 by the American Psychiatric Association in its *Diagnostic and Statistical Manual of Mental Disorders*—or *DSM-III.* The manual presents detailed descriptions of patterns of abnormal behavior. The patterns cover a broad spectrum ranging from those popularly known as neurotic to more devastating ones often referred to as psychotic. A few examples of the more than 230 disorders described in *DSM-III* are provided in Figure 12-1.

No classification system is likely to be acceptable to all those who deal with people displaying abnormal behavior. Most people in the mental health field, however, view the development of the current system as a forward step. There is some evidence, for example, that its clearer definitions allow more reliable diagnoses to be made of the problems presented by various clients (Williams and Spitzer, 1981). The five major types of disorders discussed in this section are the major ones included in *DSM-III.* Together, they account for most of the people whose personalities can clearly be described as abnormal.

Schizophrenia: no. 1 crippler

The symptoms began to appear when Ralph was 19 years old. He became suspicious of his classmates, insisting that they were developing a special language so that they could carry out their secret plans to destroy him. His dress became slovenly, and sometimes, even in the heat of summer, he would wear three sweaters to protect him from "the poisonous rays that will appear at noon." His few friends would often find him in a corner of the library, mumbling to himself. Once Ralph refused to eat for an entire week. He was convinced that the food was poisoned to punish him for his grandmother's death. He imagined that she had died as a result of a magic word he had secretly thought of in his own mind.

As time passed, Ralph's behavior became even more bizarre. He would stand at the window for hours on end, staring at passers-by and mumbling nonsensical phrases like "gloop-in-the-soup" or "brangle my strangle." Sometimes he would pull his long hair over his face and kiss it passionately. He complained that the neighbors were spying on him, and he would scream obscenities at them. He believed he had enormous powers and wrote letters to the President to offer solutions for all the world's problems. He was chosen, he said, to act as peacemaker not only between nations but also between the United States government and the creatures who were about to arrive from outer space.

By the time he was hospitalized, nothing Ralph said or did made any sense. Once he tried to climb into the toilet and have a nurse flush him away. He ordered his doctors to leave the room because, as he explained it, "I am attending a conference with God, George Washington, and IBM." Eventually he began to soil himself and to swallow stones or pieces of garbage he found on the hospital grounds.

Ralph is one of the two million people in the United States who at one time or another have suffered from *schizophrenia,* the most devastating of all mental disorders. About 40 percent of the beds in American mental hospitals are now occupied by patients with schizophrenia. The disorder is particularly common among young adults in their twenties and occurs more often among men than among women. Overall the chances that a person will develop the disease are roughly 1 in 100 (Torrey, 1980).

Behavior patterns of schizophrenics

A survey sponsored by the World Health Organization in nine different countries found that therapists generally consider individuals to be schizophrenic when they display the following behavior (Carpenter, Strauss, and Bartko, 1973):

1. *Poor insight*
2. *Incoherent speech* (often a spontaneous flow of conversation that cannot be understood)
3. *Delusions* (frequent and often extremely bizarre; schizophrenics may believe that they no longer exist or that their heads or arms are missing)
4. *Absence of emotion* (blank and expressionless face; little or no emotion shown in situations where a normal person would be upset or elated)
5. *Remoteness* (making it difficult for the therapist or others to establish any rapport)
6. *Worry about thoughts* (Schizophrenics may seem to hear their own thoughts as if they were spoken aloud and could be heard by others. They may also feel that their thoughts are somehow being broadcast so that everyone knows about them.)

In schizophrenia all the processes described in this book—perception, language, emotion, interpersonal relationships—appear to go completely haywire. People with the disorder lose touch with the real

Psychology and Society: Helping victims of schizophrenia decide about parenthood

Because schizophrenia tends to run in families, couples who have been affected must often decide whether or not to have a child who might inherit this crippling disorder. To help them resolve their dilemma, they can turn to a genetic counselor who is trained to assist people in handling just such difficult problems.

Suppose that a genetic counselor were asked by a couple, one of whom had suffered from schizophrenia, whether they should plan to conceive a child. There are a number of reasons for a negative answer. To begin with, the odds are one in ten that any child born to them will develop schizophrenia—and even higher still that the child will develop either the actual disorder or troublesome symptoms very much like it. Moreover, the chances that a person recovered from schizophrenia will suffer a relapse are often increased by the stresses of becoming a parent. This means that a child already vulnerable to schizophrenia would face an even greater risk as a result of living in a highly disorganized and disturbed home environment. For all these reasons some experts feel that people who have had schizophrenia might well be advised against parenthood—or adding to their families (Erlenmeyer-Kimling, 1976).

But there are arguments on the other side as well. After all, the majority of children born to schizophrenics are not likely to develop the disorder despite their genetic background. Such children can go through life altogether unscathed if their environment remains stable and free of unusual stress. And there is no way to identify before birth whether a particular child will be in danger. Moreover, what about the possibility that a child born to a schizophrenic parent may come into the world destined for greatness rather than disability? The offspring of schizophrenics who do not break down often show signs of unusual creativity (Schulsinger, 1976).

It is rarely possible for genetic counselors to provide simple, yes-or-no answers to couples concerned about passing on schizophrenia to their offspring. According to the Society for Human Genetics, they can serve their clients best by helping them (a) understand the facts about the disorder and the treatments available, and (b) appreciate the role that heredity plays and the risks they face that the disorder might one day appear in a child of theirs. Armed with such information, couples can more readily deal with their anxiety and arrive at an informed decision.

world. They hear voices that are not there, speak a language that does not exist, laugh for no reason, or sit motionless for hours on end. What could possibly cause the human personality to become so completely disorganized?

The search for schizophrenia's roots

Some investigators have concluded that schizophrenia is not just a single disturbance but many types that have been grouped together merely because they exhibit certain resemblances. As evidence, they cite the fact that the symptoms occur in different forms and degrees of intensity. If this is true, then it would seem futile to seek a common cause or common cure. Other investigators, however, believe that all the various forms of schizophrenia have a common basis, probably some hereditary defect. These investigators suggest that there is a *schizophrenia spectrum,* on which people with an inherited vulnerability range from a mere tendency to develop minor symptoms, through borderline behavior, and all the way to a display of the disturbance in its most severe and bizarre form (Reich, 1976).

The nature of the possible underlying defect is not known, but some clues do exist. Schizophrenics seem to have an abnormal pattern of metabolism that would affect the brain's neurotransmitters. The symptoms of many schizophrenics are associated especially with an excess of the neurotransmitter dopamine. Virtually all drugs that are effective in treating schizophrenic symptoms interfere with the action of dopamine. At the same time, certain drugs that intensify the symptoms release dopamine. Among the latter are amphetamines. Indeed many drug users who overdose on amphetamines may display symptoms that resemble schizophrenia (Snyder et al., 1974). As is shown in Figure 12-2, recently developed techniques for observing the brain in action offer further indications that schizophrenics differ from normal people in brain metabolism (Buchsbaum et al., 1982).

It has also been found that schizophrenics show abnormal patterns of eye movements when they try to track a moving object, such as a swinging pendulum (Holzman, Proctor, and Hughes, 1973). Many of their close relatives, though not themselves victims of schizophrenia, display the same unusual tracking pattern (Holzman et al., 1974), as if there were a family tendency to do so. The unusual patterns might indicate some defect in parts of the nervous system responsible for perception—which might in turn account for the fact that schizophrenics seem out of touch with reality as perceived by normal people.

Evidence for the genetic origin of schizophrenia is strong, as indicated in Figure 12-3. Even if some inherited defect is the basis for the disorder, however, the fact that not all people from the same family become schizophrenic points to the influence of environment, anxiety, and stress in determining whether the inborn tendency will actually affect behavior. The concern that children of schizophrenics might inherit the disorder is discussed in a box on Psychology and Society.

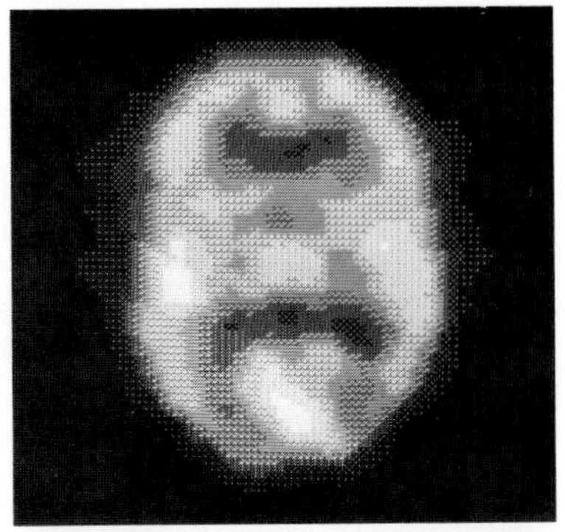

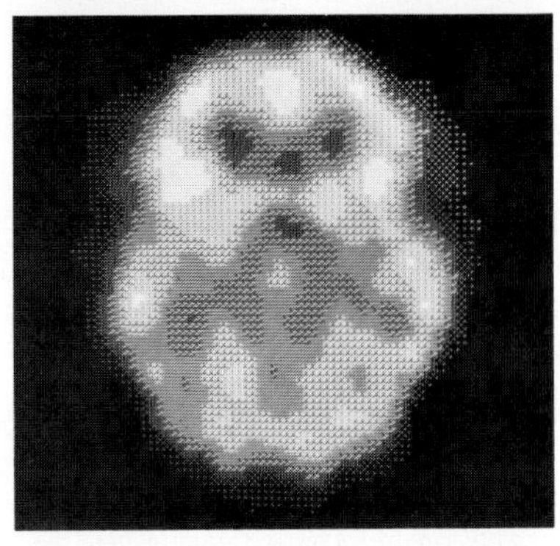

Figure 12-2 The schizophrenic and normal brain: a difference in metabolic activity *The photos were produced by the brain-scan technique known as* positron emission tomography, *or* PET. *The technique produces an image of the brain containing various colors (not shown here) that reflect the level at which glucose—the brain's main fuel—is being metabolized. The more active a particular part of the brain, the more glucose is being burned up. The most active areas are indicated by the lighter shading. In the schizophrenic patient (top), the level of glucose metabolism appears highest in the rear portions of the brain that contain the visual centers, suggesting that a hallucination may be under way. But the brain of the normal subject (bottom) is burning up the most glucose in the frontal area, where higher level thought processes are organized. When the PET scans were made, neither the patient nor the normal subject was being stimulated in any way. They were unmedicated and resting with their eyes closed in a dark, accoustically insulated room.*

Affective disorders: abnormalities of mood

All of us know from personal experience that events can alter our mood, or what psychologists call our *affect.* Even minor crises—a dented fender, a poor exam grade, a stolen wallet—can cloud the way we feel. There are times when life is marred by grief—when a friend dies, a treasured relationship breaks up, or the job you worked so hard to get is given instead to someone else.

The intensity of the sadness we feel is usually proportionate to the significance of the event. The loss of a favorite book and the loss of a child normally are not expected to evoke the same dip in mood. And however difficult the stress, we can expect after a reasonable period to bounce back and feel like our "old self" again. Many people, however, react to stress with abnormal *depression*—a plunge in mood so severe and prolonged that it can ultimately overwhelm the entire personality and cause many of life's functions to grind to a halt.

A case of depression—and how it differs from "the blues"

For Susan, a bright college sophomore, episodes of disabling depression occurred whenever she felt she was being rejected. She began to show her most recent signs of the disorder soon after she failed to win a place on the school newspaper. Susan's friends noticed that her voice became

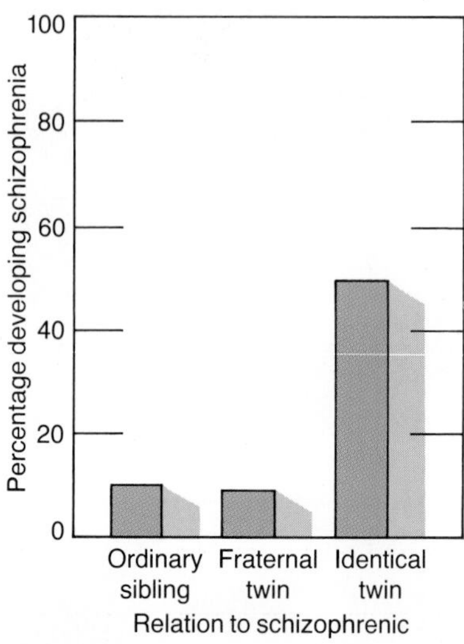

Figure 12-3 Vulnerability to schizophrenia: the difference heredity makes *The fraternal twin of a schizophrenic has about the same chance of developing the disease as an ordinary sibling—about one in ten. But for an identical twin of a schizophrenic, who has inherited exactly the same genes, the chances increase to fifty-fifty (Gottesman and Shields, 1972).*

flat and lifeless, her face gray and strained, her eyes clouded and always on the verge of tears. She lacked energy for even the most routine tasks—getting up for school, shopping, going to the library. Though she had always been a fan of the movies, she completely lost interest in them. She began to withdraw from her friends. Instead of having lunch with them, she would now go off by herself and walk aimlessly around the park. She could no longer concentrate, often staring at the same line in a magazine for minutes on end. In the evening, she would skip dinner and sit alone in front of the TV set, hardly aware of what was on the screen.

Susan's case demonstrates many of the ways that depression differs from the passing feelings of unhappiness we often call "the blues." Severely depressed people experience not only unrelenting sadness but intense helplessness and hopelessness as well. They lose all semblance of self-esteem and are filled instead with grinding self-recriminations and guilt. They have no zest for either work or play. They may find that even routine acts of thinking and speaking are slowed and take enormous effort. In the most severe cases they may suffer delusions and hallucinations. Depression causes physical problems as well. Sleep is disturbed—especially by early morning awakenings—and the appetite for food and sex tends to diminish or disappear. Depressed people often complain of poor digestion, heart palpitation, headache, visual disturbances, and dizziness. Other indicators of depression are identified in Figure 12-4.

Escaping the pain through suicide

Although the most prominent signs of depression may differ from one person to another, all abnormally depressed people share an inability to experience any pleasure whatsoever—or to imagine that they ever will again. As one depressed person put it:

> Everything I see, say, or do seems extraordinarily flat and pointless; there is no color, there is no point to anything. Things drag on and on, interminably. I am exhausted, dead inside. I want to sleep, to escape somehow, but there is always the thought that if I really could sleep, I must always and again awake to the dullness and apathy of it all (Goldstein, Baker, and Jamison, 1980).

It would be difficult to convince this individual that depression is actually a self-limiting disorder, meaning that most people eventually recover even without treatment (Zung, 1981). Those in the grip of depression feel hopeless about literally everything in the future—as illustrated by the answer to item 14 in Figure 12-4. With the outlook so dark, some choose self-destruction as a way out of their misery. Of all the symptoms of depression, it is the inability to hope that appears most likely to awaken suicidal thoughts (Beck, 1967). Only a small percentage of depression sufferers actually do commit suicide, but as shown in Figure 12-5, the risk appears higher among them than among victims of other types of mental disorders.

	None or a Little of the Time	Some of the Time	Good Part of the Time	Most or All of the Time
1. I feel down-hearted, blue, and sad				✓
2. Morning is when I feel the best	✓			
3. I have crying spells or feel like it				✓
4. I have trouble sleeping through the night				✓
5. I eat as much as I used to	✓			
6. I enjoy looking at, talking to, and being with attractive women/men	✓			
7. I notice that I am losing weight				✓
8. I have trouble with constipation				✓
9. My heart beats faster than normal				✓
10. I get tired for no reason				✓
11. My mind is as clear as it used to be	✓			
12. I find it easy to do the things I used to	✓			
13. I am restless and can't keep still				✓
14. I feel hopeful about the future	✓			
15. I am more irritable than usual				✓
16. I find it easy to make decisions	✓			
17. I feel that I am useful and needed	✓			
18. My life is pretty full	✓			
19. I feel that others would be better off if I were dead				✓
20. I still enjoy the things I used to do	✓			

Figure 12-4 A brief test for depression *The items are from a test called the Self Rating Depression Scale. The checks in the boxes would be made by a person who is depressed in the most extreme way. Note that such a person would feel that all the positive emotions and experiences mentioned in the test apply "none or a little of the time," while all the negative ones apply "most or all of the time."*

The two poles of manic-depressive illness

When episodes of depression recur without other abnormalities of mood, the disorder is called *unipolar depression.* We know from our own experience, however, that moods often vary. Some days we feel "blah," but soon enough we are on top of the world again. In extremely exaggerated form, such mood fluctuations constitute the most severe mood disturbance, known as *bipolar depression* or *manic-depressive illness.* For victims of this disorder, the emotional pendulum swings wildly from intense excitement to deep melancholy.

Figure 12-5 The chances of suicide among mental disorder victims *A person with an affective disorder whose mood is depressed is three times more likely to commit suicide than a person with schizophrenia. The contrast in suicide rates is even sharper between depression victims and those with other types of disorders (Pokorny, 1964).*

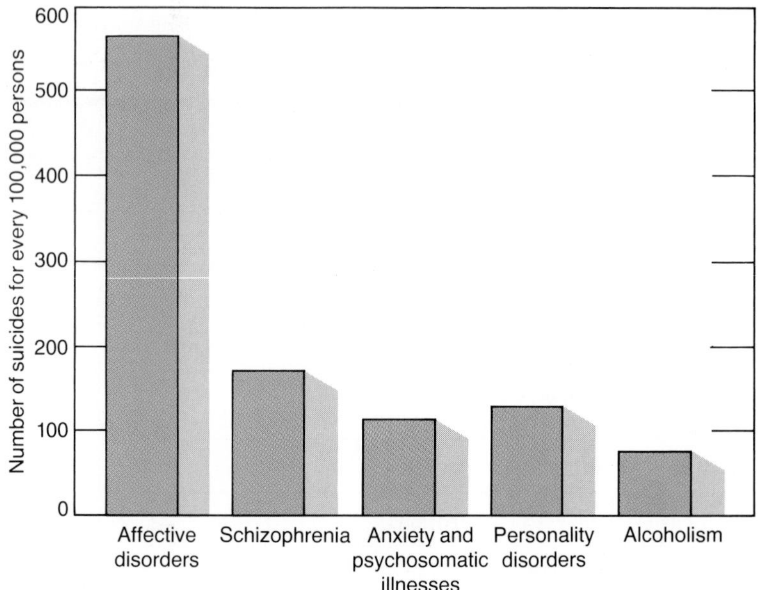

In the manic phase, people with manic-depressive illness tend to be talkative, restless, aggressive, boastful, and often destructive. They develop a feeling of intense well-being and even ecstacy. Sexual and moral inhibitions disappear and life is one uninterrupted "high." The manic person needs little sleep and is filled with abundant energy and grandiose notions. A professional golfer who suffered manic episodes has described one of them in which he believed he was a messiah handpicked by God to save the world from evil, put an end to racial prejudice, and discover a cure for cancer. He was thrilled by the assignment and intended to complete it (Kindred, 1978).

Like this man, people in the grip of mania feel capable of any undertaking, ignoring any harmful consequences. On the spur of the moment they may suddenly give away all their possessions, or embark on outlandish trips. In extreme cases, their thoughts become disconnected, jumping from one idea to another without any apparent logic. Sometimes the condition becomes difficult to differentiate from schizophrenia, and indeed some manic-depressives are mistakenly diagnosed as schizophrenics (Carpenter and Stephens, 1980). Soon, however, most manic individuals plummet back to the depressed phase, becoming so gloomy and hopeless that they are virtually immobilized. Only in rare cases—called *hypomania*—is the depressed phase never very prominent.

Origins of mood disorders

As with schizophrenia, some evidence suggests that mood disorders have a genetic basis. The risk of developing manic-depressive illness is less than 1 percent in the population at large. But it rises to around 15 percent among the close relatives—parents, siblings, and children—of manic-depressives. One study of adopted individuals who had a mood

Two famous suicides—Marilyn Monroe, Freddie Prinze.

disorder found that similar problems were three times more prevalent among their blood relatives than among their adopted relatives (Nurnberger and Gershon, 1982).

There is evidence also that mood disorders are related to disturbances in the brain—to such an extent that the symptoms sometimes appear without any apparent provocation. Neither the depressed individual nor the close family and friends can point to any unusually stressful event that might have caused a depression. The neurotransmitter noradrenalin appears to be of particular importance. Depression is associated with too little activity of the neurotransmitter, mania with too much activity. Drugs that fight depression seem to work by increasing its availability. *Lithium*—a drug that is effective in treating the wide mood swings of manic-depression—appears to work by reducing the amount.

Many people suffering from severe depression also have an excess amount of *cortisol,* a hormone secreted by the pituitary gland under stress or during emotional upset. Moreover the high level of cortisol seems to persist for an unusually long time (Carroll et al, 1981). It is not yet clear whether mood disorders are caused by these various biochemical factors or whether the disorder causes the biochemical changes. The most widely held theory is that some people are genetically vulnerable to biochemical imbalances, which are likely to occur in response to levels of stress that other people would not find disrupting.

Sex differences in depression

Mood disorders are reported more often by women than by men, and twice as many women as men take antidepressant drugs (Mellinger and Balter, 1981). The reason is not entirely clear. It may be that females are biologically more vulnerable—a possibility suggested by the fact that many women experience depression just before menstruation or after the birth of a child. Or the reason may be psychological as well, related to the more dependent and helpless role that women have been expected to play in our society. Some investigators believe that the sex

Psychology and Society: Depression in childhood: how vulnerable are the young?

Numerous studies have found that the risk of serious depression increases in the later years of life. But does this mean that children are free of the disorder?

For many years the answer was assumed to be yes. Indeed until the early 1960s, the term "childhood depression" did not appear in American textbooks on child psychiatry (Cytryn, McKnew, and Bunney, 1980). Now, however, it has become clear that children as well as adults can suffer from depression. Yet the ailment still goes unrecognized—and untreated—in too many cases.

The major reason is that by far the most common form of depression in children does not appear to be depression at all. Three types of problems often hide an underlying decay of mood in children:

1. Conduct disorders including hyperactivity, delinquency, irritability, and aggressiveness.
2. Physical complaints such as headaches, stomachaches, and bed-wetting.
3. School problems including school phobia, truancy, and poor scholastic performance.

Most parents and pediatricians are likely to overlook the possibility that such conditions may actually be masking a pervasive mood of depression. But careful observation of children by informed child psychiatrists and psychologists can often strip away the mask (Petti, 1981).

Even when the signs of depression are more obvious, the disorder is still easy to overlook in children. Because children are unaware of the meaning of depression, they do not complain of it openly in the same way that adults do. Moreover, many children can still be active and show some interest in their environment even while quite depressed. Closer attention, however, shows that depression produces symptoms in them comparable to those found among severely depressed adults.

Childhood depression, as in the case of adults, is likely to occur as a result of both genetic vulnerability and a stressful environment. Some cases are of long standing, arising when children are subjected to continuous stress. Their lives are filled, for example, with repeated separations from loved ones, abuse, family strife and violence, or the day-in and day-out trauma of being reared by an emotionally disturbed parent. Other cases last for a much briefer time, usually triggered by an identifiable, immediate cause. It could be the sudden death of a parent, an unexpected and uprooting move to a new city, or the arrival of a new sibling who seems to capture all of mother's love and attention.

In cases of either type, children suffer sharp downswings in mood like those endured by adults. They look sad and feel even sadder, are moody, cry easily, and sleep and eat poorly. They are burdened with a sense of worthlessness, hopelessness, and guilt. Finding no pleasure in life, some entertain thoughts of suicide, and a small but increasing number actually commit the act (Frederick, 1978).

The line between abnormal depression and everyday cases of "the blues" is as difficult to draw among children as among adults. But this much is certain: Youth is no shield against the ravages of depression, long regarded to be a painful consequence only of adult stress. More pediatricians, teachers and parents need to learn to recognize the condition. A more widespread awareness of the signs of childhood depression would bring children the appropriate medical treatment they need—and restore to them their lost well-being and productivity.

difference in prevalence of depression is more apparent than real. These investigators point out that women are more likely than men to express their feelings of depression and to seek help. Moreover, depression in men may be masked more often by alcoholism. One study showed that the higher rate of depression among women cancels out when alcoholics are counted as depressed (Bucher et al., 1981). For both sexes, the chances of experiencing severe episodes of depression increase with age. But this does not mean that young people are free of the disorder—as is discussed in a box on Psychology and Society.

Anxiety disorders

Abnormal behavior is typically the result of a failure to cope with anxiety. Thus it is not surprising that anxiety is a characteristic of most forms of mental disorder. But sometimes it is such an obvious and outstanding symptom that it constitutes what has been termed an *anxiety disorder.* Anxiety disorders can take a number of forms, all of them arising when situations that produce conflict and frustration remain unresolved. In some cases, anxiety itself is clearly the most prominent symptom. In other cases, individuals develop disabling patterns of behavior—such as staying home to avoid crowds or washing their hands every half hour—as a way of keeping their underlying anxiety under control.

Many victims of anxiety disorders function well enough so that even their close friends may not become aware of their symptoms. Moreover, unlike schizophrenics and manic-depressives, they stay in touch with reality and can admit that their feelings and behavior are illogical. There are four common forms of anxiety disorder.

Generalized anxiety disorder

As the name implies, victims of *generalized anxiety* attach the way they feel not to anything in particular, but rather to everything in general. Freud described the condition as "free-floating anxiety." Each day is filled with an unfocused feeling of tension, uneasiness, and vague fear. People displaying such anxiety feel irritable and jumpy, and they are uncomfortable with other people. They are constantly "on edge," unable to concentrate and filled with doubts about their ability to work or study. They go around with a furrowed brow and a strained face, and sometimes their eye muscles twitch. Their level of anxiety is likely to shoot up as a result of minor events that would not affect a normal person (Hamilton, 1982).

Many anxious people are constantly concerned about their health—partly because they actually do tend to develop physical symptoms. Their autonomic nervous system is overactive, producing heart palpitations, shortness of breath, hot flashes, cold sweats, nausea, diarrhea, and frequent urination. Because they find it difficult to "turn off" at night, they wake up feeling as tired as when they went to bed. Friends may point out that it makes no sense to live continuously as if the world were about to cave in, but victims cannot seem to control the apprehension that hovers menacingly over them and clouds virtually every aspect of their lives.

Panic disorder

Some people living in a state of anxiety experience periodic episodes when their undercurrent of tension turns into a flood of terror. They are then said to be suffering from a *panic disorder.* Often for no apparent reason, they are suddenly overwhelmed with a sense of disaster and imminent death. They also may have feelings of unreality, or believe that they are about to lose control and "go crazy." One man has described his transition from anxiety to panic this way:

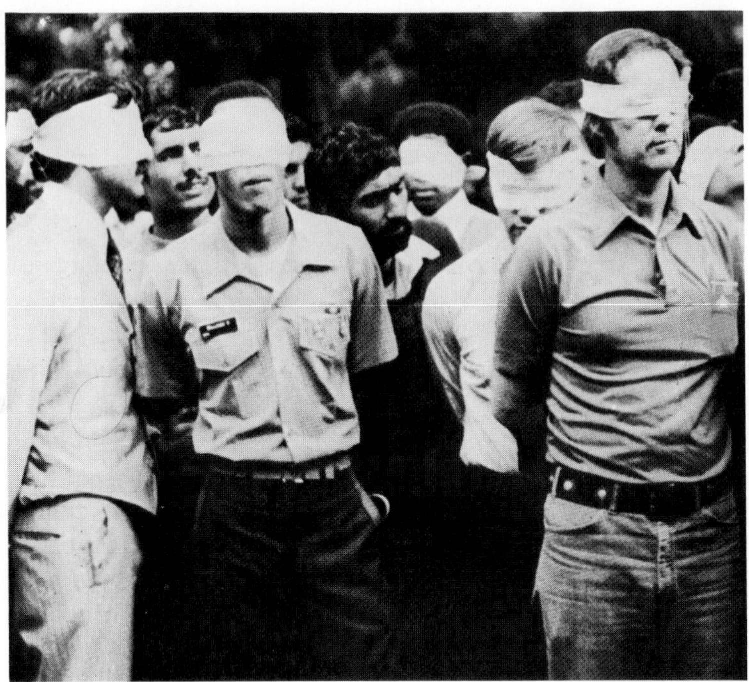

American hostages held captive in Iran and upon their release. They suffered the kind of traumatic experience that can lead to severe stress and anxiety.

> I feel anxious and fearful most of the time; I keep expecting something to happen but I don't know what. It's not the same all the time. Sometimes I only feel bad—then suddenly for no reason it happens. My heart begins to pound so fast that I feel it's going to pop out. My hands get icy and I get a cold sweat all over my body. My forehead feels like it is covered with sharp needles. I feel like I won't be able to breathe and I begin panting and choking. It's terrible—so terrible. I can go along for a while without too much difficulty and then suddenly without any warning it happens (Denike and Tiber, 1968).

Many generally anxious people have their lives pretty much under control until a panic attack erupts. One perplexed college senior is a case in point. She describes her attacks as coming "out of the blue" and making her feel suddenly as if a rapist had a knife at her throat or she was being buried alive. "But," she admits, "there's absolutely no reason in sight. I might be driving the car to school feeling pretty good and wham—all I can think about is racing home and ducking under the covers until the crisis passes."

Unlike victims of panic attacks who face no real threat to explain their terror, some people do experience shocking events that are frightfully stressful. These can result in anxiety problems that have been grouped under a special category called *post-traumatic stress disorder*—described in a box on Psychology and Society.

Phobic disorder

Anxiety states sometimes become attached to a specific object, situation, or activity. The victim is then regarded as suffering from a *phobic disorder*—in other words, displaying an unreasonable fear. Many of us

Psychology and Society: The emotional scars left by shocking life experiences

Some people are unlucky enough to endure traumatic stresses that lie far outside the range of usual human experience. They include victims not only of natural disasters such as floods and earthquakes, but also of shockingly stressful experiences that human beings themselves devise—among them rape, assault, and kidnapping. Victims of human-induced stress on a large scale can be found among survivors of military combat and of captivity and torture in prisoner-of-war and concentration camps. Indeed most people who suffer psychological trauma do so at the hands of one another rather than from events totally outside human control.

Survivors of extremely traumatic experiences are sometimes left with special anxiety problems. Some act as if they have been numbed by the shock of their ordeal. Their interest in life is diminished, and they feel alienated from the people around them (Walker, 1981). Others develop a tendency to remain constantly on the alert—as if disaster is sure to strike again at any moment. They tend also to startle easily. People who have lived through auto crashes may panic at the sound of cars in the night. Those who have endured a mugging or rape may respond with a start whenever they hear strange sounds, and some former POWs and hostages report similar reactions whenever they hear approaching footsteps. Survivors of psychological trauma are likely also to keep reliving their experience. They suffer from nightmares in which the shattering episode is reenacted in all its terrifying detail, and by day they find themselves suddenly overwhelmed by harrowing memories whenever they are exposed to situations that even remotely resemble the original event.

Post-traumatic stress reactions can occur at any age. In 1976, 26 California children were kidnapped at gunpoint by three masked men who took over the bus on which they were returning from school. The victims, ranging from 5 to 14 years of age, were first driven around in total darkened vans for 11 hours. Then they were buried in a "hole," which was actually a truck-trailer placed underground and covered with a layer of earth. After 16 hours, the kidnappers finally left and the terrorized children dug themselves out.

Follow-up studies of 23 of the children showed that each of them was still painfully affected by the trauma as long as a year later. They all lived in fear that something terrible would happen to them again. A number of them were sure that the kidnappers, although long since arrested, would be back—and indeed they found themselves being kidnapped repeatedly in their dreams. All the children now listened and watched in fear for signs of danger—in the dark, when alone, near strangers or cars, or when they felt confined. Eight of them, although perfectly safe, suffered attacks of such overwhelming anxiety that they screamed and ran for help. An 11-year-old boy refused to sleep in his bedroom for nights on end because he believed the ceiling was about to collapse, and an 8-year-old girl who now depended on a nightlight for security jumped out of bed in panic every time the heater in her room turned on (Terr, 1981).

Some people get over a traumatic experience soon enough, but others are troubled by symptoms for years on end. One team of investigators studied 27 women who had been raped as long ago as 16 years. The victims continued to suffer from episodes of depression, tension, and fatigue. They experienced not only sexual problems, but difficulties in developing any close personal relationships. Two of the women eventually became so disturbed that they had to be hospitalized, and four reported that they subsequently returned to long-abandoned patterns of alcohol and drug abuse (Ellis, Atkeson, and Calhoun, 1981). A number of elderly concentration camp survivors broke down completely decades after their ordeal was over when they had to be hospitalized for medical reasons. The experience was sufficiently similar to imprisonment to reopen fully the old psychological wounds (Edelstein, 1982).

There is some evidence that traumatic episodes inflicted by others leave worse scars than those occurring by accident or as a result of a natural catastrophe (American Psychiatric Association, 1980). Crime victims, hostages, and combat veterans are examples of those likely to suffer especially from their ordeals. Whether or not this is actually so in every case, it seems clear enough that untold psychological pain could be prevented if somehow human beings were able to learn one day to avoid making victims of each other.

refer to ourselves casually as having one sort of phobia or another. "I have a phobia about spiders," you might hear some people say as they scrupulously survey the back yard before a picnic. Others will tell you that they cannot stand thunderstorms, and so they carefully check and recheck the weather forecast before starting out on a trip. Most of us manage to function quite well despite such fears. Victims of a phobic disorder, in contrast, find that their morbid fears recur so frequently and are so intense that they interfere with day-to-day activities and even become the controlling factor in their lives.

Two common phobias are *claustrophobia* (fear of confinement in small places, which makes some people unable to ride in elevators) and *acrophobia* (fear of high places, which affects some people when they have to climb to the top of a theater balcony). Phobias can be acquired through simple conditioning in childhood, as the child Albert acquired his fear of furry animals. But they can also develop in more complex ways—for example, as a means for displacing basic anxieties about sex or social interactions onto something more tangible.

The most crippling of all phobias is *agoraphobia,* or fear of public places that can include streets, stores, buses, trains, or virtually anywhere outside the house. In fact, victims often become imprisoned in their own homes, which they perceive as the only safe place to be. Agoraphobia typically takes hold after a number of severe panic attacks. The person then begins to avoid situations in which the attacks happened, but soon this avoidance response spreads to other situations. Eventually it becomes impossible to go anywhere at all—certainly not alone. In many ways the individual with agoraphobia behaves very much like the young child suffering from *school phobia* who desperately clutches mother's hand and screams in terror at the thought of venturing out into the world.

Phobias are more likely to be found among adolescents and young adults than among older people. They are also more common among females than males. One possible explanation of this sex difference is that fearfulness has long been more acceptable among women than men (Coleman, 1976).

Obsessive-compulsive disorder

Obsessions are thoughts that keep cropping up in a persistent and disturbing fashion. Some anxiety-ridden people are obsessed with the idea that they have heart trouble or that they are going to die by a certain age. A common and mild form of obsession is the feeling of people starting out on a trip that they have left the door unlocked or the stove turned on.

Compulsions are irresistible urges to perform some act over and over again, such as washing one's hands dozens of times a day. The hostess who cannot bear to see a knife or fork out of line at the table and keeps emptying her guests' ashtrays is exhibiting mild forms of compulsion. So is the businesswoman who cannot get any work done unless her papers are arranged in neat piles on her desk and she has a half-dozen freshly sharpened pencils waiting all in a line. Or the child who steps on every crack in the sidewalk.

Obsessive-compulsive reactions sometimes serve the purpose of covering up underlying feelings of hostility. This was the case for one woman whose marriage was on the rocks, but who could never express her intense feelings of anger toward her husband. Instead she developed compulsions that made her home life a shambles. She continually scrubbed, cleaned and washed so that her housework was never done. She developed a long and rigid set of procedures for ordering groceries, making list after list until the stores were already closed. Her preparations for dinner were so elaborate that the meal was fixed—if at all—only long after bedtime. Victims of obsessive-compulsive disorder tend to use up energy in repetitious thoughts or acts instead of spontaneous expressions of feeling. As a result, many of them appear to others as cold and remote individuals.

Personality disorders

People suffering from episodes of schizophrenia, periods of depression, or attacks of anxiety are in one sense like those who are vulnerable to a physical illness such as migraine headaches. While they are in the grip of their symptoms, they are often described as "not themselves." But when they recover, they are "back to their old selves."

In contrast, some forms of abnormal behavior appear to exist as part of the entire personality rather than being expressed in specific symptoms. Although these forms of behavior may arise out of some underlying stress or deep-seated anxiety, they are displayed by individuals who may actually not feel any particular discomfort such as depression or panic. Instead such people behave in ways that are often painful to others. They seem to lack any desire—or perhaps ability—to act in ways that are socially acceptable, and they rarely seek to change by getting help. Their patterns of behavior, called *personality disorders,* often surface at an early age and become so deeply ingrained that even friends or family members would find it difficult to distinguish the disorder from the person.

Although personality disorders are not easy to classify, it is possible to differentiate over a dozen different types (American Psychiatric Association, 1980). Discussions of three of them follow, and others are described in Figure 12-6.

Antisocial personality: reckless and ruthless

An extreme form of personality disorder is *antisocial personality.* People with this type of personality seem to lack any normal conscience or sense of social responsibility and to have no feeling for other people. Some of these sociopaths, as they are called, may seem on the surface to be quite charming, candid, and generous—but in truth they are selfish, ruthless, and addicted to lying. They have no affection for anyone but themselves and take advantage of others without a shred of guilt (McCord and McCord, 1964). Indeed the apparent absence of anxiety of any kind is one of the outstanding characteristics of the sociopath—and of course a factor that makes antisocial personality completely different from most other disorders.

The antisocial personality at its extreme, Sirhan Sirhan, assassin of Presidential candidate Robert Kennedy.

Figure 12-6 **Characteristics of people with personality disorders** *We all know people who have traits somewhat like the ones listed. But for people with personality disorders, the patterns are so pervasive that it becomes virtually impossible for them to adapt to the demands of the real world. As a result, their social relationships and their work are likely to suffer significantly.*

Type of personality disorder	What the person is like
Histrionic	Highly excitable, often reacting to tiny events with gigantic displays of emotion; shallow and not very genuine; quick to form friendships—but soon becomes demanding and inconsiderate; seductive and tries to dominate the opposite sex; egocentric and needs to control others, sometimes even by threatening or actually attempting suicide
Passive-aggressive	Aggressive and resentful toward others—but only indirectly through such annoying techniques as procrastination, stubbornness, and intentional inefficiency; lacks self-confidence and has a pessimistic attitude
Avoidant	Extremely sensitive to possible rejection, avoiding close relationships unless dead certain of total acceptance and approval; crushed by even the slightest hint of criticism; feels inferior and broods about personal imperfections; yearns for affection—yet cannot take the chance of being rebuffed
Dependent	Lacks self-confidence and initiative; manages to let other people take responsibility for everything in life—even for major decisions about job or career; cannot stand the idea of being self-reliant; needs to depend on others at all costs—even if the other person is mean and abusive; sees self as dumb and helpless
Compulsive	Perfectionistic and so absorbed in trivial details as to be unable to see "the big picture"; overly serious and stingy and rarely does anything spontaneously; intent on having others conform to "my way of doing things"; indecisive, afraid of making a mistake, and unable to establish priorities; puts even routine work ahead of friends
Schizoid	Unable to build close social relationships or even to feel any warmth toward others; indifferent to almost everything, including the feelings of people; reserved and withdrawn—a true "loner"; humorless, dull, and aloof; vague and indecisive; absentminded and given to daydreaming; sometimes seems removed from the real world—but without the seriously abnormal symptoms of schizophrenia
Borderline	Impulsive, unpredictable, and easily upset; gets uncontrollably angry for little reason; quickly shifts mood—from depression to irritability to anxiety; feels empty and bored inside and is unable to establish a firm sense of identity; lives on the border of reality, slipping beyond it during periods of heavy pressure and stress

Sociopaths are likely to be in and out of trouble all their lives, for they do not learn from experience and appear to have no desire to help themselves. They are people who just "never grow up" and never become independent, self-supporting adults. Instead they are impulsive and reckless—unable to keep a job, maintain an enduring marital or sexual relationship, or act as a responsible parent. Lacking respect for the law, they often end up spending periods of their lives in prison. Such a person is sometimes also referred to as a "psychopath," a word that comes up frequently in court cases to describe criminals who appear to experience no remorse for even the most cruel deeds. They are good examples of the antisocial personality in its most extreme form.

The causes remain a mystery, but antisocial behavior patterns usually begin in childhood. It is rare for people to be diagnosed as having an antisocial personality unless they displayed similar problems before they reached 18 years of age. One study followed up over 500 adults seen in a child guidance clinic 30 years earlier. Most of those with antisocial personality had already been in trouble as children—with their parents, teachers, and often the law. They had a history of school truancy, stealing, lying, irresponsibility about money, heavy involvement in sex, staying out late, or running away from home. The more antisocial symptoms children displayed, the more likely they were to grow up as antisocial adults. The chances of developing an antisocial personality disorder are high for those raised by a parent who has the disorder. Growing up with antisocial companions and in high-crime neighborhoods are also factors—but these carry much less weight if the parents themselves are free of antisocial behavior (Robins, 1978).

Some studies have indicated that sociopaths tend to have an autonomic nervous system that is especially insensitive and difficult to arouse (Hare, 1970). This biological characteristic might lead them to seek emotional excitement and at the same time to be oblivious to danger (such as the consequences of committing a serious crime). But as in most other forms of abnormal behavior, it is unlikely that biological factors alone account for an antisocial personality. Family environment appears to weigh very heavily in the development of the disorder.

Paranoid personality: always suspicious, always threatened

All of us feel suspicious at times—and it is a good thing that we do. You would be ignoring your own best interests if you did not feel suspicious on hearing strange sounds of footsteps in your basement at night or on finding that an essay very much like the one you left in your locker appeared under someone else's name. For normal people, such suspicions are washed away once there is evidence that they are not warranted. The sounds in the night may turn out to be made by a furnace instead of a prowler, and a supposedly clear case of plagiarism may turn out to be a complete coincidence.

In contrast, people with a *paranoid personality* are unable to give up their constant suspicions and mistrust of other people—even when the facts clearly point the other way. Worse yet, they may even become suspicious of anyone who tries to reason with them. They expect at any moment to be tricked, and they are always on guard and worried about the hidden motives of others. Paranoid individuals often seem to be devious and scheming. They also appear hostile and defensive—and so stubborn and rigid that they are unable to compromise on anything.

They always manage to find in life what they expect to find, and so they go around with an "I told you so" attitude.

It is extremely hard to build a satisfying relationship with paranoid individuals. At work such people tend to be intensely concerned with rank, always needing to know who is in control. Moreover, everything is taken personally—so that if a company established a new regulation that required all employees to sign in and out of work, paranoid individuals would feel that the rule was specifically devised only to get at them. In marriage they can become insanely jealous for no reason, yet they are unable to develop feelings of intimacy because they can trust no one. It is impossible for a person to be suspicious all the time and still have the capacity to be yielding, tender, or sentimental.

People with a paranoid personality disorder are often quite bright. In their own distorted way, they display highly prized capacities such as sensitivity, quickness of thought, and great consistency (Swanson, Bohnert, and Smith, 1970). Yet underneath, paranoid persons feel grossly inferior. Because they are always fighting off feelings of inadequacy, they tend to blame everything on others. In extreme cases, this process results in delusions of persecution. Sometimes paranoid individuals manage to compensate for their feelings of inferiority by developing the conviction that they are much greater than anyone else—but that the world just does not appreciate them. The result can be delusions of power and grandeur. Some extremely disturbed paranoid individuals end up actually believing that they are the Pope or the President.

Narcissistic personality: loving yourself too much

In an ancient Greek legend, Narcissus was a beautiful young man who fell in love with his own reflection in a pool—so much so that he remained glued there until he died. His name is the basis for a trait known as narcissism—or self-love—which in extreme form dominates the personality of those with a *narcissistic personality*.

People with this disorder are often quite charming and attractive, but once you get to know them, they are easy to dislike. They go around with an inflated sense of their own importance, acting as if they are God's gift to humanity. Unlike obsessive-compulsive individuals who constantly seek perfection, narcissistic people claim it (Akhtar and Thomson, 1982). They feel entitled to everything and end up using people for their own purposes, including sex. Often they give the impression that they really like you when all they actually want is to get you to do something for them. They offer little in return, and worse still, can excuse nothing of others. For example, if you chance to have an accident and as a result miss an appointment with such a person, it is not likely that you will be forgiven. Narcissists can rarely manage to put themselves in another's place.

Narcissistic individuals crave constant attention and admiration because they are trying desperately to compensate for painful feelings of emptiness and worthlessness lurking beneath the surface. That is also why they tend to daydream of incredible successes in their work or their love affairs. They are extremely superficial, totally preoccupied with appearances. They would rather be seen with the "right people" than enjoy the company of close friends. They also fake the feelings they think are appropriate in any situation to impress others. How they look is so important to them that they can easily spend hours grooming themselves. The narcissist of today stands transfixed at the mirror instead of the reflecting pool.

Some claim that this disorder is becoming more common because there is a greater acceptance in our culture of narcissistic behavior (Lasch, 1980). For example, books intended to teach us how to look out for ourselves first—or how to get everything we want out of life at any cost—tend to become best-sellers. But there is no evidence from research that narcissistic behavior is any more prevalent today than in the days of Narcissus.

Substance abuse: abnormal use of alcohol and drugs

The use of alcohol or drugs cannot itself be viewed as a psychological disorder. Otherwise countless people would be considered abnormal for sipping a cocktail to relax before dinner or taking a sedative to get to sleep when upset. The use of substances that affect the central nervous system is considered abnormal when it becomes so frequent and heavy that users can no longer function normally—whether in the family, at school, or at work. Moreover such people continue to seek alcohol and drugs despite damage tu their health and the threat to life itself.

The development of dependence

An indication that alcohol or drug use is departing from normal is the development of psychological dependence. When this happens, users no longer view the substance as an incidental feature of life or as a way to promote pleasure and well-being. Instead they believe it to be essential in order to handle the day-to-day stresses of life. An executive might come to believe that he could not possibly endure the daily grind of corporate life without gulping a few swallows of the gin hidden in the desk drawer for "emergencies." Or a student might be convinced that without marijuana there would be no way to survive the tensions of school.

Many people who are psychologically dependent on alcohol and certain drugs become physically dependent—or *addicted*—as well. Their bodies develop a *tolerance* for the substance, meaning that they now require increasingly large doses to produce anything like the desired effect. Moreover they will now suffer from *withdrawal symptoms*—painful physical and psychological reactions—when they stop using the substance. Withdrawal from alcohol results in *delirium tremens*, popularly known as the "DTs," which is a state of intense panic that includes agitation, tremors, confusion, horrible nightmares, and even hallucinations. It is not unusual for alcoholics in the throes of the DTs to be convinced that bugs are crawling all over their bodies. Withdrawal from stimulants such as cocaine produces depression, disorientation, and irritability.

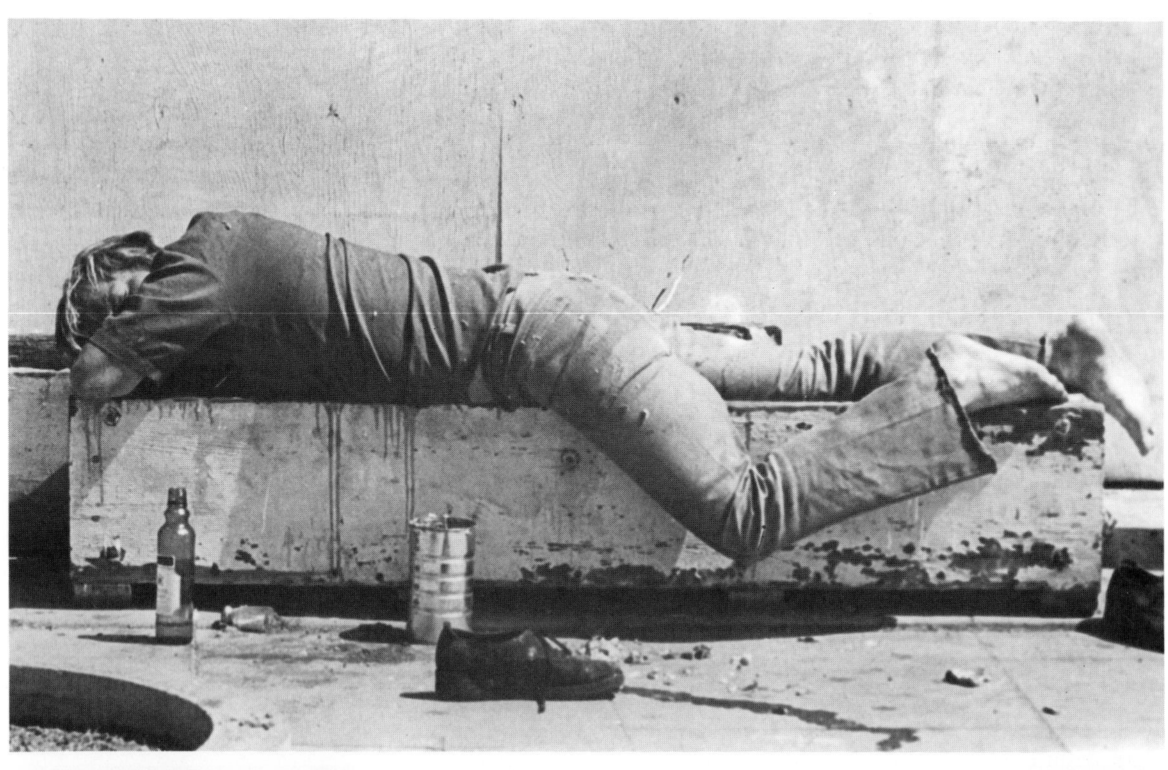

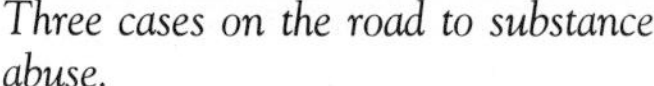

Three cases on the road to substance abuse.

The suffering produced by withdrawal is usually so great that addiction victims will go to any lengths to return once again to using the substance. Many do so despite a strong wish to be liberated from their dependence and to return to a more normal existence.

Alcoholism: trying to drown problems while creating more

Most people drink alcoholic beverages in conjunction with other activities—to be sociable at parties, celebrate an occasion with friends or relatives, take part in religious ceremonies, or enhance the taste of food at dinner. Some people, however, drink to forget their worries, escape from reality, or gather the courage to face the stresses of life. They crave alcohol to drown feelings of tension, anxiety, and depression. Such people are in danger of becoming victims of *alcoholism,* which means that they not only develop a strong dependence on alcohol but also lose control over the act of drinking. Alcoholics continue to drink despite the fact that the habit causes serious physical and psychological problems. Moreover they often either cannot or will not admit that their drinking and the problems are related.

All these symptoms of alcoholism applied to Cathy who, at age 24, appeared at a treatment center. She was ordered there by a judge after she was caught driving while drunk. But she did not admit that she was at fault. "The cops only stopped me because they have a thing about young people," Cathy said. "I wasn't weaving across the highway at all. Besides, I've driven home in much worse shape and nothing ever happened." She would not acknowledge how blurred her vision was that night, how clouded her judgment, how slowed her reflexes—and how close she came to having a tragic traffic accident.

Cathy did not admit either that it was her alcohol problem that caused her to lose her job as a waitress. "My boss was just too picky," she said. "He wouldn't give me a break. Everyone drops a tray once in a while or yells at customers when they're giving you a hard time. And sometimes things come up and you just can't call in to say that you'll be late for work." She would not concede that her morning gulps of Scotch would leave her so shaky she could not possibly hold a tray straight, or that some days she awoke with such a deadly hangover that she felt too sick to reach for the phone and call her supervisor.

As Cathy talked to her counselor, she revealed many of the telltale signs of alcoholism. At parties she would mix especially strong drinks for herself so that her friends would not know how much she was drinking. She sometimes turned down invitations to social events where she knew there would be no liquor served. She would angrily move on to another bar if a bartender refused to serve her another drink. And she abandoned friends who did not drink heavily because, in her view, they were "no fun."

After a few weeks of treatment, Cathy relaxed her defenses and admitted that she had a problem. She owned up to the fact that she often did feel guilty about her drinking, and that when sober, she regretted the things she said or did while drunk. From time to time she

Former First Lady Betty Ford, who recovered from her dependence on alcohol.

had promised herself to cut down, but she could never follow through. There were also many times when she felt so depressed that she wondered whether life was worth living. But always after a few drinks, nothing mattered any more except having still another.

From relaxation to blackouts

Cathy had her first drink when she was 15 years old, and like many alcoholics, she bagan to drink often because she found that it helped her get rid of that "uptight" feeling and gave her a better self-image. Under the influence of a drink or two, many people find they can socialize more easily, be less on guard about what they might say, and worry less about what others might think. That is because alcohol actually does suppress nerve impulses in areas of the brain that control our social behavior.

Heavier drinking, however, can transform a pleasantly "high" state into intoxication. After a number of drinks, speech becomes slurred, and memory and motor coordination deteriorate. Heavy drinkers begin to shed their inhibitions altogether, and their moods tend to swing to one extreme or the other. Past a certain point, they may enter periods of blackout. During such periods, they behave as if they are conscious of their actions, yet later they have no recollection whatsoever of the events that took place. For example, an alcoholic may awaken the morning after a drinking binge to find the car smashed, but remember nothing about hitting a tree on the way home. Cathy's friends once told her that on a previous night, she had undressed and danced on a bar table—but she could recall nothing of the episode. Alcohol had begun to affect the normal functions of her brain.

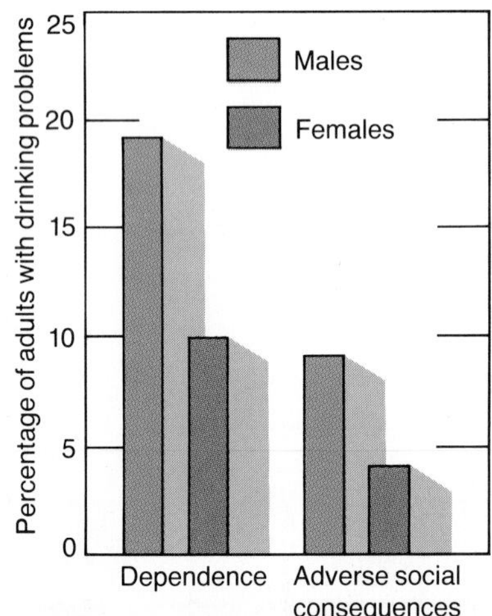

Figure 12-7 Sex differences in the extent of alcohol-related behavioral problems *Males are twice as likely as females to show signs of dependence on alcohol. Among such signs are skipping meals when drinking, sneaking drinks, drinking in the morning, drinking before a party to make sure to get enough, gulping drinks, hands shaking after drinking, morning drinking to get rid of a hangover, and blackouts. Males are also twice as likely to suffer adverse consequences from alcohol such as problems in family and social relationships, encounters with police, and auto accidents (Clark and Midanik, 1982).*

The heavy penalties of heavy drinking

Cathy's treatment helped her recover—and probably also prolonged her life. Over the long haul, alcoholics run into serious health problems. Alcohol itself has little food value, and because heavy drinkers also usually eat poorly, they often suffer severe malnutrition. *Cirrhosis* of the liver—meaning that the liver has become scarred and hardened—may result from this poor nutrition as well as from the irritating effects of alcohol. Alcoholics run a greater than normal risk also of suffering heart problems, high blood pressure, anemia, impotence, gastrointestinal disorders, and cancers of the tongue, mouth, larynx, esophagus, and liver (Eckardt et al., 1981).

Heavy drinking for long periods leads to cognitive and emotional problems as well. Alcohol destroys brain cells—which is why studies of alcoholics show that their perceptual skills and problem-solving abilities are weakened (Silberstein and Parsons, 1981). Although alcohol at first gives users the idea that their feelings of depression are lighter, it actually deepens them—as it did in Cathy's case. An unusually large number of people with drinking problems commit suicide, and more than a third of all suicides involve alcohol. A significant number of industrial accidents, drownings, burns, and falls have also been attributed to drinking. So, too, have many cases of assault, rape, child abuse and neglect, and family violence.

Male and female drinking patterns

Among Americans who drink, roughly 10 percent suffer problems associated with the habit or are actually alcoholics. Surveys consistently indicate that males are heavier drinkers than females. The percentage of adult drinkers who consume 120 or more drinks per month is five times higher for men than for women (Clark and Midanik, 1982). As shown in Figure 12-7, problems associated with the use of alcohol are much more prevalent among men.

One reason may be that heavy drinking by women is less acceptable in our culture. Women may be less prone than men to try to fight off their feelings of depression and anxiety by drinking. To handle the same complaints, they are more likely instead to receive prescription drugs from their physicians—as shown in Figure 12-8. Some researchers believe that the actual number of female alcoholics is greater than the statistics show. Because drinking by women is less acceptable, many cases are kept from the attention of doctors and the staffs of clinics treating alcoholics (Sandmaier, 1980).

Origins of alcoholism

Alcoholism has no single cause, but heredity apparently plays some role. As in the case of schizophrenia, the chances that identical twins will both become alcoholics is much greater than for fraternal twins. One study focused on children who were adopted in the first few weeks of life. Those who had been fathered by alcoholics were four times more likely to develop the disorder later in life than were similar adoptees born to fathers who were not alcoholics. Factors in the children's upbringing—including being raised by an alcoholic or living in a home broken by death or divorce—did not affect the results (Goodwin et al., 1973).

Researchers have not identified an "alcoholic personality." Many alcoholics do tend to be immature, dependent, and lacking in self-esteem, but such traits are by no means common to most alcoholics. Similarly, many alcoholics come from broken and unhappy homes, but there is no consistent pattern (National Institute on Alcohol Abuse and Alcoholism, 1980). Nor does the popular image of the alcoholic as a "skid row drunk" hold up in real life. It is estimated that only 5 percent of all alcoholics fit this stereotype. People from all walks of life can fall victim, including hard-driving politicians, high-strung performers, harried waitresses, and anxious college students.

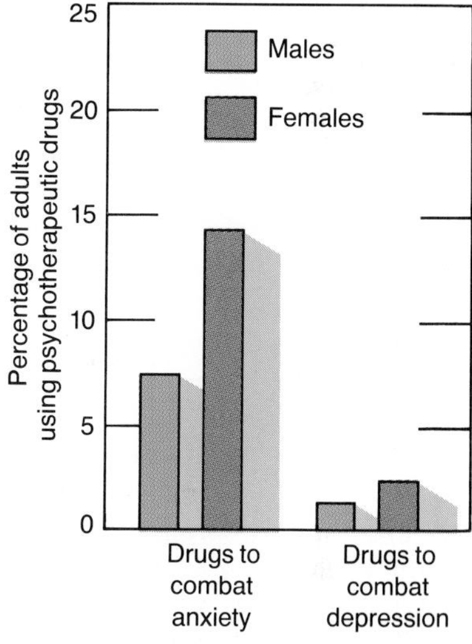

Figure 12-8 Sex differences in the number of patients taking medicine for psychological complaints *Over 11 percent of the adult population in the United States takes medicines prescribed by their doctors to relieve anxiety. The proportion of women who do so, however, is nearly double that of men. The same pattern applies to drugs prescribed for the relief of depression—although the overall percentages are smaller (Mellinger and Balter, 1981).*

Slipping from drug use to abuse

The power of various drugs to alter states of consciousness was described in the supplement to Chapter 8. Some people have a much greater need than others for the gratifying experiences drugs can produce. Among

Type of drug	Examples	Effects of use	Effects of overdose	Effects of withdrawal
Hallucinogens	LSD Phencyclidine (PCP)	Hallucinations, paranoid behavior, distorted body image, anxiety, tremors, nausea, chills, increased pulse and heart rates, amnesia	Loss of contact with reality, seizures, coma	None
Inhalants	Nitrous oxide (whippets, laughing gas) Hydrocarbons (glue)	Feelings of euphoria, giddiness, excitement, loss of inhibitions, aggressiveness, delusions, headache, depression, nausea, drowsiness	Weak memory, confusion, unsteady walk, erratic pulse and heart beat, death	Insomnia, loss of appetite, depression, headache, irritability
Narcotics	Heroin Morphine	Feelings of euphoria, drowsiness, slowed breathing, nausea	Slow and shallow breathing, clammy skin, convulsions, coma, death	Watery eyes, runny nose, loss of appetite, irritability, panic, tremors, chills, sweating, cramps, nausea
Cannabis	Marijuana Hashish	Feelings of euphoria, relaxed inhibitions, increased appeitite, disoriented behavior, increased heart and pulse rates, dizziness	Anxiety, paranoid behavior, loss of concentration, slowed movements, distorted sense of time, hallucinations	Insomnia, hyperactivity
Depressants	Barbiturates Tranquilizers	Slurred speech, drowsiness, disorientation, drunken behavior	Shallow breathing, cold and clammy skin, weak and rapid pulse, coma, death	Anxiety, insomnia, tremors, delirium, convulsions, death
Stimulants	Cocaine Amphetamines	Hyperactivity, euphoria, increased pulse rate and blood pressure, insomnia, loss of appetite, irritability, aimless behavior	Agitation, increased body temperature, panic, convulsions, hallucinations, tremors, death	Apathy, long spells of sleep, irritability, depression

Figure 12-9 Commonly used drugs and their possible effects *Many of the drugs listed may be therapeutic when prescribed in appropriate doses by a physician—but lethal when they are taken in larger quantities without medical supervision. Individuals vary considerably in their responses to drugs. How quickly a person becomes addicted depends on the availability of the drug, how often and in what doses it is used, and the user's physical condition and psychological makeup (Vaillant, 1978).*

such people are those who become victims of *drug abuse*—the repeated use of drugs for other than medical purposes in ways that result in physical and psychological disturbances. The most commonly abused drugs and some of their abnormal effects are listed in Figure 12-9.

There are many theories as to why some people get "hooked" on drugs. According to one theory, it all depends on the view they have of themselves (Gold, 1980). After experimenting with drugs, some people develop a belief that they are unable to cope without them. Continued use sets up a vicious circle. As these users rely more and more on drugs to feel in control, they repeatedly confirm their belief that they are powerless to cope on their own. Each failure to function without drugs strengthens that belief until they become addicted and are in actual fact unable to face life without chemical assistance.

Another theory is that people who slip across the line from occasional experimentation with drugs to abuse have difficulty handling their anxieties about achievement (Misra, 1980). According to this theory, such individuals turn to drugs in the first place to find temporary relief from the pressure to achieve and the fear of failure. Once the effects of the drug wear off, their anxieties return and they again seek the relief they know the drug will bring. Soon they begin to depend on the drug to block out their anxieties. The process continues to spiral until the effect of the drug becomes an end in itself. The goal now is no longer only freedom from tension but a state of uninterrupted contentment. In effect, the drug abuser seems to be saying: "I may not amount to as much as my friends, but I have something they do not have—an existence without pressures or responsibilities."

In the case of heroin, which poses perhaps the most serious drug abuse problem, one investigator found that people who became addicts were especially likely to have the following six personality traits (Nurco, 1979):

1. Inability to cope with intense feelings of anger, usually generated by frustration.
2. Need to experience immediate sense of gratification. (As children, many addicts were severely deprived of their basic needs, and they began to find waiting intolerable.)
3. Inability to establish adequate sexual identification. (Many addicts are gratified by the fact that heroin "wipes out" sexual desire, and they take pleasure in being a member of a group in which no one is expected to pursue the traditional heterosexual role.)
4. Rejection of society's goals and the means typically used to achieve them.
5. Proneness to take risks as a way of proving themselves adequate.
6. Need to deal with boredom. (Addicts fight boredom in two ways. They fill their days with activities designed to secure a needed drug, and once they take it, their sense of boredom is erased for a time.)

In some ways heroin addicts resemble people with antisocial personalities. They generally have trouble conforming to society's rules, and they live without attachments to work, family, or religion (Robins, 1980). It is sometimes hard to tell whether the complications of addiction—such as marital problems, unemployment, and crime—are the result of drugs or the sources of psychological stress leading to drug use in the first place. Since only a small percentage of those who experiment with drugs ever become addicted despite the stress in their lives, some investigators assume that a specific biochemical abnormality may exist among those who suffer addiction.

The special hazards of mixing drugs

Very few drug abusers confine themselves only to one drug. It has been estimated that over two million people in the United States use two or or more drugs simultaneously (Kaufman, 1976). A national study showed that persons 18 years old and younger requiring treatment for drug-related problems used an average of four different drugs on a regular basis (Farley, Santo, and Speck, 1979).

Exactly how drugs interact in the brain and body is still unknown, but it is clear enough that abusers of multiple drugs are likely to fall victim to various medical complications (Wesson and Smith, 1979). Many of them eventually suffer from malnutrition, others from severe brain disorders. Moreover, doses of substances that are not in themselves dangerous can be fatal when combined. The combination of alcohol and sedatives produces a large number of the drug-induced deaths we read about so often in the newspapers.

Victims are usually beset by extremely difficult psychological and social problems. They are likely to be financially strapped—not only because the habit is so expensive, but also because it interferes with productive work. Despite their abilities, they tend to make little progress either in school or at work, and they may be in deep trouble with the law. The tend also to be outcasts from both the family and society at large. Often the only persons willing to give them serious attention are drug suppliers or fellow users. Under such oppressive circumstances, they need considerable help to break free from the drug culture and get a fresh start in life (National Institute on Drug Abuse, 1977).

Attitudes toward abnormal behavior: how they can hurt or heal

People have always tended to harbor negative feelings toward those considered to be psychologically abnormal. In the Middle Ages, it was commonly believed that victims of mental disorders were possessed by the devil, and they were flogged, put in chains, or starved to root out evil influences. Centuries later, early American settlers ran the risk of being put to death as witches if they displayed the symptoms of schizophrenia or depression described in this chapter.

Attitudes toward those with mental disorders have improved over time. Today, seriously disturbed individuals are fortunate enough to be treated in hospitals and clinics instead of being put away in prisons or asylums. But they are still far from universally accepted either within the family or community. How they are viewed by others can be critical. It can help determine whether they will recover sufficiently to function in society, or continue to be overwhelmed by their symptoms and even get worse.

The importance of family supports

An international study showed that people in underdeveloped countries who suffer from serious mental disorders tend to recover more quickly and suffer fewer recurrences than do those in industrially advanced countries (World Health Organization, 1979). A major reason given for the difference is that family members in underdeveloped countries are more likely to take responsibility for caring for victims. With few mental health professionals available, they are more prone to stay close to those relatives who become psychologically disabled and offer them the kind of support and encouragement they need to increase their chances of recovery.

Family support appears to be especially important for victims of serious disorders such as schizophrenia and severe depression. One study shows that the risk of suicide is considerably less for deeply depressed persons who have close ties with relatives (Slater and Depue, 1981). Other studies reveal that recovered schizophrenics are less likely to suffer a relapse if family members play down any anxiety they might have and instead exert a calming influence. It appears critical also that relatives not blame the victim for succumbing to schizophrenia, but rather indicate their belief that schizophrenia is a legitimate and acceptable condition (Vaughn and Leff, 1976).

The taint of mental disorder

Many people who have suffered from a mental disorder find their reputations tainted by the experience. Often they hear themselves referred to as "kooks," "weirdos," or "crazies." In movies they see themselves characterized as unpredictable and dangerous. In television dramas, they are twice as likely as other characters to be portrayed as perpetrators of violent acts (Gerbner et al., 1981). And even though they have fully recovered from a mental disorder, they tend to run into difficulties in landing jobs or places to live. One study actually showed them to be less preferred in the community than ex-convicts (Lamy, 1966). Little wonder that many people who could use help do not seek it because of the shame they would feel in revealing their abnormal symptoms.

The tendency to feel prejudiced against people identified as abnormal appears to be universal. Age and intelligence make little difference. Unreasonable attitudes are found among college students and political figures as well as blue-collar workers and laborers. People who have suffered from a mental disorder face problems even in their relationships with professionals trained to help them. As an experiment, one man visited 32 doctors and complained of ulcer symptoms. He told half of them, however, that he had a history of mental illness. These doctors were less inclined to accept the complaints of their "patient," and they viewed him as physically healthier than did the others (Farina, Hagelauer, and Holzberg, 1976).

Individuals identified as having had a mental disorder are often caught in a vicious cycle. When they work together with others on a task, they are unfairly perceived as incompetent and their performance is rated as poor for no tangible reason. Feeling alienated and unappreciated, their anxieties begin to rise, and as a result their performance actually does deteriorate (Farina, 1982). Many investigators have concluded that if we could remove the disgrace associated with abnormal behavior, it would help bring people who have recovered from a breakdown back into the routine of normal life and keep them from succumbing once again to their symptoms. The importance of erasing negative attitudes is heightened by the fact that most people

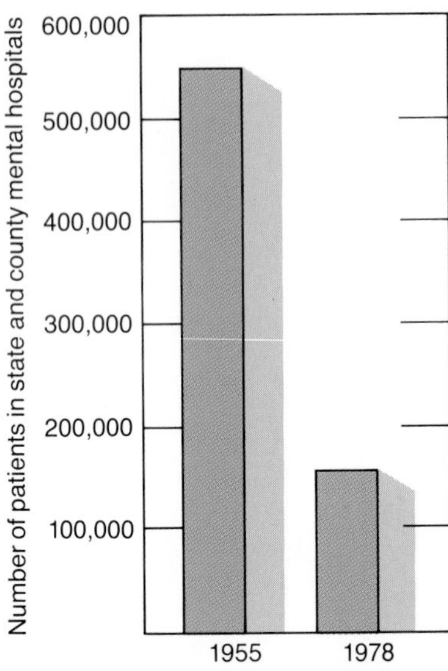

Figure 12-10 A dramatic drop in the United States mental hospital population *In 1955, there were over a half-million people in United States state and county mental hospitals. By 1978, the total was reduced to one-fourth that number. The sharp decline is due primarily to the development of medicines that eliminate the most disabling symptoms of mental disorder and the introduction of mental health treatment centers in communities across the nation (Regier and Taube, 1981).*

with a history of severe mental disorder now live in close contact with their fellow citizens in the community. As shown in Figure 12-10, the tendency is no longer to keep them locked away in institutions where they could never experience what others on the outside feel about them.

Abnormal behavior and creativity

It has long been a popular belief that very creative people are likely to be psychologically abnormal. The phrase "mad genius," for example, is widely used to describe individuals who are viewed as unusually brilliant—but only at the cost of also being quite odd. The belief probably arose because many famous and gifted individuals did in fact suffer from mental disorders. Among them are the scientist Sir Isaac Newton, artists Vincent van Gogh and Leonardo da Vinci, writers Jonathan Swift and Edgar Allan Poe, and composers Robert Schumann and Maurice Ravel.

The existence of such cases does not mean, however, that in order to be creative you must have some abnormality. Most people who have special talents go through life without ever enduring symptoms of mental disorder. What is true, however, is that having a mental disorder is no bar to a successful and productive existence. Millions of people—ordinary as well as famous—have lived accomplished and satisfying lives despite sometimes brutal encounters with abnormal symptoms. In one study, a group of men hospitalized with mental disorders were followed up 20 years later. The experience did not necessarily affect the careers even of those who still showed some signs of their disorder (Huffine and Clausen, 1979).

Some psychologists believe that experiences with conditions such as crippling anxiety and overwhelming depression can actually deepen our appreciation of life and make us more compassionate and understanding. In any case, episodes of mental disorder certainly are no longer occasions for despair. Psychology is providing a vast body of knowledge about not only the intricate roots of the human personality,

These gifted individuals—artist Vincent Van Gogh and writer Edgar Allan Poe, suffered from mental disorder. Most talented people, however, have no abnormalities.

but also the various methods of therapy that can help many people overcome seemingly insurmountable symptoms—and even substantially improve the quality of their lives.

SUMMARY

The scope of abnormal behavior

1. *Abnormal behavior,* though difficult to define, is generally considered to be behavior that is: (a) statistically unusual, (b) considered undesirable by most people, and (c) a source of unhappiness to the person who displays it.
2. It is estimated that at least 15 percent of the United States population is affected by mental disorders during any one-year period. The economic cost—including loss of earnings and expense of care and treatment—has been estimated at close to 40 billion dollars a year.

Origins and types of abnormal behavior

3. Abnormal behavior hinges on two factors: (a) the amount of stress and anxiety a person experiences and (b) the person's ability to handle this amount.
4. The ability to handle stress and anxiety appears to be determined by (a) biological factors (such as glandular activity and sensitivity of the autonomic nervous system), (b) psychological factors (such as motives and anxiety over failure to fulfill them), and (c) environmental influences.

Schizophrenia: no. 1 crippler

5. *Schizophrenia* is characterized by an extreme disorganization of personality. Schizophrenics typically display (a) poor insight, (b) incoherent speech, (c) delusions, (d) absence of emotion, (e) remoteness, and (f) worry that their thoughts are known by others.
6. Schizophrenics appear to have defects in brain metabolism and in parts of the nervous system responsible for perception. Evidence for the genetic origin of the disorder is strong.

Affective disorders: abnormalities of mood

7. Abnormal *depression* is marked by a severe and prolonged mood of sadness, helplessness, and hopelessness. Depressed individuals suffer from lowered self-esteem and motivation, guilt, sleep difficulties, physical complaints, and disturbances of perception and thought. The risk of suicide is especially high in depression.
8. When episodes of depression recur without other abnormalities of mood, the disorder is called *unipolar depression.* Exaggerated mood fluctuations from intense excitement to deep melancholy are characteristic of *bipolar depression,* or *manic-depressive illness.* In rare cases, called *hypomania,* the depressed phase is never very prominent. Evidence exists that genetic and biochemical factors are involved in the development of these disorders.

Anxiety disorders

9. *Anxiety disorders* arise when situations that produce conflict and frustration remain unresolved. Four common types of anxiety disorders are *generalized anxiety disorder, panic disorder, phobic disorder,* and *obsessive-compulsive disorder.*

Personality disorders

10. Some forms of abnormal behavior, difficult to classify, are called *personality disorders.* Unlike other forms, they are not expressed in specific symptoms or clearly related to anxiety and stress. People with these disorders seem to lack the desire or ability to act in socially acceptable ways. Three major types are *antisocial personality, paranoid personality,* and *narcissistic personality.*

Substance abuse: abnormal use of alcohol and drugs

11. Indications that alcohol or drug use is departing from normal are the development of *psychological dependence* and *physical dependence,* or *addiction.* Addiction victims develop *tolerance* for the substance (meaning that they require increasingly large doses to produce the desired effect), and they suffer *withdrawal symptoms* (painful physical and psychological reactions when they stop using the drug).
12. Persons who suffer from *alcoholism* become strongly dependent on alcohol and lose control over the act of drinking. They continue to drink despite the serious physical and psychological problems alcohol produces, including brain and liver damage, malnutrition, impaired problem-solving abilities, and disruption of family life. Alcoholism has no single cause, but heredity apparently plays some role.
13. *Drug abuse* is the repeated use of drugs for other than medical purposes resulting in severe physical and psychological disturbances. Abusers of multiple drugs are likely to have especially serious medical, personal, and social problems.

Attitudes toward abnormal behavior: how they can hurt or heal

14. Attitudes toward people with mental disorders can be critical in determining whether or not such individuals will recover sufficiently to function in society. Family support is particularly important.
15. There is a universal tendency to treat unfairly people identified as abnormal. This is so despite the fact that millions of those with a history of mental disorder have lived accomplished and satisfying lives.

IMPORTANT TERMS

abnormal behavior
acrophobia
addiction
affective disorder
agoraphobia
alcoholism
antisocial personality
anxiety disorder
bipolar depression
blackout
cirrhosis
claustrophobia

compulsion
cortisol
delirium tremens
depression
drug abuse
DSM-III
generalized anxiety disorder
hypomania
lithium
manic-depressive illness
narcissistic personality
noradrenalin
obsession
obsessive-compulsive disorder
panic disorder
paranoid personality
personality disorder
phobic disorder
physical dependence
post-traumatic stress disorder
psychological dependence
schizophrenia
schizophrenia spectrum
school phobia
stress
substance abuse
suicide
tolerance
unipolar depression
withdrawal symptoms

RECOMMENDED READINGS

Altrocchi, J. *Abnormal behavior.* New York: Harcourt Brace Jovanovich, 1980.

Berger, G. *Mental illness.* New York: Watts, Franklin, 1981.

Eisdorfer, C., et al. *Models for clinical psychopathology.* Jamaica, N.Y.: Spectrum Publications, 1981.

Estes, N. J., and Heinemann, M. E., eds. *Alcoholism: development, consequences, and interventions.* St. Louis: C. V. Mosby, 1977.

Goldstein, M. J., Baker, B. L., and Jamison, K. R. *Abnormal psychology: experiences, origins, and interventions.* Boston: Little, Brown, 1980.

Hamburg, D. A., Elliott, G. R., and Parron, D. L., eds. *Health and behavior: frontiers of research in the biobehavioral sciences.* Washington, D.C.: National Academy Press, 1982.

Klein, D. F., and Rabkin, J. G., eds. *Anxiety: new research and changing concepts.* New York: Raven Press, 1981.

Leavitt, F. *Drugs and behavior,* 2d ed. New York: John Wiley & Sons, 1982.

Rachman, S. J., and Hodgson, R. J. *Obsessions and compulsions.* Englewood Cliffs, N.J.: Prentice-Hall, 1980.

Winokur, G. *Depression: the facts.* New York: Oxford University Press, 1981.

Wynne, L. C., Cromwell, R. L., and Matthysse, S., eds. *The nature of schizophrenia: new approaches to research and treatment.* New York: John Wiley & Sons, 1978.

CHAPTER 13

Personality theories 468
- A definition of personality
- The personality hierarchy
- The three elements of personality theory

Freud's psychoanalytic theory 471
- Anxiety, repression, and the unconscious mind
- Id and pleasure principle
- Ego and reality principle
- Superego and Oedipus conflict
- Superego versus ego versus id
- Psychoanalysis: the therapy
- Other schools of psychoanalytic theory: Jung and Adler
- Some current trends in psychoanalysis

Humanistic theories of personality 479
- Rogers's "phenomenological self"
- The phenomenological self and maladjustment
- Humanistic therapy

Social learning theories and behavior therapy 482
- Conditioning and cognitive learning
- Behavior therapy and relearning
- New trends in behavior therapy: encouraging assertive coping
- Learning to cope through observation and guided participation

Other therapies (including medical) 486
- Interpersonal therapies
- Group therapies
- Medical therapy
- The question of self-therapy

Summary 493

Important terms 495

Supplement: Tests of personality 497
- Objective tests
- Situational tests
- Projective tests

Summary of supplement 500

Important terms 501

Recommended readings 501

Psychology and society
- How well—and for whom—does psychotherapy work? 490

Personality and Psychotherapy

"She has such a nice personality."
"I wonder why he doesn't do something about his personality."
"Our personalities just don't mix."

You have probably heard such observations—or made them yourself—countless times. The word *personality* crops up frequently in everyday conversation. But if you were asked to explain in detail what you actually mean by the word, you would probably run into difficulty. The traits that define personality are based on all the intricate processes covered in this book—the infinitely varied perceptions we have of the world, the wide range of styles we display in thinking and using language, the gamut of our emotions and motives, the tides of anxiety and stress we experience and the diverse efforts we make to cope with them, some successful and some not. What we casually refer to as personality is actually such a complex phenomenon that the English language has at least 18,000 words to describe the myriad traits that comprise it.

To get some idea of the complexity, try rating yourself on one side or the other on the list of personality opposites in the box on this page. Those 10 traits can occur in any combination. You may fall at the left in all of them, at the right in all of them, or at the left in some and the right in others. Thus this short list alone can account for a great variety of individual personalities: $2 \times 2 \times 2 \times 2 \times 2 \times 2 \times 2 \times 2 \times 2 \times 2$, or 1,024. Moreover you may not belong clearly at the left or the

Motives

ambitious, hard-working *or* unambitious, lazy
independent *or* dependent
friendly, a joiner *or* unfriendly, a loner
like certainty *or* prefer novelty, risk

Emotions

high in anxiety *or* low in anxiety
slow to anger *or* hot-tempered
joyous *or* gloomy

Cognitive styles

thoughtful *or* impulsive
down-to-earth *or* dreamy, impractical
talkative, eloquent *or* quiet, tongue-tied

right but somewhere in between, again multiplying the possiblities. And those 10 traits are just a small sample of all that exist. Small wonder that there are so many personalities in the world—and that personality is so difficult to understand and describe.

Personality theories

Since almost everything psychologists study is related in some way to human personality, it might be said that the entire science represents an attempt to create a comprehensive theory of personality—in other words, a set of general principles that will explain why people are alike in some ways and very different in others. But some psychologists have been especially interested in seeking these general principles. They have developed a number of theories that try to explain which personality traits are most important, the likeliest patterns of relationships among traits, the manner in which these patterns become established in individuals, and (at least by implication) how they can be changed. Personality theory has gone hand in hand with psychotherapy. Each of the main theories developed over the years has been accompanied by its own technique of treating people suffering from personality disturbances, as will be seen in a moment. First, however, we must define personality and explain what all personality theories try to accomplish.

A definition of personality

Personality can best be defined as the *total pattern of characteristic ways of thinking, feeling, and behaving that constitute the individual's distinctive method of relating to the environment.* There are four key words in the definition: (a) *characteristic,* (b) *distinctive,* (c) *relating,* (d) *pattern*.

To be considered a part of personality, a way of thinking, feeling, or behaving must have some continuity over time and circumstance. It must be *characteristic* of the individual. We do not call a man bad

A display of the positive personality trait of friendliness.

tempered if he "blows up" only once in 10 years. We say that a bad temper is part of his personality only if he shows it often and in many different circumstances.

The way of thinking, feeling, or behaving must also be *distinctive*—that is, it must distingiush the individual from other individuals. This eliminates such common American traits as eating with a knife and fork, placing adjectives before rather than after nouns, and carrying a driver's license—all of which are more or less the same for every American and do not distinguish one person from others.

Though these first two elements are essential, they are not the whole story. For example, a woman might always wear a ring that is a family heirloom and the only one of its kind in the world. Wearing the ring is therefore both characteristic and distinctive. But this would hardly be considered part of her personality (unless perhaps she attached some deep significance to the ring, regarding it as a symbol of self-esteem and social acceptance). To be a part of personality, a trait must play a part in how a person goes about *relating* to the world, especially to other people. It is because of this element of relating that personality traits are often thought of as positive or negative. A positive trait, such as friendliness, helps the individual relate to people and events in a constructive manner. A negative characteristic, such as fear of social contacts, may produce anxiety, failure, and loneliness.

Of the multitude of possible personality traits, all of us possess some but not others. It is the particular *pattern* of characteristics we possess and display—the sum total and organization—that is the final element in the definition of personality.

The personality hierarchy

The various traits that make up the personality—all the characteristic and distinctive ways of relating to the environment—exist in a hierarchy from strong to weak. Some ways of thinking, feeling, and behav-

An example early in life of a negative trait—fear of social contact?

ing are easily and frequently aroused. Others are less likely to occur. In a social situation, for example, there are many ways an individual can relate to the others in the group. The individual can be talkative or quiet, friendly or reserved, boastful or modest, bossy or acquiescent, more at ease with men or more at ease with women. One person may characteristically withdraw into the background, and we say that such a person is shy. Another may characteristically display warmth and try to put the others at their ease, and we say that such a person is outgoing. Another may be talkative, boastful, and domineering, and we say that such a person is aggressive or "pushy." In each of the three individuals, certain responses are strong in the personality hierarchy and easily aroused.

Each person's hierarchy has a certain amount of permanence. The shy person behaves shyly under many circumstances, and the aggressive person has a consistent tendency to be boastful and domineering. However, the hierarchy may change considerably depending on the circumstances. A young woman who is aggressive around people her own age may behave shyly in the presence of older people. A man who is usually shy may have one close friend with whom he is completely at ease. All of us, no matter how friendly or reserved we may be, are likely to have a strong tendency to make friends if we have been isolated for a long time, such as after an illness or a stretch at a lonely job. After a round of parties, on the other hand, we are likely to want some solitude. The businessman who is ordinarily interested in his job and eager to talk about it may shun conversation when he gets home late at night after a hard day's work.

The three elements of personality theory

Many general theories of personality have been proposed over the years. They differ in many respects, but they all have three things in common (Maddi, 1972):

1. Every theory is based on some fundamental viewpoint toward the basic quality of human nature. It assumes that there is a *core personality* composed of tendencies and traits common to all of us. Different theories take different views of this common core, as will be seen, but all of them take for granted that it exists and is a force in shaping personality.
2. Every theory maintains that the tendencies and traits that make up the common core of personality are channeled in various different directions in different individuals by the process of *development*—all the experiences we encounter, from our childhood relationships with our parents throughout the rest of our lives. Thus all theories agree that personality is the product of both nature (the common core that is part of our heritage) and nurture (the effect of individual development), though they do not necessarily agree on whether nature or nurture is more influential.
3. Every theory is concerned with what are called *peripheral traits*—that is, all the distinctive ways in which people relate to the environ-

ment. The peripheral traits are viewed as the inevitable result of the way individual development has acted on the common core of personality.

Freud's psychoanalytic theory

The most famous of all views of personality is Sigmund Freud's *psychoanalytic theory.* Freud's writings about personality development and the treatment of psychological disorders have been widely read and debated. Oddly, his method of treatment—called *psychoanalysis*—has never attracted a large following. The American Psychoanalytic Association, to which most practitioners of psychoanalysis belong, has recently had only about 2,700 members (Magelowitz, 1982). Nonetheless his views have had a profound influence on many psychologists, including some who disagree with his therapy, and on literature, especially in the United States.

Anxiety, repression, and the unconscious mind

Some of Freud's ideas have already been prominently mentioned in preceding chapters. One was his concept of the defense mechanisms (Chapter 11) as a technique for relieving anxiety. Freud believed that anxiety is the central problem in mental disturbance, so painful an emotion that we will go to almost any length to get rid of it. He regarded the defense mechanisms as a method of eliminating from conscious awareness any motive or thought that threatens to cause anxiety.

The unconscious mind, composed in part of repressed motives and thoughts, was another of Freud's most influential concepts. He was the first to suggest the now widely held theory that the human mind and

Freud at work in his office in Vienna, about 1930, when he was still highly productive at the age of 74.

personality are like an iceberg, with only a small part visible and the rest submerged and concealed. All of us, he maintained, have many unconscious motives that we are never aware of but that nonetheless have a powerful influence on our behavior.

The details of Freudian theory are difficult to summarize. For one thing, he revised and enlarged on them throughout a prolific writing career that spanned four decades. Morever his followers have continued to make refinements, especially of the new ideas he developed late in life. The discussion here is confined to the basic principles (especially those that have had the greatest influence on psychologists) as they are now viewed by psychoanalytic theorists who regard themselves as classical Freudians. To begin the discussion, let it be said that Freud conceived of the human personality and mind as composed of three major parts that he called the *id, ego,* and *superego*.*

Id and pleasure principle

The *id,* or most basic and primitive of the three parts, springs from what Freud held to be two inborn drives that all human beings possess. One of these drives is the *libido,* consisting of sexual urges and such related desires as to be kept well-fed, warm, and comfortable. The other is a drive toward aggression—to attack anyone or anything that interferes with gratification.

The drives arouse the id to a state of excitement and tension. In seeking to relieve the tension, the id operates on what Freud called the *pleasure principle,* imperiously seeking results and tolerating no delay. To satisfy the libido, the id seeks complete possession of everything desired and loved. To satisfy the drive for aggression, it wants to destroy everything that gets in the way. As we grow up, we learn to control the demands of the id, at least after a fashion. But it remains active and powerful throughout life—a sort of beast within. Although it is unconscious and we are not aware of its workings, it continues to struggle to relieve its tensions and find instant gratification.

In regard to the libido, Freud believed that human sexual development takes place in a series of stages in which the drive focuses on different parts of the body. During about the first year and a half of life, or what he called the *oral stage,* the desires and gratifications concern the mouth, tongue, and such activities as sucking and eating. This is followed by the *anal stage,* from about 1½ to 3, in which the desires and gratifications move to the other end of the alimentary canal and are concerned with the act of emptying the lower bowel or refraining from the act. This is followed by the *phallic stage,* in which the libido is principally interested in the external sex organ, male or female. At puberty the child then enters the *genital stage,* which represents the adult and final step in sexual development, characterized by love for another person.

---

*The three terms have been standard since they appeared in the first translation of Freud's writings into English. For greater accuracy and help in understanding the meaning, it has been suggested that the id might better be called the *it*, the ego the *I*, and the superego the *upper-I* (Bettelheim, 1983). You may find it useful to keep these alternative terms in mind while reading the next pages.

Incomplete sexual development may create what Freud called a fixation, in which the original focus of the drive persists to an abnormal degree into adult life. A fixation at the oral stage may be displayed in passivity, dependence, and excessive concern with eating or smoking. An anal fixation may cause either excessive messiness or an abnormal passion for cleanliness and order, or it may create a miser who hoards money.

Ego and reality principle

The conscious part of the mind that develops as we grow up is called the *ego.* This is the "real" us as we like to think of ourselves, including our knowledge, skills, beliefs, and conscious motives. The ego operates on the *reality principle.* It does our logical thinking and tries to help us get along in the world. To the extent that the demands of the id can be satisfied in some reasonable way, the ego permits satisfaction. But when the id's demands threaten to get us rejected by society, the ego represses them or tries to provide substitutes that are socially acceptable. Freud held that artistic creativity, for example, represents a channeling of the libido away from open sexual expression and into the production of paintings and literature.

Superego and Oedipus conflict

The ego, in its constant struggle to meet the irrational demands of the id in some rational way, has a strong but troublesome ally in the *superego,* the third part of the mind as conceived by Freud. In a sense the superego is our conscience, our sense of right and wrong. But Freud's concept of the superego is much stronger and more dynamic than the word "conscience" implies. Much like the id, the superego is mostly unconscious, exerting a far greater influence over our behavior than we realize. It is largely acquired as a result of the *Oedipus complex,* an important element in Freudian thinking.

According to psychoanalitic theory, all children between the ages of about 2½ and 6 are embroiled in a conflict of mingled affection and resentment toward their parents. The male child has learned that the outer world exists and that there are other people in it, and the id's demands for love and affection reach out insatiably toward the person he has been closest to—the mother. Although the child has only the haziest notion of sexual feelings, his libido drives him to want the total love of his mother and take the place of his father with her. But his anger against his father, the rival with whom he must share her, makes him fearful that his father will somehow retaliate. To further complicate matters, his demands for total love from his mother are of course frustrated—and he also wants to get rid of her and take her place in the affections of his father. Thus he becomes overwhelmed with strong feelings of mingled love, rage, and fear toward both parents.

This period of turmoil takes its name from the Greek legend in which Oedipus unwittingly killed his father and married his own mother and then, when he discovered what he had done, blinded himself as penance. Girls, according to Freudian theory, go through very similar torments in the years from 2½ to 6, except that their love becomes directed mostly toward their father. (This is sometimes called the Electra complex, after another Greek legend of a woman who loved her father and conspired to kill her mother—but Freud himself never used the term, because he believed the conflict took basically the same form for both sexes.)

Resolving the Oedipus complex through identification?

The Oedipus complex must somehow be resolved. This is accomplished through the process of identification with the parents. That is to say, we resolve our feelings of mingled love and hate for our parents by becoming like them, by convincing ourselves that we share their strength and authority and the affection they have for each other. In this process of identification, we adopt what we believe to be the standards of our parents, behaving in ways that are likely to bring their approval. Their moral judgments, or what we conceive to be their moral judgments, become our superego. This helps us hold down the demands of the id, which have caused us such intense discomfort during the Oedipal period. But, forever after, the superego tends to oppose the ego. As our parents once did, our superego punishes us or threatens to punish us for our transgressions.

In their own way, the demands of the superego are just as insatiable as the demands of the id. Its standards of right and wrong and its rules for punishment are far more rigid, relentless, and vengeful than anything in our conscious minds. Formed at a time when we were too young to distinguish between a bad wish and a bad deed, the superego may sternly disapprove of the merest thought of some transgression—which explains why some people who have never actually committed a bad deed still have strong feelings of guilt throughout life.

Superego versus ego versus id

The three parts of the mind are often in conflict, and Freud regarded conflict as the core of human personality. One result of the three-way struggle is anxiety, which is produced in the ego whenever the demands of the id threaten to create danger or when the superego threatens to impose disapproval or punishment. Anxiety arouses the ego to fight the impulses or thoughts that have created it. In one way or another—by using repression and the other defense mechanisms, by turning the mind's attention elsewhere, by gratifying some other impulse of the id—the ego defends itself against the threat posed by the id or the superego and gets rid of the anxiety.

In a sense the conscious ego is engaged in a constant struggle to satisfy the insatiable demands of the unconscious id without incurring the wrath and vengeance of the largely unconscious superego. To the extent that our behavior is controlled by the ego, it is realistic and socially acceptable. To the extent that it is governed by the passions of the id and the unrelenting disapproval of the superego, it tends to be maladjusted and neurotic.

If the ego is not strong enough to check the id's drives, a person is likely to be selfish, impulsive, and antisocial. But if the ego checks the id too severely, other problems may arise. Too much repression of the libidinal force can make a person incapable of enjoying a normal sex life or giving a normal amount of affection. Too much repression of aggression can seriously handicap a person in the give and take of competition. If the ego is not strong enough to check the superego, the result may be vague and unwarranted feelings of guilt and unworthiness, even an unconscious need for self-punishment. Thus it is the three-way conflict among ego, id, and superego, according to Freud, that often results in abnormal behavior.

Psychoanalysis: the therapy

The method of treatment developed by Freud was designed to dredge up into awareness the unconscious desires and conflicts that he considered the source of neurotic anxiety and guilt. The chief tool in psychoanalysis is *free association,* which often produces insights into hidden psychological processes. If you were to undertake psychoanalysis, you would be asked to lie on a couch, as relaxed as possible, and speak out every thought that occurred to you—no matter how foolish it might seem, how obscene, or how insulting to the analyst. In this situation, as when drifting off to sleep, conscious control of mental processes is reduced to a minimum and unconscious forces become more apparent.

The analyst would pay particular attention to occasions when your thoughts seemed to encounter what is called *resistance*—that is, when your train of thought seemed to be blocked by anxiety and repressions indicating unconscious conflicts. The analyst would also study your fantasies, slips of the tongue, and dreams in a search for clues to unconscious desires and conflicts. Freud believed that dreams, in particular, often reveal deeply hidden motives and conflicts, though in disguised ways that require painstaking psychoanalytic interpretation.

Another clue to the unconscious is what analysts call *transference.* Freud believed that in a sense none of us ever completely grows up. Neurotic people in particular tend to retain their childhood emotional attitudes toward such well-loved and much-hated persons as their parents and their brothers and sisters, and they often display or transfer these attitudes to the people they know as adults. If you were being analyzed, you might transfer many such attitudes to the analyst. At times you might display an overwhelming desired to please the analyst, as you once wanted to please your parents. At other times you might display resentment and hatred, even though the analyst had done nothing to provoke them.

Through your transferences, free associations, dreams, and reports of your everyday behavior, a pattern would gradually emerge of the unconscious problems that the analyst would say represented your real difficulties. The analyst would then interpret the problems and help you acquire insights into the unconscious processes and gain control over them. The goal in analysis is to strengthen the ego and provide what one analyst calles "freedom from the tyranny of the unconscious" (Kubie, 1950).

In its classic form, psychoanalysis is a long process, requiring three to five visits a week for two to five years or more, and is therefore very expensive. In recent years, however, many analysts have attempted to shorten the treatment period. They have adopted various new and faster techniques for helping people achieve, if not full "freedom from the tyranny of the unconscious," at least enough insight to cope with their more serious problems.

Other schools of psychoanalytic theory: Jung and Adler

Freud was an important innovator who made many contributions to understanding the human personality. He was the first to recognize the role of the unconscious and the importance of anxiety and defenses against it. He also dispelled the myth, widely accepted before his time, that children do not have sexual urges or hostile impulses. He was a pioneer in recognizing the effect of childhood experiences on personality development.

His theory, however, has many critics. It is impossible to demonstrate the existence of an id, an ego, or a superego, which some psychologists regard as merely fancy terms for processes that have a simpler explanation (for example, conflicts between motives and inner standards). Some critics believe that Freud overemphasized the role of sexual motivation by generalizing from the conflicts of patients who had

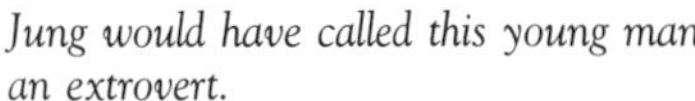
Jung would have called this young man an extrovert.

grown up during the repressive Victorian age. Even some of Freud's early disciples broke away from him and founded competing schools of psychoanalytic thought.

One Freudian who broke away was Carl Jung, inventor of the famous words *introvert* and *extrovert*. Introverts are people who tend to live with their own thoughts and to avoid socializing. Extroverts are people whose chief interest is in other people and the events around them. Jung felt that fulfillment of the human personality requires the expression of both introversion and extroversion—but that one tends to develop at the expense of the other, making people either too concerned with themselves or too preoccupied with external events.

Jung strongly believed that Freud had overestimated the importance of sexuality. He felt that the libido was far richer than Freud assumed—an all-encompassing life force that included deep-seated attitudes toward life and death, virtue and sin, and religion. Jung's theories place more emphasis than Freud's on the intellectual and especially the spiritual qualities of the human personality, less on the urges toward sex and aggression.

A key element in Jung's theories was the idea that human beings possess a *collective unconscious*—an inheritance from all the events that have occurred in human history, and perhaps even in the days before humanity appeared and only lower animals roamed the world. In the

Carl Jung

collective unconscious lie traces of primitive humanity's fears and superstitions, the belief in magic, and search for gods. There also are memories of the great events in which humanity has participated—its disasters, its conquests and defeats, its happy and unhappy love affairs, its moving experiences with birth and death. Because of the collective unconscious, every person embodies in a sense the entire gamut of human experience. Jung believed that each of us, of whatever sex, possesses elements of both woman and man, mother and father, hero, prophet, sage, and magician.

To Jung, the collective unconscious was a significant part of the core of personality, a universal aspect of the human condition. It influences our behavior in ways that we can understand only dimly or not at all. It finds expression in the work of the artist and accounts for the strong emotions we sometimes feel, without knowing why, when we look at a great painting or statue. It crops up in our dreams, often giving them a strange and mystical quality that we find beautiful or frightening. This mystical aspect makes Jung's ideas difficult to grasp and impossible to test scientifically.

Another early disciple who rejected Freud's emphasis on sexuality was Alfred Adler, who proposed instead a theory that is as simple as Jung's is complicated. It was Adler who coined the term *inferiority complex,* which he regarded as the basis for most abnormal behavior. Adler believed that the core of personality is a universal human desire to be superior and to attain perfection. When this desire is thwarted, as it must often be, the result is feelings of inferiority that sometimes are crippling.

Some current trends in psychoanalysis

In recent years, new generations of psychoanalysts have added to and in some ways revised Freud's theories—as indeed he himself was constantly doing throughout his lifetime. These *neopsychoanalysts,* or new psychoanalysts, have tended to move away from Freud's emphasis on the id and its biologically determined instincts and toward greater concern with the ego and its attempts to deal with reality. One group, led by Heinz Hartmann, has concentrated on such ego processes as perception, attention, memory, and thinking. They regard the ego as an important force in itself rather than a mere mediator between the id and the superego (Hartmann, 1951).

Erich Fromm

Another group of neopsychoanalysts have turned their attention to cultural and social influences on personality, which were largely neglected by Freud. One prominent member of this group was Erich Fromm, who suggested that personality problems are caused by conflicts between the basic human needs and the demands of society. The core of personality, according to Fromm, is the desire to fulfill oneself as a human being—that is, to achieve a kind of unity with nature in the special way that is dictated by the human ability to think. Lower animals have no need to seek such unity, for they are simply a part of nature. They are not aware of any separation between themselves and their environment, including their fellow animals. But people must

1. Relatedness	This need stems from the fact that human beings have lost the union with nature that other animals possess. It must be satisfied by human relationships based on productive love (which implies mutual care, responsibility, respect, and understanding).
2. Transcendence	The need to rise above one's animal nature and to become creative.
3. Rootedness	The need for a feeling of belonging, best satisfied by feelings of affiliation with all humanity.
4. Identity	The need to have a sense of personal identity, to be unique. It can be satisfied through creativity or through identification with another person or group.
5. A frame of orientation	The need for a stable and consistent way of perceiving the world and understanding its events.

Figure 13-1 Fromm's five basic human needs *The neopsychoanalytic theory of Erich Fromm holds that the core of human personality is the desire to fulfill these needs. Personality problems arise when the attempt to gratify them is frustrated. (From* The sane society *by Erich Fromm. Copyright © 1955 by Erich Fromm. Reprinted by permission of Holt, Rinehart and Winston Publishers.)*

seek the unity through their own efforts; they must fulfill what Fromm regarded as the five basic and unique human needs (listed in Figure 13-1).

It would be possible, Fromm believed, to create a society in which these needs could be harmoniously fulfilled. But no such society has ever existed. Therefore all of us tend to experience frustrations and personality problems. It is society, Fromm said, that is "sick"—and it will remain so until people can relate to one another "lovingly" and "in bonds of brotherliness and solidarity," can transcend nature "by creating rather than by destroying," and can gain a sense of selfhood through their own individual powers "rather than by conformity" (Fromm, 1955).

Humanistic theories of personality

Much closer to Fromm's than to Freud's are the humanistic theories of personality. Indeed these theories assume a core of personality almost opposite to the Freudian assumption. Freud believed that the core was conflict, springing in large part from the ruthless and pleasure-seeking demands of the id. Humanistic theories, on the contrary, hold that human nature is basically good and that the core of personality is the desire to perfect our skills and find peace and happiness, rather than to fulfill urges toward sexuality and aggression. They stress the importance of Maslow's motive for self-actualization, which was discussed in Chapter 10. Their therapy is based on the belief that all people want to grow in positive ways and will do so if only they have the chance and the proper encouragement.

Rogers's "phenomenological self"

Among the prominent humanistic theorists is Carl Rogers, who stresses the importance of the self-image all of us carry around. This self-image, or *phenomenological self,* represents the way we preceive ourselves as functioning human beings. It consists of our judgments about our abilities, accomplishments, attractiveness, and relationships with other

Carl Rogers (with glasses) leading an encounter group.

people. In part it is based on our own observations of our behavior and the reactions of other people. But it is also highly subjective, depending on our feelings about ourselves and the way we evaluate ourselves from good to bad.

Thus the phenomenological self does not necessarily correspond to reality. Many people who are considered successful and highly respected by others perceive themselves as unworthy failures. Nor does the phenomenological self necessarily resemble the kind of person we would like to be. Neurotic people, in particular, often display striking differences when asked to describe first what they consider to be their real self, then the ideal self they wish they were (Butler and Haigh, 1954).

To a considerable extent, our phenomenological self depends on the way we believe ourselves to be accepted and esteemed by other people. We need to feel approved if we are to lead meaningful lives in harmony with ourselves and with others, displaying a personality that is trusting, spontaneous, and flexible. We must grow up in a family and social environment that treat us with what Rogers calls *unconditional positive regard.* That is to say, we must be valued and trusted. Our opinions and behavior must be respected. We must be accepted and loved for what we are, even when we do things of which others may disapprove.

Unfortunately, few people grow up in such a completely favorable atmosphere. Most are treated with what Rogers called *conditional positive regard.* Their families and later society at large respond warmly to only some of their thoughts and actions, disapprovingly to others. The "forbidden" thoughts and actions are likely to become a source of maladjustment.

The phenomenological self and maladjustment

Maladjustment and abnormal behavior, in Roger's view, are caused by people's failure to integrate all their experiences, desires, and feelings into their phenomenological image of self—a failure that often stems from conditional positive regard with its accompanying criticism and punishment. This idea can best be explained by an example. A young boy thinks of himself as being good and as being loved by his parents. However, he also feels hostility toward a younger brother, which he expresses one day by breaking his brother's toys. His parents punish him, and he now faces a crises in integrating the experience into his image of self. He is forced to change his image in some way. What will he do?

All of us, says Rogers, try to perceive our experiences and to behave in a way that is consistent with our images of ourselves. When we are confronted with new experiences or new feelings that seem inconsistent with the image, we can take one of two courses:

1. We can recognize the new experiences or feelings, interpret them clearly, and somehow integrate them into our image of self. This is a healthy reaction. The boy just mentioned, for example, could under ideal circumstances decide that he does feel hostility toward his brother. This is something he must reckon with, but it does not make him "bad" or doom him to the scorn of his parents and society.
2. We can deny the experiences or feelings or interpret them in distorted fashion. Thus the boy may deny that he feels any hostility toward his brother and maintain that he broke the toys in retaliation for his brother's hostility (thus adopting the defense mechanism of projection). Or he may interpret the experience as proving that he is not a good boy but a bad boy, thus acquiring feelings of shame and guilt. He may decide that his parents do not love him and therefore feel rejected.

This second course of action is likely to cause trouble. Indeed Rogers believes that maladjustment represents an ever-widening gulf between phenomenological self-image and reality. Maladjusted people tend to regard any experience that is not consistent with their self-image as a threat. Their phenomenological self, as they conceive of it, does not match their true feelings and the actual nature of their experiences. Sometimes they find ways of banishing the experience from their conscious thoughts. In any case they must set up more and more defenses against the truth, and more and more tension results.

Well-adjusted people, on the other hand, are those whose self-image is consistent with what they really think, feel, do, and experience—and who are willing to accept themselves as they are. Instead of being rigid, their phenomenological self is flexible and changes constantly as new experiences occur.

Humanistic therapy

The method of therapy developed by Rogers, which is typical of humanistic therapy in general, is to provide an atmosphere of unconditional positive regard. The therapist displays great warmth and acceptance toward clients, thus creating a nonthreatening situation in which they are free to explore all their thoughts and feelings, including those they have been unable to perceive clearly for fear of condemnation by other people or by their own consciences.

Originally Rogers refrained from expressing any reactions he might have toward the conduct of the people he treated. Later, however, he concluded that he should be more "genuine"—that is, should frankly describe his own feelings, including disapproval of some of the client's actions. But humanistic therapists are always careful to distinguish between criticism of an action and criticism of the person. The core of humanistic treatment is for the therapist to be genuinely understanding and empathetic at all times.

In the safety of this relationship with an understanding and accepting therapist, clients are expected to acquire gradually the ability to resolve their conflicts. The process, Rogers has said, takes three steps: (a) they begin to experience, understand, and accept feelings and desires (such as sexuality and hostility) that they had previously denied to consciousness; (b) they begin to understand the reasons behind their behavior; and (c) they begin to see ways in which they can undertake more positive forms of behavior. In a word, they learn to be themselves.

Many who hear about humanistic therapy for the first time ask the question: If all people were encouraged to be completely themselves, would the world not suddenly be filled with aggressive, brawling, murderous, sexually unrestrained, self-seeking egoists? Rogers answers with an unqualified no. Indeed he finds that when people accept themselves, they tend to be more accepting of others.

Social learning theories and behavior therapy

Humanistic theories hold that the core of personality is the urge to grow in a constructive way. Freud's psychoanalytic theory holds that the core is conflict. Another prominent group of theories take still another view. These are the *social learning theories,* which reject Freud's notion of the primitive drives of the id and do not necessarily take any stand at all on the question, so vital to the humanistic approach, of whether human nature is basically good or evil. Instead, the social learning theories regard personality as largely composed of habits—that is to say, of habitual ways of responding to the situations that arise in one's life. Beginning at birth, our experiences mold us in accordance with the principles of learning that were discussed in Part 2 of the book. Depending on what responses we have learned to display to events in the environment, we may either cope successfully or become helpless and neurotic.

Conditioning and cognitive learning

When social learning theories of personality were first formulated, most of psychology's knowledge of learning was confined to classical and operant conditioning. Thus the theories originally stressed the way unreasonable fears can be acquired through classical conditioning and the role of reinforcement in molding operant behavior. Considered especially important were the rewards and punishments provided first by the family and later by society in general. It was suggested that an individual moving through the cultural environment resembled a complicated version of a rat moving through a T-maze. We can predict the rat's behavior if we know in which arm of the T it has been rewarded with food and in which arm it has been punished by shock. Similarly, we could predict a human being's behavior if only we knew the full story of which this person's actions had been rewarded by society and which had been punished (Miller and Dollard, 1941).

Most social learning theorists today take a more cognitive view of the manner in which experience creates habitual forms of behavior. They agree that rewards and punishments influence learning, but they believe that factors inside the person—such as inner standards—are also important. One prominent member of this group, Albert Bandura, says:

> Humans [have] a capacity for self-direction. They do things that give rise to self-satisfaction and self-worth, and they refrain from behaving in ways that evoke self-punishment. . . . To ignore the influential role of covert self-reinforcement in the regulation of behavior is to disavow a uniquely human capacity (Bandura, 1974).
>
> External consequences, influential as they often are, are not the sole determinants of human behavior. . . . People adopt certain standards of conduct and respond to their own actions in self-reinforcing or self-punishing ways. As a result behavior is regulated by the interplay of self-generated and external sources of influence (Bandura, 1976).

Behavior therapy and relearning

Like social learning theories themselves, the therapies associated with them were originally based on classical and operant conditioning. *Behavior therapy*, as first practiced by learning theorists, tried to eliminate whatever conditioned reflex or conditioned response was causing trouble—for example, an unreasonable fear produced by heights or confined spaces, or the habit of responding to certain situations with anxiety or anger. The behavior therapists made a direct attack on any such symptom of abnormal behavior by trying to break the old stimulus-response connection and substitute a more effective response. Among the techniques they developed and still use in many cases are the following:

Desensitization A method often used to eliminate phobias is *desensitization,* which originally consisted of attempts to associate the stimulus that causes the fear with relaxation rather than with panic. If you sought relief from an unreasonable fear of snakes, for example, the therapist would ask you to relax as much as possible, then to imagine you were looking at a snake in a mildly fear-producing situation, such as from far away. If you could do this without losing your feeling of relaxation, you would then be asked to imagine a slightly more threatening sight of a snake—and so on until you could remain relaxed while imagining that you held a snake.

Actual relaxation, it has now been found, is not essential. Phobias can be desensitized and eliminated simply by imagining yourself in situations that have caused fear, in the presence of a therapist who encourages the process and praises improvement in the ability to respond calmly (Wilkins, 1971). Apparently just thinking about the fearful stimulus, in an atmosphere that offers support and promises relief, is enough to produce results.

Extinction The method of *extinction* is a direct attempt to break a troublesome stimulus-response connection. In one case, it produced spectacular results with a 9-month-old boy who had somehow acquired the habit of vomiting shortly after every meal, weighed only 12 pounds, and was in danger of starving to death. An electrode was attached to his leg and shocks were administered whenever he began to vomit, continuing until he stopped. After a few experiences, the boy learned to stop vomiting as soon as the shock occurred, then soon quit altogether. After a few weeks he weighed 16 pounds, was released from the hospital, and continued to gain weight at home, showing no sign of going back to the old habit (Lang and Melamed, 1969).

The extinction of a response by pairing undesirable behavior with a disagreeable stimulus, such as shock, is called *aversive conditioning.* The person under treatment learns to abandon the undesirable action in order to avoid the unpleasant consequences with which the therapist associates it. Aversive conditioning is always used with caution—or when nothing else seems possible, as in the case of the starving boy—but has proved effective in a number of situations, such as treating men who were sexually incapacitated by sadistic fantasies (Davison, 1968) or by transvestism (Marks, 1968), which is the desire to dress in the clothing of the other sex.

Reinforcement Behavior therapists also use a technique that is the direct opposite of aversive conditioning. Often they employ *reinforcement* of a positive kind as a reward for more effective and more desirable behavior. For example, one group of behavior therapists, dealing with disturbed adolescents who had never learned to talk well or to sit quietly at a school desk, treated them by withholding breakfast and lunch, then rewarding them with small amounts of food every time they showed any signs of constructive behavior. Given this kind of push toward acceptable behavior—with food as the reinforcement—the adolescents improved rapidly (Martin et al., 1968). The technique of reinforcement, as this example indicates, is the basis of behavior modification, which was discussed on pages 94–98. It is also used in the form of a token economy, which has produced dramatic improvement in the behavior of mental hospital patients rewarded with tokens good for movies and other privileges.

New trends in behavior therapy: encouraging assertive coping

Some of the original practitioners of behavior therapy continue to believe that classical or operant conditioning produces the ineffective responses characteristic of most neurotics (Wolpe, 1976). Accordingly they rely on such techniques as desensitization, extinction, and reinforcement to change the responses. But many of today's behavior therapists, like the social learning theories on which their methods are based, have moved in a more cognitive direction. They now seek to change their clients' basic thought patterns. In treating depression, for example, therapists who practice *cognitive behavior therapy* try to bring to light the unrealistically negative views that depressed people tend to develop about their own capacities, the world about them, and the future. They attempt to help their clients by entirely altering such self-defeating habits of thinking (Rush and Beck, 1978).

The difference between normal and abnormal behavior, according to the current view of behavior therapy, often lies in a person's own convictions about ability or lack of ability to cope successfully with anxiety-producing or stressful situations. These convictions about "self-efficacy," as Bandura terms it, determine whether people will make any effort at all to cope, how hard they will try, and how long they will persist. Thus the key to therapy and behavior change is regarded as an enhanced regard for one's own self-efficacy. The key to this better feeling about oneself, in turn, is successful performance in situations that have previously caused anxiety or stress (Bandura, 1977). The behavior therapist makes every effort to foster success, using any method that seems promising.

Learning to cope through observation and guided participation

One method now used by behavior therapists is based on observation learning. Subjects with a phobia for snakes, for example, have been asked to watch a movie of other people approaching and eventually playing with a snake (see Figure 13-2). The subjects can stop the movie and turn it back at any time they begin to feel fearful. By eventually seeing the movie through to the end, they can observe that all people shown, though perhaps frightened at first, were finally able to pick up a snake and even drape it around their neck—all without suffering any harm. If others could do this, why not the subjects?

The observation learning provided by the movie helps considerably to relieve the snake phobia, as can be seen in Figure 13-3. Even more effective, however, is the further step of watching a live model handle a snake, then joining the model—who again suffers no harm and indeed actually enjoys the experience—in playing with the snake. This *guided participation* in a previously anxiety-producing activity is another method used by behavior therapists.

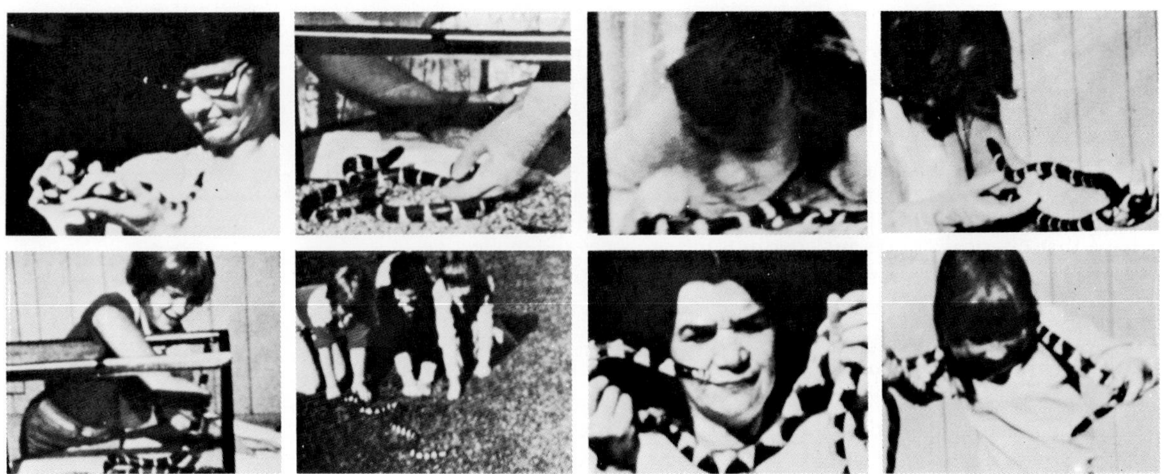

Figure 13-2 Scenes from a movie that cures the fear of snakes *The photographs are stills from a motion picture that has successfully applied observation learning to the treatment of snake phobia, as described in the text.*

In most attempts to enhance feelings of self-efficacy, therapists try to arrange real-life situations in which the client can practice assertive coping with successful results. People suffering from intense stage fright have been treated effectively by guiding them step by step through the delivery of a make-believe speech (with the therapist being the only audience), to brief comments made before just a few listeners (with the therapist again present to provide support and encouragement), to a full-scale address delivered in a large auditorium. People afraid to fly in airplanes have been taken by the therapist on inspection tours of a plane motionless on the ground during servicing, then on brief flights with the therapist alongside, then on longer flights—which finally they managed alone. One study evaluated the progress of people treated in this manner for severe phobias about public speaking, travel, shopping trips, heights, crowds, and other such matters. It was found that 80 percent got over their fears within a few days, though about half required some additional guidance and practice to make the cure permanent (Hardy, 1969). Moreover enhanced feelings of self-efficacy created by successful performance in one situation tend to improve the ability to cope with other situations as well (Bandura, Jeffery, and Gajdos, 1975).

Other therapies (including medical)

There are many other forms of psychotherapy, not all of them associated with personality theories. One estimate is that there are over 350 distinct approaches to helping people who are experiencing psychological problems or who merely want to enrich their life—plus countless more variations on these approaches (Herink, 1980). Some examples are provided in Figure 13-4. There are also many forms of medical treatment, based chiefly on the prescription of drugs developed to produce specific changes in mood or behavior. These medicines are helpful in combating anxiety, depression, and the disoriented behavior and hallucinations of schizophrenia. They all affect brain chemistry, chiefly by regulating the amount and effectivensss of neurotransmitters.

Many forms of psychotherapy are very new, and their value has not yet been established. But it appears that the particular type of psychotherapy is less important than the personality and skill of the therapist and the establishment of a strong and trusting bond between therapist and client—as is explained in a box on Psychology and Society. Thus many therapists no longer limit themselves to any one method. Instead they choose whichever technique seems most promising in each case. They may at times practice humanistic therapy, and at other times they may use behavioral therapy. Or they may combine the two—and perhaps supplement their treatment by referring the client to a physician for medical therapy. In the treatment of acute depression, the mixture of psychotherapy and medication appears to be more effective in many cases than either approach used alone (Dimascio et al., 1979).

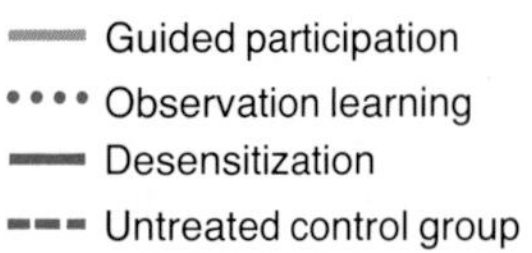

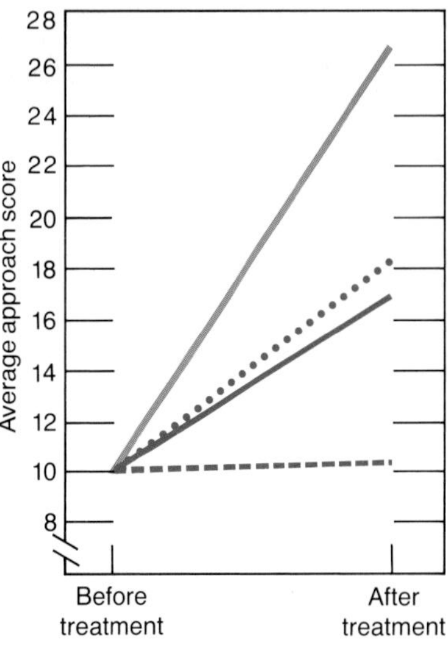

Figure 13-3 Snake phobia: different treatments, different results *Three groups of subjects suffering from snake phobia were treated through different techniques of behavior therapy: desensitization, observation learning (watching the movie illustrated in Figure 13-2), and guided participation in handling a snake. All three methods produced improvement, but in varying degrees (Bandura, Blanchard, and Ritter, 1969). A score of zero meant that a subject could not even enter a room in which there was a snake. To achieve a perfect score of 29, subjects had to let a snake crawl over their lap while holding their hands passively at their sides.*

Interpersonal therapies

Among the alternatives to psychoanalysis, humanistic therapy, and behavior therapy is a group of techniques called *interpersonal therapies* that emphasize primarily the client's relationship with others—family, friends, schoolmates, fellow workers, and society as a whole. Progress in treatment depends heavily on the relationship built up between therapist and client, which is used as a springboard for changing the client's interpersonal relationships in the real world. In one such approach known as *interactional psychotherapy*, the therapist exposes the self-defeating "strategies" developed in dealing with others, and helps the client learn to relate in a more positive and mature way (Cashdan, 1980). Probably the best known therapy of this type is *transactional analysis*, the main goal of which is to eliminate the sham and self-deceit that are viewed as interfering with healthy relationships. Clients are taught to recognize what actually lies behind their communications to others, and to replace childish and unrewarding social interactions with new ones that are more adult and satisfying.

Techniques to improve interpersonal relationships are sometimes quite direct and practical. In effect, therapists tell their clients: "In your interactions with people, you are now doing this and this and this. What you are doing is not working. Give it up for a while and try the following." Other aproaches are more indirect. Clients may be asked to play games in which they pretend to act like other people or to behave in extremely selfish or generous ways, pointing the way to types of interaction they have never tried before (Zweben and Miller, 1968).

Among the interpersonal approaches is *family therapy*, in which the therapist attacks an individual's problems by trying to change the behavior patterns of the entire family. Some therapists make videotapes of family interactions to help the members see why their behavior is unsuccessful and how it can be improved (Bernal et al., 1968). An even broader approach is taken by therapists schooled in *community psychology*. Here the therapist seeks to set up new forms of interaction to replace existing patterns that are causing trouble between employers and workers, between public officials and citizens, and so on (Gibbs, Lachenmeyer, and Sigal, 1980).

Figure 13-4 A sampling of therapies and self-improvement programs *The approaches listed here make up only a small fraction of those in use today. Some reflect a carefully developed theory of human personality, others simply the therapist's philosophy of life. A number of them are popular for a time and then are replaced by newer ones. All are intended in one way or another to reduce psychological suffering and improve well-being, but the actual rate of success of any one approach with particular types of problems remains largely untested (Parloff, 1980).*

Approach	Goal	Technique
Transpersonal therapy	To help the client achieve a sense of harmony with the world through spiritual growth, enlightenment, and self-knowledge.	Adapted from the teachings of the Orient and Middle East, and includes such features as meditation, diet, and exercises to increase sensory awareness and generate energy.
Reality therapy	To encourage the client to feel worthwhile—and capable, therefore, of receiving and giving love—by inducing a sense of self-respect. Forces a confrontation with reality, the acceptance of personal responsibility, and the recognition that well-being comes from living by clearly defined goals and values.	Focuses on the here-and-now rather than on past events, and involves the client in concrete and practical plans of action, including signed contracts.
Implosion therapy	A form of behavior therapy designed to extinguish the association between fear-provoking stimuli and anxiety typically developed by victims of phobias and obsessions.	Through graphic stories or real-life experiences, floods the client with heavy doses of the very stimuli (such as snakes, heights, or dirt) that induce anxiety. Persuades the client to face the fearsome stimuli head-on, and eventually to develop a response of boredom rather than terror.
Hypnotherapy	With no outside distractions, to focus attention entirely on the specific problem at issue, and to persuade the client to change the actual behaviors leading to such conditions as obesity, insomnia, or addiction to cigarettes and alcohol.	Uses hypnosis to put the client in a trance-like state, and then applies the power of suggestion to strengthen the capacity to break undesirable habits, behave in new ways, and improve coping skills.

Approach	Goal	Technique
Primal therapy	To expel psychological pain by reliving the intensely painful, "primal" experiences of infancy and early childhood.	Focuses on feelings instead of words. The therapist encourages an awakening of memories and goads the client into re-experiencing scenes that took place in the opening months of life—including screaming, weeping, thrashing about, and even baby talk.
Psychodrama	To help clients gain insight into their conflicts and problems by dramatizing them as if in a play.	The therapist serves as "stage director," and each member of the group acts out a problem situation in turn. Other members play supporting roles, and then everyone discusses the episode.
Assertiveness training	To teach people to stand up for their rights without violating the rights of others.	Emphasizes not only what the client says but the voice quality and "body language" used to say it. The group leader employs exhortation, advice, and modeling, and asks the client to role-play real-life situations.
est	To persuade people that they can be fully responsible for their own lives and in control of their future.	Seminars are held for a 60-hour period for two weekends. About 250 persons typically attend, who are led by a "trainer" through a variety of experiences—among them aggressive confrontations, relaxation exercises, and episodes designed to induce trust in others. Includes deprivation of bathroom privileges and food to foster a sense of reliance on the leader.

Psychology and Society: How well—and for whom—does psychotherapy work?

Especially in the United States, where psychotherapy has flourished more vigorously than anywhere else, it represents a large investment by society. It is impossible to estimate how many millions of hours have gone into the training of psychotherapists, the practice of various treatment methods, and research into new and better methods. Certainly people who undertake psychotherapy spend millions of dollars every year. Are the time and money a good investment? How much does psychotherapy contribute to society?

Except in the case of clearly defined problems such as specific phobias, the results of therapy, unfortunately, are very difficult to assess. It is hard to determine whether a client has improved at all, much less to exactly what extent. Often different opinions are held by the therapist, the client, and outside observers such as the client's family and friends. Moreover many people who experience troublesome symptoms—for example, mild anxiety or depression—get over them eventually without any treatment at all.

One severe critic of psychotherapy is the British psychologist H. J. Eysenck, who became famous in the 1950s for a series of studies that led him to conclude therapy is no more helpful than the passage of time. But subsequent investigations have swayed most psychologists—including those who do not themselves practice therapy—to a very different conclusion. A recent survey of the best available evidence gathered over the years indicates that there can no longer be much doubt about the overall value of psychotherapy. Data from 475 controlled studies of about 25,000 clients who had undergone therapy showed that on the average they were better off at the end of the treatment than about 80 percent of those with comparable complaints who went without help (Smith, Glass, and Miller, 1980).

Is one method of therapy better than another? One survey found no real evidence that the type of treatment makes any difference. Therapists are about equally helpful regardless of their theoretical background or the techniques they use. Their personal qualities seem to be more important than their methods. They are most effective if they themselves are well adjusted, if they are experienced, and if they establish a warm and close relationship with the client. Men and women appear to be equally successful as therapists (Gomes-Schwartz, Hadley, and Strupp, 1978).

Do some clients have a better chance for improvement than others? It does not seem to matter whether the client is young or old, male or female. But the nature of the problem makes considerable difference. The less serious the disturbance, the greater the likelihood of improvement. Thus people with minor maladjustments of recent origin usually do better than people with severe and long-standing maladjustments. Those who are troubled only by reactions of anxiety or depression are much more likely to benefit than victims of schizophrenia. Cases of sociopathic personality are extremely resistant to treatment—perhaps because sociopaths do not experience the intense anxiety that most other disturbed people are eager to escape.

A desire to get rid of the psychological problem is one of the most important of all factors increasing the likelihood of success. Just as strong motivation for change is highly favorable, so is a willingness to work hard at eliminating the difficulties and a belief that the treatment will help. Clients do best when they trust and like their therapist and are convinced that the therapist understands their predicament, sympathizes with them, and is going about the treatment in a way that promises relief.

Group therapies

Group therapy is the treatment of several patients at the same time. It has been used by therapists of various schools of thought, including some psychoanalysts. The method is in part the child of necessity, for there are not enough trained therapists to treat all prospective clients individually. But it also seems to have genuine advantages with some

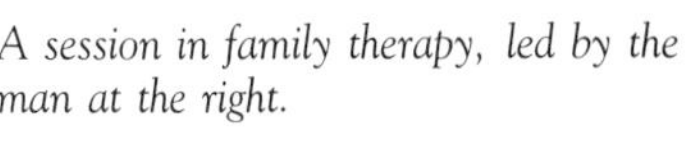

A session in family therapy, led by the man at the right.

clients. Joining a group may relieve the individual's anxieties by demonstrating that other people have the same problems. It also creates an interactional or social give-and-take that is impossible in a face-to-face session with a therapist. Some psychologists believe many clients show the greatest progress when treated through a combination of group and individual therapy (Luborsky et al., 1971).

In an *encounter group,* a number of people meet with the goal of shedding the masks they usually wear in public and presenting their true feelings. Encounters are usually led by a trained therapist, though sometimes they meet without a leader. The emphasis is on activities, games, and conversations that encourage members to interact with open displays of emotion, approval, criticism, affection, and hostility. The goal is to throw off the ordinary social restraints and explore what are often called "gut feelings." The assumption is much the same as in humanistic therapy—namely, that people will grow in a positive direction if freed of artificial barriers against perceiving their true self and interacting with others honestly and openly. The humanistic psychologist Carl Rogers has himself led numerous encounter groups.

Although encounter groups have been very popular in recent years, their effectiveness is controversial. Rogers considers them superior in some ways to his humanistic therapy as practiced on a one-to-one basis (Rogers, 1969). Abraham Maslow, who devised the humanistic concept of self-actualization, concluded that encounter groups are highly useful in encouraging self-awareness and self-expression but can help relieve only minor difficulties, not serious neurotic problems (Maslow, 1969). One study of the effects on some 200 college students who had taken part in encounter groups found that about a third changed for the better, a third were unchanged, and a third changed for the worse (Lieberman, Yalom, and Miles, 1973). The possibility of harm rather than improvement, it has been suggested, is especially great for people who have low self-esteem and cannot cope with group criticism (Kirsch and Glass, 1977).

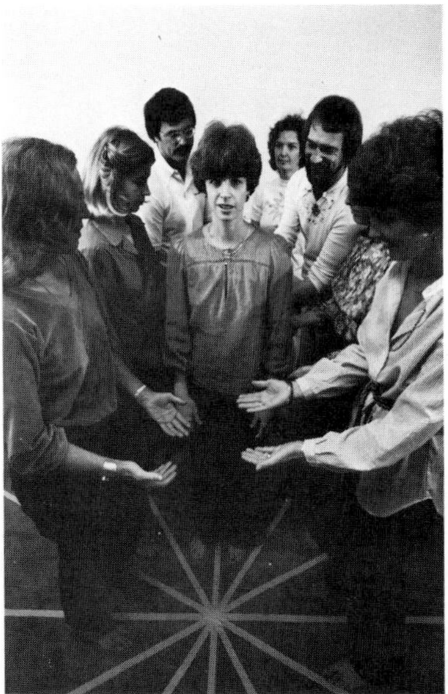

An encounter group practicing the open expression of support.

Medical therapy

One highly controversial medical treatment for personality disorders is *psychosurgery*, in which parts of the brain are severed, removed, or destroyed. At one time many physicians regarded psychosurgery as the quickest and most effective solution for many severe disorders, including uncontrollable urges toward violence. But it was found that many patients, though improved in some ways, lapsed into a vegetable-like existence, unable to function effectively. The technique is seldom used today except as a last resort for patients who are hopelessly suicidal or who suffer from crippling forms of epilepsy.

In *electroshock therapy*, sometimes used to relieve severe depression, an electric current is passed through the head for a fraction of a second. New techniques make it possible to apply the shock to just one hemisphere of the brain (Belensky, 1976). People treated in this manner go into a brief convulsion and then are unconscious for a time. When they wake up they are drowsy and somewhat confused, but advocates of electroshock believe that no permanent ill effects occur. The treatment seems to combat depression by producing a long-term increase in the amount of noradrenalin in the brain (Kety et al., 1967). As with psychosurgery, most psychologists shun the treatment except in cases of extreme emergency.

Many medications are used to treat mental disorders. Several relieve the seizures of epilepsy—including a new drug called clorazepate, approved by the Food and Drug Administration in 1981. *Amphetamines* are sometimes used to treat the abnormality called *hyperkinesis*, which affects about 3 million American children, making them overactive, irritable, and unable to concentrate. Although amphetamines ordinarily act as stimulants, they seem to have a calming effect on some hyperkinetic children.

Tranquilizers The most widely used of all medications affecting the nervous system are the *tranquilizers*, which reduce the amount and effectiveness of the brain's neurotransmitters. Tranquilizers are especially valuable in relieving some of the symptoms of schizophrenic patients, such as hallucinations and delusions. They have greatly improved the atmosphere of mental hospitals by calming patients who were previously unmanageable. They have also enabled some patients, though by no means all, to return to a more or less normal life. In milder forms and doses, tranquilizers are frequently prescribed for people with less serious disturbances associated with anxiety and stress. Though they often serve as a crutch in times of crisis, their overuse may interfere with serious attempts to cope with the causes of anxiety and stress.

Antidepression drugs Medications used to combat depression are known collectively as *psychic energizers*. Of the many types available, each works in a slightly different manner and may help some depressed people but not others. All seem to increase the brain's effective supply of noradrenalin and possibly other neurotransmitters (Janowsky, Khaled El-Yousef, and Davis, 1974). Also sometimes used in treating depression, especially when it is accompanied by swings toward manic states, are the salts of the metallic element *lithium*. This medication, taken regularly, prevents the ups and downs of mood in some people but not all. As in the case of all medications affecting the nervous system, the dosage and possible side effects must be carefully monitored (Baastrup, 1980).

All medical therapies are attempts to remedy the first of the factors mentioned in the preceding chapter as working together to produce abnormal behavior—biological, psychological, and environmental. Since the search for medications is still in its infancy, it seems likely that the future will bring many new drugs that relieve the biological causes of personality problems. It may even turn out that some disorders are primarily biological, in which case new medications may prove to be a specific cure. The great majority of psychologists, however, believe that most disorders spring from psychological as well as biological causes and that psychotherapy should always accompany medical therapy.

The question of self-therapy

The techniques of medical therapy have to be prescribed and monitored by a physician. But what about psychotherapy? Can we serve as our own psychotherapists—solving our own problems and correcting any tendencies toward abnormal behavior? How helpful are all the popular books that suggest ways to better mental health and greater self-fulfillment?

These questions are not easy to answer. For one thing, advice on self-help techniques varies widely—from articles written by untrained people to carefully documented books in which serious therapists explain their theories and methods. The former are worthless and potentially harmful. The latter seem to help some readers but not others. One difficulty with all attempts at self-therapy is that they lack the support of a warm, close, and encouraging relationship with an understanding and sympathetic therapist—which is probably the most important ingredient of success.

All psychologists agree that sound knowledge about psychological processes encourages the development of normal, healthy, and effective personality. Thus everything in this course is potentially helpful. Some topics of particular value as signposts toward mental health are psychology's knowledge about the way unreasonable fears can be acquired through conditioning, learned helplessness and how it can be counteracted, emotions, motives, anxiety, stress, assertive coping with anxiety and stress, and the wellsprings of abnormal behavior, as well as the personality theories and methods of therapy described in this chapter. Also highly pertinent are many of the topics still to come—especially the manner in which personality develops and changes throughout life (Chapter 14) and the ways in which behavior is molded for better or for worse by relationships with other people (Chapter 15).

SUMMARY

Personality theories

1. *Personality* is the total pattern of characteristic ways of thinking, feeling, and behaving that constitute the individual's distinctive method of relating to the environment.

2. *Personality theories* are concerned with three aspects of human behavior. They assume (a) that there is some *core of personality* common to all human beings, (b) that these common tendencies and characteristics of human beings are channeled in various directions by the process of *development,* and (c) that the core of personality as modified by development makes each person a unique individual displaying a unique pattern of the *peripheral traits* that are generally known as personality.

Freud's psychoanalytic theory

3. Freud's *psychoanalytic theory* assumes that the core of personality is conflict—for example, conflicts between incompatible desires (many of which are unconscious) and fears of punishment for attempts to gratify them.
4. Psychoanalytic theory holds that the human mind has three parts or forces: (a) the unconscious *id,* containing the person's instinctive drives toward sexuality (the *libido*) and aggression; (b) the largely conscious *ego,* which is the person's contact with reality; and (c) the largely unconscious *superego,* which punishes transgressions.
5. The superego is acquired largely as a result of the *Oedipus complex,* a conflict of mingled love and hate toward the parents that all children are assumed to undergo between the ages of 2½ and 6. Children resolve the conflict by identifying with their parents and adopting what they consider to be their parents' moral judgments, which form the superego.
6. The central problem in mental disturbances, according to psychoanalytic theory, is anxiety—produced in the ego when the demands of the id threaten to create danger or when the superego threatens to impose disapproval or punishment.
7. *Psychoanalysis,* the method of therapy used by followers of Freud, is designed to dredge up into awareness the unconscious desires and conflicts that Freud considered the source of neurotic anxiety and guilt. It uses the techniques of *free association* and examines *transference,* dreams, and slips of the tongue to provide insights and thus achieve "freedom from the tyranny of the unconscious."
8. Among the successors of Freud who have proposed variations of his theories are Jung, who introduced the concepts of *introvert* and *extrovert* and of a *collective unconscious*; Hartmann, who has emphasized the role of such ego processes as perception, attention, and thinking in dealing with reality; and Fromm, who stressed the importance of cultural and social influences on personality.

Humanistic theories of personality

9. *Humanistic theories* hold that human nature is basically good and that the core of personality is the desire to perfect our skills and find peace and happiness.
10. Rogers's humanistic theory stresses the self-image, or *phenomenological self,* which represents the way we see ourselves, our abil-

ities, and our relationships with other people. Maladjustments occur when people fail to integrate all of their experiences, desires, and feelings into the phenomenological self, which is therefore at odds with reality.

11. Rogers's therapy provides an atmosphere of *unconditional positive regard* in which clients are free to explore all their thoughts and feelings, including those they have been unable to perceive clearly for fear of condemnation by others or by their own consciences.

Social learning theories and behavior therapy

12. *Social learning theories* hold that the core of personality is the habitual ways we have learned to respond to events in the environment. The theories originally stressed classical and operant conditioning and reinforcement through rewards or punishments. Many of today's social learning theorists take a more cognitive view and emphasize inner standards, self-reinforcement, and self-punishment.
13. *Behavior therapy* regards pesonality disturbances as learned responses that can be changed through relearning. Its techniques include *desensitization, extinction* of undesired behavior (sometimes through *aversive conditioning*), *reinforcement* of more desirable behavior, *cognitive behavior therapy, observation learning,* and *guided participation* to help encourage assertive coping.

Other therapies (including medical)

14. *Interpersonal therapies* concentrate on changing the disturbed individual's behavior toward other people. Some examples are *transactional analysis* and *family therapy. Community psychology* is a broader form of this approach.
15. *Group therapy* is the treatment of several patients at the same time. *Encounter groups* are one example.
16. Methods of *medical therapy* include: (a) *psychosurgery,* (b) *electroshock,* (c) *tranquilizers,* and (d) *antidepresssion medications.*

IMPORTANT TERMS

antidepression medications
aversive conditioning
behavior therapy
cognitive behavior therapy
collective unconscious
community psychology
conditional positive regard
core of personality
defense mechanism
desensitization
development
ego
electroshock therapy
encounter group
extinction
extrovert
family therapy
free association
group therapy
guided participation
humanistic therapy
id
inferiority complex
interactional psychotherapy
interpersonal therapy
introvert
libido
neopsychoanalysts

observation learning
Oedipus complex
peripheral traits
personality
phenomenological self
pleasure principle
psychic energizers
psychoanalysis
psychoanalytic theory
psychosurgery
reality principle
reinforcement
resistance
social learning theories
superego
tranquilizers
transactional analysis
transference
unconditional positive regard
unconscious mind

SUPPLEMENT:
Tests of Personality

If psychologists had a test that measured personality accurately and reliably, it would be one of their most valuable tools. Clinical psychologists could quickly analyze their clients' strengths and weaknesses, pinpoint sources of stress and anxiety, and determine the most effective way of helping in the struggle to cope. Guidance counselors would have a surefire guide to jobs and careers, for personality is a major factor in determining whether a person will be happy and successful as a salesperson, teacher, police officer, or accountant. Marriage counselors could quickly discover sources of friction and ways to relieve them—or spot couples so incompatible that the situation is hopeless. Research psychologists would have an invaluable aid in studying the conditions that foster or inhibit the flowering of personality.

Thus psychologists have spent a great deal of time, effort, and ingenuity on the creation of personality tests. Their goal, unfortunately, has been elusive. They have devised several hundred tests that are useful in many ways, but they have yet to find the perfect test. Perhaps they never will. Personality is such a complex matter—the product of a tangled and endless weaving together of experiences beginning at birth, continuing throughout life, and unique for each individual—that the difficulties in measuring it are staggering.

All the personality tests now in use have some virtues but also many limitations. The tests fall into three classes: (a) *objective tests,* (b) *situational tests,* and (c) *projective tests.*

Objective tests

Many people have attempted to devise a measure of personality that meets the standard of objectivity considered ideal in any psychological test. They have come up with some *objective tests* whose scores are not seriously affected by the opinions or prejudices of the examiner. Since these tests are administered according to a standard procedure, the results should be the same regardless of who gives or scores them.

The most widely used objective test is the *Minnesota Multiphasic Personality Inventory,* or MMPI for short. The test is made up of nearly 600 statements like those shown in Figure 13-5. For each statement, subjects are asked to check whether or not it is true of their own behavior or to mark "cannot say." The method of scoring compares the individual subject's responses with those made in the past by large numbers of other people—especially with the scores made by people known to have such personality traits as tendencies to pessimism and depresssion, anxiety over health, emotional excitability, delinquency, or tendencies toward schizophrenia and paranoia.

Figure 13-5 **Some items from a personality test** *The Minnesota Multiphasic Personality Inventory is made up of statements like these, which subjects are asked to mark true, false, or cannot say of their own behavior.*

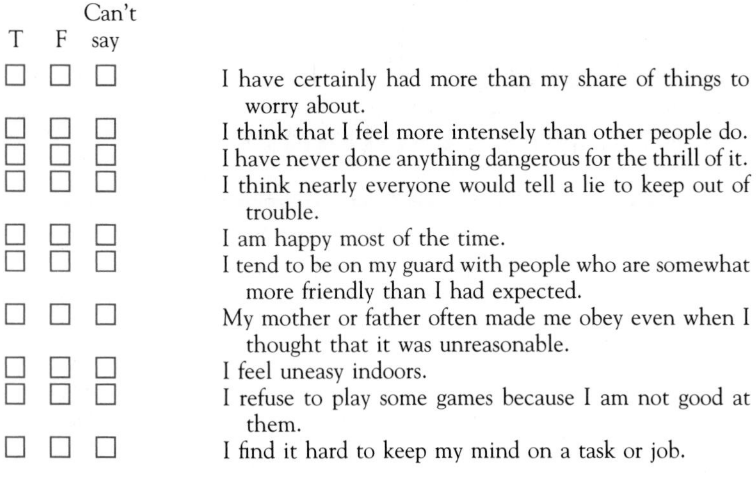

T	F	Can't say	
☐	☐	☐	I have certainly had more than my share of things to worry about.
☐	☐	☐	I think that I feel more intensely than other people do.
☐	☐	☐	I have never done anything dangerous for the thrill of it.
☐	☐	☐	I think nearly everyone would tell a lie to keep out of trouble.
☐	☐	☐	I am happy most of the time.
☐	☐	☐	I tend to be on my guard with people who are somewhat more friendly than I had expected.
☐	☐	☐	My mother or father often made me obey even when I thought that it was unreasonable.
☐	☐	☐	I feel uneasy indoors.
☐	☐	☐	I refuse to play some games because I am not good at them.
☐	☐	☐	I find it hard to keep my mind on a task or job.

Source: Minnesota Multiphasic Personality Inventory.

The MMPI has served as the basis for the development of other widely used objective tests of personality. One example is the *California Personality Inventory*, or CPI for short. This test contains nearly 500 items, yielding scores that measure such dimensions of personality as dominance, sociability, self-acceptance, self-control, and responsibility. Various combinations of scores on the scales of the CPI have been found to be typical of persons who succeed in school and various fields of work (Anastasi, 1982).

Situational tests

In a *situational test,* the examiner observes the behavior of the subject in a situation deliberately created to bring out certain aspects of personality. For example, subjects might be asked to carry out some difficult mechanical task with the assistance of "helpers" who are in fact stooges and who behave in an uncooperative and insulting fashion (U.S. Office of Strategic Services, 1948). Or subjects might be put through what is called a stress interview, in which the people asking the questions are deliberately hostile and pretend to disbelieve the answers (Mackinnon, 1967).

Situational tests have been widely applied in efforts to select people with personality traits that are appropriate for particular jobs—as counselors, police officers, or spies. One weakness of these tests is that it is difficult to know whether the situation actually seems real to the subjects and whether their motivation and behavior are the same as in real life. Moreover, two different examiners watching a subject's behavior may reach different conclusions about it. Thus situational tests, though they may give valuable clues to personality traits, must be used and interpreted with caution.

Projective tests

The term *projection* was mentioned in the preceding chapter as a defense mechanism in which people attribute to others some of their own anxiety-causing motives. *Projective tests* of personality assume that a similar mental process can be observed and measured, even in people who are not using it as a defense mechanism, by providing conditions that encourage it. In the *Thematic Apperception Test,* or TAT for short, these conditions are created by asking the subject to make up stories about pictures like the one in Figure 13-6, which you should examine before reading on.

The picture in Figure 13-6 is deliberately ambiguous. It could mean almost anything. Thus, in responding to it, you are likely to project some of your own personality traits. The story you make up may very well reveal something about your own motives, feelings, anxieties, and attitudes. Sometimes the amount of self-revelation is clear and dramatic, as in this story made up by one subject:

> The older woman represents evil and she is trying to persuade the younger one to leave her husband and run off and lead a life of fun and gaiety. The younger one is afraid to do it—afraid of what others will think, afraid she will regret the action. But the older one knows that she wants to leave and so she insists over and over again. I am not sure how it ends. Perhaps the younger woman turns and walks away and ignores the older woman.

Figure 13-6 A projective test: what is happening here? *What story does this picture tell? What led up to the situation? What is happening? How will events turn out? These are the questions asked in the Thematic Apperception Test, which uses drawings similar to this one. Try making up your own story before reading the discussion of the TAT in the text.* (*©Murray, 1971. Reprinted by permission of the Harvard University Press.*)

The TAT technique has found extensive and successful use in measuring the strength of the achievement motive (McClelland, Clark, and Lowell, 1953). A tendency to invent stories that contain frequent, intense elements of striving and ambition—or that on the contrary show little concern with success—appears to be a better measure of the achievement motive than the judgment of people who know the subjects well (French, 1959) or even the subjects' own assessment of their desire to achieve (DeCharms et al. 1955).

The *Rorschach Test* uses inkblots like the one shown in Figure 13-7. When subjects are asked what they see in the blots, they ordinarily mention 20 to 40 things of which they are reminded. Their responses are scored for various characteristics that seem to reveal personality. For example, a tendency to respond to the blot as a whole may indicate that the subject thinks in terms of abstractions and generalities, while a tendency to pick out many minor details that most people ignore may indicate an overconcern for detail.

A number of other less formal projective techniques have been developed (Garfield, 1974). In a *word association test,* the examiner calls out a word, such as "mother" or "bad" or "money," and the subject is asked to respond as quickly as possible with the first word that comes to mind. The examiner notes the nature of the associations that the test words suggest and also the speed with which the subject responds. Any unusual delay in responding is taken to indicate that the test word arouses

Figure 13-7 Another projective test: what do you see? *This is an inkblot like those used in the Rorschach Test. Subjects are asked to examine it and report everything they see in it (Klopfer and Davidson, 1962).*

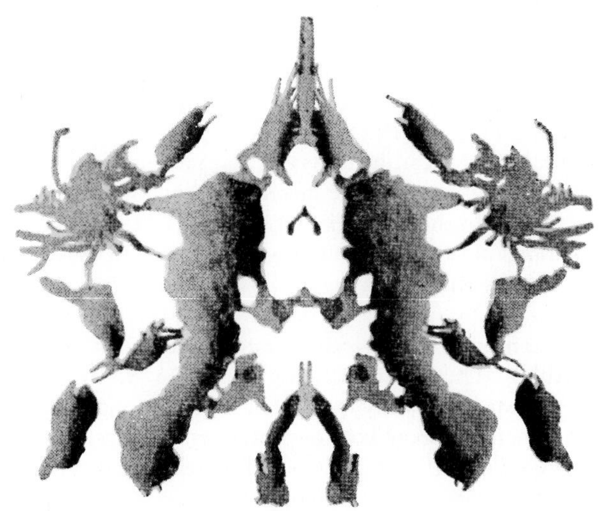

some kind of conflict. In a *draw-a-person test,* the subject is simply asked to draw a picture of a person on a blank sheet of paper. The sex of the drawing, its size, the facial expression, and other characteristics may contain personality clues. In a *sentence completion test,* the examiner gives the subject a series of partially completed sentences such as the following:

> I sometimes feel. . . .
> When by myself. . . .
> When I was young. . . .

The subject is asked to complete the sentences with the first thoughts that come to mind. The responses, like the TAT stories, may suggest motives and conflicts.

SUMMARY OF SUPPLEMENT

1. There are three types of *personality tests:*
   a. *Objective tests,* such as the Minnesota Multiphasic Personality Inventory (MMPI) and the California Personality Inventory (CPI).
   b. *Situational tests,* in which the examiner observes the behavior of the subject in a situation deliberately created to reveal some aspect of the subject's personality.
   c. *Projective tests,* such as the Thematic Apperception Test and the Rorschach Test, in which subjects supposedly insert or project aspects of their own personality into the stories they make up about ambiguous pictures or into the kinds of objects they see in inkblots. Other more informal types of projective techniques include *word association, draw-a-person,* and *sentence completion tests.*

IMPORTANT TERMS

CPI
draw-a-person test
MMPI
objective test
projective test
Rorschach test
sentence completion test
situational test
TAT
word association test

RECOMMENDED READINGS

Bandura, A. *Social learning theory.* Englewood Cliffs, N.J.: Prentice-Hall, 1976.

Campbell, J., ed. *Portable Jung.* New York: Penguin Books, 1976.

Frank, J. D. *Persuasion and healing: a comparative study of psychotherapy,* rev ed. New York: Schocken Books, 1974.

Freud, S. *New introductory lectures on psychoanalysis.* Edited by Stachey, J. New York: Norton, 1965.

Garfield, S. L. *Psychotherapy: an eclectic approach.* New York: Wiley, 1980.

Hall, C. S., and Lindzey, G. *Theories of personality,* 3d ed. New York: Wiley, 1978.

Redd, W. H., Porterfield, A. L., and Anderson, B. L. *Behavior modification: behavioral approaches to human problems.* New York: Random House, 1979.

Rogers, C. *On becoming a person: a therapist's view of psychotherapy.* Boston: Houghton Mifflin, 1970.

Rychlak, J. F. *Introduction to personality and psychotherapy: a theory-construction approach,* 2d ed. Boston: Houghton Mifflin, 1981.

Whitaker, C. A., and Malone, T. P. *The roots of psychotherapy.* New York: Brunner-Mazel, 1981.

Yalom, I. D. *The theory and practice of group psychotherapy,* 2d ed. New York: Basic Books, 1975.

PART

7

Becoming a Person and Relating to Others

Up to this point the book has discussed human behavior without much concern for when it develops and how it is sometimes transformed over the course of a lifetime. The chapters have in a way resembled still photographs, allowing detailed examination of such complex subjects as learning, memory, emotions, and motivation. In this final section the photographs will merge into a sort of motion picture, portraying behavior and personality not as frozen in time but as unfolding and changing over the years. The chapters will show, in particular, the important roles that other people play in the constantly shifting scenario of our lives.

Most of us are aware that other people can have a critical impact on us when we are young. Indeed many of us can point to one or two individuals, sometimes from within the family and sometimes from without, who made an enormous difference in our early lives—altering our values and career plans, helping us overcome a destructive habit, or seeing us through a personal crisis. But the influence of others does not by any means

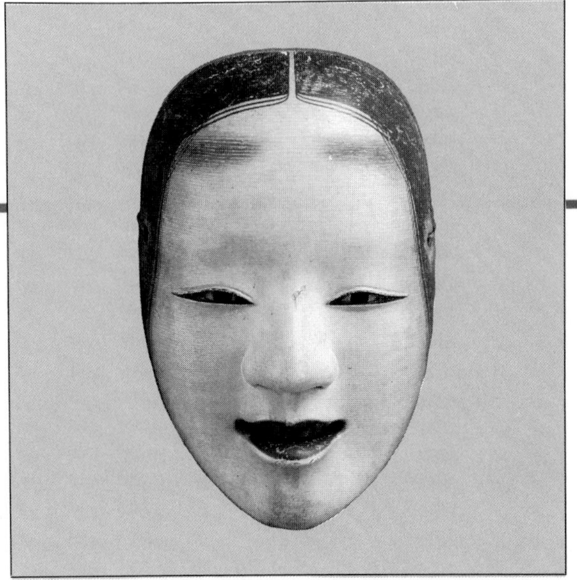

end with youth. At every stage of our existence, people move into and out of our lives—family members, all our teachers, friends, fellow workers, lovers, spouses, and ultimately our own children and their children. What these people say and do—even what we think they feel—continues to affect us profoundly until the very end.

Chapter 14 deals with *human development,* the branch of psychology that studies the way our mental and physical abilities blossom in childhood and the way both inner traits and outside influences shape and reshape our personalities from our beginnings in the womb until our existence draws to a close. Chapter 15 covers *social psychology,* which studies the dynamics of human interaction—all the varied and important ways in which we human beings meet, mingle, communicate, use other people's actions as a guide to our own, and help mold each other's behavior, life-styles, and even thoughts and feelings. The chapter completes the explanation of how and why our personalities depend so heavily on the other people with whom we live.

CHAPTER 14

Babies at birth: alike yet different 506
- Differences in sensitivity and adaptation
- Differences in activity and irritability
- Easy, slow-to-warm-up, and difficult babies
- How long do early traits persist?
- Effects of unfavorable environment: the neglected child

Physical and mental development 513
- Physical maturation
- Intellectual development

Personality development: birth to eighteen months 518
- The importance of attachment
- Attachment and exploration
- The beginnings of anxiety

The first social demands: eighteen months through three years 521
- Social demands and inner standards
- The place of rewards and punishments

The preschool years: four and five 524
- The identification process

The period of teachers and peers: six to ten 525
- The new world of the classroom
- Finding a place among peers
- The road to being dominant or submissive
- New emphasis on inner standards
- The 10-year-old as a future adult

Adolescence: fun or fury? 529
- The adolescent growth spurt
- The search for identity
- Sexual and moral development

Development—and sometimes about-face—in adulthood 536
- What becomes of the unhappy adolescent?
- Is trouble a blessing in disguise?
- Erikson's theory of psychosocial development
- Early adulthood, commitment, and marriage
- Middle age and its responsibilities

The challenges and triumphs of growing old 541
- Is it as bad as they say?
- The psychology of dying

Summary 543

Important terms 545

Recommended readings 545

Psychology and society
- Is there a magic formula for bringing up children? 511
- Psychology's message to parents: optimism—and patience—often pay off 512
- Being a good parent to the 2-year-old 523
- Does society value its teachers enough? 527
- Adolescents and parents: enemies or friends? 533

Human Development

As parents gaze for the first time at a newborn infant, they often wonder about the future. What will this tiny creature be like over time—as a toddler, a schoolchild, an adolescent, and adult? What strengths will emerge, what limitations, what problems? The influences that will mold the baby's psychological traits are the domain of *developmental psychology*—chiefly devoted to the study of the ways in which children gradually acquire all of the patterns of behavior described in this book. These include the ways in which they perceive the world, learn, think, use language, experience emotions, and develop the motives, conflicts, and methods of coping with conflicts that will help determine their adult personalities.

Developmental psychologists recognize that the future of newborns is already influenced to a degree before their parents meet them for the first time. To begin with, the impact of heredity is exerted once and for all at the moment of union between mother's egg cell and father's sperm cell. The genes and chromosomes packed into these cells tend to program the child's future along certain lines, contributing to the development of psychological characteristics such as sociability, intelligence, and the various forms of abnormal behavior described in Chapter 12. Then, from the instant of conception, the impact of the environment begins to leave its mark. Indeed when babies give up their home in the womb, they have already experienced an environment that can heavily influence how their inherited characteristics will actually unfold in the outside world.

If the mother's diet during pregnancy lacks nutritional values and vitamins, the baby may have difficulty attaining the IQ level that its genes might otherwise have made possible. Mothers who experience prolonged anxiety or anger during pregnancy may have babies who are of less than average size, overactive, and inclined to have digestive problems—as if they, too, had been subjected to damaging stress. Mothers who smoke constantly may pollute the unborn baby's blood supply with carbon monoxide and thus deprive the baby of the oxygen and nutrients essential for healthy development. Some babies, born to mothers who use sedatives and tranquilizers, appear sluggish and withdrawn. Others, born to women who use narcotics, are themselves full-fledged addicts at birth. And heavy drinking of alcohol by the pregnant mother may damage the baby's central nervous system, producing a pattern of physical and psychological abnormalities that limit at the very start the infant's chances for reaching its potential (Segal and Segal, 1984).

At birth a new set of influences begins to operate and to mold the infant's psychological traits. These influences change as the years pass, but in one way or another they continue to affect development during the entire life span. The study of development, once confined to the growing child, is now viewed as a process that continues throughout our existence, from cradle to grave. The effects of stresses suffered in the womb, it has been found, can often be reversed if remedial steps are taken early in infancy. Even the most drastic handicaps caused by a deprived childhood can often be overcome if the environment improves dramatically in later life. The angry, aggressive 7-year-old may blossom into a well-adjusted adult. The troubled adolescent may become a perfectly well-adjusted 30-year-old. Thus developmental psychology has expanded to the study not only of infancy and childhood, but of adolescence, young adulthood, and the experiences of old age that complete the full spectrum of human development. All the future characteristics of a child that new parents wonder about will continue to be shaped by the environment—from the moment the infant arrives until its life has come to a close.

Babies at birth: alike yet different

The human baby, though more helpless at birth than most other newborn organisms, is nonetheless a miraculous creation. From the moment the first breath is drawn, all normal babies are sensitive to stimuli in their environments. They can learn to distinguish between musical tones as close as C and C-sharp, the colors red and green, or the taste of plain and sugar water—as is evident in Figure 14-1. Even babies a few hours old follow a moving object with their eyes. After only a few days, newborns can differentiate between the smell of their own mother's milk and the smell of milk from another mother (Werner and Lipsitt, 1981).

Babies respond to stimuli with a wide range of inborn reflex behavior. When the sides of their mouths are tickled, they display the reflex illustrated in Figure 14-2—the so-called rooting response that enables them to find food at the mother's breast. If the sole of the foot is gently pricked with a pin, they draw the foot away as shown in Figure 14-3—a reflex that enables them to escape from pain. If a bright light is flashed, they protect themselves by closing their eyelids.

Though all normal babies are aware of their environment and can react to the stimuli it presents, they differ in their sensitivity and responses. They differ also in level of activity, mood, friendliness, and other ways that parents are quick to recognize and describe as their

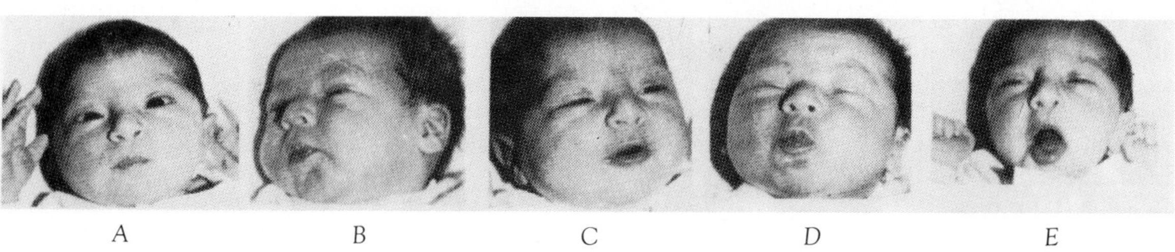

Figure 14-1 The newborn's reactions to different taste stimuli *These photos were taken before the infant had ever received a full feeding. The facial reactions are to no taste stimulus (A), distilled water (B), a sweet stimulus (C), a sour stimulus (D), and a bitter stimulus (E). Similar reactions can be produced by different odors (Steiner, 1979).*

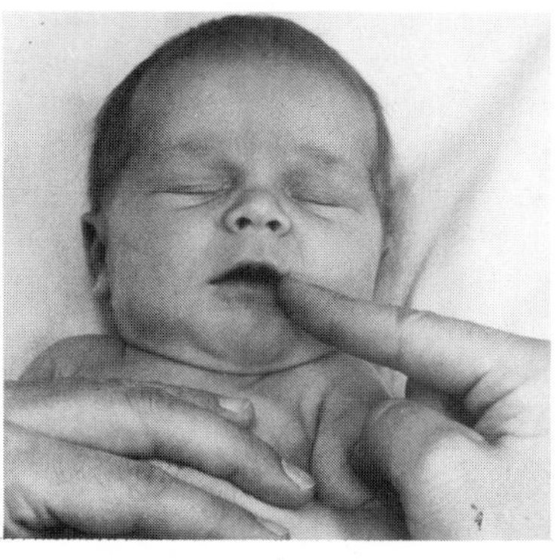

A

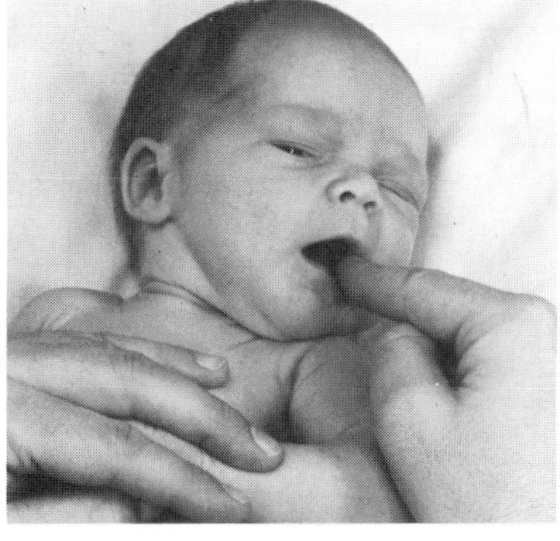

B

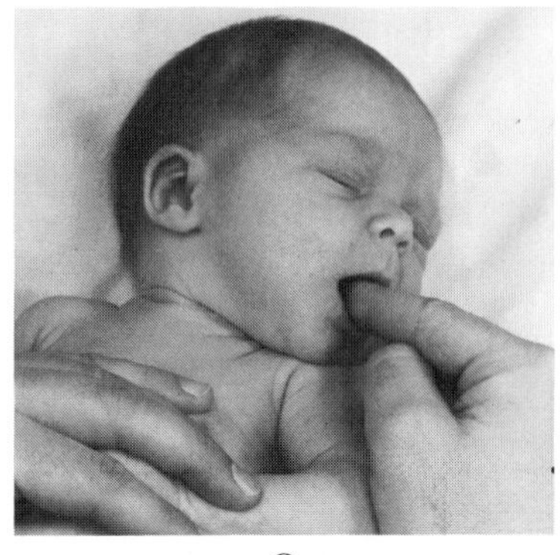

C

Figure 14-2 The newborn's rooting response *When the side of an infant's mouth is tickled (A), the reflex response is to turn the head toward the stimulus (B) and then try to suck the finger (C), as if it were a source of food.*

baby's "nature." These characteristic styles of behavior are displayed so early that they almost surely represent inborn traits. To what extent are such traits likely to persist and to what extent are they modified by environment and experience?

Differences in sensitivity and adaptation

Studies have shown wide individual differences in sensory threshold. With some babies, even the most gentle stroking of the skin produces a muscular reflex. Other babies do not respond unless the stroking is fairly firm. Some babies cry when exposed to sounds or light flashes of low intensity, others only when the intensity is much higher.

There are also differences in how rapidly babies display sensory adaptation and quit responding. When a sound loud enough to produce crying is repeated over a period of time, some babies get used to it very quickly. Others continue to show distress even at the thirtieth repetition (Bridger, 1961). Similiarly, some babies appear to become bored with a stimulus more quickly than others. If a series of pictures of the human face is projected on a screen above the crib, some infants pay close attention for a long time. Others soon stop looking, as if they had rapidly tired of the repetitive stimulus.

Figure 14-3 Reflex escape from pain *When the sole of the infant's foot is touched by a sharp object, the reflex response is to pull the foot away from the offending stimulus.*

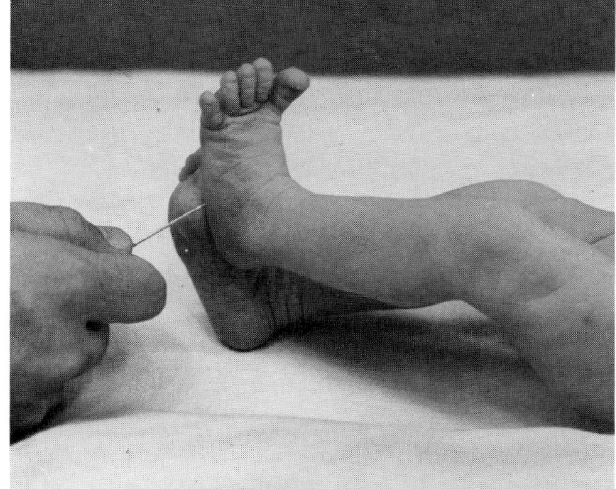

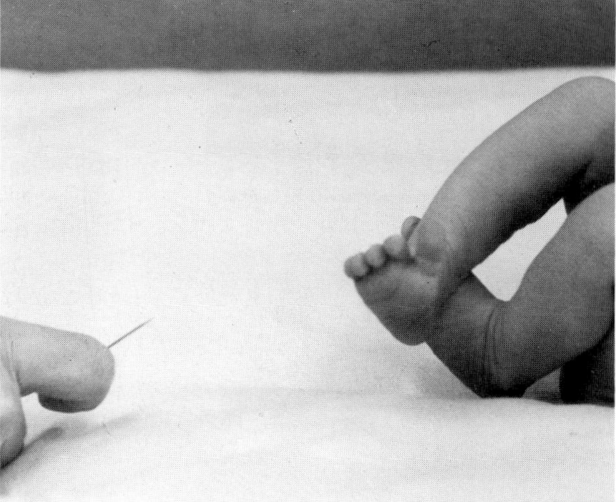

Differences in activity and irritability

Even in the very early days of life, some babies are much more active than others. They move their arms and legs with considerable force, tend to be restless when asleep, suck vigorously when nursing, and appear to have above-average appetites. As they get a little older, they tend to make loud noises when they babble, bang their toys together, and kick at the sides of their crib. Other babies are much more placid in these respects (Wolff, 1959).

Another important difference among infants is in what might be called irritability. Some babies begin to fret, whine, or cry at the slightest provocation. Once they begin to fret, they often work themselves up into what looks like a temper tantrum and soon are bellowing at the top of their lungs. Other babies do not fret unless their discomfort or pain is intense. Even then, they may fret only for a half-minute or so and then stop, as if possessing some mechanism that inhibits the buildup of extreme upset.

Some pronounced differences have been found among babies of different ethnic backgrounds. If placed face down in their cribs, Caucasian infants immediately turn their heads to the side, whereas Chinese babies leave their face placidly buried in the sheets. An even more striking difference has been demonstrated by pressing a cloth briefly against the baby's nose. Caucasian and black babies try to fight off the cloth by turning away or trying to dislodge it with their hands. Chinese babies simply accept the situation and start breathing through their mouths. Such differences in response may reflect a tendency of Chinese babies to be less active and less easily distracted than their American counterparts (Hsu et al., 1981). A notable difference between Americans of Caucasian and Indian descent is illustrated in Figure 14-4.

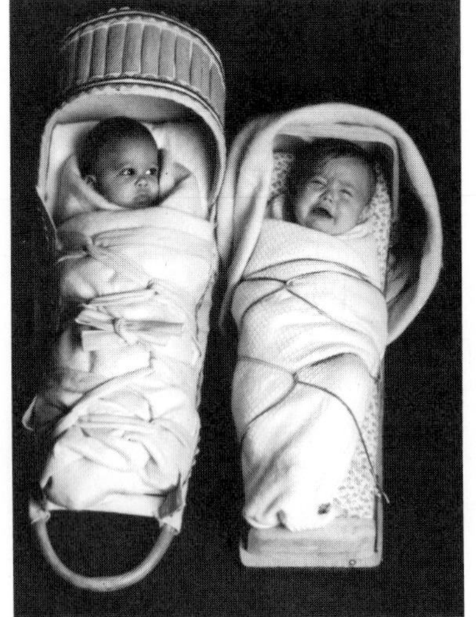

Figure 14-4 Happy Indian baby, unhappy Caucasian *These two infants have been placed on a cradle board, which Navaho Indian mothers have used for generations to carry their young. The Navaho baby is perfectly content. The Caucasian baby lodges a vigorous protest.*

Easy, slow-to-warm-up, and difficult babies

One group of investigators, after studying more than a hundred children from birth through elementary school, came to the conclusion that most newborn Americans fall into three distinct classes of temperament:

1. *Easy* children are generally cheerful. Their reactions to stimuli show a low to moderate intensity. They establish regular habits of eating and sleeping and are quick to adapt to new schedules, foods, and people.
2. *Slow-to-warm-up* children are less cheerful; indeed their mood seems slightly negative. Their responses are low in intensity. Their eating and sleeping habits vary and they tend to withdraw from their first exposure to a new experience. They take time to adjust to change.
3. *Difficult* children seem unfriendly and hard to please. They are given to unusually intense reactions, such as loud laughter, frequent loud crying, and temper tantrums. They show little regularity in eating and sleeping and are easily upset by new experiences.

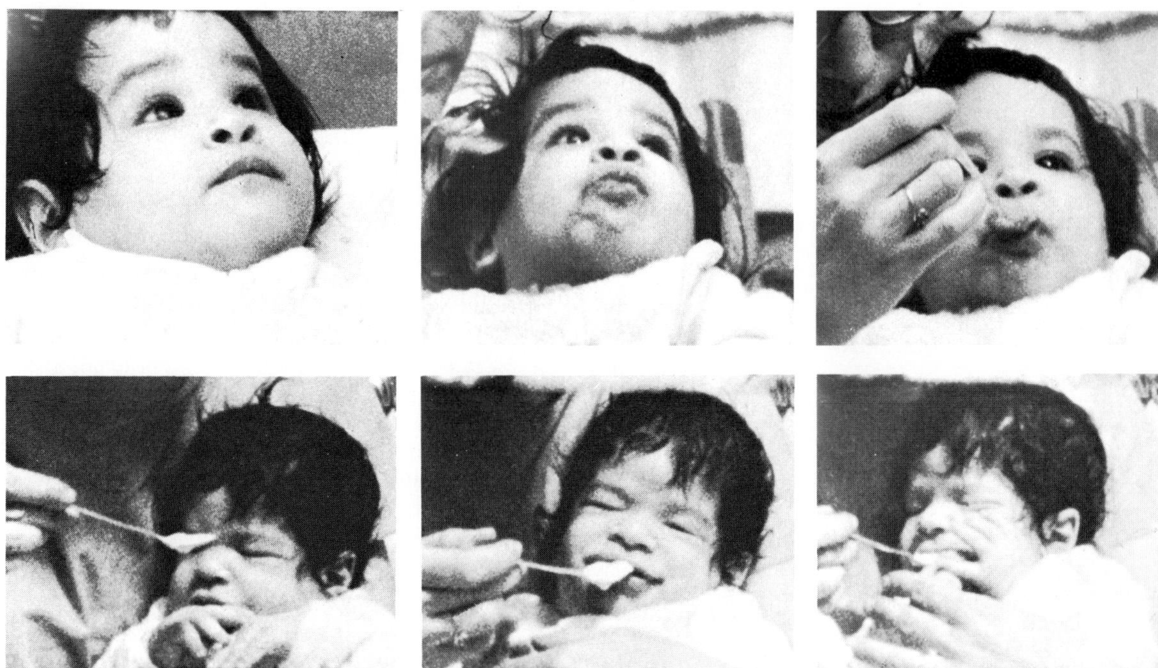

Figure 14-5 **A contrast in infant temperament** *Both these babies are 3 months old and are being offered a new kind of cereal for the first time. The girl at the top, an easy baby, eagerly accepts the new experience. The boy at the bottom, a difficult baby, fights it.*

A striking example of the difference between an easy and a difficult baby is shown in Figure 14-5. The photographs, which were made several years apart, are of an older sister and a younger brother—an indication that early differences in temperament do not necessarily reflect the parents' personalities or child-rearing methods. Regardless of the parents' behavior or the general atmosphere of the home, about 40 percent of the children in the study were easy, 15 percent slow-to-warm-up, and 10 percent difficult. The remaining 35 percent showed a mixture of the three different kinds of temperament (Thomas, Chess, and Birch, 1970).

The investigators concluded that the three types require very different treatment during infancy and in the early years of school. Easy children thrive under almost any kind of treatment in early childhood—but, having adapted so well to the home environment, they may have trouble when their teacher and schoolmates make different demands. Slow-to-warm-up children require considerable patience. They do their best when encouraged to try new experiences but allowed to adapt at their own pace. Too much pressure heightens their natural inclination to withdraw.

Difficult children present a special problem. Because of their irregular habits, their resistance to adjustment, and their negative attitude, they are hard to live with—a trial to their parents and later their teachers. Attempts to force them to behave like other children may only make them more negative and difficult. Their parents must exercise exceptional understanding and tolerance to bring them around—slowly and gradually—to getting along with other individuals.

These findings about inborn differences in temperament, together with the other new knowledge about variations in sensitivity, activity, and irritability, are of great potential value to parents, the staffs of day-care centers, and teachers, especially in the early grades. The findings disprove the popular assumption that all young children are more or less alike and should behave as if cut from the same pattern. Developmental psychology has established that infants are individuals who require individual treatment if they are to develop to their maximum capability. The search by many parents for all-purpose techniques to use in rearing their children is discussed in a box on Psychology and Society.

How long do early traits persist?

The traits displayed by babies in the early weeks and months of life endure for varying periods of time. One trait that appears to be relatively persistent is timidity. When faced with an unfamiliar event—a new face or a new toy—some babies show signs of considerable anxiety. They stop playing, turn quiet, and look wary. Their heart rate is also different from that of other babies in similar situations. It goes up slightly and remains stable—a sign that these babies may be trying unsuccessfully to understand a strange and troubling event. Timid babies go on to display signs of the trait for several years when they find themselves in novel predicaments. In one follow-up study, a small group of children who were extremely shy during the first three years of life continued to stand out as such throughout childhood and adolescence (Kagan, 1983).

Most early traits, however, show little staying power as the environment begins to exert its influence. In the follow-up of easy, slow-to-warm-up, and difficult babies, it was found that they tended to show the same differences in personality at the age of 2 that they had shown in the cradle. But the pattern no longer existed by the time they were 6 to 12 (Thomas and Chess, 1972). Many comparable findings support the theme of change rather than constancy in human development.

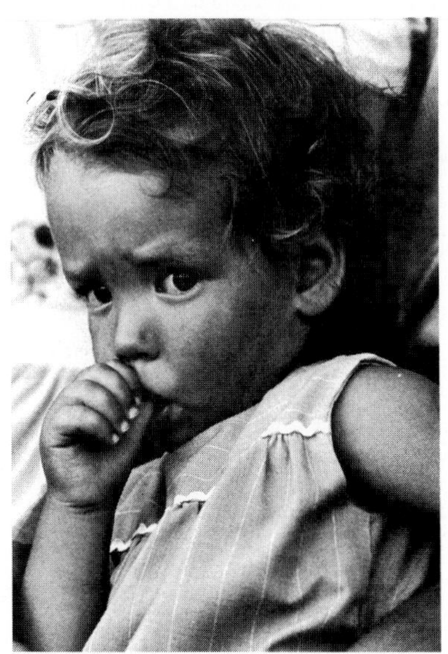

Will this shy child become a shy adolescent?

Numerous studies have shown how rapidly change can occur in early childhood. One study explored such traits as irritability, readiness to smile, attentiveness, activity level, and vocal excitability. No significant relationship was found between the way babies scored on these psychological attributes before they were a year old and the way they scored at 27 months. Indeed there were some spectacular reversals of behavior. One boy, as an infant, worried the investigators because he kept rocking his body and sucking on his forearm. By the time he was just a few months over 2 years old, his behavior was perfectly normal. A follow-up of the children, moreover, found no meaningful relationship between their 27-month-old behavior (in regard to irritability, attentiveness, activity level, and vocal excitability) and the scores they made at age 10 on reading and intelligence tests. What such studies have to say to parents concerned aout the development of their children is discussed in a box on Psychology and Society.

Psychology and Society: Is there a magic formula for bringing up children?

As you know if you have been a parent—or will discover if you become one—our society does not lack for advice about bringing up children. Grandparents, in-laws, neighbors, and friends all have firm opinions. Bookstores are full of volumes of counsel, many claiming to present the only surefire formula for success. You can hear or read that babies have to be pampered or should not be pampered, they they need or do not need a firm schedule of eating and sleeping, that they require a constant diet of hugging and kissing or of firm discipline, that spanking will doom them to lifelong mental health problems or is the only way to turn them into upright and responsible adults.

To add to the confusion, the formulas have had a way of changing over the years. Ideas about discipline, for example, have run the gamut. Parents used to be advised not to pick up a crying infant since this might spoil the child. But soon enough the pendulum swung in the other direction, and one authority on child rearing wrote that "it is impossible to spoil an infant," and that "babies are absolutely unable to put off any gratification without some sense of frustration" (Salk, 1973). How can a conscientious parent, eager to give the child the best possible start in life, know which view is right and which is wrong?

One clue to the answer comes from studies of child-rearing practices around the world—which, it turns out, show a remarkable diversity. Do babies need to be held a lot? Among some of the Indian people in Guatemala, they are held by an adult for more than six hours a day. But in parts of the Netherlands, they are held only while feeding and spend the rest of the day tightly bound in bassinets, alone in a little room of their own (Rebelsky, 1967). In some places children are encouraged to stand up for their rights—but among some of the Eskimos any display of aggression is immediately squelched (Briggs, 1970). In the United States parents are usually urged to communicate with their children and explain their actions to avoid any hint of rejection—but in rural sections of Norway a mother who finds her 4-year-old son blocking her way simply picks him up and moves him, without saying a word (Baldwin, 1975). There are parts of the world where parents generally assume that the child's personality will thrive on sympathy and affection, others where the child is regarded as an untamed creature whose natural instincts must be curbed, and still others where it is believed that the child's nature is determined at birth and that parents should stand aside and let nature take its course.

There are all kinds of theories and methods—yet it appears that the outcome, by and large, is very much the same. By any tests or standards of emotional well-being or intelligence, no significant differences have been found among the children of various countries by the time they reach later childhood. The oft-held babies of Guatemala grow up no more secure than the seldom-held babies of the Netherlands. The Eskimo and Norwegian children turn out to be similar to each other and to children everywhere.

The worldwide studies show that no magic formula exists. If there are any specific rules for successful child rearing, they have not yet been discovered. Developmental psychologists know of no specific actions a parent can take—holding, cuddling, kissing, spanking, other forms of discipline—that will guarantee a happy and productive future. Children thrive on acceptance—but there are many different ways to demonstrate acceptance. Children wither under rejection—but what seems like rejection to an outside observer, or by the rules set out in a manual, may not be considered rejection by the child or the parents.

Effects of unfavorable environment: the neglected child

One topic that has always interested developmental psychologists is the effect of an extremely unfavorable early environment. If children grow up in circumstances that seriously retard their progress, are they doomed to be ineffective and unhappy throughout life? Or do they have a

Psychology and Society: Psychology's message to parents: optimism—and patience—often pay off

What conclusion can parents and prospective parents draw from the findings of developmental psychologists about the individual differences displayed by babies and the way these differences persist or vanish as years go by? What do the facts tell us about rearing our children?

The studies described in the text point to one message above all: It is very difficult to predict, from the way children behave in the early months or years, how they will behave even in the elementary school years, much less as adolescents or adults. This is hardly surprising, for development depends on many complex interactions between children and the people and events in their environment. We cannot know, at any given moment, what form these interactions will take in the months and years to come (Horowitz, 1977). Moreover psychologists do not yet fully understand how different experiences mold development along different lines. The child's future, like life itself, defies attempts at prediction. All we can be sure of is that the years between infancy and adulthood will be full of unforeseen events—and that these events will often bring striking changes in the patterns of temperament and behavior seen in the cradle.

Yet there is a natural tendency for parents to be wrapped up in the events of the moment, and to become discouraged and pessimistic if a child is difficult, irritable, overactive, or seemingly unable to pay attention. As a result they may treat the child with too little affection and sympathy, too much criticism and punishment. Out of such a relationship, the child may acquire the learned helplessness discussed in Chapter 3 as a serious handicap to progress in school, normal adjustment to life in general, and self-fulfillment.

The findings of developmental psychology suggest not pessimism but optimism about children and their potentialities. Difficult babies—boisterous, stubborn, and headstrong—often quiet down as they get older. Babies who seem restless and inattentive in the cradle often learn to concentrate and become star pupils in school. Even babies who seem anxious may turn out to be perfectly normal. If parents can remember that babies show a wide range of individual differences, need individual treatment, and thrive on warmth and love—and if they can tolerate behavior that at the moment may hardly be ideal—their patience will usually be rewarded.

chance to throw off their early handicaps? To put this another way: What chance does the neglected child have to develop into a normal adult?

Many of the first studies bearing on this problem produced pessimistic results. In the animal world, it was found that monkeys raised in isolation—a form of total neglect—grew up with many symptoms of maladjustment. They were unfriendly, aggressive, and sexually incompetent (Harlow and Harlow, 1966). Among human babies with a severely deprived childhood, many lasting effects of deprivation were observed (Spitz, 1946). One investigator made a study of children who had spent the first 3 years of their lives in the impersonal atmosphere of an orphanage, then had gone on to foster homes. Later these children were compared with a control group of children of the same age and sex who had been brought up from the very start in foster homes, where presumably they received more care and encouragement than is possible in an institution. Even after some years had passed, the orphanage children were found to be notably more aggressive, with strong tendencies to have temper tantrums, to kick and hit other children, and to lie, steal, and destroy property. They tended to be emotionally cold, isolated, and incapable of affectionate relationships (Goldfarb, 1944).

There seems to be no doubt that deprivation seriously retards development. However, other studies have indicated that the ill effects are often reversible. In one animal experiment, monkeys were isolated inside black boxes from birth until they were 6 months old. When they were permitted to leave the boxes, their behavior was decidedly abnormal. But they were then permitted to associate with other infant monkeys who had a normal social background. Within a few months the black-box monkeys began to improve and after six months they seemed almost completely normal in their social behavior (Suomi and Harlow, 1972).

Human subjects have also been found to display a remarkable ability to bounce back from the numbing effects of an unstimulating early environment. One study was made in an isolated Indian village in Guatemala, where babies are kept inside the family's windowless hut for most of the first year of life. (The tribe members believe that sunlight, air, and the stares of certain people cause illness in the young.) It was found that the babies, when they emerge from the hut, appear severely retarded by the standards of other societies. But they soon catch up in the development of physical skills, and by adolescence they do as well as most children on some tests of perception and memory (Kagan and Klein, 1973).

Perhaps the most dramatic example of overcoming deprivation comes from Czechoslovakia, where a psychologist has reported the case of twin boys who spent most of the first six years of their lives under cruelly inhuman circumstances. They lived with a mentally subnormal father and an apparently psychopathic stepmother who totally excluded them from the family circle. They were never permitted outside the house but were kept in the cellar or in a small closet. None of the other children in the family was permitted to talk to them. Thus they grew up in almost total isolation except for their own company.

When the case was discovered, the twins looked more like 3-year-olds than 6-year-olds. They were barely able to walk or speak. They were so retarded, in fact, that it was impossible to test their intelligence. Yet, after they were moved to a favorable environment, they soon began to make progress. By the time they were 11, their IQs were about average and their social and emotional development also appeared to be normal (Koluchova, 1972).

Much remains to be learned about the effects of early neglect and deprivation. The evidence to date, however, suggests these tentative conclusions: Human infants are extremely impressionable, and their environment has a profound effect on their development from the moment they are born. A highly unfavorable environment can produce drastic damage. But infants often prove to be resilient and malleable, that is, capable of changing when circumstances change. Under the proper conditions for growth, early handicaps can sometimes be overcome.

Physical and mental development

One of nature's most spectacular events is the growth of the helpless newborn baby into eager toddler (sometime after the first birthday), experimenter with language (starting near the end of the second year), and eventually 6-year-old schoolchild, about to solve the mysteries of reading and writing. How many and varied are the accomplishments of those early years. How many new worlds are faced and conquered.

Part of this rapid early development is the result of *maturation*—the physical changes, taking place after birth, that continue the biological growth of the organism from fertilized egg cell to adult. Almost day by day, simply as the result of getting older, babies become capable of new feats of physical, perceptual, and mental skill.

Physical maturation

Even before birth, babies begin to use their muscles. Their movements can usually be felt in the womb in about the twentieth week of pregnancy. Newborn babies have all the muscle fibers they will ever possess, but the fibers still have a lot of growing to do. Eventually, at full maturity, the muscles will weigh about 40 times as much as they weighed at birth. The muscles of posture, creeping, and standing must mature as shown in Figure 14-6 before the baby can walk alone, at around the age of 15 months. The muscles of the hands and arms, as they mature, produce increased skill at reaching and grasping, as shown in Figure 14-7.

The skeleton at birth is largely composed of cartilage, which is softer and more pliable than bone but gradually hardens. The fibers of the nervous system grow and form additional synaptic connections to other fibers, and some of them develop protective sheaths that make them faster and more efficient conductors of nervous impulses. The brain, in particular, grows in size and weight—very rapidly during the first two years, then more slowly until growth is complete.

Much of the baby's remarkable progress in the early months of life reflects maturation of the body and the nervous system. Thus children all over the world, regardless of child-rearing practices, tend to display various skills at about the same age. They begin to smile at the sight of a human face at about 4 months, show vocal excitement to a new voice at 9 months, and search for a hidden object that they saw being covered by a piece of cloth at about 12 months. They begin to utter some of the basic sounds of language in the first few days of life—but they cannot really use speech until around 18 months. Evidence suggests that their brains may be mature enough earlier, but their voice boxes are not yet ready (Bonvillian, Orlansky, and Novack, 1983).

The process of maturation cannot be speeded up to any great extent. Indeed attempts to push children far beyond their level of maturation may be harmful (McGraw, 1943). Their environment does have some effect, however. Encouraging infants to perform skills—though without forcing them—is likely to produce the appearance of these skills at a somewhat earlier age. Infants whose parents talk to them a great deal may themselves begin speaking as early as the first birthday or shortly thereafter. Infants with less encouragement may not start until the age of 2 or even later. Skill at such cognitive tasks as remembering long lists of objects develops much earlier in societies that consider such activities important for young children than in societies that consider them unimportant.

Figure 14-6 How the muscles of movement mature *As is explained in the text, the process of maturation accounts for the increasing ability of babies to move around. Shown here are the progress from birth to walking alone and the average age at which each stage of development occurs.*

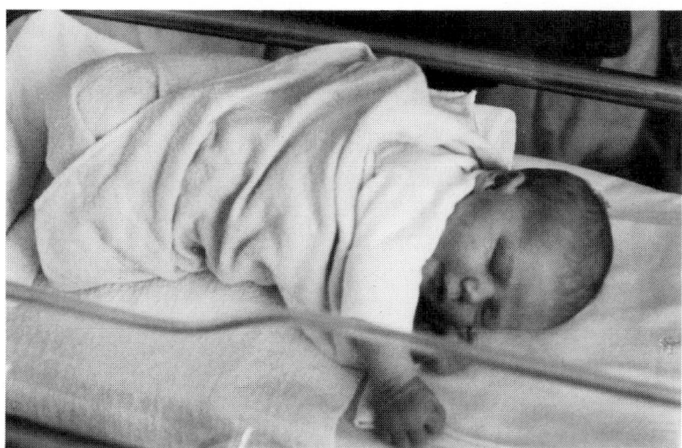

newborn

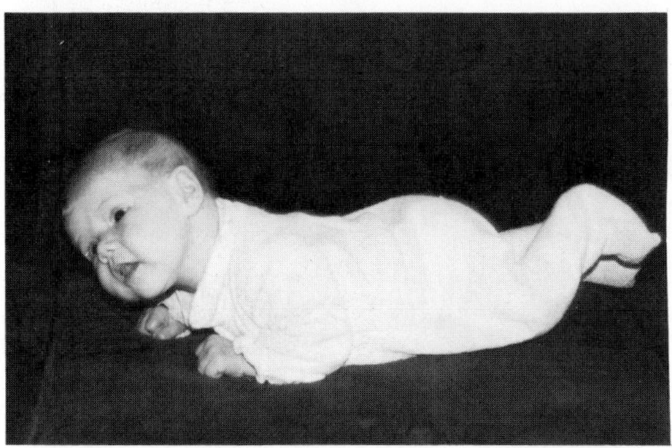

chin up: 2 months

sit in high chair, grasp: 6 months

stand: 9 months

climb: 13 months

walk alone: 15 months

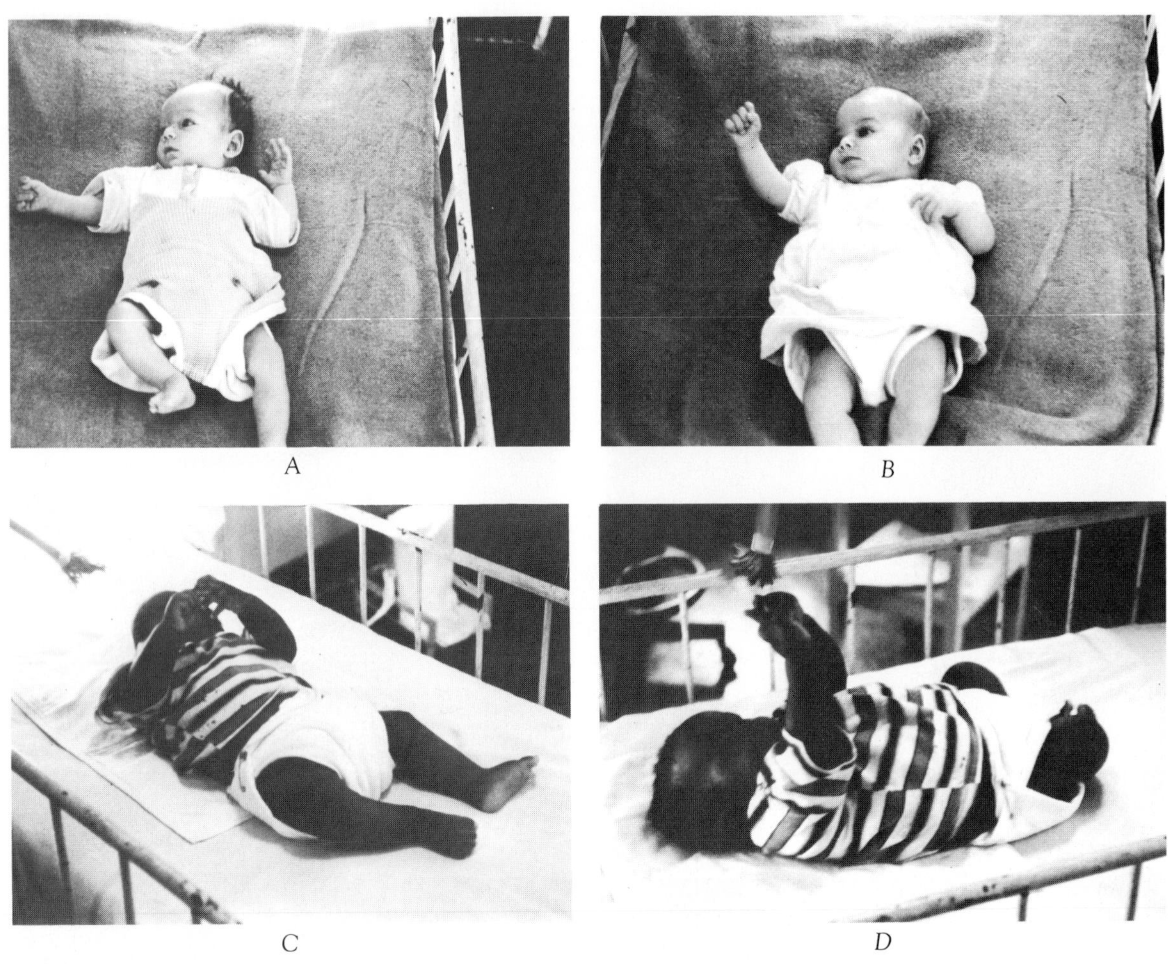

Figure 14-7 First attempts at reaching *Maturation produces rapid changes in what happens when a bright toy is held over a baby's crib. Very young babies (A), typically lying with head to one side, pay only slight attention. Later (B) they occasionally watch the hand that is extended in the same direction the head is turned. At about 3½ months (C) they no longer hold the head to the side and may clasp their hands together beneath the toy. Soon they begin to raise their clasped hands toward the object (D). This is the final stage before they actually reach for the object with an open hand and try to grasp it (White, Castle, and Held, 1964).*

Intellectual development

During the opening years of life, children display a dazzling succession of intellectual capacities, each more intricate and advanced than the one before. Some of the most important of them are listed in Figure 14-8. While we take such skills for granted in adults, they are remarkable in infants who have just begun to function in the real world. Equally remarkable is the rapid and steady pace at which a given skill develops. The ability to recognize a familiar stimulus, for example, gets stronger with the passage of only a brief time. One-month-old infants who have learned to recognize a frequently repeated word lose the ability if a day passes without their hearing that word spoken. Only three months later, however, they can recognize a familiar word after interruptions of as long as a week or two. The ability of babies to recall past events also becomes more solidly entrenched over the space of only a few months as is shown in Figure 14-9.

Skill	Age at which it emerges	What the baby seems to be thinking
Recognition	First 6 months	I recognize that the rattle I am looking at is different from the one I just saw a second or two ago.
Retrieval of past events	8–12 months	I recall that a little while ago you hid my rattle under that blanket.
Juggling the present with memories of the past	8–18 months	I am aware of that bright, round thing across the room, but I also remember that dad can reach it and bounce it to me.
Imitation	9–24 months	I am going to dial a number on that phone just as mom did yesterday.
Use of symbols	12–24 months	I think I'll use this sand to feed my doll.
Language	18–24 months	I don't have to point and cry anymore to get a drink. I can just say "milk" and get the same result.
Self-awareness	18–24 months	I just saw mom put that puzzle together, and I'm getting terribly upset because I think she wants me to do the same thing—but I can't.

Figure 14-8 Some intellectual skills that emerge early in life *The appearance and growth of these skills reflect a progressive maturation of the young child's central nervous system as described in the text (Kagan, 1981).*

Many factors contribute to intellectual development. One is improvement in the process of perception. As children grow older, they begin to know what to search for in the environment and how to go about it. They develop strategies for seeking important information and ignoring irrelevant information. Their attention becomes more selective and they are able to maintain it over a longer time span. Their scanning of the environment becomes more systematic and orderly.

Progress in perceptual efficiency has been charted by recording children's eye movements, as shown in Figure 14-10. When 1-month-olds are shown a design, they are likely to scan whatever feature their eyes first encounter—usually part of the external border. Only one month later, they scan the essential elements of the design. As children get older, they become increasingly efficient in using visual perception to search for information. They also become more adept at perceiving details (Gibson, 1969) and organizing them into meaningful patterns and entities.

Another important factor in intellectual development is a growing skill at understanding and using language. In turn, adeptness with language facilitates the formation of concepts—which helps organize information into categories and facilitates the deep processing that creates long-lasting memory.

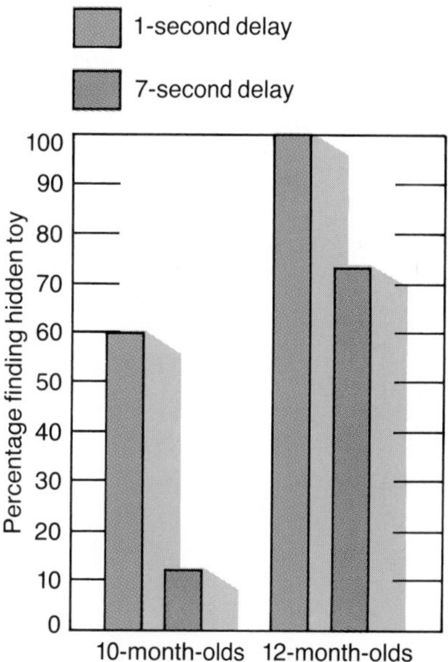

Figure 14-9 The baby's progress in short-term memory *The bars show the percentages of 10- and 12-month-old babies who could recall where a toy was hidden after brief delays. The babies watched a toy being placed under one of two cloths, and a screen was then lowered to block their view for 1 second or 7 seconds. The task of finding the toy gets harder, of course, as the delay gets longer. But more important, no matter how long the delay, note how sharply the ability to find the toy improves with the passage of only two months (Kagan, Kearsley, and Zelazo, 1978).*

Figure 14-10 **Early advances in eye movements and scanning** *When babies were shown the design at the left, a typical 1-month-old scanned only one part of the outer border. A typical 2-month-old quickly arrived at the "heart of the matter" with the scanning pattern shown at the right (Salapatek, 1975).*

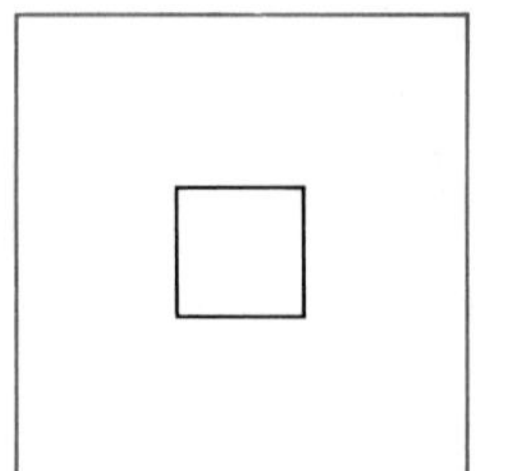

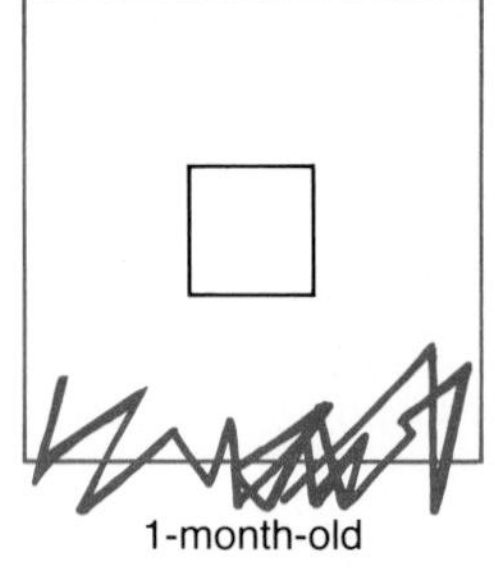

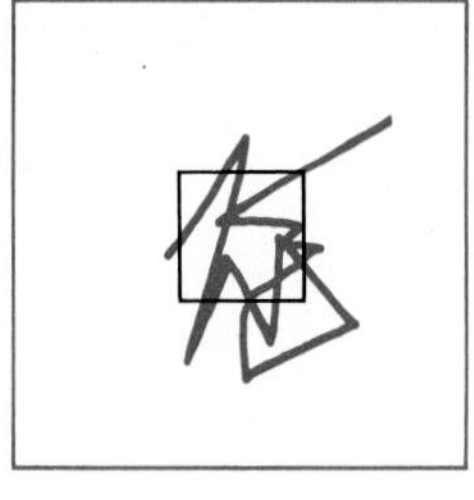

Personality development: birth to eighteen months

As with intellectual progress, the development of personality also seems to proceed in an orderly way, through a series of stages merging one into another. All the aspects of personality—emotions, motives, and ways of coping with conflicts—begin to appear and undergo change. As children grow from the crib to the age when they can move about, then to the preschool age, and later into schoolchildren interacting closely with their classmates and teachers, they enter into new and widening circles of influence. Their changing social experiences mold their personalities in many different ways, for better or for worse. So do their developing intellectual skills, which allow them to become increasingly aware of themselves and the meaning of events around them—often with strong emotional impact.

The first stage of personality development lasts from birth to about the age of 18 months. During this period the infant has only limited social experiences, usually centering on one person who constitutes the greatest influence. Usually this person is the mother. It can, however, be someone else—the father, a grandparent, a baby-sitter, or a day-care teacher who takes care of the baby's first needs. Personality development is affected by the establishment of *attachment* to the person who constitutes the main source of interaction, comfort, and care.

The importance of attachment

Much psychological thinking about the very earliest development of attachment stems from a famous series of experiments by Harry F. Harlow, who took baby monkeys from their own mothers and placed them with doll-like objects that he called "surrogate mothers." As is shown in Figure 14-11, Harlow gave his baby monkeys two such surrogate mothers. One was made of wire, with a bottle and nipple from which the monkey received milk. The other was made of sponge rubber and terry cloth; it was an object to which the baby monkey could cling.

As the photographs show, the baby monkeys strongly preferred the terry-cloth doll to the wire doll. Indeed they clung to the terry-cloth mother even when feeding from the other. When a new object was

Figure 14-11 Baby monkey and surrogate mothers *The baby monkey has been taken from its own mother and placed with two surrogate mothers. Note how it clings to the terry-cloth mother, even when feeding from the wire mother and especially when exploring a new and unfamiliar object that has been placed in the cage.*

placed in the cage, they clung to the terry-cloth mother while making their first hesitant and tentative attempts to discover what this strange and at first frightening object might be (Harlow, 1961). Obviously something about the terry-cloth surrogate provided the baby monkey with what humans would call comfort, protection, and a secure base from which it could explore new aspects of the environment.

In human infants during the first two years of life, attachment takes the form of a strong tendency to approach particular people, to be receptive to care and consolation from them, and to be least afraid when in their presence. Human babies, like monkeys, seem to be born with an innate tendency to become attached to the adults who care for them. They show a strong preference for those who have served as continuous caretakers. This preference is particularly noticeable when they are bored, frightened, or distressed by the unfamiliar and unexpected.

Attachment and exploration

The inborn tendency to attachment is a valuable asset in survival. It helps infants find nurturance and protection from distress and dangers, real or imagined. It also seems to make them more receptive to parental standards—probably in order to make sure that their sources of attachment remain undisturbed. One study found that strongly attached 1-year-olds were more likely than others to obey the requests and commands of their mothers nearly a year later (Londerville and Main, 1981). But if the tendency to remain closely attached to a parent persisted, children would never outgrow their dependency on their caretakers. To become self-sufficient, they must explore the environment, encounter new objects and new experiences, and learn how to cope with them.

Oddly, though attachment and exploration seem to be conflicting tendencies, they actually work hand in hand. Note in Figure 14-11 how the baby monkey engages in both activities at once—cautiously exploring a new object while clinging to its terry-cloth surrogate mother.

Human babies also seem to gather courage for exploration from their attachment to their mothers. In one experiment, babies just under a year old were placed in a strange room that contained a chair piled high with and surrounded by toys. When baby and mother were in the room together, the baby actively looked at the toys, approached them, and touched them. All this exploratory behavior dropped off, however, if a stranger was present or if the mother left the room (Ainsworth and Bell, 1970).

The beginnings of anxiety

The experiment just described also produced results that point to another phase of development in the first 18 months—namely, the first appearance of signs of anxiety. When the babies were left alone in the room, many of them very quickly began to cry, make what appeared to be a rather frantic search for the mother, or do both. They were exhibiting *separation anxiety,* which rarely appears among American babies until around the age of 8 months.

Separation anxiety seems to emerge as an outgrowth of some of the newly developed intellectual skills described in Figure 14-8 (page 517). At 8 months, most babies are able for the first time not only to call to mind past events, but also to compare them with the here and now. When mother departs, they can now recall her former presence—and at the same time realize that she is no longer there. Not being able to understand the inconsistency, they become anxious and cry. Later, when babies can also anticipate that mother will return, the inconsistency is more easily resolved, and separation anxiety begins to fade.

It might seem simpler to regard separation anxiety as reflecting the child's attachment to the caretaker, but this does not seem to be the case. Babies brought up at home, with their mothers almost always around and with opportunities for attachment at a maximum, are no

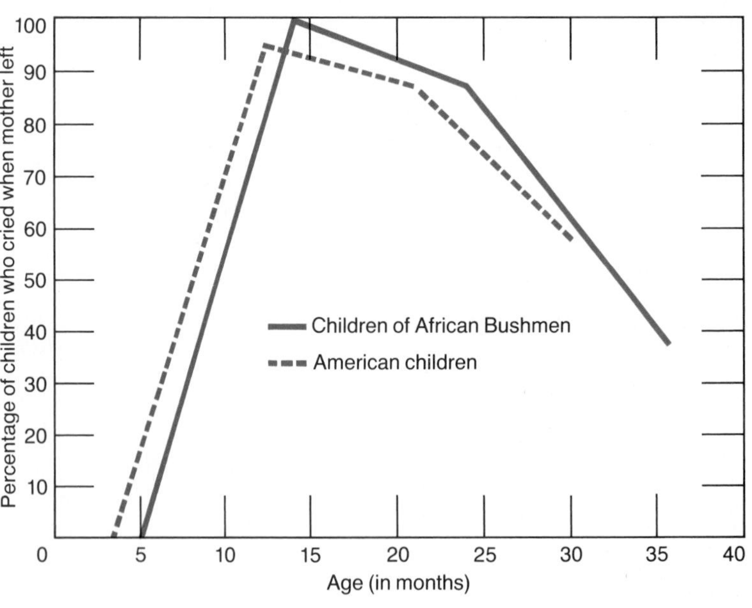

Figure 14-12 The emergence of separation anxiety: a universal pattern *In widely different cultures, babies younger than 7 months rarely cry when their mothers leave them. Between 12 and 15 months, however, the experience is almost sure to being distress and tears—and then the impact begins to weaken. The pattern shown here applies equally everywhere children have been studied, including isolated villages in the Guatemalan highlands and remote areas of the African Kalahari Desert (Kagan, Kearsley, and Zelazo, 1978).*

more likely to show separation anxiety than children who spend much of their time at day-care centers (Kearsley et al., 1975). American children reared by their mothers display no more separation anxiety than children brought up in Israeli kibbutzim, where the mothers are absent for most of the day (Maccoby and Feld, 1972). As is shown in Figure 14-12, separation anxiety appears to be a universal experience regardless of child-rearing practices.

Even before separation anxiety becomes apparent, babies show what is called *stranger anxiety*. They will usually smile if the mother shows her face above the crib. But if a stranger's face appears, they often show anxiety by turning away and perhaps breaking into tears. Again, the explanation may be that the appearance of the strange face creates uncertainty. The baby has acquired some sort of mental representation or perceptual expectation of the familiar face, which is violated by the unfamiliar face. Indeed behavior that seems to indicate stranger anxiety can sometimes be produced by showing the baby a distorted mask of the human face, as is shown in Figure 14-13. Among children everywhere, stranger anxiety first appears at about the age of 7 months, increases to around the first birthday, then declines.

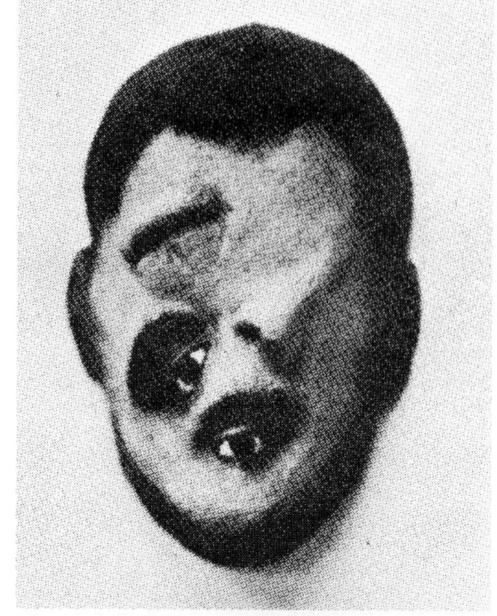

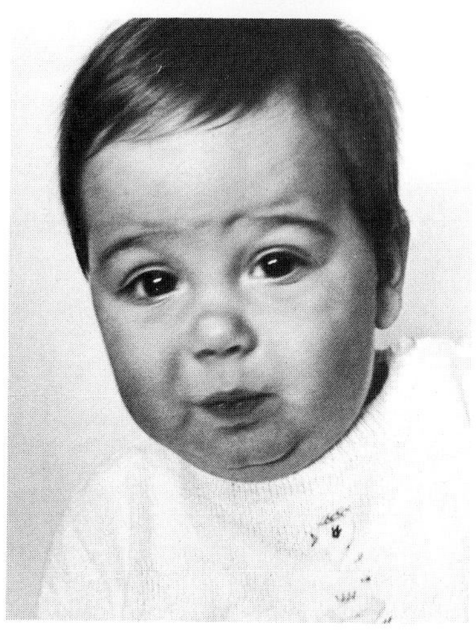

Figure 14-13 A weird "stranger" and infant anxiety *The baby is reacting to the sight of the distorted mask—perhaps because it violates perceptual expectancies. At an earlier age, before learning what the human face is supposed to look like, the baby might have smiled instead of showing anxiety.*

The first social demands: eighteen months through three years

The second important period in personality development, roughly from 18 months through the third year, is dominated by children's first important experiences with the demands of society. When they leave the crib and begin walking about the house, they find innumerable objects that look like toys provided for their own special delight but that in fact are expensive and fragile pieces of household equipment—or, like knives and electric light cords, are dangerous. They discover that they can no longer do whatever they please. The rules of the home say that they must not destroy valuable property and must not get into dangerous situations. At the same time they encounter a rule of society holding that the elimination drive must be relieved only in the bathroom. They undergo that much-discussed process called toilet training. In one situation after another, they find that life is filled with prohibitions and regulations. All the while, their developing intellectual ability allows them to become aware of what their parents and other caretakers expect, sometimes reinforced by their first experiences with adult displeasure.

The horizons of children at this age widen greatly. They leave the self-centered environment of the crib and begin to take their place in a world where people and their property rights must be respected. When the attachment to parent or other caretaker is strong and the relationship between them is good, children seem to want to comply (Maccoby, 1979). Others must learn the hard way to control the aggressive feelings sometimes ignited by the imposition of new limits on their behavior. Whether smoothly or with stormy difficulty, these children—just yesterday cradled in infancy—begin to become disciplined members of society.

Social demands and inner standards

In toilet training, children must learn *not* to do something—not to respond immediately to the bodily sensations that call for relief of the elimination drive. They must also learn *not* to respond to such external stimuli as the cupboard full of dishes that they would like to explore or the lamp that they would like to smash to the floor. In other words, they begin in this period to control and forgo forms of behavior that would ordinarily be their natural responses to internal or external stimuli.

The process through which parents impose discipline—and teach children to live by the rules of society—is helped along considerably by a dramatic change from within as well. Around the age of 2, children first develop inner standards and the desire to live up to them, one of the most powerful motives. In one study, 2-year-olds watched someone play in a complicated manner—such as pretending to use toy kitchenware to cook a meal for a family—and then were told that it was their turn to play with the toys. Just a few months earlier, the process passed without incident. Now, however, many of them broke into tears or ran to their mother. Apparently they felt obligated to play with the toys in an equally sophisticated manner, yet they were unsure of their ability. This newly developed uncertainty over living up to a standard that was entirely self-imposed—since nobody taking part in the experiment suggested that they imitate the cooking—created anxiety and distress (Kagan, 1981). The study indicates that children at the end of the second year have a remarkable understanding about their conduct and their abilities—and the way these may or may not live up to what other people seem to expect of them and to their own standards of doing the right thing.

Even subtle violations of standards appear to be disturbing for the first time at this age. Children will now point to a cracked toy, dirty hands, torn clothing, or a missing button and show their concern. They can discern—even from changes in the sound of father's voice or the shape of mother's eyes—that their own behavior elicits judgmental responses in others. Younger children do not yet have these standards or insights. They cannot yet make the link between their own actions and the reactions of others. Only now do they begin to show signs of the distress that is the price of self-awareness—and the capacity to sense how that self stacks up against adult standards.

The place of rewards and punishments

In learning to meet the social demands first encountered during the period from 18 months to 3 years, rewards and punishments probably also play a part. Children are usually rewarded with praise and fondling when they are successful at toilet training or refrain from playing with a lamp after being told "No." And they may be punished, with disapproval if not physically, when they soil themselves, break something, or get into forbidden places. But the desire to live up to inner standards of proper conduct seems to appear even before children have learned to become anxious over possible punishment—and to have a stronger influence on behavior.

Psychology and Society: Being a good parent to the 2-year-old

Parents face a difficult problem with 2-year-olds. Certainly they must teach children to avoid danger. They must also try to curb any inclinations to let exploration turn into destruction. But there is a fine line to be drawn. At what point do constructive attempts to preserve children's safety and responsibility turn into harmful repression that may thwart normal development?

Psychology's findings about the inner standards of 2-year-olds emphasize the problem. As children grow increasingly conscious of themselves and their world, they spontaneously become aware of what is expected of them. They can distinguish between right and wrong. They become concerned over their ability to perform and the possibility of failure. They want to live up to their own standards of competence and goodness. The danger is that they may become overconcerned, overfearful, and inhibited. In Freudian terms, they may develop superegos so strong as to be crippling.

Some parents are overprotective of their 2- to 3-year-olds. They try to keep their children "tied to their apron strings" and object to any attempt by the children to undertake activities on their own. Other parents are too concerned with neatness and order. They are upset when children make the slightest mess, get the least bit dirty, or merely touch a newly polished table. When parents are overprotective or overneat—and convey their concern either through punishment or in more subtle ways—children can acquire too much anxiety. Their fear of being disapproved of by their parents or violating their own rapidly shaping inner standards may generalize to all new objects or new activities. As a result they may develop strong inhibitions against trying anything new or challenging, including attempts to adjust to other people.

Parents who are more permissive during this difficult period, on the other hand, can set the stage for spontaneous, self-reliant, and effective behavior. Though they must stop their children at times, they do so only when absolutely necessary. They encourage attempts at anything new and constructive, such as drawing pictures or riding a tricycle. Thus their children learn that only some kinds of exploratory behavior are forbidden, not all. They discover that curiosity and attempts to operate on the environment are generally approved. They are likely to make a good start toward independence and self-confidence.

Punishment can actually upset the delicate balance between children's natural, constructive urge to explore the environment and the requirement of social discipline. This early period of life holds exciting possibilities for children and their self-image as active, competent, and increasingly self-sufficient human beings. By moving about in the world for the first time, they acquire all kinds of fascinating information about the environment. By handling objects—and sometimes, unfortunately, destroying them—they learn that they have some power over the environment. They discover that they can roam about the world and perhaps rearrange it to their liking. They can reach for objects they want. They can move objects around. They learn that they can satisfy many of their own desires. By reaching into the cookie jar, they can relieve hunger. By crawling under the coat a visitor has thrown on the sofa, they can find warmth. One of the responsibilities of parents is to aid children in their explorations and discoveries while at the same time setting appropriate limits on their behavior. The balance is critical—for behaving independently without infringing on the rules of society will continue as a challenging task throughout life. How parents can best aid their children in achieving this balance is discussed in a box on Psychology and Society.

The preschool years: four and five

By the time children are 4, they begin to venture outside the home and play with other children. They may go to nursery school or kindergarten. This increasing social experience appears to be essential to normal development. Even monkeys, if raised solely in the company of the mother, with no opportunity to interact with other young monkeys, often turn out to be overfearful or overaggressive (Suomi, 1977). As children move into broader social circles, they learn among other things that the world is made up of males and females, for whom society decrees different kinds of behavior. Boys begin to take on the characteristics that society considers appropriate to males, and girls to take on the characteristics considered appropriate to females.

Children of 4 and 5 become adept at using language and concepts. They continue to acquire inner standards and the urge to live up to them—and this process gives them their first feelings of guilt, representing that mysterious mechanism called conscience. Moreover a new factor begins to influence their personalities. This is the period in which children begin to identify with their parents.

The identification process

Exactly what identification means and how it takes place are matters of debate. To psychoanalysts, it is a complex process involving the Oedipus complex and the superego, as was explained in Chapter 13. To many psychologists it means that children come to feel that they and their parents share a vital bond of similarity. Children bear the family name. They are often told that they look like their parents. Thus they consider themselves in many significant ways to be similar to their parents. Consequently they feel more secure, for they view their parents as stronger and more competent than themselves. They begin to imitate their parents' behavior to increase this similarity—and to share vicariously in the parents' strengths, virtues, skills, and triumphs.

Children with intelligent parents often come to think of themselves as intelligent. A boy whose father holds a job requiring physical strength usually begins to think of himself as being strong, and a girl with an attractive mother thinks of herself as being attractive. Unfortunately, children identify with their parents' faults as well as their virtues, and it is not unusual for children to become aware of their parents' defects. They may see that their father is unable to hold a job and is the object of ridicule in the community or that their mother drinks too much and is unwelcome in the neighbors' house. They may hear relatives criticize their parents. Or they may hear divorced parents bitterly criticize each other's conduct. Under such circumstances many children begin to believe that they too are unworthy, unlovable, hateful, stupid, lazy, or mean. Many children treated in guidance clinics for psychological problems exhibit identification with a "bad" parent.

Children may also be affected adversely by the loss of a parent. This is true when the loss occurs at any time in childhood, but especially

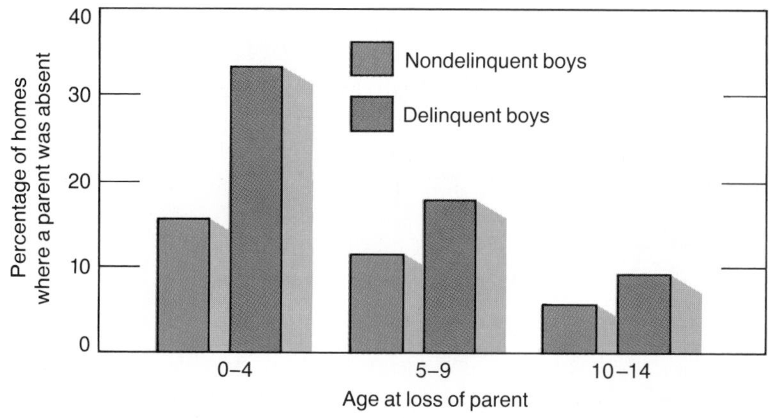

Figure 14-14 Delinquency and loss of a parent *A study of the home backgrounds of delinquent boys, as compared with a matched control group of nondelinquent boys, found that considerably more of the delinquents had lost a parent through death, divorce, or other causes—particularly when they were very young (Bowlby, 1961).*

when it happens before the end of the preschool years. As Figure 14-14 shows, a substantial number of deliquent boys come from homes in which a parent died or was absent for other reasons, with the percentage of delinquency greatest among the boys who were youngest when the absence began. Of the many ways in which the death of a parent or divorce can hamper a child's development, one is interference with the normal workings of the identification process.

The period of teachers and peers: six to ten

The social influences that begin in the preschool years expand dramatically when children enter elementary school. Suddenly they spend much of their time with new teachers. They come into close contact with large numbers of their peers—boys and girls of the same age with whom they share work and play. They have to prove their competence at school tasks and at skills admired by fellow pupils. Although the home continues to be important in development, outside factors begin to play an increasingly influential role.

The new world of the classroom

In the world that children enter at 6 there is a new adult—the teacher—whose discipline they must conform to and whose acceptance they must court. Ordinarily the teacher is a woman, like the mother, and children's behavior toward their mother can be generalized toward her. But boys who are identifying with their father and rebelling against their mother often have trouble in the early grades. They may be less fearful of rejection by the teacher and therefore more reluctant to accept her influence. They typically get lower marks and cause more disciplinary problems than do girls.

The teacher usually plays a dual role in pupils' development. First, she teaches the intellectual skills appropriate to our society. Second, and perhaps even more important to personality development, she tries to encourage a motive for intellectual mastery. It is in the early years of school that children crystallize their inner standards of intellectual

A new and powerful influence—the teacher has entered this child's life.

mastery and begin to feel anxiety if they do not live up to the standards. By the age of 10, some children have developed an expectancy of success that is likely to bolster their self-confidence throughout life. Others have developed expectations and fears of failure—even the signs of learned helplessness. Such outcomes depend largely on the school experience, the impact of which is discussed in a box on Psychology and Society.

Finding a place among peers

Besides adjusting to teachers and schoolwork, children must also learn to live with their schoolmates. During the years from 6 to 10 these peers have a particularly strong influence. For one thing, children beginning school can now evaluate themselves in relation to their classmates. They can determine their rank on such attributes as intelligence, strength, and skills of various kinds. For another thing, they can more freely express among their peers the rebelliousness and hostility they so commonly feel toward the adult world. At the same time, it is in the company of their peers that they can best satisfy their need for unqualified acceptance. Even when young children acknowledge each other's faults, they manage to do so without conveying rejection. They typically grant each other sufficient "idiosyncracy credits" to permit them to behave inappropriately at times without losing face (Fine, 1981).

Peers often serve effectively to advance each other's development. They can provide models for learning such positive traits as generosity, empathy, and helpfulness. They can teach other academic skills with surprising effectiveness, and sometimes do a better job than parents of relieving the anxieties and agitation encountered in growing up (Furman, Rahe, and Hartup, 1981). Indeed those young children who remain socially isolated—or whose peer relationships are constantly turbulent and unsatisfactory—appear more likely than others to have a

Psychology and Society: Does society value its teachers enough?

Many of us remember from our own childhood how much difference a teacher could make in our motivation and school performance. Some teachers never seemed to communicate or inspire, while others seemed to care a great deal and bring out the best in us. Dramatic cases even exist of children who were once given up as failures—but who were later transformed into competent and achieving individuals by a charismatic teacher who was able to give them self-confidence and a sense of purpose (Segal and Yahraes, 1978).

Studies show just how much children can be affected in the classroom. Teachers who are punitive, hostile, narcissistic, and preoccupied with their own problems are likely to dampen the potential of students and hamper their adjustment. In contrast, those who are flexible, warm, democratic in their approach and truly interested in children are inclined to produce students who are more motivated in the classroom and achieve more. An extensive study of schools in London found that physical factors—the size of the school, the age of the buildings, or the space available—do not seem to matter much. What does matter are the ways students are dealt with in the school. They accomplish more and display fewer behavior problems when they are given positions of responsibility and opportunities to help run the school, when they are rewarded and praised for their work, and when staff members are available for consultation and help. Students also do better when their teachers emphasize their successes and good potential rather than focus on their shortcomings (Rutter, 1983).

Given the critical role that teachers play in children's lives, it would seem logical for the teaching profession to be held in very high esteem. But this does not seem to be the case. A recent study by the National Institute for Education concluded that the relative status of teaching among American occupations has declined over the past 30 years, and that its standing as a white-collar job is even more marginal than in the past. While an unusually large number of young people who want to be community leaders and are concerned with social justice train to become teachers, it is precisely those who have such aspirations and concerns who are most likely to abandon the profession. Most of those who stay on as teachers are looking only for job security and favorable working hours (Vance and Schlechty, 1982).

How motivated are today's teachers, how committed to their work? Two surveys, made 20 years apart, provide a disappointing answer. In 1961, 50 percent of teachers said they would certainly become teachers again if they could start all over. In 1981, only 21 percent gave the same positive response. The National Institute for Education study reaches a somber conclusion: The quality of those entering teaching is falling fast and will continue to fall unless somehow the teaching profession is accorded a status comparable to other human service occupations. Could we be ignoring one of society's most precious assets?

Peer relationships—one of the most powerful influences in human development.

rocky road ahead. They are more prone to drop out of school, to become delinquents, or to suffer psychological problems requiring professional help (Asher, Oden, and Gottman, 1981).

The road to being dominant or submissive

One personality trait that is partially set by the end of the early school years is the tendency to be dominant or submissive in relations with other people. Children of 10 who actively make suggestions to the group, try to influence and persuade others, and resist pressure from others often tend to remain dominant in their social relations. Children who are quiet and like to follow the lead of others often remain passive and submissive.

The tendency to be dominant or submissive is in part a function of group acceptance. Children who believe that they are admired by the group are likely to develop enhanced self-confidence and dominance over others. Children who do not consider themselves admired by the group are likely to develop feelings of inferiority and to be submissive. Physical attributes play an important part. The large, strong boy and the attractive girl are more likely to be dominant. The small, frail boy and the unattractive girl are likely to be submissive. Other factors are identification with a dominant or submissive parent and the kind of control exercised by the parents. Permissive parents tend to influence their children in the direction of dominance, while parents who restrict their children's activities tend to influence them in the direction of submissiveness.

New emphasis on inner standards

Although the motive to live up to inner standards appears by about the age of 2, it plays a relatively minor part in behavior for some years. A preschool girl, for example, does not think of a kiss from her mother in terms of inner standards. She values the kiss for its own sake, because it satisfies the motive for affiliation and affection. By the time she is about 8, however, she takes a different view. She is likely to have developed an inner standard that says in effect, "I should be valued by my parents"—and she values a kiss as evidence that she is living up to this standard.

In general, in the early school years the desire to live up to inner standards begins to take a top position in the hierarchy of motives. Three standards that become especially important at this time are these:

1. Being valued by parents, teachers, and peers.
2. Mastering physical and mental skills.
3. Achieving harmony between thoughts and behavior. (Children develop a standard that calls for them to behave rationally and sensibly—and in a way that confirms their self-concept and their identification with their parents and their other heroes.)

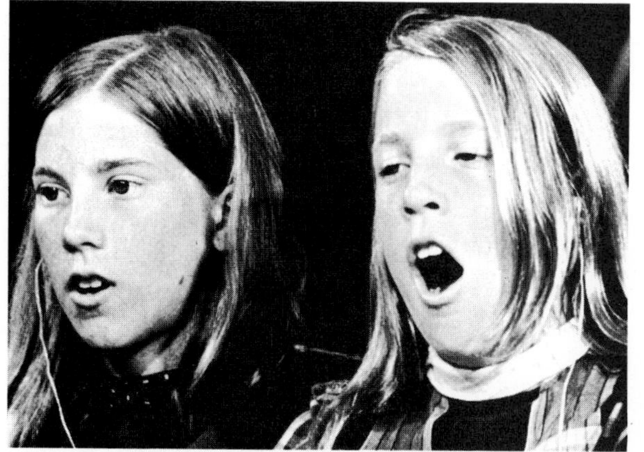

Figure 14-15 Two sisters, two different personalities *The two young daughters of an astronaut exhibit very different reactions while watching their father on a space-walk broadcast over television. The girl at right stifles a yawn while her older sister casts a reproachful glance.*

For children who have been sex typed in the traditional manner, a fourth standard assumes prominence. These children want to behave in a manner appropriate to the sex typing—boys by exhibiting strength, independence, and athletic skills; girls by demonstrating social skills and suppressing any urges toward aggression.

The 10-year-old as a future adult

By the age of 10, children have made spectacular progress from their helpless days in the crib. Their body and nervous system have grown to near maturity. They are capable of many physical skills. Intellectually, they are well along in Piaget's stage of concrete operations and about to embark on the final stage of formal operations. Their personality has changed and blossomed. They now display many individual differences in personality—like those apparent in Figure 14-15.

In some ways, the 10-year-old child offers a reasonably accurate preview of the future adult. The trend of physical development and the pattern of mental processes have been established. Personality traits have emerged and may persist through adolescence and into adulthood, as indicated by the correlations shown in Figure 14-16. But note that the correlations are by no means perfect. Some are indeed very low. The child's personality is still subject to change—for development, though it proceeds rapidly and dramatically through the first 10 years, does not end at that point. Adolescence and adulthood, as will now be seen, may switch development into entirely new channels.

Adolescence: fun or fury?

The question of whether adolescence is a joy or a burden has been pondered by many psychologists (as well as by many adolescents). The first American psychologist to become concerned with the problems of growing up concluded that adolescence was all in all a difficult time of life—a period of "storm and stress" (Hall, 1904). Many other psychologists agree. One study found that substantial numbers of people, looking back on their lives when they had reached the age of 30, felt that

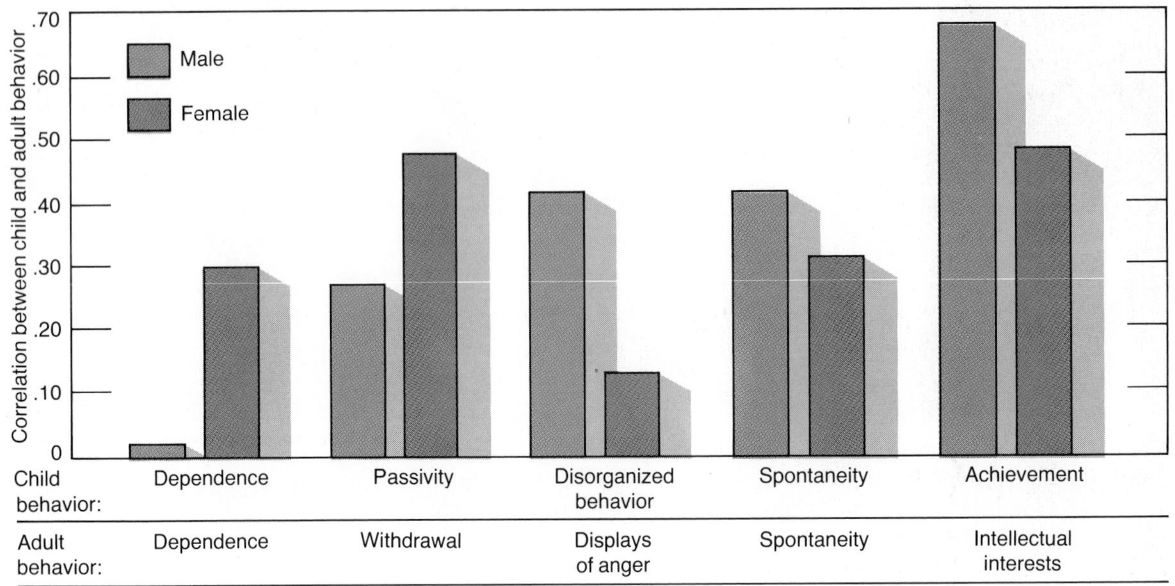

Figure 14-16 Some relationships between childhood traits and adult personality *The correlations were obtained by rating the behavior of children aged 6 to 14, then making ratings of the same subjects after they had become young adults. For males, note that dependence in childhood shows almost no correlation with dependence as an adult—but striving for achievement shows a high correlation. For females, disorganized behavior in childhood shows little correlation with displays of anger in adulthood—but striving for achievement shows a fairly high correlation (Kagan and Moss, 1962).*

their adolescent years were the time when they were most confused and their morale was at its lowest ebb. They mentioned such difficulties as striving for recognition from peers of their own and the opposite sex, being under anxiety-producing pressures from their parents for scholastic and social achievement, and trying to establish their independence while still financially dependent on their parents (Macfarlane, 1964).

Other psychologists, however, have reached different conclusions. Some studies have found that most adolescents, far from being in bitter rebellion, have a warm and mutually respectful relationship with their parents (Sorenson, 1973). Some investigators have even concluded that most adolescents, far from being hopelessly confused and demoralized, are actually well-adjusted (Offer, Ostrov, and Howard, 1982). The conflicting evidence may reflect the vast range of individual differences—in both experiences and reactions to these experiences—that mark a period when all of us undergo rapid and intense growth, both physical and psychological.

The adolescent growth spurt

Adolescence is not so much a natural state of events as an invention of the modern industrial society. In simpler societies, even today in many parts of the world, the transition from childhood to full membership in the community is so smooth and imperceptible that it does not have a name. Children begin helping with the work of the community as soon as they can—and one day, without fuss, they quietly become self-sufficient and independent of their parents. They start rearing their own families and the cycle starts over again.

But the work of an industrial society requires a prolonged education. Most Americans remain in school at least until they are around 18. Many go to college until their early twenties. Some people who train for professions—for example, physicians—may not be able to earn a living

A stormy day in the struggle for independence

until they are 30. It is difficult to determine at exactly what point, in this extended preparation for full participation in society, the child becomes an adolescent and the adolescent becomes an adult.

Adolescence is usually defined as beginning with the onset of puberty—marked by menstruation in the female and the production of sperm in the male. This can occur at any time between the ages of 11 and 18, usually a year or two earlier in girls than in boys. The onset of puberty is almost invariably accompanied by rapid physical growth. A girl may suddenly grow 3 to 5 inches in height in a single year, a boy 4 to 6 inches. Along with the growth comes a change in physical proportions and strength. The girl begins to look like a woman, the boy like a man. All these changes are set into motion by increased activity of the pituitary gland, stimulating the sex glands to produce large quantities of estrogen in the female and androgens in the male.

For boys, early puberty is a distinct advantage. These boys quickly become physically stronger and thus better athletes than classmates who are slower to mature. It has been found that they are more highly regarded by their peers (Conger, 1977) and by adults. They tend to develop a great deal of self-confidence, social poise, and leadership abilities. Boys who are slow to show the growth spurt, on the other hand, continue to be treated as "little boys" while their bigger and more mature classmates are gaining this new respect. Sometimes they try to make up for their physical and social disadvantages by working too hard to attract attention. Sometimes they draw into a shell. Though they catch up later in physical development, they may continue as adults to be less confident, sociable, and enterprising, and more rebellious (Jones and Bayley, 1950).

For girls, reaching puberty at about the same time as others in the class seems to permit the smoothest transition (Petersen, 1981). Early puberty is a mixed blessing. It is awkward to look like an adult in a schoolroom full of children—especially to tower over the boys in the class. Moreover early puberty makes a girl seem sexually provocative at a time when she is still unable psychologically to cope with such reactions (Clausen, 1975). Later, however, girls who mature early seem to benefit. By the time they reach junior high school they seem to have a better opinion of themselves and better relations with both their classmates and their parents than girls who were late in starting puberty (Weatherly, 1964).

The search for identity

Adolescents typically begin to feel very grown-up and to crave independence. They seek to establish a sense of *identity*—that is, to think of themselves as possessing a distinct and unique character, of being people in their own right. But the search is surrounded by troublesome questions: *Who am I? What am I? What do I want to do with my life?*

Adolescents are concerned about the practical matter of choosing a career—a task complicated by the fact that today's society, though it seems to offer a bewildering number of possibilities, has few desirable positions open to young people. (The number of unemployed or underemployed has been greater in recent years for young people than for any other group.) They are also concerned about such intangible issues as moral values and religion. Their cognitive development has advanced to the stage in which they can think in abstractions, form theories of what life is all about, and contemplate what society might be rather than what it seems to be. Often their thinking makes them critical of the values held by society and by their parents. Indeed the relationship between adolescents and parents is fraught with difficulties (but also rich in opportunities), as discussed in a box on Psychology and Society.

Friendships are highly valued throughout life, but rarely more than in adolescence.

Psychology and Society: Adolescents and parents: enemies or friends?

Adolescents often complain that parents are impossible to live with. Parents complain that adolescents are impossible. Are they both right? Is this an inescapable fact of life?

Clashes are inevitable. Adolescents, in the midst of their struggle to establish identity, tend to be wrapped up in their own thoughts—preoccupied with their emerging view of the world, their behavior, and their appearance. They sometimes seem oblivious to anything else, including clocks, chores, and social amenities. Parents, as it happens, are often going through an identity crisis of their own. At the time their children are in adolescence, parents are at an age when some of them are inclined to feel that the world is closing in, shutting off the options of life-style and career they had when younger (Conger, 1977).

The adolescent search for independence often takes the form of struggle against authority and discipline. To parents, surrendering authority often comes hard. After regarding daughters and sons as children for so many years, it is difficult to start treating them as adults. How can all the problems be made more bearable?

A great deal, it turns out, depends on the parents. Studies have shown that two kinds of parents aggravate the difficulties. The first insist that their word is law and that adolescents have no right to make any decisions. The second take a totally hands-off position—either because they do not really care or because they have exaggerated notions about the wisdom of letting children "do their own thing." In the first case, adolescents frequently display continued dependency, lack of confidence, and low self-esteem (Kandel and Lesser, 1972). In the second case, they may fail to develop a sense of responsibility for their own actions.

A study of high school students and their mothers found that students who displayed the fewest behavior problems tended to have a very similar home background. Their mothers had a firm and fairly conservative set of values and clearly expressed their disapproval of using drugs, alcohol abuse, lying, and stealing. They enforced rules about doing homework and getting home at a set hour. But they also had a warm and affectionate relationship with the adolescents and offered them a good deal of independence and support (Jessor and Jessor, 1977). It appears that the best antidote to adolescent aches and pains is the opportunity to identify with and imitate parents who are not too strict, not too permissive—but reasonable, fair, respectful, and eager to show the road to adult responsibility and happiness.

Studies of the mood of today's adolescents indicate that they tend to emphasize such values as love, friendship, privacy, tolerance, self-expression, and self-fulfillment. Although perhaps less so than in recent decades, many are skeptical of the ethics and efficiency of government, business, and other social institutions. Some feel alienated from society—a fact that may help explain why such signs of psychological distress as delinquency, suicide, and adolescent pregnancies have increased in the last 20 years. Yet, despite the problems and the casualties, the majority of adolescents are at least reasonably well-adjusted, confident about their future, and resilient enough to work through the stresses they encounter in their transition to adulthood.

Sexual and moral development

One activity of overriding importance revolves around the first serious attempts to establish relationships with the opposite sex. Adolescents must try to establish their sexual identities at the same time they are coping with all the other difficulties of becoming adults. Society's sexual

Building relationships with the opposite sex—still a difficult hurdle in growing up.

attitudes are more permissive today than in the past, as was discussed in the supplement to Chapter 9. But despite this more lenient atmosphere—or perhaps because of it—adolescents face many confusions and self-doubts. In the words of one group of investigators who have spent much time studying the sexual behavior of teenagers, "coping with sexual development remains a lonely and overly silent experience" (Simon, Berger, and Gagnon, 1972).

Moral standards in general—not only of sexual but of other types of behavior as well—usually undergo rapid and often lasting change during adolescence. Though such standards appear much earlier, they are originally based mostly on a desire to obtain approval and avoid criticism. In adolescence, the standards take a new form—dictated not by mere self-interest but by principles.

The manner in which moral judgments develop has been studied extensively by Lawrence Kohlberg, who questioned boys 7 years old through adolescence. Kohlberg presented his subjects with a number of

Preconventional level Seven-year-old children are oriented to the consequences of their behavior.	Stage 1. Defer to the power of adults and obey rules to avoid trouble and punishment. Stage 2. Seek to satisfy their own needs by behaving in a manner that will gain rewards and the return of favors.
Conventional level At around 10, children begin to become oriented to the expectations of others and to behave in a conventional fashion.	Stage 3. Want to be "good" in order to please and help others and thus receive approval. Stage 4. Want to "do their duty" by respecting authority (parents, teachers, God) and maintaining the social order for its own sake.
Postconventional level Adolescents become oriented to more abstract moral values and their own consciences.	Stage 5. Think in terms of the rights of others, the general welfare of the community, and a duty to conform to the laws and standards established by the will of the majority. Behave in ways they believe would be respected by an impartial observer. Stage 6. Consider not only the actual laws and rules of society but also their own self-chosen standards of justice and respect for human dignity. Behave in a way that will avoid condemnation by their own consciences.

Figure 14-17 Kohlberg's stage theory of moral development
Summarized in the table are the six stages in moral development *found by Kohlberg. Among 7-year-olds, almost all moral judgments are made at the preconventional level. By 16, only a few are made at this level, and judgments made at the postconventional level become important (Kohlberg, 1963, 1967).*

hypothetical situations involving moral questions like these: If a man's wife is dying for lack of an expensive drug that he cannot afford, should he steal the drug? If a patient who is fatally ill and in great pain begs for a mercy killing, should the physician agree? By analyzing the answers and particularly the reasoning by which his subjects reached their answers, Kohlberg determined that moral judgments develop through a series of six stages, as shown in Figure 14-17. Children in the two stages of what he calls the preconventional level base their ideas of right and wrong largely on self-interest. They are concerned chiefly with avoiding punishment and gaining rewards. Later, in the two stages of what he calls the conventional level, they become concerned about the approval of other people. Finally, in the two stages of the postconventional level, they become concerned with abstract moral values and the dictates of their own consciences.

Thus children's reasons for good behavior progress from sheer self-interest to a desire for the approval of others and finally to a concern for their own moral values and the approval of their own consciences. Apparently this stage-by-stage development takes place in other societies as well as our own. Kohlberg has found a similar progression among children in Mexico and Taiwan (Kohlberg and Kramer, 1969).

Development—and sometimes about-face—in adulthood

Though adolescence is in a sense the last step in the transformation of the infant into the adult, development does not end when we become old enough to vote, earn our own living, and marry if we wish. At 18, we have lived only about a quarter of today's average lifetime. If male, we can expect to live another 52 years; if female, another 59. We will face new crises and either solve or fail at them. We may still change spectacularly in many respects.

The long period from adolescence to old age brings about many physical alterations, as is shown in Figure 14-18. We may continue to look the same to ourselves, but not to our acquaintances. (Indeed people who attend a fortieth college reunion often have difficulty recognizing old classmates.) At the same time we change on the inside. Personality patterns may become as unrecognizable as faces.

What becomes of the unhappy adolescent?

One of the most startling about-faces in personality has been observed among people who seemed badly maladjusted as adolescents. It has been found that even the most troubled adolescent—a failure in school, unsuccessful in social contacts, unpopular and despondent—may turn into a successful, happy, well-liked, and highly respected adult. In one study, 166 boys and girls were observed from shortly after birth until they were 18 years old, then observed again at the age of 30. As an example of the kind of change that some of them displayed between adolescence and adulthood note this finding:

> [One subject]—a large, awkward, early-maturing girl who labored under the weight of her size and shyness, feeling that she was a great disappointment to her mother—worked hard for her B average to win approval and was a pedestrian, uninteresting child and adolescent. She had periods of depression, when she could see no point of living. Then, as a junior in college, she got excited over what she was learning (not just in grades to please her mother) and went on to get an advanced degree and to teach in college. Now she has taken time out to have and raise her children. . . . [She is] full of zest for living, married to an interesting, merry, and intelligent man she met in graduate school.

Similarly, a girl who was expelled from school at 16 and a boy expelled at 15—for failing grades and misbehavior—were found to have developed into "wise, steady, understanding parents who appreciate the complexities of life and have both humor and compassion for the human race." An adolescent boy who could only be described as a "listless oddball" had turned into a successful architect and excellent husband and parent who called his adult life "exciting and satisfying." All told, just about half the subjects were living richer and more productive lives as adults than could have been predicted from their adolescent personalities (Macfarlane, 1963).

Figure 14-18 Adolescence to old age *The camera recorded these changes as a women progressed from 16 to nearly 90 years old.*

Is trouble a blessing in disguise?

What causes such marked changes between adolescence and the age of 30? One conclusion reached by the psychologists who conducted the study is that some people are just naturally "late bloomers." It takes them a long time—and often a change of environment that gets them away from their parents or even to a new community—to find themselves. Taking on a meaningful job may help. So may marriage and especially parenthood, with all its responsibilities and opportunities.

The authors of the study have also concluded that even the problems of a troubled adolescence may sometimes prove a blessing in disguise as the years go by. If adolescents go through a period of "painful, strain-producing, and confusing experiences" but manage to survive them, these experiences may in the long run produce greater insight and stability (Macfarlane, 1964).

It is interesting to note that subjects in the study who seemed perfectly well adjusted in adolescence did not always turn out well as adults. About 20 percent of the subjects were found to have less fulfilling lives at 30 than would have been expected from the promise they showed at 18. Included in this group were a number of men and women whose early lives had been smooth, free from any severe strains, and marked by success in both school and social relations. At 18 these subjects seemed well poised and self-confident. The boys tended to be much-admired leaders in athletics, the girls to be good-looking and socially skillful. Yet at 30 they were found to be "brittle, discontented, and puzzled." Perhaps too easy a childhood and adolescence, creating no need to face and overcome problems, can sometimes hinder future development.

Erikson's theory of psychosocial development

The idea that personality growth depends on facing and meeting crises is the basis of an influential theory proposed by Erik Erikson, a psychoanalyst who bases his conclusions on observations of people he has treated at all ages, some in childhood and others at various stages of adulthood. Erikson speaks in terms of *psychosocial development.* That is to say, he holds that development is a twofold process in which the psychological development of individuals (their personalities and view of themselves) proceeds hand in hand with the social relations they establish as they go through life. He has suggested that this development can be divided into eight stages, in each of which individuals face new social situations and encounter new problems (or "psychosocial crises"). They may emerge from the new experiences with greater maturity and richer personalities—or they may fail to cope successfully with the problems and their development may be warped or arrested.

Erikson's eight stages are shown in Figure 14-19. They begin with the child in the first year of life. At this stage the child's social relations are confined to the caretaker. Out of this relationship, Erikson believes, the child learns either to trust the social environment and what it will bring in the future or to be suspicious and fearful of others. In later stages the social environment widens and new psychosocial crises occur, again with outcomes that may be favorable or unfavorable.

Early adulthood, commitment, and marriage

Early adulthood demands many new adjustments. One entails choice of job and career, and often intense preoccupation with efforts to start up the promotional ladder. For women, these years may also require a decision as to whether to pursue a career, marry and have children, or do both.

Erikson believes that the really critical event, however, centers on moving into a relationship marked by intimacy, commitment, and love. For most of us, this means marriage—despite all the recent outpouring

Stage	Crisis	Favorable outcome	Unfavorable outcome
		Childhood	
First year of life	Trust versus mistrust	Faith in the environment and future events	Suspicion, fear of future events
Second year	Autonomy versus doubt	A sense of self-control and adequacy	Feelings of shame and self-doubt
Third through fifth years	Initiative versus guilt	Ability to be a "self-starter," to initiate one's own activities	A sense of guilt and inadequacy to be on one's own
Sixth year to puberty	Industry versus inferiority	Ability to learn how things work, to understand and organize	A sense of inferiority at understanding and organizing
		Transition years	
Adolescence	Identity versus confusion	Seeing oneself as a unique and integrated person	Confusion over who and what one really is
		Adulthood	
Early adulthood	Intimacy versus isolation	Ability to make commitments to others, to love	Inability to form affectionate relationships
Middle age	Generativity versus self-absorption	Concern for family and society in general	Concern only for self—one's own well-being and prosperity
Aging years	Integrity versus despair	A sense of integrity and fulfillment; willingness to face death	Dissatisfaction with life; despair over prospect of death

Figure 14-19 Erikson's stage theory of "psychosocial crises" *Erikson views the life cycle of development, from cradle to grave, as passing through eight stages. Each stage brings new social experiences and new crises—which, if surmounted successfully, lead to constant growth and a steadily enriched personality (Erikson, 1963).*

of books and magazine articles called *What's Killing Our Marriages?* and *Death of the Family.* Statistics show that between 90 and 95 percent of Americans get married sooner or later (Bane, 1976). Among the college educated, the number is probably even higher. A survey of 2,500 students in the Boston area showed that 94 percent believed they would marry within 10 years and 98 percent of them eventually (Rubin, 1973).

It is true that far more marriages break up today than in the past. The divorce rate has increased eightfold since the early part of the century and doubled just since 1965, to the point where about 2.5 million Americans go through the divorce courts every year (National Center for Health Statistics, 1982). But about four out of every five people who get divorced marry again (Norton and Glick, 1976), and many second marriages seem to be quite successful. A survey made in Canada found that about 80 percent of husbands and wives described their remarriages as very satisfactory, 10 percent as satisfactory, and only 10 percent as unsatisfactory (Schlesinger, 1970).

In one way or another, most people seem to cope with the crises of early adulthood in a reasonably satisfactory manner. They form affectionate and nourishing relationships—in most cases with marriage partners, sometimes with close friends, and often with both. Most of them also commit themselves to children. A 1976 survey showed that about

Most young women look forward to becoming mothers.

90 percent of young adult women expected to become mothers (U.S. Bureau of the Census, 1982).

Middle age and its responsibilities

The crisis of middle age, in Erikson's terms, centers on a conflict between "self-absorption" and "generativity." Self-absorption means a narrow concentration on one's own interests—especially in matters of getting ahead in life, making money, and enjoying material comforts. Generativity means a concern for others—partly for the psychological welfare of one's children, partly for humanity in general.

Ideally, Erikson believes, this crisis produces a wider outlook on the meaning of life—a sense of kinship with one's fellow human beings, with the ebb and flow of history, with nature itself. Old goals, especially selfish ones, may be abandoned. New satisfactions of the spirit may be found. People sometimes make radical changes in their life-style. Men may switch careers—moving from a job they have held because of accident or habit, or for financial reasons, into something they have always wanted to do. Women who have spent their early years working as homemakers and mothers may take an outside job for the first time, thus encountering new problems but also finding new satisfactions. While such changes sometimes involve stress, adults at middle age are often able by virtue of their experience to cope more successfully than are younger people (Pruett, 1980). When the crisis of middle age is met successfully—and a quieter and deeper attitude toward the rhythm of life established—people are prepared to grow old with grace and contentment. The process of development, from its seeds in the newborn baby, has come full flower.

The challenges and triumphs of growing old

Until recently, the average life expectancy in the United States was about 50 years. This is still true in parts of the world that have not caught up with today's advanced techniques of sanitation, nutrition, and medical science. But thanks to modern knowledge and technology, the average life expectancy of Americans is up to 73 years, and further strides in curing disease are soon expected to add a dozen more years (Fries and Crapo, 1981).

When our country declared its independence, only 2 percent of the population was 65 or over, and as recently as a century ago, old people were still a rarity. Typically, men died while they still had an unmarried child living at home. Women, because their genes incline them to greater longevity, lived a few years longer—but usually only until just after the last child married (Bane, 1976). Except for a small minority, the psychology of aging was not a matter of concern in the past. As shown in Figure 14-20, however, the percentage of persons in the United States who have passed what is generally considered to be the retirement age of 65 has virtually tripled since the turn of the century. With over 25 million such older persons among us—one out of every nine Americans—the problems and pleasures of the retirement years have become very much a part of psychological investigation.

To Erikson, the aging years represent a fork in the road that can lead either to a heartwarming sense of integrity or to feelings of despair. People who succeed in negotiating this crisis live out the final years of their lives with a sense of self-fulfillment and wisdom. They face the inevitability of death without fear or regret. Those who fail—often because they have not surmounted life's earlier crises—wind up embittered. They are dissatisfied with the way they have lived their lives. They regret what might have been. The prospect of dying fills them with despair.

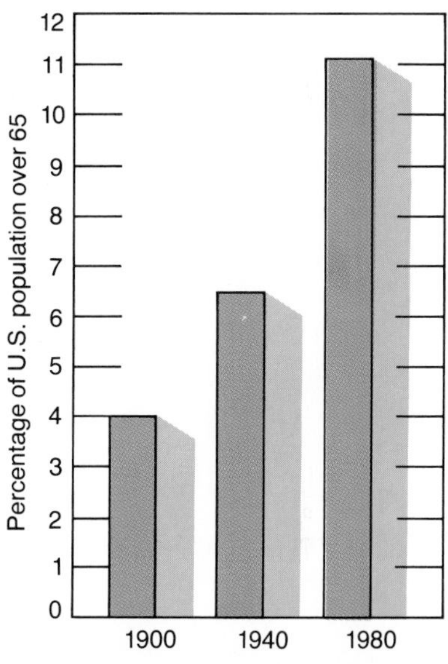

Figure 14-20 The increasing United States population over 65
In 1900, the number of Americans over 65—3.1 million persons—made up only 4 percent of the population. In the next 80 years, their number swelled to 25.5 million, or over 11 percent of the population—and this percentage is expected still to rise further before the end of the century (Brotman, 1981).

Is it as bad as they say?

How many people find happiness in their aging years, and how many fail? Psychology's findings are contrary to what is generally assumed. Our society has been described as youth-oriented—and old age is often thought of as a period of decrepitude and dissatisfaction. One study showed that younger people assume that life will become less and less zestful with the passage of time, and they give the aging years the lowest rating of all for happiness and quality of life. But the study also showed that older people themselves tend on the average to give the period a much higher rating. They do not, as is commonly assumed, tend to "live in the past" (Cameron, 1972).

There are problems, of course. Some people, after retiring, are plagued by financial difficulties. Some suffer from chronic illnesses. Among people over 65 are about 1.9 million widowers and 10.8 million widows (U.S. Bureau of the Census, 1982), and the stresses they encounter in adjusting to their loneliness are reflected in their own sub-

One of the supreme pleasures of growing old.

sequent mortality rates. Men especially seem to have a difficult time. One study showed that the mortality rate was 61 percent higher for widowers between the ages of 55 and 64 than for those in the same age range who were married. Among both men and women who lost their mates, the death rate was higher for those who lived alone than for those who shared a household with someone else (Helsing, Szklo, and Comstock, 1981).

But in one way or another, most people seem to cope with the problems. A study of men and women in their seventies found that three out of every four were satisfied with their lives. Most of these septuagenarians were still active, at least to the extent they found suitable to their physical endurance, and were not especially troubled by loneliness. Only a few showed signs of senility, which is mental impairment caused by brain damage that sometimes occurs with aging (Neugarten, 1971). Indeed older persons often remain vibrant, sharp, and capable of achievement—especially those whose motivation continues undiminished (National Institute on Aging, 1981). Most people seem to find that the retirement years are not nearly so bad as they were led to expect—surprisingly full of pleasures that may differ in kind and intensity but are nonetheless as fullfilling as the joys of youth.

The psychology of dying

The chief reason for today's increased life expectancy is that science has conquered diseases such as pneumonia that formerly killed many people in the prime of life. Most deaths today result from chronic, long-lasting conditions such as cancer and ailments of the heart and circulatory system. Thus people are more likely to be aware that they are approaching the end of life—and must somehow reconcile themselves.

Psychologists have only recently begun to study the cognitive and emotional processes that occur with the knowledge that death is imminent. Their findings thus far are sparse and inconclusive. But the search goes on for information that may help ease this final episode and surround dying with a grace and dignity befitting the human spirit and the remarkable flow of events from cradle to grave.

SUMMARY

Babies at birth: alike yet different

1. *Developmental psychology* studies the ways in which children gradually acquire their patterns of thinking, emotions, motives, and other aspects of personality—and the ways in which these patterns may change in later life.
2. Babies at birth differ in (a) sensory thresholds and adaptation, (b) activity and irritability, and (c) temperament. Most appear to be *easy children,* some *slow-to-warm-up,* and some *difficult.*
3. Traits displayed in infancy endure for varying periods of time. Most early traits are altered by childhood environment.
4. Human infants are extremely impressionable. An unfavorable environment may produce drastic and sometimes long-lasting abnormalities. But infants are also resilient and malleable—capable of changing when circumstances change.

Physical and mental development

5. Physical development, including the acquisition of such skills as walking and talking, depends largely on the process of *maturation*—the physical changes, taking place after birth, that continue biological growth from fertilized egg cell to adult.
6. Factors contributing to intellectual development include improvement in the process of perception and growing skill at understanding and using language.

Personality development: birth to eighteen months

7. Personality development from birth to 18 months is characterized by *attachment* to the mother or other caretaker. This period is marked by the appearance of *separation anxiety* and *stranger anxiety.*

The first social demands: eighteen months through three years

8. *Socialization* is the process through which children are taught to live by the ways of society. Too much discipline or protection during this period may instill a crippling amount of anxiety and create lifelong inhibitions against trying anything new or challenging. The motive to live up to inner standards first appears at about the age of 2.

The preschool years: four and five

9. The preschool years, 4 and 5, are characterized by (a) the first notions of *sex typing* and conduct appropriate to males and females,

(b) the first feelings of guilt and conscience, and (c) *identification* with the parents.

The period of teachers and peers: six to ten

10. From 6 to 10, children come under the strong influence of their peers—that is, other children. Peers provide (a) evaluation, (b) a social role, and (c) an opportunity for rebellion against the adult world. During this period children acquire a tendency to be dominant or submissive and strong inner standards calling for (a) being valued by parents, teachers, and peers; (b) mastering physical and mental skills; and (c) achieving harmony between thoughts and behavior.

Adolescence: fun or fury?

11. Adolescence is characterized physically by the sudden growth spurt that accompanies puberty. Psychologically, this may be a period of "storm and stress"—with much confusion over establishing independence and a sense of *identity*, striving for recognition, and being under anxiety-producing scholastic and social pressures. However, some studies have shown that most adolescents are well-adjusted.
12. Moral standards—of sexual and other types of behavior—usually undergo rapid change during adolescence. Kohlberg has suggested that *moral development* occurs in six stages, in which children's reasons for good behavior progress from sheer self-interest to a desire for the approval of others and finally to a concern for their own values and the approval of their own consciences.

Development—and sometimes about-face—in adulthood

13. Continuing development in the years after adolescence often produces striking changes. Some of the most troubled and despondent adolescents turn out to lead happy and fulfilling lives as adults, while some untroubled and self-confident adolescents do not live up to their early promise.
14. One of the prominent proponents of the idea that development is a lifelong process is Erikson, who holds that *psychosocial development* (psychological changes occurring with changes in the social environment) proceeds in eight stages extending from infancy to old age.
15. According to Erikson, the critical event in early adulthood is moving into a relationship (usually marriage) marked by intimacy, commitment, and love. Middle adulthood brings a conflict between "self-absorption" (a narrow concentration on one's own interests) and "generativity" (a concern for others).

The challenges and triumphs of growing old

16. Old age, in Erikson's terms, results in either integrity or despair. Most people seem to cope with the problems of the retirement years and to find them fufilling.

IMPORTANT TERMS

attachment
caretaker
difficult children
easy children
exploration
identification
identity
maturation
moral development
psychosocial development
rooting response
separation anxiety
sex typing
slow-to-warm-up children
stranger anxiety
surrogate mother

RECOMMENDED READINGS

Biehler, R. F. *Child development: an introduction,* 2d ed. Boston: Houghton Mifflin, 1981.

Birren, J. E. et al. *Developmental psychology: a life-span approach.* Boston: Houghton Mifflin, 1981.

Conger, J. J. *Adolescence and youth: psychological development in a changing world,* 2d ed. New York: Harper & Row, 1977.

Erikson, E. H. *Identity and the life cycle.* New York: Norton, 1980.

Mussen, P. H., Conger, J. J., and Kagan, J. *Child development and personality,* 5th ed. New York: Harper & Row, 1979.

Schaie, K. W., and Geiwitz, J. *Adult development and aging.* Boston: Little, Brown, 1982.

Wolman, B., ed. *Handbook of developmental psychology.* Englewood Cliffs, N. J.: Prentice-Hall, 1982.

For practical guidance to parents and prospective parents:

For physical welfare

Spock, B. *Baby and child care.* New York: Pocket Books, 1968

For psychological welfare

McCall, R. B. *Infants.* Cambridge, Mass.: Harvard University Press, 1979

CHAPTER 15

Learning—and conforming to—the ways of society 547
- The socialization process
- Obedience and conformity
- Conformity as a part of everyday life
- The Asch experiment: agreeing that a wrong answer is right
- The Milgram experiment: turning ordinary people into torturers
- Why we conform
- The theory of social comparison and our opinion of ourselves
- Expedient conformity and true conformity

Our attitudes toward life: how we acquire, cling to, and sometimes change them 557
- Why attitudes, though persistent, are not necessarily consistent
- Prejudices and stereotypes
- New experiences, new socialization, new attitudes
- Attitude change and the theory of cognitive dissonance
- Do attitudes change behavior—or vice versa?
- Making a decision as a form of behavior change

"Persuasive communications" and attitude change 562
- Is anybody listening? If so, who?
- And who are you to tell me to change?
- What kinds of communications are most effective?
- The communication and the listener

Our search for the reasons people act as they do: attribution theories 566
- Dispositional and situational factors and the "fundamental attribution error"
- An attribution theorist's quiz game and its strange results
- Compounding the error: guessing people's dispositions by guessing how they feel
- Ignoring our own influence on other people's actions
- Some everyday applications
- Self-perception theory—or "Why did I do that?"

How we form our social relationships: the forces of attraction and liking 572
- Propinquity and familiarity: "I like you because I know you"
- Similarity: "I like you because we seem so alike"
- "I like you because you like me—and are good at what you do"
- Physical attractiveness: "I like you because I like your looks"
- Why physical attractiveness counts: the matter of first impressions
- Why first impressions persist: implicit personality theory

Summary 577

Important terms 579

Supplement: Aggression, altruism, and bystander apathy 580
- Is aggression bred into our genes?
- Or is aggression learned?
- Aggression's opposite: studies of altruism
- Bystander apathy: treating others with benign (or not so benign) neglect
- Apathy, anonymity, and intimacy
- You can't be a Good Samaritan if you're in a hurry

Summary of supplement 585

Important terms 585

Recommended readings 585

Psychology and society
- Change for the better: it is easier than many people think 565
- How self-fulfilling prophecies can cause damage 570

Social Psychology

What was perhaps the first experiment in social psychology was reported in 1898, when the science was a mere two decades old. Using the aptitude tests that psychologists were beginning to develop, the experimenter measured some skills of his subjects as exhibited in the privacy of the testing situation. Then he observed how well they performed similar tasks when they were in a social situation, in the company of and in competition with other people. He found some striking differences between test scores and actual performances (Triplett, 1898).

The experiment opened the gates to a whole field of psychological inquiry by demonstrating that human behavior cannot be entirely understood by studying the individual in isolation. The influence of other people, exerted in various ways in various different situations, must also be examined. Indeed it was soon established that an individual's actions often display startling inconsistencies from one social setting to another. A person may be scrupulously honest in dealing with business associates yet cheat when playing cards with friends, generous toward some people but stingy toward others, domineering around close relatives but meekly submissive around in-laws. Even children, it has been found, may be chronic liars at school yet always tell the truth at home (Horowitz and Horowitz, 1938).

So wide-ranging is the influence of other people that social psychology is called *the study of the manner in which the human being "thinks, feels, and behaves in social situations"* (Aronson, 1972)—a definition that covers cognitive processes and emotions as well as actions. The relationship between social situation and the individual, it should be added, is a two-way street. Other people influence us and we influence them. That is to say, how we feel and what we do is determined at least in part—and often to a great extent—by what other people are doing or what we think they expect us to do. At the same time, what we do or seem to expect helps determine what they do (Secord and Backman, 1964).

Learning—and conforming to—the ways of society

Other people are important to us and influence us because we human beings are social animals. We do not prowl the world alone or in the company of only a mate, as some other organisms do. Indeed we do not seem capable of existing in isolation. We need the company and help of other human beings to acquire even such necessities as food, clothing, shelter, and protection against enemies. We can survive only by establishing some kind of *society*—which is the term applied to any group of people who occupy the same geographical area and cooperate in an accepted pattern of living together.

Ever since human beings appeared on earth they appear to have lived in societies, probably starting with the ancient cave communities. The people who live today in the most undeveloped parts of the world are banded together in some sort of society, like the tribes who occupy thatched huts in the jungles of South America. The people who live in a small rural town or in Chicago constitute a society. The United States itself is a society. Big or little, simple or complex, the society is a universal way of human life.

The socialization process

The society into which we are born begins to influence us almost from the moment of birth. We develop from child to adult not in a vacuum but in close interaction with our parents, family, teachers, and schoolmates. From all these people, we learn the ways of our own society. We learn the English language. We learn how Americans speak, behave toward one another, and express or conceal their emotions. Later we learn what the people in our society believe and what they value. We learn the customs and laws that dictate a whole host of activities, from finding a mate to conducting a business deal. This process is called *socialization*—the way children are integrated into the society through exposure to the actions and opinions of other members of the society. In many ways, children become creatures of their society (Benedict, 1959), molded by the customs and rules that make up its *culture*, or established way of life.

The term "culture" embraces all the physical objects the society produces as part of its life-style—its clothing, shelter, tools, and artistic creations. The term also includes the society's language, beliefs, politi-

A jubilant crowd at an outdoor concert, one of society's shared experiences—though the young man at center seems unmoved.

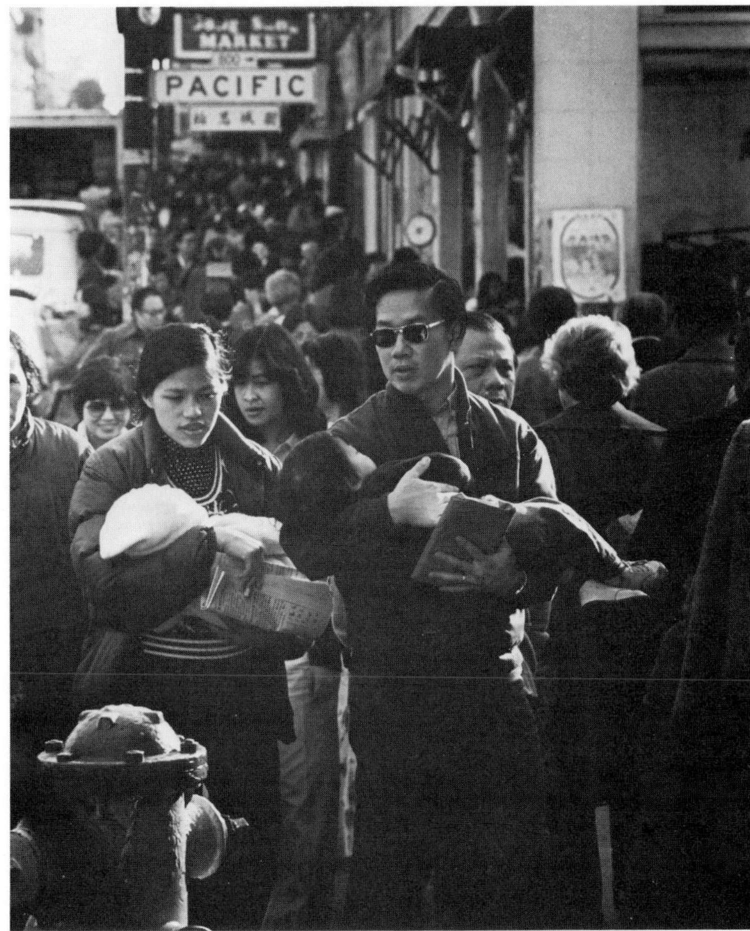

An American subculture: the Chinese community in San Francisco.

cal structure, family relationships, rules, and customary patterns of behavior. All these aspects of culture vary greatly around the world. The way of life in England calls for driving on the left side of the road, in the Orient for eating with chopsticks, in some countries for disregarding clocks and appointment times. There are societies where the women do all the work and the men devote themselves to ceremony and self-adornment (Mead, 1935), where two friends would never dream of competing against each other in games or athletic contests (McGrath, 1964), and even where cannibalism is approved.

In a society as complex as ours, not every child is socialized to follow the same customs and rules. Within our society there exist many *subcultures,* or ways of life that differ from one another in many important respects. Some of these subcultures exist partly because the nation has been settled over the years by people from many different parts of the world, bringing with them their own particular customs and values. Other subcultures have a religious basis. Still others depend on occupation and social class. All in all the United States is a nation of many subcultures holding very different views on religion, politics, militarism, sexual behavior, and lifestyles in general.

Obedience and conformity

Whatever the customs and rules may be, every culture and every subculture molds its children accordingly. Socialization is a universal process. It is a form of learning that everyone undergoes—and that probably has a more pervasive and lasting effect than anything learned in school (although school also serves to socialize pupils). In one way or another, socialization gives all of us a lifelong tendency to think and act like the people with whom we have grown up.

There are always rebels, of course, who resist the influence of socialization and break the rules. Some of them become criminals, at war with the society. Others are innovators who sometimes reshape history by jolting society out of its old ways and into better ones—like such great figures, martyred for daring to suggest changes, as Socrates, Christ, Joan of Arc, and Galileo. Despite the exceptions, however, most people follow the customs and rules they have learned and behave as they believe they are expected to behave. Social psychologists have found that most human beings everywhere display strong tendencies toward (a) *obedience,* or submission to authority, and (b) *conformity,* which is defined as the yielding by individuals to pressures from the group in which they find themselves. The group applying the pressure may be the society as a whole or any part of it, such as our family, friends, classmates, or business associates. It may even be made up of total strangers, such as the people sitting around us on a bus or in a theater.

Conformity as a part of everyday life

The tendencies toward obedience and conformity—and the difference between them—were once demonstrated in a simple little experiment built around a campus doorway that was in frequent use. On the doorway an urgent sign suddenly appeared:

ABSOLUTELY NO ADMITTANCE
USE ANOTHER ENTRANCE

The sign, of course, was put up by a psychologist, who then sat by to see what happened. One person after another, even those who had been walking through the doorway every day, turned back—thus exhibiting obedience to society's rules. But then the experimenter arranged for confederates to appear, ignore the sign, and march right in. Given this example, others walked in too (Freed et al., 1955). They were now exhibiting conformity to the behavior of the confederates.

If you make a point of looking for similar examples, you will see them all around you. If a traffic light sticks, showing red to motorists approaching from all four directions, the drivers all come to a halt and wait patiently for a change. But when at last one or two venture across the intersection, others follow. When a pedestrian on a crowded city sidewalk stops to stare at the upper floor of a tall building, others are likely to stop and stare too, even if they find nothing worth watching. (If you and some companions want to try it, you may soon find quite a crowd of imitators.) People even manage to resemble one another in appearance. As the street scenes in Figure 15-1 show, styles change over

1910

mid-1930s

mid-1980s

Figure 15-1 Styles change over the years—but people remain look-alikes *These street scenes photographed over a span of three-quarters of a century show how the way Americans look has shifted since 1910. Yet, no matter when the camera records them, they all look more or less like their contemporaries.*

the years—but at any given moment in history, everybody looks pretty much like everybody else.

It is amusing but not very significant that all of us tend to gawk at a building when others are doing it—or that we follow the dictates of fashion in clothing, hair styles, and growing or not growing beards. Often, however, obedience and conformity have a much more profound effect on behavior.

Figure 15-2 Asch's famous study: will student 6 conform to the group? *Of these seven students in the Asch experiment, student 6 is the only real subject. All the others are in league with the experimenter. Student 6 believes the experiment is about discrimination among lines like those shown in Figures 15-3 and 15-4—but in fact it is designed to find out how far he and other subjects will go in conforming to the group.*

The Asch experiment: agreeing that a wrong answer is right

One of the classic experiments on conformity was performed in the 1950s at Swarthmore College by Solomon Asch. It used the method illustrated in Figure 15-2, in which one real subject, who thought he was taking part in a study of perceptual discrimination, sat at a table with a group of confederates of the experimenter. The experimenter showed pairs of white cards with black lines of varying length, such as the lines shown in their relative sizes in Figures 15-3 and 15-4, and asked the group which of the lines in Figure 15-4 matched the test line.

For what the experimenter claimed were reasons of convenience, the people sitting around the table were asked to call out their judgments in order, beginning with the student at the experimenter's left. The real subject was always placed near the other end so that he would hear the judgments of several confederates before making his own. Sometimes the confederates gave the right answer, but on some trials they deliberately called out the wrong answer. On these trials 37 percent of the answers given by the real subjects who took part in the experiment were also incorrect. In other words, the subjects conformed with the group's wrong judgment much of the time.

Some of the subjects conformed on all trials, others on some but not all. Only one subject out of four remained completely independent and did not conform at any time. Even the subjects who showed independence, however, experienced various kinds of conflict and anxiety, as is readily apparent from the photographs of the subject in Figure 15-5. Some of their comments later were: "Despite everything, there was a lurking fear that in some way I did not understand I might be wrong." "At times I had the feeling, to heck with it, I'll go along with the rest." "I felt disturbed, puzzled, separated, like an outcast from the rest." Thus the urge to conform—to go along with the group—was strong even among the most independent subjects (Asch, 1956).

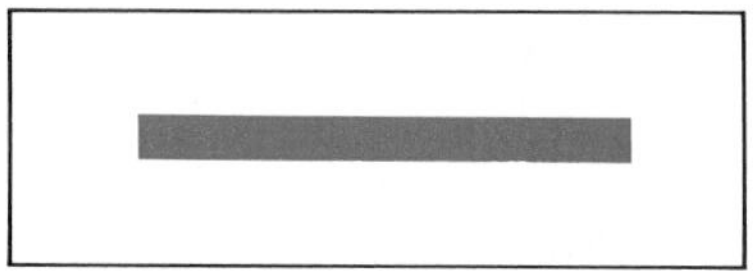

Figure 15-3 A test line in the Asch experiment *This is a scaled-down version of one of the lines Asch showed to the group. Which of the lines in Figure 15-4, he asked, matches it?*

The Milgram experiment: turning ordinary people into torturers

Another experiment that produced even more dramatic results—and in this case frightening ones—was performed by Stanley Milgram in a laboratory at Yale. Milgram selected 80 men of various ages and occupational backgrounds and asked them to take part in what he said was an important experiment in learning. Each subject was assigned to a group of four people—the other three of whom, unknown to the subject, were Milgram's assistants. One of the assistants was the "learner" in the make-believe experiment. The other two assistants and the subject were the "teachers," and their job was to instruct the "learner" by punishing him with an electric shock when he made an error. The subject was put at the controls that regulated the amount of shock (see Figure 15-6). Actually, no electricity was hooked up to the controls and no learning took place. The "learner" deliberately made errors and only pretended to feel pain when punished.

Of the 80 subjects, half were placed in a control group. These subjects were not subjected to any pressure to raise the shock levels and did not raise them very high. Thirty-four of these 40 control subjects stopped at shock levels listed as "slight" or "moderate." Only six went above 120 volts. But it was a far different story with the other 40 subjects. These 40 were strongly urged by their fellow "teachers" to raise the amount of electricity higher and higher—and they did. Only six of them refused to go above 120 volts. The other 34 went right on, even though the "learner" at first shouted that the shocks were becoming painful and later began to groan and finally scream in pain. Seven of the subjects

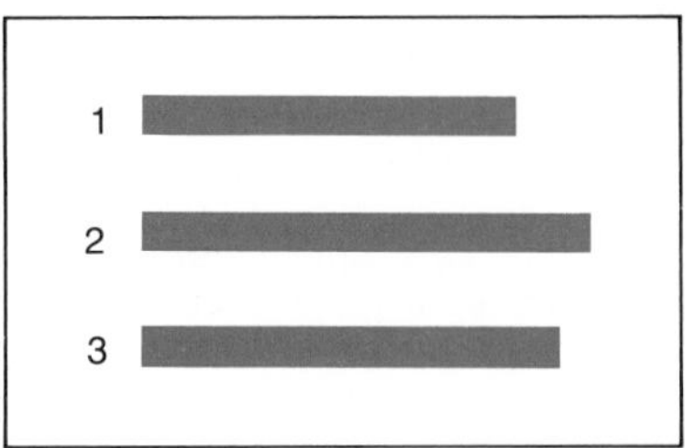

Figure 15-4 Which line matches?
The group was asked to judge which of these lines was the same as the line in Figure 15-3. The correct answer is 2. But the experimenter's six confederates at the table insisted unanimously that it was line 1—which is in fact the least like the test line.

Figure 15-5 An "independent" subject—shaken but unyielding
In the top photo, student 6 is making his first independent judgment, disagreeing with the group's otherwise unanimous but incorrect verdict. In the other photos his puzzlement and concern seem to increase until, preserving his independence despite the pressure from the group, he announces (bottom), "I have to call them as I see them."

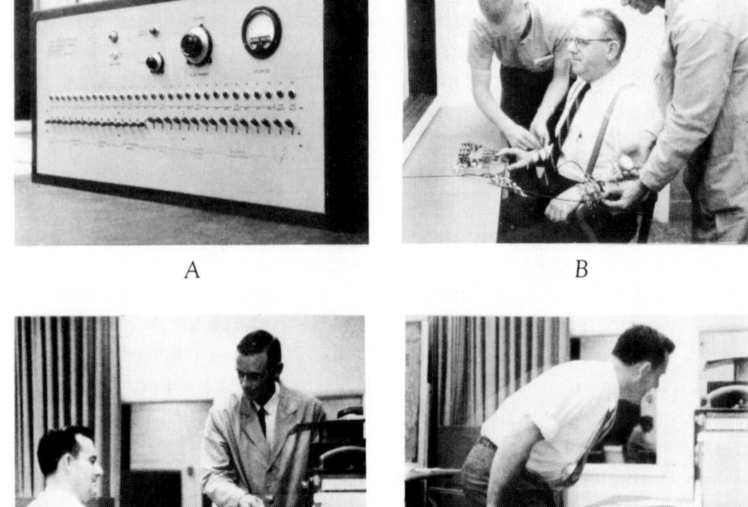

Figure 15-6 The Milgram experiment *In these scenes from a film on the Milgram experiment, A shows the panel, which subjects believed to control the level of shock. In B, electrodes are attached to the wrists of a "learner." In C, a subject who will be at the control panel receives a sample shock of the kind he believes he will administer. In D, a subject breaks off the experiment after reaching as high a shock level as he is willing to administer.*

went up to what they thought was the maximum they could deliver—a "highly dangerous" shock of 450 volts. Many of the experimental subjects showed signs of doubt and distress about engaging in such a cruel act, yet they went along with the group anyway (Milgram, 1964).

Why we conform

Milgram's subjects were just ordinary people who presumably would never be guilty of cruelty under ordinary circumstances. The fact that they were willing to go to such outrageous lengths under group pressure is eloquent and even frightening proof of just how strong the human tendency to conform is. The question, of course, is why do we have this tendency? Why is it so powerful that it can sometimes make us behave in unexpected and almost unbelievable ways?

(1) Our dependence on approval One reason seems to be that we depend on the people around us for many of our psychological satisfactions. It is pleasant to win approval as an accepted, well-liked member of the group. It is highly unpleasant to be rejected by the group and perhaps even subjected to ridicule (Aronson, 1972). Thus it is generally easier and more rewarding to conform. It can be very difficult to stand alone as a single dissenter.

Studies have shown, indeed, that unanimity within the group is the most powerful factor of all in producing conformity. If we are in a group that expresses unanimous agreement, we are under much stronger pressure to conform than if even one person disagrees. This was demonstrated in an ingenious variation of the Asch experiment in which one

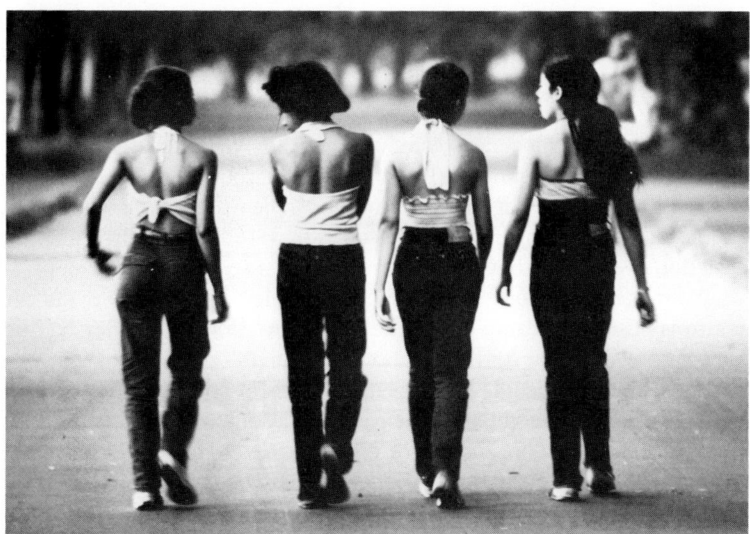

Four dress-alikes display one kind of conformity.

of the confederates sitting around the table was a black and some of the actual subjects were known to be prejudiced against blacks. When the confederates were unanimous in the incorrect answers they gave, all the subjects showed the usual tendency to conform. But when the black confederate broke the unanimity of the group by giving the correct answer, the subjects were much less likely to conform (Malof and Lott, 1962). Even those who might have been expected to reject the black confederate's opinion seemed to welcome the excuse he gave them for breaking away from the others.

(2) Our need for guidance Another reason for conformity is that we need the help of other people in developing an accurate view of our physical and social environment. We cannot get through life successfully, and may not even survive, unless we understand ourselves and our world—and often other people are the only guide we have. To cite some extreme examples, you can get killed if you venture out in a boat at a time when a more experienced mariner would know a storm is about to churn up waves that may swamp you, or if you eat a mushroom that an expert would immediately recognize as poisonous. In dealings with other people, you can come to grief if you misjudge the reaction of an armed mugger to a show of resistance. On a more commonplace level, you are not likely to get past a job interview if you misjudge the interviewer's concern for promptness and neat appearance—or hold a job very long if you have a false notion of its requirements or your talent for it.

The need for guidance to successful behavior is the basis of an important psychological concept called the *theory of social comparison.* The theory holds that we usually have no objective and scientific way to evaluate our abilities, opinions, or the propriety of our actions (Horowitz and Horowitz, 1938). Therefore we can only judge ourselves by comparing ourselves with other people—usually our friends or other people we believe to be similar to ourselves, but sometimes strangers whom we happen to be around. The more uncertain we are of where we stand and how we should act, the more likely we are to make and rely on the comparisons (Radloff, 1959). For example, if you go to a party where you are the only stranger, how can you fit in without seeing how the others act? On a new campus, how are you expected to dress, behave in the classroom, and get along with your fellow students?

The result of the Milgram experiment can be readily explained by the theory of social comparison. The subjects were in a highly uncertain situation. After all, they were taking part in a scientific experiment. If they were supposed to stop at a low level of electric shock, why did the controls on the machine go all the way up to 450 volts? They had no way of knowing what to think or how to behave—so they looked to the other "teachers," people who seemed to be just like themselves, for information. They compared their own opinions with the opinions of the others in the group. When the others proved to be so positive about raising the shock levels, who were they to argue otherwise?

The theory of social comparison and our opinion of ourselves

The theory of social comparison also holds that our search for guidance strongly influences our self-esteem—indeed our entire self-image. We judge our abilities and our worth, the theory maintains, mostly by comparing ourselves with other people. We cannot state for sure, as a proven fact, that we are good students, good teachers, good athletes, or anything else. We have to try to decide how we rank in comparison with other people. We must also ask ourselves, "What do other people think of me?"

The opinions of other people play a far greater part in self-esteem than could ever be imagined by a person who has never been exposed to social psychology and its emphasis on social influences. For dramatic evidence, note this experiment and its surprising results:

The subjects were women attending high school or college. They were asked to try their hand at a problem-solving task containing 25 items. After they had finished, the experimenters pretended to grade their attempts and then told them how they had scored. Actually, no grading was ever done. The experimenters simply decided arbitrarily to tell half the subjects that they had done badly, the other half that they had done very well.

This false information about performance was allowed to "sink in" for a time. Then the experimenters flatly admitted their deception. The women were told that their scores had never actually been compiled and that there was no truth at all in the information that they had done badly or well. Once the truth was out, the women were asked to rate their own ability at that kind of problem solving, estimate how many problems they had in fact solved correctly, and also predict how many they would solve correctly on a future trial.

As is shown in Figure 15-7, the results were startling. Apparently the women who had been told they did badly were never quite able to get over the loss of self-esteem they suffered—even though they knew that the unfavorable rating bore no relation to the facts and meant absolutely nothing. The women who had been told they did well, on the

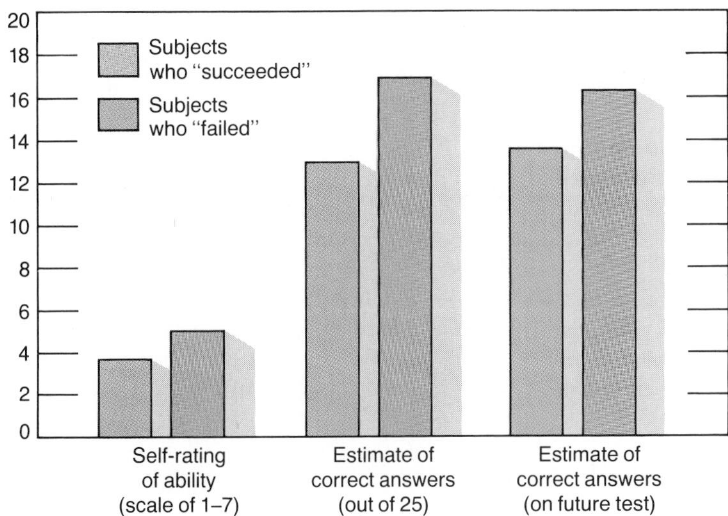

Figure 15-7 It is not true—but I believe it! *The graph illustrates the results of the experiment with high school and college women discussed in the text. Subjects who were told they failed at a problem-solving task had a significantly lower opinion of their ability than subjects who were told they succeeded—even though they knew that the information about their performance had no relation to the facts (Ross, Lepper, and Hubbard, 1975).*

other hand, were much more confident—even though they too knew that the information was meaningless. There could hardly be a more convincing demonstration of the way other people's opinions shape our own views—even of ourselves.

Expedient conformity and true conformity

Sometimes, it should be added, we merely pay lip service to the opinions and ideas expressed by others—thus engaging in what social psychologists called *expedient conformity.* For example, a woman who strongly favors the Democratic candidate in a coming election may find herself at a party where everybody else is enthusiastic about the Republican. She may conform and go along with the others even though she is convinced they are wrong, just to avoid argument and win acceptance.

Often, however, we change not only our outward behavior but also our private beliefs in response to group pressure—thus engaging in *true conformity.* For example, a man who has always opposed strict pollution control laws as bad for business and employment moves to another community. There his new business associates and neighbors strongly favor pollution control. Eventually he may come to agree wholeheartedly. One might say that he has internalized the group opinion and made it his own. True conformity means we have made our social comparisons and decided that we were wrong and the group is right—a process that bears on another important aspect of social psychology that will now be discussed.

Our attitudes toward life: how we acquire, cling to, and sometimes change them

All of us, as we grow up, acquire many strong beliefs and feelings, or what social psychologists call *attitudes,* toward people and situations. We have favorable or unfavorable attitudes toward members of various ethnic groups, foreigners, rich people, poor people, males, females, homosexuals, children, teenagers, and old people. We have strong attitudes toward the nation's political parties, national defense, taxation, welfare, crime, unions, religion, and all the other issues and institutions in society.

Attitudes are not just mere off-the-cuff judgments that we make casually and can easily change. Instead they are deeply ingrained—as if constituting a basic part of our personality. We acquire many of them as part of the socialization process, and they tend to influence us throughout life. We are very much in favor of things toward which we have a positive attitude—and very much against things toward which we have a negative attitude.

It is chiefly this "for" or "against" quality that distinguishes attitudes from more superficial and less influential opinions. Our belief that the earth is round is an example of a mere opinion, not an attitude. We are neither for nor against roundness—and in the unlikely event science suddenly discovered that the earth is in fact shaped like a football, we would not hesitate to change our opinion. An attitude, because it concerns something that really matters to us, is far more resistant to change. A congresswoman with a strongly disapproving attitude toward abortion is not easily persuaded, even by her most influential colleagues, to vote for federal funding of abortion clinics. A man with a strongly favorable attitude toward gun control is hardly likely to accept a co-worker's invitation to join the National Rifle Association.

Since attitudes are so enduring, and can be powerful forces in determining behavior, they have always been a key topic in social psychology. Investigators have devoted considerable study to how people acquire them, cling to them, but sometimes change them—and when, under what circumstances, and to what extent they predict what the individual will do (Brigham and Wrightsman, 1982).

Why attitudes, though persistent, are not necessarily consistent

Attitudes are not necessarily based on evidence. Some of them simply represent the effects of socialization and conformity to the social group. We have taken them over lock, stock, and barrel from the people around us—without ever looking at the evidence at all. Nor are they necessarily logical or consistent. Some psychologists have concluded, indeed, that the most remarkable thing about our attitudes is the amount of inconsistency we manage to tolerate (Bem, 1970).

For example, Mayor Smith is running for reelection. Mr. and Mrs. Jones, like their friends and neighbors, have a strongly favorable attitude toward Mayor Smith and the mayor's political party. But one day something rather upsetting occurs. The local newspaper publishes a strong and extremely persuasive editorial that describes in detail how Mayor Smith has failed to solve a number of urgent city problems. In fact the mayor has accepted graft as an inducement to permit gambling and to tolerate inferior performance on building contracts.

Will Mr. and Mrs. Jones change their attitude toward Mayor Smith? Not necessarily. Instead, they may do any one of several things. They may convince themselves that the newspaper is simply biased against the mayor. They may engage in a mental debate with the editorial and disprove its allegations, at least to their own satisfaction. Or they may put the whole editorial right out of their mind and simply refuse to think about it. Our ingenuity at finding ways of maintaining our attitudes despite strong opposing arguments seems almost boundless.

Prejudices and stereotypes

Two kinds of attitudes that often fly in the face of fact are so common that social psychologists have given them special names:

1. A *prejudice* is an attitude that an individual maintains so stubbornly as to be virtually immune to any information or experiences that would disprove it. In our society, one of the most common prejudices is held by some whites against blacks and by some blacks against whites.
2. A *stereotype* is an attitude, shared by large numbers of people, that disregards individual differences and holds that all members of a certain group behave in the same manner. People are making judgments on the basis of stereotypes when they claim that all women are flighty or that all men are male chauvinists.

Prejudices and stereotypes affect many forms of human behavior. Even scientists are not always free of their influence. The best-trained scientists sometimes become so enamored of a particular theory that they refuse to abandon it even in the face of mounting proof that it is wrong. Even in their personal relationships they may judge new acquaintances on the basis of stereotypes that make them suspicious of certain kinds of people who might prove highly congenial if only given a chance.

New experiences, new socialization, new attitudes

We tend to cling to our attitudes in general like a child to a security blanket—and perhaps for some of the same reasons. Yet attitudes are not entirely permanent and unyielding. Sometimes the dyed-in-the-wool Republican switches to the Democratic party. Or a confirmed atheist joins a church—and a devout churchgoer drops out. Public opinion polls taken at intervals over recent decades have shown sharp changes in prevailing attitudes toward many institutions and issues.

One reason attitudes change is that the socialization process continues throughout life. In our early years, our parents are the chief instruments of socialization and we tend to adopt their attitudes as our own. Studies have shown, for example, that prejudices against minority groups are often passed along from parent to child (Horowitz and Horowitz, 1938). Similarly, a very large majority of children in elementary school have been found to favor the same political party as their parents (Hess and Torney, 1967). But as we grow older and are exposed to other socializing influences, the early influence of our parents begins to weaken. Although about 80 percent of elementary school children prefer the same political party as their parents, one study found that the number drops to only about 55 percent among college students (Goldsen et al., 1960).

The freshman year in college is particularly likely to produce attitude change (Freedman, Carlsmith, and Sears, 1970). Up to that time many students have lived in an environment where most people are quite alike in their attitudes. Then as freshmen they suddenly find themselves in the company of teachers and fellow students who hold attitudes they had not previously encountered. Students from a religious and politically conservative background may find themselves exposed to new attitudes of religious skepticism and political liberalism. Students whose family and friends have scoffed at literature and art may find themselves around people who admire Shakespeare and Rembrandt. These new socialization influences may have pronounced effects. Moreover, attitudes acquired in college tend to be long lasting (Newcomb, 1963).

Experiences that come after college can also have an effect. When we take a job, we undergo a new kind of socialization. Each time we change jobs or get a promotion, each time we move to a new neighborhood or a new community, we come under new influences. We can also be swayed by what we read and by what we see on television. The world changes and we change with it. Our attitudes can be compared to a house that undergoes frequent remodeling, expansion, and repainting over the years. In some ways the house never changes, yet it is never really the same.

Attitude change and the theory of cognitive dissonance

What kinds of new experiences and new information are most likely to produce attitude changes? One answer comes from proponents of what is called the *theory of cognitive dissonance.* This theory maintains that we have a strong urge to be consistent and rational in our thinking and to preserve agreement and harmony among our beliefs, feelings, and behavior—and therefore our attitudes. When consistency and harmony are broken, we experience cognitive dissonance. We may manage to tolerate the inconsistency, as the Joneses did in the case of Mayor Smith. But cognitive dissonance tends to be highly uncomfortable, and we may be strongly motivated to restore harmony by making some kind of adjustment.

In some cases, new factual information is enough to create cognitive dissonance and bring about a change in attitude. For example, many people who were once strongly opposed to birth control have been greatly influenced by all the factual information that has appeared in recent years about the population explosion and the danger of worldwide overcrowding. They once had the cognitive belief that a growing population is a good thing. This cognitive belief has now changed, and their attitude toward birth control has changed with it.

Events that have a strong emotional impact may also create an inconsistency that calls for change. For an example, imagine what would happen if a man who had always regarded women as second-class citizens found himself in love with a woman who was an ardent feminist. Or consider an actual laboratory experiment in which college women underwent a deeply emotional experience related to cigarette smoking. The women, all heavy smokers, were asked to act out a scene in which the experimenter pretended to be a physician and they his patients. Each subject, visiting the "doctor," got bad news about a persistent cough from which she had been suffering; her X ray had shown lung cancer; immediate surgery was required; before the operation she and the doctor would have to discuss the difficulty, pain, and risk. The experimenter tried to keep the scene as realistic as possible and to involve each subject emotionally to the greatest possible degree. As a result, almost all the women quit or drastically cut down on smoking. A follow-up 18 months later found that they continued to show a significant change in their smoking habits (Mann and Janis, 1968).

Do attitudes change behavior—or vice versa?

It seems logical that a change in an attitude, caused by new beliefs or new emotional responses, should cause a change in behavior. Yet, strangely enough, the sequence of events is often exactly the opposite. In many cases, the change in behavior comes first, and this new behavior creates the change in attitude.

Many studies have shown that experimental manipulation of behavior can produce remarkable results. One such experiment concerned the highly controversial action of President Gerald Ford in extending a blanket pardon to his predecessor, Richard Nixon, for any crimes committed during the Watergate incident. College students who strongly opposed the pardon were asked to write essays taking the opposite view and justifying Ford's action. This simple act of writing an essay tended to create a more favorable attitude toward the pardon (Cooper, Zanna, and Taves, 1978). A similar experiment was conducted with students who favored the legalization of marijuana. After they were asked to write an essay opposing legalization, their attitudes tended to show considerable change (Fazio, Zanna, and Cooper, 1977).

In our everyday lives, new social situations often push us in the direction of changes in behavior, and these in turn often lead to changes in attitudes. This has been especially noticeable in recent years in the attitudes of whites toward blacks and of blacks toward whites. In general, it has been found that people who have attended school or worked with members of the other race hold more favorable attitudes, while those who have had no interracial contacts tend to feel less favorable (Pettigrew, 1969). Undoubtedly the explanation is that new forms of behavior—that is, dealing with members of the other race, studying or working with them, and treating them as friendly companions—have produced attitude changes. The theory of cognitive dissonance maintains that the friendly behavior produced an imbalance that was remedied by abandoning the disapproving attitude.

Making a decision as a form of behavior change

One type of behavior likely to produce attitude change is the mere act of making a decision. In a classic experiment, a psychologist posing as a market researcher asked a woman to examine eight electrical appliances (a toaster, coffee maker, and so on) and rate them in terms of how attractive she found them. Once she had done this, the psychologist picked out two appliances that she liked equally well and asked her to choose one of them as a reward for helping in the study. Her choice was wrapped up and presented to her. Then she was asked to rate the eight appliances once more. This procedure was repeated with a number of different subjects—always with the same results. On the second rating, the women gave a higher mark than before to the appliance they had selected and received as a gift. But they gave a lower mark to the other appliance that had been offered to them—the one they had rejected (Brehm, 1956). Once they had made their decision between the two appliances, they emphasized the good points of the one they had chosen and looked unfavorably on the one they had turned down.

People who buy an automobile often find themselves in a similar situation. In the advertisements and in the showrooms a number of models look extremely attractive. But only one of them can be purchased. Once the decision has been made, automobile buyers behave very much like the women in the appliance study. One study showed that they tended to take pleasure in continuing to read ads for that particular model but avoided advertisements for others (Ehrlich et al., 1957). They seemed to be looking for praise of their car, confirming the wisdom of their decision to buy it. They shunned any conflicting claims that might have raised doubts. In the case of both cars and appliances, dissonance theory would hold that choosing between attractive alternatives made these people uncomfortable. They relieved the dissonance by deciding that the alternative they chose was clearly superior, and they were determined to cling to this new attitude.

"Persuasive communications" and attitude change

Up to this point, the discussion has been confined to attitude changes that occur as the result of our own experiences. But all of us are under constant outside pressure as well. Politicians bombard us with speeches and press releases intended to foster favorable attitudes toward them and their party. Advertisers spend millions of dollars every year to try to create favorable attitudes toward their products. Many organizations work hard to win support for such causes as conservation, kindness to animals, and pollution control.

To social psychologists, all such attempts to change attitudes by transmitting information and making emotional appeals are known as *persuasive communications.* Because persuasive communications potentially have a great effect on our society, they have been studied in considerable depth.

Is anybody listening? If so, who?

Any attempt to influence the attitudes of large numbers of people faces many handicaps. For one thing, persuasive communications do not ordinarily reach very many people. A politician may make the most impassioned and convincing plea for support—yet his speech will be

Handing out a persuasive communication: Whom will it reach? What effect will it have?

heard in person by only a few thousand people at most. Even if part of the speech is shown on television, it will still reach only a small proportion of Americans. One study indicates that only about one person in four watches national television news on any given evening (Robinson, 1971). Moreover those who do watch seem to pay only casual attention, for they remember very little of what they have seen. A study found that viewers questioned later in the evening could recall only 6 percent of the news items they had seen (Neuman, 1976). Newspaper accounts of a political speech reach and impress an even smaller audience, and editorials have a smaller readership still.

It has also been found that the audience likely to watch or read any appeal for attitude change—and to pay attention to it—is determined largely by a factor called *selective exposure.* This means that, by and large, persuasive communications reach only people who are already persuaded. The audience that turns out for a Democratic rally is overwhelmingly composed of confirmed Democrats. The people who read magazines favoring the conservation of natural resources are already dedicated to conservation. Since we all tend to associate with people we like and to read or listen to communications we find interesting, we are exposed mostly to people and communications we already agree with.

And who are you to tell me to change?

Let us now assume that a persuasive communication does succeed in reaching us, despite the handicaps. It argues for a viewpoint to which we are opposed. To adopt it, we will have to change an attitude. Will the persuasive communication actually persuade us?

Several factors help determine the answer. One of the most important is the matter of who is trying to persuade us—in other words, *the source of the communication.* Some sources are likely to have considerable influence. Others are less likely to convince us and may in fact only make us more opposed to what they are proposing.

The importance of the source was convincingly demonstrated in one of the very first experiments on the effectiveness of persuasive communications. Subjects in this study were asked to read a controversial argument on the development of an atomic energy project. Half the subjects were told that the argument was written by a well-known atomic scientist. The other half were told that it came from the Soviet newspaper *Pravda.* As might be expected, there was a great deal more attitude change among subjects who believed that the scientist was the source (Hovland and Weiss, 1951).

Of great significance here is the *credibility of the source.* If the communication comes from someone whose knowledge or motives are suspect—in other words, from a source of low credibility—we tend to disregard it. If it comes from people who clearly know what they are talking about—in other words, from a source of high credibility—we are much more likely to accept it. The effectiveness is enhanced if the source seems to be fair, objective, and not particularly interested in wielding influence. A statement that Car X is superior is more impressive coming from a friend who understands mechanics than coming from a dealer who is trying to sell Car X.

What kinds of communications are most effective?

Just as the source influences effectiveness, so does the nature of the communication—that is, what kinds of arguments it presents and how and when. In general, appeals to the emotions tend to be especially effective (Weiss and Fine, 1958). One experimenter, dealing with actual voters in an actual election campaign, found that an appeal to vote for a candidate was considerably more successful when it was primarily emotional than when it was primarily logical (Hartman, 1936). Appeals to fear are often particularly effective, as was shown by the experiment cited earlier in which women acted out the role of patients suffering from lung cancer. But sometimes the arousal of fear may backfire (Janis and Feshbach, 1953), presumably because the listener becomes so upset as to try to forget the whole matter.

The effectiveness of a communication addressed to an intelligent audience appears to be increased if it presents a fair rather than a one-sided argument, admitting that the other side also has its points (Hovland, Lumsdaine, and Sheffield, 1949). With a less intelligent audience, a one-sided argument may be more effective, perhaps because the listeners would be confused by hearing both sides (Aronson, 1972). The one-sided argument also has a greater influence on an audience already leaning toward that side, while a fair argument is more likely to influence people leaning in the opposite direction (Hovland, Lumsdaine, and Sheffield, 1949).

The communication and the listener

A final factor that helps determine the effectiveness of a persuasive communication is the audience it reaches. Who is listening may be just as important as what is said and the source of the communication. For

Psychology and Society: Change for the better: it is easier than many people think

One of the great barriers to progress—for both individuals and society as a whole—is the fact that many people take a pessimistic view of the nature-nurture argument. Although there is strong evidence that most human behavior is influenced just as much by environment and learning as by heredity—and often more so—many people still cling to the belief that human nature is determined at birth and resists any attempt to alter or improve it. This belief is evident in such familiar expressions as "People don't change," "That's just human nature," or "That kid was born to be bad." About themselves, people often say, "I can't help it; I'm just built thay way," or "I was born unlucky."

The belief that human nature is largely inherited is a powerful deterrent to change in attitudes and behavior. In one experiment, university students were asked whether they thought the next five years might change their attitudes about some of their personality characteristics (such as whether they regarded themselves as trusting, curious, and so on) and toward various social issues (such as capital punishment and legalization of marijuana). It turned out that their answers depended largely on whether they thought their present attitudes were the result of nature or nurture (Festinger, 1954). If they considered an attitude to be largely a matter of learning (as a majority did for being trusted or for favoring legalization of marijuana) they were significantly more likely to foresee possible change than if they regarded the attitude as something innate (as a majority did for the trait of curiosity).

Unfortunately our society has a way of implying that personality traits—and especially any undesirable ones—are inborn and immutable. Many people become convinced that they are just naturally "dumb," or "awkward," or "bad." Accepting these labels as representing their inherited nature makes it unlikely that they will even consider change possible, much less try to achieve it. Suppose, for example, that an adolescent boy who is in constant trouble feels he was "born" to be a delinquent. He is likely to be totally unresponsive to any appeals to change his attitudes and behavior. If he could be convinced that his delinquency is the result of environmental influences, as it probably is, he would be much more receptive to the possibility of change.

Perhaps the greatest potential contribution of the social psychologists to human happiness and progress is the evidence they have accumulated about the influence of nurture in the form of the social environment. The findings indicate that personality, attitudes, and behavior are more elastic than is generally realized and that change for the better—in both human happiness and the way society functions—is always possible.

example, some people are much more easily persuaded than others. Indeed experiments have shown that people who tend to change their attitudes under one set of circumstances and in response to one kind of communication are also likely to change under different circumstances and in response to different kinds of communications (Hovland and Janis, 1959). The crucial factor seems to be one's own opinion of oneself. People who are low in self-esteem tend to be much more easily persuaded than people who are high in self-esteem (Cohen, 1959). Similarly, people who are anxious about social acceptance are more easily persuaded than those who have little anxiety (Sears, 1967).

In an odd way, the possibility that listeners will change their attitudes is also affected by their beliefs about the nature-nuture argument. This fact is so significant—especially as an influence that can discourage change for the better—that its implications are discussed in a box on Psychology and Society.

Our search for the reasons people act as they do: attribution theories

You have probably heard this old joke: A psychoanalyst runs into a woman acquaintance who greets him with a cheery "Good morning"—and he walks away asking himself, "I wonder what she meant by that?" Like many jokes, it contains a glimmer of wisdom. All of us spend a good deal of our time trying to analyze why other people acted as they did, because only if we know their reasons can we respond appropriately.

A friend pays you a compliment. If you decide the words were sincere, you respond with pleasure. If you decide that the compliment was merely a hypocritical prelude to a request for a favor, you are turned off. At a family reunion an elderly uncle slumps into a chair and grasps at his chest, complaining of severe pain. You may rush him to a hospital emergency room—or, if you suspect he is merely bidding for attention and sympathy, do nothing.

The search for the causes of behavior is the basis of what are called *attribution theories,* which attempt to explain why and how we go about making the search. The various theories all assume that we want to know why people act as they do because we want our social interactions to have the most favorable possible outcome (Heider, 1944)—that is, we hope to avoid embarrassing and possibly costly mistakes and maximize the satisfactions and rewards. If we can attribute behavior to some underlying motive or other cause, we have a valuable clue to where we stand, what is likely to happen next, and how we can best deal with the situation. Thus we all perform a good deal of amateur psychoanalysis, seeking in various ways and as best we can to interpret the meanings and future implications of behavior.

Dispositional and situational factors and the "fundamental attribution error"

For almost any action, there are a number of possible explanations. Note these simple examples: One morning a waitress smiles at us and says she hopes we enjoy our meal. On the other hand the man at the filling station scowls as he takes our money. One possibility is that the waitress is a basically warm and friendly person, and the man at the filling station is hostile and bad tempered. In that event their behavior was due to what are called *dispositional factors,* or deep-seated and consistent personality traits. There is also the possibility, however, that the waitress acted as she did only because her boss had just warned her against being her natural surly self around customers—and the man at the filling station, though ordinarily good-humored, had a bad headache. In that event their behavior was caused by *situational factors,* or circumstances that forced them in that direction.

We usually attribute other people's actions to dispositional factors, thus ignoring social psychology's evidence that people are not nearly so consistent as generally assumed, and that their behavior so often depends on the circumstances. This tendency to favor dispositional factors—rather than aspects of the situation that may provide a far better explanation—is so powerful and widespread that it has been called the *fundamental attribution error* (Ross, 1977).

Why we should fall into this mistake—often in judging others, sometimes even in judging ourselves—is difficult to explain. Perhaps, as one investigator has suggested, thinking that we know what people are really like gives us at least an illusion of being able to predict their behavior and is therefore comforting (Jones, 1979).

An attribution theorist's quiz game and its strange results

To demonstrate the fundamental attribution error, a group of psychologists devised an experiment that produced almost unbelievable results. The subjects participated as pairs in a laboratory quiz game. By lot, one member of each pair was assigned to make up the questions, the other to try to answer them. In front of both of them, the experimenters told the quiz maker to try to stump the quiz taker by posing questions that, though not impossible for someone possessing a great deal of general information, were difficult and challenging. Obviously, the situation was rigged in favor of the questioner, for everyone has acquired obscure pieces of information that another person could hardly be expected to know. The quiz maker could easily come up with questions that were almost sure to baffle the quiz taker. That is exactly what happened—the quiz takers, by and large, did very badly in the game.

The strange thing was how the game affected the quiz takers' opinion of the quiz makers. Typically, they ignored the unfair circumstances and decided that the quiz makers were people who possessed knowledge far superior to their own. In other words, they proved to be victims of the fundamental attribution error—explaining the behavior of the quiz makers in dispositional rather than situational terms. So, likewise, did other subjects who watched the quiz game, even though they too knew how it favored the quiz maker (Ross, Amabile, and Steinmetz, 1977).

Drawing inferences about the personalities of other people from their behavior—regardless of how much the situation might have affected that behavior—leads to many unwarranted assumptions by teachers about their students, by family members about other members of the family, probably even by psychotherapists and counselors about their clients (Jones, 1979). It helps explain why "con artists," who are often psychopaths adept at exuding a false charm, find so many willing victims.

Compounding the error: guessing people's dispositions by guessing how they feel

The fundamental attribution error sometimes gets compounded because we reach our mistaken conclusions on the basis of mistaken impressions. An example occurred in an experiment in which psychologists made a videotape, without a sound track, of a college woman being interviewed. They then showed the videotape to two groups of male subjects. One group was told that the subject of the interview was sex, the other that the subject was politics. Afterward the subjects were asked to rate the woman on a scale of how nervous and anxious she seemed to be. Their ratings turned out to depend on what they had been told about the interview. If they thought the subject was sex, they found that the woman showed considerable anxiety. If they thought the subject was politics, they found that she showed less anxiety. Thus exactly the same behavior—the same videotape of the same woman—created two very different impressions.

Next the two groups of subjects were asked to rate the woman's general tendency to be calm or flustered—in other words, her basic disposition. The results followed the same pattern. Subjects who believed that the interview was about sex, and that it had flustered her, decided she was just naturally inclined to be apprehensive, nervous, and anxious. The other subjects did not (Snyder and Frankel, 1976).

In part, the experiment provided another demonstration of what was shown in the make-believe quiz game. The subjects jumped to the erroneous conclusion that acting flustered during a sex interview—a situation that might produce a certain amount of anxiety in almost everyone—indicated a disposition to be easily flustered in general. But the mistake was compounded by the fact that they only *thought* the woman acted flustered.

Why did this happen? We can assume that the subjects took the situation into account in judging the woman's behavior. They felt that a sex interview would naturally produce anxiety. Therefore they interpreted her behavior during the interview as showing anxiety. But in judging her general disposition, they fell into the fundamental attribution error and ignored situational factors. Thus they made a double error. They inferred her basic disposition from behavior that was itself only inferred. They made two guesses—either or both of which may have been totally wrong.

All of us are probably guilty at times of this compounded error. We watch person A being treated by person B in what we consider an abusive manner. Such treatment would make us angry—so we assume that A is angry. Then, on the basis of this assumption, we further assume that A tends to be hot-tempered in general. We watch person C making a fuss over person D. Such attention from C, whom we like very much, would greatly please us—so we assume that D is pleased. Then, on the basis of this assumption, we further assume that D is friendly and easily pleased in general. We could be dead wrong in thinking that A is angry or that D is pleased—and how they happen to feel in this particular situation does not necessarily reflect their basic disposition anyway.

Ignoring our own influence on other people's actions

One situational factor we often ignore, in committing the fundamental attribution error, is the effect of our own behavior on the behavior of others. We do not fully recognize that we ourselves, by the way we act, may produce the very actions that we then incorrectly interpret as indicating another person's deep-seated personality traits. This fact was best demonstrated in an experiment that was simple in design but had some surprising and significant results.

The subjects were college men. Each of them was merely asked to become acquainted over the telephone, in a ten-minute conversation, with a college woman he had never met. Before the call was made, the subject saw what he was told was a photograph of the woman. Actually the photograph was of someone else. Half the subjects saw the picture of a woman who had been judged particularly attractive by an independent panel. The other subjects saw the picture of a woman who had been judged physically unattractive.

The phone calls were made and recorded on tape. In analyzing the tapes, the experimenters found something that seems utterly baffling. There seemed to be two completely different types of women on the phone. One type—those believed by the male students to be the person in the attractive photo—sounded warm, charming, and humorous. The other type—those believed by the men to be the person in the unattractive photo—sounded cold, clumsy, and humorless. How could this be?

The answer is simple. There also seemed to be two very different types of men on the tapes. If the male subjects thought their telephone partner was attractive, they expected her to be warm and charming—and they themselves were friendly, eager, and easy to respond to. If they thought she was unattractive, they expected her to be cold and humorless—and they themselves cast a pall over the phone call, inviting a chilly and stilted response. By thus setting the tone of the conversation, they pushed their partner into the very kind of behavior they expected (Snyder, Tanke, and Berscheid, 1977).

The psychologists who conducted the experiment call it a conspicuous example of a *self-fulfilling prophecy*—that is, a prediction that comes true not because it was right but simply because it was made in the first place. In this case the gloomy prophecy made by half the male subjects was that their telephone partner would be unsociable—and since they acted accordingly, the prophecy was fulfilled. The other half of the men did exactly the opposite—and made their optimistic prediction come true. Self-fulfilling prophecies based on false attributions and other mistaken impressions are commonplace, with often dangerous implications discussed in a box on Psychology and Society.

Some everyday applications

The telephone experiment makes a point worth remembering in social relationships: In everyday dealings with other people, it pays to be an optimist. When you have high hopes that the other person will be likable, your own friendly and accepting actions go a long way toward guaranteeing that the person will indeed behave in a likable manner. But if you expect to dislike someone, your own pessimistic and sour actions almost guarantee a cold and unsympathetic response. It is probably equally true that expecting other people to like us also tends to be a self-fulfilling prophecy. If we expect to be liked, we behave in a likable fashion. If we fear rejection, we tend to act tense, guarded, and not likable at all—and thus bring about the very thing we dreaded. By and large, people treat us not only as we treat them but also as we expect to be treated.

Psychology and Society: How self-fulfilling prophecies can cause damage

The elementary schoolroom is one place where the self-fulfilling prophecy flourishes—often with harmful effects on some of the pupils. Teachers, it has been found, frequently decide very early on that some pupils can be expected to do well, while others are not worth much attention. They may make this decision on the basis of personal appearance and social class (Rist, 1970). Or they may have taught a pupil's older brother or sister and expect the younger child to be cut from the same cloth (Seaver, 1973). Once teachers have made their prophecy, for whatever reason, they tend to ignore their "dull" pupils and provide much more attention and help to the "bright" ones (Cooper, 1979). This behavior has a considerable effect on the pupils' actual progress in the classroom (Crano and Mellon, 1978). The ones tagged as "dull," possibly through no fault of their own, have little opportunity or encouragement to change that reputation.

Compounding the problem is the fact that a prophecy about another person's behavior may seem to come true, in the eyes of the prophecy maker, regardless of how the other person actually does behave. Once we have decided that people are likely to be "bright" or "dull" (or friendly, hostile, charming, humorless, or anything else) we are likely to interpret whatever they do as evidence of that trait. Many actions do not in themselves tell very much about the person who performs them—and an observer who starts with a bias is free to assign whatever meaning the bias dictates (Darley and Fazio, 1980). Teachers may find the very same action to be a sign of stupidity in a "dull" pupil but of intelligence in a "bright" pupil.

Self-fulfilling prophecies and other aspects of attribution theories, along with the power of first impressions, influence our society in many ways. All of us are inclined to judge behavior—and sometimes create it—on the basis of what we expect others to do. Our expectation can be created by a stereotype claiming that certain types of behavior are characteristic of members of racial or ethnic groups, or of social classes or the two sexes. Or the expectation can represent a hasty first impression—or even what we have heard, true or not, of the other person's reputation. Unfortunately, such an expectation can have far-reaching and drastic results, especially when it is held by a person with the power of a teacher, employer, police officer, or psychiatrist. As one study of the matter has concluded, an expectation about another person can "significantly affect the life" of that person—"perhaps for the better, but as many who do this research fear, often for the worse" (Darley and Fazio, 1980).

The attribution theories in general offer another guide to everyday living. They tell us that we had best be cautious and tentative when we act as amateur analysts looking for the reasons behind other people's actions. Yet the attempt at analysis, it should be added, is often useful and not necessarily doomed to failure. Despite the difficulties, we often manage to make a careful enough study to judge people more or less correctly. We take account, when we can, of situational factors. (If a woman tells us she likes her job, we try to determine whether her words reflect her real opinion or merely the fact that the boss may be listening.) We search for any information that would indicate whether an act is typical or just an uncharacteristic incident. (We do not necessarily decide that a man is hot tempered because of a single display of anger.) When possible we seek and consider the opinions of other observers (which can help us determine whether the woman really likes her job and whether the man is generally hot tempered). Other people are so important to us that we simply have to try to understand them—we have to make attributions of some kind—and we do the best we can.

Self-perception theory—or "Why did I do that?"

Besides seeking the reasons for other people's behavior, we also make frequent attempts to analyze our own actions—especially on occasions when we find ourselves doing something we cannot quite understand. We try to gain some perception of what it was about ourselves or the situation that made us act as we did (Bem, 1972). The way we make the search is the basis of a special kind of attribution theory called *self-perception theory*.

Some examples you may have experienced are these: You are playing a friendly game of tennis, lose your temper, and throw your racket into the net—even though the outcome of the game means very little to you. Watching a charity telethon, you impulsively call the number shown on the screen and pledge a contribution much larger than you can really afford. You are puzzled. You are likely to ask yourself, "Why did I do that?"

Again, as in the case of other people's behavior, we can decide that we were pushed into our behavior by situational factors: We lost our temper because our tennis opponent or the spectators did something that was bound to provoke us. We pledged too much to the charity because the people on the telethon were so attractive and persuasive. Or we can decide on dispositional factors: We lost our temper because we hate to lose and are sometimes easily angered. We were overgenerous to the charity because we are generous at heart and do not always stop to think before we act.

Strangely, when we look for the causes of our own behavior we tend to look for situational rather than dispositional factors—just the opposite of what we do when analyzing other people. If we do badly in school, for example, our faculty advisor is likely to attribute our failure to laziness or lack of ability. We ourselves are likely to attribute it to too heavy a course load, emotional strain over personal problems, or some other situational factor (Jones and Nisbett, 1972). Even if we do something rather praiseworthy, such as stopping on a highway to help an elderly couple change a tire, the same thing is likely to happen. An outsider watching our behavior would probably attribute it to a consistent disposition to be friendly and helpful. We ourselves would be inclined to emphasize the situational factors. We would say that the couple seemed very nice, unable to cope with their problem, and badly in need of help.

Attribution theorists believe that our self-perceptions have an important bearing on changes in attitude. When we manage to find situational factors, as we usually try to do, we have no reason to question or change our attitudes. When we are forced to decide that dispositional factors caused our behavior, however, we may be forced to reexamine and revise our attitudes (Nisbett and Valins, 1972). For example, if we have to admit that our poor grades were indeed caused by our lackadaisical attitude toward study, rather than by circumstances that were beyond our control, we may very well find ourselves jolted into making a change.

How we form our social relationships: the forces of attraction and liking

Much of the chapter has stressed how other people influence our behavior—sometimes through persuasive communications, more often simply because of the example they set and our tendency to conform to the group in which we find ourselves. The question now arises: What determines the kinds of people who influence us most? In particular, in this diverse society, why do we become members of one group and not another?

It is of course the people around us—those with whom we have our closest and most frequent social relationships—who have the greatest impact on our attitudes and our behavior. Therefore, social psychology has extensively studied the forces that attract us to others and make us like them and associate with them. The key finding has been aptly summarized in a single sentence: "We like those who reward us, and the more they reward us the better we like them" (Berscheid and Walster, 1974). But fully understanding that sentence requires an examination of what it is that we find rewarding about other people—and why.

Propinquity and familiarity: "I like you because I know you"

To a considerable extent, social relationships are dictated by sheer chance. The family you happen to be born into determines the culture and subculture into which you are socialized, which in turn helps shape your attitudes. The neighborhood you happen to grow up in provides the playmates, classmates, and teachers who influence your childhood. Even in later life, you do not have full freedom of choice. Going to college because it is close to your home or offers you a scholarship can place you in a group of students and instructors very different from those you might find on another campus. Taking a job puts you into a group of co-workers who already happen to be there. Once you have your own home, the people next door move in or out without your permission.

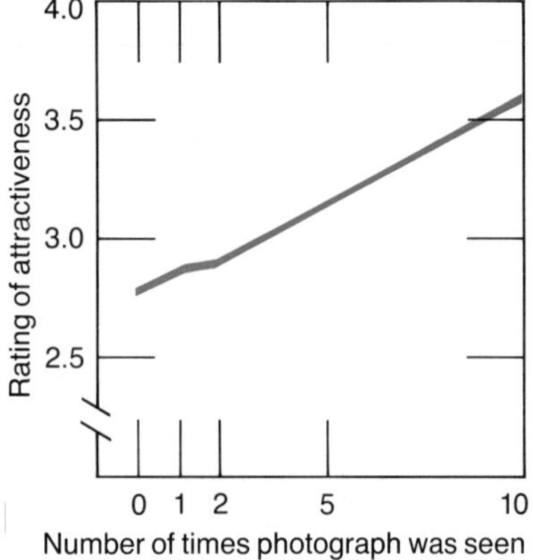

Figure 15-8 Even a photograph looks better the more familiar it becomes *The ratings of attractiveness were made by subjects asked to look at the photograph of another person. The lowest ratings were made by subjects who had never seen the photo before, the highest by subjects who had seen it most often (Zajonc, 1968).*

Some social psychologists have concluded that *propinquity*—or nearness—is the most powerful factor of all determining our associates. Obviously we cannot become part of a group whose members we never even see. Moreover it has been found that just being around other people—knowing them and getting used to them—inclines us to consider them attractive and likable. One experiment on the effect of such *familiarity* brought together pairs of subjects who did not know each other. They did not speak but merely sat across from each other in the laboratory. Some pairs saw each other on only a few occasions, others as many as a dozen times. Afterward they were asked how much they liked each other. The more often they had been together—even in this casual fashion—the greater was the mutual attraction (Freedman, Carlsmith, and Suomi, 1970). Similar results have been obtained merely by exposing subjects to a photograph of another person, as is shown in Figure 15-8.

Other studies show that people are likely to be most friendly with those who are familiar because they live next door in a college dor-

A track meet has provided these two athletes with two of the factors that help create interpersonal attraction—propinquity and similarity.

mitory, an apartment building, or a row of houses (Festinger, Schachter, and Back, 1950). On some occasions the mere prospect of becoming familiar seems to make other people more attractive. One study found that strangers introduced in a laboratory were more attracted to one another if told they would work together in the future than if they thought they probably would never meet again.

Similarity: "I like you because we seem so alike"

Though propinquity and familiarity are powerful forces in determining social interaction, they are by no means the only factors. Even among the people with whom you have frequent contacts, you manage to pick and choose. You spend a great deal of your time with companions of your own selection and deliberately create your closest friendships. You join groups you like and stay away from groups you find uncongenial.

One important factor in this picking and choosing is *similarity*. Given the opportunity, and all other things being equal, we tend to be attracted to people who are very much like us—or at least whom we perceive to be similar. The best demonstration was an experiment performed by a psychologist who arranged to operate a men's dormitory at a large university. The assignment of roommates was based on questionnaires and interviews about attitudes, interests, and tastes. Some roommates were put together because their replies showed them to be very similar, others because they were sharply different in many respects. As the term went on, it developed that roommates who were much alike usually got along well and became good friends. Those who were dissimilar were less likely to develop a very close relationship (Newcomb, 1961).

Indeed one reason propinquity and familiarity breed attraction is that most of the people we happen to know are usually similar to us to at least some extent. If nothing else, we have a mutual interest in the course

In choosing their companions, these men have obviously been birds of a feather.

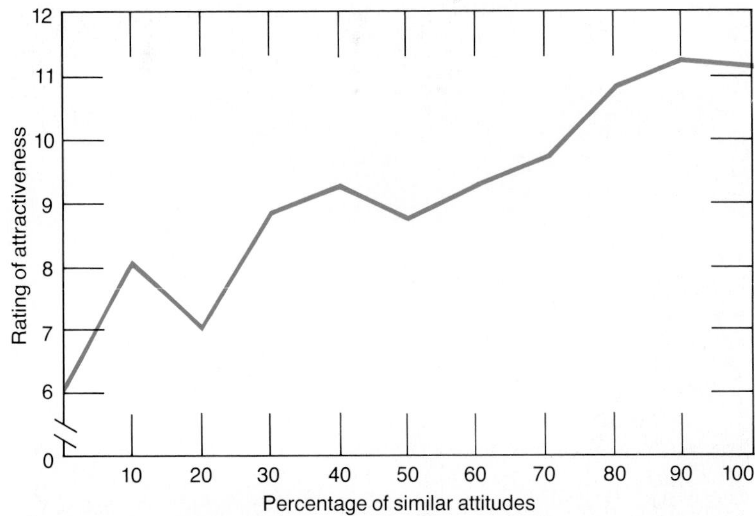

Figure 15-9 The more similar the attitudes, the greater the attraction *The graph shows the results of an experiment in which college students were asked to rate a stranger on a scale of attractiveness. Their only information about the stranger came from reading a set of replies supposedly given to a questionnaire about attitudes toward politics and other issues. When the experimenter rigged the stranger's answers to indicate attitudes different from those of the subjects, the attractiveness rating was low. But it went up steadily as the percentage of shared attitudes seemed to increase, forming an almost perfect correlation (Byrne, 1969).*

that we and our college classmates are taking or in the job we share with co-workers. Usually we find ourselves thrown together with people of roughly the same age, education, and socioeconomic class. Often, therefore, we have many attitudes in common—and it has been found that the degree to which we find another person attractive shows a high correlation with the number of similar attitudes we share or think we share. Note the almost straight-line relationship shown in Figure 15-9.

"I like you because you like me—and are good at what you do"

Many studies have shown that we tend to be attracted to people who seem to be attracted to us (Tagiuri, 1958) or who hold a high opinion of us (Worchel, 1961). We also tend to like people in whose company we have achieved satisfactions, as can be observed in the camaraderie that usually flourishes among members of a winning athletic team.

We seem to be especially attracted to people who at first do not seem to like us or hold us in high regard, then later change their mind (Aronson and Linder, 1965). Apparently there is a special reward—and thus a strong tendency toward attraction—in winning over a person who was originally critical. In general, we also have a tendency to be attracted to competent people—those who are good at what they do, whether it is singing, solving mathematical problems, playing basketball, or driving a car. We seem, however, to like very competent people to display a few obvious human frailties (Bales and Slater, 1955), so that they do not put us to shame.

Physical attractiveness: "I like you because I like your looks"

Most of us like to deny that physical appearance has anything to do with our feelings toward other people. Beauty, we have been told, is only skin deep. Some of the greatest men and women in history have been physically unprepossessing or downright ugly. It seems unfair to like or dislike someone just because of facial features resulting from an accident

The camaraderie of a winning basketball team—an example of liking people in whose company we have achieved satisfaction.

of heredity. For more than a half-century psychologists have been asking college students what they value most in a person of the opposite sex, and *physical attractiveness* has always wound up near the bottom of the list (Tesser and Brodie, 1971).

In actual fact, however, physical attractiveness is more influential than most people care to admit. Even children judge one another on the basis of appearance. As early as the nursery school years, it has been found, the attractive boys are the most popular, the unattractive boys the least popular (Dion and Berscheid, 1972). Attractive children also receive preferential treatment from adults (Dion, 1972).

Many studies have demonstrated the ways in which adult relationships are influenced by physical attractiveness. In one study, college men were asked to rate the quality of an essay supposedly written by a college woman. When they believed that the writer was an unusually attractive woman, they gave the essay the highest marks. When they had no clues about her appearance, their marks fell in the middle range. When they believed she was unattractive, they gave the lowest marks (Landy and Sigall, 1974).

Standards of physical attractiveness have changed through history, as can be seen from old sculptures and paintings, and differ widely from one society to another. At any given time and place, however, there seems to be general agreement. In our own society, studies of ratings of photographs made by numerous subjects—from most attractive to least attractive—have shown fairly high correlations (Freedman and Suomi, 1970). Fortunately for those of us who have never won beauty contests, however, the correlations are by no means perfect. In one study that

What broke the ice? A mutual feeling of physical attractiveness?

used a number of photographs of children, teenagers, and adults, every one of the photos was ranked first by at least one subject (Cross and Cross, 1971).

Why physical attractiveness counts: the matter of first impressions

Why is physical attractiveness so influential? One reason seems to be that it is immediately and obviously apparent. When we meet someone for the first time, we can only guess whether this person is similar to us in attitudes, interests, and tastes. We have no clear clues about competence. We can see at a glance, however, how well the person meets our own standards of attractiveness—and thus move toward acceptance or rejection.

First impressions, it has been found, have a strong and lasting influence. If we like people from the start, even merely because of their physical appearance, we tend to keep on liking them—no matter if some of their subsequent behavior is objectionable. If we dislike them at the start, we are likely to continue to dislike them—even if their subsequent behavior is above reproach.

In one experiment, subjects first saw a stranger—actually a man who was an accomplice of the experimenter—in a laboratory waiting room. In his dealings with a secretary who was in charge of the waiting room, the stranger was at times extremely impolite, belligerent, and demanding. At other times, in the presence of other subjects, he was polite and pleasant. Later the subjects met the accomplice-stranger on three to twelve other occasions. As would be expected from what is known about the effect of familiarity, they liked the "pleasant" stranger better when they saw him twelve times than when they saw him only three times. But increased contact did not change their ratings of the "unpleasant" stranger (Freedman and Suomi, 1970). The effect of the bad first impression outweighed familiarity.

Why first impressions persist: implicit personality theory

Why are first impressions of people so strong and long lasting? Social psychologists say the reason is that we carry around a sort of working theory about people and their personalities. We have concluded that certain personality traits generally go together. If something convinces us at the start that a new acquaintance is "cold," for example, we automatically assume that this person is also likely to be irritable, humorless, unsociable, and self-centered. But if we perceive the new acquaintance as "warm," we expect this warmth to be accompanied by a good disposition, a sense of humor, friendliness, and generosity (Kelley, 1950). This belief that personality traits come in clusters is called an *implicit personality theory.* All of us seem to hold such a theory, without being aware of it.

Most of us believe, as part of our implicit personality theory, that physically attractive people also have many other attractive qualities. In one study in which subjects were asked to judge the personality characteristics of people shown in photographs, the subjects read all kinds of virtues into photos of attractive people. They judged the attractive people, as compared with the unattractive ones, to be considerably more interesting, strong, sensitive, sociable, poised, modest, outgoing, and sexually responsive. This was true of both male or female judges (Dion, Berscheid, and Walster, 1972).

Not all physically attractive people, of course, are admirable in every other respect—and the theory that desirable traits always come in clusters can lead us into error in other ways as well. For one thing, it inclines us to think of people as more consistent than they really are. But our theory has been developed through experience and is probably right a good deal more often than it is wrong. Right or wrong, it is one of the tools we use in conducting the social relationships that—as everything in this chapter has emphasized—are such an important part of our lives.

SUMMARY

Learning—and conforming to—the ways of society

1. *Social psychology* is the study of how the human being "thinks, feels, and behaves in social situations"—or, in broader terms, the study of how people influence and are influenced by other people.
2. *Socialization* is the process through which children are integrated into the *society* through exposure to the actions and opinions of other members of the society.
3. Children are socialized into the society's *culture,* or way of life—including its language, beliefs, political structure, rules, patterns of behavior, and the physical objects it produces and uses as part of its life-style.
4. A complex society like ours also has many *subcultures,* or ways of life dictated by different national and ethnic backgrounds, religions, occupations, and social classes.
5. Most people follow the customs they have learned and behave as they believe they are expected to behave. They display strong tendencies toward (a) *obedience,* or submission to authority, and (b) *conformity,* or the yielding by individuals to pressures from the group in which they find themselves.
6. One reason for conformity is that we depend on the people around us for many of our psychological satisfactions. It is pleasant to win approval as an accepted member of the group—and highly unpleasant to be rejected.
7. Another reason for conformity is that we need guidance from other people in developing an accurate view of our physical and social environment.
8. The need for guidance is the basis of the *theory of social comparison,* which holds that to live successfully we must evaluate our own conduct, abilities, and opinions—and often can do so only by comparing ourselves with other people.
9. There are two kinds of conformity: (a) In *expedient conformity,* we merely pay lip service to the opinions and standards of other people, without changing our real feelings. (b) In *true conformity,* we change both our behavior and our private beliefs because we have made our social comparisons and decided that the group is right.

Our attitudes toward life: how we acquire, cling to, and sometimes change them

10. *Attitudes* are strong, deeply ingrained opinions and feelings that we think of as principles that shape our conduct. We are very much "for" things toward which we have a positive attitude, and very much "against" things toward which we have a negative attitude.
11. Attitudes, though powerful, are not necessarily consistent or based on evidence. Two kinds of attitudes that often fly in the face of fact are (a) *prejudices* (for example, against other ethnic groups or religions) and (b) *stereotypes,* which assume that all members of a certain group behave in the same manner.
12. Though attitudes tend to persist, they sometimes change. One explanation for change is the *theory of cognitive dissonance,* which maintains that we have a strong desire to preserve agreement and harmony among our beliefs, feelings, and behavior. When there is a conflict—caused by factual information, the arousal of emotions, or the fact that circumstances push us into different behavior—we experience cognitive dissonance and may relieve it by changing our attitude.

"Persuasive communications" and attitude change

13. Attempts by other people to change our attitudes—by transmitting information or making emotional appeals—are called *persuasive communications*.
14. The effectiveness of persuasive communications is affected by *selective exposure*—the fact that most such communications reach only people who are already persuaded. It also depends on (a) the *source of the communication,* (b) the *credibility of the source,* (c) the nature of the communication, and (d) the listener. Listeners who are low in self-esteem or anxious about social acceptance are more easily persuaded.

Our search for the reasons people act as they do: attribution theories

15. All of us spend considerable time seeking the reasons other people acted as they did. Why and how we make the search is the subject of various *attribution theories.*
16. Attribution theories all assume that we want to know the reasons behind other people's behavior because we want our social interactions to have the most favorable possible outcome; therefore we seek clues to where we stand, what is likely to happen next, and how best to handle the situation.
17. We have a strong tendency to attribute other people's behavior to *dispositional factors* rather than to *situational factors* that may provide a far better explanation. Because this tendency is so common—and ignores social psychology's finding that people's behavior is not necessarily consistent and often depends on circumstances—it is called the *fundamental attribution error.*

18. One situational factor we often ignore is the influence of our own behavior on the behavior of others. So strong is this influence that often, because we expect another person to act in a certain way (for example, be friendly or unfriendly), we push the person into exactly the kind of behavior we expected—thus turning our expectation into a *self-fulfilling prophecy*.
19. In seeking the reasons for our own behavior—the subject of *self-perception theory*—we tend to look for situational rather than dispositional factors. When we are forced to accept a dispositional cause, we may change our attitudes accordingly.

How we form our social relationships: the forces of attraction and liking

20. The forces that attract us to other people—and make us like them and associate with them—are important in social psychology because it is our closest associates who have the greatest effect on our attitudes and behavior. It is a general principle that "we like those who reward us, and the more they reward us the better we like them."
21. The most powerful factor may be *propinquity*, or nearness, which occurs by chance because of the family into which we are born, neighborhood, school companions, and co-workers we find on the job. Propinquity is influential because of the effect of *familiarity*—for, in general, the better we know people the better we like them.
22. We are also attracted to people because of (a) *similarity*, especially in attitudes; (b) an indication that they like us; (c) their competence; and (d) *physical attractiveness*.
23. *First impressions* of other people have a strong and lasting effect. The reason is that we seem to hold an *implicit personality theory* that personality traits come in clusters—for example, that physically attractive people are also likely to be warm, sociable, poised, and interesting.

IMPORTANT TERMS

attitude
attribution theory
cognitive dissonance
conformity
credibility of the source
culture
dispositional factors
expedient conformity
familiarity
first impressions
fundamental attribution error
implicit personality theory
obedience
persuasive communications
physical attractiveness
prejudice
propinquity
selective exposure
self-fulfilling prophecy
self-perception theory
similarity
situational factors
social comparison theory
socialization
society
source of the communication
stereotype
subculture
true conformity

SUPPLEMENT:

Aggression, Altruism, and Bystander Apathy

Many questions about social behavior continue to puzzle scientists. One of them has to do with the basic quality of human nature. Is it essentially "good," as the humanistic psychologists maintain? Or is it essentially "evil," as crime statistics and history's records of war and cruelty might indicate? Is it perhaps even neutral—neither good nor evil but capable of being molded in either direction?

Perhaps we will never know the answer. The question may lend itself only to philosophical speculation, not to scientific proof. But science is learning more all the time about the way people sometimes treat each other with aggression and violence, sometimes with great kindness and generosity, and sometimes with thoughtless disdain.

Is aggression bred into our genes?

Some scientists, especially those in fields such as biology, have concluded that *aggression* is a part of our inheritance—indeed, as one of them describes it, "an essential part of the life-preserving organization of instincts" (Lorenz, 1966). They point out that human beings are just another form of animal life, and that the "law of the jungle" dictates that animals must often kill to survive.

Certainly aggression is common and apparently instinctive among lower animals. Even if a rat is raised in isolation—without any chance to observe and learn aggression from others—it will immediately show hostility toward any other rat that enters its cage. It uses the same aggressive tactics employed by other rats of its species (Eibl-Eibesfeldt, 1963).

Observations of fish in their natural environment have shown that certain males ordinarily attack only other males of the same species—presumably to protect their territories and their mates. But, if no other males of the species are around, these fish will attack the males of other species. If there are no males of any kind available, the fish will attack females—and sometimes even kill their own mates. This behavior has been cited as proof that the fish has an instinct or drive for aggression so powerful that it has to find some outlet, even if this means violent destruction of the family (Lorenz, 1966).

Or is aggression learned?

Do these fish and rats, which seem obviously programed for violent behavior, tell us anything about human beings? Perhaps. But many psychologists—probably most of them—believe otherwise. They have concluded that human aggression, though it may have some relation to heredity, is largely the result of learning. Many experimental findings point in this direction. You may recall the photographs on page 113 showing how children tend to imitate an adult who attacks a life-size doll—an indication that learning through observation can produce aggressive behavior. Similarly, it has been found that adults tend to behave more aggressively after watching a film showing acts of aggression (Hartmann, 1969)—or even after watching a football game with its violent bodily contact (Goldstein and Arms, 1971).

It has also been found that many aggressive people come from aggressive families and were punished severely for childhood misconduct. They may be imitating the behavior of their parents, even though it was once painful to them. Others seem somehow to have decided, from experience, that aggression serves in some way to bring social rewards. Having used it successfully on one occasion, they may adopt it as a way of life.

Even a monkey's display of aggression may depend greatly on learning and on the social situation. This fact has been observed in an animal that behaved aggressively in response to electrical stimulation through an electrode planted in the limbic system of the brain. When this stimulus was applied, the monkey would attack other monkeys who ranked lower in the social hierarchy. But if the monkey was in the presence of others who ranked higher, it did not attack. Instead, it ran away. If even a monkey experiencing "brain control" modifies its aggressive behavior so drastically in accordance with the social situation, it seems only logical to many psychologists that social influences and learning must certainly affect human aggression.

There seems to be no way, at this stage of psychology's development, to say for sure whether violence is learned or is programed by heredity—or both. Whatever its origin, many scientists agree that it once had undoubted value in helping the human race survive but has become obsolete and counterproductive in our present civilization. As one biologist states: "The need now is for a gentler, a more tolerant people than those who won . . . against the ice, the tiger, and the bear" (Eiseley, 1946).

Aggression's opposite: studies of altriusm

For behavior that is the opposite of aggression—being kind, generous, and helpful to others—social psychologists use the word *altruism.* Cases of altruism are not reported in the newspapers so often as incidents of violence, but they take place with great frequency. People go to considerable trouble to help a sick neighbor, take in a family left homeless by a fire, and serve as volunteer firemen and hospital attendants. The amounts donated each year to charities are staggering.

As in the case of aggression, it can be argued that the behavior of lower animals points to a hereditary basis for altruism. Chimpanzees, for example, have been observed to share their food with another hungry chimpanzee in an adjoining cage—though they do so somewhat grudgingly (Nissen and Crawford, 1936). Many other animal studies have also produced evidence of an altruistic concern for others (Hebb and Thompson, 1968).

Some scientists maintain that altruism is an innate trait that has been passed along through the process of evolution. They point out that human beings have always had a better chance of survival when living with other people than when trying to make it alone. So it seems likely that those who were willing to cooperate with others had a better chance of surviving and passing along their characteristics to future generations (Campbell, 1965). Again, as in the case of aggression, it is impossible either to prove or disprove this theory.

Other psychologists believe the explanation lies not in heredity but in learning. They point out that there are wide individual differences in tendencies toward altruism. Studies have shown that the people most likely to be altruistic are those who have somehow come to feel a personal responsibility for others (Schwartz, 1970) and have learned to *empathize* (Aronfreed, 1970)—that is, to feel the joys and pains of other people as if these emotions were their own. Having altruistic parents to imitate and identify with also plays a part. One study of boys who were regarded as generous found that they usually had fathers whom they perceived to be warm and helpful (Rutherford and Mussen, 1968). Another study, looking into the backgrounds of a group devoted to promoting civil rights, found that the members were characterized by a close relationship with an altruistic parent—at least one and sometimes both (Rosenhan, 1970). Whether altruism is or is not a basic and innate human trait, there seems to be no doubt that it can be at least encouraged or discouraged by learning and social influences.

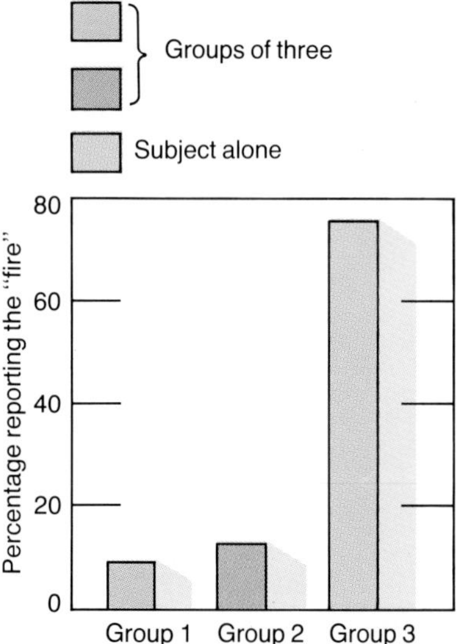

Figure 15-10 The more spectators, the more apathy *How many students, sitting in the waiting room of a psychology laboratory, would report the presence of smoke that seemed to indicate a fire? The answer seems to depend on how many people are present. In group 1, there were three people in the room—one actual subject and two confederates of the experimenter who were instructed to ignore the smoke. In group 2, three actual subjects were waiting in company. In group 3—the only one in which a majority took action—the subject was alone in the room and presumably felt a greater sense of personal responsibility (Latané and Darley, 1970).*

Bystander apathy: treating others with benign (or not so benign) neglect

Closely related to studies of altriusm and aggression is a line of investigation that was inspired by a well-publicized incident in New York City some years ago. A young women named Kitty Genovese was murdered on the street one night in sight of 38 neighbors who heard her cries and ran to their apartment windows. Although the assault went on for half an hour and many of the spectators watched for the entire time, no one called the police or took any other action. Why? Why do people sometimes help others who are in trouble but sometimes, as in the Genovese case, show a remarkable degree of what social psychologists term *bystander apathy?*

Experiments show a close relationship between the number of people who witness an incident—such as the Genovese murder, a theft, a fire, or a call for help—and the likelihood that anyone will offer assistance. In a typical experiment, men students arriving at a psychology laboratory were asked to sit in a small waiting room until they could be interviewed. Some of the subjects waited alone, others in groups of three, and still others in groups of three that contained only one actual subject and two confederates of the experimenter. Soon smoke began to seep into the room through a ventilator in the wall. The smoke continued until someone took steps to report a fire, or, if no one made any move, for six minutes.

As Figure 15-10 shows, most of the subjects who were alone took action to report the smoke, usually very promptly. But when three

Walking past a man who lies on a city street: a common case of bystander apathy.

subjects were waiting together, only 13 percent ever reported the smoke. Of the subjects who were sitting with the two confederates—who were instructed to pay no attention to the smoke—only 10 percent took action.

Kitty Genovese may have been a victim of the fact that, contrary to popular belief, there is no safety in numbers. Apparently a person who needs help is more likely to receive it if there is only one person around than if there are many. Several reasons have been suggested. First, the presence of others may relieve any single member of the group from feelings of personal responsibility. Second, apparent indifference on the part of other spectators may cause the individual bystander to downgrade the seriousness of the situation. In some cases, bystander apathy may even represent a type of conformity. If a group of people seems to be ignoring the plight of a person in need, individual members may feel strong pressure to behave as the group is behaving.

Apathy, anonymity, and intimacy

Kitty Genovese may also have been a victim of the anonymity of big-city life. Studies have shown that people who need help are much more likely to receive it in a small town than in a city (Altman et al., 1969). In a large city, people can walk for blocks without meeting anyone they know. They are mere faces in the crowd. They do not have the intimate contacts with friends and neighbors that might produce offers of help.

Any increase in the degree of intimacy—even in just the matter of physical closeness—serves to reduce the tendency toward bystander apathy. Thus a person who collapses in the close confines of a subway car is much more likely to receive help than someone who collapses in the open spaces of a city street. This was demonstrated by investigators who fell to the floor of a New York subway car, as if suddenly stricken. When they were carrying a cane, as if they had a physical ailment, someone tried to help them in 95 percent of the cases. Even if they smelled of alcohol and carried a whisky bottle in a paper bag, indicating that they might merely have been drunk, someone went to their assistance half the time (Piliavin, Rodin, and Piliavin, 1969). The results were doubtless due to the fact that the bystanders were in a face-to-face situation with the victims and in a confined space where they could not just ignore the incident and walk right past.

You can't be a Good Samaritan if you're in a hurry

One experiment on bystander apathy was particularly ingenious. The subjects were men attending a theological seminary—people who might be expected to lend a helping hand to anyone in trouble. The subjects had volunteered to make a brief talk that would be recorded and distributed. When they arrived at the experimenter's office they received some printed material that was to be the basis of the talk. After studying it, they were directed to proceed to a recording studio in a nearby building. The route, as shown on a map given to each of them, took them through an alley in which they passed a confederate of the experimenter who was lying in a doorway, coughing and groaning as if in pain. The question, of course, was how many of them would stop to help the man in trouble—as did the subject shown in Figure 15-11.

Figure 15-11 A "Good Samaritan" offers help *One of the subjects in an experiment on bystander apathy stops to help a man lying in an alley doorway. Was he really a "Good Samaritan"—or did he just stop because he was in no special hurry to get anywhere? For the answer, see the text.*

The printed material that half the subjects studied was the story of the Good Samaritan, which, it seemed, might remind them of their duty to help others. The other half studied a discussion of job opportunities for seminary graduates, which, it was presumed, would have no effect one way or the other. In addition, an attempt was made to determine whether the men might be influenced by how much of a hurry they were in to reach the recording studio. Some of the men were told that they were early and should take their time, others that they were just about on schedule, and still others that they were late and should rush to the studio as fast as possible. In other words, a third of the subjects were put in what the experimenter deemed a "low hurry" situation, a third in an "intermediate hurry," and a third in a "high hurry" situation.

Which subjects offered to help the man in pain and which did not? It turned out that it made no difference whether the subjects had just read the Good Samaritan parable or the material on job opportunities. What did make a difference was whether or not they were in a hurry. Of the "low hurry" subjects, 63 percent offered help; of the "intermediate hurry" subjects, 45 percent; and of the "high hurry" subjects only 10 percent (Darley and Batson, 1971). The study suggests that it is difficult to be a Good Samaritan when you are in a hurry—an indication that the rush of big-city life, as well as the lack of intimacy, may contribute to bystander apathy.

SUMMARY OF SUPPLEMENT

1. The question of whether human beings have an inborn tendency to display *aggression*—or whether aggression is the result of learning—is one of the unresolved issues in psychology.
2. The people most likely to display *altruism* (a tendency to be kind, generous, and helpful to others) are those who feel a personal responsibility for others and have learned to *empathize* (feel the joys and pains of others as if these emotions were their own).
3. *Bystander apathy* is a failure to assist another person who appears in need of help. Bystander apathy tends to be greatest when there are large numbers of other people around. It is encouraged by the anonymity, lack of intimacy, and the rush of big-city life.

IMPORTANT TERMS

aggression
altruism
bystander apathy
empathize

RECOMMENDED READINGS

Aronson, E. *The social animal,* 2d ed. San Francisco: Freeman, 1976.

Bandura, A. *Social learning theory.* Englewood Cliffs, N.J.: Prentice-Hall, 1976.

Bem, D. J. *Beliefs, attitudes, and human affairs.* Belmont, Calif.: Brooks/Cole, 1970.

Berkowitz, L., ed. *Advances in experimental social psychology,* Vol. 10. New York: Academic Press, 1977.

Berscheid, E., and Walster, E. C. *Interpersonal attraction,* 2d ed. Reading, Mass.: Addison-Wesley, 1978.

Brigham, J. C., and Wrightsman, L. S., eds. *Contemporary issues in social psychology,* 4th ed. Monterey, Calif: Brooks/Cole, 1982.

Carlsmith, J. M., Ellsworth, P. C., and Aronson, E. *Methods of research in social psychology.* Reading, Mass.: Addison-Wesley, 1976.

Gergen, K. J., and Gergen, M. M. *Social psychology.* New York: Harcourt Brace Jovanovich, 1981.

Jones, E. E., et al. *Attribution: perceiving the causes of behavior.* Morristown, N.J.: General Learning Press, 1972.

Milgram, S., *Obedience to authority.* New York: Harper & Row, 1974.

Shaver, K. C. *An introduction to attribution process.* Cambridge, Mass. Winthrop, 1975.

APPENDIX

Probability and normal distribution 587
Dreams and prophecies: why they often come true
What happens when you toss coins: a normal curve of distribution

Descriptive statistics 590
Number in group
The statistical average (or mean)
Variability and standard deviation
Percentiles

Inferential statistics: the science of making generalizations 593
Population and sample
Choosing valid control groups
Comparing two groups
Standard error of the mean
Probability and significance

The technique and significance of correlation 597
Scatter plots
Correlation coefficients
Correlation and prediction
Correlation, cause, and effect

The mathematical computations 599
The mean
The standard deviation
The standard error of the mean
Differences between groups
Correlation coefficients
Contingency

Summary 605

Statistical Methods

The use of statistics as a tool in psychology began with Sir Francis Galton, an Englishman who did his most important work in the 1880s. Sir Francis was interested in individual differences—how people vary in height, weight, and such characteristics as color vision, sense of smell, hearing, and ability to judge weights. He was also interested in the workings of heredity. One of the questions that fascinated him was whether taller-than-average people tend to have taller-than-average children. Another was whether successful people tend to have successful children.

Since Galton's time, many investigators have pursued similar questions, such as: Do parents of above-average intelligence tend to have children of above-average intelligence? Do strict parents tend to produce children who are more or less aggressive than the children of lenient parents? Do people of high intelligence tend to be more or less neurotic than people of low intelligence?

To answer these questions, as Galton discovered, one must first make some accurate measurements. Galton himself devised a number of tests for such abilities as vision and hearing. Newer generations of psychologists have tried to perfect tests for intelligence and personality traits. But the results of the tests are meaningless unless they can be analyzed and compared in accordance with sound statistical practices.

Psychological statistics is the application of mathematical principles to the interpretation of the results obtained in psychological studies. It has been aptly called a "way of thinking" (Hebb, 1958)—a problem-solving tool that enables us to summarize our knowledge of psychological events and make legitimate inferences from what we discover.

Probability and normal distribution

As an example of how we can profit from thinking in terms of statistical methods, suppose someone shows you two possible bridge hands. One is the bridge player's dream—13 spades. The other is a run-of-the-mill hand containing one ace, a few face cards, and many cards of no special value. The person who has put the hands together asks: "If you play bridge tonight, which of these hands are you less likely to pick up?"

Your first impulse would surely be to say, "The 13 spades." When a bridge player gets such a hand, the newspapers report it as a great rarity. The player is likely to talk about it forever afterward. And, in all truth, a hand of 13 spades is extremely rare. It occurs, as a statistician can quickly calculate, on an average of only once in about 159 billion deals.

But the other hand, whatever it is, is equally rare. The rules of statistical probability say that the chance of getting any particular combination of thirteen cards is only one in about 159 billion deals. The reason a hand of 13 spades seems rarer than any other is that bridge players pay attention to it, while lumping all their mediocre hands together as if they were one and the same.

Think about the hand of 13 spades in another way. Since it occurs only once in 159 billion deals, is it not a miracle that it should ever occur at all? No, it is not. It has been estimated that there are about 25 million bridge players in the United States. If each of them deals 20 times a week, that makes 26 billion deals a year. The statistical method tells us that we should expect a hand of 13 spades to be dealt on the average of about once every six years.

Dreams and prophecies: why they often come true

The fact that we can expect a hand of 13 spades to occur with some regularity explains some events in life that seem baffling to people who do not understand statistics. For example, every once in a while the newspapers report that someone shooting dice in Las Vegas has made 28 passes (or winning throws) in a row. This seems almost impossible, and in fact the mathematical odds are more than 268,000,000 to 1 that it will not happen to anyone who picks up the dice. These are very high odds indeed. Yet, considering the large number of people who step up to all the dice tables in Las Vegas, it is very likely that sooner or later someone will throw the 28 passes.

The laws of probability also explain many of the coincidences that seem—to people unfamiliar with the laws—to represent the working of supernatural powers. A woman in Illinois dreams that her brother in California has died and the next morning gets a telephone call that he was killed in an accident. This many sound like an incredible case of mental telepathy, but the laws of probability offer a much simpler explanation. Most people dream frequently. Dreams of death are by no means rare. In the course of a year millions of people dream of the death of someone in the family. Sooner or later, one of the dreams is almost sure to coincide with an actual death.

Astrologers and other seers also profit from the rules of probability. If an astrologer keeps predicting that a catastrophe will occur, the forecast is bound to be right sooner or later, because the world is almost sure to have some kind of tragedy, from airplane accident to tornado, in any given period. And a prophet who makes a reputation by predicting the death of a world leader knows that there are many world leaders and that many of them are so advanced in age that their death would not be unusual.

In a world as big as ours, all kinds of coincidences are likely to occur. The rules of statistics say that we should expect and not be surprised by them. Statistical analysis lets us view these coincidences for what they are and helps us recognize that they have no real significance.

What happens when you toss coins: a normal curve of distribution

One of the principles of probability, as Galton was the first to notice, has to do with the manner in which many things, including psychological traits, are distributed in the normal course of natural events. The principle can best be demonstrated by a simple experiment. Drop 10 coins into a cup, shake them, throw them on a table, and count the number of heads. Do this a number of times, say 100. Your tally will almost surely turn out to be very much like the one shown in Figure A-1.

What you have come up with is a simple illustration of normal distribution. When you toss 10 coins 100 times—a total of 1,000 tosses—you can expect 500 heads to come up, an average of five heads per toss. As the tally shows, this number came up most frequently. The two numbers on either side, four and six, were close seconds. The numbers farther away from five were increasingly infrequent. Ten came up only once, and zero did not come up at all. (Over a long period, both 10 and zero would be expected to come up on an average of once in every 1,024 tosses.)

The tally shown in Figure A-1 can be converted into the bar graph shown in Figure A-2, which provides a more easily interpreted picture of what happened in the coin tossing. Note its shape—highest in the middle, then tapering off toward the extreme left and the extreme right. If a curve is drawn to connect the tops of the bars, we have a good example of the *normal curve of distribution*—which, as was explained in Chapter 1, is typical of the results generally found in all tests and measurements, of both physical and psychological traits. The curve for distribution of IQs, which was presented in Chapter 1, is repeated in Figure A-3. Note again that most people fall around the average of 100 and that only a few are found at the far extremes below 40 or above 160. The message of the curve is that in IQ (or height or weight or almost anything else) the people who are about average are in the majority—while some are as rare as those 28 passes in a dice game.

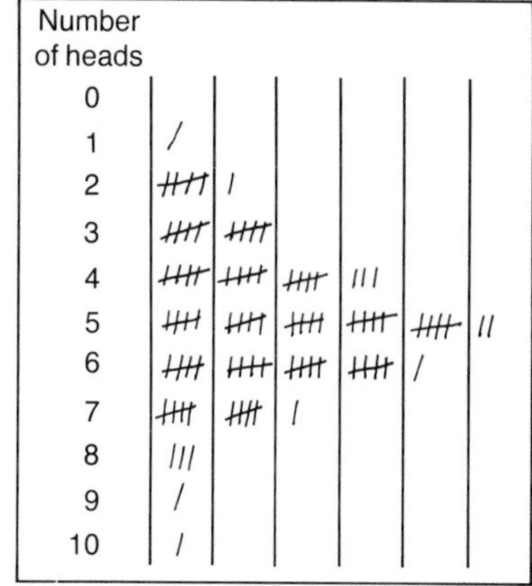

Figure A-1 A tally of coin tosses
Ten coins were shaken in a cup and tossed on a table 100 times. This is a tally of the number of heads that appeared on each toss.

Figure A-2 The tally in bar form
Here the tally of the coin-tossing experiment has been converted into a bar graph. Note the peak at the center and the rapid falling off toward each extreme.

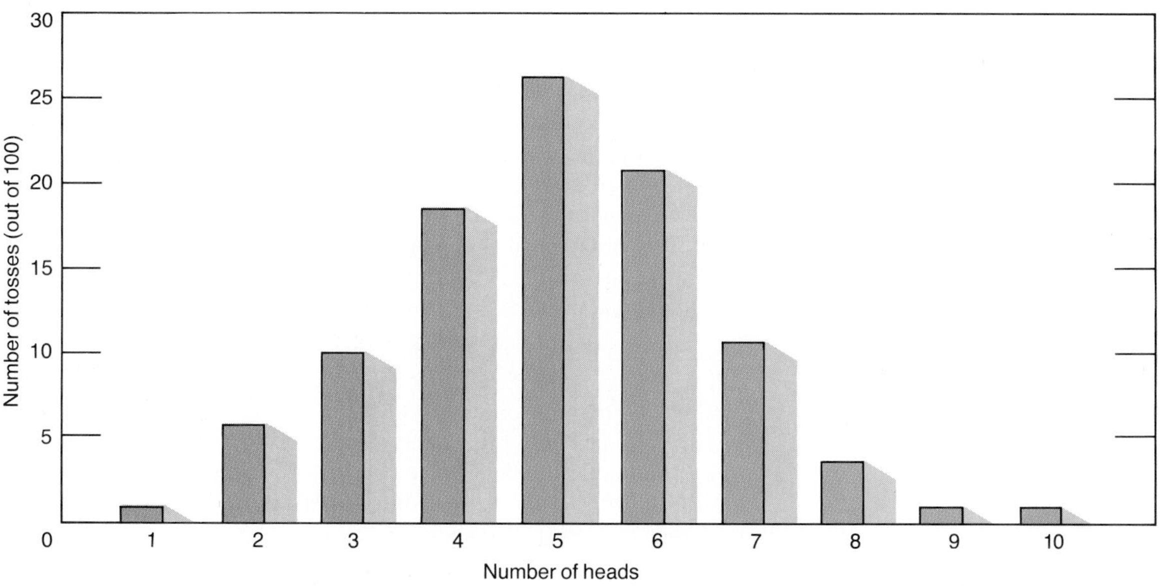

Figure A-3 The normal curve of IQ distribution The graph was constructed from IQs found in large-scale testing (Terman and Merrill, 1937). Note that it looks very much like a line connecting the peaks of the bars in Figure A-2.

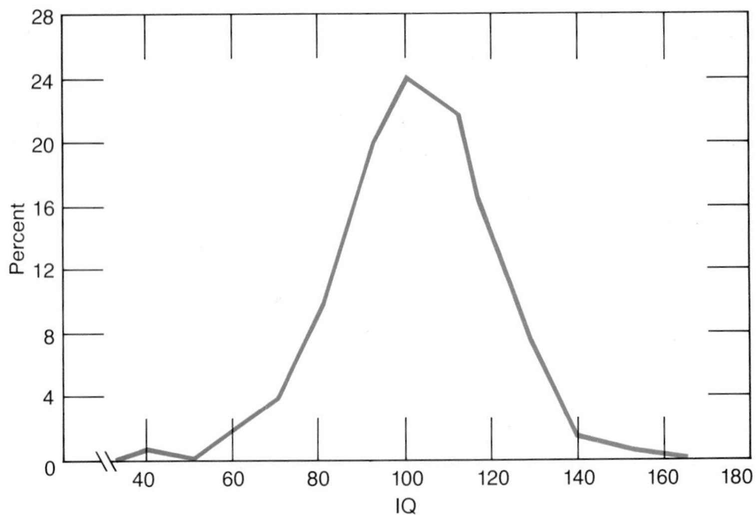

Descriptive statistics

As a quick and convenient method of summarizing the characteristics of any group under study—as well as the distribution of these characteristics—psychologists use a technique called *descriptive statistics.* For example, suppose we draw up a new intelligence test and administer it to 10,000 college students. We wind up with 10,000 raw scores. To pass along what we have learned about the test, however, we need not quote every one of the 10,000 scores. Through the use of descriptive statistics we can summarize and condense. With just a few well-chosen numbers, we can tell other people what they need to know in order to understand our results. Among the most commonly used forms of descriptive statistics are the following.

Number in group

Number in group is simply the total number of subjects we have studied. It is important because the chances of obtaining accurate results are greater if we study a large group than if we study only a small group. If we test only three people on our new intelligence test, we may happen to select three geniuses or three morons. A large sample is likely to be more representative of the population as a whole.

The statistical average (or mean)

Another useful piece of information is what in everyday language is called the *average.* For example, six students take an examination containing 100 true-false questions and get test scores of 70, 74, 74, 76, 80, and 82. The average score—or in technical language, the *mean*—is the sum of the scores divided by the number of subjects who took the test. In other words, it is 456 divided by 6—or 76. Knowing that the mean is 76 tells us a great deal about the curve of distribution that could be drawn up from the scores. We know that the curve would center on a figure of about 76—and that the majority of scores would be somewhere in this neighborhood.

Another measure of central tendency, or the point around which the scores tend to cluster, is the *median.* This is the halfway point that separates the lower 50 percent of scores from the higher 50 percent. In the example just given, the median would be 75, because half the scores fall below 75 and the other half fall above. The median is an especially useful figure when the data include a small number of exceptionally low or exceptionally high measurements. Let us say, for example, that the six scores on the true-false examination were 70, 74, 74, 76, 80, and 100. The one student who scores 100 brings up the mean score quite sharply to 79. But note that 79 is hardly an "average" score, because only two of the six students scored that high. The median score, which remains at 75, is a better description of the data.

A third measure of central tendency is the *mode*—the measurement or score that applies to the greatest number of subjects. In the case of the true-false examination it would be 74, the only score made by as many as two of the students. The mode tells us where the highest point of the curve of distribution will be found. In a perfectly symmetrical normal curve the mode, the median, and the mean are the same. If the distribution is not symmetrical, but on the contrary tails off more sharply on the below-average side than on the above-average side, or vice versa (as often happens), it is useful to know all three of these figures.

Variability and standard deviation

Even when the normal curve is perfectly symmetrical, it may take different forms. Sometimes it is high and narrow. At other times it is shorter and wider. This depends on the *variability* of the measurements, which means the extent to which they differ from one another.

A crude way to describe the variability of scores made on a psychological test is simply to give the *range* of the scores—the highest minus the lowest. A much more sensitive description is provided by what is called the *standard deviation,* often abbreviated to *SD.* The standard deviation, which is computed from the data by a formula that will be explained later, is an especially useful tool because it indicates the proportion of scores or measurements that will be found under any part of the curve. As Figure A-4 shows, the rule is that 34.13 percent of all the scores lie between the mean and a point 1 *SD* above the mean; 13.59 percent lie between 1 *SD* and 2 *SD*s above the mean; and 2.14 percent lie between 2 *SD*s and 3 *SD*s above the mean. Thus the *SD* gives a clear description of the variability of the measurements.

With intelligence quotients, for example, the mean is 100 and the *SD* is approximately 15. That is to say, an IQ one *SD* above the mean is 115. Armed with this knowledge alone, plus the general statistical rule illustrated in Figure A-4, we know that human intelligence tends to be distributed according to the figures in the following table:

IQ	Percentage of people
over 144	0.14
130–144	2.14
115–129	13.59
100–114	34.13
85–99	34.13
70–84	13.59
55–69	2.14
under 55	0.14

The *SD* is also used to compute what are called *standard scores,* or *z-scores,* which are often more meaningful than the raw scores made on a test. The *z*-score tells how many *SD*s a score is above or below the mean. It is obtained very simply by noting how many points a score is above or below the mean and then dividing by the *SD.* A *z*-score of 1 is one *SD* above the mean. A *z*-score of −1.5 is one-and-a-half *SD*s below the mean.

Percentiles

The meaning of *percentile* can best be explained by an example. A college man, a senior who wants to go on to graduate school, is asked to take the Graduate Record Examinations, which are nationally administered aptitude tests often used to screen applicants. He makes a score of 460 on the verbal test and 540 in mathematics. By themselves, these scores do not mean much either to him or to the faculty of the school he wants to attend. But records of other people's results on the test provide a means of comparing his scores with those of other college seniors. A score of 460 on the verbal test, the records show, lies on the 40th percentile for men. This means that 40 percent of all senior men who take the test make a lower score and 60 percent make higher score. The 540 score in math lies on the 66th percentile for men. In other words, 66 percent of senior men make a lower score, and only 34

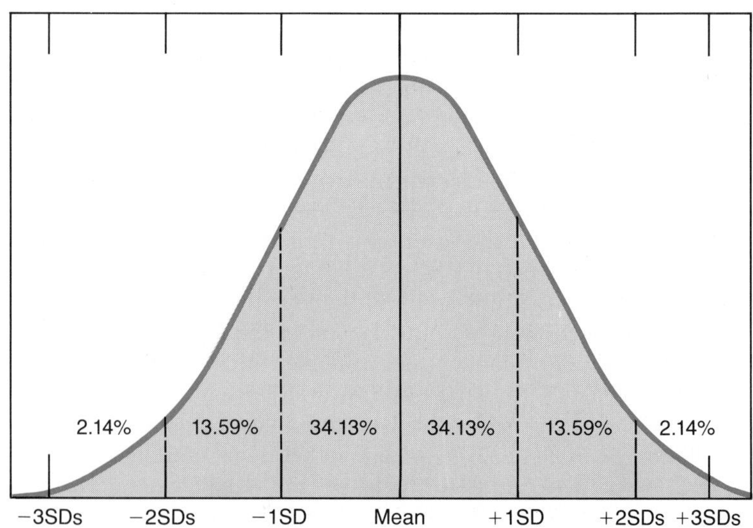

Figure A-4 Using the *SD* to analyze data In a normal curve of distribution, the standard deviation indicates how many measurements of scores will be found at various distances from the mean. As shown here, 34.13 percent of all measurements lie between the mean and 1 *SD* above the mean. Measurements that are between 1 *SD* and 2 *SD*s above the mean make up 13.59 percent of the total. Measurements between 2 *SD*s and 3 *SD*s above the mean make up 2.14 percent. The same percentages are found below the mean. Note that the figures do not quite add up to 100 percent. This is because 0.14 percent of measurements are found more than 3 *SD*s above the mean and another 0.14 percent are found more than 3 *SD*s below the mean. These various percentages hold for any normal distribution, although the size of the *SD* differs from one curve to another.

percent make higher scores. These percentile figures show the student and the school he hopes to attend how his ability compares with that of other prospective graduate students: He is well above average in mathematical ability (only a third of male college seniors make better scores) but below average in verbal aptitude.

Percentile ratings can be made for any kind of measurement, whether or not it falls into a normal pattern of distribution. A percentile rating of 99—or, to be more exact, 99.99—means that no one had a higher score. A percentile rating of 1—or, to be more exact, 0.01—is the lowest in the group.

Inferential statistics: the science of making generalizations

Descriptive statistics permits psychologists to summarize the findings of their studies and determine how one individual compares with the others. But psychologists need another tool to help them interpret and make generalizations from their studies. When psychologists study the behavior of a rat in a Skinner box, for example, they are not especially interested in how rapidly that particular animal demonstrates learning. Rather, their primary concern is to discover a general principle of behavior that says something about the learning processes of all rats—and, by implication, perhaps about the learning process in general. Psychologists studying the performance of a group of human subjects who memorize nonsense syllables—or who take part in an experiment on physical attractiveness—are not especially interested in those particular people. Their ultimate goal is to learn something about the behavior of people in general.

The mathematical tool they use is called *inferential statistics*—a set of techniques that enable them to make valid generalizations from their measurements of behavior.

Population and sample

Inferential statistics is important because science is interested in what is called the *population,* or sometimes the *universe*—that is to say, all people or all events in a particular category. But we cannot study or measure the entire population. We cannot give an intelligence test, for example, to every human being on the face of the earth. Even if we could, we still would not have reached the entire population, because many people would have died and many new people would have been born while we were conducting our test. We must settle for a *sample,* a group of convenient size taken from the population as a whole.

The rules of inferential statistics hold that we can make valid generalizations only if the sample we use is *representative* of the population we want to study. If we are seeking some general conclusions about the intelligence of the American population, we cannot use a sample made up entirely of college students or a sample made up of high-school dropouts. If we want to learn about political attitudes, we cannot poll only Republicans or people who live in big cities or people who belong to one church or one social class. Our sample must be representative of all kinds of Americans.

One way to ensure a representative sample is to choose it entirely at *random*. If each member of the total population has an absolutely equal chance of being studied—and if our sample is large enough—then it is very likely that the sample will represent all segments of the population. For example, the experimenter who wants to study the emotional behavior of rats in a laboratory cannot just reach into a cage and pull out the first dozen animals that are closest at hand. The very fact that they are close at hand may mean that they are tamer than the others and have a different emotional temperament. To achieve a more valid sampling, the experimenter might take the first rat, reject the second, take the third, reject the fourth, and so on. An investigator interested in student attitudes toward marijuana on a particular campus might draw up an alphabetical list of all students, then interview every tenth person on the list.

In the Gallup election polls, the random sampling starts with a list of the approximately 200,000 election districts and precincts in the nation. From this master list, about 300 districts are chosen at random. Then a map of each of the 300 districts is drawn up. On the map, one house is chosen as a starting point—again at random. Beginning at that point, and proceeding along a path drawn through the district, the pollsters collect interviews at each third residence or sometimes each fifth or twelfth residence, depending on the size of the sample they want (Gallup, 1972).

Choosing valid control groups

The random technique of obtaining a representative sample is also standard procedure in selecting experimental and control groups. Ideally, every individual in the control group should be identical with a member of the experimental group. But this is of course impossible, because not even identical twins (who are too scarce anyway) are alike in every respect. To ensure as much similarity as possible between the experimental and control groups, subjects are usually assigned to one group or the other at random. Each individual who arrives at the laboratory has a 50-50 chance of being assigned to the experimental group and a 50-50 chance of being assigned to the control group.

Comparing two groups

For an example of how inferential statistics is used to compare two groups, such as an experimental group and a control group, let us imagine an experiment in which we try to determine whether physical health affects the learning ability of high school students. We select an experimental group of 16 representative, randomly chosen students who agree to take part in a rigorous health program. We arrange a supervised diet and exercise schedule, give them regular physical examinations, and promptly treat any illnesses or defects such as impaired vision or hearing. We also select a control group of 16 similar students who do not receive any special treatment. At the end of a year, we find that the experimental group has a grade-point mean of 89, with a standard deviation of 3. The control group has a grade-point mean of 85, with a standard deviation of 4. Question: Is this difference of four points between the mean of the experimental group and the mean of the control group just a statistical accident? Or does it really mean that good health produces better grades?

Although four points may sound like a lot, the question is not easy to answer. The reason is that *any* two samples of 16 people each, taken from the highschool population or any other population, are likely to have somewhat different means. Suppose we write the names of all the students in the high school (or in the city) on slips of paper and draw the slips from a hat. The grade-point mean for the first 16 names we draw may be 85, for the next 16 names 88, for the next 16 names 87. If we pull 20 different samples of 16 students each from the hat, we will find that the means vary from sample to sample, perhaps by as much as several points. So the question now becomes: Is the difference between the mean score of 89 for the experimental group and the mean score of 85 for the control group just an accidental result such as we might get by pulling samples from a hat? Or is it *statistically significant*—that is, does it indicate a real difference between our two groups?

Standard error of the mean

Helping answer the question is the fact that the means of randomly chosen samples, like raw measurements or scores themselves, tend to fall into a pattern of normal distribution. From our control group of 16 with a grade-point mean of 85 and a standard deviation of 4, we can

Figure A-5 How means are distributed These graphs show how the standard error of the mean of a sample is used to infer the true mean that would be found if the entire population could be measured. In the control group of high school students, at left, the mean is 85 and the standard error of the mean is 1.0. Thus we know that the chances are 68.26 percent that the true mean for the population lies between 84 and 86 (1 standard error above or below the mean of our sample), 95.44 percent that the true mean lies between 83 and 87 (2 standard errors above or below), and 99.72 percent that the true mean lies between 82 and 88 (3 standard errors above or below). In the experimental group, at right, the mean is 89 and the standard error of the mean is 0.75. Therefore the chances are 68.26 percent that the true mean of the experimental population would fall between 88.25 and 89.75; the chances are 95.44 percent that the mean would fall between 87.50 and 90.50; and they are 99.72 percent that the mean would fall between 86.75 and 91.25.

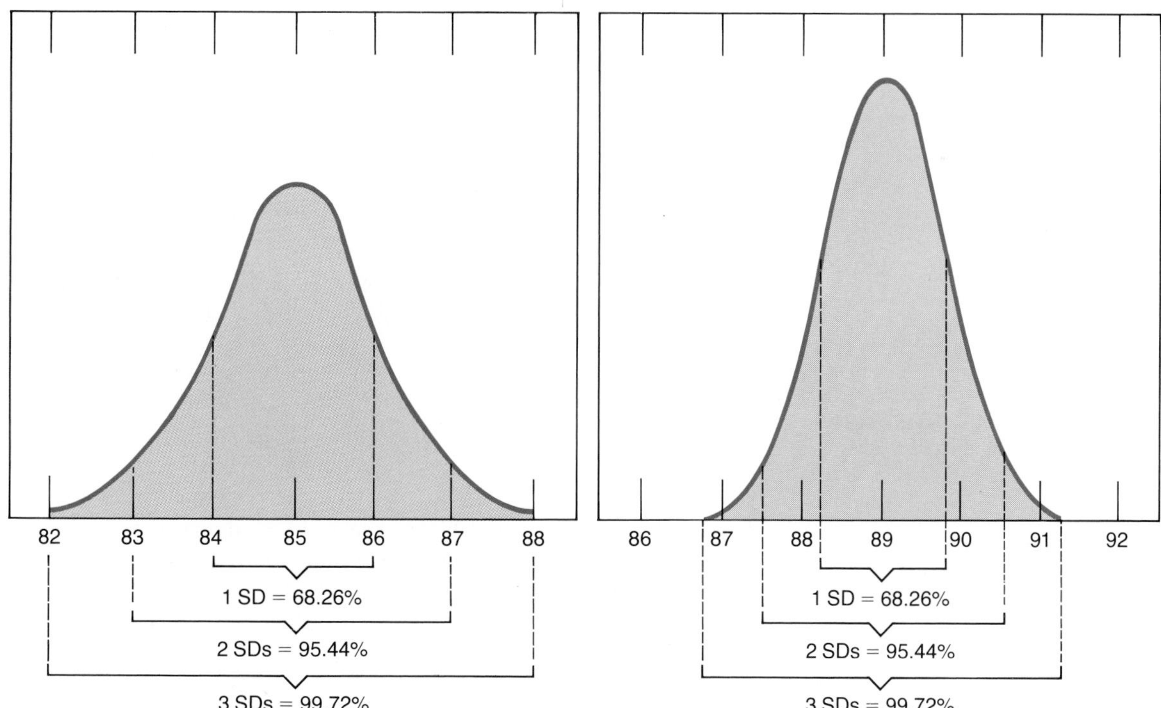

figure out the distribution of all the means we would be likely to get if we continued to pick samples of 16 students at random, and we find that the curve looks like the one shown on the left in Figure A-5. We get the curve by using the formula (shown later) for the *standard error of the mean.* For the control group, the standard error of the mean turns out to be 1.0. For the experimental group, we get the curve shown at the right in Figure A-5. For this group the standard error of the mean turns out to be .75.

Having found the two curves, we can put them together as in Figure A-6, which shows a very high probability that there is a true difference between the grades of students who receive special medical care and the grades of students who do not. The possibility that the difference we found is merely a matter of chance is represented by the small area that lies beneath the extreme right-hand end of the control curve and the extreme left-hand of the curve for the experimental group.

Probability and significance

In actual statistical calculation the curves shown in Figures A-5 and A-6 need not be constructed. We can use the two means and the standard error of each mean to work out what is called *the standard error of the difference between two means.* We can then use this figure to work out the probability that the difference we found was due merely to chance. In the case of the hypothetical experiment we have been describing, the probability comes to less than .01.

It is an arbitrary rule of thumb in experimental work that a difference is considered *statistically significant* only when the probability that it might have been obtained by chance is .05 (5 chances in 100, or 1 chance in 20) or less than .05.

In reports on experiments that can be analyzed with this kind of inferential statistics, the probability figure is always given. You will frequently find the note

$$p \leq .05$$

This means that the difference would be found by chance only 5 times

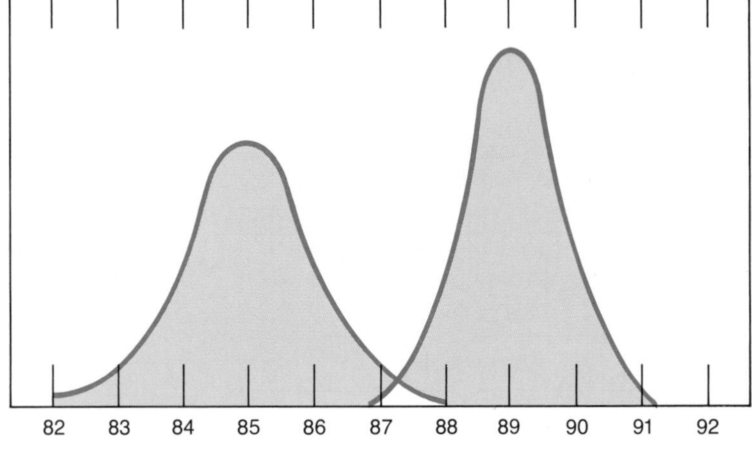

Figure A-6 Is the difference between the means significant? When we superimpose the curves shown in Figure A-5, we find that they have only the small white area in common. This area represents the probability that the difference between the two means was due solely to chance. The probability that the difference is a real one is represented by the colored areas.

or less out of 100 and is therefore statistically significant. In virtually all the experiments cited in this book, p was .05 or less.

The technique and significance of correlation

As was said in Chapter 1, *correlation* is a statistical tool used to examine two different measurements (such as the IQs of parents and the IQs of their children)—and to determine, from what would otherwise seem hopelessly jumbled numbers, what relationship if any exists between the two measurements.

Some correlations are *positive.* This means that the higher a person measures on scale X (for example, IQ) the higher that person is likely to measure on scale Y (for example, grades). Other correlations are *negative.* This means that a high score on scale X is likely to be accompanied by a low score on scale Y. For example, the frequency of premature births has been found to be negatively correlated with social class—meaning that there tends to be less prematurity among upper-income families than lower-income families. Negative correlations also exist between aggressive behavior in children and social class and between test anxiety and grades made in schools.

Scatter plots

A rough idea of the degree of correlation between two traits can be obtained by plotting each subject's score on scale X against the subject's score on scale Y. For each person, a dot is entered at a point corresponding to the scores on both scales, as shown in Figure A-7. The result is what is called a *scatter plot.* If the dots are scattered completely at random, we can see that the correlation is 0. If we should happen on one of those extremely rare cases where the dots form a perfectly straight line, running diagonally up or diagonally down, we know that we are dealing with a perfect correlation, either positive or negative. Most scatter diagrams fall somewhere in between. If a fairly narrow diagonal oval would enclose most of the dots, the correlation is rather high. If the oval must be fatter, the correlation is lower.

Correlation coefficients

A more precise measure of the relationship between scores on the X-scale and scores on the Y-scale can be obtained—without the need for constructing a scatter plot—by using various statistical formulas for

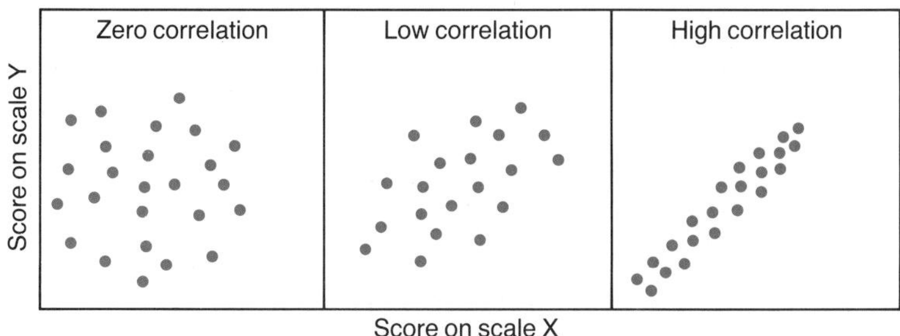

Figure A-7 Scatter plots of correlations For each subject, a dot has been placed at the point indicating both score on scale X and score on scale Y (Ferguson, G. A. *Statistical analysis in psychology and education.* New York: McGraw-Hill, 1959. Copyright © 1959 by McGraw-Hill Book Co.).

calculating a *correlation coefficient.* (The formulas are presented later.) A correlation coefficient can range from 0 (no correlation at all) to +1 (a perfect positive correlation) or −1 (a perfect negative correlation). But correlations of +1 or −1 are very rare. Even such physical traits as height and weight, which would seem to go together in almost perfect proportion, do not reach a correlation of +1. Some typical correlations that have been found in various studies are the following:

Between IQ and college grades	.50
Between parents' IQ and child's IQ	.49
Between IQ and ability at pitch discrimination	.00
Between boys' height at age 2 and height at age 18	.60
Between boys' height at age 10 and height at age 18	.88

Correlation and prediction

The correlation coefficients in the above table show that there is a considerable relationship between boys' height at age 2 and at age 18—and an even greater relationship between height at age 10 and at age 18. Knowing that these relationships exist, we can make some predictions. We can say that a boy who is taller than average at 2—or especially at 10—has a pretty good chance of also being taller than average at 18. Because of the .50 correlation coefficient between IQ and college grades, we can suggest that high-school seniors who make high scores on intelligence tests have a good chance of getting high grades in college, and that students with very low scores run the risk of failure.

It must always be kept in mind, however, that a coefficient of correlation is less accurate in making predictions than it sounds. Only when the correlation is very close to 1, as in the scatter plot that is shown in Figure A-7, does every subject tend to show a close relationship between score on scale X and score on scale Y. Even in a correlation of .75, which sounds high, there is a considerable amount of scatter, representing subjects who scored relatively low on scale X but relatively high on scale Y, or vice versa. Since most correlations found in psychological studies are lower than .75, we must be quite tentative in making predictions.

Correlation, cause, and effect

Just knowing the degree of relationship implied by a correlation coefficient is often of value to psychologists. For example, it has been found that there is a positive correlation between strict discipline on the part of parents and the amount of aggressive behavior displayed by children.

Again, however, it is important not to exaggerate the degree of relationship expressed by a correlation coefficient. We cannot say that strict discipline always—or even usually—is accompanied by aggressive behavior. Moreover we must avoid jumping to conclusions about cause and effect. Did the children become aggressive because the parents were strict, or were the parents strict because the children were aggressive? Is it possible that some third factor caused both the parents' strictness and the children's aggression? (For example, it may be that parents who are generally cold and rejecting of their children tend to be strict and that it is the coldness and rejection, rather than the strictness, that make the children aggressive.)

To avoid the danger of jumping to false conclusions on the basis of correlations, keep in mind that there is a very high correlation between the number of permanent teeth that have erupted through the schoolchild's gums and the child's raw scores for questions answered correctly on any kind of intelligence or aptitude test. But it would be foolish to conclude that more teeth make the child smarter or that better scores make more teeth appear. Increased maturity produces both the teeth and the higher scores.

The mathematical computations

The use of correlations and other descriptive and inferential statistics is not nearly so difficult as might be assumed. The mathematical knowledge required for these kinds of analysis is really not complicated at all. One need only be able to manipulate mathematical symbols, the most frequently used of which are explained in Figure A-8, and to apply the few basic formulas presented in Figure A-9.

The symbols and formulas are given at the start of this section on computations so that they can be found all in one place for future

N	Number of subjects from whom a measurement or score has been obtained
X	The numerical value of an individual score
Y	If each subject is measured on two scales, the numerical value of an individual score on the second scale
Σ	The Greek capital letter sigma, standing for "sum of"
ΣX	The sum of all the individual scores on scale X
M	The mean, which is the sum of the scores divided by the number of subjects
x	A deviation score; that is, the difference between an individual score and the mean for the group of which the individual is a member
y	A deviation score on the second scale, or Y-scale
SD	The standard deviation of the scores
SE_M	The standard error of the mean; also called the standard deviation of the mean
D_M	The difference between two means; for example, the difference between the mean (M) of scale X and the mean of scale Y
SE_{D_M}	The standard error of the difference between two means, used as a measure of whether the difference is significant
p	Probability, expressed in decimals ranging from .00 (no chance) through .50 (50-50 chance) to 1.00 (100 percent chance). A result is considered statistically significant when $p \leq .05$, meaning that there are only 5 chances in 100 (or fewer) that it was obtained by chance
r	Correlation coefficient obtained by the product-moment method
ρ	Correlation coefficient obtained by the rank-difference method
z	A standard score, expressed in numbers of SDs above or below the mean
C	Coefficient of contingency; type of correlation used to find relationships between events on a nominal scale

Figure A-8 Some useful mathematical symbols These are the symbols used in the statistical formulas discussed in this appendix.

Figure A-9 Some statistical formulas These are some of the formulas most frequently used in psychological statistics. Their use is explained in the text and in the following figures.

1. For determining the mean:

$$M = \frac{\Sigma X}{N}$$

2. For determining a deviation score:

$$x = X - M$$

3. For determining the standard deviation:

$$SD = \sqrt{\frac{\Sigma x^2}{N - 1}}$$

4. For determining a z-score:

$$z = \frac{x}{SD}$$

5. For determining the standard error of the mean:

$$SE_M = \frac{SD}{\sqrt{N}}$$

6. For determining the difference between two means:

$$D_M = M_1 - M_2$$

7. For determining the standard error of the difference between two means:

$$SE_{D_M} = \sqrt{(SE_{M1})^2 + (SE_{M2})^2}$$

8. For determining the critical ratio:

$$\text{Critical ratio} = \frac{D_M}{SE_{D_M}}$$

9. For determining the coefficient of correlation by the product-moment method:

$$r = \frac{\Sigma xy}{(N - 1)SD_x SD_y}$$

10. For determining the coefficient of correlation by the rank-difference method:

$$\rho = 1 - \frac{6(\Sigma D^2)}{N(N^2 - 1)}$$

reference. They may seem rather difficult when shown all together in this fashion, but their application should be apparent from the examples that will be presented as we go along.

The kind of measurement that an investigator often wants to analyze is illustrated in Figure A-10. Here 17 students have taken a psychological test and have made scores ranging from 60 to 97. The raw scores are a jumble of figures, from which we now want to determine the mean, the standard deviation, and the standard error of the mean.

The mean

The formula for computing the mean, as shown in Figure A-9, is

$$M = \frac{\Sigma X}{N}$$

1. 78	4. 74	7. 92	10. 74	13. 70	16. 82
2. 97	5. 80	8. 72	11. 85	14. 84	17. 78
3. 60	6. 77	9. 79	12. 68	15. 76	

Figure A-10 The raw material of statistical analysis: test scores of 17 students These raw scores, obtained by students on a psychological test, are analyzed in the text.

These symbols denote, as Figure A-8 shows, that the mean equals the sum of the individual scores divided by the number of subjects.

The way the formula is applied is illustrated in Figure A-11. The sum of the individual scores, which are shown in column one, is 1,326. The number of subjects is 17. Thus the mean is 1,326 divided by 17, or 78.

The standard deviation

The method of finding the standard deviation is also illustrated in Figure A-11. The formula for the standard deviation is

$$SD = \sqrt{\frac{\Sigma x^2}{N - 1}}$$

This means that we square each of the deviation scores, add up the total, and divide the total by the number of subjects minus 1. The square root of the figure thus obtained is the standard deviation.

The deviation scores shown in column two have been obtained by the formula $x = X - M$—that is, by subtracting the mean, which is 78, from each individual score. These figures in column two have then been squared to give the figures in column three. The sum of the x^2 figures is 1,224, and this figure divided by 16 (our $N - 1$) comes to 76.5. The standard deviation is the square root of 76.5 or 8.75.

Test scores (X)	Deviation scores (x)	Deviation scores squared (x^2)
78	0	0
97	+19	361
60	−18	324
74	− 4	16
80	+ 2	4
77	− 1	1
92	+14	196
72	− 6	36
79	+ 1	1
74	− 4	16
85	+ 7	49
68	−10	100
70	− 8	64
84	+ 6	36
76	− 2	4
82	+ 4	16
78	0	0
$\Sigma X = 1{,}326$		$\Sigma x^2 = 1{,}224$

$$M = \frac{\Sigma X}{N} = \frac{1{,}326}{17} = 78$$

$$SD = \sqrt{\frac{\Sigma x^2}{N - 1}} = \sqrt{\frac{1{,}224}{16}} = \sqrt{76.5} = 8.75$$

Figure A-11 Computing the mean and *SD* of the 17 scores Using the formulas in Figure A-9, we first compute the mean score (M) for the 17 students, which comes out to 78. Once we have the mean, we can work out the standard deviation (SD). We start by obtaining the deviation scores ($x = X - M$), then squaring these deviation scores to get x^2.

The standard error of the mean

Finding the standard error of the mean for our group is extremely simple. The formula is

$$SE_M = \frac{SD}{\sqrt{N}}$$

We have found that the *SD* of our sample is 8.75 and our $N = 17$. The formula yields

$$SE_M = \frac{8.75}{\sqrt{17}} = \frac{8.75}{4.12} = 2.12$$

Differences between groups

For an example of how to apply the formulas for analyzing differences between groups, let us return to the hypothetical experiment mentioned earlier. We had the school grades, you will recall, of an experimental group of 16 students who took part in a health program; the mean was 89 and the standard deviation was 3. We also had the grades of a control group of 16 students; the mean for this group was 85 and the standard deviation was 4.

The difference between the two means is easily computed from the formula

$$D_M = M_1 - M_2$$

which means that the difference between the means is the mean of the first group minus the mean of the second group—in this case, 89 minus 85, or 4. To know whether this difference is statistically significant, however, we must calculate the standard error of the difference between the two means. To do so, as figure A-9 shows, we must use the fairly complex formula

$$SE_{D_M} = \sqrt{(SE_{M1})^2 + (SE_{M2})^2}$$

Our first step is to compute SE_{M1}, the standard error of the mean of our first or experimental group. We do so as shown earlier, this time with 3 as our standard deviation and 16 as our number of subjects.

$$SE_{M1} = \frac{SD}{\sqrt{N}} = \frac{3}{\sqrt{16}} = \frac{3}{4} = 0.75$$

We also compute SE_{M2}, the standard error of the mean of our second or control group, where the standard deviation is 4 and the number of subjects is 16.

$$SE_{M2} = \frac{SD}{\sqrt{N}} = \frac{4}{\sqrt{16}} = \frac{4}{4} = 1.00$$

Thus SE_{M1} is 0.75 and SE_{M2} is 1.00, and the standard error of the difference between the two means is computed as follows:

$$\begin{aligned} SE_{D_M} &= \sqrt{(SE_{M1})^2 + (SE_{M2})^2} \\ &= \sqrt{(0.75)^2 + (1)^2} \\ &= \sqrt{.5625 + 1} \\ &= \sqrt{1.5625} \\ &= 1.25 \end{aligned}$$

To complete our analysis of the difference between the two groups, we need one more statistical tool—the *critical ratio.* This is given by the formula

$$\text{Critical ratio} = \frac{D_M}{SE_{D_M}}$$

In the case of our hypothetical experiment we have found that D_M is 4 and that SE_{D_M} is 1.25. Thus

$$\text{Critical ratio} = \frac{4}{1.25} = 3.2$$

This critical ratio gives us a measure of the probability that our difference was due merely to chance. For reasons that mathematically minded students may be able to work out for themselves but that need not concern the rest of us, the magic numbers for the critical ratio are 1.96 and 2.57. If the critical ratio is as high as 1.96, then $p \leq .05$, and the difference is considered statistically significant. If the critical ratio is as high as 2.57, then $p \leq .01$, and the difference is considered highly significant. The critical ratio we found for our two groups, 3.2, is well over 2.57; thus we can have some confidence that the difference was not the result of chance.

Correlation coefficients

There are a number of ways of computing correlation coefficients, depending on the type of data that are being studied. The most frequently used is the *product-moment method,* which obtains a coefficient of correlation designated by the letter r for the relationship between two different measurements. The formula is

$$r = \frac{\Sigma xy}{(N - 1)SD_x SD_y}$$

To use the formula we have to determine the amount by which each subject's score on scale X differs from the mean for all scores on scale X—in other words the value for x, the deviation score, which may be plus or minus. We must also determine the amount by which the subject's score on the second test, or scale Y, differs from the mean for all scores on scale Y—in other words, the value for y, which also may be plus or minus. We then multiply x by y for each subject and add the xy products for all the subjects in the sample. This gives us the top line, or numerator, of the formula. The bottom line, or denominator, is found by multiplying the number of subjects minus 1 $(N - 1)$ by the standard deviation of the scores on the X-scale (SD_x) and then multiplying the product by the standard deviation of the scores on the Y-scale (SD_y). An example is shown in Figure A-12.

In some cases it is convenient to use the *rank-difference method,* which produces a different coefficient of correlation called ρ (the Greek letter *rho*), which is similar to but not exactly the same as r. The formula is

$$\rho = 1 - \frac{6(\Sigma D^2)}{N(N^2 - 1)}$$

The method of applying the formula is demonstrated in Figure A-13.

Figure A-12 A product-moment correlation Shown here are the calculations required to determine the product-moment correlation between the scores made by 10 subjects on two different tests, X and Y. First we compute the mean and *SD* for scales X and Y as was described in Figure A-11. Then we calculate each subject's deviation scores (x and y) for each scale and multiply them together to produce the product of the deviation scores (xy). Note that four subjects who scored above the mean on scale X also scored above the mean on scale Y (subjects 2, 5, 6, and 10). Four students who scored below the mean on scale X also scored below the mean on scale Y (subjects 3, 4, 7, and 9). Only two subjects (1 and 8) scored above the mean on one test and below the mean on the other. Thus multiplying the x deviations times the y deviations gives us eight positive products and two negative products. Σxy, the total of the positive products minus the negative products, comes to 600. The correlation coefficient works out to .78.

Subject	Test scores X	Test scores Y	Deviation scores x	Deviation scores y	Product of deviation scores (xy)
1	60	81	−12	+ 1	− 12
2	80	92	+ 8	+12	+ 96
3	70	76	− 2	− 4	+ 8
4	65	69	− 7	−11	+ 77
5	75	88	+ 3	+ 8	+ 24
6	85	96	+13	+16	+208
7	60	64	−12	−16	+192
8	75	75	+ 3	− 5	− 15
9	70	77	− 2	− 3	+ 6
10	80	82	+ 8	+ 2	+ 16
					Σxy = 600

N = 10
For scale X, M = 72, and SD_x = 8.56
For scale Y, M = 80, and SD_y = 9.98

Thus

$$r = \frac{\Sigma xy}{(N-1)SD_xSD_y} = \frac{600}{(10-1) \times 8.56 \times 9.98}$$
$$= \frac{600}{768.9} = .78$$

Figure A-13 Computing a rank-difference correlation Here the same scores that were shown in Figure A-12 have been used to find the rank-difference correlation, which comes to .76—very close to the .78 found in Figure A-12 for the product-moment correlation. Note that here we disregard the individual scores on scale X and scale Y and use merely the rank of each score as compared with the others on the scale. Subjects 2 and 10 are tied for second place on the X scale. Their rank is therefore considered to be 2.5, halfway between second and third place.

Subject	Test scores X	Test scores Y	Rank X	Rank Y	Difference in rank (D)	Difference squared (D^2)
1	60	81	9.5	5	−4.5	20.25
2	80	92	2.5	2	−0.5	0.25
3	70	76	6.5	7	+0.5	0.25
4	65	69	8.0	9	+1.0	1.00
5	75	88	4.5	3	−1.5	2.25
6	85	96	1.0	1	0.0	0.00
7	60	64	9.5	10	−0.5	0.25
8	75	75	4.5	8	−3.5	12.25
9	70	77	6.5	6	−0.5	0.25
10	80	82	2.5	4	+1.5	2.25
						ΣD^2 = 39.00

N = 10
Thus

$$\rho = 1 - \frac{6(\Sigma D^2)}{N(N^2-1)} = 1 - \frac{6(39)}{10(10^2-1)}$$

$$= 1 - \frac{234}{990} = 1 - .24 = .76$$

Note that the D in the formula refers to the difference between a subject's rank on scale X—that is, whether first, second, third, or so on among all the subjects—and the subject's rank on scale Y. ΣD^2 is found by squaring each subject's difference in rank and adding to get the total for all subjects.

Contingency

One other frequently used type of correlation is known as the *coefficient of contingency,* symbolized by the letter C. This is used to find relationships between events that can be measured only on what is called a *nominal scale*—where all we can say about them is that they belong to certain groups. For example, we can set up a nominal scale on which all college students taking a humanities course are grouped in class 1, all taking engineering are grouped in class 2, and all taking a preparatory course for one of the professional schools such as law or medicine are grouped in class 3. We might set up another nominal scale on which we designate the students as males or females. If we then want to determine whether there is any relationship between a student's sex and the kind of college course the student is likely to take, we use the coefficient of contingency. Its meaning is roughly the same as that of any other coefficient of correlation.

SUMMARY

Probability and normal distribution

1. *Psychological statistics* is the application of mathematical principles to the interpretation of results obtained in psychological studies.
2. The statistical method is of special importance as a *way of thinking*—reminding us that many events take place in accordance with the laws of probability and that remarkable coincidences can often be explained as occurring by mere chance.
3. Many events in nature, including many human traits, fall into the pattern of the *normal curve of distribution.* In this curve, most such events or traits cluster around the average measurement, and the number then gets smaller toward the lower and upper extremes.

Descriptive statistics

4. *Descriptive statistics* provides a convenient method of summarizing scores and other psychological measurements. Important types of descriptive statistics are
   a. The *number of subjects,* or N.
   b. Measures of central tendency, including the arithmetic average, or *mean* (total of all scores divided by N), *median* (point separating the lower half of scores from the upper half), and *mode* (most frequent score in the group).
   c. Index of *variability,* including *range* (obtained by subtracting the lowest score from the highest) and *standard deviation,* symbolized by *SD.* In a normal distribution, 34.13 percent of the scores lie between the mean and 1 *SD* above the mean, 13.59 percent

between 1 *SD* and 2 *SD*s above the mean, and 2.14 percent between 2 *SD*s and 3*SD*s above the mean, while 0.14 percent lie more than 3 *SD*s above the mean. The same pattern of distribution exists below the mean.

5. *Percentiles* are used to describe the position of an individual score in the total group. A measurement on the 75th percentile is larger than 75 percent of the measurements, or, to put it another way, 25 percent of measurements lie on or above the 75th percentile.

Inferential statistics: the science of making generalizations

6. *Inferential statistics* is made up of procedures that allow us to make generalizations from measurements. It enables us to infer conclusions about a *population* or *universe,* which is the total of all possible cases in a particular category, by measuring a relatively small *sample.* To permit valid generalization, however, the sample must be *representative.* One way to ensure that the sample is representative is to choose it entirely at *random,* with each member of the population having an equal chance of being selected.
7. A set of findings is considered *statistically significant* when the probability that the findings might have been obtained by chance is only 5 in 100 or less. The figure is expressed mathematically as $p \leq .05$.

The technique and significance of correlation

8. *Correlations* between two measurements—such as scores on two different tests—range from 0 (no relationship) to +1 (perfect positive relationship) or −1 (perfect negative relationship).

The mathematical computations

9. The symbols and formulas for the statistical analyses are shown in Figures A-8 and A-9.

Glossary

A

abnormal behavior Behavior that is statistically unusual, considered strange or undesirable by most people, and a source of unhappiness to the person who displays it.

abnormal psychology The study of mental and emotional disturbances, their origins, and treatment.

absolute threshold The minimum amount of stimulus energy to which a receptor will respond 50 percent of the time.

accommodation The process of changing one's cognitive view when new information dictates such a change; one of the processes emphasized in Piaget's theory of intellectual development.

achievement motive The desire for success.

achievement test A test that measures the individual's present level of either skill or knowledge.

acrophobia An abnormal fear of heights.

active processing The mental work performed by a listener in interpreting speech. The listener tries to recognize sounds, identify words, look for syntactic patterns, and search for semantic meaning.

acuity A scientific term for sharpness of vision.

adaptation The tendency of the sensory apparatus to adjust to any steady and continued level of stimulation and to stop responding.

addiction *See* **physical dependence.**

adjustment Living in harmony with oneself and outside events.

adrenal glands A pair of endocrine glands, lying atop the kidneys.

adrenalin (*also called* **epinephrine**) A hormone secreted by the adrenal glands, associated with the bodily states of fear or "flight" situations.

aerial perspective A clue to distance perception; refers to the fact that distant objects appear less distinct and less brilliant in color than nearby objects.

affective disorder A form of mental disorder characterized by abnormalities of mood, including severe depression and swings of mood from one extreme to the other.

afferent neuron A neuron that carries impulses from the sense organs toward the central nervous system.

affiliation motive The desire to be closely associated with other people.

afterimage The visual phenomenon produced by withdrawal of a stimulus. Withdrawal is followed briefly by a positive afterimage, then by a negative afterimage.

aggression A type of behavior arising from hostile motives; it takes such forms as argumentativeness and fighting.

agoraphobia Abnormal fear of public places or of being virtually anywhere outside the home.

alcoholism The abnormal use of alcohol characterized by a strong dependence on alcohol and loss of control over the act of drinking. Usually results in serious physical, psychological, and social problems.

algorithm A problem-solving technique, for example a mathematical formula, that will produce a correct solution without fail.

all or none principle The fact that a neuron, if it fires at all, fires as intense an impulse as it can.

alpha waves A pattern of regular waves of seven to ten cycles per second characteristically found when the brain is at rest.

altered states of consciousness States of consciousness different from normal waking experience, such as those produced by sleep, hypnosis, or drugs.

altruism Behavior that is kind, generous, and helpful to others.

amnesia Loss of memory. It may be caused by physical injury or it may be a defense mechanism—an exaggerated form of repression.

amphetamine Any of a group of drugs that excite the central nervous system.

amplitude The characteristic of a sound wave that determines the loudness we hear.

androgens The male hormones, secreted by the testes.

androgynous Behaving in some ways society considers appropriate for females and in other ways considered appropriate for males.

antisocial personality An extreme form of personality disorder characterized by the absence of any conscience or sense of social responsibility or feeling for other people; also by selfishness, ruthlessness, and lying. People with this disorder are sometimes referred to as sociopaths or psychopaths.

anxiety An emotion characterized by a vague fear or premonition that something undesirable is going to happen.

anxiety disorder A form of abnormal behavior in which anxiety is the most obvious and outstanding symptom, or in which abnormal patterns of behavior such as obsessions and compulsions are developed to keep underlying anxiety under control.

apathy A state of indifference in which people lose all interest in what happens to them.

apparent motion The perception of motion in stimuli that do not actually move, as in *stroboscopic motion* or the *phi phenomenon.*

applied psychology The application of psychological knowledge and principles to practical situations in school, industry, social situations, and treatment of abnormal behavior.

approach-approach conflict A conflict in which the aroused motives have two incompatible goals, both of which are desirable.

approach-avoidance conflict A conflict in which the individual has a single goal with both desirable and undesirable aspects, causing mixed feelings.

aptitude A capacity to learn or to perform, such as mechanical or musical aptitude; an inborn ability that exists and can be measured even though the individual has had no special training to develop the skills (such as at mechanical or musical tasks).

aptitude test A test that measures the individual's *capacity* to perform, not the present level of skill or knowledge.

artificial intelligence The information-processing ability of electronic computers.

assertive coping A constructive attempt to get rid of anxiety and stress in a meaningful way that has some chance of success.

assimilation The process of incorporating a new stimulus into one's existing cognitive view; one of the processes emphasized in Piaget's theory of intellectual development.

associative network The manner in which knowledge is believed to be stored in memory in a complex network in which words and ideas are connected and interconnected by strands of associations that make them easy to retrieve.

attachment The inborn tendency of babies to approach caretakers, to be receptive to their help and to be least afraid when in their presence.

attention The process of focusing perception on a single stimulus or limited range of stimuli.

attitude An organized and enduring set of beliefs and feelings toward some object or situation and a predisposition to behave toward it in a particular way.

attribution theory The theory that social behavior is often influenced by our attempts to attribute behavior to a motive or other cause.

autokinetic illusion The illusion of self-generated movement that a stationary object, such as a point of light seen in an otherwise dark room, sometimes creates.

autonomic nervous system A complicated nerve network that connects the central nervous system with the glands and the smooth muscles of the body.

aversive conditioning A type of behavior therapy that attempts to associate a behavioral symptom with punishment rather than with pleasure and reward.

avoidance-avoidance conflict A conflict in which there is simultaneous arousal of motives to avoid alternatives, both of which are undesirable.

axon The fiber of the neuron that carries the nervous impulses to the end branches or "senders."

B

basilar membrane A piece of tissue dividing the cochlea more or less in half for its entire length. The organ of Corti, containing the hearing receptors, lies on this membrane.

behavior The activities of an organism, both overt, or observable (such as motor behavior), and covert, or hidden (such as thinking).

behavior genetics The study of how human beings and other organisms inherit characteristics that affect behavior.

behavior modification The technique of changing the behavior, especially of disturbed people, by manipulating rewards and punishments.

behavior therapy A type of psychotherapy that concentrates on eliminating abnormal behavior, which is regarded as learned, through new forms of learning.

behaviorism A school of thought maintaining that psychologists should concentrate on the study of overt behavior rather than on "mental life" or consciousness.

binocular vision A clue to distance perception; refers to the fact that the two eyes, being about two and a half inches apart, receive slightly different images of any seen object.

biofeedback A method of achieving control of bodily and brain functions through the feedback of information about these functions.

bipolar depression *See* **manic-depressive illness.**

blind spot The point at which the optic nerve exits from the eyeball, creating a small and mostly insensitive gap in the retina.

bodily movement The sense that keeps us informed of the position of our muscles and bones.

brain control A term for control of behavior through drugs or electrical stimulation of the brain.

breathing drive A biological drive aroused by physiological requirements for oxygen.

brightness One dimension of the visual sensation; dependent on intensity.

brightness constancy The tendency to perceive objects to be of consistent brightness regardless of the amount of light they actually reflect under different conditions of illumination.

broad-tuned receptors The receptor cells of the sense organs, sensitive to a wide range of stimuli.

bystander apathy The tendency of people, especially under crowded conditions, to ignore others who need help or situations that call for action.

C

Cannon-Bard theory A neurological theory of emotion holding that stimuli in the environment set off patterns of activity in the hypothalamus and thalamus; these patterns are then relayed both to the autonomic nervous system, where they trigger the bodily changes of emotion, and to the cerebral cortex, where they result in the feelings of emotion.

caretaker period The first eighteen months of life, during which babies' personality development depends chiefly on a close relationship with the mother or other caretaker.

case history An attempt to reconstruct a person's life to show how patterns of behavior have developed.

categories Logical groups into which materials can be lumped together; an aid to long-term memory.

cell body (of a neuron) The portion of a neuron containing its genes, as opposed to the fiber portion of the neuron.

central nervous system The spinal cord and the brain.

cerebellum The brain structure that controls body balance and helps coordinate bodily movements.

cerebral cortex The highest part of the brain, the surface of the cerebrum; a dense and highly interconnected mass of neurons.

cerebrum The large brain mass of which the cerebral cortex is the surface. It is divided into two separate halves called the left hemisphere and the right hemisphere.

certainty motive The desire to know where one stands and to be able to predict the course of events.

character disorder *See* **personality disorder.**

chromosome The mechanism of human heredity. There are 23 pairs of these tiny structures, 46 in all, found in the fertilized egg cell and repeated through the process of division in every cell of the body.

chronological age A person's actual age in years and months; compared with mental age to produce IQ.

ciliary muscles The muscles that control the shape of the lens of the eye.

cirrhosis The hardening and scarring of an organ—in the case of the liver, often as a result of heavy and prolonged use of alcohol.

clairvoyance The supposed ability to perceive something that is not apparent to the sense organs; a form of extrasensory perception.

classical conditioning A type of learning process through which a response becomes attached to a conditioned (or previously neutral) stimulus.

claustrophobia Abnormal fear of being in enclosed places, such as elevators.

client A term used, in preference to "patient," by clinical psychologists to refer to the people they treat.

clinical psychology The branch of applied psychology concerned with the application of psychological knowledge to the treatment of personality problems and mental disorders.

closure The tendency to perceive an object in its entirety even when some details are missing.

clustering The organization of materials into groups, such as categories; an aid to long-term memory and retrieval.

cochlea A bony structure of the inner ear shaped like a snail's shell; contains the receptors for hearing.

codeine A narcotic drug derived from the poppy plant.

cognition All the mental processes entailed in thinking.

cognitive consonance Consistency and agreement among one's beliefs, feelings, and behavior.

cognitive dissonance Lack of consistency among beliefs, feelings, and behavior. The theory of cognitive dissonance maintains that people are stongly motivated to relieve such dissonance, often by changing attitudes.

cognitive map Tolman's term for one type of "model of reality"; knowledge of the spatial features of the environment acquired, for example, by rats running a maze.

cognitive psychology A school of thought maintaining that the mind does not merely react to stimuli but actively processes the information it receives into new forms and categories.

collective unconscious In Jung's theory, a repository for the events of human history, superstitions, fears, and so on, which influence all people.

color blindness A visual defect involving deficiency in color discrimination.

color constancy The tendency to perceive a familiar object as being of constant color, regardless of changes in illumination that alter its actual stimulus properties.

communication A general term for exchanges of information and feelings between two (or more) people. For its special meaning in social psychology, *see* **persuasive communications.**

community therapy A type of interactional therapy in which the therapist attempts to change conflicts and patterns of behavior through alteration of behavior in the community.

complementary hues Two hues that, when added one to the other, yield gray.

complex cell A feature detector cell that receives messages from a number of simple cells and can therefore respond to several kinds of stimuli.

complexity The characteristic of a sound wave that determines the timbre we hear; caused by the number and strength of the overtones.

compulsion An irresistible urge to perform some act over an over again.

concept A mental grouping of objects or ideas on the basis of similarity.

conceptual intelligence The term used by Piaget to describe the developmental process after 2 years of age, in which the child increasingly uses concepts to organize the evidence of the senses and to engage in ever more complex thinking and problem solving.

concrete operations The term applied by Piaget to the stage of intellectual development (7–11 years of age) when children can reason logically about objects they see but have yet to learn to deal with rules in the abstract.

conditional positive regard In Rogers' personality theory, the cause of maladjustments; approval of some but not all aspects of an individual's behavior.

conditioned operant Behavior learned through operant conditioning; a type of behavior with which the organism "operates" on its environment to obtain a desired result.

conditioned response A response that has become attached through learning to a conditioned (or previously neutral) stimulus; an example is the salivation by Pavlov's dog to the sound of the metronome.

conditioned stimulus In classical conditioning, a previously neutral stimulus (such as a sound) that through pairing with an unconditioned stimulus (such as food) acquires the ability to set off a response (such as salivation).

cones One of two types of receptors for vision located in the retina. The cones are receptors for color and are also sensitive to differences in light intensity resulting in sensations of black, white, and gray.

conflict The simultaneous arousal of two or more incompatible motives, resulting in unpleasant emotions.

conformity The yielding by an individual to pressures from another person or, more usually, from a group.

connecting neuron A neuron that is stimulated by another neuron and passes its message along to a third neuron.

conservation The principle that such qualities as mass, weight, and volume remain constant regardless of changes in appearance; learned by the child during Piaget's stage of concrete operations.

consolidation A process, requiring time, during which the memory trace becomes more resistant to extinction.

constant reinforcement Provision of reinforcement for every desired response.

constructive processing The manner in which information is encoded into memory in the form of meanings and associations rather than as an exact copy.

continuity The tendency to perceive continuous lines and patterns.

contour In perception, the dividing line between figure and ground.

control group A group used for comparison with an experimental group. The two groups must be alike in composition and must be observed under the same circumstances except for the one variable that is manipulated in the case of the experimental group.

coping An attempt, constructive or destructive, to relieve anxiety and stress.

core of personality To personality theorists, the tendencies and characteristics common to all people.

cornea The transparent bulge in the outer layer of the eyeball through which light waves enter.

corpus callosum A large nerve tract that connects the left and right hemispheres of the cerebrum and enables the two hemispheres to cooperate and share in duties.

correlation The degree of relationship between two different factors; measured statistically by the correlation coefficient.

correlation coefficient A statistic that describes in numbers ranging from -1 to $+1$ the degree of relationship between two different factors.

cortisol A hormone secreted by the pituitary gland under stress or during emotional upset. Many people suffering from depression have excessive amounts of the hormone, which seems to persist in them for an unusually long time.

counseling psychology The branch of psychology that concentrates on vocational guidance, assistance with marital problems, and advice in other situations regarded as less serious or deepseated than the behavioral problems usually treated by clinical psychologists.

creative thinking A highly imaginative and rare form of thinking in which the individual discovers new relationships and solutions to problems and may produce an invention or an artistic creation.

credibility of the source A factor in the effectiveness of a persuasive communication.

critical ratio A measure of the degree of difference between two groups.

culture The ways of a given society, including its customs, beliefs, values, and ideals.

curve of forgetting A graph plotting the course of forgetting.

D

decibel A measure of the amplitude of sound.

defense mechanism A process, generally believed to be unconscious, in which the individual maintains that a frustration or conflict and the resulting anxiety do not exist or have no importance.

delirium tremens A condition popularly known as the "DTs" that occurs when an alcoholic suddenly withdraws from drinking; a state of intense panic characterized by agitation, tremors, confusion, horrible nightmares, and hallucinations.

delusion A false belief, such as imagining that one is already dead.

dendrite The part of the neuron, usually branched, that has the special function of being sensitive to stimuli and firing off a nervous impulse; the "receiving" portion of the neuron.

dendritic spines Outgrowths of a dendrite, capable of being stimulated by the axon of another neuron.

denial A defense mechanism, closely related to repression, in which the individual simply denies the existence of the events that have aroused anxiety.

dependency motive The desire to rely on others.

dependent variable A change in behavior that results from changes in the conditions that affect the organism—that is, from changes in an *independent variable*.

depressant A drug that reduces activity of the central nervous system.

depression A feeling of severe and prolonged sadness, sometimes accompanied by total apathy, that occurs as a reaction to stress; possibly influenced by chemical imbalances in the brain.

descriptive statistics A quick and convenient method of summarizing measurements. Important figures in descriptive statistics are the number of subjects; measures of central tendency, including the mean, median, and mode; and measurements of variability, including range and standard deviation.

desensitization An attempt to eliminate phobias by associating the stimulus that has caused the fear with relaxation rather than with fearful behavior; a technique used in behavior therapy.

development In personality theory, the way the common core of human personality is channeled into individual patterns by learning and experience.

developmental psychology The study of changes that take place, physically and psychologically, beginning at birth and continuing throughout life.

difference threshold (*also called* **just noticeable difference** *or* **j.n.d.**) The smallest difference in intensity or quality of stimulation to which a sensory receptor will respond 50 percent of the time.

difficult children Those who seem to display an inborn tendency to negative and stubborn behavior.

direct aggression Aggressive behavior focused directly on the obstacle that has caused frustration.

displaced aggression Aggressive behavior directed against an "innocent bystander" because the cause of frustration or conflict cannot itself be attacked.

dispositional factors Behavior-producing factors that represent lasting and consistent personality traits.

dissonance theory A theory maintaining that inconsistencies among one's beliefs, feelings, and behavior create a state of cognitive dissonance that the individual then tries to relieve, often by changing an attitude.

DNA (deoxyribonucleic acid) The complex chemical of which genes are composed.

double approach-avoidance conflict A conflict aroused by motives toward two goals that both have their good and bad points.

double blind An experimental technique in which neither the subjects nor the experimenter knows which subjects are in the control group and which are in the experimental group.

drive A psychological urge created by the body's demands for homeostasis.

drug abuse The repeated and excessive use of drugs, resulting in physical and psychological disturbances.

DSM-III An abbreviation for the *Diagnostic and Statistical Manual of Mental Disorders* established by the American Psychiatric Association in 1980 for the classification of various forms of abnormal behavior. The manual provides detailed descriptions of the symptoms of more than 230 mental disorders.

ductless gland *See* **endocrine gland.**

E

eardrum A membrane between the outer part of the auditory canal and the middle ear.

easy children Those who display an inborn tendency to be cheerful and adapt quickly.

EEG See **electroencephalograph.**

efferent neuron A neuron that carries impulses from the central nervous system toward the muscles or glands.

ego According to psychoanalytical theory of personality, the conscious, logical part of the mind that develops as we grow up and that is our operational contact with reality.

ego ideal Our notion of how we would always think and behave if we were as perfect as we would like to be.

electroencephalograph (EEG) A delicate instrument that measures the electrical activity of the brain.

electroshock A medical method of treating behavior disorders, especially depression, by passing an electric current through the patient's brain.

elimination drive A drive aroused by physiological requirements to get rid of the body's waste products.

emotion A feeling created by brain patterns accompanied by stirred-up or toned-down bodily changes.

emotional stress Wear and tear on the body created by the physical changes during emotional states.

empathy Understanding other people by putting yourself in their place and sharing their thoughts and feelings.

encoding The process through which information is transformed in a way that makes it simple and easy to handle and is then transferred to and stored in long-term memory.

encounter group A group of people who meet, usually under the leadership of a psychotherapist, with the goal of throwing off the masks they usually present in public and airing their true feelings.

end branches The part of the neuron that acts as the "sender" of messages to other neurons or to muscles and glands.

endocrine gland (*also called* **ductless gland**) A gland that discharges chemical substances known as *hormones* directly into the bloodstream, which then carries them to all parts of the body, resulting in many kinds of physiological changes.

endorphins A group of brain chemicals, similar in structure and effect to the painkiller morphine, that seem to affect parts of the brain associated with pain and with emotion and mood.

environmental psychology Study of the effects of the physical environment on physical and psychological well-being.

epinephrine *See* **adrenalin.**

equilibrium The sense that gives us the information needed to keep us in balance and oriented to the force of gravity.

ESP *See* **extrasensory perception.**

estrogen The chief female hormone, secreted by the ovaries.

Eustachian tube A passage between the middle ear and the air chambers of the mouth and nose; it keeps the pressure on both sides of the eardrum constant.

existential psychology A school holding that our own attitudes toward events in our life are more important than the events themselves.

expectancy One type of knowledge acquired through learning; the awareness that one event in the environment will be followed by another—in other words, "what leads to what."

expedient conformity Mere lip service to the opinion of the group.

experiment A scientific method in which the experimenter makes a careful and rigidly controlled study of cause and effect, by manipulating an independent variable (or condition affecting the subject) and observing its effect on a dependent variable (or the subject's behavior in response to changes in the independent variable).

experimental group A group of subjects whose behavior is observed while the experimenter manipulates an independent variable.

exploration The baby's early attempts to examine new aspects of the environment.

extinction The disappearance of a conditioned response (or other learned behavior) when reinforcement is withdrawn.

extrasensory perception (ESP) Any of several forms of supposed ability to perceive stimuli through some means other than the sense organs.

extrovert An individual who dislikes solitude and prefers the company of other people.

F

family therapy A type of interactional therapy that attempts to change the patterns of behavior that various members of a family display toward one another.

fantasy Images; daydreams.

"fast" fibers Neurons that carry sensory messages signaling sharp, localized pains.

fat cells Cells scattered throughout the body that are designed for the storage of fatty compounds. An excess of such cells is believed to be a common cause of obesity.

feature analysis Perceptual interpretation through examination of the individual features of an object.

feature detector A nerve cell that responds to special features of a stimulus reaching the sense organs—for example, to a horizontal line but not to a vertical line.

feedback In learning, information about how much progress is being made.

feminine The type of behavior society considers appropriate for females.

figure-ground In perception, the tendency to see an object as a figure set off from a neutral ground.

formal operations The term applied by Piaget to the stage of intellectual development (beginning at about 11 or 12 years of age) at which the child becomes capable of thinking in the abstract.

fovea The most sensitive part of the retina; contains only cones, which are packed together more tightly than anywhere else in the retina.

free association A tool of psychoanalysis in which patients, lying as relaxed as possible on a couch, are encouraged to let their mind wander where it will and to speak out every thought that occurs to them.

frequency The characteristic of a sound wave determining the tone or pitch that we hear; measured in number of cycles per second.

frustration The blocking of motive satisfaction by some kind of obstacle. (In popular usage, also the unpleasant feelings caused by the blocking of motive satisfaction.)

functional autonomy A principle holding that an activity that is originally a means to an end frequently acquires an independent function of its own and becomes an end in itself.

functional fixedness The tendency to think of an object in terms of its usual functions, not other possible functions; a common barrier to problem solving.

fundamental attribution error The common tendency to attribute the behavior of others to dispositional rather than situational factors.

G

galvanic skin reflex (GSR) A change in the electrical conductivity of the skin caused by activity of the sweat glands.

ganglion (*plural:* **ganglia**) A mass of nerve cells and synapses forming complex and multiple connections.

gate control mechanism A theoretical part of the spinal cord that lets pain messages through or shuts them off.

gene A tiny substance that is a molecule of *DNA.* The genes, grouped together into chromosomes, direct the growth of cells into specific parts of the body and account for inherited individual differences.

general adaptation syndrome A phrase coined by Selye for the sequence of events involved in prolonged stress; the initial shock or alarm, the recovery or resistance period, and at last exhaustion and death.

general anxiety The tendency to be anxious in many different kinds of situations.

general factor An intellectual ability posited by Thurstone as common to all the seven primary mental abilities.

generalized anxiety disorder A type of anxiety disorder marked by unfocused feelings of tension, uneasiness, and vague fear.

Gestalt psychology A school of thought holding that all psychological phenomena must be studied as a whole (rather than broken down into parts) and in the context in which they occur.

global processing Perceptual interpretation made by viewing the total pattern formed by the various individual features of an object.

gradient of texture A clue to distance perception; refers to the fact that nearby objects are seen more sharply and therefore appear grainier in texture than more distant objects.

grammar The rules of language for combining words into meaningful sentences.

group test A psychological test that can be given to many individuals at the same time.

group therapy A type of psychotherapy in which several patients are treated simultaneously.

GSR *See* **galvanic skin reflex.**

guided participation A technique used by behavior therapists for the practice of assertive coping.

H

hallucination An imaginary sensation, such as seeing nonexistent animals in the room or feeling bugs crawling under the skin.

hemispheres The two halves of the cerebrum and cerebral cortex. The left hemisphere appears to control language and logical thinking about details, the right hemisphere to be concerned with forms, patterns, and the "big picture."

Hering theory An early theory of color vision, holding that nervous messages must be paired as black-white, red-green, and blue-yellow; now believed to be generally true of the neurons from eye to cerebral cortex.

heroin A narcotic drug derived from the poppy plant.

heterosexuality Sexual attraction to members of the opposite sex.

heuristics A problem-solving technique; applying rules of thumb that have worked in similar situations and may—or may not—succeed again.

hippocampus A part of the brain that appears essential to the transfer of information from short-term memory to long-term memory.

homeostasis An internal environment in which such bodily states as blood circulation, blood chemistry, breathing, digestion, temperature, and so on, are kept at optimal levels for survival of the living organism.

homosexuality Sexual attraction to

members of the same sex.

hormones Substances produced by the endocrine glands and secreted into the bloodstream; complicated chemicals that trigger and control many kinds of bodily activities and behavior.

hostility motive The desire to cause physical or psychological discomfort in others.

hue The sensation of color, determined by the length of the light wave.

human engineering A branch of applied psychology concerned with the design of equipment and machinery to fit the size, strength, and capabilities of the people who will use it.

humanistic therapy A form of psychotherapy based on the assumption that people will grow in a positive direction if only they have the chance.

hunger drive A biological drive caused by deprivation of food.

hypercomplex cell The highest type of feature detector cell, capable of making fine distinctions among stimuli.

hypnosis The act of inducing the hypnotic state, in which the subject is in a sort of dreamlike trance and highly susceptible to suggestions from the hypnotist; sometimes used in psychotherapy.

hypomania A rare form of manic-depressive illness in which the individual remains primarily in a state of manic excitement, and the depressed phase of the illness never becomes very pronounced.

hypothalamus The portion of the brain that serves as a mediator between the brain and the body, helping control metabolism, sleep, hunger, thirst, body temperature, and sexual behavior, and that is also concerned with emotions.

I

id According to psychoanalytical theory, the unconscious part of the human mind comprising the individual's primitive instinctive forces toward sexuality (the *libido*) and aggression.

identification (a) A process in which children try to imitate the behavior of their parents or other "heroes." (b) In psychoanalytical theory, the process through which children resolve the Oedipus complex by absorbing their parents' characteristics into themselves. (c) As a defense mechanism, an attempt to relieve anxiety by becoming like another person or group.

illusion A perception that is a false interpretation of the actual stimuli.

illusory motion The perception of motion in an unchanging stimulus, such as in the *autokinetic illusion.*

imagery Forming a mental picture of events; an aid to long-term memory.

imitation *See* **learning through observation.**

implicit personality theory The assumption, held by most people, that certain personality traits are correlated with others—for example, that "warmth" of personality is accompanied by sociability and a good sense of humor.

incentive object A stimulus that arouses a drive or motive.

incentive value The particular desirability of any object or event that arouses a motive.

independence As used in social psychology, the tendency to make up one's own mind and decide on one's own behavior and thinking regardless of society's pressures.

independent variable A condition, affecting an experimental subject, that is controlled and varied by the experimenter, thus producing changes in the subject's behavior, called the *dependent variable.*

individual difference Any difference —as in physical size or strength, intelligence, sensory threshold, perceptions, emotions, personality, and so on—between the individual organism and other members of the species.

individual test A psychological test that is given by a trained examiner to one person at a time.

industrial psychology A branch of applied psychology, embracing the use of psychological knowledge in setting working hours and rest periods, improving relations between employer and employees, and so on.

inference A form of thinking; drawing logical conclusions from facts already known.

inferential statistics Statistics that are used to make generalizations from measurements.

inferiority complex A concept introduced by Adler to describe the condition of a person who for some reason has been unable to develop feelings of adequacy, independence, courage, and wholesome ambition.

information processing A description used by cognitive psychologists for the mental processes entailed in perception, learning, and thinking.

inhibition (a) The action of a neuron whose messages tend to stop another neuron from firing. (b) The suppression of behavior or emotional barriers to action, such as an inhibition against competitive or sexual activity.

"innate mechanism" Chomsky's term for a species-specific quality of the brain that enables us to learn and use language.

inner ear The portion of the ear inward from the oval window; contains the cochlea, vestibule, and semicircular canals.

inner standards The principles we develop—and are motivated to live up to—of how we are supposed to behave.

insight (a) In problem solving, the sudden "flash of inspiration" that results in a successful solution (*compare* trial and error learning). (b) In psychotherapy, the discovery by the patient of psychological processes that have caused difficulties.

instinct An elaborate and inborn pattern of activity, occurring automatically and without prior learning in response to certain stimuli in the environment.

insulin A hormone, secreted by the pancreas, that burns up blood sugar to provide energy.

intellectualization A defense mechanism in which the individual tries to explain away anxiety by intellectually analyzing the situations that produce the unpleasant feelings and making them a matter of theory rather than of action.

intelligence The ability to profit from experience, to learn new pieces of information, and to adjust to new situations.

intelligence quotient (IQ) A numerical value assigned to an individual as a result of intelligence testing. The average intelligence quotient is set at 100.

intelligence test A test measuring the various factors that make up the capacity called intelligence. It measures chiefly the individual's ability to use acquired knowledge in a novel way.

intensity The strength of light waves, accounting for sensations of brightness.

interactional therapies Types of psychotherapy that concentrate on changing the individual's behavior toward other people.

interest test A test measuring the individual's interest or lack of interest in various kinds of amusements, literature, music, art, science, school subjects, social activities, kinds of people, and so on.

interference Failures of memory caused by the effect of old learning on new or new learning on old.

intermittent reinforcement *See* **partial reinforcement.**

interpersonal attraction A person's tendencies to like other people, largely determined by such factors as similarities in attitudes, interests, and personality.

interpersonal therapies Types of psychotherapy that concentrate on changing the individual's behavior toward other people.

interposition A clue to distance perception; refers to the fact that nearby objects interpose themselves between our eyes and more distance objects.

interpretation In perception, the meaning we attach to stimuli affecting the sense organs.

interview A scientific method in which the investigator obtains information through careful and objective questioning of the subject.

introspection Inward examination of a "mental life" or mental process that nobody but its possessor can see in operation.

introvert A term for people who tend to be preoccupied with their own thoughts and activities and to avoid social contact.

intuitive thought The term applied by Piaget to the stage of intellectual development (4–6 years of age) when the child is developing concepts that become more and more elaborate but are still based largely on the evidence of the senses.

IQ *See* **intelligence quotient.**

iris A circular arrangement of smooth muscles that contract and expand to make the pupil of the eye smaller in bright light and larger in dim light.

J

James-Lange theory of emotion A physiological theory holding that stimuli in the environment set off physiological changes in the individual, that the changes in turn stimulate sensory nerves inside the body, and that the messages of these sensory nerves are then perceived as emotion.

just noticeable difference (j.n.d.) *See* **difference threshold.**

L

latent learning Learning that takes place without reinforcement, almost as if by accident, then lies latent until reinforcement is provided.

learned helplessness A condition in which the organism has been subjected to punishment over which it has no control, leading to an impairment of the ability to learn or use old habits.

learning The process by which behavior becomes altered or attached to new stimuli.

learning by imitation *See* **learning through observation.**

learning through modeling *See* **learning through observation.**

learning through observation (*also called* **learning through modeling, learning by imitation**) A type of learning in which the behavior of another organism is observed and imitated.

lens A transparent structure of the eye that changes shape to focus images sharply on the retina.

levels of processing A theory that long-term memory depends on how well we have analyzed and organized the material we learned.

libido According to psychoanalytic theory, a basic instinctual force in the individual, embracing sexual urges and such related desires as to be kept warm, well-fed, and happy.

lie detector A device designed to reveal whether a subject is telling the truth by measuring physiological changes, usually in heart rate, blood pressure, breathing, and galvanic skin reflex.

limbic system A set of interconnected pathways in the brain, including the hypothalamus, some primitive parts of the cerebrum that have to do with the sense of smell, eating and emotion, and other structures.

linear perspective A clue to distance perception; refers to the fact that parallel lines seem to draw closer together as they recede into the distance.

lithium A drug that is effective in treating the wide mood swings of manic-depression. It appears to work by reducing the amount of the neurotransmitter noradrenalin in the brain.

location constancy The tendency to perceive objects as being in their rightful and accustomed place and remaining there even when we move and their images therefore move across our eyes.

locus of control The belief that we are in control of our own life (inner locus) or at the mercy of outside events (external locus).

logical thinking An objective and disciplined form of thinking in which facts are carefully examined and conclusions consistent with the facts are reached.

long-term memory The permanent storehouse from which information can be retrieved under the proper circumstances.

loudness The hearing sensation determined by the amplitude of the sound wave.

LSD (lysergic acid diethylamide) A psychedelic drug.

M

made-up stories The organization of new materials by weaving them into narratives; an aid to long-term memory.

manic-depressive illness (*also called* **bipolar depression**) A type of mood disorder in which the person's mood swings from deep melancholy to wild excitement.

marijuana The dried leaves and flowers of the hemp plant; a drug that affects different users in different ways, often interfering with short-term memory and concentration and producing feelings of elation.

masculine The type of behavior society considers appropriate for males.

maturation The physical changes, taking place after birth, that continue the biological development of the organism from fertilized egg cell to complete adult.

mean A measure of central tendency obtained by dividing the sum of all the measurements by the number of subjects measured.

measurement The assignment of numbers to traits, events, or subjects according to an orderly system.

median A measure of central tendency; the point separating the lower half of measurements from the upper half.

meditation A technique for producing an altered state of consciousness.

medulla The connection between the spinal cord and the brain; an important connecting link that is vital to life because it helps regulate heartbeat, blood pressure, and breathing.

memory trace The basis of a theory of remembering, maintaining that learning left some kind of trace in the nervous system that could be kept active through use but tended to fade away or become distorted through lack of practice.

mental age A person's age as measured by performance on an intelligence test; a person who scores as well as the average 10-year-old has a mental age of 10 regardless of chronological age.

mental health A state of psychological well-being.

mentally gifted Having an IQ over 130.

mentally retarded Having an IQ below 70.

"mental models of reality" A key idea in cognitive psychology: the patterns of knowledge about the world that the brain builds through its information processing, stores, and uses as a guide to intelligent behavior.

mental telepathy The supposed ability of one person to know what is going on in another person's mind; a form of extrasensory perception.

metabolism The bodily process that maintains life by turning food and oxygen into living tissue and energy.

middle ear The portion of the ear between the eardrum and the oval window of the inner ear; contains three bones that aid transmission of sound waves.

mnemonic device A form of memory aid in which memorized symbols provide organization for otherwise unrelated material.

mode A measure of central tendency; the measurement at which the greatest number of subjects fall.

modeling *See* **learning through observation.**

moral development The child's acquisition of standards of right and wrong, extensively studied by Kohlberg.

morpheme The smallest meaningful unit of language, made by combining *phonemes* into a prefix, word, or suffix.

morphine A narcotic drug derived from the poppy plant.

motion parallax A term describing the fact that when we move our heads, near objects move across our field of vision more rapidly than objects that are farther away.

motivated forgetting Forgetting because we want to forget.

motivation A general term referring to the forces regulating behavior that is undertaken because of drives, needs, or desires and is directed toward goals.

motive A desire for a goal or incentive object that has acquired value for the individual.

motive hierarchy The pattern of motive strength, from strongest to weakest.

motive targets The people to whom motives are directed. People may exhibit strong motives of affiliation toward a "target" such as their parents and of hostility toward other "targets."

muscle tension Contractions of a muscle; one of the bodily changes often observed in emotion.

myelin sheath A fatty sheath, white in appearance, that covers many neuron fibers and speeds the transmission of nervous impulses.

N

narcissistic personality A personality disorder characterized by extreme narcissism, or self-love. Narcissistic individuals crave constant attention and admiration, and they use people for their own purposes.

narcotic A term applied to a group of drugs that produce repose or sleep.

naturalistic observation A scientific method in which the investigator does not manipulate the situation and cannot control all the variables; the investigator tries to remain unseen or as inconspicuous as possible.

nature-nurture The argument over the relative importance of heredity and environment.

negative reinforcement Rewarding learning through the termination of an unpleasant stimulus, for example, an electric shock.

negative transfer A process in which learning is made more difficult by interference from previous learning.

neopsychoanalysts The recent psychoanalytical theorists who have changed Freud's original ideas in various ways; "neo" means new.

nerve A group of neurons, small or very large in number, traveling together to or from the central nervous system; in appearance, a single large fiber that is in fact made up of many fibers.

nervous impulse A tiny charge of electricity passing from the dendrite end of the neuron to the end of the axon.

neuron The individual nerve cell; basic unit of the nervous system.

neurotransmitter A chemical released by one neuron that stimulates another neuron to fire; also sometimes inhibits the second neuron from firing.

nodes Booster stations along the axon of a neuron, helping speed transmission of the nervous impulse.

nonsense syllable A meaningless syllable, such as XYL or GEF, used in the study of learning.

noradrenalin One of the neurotransmitters. Also a hormone, secreted by the adrenal gland, that produces bodily changes associated with anger or "fight" situations.

norepinephrine *See* **noradrenalin.**

normal behavior Behavior that is relatively well adjusted, successful, and productive of happiness.

normal curve of distribution A bell-shaped curve that describes many events in nature; most cases cluster around the average, and the number declines approaching either the lower or the upper extreme.

O

obedience In social psychology, conformity to a figure of authority.

object constancy The tendency to perceive objects as constant and unchanging, even under varying conditions of illumination, distance, and position.

objective personality test A paper-and-pencil test administered and scored according to a standard procedure, giving results that are not affected by the opinions or prejudices of the examiner.

obsession A thought that keeps cropping up in a persistent and disturbing fashion.

obsessive-compulsive disorder A type of anxiety disorder marked by repetitious thoughts (obsessions) or acts (compulsions).

Oedipus complex According to Freud, the conflict of mingled love and hate toward the parents that every child undergoes between 2½–6 years of age.

operant avoidance Behavior, learned through operant conditioning, by which the organism attempts to avoid something unpleasant.

operant behavior Behavior that is not initially associated with or normally elicited by a specific stimulus.

operant conditioning The process by which, through learning, free operant behavior becomes attached to a specific stimulus.

operant escape Behavior, learned through operant conditioning, by which the organism seeks to escape something unpleasant.

operational rules A key concept in Piaget's theory of intelligence; a mental formula for manipulating ideas or objects into new forms and back to the original.

opium A drug derived from the poppy plant, most commonly used in the United States in the form of heroin.

opponent-process theory (of color vision) A type of pattern theory maintaining that our visual sensation of color results from three types of cones plus nerve cells. Messages they pick up from the eye are sent along as signals paired as red-or-green, blue-or-yellow, and black-or-white.

ordinary sleep A state of the organism in which brain activity is different from that in the waking state and the muscles of the body are quite relaxed.

organ of Corti The collection of hair cells, lying on the basilar membrane, that are the receptors for hearing.

organism An individual animal, either human or subhuman.

organization In learning, a form of processing; an aid to long-term memory. In perception, the tendency to find a pattern in stimuli reaching the sense organs.

outer ear The visible portion of the ear; collects sound waves and directs them toward the hearing receptors.

oval window The membrane through which sound waves are transmitted from the bones of the middle ear to the cochlea.

ovaries Glands that, in addition to producing the female egg cells, secrete hormones that bring about bodily changes known as secondary female sex characteristics.

overlearning The process of continuing to practice at learning after bare mastery has been attained.

overlearning, law of The principle that overlearning increases the length of time the material will be remembered.

overt behavior Observable behavior, such as motor movements, speech, and signs of emotion such as laughing or weeping.

overtones The additional vibrations of a source of sound, at frequencies higher than the fundamental tone it produces; the overtones account for the complexity and timbre of the sound.

P

pain drive A biological drive aroused by unpleasant or noxious stimulation, usually resulting in behavior designed to escape the stimulus.

pancreas The endocrine gland that secretes insulin.

panic disorder A type of anxiety disorder characterized by eposides of extreme terror during which the person suddenly feels overwhelmed with a sense of impending disaster and imminent death.

paradoxical sleep A state of the organism in which the brain's activity is similar to that in the waking state but the muscles are extremely relaxed; also known as REM sleep because it is accompanied by the rapid eye movements that characterize dreaming.

paranoid personality A type of personality disorder marked by constant and unwarranted suspicions and mistrust of other people.

parapsychology The study of psychological phenomena that cannot be explained in ordinary ways.

parasympathetic nervous system A division of the autonomic nervous system, composed of scattered ganglia that lie near the glands and muscles they affect. The parasympathetic system is most active in helping maintain heartbeat and digestion under normal circumstances.

parathyroids A pair of endocrine glands, lying atop the larger thyroid gland, that regulate the balance of calcium and phosphorus in the body, an important factor in maintaining a normal state of excitability of the nervous system.

partial reinforcement Reinforcement provided on some but not all occasions.

participant observation A scientific method in which the investigator takes part in a social situation, encounter group, or the like in order to study the behavior of others.

pattern theory A theory of the operation of the sense organs; it holds that our sensations are the result of the entire pattern of nervous impulses sent to the brain by many "broadly tuned" sensory receptors that respond in different ways to different stimuli.

peers For any individual, other people of about the same age and standing in the community; equals.

percentile A statistical term used to describe the position of an individual score in the total group.

perception The process through which we become aware of our environment by organizing and interpreting the evidence of our senses.

perceptual constancy The tendency to perceive a stable and consistent world even though the stimuli that reach the senses are inconsistent and potentially confusing.

perceptual expectation A form of mental set that influences interpretation.

performance Overt behavior; used as a measure of learning.

performance test An intelligence test or part of an intelligence test that measures the individual's ability to perform such tasks as completing pictures, making designs, and assembling objects.

peripheral nervous system The outlying nerves of the body and the individual neurons that make up these nerves.

peripheral traits To personality theorists, the observable traits that spring from the core of personality as channeled by individual development.

persistence of set In problem solving, the tendency to continue to apply a certain hypothesis because it has worked in other situations, often at the expense of trying different and much more efficient hypotheses.

personality The total pattern of characteristic ways of thinking, feeling, and behaving that constitute the individual's distinctive method of relating to the environment.

personality disorder A form of abnormal behavior characterized by failure to acquire mature and socially acceptable ways of coping with the problems of adult life; appears as part of the entire personality rather than being expressed in specific symptoms.

personality test A test designed to measure the various characteristics that make up the individual's personality.

perspective A clue to distance perception; refers to the fact that three-dimensional objects can be delineated on a flat surface, such as the retina of the eye.

persuasive communications The transmission of information and appeals to emotion in an attempt to change another person's attitudes.

phenomenological self A concept proposed by Rogers in his theory of personality; one's uniquely perceived self-image, based on the evidence of one's senses but not necessarily corresponding to reality.

pheromone Bodily secretions whose odor affects the behavior of other members of the species.

phi phenomenon Motion produced by a rapid succession of images that are actually stationary; the simplest form of *stroboscopic motion.*

phobic disorder A type of anxiety disorder in which the person's anxiety becomes attached to a specific object, situation, or activity—resulting in an unreasonable fear, or phobia.

phonemes The building blocks of language; basic sounds that are combined into *morphemes* and words.

physical attractiveness A stronger influence than generally supposed on interpersonal attraction.

physical dependence (*also called* **addiction**) A term used to describe the condition reached by heavy users of alcohol and drugs when they require increasingly large doses to produce the desired effect, and suffer painful psychological and physical symptoms if they stop using the substance.

pitch The property of being high or low in tone, determined by the frequency (number of cycles per second) of the sound wave.

pituitary gland The master endocrine gland that secretes hormones controlling growth, causing sexual development at puberty, and also regulating other endocrine glands.

placebo A "sugar pill" that relieves illness through psychological suggestion, although it has no medical value.

pleasure principle According to psychoanalytic theory, the demand of the unconscious id for immediate and total satisfaction of all its demands.

pons A structure of neurons connecting the opposite sides of the cerebellum; it helps control breathing and is apparently the origin of the nervous impulses that cause rapid eye movements during dreaming.

population In statistics, the term for all people or all events in a particular category—such as all male college students in the United States.

positive reinforcement Encouraging desired behavior through reward.

positive transfer A process in which learning is made easier by something learned previously.

posthypnotic suggestion A suggestion made during hypnosis, urging the subject to undertake some kind of activity after the hypnotic trance ends.

post-traumatic stress syndrome A special category of anxiety disorder suffered as a result of extremely shocking and stressful events—with symptoms that include loss of interest in life, insomnia and nightmares, and a tendency to keep reliving the experience.

power motive The desire to be in charge and control other people.

precognition The supposed ability to forecast events; a form of *extrasensory perception.*

preconceptual thought The term applied by Piaget to the stage of intellectual development (2–3 years of age) at which the child begins to use language to attach new meanings to stimuli in the environment and to use one stimulus as a symbol for another.

prejudice A deep-seated attitude that an individual maintains so stubbornly as to be uninfluenced by any information or experiences that might disprove it.

premise A basic belief that we use in thinking although it cannot be proved.

preoperational stage The term applied by Piaget to the period (2–7 years of age) when the child's ability to use language begins to dominate intellectual development.

primary mental abilities According to Thurstone, the seven basic abilities that make up intelligence. They are verbal comprehension, word fluency, number, space, associative memory, perceptual speed, and general reasoning.

primary reinforcement Reinforcement provided by a stimulus that the organism finds inherently rewarding—usually stimuli that satisfy biological drives such as hunger or thirst.

proactive interference Interference by something learned in the past with the ability to remember new materials.

problem solving Thinking that is directed toward the solution of a problem.

programed learning A system of instruction in which the subject matter is broken down into very short steps, mastered one at a time before going on to the next.

projection A defense mechanism in which the individual hides anxiety-producing motives by accusing other people of having them.

projective personality test A test in which subjects are expected to project aspects of their own personality into ambiguous pictures or inkblots.

propinquity Physical nearness to other people, often dictated by chance; a factor in attraction.

protoplasm The basic structure of living tissue, the "stuff of life."

prototype Another term for *schema.* Also the model on which a concept is based; the ideal example of a category, to which other items included in the category bear a family relationship.

proximity In perception, one of the factors affecting organization.

psychedelic drugs Drugs, such as LSD, that often produce hallucinations and a sense of detachment from one's body.

psychiatrist A physican who has had special training in treating behavior disturbances.

psychic energizer Any of a number of drugs used to relieve depression by increasing brain activity.

psychoanalysis A type of psychotherapy developed by Freud, in which the chief tools are free association, study of dreams and slips of the tongue, and transference. Psychoanalysis attempts to give the patient insight into unconscious conflicts.

psychoanalyst A person, usually a physician, who practices psychoanalysis.

psychoanalytical theory of personality A theory originally formulated by Freud that emphasizes three parts of the personality (a) the unconscious *id,* (b) the conscious *ego,* and (c) the largely unconscious *superego.*

psychokinesis (PK) The supposed ability of some people to influence physical events through exercise of the mind—for example, to make dice turn up as they wish.

psychological dependence The feeling that the use of alcohol or drugs is no longer an incidental feature of life, but instead is absolutely essential in order to handle day-to-day stress.

psychological statistics The application of mathematical principles to the description and analysis of psychological measurements.

psychology The science that systematically studies and attempts to explain observable behavior and its relationship to the unseen mental processes that go on inside the organism and to external events in the environment.

psychophysical methods Techniques of measuring how changes in the intensity or quality of a stimulus affect sensation.

psychosexual development The Freudian theory that psychological development goes through oral, anal, phallic, and genital stages.

psychosocial development A term used by Erikson in his theory that psychological development goes hand in hand with changing social relations.

psychosomatic illness An illness in which the physical symptoms seem to have mental and emotional causes.

psychosurgery A controversial treatment for mental disturbance; cutting or destroying parts of the brain.

psychotherapy A technique used by clinical psychologists, psychiatrists, and psychoanalysts in which a person suffering from personality disorder or mental disturbance is treated by the application of psychological knowledge.

public opinion survey A scientific sampling of attitudes (for example, the Gallup poll).

punishment An attempt to eliminate undesired behavior by providing unpleasant or painful consequences.

pupil The opening in the iris that admits light waves into the eyeball.

pure science The seeking of knowledge for the sake of knowledge.

Q

questionnaire A scientific method similar to the interview but in which information is obtained through written questions.

R

random sample A statistical sample that has been obtained by chance methods that avoid any bias.

range A measurement of variability obtained by subtracting the lowest measurement from the highest.

rapid eye movement (REM) Small movements of a sleeper's eyes that occur during paradoxical sleep and dreaming.

rationalization A defense mechanism in which people maintain that a goal they were unable to attain was not desirable or that they acted out of "good" motives rather than "bad."

reaction formation A defense mechanism in which people behave as if their motives were the opposite of their real motives; often characterized by excessive display of a "good" trait such as politeness.

reality principle According to psychoanalytic theory, the principle on which the conscious ego operates as it tries to mediate between the demands of the unconscious id and the realities of the environment.

recall A way of measuring learning. Subjects are asked to repeat as much of what they have learned as they can.

receptor A specialized nerve ending of the senses, capable of responding to an environmental stimulus.

receptor site A spot on the cell body of a neuron that can be stimulated by the axon of another neuron.

recognition A way of measuring learning. Subjects are asked to recognize what they have learned—for example, by picking out the right answer in a multiple-choice test.

reflex An automatic and unthinking reaction to a stimulus by the organism. A reflex is inborn, not learned, and depends on inherited characteristics of the nervous system.

regression A retreat toward types of activity appropriate to a lower level of maturity; a result of anxiety and stress.

rehearsal Repeating information to keep it alive in short-term memory.

reinforcement In classical conditioning, the pairing of an unconditioned stimulus (such as food) with a conditioned stimulus (such as sound). (Here, the food is the reinforcement.) In general, the process of assisting learning by pairing desired behavior with something the organism finds rewarding.

relearning A sensitive method of measuring learning. Subjects are asked to relearn to perfection something they have learned and partially forgotten, and the time this takes is noted.

reliable test A test that gives consistent scores when the same individual is tested on different occasions.

REM *See* **rapid eye movement, paradoxical sleep.**

replicate To repeat an experiment at a different time with a different experimenter and different subjects but with the same results.

representative sample A statistical sample in which all parts of the population are represented.

repression A defense mechanism in which people suffering anxiety over motives seem to banish the motives from conscious thought, pushing them into the unconscious.

resistance In psychoanalysis, a blocking of the patient's thoughts by anxiety and repressions.

response A general term used to describe any kind of behavior produced by a stimulus.

reticular activating system A network of nerves in the brain stem and hypothalamus, serving as a way station for messages from the sense organs.

retina A small patch of tissue at the back of the eyeball; contains the nerve endings called rods and cones that are the receptors for vision.

retrieval The process of extracting information from long-term memory.

retroactive interference Partial or complete blacking out of old memories by new learning.

rods One of the two types of receptors for vision located in the retina. The rods are receptors for light intensity, resulting in sensations of black, white, and gray.

rooting response One of the infant's inborn reflexes; an aid to finding food.

S

sample A relatively small group whose measurements are used to infer facts about the population or universe. To permit valid generalization the sample must be representative and random.

saturation The amount of pure hue present in a color as compared to the amount of other light wave lengths mixed in; thus the complexity of the mixture of waves determines saturation.

scanning A process that takes place in short-term memory; the study of information that has arrived in sensory memory from the sense organs. Also the controlled movement of the eyes when the person is studying a stimulus.

scapegoating Blaming other people, often members of minority groups, for feelings of frustration or conflict of which they are not the cause.

schema A generalized model, stored in memory, of the qualities of objects and events in the environment; also called *prototype.*

schizophrenia The most devastating of all mental disorders, in which the victim loses touch with reality and personality functioning breaks down and becomes completely disorganized.

schizophrenia spectrum According to one theory, a group of symptoms ranging from very mild to extreme, to which people may have tendencies because of an inherited defect.

school phobia An abnormal fear of leaving home to go to school experienced by children who are terrorized at the thought of venturing out into the world.

school psychology The application of psychological findings to methods of education.

secondary reinforcement Reinforcement provided by a stimulus that has acquired reward value through association with a primary reinforcing stimulus.

sedative A drug that reduces activity of the central nervous system.

selection In perception, the tendency to pay attention to only some of the stimuli that reach our senses.

selective exposure A term used by social psychologists to describe the fact that persuasive communications usually reach mostly people who already agree with them.

self-actualization Maslow's name for the human desire for self-fulfillment and harmony.

self-fulfilling prophecy An expectation about another person's behavior, leading to actions that cause the person to behave that way.

self-perception theory The theory that we often take the role of an outside observer trying to find the reasons for our own behavior.

semantics The meaning of the morphemes and words in language.

semicircular canals Three liquid-filled canals in the inner ear, containing receptors for the sense of equilibrium.

sense of identity The feeling sought by adolescents that they possess a distinct and unique character and are persons in their own right.

sensorimotor stage The term applied by Piaget to the period of intellectual development during the first two years of life, when the child knows the world only in terms of sensory impressions and motor activities.

sensory adaptation The tendency of sensory receptors to adjust to a stimulus and stop responding after a time.

sensory memory A memory system of very brief duration, composed of lingering traces of information sent to the brain by the senses.

sensory-motor area A part of the brain's cortex serving as a control point for sensory impressions and motor movements of the body.

sensory register *See* **sensory memory.**

separation anxiety Fear of being separated from the caretaker; a form of anxiety that develops in the infant of about 10 to 18 months.

set A tendency to respond in a certain way; to be prepared or "set" so to respond.

sex drive A biological drive aroused by physiological requirements for sexual satisfaction.

sex typing The process through which society molds its members into its traditional patterns of femininity or masculinity.

shadowing The pattern of light and shadow on a object; often a clue to perception of three-dimensional quality.

shape constancy The tendency to perceive objects as retaining their shape regardless of the true nature of the image that reaches the eyes because of the viewing angle.

shaping The learning of complicated tasks through operant conditioning, in which complex actions are built up from simpler ones.

short-term memory A memory system in which information is held briefly, then either transferred to long-term memory or forgotten.

similarity In perception, one of the factors affecting organization.

simple cell A feature detector cell at the lowest level.

single blind An experimental technique that keeps subjects in the dark as to whether they are in the control group or the experimental group.

situational factors Behavior-producing factors that depend on the situation of the moment, particularly the other people who are in the situation.

situational personality test A test in which the examiner observes the behavior of the subject in a situation deliberately created to reveal aspects of personality.

size constancy The tendency to perceive objects in their correct size regardless of the size of the actual image they cast on the eyes when near or far away.

sleep drive A biological drive aroused by the physiological requirements for sleep.

sleepwalking A form of dissociative reaction.

"slow" fibers Neurons that carry sensory messages signaling dull, unlocalized pain.

slow-to-warm-up children Those with an inborn tendency to need time to adjust to new situations.

smooth muscle A muscle of the internal organs, such as the stomach and intestines, or of the pupil of the eye, over which the individual ordinarily has no conscious control.

social behavior Actions taken in relation to another person or persons.

social class A subdivision of society characterized by the access it has or believes it has to power, determined in Western society largely by income and education.

social comparison theory The theory that often we can only evaluate our own abilities, opinions, and behavior by comparing ourselves with other people.

social learning theories of personality Theories maintaining that personality is made up of learned, habitual ways of responding to the environment.

social psychology The study of our behavior as members of society and the influence that the actions and attitudes of other people have on our behavior and thinking.

socialization The training of the young in the ways of the society.

society Any organized group of people, large or small.

species-specific behavior A type of behavior toward which members of a species have an inborn tendency.

specific anxiety Being anxious in one particular situation although not in others.

spinal cord The thick cable of neurons connecting with the brain; a part of the central nervous system.

spontaneous recovery The tendency of a conditioned response that has undergone extinction to occur again after a rest period.

SQ3R system An efficient five-step study method (survey, question, read, recite, review).

standard deviation (SD) A statistical device for describing the variability of measurements.

standardized test A test that has been pretested on a large and representative sample so that one person's score can be compared with the scores of the population as a whole.

stereotype An attitude that disregards individual differences and holds that all people of a certain group behave in the same manner.

stereotyped behavior A tendency to repeat some action over and over again, almost as a ritual; a result of frustration.

stimulant A drug that increases activity of the central nervous system.

stimulus Any form of energy capable of exciting the nervous system.

stimulus complexity The relative level of simplicity or complexity possessed by a sensory stimulus. The organism apparently has stimulus needs for stimuli of a particular level of complexity found the most "comfortable."

stimulus discrimination The ability, acquired through learning, to make distinctions between stimuli that are similar but not exactly alike.

stimulus generalization The tendency of an organism that has learned to associate a stimulus with a certain kind of behavior to display this behavior toward stimuli that are similar though not exactly identical to the original stimulus.

stimulus need The tendency of an organism to seek certain kinds of stimulation. The tendency does not have the life-and-death urgency of a drive, nor is its goal as specific and clear-cut. Examples are the needs for stimulation, stimulus variability, and physical contact (or tactual comfort).

stimulus variability Change and variety in stimulation; believed to be one of the organism's inborn stimulus needs.

stranger anxiety Fear of unfamiliar faces, one of the first forms of anxiety, that develops in the child at about 8 months of age.

stress The bodily wear and tear caused by physical or psychological arousal by outside events.

stress interview A form of situational personality test in which the subject is asked deliberately hostile questions and the interviewers pretend to disbelieve the answers.

stroboscopic motion Motion produced by a rapid succession of images that are actually stationary, as in motion pictures.

subculture A culture within a culture —that is, the ways of life followed by a group in a society that does not adhere to all the practices of the society as a whole.

sublimation A defense mechanism in which a forbidden motive is channeled toward a more acceptable goal, as when an artist directs sexual urges into the creation of paintings.

substance abuse The heavy and frequent use of alcohol and drugs to the point that the user can no longer function normally and continues to seek the substance despite damage to health and threat to life.

superego According to psychoanalytical theory, a largely unconscious part of the mind that threatens punishment for transgressions.

sympathetic nervous system A division of the autonomic nervous system, composed of long chains of ganglia lying along both sides of the spinal column. It activates the glands and smooth muscles of the body and helps prepare the organism for "fight" or "flight."

synapse A junction point between the axon of one neuron and the dendrite or cell body receptor site of another neuron.

synaptic cleft The tiny space between the axon of one neuron and the dendrite or receptor site of another neuron.

synaptic knob A swelling at the end of a dendrite; an important structure in the transmission of messages across the synapse.

synaptic vesicles Tiny sacs in the synaptic knob, containing neurotransmitters.

syndrome A medical term meaning the entire pattern of symptoms and events that characterize the course of a disease.

syntax The rules of language for sentence structure.

T

tabula rasa A "blank tablet"; a phrase used to describe the theory that the mind of a human baby is a "blank tablet" on which anything can be written through learning and experience.

tactual comfort Physical contact; one of the stimulus needs.

taste buds The receptors for the sense of taste; found on the tongue, at the back of the mouth, and in the throat.

teaching machine A device used in programed learning; the machine presents the program one step at a time and asks a question that the learner answers before going on to the next step.

temperature drive A biological drive aroused by physiological requirements that the body temperature be kept at a constant level (in human beings, around 98.6° Fahrenheit).

test A measurement of a sample of individual behavior. Ideally, a scientific test should be: (a) objective, (b) standardized, (c) reliable, and (d) valid.

test anxiety A form of specific anxiety common among students, centering on taking exams.

testes Glands that, in addition to producing the male sperm cells, secrete hormones that bring about secondary male sex characteristics, such as the growth of facial hair and change of voice.

thalamus The brain's major relay station, connecting the cerebrum with the lower structures of the brain and the spinal cord.

theory A statement of general principles that explains events observed in the past and predicts what will happen under a given set of circumstances in the future.

thinking The covert manipulation of images, symbols, and other mediational units, especially language, concepts, premises, and rules.

thirst drive A biological drive aroused by deprivaton of water.

threshold The minimum amount of stimulation or difference in stimulation to which a sensory receptor will respond 50 percent of the time.

thyroid gland An endocrine gland that regulates the rate of metabolism and affects the body's activity level.

tic The involuntary twitching of a muscle.

timbre The quality of a sound, determined by the number and strength of the overtones that contribute to the complexity of the sound wave.

tip of the tongue phenomenon A partially successful attempt at retrieval in which we cannot quite remember a word (for example) but seem to have it almost available or "on the tip of the tongue."

token economy An arbitrary economic system, often used in mental hospitals, in which patients are rewarded for good behavior with tokens that they can exchange like money for various privileges.

tolerance A sign of addiction to alcohol or drugs when the user begins to require increasingly large doses to produce anything like the desired effect.

tranquilizer A drug that reduces anxiety and often eliminates the hallucinations and delusions of schizophrenics, apparently by slowing down the activity of the brain.

transfer of learning The effect of prior learning on new learning.

transference A psychoanalytic term for the tendency of the patient to transfer to other people (including the psychoanalyst) the emotional attitudes felt as a child toward such much loved and hated persons as parents and siblings.

tremor A shaking produced when two sets of muscles work against each other; one of the bodily changes observed in emotion.

trial and error learning A form of learning in which one response after another is tried and rejected as unsuitable, until at last a successful response is made.

true conformity Changing one's true beliefs to agree with the group.

U

unconditional positive regard The basis of Rogers' humanistic therapy; total acceptance of clients as people if not all their behavior.

unconditioned response An automatic, unlearned reaction to a stimulus—such as the salivation of Pavlov's dog to food.

unconditioned stimulus A stimulus that is innately capable of causing a reflex action—such as the food that originally caused Pavlov's dog to respond with salivation.

unconscious mind In psychoanalytical theory, the bulk of the human mind, though we are not usually aware of it.

unconscious motives Desires of which we are unaware but which nonetheless influence our behavior.

unipolar depression A type of mood disorder that recurs without the swings in mood experienced in bipolar depression.

V

valid test A test found to actually measure the characteristic that it is designed to measure.

variability In statistics, the amount of variation found in a group of measurements, described by the range and standard deviation.

variable A condition that is subject to change, especially in an experiment.

verbal test An intelligence test or part of an intelligence test that measures the individual's ability to deal with verbal symbols; it may include items measuring vocabulary, general comprehension, mathematical reasoning, ability to find similarities, and so on.

vestibule A chamber in the inner ear containing receptors for the sense of equilibrium

visceral organs The internal organs, such as the stomach, intestines, liver, kidneys, and so on.

visual purple A light-sensitive substance associated with the rods of the retina.

vocational aptitude test A test that measures the ability to perform specialized skills required in various kinds of jobs.

vocational guidance The technique of helping a person select the right lifetime occupation, often through tests of aptitudes and interests.

W

wavelength The characteristic of light waves that determines hue.

Weber's Law The rule that the difference threshold, or just noticeable difference, is a fixed percentage of the original stimulus.

withdrawal In the process of coping, a reaction in which people try to relieve feelings of frustration by withdrawing from the attempt to attain their goals. In alcoholism and drug abuse, the painful physical and psychological reactions experienced by individuals after they stop using the substance to which they are physically addicted.

X

X-chromosome One of the two chromosomes that determine sex; an X-X pairing produces a female; an X-Y pairing, a male.

Y

Y-chromosome One of the two chromosomes that determine sex.

Young-Helmholtz theory A theory stating that, since the entire range of hues can be produced by combining red, green, and blue, there must be three kinds of cones differentially sensitive to these wave lengths.

References and Acknowledgments

AACRAO (American Association of Collegiate Registrars and Admissions Officers) and the College Board. *Undergraduate admissions, 1980.* New York: College Entrance Examination Board, 1980.

Abelson, H. C., and **Fishburn, P. M.** *Nonmedical use of psychoactive substances.* Princeton, N.J.: Response Analysis Corp., 1976.

Abernathy, T. J., Jr., et al. A comparison of the sexual attitudes and behavior of rural, suburban, and urban adolescents. *Adolescence,* 1979, *14,* 289–95.

Abramson, L. Y., Seligman, M. E. P., and **Teasdale, J. D.** Learned helplessness in humans. *Journal of abnormal psychology,* 1978, *87*, 49–74.

Adler, A. Characteristics of the first, second, and third child. *Children,* 1928, *3,* 14–52.

Aigner, T. G., and **Balster, R. L.** Choice behavior in rhesus monkeys. *Science,* 1978, *201,* 234–35.

Ainsworth, M. D. S., and **Bell, S. M.** Attachment, exploration, and separation. *Child development,* 1970, *41*, 49–68.

Akhtar, S., and **Thomson, J. A., Jr.** Overview: narcissistic personality disorder. *American journal of psychiatry,* 1982, *139*, 12–20.

Alexander, C. N. Unpublished doctoral dissertation. Harvard University, 1982.

Altman, D., et al. *Trust of the stranger in the city and the small town.* Unpublished research, Graduate Center, City University of New York, 1969.

American Psychiatric Association. *Diagnostic and statistical manual of mental disorders,* 3d ed. Washington, D.C., 1980.

Anand, B. K., and **Brobeck, J. R.** Hypothalamic control of food intake in rat and cat. *Yale journal of biology and medicine,* 1951, *24,* 123–40.

Anastasi, A. Coaching, test sophistication, and developed abilities. *American psychologist,* 1981, *36,* 1086–93.

Anastasi, A. *Psychological testing,* 5th ed. New York: Macmillan, 1982.

Anderson, F. Personal communication, 1981.

Anderson, J. R., and **Bower, G. H.** *Human associative memory.* Washington, D.C.: Winston, 1973.

Andrew, R. J. The origins of facial expressions. *Scientific American,* 1965, *213,* 88–94.

Arnold, M. B. *Emotion and personality,* Vol. 1. New York: Columbia University Press, 1960.

Aronfreed, J. The socialization of altruistic and sympathetic behavior. In J. Macauley and L. Berkowitz, eds. *Altruism and helping behavior.* New York: Academic Press, 1970.

Aronson, E. *The social animal.* San Francisco: Freeman, 1972.

Aronson, E., and **Linder, D.** Gain and loss of esteem as determinants of interpersonal attractiveness. *Journal of experimental social psychology,* 1965, *1,* 156–71.

Asch, S. E. Studies of independence and submission to group pressure. I. A minority of one against a unanimous majority. *Psychological monographs,* 1956, *70* (No. 416), Fig. 2, p. 7.

Ashear, J. B. Study cited in E. H. Hess. The role of pupil size in communication. *Scientific American,* 1975, *233,* 110–19.

Asher, S. R., Oden, S. L., and **Gottman, J. M.** Children's friendships in school settings. In E. M. Hetherington and R. D. Parke, eds. *Contemporary readings in child psychology,* 2d ed. New York: McGraw-Hill, 1981.

Astin, A. W. *Minorities in American higher education.* San Francisco: Jossey-Bass, 1982.

Atkinson, J. W. The mainsprings of achievement-oriented activity. In J. W. Atkinson and J. O. Raynor, eds. *Personality, motivation, and achievement.* Washington, D.C.: Winston, 1974.

Atkinson, J. W. Resistance and overmotivation in achievement-oriented activity. In G. Serban, ed. *Psychopathology of human adaptation. Proceedings of the Third International Symposium of the Kittay Scientific Foundation.* New York: Plenum Press, 1976.

Atkinson, J. W., and **Litwin, G. H.** Achievement motive and test anxiety conceived as motive to approach success and motive to avoid failure. *Journal of abnormal and social psychology,* 1960, *60,* 53–62.

Atkinson, J. W., and **Raynor, J. O.** *Personality, motivation, and achievement.* Washington, D.C.: Winston, 1974.

Atkinson, J. W., et al. The achievement motive, goal setting, and probability preferences. *Journal of abnormal and social psychology,* 1960, *60*, 27–37.

Atkinson, K., MacWhinny, B., and **Stoel C.** An experiment on recognition of babbling. In *Papers and reports on child language development.* Stanford, Calif.: Stanford University Press, 1970.

Ayllon, T., and **Azrin, N. H.** *The token economy.* New York: Appleton-Century-Crofts, 1968.

Ayoub, D. M., Greenough, W. T., and **Juraska, J. M.** Sex differences in dendritic structure in the preoptic area of the juvenile macaque monkey brain. *Science,* 1983, *219,* 197–98.

Baastrup, P. C. Lithium in the treatment of recurrent affective disorders. In F. N. Johnson, ed. *Handbook of lithium therapy.* Baltimore: University Park Press, 1980.

Baddeley, A. D. The trouble with levels: a reexamination of Craik and Lockhart's framework for memory research. *Psychological review,* 1978, *85,* 139–52.

Baddeley, A. The cognitive psychology of everyday life. *British journal of psychology,* 1981, *72,* 257–69.

Baer, D. M. The control of developmental process. In J. R. Nesselroade and H. W. Reese, eds. *Life-span developmental psychology.* New York: Academic Press, 1973.

Balagura, S. *Hunger.* New York: Basic Books, 1973.

Baldwin, A. L. Personal communication, 1975.

Bales, R., and **Slater, P.** Role differentiation in small decision-making groups. In T. Parsons and R. Bales, eds. *The family, socialization, and interaction process.* Glencoe, Ill.: Free Press, 1955.

Ball, G. G. Vagotomy. *Science,* 1974, *184,* 484–85.

Baltes, P. B., and **Schaie, K. W.** Aging and IQ: the myth of the twilight years. *Psychology today,* March 1974, *7,* 35–40.

Bander, R. S., Russell, R. K., and **Zamostny, K. P.** A comparison of cue-controlled relaxation and study-skills counseling in the treatment of mathematics anxiety. *Journal of educational psychology,* 1982, *74,* 96–103.

Bandura, A. *Aggression.* Englewood Cliffs, N.J.: Prentice-Hall, 1973.

Bandura, A. Behavior theory and the models of man. *American psychologist,* 1974, *29,* 859–69.

Bandura, A. Social learning perspective on behavior change. In A. Burton, ed. *What makes behavior change possible.* New York: Brunner/Mazel, 1976.

Bandura, A. Self-efficacy. *Psychological review,* 1977, *84,* 191–215.

Bandura, A., Blanchard, E. B., and **Ritter, B.** Relative efficacy of desensitization and modeling approaches for inducing behavioral, affective, and attitudinal changes. *Journal of personality and social psychology,* 1969, *13,* 173–99.

Bandura, A., Jeffery, R. W., and **Gajdos, E.** Generalizing change through self-directed performance. *Behavior research and therapy,* 1975, *13,* 141–52.

Bane, M. J. *Here to stay.* New York: Basic Books, 1976.

Banquet, J. P. Spectral analysis of the EEG in meditation. *EEG clinical neurophysiology,* 1973, *35,* 143–51.

Barber, J. D. *The presidential character.* Englewood Cliffs, N.J.: Prentice-Hall, 1972.

Bardwick, J. M. *Psychology of women.* New York: Harper & Row, 1971.

Barker, R. G., Dembo, T., and **Lewin, K.** Frustration and regression. *University of Iowa studies in child welfare,* 1941, *18* (No. 386).

Baron, R. A., and **Lawton, S. F.** Environmental influences on aggression. *Psychonomic science,* 1972, *26,* 80–82.

Barron, F. The psychology of imagination. *Scientific American,* 1958, *199,* 50.

Barron, F., Jarvik, M., and **Bunnell, S., Jr.** The hallucinogenic drugs. In *Altered states of awareness.* San Francisco: Freeman, 1972.

Barron, F. H. *Creativity and personal freedom.* New York: Van Nostrand Reinhold, 1968.

Baumrind, D. From each according to her ability. *School review,* 1972, *80,* 161–97.

Bayley, N. Development of mental abilities. In P. Mussen, ed. *Carmichael's manual of child development.* New York: Wiley, 1970.

Beach, F. A. Hormonal control of sex-related behavior. In F. A. Beach, ed. *Human sexuality in four perspectives.* Baltimore: Johns Hopkins University Press, 1976.

Beary, J. F., and **Benson, H.** A simple psychophysiologic technique which elicits the hypometabolic changes of the relaxation response. *Psychosomatic medicine,* 1974, *36,* 115–20.

Beck, A. T. *Depression: causes and treatment.* Philadelphia: University of Pennsylvania Press, 1967.

Beeler, N. F., and **Branley, F. M.** *Experiments in optical illusion.* New York: Crowell, 1951.

Bekerian, D. A., and **Baddeley, A. D.** Saturation advertising and the repetition effect. *Journal of verbal learning and verbal behavior,* 1980, *19,* 17–25.

Békésy, G. V. *Experiments in hearing.* New York: McGraw-Hill, 1960.

Belensky, G. L. Presentation to a section of the Society of Neuroscience, Potomac, Md., 1976.

Belmont, L., and **Marolla, F. A.** Birth order, family size, and intelligence. *Science,* 1973, *182,* 1096–101.

Belmont, L., Stein, Z., and **Zybert, P.** Child spacing and birth order. *Science,* 1978, *202,* 995–96.

Bem, D. J. *Beliefs, attitudes, and human affairs.* Belmont, Calif.: Brooks/Cole, 1970.

Bem, D. J. Self-perception theory. In L. Berkowitz, ed. *Advances in experimental social psychology,* Vol. 6. New York: Academic Press, 1972.

Bem, S. L. The measurement of psychological androgyny. *Journal of consulting and clinical psychology,* 1974, *42,* 155–62.

Bem, S. L. Gender schema theory: a cognitive account of sex typing. *Psychological review,* 1981, *88,* 354–64.

Benedict, R. *Patterns of culture,* 2d ed. Boston: Houghton Mifflin, 1959.

Benjamin, M., et al. Test anxiety: deficits in information processing. *Journal of educational psychology,* 1981, *73,* 816–24.

Bennett, E. L., et al. Chemical and anatomical plasticity in the brain. *Science,* 1964, *146,* 610–19.

Benson, H. *The relaxation response.* New York: William Morrow, 1975.

Benson, H., Rosner, B. A., and **Marzetta, B. R.** Decreased systolic blood pressure in hypertensive subjects who practiced meditation. *Journal of clinical investigations,* 1973, *52,* 8.

Benson, H., and **Wallace, R. K.** Decreased drug abuse with transcendental meditation—a study of 1,862 subjects. In C. J. Zarafonetis, ed. *Drug abuse.* New York: Lea and Febiger, 1972.

Berg, I. *Education and jobs.* New York:

Praeger, 1970.

Berger, R. J. The sleep and dream cycle. In A. Kales, ed. *Sleep, physiology, and pathology.* Philadelphia: Lippincott, 1969.

Bernal, M. E., et al. Behavior modification and the brat syndrome. *Journal of consulting and clinical psychology,* 1968, *32,* 447–55.

Berscheid, E., and **Walster, E.** Physical attractiveness. In L. Berkowitz, ed. *Advances in experimental social psychology,* Vol. 7. New York: Academic Press, 1974.

Bersoff, D. N. Testing and the law. *American psychologist,* 1981, *36,* 1047–56.

Bettelheim, B. Individual and mass behavior in extreme situations. *Journal of abnormal and social psychology,* 1943, *38,* 417–52.

Bettelheim, B. *Freud and man's soul.* New York: Knopf, 1983.

Bexton, W. H., Heron. W., and **Scott, T. H.** Effects of decreased variation in the sensory environment. *Canadian journal of psychology,* 1954, *8,* 70–76.

Bjork, R. A. Theoretical implications of directed forgetting. In A. W. Melton and E. Martin, eds. *Coding processes in human memory.* Washington, D.C.: Winston, 1972.

Björntorp, P. Disturbances in the regulation of food intake. *Advances in psychosomatic medicine,* 1972, *7,* 116–47.

Black, J. B., and **Bern, H.** Causal coherence and memory for events in narratives. *Journal of verbal learning and verbal behavior,* 1981, *20,* 267–75.

Black, J. B., Turner, T. J., and **Bower, G. H.** Point of view in narrative comprehension, memory, and production. *Journal of verbal learning and verbal behavior,* 1979, *18,* 187–98.

Blass, E. M., and **Hall, W. G.** Drinking termination. *Psychological review,* 1976, *83,* 356–74.

Block, J., Von Der Lippe, A., and **Block, J. H.** Sex-role and socialization patterns. *Journal of consulting and clinical psychology,* 1973, *41,* 321–41.

Block, N. J., and **Dworkin, G.,** eds. *The IQ controversy.* New York: Pantheon, 1976.

Bloom, W., and **Fawcett, D. W.** *A textbook of histology,* 9th ed. Philadelphia: Saunders, 1968.

Blum, J. E., Jarvik, I. F., and **Clark, E. T.** Rate of change on selective tests of intelligence. *Journal of gerontology,* 1970, *25,* 171–76.

Bogen, J. Drawings by a patient. *Bulletin of the Los Angeles Neurological Society,* 1969, *34,* 73–105.

Bolles, R. C. Reinforcement, expectancy, and learning. *Psychological review,* 1972, *79,* 394–409.

Bond, E. A. *Tenth-grade abilities and achievements.* New York: Columbia University Teachers College, 1940.

Bonvillian, J. D., Orlansky, M. D., and **Novack, L. L.** Early sign language acquisition and its relation to cognitive and motor development. In J. G. Kyle and B. Woll. *Language in sign: an international perspective on sign language.* London: Croom Helm, 1983.

Boring, E. G. Size constancy in a picture. *American journal of psychology,* 1964, *77,* 494–98.

Bower, G. H. Organizational factors in memory. *Cognitive psychology,* 1970, *1,* 18–46.

Bower, G. H. Mental imagery and associative learning. In L. Gregg, ed. *Cognition in learning and memory.* New York: Wiley, 1972.

Bower, G. H. Improving memory. *Human nature,* 1978, *1,* 64–72.

Bower, G. H. Mood and memory. *American psychologist,* 1981, *36,* 129–48.

Bower, G. H., and **Clark, M. C.** Narrative stories as mediators for serial learning. *Psychonomic science,* 1969, *14,* 181–82.

Bower, G. H., et al. Hierarchical retrieval schemes in recall of categorized word lists. *Journal of verbal learning and verbal behavior,* 1969, *8,* 323–43.

Bowerman, M. Learning the structure of causative verbs. *Papers and reports on child language development,* Stanford University, 1974, *8,* 142–78.

Bowerman, M. Systematizing semantic knowledge. *Child development,* 1978, *49,* 977–87.

Bowlby, J. Childhood mourning and its implications for psychiatry. *American journal of psychiatry,* 1961, *118,* 481–98.

Braestrup, C. Neurotransmitters and CNS disease: anxiety. *Lancet,* 1982, *11,* 8306, 1030–34.

Brecher, E. M. *Licit and illicit drugs.* Boston: Little, Brown, 1972.

Brehm, J. Postdecision changes in the desirability of alternatives. *Journal of abnormal and social psychology,* 1956, *52,* 384–89.

Breland, K., and **Breland, M.** The misbehavior of organisms. *American psychologist,* 1961, *61,* 681–84.

Bridger, W. N. Sensory habituation and discrimination in the human neonate. *American journal of psychiatry,* 1961, *117,* 991–96.

Briggs, J. *Never in anger.* Cambridge, Mass.: Harvard University Press, 1970.

Brigham, J. C., and **Wrightsman, L. S.** *Contemporary issues in social psychology.* Monterey, Calif.: Brooks/Cole, 1982.

Broadbent, D. E. The hidden preattentive process. *American psychologist,* 1977, *32,* 109–18.

Broen, P. The verbal environment of the language-learning child. *Monographs of the American Speech and Hearing Association,* 1972, p. 17.

Brooks, J., and **Lewis, M.** Attachment behavior in thirteen-month-old, opposite-sex twins. *Child development,* 1974, *45,* 243–47.

Bross, I. D. J. Language in cancer research. In G. P. Murphy, D. Pressman, and E. S. Mirand, eds. *Perspectives in cancer research and treatment.* New York: Liss, 1973.

Brotman, H. B. Supplement to chartbook on aging in America. The White House Conference on Aging, 1981.

Broverman, I. K., et al. Sex-role stereotypes. *Journal of social issues,* 1972, *28,* 59–79.

Brown, G. W., and **Harris, T.** *Social*

origins of depression: a study of psychiatric disorder in women. London: Tavistock Publications, 1978.

Brown, M. D. *The effectiveness of the personality dimensions of dependency, power, and internal-external locus of control in differentiating among unremitted and remitted alcoholics and non-alcoholic controls.* Unpublished doctoral dissertation, University of Windsor, 1975.

Brown, R. The first sentences of child and chimpanzee. In R. Brown, ed. *Psycholinguistics,* New York: Free Press, 1970.

Brown, R. *A first language.* Cambridge, Mass.: Harvard University Press, 1973.

Brown, R., and **Bellugi, U.** The three processes in the child's acquisition of syntax. *Harvard educational review,* 1964, *34,* 133–51.

Brown, R., Cazden, C., and **Bellugi-Klima, U.** The child's grammar from I to III. In J. P. Hill, ed. *Minnesota symposia on child psychology,* Vol. 2. Minneapolis: University of Minnesota Press, 1969.

Brown, R., and **McNeill, D.** The "tip of the tongue" phenomenon. *Journal of verbal learning and verbal behavior,* 1966, *5,* 325–37.

Brown, R. W. *Social psychology.* New York: Free Press, 1965.

Bruner, J. S. Learning the mother tongue. *Human nature,* 1978, *1,* 42–49.

Bruner, J. S., Goodnow, J. J., and **Austin, G. A.** *A study of thinking.* New York: Wiley, 1956.

Bucher, K. D., et al. The transmission of manic depressive illness. II. Segregation analysis of three sets of family data. *Journal of psychiatric research,* 1981, *16,* 65–78.

Buchsbaum, M. S., et al. Cerebral glucography with positron tomography: use in normal subjects and in patients with schizophrenia. *Archives of general psychiatry,* 1982, *39,* 251–59.

Bugelski, B. R., and **Alampay, D. A.** The role of frequency in developing perceptual sets. *Canadian journal of psychology,* 1961, *15,* 205–11.

Bugelski, B. R., Kidd, E., and **Segmen, J.** Image as a mediator in one-trial paired-associative learning. *Journal of experimental psychology,* 1968, *76,* 69–73.

Bühler, C. Psychotherapy and the image of man. *Psychotherapy,* 1968, *5,* 89–94.

Bullen, B. A., Reed, R. B., and **Mayer, J.** Physical activity of obese and nonobese girls appraised by motion picture sampling. *American journal of clinical nutrition,* 1964, *14,* 211–23.

Bureau of the Census. *See* **U.S. Bureau of the Census**

Butler, J. M., and **Haigh, G. V.** Changes in the relation between self-concepts and ideal concepts consequent upon client-centered counseling. In C. R. Rogers and R. F. Dymond, eds. *Psychotherapy and personality change.* Chicago: University of Chicago Press, 1954.

Butler, R. A. Discrimination learning by rhesus monkeys to visual-exploration motivation. *Journal of comparative and physiological psychology,* 1953, *46,* 95–98.

Butterfield, F. University exams exalt or banish 3 million in China. *New York Times,* July 19, 1980, p. 3.

Byrne, D. Attitudes and attraction. In L. Berkowitz, ed. *Advances in experimental social psychology,* Vol. 4. New York: Academic Press, 1969.

Byrne, W. L., et al. Memory transfer. *Science,* 1966, *153,* 658.

Califano, J. A., Jr. Report to the governor of New York, 1982.

Calne, D. B. *The brain.* Publication no. 81–1813, National Institutes of Health, Rockville, Md., 1981.

Cameron, P. The generation gap. *Gerontologist,* 1972, *12,* 117–19.

Campbell, B. A., and **Church, R. M.,** eds. *Punishment and aversive behavior.* New York: Appleton-Century-Crofts, 1969.

Campbell, D. Ethnocentrism and other altruistic motives. In D. Levine, ed. *Nebraska symposium on motivation, 1965.* Lincoln: University of Nebraska Press, 1965.

Carmen, E. H., Russo, N. F., and **Miller, J. B.** Inequality and women's mental health. *American journal of psychiatry,* 1981, *138,* 1319–30.

Carpenter, W. T., Jr., and **Stephens, J. H.** The diagnosis of mania. In R. H. Belmaker and H. M. van Praag, eds. *Mania: an evolving concept.* Jamaica, New York: Spectrum Publications, 1980.

Carpenter, W. T., Jr., Strauss, J. S., and **Bartko, J. J.** Flexible system for the diagnosis of schizophrenia. *Science,* 1973, *182,* 1275–78.

Carroll, J. B., and **Horn, J. L.** On the scientific basis of ability testing. *American psychologist,* 1981, *36,* 1112–19.

Carroll, J. B., et al. A specific laboratory test for the diagnosis of melancholia. Standardization, validation, and clinical utility. *Archives of general psychiatry,* 1981, *38,* 15–22.

Cashdan, S. Interactional psychotherapy. In R. Herink, ed. *The psychotherapy handbook.* New York: The New American Library, 1980.

Chechile, R., and **Butler, K.** Storage and retrieval changes that occur in the development and release of PI. *Journal of verbal learning and verbal behavior,* 1975, *14,* 430–37.

Chomsky, N. *Aspects of the theory of syntax.* Cambridge, Mass.: M.I.T. Press, 1965.

Christiaansen, R. E. Prose memory: forgetting rates for memory codes. *Journal of experimental psychology: human learning and memory,* 1980, *6,* 611–19.

Clark, H. H., and **Clark, E. V.** *Psychology and language.* New York: Harcourt Brace Jovanovich, 1977.

Clark, L. D., and **Nakashima, E. N.** Experimental studies of marihuana. *American journal of psychiatry,* 1968, *125,* 379–84.

Clark, W. B., and **Midanik, L.** *Report of the 1979 national survey.* National Technical Information Service, Port Royal, Va., PB No. 82–156514, 1982.

Clausen, J. A. The social meaning of differential physical and sexual maturation. In S. E. Dragastin and G. H.

Elder, Jr., eds. *Life cycle.* New York: Wiley, 1975.

Cofer, C. N. *Motivation and emotion.* Glenview, Ill.: Scott, Foresman, 1972.

Cohen, A. R. Some implications of self-esteem for social influence. In C. I. Hovland and I. L. Janis, eds. *Personality and persuasibility.* New Haven, Conn.: Yale University Press, 1959.

Cohen, H. Study reported in *Behavior today,* 1970, *1,* 2.

Cohen S., Glass, D. C., and **Singer, J. E.** Apartment noise, auditory discrimination, and reading ability in children. *Journal of experimental social psychology,* 1973, 9, 407–22.

Cohen, S., et al. Physiological, motivational, and cognitive effects of aircraft noise on children. *American psychologist,* 1980, *35,* 231–43.

Coleman, J. C. *Abnormal psychology and modern life,* 5th ed. Glenview, Ill.: Scott, Foresman, 1976.

Coleman, J. S. *Equality of educational opportunity.* Washington, D.C.: U.S. Government Printing Office, 1966.

Coles R. Like it is in the alley. In J. Kagan, M. M. Haith, and C. Caldwell, eds. *Psychology.* New York: Harcourt Brace Jovanovich, 1971.

Collins, A. M., and **Quillian, M. R.** How to make a language user. In E. Tulving and W. Donaldson, eds. *Organization of memory.* New York: Academic Press, 1972.

Conger J. J. *Adolescence and youth,* 2d ed. New York: Harper & Row, 1977.

Conry, R., and **Plant, W. T.** WAIS and group test predictions of an academic success criterion. *Educational and psychological measurement,* 1965, *25,* 493–500.

Cooper, H. Pygmalion grows up: a model for teacher expectation communication and performance influence. *Review of educational research,* 1979, *49,* 389–410.

Cooper, J. Deception and role-playing. *American psychologist,* 1976, *31,* 605–10.

Cooper, M., Zanna, M. P., and **Taves, P. A.** Arousal as a necessary condition for attitude change following induced compliance. *Journal of personality and social psychology,* 1978, *36,* 1101–06.

Craik, F. I. M., and **Kirsner, K.** The effect of speaker's voice on word recognition. *Quarterly journal of experimental psychology,* 1974, *26,* 274–84.

Craik, F. I. M., and **Lockhart, R. S.** Levels of processing. *Journal of verbal learning and verbal behavior,* 1972, *11,* 671–84.

Craik, F. I. M., and **Tulving, E.** Depth of processing and the retention of words in episodic memory. *Journal of experimental psychology: general,* 1975, *104,* 268–94.

Craik, K. *The nature of explanation.* Cambridge, England: Cambridge University Press, 1952.

Crandall, V. J. Sex differences in expectancy of intellectual and academic reinforcement. In C. P. Smith, ed. *Achievement-related motives in children.* New York: Russell Sage Foundation, 1969.

Crano, W. D., and **Mellon, P. M.** Causal influence of teachers' expectations on children's academic performance. *Journal of educational psychology,* 1978, *70,* 39–49.

Crockenburg, S. B. Creativity tests: a boon or boondoogle for education? *Review of educational research,* 1972, *42,* 27–45.

Crockett, H. J. The achievement motive and differential occupational mobility in the United States. *American sociological review,* 1962, *27,* 191–204.

Cronbach, L. J. *Essentials of psychological testing.* New York: Harper, 1949.

Crosby, E., Humphrey, T., and **Lauer, E. W.** *Comparative anatomy of the nervous system.* New York: Macmillan, 1962.

Cross, J. F., and **Cross, J.** Age, sex, race, and the perception of facial beauty. *Developmental psychology,* 1971, *5,* 433–39.

Cross, T. G. Mothers' speech adjustments. In C. Ferguson and C. Snow, eds. *Talking to children.* Cambridge, England: Cambridge University Press, 1977.

Cytryn, L., McKnew, D. H., and **Bunney, W. E.** Diagnosis of depression in children: a reassessment. *American journal of psychiatry,* 1980, *137,* 22–25.

Darley, J. M., and **Batson, C. D.** *From Jerusalem to Jericho.* Unpublished study, 1971.

Darley, J. M., and **Fazio, R. H.** Expectancy confirmation processes arising in the social interaction sequence. *American psychologist,* 1980, *35,* 867–81.

Davidson, R. J., and **Schwartz, G. E.** Patterns of cerebral lateralization during cardiac biofeedback versus the self-regulation of emotion. *Psychophysiology,* 1976, *13,* 62–68.

Davis, K. L., et al. Physostigmine. *Science,* 1978, *201,* 272–74.

Davison, G. C. Elimination of a sadistic fantasy by a client-controlled counterconditioning technique. *Journal of abnormal psychology,* 1968, *73,* 84–90.

Deaton, J. E., et al. Coping activities in solitary confinement of U.S. Navy POWs in Vietnam. *Journal of applied social psychology,* 1977, *7,* 239–57.

Deaux, K., White, L., and **Farris, E.** Skill versus luck. *Journal of personality and social psychology,* 1975, *32,* 629–36.

DeCharms, R., and **Muir, M. S.** Motivation. *Annual review of psychology,* 1978, *29,* 91–113.

DeCharms, R. C., et al. Behavioral correlates of directly measured achievement motivation. In D. C. McClelland, ed. *Studies in motivation.* New York: Appleton-Century-Crofts, 1955.

Deikman, A. J. Deautomatization and the mystic experience. In R. E. Ornstein, ed. *The nature of human consciousness.* San Francisco: Freeman, 1973.

Dekker, E., Pelser, H. E., and **Groen, J.** Conditioning as a cause of asthmatic attacks. *Journal of psychiatric research,* 1957, *2,* 97–108.

Dember, W. N. Birth order and need

affiliation. *Journal of abnormal and social psychology,* 1964, *68,* 555–57.

Dember, W. N. The new look in motivation. *American scientist,* 1965, *53,* 409–27.

Denike, L. D., and **Tiber, H.** Neurotic behavior. In P. London and D. Rosenhan, eds. *Foundations of abnormal psychology.* New York: Holt, Rinehart and Winston, 1968.

Depue, R. A., and **Monroe, S. M.** Learned helplessness in the perspective of the depressive disorders. *Journal of abnormal psychology,* 1978, *87,* 3–20.

De Valois, R. L. Neural processing of visual information. In R. W. Russell, ed. *Frontiers in physiological psychology.* New York: Academic Press, 1966.

De Valois, R. L., and **De Valois, K. K.** Neural coding of color. In E. C. Carterette and M. P. Friedman, eds. *Handbook of perception,* Vol. 5. New York: Academic Press, 1975.

De Valois, R. L., and **Jacobs, G. H.** Primate color vision. *Science,* 1968, *162,* 533–40.

de Villiers, J. G., and **de Villiers, P. A.** *Language acquisition.* Cambridge, Mass.: Harvard University Press, 1978.

Diamond, M. C. The aging brain. *American scientist,* 1978, *66,* 66–71.

Dimascio, A., et al. Differential symptom reduction by drugs and psychotherapy in acute depression. *Archives of general psychiatry,* 1979, *36,* 1450–56.

Dion, K. K. Physical attractiveness and evaluations of children's aggressions. *Journal of personality and social psychology,* 1972, *24,* 207–13.

Dion, K. K., and **Berscheid, E.** *Physical attractiveness and social perception of peers in preschool children.* Unpublished research report, 1972.

Dion, K. K., Berscheid, E., and **Walster E.** What is beautiful is good. *Journal of personality and social psychology,* 1972, *24,* 285–90.

Dollard, J., et al. *Frustration and aggression.* New Haven, Conn.: Yale University Press, 1939.

Doob, A. N., and **Gross, A. E.** Status of frustrator as an inhibitor of horn-honking responses. *Journal of social psychology,* 1968, *76,* 213–18.

Dooling, D. J., and **Lachman, R.** Effects of comprehension on retention of prose. *Journal of experimental psychology,* 1971, *88,* 216–22.

Doyle, K. O. Theory and practice of ability testing in ancient Greece. *Journal of the history of the behavioral sciences,* 1974, *10,* 202–12.

Duncan, O. D., Featherman, D. L., and **Duncan, B.** *Socioeconomic background and achievement.* New York: Seminar Press, 1972.

Duncker, K. On problem solving. *Psychological monographs,* 1945, *58,* 1–113.

Dunn, R. Personal communication, 1983.

Dweck, C. S., Goetz, T., and **Strauss, N.** *Sex differences in learned helplessness.* Unpublished manuscript, University of Illinois, 1977.

Ebbinghaus, H. *Memory.* New York: Columbia University Teachers College, 1913.

Eccles, J. C. *The physiology of synapses.* New York: Academic Press, 1964.

Eckhardt, M. J., et al. Health hazards associated with alcohol consumption. *Journal of the American Medical Association,* 1981, *246,* 648–66.

Edelson, E. The neuropeptide explosion. *Mosaic,* May/June 1981, pp. 15–18.

Edelstein, E. L. Reactivation of concentration camp experiences as a result of hospitalization. In C. D. Spielberger, I. G. Sarason, and N. A. Milgram, eds. *Stress and anxiety,* Vol. 8. Washington, D.C.: Hemisphere Publishing, 1982.

Ehrhardt, A. A., and **Baker, S. W.** Fetal androgens, human central nervous differentiation, and behavior sex differences. In R. C. Friedman, R. M. Richart, and R. L. Van de Wiele, eds. *Sex differences in behavior.* New York: Wiley, 1973.

Ehrlich, D., et al. Postdecision exposure to relevant information. *Journal of abnormal and social psychology,* 1957, *54,* 98–102.

Ehrmann, W. Marital and nonmarital sexual behavior. In H. T. Christensen, ed. *Handbook of marriage and the family.* Chicago: Rand McNally, 1964.

Eibl-Eibesfeldt, I. Aggressive behavior and ritualized fighting in animals. In J. H. Masserman, ed. *Science and psychoanalysis, Vol.* 6 *(Violence and war).* New York: Grune & Stratton, 1963.

Eiseley, L. *The immense journey.* New York: Random House, 1946.

Ekman, P. Universals and cultural differences in facial expressions of emotion. In J. K. Cole, ed. *Nebraska symposium on motivation,* Vol. 19. Lincoln: University of Nebraska Press, 1971.

Ellis, E. M., Atkeson, B. M., and **Calhoun, K. S.** An assessment of long-term reaction to rape. *Journal of abnormal psychology,* 1981, *90,* 263–66.

Elmadjian, F. Excretion and metabolism of epinephrin. *Pharmacological reviews,* 1959, *11,* 409–15.

Elton, C. F., and **Shevel, L. R.** *Who is talented? An analysis of achievement.* Iowa City: American College Testing Program, 1969.

England, P. Women and occupational prestige: a case of vacuous sex equality. *Journal of women in culture and society,* 1979, *5,* 252–65.

Epstein, A. N., Fitzsimons, J. T., and **Simons, B.** Drinking caused by the intercranial injection of angiotensin into the rat. *Journal of physiology* (London), 1969, *200,* 98–100.

Epstein, A. N., Kissileff, H. R., and **Stellar, E.,** eds. *The neuropsychology of thirst.* Washington, D.C.: Winston, 1973.

Epstein, A. N., and **Teitelbaum, P.** Regulation of food intake in the absence of taste, smell, and other oropharyngeal sensations. *Journal of comparative and physiological psychology,* 1962, *55,* 155.

Epstein, S., and **Roupenian, A.** Heart rate and skin conductance during experimentally induced anxiety. *Journal of personality and social psychology,* 1970, *16,* 20–28.

Erikson, E. H. *Childhood and society,*

2d ed. New York: Norton, 1963.

Erikson, E. H. *Identity, youth, and crisis.* New York: Norton, 1968.

Erlenmeyer-Kimling, L. Schizophrenia: a bag of dilemmas. *Social biology,* 1976, *23,* 123–34.

Erlenmeyer-Kimling, L., and **Jarvik, L. F.** Genetics and intelligence. *Science,* 1963, *142,* 1477–79.

Eron, L. D., and **Huesmann, L. R.** Adolescent aggression and television. *Annals of the New York Academy of Sciences,* 1980, *347,* 319–31.

Evarts, E. V. Brain mechanisms of movement. In Scientific American's *The brain.* San Francisco: Freeman, 1979.

Eysenck, H. J. (with **Kamin, L.**). *The intelligence controversy.* New York: Wiley, 1981.

Facklam, M., and **Facklam, H.** *The brain: magnificent mind machine.* New York: Harcourt Brace Jovanovich, 1982.

Falbo, T. Relationships between birth category, achievement, and interpersonal orientation. *Journal of personality and social psychology,* 1981, *41,* 121–31.

Farb, P. *Word play.* New York: Knopf, 1974.

Farina, A. The stigma of mental disorders. In A. G. Miller. *In the eye of the beholder: contemporary issues in stereotyping.* New York: Praeger, 1982.

Farina, A., Hagelauer, H. D., and **Holzberg, J. D.** The influence of psychiatric history on physicians' responses to a new patient. *Journal of consulting and clinical psychology,* 1976, *44,* 499.

Farley, E. C., Santo, Y., and **Speck, D. W.** Multiple drug-abuse patterns of youths in treatment. In G. M. Beschner and A. S. Friedman, eds. *Youth drug abuse: problems, issues, and treatment.* Lexington, Mass.: Heath, 1979.

Fazio, R. H., Zanna, M. P., and **Cooper, J.** Dissonance and self-perception. *Journal of experimental social psychology,* 1977, *13,* 464–79.

Feinman, S. Approval of cross-sex-role behavior. *Psychological reports,* 1974, *35,* 643–48.

Feshbach, S. The dynamics and morality of violence and aggression. *American journal of psychology,* 1971, *26,* 281–92.

Festinger, L. A. A theory of social comparison processes. *Human relations,* 1954, *7,* 117–40.

Festinger, L., Schachter, S., and **Back, K.** *Social pressures in informal groups.* New York: Harper & Row, 1950.

Fine, G. A. Friends, impression management, and preadolescent behavior. In S. R. Asher and J. M. Gottman. *The development of children's friendships.* London: Cambridge University Press, 1981.

Fodor, E. M., and **Smith, T.** The power motive as an influence on group decision making. *Journal of personality and social psychology,* 1982, *42,* 178–85.

Forward, J., Canter, R., and **Kirsch, N.** Role-enactment and deception methodologies. *American psychologist,* 1976, *31,* 595–604.

Foulkes, D. *Children's dreams.* New York: Wiley, 1982.

Frederick, C. Current trends in suicidal behavior in the United States. *American journal of psychotherapy,* 1978, *32,* 172–200.

Freed, A., et al. Stimulus and background factors in sign violation. *Journal of personality,* 1955, *23,* 499.

Freedman, J. L., Carlsmith, J. M., and **Sears, D. O.** *Social psychology.* Englewood Cliffs, N.J.: Prentice-Hall, 1970.

Freedman, J. L., Carlsmith, J. M., and **Suomi, S.** Unpublished study, cited in J. L. Freedman, J. M. Carlsmith, and D. O. Sears. *Social psychology.* Englewood Cliffs, N.J.: Prentice-Hall, 1970.

Freedman, J. L., and **Suomi, S.** Unpublished study, cited in J. L. Freedman, J. M. Carlsmith, and D. O. Sears. *Social psychology.* Englewood Cliffs, N.J.: Prentice-Hall, 1970.

French, E. G. Development of a measure of complex motivation. In J. W. Atkinson, ed. *Motives in fantasy, action, and society.* Princeton, N.J.: Van Nostrand, 1959.

French, E. G., and **Thomas, F. H.** The relation of achievement to problem-solving effectiveness. *Journal of abnormal and social psychology,* 1958, *56,* 45–48.

Friedman, M. I., and **Stricker, E. M.** The physiological psychology of hunger. *Psychological review,* 1976, *83,* 409–31.

Fries, J. F., and **Crapo, L. M.** *Vitality and aging, implications of the rectangular curve.* San Francisco: Freeman, 1981.

Frieze, I. H. Women's expectations for and causal attributions of success and failure. In M. T. S. Mednick, S. S. Tangri, and L. W. Hoffman, eds. *Women and achievement.* New York: Halsted, 1975.

Fromkin, V. *Speech errors as linguistic evidence.* The Hague: Mouton, 1973.

Fromm, E. *The sane society.* New York: Holt, Rinehart and Winston, 1955.

Fuller, J. L. Experimental deprivation and later behavior. *Science,* 1967, *158,* 1645–52.

Furman, W., Rahe, D. F., and **Hartup, W. W.** Rehabilitation of socially-withdrawn preschool children through mixed-age and same-age socialization. In E. M. Hetherington and R. D. Parke, eds. *Contemporary readings in child psychology,* 2d ed. New York: McGraw-Hill, 1981.

Galaburda, A. M., et al. Right-left asymmetries in the brain. *Science,* 1978, *199,* 852–56.

Gallagher, E. J. Personal communication, 1983.

Ganzer, V. J. Effects of audience presence and test anxiety on learning and retention in a serial learning situation. *Journal of personality and social psychology,* 1968, *8,* 194–99.

Garber, J., and **Hollon, S.** *Depression and the expectancy of success for self and for others.* Unpublished manuscript, University of Minnesota, 1977.

Garcia, J., and **Koelling, R.** Relation of cue to consequence in avoidance learning. *Psychonomic science,* 1966, *4,* 123–24.

Gardner, R. A., and **Gardner, B. T.** Communication with a young chimpanzee. In R. Chauvin, ed. *Edition du centre national de la recherche scientific.* Paris: 1972.

Garfield, S. L. *Clinical psychology.* Chicago: Aldine, 1974.

Gass, G. Z. Equitable marriage. *Family coordinator,* 1974, *23,* 369–72.

Gates, A. L. Recitation as a factor in memorizing. *Archives of psychology,* New York, 1917, No. 40. Columbia University.

Gatz, A. J. *Manter's essentials of clinical neuroanatomy and neurophysiology.* Philadelphia: Davis, 1970.

Gebhard, P. H. Personal communication, 1979.

Gebhard, P. H. Personal communication, 1980.

Geen, R. G. *Personality.* St. Louis: Mosby, 1976.

Geen, R. G., and **O'Neal, E. C.** Activation of cue-elicited aggression by general arousal. *Journal of personality and social psychology,* 1969, *11,* 289–92.

Gellhorn, E., and **Miller, A. D.** Methacholine and noradrenaline tests. *Archives of general psychiatry,* 1961, *4,* 371–80.

Gerbner, G., and **Gross, L.** The scary world of TV's heavy viewer. *Psychology today,* 1976, 9, 41–45.

Gerbner, G., et al. The "mainstreaming" of America: violence profile no. 11. *Journal of communication,* 1980, *30,* 10–29.

Gerbner, G., et al. Health and medicine on television. *New England journal of medicine,* 1981, *305,* 901–04.

Geschwind, N. Personal communication, 1980.

Gevins, A. S., et al. Electroencephalogram correlates of higher cortical functions. *Science,* 1979, *203,* 665–67.

Geyer, L. H., and **DeWald, C. G.** Feature lists and confusion matrices. *Perception and psychophysics,* 1973, *14,* 471–82.

Gibbs, M. S., Lachenmeyer, J. R., and **Sigal, J.,** eds. *Community psychology.* New York: Gardner Press, 1980.

Gibson, E. J. *Principles of perceptual learning and development.* New York: Appleton-Century-Crofts, 1969.

Gibson, E. J., and **Walk, R. D.** The "visual cliff." *Scientific American,* 1960, *202,* 64–71.

Ginsburg, H. J., and **Miller, S. M.** Sex differences in children's risk-taking behavior. *Child development,* 1982, *53,* 426–28.

Glaser, R., and **Bond, L.** Introduction to a special issue on Testing: concepts, policy, practice, and research. *American psychologist,* 1981, *36,* 997–1000.

Glass, D. C. Stress, behavior patterns, and coronary disease. *American scientist,* 1977, *65,* 177–87.

Glass, D. C., and **Singer J. E.** Experimental studies of controllable and uncontrollable noises. *Representative research in social psychology,* 1973, *4,* 165–83.

Gold, S. R. The CAP control theory of drug abuse. In D. J. Lettieri, M. Sayers, and H. W. Pearson, eds. *Theories on drug abuse: selected contemporary perspectives.* National Institute on Drug Abuse, DHHS Publication No. (ADM) 80–967, 1980, pp. 8–11.

Goldberg, S., and **Lewis, M.** Play behavior in the year-old infant. *Child development,* 1969, *40,* 21–30.

Goldfarb, W. Effects of early institutional care on adolescent personality. *American journal of orthopsychiatry,* 1944, *14,* 441–47.

Goldman, P. An alternative to developmental plasticity: heterology of CNS structures in infants and adults. In D. G. Stein, J. J. Rosen, and N. Butters, eds. *Plasticity and recovery of function in the central nervous system.* New York: Academic Press, 1974.

Goldsen, R., et al. *What college students think.* Princeton, N.J.: Van Nostrand, 1960.

Goldstein, J. H., and **Arms, R. L.** Effects of observing athletic contests on hostility. *Sociometry,* 1971, *34,* 83–90.

Goldstein, M. J., Baker, B. L., and **Jamison, K. R.** *Abnormal psychology: experiences, origins, interventions.* Boston: Little, Brown, 1980.

Goleman, D. Hypnosis comes of age. *Psychology today,* July 1977, *11,* 54–56+.

Gomes-Schwartz, B., Hadley, S. W., and **Strupp, H. H.** Individual psychotherapy and behavior therapy. *Annual review of psychology,* 1978, *29,* 435–71.

Goode, W. J. *The family.* Englewood Cliffs, N.J.: Prentice-Hall, 1965.

Goodnow, J. J., and **Bethon, G.** Piaget's tasks. *Child development,* 1966, *37,* 573–82.

Goodwin, D. W., et al. Loss of short-term memory as a predictor of the alcoholic "blackout." *Nature,* 1970, *227,* 201–02.

Goodwin, D. W., et al. Alcohol problems in adoptees raised apart from biological parents. *Archives of general psychiatry,* 1973, *28,* 238–43.

Gottesman, I. I. Biogenetics of race and class. In M. Deutsch, I. Katz, and A. B. Jensen, eds. *Social class, race, and psychological development.* New York: Holt, Rinehart, and Winston, 1963.

Gottesman, I. I., and **Shields, J.** *Schizophrenia and genetics: a twin study vantage point.* New York: Academic Press, 1972.

Graf, R. C. Speed reading. *Psychology today,* December, 1973, pp. 112–13.

Granzberg, G., and **Steinbring, J.** *Television and the Canadian Indian.* Technical report, Department of Anthropology, University of Winnipeg, 1980.

Gray, J. A. Anxiety. *Human nature,* 1978, *1,* 38–45.

Greene, W. A., Goldstein, S., and **Moss, A. J.** Psychosocial aspects of sudden death. *Archives of internal medicine,* 1972, *129,* 725–31.

Greenough, W. T. Enduring brain effects of differential experience and training. In M. R. Rosenzweig and E. L. Bennett, eds. *Neural mechanisms of learning and memory.* Cambridge, Mass.: M.I.T. Press, 1976.

Greenough, W. T. Lecture to the developmental Psychology Research Group, Estes Park, Colo.: June, 1982.

Grinker, J. A. Physiological and behavioral basis of human obesity. In D. W. Pfaff, ed. *The physiological mechanisms of motivation.* New York: Springer-Verlag, 1982.

Guilford, J. P. A factor analytic study across the domains of reasoning, creativity, and evaluation. *Reports from the psychology laboratory,* University of Southern California, 1954.

Guilford, J. P. *The nature of human intelligence.* New York: McGraw-Hill, 1967.

Gunter, B., Berry, C., and **Clifford, B. R.** Proactive interference effects with television news items: further evidence. *Journal of experimental psychology: human learning and memory,* 1981, *7,* 480–87.

Hall, G. S. *Adolescence,* Vol. 1. New York: Appleton, 1904.

Hall, R. C. W. Anxiety. In R. C. W. Hall, ed. *Psychiatric presentations of medical illness: somatopsychic disorders.* New York: Spectrum Publications, 1980a.

Hall, R. C. W. Medically induced psychiatric disease—an overview. In R. C. W. Hall, ed. *Psychiatric presentations of medical illness: somatopsychic disorders.* New York: Spectrum Publications, 1980b.

Hall, R. C. W., Stickney, S. K., and **Gardner, E. R.** Behavioral toxicity of nonpsychiatric drugs. In R. C. W. Hall. *Psychiatric presentations in medical illness: somatopsychic disorders.* New York: Spectrum Publications, 1980.

Hamilton, M. Diagnosis of anxiety states. In R. J. Mathew, ed. *The biology of anxiety.* New York: Bruner/Mazel, 1982.

Hansel, C. E. M. *ESP.* New York: Scribners, 1966.

Hardy, A. B. *Exposure therapy as a treatment for agoraphobia and anxiety.* Unpublished manuscript, Palo Alto, Calif., 1969.

Hare, R. D. *Psychopathy.* New York: Wiley, 1970.

Hargadon, F. Tests and college admissions. *American psychologist,* 1981, *36,* 1112–19.

Harlow, H. F. The formation of learning sets. *Psychological review,* 1949, *56,* 51–65.

Harlow, H. F. The development of affectional patterns in infant monkeys. In B. M. Foss, ed. *Determinants of infant behaviour.* London: Methuen, 1961.

Harlow, H. F., and **Harlow, M. K.** Social deprivation in monkeys. *Scientific American,* 1962, *207,* 136–46.

Harlow, H. F., and **Harlow, M. K.** Learning to love. *American scientist,* 1966, *54,* 244–72.

Harrell, T. W., and **Harrell, M. S.** Army general classification test scores for civilian occupations. *Educational and psychological measurement,* 1945, *5,* 229–39.

Harris, B. Whatever happened to little Albert? *American psychologists,* 1979, *34,* 151–60.

Harris, F. R., et al. Effects of positive social reinforcement on regressed crawling of a nursery school child. In L. Ullmann and L. Krasner, eds. *Case studies in behavior modification.* New York: Holt, Rinehart and Winston, 1965.

Hartley, R. E. Sex-role pressures and the socialization of the male child. *Psychological reports,* 1959, *5,* 457–68.

Hartman, G. A field experiment on the comparative effectiveness of "emotional" and "rational" political leaflets in determining election results. *Journal of abnormal and social psychology,* 1936, *31,* 336–52.

Hartmann, D. P. Influence of symbolically modeled instrumental aggression and pain cues on aggressive behavior. *Journal of personality and social psychology,* 1969, *11,* 280–88.

Hartmann, E. L. *The functions of sleep.* New Haven, Conn.: Yale University Press, 1973.

Hartmann, H. Ego psychology and the problem of adaptation. In D. Rapaport, ed. *Organization and pathology of thought.* New York: Columbia University Press, 1951.

Hauri, P. Dreams in patients remitted from reactive depression. *Journal of abnormal psychology,* 1976, *72,* 16–22.

Hebb, D., and **Thompson, W.** The social significance of animal studies. In G. Lindzey and E. Aronson, eds. *The handbook of social psychology,* 2d ed., Vol. 2 (Research methods). Reading, Mass.: Addison-Wesley, 1968.

Heider, F. Social perception and phenomenal causality. *Psychological review,* 1944, *51,* 358–74.

Helsing, K. L., Szklo, M., and **Comstock, G. W.** Factors associated with mortality after widowhood. *American journal of public health,* 1981, *71,* 802–09.

Hendrick, G. When television is a school for criminals. *TV guide,* Jan. 29, 1977, pp. 4–10.

Herink, R., ed. *The psychotherapy handbook.* New York: The New American Library, 1980.

Herrnstein, R. J., and **de Villiers, P. A.** Fish as a natural category for people and pigeons. In G. H. Bower, ed. *Psychology of learning and motivation,* Vol. 14, New York: Academic Press, 1980.

Hervey, G. R. Regulation of energy balance. *Nature,* 1969, *222,* 629–31.

Herzog, E., and **Lewis, H.** Children in poor families. *American journal of orthopsychiatry,* 1970, *40,* 375–87.

Hess, E. H. Attitude and pupil size. *Scientific American,* 1965, *212,* 46–54.

Hess, E. H. The role of pupil size in communication. *Scientific American,* 1975, *233,* 110–19.

Hess, R., and **Torney, J.** *The development of political attitudes in children.* Chicago: Aldine, 1967.

Hess, R. D., and **Bear, R. M.** *Early education.* Chicago: Aldine, 1968.

Hesselund, H. On some sociological sex differences. *Journal of sex research,* 1971, *7,* 263–73.

Heston, L. L. The genetics of schizophrenic and schizoid disease. *Science,* 1970, *167,* 249–55.

Hetherington, A. W., and **Ranson, W. W.** Hypothalamic lesions and adiposity in the rat. *Anatomical record,* 1940, *78,* 149–72.

Hilgard, E. R. *Hypnotic suggestibility.* New York: Harcourt Brace Jovanovich, 1965.

Hilgard, E. R., and **Hilgard, J. R.** *Hypnosis in the relief of pain.* Los Altos, Calif.: William Kaufmann, 1975.

Hilgard, J. R. *Personality and hypnosis.* Chicago: University of Chicago Press, 1970.

Hilton, I. Differences in the behavior of mothers toward first- and later-born children. *Journal of personality and social psychology*, 1967, *7*, 282–90.

Hinkle, L. E. The effect of exposure to cultural change, social change, and change in interpersonal relationships on health. In B. S. Dohrenwend and B. P. Dohrenwend. *Stressful life events: their nature and effects.* New York: Wiley, 1974.

Hintzman, D. L., Block, R. A., and **Inskeep, N. R.** Memory for mode of input. *Journal of verbal learning and verbal behavior*, 1972, *11*, 741–49.

Hiroto, D. S. Locus of control and learned helplessness. *Journal of experimental psychology*, 1974, *102*, 187–93.

Hirsch, J., and **Knittle, J. L.** Cellularity of obese and nonobese human adipose tissue. *Federal proceedings*, 1970, *29*, 1516–21.

Hochberg, J. *Perception*, 2d ed. Englewood Cliffs, N.J.: Prentice-Hall, 1978.

Hoffman, J. E. Interaction between global and local levels of a form. *Journal of experimental psychology: human perception and performance*, 1980, 6, 222–34.

Hohmann, G. W. Some effects of spinal cord lesions on experienced emotional feelings. *Psychophysiology*, 1966, *3*, 143–56.

Hollingshead, A. B., and **Redlich, F. C.** *Social class and mental illness, a community study.* New York: Wiley, 1958.

Hollister, L. E. Marihuana in man. *Science*, 1971, *172*, 21–29.

Holmes, T. H., and **Rahe, R. H.** The social readjustment rating scale. *Journal of psychosomatic research*, 1967, *11*, 213–18.

Holyrod, K. A., et al. Performance, cognition, and physiological responding in test anxiety. *Journal of abnormal psychology*, 1978, *87*, 442–51.

Holzman, P. S., Proctor, L. R., and **Hughes, D. W.** Eye tracking patterns in schizophrenia. *Science*, 1973, *181*, 179–81.

Holzman, P. S., et al. Eye tracking dysfunctions in schizophrenic patients and their relatives. *Archives of general psychiatry*, 1974, *31*, 143–51.

Honzik, M. P., Macfarlane, J. W., and **Allen, L.** The stability of mental test performance between two and eighteen years. *Journal of experimental education*, 1948, *17*, 454–55.

Hormuth, S. Sex differences in horse trading: a replication of Maier and Burke. *Replications in social psychology*, 1982, *2*, 24–26.

Horowitz, E. L., and **Horowitz, R. E.** Development of social attitudes in children. *Sociometry*, 1938, *1*, 301–38.

Horowitz, F. C. *Stability and instability in the newborn infant.* Paper presented at meeting of the Society for Research in Child Development, New Orleans, La., 1977.

Hovland, C., and **Weiss, W.** The influence of source credibility. *Public opinion quarterly*, 1951, *15*, 635–50.

Hovland, C. I., and **Janis, I. L,** eds. *Personality and persuasibility.* New Haven, Conn.: Yale University Press, 1959.

Hovland, C. I., Lumsdaine, A. A., and **Sheffield, F. C.** *Experiments on mass communication.* Princeton, N.J.: Princeton University Press, 1949.

Howe, F. Sexual stereotypes start early. *Saturday review*, 1971, *54*, 76–82.

Hoyos, C. G. Motivationpsychologische Untersuchungen von Kraftfahrern mit dem TAT nach McClelland. *Archiv für die gesamte psychologie*, 1965. Supp. No. 7.

Hsu, C., et al. The temperamental characteristics of Chinese babies. *Child development*, 1981, *52*, 1337–40.

Hubel, D. H. The visual cortex of the brain. *Scientific American*, 1963, *209*, 54–62.

Hubel, D. H. Vision and the brain. *Bulletin of the American Academy of Arts and Sciences*, 1978, *31*, 17–28.

Hubel, D. H. The brain. In Scientific American's *The brain.* San Francisco: Freeman, 1979.

Hubel, D. H., and **Wiesel, T. N.** Receptive fields and functional architecture in two non-striate visual areas (18 and 19) of the cat. *Journal of neurophysiology*, 1965, *28*, 229–89.

Hubel, D. H., and **Wiesel, T. N.** Brain mechanisms of vision. In Scientific American's *The brain.* San Francisco: Freeman, 1979.

Huffine, C. L., and **Clausen, J. A.** Madness and work: short- and long-term effects of mental illness on occupational careers. *Social forces*, 1979, *57*, 1049–62.

Hutt, M. L. "Consecutive" and "adaptive" testing with the revised Stanford-Binet. *Journal of consulting psychology*, 1947, *11*, 93–103.

Hyden, H. Biochemical and molecular aspects of learning and memory. *Proceedings of the American Philosophical Society*, 1967, *111*, 347–51.

Ilfeld, F. W. Coping styles of Chicago adults: description. *Journal of human stress*, 1980, 6, 2–10.

Iversen, L. L. The chemistry of the brain. *Scientific American*, 1979, *241*, 14+, 134–35+.

Iversen, L. L. Neurotransmitters and CNS disease: introduction. *Lancet*, 1982, II, 8304, 914–16.

Izard, C. E. *Human emotions.* New York: Plenum, 1977.

Izard, C. E., and **Dougherty, L. M.** Two complementary systems for measuring facial expressions in infants and children. In C. E. Izard, ed. *Measuring emotions in infants and children.* Cambridge, England: Cambridge University Press, 1982.

James, W. *Principles of psychology.* New York: Holt, 1890.

Jamison, K. R. Personal communication, 1982.

Janis, I. L., and **Feshbach, S.** Effects of fear-arousing communications. *Journal of abnormal and social psychology*, 1953, *48*, 78–92.

Janis, I. L., and **Frick, F.** The relationship between attitudes toward conclusions and errors in judging logical validity. *Journal of experimental psychology*, 1943, *33*, 73–77.

Janis, I. L., and **Mann, L.** *Decision*

making. New York: Free Press, 1977.

Janke, L. L., and **Havighurst, R. J.** Relation between ability and social-status in a midwestern community. II. Sixteen-year-old boys and girls. *Journal of educational psychology,* 1945, *36,* 499–509.

Janowsky, D. S., Khaled El-Yousef, M., and **Davis, J. M.** Acetylcholine and depression. *Psychosomatic medicine,* 1974, *36,* 248–57.

Jencks, C., et al. *Inequality.* New York: Basic Books, 1972.

Jensen, A. R. How much can we boost IQ and school achievement? *Harvard educational review,* 1969, *39,* 1–123.

Jensen, A. R. The heritability of intelligence. *Saturday evening post,* 1972, *244,* 9.

Jessor, R., and **Jessor, S. L.** *Problem behavior and psychosocial development.* New York: Academic Press, 1977.

Joffe, C. Sex role socialization and the nursery school. *Journal of marriage and the family,* 1971, *33,* 467–75.

John, E. R., et al. Observation learning in cats. *Science,* 1968, *159,* 1489–91.

Johnson, F. N. The effects of chlorpromazine on the decay and consolidation of short-term memory traces in mice. *Psychopharmacologia,* 1969, *16,* 105–14.

Johnson, L. C., and **MacLeod, W. L.** Sleep and wake behavior during gradual sleep reduction. *Perceptual motor skills,* 1973, *36,* 87–97.

Johnson, P. B. Achievement motivation and success: does the end justify the means? *Journal of personality and social psychology,* 1981, *40,* 374–75.

Johnston, L. D., Bachman, J. G., and **O'Malley, P. M.** *Student drug use in America, 1975–1980.* Rockville, Md.: National Institute on Drug Abuse, 1981.

Johnston, L. D., Bachman, J. G., and **O'Malley, P. M.** *Student drug use in America, 1975–1981.* Rockville, Md.: National Institute on Drug Abuse, 1982.

Jones, D. R. *Psychologists in mental health: 1966.* Washington, D.C.: National Institute of Mental Health. Public Health Service Publication, No. 1984, 1969.

Jones E. E. The rocky road from acts to dispositions. *American psychologist,* 1979, *34,* 107–17.

Jones, E. E., and **Nisbett, R. E.** The actor and the observer. In E. E. Jones, et al., eds. *Attribution.* Morristown, N.J.: General Learning Press, 1972.

Jones, J. C. A laboratory study of fear. *Pedagogical seminary,* 1924, *31,* 308–15.

Jones, M. C., and **Bayley, N.** Physical maturity among boys as related to behavior. *Journal of educational psychology,* 1950, *41,* 129–48.

Kagan, J. Inadequate evidence and illogical conclusions. *Harvard educational review,* 1969, *39,* 274–77.

Kagan, J. *The second year: the emergence of self-awareness.* Cambridge, Mass.: Harvard University Press, 1981.

Kagan, J. Stress and coping in early development. In N. Garmezy and M. Rutter, eds. *Stress, coping, and development in children.* New York: McGraw-Hill, 1983.

Kagan, J., Kearsley, R. B., and **Zelazo, P. R.** *Infancy: its place in human development.* Cambridge, Mass.: Harvard University Press, 1978.

Kagan, J., and **Klein, R. E.** Cross-cultural perspectives on early development. *American psychologist,* 1973, *28,* 947–61.

Kagan, J., and **Moss, H. A.** *Birth to maturity.* New York: Wiley, 1962.

Kales, A., moderator. Drug dependency. University of California at Los Angeles Interdepartmental Conference. *Annals of internal medicine,* 1969, *70,* 591.

Kales, A., et al. Chronic hypnotic-drug use—ineffectiveness, drug withdrawal insomnia, and dependence. *Journal of the American Medical Association,* 1974, *227,* 513–17.

Kales, A., et al. Personality patterns in insomnia. *Archives of general psychiatry,* 1976, *33,* 1128–34.

Kamin, L. Presidential address, Eastern Psychological Association, 1979.

Kamin, L. (with **Eysenck, H. J.**). *The intelligence controversy.* New York: Wiley, 1981.

Kandel, D. B., and **Lesser, G. S.** *Youth in two worlds.* San Francisco: Jossey-Bass, 1972.

Kandel, E. R. Nerve cells and behavior. *Scientific American,* 1970, *223,* 57–68.

Kaplan, R. M., and **Singer, R. D.** Television violence and viewer aggression. *Journal of social issues,* 1976, *32,* 35–70.

Katona, G. *Organizing and memorizing.* New York: Columbia University Press, 1940.

Kaufman, E. The abuse of multiple drugs: I. Definition, classification, and extent of problem. *American journal of drug and alcohol abuse,* 1976, *3,* 279–92.

Kay, P. Synchronic variability and diachronic changes in basic color terms. *Language in society,* 1975, *4,* 257–70.

Kearsley, R. B., et al. Differences in separation protest between day care and home reared infants. *Pediatrics,* 1975, *55,* 171–75.

Kelley, H. H. The warm-cold variable in the first impressions of persons. *Journal of personality,* 1950, *18,* 431–39.

Kelly, J. G., Snowden, L. R., and **Munoz, R. F.** Social and community interventions. *Annual review of psychology,* 1977, *28,* 323–61.

Kenny, R. Survey for Spencer Stuart and Associates, quoted in *Wall Street Journal,* July 25, 1980.

Kety, S. S. The impact of neurobiology in the concept of the mind. Paper presented at European Neuroscience Congress, Malaga, Spain, September 1982.

Kety, S. S., et al. A sustained effect of electroconvulsive shock on the turnover of norepinephrine in the central nervous system of the rat. *Publication of the proceedings of the National Academy of Science,* 1967, *58,* 1249–54.

Kimble, G. A. *Hilgard and Marquis' conditioning and learning.* New York: Appleton-Century-Crofts, 1961.

Kindred, D. Yancey: fall into darkness. *The Washington Post,* March 24, 1978.

Kinsey, A. C., Pomeroy, W. B., and **Martin, C. E.** *Sexual behavior in the human male.* Philadelphia: Saunders, 1948.

Kinsey, A. C., et al. *Sexual behavior in the human female.* Philadelphia: Saunders, 1953.

Kintsch, W. *Learning, memory, and conceptual processes.* New York: Wiley, 1970.

Kintsch, W. *Memory and cognition,* 2d ed. New York: Wiley, 1977.

Kirsch, M. A., and **Glass, L. L.** Psychiatric disturbances associated with Erhard Seminars Training. *American journal of psychiatry,* 1977, *134,* 1254–58.

Klatzky, R. L. *Human memory: structures and processes,* 2d ed. San Francisco: Freeman, 1980.

Kline, N. S. *From sad to glad.* New York: Putnam's, 1974.

Klopfer, B., and **Davidson, H. H.** *The Rorschach technique.* New York: Harcourt Brace Jovanovich, 1962.

Knapp, R. R. Relationship of a measure of self-actualization to neuroticism and extraversion. *Journal of consulting psychology,* 1965, *29,* 168–72.

Knittle, J. L., and **Hirsch, J.** Effect of early nutrition on the development of rat epididymal fat pads. *Journal of clinical investigations,* 1968, *47,* 2091.

Kobasa, S. C. Stressful life events, personality and health. *Journal of personality and social psychology,* 1979, *37,* 1–11.

Kohlberg, L. The development of children's orientations toward a moral order. I. Sequence in the development of moral thought. *Vita humana,* 1963, 6, 11–33.

Kohlberg, L. Moral and religious education and the public schools. In T. Sizer, ed. *Religion and public education.* Boston: Houghton Mifflin, 1967.

Kohlberg, L., and **Kramer, R.** Continuities and discontinuities in child and adult moral development. *Human development,* 1969, *12,* 93–120.

Kohler, W. *The mentality of apes.* Harcourt, Brace, 1925.

Koluchova, J. Severe deprivation in twins. *Journal of child psychology and psychiatry,* 1972, *13,* 107–14.

Komarovsky, M. Cultural contradictions and sex roles. *American journal of sociology,* 1973, *78,* 873–84.

Krantz, D., et al. *Behavior and health.* Paper commissioned by NRC/ABASS Committee on Basic Research in Behavioral and Social Sciences and Social Science Research Council, 1981.

Kripke, D. F., and **Simons, R. N.** Average sleep, insomnia, and sleeping pill use. *Sleep research sociometry,* 1976, *5,* 110.

Krippner, S. *Experimentally induced effects in dreams and other altered conscious states.* 20th International Congress of Psychology, Tokyo, August 1972.

Kubie, L. S. *Practical and theoretical aspects of psychoanalysis.* New York: International Universities Press, 1950.

Kuffler, S. W. Discharge pattern and functional organization of mammalian retina. *Journal of neurophysiology,* 1953, *16,* 37–68.

Labov, W. *The study of nonstandard English.* Urbana, Ill.: National Council of Teachers of English, 1970.

Lacey, J. I., Bateman, D. E., and **Van Lehn, R.** Autonomic response specificity. *Psychosomatic medicine,* 1953, *15,* 8–21.

Lacey, J. I., and **Lacey, B. C.** Verification and extension of the principle of autonomic response-stereotypy. *American journal of psychology,* 1958, *71,* 50–73.

Lacey, J. I., and **Van Lehn, R.** Differential emphasis in somatic response to stress. *Psychosomatic medicine,* 1952, *12,* 73–81.

Ladner, J. A. *Tomorrow's tomorrow.* Garden City, N.Y.: Doubleday, 1971.

Laing, R. D. *The divided self.* Baltimore: Penguin, 1960.

Laird, J. D. Self-attribution of emotion. *Journal of personality and social psychology,* 1974, *29,* 475–86.

Lamy, R. E. Social consequences of mental illness. *Journal of consulting and clinical psychology,* 1966, *30,* 450–54.

Landy, D., and **Sigall, H.** Beauty is talent. *Journal of personality and social psychology,* 1974, *29,* 299–304.

Lang, P. J., and **Melamed, B. G.** Avoidance conditioning therapy of an infant with chronic ruminative vomiting. *Journal of abnormal psychology,* 1969, *74,* 1–8.

Lasch, C. The culture of narcissism. *Bulletin of the Menninger Clinic,* 1980, *44,* 426–40.

Latané, B., and **Darley, J. M.** *The unresponsive bystander.* Englewood Cliffs, N.J.: Prentice-Hall, 1970.

Lazarus, R. S. *The stress and coping paradigm.* Paper delivered at the University of Washington conference on the critical evaluation of behavioral paradigms for psychiatric science, 1978.

Lazarus, R. S. Thoughts on the relations between emotion and cognition. *American psychologist,* 1982, *37,* 1019–24.

Lazarus, R. S., and **Averill, J. R.** Emotion and cognition. In C. D. Spielberger, ed. *Anxiety.* New York: Academic Press, 1972.

Lefcourt, H. M., et al. Locus of control as a modifier of the relationship between stressors and moods. *Journal of personality and social psychology,* 1981, *41,* 357–69.

Leibowitz, S. F. Hypothalamic β-adrenergic "satiety" system antagonizes an α-adrenergic "hunger" system in the rat. *Nature,* 1970, *226,* 963–64.

Leiffer, A. D., Gordon, N. J., and **Graves, S. B.** Children's television. *Harvard educational review,* 1974, *44,* 213–45.

Lenneberg, E. H. *Biological foundations of language.* New York: Wiley, 1967.

Lepper, M. R., Greene, D., and **Nisbett, R. E.** Undermining children's interest with extrinsic awards. *Journal* *of personality and social psychology,* 1973, *28,* 129–37.

Leukel, F. A comparison of the effects of ECS and anesthesia on acquisition of the maze habit. *Journal of comparative and physiological psychology,* 1957, *50,* 300–06.

Levine, F. M., and **Fasnacht, G.** Token rewards may lead to token learning. *American psychologist,* 1974, *29,* 816–20.

Levine, M. W., and **Shefner, J. M.** *Fundamentals of sensation and perception.* Reading, Mass.: Addison-Wesley, 1981.

Levinson, B., and **Reese, H. W.** Patterns of discrimination learning set in preschool children, fifth-graders, college freshmen, and the aged. *Monographs of the Society for Research in Child Development,* 1967, *32* (No. 7), 1–92.

Levy, J., Trevarthen, C., and **Sperry, R. W.** Perception of bilateral chimeric figures following hemisphere deconnection. *Brain,* 1972, *95,* 61–78.

Lewin, K. *A dynamic theory of personality.* New York: McGraw-Hill, 1935.

Lewin, R. *The nervous system.* Garden City, N.Y.: Anchor Books, 1974.

Lewis, E. R., Zeevi, Y. Y., and **Everhart, T. E.** Studying neural organization in *Aplysia* with scanning electron microscope. *Science,* 1969, *165,* 1140–42.

Lewis, M., and **Als, H.** *The contribution of the infant to the interaction with his mother.* Paper presented at the meetings of the Society for Research in Child Development, Denver, April 1975.

Lewontin, R. C. Race and intelligence. In N. J. Block and G. Dworkin, eds. *The IQ controversy.* New York: Pantheon, 1976.

Lieberman, M. A., Yalom, I. D., and **Miles, M. B.** *Encounter groups.* New York: Basic Books, 1973.

Liebeskind, J. C., and **Paul, L. A.** Psychological and physiological mechanisms of pain. *Annual review of psychology,* 1977, *28,* 41–60.

Linn, S., et al. Salience of visual patterns in the human infant. *Developmental psychology,* 1982, *18,* 651–57.

Lipscomb, D. M. High intensity sounds in the recreational environment: hazard to young ears. *Clinical pediatrics,* 1969, 8, 63–68.

Loehlin, J. C., Lindzey, G., and **Spuhler, J. N.** *Race differences in intelligence.* San Francisco: Freeman, 1975.

Loftus, E. F., Miller, D. G., and **Burns, H. J.** Semantic integration of verbal information into a visual memory. *Journal of experimental psychology,* 1978, *4,* 19–31.

Londerville, S., and **Main, M.** Security of attachment, compliance, and maternal training methods in the second year of life. *Developmental psychology,* 1981, *17,* 289–99.

Lopata, H. Z. *Occupation: housewife.* New York: Oxford University Press, 1972.

Lorenz, K. *On aggression.* New York: Harcourt Brace Jovanovich, 1966.

Lowell, E. L. The effect of need for achievement on learning and speed of performance. *Journal of psychology,* 1952, *33,* 31–40.

Lubin, A., et al. The effects of exercise, bedrest, and napping on performance decrement during 40 hours. *Psychophysiology,* 1976, *13,* 334–39.

Luborsky, L., Docherty, J. P., and **Penick, S.** Onset conditions for psychosomatic symptoms. *Psychosomatic medicine,* 1973, *35,* 187–201.

Luborsky, L., et al. Factors influencing the outcome of psychotherapy. *Psychological bulletin,* 1971, *75,* 145–61.

Lutz, C. The domain of emotion words on Ifaluk. *American ethologist,* 1982, 9, 113–28.

Lykken, D. T. *A tremor in the blood: uses and abuses of the lie detector.* New York: McGraw-Hill, 1981.

Lyon, D. O. The relation of length of material to time taken for learning and the optimum distribution of time. *Journal of educational psychology,* 1914, *5,* 1–9, 85–91, and 155–63.

Maccoby, E. E. Personal communication, 1979.

Maccoby, E. E., and **Feld, S. S.** Mother attachment and stranger reactions in the third year of life. *Monographs of the Society for Research in Child Development,* 1972, *37,* Serial No. 146.

Maccoby, E. E., and **Jacklin, C. N.** *The psychology of sex differences.* Stanford, Calif.: Stanford University Press, 1974.

MacFarlane, D. A. The role of kinethesis in maze learning. *University of California publications in psychology,* 1930, *4,* 277–305.

Macfarlane, J. W. From infancy to adulthood. *Child education,* 1963, *39,* 336–42.

Macfarlane, J. W. Perspectives on personality consistency and change from the guidance study. *Vita humana,* 1964, *7,* 115–26.

MacKinnon, D. W. The nature and nurture of creative talent. *American psychologist,* 1962, *17,* 484–95.

MacKinnon, D. W. The personality of correlates of creativity. In G. S. Neilson, ed. *Proceedings of the XIV international congress of applied psychology,* Copenhagen, 1961. Copenhagen: Munksgaard, 1962.

MacKinnon, D. W. Stress interview. In D. N. Jackson and S. Messick, eds. *Problems in human assessment.* New York: McGraw-Hill, 1967.

Macklin, E. D. Heterosexual cohabitation among college students. *Family coordinator,* 1972, *21,* 463–72.

MacNichol, E. F., Jr. Three-pigment color vision. *Scientific American,* 1964, *211,* 48–56.

Maddi, S. R. *Personality theories,* rev. ed. Homewood, Ill.: Dorsey Press, 1972.

Magelowitz, E. Personal communication, 1982.

Magoun, H. W. *The waking brain,* 2d ed. Springfield, Ill.: Thomas, 1963.

Maier, S. F., Seligman, M. E. P., and **Solomon, R. L.** Pavlovian fear conditioning and learned helplessness. In B. A. Campbell and R. M. Church, eds. *Punishment and aversive behavior.* New York: Appleton-Century-Crofts, 1969.

Malof, M., and **Lott, A. J.** Ethnocentrism and the acceptance of Negro support in a group pressure situation. *Journal of abnormal and social psychology,* 1962, *65,* 254–58.

Mandler, G. Emotion. In R. Brown, et al. *New directions in psychology.* New York: Holt, Rinehart, and Winston, 1962.

Mankiewicz, F., and **Swerdlow, J.** *Remote control.* New York: Quadrangle, 1977.

Mann, L., and **Janis, I. L.** A followup study on the long-term effects of emotional role playing. *Journal of personality and social psychology,* 1968, *8,* 339–42.

Marks, I. M. Aversion therapy. *British journal of medical psychology,* 1968, *41,* 47–52.

Martin, M., et al. Programing behavior change and reintegration into school milieux of extreme adolescent deviates. *Behavior research and therapy,* 1968, *6,* 371–83.

Maslach, C. The emotional consequences of arousal without reason. In C. E. Izard, ed. *Emotion, conflict, and defense.* New York: Plenum, 1978.

Maslow, A. Personal communication, 1969.

Maslow, A. H. *Motivation and personality,* 2d ed. New York: Harper & Row, 1970.

Masserman, J. H. *Behavior and neurosis.* Chicago: University of Chicago Press, 1943.

Masserman, J. H. *Principles of dynamic psychiatry,* 2d ed. Philadelphia: Saunders, 1961.

Masters, W. H., and **Johnson, V. E.** Personal communication, 1963.

Masters, W. H., and **Johnson, V. E.** *Human sexual inadequacy.* Boston: Little, Brown, 1970.

Matarazzo, J. D. *Wechsler's measurement and appraisal of adult intelligence,* 5th ed. Baltimore: Williams & Wilkins, 1972.

Matson, F. W. Humanistic theory: the third revolution in psychology. *The humanist,* March/April 1971, 7–11.

Maugh, T. M., II. Sleep-promoting factor isolated. *Science,* 1982, *216,* 1400.

McBurney, D., and **Collings, V.** *Introduction to sensation/perception.* Englewood Cliffs, N.J.: Prentice-Hall, 1977.

McCaul, K. D. Sensory information, fear level, and reactions to pain. *Journal of personality,* 1980, *48,* 494–504.

McCaul, K. D., Holmes, D. S., and **Solomon, S.** Voluntary expressive changes in emotion. *Journal of personality and social psychology,* 1982, *42,* 145–52.

McCaul, K. D., Solomon, S., and **Holmes, D. S.** Effects of paced respiration and expectations on physiological and psychological responses to threat. *Journal of personality and social psychology,* 1979, *37,* 564–71.

McClelland, D. C. Inhibited power motive and high blood pressure in men. *Journal of abnormal psychology,* 1979, *88,* 182–90.

McClelland, D. C., and **Atkinson, J. W.** The projective expression of needs. I. The effect of different intensities of the hunger drive on perception. *Journal of psychology,* 1948, *25,* 205–22.

McClelland, D. C., Clark, R. A., and **Lowell, E. L.** *The achievement motive.* New York: Appleton-Century-Crofts, 1953.

McClelland, D. C., and **Liberman, A. M.** The effect of need for achievement on recognition of need-related words. *Journal of personality,* 1949, *18,* 236–51.

McClelland, D. C., and **Teague, G.** Predicting risk preferences among power-related acts. *Journal of personality,* 1975, *43,* 266–85.

McClelland, D. C., et al. *The drinking man.* New York: Free Press, 1972.

McClintock, M. K. Menstrual synchrony and suppression. *Nature,* 1971, *229,* 244–45.

McCord, W., and **McCord, I.** *The psychopath.* Princeton, N.J.: Van Nostrand, 1964.

McCullough, C. Color adaptation of edge-detectors in the human visual system. *Science,* 1965, *149,* 1115–16.

McDermott, M. J. *Rape victimization in 26 American cities.* Washington, D.C.: U.S. Department of Justice, 1979.

McGaugh, J. L., and **Dawson, R. G.** Modification of memory storage processes. *Behavioral science,* 1971, *16,* 45–63.

McGeoch, J. A. The influence of associative value upon the difficulty of nonsense-syllable lists. *Journal of genetic psychology,* 1930, *37,* 421–26.

McGeoch, J. A., and **McDonald, W. T.** Meaningful relation and retroactive inhibition. *American journal of psychology,* 1931, *43,* 579–88.

McGrath, J. W. *Social psychology.* New York: Holt, Rinehart, and Winston, 1964.

McGraw, M. B. *The neuromuscular maturation of the human infant.* New York: Columbia University Press, 1943.

McNemar, Q. *The revision of the Stanford-Binet scale.* Boston: Houghton Mifflin, 1942.

Mead, M. *Sex and temperament.* New York: Morrow, 1935.

Meddis, R., Pearson, A. J. D., and **Langford, G.** An extreme case of healthy insomnia. *EEG clinical neurophysiology,* 1973, *35,* 213–24.

Meece, J. L., et al. Sex differences in math achievement: toward a model of academic choice. *Psychological bulletin,* 1982, *91,* 324–48.

Mellinger, G. D., and **Balter, M. B.** Prevalence and patterns of use of psychotherapeutic drugs: results from a 1979 national survey of American adults. In G. Tognoni, C. Bellantuono, and M. Lader, eds. *Epidemiological impact of psychotropic drugs.* Amsterdam: Elsevier/North Holland Biomedical Press, 1981.

Melzack, R. *The puzzle of pain.* New York: Basic Books, 1973.

Messenger, J. Personal communication, 1979.

Meyer, R. J., and **Haggerty, R. J.** Streptococcal infections in families: factors altering individual susceptibility. *Pediatrics,* 1962, *29,* 539–49.

Milgram, S. Group pressure and action against a person. *Journal of abnormal and social psychology,* 1964, *69,* 137–43.

Miller, G. A. *Language and communication.* New York: McGraw-Hill, 1951.

Miller, G. A. The magical number seven, plus or minus two: some limits on our capacity for processing information. *Psychological review,* 1956, *63,* 81–97.

Miller, G. A. Language and psychology. In E. H. Lenneberg, ed. *New directions in the study of language.* Cambridge, Mass.: M.I.T. Press, 1964.

Miller, G. A. *Language and speech.* San Francisco: Freeman, 1981.

Miller, G. A. Personal communication, 1983.

Miller, N. E. *From the brain to behavior.* Invited lecture at XII Interamerican Congress of Psychology, Montevideo, Uruguay March 30 to April 6, 1969.

Miller, N. E. *Behavioral sciences report for the overview cluster of the President's biomedical research panel,* 1975.

Miller, N. E. The role of learning in physiological response to stress. In G. Serban, ed. *Psychopathology of human adaptation.* New York: Plenum, 1976.

Miller, N. E., and **Dollard, J.** *Social learning and imitation.* New Haven, Conn.: Yale University Press, 1941.

Milner, B. The memory defect in bilateral hippocampal lesions. *Psychiatric research reports,* 1959, *11,* 43–52.

Minuchin, S., et al. A conceptual model of psychosomatic illness in children: family organization and family therapy. *Archives of general psychiatry,* 1975, *32,* 1031–38.

Misra, R. K. Achievement, anxiety, and addiction. In D. J. Lettieri, M. Sayers, and H. W. Pearson, eds. *Theories on drug abuse: selected contemporary perspectives.* National Institute on Drug Abuse, DHHS Publication No. (ADM) 80–967, 1980, 212–14.

Money, J., and **Ehrhardt, A. A.** *Man and woman, boy and girl.* Baltimore: Johns Hopkins University Press, 1973.

Moore, R. Y. Synaptogenesis and the morphology of learning and memory. In M. R. Rosenzweig and E. L. Bennett, eds. *Neural mechanisms of learning and memory.* Cambridge, Mass.: M.I.T. Press, 1976.

Morgan, C. T., and **Morgan, J. D.** Studies in hunger. II. The relation of gastric denervation and dietary sugar to the effect of insulin upon food-intake in the rat. *Journal of genetic psychology,* 1940, *57,* 153–63.

Morgan, H. H. *An analysis of certain structured and unstructured test results of achieving and nonachieving high ability college students.* Unpublished doctoral dissertation, University of Michigan, 1951.

Morris, J. L. Propensity for risk taking as a determinant of vocational choice. *Journal of personality and social*

Moruzzi, G. The sleep-waking cycle. In R. H. Adrian, et al., eds. *Reviews of psychology* 64. Berlin: Springer-Verlag, 1972.

Moruzzi, G., and **Magoun, H. W.** Brain stem reticular formation and activation of the EEG. *Electroencephalography and clinical neurophysiology,* 1949, *1,* 455–73.

Moss, C. S. *Hypnosis in perspective.* New York: Macmillan, 1965.

Munn, N. L., Fernald, L. D., Jr., and **Fernald, P. S.** *Introduction to psychology,* 2d ed. Boston: Houghton Mifflin, 1969.

Murray, H. A. *Thematic Apperception Test.* Cambridge, Mass.: Harvard University Press, 1971.

Mussen, P. H., Conger, J. J., and **Kagan, J.** *Child development and personality,* 4th ed. New York: Harper & Row, 1974.

Mussen, P. H., Conger, J. J., and **Kagan, J.** *Child development and personality,* 5th ed. New York: Harper & Row, 1979.

National Academy of the Sciences. *Marijuana and health.* Washington, D.C., 1982.

National Assessment of Educational Progress. *Report on trends in the nation's schools,* 1981.

National Center for Health Statistics. *Annual summary of births, deaths, marriages, and divorces, United States, 1981.* Monthly vital statistics report, Vol. 30, no. 13. DHHS Pub. No. (PHS) 83–1120, December 20, 1982.

National Institute on Aging. *Special report on aging.* NIH Publication No. 81–2328, September 1981.

National Institute on Alcohol Abuse and Alcoholism. *Facts about alcohol and alcoholism.* DHHS Publication No. (ADM) 80–31, 1980.

National Institute on Drug Abuse. *Treatment manual 3: referral strategies for polydrug abusers.* DHEW Publication No. (ADM) 77–515, 1977.

National Research Council. *Ability testing: uses, consequences and controversies.* Washington, D.C.: National Academy Press, 1982.

Nauta, W. J. H. Hypothalamic regulations of sleep in rats. *Journal of neurophysiology,* 1946, 9, 285–316.

Neisser, U. John Dean's memory: a case study. *Cognition,* 1981, 9, 1–22.

Neisser, U., and **Becklen, R.** Selective looking. *Cognitive psychology,* 1975, *7,* 480–94.

Neugarten, B. Grow old with me: the best is yet to be. *Psychology today,* 1971, 97, 45–49.

Neuman, W. R. Patterns of recall among television news viewers. *Public opinion quarterly,* 1976, *40,* 115–23.

Neuringer, A. J. Superstitious key pecking after three peck-produced reinforcements. *Journal of the experimental analysis of behavior,* 1970, *13,* 127–34.

Newcomb, T. M. *The acquaintance process.* New York: Holt, Rinehart and Winston, 1961.

Newcomb, T. M. Persistence and regression of changed attitudes. *Journal of social issues,* 1963, *19,* 3–14.

Newport, E. L. Motherese. *Technical report no.52. Center for Human Information Processing.* San Diego, Calif.: University of California, 1975.

Nickerson, R. S., and **Adams, M. J.** Memory for a common object. *Cognitive psychology,* 1979, *11,* 387–407.

Nielsen, S. L., and **Sarason, I. G.** Emotion, personality, and selective attention. *Journal of personality and social psychology,* 1981, *41,* 945–60.

Nisbett, R. E. Taste, deprivation, and weight determinants of eating behavior. *Journal of personality and social psychology,* 1968, *10,* 107–16.

Nisbett, R. E. Hunger, obesity, and the ventromedial hypothalamus. *Psychological review,* 1972, *79,* 433–53.

Nisbett, R. E., and **Platt, J.** Unpublished data referred to in R. E. Nisbett. Hunger, obesity, and the ventromedial hypothalamus. *Psychological review,* 1972, *79,* 433–53.

Nisbett, R. E., and **Valins, S.** Perceiving the causes of one's own behavior. In E. E. Jones, et al., eds. *Attribution.* Morristown, N.J.: General Learning Press, 1972.

Nissen, H., and **Crawford, M.** A preliminary study of food-sharing behavior in young chimpanzees. *Journal of comparative psychology,* 1936, *22,* 283–419.

Norton, A. J., and **Glick, P. C.** Marital instability. *Journal of social issues,* 1976, *32,* 5–20.

Nurco, D. N. Etiological aspects of drug abuse. In R. I. Dupont, A. Goldstein, and J. O'Donnell, eds. *Handbook on drug abuse.* Washington, D.C.: U.S. Government Printing Office, January 1979, pp. 315–34.

Nurnberger, J. I., and **Gershon, E. S.** Genetics. In E. S. Paykel, ed. *Handbook of affective disorders.* London: Churchill Livingston, 1982.

Offer, D., Ostrov, E., and **Howard, K. I.** *The adolescent: a psychological self-portrait.* New York: Basic Books, 1982.

O'Kelly, C. G. Sexism in children's television. *Journalism quarterly,* 1974, *51,* 722–24.

O'Leary, K. D. Behavior modification in the classroom. *Journal of applied behavior analysis,* 1972, *5,* 505–11.

O'Leary, K. D., and **Drabman, R.** Token reinforcement programs in the classroom. *Psychological bulletin,* 1971, *75,* 379–98.

Ollison, L. *Socialization.* Unpublished study, San Diego State University, 1975.

O'Neil, H. F., Jr., Spielberger, C. D., and **Hansen, D. N.** Effects of state anxiety and task difficulty on computer-assisted learning. *Journal of educational psychology,* 1969, *60,* 343–50.

Opler, M. K. Cultural induction of stress. In M. H. Appley and R. Trumbull, eds. *Psychological stress.* New York: Appleton-Century-Crofts, 1967.

Orne, M. Lecture to American Association for the Advancement of Science. Washington, D.C., 1982.

Ornstein, R. The split and the whole brain. *Human nature,* 1978, *1,* 76–83.

Ornstein, R. E. The techniques of meditation and their implications for modern psychology. In C. Naranjo and R. E. Ornstein, eds. *On the psychology of meditation.* New York: Viking, 1971.

Owens, W. A., Jr. Age and mental abilities. *Journal of educational psychology,* 1966, *57,* 311–25.

Oyama, S. *A sensitive period for the acquisition of a second language.* Unpublished doctoral dissertation, Harvard University, 1973.

Paddock, J., O'Neill, C. W., and **Haver, W.** *Faces of anti-violence.* International Society for Research on Aggression, Washington, D.C., Sept. 1978.

Paivio, A. *Imagery and verbal processes.* New York: Holt, Rinehart and Winston, 1971.

Parelius, A. P. Emerging sex-role attitudes, expectations, and strains among college women. *Journal of marriage and the family,* 1975, *37,* 146–53.

Parloff, M. B. Psychotherapy and research: an anaclytic depression. *Psychiatry,* 1980, *43,* 279–93.

Parsons, T., and **Bales, R. F.** *Family, socialization, and interaction process.* Glencoe, Ill.: Free Press, 1953.

Patterson, G. R., Hops, H., and **Weiss, R. L.** Interpersonal skills training for couples in early stages of conflict. *Journal of marriage and the family,* 1975, *37,* 295–303.

Patterson, M. M., Cegavske, C. F., and **Thompson, R. F.** Effectiveness of a classical conditioning paradigm on hind-limb flexor nerve response in immobilized spinal cats. *Journal of comparative and physiological psychology,* 1973, *84,* 88–97.

Pavlov, I. P. *Conditioned reflexes.* London: Oxford University Press, 1927 (reprinted by Dover, New York, 1960).

Paykel, E. S. Contribution of life events to causation of psychiatric illness. *Psychological medicine,* 1978, *8,* 245–53.

Pearson, C. Intelligence of Honolulu preschool children in relation to parents' education. *Child development,* 1969, *40,* 647–50.

Peele, S. Reductionism in the psychology of the eighties: can biochemistry eliminate addiction, mental illness, and pain? *American psychologist,* 1981, *36,* 807–18.

Peele, T. L. *The neuroanatomic basis for clinical neurology.* New York: McGraw-Hill, 1961.

Perin, C. T. A quantitative investigation of the delay of reinforcement gradient. *Journal of experimental psychology,* 1943, *32,* 37–51.

Petersen, A. C. *Menarche: meaning of measures and measuring meaning.* Presented at meeting of Society for Menstrual Cycle Research, New Rochelle, N.Y., June, 1981.

Peterson, C., Schwartz, S. M., and **Seligman, M. E. P.** Self-blame and depressive symptoms. *Journal of personality and social psychology,* 1981, *41,* 253–59.

Peterson, L. R., and **Peterson, M. J.** Short-term retention of individual items. *Journal of experimental psychology,* 1959, *58,* 193–98.

Petti, T. A. Depression in children: a significant disorder. *Psychosomatics,* 1981, *22,* 444–47.

Pettigrew, T. F. Racially separate or together? *Journal of social issues,* 1969, *25,* 43–69.

Pfaffman, C. Gustatory nerve impulses in rat, cat, and rabbit. *Journal of neurophysiology,* 1955, *18,* 429–40.

Phares, E. J., and **Lamiell, J. T.** Internal-external control, interpersonal judgments of others in need, and attribution of responsibility.

Journal of personality, 1975, *43,* 23–38.

Piaget, J. *The origins of intelligence in children.* New York: International Universities Press, 1952.

Piliavin, I. M., Rodin, J., and **Piliavin, J. A.** Good Samaritanism: an underground phenomenon? *Journal of personality and social psychology,* 1969, *13,* 289–99.

Pogrebin, L. C. Down with sexist upbringing. *Ms. magazine,* Spring 1972, 18+.

Pokorny, A. D. Suicide rates in various psychiatric disorders. *The journal of nervous and mental disease,* 1964, *139,* 499–506.

Polivy, J. On the induction of emotion in the laboratory: discrete moods or multiple affect states? *Journal of personality and social psychology,* 1981, *41,* 803–17.

Pollack, I., and **Pickett, J. M.** Intelligibility of excerpts from fluent speech. *Journal of verbal learning and verbal behavior,* 1964, *3,* 79–84.

Pope, H. G., Jr., Ionescu-Pioggia, M., and **Cole, J. O.** Drug use and life-style among college undergraduates. *Archives of general psychiatry,* 1981, *38,* 588–91.

Post, F. *Persistent prosecutory states of the elderly.* London: Pergamon, 1966.

Postman, L., Bruner, B., and **McGinnies, E.** Personal values as selective factors in perception. *Journal of abnormal and social psychology,* 1948, *43,* 142–54.

Premack, D. *Intelligence in ape and man.* Hillsdale, N.J.: Erlbaum, 1976.

President's Commission on Mental Health. *Task panel reports,* Vol. 2. Washington, D.C.: U.S. Government Printing Office, 1978.

Pritchard, R. M. Stabilized images on the retina. *Scientific American,* 1961, *204,* 72–78.

Pruett, H. L. Stressors in middle adulthood. *Family and community health,* 1980, *2,* 53–60.

Rabkin, J. G., and **Struening, E. L.** Life events, stress, and illness. *Science,* 1976, *194,* 1013–20.

Radecki, C., and **Jennings, J.** Sex as a status variable in work settings: female and male reports of dominance behavior. *Journal of applied social psychology,* 1980, *10,* 71–85.

Radloff, R. *Opinion and affiliation.* Unpublished doctoral dissertation, University of Minnesota, 1959.

Radtke, R. C., and **Grove, E. K.** Proactive inhibition in short-term memory: availability or accessibility? *Journal of experimental psychology: human learning and memory,* 1977, *3,* 78–91.

Raloff, J. Occupational noise—the subtle pollutant. *Science news,* 1982, *121,* 347–50 and 377–81.

Rebelsky, F. Infancy in two cultures. *Nederlands tijdschrift voor de psychologie,* 1967, *22,* 379–85.

Regier, D. A., and **Taube, C. A.** The delivery of mental health services. In S. Arieti and H. K. H. Brodie. *American handbook of psychiatry,* 1981, *7,* 715–33.

Reich, W. The schizophrenia spectrum. *The journal of nervous and mental disease,* 1976, *162,* 3–12.

Reisman, B. Conflict in an Israeli collective community. *Journal of conflict resolution,* 1981, *25,* 237–58.

Rhine, J. B., and **Pratt, J. G.** *Parapsychology.* Springfield, Ill.: Thomas, 1957.

Rice, K. M., and **Blanchard, E. B.** Biofeedback in the treatment of anxiety disorders. In R. J. Mathew, ed. *The biology of anxiety.* New York: Brunner/Mazel, 1982.

Richlin, M., et al. Five-year medical followup of Vietnam POWs: preliminary results. *U.S. Navy medicine,* August 1980, *71,* 19–26.

Riger, S., and **Gordon, M. T.** The fear of rape: a study in social control. *Journal of social issues,* 1981, *37,* 71–92.

Riley, J. N., and **Walker, D. W.** Morphological alterations in hippocampus after long-term alcohol consumption in mice. *Science,* 1978, *201,* 646–48.

Rist, R. C. Student social class and teacher expectations: the self-fulfilling prophecy in ghetto education. *Harvard educational review,* 1970, *40,* 411–51.

Rizley, R. Depression and distortion in the attribution of causality. *Journal of abnormal psychology,* 1978, *87,* 32–48.

Robbins, D. Partial reinforcement. *Psychological bulletin,* 1971, *76,* 415–31.

Robertson, I. *Sociology.* New York: Worth, 1977.

Robins, L. N. Sturdy childhood predictors of adult outcomes: replications from longitudinal studies. *Psychological medicine,* 1978, *8,* 611–22.

Robins, L. N. The natural history of drug abuse. In D. J. Lettieri, M. Sayers, and H. W. Pearson, eds. *Theories on drug abuse: selected contemporary perspectives.* National Institute on Drug Abuse, DHHS Publication No. (ADM) 80–967, 1980, 215–24.

Robinson, F. P. *Effective reading.* New York: Harper & Row, 1962.

Robinson, J. P. The audience for national TV news programs. *Public opinion quarterly,* 1971, *35,* 403–05.

Rodin, J. *Shock avoidance behavior in obese and normal subjects.* Unpublished manuscript, Yale University, 1972.

Rodin, J., Elman, D., and **Schachter, S.** *Emotionality and obesity.* Unpublished manuscript, Yale University, 1972.

Rogers, C. Personal communication, 1969.

Roper Organization. *Virginia Slims American women's opinion poll,* 1980.

Rosch, E. H. Natural categories. *Cognitive psychology,* 1973, *4,* 328–50.

Rosch, E. H. Human categorization. In E. Warren, ed. *Advances in cross-cultural psychology,* Vol. 1. London: Academic Press, 1977.

Rosch, E., and **Mervis, C. B.** Family resemblances: studies in the internal structure of categories. *Cognitive psychology,* 1975, *7,* 573–605.

Rose, J. E., et al. Some effects of stimulus intensity on response of auditory nerve fibers in the squirrel monkey. *Journal of neurophysiology,* 1971, *34,* 685–99.

Rose, R. M. Endocrine responses to

stressful psychological events. *Psychiatric clinics of North America*, 1980, *3*, 251–76.

Rosenhan, D. The natural socialization of altruistic autonomy. In J. Macauley and L. Berkowitz, eds. *Altruism and helping behavior.* New York: Academic Press, 1970.

Ross, G. Concept categorization in one to two-year-olds. *Developmental psychology*, 1980, *16*, 391–96.

Ross, L. The intuitive psychologist and his shortcomings. In L. Berkowitz, ed. *Advances in experimental social psychology*, Vol. 10. New York: Academic Press, 1977.

Ross, L., Lepper, M. R., and **Hubbard, M.** Perseverance in self-perception and social perception. Stanford, Calif.: Stanford University. *Journal of personality and social psychology*, 1975, *32*, 880–92.

Ross, L. D., Amabile, T. M., and **Steinmetz, J. L.** Social roles, social control, and biases in social-perception processes. *Journal of personality and social psychology*, 1977, *35*, 485–94.

Rozin, P., and **Kalat, J. W.** Specific hungers and poisoning as adaptive specializations of learning. *Psychological review*, 1971, *78*, 459–86.

Rubin, D. C. Very long-term memory for prose and verse. *Journal of verbal learning and verbal behavior*, 1977, *16*, 611–21.

Rubin, J. Z., Provenzano, F. J., and **Luria, Z.** The eye of the beholder. *American journal of orthopsychiatry*, 1974, *44*, 512–19.

Rubin, Z. *Liking and loving.* New York: Holt, Rinehart, and Winston, 1973.

Rush, A. J., and **Beck, A. T.** Adults with affective disorders. In M. Hersen and A. S. Bellack, eds. *Behavior therapy in the psychiatric setting.* Baltimore: Williams and Wilkins, 1978.

Rutherford, E., and **Mussen, P.** Generosity in nursery school boys. *Child development*, 1968, *39*, 755–65.

Rutter, M. School effects on pupil progress: research findings and policy implications. *Child development*, 1983, *54*, 1–29.

Rutter, M. Stress, coping, and development: some issues and some questions. In N. Garmezy and M. Rutter, eds. *Stress, coping, and development in children.* New York: McGraw-Hill, 1983.

Sachs, J. S., and **Johnson, M.** Language development in a hearing child of deaf parents. In W. von Raffler Engel and Y. LeBrun, eds. *Baby talk and infant speech* (neolinguistics 5). Amsterdam: Swets and Zeitlinger, 1976.

Sackheim, H. A., Gur, R. C., and **Saucy, M. C.** Emotions are expressed more intensely on the left side of the face. *Science*, 1978, *202*, 434–36.

Sadacca, R., Ricciuti, H. N., and **Swanson, E. O.** *Content analysis of achievement motivation protocols.* Princeton, N.J.: Educational Testing Service, 1956.

Salapatek, P. Pattern perception in early infancy. In L. Cohen and P. Salapatek, eds. *Infant perception: from sensation to cognition, Vol I: Basic visual processes.* New York: Academic Press, 1975.

Salapatek, P., and **Kessen, W.** Visual scanning of triangles by the human newborn. *Journal of experimental child psychology*, 1966, *3*, 155–67.

Salk, L. *What every child would want his parents to know.* New York: Warner Books, 1973.

Sampson, E. A., and **Hancock, F. T.** An examination of the relationship between ordinal position, personality, and conformity. *Journal of personality and social psychology*, 1967, *5*, 398–407.

Sandmaier, M. *The invisible alcoholics: women and alcohol abuse in America.* New York: McGraw-Hill, 1980.

Sands, S. F., and **Wright, A. A.** Monkey and human pictorial memory scanning. *Science*, 1982, *216*, 1333–34.

Savage-Rumbaugh, E. S., Rumbaugh, D. M., and **Boysen, S.** Symbolic communication between two chimpanzees. *Science*, 1978, *201*, 641–44.

Sawrey, W. L., Conger, J. J., and **Turrell, E. S.** An experimental investigation of the role of psychological factors in the production of gastric ulcers of rats. *Journal of comparative and physiological psychology*, 1956, *49*, 457–61.

Scarr, S. Social introversion-extroversion as a heritable response. *Child development*, 1969, *40*, 823–32.

Scarr, S. Testing for children. *American psychologist*, 1981, *36*, 1159–66.

Scarr, S., and **Weinberg, R. A.** IQ test performance of black children adopted by white families. *American psychologist*, 1976, *31*, 726–39.

Scarr-Salapatek, S. Race, social class, and IQ. *Science*, 1971, *174*, 1286–95.

Scarr-Salapatek, S. Unknowns in the IQ equation. *Science*, 1971, *174*, 1223–28.

Schachter, S. *Psychology of affiliation.* Stanford, Calif.: Stanford University Press, 1959.

Schachter, S. Some extraordinary facts about obese humans and rats. *American psychologist*, 1971, *26*, 129–44.

Schachter, S., and **Gross, L. P.** Manipulated time and eating behavior. *Journal of personality and social psychology*, 1968, *10*, 98–106.

Schachter, S., and **Singer, J. E.** Cognitive, social and physiological determinants of emotional state. *Psychological review*, 1962, *69*, 379–99.

Schaie, K., and **Strother, C.** A cross-sequential study of age changes in cognitive behavior. *Psychological bulletin*, 1968, *70*, 671–80.

Schapiro, S., and **Vukovich, K. R.** Early experience effects upon cortical dendrites. *Science*, 1970, *167*, 292–94.

Scheibel, M. E., et al. Dendritic changes in aging human cortex. *Experimental neurology*, 1975, *47*, 392–403.

Scheils, D. A cross-cultural study of beliefs in out-of-the-body experiences, waking and sleeping. *Journal of the society for psychical research*, 1978, *49*, 697–741.

Schemmel, R., Michelsen, O., and **Gill, J. L.** Dietary obesity in rats. Journal of nutrition, 1970, *100*, 1041–48.

Scherer, K. R. Speech and emotional states. In J. Darby, ed. *The evaluation of speech in psychiatry.* New York: Grune and Stratton, 1981.

Schiff, M., et al. Intellectual status of working-class children adopted early into upper middle-class families. *Science,* 1978, *200,* 1503–04.

Schildkraut, J. J. *Neuropsychopharmacology and the affective disorders.* Boston: Little, Brown, 1969.

Schlesinger, B. Remarriage as family organization for divorced persons—a Canadian study. *Journal of comparative family studies,* 1970, *1,* 101–18.

Schulsinger, H. A 10-year follow-up of children of schizophrenic mothers: clinical assessment. *Acta psychologica et neurologica Scandanavica.* 1976, *53,* 371–86.

Schwab, J. J. Psychiatric manifestations of infectious diseases. In R. C. W. Hall, ed. *Psychiatric presentations of medical illness: somatopsychic disorders.* New York: Spectrum Publications, 1980.

Schwartz, G. E. Psychophysiological patterning and emotion revisited: a system perspective. In C. E. Izard, ed. *Measuring emotions in infants and children.* Cambridge, England: Cambridge University Press, 1982, 67–93.

Schwartz, S. Moral decision making and behavior. In J. Macauley and L. Berkowitz, eds. *Altruism and helping behavior.* New York: Academic Press, 1970.

Schweinhart, L. J., and **Weikart, D. P.** *Young children grow up: the effects of the Perry preschool program on youths through age 15.* Ypsilanti, Mich.: The High/Scope Press, 1980.

Sears, D. O. Social anxiety, opinion structure, and opinion change. *Journal of personality and social psychology,* 1967, *7,* 142–51.

Seaver, W. B. Effects of naturally induced teacher expectancies. *Journal of personality and social psychology,* 1973, *28,* 333–42.

Secord, P. F., and **Backman, C. W.** *Social psychology.* New York: McGraw-Hill, 1964.

Segal, J., and **Segal, Z.** *Helping Children Succeed.* New York: McGraw-Hill, 1984.

Segal, J., and **Yahraes, H.** *A child's journey: forces that shape the lives of our young.* New York: McGraw-Hill, 1978.

Seidenberg, R. *Marriage in life and literature.* New York: Philosophical Library, 1970.

Sekuler, R., and **Levinson, E.** The perception of moving targets. *Scientific American,* 1977, *236,* 60–73.

Selfridge, O. G., and **Neisser, U.** Pattern recognition by machine. *Scientific American,* 1960, *203,* 60–68.

Seligman, M. E. P. Phobias and preparedness. *Behavior therapy,* 1971, *2,* 307–20.

Selye, H. *The stress of life.* New York: McGraw-Hill, 1956.

Selye, H. Stress without distress. In G. Serban, ed. *Psychopathology of human adaptation.* New York: Plenum, 1976.

Serbin, L. A., and **O'Leary, K. D.** How nursery schools teach girls to shut up. *Psychology today,* 1975, *9,* 56–58.

Shaffer, L. F. Fear and courage in aerial combat. *Journal of consulting psychology,* 1947, *11,* 137–43.

Shapiro, J., et al. Isolation of pure *lac* operon DNA. *Nature* (London), 1969, *224,* 768–74.

Shepherd, R. N. Recognition memory for words, sentences, and pictures. *Journal of verbal learning and verbal behavior,* 1967, *6,* 156–63.

Sherman, S. J. Internal-external control and its relationship to attitude change under different social influence techniques. *Journal of personality and social psychology,* 1973, *26,* 23–29.

Shiffrin, R. M., and **Atkinson, R. C.** Storage and retrieval processes in long-term memory. *Psychological review,* 1969, *76,* 179–93.

Shigetomi, C. C., Hartmann, D. P., and **Gelfand, D. M.** Sex differences in children's altruistic behavior and reputations for helpfulness. *Developmental psychology,* 1981, *17,* 434–37.

Silberman, C. E. *Crisis in the classroom.* New York: Random House, 1970.

Silberstein, J. A., and **Parsons, O. A.** Neuropsychological impairment in female alcoholics: replication and extension. *Journal of abnormal psychology,* 1981, *90,* 179–82.

Simon, H. A. Unity of the arts and sciences: the psychology of thought and discovery. *Bulletin of the American Academy of Arts and Sciences,* March 1982, *35,* 26–53.

Simon, W., Berger, A. S., and **Gagnon, J. H.** Beyond anxiety and fantasy. *Journal of youth and adolescence,* 1972, *1,* 203–22.

Simons, R. G., and **Rosenberg, F.** Sex, sex roles, and self-image. *Journal of youth and adolescence,* 1975, *4,* 229–58.

Sims, E. A., et al. Experimental obesity in man. *Exerpta medica monograph,* 1968.

Singer, J. L., and **Singer, D. G.** *Television, imagination, and aggression: a study of preschoolers.* Hillsdale, N.J.: Erlbaum, 1980.

Singh, B. K. Trends in attitudes toward premarital sexual relations. *Journal of marriage and the family,* 1980, *42,* 387–93.

Skinner, B. F. *The behavior of organisms.* New York: Appleton-Century-Crofts, 1938.

Skinner, B. F. *Verbal behavior.* Englewood Cliffs, N.J.: Prentice-Hall, 1957.

Skinner, B. F. *Beyond freedom and dignity.* New York: Knopf, 1971.

Skolnick, A., and **Skolnick, J. H.** *Intimacy, family, and society.* Boston: Little, Brown, 1974.

Slaby, R. G., Quarforth, G. R., and **McConnachie, G. A.** Television violence and its sponsors. *Journal of communication,* 1976, *26,* 88–96.

Slater, J., and **Depue, R. A.** The contribution of environmental events and social support to serious suicide attempts in primary depressive disorder. *Journal of abnormal psychology,* 1981, *90,* 275–85.

Slobin, D. I. *Psycholinguistics.* Glenview Ill.: Scott, Foresman, 1971.

Slobin, D. I. Cognitive prerequisites for the acquisition of grammar. In C. A. Ferguson and D. I. Slobin, eds. *Studies of child language development.* New York: Holt, Rinehart, and Winston, 1973.

Smith, E. E., and **Medin, D. L.** *Categories and concepts.* Cambridge, Mass.: Harvard University Press, 1981.

Smith, M. E. An investigation of the development of the sentence and the extent of vocabulary in young children. *University of Iowa studies in child welfare,* 1926, 3(5).

Smith, M. L., Glass, G. V., and **Miller, T. I.** *The benefits of psychotherapy.* Baltimore: Johns Hopkins University Press, 1980.

Smith, S. M. Remembering in and out of context. *Journal of experimental psychology,* 1979, *5,* 460–71.

Snow, C. E. Mothers' speech to children learning language. *Child development,* 1972, *43,* 549–65.

Snow, C. E., et al. Mothers' speech in three social classes. *Journal of psycholinguistic research,* 1976, *5,* 1–20.

Snyder, M., Tanke, E. D., and **Berscheid, E.** Social perception and interpersonal behavior. *Journal of personality and social psychology,* 1977, *35,* 656–66.

Snyder, M. L., and **Frankel, A.** Observer bias. *Journal of personality and social psychology,* 1976, *34,* 857–64.

Snyder, S. H. Brain peptides as neurotransmitters. *Science,* 1980, *209,* 976–83.

Snyder, S. H. Neurotransmitters and CNS disease: schizophrenia. *Lancet,* 1982, II, 8305, 970–73.

Snyder, S. H., et al. Drugs, neurotransmitters, and schizophrenia. *Science,* 1974, *184,* 1243–53.

Solomon, R. L. Punishment. *American psychologist,* 1964, *19,* 239–53.

Solomon, R. L., and **Turner, C. H.** Discriminative classical conditioning in dogs paralyzed by curare can later control discriminative avoidance response in the normal state. *Psychological review,* 1962, *69,* 202–19.

Sommers, R. *Personal space: the behavioral analysis of design.* Englewood Cliffs, N.J.: Prentice-Hall, 1969.

Sontag, L. W., Baker, C. T., and **Nelson, V. L.** Mental growth and personality development. *Monographs of the society for research in child development,* 1958, *23* (No. 2).

Sorenson, R. C. *Adolescent sexuality in contemporary America.* New York: World, 1973.

Sorrentino, R. M., and **Sheppard, B. H.** Effects of affiliation-related motives on swimmers in individual versus group competition. *Journal of personality and social psychology,* 1978, *36,* 704–14.

Spearman, C. *The abilities of man.* London: Macmillan, 1927.

Sperling, G. The information available in brief visual presentations. *Psychological monographs,* 1960, *74,* (No. 11, Whole no. 498).

Sperling, G. Successive approximations to a model for short-term money. *Acta psychologica,* 1967, *27,* 285–92.

Sperry, R. Some effects of disconnecting the cerebral hemispheres. *Science,* 1982, *217,* 1223–26.

Spielberger, C. D. The effects of manifest anxiety on the academic achievement of college students. *Mental hygiene,* 1962, *46,* 420–26.

Spielberger, C. D. Anxiety as an emotional state. In C. D. Spielberger, ed. *Anxiety.* New York: Academic Press, 1971.

Spielberger, C. D., Denny, J. P., and **Weitz, H.** The effects of group counseling on the academic performance of anxious college freshmen. *Journal of counseling psychology,* 1962, *9,* 195–204.

Spitz, R. A. Hospitalism. In R. S. Eissler, et al., eds. *Psychoanalytic study of the child,* Vol. 2. New York: International Universities Press, 1946.

Stake, J. E., and **Levitz, E.** Career goals of college women and men and perceived achievement-related encouragement. *Psychology of women quarterly,* 1979, *4,* 151–59.

Steiner, J. E. Human facial expressions in response to taste and smell stimulation. In H. W. Reese and L. P. Lipsitt, eds. *Advances in child development and behavior,* Vol. 13. New York: Academic Press, 1979.

Stellar, E., and **Corbit, J. B.,** eds. Neural control of motivated behavior. *Neuroscience research program bulletin, 11* (No. 4), Sept. 1973.

Stern, M. Personal communication, 1983.

Stern, W. Wirklichkeitsversuche. *Beitrage zur psychologie der aussage,* 1904, *2,* 1–31.

Stevens, B. The sexually oppressed male. *Psychotherapy,* 1974, *11,* 16–21.

Stevens, C. F. The neuron. In Scientific American's *The brain.* San Francisco: Freeman, 1979.

Stevenson, H. W., and **Bitterman, M. E.** The distance effect in the transposition of intermediate size by children. *American journal of psychology,* 1955, *68,* 274–79.

Stevenson, H. W., Friedrichs, A. G., and **Simpson, W. E.** Interrelations and correlates over time in children's learning. *Child development,* 1970, *41,* 625–37.

Stewart, A. J. *Longitudinal prediction from personality to life outcomes among college-educated women.* Unpublished doctoral dissertation, Harvard University, 1975.

Stewart, A. J., and **Rubin, Z.** Power motivation in the dating couple. *Journal of personality and social psychology,* 1976, *34,* 305–09.

Stock, M. B., and **Smythe, P. M.** Does undernutrition during infancy inhibit brain growth and subsequent intellectual development? *Archives of disorders in children,* 1963, *38,* 546–52.

Stoller, R. J. The bedrock of masculinity and femininity—bisexuality. *Archives of general psychiatry,* 1972, *26,* 207–12.

Stolz, S. B., Wienckowski, L. A., and **Brown, B. S.** Behavior modification. *American psychologist,* 1975, *30,* 1027–48.

Strauss, J. S. Social and cultural influences on psychopathology. *Annual review of psychology,* 1979, *30,* 397–415.

Strickland, B. R. Internal-external control of reinforcement. In T. Blass, ed. *Personality variables in social behavior.* Hillsdale, N.J.: Erlbaum, 1977.

Suedfeld, P. Sensory deprivation stress. *Journal of personality and social psychology,* 1969, *11,* 70–74.

Suedfeld, P. The benefits of boredom. *American scientist,* 1975, *63,* 60–69.

Suomi, S. J. Peers, play, and primary prevention in primates. *Proceedings of the Third Vermont Conference on the Primary Prevention of Psychopathology: Promoting Social Competence and Coping in Children.* Hanover, N.H.: University Press of New England, 1977.

Suomi, S. J., and **Harlow, H. F.** Social rehabilitation of isolate-reared monkeys. *Developmental psychology,* 1972, *6,* 487–96.

Swanson, D. W., Bohnert, P. J., and **Smith, J. A.** *The paranoid.* Boston: Little, Brown, 1970.

Symonds, A. The liberated woman. *American journal of psychoanalysis,* 1974, *34,* 177–83.

Tagiuri, R. Social preference and its perception. In R. Tagiuri and L. Petrullo, eds. *Person perception and interpersonal behavior.* Stanford, Calif.: Stanford University Press, 1958.

Tanner, J. M. *Foetus into man.* Cambridge, Mass.: Harvard University Press, 1978.

Tarler-Benlolo, L. The role of relaxation in biofeedback training. *Psychological bulletin,* 1978, *85,* 727–55.

Tarnopolsky, A., Watkins, G., and **Hand, D. J.** Aircraft noise and mental health. I. Prevalence of individual symptoms. *Psychological medicine,* 1980, *10,* 683–98.

Tarpy, R. M., and **Mayer, R. E.** *Foundations of learning and memory.* Glenview, Ill.: Scott, Foresman, 1978.

Tavris, C., and **Offir, C.** *The longest war.* New York: Harcourt Brace Jovanovich, 1977.

Taylor, C., Smith, W. R., and **Ghiselin, B.** The creative and other contributions of one sample of research scientists. In C. Taylor and F. Barron, eds. *Scientific creativity.* New York: Wiley, 1963.

Teasdale, J. D. Effects of real and recalled success on learned helplessness and depression. *Journal of abnormal psychology,* 1978, *87,* 155–64.

Tecce, J. J. Contingent negative variation and individual differences. *Archives of general psychiatry,* 1971, *24,* 1–16.

Tennen, H., and **Eller, S. J.** Attributional components of learned helplessness and facilitation. *Journal of personality and social psychology,* 1977, *35,* 265–71.

Tennes, K. H., and **Mason, J. W.** Developmental psychoendocrinology: an approach to the study of emotions. In C. E. Izard, ed. *Measuring emotions in infants and children.* Cambridge, England: Cambridge University Press, 1982.

Terman, L. M., and **Merrill, M. A.** *Stanford-Binet intelligence scale: manual for the third revision, form L-M,* 1937.

Terr, L. C. Psychiatric trauma in children: observations following the Chowchilla school bus-kidnapping. *American journal of psychiatry,* 1981, *138,* 14–19.

Terrace, H. S. *Nim: a chimpanzee who learned sign language.* New York: Knopf, 1979.

Tesser, A., and **Brodie, M.** A note on the evaluation of a "computer date." *Psychonomic science,* 1971, *23,* 300.

Thomas, A., and **Chess, S.** Development in middle childhood. *Seminars in psychiatry,* 1972, *4,* 331–41.

Thomas, A., Chess, S., and **Birch, H. G.** The origin of personality. *Scientific American,* 1970, *223,* 106–07.

Thomas, M. H., et al. Toleration of real life aggression as a function of exposure to television violence. *Journal of personality and social psychology,* 1977, *35,* 450–58.

Thompson, R. F. *Foundations of physiological psychology.* New York: Harper & Row, 1967.

Tinklepaugh, O. L. An experimental study of representative factors in monkeys. *Journal of comparative psychology,* 1928, *8,* 197–236.

Tolman, E. C. Cognitive maps in rats and men. *Psychological review,* 1948, *55,* 189–208.

Tolman, E. C., and **Honzik, C. H.** Introduction and removal of reward and maze performance in rats. *University of California publications in psychology,* 1930, *4,* 257–75.

Tomkins, S. S. *Affect, imagery, consciousness, Vol. 1. The positive affects.* New York: Springer, 1962.

Torrance, E. P. *Torrance tests of creative thinking.* Princeton, N.J.: Personnel Press, 1966.

Torrey, E. F. *Schizophrenia and civilization.* New York: Jason Aronson, 1980.

Treisman, A. M. Strategies and models of selective attention. *Psychological review,* 1969, *76,* 282–99.

Treisman, A. M., and **Gelade, C.** A feature-integration theory of attention. *Cognitive psychology,* 1980, *12,* 97–136.

Triplett, N. The dynamogenic factors in pace making and competition. *American journal of psychology,* 1898, *9,* 507–33.

Trusheim, D., and **Crouse, J.** The DTS admissions formula: does the SAT add useful information? *Phi Delta Kappa,* September 1982, pp. 59–61.

Tsang, Y. C. Hunger motivation in gastrectomized rats. *Journal of comparative psychology,* 1938, *26,* 1–17.

Tschukitscheff, I. P. Über den Mechanismus der Hungerbewegungen des Magens. I. Einfluss des "satten" und "Hunger" -Blutes auf die periodische Tatigkeit des Magens. *Archiv für die gesamte psychologie,* 1930, *223,* 251–64.

Tsuang, M. T., and **Vandermey, R.** *Genes and the mind: inheritance of mental illness.* New York: Oxford University Press, 1980.

Tversky, A., and **Kahneman, D.** Availability: a heuristic for judging frequency and probability. *Cognitive psychology,* 1973, *5,* 207–32.

Tversky, A., and **Kahneman, D.** Judgment under uncertainty: heuristics and biases. *Science,* 1974, *185,* 1124–31.

Tyhurst, J. S. Individual reactions to community disaster. *American journal of psychiatry,* 1951, *10,* 746–69.

Tyler, L. E. The intelligence we test—an evolving concept. In L. B. Resnick, ed. *The nature of intelligence.* New York: Erlbaum, 1976.

Tyler, R. W. Permanence of learning. *Journal of higher education,* 4 (April 1933), Table 1, p. 204.

Underwood, B. J. Interference and forgetting. *Psychological review,* 1957, *64,* Fig. 1, p. 61.

U.S. Bureau of the Census. *Current population reports,* Series P-25. No. 917, 1980.

U.S. Bureau of the Census. *Population characteristics,* Series P-20. No. 369, 1982.

U.S. Bureau of the Census. *Current population reports,* Series P-20. No. 372, 1982.

U.S. Bureau of Labor Statistics. *Monthly employment and earnings,* Vol. 27. 1980.

U.S. National Center for Education Statistics. *Digest of education statistics,* 1983.

U.S. Office of Strategic Services, Assessment Staff. *Assessment of men.* New York: Holt, Rinehart, and Winston, 1948.

Uttal, W. R. *The psychobiology of sensory coding.* New York: Harper & Row, 1973.

Vaillant, G. E. Alcoholism and drug dependence. In A. M. Nicholi, Jr., ed. *The Harvard guide to modern psychiatry.* Cambridge, Mass.: Harvard University Press, 1978.

Valenstein, E. S. *Brain control.* New York: Wiley, 1973.

Valenstein, E. S. Stereotyped behavior and stress. In G. Serban, ed. *The psychopathology of human adaptation.* New York: Plenum, 1976.

Valenstein, E. S., Cox, V. C., and **Kakolewski, J. W.** Re-examination of the role of the hypothalamus in emotion. *Psychological review,* 1970, *77,* 16–31.

Valenta, J. G., and **Rigby, M. K.** Discrimination of the odor of distressed rats. *Science,* 1968, *161,* 599–601.

Vance, V. S., and **Schlechty, P. C.** *The structure of the teaching occupation and the characteristics of teachers.* Report prepared for the National Institute of Education, Contract No. NIE–81–0100, 1982.

Van Dyke, C., and **Byck, R.** Cocaine. *Scientific American,* 1982, *246,* 3, 128–41.

Vaughn, C. E., and **Leff, J. P.** The influence of family and social factors on the course of psychiatric illness: a comparison of schizophrenic and depressed neurotic patients. *British journal of psychiatry,* 1976, *129,* 125–37.

Vennemann, T. An explanation of drift. In C. N. Li, ed. *Word order and word order change.* Austin: University of Texas Press, 1975.

Verhave, T. The pigeon as a quality-control inspector. *American psychologist,* 1966, *21,* 109–15.

Vierling, J. S., and **Rock, J.** Variations of olfactory sensitivity to exaltolide during the menstrual cycle. *Journal of applied physiology,* 1967, *22,* 311–15.

Vincent, C. E. Social and interpersonal sources of symptomatic frigidity. *Marriage and family living,* 1956, *18,* 355–60.

Von Frisch, W. *Bees.* Ithaca, N.Y.: Cornell University Press, 1950.

Vorster, J. Mothers' speech to children. *Publications of the Institute for General Linguistics,* No. 8. Amsterdam: University of Amsterdam, 1974.

Wagner, M. W., and **Monnett, M.** Attitudes of college professors toward extrasensory perception. *Zetetic scholar,* 1979, *5,* 7–16.

Wald, G. The photochemical basis of rod vision. *Journal of the Optical Society of America,* 1951, *41,* 949–56.

Walker, J. I. The psychological problems of Vietnam veterans. *Journal of the American Medical Association,* 1981, *246,* 781–82.

Wallace, R. K., and **Benson, H.** The physiology of meditation. *Scientific American,* 1972, *226,* 84–90.

Wallach, M. A. Tests tell us little about talent. *American scientist,* 1976, *64,* 57–63.

Wangensteen, O. H., and **Carlson, A. J.** Hunger sensations in a patient after total gastrectomy. *Proceedings of the Society for Experimental Biology and Medicine,* 1931, *28,* 545–47.

Warren, R. M., and **Warren, R. P.** Auditory illusions and confusions. *Scientific American,* 1970, *223,* 30–36.

Warrington, E. K., and **Sanders, H. I.** The fate of old memories. *Quarterly journal of experimental psychology,* 1971, *23,* 232–42.

Wason, P. C. Problem solving and reasoning. *Cognitive psychology,* British Medical Bulletin, 1971, *27.*

Watkins, O. C., and **Watkins, M. J.** Buildup of proactive inhibition as a cue-overload effect. *Journal of experimental psychology: human learning and memory,* 1975, *1,* 442–52.

Watson, J. B., and **Rayner, R.** Conditioned emotional reactions. *Journal of experimental psychology,* 1920, *3,* 1–14.

Weatherly, D. Self-perceived rate of physical maturation and personality in late adolescence. *Child development,* 1964, *35,* 1197–1210.

Webb, W. B., and **Cartwright, R. D.** Sleep and dreams. *Annual review of psychology,* 1978, *29,* 223–52.

Wechsler, D. Intelligence defined and undefined. *American psychologist,* 1975, *30,* 135–59.

Weiner, B. *Achievement motivation and attribution theory.* Morristown, N.J.: General Learning Press, 1974.

Weiner, H. Psychobiology of essential hypertension. In R. J. Mathew, ed. *The biology of anxiety.* New York: Brunner/Mazel, 1982.

Weingartner, H., et al. Effects of vasopressin on human memory functions. *Science,* 1981, *211,* 601–03.

Weiskrantz, L. Experimental studies of amnesia. In C. W. M. Whitty and O. L. Zangwill, eds. *Amnesia.* London: Butterworths, 1966.

Weiss, J. M. Somatic effects of predictable and unpredictable shock. *Psychosomatic medicine,* 1970, *32,* 397–408.

Weiss, J. M., Glazer, H. I., and **Po-**

horecky, L. A. Coping behavior and neurochemical changes. In G. Serban and A. Kling, eds. *Animal models in human psychobiology.* New York: Plenum, 1976.

Weiss, J. M., et al. Effects of acute and chronic exposure to stressors on avoidance behavior and brain norepinephrine. *Psychosomatic medicine,* 1975, *37,* 522–34.

Weiss, W., and **Fine, B. J.** The effect of induced aggressiveness on opinion change. In E. E. Maccoby, T. M. Newcomb, and E. L. Hartley, eds. *Readings in social psychology,* 3d ed. New York: Holt, Rinehart, and Winston, 1958.

Weitzman, L. J. Sex-role socialization. In J. Freeman, ed. *Women.* Palo Alto, Calif.: Mayfield, 1975.

Weitzman, L. J., et al. Sex role socialization in picture books for pre-school children. *American journal of sociology,* 1972, *77,* 1125–50.

Werner, J. S., and **Lipsitt, L. P.** The infancy of human sensory systems. In E. S. Gollin, ed. *Developmental plasticity.* New York: Academic Press, 1981.

Wessels, M. G. *Cognitive psychology.* New York: Harper & Row, 1982.

Wesson, D. R., and **Smith, D. E.** Treatment of the polydrug abuser. In R. I. Dupont, et al., eds. *Handbook on drug abuse.* Rockville, Md.: National Institute on Drug Abuse, January 1979, 151–57.

Whalen, R. E. Brain mechanisms controlling sexual behavior. In F. A. Beach, ed. *Human sexuality in four perspectives.* Baltimore: Johns Hopkins University Press, 1976.

White, B. L., Castle, P., and **Held, R.** Observations on the development of visually directed reaching. *Child development,* 1964, *35,* 349–64.

Whitfield, I. C., and **Evans, E. F.** Responses of auditory cortical neurons to stimuli of changing frequency. *Journal of neurophysiology,* 1965, *28,* 655–72.

Whorf, B. L. Science and linguistics. In J. B. Carroll, ed. *Language, thought, and reality.* Cambridge, Mass.: M.I.T. Press, 1956.

Wickelgren, W. A. *Learning and memory.* Englewood Cliffs, N.J.: Prentice-Hall, 1977.

Wickelgren, W. A. Human learning and memory. *Annual review of psychology,* 1981, *32,* 21–52.

Wickert, F. *Psychological research on problems of redistribution.* Washington, D.C.: Government Printing Office, 1947.

Wiesel, T. N., and **Hubel, D. H.** Comparison of the effects of unilateral and bilateral eye closure on cortical unit responses in kittens. *Journal of neurophysiology,* 1965, *28,* 1029–40.

Wiesel, T. N., and **Hubel, D. H.** Ordered arrangement of orientation columns in monkeys lacking visual experience. *Journal of comparative neurology,* 1974, *158,* 307–18.

Wilkins, W. Desensitization. *Psychological bulletin,* 1971, *76,* 311–17.

Will, J., Self, P., and **Datan, N.** Paper presented to the American Psychological Association, 1974.

Williams, H. L. The new biology of sleep. *Journal of psychiatric research,* 1971, *8,* 445–78.

Williams, J., and **Spitzer, R.** The reliability of the diagnostic criteria of DSM-III. In J. Wing, P. Bebbington, and L. Robins, eds. *What is a case? The problem of definition in psychiatric community surveys.* London: Grant-McIntyre, Ltd., 1981.

Williams, M. *Brain damage, behaviour, and the mind.* New York: Wiley, 1979.

Williams, R. J. *Biochemical individuality.* New York: Wiley, 1956.

Williams, T. M. *Differential impact of TV on children: a natural experiment in communities with and without TV.* Paper presented at meeting of the International Society for Research on Aggression, Washington, D.C., 1978.

Wilson, E. O. *Sociobiology: the new synthesis.* Cambridge, Mass.: Harvard University Press, 1975.

Wine, J. *Investigations of attentional interpretation of test anxiety.* Unpublished doctoral dissertation, University of Waterloo, Ont., 1971.

Wing, C. W., Jr., and **Wallach, M. A.** *College admissions and the psychology of talent.* New York: Holt, Rinehart, and Winston, 1971.

Winget, C., Kramer, M., and **Whitman, R.** Dreams and demography. *Canadian Psychiatric Association journal,* 1972, *17,* 203–08.

Winokur, G. *Depression: the facts.* New York: Oxford University Press, 1981.

Winter, D. G. *The power motive.* New York: Free Press, 1973.

Winter, D. G., and **Stewart, A. J.** The power motive. In H. London and J. E. Exner, eds. *Dimensions of personality.* New York: Wiley, 1978.

Winterbottom, M. R. *The relation of childhood training in independence to achievement motivation.* Unpublished doctoral dissertation, University of Michigan, 1953. Summarized in D. C. McClelland, et al. *The achievement motive.* New York: Irvington Publishers, 1953.

Wolf, R. M. *The identification and measurement of environmental process variables related to intelligence.* Unpublished Ph.D. dissertation, University of Chicago, 1963.

Wolff, P. H. Observations on newborn infants. *Psychosomatic medicine,* 1959, *21,* 110–18.

Wolpe, J. *Theme and variations.* Elmsford, N.Y.: Pergamon, 1976.

Woolfolk, A. E., Woolfolk, R. L., and **Wilson, G. T.** A rose by any other name. . . .labeling bias and attitudes toward behavior modification. *Journal of consulting and clinical psychology,* 1977, *45,* 184–91.

Worchel, P. *Self-enhancement and interpersonal attraction.* Paper read at the American Psychological Association, August, 1961.

World Health Organization. *Schizophrenia: an international follow-up study.* New York: Wiley, 1979.

Wyatt, R. J., and **Freed, W. J.** Progress in neurografting as a treatment for degenerative brain disease: the Parkinson's model. In W. Regelson, ed. *Intervention in the aging process.* New York: Alan R. Liff, 1983.

Yankelovich, Skelly, and **White.** Public opinion poll for *Time Magazine,* Nov. 21, 1977, 111+.

Yankelovich, Skelly, and **White.** *The Yankelovich monitor,* 1983.

Yarbus, A. L. *Eye movements and vision.* Translated by L. A. Riggs. New York: Plenum, 1967.

Yates, F. A. *The art of memory.* Chicago: University of Chicago Press, 1966.

Yerkes, R. M., and **Morgulis, S.** The methods of Pavlov in animal psychology. *Psychological bulletin,* 1909, *6,* 257–73.

Young, P. T. *Motivation and emotion.* New York: Wiley, 1961.

Zajonc, R. B. Attitudinal effects of mere exposure. *Journal of personality and social psychology,* 1968, *8,* 18.

Zajonc, R. B., and **Markus, G. B.** Birth order and intellectual development. *Psychological review,* 1975, *82,* 74–88.

Zelnick, M., and **Kantner, J. F.** Sexual activity, contraceptive use and pregnancy among metropolitan-area teenagers: 1971–1979. *Family planning perspectives,* 1980, *12,* 5, 230–37.

Zigler, E., and **Trickett, P. K.** IQ, social competence, and evaluation of early childhood intervention programs. *American psychologist,* 1978, *33,* 789–98.

Zillman, D., Katcher, A. H., and **Milavsky, B.** Excitation transfer from physical exercise to subsequent aggressive behavior. *Journal of experimental social psychology,* 1972, *8,* 247–59.

Zimbardo, P. G., Andersen, S. M., and **Kabat, L. G.** Induced hearing deficit generates experimental paranoia. *Science,* 1982, *212,* 1529–31.

Zipf, G. K. *Human behavior and the principle of least effort.* Cambridge, Mass.: Addison-Wesley, 1949.

Zola-Morgan, S., Squire, L. R., and **Mishkin, M.** The neuroanatomy of amnesia: amygdala-hippocampus versus temporal stem. *Science,* 1982, 218, 1337–39.

Zung, W. W. K. *How normal is depression? Current concepts.* The Upjohn Co., December 1981.

Zweben, J. E., and **Miller, R. L.** The systems game. *Psychotherapy,* 1968, *5,* 73–76.

Picture Credits

Chapter 1

PAGE	SOURCE
3	top © Melanie Kaestner; bottom, left, © B. Uzzle/Woodfin Camp & Assoc.; right, © Harvey Stein
9	© Sepp Seitz/Woodfin Camp & Assoc. 1982
10	© Bohdan Hrynewtych/Stock, Boston
11	Plate 11, "The Consulting Room" from Berggasse 19: Sigmund Freud's Home and Office, Vienna, 1938, The Photographs of Edmund Engelman. Captions to the photographs © 1976 by Basis Books, Inc.; the photographs of Berggasse 19 © 1976 by Edmund Engelman. Used with permission
13	© Marcia Weinstein
14	Photo by Dellenbach. Reproduced by permission of the Kinsey Institute for Research in Sex, Gender, and Reproduction, Inc.
19	© David McKinley
22	Brown Brothers
23	top, Culver Pictures, Inc.; bottom, Historical Picture Service
24	Harvard University
30	© Bill Hayward
31	top, Courtesy of Dr. Landrum B. Shettles; bottom, Dr. J. H. Tjio
32	Dr. Lorne MacHattie
33	© Robert Burroughs

Chapter 2

PAGE	SOURCE
48	© Martin M. Rotker/Taurus Photos
50	© 1979 Karen R. Preuss/Jeroboam
55	top, © William Rosenthal/Jeroboam; right, © Thomas Hopker/Woodfin Camp & Assoc.
56	© 1979, Sharon Fox/The Picture Cube
58	R. W. Sperry
61	Erik Arneson
62	© Melanie Kaestner
63	Arthur Leipzig
64	© Don Bartletti/Focus West
66	top, © Robert V. Eckert/EKM-Nepenthe; bottom, © Marcia Weinstein

Chapter 3

PAGE	SOURCE
81	© Max and Kit Hunn/Photo Researchers, Inc.
83	© Robert Burroughs
85	Sovfoto/Eastfoto
91	top, © Reed D. Brugger/The Picture Cube; bottom, © Sibyl/ Shelton/Monkmeyer Press Photo
92	H. S. Terrace
93	U.P.I.
94	Yerkes Primate Research Center, Emory University
95	© Michael Weisbrot/Stock, Boston
97	© Merrim/Monkmeyer Press Photo
100	© Anna Kaufman Moon/Stock, Boston
102	© Harvey Stein
112	© Eugene Richards/The Picture Cube
113	Albert Bandura

Chapter 4

PAGE	SOURCE
120	David Moskowitz
126	© Ken Karp
137	© Melanie Kaestner
145	© Ken Karp

Chapter 5

PAGE	SOURCE
161	© Marjorie Pickens
162	© Kent Reno/Jeroboam
164	Editorial Photocolor Archive
169	Tzovaras/U.N.
175	B. T. Gardner
176	E. Sue Savage-Rumbaugh, Yerkes Regional Primate Research Center, Emory University

PAGE	SOURCE
178	Dr. Nicholas Pastore, New York City
185	© Kent Reno/Jeroboam
191–2	Joel Havemann

Chapter 6

204	© Elizabeth Crews
205	© Marcia Weinstein
206	© E. F. Bernstein/Black Star
208	Courtesy of Georgette and Geraldine Binet, *Time,* Paris
209	This illustration of the Stanford-Binet Kit shows materials included in the 1973 edition. An illustration of the 1985 edition was not available at the time of publication. Both are published by the Riverside Publishing Company
212	© Nancy Hays/Monkmeyer Press Photo
213	U.S. Signal Corp. in the National Archive
224	© Peter Vandermark/Black Star
227	© Melanie Kaestner
228	© Bettye Lane

Chapter 7

247	© Marcia Weinstein
248	© Manfred Kage/Peter Arnold
251	© Russ Kinne/Photo Researchers
258	© Charles Gatewood
261	Edwin R. Lewis

Chapter 8

277	American Museum of Natural History
278	© Mitchell Payne/Jeroboam
285	David Moskowitz
286	© Melanie Kaestner
287	Wm. Vandivert
289	top, © Michael Weisbrot, bottom, United Nations
290	© Melanie Kaestner
301	© Jean-Claude LeJeune/EKM-Nepenthe
303	© Ira Berger

Chapter 9

313	© Michael Hayman/Black Star
314	left, Walter Chandoha; right, David Moskowitz

PAGE	SOURCE
315	© Ken Karp
317	Gary Schwartz, Harvard University
318	Ed Gallob
319	top, from Measuring Emotions in Infants and Children, Izard, C. E., ed., Cambridge University Press, Reproduced by permission; bottom, Sackheim, H. A., Gur, R. C. and Saucy, M. C. *Science,* 1978, 202, 434–36 with the permission of the American Association for the Advancement of Science
320	Dr. Eckhard N. Hess
321	© Melanie Kaestner
325	© Dennis Brack/Black Star
330	© Cary Wolinsky/Stock, Boston
334	Museum of Art, Rhode Island School of Design, Nancy Sayles Day Collection
335	© Watson/Monkmeyer Press Photo
336	Bell Laboratories
338	Fred Sponholz
339	© Kent Reno/Jeroboam
345	© Charles Gatewood
348	© Don Bartletti/Focus West

Chapter 10

355	© Don Bartletti/Focus West
356	© Frank Siteman/The Picture Cube
359	© Jean-Claude LeJeune/EKM-Nepenthe
360	© Olive Pierce/Stock, Boston
361	right bottom, center, The Bettmann Archive; all others, U.P.I.
364	U.P.I.
367	top, U.N. Photo; middle, Crown Publishers; bottom, American Foundation for the Blind
373	© Melanie Kaestner
385	© Doug Wilson/Black Star
388	© Janice Fullman/The Picture Cube
391	© John Maher/EKM-Nepenthe

Chapter 11

398	© Robert V. Eckert/EKM-Nepenthe
401	© Arthur Grace/Stock, Boston
405	© Michael O'Brien/Archive
409	©Tom Sobolik/Black Star

PAGE	SOURCE
415	from a study by Simon Goldberg and Michael Lewis
420	© Peter Southwick/Stock, Boston
422	© Paul Conklin
423	© Andy Levin/Black Star
424	J. H. Masserman

Chapter 12

430	© Frank Siteman/Stock, Boston
439	Monte S. Buchsbaum, Department of Psychiatry, University of California, Irvine
443	U.P.I.
446	U.P.I.
449	U.P.I.
454	top, © Melanie Kaestner; bottom, left, © Michael Weisbrot/Stock, Boston; right, © Jim Anderson/Woodfin Camp & Assoc.
455	U.P.I.
462	left, Stedelijh Museum, Amsterdam; right, The Bettmann Archive

Chapter 13

468	© Karen R. Preuss/Jeroboam
469	© Marion Bernstein
471	The Bettmann Archive
474	© Ann Hagen Griffiths/DPI
477	top, © Ira Berger; bottom, The Bettmann Archive
478	HBJ Picture Library
480	Ted Lau
486	Albert Bandura
491	top © Linda Ferrer/Woodfin Camp & Assoc., bottom, Watriss/Baldwin/Woodfin Camp & Assoc.

Chapter 14

PAGE	SOURCE
507	H. F. R. Prechtl, 1977. The Neurological examination of the full-term newborn infant. Second revised and enlarged edition. Heinemann, London Clinics in Developmental Medicine, No. 60
508	© Doris Pinney
509	Drs. Lillian and Edwin Robbins
510	© Marjorie Pickens
515	Joel Havemann
519	Fred Sponholz
521	Jerome Kagan
526	© George Bellerose/Stock, Boston
527	© Bonnie Griffith/The Picture Cube
529	U.P.I.
531	© Mimi Cotter/International Stock Photography
532	© Marcia Weinstein
534	©Melanie Kaestner
537	Steven J. Kaiser
540	© B. Kliewe/Jeroboam
542	© Marjorie Pickens

Chapter 15

548	© Ken Karp
549	© John Maher/EKM-Nepenthe
551	top and center, The Bettmann Archive; bottom, © Ken Karp
552–3	William Vandivert
554	© 1965 by Stanley Milgram from the film "Obedience" distributed by N.Y. University Film Library
555	© Joel Gordon
563	© Martin Levick/Black Star
573	top, © Marjorie Pickens; bottom, © Rosemary Ranck
575	top, © Bob Daemmrich/Sullivan Associates; bottom, Barbara Pfeffer/Peter Arnold
583	© Ivan Massar/Black Star
584	Dr. John Darbey

Part Opening Photos

PAGE	PART AND SOURCE
3	One: Teotihuacan mask, Mexico, Photograph by Ken Hughes, San Diego Museum of Man
79	Two: Dan mask, Africa, © Zoological Society of San Diego
159	Three: Tlingit mask, North America, Courtesy of Exxon Company, U.S.A.
241	Four: Wayang dance mask, Java, Photograph by Ken Hughes, San Diego Museum of Man

PAGE	PART AND SOURCE
311	Five: Oaxacan mask, Mexico, Rollins Collection
395	Six: Tlingit mask, North America, Courtesy of Exxon Company, U.S.A.
503	Seven: Noh mask, Japan, Sekai Bunka Photo

Color Section

Plate IV, American Optical Corporation
Plate VII, Jasper Johns

Name index

This index lists all the studies cited in the book by page number. "Ayllon and Zarin (1968), *97*" means that the study is cited on page 97. The fact that the 97 is in italics indicates that the study is cited in an illustration. Where a full name is given, as in "Adler, Alfred, 362, 478," the individual is discussed in the text.

A

AACRAO (American Association of Collegiate Registrars and Admissions Officers) and the College Board (1980), 213
Abelson and Fishburn (1976), 303
Abernathy, et al. (1979), 343
Abramson, Seligman, and Teasdale (1978), 106
Adler, Alfred, 362, 478
Adler (1928), 362
Aigner and Balster (1978), 306
Ainsworth and Bell (1970), 520
Akhtar and Thomson (1982), 452
Alexander (1982), 301
Altman, et al. (1969), 583
American Psychiatric Association (1980), *434*, 447, 449
American Psychological Association, 86
Anand and Brobeck (1951), 330
Anastasi (1981), 214
Anastasi (1982), 498
Anderson, F. (1981), 392
Anderson, J. R., and Bower (1973), 138
Andrew (1965), 317
Arnold (1960), 324
Aronfreed (1970), 582
Aronson (1972), 547, 554, 564
Aronson and Linder (1965), 574
Asch, Solomon, 552
Asch (1956), 552
Ashear (1975), 320
Asher, Oden, and Gortman (1981), 528
Astin (1982), 217
Atkinson, J. W. (1976), 371
Atkinson, J. W., and Litwin (1960), 405
Atkinson, J. W., and Raynor (1974), 371
Atkinson, J. W., et al. (1960), 404
Atkinson, K., MacWhinny, and Stoel (1970), 170
Ayllon and Azrin (1968), 97
Ayoub, Greenough, and Juraska (1983), 381

B

Baastrup (1980), 493
Baddeley (1978), 138
Baddeley (1981), 20
Baer (1973), 97
Balagura (1973), 330
Baldwin (1975), 511
Bales and Slater (1955), 574
Ball (1974), 329
Baltes and Schaie (1974), 228
Bander, Russell, and Zamostry (1982), 403
Bandrua, Albert, 112–13, 483
Bandura (1973), 364, 366
Bandura (1974), 113, 483
Bandura (1976), 483
Bandura (1977), 485
Bandura, Jeffery, and Gajdos (1975), 107, 486
Bane (1976), 539, 541
Banquet (1973), 301
Barber (1972), 358
Bardwick (1971), 381
Barker, Demko, and Lewin (1941), 374
Baron and Lawton (1972), 365
Barron, F. (1958), *230*
Barron, F., Jarvik, and Bunnell (1972), 304
Barron, F. H. (1968), 229
Baumrind (1972), 385
Bayley (1970), 224
Beach (1976), 345
Beary and Benson (1974), 301
Beck (1967), 440
Beeler and Branley (1951), *290*
Bekerian and Baddeley (1980), 142
Békésy (1960), 254
Belensky (1976), 492
Belmont and Marolla (1973), 225
Belmont, Stein, and Zybert (1978), 225
Bem, D. J. (1970), 558
Bem, D. J. (1972), 571
Bem, S. L. (1974), 380
Bem, S. L. (1981), 386
Benedict (1959), 548
Benjamin, et al. (1981), 404
Bennett, et al. (1964), 57, 127
Benson (1975), 301
Benson, Rosner, and Marzetta (1973), 301
Benson and Wallace (1972), 301
Berg (1970), 219
Berger (1969), 298
Bernal, et al. (1968), 487
Berscheid and Walster (1974), 572
Bersoff (1981), 217
Bettelheim (1943), 421
Bexton, Heron, and Scott (1954), 336
Binet, Alfred, *208*, 209, 210, 215, 217
Bjork (1972), 122
Björntorp (1972), 333
Black and Bern (1981), 150
Black, Turner, and Bower (1979), 150
Blass and Hall (1976), 334
Block, J., Von Der Lippe, and Block (1973), 388
Block, N. J., and Dworkin (1976), 222
Bloom and Fawcett (1968), *260*
Blum, Jarvik, and Clark (1970), 228
Bogen (1969), 59
Bolles (1972), 111
Bond (1940), *215*
Bonvillian, Orlansky, and Novack (1983), 514
Boring (1964), *290*

Bower (1970), 136
Bower (1972), 151
Bower (1978), 141, *151, 153*
Bower (1981), *132,* 132
Bower and Clark (1969), 152
Bower, et al. (1969), 149
Bowerman (1974), 172
Bowerman (1978), 186
Bowlby (1961), 525
Braestrup (1982), 73
Brecher (1972), 305
Brehm (1956), 562
Breland and Breland (1961), 113
Briggs (1970), 511
Broadbent (1977), 292
Broen (1972), 173
Brooks and Lewis (1974), 384
Bross (1973), 181
Brotman (1981), 541
Broverman, et al. (1972), 379
Brown, G. W., and Harris (1978), 413
Brown, M. D. (1975), 358
Brown, R. (1970), 161
Brown, R. (1973), 173, 174
Brown, R., and Bellugi (1964), 172
Brown, R., Cazden, and Bellugi-Klima (1969), *173*
Brown, R., and McNeill (1966), 138
Brown, R. W. (1965), 208
Bruner (1978), 170
Bruner, Goodnow, and Austin (1956), 179
Bucher, et al. (1981), 444
Buchsbaum, et al. (1982), 439
Bugelski and Alampay (1961), *292*
Bugelski, Kidd, and Segmen (1968), 155
Bühler (1968), 418
Bullen, Reed, and Mayer (1964), 333
Butler, J. M., and Haigh (1954), 480
Butler, R. A. (1953), 338
Butterfield (1980), 213
Byrne, D. (1969), 574
Byrne, W. L., et al. (1966), 128

C

Califano (1982), 307
Calne (1981), 47
Cameron (1972), 541
Campbell, B. A., and Church (1969), 101
Campbell, D. (1965), 582
Carmen, Russo, and Miller (1981), 388
Carpenter and Stephens (1980), 442
Carpenter, et al. (1973), 437
Carroll (1981), 443
Carroll and Horn (1981), 217
Cashdan (1980), 487
Chechile and Butler (1975), 134
Chomsky, Noam, 174–75, 177
Chomsky (1965), 165
Christiaansen (1980), 134
Clark and Clark (1977), 141, 162, 164, 167, 169, 173, 181, 184
Clark and Midanik (1982), 456, 457
Clark and Nakashima (1968), 304
Clausen (1975), 532
Cofer (1972), 334
Cohen, A. R. (1959), 566
Cohen, H. (1970), 97
Cohen, S., Glass, and Singer (1973), 256
Cohen, S., et al. (1980), 256
Coleman, J. C. (1976), 448
Coleman, J. S. (1966), 106
Coles (1971), 106
Collins and Quillian (1972), 180
Conger (1977), 531, 533
Conry and Plant (1965), 215
Cooper, H. (1979), 570
Cooper, J. (1976), 86
Cooper, M., Zanna, and Taves (1978), 561
Cowan (1979), 57
Craik, F. I. M., and Kirsner (1974), 152
Craik, F. I. M., and Lockhart (1972), 138
Craik, F. I. M., and Tulving (1975), 140, 144
Craik, Kenneth, 27
Craik, K. (1952), 27
Crandall (1969), 381
Crano and Mellon (1978), 570
Crockenburg (1972), 229
Crockett (1962), 355
Cronbach (1949), 209
Crosby, Humphrey, and Lauer (1962), *67*
Cross, J. F., and Cross (1971), 576
Cross, T. G. (1977), 173
Cytryn, McKnew, and Bunney (1980), 444

D

Darley and Batson (1971), 584
Darley and Fazio (1980), 570
Davidson and Schwartz (1976), 319
Davis (1978), 127
Deaton, et al. (1977), 416
Deaux, White, and Farris (1975), 387
DeCharms, R., and Muir (1978), 370
DeCharms, R. C., et al. (1955), 499
Deikman (1973), 301
Dekker, Pelser, and Groen (1957), 87
Dember (1964), *361*
Dember (1965), *337*
Denike and Liber (1968), 446
Depue and Monroe (1978), 105
De Valois (1966), 268
De Valois and De Valois (1975), *262*
De Valois and Jacobs (1968), 262
de Villiers and de Villiers (1978), 171, 174
Diamond (1978), 56
Dimascio, et al. (1979), 487
Dion (1972), 575
Dion and Berscheid (1972), 575
Dion, Berscheid, and Walster (1972), 577
Dollard, et al. (1939), 366
Doob and Gross (1968), 12
Dooling and Lachman (1971), 139
Doyle (1974), 235
Duncan, Featherman, and Duncan (1972), 218
Duncker (1945), 191
Dunn (1983), 107
Dweck, Goetz, and Strauss (1977), 104

E

Ebbinghaus, Hermann, 129–30
Ebbinghaus (1913), *130*
Eccles, John, 72
Eccles (1964), 69
Eckardt, et al. (1981), 456
Edelson (1981), 50
Edelstein (1982), 447
Ehrhardt and Baker (1973), 381
Ehrlich, et al. (1957), 562
Ehrmann (1964), 342
Eibl-Eibesfeldt (1963), 580
Einstein, Albert, 60, *367*
Eiseley (1946), 587
Ekman (1971), 317
Ellis, Arkeson, and Calhoun (1981), 447
Elmadjian (1959), 316
Elton and Shevel (1969), 236
England (1979), 387
Epstein, A. N., Fitzsimons, and Simons (1969), 334

Epstein, A. N., Kissileff, and Stellar (1973), 334
Epstein, S., and Roupenian (1970), 401
Erickson, Erik, 538, *539*
Erickson (1963), 539
Erickson (1968), 418
Erlenmeyer-Kimling (1978), 439
Erlenmeyer-Kimling and Jarvik (1963), *220*
Eron and Huesmann (1980), 366
Evarts (1979), 53, 54
Eysenck, H. J., 490
Eysenck (1981), 219, 222

F

Facklam and Facklam (1982), 51, 72
Falbo (1981), 361
Farb (1974), 171
Farina (1982), 461
Farina, Hagelauer, and Holzberg (1976), 461
Farley, Santo, and Speck (1979), 460
Fazio, Zanna, and Cooper (1977), 561
Feinman (1974), 390
Ferguson (1959), *597*
Feshbach (1971), 362
Festinger (1954), 565
Festinger, Schachter, and Back (1950), 573
Fodor and Smith (1982), 358
Ford, Gerald, 561
Forward, Canter, and Kirsch (1976), 86
Foulkes (1982), 298
Freed, et al. (1955), 550
Freedman, Carlsmith, and Sears (1970), 561
Freedman, Carlsmith, and Suomi (1970), 572
Freedman and Suomi (1970), 575, 576
French (1959), 499
French and Thomas (1958), 354
Freud, Sigmund, 10–11, 28, 297, 471–79
Friedman and Stricker (1976), 329
Fries and Crapo (1981), 541
Frieze (1975), 387
Fromkin (1973), 167
Fromm, Erich, *478*, 478
Fromm (1955), 479
Fuller (1967), 405
Furman, Rahe, and Hartup (1981), 526

G

Galaburda, et al. (1978), 59
Gallagher (1983), 305
Gallup (1972), 594
Galton, Sir Francis, *22*, 22, 587
Ganzer (1968), 402
Garber and Hollon (1977), 105
Garcia and Koelling (1966), 114
Gardner, Allen, 175
Gardner, Beatrice, 175
Gardner and Gardner (1972), 175
Garfield (1974), 499
Gass (1974), 388
Gates (1917), 21, 40
Gatz (1970), 319
Gebhard, Paul, 343, 349–50
Gebhard (1979), 348, 350
Gebhard (1980), 344
Geen (1976), 365
Geen and O'Neal (1969), 365
Gellhorn and Miller (1961), 327
Genovese, Kitty, 582–83
Gerbner and Gross (1976), 366
Gerbner, et al. (1980), 366
Gerbner, et al. (1981), 461
Geschwind (1979), 53
Geschwind (1980), 60
Gevins, et al. (1979), 61
Geyer and DeWald (1973), 291
Gibbs, Lachenmeyer, and Sigal (1980), 487
Gibson (1969), 273, 517
Gibson and Walk (1960), 287
Ginsburg and Miller (1982), 385
Glaser and Bond (1981), 217
Glass (1972), 411
Glass and Singer (1973), 256
Gold (1980), 458
Goldberg and Lewis (1969), 384
Goldfarb (1944), 511
Goldman (1974), 56
Goldsen, et al. (1960), 560
Goldstein, J. H., and Arms (1971), 581
Goldstein, M. J., Baker, and Jamison (1980), 440
Goleman (1977), 250
Gomes-Schwartz, Hadley, and Strupp (1978), 490
Goode (1965), 387
Goodnow and Bethon (1966), 208
Goodwin, et al. (1970), 126
Goodwin, et al. (1973), 457
Gottesman (1963), 221
Gottesman and Shields (1972), 440
Graf (1973), 145
Granzber and Steinbring (1980), 366
Gray (1978), 402
Greene, Goldstein, and Moss (1972), 408
Greenough (1976), 127
Greenough (1982), 57, 127n
Grinker (1982), 331
Guilford, J. P., 201–02, *201*, 203
Guilford (1954), 230
Guilford (1967), 201
Gunter, Berry, and Clifford (1981), *133*

H

Hall, G. S. (1904), 529
Hall, R. C. W. (1980a), 433
Hall, R. C. W. (1980b), 433
Hall, R. C. W., Stickney, and Gardner (1980), 433
Hamilton (1982), 445
Hansel (1966), 297
Hardy (1969), 486
Hare (1970), 451
Hargadon (1981), 213
Harlow, Harry F., 518
Harlow (1949), *147*
Harlow (1961), 519
Harlow and Harlow (1962), 344
Harlow and Harlow (1966), 512
Harrell and Harrell (1945), *216*
Harris, B. (1979), 86
Harris, F. R., et al. (1965), 96
Hartley (1959), 390
Hartman (1936), 564
Hartmann, D. P. (1969), 581
Hartmann, E. L. (1973), 299
Hartmann, G. (1969), 366
Hartmann, Heinz, 478
Hartmann, H. (1951), 478
Hauri (1976), 297
Hebb (1958), 587
Hebb and Thompson (1968), 581
Heider (1944), 566
Helsing, Szklo, and Comstock (1981), 542
Hendrick (1977), 366
Herink (1980), 486
Herrnstein and de Villiers (1980), 178
Hervey (1969), 331
Herzog and Lewis (1970), 214
Hess, E. H. (1965), 283, 320
Hess, E. H. (1975), 320, 321
Hess, R., and Torney (1967), 559
Hess, R. D., and Bear (1968), 106
Hesselund (1971), 349
Heston (1970), 34

Hetherington and Ranson (1940), 330
Hilgard, E. R. (1965), 300
Hilgard, E. R., and Hilgard (1975), 300
Hilgard, J. R. (1970), 300
Hilton (1967), 362
Hinkle (1974), 411
Hintzman, Block, and Inskeep (1972), 152
Hiroto (1974), 104
Hirsch and Knittle (1970), 333
Hochberg, Julian, 281
Hockberg (1978), 273, 280, 281, 286, 287
Hoffman (1980), 292
Hohmann (1966), 328
Hollingshead and Redlich (1958), 35
Hollister (1971), 304
Holmes and Rahe (1967), 409
Holyrod, et al. (1978), 402
Holzman, et al. (1973), 439
Holzman, et al. (1974), 439
Honzik, Macfarlane, and Allen (1948), 226
Hormuth (1983), 190
Horowitz, E. L., and Horowitz (1938), 547, 555, 559
Horowitz, F. C. (1977), 512
Hovland, C., and Weiss (1951), 564
Hovland, C. I., and Janis (1959), 566
Hovland, C. I., Lumsdaine, and Sheffield (1949), 564
Howe (1971), 385
Hoyos (1965), 356
Hsu, et al. (1981), 508
Hubel, David, 274, 275
Hubel (1963), *274*
Hubel (1978), 50
Hubel (1979), 49, 54
Hubel and Wiesel (1965), 274
Hubel and Wiesel (1979), 50
Huffine and Clausen (1979), 462
Hutt (1947), 374
Hyden (1967), 128

I

Ilfield (1980), 417
Institute of Medicine, 304
Iverson (1979), 250
Iverson (1982), 51, 73
Izard (1977), 317, 324, 326
Izard and Dougherty (1982), 317, 322

J

James, William, 22–23, *23*, 25, 30, 146–47, 321, 325–26, 353–54
James (1890), 23, 147, 321, 353
Jamison (1982), 431
Janis and Feshbach (1953), 564
Janis and Frick (1943), 190
Janke and Havighurst (1945), 214
Janowsky, Khaled El-Yousef, and Davis (1974), 492
Jencks (1972), 219
Jencks, et al. (1972), *220*
Jensen, (1969), 222
Jensen (1972), 219
Jessor and Jessor (1977), 533
Joffe (1971), 385
John, et al. (1968), 112
Johnson, F. N. (1969), 127
Johnson, L. C., and MacLeod (1973), 299
Johnson, P. B. (1981), 369
Johnston, Bachman, and O'Malley (1981), 302
Johnston, Bachman, and O'Malley (1982), 303, 305
Jones, D. R. (1969), 9
Jones, E. E. (1979), 567
Jones E. E., and Nisbett (1972), 571
Jones, J. C. (1924), 88
Jones, M. C., and Bayley (1950), 531
Jung, Carl, 477–78

K

Kagan (1981), *517*, 522
Kagan (1983), 510
Kagan, Kearsley, and Zelazo (1978), 517, 520
Kagan and Klein (1973), 512
Kagan and Moss (1962), *530*, 530
Kales (1969), 305
Kales, et al. (1974), 299
Kales, et al. (1976), 299
Kamin, Leon, 221, 222
Kamin (1979), 220
Kamin (1981), 219, 221, 222
Kandel, D. B., and Lesser (1972), 533
Kandel, E. R. (1970), 127
Kaplan and Singer (1976), 366
Katona (1940), 144
Kaufman (1976), 460
Kay (1975), 184
Kearsley, et al. (1975), 521
Keller, Helen, 240–41, *367*, 417
Kelley (1950), 576
Kelly, Snowden, and Munoz (1977), 433
Kenny (1980), 387
Kety, Seymour, 72
Kety (1982), 72
Kety, et al. (1967), 492
Kimble (1961), 110
Kindred (1978), 442
Kinsey, Alfred, 12–13, *14*, 343, 345, 346
Kinsey, Pomeroy, and Martin (1948), 346, 347, 348
Kinsey, et al. (1953), 343, 346, 347
Kintsch (1970), 123
Kintsch (1977), 131, 142
Kirsch and Glass (1977), 491
Klatzky (1980), 27, 82, 111, 132
Kline (1974), 413
Knittle and Hirsch (1968), 333
Kobasa (1979), 411
Kohlberg, Lawrence, 534, 535
Kohlberg (1963), 535
Kohlberg (1967), 535
Kohlberg and Kramer (1969), 535
Köhler, Wolfgang, 108
Köhler (1925), *108*
Koluchova (1972), 512
Komarovsky (1973), 392
Krantz, et al. (1981), 412
Krech and Crutchfield (1969), 288
Kripke and Simons (1976), 299
Krippner (1972), 297
Kubie (1950), 476
Kuffler (1953), 246, 267, 279

L

Labov (1970), 171
Lacey, Bateman, and Van Lehn (1953), 316
Lacey and Lacey (1958), 327
Lacey and Van Lehn (1952), 316
Ladner (1971), 385
Laing (1960), 418
Laird (1974), 314
Lamy (1966), 461
Landy and Sigall (1974), 575
Lang and Melamed (1969), 484
Lange, Carl, 322, 325–26
Lasch (1981), 453
Latané and Darley (1970), *582*
Lazarus (1978), 414, 417
Lazarus (1982), 323
Lazarus and Averill (1972), 324
Lefcourt, et al. (1981), 370
Leibowitz (1970), 72

Leiffer, Gordon, and Graves (1974), 366
Lenneberg (1967), 169
Lepper, Greene, and Nisbett (1973), 98
Leukel (1957), 127
Levine, F. M., and Fasnacht (1974), 98
Levine, M. W., and Shefner (1981), 273, 276
Levinson and Reese (1967), 148
Levy, Trevarthen, and Sperry (1972), 59
Lewin, K. (1935), 376
Lewin, R. (1974), 50, 53, 70
Lewis, E. R., Zeevi, and Everhart (1969), 69
Lewis, M., and Als (1975), 383
Lewontin (1976), 222
Lieberman, Yalom, and Miles (1973), 491
Liebeskind and Paul (1977), 250
Linn, et al. (1982), 178
Lipscomb (1969), 257
Locke, John, 3
Loehlin, Lindzey, and Spuhler (1975), 222
Loftus, Miller, and Burns (1978), 140
Londerville and Main (1981), 519
London (1978), 54
Lopata (1972), 388
Lorenz (1966), 363, 580
Lowell (1952), 354
Lubin, et al. (1976), 299
Luborsky, Docherty, and Penick (1973), 407
Luborsky, et al. (1971), 491
Lutz (1982), 326
Lykken (1981), 315
Lyon (1914), *144*

M

Maccoby (1979), 521
Maccoby and Feld (1972), 521
Maccoby and Jacklin (1974), 385
MacFarlane (1930), 110
Macfarlane (1963), 536
Macfarlane (1964), 530, 532, 538
MacKinnon (1962), 229
MacKinnon (1967), 498
Macklin (1972), 349
MacNichol (1964), 246, *261*
Maddi (1972), 470
Magelowitz (1982), 471
Magoun (1963), 337
Maier, Seligman, and Solomon (1969), 104
Malof and Lott (1962), 555
Mandler (1962), 316
Mankiewicz and Swerdlow (1977), 366
Mann and Janis (1968), 561
Marks (1968), 484
Martin, et al. (1968), 484
Maslach (1978), 325
Maslow, Abraham, 365–67, 418, 479
Maslow (1969), 491
Maslow (1970), 367
Masserman (1943), 431
Masserman (1961), 424
Masters, W. H., and Johnson, V. E., 12
Masters and Johnson (1963), 349
Masters and Johnson (1970), 348
Matarazzo (1972), 215
Matson (1971), 27
Maugh (1982), 299
McBurney and Collings (1977), 243
McCaul (1980), 401
McCaul, Holmes, and Solomon (1982), 322
McCaul, Solomon, and Holmes (1979), 401
McClelland (1979), 411
McClelland and Atkinson (1948), 293
McClelland, Clark, and Lowell (1953), 499
McClelland and Liberman (1949), 280
McClelland and Teague (1975), 358
McClelland, et al. (1972), 358
McClelland, et al. (1981), 411
McClintock (1971), 249
McCord and McCord (1964), 449
McCullough (1965), 275
McDermott (1979), 402
McGaugh and Dawson (1971), 127
McGeoch (1930), 143
McGeoch and McDonald (1931), *134*
McGrath (1964), 549
McNemar (1942), 214
Mead, Margaret, 382
Mead (1935), 382, 549
Meddis, Pearson, and Langford (1973), 299
Meece, et al. (1982), 388
Mellinger and Balter (1981), 443, 457
Melzack (1973), 250
Messenger (1979), 347
Meyer and Haggerty (1962), 408
Milgram, Stanley, 550–51
Milgram (1964), 554
Miller, George, 231
Miller, G. A. (1951), 170
Miller, G. A. (1956), 122, 136
Miller, G. A. (1964), 121
Miller, G. A. (1981), 161, 175
Miller, G. A. (1983), 231
Miller, N. E. (1969), 48, 55, 336
Miller, N. E. (1975), 102, 332, 333, 407
Miller, N. E. (1976), 413, 414
Miller, N. E., and Dollard (1941), 108, 483
Milner (1959), 56
Minuchin, et al. (1975), 408
Misra (1980), 459
Money and Ehrhardt (1973), 381
Moore (1976), 127
Morgan, C. T., and Morgan (1940), 329
Morgan, H. H. (1951), 354
Moruzzi (1972), 299
Moruzzi and Magoun (1949), 54
Moss (1965), 300
Munn, Fernald, and Fernald (1969), 103

N

National Academy of Sciences, 217, 304
National Academy of Sciences (1982), 304
National Assessment of Educational Progress (1981), 107
National Center for Health Statistics (1982), 539
National Institute on Aging (1981), 542
National Institute on Alcohol Abuse and Alcoholism (1980), 457
National Institute on Drug Abuse (1977), 460
National Research Council (1982), 217
Nauta (1946), 72
Neisser (1981), 140
Neisser and Becklen (1975), 281
Neuman (1976), 563
Neuringer (1970), 94
Newcomb (1961), 573
Newcomb (1963), 560

Newport (1975), 173
Nickerson and Adams (1979), 142
Nielsen and Sarason (1981), 324
Nisbett (1968), 332
Nisbett (1972), 330, 331, 333
Nisbett and Platt (1972), 333
Nisbett and Valins (1972), 571
Nissen and Crawford (1936), 581
Nixon, Richard M., 561
Norton and Glick (1976), 539
Nurco (1979), 459
Nurnberger and Gershon (1982), 443

O

Offer, Ostrow, and Howard (1982), 530
O'Kelly (1974), 385
O'Leary (1972), 97
O'Leary and Drabman (1971), 97
Ollison (1975), 387
O'Neil, Spielberger, and Hansen (1969), 402
Opler (1967), 327
Orne (1982), 300
Ornstein, Robert, 60
Ornstein, R. (1978), 60, 61
Ornstein, R. E. (1971), 301
Owens (1966), *229*
Oyama (1973), 171

P

Paddock, O'Neill, and Haver (1978), 364
Paivio (1971), 152
Parelius (1975), 389
Parloff (1980), 488
Parsons and Bales (1953), 386
Patterson, G. R., Hops, and Weiss (1975), 101
Patterson, M. M., Cegavske, and Thompson (1973), 126
Pavlov, Ivan, 84–85, 88–90, 103, 282, 431
Pavlov (1927), 85, 90, 431
Pearson (1969), 224
Peele, S. (1981), 72
Peele, T. L. (1961), 319
Perin (1943), 95
Petersen (1981), 532
Peterson, C., Schwartz, and Seligman (1981), 105
Peterson, L. R., and Peterson (1959), *121*
Petti (1981), 444
Pettigrew (1969), 561
Pfaffman (1955), *71*
Phares and Lamiell (1975), 370
Piaget, Jean, 202–08, 339
Piaget (1952), 204
Piliavin, Rodin, and Piliavin (1969), 584
Pogrebin (1972), 385
Pokorny (1964), 442
Polivy (1981), 324
Pollack and Pickett (1964), 168
Pope, Ionescu-Pioggia, and Cole (1981), 303
Post (1966), 257
Postman, Bruner, and McGinnies (1948), 280
Premack, David, 177
Premack (1976), 177
President's Commission on Mental Health (1978), 431
Pritchard (1961), 245

R

Rabkin and Struening (1976), 410
Radecki and Jennings (1980), 387
Radloff (1959), 556
Radtke and Grove (1977), 134
Raloff (1982), 257
Rebelsky (1967), 511
Regier and Taube (1981), 431, 462
Reich (1976), 438
Reisman (1981), 376
Rhine and Pratt (1957), 297
Rice and Blanchard (1982), 401
Richlin, et al. (1980), 416
Riger and Gordon (1981), *402*
Riley and Walker (1978), 56
Rist (1970), 570
Rizley (1978), 105
Robbins (1971), 95
Robertson (1977), 386
Robins (1978), 451
Robins (1980), 459
Robinson, F. P. (1962), 39
Robinson, J. P. (1971), 563
Rodin (1972), 333
Rodin, Elman, and Schachter (1972), 333
Rogers, Carl, 479–80
Rogers (1969), 491
Roosevelt, Eleanor, *367*
Roper Organization (1980), 384, *389*, 389, 390
Rosch, Eleanor, 182–83, 184
Rosch (1973), 183
Rosch (1977), 184
Rosch and Mervis (1975), 182
Rose, J. E., et al. (1971), 246, *255*
Rose, R. M. (1980), 316
Rosenhan (1970), 582
Ross, G. (1980), 179
Ross, L., Lepper, and Hubbard (1975), *557*
Ross, L. D., Amabile, and Steinmetz (1977), 567
Rozin and Kalat (1971), 114
Rubin, D. C. (1977), 139
Rubin, J. Z., Provenzano, and Luria (1974), 383
Rubin, Z. (1973), 539
Rush and Beck (1978), 485
Rutherford and Mussen (1968), 582
Rutter (1983), 410, 413, 527

S

Sachs and Johnson (1976), 170
Sackheim, Gur, and Saucy (1978), 318
Sadacca, Ricciuri, and Swanson (1956), 354
Salapatek (1975), 518
Salapatek and Kessen (1966), 278
Salk (1973), 511
Sampson and Hancock (1967), 362
Sandmaier (1980), 457
Sands and Wright (1982), 152
Savage-Rumbaugh, Rumbaugh, and Boysen (1978), 177
Sawrey, Conger, and Turrell (1956), 87
Scarr, Sandra, 222–23
Scarr (1969), 34
Scarr (1981), 215, 223, 227
Scarr and Weinberg (1976), 225
Scarr-Salapatek (1971), 221, 222
Schachter (1959), 360
Schachter (1971), 332, 333
Schachter and Gross (1968), 332
Schachter and Singer (1962), 325
Schaie and Strother (1968), 228
Schapiro and Vukovich (1970), 57
Scheibel, et al. (1975), 56
Scheils (1978), 297
Schemmel, Michelson, and Gill (1970), 333
Scherer (1981), *317*
Schiff, et al. (1978), 225
Schildkraut (1969), 73, 413
Schlesinger (1970), 539

Schulsinger (1976), 439
Schwab (1980), 433
Schwartz, G. E. (1982), 317
Schwartz, S. (1970), 582
Schweinhart and Weikart (1980), 107
Sears (1967), 566
Seaver (1973), 570
Secord and Backman (1964), 547
Segal and Segal (1984), 505
Segal and Yahraes (1975), 527
Seidenberg, Robert, 391
Seidenberg (1970), 392
Sekuler and Levinson (1977), 278
Selfridge and Neisser (1960), *293*
Seligman (1971), 114
Selye, Hans, 406–07
Selye (1956), 407
Selye (1976), 328, 412
Serbin and O'Leary (1975), 385
Shaffer (1947), 315
Shapiro, et al. (1969), *32*
Shepherd (1967), 151
Sherman (1973), 370
Shiffrin and Atkinson (1969), *121*, 121
Shigetomi, Hartmann, and Gelfand (1981), 385
Silberman (1970), 106
Silberstein and Parsons (1981), 456
Simon, H. A. (1982), 230
Simon, W., Berger, and Gannon (1972), 348, 534
Simons and Rosenberg (1975), 387
Sims, et al. (1968), 333
Singer and Singer (1980), 366
Skinner, B. F., 24–25, *24*, 91–93
Skinner (1938), 92
Skinner (1957), 174
Skinner (1971), 7
Skolnick and Skolnick (1974), 391
Slaby, Quarforth, and McConnachie (1976), 366
Slater and Depue (1981), 461
Slobin (1971), 173
Slobin (1973), 173
Smith, E. E., and Medin (1981), 179, 182
Smith, M. E. (1926), 169
Smith, M. L., Glass, and Miller (1980), 490
Smith, S. M. (1979), 132
Snow (1972), 173
Snow, et al. (1976), 170
Snyder, M., Tanke, and Bercheid (1977), 569
Snyder, M. L., and Frankel (1976), 568
Snyder, S. H. (1980), 50, 51
Snyder, S. H. (1982), 51, 73
Snyder, S. H., et al. (1974), 439
Solomon (1964), 101
Solomon and Turner (1962), 110
Sommers (1969), 20
Sontag, Baker, and Nelson (1958), 226
Sorenson (1973), 530
Sorrentino and Sheppard (1978), 372
Spearman, Charles, 200
Spearman (1927), 200
Sperling (1960), 120
Sperling (1967), 122
Sperry, Roger, 72
Sperry (1982), 61, 72
Spielberger (1962), 403
Spielberger (1971), 401
Spielberger, Denny, and Weitz (1962), 403
Spitz (1946), 512
Stake and Levitz (1979), 392
Steiner (1979), 506
Stellar and Corbit (1973), 331
Stern, M. (1983), 344
Stern, W. (1904), 140
Stevens, B. (1974), 390, 391
Stevens, C. F. (1979), 50, 68
Stevenson and Bitterman (1955), 205
Stevenson, Friedrichs, and Simpson (1970), 201
Stewart (1975), 358
Stewart and Rubin (1976), 358
Stock and Smythe (1963), 223
Stoller (1972), 382
Stolz, Wienckowski, and Brown (1975), 96, 97
Strauss (1979), 106
Strickland (1977), 370
Suedfeld (1969), 362
Suedfeld (1975), 337
Sullivan, Anne, 241
Suomi (1977), 524
Suomi and Harlow (1972), 512
Swanson, Bohnert, and Smith (1970), 452
Symonds (1974), 388

T

Tagiuri (1958), 574
Tanner (1978), 57
Tarler-Benlolo (1978), 99
Tarnopolsky, Watkins, and Hand (1980), 400
Tarpy and Mayer (1978), 82
Tavris and Offir (1977), 379, 386
Taylor, Smith, and Ghiselin (1963), 219
Teasdale (1978), 107
Tecce (1971), 283
Tenner and Eller (1977), 104
Tennes and Mason (1982), 327
Terman, Lewis M., 218–19
Terman and Merrill (1937), *16*, *590*
Terr (1981), 447
Terrace, Herbert, 177
Terrace (1979), 177
Tesser and Brodie (1971), 575
Thomas, A., and Chess (1972), 510
Thomas, A., Chess, and Birch (1970), 509
Thomas, M. H., et al. (1977), 366
Thurstone, L. L., 200–01, 203
Tinklepaugh (1928), 98
Tolman, Edward, 111
Tolman (1948), 111
Tolman and Honzik (1930), *109*
Tomkins (1962), 322
Torrance (1966), 230
Torrey (1980), 437
Treisman (1969), 281
Treisman and Gelade (1980), 293
Triplett (1898), 547
Trusheim and Crouse (1982), 213
Tsang (1938), 329
Tschukitscheff (1930), 360
Tsuang and Vandermey (1980), 34, 432
Tversky and Kahneman (1973), 192
Tversky and Kahneman (1974), 193
Tyhurst (1951), 322
Tyler, L. E. (1976), 217
Tyler, R. W. (1933), *135*

U

Underwood (1957), *133*
U.S. Bureau of the Census (1980), 368
U.S. Bureau of the Census (1982), 106, 540, 541
U.S. Bureau of Labor Statistics (1980), 388
U.S. Commission on the Higher Education of Minorities, 217
U.S. Environmental Protection Agency, 257
U.S. National Center for Education Statistics (1983), 106
U.S. Office of Strategic Services (1948), 498
Uttal (1973), 246, 255

V

Vaillant (1978), 458
Valenstein, Elliot, 72
Valenstein (1973), 330
Valenstein (1976), 330
Valenstein, Cox, and Kakolewski (1970), 330
Valenta and Rigby (1968), 248
Vance and Schlechty (1982), 527
Van Dyke and Byck (1982), 302, 306
Vaughn and Leff (1976), 461
Vennemann (1975), 165
Verhave (1966), 93
Vierling and Rock (1967), 249
Vincent (1956), 348, 350
Von Frisch (1950), 162
Vorster (1974), 173

W

Wagner and Monnett (1979), 297
Wald (1951), 261
Walker (1981), 447
Wallace and Benson (1972), 301
Wallach (1976), 219
Wangensteen and Carlson (1931), 329
Warren and Warren (1970), 168
Warrington and Sanders (1971), 228
Wason (1971), *189*, 189
Watkins and Watkins (1975), 133
Watson, John, 23–24, *23*, 28, 30, 85, 113
Watson and Rayner (1920), 86
Weatherly (1964), 532
Webb and Cartwright (1978), 298, 299
Wechsler, David, 199–200, 211
Wechsler (1975), 199
Weiner, B. (1974), 370
Weiner, H. (1982), 412
Weingartner, et al. (1981), 72
Weiskrantz (1966), 131
Weiss, J. M. (1970), 414
Weiss, J. M., Glazer, and Pohorecky (1976), 73, 413
Weiss, J. M., et al. (1975), 414
Weiss, W., and Fine (1958), 564
Weitzman (1975), 383, 384, 385
Weitzman, et al. (1972), 385
Werner and Lipsitt (1981), 506
Wesson and Smith (1979), 460
Whalen (1976), 345
White, Castle, and Held (1964), 516
Whitfield and Evans (1965), 274
Whorf, Benjamin, 183, 184
Whorf (1956), 183
Wickelgren, Wayne A., 124
Wickelgren (1977), 95, 111, 124, 128, 131, 143
Wickelgren (1981), 125, 126, 181
Wickert (1947), 328
Wiesel, Torsten, 274, 275
Wiesel and Hubel (1965), 275
Wiesel and Hubel (1974), 275
Wilkins (1971), 484
Will, Self, and Datan (1974), 384
Williams, H. L. (1971), 296, 298
Williams, J., and Spitzer (1981), 436
Williams, M. (1979), 52
Williams, R. J. (1956), 34, 327
Williams, T. M. (1978), 366
Wilson (1975), 336
Wine (1971), 401
Wing and Wallach (1971), 215
Winget, Kramer, and Whitman (1972), 298
Winokur (1981), 413
Winter (1973), 357, 358
Winter and Stewart (1978), 357, 358, 359
Winterbottom (1953), *356*
Wolf (1963), 224
Wolff (1959), 508
Wolpe (1976), 485
Woolfolk, Woolfolk, and Wilson (1977), 98
Worchel (1961), 574
World Health Organization (1979), 460
Wundt, Wilhelm, *22*, 22
Wyatt and Freed (1983), 72

Y

Yankelovich, Skelly, and White (1977), 342
Yankelovich, Skelly, and White (1983), 344
Yarbus (1967), *282*
Yates (1966), 152
Yerkes and Morgulis (1909), *84*
Young (1961), 314

Z

Zajonc (1968), *572*
Zajonc and Markus (1975), 225
Zelnick and Kanter (1980), 343
Zigler and Trickett (1978), 219
Zillman, Katcher, and Milavsky (1972), 365
Zimbardo (1979), 62
Zimbardo, Andersen, and Kabat (1981), 257
Zipf (1949), 184
Zola-Morgan, Squire, and Mishkin (1982), 56
Zung (1981), 440
Zweben and Miller (1968), 487

Subject Index

(Page numbers in *italics* refer to illustrations)

A

ANS. *See* Autonomic nervous system
Absolute threshold of senses, 244
Acceptance, approval and, 554–55
Accommodation, 202–04
Acetylcholine, 127
Achievement, women and, 387–88
Achievement in school: IQ and, 214–16, *215*
Achievement motive, 354–57
Achievement tests, 213–14
Acrophobia, 83, 448
Acuity, 268
Acupuncture, 50–51, 250
Addictions, 453–59
Adjustment, 417–18
Adolescence, 528–29, 530–35; definition of, 531; parents and, 533; physical changes in, 531–32; psychological changes in, 533–34
Adrenal glands, 65, 66
Adrenalin, fear and, 316
Adulthood; development into, 536–38; early, 538–40
Aerial perspective, 288
Affection, 528; in child-rearing, 511
Affective disorders, 439–40
Afferent neurons, 51–52
Affiliation, 359–60, 528
Afterimages, 269
Age: intelligence and, 210–11, 228–29, *229*
Aggression, 423, 580–81; id and, 472–73; in infants, 511; limbic system and, 62, *63*; observation learning of, 112, *113*
Agoraphobia, 83, 448
Albert experiment, 85–86, 324–25, 326
Alcohol, 302; abuse, 453–59; effects on human development, 505
Alcoholism. *See* Alcohol, abuse
Algorithms, 188–89
All or none principle, 71
Alpha waves, during meditation, 301
Altered states of consciousness. *See* Consciousness, altered states of
Altruism, 581–82
American Psychiatric Association, Diagnostic and Statistical Manual of Mental Disorders (DSM-III), 436
Amnesia, 131. *See also* Forgetting
Amphetamines, 303, 305, 492
Amplitude of sound waves, 252–53, *253*
Anal stage, of human sexual development, 472–73
Androgens, 381, 531
Androgynous, 380
Angel dust (PCP), 302, 305
Anger, physical reactions to, 314–15. *See also* Anxiety; Emotions
Anonymity, 583–84
Antianxiety drugs, 402
Antidepression drugs, 492–93
Antisocial personality, 449–50
Anxiety, 397–427, 471–72, 520–21; behavior and, 398–414; coping and, 418–25; defense mechanisms, 418–25; definition of, 398; disorders, 445–49; general, 401–02, 445; specific, 401–02; testing and, 401. *See also* Fears; Phobias
Apathy, 423–24; bystander, 582–83, *582*
Applied science, 9
Approach and avoidance. *See* Conflict
Approval, 554
Aptitude tests, 10, 213–14; vocational, 237. *See also* Intelligence tests
Asch experiments, 552
Aspirations, 310–50
Assertive coping, 414–17
Assertiveness training, 489
Assimilation, 202–04
Associative network theory of memory, 138–39, 141–42
Attachment, in infants, 518–19
Attention, perception and, 279–83
Attitudes, 557–62; changing, 559–61; decisions and, 561–62; formation of, 558; heredity and changing, 565; inconsistency in, 558; prejudice, 559; stereotypes and, 559
Attraction: physical attractiveness and, 574–75; similarities of attitudes and, *574*
Attractiveness, 572, *572*
Attribution theories, 566–71
Auditory canal, *254*
Auditory nerve, *254*, 255, *255*
Autokinetic illusion, 276
Autonomic nervous system (ANS), 64–67, *67*, 316, 327; parasympathetic division, 66, *67*; sympathetic division, 66–67, *67*
Average (statistical), 590–91
Axon, 68, *68*

B

Babbling, 169–70
Babies. *See* Infants
Bait shyness, 114
Basilar membrane, 254–55
Behavior, 568–69; abnormal, 429–63; anxiety and, 398–414; attitude and, 561; control of, as goal of psychology, 6–7; dispositional factors of, 566; drives and, 313–50; emotions and, 339; environment and, 34–35; fundamental attribution error, 567; heredity and, 34; infants and, 509; influence of people and, 547–72; normal, 417–18; patterns and schizophrenics, 437–38; situational factors and, 517–72; therapy 482–86; Type A and Type B, 411
Behavior genetics, 29, 34
Behavior modification, 96–97, *97*, 98
Behavior therapy, 98
Behaviorism, 23–25

Binocular vision, 288
Biofeedback, 97–99; anxiety and, 401–02
Bipolar cell, 266, *267*
Bipolar depression. *See* Manic-depressive illness
Birth, 506
Birth control, and sexual feelings, 343
Birth order, 361–62
Blind spot, 259–60, *260*
Bodily movement: brain function and, 53; sense of, 250–51
Brain, 47–73, *48, 54*; cerebellum, 54–55; cerebral cortex, 48–50, *49,* 52, *53,* 57–58; cerebrum, *49,* 57–58; cognitive processes and, 55–61; emotions and, 61–63, 322–25; evolution, *49*; functions of, 52–73, *53*; glands and, 61–63; growth of, *57*; hippocampus, 56; hormones and chemicals produced by, 50–51; language and, 52, 53; left and right hemispheres, *48, 49,* 57–61, *61,* 318–19; limbic system and, 323; memory and, 51, 56; neurons, *see* Neurons; neurotransmitters, 439; physical well-being and, 63–64; reticular activating system of, 53–54; schizophrenia and, *439*; senses and, 52–55; split–brain experiments, *58,* 58–59, *59,* 72; thalamus, 53–54
Brightness, 259
Brightness constancy, 286
Broad-tuned receptors, 246

C

CA. *See* Chronological age
Caffeine, 302
California Personality Inventory (CPI), 498
Cancer, 542
Cannon-Bard theory of emotion, 324–25
Case histories, 13
Categories: concepts as, 180–82, *181*; learning and, *148,* 148–49, *149*
Cause-and-effect, memory and, *150,* 150
Cell body, 68, 68
Central nervous system, 51
Cerebellum, 54–55
Cerebral cortex, 48–50, *49,* 52, *53,* 57–58
Cerebrum, 49, 57–58
Certainty, as a motive, 362–63
Childhood: depression in, 444; early, 510. *See also* Adolescence; Infancy
Child-rearing, 509, 511
Children: behavior modification and, 97; inellectual development of, 202–08, *205*; language learning by, 169–74, *172*; learned helplessness in, 104–07; punishment of, 101–03. *See also* Adolescence; Infants
Chromosomes, 30–34, *31,* 381; human development and, 505; pairs, 382; sex determination and, 33–34; tests for, 382–83
Chronological age (CA), 210–11
Chunking, memory and, 136, *137,* 149
Ciliary muscles, 259, *260*
Clairvoyance, 297
Classical conditioning, 82–90; elements of, 88; of fears, 83–88; neuroses and,-90; Pavlov's experiments with dogs, *84,* 84–85; 88–90, *89, 103,* 103–04; of physical symptoms, 87–88; reinforcement, extinction, and spontaneous recovery, 88–89, *89*; stimulus generalization and discrimination, 89–90; of unreasonable preferences, 83–84; Watson's Albert experiment, 85–86, 324–25, 326
Claustrophobia, 83, 448
Clinical psychology, 9–11
Closure, perception of, 283, *284*
Clustering, memory and, 149–50
Cocaine, 303, 306
Cochlea, *254,* 254, 255
Codeine, 307
Coefficient of correlation, 17. *See also* Correlation
Cognition: emotion and, 324–25; James-Lange theory and, 325–26; language and, 177–84. *See also* Thinking
Cognitive maps, 111
Cognitive processes, 55–61
Cognitive psychology, 26–27, 111–12
Cognitive theory of emotion, 323–24
Cognitive theory of learning, 108–14, 483
Cold, sensation of, 249, *249*
Color blindness, 269
Color mixture, 269
Color vision, 261–62
Colors: adding and substracting, 268; complementary, 268
Communication: attitude change and, 562–65; effective, 564; language and, 162–63, 165–69; listener and, 564–65; sexual relationships and, 349–50
Community psychologists, 9
Complementary colors, 268
Complex cell, in visual cortex, 275
Complexity of light waves, 259
Complexity of sound waves, 253, *254*
Compulsions. *See* Obsessive-compulsive disorders
Computers, thinking of, 230–31
Concepts, language and, 177–84, *178, 181*
Concrete operations, stage of, 206–07
Conditional positive regard, 481
Conditioned reflex, 24
Conditioned response, 88, *89*
Conditioned stimulus, 88
Conditioning, 483
Cones, 260–61, *261,* 267, *267*
Conflict, 353–92: definition of, 372; group, 375–76; physical well being and, 433; sex and, 379–92; sources of, 372–73; women and, 388–89
Conformity, 550; expedient, 557; true, 557
Connecting neurons, 51–52
Conscience, 524
Consciousness: altered states of, 276, 296–307; brain and, 55–56; drugs and, 301–07; hypnosis and, 300; meditation and, 301; sleep and dreams, 296–99
Conservation, rule of, 206
Constancy, perceptual, 284–86, *285, 286*
Constructive processing, memory and, 139–41
Context, and perception, *293,* 293
Contigency, 605
Continuity, perception of, *284,* 284
Contour, in perception, 283
Contrast, perception of, 277–79
Control groups, 20–21
Coping, 397–427, 485–86; forms of, 418–25; stress and, 414–18
Cornea, *260*
Corpus callosum, 58
Correlation, 16–18, 597–99, 603–04; product moment, 603–04; rank difference, 603–04
Cortisol, 443

Counseling, 9–11
Cranial nerves, *51*
Creativity: intelligence and, 229–30, *230*
Credibility, of source, 564
Culture, 548

D

DNA (Deoxyribonucleic acid), 31
DSM-III. *See* Diagnostic and Statistical Manual of Mental Disorders
Dark adaptation, 262–63
Deafness, 257
Death, psychology of, 542–43
Decibels, 255–56, *256*
Defense mechanisms, 418–24, 471–72
Deliquency, 525
Dendrites, 68, *68*
Deoxyribonucleic acid. *See* DNA
Dependency, 360–61
Dependent variables, 18–20
Depression: definition of, 413; heredity and, 413, 414; in childhood, 444; insomnia and, 299; manic, 441–42; sex differences in, 443–44; suicide and, *442*; tests for, *441*
Deprivation, effects on development, 511–12
Depth, perception of, 286–87, *286*
Descriptive statistics, 590–93
Desensitization, 484
Development: human, 505–43; mental, 513–17; of personality, 470–71; physical, 513–17; psychosocial, 538; social, 522
Developmental psychology, 505–06
Diagnostic and Statistical Manual of Mental Disorders (DSM-III), 436
Difference threshold of senses, 244
Direct-access retrieval, 125
Discipline, in child-rearing, 511
Displaced aggression, 423
Distance, perception of, 286–89, *287–89*
Dopamine, 439
Double-blind technique, 21
Draw-a-person test, 500
Dreams: meaning of, 296–98; in psychoanalysis, 297
Drives, 313–50; elimination, 336; hunger, 329–36; temperature, 335; thirst, 334; sleep, 335
Drugs: hazards of, 450–60; memory and, 127; neurotransmitters and, 73; perception and, 301–07; reduction of anxiety and, 402; types of, 453–59; young people's use of, 302–04. *See also specific drugs*
Dyslexia, 60

E

EEG. *See* Electroencephalograph
ESP. *See* Extrasensory perception
Ear: structure of, 253–55, *254*. *See also* Hearing
Eardrum, 254, *254*
Efferent neurons, 51–52
Egg cell, human, *31*, 31–34
Electroencephalograph (EEG), *61*
Electroshock therapy, 492
Elimination drive, 336
Emotions, 310–12; 313–50; autonomic nervous system and, 316; basic, 326; brain and, 61–62; Cannon-Bard theory of, 322–23; cognitive theory of, 323–24; differences in, 326–28; facial expressions and, 316–17; James-Lange theory of, 322; physical aspects of, 313–22; speech and, 317; theories of, 316, 321–23. *See also specific emotions*
Empathy, 580–84
Encoding: aids to, *147*, 147–54; and learning, 141–47, *144*; long-term memory and, 135–41; short-term memory and, 122–23
Encounter group, 491
End branches, 68–69
Endocrine glands, 65, 327
Endorphines, 50–51
Environment: cerebral cortex and, 52; effects on infants, 510, 514; IQ and, 34, 221–22; personality and, 394–427. *See also* Nature-nurture argument
Environmental psychology, 8, 9
Equality, women and, 386–87
Equilibrium, cerebellum and, 55; sense of, *251*, 251–52
Escape, operant, 99–100
Estrogen, 381
Ethics, 86
Ethnicity, infants and, 508
Eustachian tube, *254*
Existential psychology, 28
Expectancies, 111
Expectations, perceptual, *292*, 293
Experimental groups, 20–21
Experiments, 18–21, *19*, *20*; control groups and experimental groups, 20–21, *21*, replication of, 21; single-blind and double-blind, 21; variables in, 18–20
Extinction, 484; of conditioned response, 89, *89*; memory trace's resistance to, 131; in operant conditioning, 92
Extrasensory perception (ESP), 296, 297
Extroverts, 34, 477
Eye, 266; emotions and, 320–21; movements and scanning, *281*, 281–83; structure of, 259–61, *260*, *261*. *See also* Vision
Eye movements: distance perception and, 287–88; in infants; *518*; scanning, *281*, 281–83. *See also* REM sleep

F

Failure: fear of, 371–72; learned helplessness as a result of, 104–07
Familiarity, 572–73
"Fast" fibers, and skin sensation, 250
Fat. *See* Obesity
Fears, 66, 114; anxiety and, 398; conditioned, 83–88; of failure, 371–72. *See also* Anxiety; Phobias
Feature analysis, 291
Feature detector cells, *274*, 274–75
Feedback theories of emotion, 321–22
Feelings. *See* Emotions
Feminine, definition of, 379–86; sex-typing, 383–84
Figure and ground, in perception, *283*, 283
First born, 362
Forgetting, 128–35; curve of, 129–30, *130*; as fading of the memory trace, 130–31; as failure in retrieval, 131–32, *132*; interference theory of, 132–34, *133*, *134*, *135*; motivated, 135. *See also* Amnesia
Formal operations, stage of, 207
Fovea, *260*, 261, 268
Free association, as tool in psychoanalysis, 475
Frequency of sound waves, 252, *253*
Friendship, 353–61
Frustration, 353–92; definitions of, 372; sources of, 372–73
Functional fixedness, 190–92, *191–92*

G

G factor, of intelligence, 201
Galvanic skin reflex, *315*
Ganglia, 65–66
Ganglion cell, 266, *267*
Gate-control mechanism, and skin sensation, 250
Gay liberation, 343
General adaptation syndrome, 406–07
Generativity, 540
Genes, 30–34, *32*; human development and, 505–06
Genital stage, of human sexual development, 472–75
Gestalt psychology, 25–26, *25, 26*
Glands, emotions and, 316
Global processing, 291–92
Good Samaritan, 584, *584*
Gradient of texture, 288–89
Grammar, 164, 172–74
Gratification, 472–75
Group tests, 212
Group therapy, 490–91
Guidance, in behavior, 555–56
Guilt, 524

H

Hallucinations, drug-induced, 304–05
Hearing: absolute threshold of, 244; difference threshold of, 244; location of sounds, 256–58; loudness, 255–56, *256, 257*; receptors for, 253–55, *255*; stimulus for, 252–53; structure of the ear and, 253–55, *254*. *See also* Perception
Heredity, 29–35; aggression and, 580; altruism and, 581–82; chromosomes and genes and, 30–34; depression and, 413–14; environment and, 34–35; human development and, 505; IQ and, 35, 219–21, *220*; personality and, 394–427; schizophrenia and, 34, 440; sex determination and, 33–34; sex roles and, 381–82 *See also* Nature-nurture argument
Hering theory, 270
Hermaphrodites, 382
Heroin, 302, 306–07
Hertz, 252
Heuristics, 189
Hierarchies of motive, 368–69
High blood pressure, noise and, 257
Hippocampus, 56
Homeostasis, 63
Homosexuality, 342–44
Horizontal cell, 266, *267*
Hormones, 50–51, 65
Hostility, 363–65
Hue, 259, 269–70
Human, development, 505–43; interactions with others, 502–84
Humanistic psychology, 27–28
Hunger drive, 329–36; perceptual expectations and, 293
Hypercomplex cell, in visual cell, 275
Hyperkinesis, 492
Hypnosis, 250, 300; therapy and, 488
Hypomania, 442
Hypothalamus, 61, 63–64, 72, 323, 324, 329–30

I

IQ. *See* Intelligence quotient
Id, 472–73
Identification, 421, 524–25
Identity, 532–33
Illusions, perceptual, *276*, 276–79
Imitation, 524; language, 74; learning by, 112
Implicit personality theory, 576–77
Implosion therapy, 488
Impressions, 576; errors in perception of, 567–68
Incentive value, 369
Independence, adolescence and, 533
Independent variables, 18–20
Individual, relating to others, 502–84
Individual differences, 15
Individual tests, 212
Industrial psychologists, 9
Infancy, 506–21
Infants, 505; reaction to stimuli, 506–07. *See also* Infancy
Inferences, 179–80
Inferential statistics, 593–97
Inferiority complex, 478; women and, 387–88
Information processing, 26–27, 108, 159; memory and, 122–23
Innate needs, 337–38
Inner ear, 254
Insight, *108*, 108
Insomnia, 299
Instincts, 81–82; human, 353
Intellectual development, 56–57, 516–17
Intelligence, 159, 199–231; abilities constituting, 200–02; age and, 210–11; artificial, 230–31; attitudes toward, 199; definition of, 199; Guilford's theory of, *201*, 201–02; job and career choices and, 203; Piaget's theory of, 202–08, *205*; racial differences in, 222; Spearman-Thurstone view of, 200–01. *See also* Intellectual development; Intelligence quotient; Intelligence tests
Intelligence quotient (IQ), 16–17, *16*, 203, 210, *211*; age and, 228–29, *229*; creativity and, 229–30, *230*; environment and, 34, 221–22; family size and, 225; heredity and, 35, 220–21, *220*; intellectual stimulation and, 224; nature-nurture issue and, 219–27, *223*; nutrition and, 223; occupation and, *216*, 216–18; psychological environment and, 224; racial difference in, 222; school achievement and, 214–16, *215*; social class and, 224–25; spontaneous changes in, 225–26, *226*; success and, 218–19
Intelligence tests, 10, 209–19; as aptitude tests, 213–14; fairness or bias of, 214; group, 212; individual, 212; origin of, 209; Scholastic Aptitude Tests (SAT), 15, 212–13; social policy and, 217; Stanford-Binet, *209–10*, 209–11, 214, *215*; Wechsler intelligence scale, 211–12, *212*. *See also* Intelligence quotient
Intensity: of light, 259; perception of, 279
Interactional psychotherapy, 487
Interest tests, 237
Interference theory of forgetting, 132–34, *133, 134*
Internal association network, 266, *267*
Interpersonal therapy, 487–91
Interposition, distance perception and, *288*, 288
Interpretation, perception and, *291–93*, 291–93
Interviews, 12–13
Introspection, 22–23
Introverts, 34, 477
Intuitive understanding, 205
Iowa achievement test, 213–14
Iris, 259, *260*

J

James-Lange theory of emotion, 322, 325–26
Just noticeable difference, 244

K

Kibbutz, 521
Knowledge, 111

L

LSD (Lysergic acid diethylamide), 302, 304–05
Language, 158–59, 161–93; brain and, 52, 53; in children, 524; communication and, 162; concepts, cognition and, 177–84, *178*; development of, 514; flexibility of, 166; function of, 161–63; invention of, 184; learning by animals, *175*, 175–77, *176*; learning by children, 169–74, *172*; memory and, 180–82; producing and understanding, 165–69; as species-specific behavior, 174–75; structure of, 162–65; theories of learning, 174–75; thinking and, 183–88
Latent learning, *109*, 109–10
Lateral interaction, 279
Learned helplessness, 90, *103*, 103–07; as a result of failure, 104–07; intellectual development and, 208; therapy and self-therapy for, 106–07
Learning, 39, 78–79, 81–114, 158–59; anxiety and, 402–03; as building on learning, 146–47; categories and, *148*, 148–49, *149*; cognitive, 483; cognitive view of, 108–14; defined, 82; encoding and, 141–47, *144*; as information processing, 168; and instinct, 81–82; of language, 169–77; latent, *109*, 109–10; through observation, *see* Observation learning; organization, 142–43, *144*; RNA and, 128; by rule vs. rote, 143–44, *145;* without reinforcement, 109–10; without response, 110–111
Learning set, 147–48
Left hemisphere, of cerebral cortex, 49, 57–61, *61*
Lens, of the eye, 259, *260*
Levels-of-processing theory of memory, 138
Libido, 472–73
Librium, 306
Lie detector testing, 315, *315*
Life stress scale, 408–09, *409*
Life-style. *See* Culture
Light waves, 258–59, *261*; adding and subtracting, 267
Limbic system, 61–63, *62, 63*
Linear perspective, 288
Lithium, 492–93
Locus of control, 370–71; external, 387, 417
Long-term memory, *121*, 123–25, 136
Loudness, measurement of, 255–56, *256*
Lysergic acid diethylamide. *See* LSD

M

MA. *See* Mental age
Manic-depressive illness, 441–42
Marijuana, 302, 303, 304, 453
Marriage, commitment and, 538–40
Marriage counselors, 10
Masculine: definition of, 379–86; sex-typing, 383–84
Masculinity, 391
Maturity, physical, 514–15
Mean, 600
Measurements, 15–18. *See also* Statistics
Median, 591
Medical therapy, 492
Meditation, 300–01
Medulla, 64
Memory, 39, 119–54, 158–59; associative network theory of, 138–39, 141–42; brain and, 51, 56; categories and, *148*, 148–49, *149*, 180–82, *181*; cause-and-effect in, *150*, 150; chunking in, 136, *137*, 149; clustering in, 149–50; drugs and, 127; forming linkages as aid to, 139; hippocampus and, 56; language and, 180–82; levels-of-processing theories of, 138; long-term, *121*, 123–25; made-up stories and imagery as aids to, 150–52, *151, 152*; mneumonic devices and, 152–54, *153*; neurotransmitters and, 126–27; sensory, 120, *121*; short-term, *121*, 121–23, 517; tests of, 128–29; tip of the tongue phenomenon, 136–38, *138*
Memory traces, 125–28: consolidation process of, 131; fading of, 130–31; neurotransmitters and, 126–27; resistance to extinction of, 131; strength of, 130–31; synapses and, 127–28
Men: problems and, 390–92; superiority and, 391–92
Menstruation, 531
Mental age (MA), 210–11
Mental health, 417
Mental illness, 73
Mental models of reality, 27
Mental telepathy, 297
Mescaline, 305
Metabolism, 68
Middle ear, *254*, 254
Milgram experiment, 550–51
Mind, unconscious, 471–72
Minnesota Multiphasic Personality Inventory (MMPI), 497
Mnemonic devices, 152–54, *153*
Morals: development in adolescence, 533–34; stage theory of moral development, 535
Morphemes, 163–64
Morphine, 307
Motion parallax, 287
Motive targets, 361
Mood: abnormalities of, 439–40; disorders, 442–43
Motives, 353–92; achievement, 354–57; birth order and, 361–62; competing, 375–76; definition, 354; hierarchy of, 528; men and, 390–92; power, 357–58; relationship to behavior, 371; self-actualization, 365; unconscious, 367; women and, 387–88
Movement: of infants, 514; perception of, 278, sense of, 250–51
Muscles (muscular movements): cerebellum and, 54–55; cerebral cortex and, 53; during sleep, *298*, 298; facial, 316–17; sense of bodily movement and, 250
Myelin sheath, 68

N

Narcissistic personality, 452–53
Narcotics, 307; effects on human development, 505
Naturalistic observation, 12, *13*
Nature-nurture argument, 30, 35, 346–47, 354, 380–81

Need; Fromm's theory of basic human, *479*
Neopsychoanalysts, 478
Nerve cells. *See* Neurons
Nervous impulse, 69–73, *71*
Nervous system, *51*, 51–52. *See also* Autonomic nervous system; Brain; Central nervous system; Neurons; Peripheral nervous system
Neurons (nerve cells; brain cells), 50–52, 68, 68–73; feature detector, 274–75; kinds of, 51–52; neurotransmitters, *see* Neurotransmitters; synapses, 69, 69–71; synaptic knobs, 69, 69; transmission of impulses by, 69–73, *71*; visual, 260–63, *262*
Neuroses, 476; classical conditioning in, 90
Neurotransmitters, 69–73; memory and, 126–27. *See also* Noradrenalin
Newborns. *See* Infant
Nicotine, 302
Nodes, of axon, 68
Noise pollution, 257
Noradrenalin, 73, 443; anger and, 316; stress and, 413
Normal curve of distribution, 16, 588–89
Nucleus, of neuron, 68
Number in group, 590
Nurturance, 519

O

Obedience, 550
Obesity, causes of, 331–33
Objectivity in tests, 235; of personality, 497
Observation learning, 112–13, *113*; of language, 175–76
Obsessions. *See* Obsessive-compulsive disorders
Obsessive-compulsive disorders, 448–49
Occupation: Guilford's view of intelligence and, 203; IQ and, *216*, 216–18; vocational aptitude tests and, 237
Oedipus complex, 524; superego and, 473–74
Old age, *537*, 541–43
120-factor, of intelligence, 201
Operant avoidance, 99
Operant behavior, 90
Operant conditioning: behavior modification, 96–97, *97*, *98*; biofeedback, 97–99; cognitive theory of learning and, 108; escape and avoidance, 99–100; language learning and, 174–75; principles of, 92–93; punishment in, 100–103; reinforcement in, *94*, *95*, *94–96*; shaping behavior, *92*, *93*; Skinner box, *91*, 91–92, *95*; superstition and, 92–94
Operant escape, 99–100
Operations, in Piaget's theory of intelligence, 204
Opponent-process theory, *262*, 262
Optic nerve, 259, *260*
Optical illusions, *276*, 276–77
Oral stage, of human sexual development, 472–73
Ordinary sleep, 298
Organ of Corti, 254
Organization: learning and, 142–43, *144*; in perception, *see* Visual organization
Orienting reflex, in perception, 282
Otis-Lennon School Ability Test, *212*
Outer ear, *254*, 254
Oval window, *254*
Ovaries, 65
Overeating, 333. *See also* Obesity
Overlearning, 146
Overtones, 253

P

PCP. *See* Angel dust
Pain, sensation of, 249–50
Pancreas, 65
Panic disorder, 445–46
Paradoxical sleep, 298
Paranoia, deafness and, 257
Paranoid personality, 451–52
Parapsychology, 297
Parasympathetic division, of autonomic nervous system, 66, *67*
Parathyroids, 65
Parenting, 509, 523; sex-typing and, 384
Participant observation, 12
Pattern theory, 246
Peer group, 526
People, relating to others, 502–84
Percentile, 592–93
Perception, 273–93; alternate states of consciousness and, 276, 296–307; of change and contrast, 277–79; of closure, 283, *284*; constancy in, 284–86; continuity in, *284*, 284; defined, 273; of distance and depth, 286–89, *287–89*; drugs and, 301–07; expectations and, *292*, *293*; extrasensory, 296, 297; feature detector cells and, *274*, 274–75; figure and ground, *283*, 283; in hypnosis, 300; impressions and, 567–68; inborn skill, 275–76; in infants, 516; interpretation in, *291*, 291–93; organization in, 283–91; prototypes and, *291*, 291–92; selection in, 279–83, *281*, *282*; similarity and proximity, 284, *285*; of size, 290–91, *291*. *See also* Hearing; Senses; Vision
Peripheral nervous system, 51
Persistence of set, 192
Personality, 467–93, 497–500; abnormal, 429–63; core, 470; defined, 468–69; development of, 470; dominant, 528; hierarchy, 469–70; humanistic theories of, 479–82; of infants, 509; normal, 417–18; peripheral traits, 470; problems, 394–427; relationship between child and adult, *530*; sources, 394–427; submissive, 528; theories of, 468–71; types of 450
Personality development: from birth to 18 months, 518–21; from 18 months to 3 years, 521–24; from 4 to 5 years, 524–25; from 6 to 10 years, 526–29
Personality disorders, 449–53
Personality tests, 237–38, 497–500
Perspective, distance perception and, 288–89, *289*
Persuasive communication, 562; effects on attitudes, 562–64; emotions and, 564
Phallic stage, of human sexual development, 472–75
Phencyclidine. *See* Angel dust
Phenomenological self, 479–80; maladjustment and, 481–83
Pheromones, 248–49
Phobias, 83–84, 446–48, *487*. *See also* Anxieties; Fears
Phonemes, 163
Physical attractiveness, 575; impressions and, 576–77; standards of, 575–76
Physical well-being: brain and, 63–64; psychological disorders and, 433
Pineal gland, 65
Pitch, 252
Pituitary gland, 61, 65, 531

Placebo effect, 410
Pleasure principle, id and, 472–73
Pons, 55
Population: elderly, 541; (statistical), 593–94
Positron emission tomography, *439*
Post-traumatic stress disorder, 446, 447
Power motive, 357–58; avoidance of, 358–59
Precognition, 297
Pregnancy, human development and, 505; physical maturation during, 514–15
Prejudice, 559
Preoperational stage, *205*, 205
Pressure, sensation of, 249
Primal therapy, 489
Primary mental abilities, 200–01
Proactive interference, 132–34, *133*, 147
Probability, 587–89, 596–97
Problem solving, 188–93; pitfalls, of, *189–91*, 189–93; techniques of, 186–87
Projection, 421
Projective tests, of personality, 497, 499
Propinquity, 572–73
Prototypes, in perception, *291*, 291–92
Proximity, perception of, 284, *285*
Psilocybin, 305
Psychedelic drugs, 304
Psychic energizers. *See* Anti-depression drugs
Psychoanalysis, 11, 28, 471, 475–79; humanistic theory, 482; social learning theories, 482–86. *See also* Psychotherapy
Psychoanalytic theory, 471–79
Psychodrama, 489
Psychological disorders, physical well-being and, 433
Psychological statistics, application of, 587
Psychological tests. *See* Tests
Psychology: as applied science, 9; behaviorism, 23–25; clinical, 9–11; cognitive, 26–27; community, 9; defined, 5–6; environmental, 8, 9; existential, 28; experiments in, 18–21; Gestalt, 25–26, *25, 26*; goals of, 6–7; history of, 2–3; humanistic, 27–28; interviews and case histories in, 12–13; methods of, 6, 11–18; observations in, 11–12; public opinion surveys in, 14–15; as pure science, 7–8; questionnaires in, 13–14; in schools and industry, 9; tests and measurements in, 15–18; theories of, 22–29
Psychology, abnormal, 429–63: biological influences of, 432–33; characteristics of, 430–31; defined, 429; developmental, 505–06; environmental influences of, 433–34; origins and types, 431–36
Psychoneuroses. *See* Neuroses
Psychosocial development, theory of, 538, *539*
Psychosomatic illness, 407–08
Psychosurgery, 492
Psychotherapy, 10–11, *11*, 467–93, 497–500. *See also* Psychoanalysis
Puberty, 531–32; males and, 531; females and, 531–32
Public opinion surveys, 14–15
Punishment, 522–23; children and, 101–03; learned helplessness and, 104; in operant conditioning, 100–03
Pupil, 259, *260*
Pure science, 7–8

Q

Quaaludes, 303, 306
Quality of life, 541
Questionnaires, 13–14

R

REM sleep, 298
RNA, learning and, 128
Race, intelligence and, 222
Rapid eye movement. *See* REM sleep
Rationalization, 418–19
Reaction formation, 421
Reality principle, ego and, 473
Reality therapy, 488
Recall, 129
Receptor sites, 68
Receptors, sensory, 244; for bodily movement, 250–51; for equilibrium, 251–52; for hearing, 253–55, *255*; for the skin senses, 249–50; for smell, 248–49; for taste, 247–48; for vision, 245
Recitation, 39, *40*
Recognition, 129
Reflex, 84–85
Regression, 424–25
Rehearsal system, short-term memory and, 122–23
Reinforcement, 484; in classical conditioning, 88–89; constant, 95; learning without, 109–10; negative, 99; in operant conditioning, *94, 95*, 94–96; partial, 95; positive, 99; primary, 94; secondary 94
Relationships, with people, 582–84
Relaxation, anxiety and, 401–02
Relearning, 129
Reliability, in tests, 235–36
Repression, 420, 471–72
Response, 24; learning without, 110–11
Reticular activating system, 53–54
Retina, 259–60, *260, 261*; neurons of, 266–68, *267*
Retrieval, 125; forgetting as failure in, 131–32, *132*
Retroactive interference, *134*, 134, *135*, 147
Reward, 522–23
Right hemisphere, of cerebral cortex, 49, 57–61, *61*
Risk taking, anxiety and, 404–05
Rods, 260–61, *261*, 262, *267*, 267
Rooting response, *507*
Rorschach test, 499
Rote, learning by, 143–44, *145*
Rule, learning by, 143–44, *145*

S

SAT. *See* Scholastic Aptitude Test
SQ3R system of studying, 39–43, 144
S factor, of sleep, 299
Salivary reflex, *84*, 85
Sample (statistical), 593–94
Saturation, of light, 259
Scanning: eye movement and, *282*, 282–83; short-term memory and, 122–23
Scatter plots, 597
Schema. *See* Prototypes
Schizophrenia, 432, 436–39; behavior patterns of, 437–38; brain chemicals and treatment of, 51; environment and, 35; genetic origin of, 439; heredity and, 34, *440*; and parenting, *438*; roots of, 438–39
Schizophrenia spectrum, 438
Scholastic Aptitude Test (SAT), 15, 212–23. *See also* Intelligence tests
School achievement, IQ and, 214–16, *215*
School phobia, 448
School psychologists, 9

Schools: behavior modification in, 97; learned helplessness in, 106–07
Science, pure versus applied, 7–9
Seconals, 306
Sedatives, 306; effects on human development, 505
Selection, in perception, 279–83, *281, 282*
Self-absorption, 540
Self-actualization: Maslow's motive for, 479; motive and, 365–67
Self-esteem, 417; theory of social comparison and, 556
Self-fulfilling prophecy, 567
Self-perception theory, 571–72
Self-Rating Depression Scale, *441*
Self-therapy, 493
Semantics, 164
Semicircular canals, 251, *254*
Senses, 243–63; absolute threshold of, 244; adaptation of, 245; bodily movement, 250–51; brain function and, 52–55; difference threshold of, 244; equilibrium, *251,* 251–53; pattern theory of, 246; range and limits of, 244; skin, *249*, 249–50; smell, *248,* 248–49; taste, 247–48. *See also* Hearing; Perception; Vision
Sensorimotor stage, 204–05
Sensory adaptation, 245; of infants, 507
Sensory deprivation, *336*
Sensory memory, 120, *121*
Sensory threshold, 244
Sentence completion test, 500
Separation anxiety, 520
Sex: development of, in adolescence, 533; drive, 334; role and conflict, 379–92. *See also* Id; Libido
Sex determination, 33–34
Sex drive, in females, 344–45
Sex glands, 65
Sex roles, 379–92
Sex typing, 383–84, 529; influence of parents, 384; influence of society, 384–86; of men, 390–92; of women, 386–87
Sexual development: feelings and, 342–50; stages according to Freud, 472–75
Sexuality, 344–45
Shadowing, distance perception and, *289,* 289–90
Shape constancy, 285
Shaping behavior, 92, *93*
Short-term memory, *121,* 121–23, 136
Significance, 596–97
Similarity, 573–74; perception of, 284, *285*
Simple cell, in visual cortex, 275
Single-blind technique, 21
Situational tests, of personality, 497, 498
Size, perception of, 279, *290,* 290–91
Size constancy, *285,* 285–86, *286*
Skin senses, *249,* 249–50
Skinner box, *91,* 91–92, 95
Sleep: brain during, *298,* 298; effects of lack of, 299; function of, 299; hours of, 298–99; insomnia, 299; ordinary, 298; paradoxical, 298; perception during, 296–98; REM, 298
"Slow" fibers, and skin sensation, 250
Smell, *248,* 248–49
Smile: infants and, 514
Smoking: effects on human development, 505
Social behavior, anxiety and, 402
Social class, IQ and, 224–25
Social psychology, 547–84; definition of, 547
Social relationships, formation of, 572–77
Socialization, 522, 548–49
Sociobiology, 336
Sound: locating, 256–58; loudness of, 255–56, *256,* 257. *See also* Hearing
Sound waves, 252–53, *253*
Species-specific behavior, 113–14; language as, 174–75
Speech, emotions and, 317
Sperm cell: human, *31,* 31–34; production of, 531
Spinal cord, 51
Spleen, 66
Split-brain experiments, *58,* 58–59, *59,* 72
Spoken language: producing and understanding, 165–69. *See also* Language
Spontaneous recovery: of conditioned response, 88–89; in operant conditioning, 92–93
Standard deviation, 591–92, 601
Standard error, of the mean, 595, 602
Standardization, in tests, 236–37
Stanford-Binet Intelligence Scale, *209–10,* 209–11, 214, *215*
Statistical methods, 587–605
Stereotype, 559
Stimulants, 305
Stimulus (stimulation), 24; adaptation of senses to, 245; conditioned, 88; defined, 244; difference threshold and, 244; for hearing, 252–53, *253;* senses and, 244–46; unconditioned, 88, *89*; visual, 258–59
Stimulus discrimination: in conditioned response, 89–90; in operant conditioning, 93
Stimulus generalization: in classical conditioning, 89–90; in operant conditioning, 93
Stimulus variability, 337; survival and, 338–39
Stress, 397–427; coping with, 414–25; defense mechanisms, 418–25; definition of, 405–06; effects of, 405–13; emotional, 328; general adaptation syndrome, 406–07; life stress scale, 408–09; physical wellbeing and, 433; physiological changes, 328–36; psychological effects of, 413–14; tension and, 316; in the womb, 506
Stroboscopic motion, 276, *277*
Study methods: overlearning of, 146; recitation, 30, *40*; SQ3R system, 39–43
Subcultures, 549
Sublimation, 420
Success, 353–61, 370–71; birth order and, 361–62; IQ and, 218–19
Suicide, 440–41; adolescence and, 533
Superego, 472–73, 524
Superstition, 93–94
Surrogate mothers, 518–19
Survival: stimulus variability and, 338–39
Sympathetic division, of autonomic nervous system, 66–67, *67*
Synapses, 69, 69–71; memory traces and formation of new, 127–28
Synaptic cleft, 69, 70
Synaptic knobs, 69, 69
Synaptic vesicles, 70
Syntax, 164–65

T

TAT. *See* Thematic Aptitude Test
Taste, 247–48
Taste buds, 247–48
Teachers, 527
Television, learning language and, 170

Temperament: of infants, 508–09
Tension. *See* Stress
Test anxiety, 401
Testes, 65
Tests, 15–18; aptitude, *see* Aptitude tests; construction of, 235–38; of creativity, *230,* 230; of intelligence, *see* Intelligence tests; normal curve of distribution and, 16; objectivity of, 235; reliability of, 235–36; standardization of, 236–37; validity of, 21, 236
Thalamus, 53–54
Thematic Apperception Test (TAT), 499
Theory of cognitive dissonance: attitude change and, 560–61; decisions and, 562
Theory of social comparison, 555–56
Therapy: for learned helplessness, 106–07. *See also specific therapies*
Thinking, 159; by computers, 230–31; defined, 185; by inference, 179–80; language and, 183–88; logical and illogical, 187–88; rules and premises of, 186–87. *See also* Problem solving
Thirst, 334–36
Thought, in infants, 517
Thyroid, 65
Timbre, 253, *254*
Tip of the tongue phenomenon, 136–38, *138*
Token economies, *97,* 97
Traits, in infants, 510
Tranquilizers, 306; effects on human development, 505; use in therapy, 492
Transfer of information, 122–23
Transfer process, short-term memory and, 123; long-term memory and, 135–41
Transpersonal therapy, 488

U

Ulcers, noise and, 257
Uncertainty and anxiety, 399–401
Unconditional positive regard, 480
Unconditioned response, 88
Unconditioned stimulus, 88, *89*
Unconscious motives, 367
Unipolar depression, 141

V

Validity, in tests, 21, 236
Valium, 306
Variability, 591–92
Variables, 18–20
Vestibular sacs, 251
Vision, 258–63; absolute threshold of, 244, 260–61; binocular, 288; in bright and dark conditions, 262–63 color, 261–62; difference threshold of, 244; eye movements and scanning, *281,* 281–83; light waves and, 244–45, 258–59; opponent-process theory of, *262,* 262; receptors for, 245; structure of the eye and, 259–61, *260, 261.* *See also* Perception; Senses
Visual cliff, 286–87, *287*
Visual organization, 283–91; closure in, 283, *284*; continuity in, *284,* 284; distance and perception in, 286–89; figure and ground in, *283,* 283; interpretation and, *292,* 292; similarity and proximity in, 284, *285*
Visual purple, 261, 262
Vocabulary, 164, 183
Vocational aptitude tests, 237

W

WAIS. *See* Wechsler Adult Intelligence Scale
Warmth, sensation of, *249,* 249
Wavelength, 259
Weber's Law, 244
Wechsler Adult Intelligence Scale (WAIS), 211–12, *212*
Weight, hunger and, 331
Withdrawal, 423–24
Women: inferiority, 391–92; liberation and, 389; problems of sex typing, 386–87; status of, 389
Word association test, 499–500

X

X chromosome, 33–34

Y

Y chromosome, 33–34
Young-Helmholtz theory, 269–70

C
D 6
E 7
F 8
G 9
H 0
I 1
J 2